De Bourgh
"ALL AMERICAN LOCKERS"

AT&T

STANDARD CANDY COMPANY

Levi's
QUALITY NEVER GOES OUT OF STYLE.®

THE SOUTHLAND CORPORATION

CHRYSLER CORPORATION

Piccadilly Cafeteria
50th Anniversary 1944 1994

STARBUCKS COFFEE

Financial Accounting

A Focus on Decision Making

Annotated Instructor's Edition

Accounting Textbooks from West Educational Publishing

Listed alphabetically by author

Jesse T. Barfield, Cecily A. Raiborn, and Michael R. Kinney: *Cost Accounting, Traditions and Innovations, 2E*

Leonard J. Brooks: *Professional Ethics in Accounting*

John G. Burch: *Cost and Management Accounting: A Modern Approach*

Janet Cassagio, Dolores Osborn & Beverly Terry: *College Accounting*

James Doak and Christine Kloezeman: *Computerized Accounting Principles*

James A. Hall: *Accounting Information Systems*

Bart P. Hartman, Robert M.J. Harper, Jr., James A. Knobl, and Philip M. Reckers: *Intermediate Accounting*

William H. Hoffman, Jr., William A. Raabe, James E. Smith and David M. Maloney: *West's Federal Taxation: Corporations, Partnerships, Estates and Trusts, 1996 Edition*

William H. Hoffman, Jr., James E. Smith, and Eugene Willis: *West's Federal Taxation: Individual Income Taxes, 1996 Edition*

Michael C. Knapp: *Contemporary Auditing: Issues and Cases, 2E*

Michael C. Knapp: *Financial Accounting: A Focus on Decision Making*

Larry F. Konrath: *Auditing Concepts and Applications: A Risk Analysis Approach, 3E*

Joseph G. Louderback, G. Thomas Friedlob, and Franklin J. Plewa: *Survey of Accounting*

Kevin Murphy with Rick L. Crosser and Mark Higgins: *Concepts in Federal Taxation, 2E*

William A. Raabe, Gerald E. Whittenburg, and John Bost: *West's Federal Tax Research, 3E*

Cecily A. Raiborn, Jesse T. Barfield, and Michael Kinney: *Managerial Accounting, 2E*

James E. Smith: *West's Internal Revenue Code of 1986 and Treasury Regulations: Annotated and Selected, 1996 Edition*

Gerald E. Whittenburg and Martha Altus-Buller: *Income Tax Fundamentals, 1996 Edition*

Eugene Willis, William H. Hoffman, Jr., David Maloney, and William A. Raabe: *West's Federal Taxation: Comprehensive Volume, 1996 Edition*

FINANCIAL ACCOUNTING

A FOCUS ON DECISION MAKING

Annotated Instructor's Edition

Michael C. Knapp
UNIVERSITY OF OKLAHOMA

WEST PUBLISHING COMPANY

MINNEAPOLIS/SAINT PAUL

NEW YORK

LOS ANGELES

SAN FRANCISCO

DEDICATED TO Carol, John, Lindsay and Jessi

COMPOSITION	Parkwood Composition
COPYEDITOR	Joan Torkildson
INDEXER	Sonsie Conroy, Catalyst Communication
TEXT DESIGN	Kristen Weber for Metiér
ART	B. Suter Graphics and Design
PHOTO RESEARCHER	Kathy Ringrose
LOGO RESEARCHER	Michelle Oberhoffer
PAGE LAYOUT	Wendy LaChance, By Design
COVER PHOTO	Leo deWys Inc./J. B. Grant

PRODUCTION, PREPRESS, PRINTING AND BINDING BY WEST PUBLISHING COMPANY

PHOTO CREDITS FOLLOW THE INDEX

WEST'S COMMITMENT TO THE ENVIRONMENT

In 1906, West Publishing Company began recycling materials left over from the production of books. This began a tradition of efficient and responsible use of resources. Today, up to 95 percent of our legal books are printed on recycled, acid-free stock. West also recycles nearly 22 million pounds of scrap paper annually—the equivalent of 181,717 trees. Since the 1960s, West has devised ways to capture and recycle waste inks, solvents, oils and vapors created in the printing process. We also recycle plastics of all kinds, wood, glass, corrugated cardboard, and batteries, and have eliminated the use of Styrofoam book packaging. We at West are proud of the longevity and the scope of our commitment to the environment.

TEXT IS PRINTED ON 10% POST CONSUMER RECYCLED PAPER   Printed with Printwise — Environmentally Advanced Water Washable Ink

British Library Cataloguing-in-Publication Data. A catalogue record for this book is available from the British Library.

COPYRIGHT © 1996 By WEST PUBLISHING COMPANY
610 Opperman Drive
P.O. Box 64526
Saint Paul, MN 55164-0526

Library of Congress Cataloging-in-Publication Data

Knapp, Michael Chris, 1954–
  Financial accounting : a focus on decision making / Michael Chris
  Knapp
    p.   cm.
  Includes index.

  ISBN 0-314-06345-5 (hc : alk. paper)
  1. Managerial accounting. 2. Decision-making   I. Title.
HF5657.4.K647   1996
658.15'11—dc20   95-35038
    ISBN 0-314-07598-4 (loose leaf edition)   CIP
    ISBN 0-314-07164-4 (annotated instructor's edition)

ABOUT THE AUTHOR

Michael Chris Knapp, Ph.D., CPA, CMA, has been a member of the faculty of the University of Oklahoma since 1988 and taught previously at the University of Southern California and Texas Christian University. Chris Knapp has published extensively in both academic research journals and practitioner-oriented journals. Included in his more than one dozen publications in refereed academic journals are publications in *The Accounting Review, Auditing: A Journal of Practice & Theory*, the *Journal of Accounting, Auditing and Finance*, and *Behavioral Research in Accounting*. Among Knapp's publications in practice journals are articles appearing in the *Journal of Accountancy*, the *CPA Journal*, and the *Internal Auditor*. Additionally, he has served on the editorial boards of several journals including *The Accounting Review, Auditing: A Journal of Practice & Theory, Advances in Accounting*, and *Research in Accounting Regulation*. In 1993, his auditing casebook, *Contemporary Auditing: Issues and Cases*, was published by West Publishing. To date, more than two hundred colleges and universities have adopted that text which is now in its second edition. In 1994, West published Chris's *Financial Accounting: Issues and Cases*.

Finally, Professor Knapp is probably the only former *Jeopardy!* contestant among accounting textbook authors. In 1984 on the sixth *Jeopardy!* show produced by Alex Trbek, Chris failed to win the championship by not answering the $1,000 question in the "50 States" category. The answer? The state with the highest per capita American Indian population. Knapp, an Oklahoma native who is part Cherokee Indian, is reminded continually by his family that Arizona has a large Indian population but Oklahoma has the highest per capita Indian population in the nation.

CONTENTS IN BRIEF

Preface   xxi

PART I   ACCOUNTING FUNDAMENTALS   1

1   An Introduction to Accounting   3

2   Accounting Concepts and Elements   31

3   Accounting Systems and Internal Control   76

PART II   THE ACCOUNTING MODEL   111

4   The Mechanics of Double-Entry Accounting   112

5   The Accounting Cycle   154

6   Accounting for Merchandising Companies   212

PART III   ACCOUNTING FOR ASSETS   263

7   Cash and Receivables   265

8   Inventory   318

9   Property, Plant & Equipment, and Intangible Assets   366

PART IV   ACCOUNTING FOR LIABILITIES   417

10   Current Liabilities, Contingent Liabilities, and the Time
Value of Money   418

11   Long-Term Liabilities   470

**PART V   ACCOUNTING FOR OWNERSHIP
INTERESTS**   519

12   The Corporate Form of Business Organization: Accounting
for Stockholders' Equity   521

13 The Corporate Income Statement and Statement of
Stockholders' Equity   567

14 Intercorporate Investments and Accounting for International
Operations   607

15 Partnerships and Proprietorships   651

PART VI   ANALYSIS OF ACCOUNTING DATA   689

16 Statement of Cash Flows   690

17 Financial Statement Analysis   742

APPENDIX   MICHAELS STORES INC. ANNUAL
REPORT   A-1

Glossary   G-1

Company Index   I-1

Subject Index   I-4

CONTENTS

Preface   xxi

PART I   ACCOUNTING FUNDAMENTALS   1

CHAPTER 1   AN INTRODUCTION TO ACCOUNTING   3

Learning Objectives   3
- FOCUS ON DECISION MAKING: Accounting and the Allocation of Scarce Economic Resources   4

The Historical Development of Accounting   5
Double-Entry Bookkeeping and the Laws of Physics   5
The Evolution of Accounting Systems   6
Generally Accepted Accounting Principles: The Rules of the Game   7

The Nature of Accounting: A Means to an End   8
Defining the Societal Role of Accounting   8
Communicating Financial Information to External Decision Makers   8
Communicating Financial Information to Internal Decision Makers   9

Abusive Accounting Practices: Losing Sight of the Role of Accounting   10
Creative Accounting Comes to the Savings and Loan Industry   11
- SPOTLIGHT ON ETHICS: Doing the Right Thing . . . and Paying for It   12
Abusive Accounting and Abused Accountants   12

An Overview of the Accounting Profession   13
Accountant vs. CPA   13
Private vs. Public Accounting   13
Work Roles in Private Accounting   13
Public Accounting: A Closer Look   14
Regulation of the Accounting Profession   17
- FOR YOUR INFORMATION: Unconventional Accounting Services   18

Accounting: A Profession in Transition   19
Recent Trends and Events Affecting the Accounting Profession   19
The Expectations Gap and the Litigation Crisis   20
Accounting on an International Scale   20
Looking Forward to the 21st Century   21

Summary   21
Glossary   22

■ DECISION CASE   22
Questions   23
Exercises   24
Problem Set A   25
Problem Set B   27
Cases   29
Projects   30

CHAPTER 2   ACCOUNTING CONCEPTS AND ELEMENTS   31

Learning Objectives   31
■ FOCUS ON DECISION MAKING: A Stick-to-the-Basics Approach to Business and
   Accounting   32
Objectives of Financial Reporting   33
**Financial Statements: Nature, Purpose, and Definitions of
   Key Elements**   35
   The Balance Sheet   35
■ FOR YOUR INFORMATION: A Noncurrent Current Asset   40
   The Income Statement   43
■ FOR YOUR INFORMATION: The Balance Sheet: Going Dutch   46
   Statement of Stockholders' Equity   47
   Statement of Cash Flows   47
   Financial Statement Footnotes   50
Key Attributes of Accounting Information   50
   Understandability   50
   Relevance   51
   Reliability   51
■ SPOTLIGHT ON ETHICS: The Windbag Theory   52
   Attributes of Accounting Information: A Few Other Issues   52
Fundamental Accounting Concepts   53
   Entity Concept   54
   Accounting Period Concept   55
   Going Concern Assumption   56
   Unit of Measurement Concept   56
   Historical Cost Principle   56
   Revenue and Expense Recognition Rules   57
   Full Disclosure Principle   58
Summary   59
Glossary   60
■ DECISION CASE   62
Questions   63
Exercises   63
Problem Set A   67
Problem Set B   71
Cases   73
Projects   74

CHAPTER 3   ACCOUNTING SYSTEMS AND INTERNAL
             CONTROL   76

Learning Objectives   76

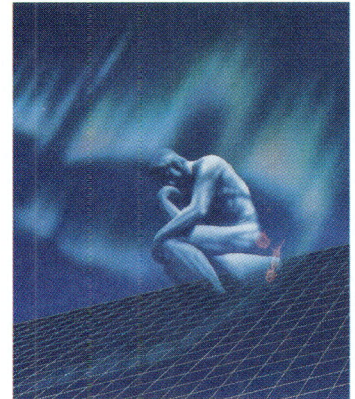

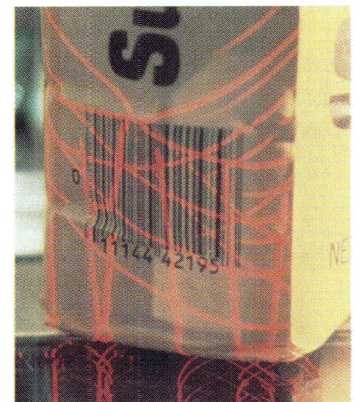

■ FOCUS ON DECISION MAKING: Internal Controls: Being Safe Not Sorry   77

Accounting Systems: An Introduction   78

    The Accounting Function as a System   78

    Accounts   79

    Chart of Accounts   81

    The General Journal and General Ledger: The Basic Accounting "Books"   81

    The Accounting Cycle   83

Internal Control Concepts and Issues   83

    Internal Control Structure: Definition and Objectives   84

    Elements of an Internal Control Structure   84

■ SPOTLIGHT ON ETHICS: Cashing in on Weak Internal Controls   85

    Internal Control Reports   87

■ FOR YOUR INFORMATION: 1994 Report of Management, Mesa Laboratories, Inc.   88

Computer Processing and Internal Control   88

    Integrating Computers into Accounting and Control Functions   88

    Computerized vs. Manual Processing of Accounting Data: Internal Control Implications   90

    Computer Processing: What the Future Holds for Accountants and Accounting   92

■ FOR YOUR INFORMATION: When in Rome . . .   94

Internal Control on an International Scale   95

Summary   96

Glossary   97

■ DECISION CASE   97

Questions   98

Exercises   98

Problem Set A   102

Problem Set B   105

Cases   107

Projects   108

PART II   THE ACCOUNTING MODEL   111

CHAPTER 4   THE MECHANICS OF DOUBLE-ENTRY ACCOUNTING   112

Learning Objectives   112

■ FOCUS ON DECISION MAKING: The Evolution of Accounting: From Clay Tokens to Computers   113

The Accounting Equation   113

Double-Entry Bookkeeping Rules   116

    Debits and Credits?   117

■ SPOTLIGHT ON ETHICS: The Pen Is Greater Than the Pistol   118

    Asset Accounts   118

    Liability Accounts   119

    Owners' Equity Accounts   119

    Temporary Accounts   119

    Contra Accounts   121

Journalizing Transactions: Applying the Bookkeeping Rules   121

    Journalizing: Easy as 1, 2, 3 . . .   121

■ FOR YOUR INFORMATION: Knowing When to Dial "B" for Bookkeeper   123
    Accounting Illustrated: Eight Real-World Journal Entries   123
    Entries, Entries, and More Entries   127
    Journalizing: A Few Helpful Hints and Reminders   128
■ FOR YOUR INFORMATION: Candy's Tortilla Factory   130
Posting and Preparation of the Trial Balance   130
    Posting   130
    Preparation of a Trial Balance   133
Summary   136
Glossary   137
■ DECISION CASE   137
Questions   138
Exercises   139
Problem Set A   145
Problem Set B   147
Cases   150
Projects   152

CHAPTER 5   THE ACCOUNTING CYCLE   154

Learning Objectives   154
■ FOCUS ON DECISION MAKING: Keeping the Books for Uncle Sam:
    Accounting for Gridlock   155
The Accounting Cycle: An Overview   156
The Accounting Cycle Illustrated   158
    Accounting Cycle, Step 1: Analyze Transactions   159
■ FOR YOUR INFORMATION: The SEC: Just Say No to Foreign Financial
    Statements   160
    Accounting Cycle, Step 2: Journalize Transactions   163
    Accounting Cycle, Step 3: Post Journal Entries   163
    Accounting Cycle, Step 4: Prepare Trial Balance   165
    Accounting Cycle, Step 5: Adjust the General Ledger Accounts   168
■ FOR YOUR INFORMATION: Beyond the Accounting Cycle: "Nonaccounting"
    Information Needs of Decision Makers   171
    Accounting Cycle, Step 6: Prepare Financial Statements   181
    Accounting Cycle, Step 7: Journalize and Post Adjusting Entries   182
    Accounting Cycle, Step 8: Journalize and Post Closing Entries   183
    Accounting Cycle, Step 9: Prepare Post-Closing Trial Balance   191
■ FOR YOUR INFORMATION: Unaccountable Accounting by State and Local
    Governments   192
Summary   193
Glossary   194
■ DECISION CASE   194
Questions   196
Exercises   196
Problem Set A   201
Problem Set B   205
Cases   209
Projects   210

CHAPTER 6   ACCOUNTING FOR MERCHANDISING COMPANIES   212

Learning Objectives   212
■ FOCUS ON DECISION MAKING: Marketing by the (Accounting) Numbers   213
An Overview of Merchandising Operations   213
    Nature of Merchandising Operations   214
    The Operating Cycle for Merchandising Companies   214
    Income Statement for a Merchandising Company   216
    Analyzing the Financial Health of Merchandising Companies   217
Accounting for Merchandising Operations   219
    Inventory Systems Used by Merchandising Companies   219
■ FOR YOUR INFORMATION: 50-Off Stores, Inc.   220
    Accounting for Sales Transactions in a Periodic Inventory System   221
    Accounting for Purchases Transactions in a Periodic Inventory System   224
    Accounting for Transportation Costs in a Periodic Inventory System   226
    Determining Cost of Goods Sold in a Periodic Inventory System   228
    Period-Ending Closing Procedures for a Merchandising Company That Uses a Periodic Inventory System   228
■ FOR YOUR INFORMATION: Cadbury Schweppes plc   230
Internal Control for Merchandising Operations   235
    General Control Procedures for Merchandising Operations   235
■ SPOTLIGHT ON ETHICS: Betty the Cashier: A Case of Misplaced Trust   237
    The Net Method of Accounting for Purchases   237
    Special Journals and Subsidiary Ledgers   239
Summary   244
Glossary   245
■ DECISION CASE   246
Questions   246
Exercises   247
Problem Set A   252
Problem Set B   255
Cases   259
Projects   260

PART III   ACCOUNTING FOR ASSETS   263

CHAPTER 7   CASH AND RECEIVABLES   265

Learning Objectives   265
■ FOCUS ON DECISION MAKING: Giving Credit to Whom Credit Is Due   266
Cash   267
    Cash, Cash Equivalents, and Cash Flows   267
    Cash: Information Needs of Decision Makers   268
    Accounting for Cash   270
    Analyzing Cash   271
■ FOR YOUR INFORMATION: Running a Business Without Cash   273
    Key Internal Control Procedures for Cash   273
Accounts Receivable   280
    Credit Makes the (Business) World Go Round   280

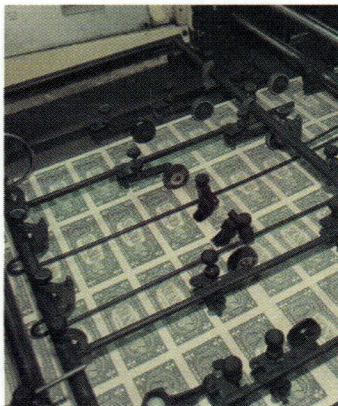

Accounts Receivable: Information Needs of Decision Makers   281
■ FOR YOUR INFORMATION: Foreign Receivables: Far Away and Tough to Collect   282
    Accounting for Accounts Receivable   282
    Analyzing Accounts Receivable   288
■ FOR YOUR INFORMATION: StarPak's Metto: Don't Give Up, Don't Ever Give Up   290
    Key Internal Control Procedures for Accounts Receivable   291
A Few Notes on Notes Receivable   292
    Notes Receivable: Characteristics and Terminology   292
    Accounting for Notes Receivable   295
Summary   297
Glossary   298
■ DECISION CASE   299
Questions   300
Exercises   301
Problem Set A   305
Problem Set B   310
Cases   314
Projects   316

CHAPTER 8   INVENTORY   318

Learning Objectives   318
■ FOCUS ON DECISION MAKING: Managing Inventory: Cabbage Patch Kids, Hot Wheels, and the Corporate Accountant   319
Inventory: An Introduction   320
    Inventory Terms   320
    Inventory: Size Equals Importance   321
    Inventory Errors and the Bottom Line   323
■ SPOTLIGHT ON ETHICS: Rocky Mount Accounting Horror   324
Inventory: Information Needs of Decision Makers   324
    Inventory Balances   325
    Information Regarding Inventory Accounting Methods   325
    "What If" Information   326
Accounting for Inventory   327
    Determining Year-End Inventory Quantities   327
    Inventory Costing Methods   327
■ FOR YOUR INFORMATION: Inventory Costing Methods in Europe   334
    Valuing Inventory at Other Than Cost   334
    Estimating Inventory   336
    The Perpetual Inventory System   337
Analyzing Inventory   341
Key Internal Control Procedures for Inventory   342
■ FOR YOUR INFORMATION: Inventory Management: Howard Knows Best   345
Summary   345
Glossary   346
■ DECISION CASE   347
Questions   348
Exercises   349
Problem Set A   353
Problem Set B   357
Cases   362
Projects   363

CHAPTER 9   PROPERTY, PLANT & EQUIPMENT, AND INTANGIBLE
             ASSETS   366

Learning Objectives   366
■ FOCUS ON DECISION MAKING: Avoiding Edsel-Land   367
Property, Plant, & Equipment: Formerly Fixed Assets   368
**Property, Plant, & Equipment: Key Information Needs of
    Decision Makers**   369
    Disclosures of Specific Types of Property, Plant & Equipment   370
    Valuation Issues   370
    Depreciation Methods   371
    Restrictions on Use   372
    Future Property, Plant & Equipment Needs   372
■ FOR YOUR INFORMATION: International Differences in Valuing Long-Term
    Assets   372
Accounting for Property, Plant & Equipment   373
    Acquisition of Property, Plant & Equipment   373
    Depreciation of Property, Plant & Equipment   374
■ FOR YOUR INFORMATION: Even a Whale of an Asset Must Be
    Depreciated   380
■ SPOTLIGHT ON ETHICS: Depreciation, Harvard Style   383
    Revenue Expenditures vs. Capital Expenditures   383
    Disposal of Property, Plant & Equipment Assets   385
Analyzing Total Assets   388
    Return on Assets   388
    Total Asset Turnover Ratio   389
Key Internal Control Procedures for Property, Plant & Equipment   390
A Few Notes on Intangible Assets   392
    Accounting for Intangible Assets: An Overview   392
    Specific Types of Intangible Assets   393
■ FOR YOUR INFORMATION: Goodwill With an Attitude   395
Summary   395
Glossary   396
■ DECISION CASE   397
Questions   398
Exercises   399
Problem Set A   405
Problem Set B   409
Cases   413
Projects   415

PART IV   ACCOUNTING FOR LIABILITIES   417

CHAPTER 10 CURRENT LIABILITIES, CONTINGENT LIABILITIES, AND
            THE TIME VALUE OF MONEY   418

Learning Objectives   418
■ FOCUS ON DECISION MAKING: Accounts Payable: A Nine-Point Management
    Plan   419
Current Liabilities: An Introduction   420

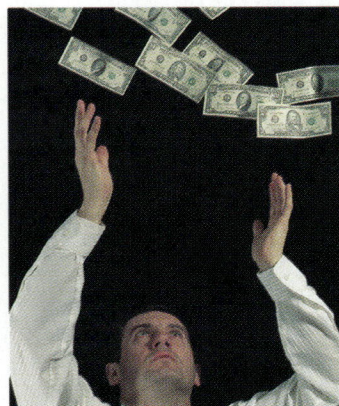

Current Liabilities: Key Information Needs of Decision Makers   421
    Completeness   421
■ FOR YOUR INFORMATION: Classification of Liabilities in Other
    Countries   422
    Valuation Methods   422
    Unusual Circumstances   423
Accounting for Current Liabilities   423
    Accounts Payable   423
    Notes Payable   423
    Current Portion of Long-Term Debt   426
    Deferred Revenues   426
    Sales Taxes Payable   427
    Accrued Expenses   427
■ SPOTLIGHT ON ETHICS: Insufficient Warranty Expense for an Exploding
    Product   429
Analyzing Current Liabilities   432
Key Internal Control Procedures for Current Liabilities   433
■ SPOTLIGHT ON ETHICS: Payroll Padding: A Case of Dodger Blue   434
Contingent Liabilities   435
The Time Value of Money   437
    Simple Interest vs. Compound Interest   438
    Future Value of a Single Amount   439
    Future Value of an Annuity   442
    Present Value of a Single Amount   445
    Present Value of an Annuity   447
Summary   449
Glossary   450
■ DECISION CASE   450
Questions   451
Exercises   452
Problem Set A   457
Problem Set B   462
Cases   466
Projects   468

CHAPTER 11   LONG-TERM LIABILITIES   470

Learning Objectives   470
■ FOCUS ON DECISION MAKING: A Mickey Mouse Organization Built on Mickey
    Mouse Loans   471
Long-Term Liabilities: An Overview   472
Long-Term Liabilities: Key Information Needs of Decision Makers   473
    Completeness   473
    Valuation Methods   473
    Unusual Circumstances   474
Accounting for Bonds Payable   474
    Corporate Bonds: An Introduction   475
    Accounting for Bonds Issued at Face Value   479
■ FOR YOUR INFORMATION: Zeroes, LYONS, TIGRS and . . . CATS?   480
    Accounting for Bonds Issued at a Discount   481
    Accounting for Bonds Issued at a Premium   483
    Using the Effective-Interest Method to Amortize Bond Discounts and
        Premiums   484

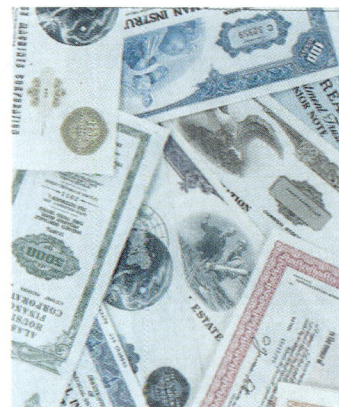

■ FOR YOUR INFORMATION: Accounting for Discounts on Long-Term Debt: A "Conservative" Approach   486
    Accounting for Bonds Payable: A Few Other Issues   487

Accounting for Long-Term Liabilities Other Than Bonds Payable   491
    Long-Term Notes Payable   491
    Long-Term Lease Obligations   491

■ FOR YOUR INFORMATION: Leasing vs. Borrowing: A Tough Decision for Small Businesses   493
    Pension Liabilities   493

■ FOR YOUR INFORMATION: Abe Lincoln on Accounting for Postretirement Employee Benefits   494
    Other Postretirement Benefit Liabilities   495

Analyzing Long-Term Liabilities   496
    Long-Term Debt to Equity Ratio   497
    Times Interest Earned Ratio   497

Key Internal Control Procedures for Long-Term Liabilities   498

Summary   499
Glossary   500
■ DECISION CASE   501
Questions   501
Exercises   502
Problem Set A   507
Problem Set B   511
Cases   515
Projects   516

PART V   ACCOUNTING FOR OWNERSHIP INTERESTS   519

CHAPTER 12   THE CORPORATE FORM OF BUSINESS ORGANIZATION: ACCOUNTING FOR STOCKHOLDERS' EQUITY   521

Learning Objectives   521
■ FOCUS ON DECISION MAKING: Going Public: The Price Is Right . . . Hopefully   522

An Introduction to the Corporate Form of Business Organization   523
    Corporations: Artificial and Invisible Beings   532
    Key Advantages of the Corporate Form of Business Organization   523
    Key Disadvantages of the Corporate Form of Business Organization   525
    Corporate Stock   525

■ SPOTLIGHT ON ETHICS: Battle Mountain Gold Company's Statement of Core Values   529

Stockholders' Equity: Key Information Needs of Decision Makers   529
    Stockholder Rights and Privileges   529
    Earnings Data   530
    Dividend Information   531

Accounting for Stockholders' Equity   532
    Stockholders' Equity in the Corporate Balance Sheet   532
    Issuance of Common Stock   533
    Sale of Preferred Stock   535

Treasury Stock Transactions   536
Dividends   537
■ FOR YOUR INFORMATION: A Yen for Dividends   539
Stock Dividends   539
■ FOR YOUR INFORMATION: Stock Dividends and the Supreme Court: A Taxing
Matter   542
Accounting for Stock Splits   542
Analyzing Stockholders' Equity   544
■ FOR YOUR INFORMATION: Zeroes Who Are Heroes   546
Key Internal Control Procedures for Stockholders' Equity   546
Summary   547
Glossary   548
■ DECISION CASE   549
Questions   550
Exercises   551
Problem Set A   556
Problem Set B   559
Cases   563
Projects   564

**CHAPTER 13   THE CORPORATE INCOME STATEMENT AND
STATEMENT OF STOCKHOLDERS' EQUITY**   567

Learning Objectives   567
■ FOCUS ON DECISION MAKING: Mixing Social Consciousness and Corporate
Profits   568
The Corporate Income Statement   569
Corporate Income Statements: Serving the Information Needs of
Decision Makers   569
The Comprehensive Approach to Income Measurement   569
Alternative Titles and Formats   571
Key Elements of the Corporate Income Statement   571
■ FOR YOUR INFORMATION: An Income Statement With a
Northern Accent   572
■ SPOTLIGHT ON ETHICS: Fully "Inflated" Earnings Per Share   577
Corporate Income Taxes   577
Statement of Stockholders' Equity   580
Statement of Stockholders' Equity Illustrated   580
Prior Period Adjustments   581
Appropriations of Retained Earnings   582
**Analyzing Corporate Common Stocks as Potential Investments: The Price-
Earnings and Market Price to Book Value Ratios**   583
Price-Earnings Ratio   583
Market Price to Book Value Ratio   585
■ FOR YOUR INFORMATION: Market Price vs. Book Value   586
Summary   588
Glossary   589
■ DECISION CASE   589
Questions   590

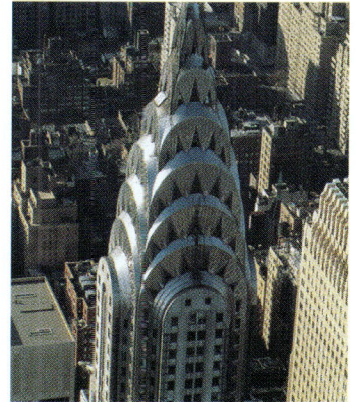

Exercises 591
Problem Set A 596
Problem Set B 600
Cases 603
Projects 605

CHAPTER 14 INTERCORPORATE INVESTMENTS AND ACCOUNTING FOR INTERNATIONAL OPERATIONS 607

Learning Objectives 607
■ FOCUS ON DECISION MAKING: LBOs and CPAs 608
Intercorporate Investments 609
■ FOR YOUR INFORMATION: Golden Parachutes and White Knights 610
    Intercorporate Investments: Key Information Needs of Decision Makers 610
    Accounting for Intercorporate Investments 612
■ FOR YOUR INFORMATION: Missing the Mark in the Mark-to-Market Debate 619
    Intercorporate Investments, Other Issues 624
Accounting for International Operations 627
    Realized Gains and Losses on Currency Exchange 628
    Unrealized Gains and Losses on Currency Exchange 630
■ FOR YOUR INFORMATION: International Ethics and Internal Controls 631
    Consolidation of Foreign Subsidiaries 631
    Financial Disclosures for International Operations 632
Summary 632
Glossary 633
■ DECISION CASE 634
Questions 634
Exercises 635
Problem Set A 640
Problem Set B 644
Cases 647
Projects 649

CHAPTER 15 PARTNERSHIPS AND PROPRIETORSHIPS 651

Learning Objectives 651
■ FOCUS ON DECISION MAKING: Sinking Partner-Ships 652
Partnerships 653
    Characteristics of Partnerships 653
■ FOR YOUR INFORMATION: Owning a (Small) Piece of the Boston Celtics 654
    Accounting for the Owners' Equity of a Partnership 655
■ FOR YOUR INFORMATION: A Partnership Gone Sour: The Sad Story of Claude and Harry 657
Proprietorships 668
    Proprietorships: Accounting on a "No Frills" Budget 668
    Accounting for the Ownership Interests of Proprietorships 668
■ FOR YOUR INFORMATION: International Opportunities for Small Businesses: Advice from the Accounting Profession 670
Summary 671
Glossary 672

■ DECISION CASE   672
Questions   673
Exercises   674
Problem Set A   678
Problem Set B   682
Cases   686
Projects   687

PART VI   ANALYSIS OF ACCOUNTING DATA   689

CHAPTER 16   STATEMENT OF CASH FLOWS   690

Learning Objectives   690
■ FOCUS ON DECISION MAKING: Slow Cash Flow: Common Nemesis of the
Rapidly Growing Small Company   691
Financial Decision Making and Cash-Flow Data   692
No Cash, No Company: The Case of W. T. Grant Company   692
Statement No. 95 to the Rescue   692
Principal Uses of the Statement of Cash Flows   692
The Statement of Cash Flows: A Closer Look   694
The Statement of Cash Flows: Two Examples   694
Three Major Types of Business Activities and Related Cash Flows   697
Direct Method vs. Indirect Method of Preparing a Statement of Cash Flows   699
■ FOR YOUR INFORMATION: A TAD Here and a TAD There Adds Up to Real
Cash   700
Indirect Method of Preparing a Statement of Cash Flows   700
Source of Data for a Statement of Cash Flows   700
Determining Cash Flows from Operating Activities: The Indirect Method   701
Determining Cash Flows from Investing and Financing Activities: The Indirect
Method   707
Cherokee Station, Inc.: The Indirect Method of Preparing a Statement of Cash
Flows   707
Direct Method of Preparing a Statement of Cash Flows   709
Determining Cash Flows from Operating Activities: The Direct Method   711
Determining Cash Flows from Investing and Financing Activities: The Direct
Method   712
Cherokee Station, Inc.: The Direct Method of Preparing a Statement of Cash
Flows   712
■ FOR YOUR INFORMATION: Cash Flows: To Report or Not to Report   713
Interpreting Cash-Flow Information   715
Comparative Analysis of an Entity's Cash Flows   715
Computing and Interpreting Cash Flow Per Share   717
■ SPOTLIGHT ON ETHICS: In Our Employees We Trust: Safeguarding Cash in a
Small Business   719
Summary   720
Glossary   721
■ DECISION CASE   722
Questions   722
Exercises   724
Problem Set A   728

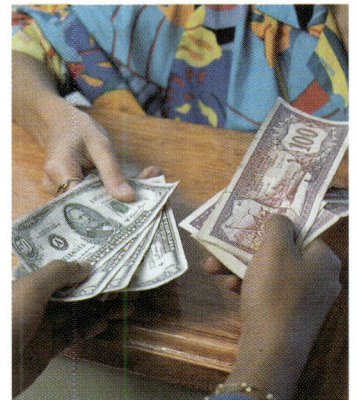

Problem Set B   733
Cases   738
Projects   740

CHAPTER 17   FINANCIAL STATEMENT ANALYSIS   742

Learning Objectives   742
■ FOCUS ON DECISION MAKING: Too-Good-to-Be True Financial Statements Are
    Usually Too Good to Be True   743
Financial Statement Analysis: Making Informed Economic Decisions   744
    Objectives of Financial Statement Analysis   744
    Information Sources for Financial Statement Analysis   745
■ SPOTLIGHT ON ETHICS: On-Line, Real-Time Financial Fraud   746
Analytical Techniques   747
    Trend Analysis   747
    Common-Sized Financial Statements   749
    Ratio Analysis   753
Assessing Earnings Quality   760
■ FOR YOUR INFORMATION: Guilders to GAAP   761
    Factors Influencing Earnings Quality   761
    Measures to Use in Assessing Earnings Quality   762
■ FOR YOUR INFORMATION: A Random Walk through the Stock Market   764
Summary   765
Glossary   765
■ DECISION CASE   766
Questions   767
Exercises   768
Problem Set A   773
Problem Set B   778
Cases   783
Projects   785

APPENDIX: MICHAELS STORES INC. ANNUAL REPORT   A-1

Glossary   G-1

Company Index   I-1

Subject Index   I-4

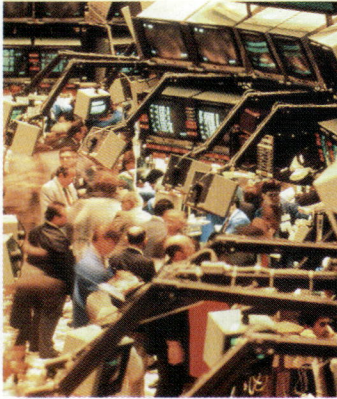

Preface

George Bernard Shaw once observed that all progress stems from the efforts of unreasonable individuals. Why? Because reasonable individuals make do with the status quo, while unreasonable individuals insist on change, on trying something new and, in doing so, accepting some risk of failure and embarrassment. Over the past few years, I came to the conclusion that there was a need for a different type of financial accounting textbook despite the fact that several rigorous and challenging financial textbooks have been available for quite some time. So, being a bit unreasonable and a bit stubborn, I set about writing that textbook. Here in your hands is the result.

THE ELUSIVE "USER" ORIENTATION

If you have been in the market for an introductory financial accounting textbook in recent years, you have certainly been peppered with the term "user orientation" by textbook sales reps. Each successive new book in this market or revision of an existing book touts itself as having a strong user orientation. Although seldom defined explicitly, the phrase "user orientation" typically implies that a financial accounting textbook downplays the procedural facets of accounting while emphasizing how accounting data can and should be used. In the olden days, textbook authors viewed accounting as an end in itself. But, clearly, an organization's accounting function is simply a means to an end, and that end is superior economic decisions. In my view, then, the key defining feature of a "user orientation" is the recognition that an organization's accounting function is a service activity designed to facilitate the economic decisions of parties both internal and external to that organization.

Few of us would disagree that a user orientation is appropriate for an introductory financial accounting course. The catch here is that you will find little agreement among financial accounting textbook authors on how to operationalize a user orientation. At the risk of oversimplification, it appears that there are two general strategies textbook authors in this market have taken to convince instructors (potential adopters) that their textbooks are truly user-oriented. An approach taken by many existing textbooks has been to retain a basic procedural, or preparer, orientation in covering the major topical areas in accounting. For example, if the topic is receivables, these textbooks will focus their coverage on the three, or five, or whatever major accounting procedures related to that item. While doing so, these textbooks typically blend in repeated "real world" examples: "Oh, by the way, Acme Supply reported total receivables of $4 billion in its most recent balance sheet compared to only $1.5 billion reported by its major competitor, Discount Suppliers." Although these examples are often at least marginally interesting, they generally do not provide students with insight on how accounting data can be, or should be, put to effective use.

A second general strategy for implementing a user orientation in a financial accounting textbook is to simply avoid any references to bookkeeping terminology. Authors adopting this strategy perceive that the true culprits in the procedural approach to teaching financial accounting are those deadly terms "debit" and "credit." The rationale here is that a book that downplays bookkeeping terminology, by definition, must be user-oriented or, at least, nonprocedural. These textbooks also tend to be oriented around the principal activities of a business entity—operating, financing, and investing. Although there are clearly advantages to this organizational scheme, one key disadvantage is a lack of coherence. If you review these textbooks, you will find that coverage of accounting issues related to major financial statement items is spread over a series of chapters. The result is that at semester-end students may have a good understanding of how business organizations operate, but they often do not have a coherent knowledge of key accounting issues.

ORIENTING FOCUS OF THIS TEXT

This textbook has a coherent theme interwoven throughout all seventeen chapters. My purpose in this textbook is to demonstrate to students how accounting data can and should be used by decision makers to make better, or at least more informed, economic decisions. This theme is operationalized in several ways and on several levels. To integrate a true decision-making orientation in an introductory financial accounting course, I believe it is necessary to take a top-down approach to covering accounting issues. Part I of this textbook provides students with a thorough understanding of the purpose of the accounting function, key accounting concepts, and how an organization's accounting function operates. In the remaining five parts of this book, students are frequently reminded of the accounting fundamentals that they were introduced to in Part I. The conceptual foundation built for students by Part I allows them to better grasp the reasoning and purpose underlying specific accounting rules discussed in subsequent chapters.

Throughout Parts II through VI of this textbook the decision-making theme is reinforced by continually focusing students' attention on how and why accounting data are needed by decision makers. Each chapter begins with a Focus on Decision Making vignette, which typically presents an explicit decision-making scenario in which accounting data are relevant. Likewise, each chapter ends with a Decision Case that requires students to analyze a decision context involving accounting data. Numerous anecdotes involving "real world" examples are also integrated into each chapter. Rather than oblique references to factual situations or financial statement data, these anecdotes typically describe situations in which accounting data are developed and/or used for a specific purpose by decision makers.

Two additional facets of the decision-making theme of this textbook are an emphasis on ethical issues related to the development and use of accounting data and the integration of international accounting issues into coverage of key accounting topics. As you are well aware, accountants and the individuals who use accounting data are often faced with ethical dilemmas. By making students aware of such dilemmas and their proper resolution they will be better prepared to face such situations in their own professional careers. Recent decades have witnessed an ever increasing trend toward multinational business organizations. To fully appreciate how decision-making contexts and related accounting issues are complicated by this trend, students must be acquainted with the often significant differences in accounting and financial reporting rules around the globe.

A final facet of the decision-making theme of this textbook is an emphasis on internal control issues. Most introductory financial accounting textbooks focus little attention on internal control issues. However, an organization's accounting function is actually one component—one major component—of an overall control structure used by management to monitor an organization's activities, safeguard its assets, and provide for reliable financial records. Both decision makers internal and external to an organization have an interest in the organization's internal controls. For example, departmental managers must establish internal controls to safeguard the assets in their areas of responsibility. Investors, on the other hand, recognize that an organization's operating results can be significantly influenced by the reliability of its internal controls. In each chapter of this textbook, students are introduced to internal control concepts and how these concepts articulate with related accounting issues.

ORGANIZATION AND CONTENT

This textbook is organized into six parts. As mentioned previously, Part I introduces students to fundamental accounting issues and concepts. Particularly important in this series of three chapters is Chapter 2, "Accounting Concepts and Elements." This chapter acquaints students with the basic elements of financial statements, the key features of the FASB's conceptual framework, and fundamental accounting concepts, such as the entity concept and the historical cost principle. Chapter 2 provides students with a coherent conceptual foundation that allows them to quickly grasp the nature of accounting issues and the purpose of the accounting rules introduced in subsequent chapters.

Part II presents another series of three chapters, Chapters 4 through 6. The role of these chapters is to acquaint students with the methods used by accountants to collect, process, summarize, and report financial data. With tongue-in-cheek apologies to those pure nonprocedural or antiprocedural types, Part II makes extensive use of such terms as debit, credit, journals, and ledgers. In my view, the primary responsibility of college-level instructors in business programs is to develop future leaders for the business world. Clearly, accounting majors have a need to understand the mechanics of double-entry bookkeeping that form the backbone of practically every modern organization's accounting system. But, just as important, nonaccounting majors who aspire to be marketing experts, human resource specialists, and chief executive officers should be familiar with the mechanical features of an accounting system if they are to assume leadership roles in their future organizations. For example, a sales manager who understands how accounting data are processed and summarized is much better equipped to stand his or her ground in meetings in which accounting data are being bandied about.

A unique feature of my coverage of the double-entry accounting system is the presentation of the entire accounting cycle in one chapter, Chapter 5. The last chapter of Part I, Chapter 3, provides students an introduction to the logic, purpose, and structure of accounting systems. Chapter 4 then presents students with an overview of double-entry accounting rules. Included in Chapter 4 is a section containing eight "real world" journal entries. This section discusses actual transactions of large public companies in recent years and illustrates a unique format that students can use to analyze such transactions and then develop appropriate journal entries. Next, Chapter 5 provides students with a comprehensive overview of the accounting cycle for a small business. Chapter 6, the final chapter of Part II, discusses accounting and control issues unique to merchandising companies. This chapter also introduces students to financial statement analysis by discussing financial ratios that can be used to interpret a merchandiser's financial statements.

Parts III through V discuss accounting issues related to assets, liabilities, and owners' equity, respectively. Yes, this is a conventional organizational scheme for the main body of a financial accounting text. However, a unique intra-chapter organizational scheme is used in these chapters to articulate the decision-making theme of this textbook. The coverage of each major topical area in these chapters, such as inventory and current liabilities, is structured around a five-point organizational scheme. First, a brief introductory section acquaints students with the financial statement item, including key terms related to that item. Next, the key information needs of decision makers regarding the specific item are presented and discussed. This section is particularly critical to establishing a true decision-making orientation for a financial accounting textbook. Before discussing accounting rules and procedures related to receivables, long-term liabilities, and so on, students are reminded that the function of accounting is to provide useful information to decision makers. Focusing students' attention on users' information needs for a financial statement item *before* discussing the relevant accounting rules allows students to better appreciate the purpose of those rules and causes them to be less likely to perceive those rules as arbitrary or capricious.

The third element of coverage for each major financial statement item presented in Parts III through V is a discussion of key accounting rules and procedures for that item. Immediately following this discussion, financial ratios and other analytical techniques related to the given item are discussed and illustrated. For example, after students learn how accounting data are processed for inventory, they are immediately exposed to methods for interpreting that data for decision-making purposes. For inventory, these methods include the computation of the inventory turnover ratio and the age of inventory. This organizational scheme reinforces that the processing of accounting data is not an end in itself but instead a means to an end, namely, the provision of accounting data that are useful to decision makers. The final element of coverage for each major financial statement item in Parts III through V is a discussion of relevant internal control issues and procedures.

Part VI contains two chapters. Chapter 16 provides a comprehensive discussion of the statement of cash flows, while Chapter 17 presents an integrative treatment of financial statement analysis. Although the comprehensive cash flow chapter is presented late in the textbook, the statement of cash flows is discussed at several points in earlier chapters. For example, Chapter 2 discusses the nature and structure of the statement of cash flows. That chapter also compares and contrasts the purpose of the statement of cash flows with the income statement and identifies the key information available in a statement of cash flows that is not available from an income statement. Likewise, the Decision Case at the end of Chapter 5 requires students to complete a statement of cash flows for a small business.

Chapter 17 provides students with a review of the key financial ratios discussed in earlier chapters and introduces them to additional techniques that can be used to analyze financial statement data. This chapter illustrates a comprehensive approach to financial statement analysis by dissecting the financial statements of a hardware retailer.

SPECIFIC PEDAGOGICAL FEATURES

This textbook contains a series of pedagogical features designed to facilitate the learning process for introductory financial accounting students. Among these features are the following:

Learning Objectives   The opening page of each chapter profiles a list of key learning objectives. Each objective is repeated at the appropriate point within the margins of a chapter. Additionally, the learning objective or objectives associated with each end-of-chapter exercise and problem are identified parenthetically following the title of the item.

Focus on Decision Making Vignette   As mentioned previously, each chapter begins with a vignette presenting a decision-making context in which accounting data are relevant. This vignette for Chapter 8 is entitled "Managing Inventory: Cabbage Patch Kids, Hot Wheels, and the Corporate Accountant." Discussed within this vignette are techniques used by accountants to help corporate executives better manage their organization's inventory.

Decision Cases   Each chapter concludes with a Decision Case that requires students to analyze a decision scenario involving accounting data. The Decision Case for Chapter 6 requires students to consider a scenario involving the company that developed and patented AZT, the drug used to combat AIDS-related symptoms. The key issue in that Decision Case is whether corporations have an obligation to publicly disclose accounting data used in arriving at pricing decisions for their goods and services.

For Your Information Vignettes   Each chapter contains one or more of these vignettes. These boxed inserts present unique methods of applying accounting methods and discussions of controversial accounting issues, among other topics. There are two types of For Your Information vignettes: general (identified by a city icon) and international, which focus exclusively on international accounting issues (identified by a globe icon). Examples of For Your Information vignettes include "The Balance Sheet: Going Dutch" found in Chapter 2, "Goodwill with an Attitude" in Chapter 9, and in Chapter 14 "International Ethics and Internal Controls."

Spotlight on Ethics Vignettes   Most chapters contain a Spotlight on Ethics vignette, which presents a real-world situation involving an ethical dilemma or issue typically related to the use, preparation, or interpretation of accounting data. Among these vignettes are "Rocky Mount Accounting Horror" (Chapter 8), "Payroll Padding—A Case of Dodger Blue" (Chapter 10), and "Fully 'Inflated' Earnings Per Share" (Chapter 13).

Summary   A chapter-ending summary provides a concise overview of the key topics presented in each chapter.

Glossary   A glossary at the end of each chapter defines the key terms introduced in the chapter.

Assignment Materials   The assignment materials for each chapter consist of five types of items: questions, exercises, two parallel problem sets, cases, and projects. The overriding decision-making theme articulated within the text is carried through to the assignment materials. In each chapter, many assignment items specifically require students to apply or relate what they have learned to a decision-making context involving accounting data. The assignment materials in each chapter also require students to address internal control issues; ethical issues related to the use, preparation, or interpretation of accounting data; and international accounting issues. To enhance the realism of the assignment materials, many of the factual backgrounds for individual items are drawn from the annual reports of public companies and other factual sources.

We have all come to recognize in recent years the need for business students to develop strong communication skills. Given this need, numerous items in each chapter's assignment materials include a written or oral communication component. The assignment materials also provide instructors with an opportunity to hone their students' computer skills. Spreadsheet software accompanying this text can be used to solve selected items in the assignment materials of each chapter. Finally, at least one project in each chapter's assignment materials is a group or team project.

To assist instructors in identifying assignment materials containing specific features, icons are included in the page margins of these materials. Icons are provided for the following specific types of assignment items:

those involving ethical issues,

those that involve an international accounting issue,

those that can be solved with the use of the textbook's spreadsheet software, and

team project assignments.

Because of the large number of assignment items that contain communication components and/or real-world financial data, icons are not provided for those items.

Annotations   A four-part series of annotations is provided in the *Annotated Instructor's Edition* as additional reference material to assist instructors in developing lecture notes for each chapter. These annotations were written by Carol Knapp of the University of Central Oklahoma. Following are the specific types of annotations and a brief description of each. All appear in the margins in blue.

Teaching Notes: Interesting or unusual ways to emphasize key material or points included in the textbook.

Focus on Ethics: Questions or points that instructors can pose to students to make then consider the ethical dimensions of accounting practices or ethical issues related to the use of accounting data.

Real World: Interesting points relating to accounting practices or real world examples of how accounting data are used.

Discussion Questions: Questions that instructors can pose to students to stimulate in-class discussion of key issues or topics from the text.

Also included in the *Annotated Instructor's Edition* are check figures, which present answers for all numerical end-of-chapter exercises and problems. These too appear in the margin in blue.

SUPPLEMENTS

Accompanying this textbook is a broad array of supplemental materials designed with the needs of both instructors and students in mind. Following is a brief description of each supplement.

Supplements for the Instructor

Instructor's Manual   This supplement, prepared by Carol Hitzfelder of Austin Community College, contains a listing of key terms introduced in each chapter and lecture outlines for each chapter. Also included in the *Instructor's Manual* is a table indicating the level of difficulty of each end-of-chapter assignment item, solutions to the Decision Case, questions, cases, and projects at the end of each chapter, and transparency masters that can be integrated into the lectures for each chapter.

Solutions Manual   Contained in the *Solutions Manual* are complete solutions to each exercise and problem in the text and a copy of the check figures for these items. The *Solutions Manual* was developed from solutions materials provided by the following individuals: Christine Schalow, CSU–San Bernadino; Dennis O'Reilly, University of South Carolina; Julia Higgs, University of South Carolina; John Reisch, University of South Carolina; Sheila Ammons, Austin Community College; Carol Hitzfelder, Austin Community College; and Barb Muller, ASU–West.

Test Bank   Sue Atkinson of Tarleton State University prepared the test bank which contains over one thousand multiple choice questions, short exercises, and discussion questions with accompanying solutions.

WesTest   This supplement is a computerized version of the multiple choice and short exercise portions of the hard copy test bank. WesTest includes edit and word processing features that allow test customization through the addition, deletion, or scrambling of test items.

Astound™   This software package contains a series of electronic transparencies for each chapter that allows instructors to make efficient and effective classroom presentations of text material. This supplement was developed by David Vicknair of Rockhurst College. *Transparency Masters* will be available from this package, as well.

Videos   This text is accompanied by a wide selection of videos that illustrate financial accounting concepts and issues.

Video Guide   This guide provides a brief overview of each available video segment, indicates segment length, discusses each segment's key points, and provides questions for classroom discussion related to each segment.

Supplements for Students

Study Guide   Lola Dudley of Eastern Illinois University prepared this supplement, which contains chapter learning objectives, chapter overviews, detailed notes for each chapter, and self-test questions.

Practice Set   The Island Nuts practice set, written by Diane Adcox of the University of North Florida, requires students to complete a monthly accounting cycle for a small business.

Student Solutions Manual   This student supplement, prepared from the instructor's solutions manual, provides complete solutions to alternate end-of-chapter exercises and problems.

Insights: Readings in Financial Accounting This readings book developed by Carol Knapp, University of Central Oklahoma, and Michael C. Knapp, is available for those faculty who wish to supplement text assignments with articles that discuss contemporary issues in financial accounting and the related business environment.

Working Papers Workpaper templates, prepared by Carol Knapp, are provided for the problem assignments within each chapter. These templates include preprinted headings identifying the name of the company and/or the title of the financial statement or other item to be completed.

Spreadsheet Templates for Financial Accounting Prepared by Bill Cummings of Northern Illinois University, this package allows students to use Lotus 1–2–3 for Windows to solve many end-of-chapter assignment items (which are identified with the computer disk icon).

Student Notetaking Guide This unique supplement includes copies of the transparencies provided to instructors. These transparencies are printed at 50 percent of normal size which provides space for students to take lecture notes. Detailed lecture outlines are also provided.

Financial Accounting: Issues and Cases This casebook, authored by Michael C. Knapp, contains twelve cases addressing important financial accounting issues. Topics covered in these cases include, among others, ethics, internal controls, and controversial accounting rules adopted in recent years.

ESL Supplement Prepared by Luis Guillen, this supplement includes a Spanish glossary of the key terms introduced in the text and is designed to aid those students for whom English is a second language.

REVIEWERS

I would like to thank each and every reviewer for their hard work, insight, and patience. So many times in reading review comments a recurring thought would pop into mind, namely, "Why didn't I think of that." Again, a heartfelt thanks to each of you.

Brian Nagle
Duquesne University

Catherine Craycraft
University of New Hampshire

John Reisch
University of South Carolina

Edward Goodhart
Shippensburg University

Christine Schalow
California State University—San Bernadino

Rene Manes
Florida State University

Johanna Lyle
Kansas State University

Robert Norman West
University of Virginia

Sue Atkinson
Tarleton State University

Marcia Niles
University of Idaho

Julia Higgs
University of South Carolina

George Sanders
University of Miami

Arnold Cirtin
Ball State University

Ken Coffey
Johnson County Community College

Sharon Walters
Morehead State University

Larry Falcetto
Emporia State College

Elliott Levy
Bentley College

Neal Ushman
Santa Clara University

Irving Mason
Herkimer County Community College

Charles T. Andrews
Cal Poly State University-San Luis Obispo

Bill Cummings
Northern Illinois University

Marcia Halvorsen
University of Cincinnati

Jane Campbell
Kennesaw State College

Joanne Rockness
University of North Carolina-Wilmington

Cathy Pitts
Highline Community College

Chandra Schorg
Texas Woman's University

Douglas Sharp
Wichita State University

Joyce C. Lambert
University of New Orleans

Vicki Rymer
University of Maryland

Linda Wade
Tarleton State University

Dean Wallace
Collin County Community College

D'Arcy Becker
University of New Mexico

Michael Akers
Marquette University

Bob DeFilippis
Fairleigh Dickinson University

Joann Noe Cross
University of Wisconsin—Oshkosh

David B. Vicknair
Rockhurst College

T. Sterling Wetzel
Oklahoma State University

Eric Carlsen
Kean College of New Jersey

Barbara Theisen
Oakland University

Vince Guide
Clemson University

Leon Hanouille
Syracuse University

Frank Gersich
Gustavus Adolphus College

Mary Alice Seville
Oregon State University

Emeka Ofobike
University of Akron

Marilyn Okleshen
Mankato State University

Ron Huefner
State University of New York—
    Buffalo

James Makofske
Fresno City College

ACKNOWLEDGEMENTS

I would like to thank all of those people who have contributed so significantly to the development and writing of this book. First, I greatly appreciate the encouragement of the wonderful folks at West Publishing. Rick Leyh, executive editor, is a tough taskmaster but thoroughly understands and constantly rises to the challenges posed by the dynamic business of college textbook publishing. Thanks also to the ever-vigilant and resourceful Deanna Quinn, my production editor. The humor, patience, and kindness of the two developmental editors who worked on this project, Cathy Story and Jessica Evans, are also greatly appreciated. I am also very grateful to Ann Hillstrom, my promotions editor, Joan Torkildson, my copyeditor, and Richard Baker, my permissions editor. To the compositor, artists, photo researcher and many other individuals who contributed to this book, I offer a collective thank you.

I have already mentioned the supplement authors, but now I extend a personal "Thanks" to them for their hard work and dedication. One ancillary author deserves special mention, my wife, Carol Knapp. Not only did Carol do an excellent job on several of the ancillaries, she also patiently endured my occasional panic attacks and was always there to offer a word of encouragement when I most needed it. Thanks Carol Ann. In the spirit of the Academy Awards, please allow me to also thank the three generations of the Knapp family who are so special to me. Big Bill Knapp and Orebel DeBurger Knapp taught me the satisfaction of a hard day's work and a job well done. Thanks to my three sisters, Paula, Suzy, and Becky, each of whom is a legend on the long-gone six-on-six basketball courts of Garvin County, Oklahoma. And, finally, thanks to my three kids, John William, Lindsay Suzanne, and Jessica Leigh. A 19th century Frenchman, Henri Amiel, said it best: "Blessed be childhood, which brings down something of heaven into the midst of our rough earthliness."

Michael C. (Chris) Knapp

I

ACCOUNTING FUNDAMENTALS

You begin your study of accounting in this textbook by becoming better acquainted with the accounting discipline. "Just who are accountants and what do they do?" is an informal title that could be applied to this opening series of chapters that includes Chapters 1 through 3. More specifically, Chapter 1 provides a brief overview of the historical development of accounting and discusses the important role of the accounting profession in our modern society. Chapter 1 also acquaints you with the two major segments of the accounting profession, private accounting and public accounting, and the specific job roles and responsibilities that accountants assume. An analysis of problems and challenges facing the accounting profession as it prepares for the next century is the final topic of the opening chapter.

Chapter 2 discusses the fundamental concepts, elements, and issues that are central to the accounting discipline. This chapter begins with an overview of the key objectives of accounting and financial reporting. Next, the four basic financial statements are discussed and illustrated. Chapter 2 also identifies the key attributes that accounting information should possess and the basic conceptual principles that underlie accounting rules and procedures. This opening series of chapters concludes with Chapter 3, which presents an introduction to accounting information systems and internal control issues and concepts. By first studying accounting systems and internal control, you will find it much easier to grasp the procedural aspects of recording and reporting accounting information that are discussed in later chapters.

AN INTRODUCTION TO ACCOUNTING

LEARNING OBJECTIVES

After studying this chapter, you should be able to do the following:

1. Provide a brief overview of the historical development of the accounting profession

2. Define the societal role of accounting

3. Identify the primary means used by accountants to communicate financial information to decision makers

4. Discuss the problems that may result when organizations are allowed to use improper accounting methods

5. Define the nature, structure, and major segments of the accounting profession

6. Identify the accounting profession's principal regulatory bodies

7. Discuss important changes presently taking place within the accounting profession

Getting the facts is the key to good decision making. Every mistake that I made came because I didn't take the time. I didn't drive hard enough. I wasn't smart enough to get the facts.

Charles F. Knight, Chief Executive Officer, Emerson Electric Company

Accounting and the Allocation of Scarce Economic Resources

To make rational economic decisions, a decision maker must have good information. A nine-year-old, freckle-faced baseball card collector obtains that information from *Beckett Baseball Card Monthly*, the nationally recognized price quotation source for sports cards. For meteorologists attempting to predict the exact time and point of landfall of an approaching hurricane, the data supplied by weather satellites, hurricane-tracking aircraft, and computer simulations are invaluable. In the business world, the quality of decisions made by corporate executives depends largely upon the relevance and reliability of the information supplied to them by their accountants.

Take the case of Jackpot Enterprises, Inc., a Nevada-based company that owns and operates several casinos. Jackpot's management must decide how much of the square footage of each casino to devote to roulette, slot machines, blackjack, and other games of chance. Additionally, the company's executives must decide the betting limits of its table games and denominations of its slot machines. If a casino's principal clientele is represented by Grandpa Sam and Grandma Suzie from Peoria, Illinois, then it will want to have few, if any, "high roller" blackjack tables and slot machines. Like all major gaming companies, Jackpot has a sophisticated accounting information system that collects a wide range of data needed by executives to make critical resource allocation decisions. A recent financial report issued by Jackpot explains how the firm's accounting information system collects and processes data needed by management to develop and then evaluate a casino's slot machine placement strategy. Following is a brief excerpt from this discussion.

> Before the installation of gaming machines at new locations, careful analysis of the location is performed. Comparison with other locations based on demographic data and trends, potential revenues and the experience of Jackpot's own personnel are considered and used to determine the type and denomination of gaming machines that would be most appropriate for that location. After the machines have been installed, Jackpot's computerized data processing system enables management to monitor results to determine the optimum mix of gaming machines so as to enhance customer satisfaction [and, more important, profits!].[1]

The managers of every organization must continually make decisions regarding how to utilize scarce economic resources. These decisions ultimately determine which companies are successful and which companies wind up in the corporate graveyard. The key scarce resource for Jackpot Enterprises and other casino companies is the square footage available for their gaming operations. Portfolio managers of The China Fund, a large mutual fund traded on the New York Stock Exchange, must decide in which companies in the People's Republic of China they will invest the capital entrusted to them by thousands of investors. Executives of General Motors must decide how much of the company's large, but limited, manufacturing capacity should be devoted to the production of Camaros, Corvettes, and other GM models. Business executives make these important resource allocation decisions only after they have spent untold hours studying data supplied to them by their accountants. Even the most skilled and insightful managers will find profits elusive if they do not have access to relevant and reliable accounting data.

---

1. Recent annual report of Jackpot Enterprises, Inc.

This chapter provides you with an introduction to the accounting profession. Chapter 1 begins with a brief overview of the historical development of the accounting profession. By becoming familiar with the origins of accounting, you can better appreciate and understand the purpose of the profession. Next, this chapter discusses the nature of accounting, with a particular emphasis on the societal role of the accounting profession and the related responsibilities of accountants. The serious consequences that abusive or "creative" accounting can have for individual business entities and for the economy, as a whole, is discussed as well. Also included in this chapter are examples of work roles in accounting, descriptions of the two major segments of the profession, and a brief introduction to the major regulatory bodies that oversee the profession. This chapter concludes with a discussion of several changes the accounting profession has been undergoing in recent years and important challenges it faces in coming years.

Discussion Question
Ask students what they use accounting information for in their personal lives.
Answer: Financial information is needed to apply for student loans and to file income tax returns.

THE HISTORICAL DEVELOPMENT OF ACCOUNTING

Financial recordkeeping, in one form or another, has existed for thousands of years. However, the origins of modern accounting can be traced to a mathematics book written in 1494 by **Luca Pacioli,**[2] a Franciscan monk who lived in what is now present-day Italy. Pacioli was a mathematics scholar and a close friend of Leonardo da Vinci. As a favor to local merchants, Pacioli included in his book a section on the mechanics of **double-entry bookkeeping,** a financial recordkeeping system that had been used for several decades in and around Venice.

Pacioli did not invent or claim to invent the "Method of Venice." Nevertheless, his book did formalize and document this recordkeeping system. This system allowed merchants to maintain financial records that summarized the operating results and financial condition of their businesses in a logical and easily understood manner. More important, double-entry bookkeeping permitted merchants to make more informed and timely decisions regarding their business affairs. Economic historians attribute the rapid spread of commerce across Europe during the sixteenth century in large part to the availability of this recordkeeping system. Five hundred years following the publication of Pacioli's book, double-entry bookkeeping serves as the backbone of accounting systems worldwide.

■ **LEARNING OBJECTIVE 1**
Provide a brief overview of the historical development of the accounting profession

Luca Pacioli

double-entry bookkeeping

Double-Entry Bookkeeping and the Laws of Physics

The key underlying premise of double-entry bookkeeping is related to a fundamental law of physics: for every action there is an equal and opposite reaction. You will discover that applying this natural law to bookkeeping is a bit of a stretch at times. Nevertheless, financial transactions are recorded as if they consist of two equal and opposite effects. A brief example may be helpful. Consider a purchase made by Chrysler Corporation from one of its suppliers. Assume that Chrysler purchases on credit $1,000 of supplies from Office Depot. From Chrysler's perspective, this transaction can be reduced to two parts: (1) the company obtains assets valued at $1,000; (2) the company assumes a liability or debt in the same amount. Action . . . reaction.

---

2. The first time that a substantive reference is made to a key term, that term is boldfaced in the text and in the margin. At the end of each chapter is a glossary of key terms introduced in the chapter.

Luca Pacioli was a mathematics scholar who collaborated with his friend, Leonardo da Vinci, on a mathematics text in the late 15th century. In 1494, Pacioli authored another mathematics text. As a favor to local merchants, Pacioli included a discussion of double-entry bookkeeping techniques in this text.

Discussion Question
Ask students to think of other examples of the "dual" nature of financial transactions.
Suggestions: Pay tuition and fees/receive education; work at a part-time job/receive paycheck.

Another example? What about a personal transaction that each of us makes periodically? When you purchase a set of tires, that transaction can be reduced to two components: (1) you give up a certain amount of cash; (2) you obtain a set of tires having a retail value equal to the cash you paid to acquire them.

Every transaction, regardless of how large or small, can be reduced by an accountant to two equal effects expressed in dollars. If a company properly records the dual nature of each of its transactions, the entity's financial records will be "in balance" at any given point in time. Failure to apply the basic premise of double-entry bookkeeping results in an "unbalanced" set of financial records. Many weary accountants have invested long and tedious overtime hours attempting to balance a set of accounting records. This frustrating exercise is very similar to reconciling your checkbook balance with your month-end bank statement balance when you have failed to record certain checks or deposits.

The Evolution of Accounting Systems

Double-entry bookkeeping provided businesses in the Middle Ages with a systematic method to record financial data. However, in addition to a basic financial record-keeping system, these early businesses needed somewhere to record their financial transactions. At some point in the history of accounting, journals and ledgers were developed to meet this need. Journals and ledgers are financial diaries in which businesses and other organizations record their transactions. In subsequent chapters, we discuss journals and ledgers at length.

Before the Industrial Revolution of the eighteenth century, accounting systems were quite simple. Most business enterprises prior to the eighteenth century were small and engaged in only a few types of routine transactions. The Industrial Revolution resulted in much larger businesses and a wider array of business transactions, which led to a need for more elaborate accounting systems. In today's business world, huge companies such as Exxon, Microsoft, and General Electric spend millions of dollars each year to process and record their transactions. Recently, an accounting executive of Citicorp, a large bank based in New York City, estimated his firm would spend approximately $3 million to implement the requirements of just one new accounting standard.[3] As you can imagine, the enormous volume of transactions engaged in by large companies and the geographical dispersion of their operating units mandates that computers be an integral part of their accounting systems.

Generally Accepted Accounting Principles: The Rules of the Game

Double-entry bookkeeping provides the foundation upon which modern accounting is based. Since Pacioli's time, successive generations of accountants have developed a series of rules, guidelines, and concepts that are helpful in applying double-entry bookkeeping to the task of recording and reporting financial information. These rules, guidelines, and concepts are known collectively as **generally accepted accounting principles.** Accountants use the acronym GAAP to refer to these basic accounting principles. Notice the term "generally accepted." Most accounting principles have become established by general acceptance or usage over time.

generally accepted accounting principles

Accounting rules developed over a period of several centuries on an industry-by-industry basis. For example, one set of accounting rules became generally accepted, or widely used, by merchants, while another set of accounting rules became generally accepted within the shipbuilding industry. Even today, there are significant differences in how similar transactions are recorded within different industries. In fact, companies within the same industry do not necessarily use the same accounting rules.

The lack of uniformity in accounting rules is a common criticism directed at the accounting profession. A prominent accountant of the twentieth century, Carman Blough, was a particularly vocal critic of the lack of uniformity in accounting principles. While serving during the 1930s as the chief accountant of the Securities and Exchange Commission, an important regulatory body in the accounting profession, Blough commented on this issue.

Discussion Question
Ask students why uniformity in accounting rules is needed. Answer: Uniformity enhances comparability and, hence, the informativeness of financial statements.

> An examination of hundreds of statements filed with our Commission leads one to the conclusion that aside from simple rules of double-entry bookkeeping, there are very few principles of accounting upon which the accountants in this country are in agreement.[4]

Eventually, the accounting profession decided that allowing accounting rules to develop strictly by general acceptance was not necessarily a good idea. As a result, during the latter part of this century the development of accounting rules or standards has been guided by several rule-making bodies. Presently, the **Financial Accounting Standards Board** (FASB) is the principal rule-making authority within the accounting profession in the United States. Before the establishment of the FASB in 1973, the Accounting Principles Board and the Committee on Accounting Procedures served as the authoritative rule-making bodies in accounting for fourteen years and twenty years, respectively.

Financial Accounting Standards Board

---

3. L. Berton, "Accounting-Board Rulings Make Business See Red," *The Wall Street Journal*, 21 March 1989, A22.

4. C. G. Blough, "Need for Accounting Principles," *Accounting Review*, March 1937, 31.

THE NATURE OF ACCOUNTING: A MEANS TO AN END

Now that you have become acquainted briefly with the historical development of accounting, let us take a closer look at the nature of accounting. Most important, we want to focus on the societal role of accounting and the related responsibilities of accountants.

Defining the Societal Role of Accounting

accounting

■ LEARNING OBJECTIVE 2
Define the societal role of accounting

In 1970, the Accounting Principles Board defined **accounting** as follows:

> Accounting is a service activity. Its function is to provide quantitative information, primarily financial in nature, about economic entities that is intended to be useful in making economic decisions—in making reasoned choices among alternative courses of action.[5]

Notice that first and foremost, accounting is a service activity. Accounting is a means to an end, that end being to assist a wide variety of parties in making economic decisions. Accountants often segregate these decision makers into two groups: external and internal decision makers. External decision makers are third parties who do not have ready access to an organization's financial records or accountants since they are not members of the organization. Internal decision makers, on the other hand, are executives or employees of a given entity.

Communicating Financial Information to External Decision Makers

financial statements

■ LEARNING OBJECTIVE 3
Identify the primary means used by accountants to communicate financial information to decision makers

Teaching Note
Emphasize to students that financial statements are the end product of an accounting system. To understand a set of financial statements requires knowledge of accounting.

Financial statements are the principal means accountants use to communicate financial information to external decision makers such as investors, suppliers, and bank loan officers. Most large companies prepare an annual financial report that they distribute to the general public. Included in an appendix to this text is the annual financial report issued in 1995 by Michaels Stores, Inc., an arts and crafts retailer. Among other items, an annual financial report contains four financial statements: a balance sheet, an income statement, a statement of stockholders' equity, and a statement of cash flows. Shown in Exhibit 1.1 is a condensed income statement for Abbott Laboratories, a pharmaceuticals firm. This income statement reports that Abbott earned $1,239,057 during the year in question. That number sounds impressive enough, but notice that Abbott's income statement, like the financial statements of most large companies, is presented in thousands. Consequently, Abbott's actual net income was more than $1.2 billion!

External decision makers use financial statements as input to a wide range of decisions. These decisions include determining whether to invest in a given company, whether to extend a loan to a company, or, in the case of a regulatory authority, deciding whether a company is complying with specific governmental regulations. In Chapter 2, we examine the four financial statements in more detail.

---

5. *Statement of Accounting Principles Board No. 4*, "Basic Concepts and Accounting Principles Underlying Financial Statements of a Business Enterprise" (New York: American Institute of Certified Public Accountants, 1970), para. 40.

■ **EXHIBIT 1.1**
Recent Income Statement (in thousands) for Abbott Laboratories

Net Sales Revenues	$7,851,912
Gain on Sale of Investment	271,986
Interest and Dividend Revenue	42,250
Operating Expenses	(6,325,900)
Miscellaneous Expenses	(101,495)
Income Tax Expense	(499,696)
Net Income	$1,239,057

Large, publicly owned companies, such as Abbott Laboratories, prepare annual financial statements that are used by a wide range of decision makers including investors, creditors, and regulatory authorities.

Communicating Financial Information to Internal Decision Makers

The form and content of financial statements prepared for external decision makers are specified by GAAP. When accountants provide financial data to internal decision makers, such as production-line superintendents and advertising managers, most of these formal rules and regulations do not apply. To assist internal decision makers, accountants develop customized financial reports designed with the specific information needs of these parties in mind.

To illustrate how accountants are called upon to satisfy the information needs of internal decision makers, consider a recent series of events involving Holly Farms, Inc., a leading producer of poultry products. In the late 1980s, Holly Farms decided to market a new product, roasted chicken, to retail grocery chains, the company's principal customers.[6] The company invested $20 million to build a production facil-

---

6. Buckler, A. "Holly Farms' Marketing Error: The Chicken That Laid an Egg," *The Wall Street Journal*, February 9, 1988, p. 34. Reprinted by permission of *The Wall Street Journal*, © 1988 Dow Jones & Company, Inc. All Rights Reserved Worldwide.

ity for this new product and then spent several million dollars advertising the product when it went on the market in the fall of 1987. No doubt, after the roasted chicken had been on the market for a few months, company executives were more than a little interested in determining whether the venture was a financial success. To answer this question, the executives relied upon their accountants to collect, process, and analyze the appropriate financial data. This data included the total or "gross" sales generated by the product, sales returns made by customers, production and production-related expenses, advertising costs, and so on.

Determining whether a new product is profitable does not sound like a particularly challenging exercise. Simply add and subtract a few numbers, right? Wrong. Holly Farms' accountants had to address several difficult issues to determine whether the roasted chicken product was profitable. One of the toughest of these issues was the allocation of so-called common costs to the new product.

Since Holly Farms ships numerous products to market in its large fleet of trucks, the company's accountants must decide how to allocate delivery costs to these various products. Common costs can be allocated in several different ways. One method of allocating common delivery costs is based upon the proportionate weight of the products in each shipment. For example, assume that a delivery truck is carrying 10,000 pounds of product and the freight bill for this shipment is $1,000. In this case, the common cost of $1,000 could be allocated to the products at a rate of $.10 per pound ($1,000/10,000 pounds). Alternatively, the relative sales value of the products can be used as the basis for distributing delivery costs or other common costs to products. All common cost allocation methods are somewhat arbitrary, including the two just mentioned. If an allocation method is extremely arbitrary, the profitability of the products or product lines affected by that method may be significantly distorted. In turn, distorted accounting data may result in company executives making improper decisions.

So, was the roasted chicken product successful? No, at least not initially. The problem was not the quality of the product but Holly Farms' inability to get the product to market on a timely basis. By the time the roasted chicken reached retail grocery outlets, it had only a few days of shelf life remaining, meaning that spoilage losses were high. To remedy this problem, Holly Farms decided to develop a new distribution system for the roasted chicken product, a decision creating more data collection, processing, and analysis problems—or opportunities—for the company's accountants.

Real World
Refer students to the opening quote for this chapter. Here is a situation in which additional information could have prevented a mistake. Point out that the information needed here was not financial, but operational. Financial information is only one source of information needed by managers to successfully perform their jobs.

ABUSIVE ACCOUNTING PRACTICES: LOSING SIGHT OF THE ROLE OF ACCOUNTING

■ **LEARNING OBJECTIVE 4**
Discuss the problems that may result when organizations are allowed to use improper accounting methods

Business executives occasionally lose sight of the purpose of accounting. As noted earlier, the primary mission of accounting is to provide useful information to financial decision makers. Accounting information, rather than the decision to be made, sometimes becomes the principal focus of attention in a decision-making context. The objective in these circumstances becomes modifying accounting information to justify a particular decision alternative instead of using accounting information to choose the most appropriate alternative. Quite often in such cases, accountants find themselves being pressured by business executives to approve an improper or "creative" accounting method.

Creative Accounting Comes to the Savings and Loan Industry

History has proven repeatedly that when business entities begin distorting their accounting information to serve a specific purpose, trouble often ensues. To prove this point, one has to look no further than the decade of the 1980s, which saw a near total collapse of the savings and loan industry. A key contributing factor to this financial disaster was the use of abusive accounting practices by many savings and loans.

For most of this century, the principal line of business of savings and loans was providing mortgage loans to individual home buyers. Legislation passed in the late 1970s and early 1980s allowed savings and loans to venture into other lending activities on a large scale for the first time. Almost immediately, many savings and loans began lending money to finance commercial development projects involving the construction of large condominium complexes, golf courses, vacation resorts, and similar properties. Unfortunately, savings and loan executives were largely unfamiliar with the economics of commercial development projects. As a result, many savings and loans were hoodwinked into financing projects that had little chance of being successful.

When savings and loans began experiencing large losses on their portfolios of commercial development loans in the early 1980s, the owners of these institutions successfully lobbied Congress to modify the industry's accounting rules. Essentially, savings and loan executives convinced Congress that the industry should be allowed to use accounting methods that concealed the deteriorating financial condition of hundreds of savings and loans. Without becoming too technical, one such accounting method allowed savings and loans to postpone the recording of losses on the sale of certain securities. For instance, assume that a savings and loan lost $5 million on the sale of a large block of securities. Under the "creative" accounting rules approved by Congress, that loss did not have to be recorded immediately. Instead, the loss could be gradually recorded over a period of several years. Even someone who has no familiarity with accounting should recognize that this accounting method is inappropriate. A loss is a loss and should be recorded when incurred, otherwise an entity's financial status is misrepresented.

Why did Congress allow savings and loans to use improper accounting methods? The answer is simple. Congress did not want a large number of savings and loans to be forced out of business. Federal legislators believed that the financial problems of the savings and loan industry would eventually go away when the national economy rebounded from the economic recession of the early 1980s. However, while waiting for the economy to recover, executives of financially distressed savings and loans began adopting a "go for broke" approach to doing business. To recover the losses suffered on earlier loans, these executives began making increasingly larger and riskier loans on commercial development projects. The federal government was eventually forced to bail out the savings and loan industry in the late 1980s, a bailout plan that cost taxpayers several hundred billion dollars.

The accounting methods used by many savings and loans during the 1980s created an impression of financial stability and profitability for these financial institutions when nothing could have been further from the truth. Here, the appropriate cliché is "allow the chips to fall where they may." If a company or even an entire industry is experiencing financial losses, the accounting data produced by that company or industry should faithfully reflect that fact. If accounting data do not reflect economic reality, then the decision makers who act on that data are likely to make inappropriate decisions. In the case of the savings and loan industry, these decision makers included individual investors and depositors from across the nation. Many of these individuals did not recover the funds that they entrusted to savings and loans during the 1980s.

Real World
Business executives want their company's financial statements to be impressive because the statements reflect on their performance. Requiring conformance with GAAP limits a manager's ability to manipulate financial statements. The S & L fiasco provides an example of a situation where GAAP were not required, thus allowing executives to easily manipulate their firms' financial statements.

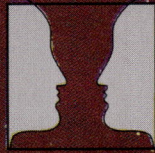

Doing the Right Thing . . .
and Paying for It

Real World
More than three-fourths of
large U.S. companies now have
a code of ethics.

Focus on Ethics
Ethical choices are encountered
frequently in the real world.
Imagine that you work in the
registrar's office of your
university or college. A friend
asks you to find out someone
else's GPA . What are your
alternative courses of action and
what would you do?

In 1984, an accountant with Allegheny International discovered several suspicious transactions in his company's accounting records. These transactions included improper
expense reimbursement requests by company executives, unreported cost overruns of
nearly $8 million on a real estate development project, and undisclosed transactions
involving the son of the company's chief executive officer (CEO). The accountant discovered that the CEO's son was living free of charge in a penthouse owned by the company,
a penthouse that had been renovated at a cost of more than $1 million. After completing
an investigation of these matters, the accountant submitted a report regarding the financial irregularities to the company's chief administrative officer (CAO) and urged him to
pass the report on to Allegheny's board of directors. To the consternation of the accountant, the CAO refused to give the report to the board of directors. The accountant then
decided to disclose the irregularities directly to the board of directors; however, before
he could do so, he was fired.

SOURCE: Securities and Exchange Commission, *Accounting and Auditing Enforcement Release No. 151*, 9
September 1987.

Abusive Accounting and Abused Accountants

Accountants who prepare and deliver financial reports that document that a company is in poor financial health often encounter a "kill the messenger" attitude on the
part of top management. That was true during the 1980s within the savings and loan
industry. Many accountants spoke out regarding the improper accounting practices
being used by savings and loans. These warnings were largely ignored, and the
accountants who voiced them were often chastised for being too conservative or pessimistic.

Consider the case of Phoenix-based Lincoln Savings and Loan, one of the nation's
largest savings and loans in the 1980s. For several years, Lincoln's accounting firm
was the large international firm of Arthur Young & Company. In 1988, the Arthur
Young accountant assigned to supervise the accounting services being provided to
Lincoln vigorously contested aggressive accounting practices used by the savings and
loan. Lincoln's chief executive, Charles Keating, did not appreciate this accountant's
point of view and pressured top officials of Arthur Young to replace that accountant.
To their credit, the executives of Arthur Young resigned from the Lincoln engagement rather than capitulate to Keating's demand.[7] Another example of an accountant
who refused to sacrifice his professional integrity to conceal improper accounting
practices can be found in the Spotlight on Ethics vignette included in this section.

---

7. See M. C. Knapp, "Lincoln Savings and Loan Association," *Contemporary Auditing: Issues and Cases*,
2d Ed. (Minneapolis/St. Paul: West Publishing Co., 1996), 55–68.

AN OVERVIEW OF THE ACCOUNTING PROFESSION

"A vocation requiring extensive education and often specialized training" defines a profession according to *Random House Webster's College Dictionary*. Given this definition, the accounting discipline clearly qualifies as a profession. In this section, we take a closer look at the accounting profession in the United States.

Accountant vs. CPA

To the proverbial man, or woman, on the street, accountant and CPA—**certified public accountant**—are essentially interchangeable terms. In fact, all CPAs are not practicing accountants, and many, many accountants are not CPAs. "Accountant" is a generic term that can be applied to anyone, including a CPA, who works in one of the fields of accounting. On the other hand, a CPA is an individual who has passed the rigorous CPA examination and met any other certification requirements established by his or her state. Most states, for example, require CPA candidates to complete an experience requirement ranging from six months to two years. (Like all professions, accounting is regulated primarily at the state level.) The CPA examination is administered twice each year by the **American Institute of Certified Public Accountants** (AICPA), a national professional organization of CPAs. By 1996, there were more than three hundred thousand CPAs in the United States.

Private vs. Public Accounting

Most businesspeople think of the accounting profession as consisting of two segments: private accounting and public accounting.[8] Accountants in private industry are employed by corporations and other business entities, not-for-profit organizations, and governmental agencies. Public accountants are employed by accounting firms or are sole proprietors or partners of their own firms. Both segments of the profession have experienced strong growth in employment levels over the past few decades. Looking toward the future, the United States Department of Labor has predicted that the number of accounting jobs will increase by approximately 40 percent during the decade of the 1990s.[9]

Work Roles in Private Accounting

Individuals in private accounting have job titles such as controller, internal auditor, cost analyst, and tax accountant. A controller is the top accounting executive of an

■ **LEARNING OBJECTIVE 5**
Define the nature, structure, and major segments of the accounting profession

certified public accountant

Real World
A CPA can also be a CMA, certified management accountant, and/or a CIA, certified internal auditor.

American Institute of Certified Public Accountants

Teaching Note
Provide students with information about the certification requirements of your state or tell them where that information can be obtained (typically the State Board of Accountancy or Public Accountancy).

Discussion Question
Discuss accounting as a career choice. Inform students where they can obtain specific information about a major in accounting.

---

8. The terms "private accounting" and "public accounting" refer to the two major employment sectors within the profession. College sophomores majoring in business tend to view the accounting domain as being segmented into "Financial Accounting" and "Management Accounting," the titles typically assigned to the two introductory level accounting courses in business programs. Financial accounting is generally concerned with the methods and procedures used to record financial data and to develop financial reports for decision makers external to organizations. Management or managerial accounting focuses on developing and communicating financial data to decision makers within given enterprises.

9. U.S. Department of Labor, Bureau of Labor Statistics, *Occupational Projections and Training Data: 1991 Edition* (Washington, D.C.: U.S. Government Printing Office, 1991).

organization. A primary responsibility of a controller is to ensure that an entity's periodic financial statements are prepared on a timely and accurate basis. A controller usually reports to his or her organization's chief financial officer (CFO), who generally has the overall responsibility for supervising an organization's finance and accounting functions.

An internal auditor monitors the compliance of an organization's employees with its operating policies and procedures. Such monitoring is important if top management is to maintain effective control over an organization and keep its employees focused on the entity's short-term and long-term goals and objectives. Take the case of Hertz, the rental car company. Hertz has a large internal audit staff. These internal auditors regularly visit the hundreds of Hertz rental car agencies. An internal audit of a Hertz agency usually requires two weeks and involves a detailed review and study of the agency's financial records and day-to-day operations. Any significant deviations from Hertz's operating policies and procedures discovered during an internal audit are referred to a Hertz regional manager, who then takes the proper corrective action.

An individual holding the job title of "cost analyst" may have any of a number of accounting-related responsibilities within an organization. These responsibilities may include maintaining production cost records for manufacturing processes, analyzing variances from budgeted expenditures, and preparing customized reports that forecast expected costs for a new operating unit. Finally, a tax accountant's principal duties involve the collection and processing of data needed to file an entity's periodic federal, state, and local tax returns.

certified management accountant

Most organizations do not require their accountants to earn the CPA designation, although doing so nearly always furthers one's career in private accounting. A person interested strictly in a career in private accounting should consider the benefits of becoming a **certified management accountant** (CMA). This professional designation is sponsored by the Institute of Management Accountants. CMAs specialize in assisting the management of business entities and other organizations in obtaining and making optimal use of accounting information. To earn the CMA designation, an individual must have a college degree, pass the CMA examination, and work for two years in a field of private (management) accounting. Although the CMA designation has only existed since the early 1970s, it is now widely recognized as an important symbol of professional expertise in the field of private accounting.

Accountants who obtain the CPA or CMA designation can usually command higher salaries than accountants who lack these professional designations. Shown in Exhibit 1.2 are the results of a 1994 survey of salaries within the accounting profession classified by professional designation.

Public Accounting: A Closer Look

Public accounting firms, like law firms, market their professional services to the general public. Among the services offered by public accounting firms to their clients are basic bookkeeping services, taxation services, auditing, and management consulting services of various types. The preparation of tax returns is the professional service most closely identified with public accounting firms. Besides preparing tax returns for their clients, public accounting firms provide a wide range of other taxation services. Most important, these firms assist their clients in structuring personal and business transactions to minimize their taxes—legally.

Although not well understood by the public, independent auditing is arguably the most important professional service provided by public accounting firms. The independent audits performed by public accounting firms are much different from the

■ **EXHIBIT 1.2**

Average Accounting Salaries by Age and Professional Designation

SOURCE: Bar graph from *The Journal of Accountancy*, September 1994, p. 16. Reprinted with permission from *The Journal of Accountancy*, copyright © 1994 by American Institute of CPAs. Opinions of the authors are their own and do not necessarily reflect policies of the AICPA.

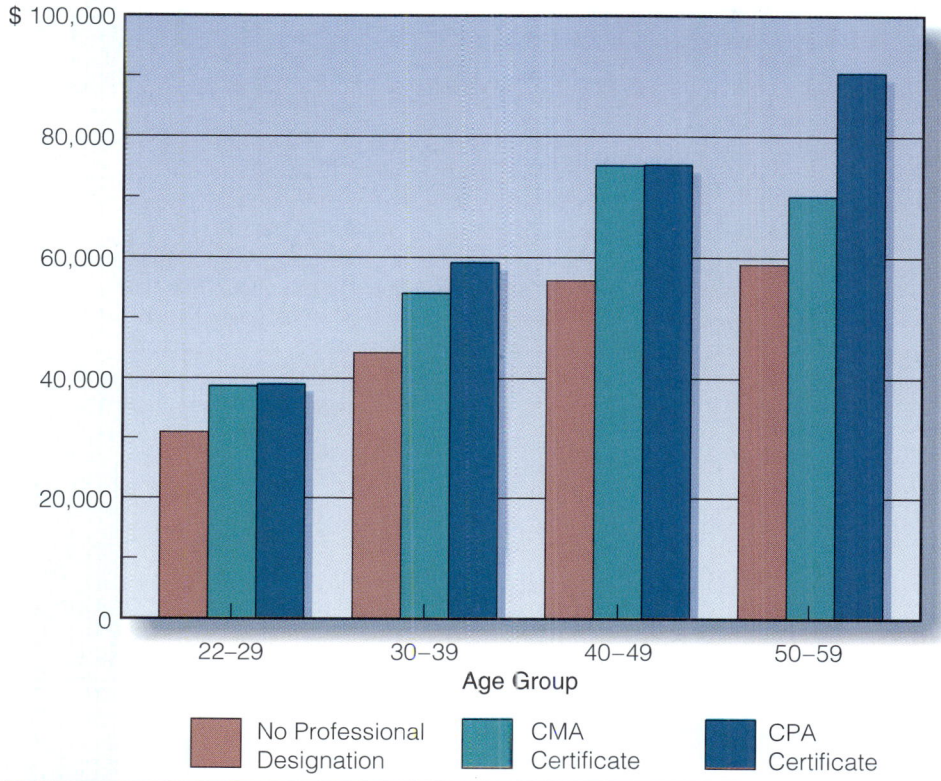

services provided by internal auditors. One key difference is that an independent audit is just that—independent. A public accounting firm that has no financial interests or other ties to an organization is brought in to perform an independent audit of that entity's financial statements. On the other hand, internal auditors are not independent when they provide audit services to their employer because the employer-employee relationship creates a strong financial bond or relationship between the two parties.

The principal objective of an independent audit is to determine whether an entity's financial statements have been prepared in accordance with GAAP. That is, auditors examine an audit client's financial statements and underlying accounting records to determine whether GAAP were used in recording the data summarized in those financial statements. If a company's financial statements have been prepared in accordance with GAAP, those statements are presumed to fairly reflect the financial affairs of the company.

In the absence of an independent audit, financial statement users would be much less likely to assume that an entity's published financial statements are honest representations of its financial affairs. Why? Because corporate executives have an economic incentive to "window-dress" financial statements to make their companies

Real World
Big Six accounting firms generally earn 60 to 65 percent of their revenues from auditing services.

EXHIBIT 1.3

Audit Report Issued by Deloitte & Touche on Recent Financial Statements of Sears, Roebuck and Co.

Report of Independent Certified Public Accountants

To the Shareholders and Board of Directors
Sears, Roebuck and Co.

We have audited the accompanying Consolidated Statements of Financial Position of Sears, Roebuck and Co. as of December 31, 1994 and 1993, and the related Consolidated Statements of Income, Shareholders' Equity and Cash Flows for each of the three years in the period ended December 31, 1994. These financial statements are the responsibility of the Company's management. Our responsibility is to express an opinion on these financial statements based on our audits.

We conducted our audits in accordance with generally accepted auditing standards. Those standards require that we plan and perform the audit to obtain reasonable assurance about whether the financial statements are free of material misstatement. An audit includes examining, on a test basis, evidence supporting the amounts and disclosures in the financial statements. An audit also includes assessing the accounting principles used and significant estimates made by management, as well as evaluating the overall financial statement presentation. We believe that our audits provide a reasonable basis for our opinion.

In our opinion, such consolidated financial statements present fairly, in all material respects, the financial position of Sears, Roebuck and Co. as of December 31, 1994 and 1993, and the results of its operations and its cash flows for each of the three years in the period ended December 31, 1994 in conformity with generally accepted accounting principles.

As discussed in note 2 to the consolidated financial statements, the Company changed its method of accounting for certain investments in debt securities in 1993 and postretirement benefits in 1992.

Deloitte & Touche LLP
Chicago, Illinois

February 24, 1995

Teaching Note
Call attention to the date of the audit opinion. Comment on the time needed to close the accounting records of the company, prepare its financial statements, and complete the audit of its financial statements.

appear more profitable and financially stable than they actually are. If corporate executives report impressive financial results for their firms, they will likely receive higher salaries in the future and benefit from an increase in the value of the stock they own in their firms. By independently examining the financial statements and accounting records of companies, public accounting firms bolster the confidence that third parties have in the accuracy of those statements. This higher level of confidence in financial statements increases the likelihood that individuals will invest in, or loan funds to, business entities and thus keep the national economy healthy and growing.

Shown in Exhibit 1.3 is an example of an audit report on a company's financial statements. This audit report was issued in 1995 by Deloitte & Touche, a large public accounting firm, on a recent set of financial statements prepared by Sears, Roebuck and Co.

Public accounting firms range in size from one-person proprietorships to huge international partnerships that have hundreds of partners and thousands of employ-

■ **EXHIBIT 1.4**

Worldwide Revenues of Big Six Accounting Firms

SOURCE: "The 500 Largest Private Companies in the U.S.," *Forbes*, 5 Dec. 5, 1994. Reprinted by permission of Forbes Magazine © Forbes Inc., 1994.

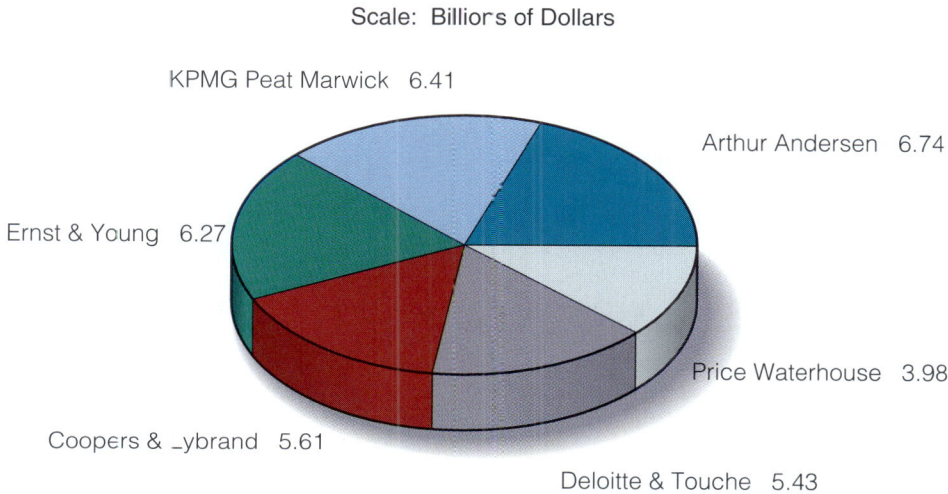

Scale: Billions of Dollars

KPMG Peat Marwick   6.41

Arthur Andersen   6.74

Ernst & Young   6.27

Price Waterhouse   3.98

Coopers & Lybrand   5.61

Deloitte & Touche   5.43

ees. The Big Six accounting firms, all of which are international in scope, dominate the public accounting profession in many respects. Shown in Exhibit 1.4 are the worldwide revenues generated by the Big Six firms in a recent year. The size and financial resources of these firms allow them to spend enormous amounts each year training their personnel and developing new and more effective means of serving the needs of their clients. In fact, the Big Six firm of Arthur Andersen & Co. operates the largest private educational center in the world. Located in St. Charles, Illinois, the Arthur Andersen & Co. Center for Professional Education is used as a training facility for the professionals that staff the several hundred Arthur Andersen offices scattered across the world.

Regulation of the Accounting Profession

In the early 1930s, the **Securities and Exchange Commission** (SEC) was formed to deter the abusive accounting and financial reporting practices that contributed to the collapse of the stock market in 1929. The SEC regulates the sale of securities, such as stocks and bonds, by publicly owned companies and the subsequent trading of those securities on stock exchanges. (Companies that market their stocks, bonds, or other securities on an interstate basis are generally referred to as "publicly owned" companies.) The SEC also oversees the financial reporting and accounting practices of publicly owned companies. "Full and fair disclosure" is the SEC's motto. This federal agency does not attempt to assess the investment quality of the securities issued by the companies that it regulates or to prohibit the sale of highly speculative securities. Instead, the SEC attempts to ensure that publicly owned companies provide third parties with sufficient information to make informed economic decisions regarding those companies and the securities they sell.

Securities and Exchange Commission

■ **LEARNING OBJECTIVE 6**
Identify the accounting profession's principal regulatory bodies

Unconventional Accounting Services

Besides bookkeeping, taxation services, auditing, and management consulting, public accounting firms provide several other less traditional or conventional professional services. For instance, Price Waterhouse has served for more than fifty years as the official vote tabulator of Hollywood's annual Academy Awards. Described in the following article is a similar "attestation" engagement performed by an accounting firm for a record company.

In a move designed to bolster the credibility of the U.S. Hispanic music industry, Sony Discos has begun using an outside accounting firm to certify album sales.

Sony Discos, the U.S. Latin division of Sony Music International, kicked off its initiative in July when it asked the Miami-based accounting firm Goldstein Schecter Price Lucas Horwitz & Co. to audit the sales for La Mafia's "Estas Tocando Fuego."

The firm certified the album as having reached the 200,000 unit level, described by Sony as "double platinum," based on the levels informally recognized in the U.S. and Puerto Rican Latin record market.

The Hispanic music industry in the U.S. and Puerto Rico accepts 50,000 units as gold and 100,000 units sold as platinum. However, independent audits for Hispanic album sales have been rare, which has led many executives of U.S. labels to question the validity of the industry's gold and platinum awards. Goldstein Schecter carried out the La Mafia certification based on the procedures used by the Recording Industry Association of America. Under those guidelines, for example, an album must have been released at least 60 days before it can be certified and at least 50% of the retail sales must have gone through regular retail chains. However, the RIAA does not certify sales of albums under the 500,000 level.

The result of La Mafia's album certification, asserts Sony Discos president Frank Welzer, is that future album sales by Sony—and the Latin industry in general—will be taken more seriously.

"One of the reasons why we're supplying these numbers," says Welzer, "is because we'd like to be noted for success and integrity rather than hype. We're now taking the first step to legitimize the sales figures. And I think now that we're doing it, I'd be very, very surprised if the other majors don't fall in line—and even the independents."

SOURCE: Lannert, John. "Sony Discos Hires Firm to Certify Album Sales," *Billboard*, August 8, 1992, © 1992 BPI Communications, Inc. Used with permission.

The accounting profession's rule-making processes are closely monitored by the SEC. The SEC has the authority to override any new accounting rules issued by the FASB, at least to the extent that those rules apply to publicly owned companies. However, the SEC has seldom interfered with the rule-making bodies within the profession.

As suggested earlier, the accounting profession is regulated most directly at the state, rather than federal, level. Each state has established an agency to regulate the practice of accounting within its borders. Typically, this agency is known as the state board of accountancy or the state board of public accountancy. The primary responsibilities of this agency include issuing and renewing CPA licenses, monitoring compliance with continuing education requirements, and sanctioning CPAs who violate the agency's rules and regulations.

ACCOUNTING: A PROFESSION IN TRANSITION

The past quarter of a century has brought extensive changes to the accounting profession, a profession often characterized as averse to change. Recent trends affecting accounting include an influx of large numbers of women and minorities into the profession, the increasing availability of computer resources, and changing educational requirements for prospective accountants. In addition to coping with these trends, the accounting profession faces other key challenges as it prepares for the next century. These challenges include mounting litigation problems facing public accounting firms and the need to "internationalize" the accounting profession.

■ **LEARNING OBJECTIVE 7**
Discuss important changes presently taking place within the accounting profession

Recent Trends and Events Affecting the Accounting Profession

One of the most noticeable changes in the accounting profession in recent years has been a large increase in the number of women choosing careers in accounting. Throughout the history of the accounting profession in the United States, both private and public accounting have been predominantly male. However, the number of women majoring in accounting in college began increasing significantly during the 1970s. In 1990, for the first time, the majority of college graduates in accounting were women rather than men. The number of minorities choosing to pursue an accounting career is also on the rise. By the early 1990s, 17 percent of accounting graduates were minorities.[10]

Another very noticeable change in accounting over the past two decades has been a rapid growth in the use of computers by accountants. Much of the tedious clerical work previously performed by accountants can now be done in a matter of nanoseconds by modern computers. Take the case of independent auditing. With the aid of computers, auditors use statistical sampling techniques to efficiently and effectively audit populations of client transactions that can easily number in the tens of millions, if not more, during a given year.

One recent trend in the accounting profession is of special significance to prospective accountants. This trend involves requiring individuals sitting for the CPA examination to have completed a minimum of 150 hours of college credit. This requirement has spread across the nation over the past decade. By the year 2000, most states are expected to have adopted this requirement. Essentially, this new rule requires prospective accountants to complete a five-year, instead of a four-year, academic pro-

Large accounting firms hire thousands of college graduates each year. In recent years, these firms have adopted measures to aggressively recruit and retain women and minority employees. One large accounting firm, Deloitte & Touche, recently spent more than $2 million to implement a program entitled "Men and Women as Colleagues."

---

10. The statistics reported here were drawn from the following source: "Female Grads Dominate New Accounting Hires," *Accounting Today*, 9 September 1991, 3.

Teaching Note
Be prepared to discuss the
150-hour requirement as it
specifically relates to your state.

gram in accounting. A perceived need for future accountants to develop better communication, computer, and interpersonal skills was a key factor that motivated the profession to move toward a five-year educational rule.

The Expectations Gap and the Litigation Crisis

The most perplexing problem facing the accounting profession as it prepares to enter the twenty-first century is a recent and dramatic increase in the number of lawsuits filed against public accounting firms. Until the 1970s, public accounting firms had little fear of being sued either by their clients or by third parties. However, lawsuits against public accounting firms are now much more common. Investors, creditors, and other parties who lose money when businesses fail often attempt to recover their losses from "deep-pocketed," or well-to-do, parties associated with the failed ventures. Since accounting firms are perceived as deep-pocketed parties and are closely associated with their clients' financial statements, they are frequently dragged into court when a company goes "belly up."

Many of the largest lawsuits filed against accounting firms during the late 1980s and early 1990s were based upon allegations of faulty audits of savings and loans. These lawsuits typically alleged that auditors discovered a savings and loan was failing but chose not to disclose this fact in their audit report. In late 1992, the Big Six accounting firm of Ernst & Young collectively settled a group of these lawsuits by paying $400 million to the federal government. Despite this settlement, Ernst & Young steadfastly maintained that the savings and loan audits in question had been performed in compliance with all professional standards.

The accounting profession's litigation problems stem most directly from an "expectations gap" that has arisen between accounting firms and the decision makers who rely on audited financial statements. These decision makers often have unrealistic expectations of independent audits. For example, many financial statement users expect independent audits to uncover management fraud. Unfortunately, management fraud is typically so well concealed that accounting firms have little chance of discovering and disclosing it.

Accounting on an International Scale

Real World
Due to the rapid globalization
of our economy, individuals
graduating from college with an
accounting degree and the
ability to speak a foreign
language are highly demanded
by Big Six firms.

The growing trend toward multinational business enterprises and international trade promises to complicate the work roles of public and private accountants in the next several decades. Cultural differences in business practices, varying governmental regulations, and a lack of uniform international accounting rules create "global-sized" headaches for accountants of multinational companies. To investigate the impact of differences in international accounting rules on business entities' reported operating results, three researchers computed the profit of a hypothetical company four times. Each time, these researchers based the profit computation on a different country's accounting rules.[11] The results, reported in United States dollars, were as follows:

COUNTRY	NET INCOME
Australia	$240,000
West Germany	10,402
United Kingdom	260,600
United States	34,600

11. D. E. Wygal, D. E. Stout, and J. Volpe, "Reporting Practices in Four Countries," *Management Accounting*, December 1987, 37–42.

The preceding data demonstrate that financial decision makers must be cautious when interpreting the financial statements of a foreign entity. Likewise, these data suggest a strong need for uniform international accounting rules.

Looking Forward to the Twenty-first Century

The accounting profession is facing several challenging problems as it prepares to enter the twenty-first century. However, these problems also pose opportunities for a new generation of accountants. Since the time of Pacioli, and before, accountants have played an integral role in the economic success of business enterprises and other organizations. Those organizations that thrive in the coming century will share several key attributes. One of these attributes will be a supporting staff of accountants who understand their organization, recognize the organization's information needs, and satisfy those needs on a timely basis with relevant and reliable accounting data.

Discussion Question
After students have read Chapter 1, ask them to discuss what they learned about accounting and accountants that surprised them.

SUMMARY

The primary role of accounting is to provide useful financial information to decision makers. The manner in which accountants communicate financial data depends upon the identity of the decision maker who will utilize that data. Financial statements are the primary means accountants use to communicate financial information to investors, creditors, regulatory agencies, and other decision makers external to a given organization. Financial data oriented toward the needs of internal decision makers, such as production-line superintendents and advertising managers, are communicated in the form of customized reports designed with the objectives of those decision makers in mind.

Accountants have a professional responsibility to ensure that an organization uses accounting practices that honestly portray its financial status. History has proven repeatedly that abusive or "creative" accounting practices can result in poor economic decisions. During the 1980s, Congress permitted financially distressed savings and loans to conceal their true financial condition by using improper accounting methods. As a result, many of these institutions incurred huge losses, ultimately absorbed by taxpayers, that would have been avoided had these savings and loans been forced out of business.

Private accounting and public accounting are the two major segments of the accounting profession. Accountants in private industry are employed by corporations, not-for-profit organizations, and other entities in various accounting-related work roles. Public accountants are employees, partners, or proprietors of accounting firms. Public accounting firms provide an array of professional services to the public including bookkeeping, taxation services, auditing, and management consulting.

The accounting profession has undergone significant changes over the past two decades and faces several challenging problems as it prepares for the next century. The most perplexing of these problems is a dramatic increase in lawsuits filed against public accounting firms in recent years. Another important challenge facing the accounting profession is posed by the increasing trend toward international trade and multinational business operations. This trend is important because the lack of uniform international accounting standards impairs the comparability of financial data prepared in different countries.

GLOSSARY

Accounting (p. 8)   A service activity designed to provide quantitative information about economic entities that is intended to be useful in making economic decisions.

American Institute of Certified Public Accountants (AICPA) (p. 13)   The national professional organization of CPAs that prepares and administers the CPA examination.

Certified management accountant (CMA) (p. 14)   An individual who has passed the CMA examination and satisfied the other requirements to qualify for this professional designation; CMAs generally specialize in private (management) accounting.

Certified public accountant (CPA) (p. 13)   An individual who has passed the CPA examination and satisfied any other requirements established by his or her state to qualify for this professional designation.

Double-entry bookkeeping (p. 5)   A method of maintaining financial records developed more than five hundred years ago that serves as the foundation of modern accounting systems worldwide.

Financial Accounting Standards Board (FASB) (p. 7)   The rule-making body that has the primary authority for establishing accounting standards in the United States.

Financial statements (p. 8)   The principal means accountants use to communicate financial information regarding business entities and other organizations to investors, creditors, and other decision makers external to these entities.

Generally accepted accounting principles (GAAP) (p. 7)   The fundamental rules, guidelines, and concepts that accountants follow in recording and reporting financial information.

Luca Pacioli (p. 5)   A Franciscan monk credited with formalizing and documenting double-entry bookkeeping in the late fifteenth century.

Securities and Exchange Commission (SEC) (p. 17)   A federal agency that regulates the sale of securities by publicly owned companies and the subsequent trading of those securities; also oversees the financial reporting and accounting practices of these companies.

DECISION CASE

In the late 1980s, Vincent Golden was the chief financial officer of Regina Company, Inc., whose principal line of business was the manufacturing and marketing of vacuum cleaners. As Regina's chief financial officer, Golden was responsible for the company's accounting function. Golden's immediate superior was Donald Sheelen, Regina's chief executive officer. Regina began experiencing financial problems in the late 1980s that stemmed primarily from poor quality controls over product development and manufacturing processes. Under Sheelen's leadership, the company introduced several new products that were initially well received by the public. However, many of these products were returned by customers since they suffered from a high rate of malfunctions.

In 1988, Sheelen became very concerned when he realized that Regina would not achieve target sales and earnings goals he had established for the company. Sheelen recognized that if Regina reported disappointing financial results, the company's stock price would decline. To prevent this from occurring, Sheelen instructed Golden to falsify Regina's accounting records. Among the steps taken by Golden to improve Regina's reported financial results were recording millions of dollars of nonexistent sales and ignoring $13 million of merchandise returned by customers.

As typically happens, Sheelen and Golden were unable to conceal Regina's financial problems indefinitely. When the fraud was revealed, both men were prosecuted and eventually pleaded guilty to federal mail fraud and securities fraud charges.

Required: Assume that in the future you are the chief financial officer of Boyd Enterprises. Near the end of a year, you realize that the company will not meet the target sales and earnings goals established at the beginning of that year by Boyd's new chief executive officer (CEO). Over the past year, you have realized that this individual has a very casual attitude toward financial reporting. When you inform the CEO that the company's financial goals will not be met, the CEO responds, "You can fix that by back-dating the sales for the first two weeks of January as if they occurred in December. That will put us right on target." When a stunned look appears on your face, the CEO continues. "This is a one-time thing only. We're turning around this company. Next year's profit figures will be much better and we won't have to get involved in any of these accounting shenanigans." What would you do at this point? Before answering, identify the parties who will be affected by your decision. What responsibility, if any, do you have to each of these parties?

QUESTIONS

1. To what fifteenth century scholar do we trace the origin of modern accounting?

2. What fundamental law of physics is reflected in double-entry accounting?

3. You just bought a new tennis racket for $125. Identify the two dimensions of this transaction and how these dimensions are equivalent in an economic sense.

4. Distinguish between external and internal decision makers.

5. What are the principal means accountants use to communicate financial information to external decision makers? To internal decision makers?

6. Identify three external decision-making groups and identify at least one way that each group might use financial statements of business entities for decision-making purposes.

7. "Accounting is a means to an end rather than the end itself." Briefly explain the meaning of this statement.

8. How did "creative" accounting contribute to the financial problems experienced by the savings and loan industry in the 1980s?

9. Complete the following two sentences from the text. "If a company or even an entire industry is experiencing financial losses, the accounting data produced by that company or industry should _____. If accounting data do not reflect economic reality, then the decision makers who act on that data are likely to make _____."

10. Is a CPA an accountant? Is an accountant a CPA? Distinguish between accountants and CPAs.

11. Distinguish between private and public accounting. Describe briefly some of the work roles in private accounting.

12. What services do public accounting firms typically offer to the public?

13. What is the principal objective of an independent audit?

14. What prompted the formation of the Securities and Exchange Commission (SEC), and what is its primary function?

15. Identify the principal rule-making body within the accounting profession in the United States today. What is its relationship to the SEC?

16. List several changes that have occurred in the accounting profession over the last two decades.

17. Describe the expectations gap that exists between public accountants and the general public. What problems does this "gap" create for accountants?

18. How has the growing trend toward the internationalization of business enterprises complicated the work roles of public and private accountants?

EXERCISES

19. **Analyzing Business Transactions** (LO 1)

"Every transaction, regardless of how large or small, can be reduced by an accountant to two equal effects expressed in dollars." As you will see in a subsequent chapter, all transactions affect either assets (things owned), liabilities (amounts owed), or owners' equity (the ownership interest in a business), or some combination of these. As an illustration, the two examples on pages 5 and 6 have the following effects:

	ASSETS	LIABILITIES	OWNERS' EQUITY
1. Chrysler's $1,000 purchase of office supplies on credit	+ $1,000	+1,000	
2. Purchase of a set of tires (assume for $200 cash)	+ $ 200 − $ 200		

Required:

For each of the following business transactions, perform a similar analysis of its effect on assets, liabilities, and owners' equity:

1. Borrowed $10,000 from a local bank
2. Purchased equipment for $12,500 cash
3. Purchased land by issuing a note payable of $40,000
4. Purchased inventory for $4,000 on credit

19. 1. A, +$10,000
       L, +$10,000
    2. A,+$12,500–$12,500
    3. A, +$40,000
       L, +$40,000
    4. A, +$4,000
       L, +$4,000

20. **Information Needs of External and Internal Decision Makers** (LO 3)

Consider the following items of information that may be obtained from a given company's accounting records.

a. Net income
b. Inventory cost per unit
c. Total liabilities (amounts owed)
d. Total sales by geographical area of business operations
e. Change in sales revenue over the past five years
f. Employee salaries by department

Required:

1. Indicate a specific type of decision maker that would have a primary interest in each of these items of information. The decision maker may be external, such as an investor or bank loan officer, or internal, such as a departmental supervisor or president of a company.
2. Briefly explain why the decision maker identified in Part 1 would have a need for the given item of information.

20. No check figures

21. **Analyzing the Financial Statements of Foreign Companies** (LO 7)

Joan wants to invest in one or more automobile manufacturers. She is considering both domestic, or U.S.-based, automobile manufacturers and foreign firms in the industry. Joan has obtained the most recent income statements of two foreign automobile manufacturers, Company A which is based in Japan and Company B which is headquartered in Germany. She has translated each firm's net income into U.S. dollars. Company A's most recent net income expressed in

U.S. dollars is $55 million, while Company B earned a net income equivalent to $702 million.

Required:
1. What additional information should Joan obtain before she can compare the translated profits of these two companies?
2. Are the translated net incomes of the two foreign companies directly comparable to the net incomes of U.S. firms such as Chrysler and General Motors? Explain.

22. **The Need for Financial Statements** (LO 3)

Jim Nelson opened a new business several months ago which he named Jim's Bike Shop. Jim sells and repairs bicycles. Since Jim took several accounting courses in college, he has decided to maintain his business's accounting records. Although the bike shop has been in operation for more than three months, Jim has not yet prepared any financial statements for the business. Jim has several friends who are business owners and is aware that they prepare monthly financial statements for their businesses. Nevertheless, Jim has decided that it is too much of a "hassle" to prepare monthly financial statements for Jim's Bike Shop.

Required:
Write a memo to Jim explaining why financial statements would help him operate his business more effectively and efficiently.

21. No check figures

22. No check figures

PROBLEM SET A

23. **Use of Income Statement Information** (LO 3)

The following condensed income statement was taken from the 1994 annual report of Carl Karcher Enterprises, Inc. This company operates Carl's Jr. fast-food restaurants in the western United States and Mexico. Amounts are in thousands.

Sales by Company-Operated Restaurants	$381,733
Revenues from Franchised and Licensed Restaurants	78,635
Other Income	6,148
Operating Expenses	(449,860)
Interest Expense	(10,387)
Income Tax Expense	(1,836)
Other Expenses	(768)
Net Income	$ 3,665

Required:
Different financial statement users concentrate on different aspects of financial statements. For example, stockholders (a company's owners), company management, and bankers concentrate on different components of an income statement. Describe how each of these three groups of decision makers would use Carl Karcher's income statement data. Be specific in your descriptions. For example, identify the questions or issues that each type of decision maker would address with the information reported in this income statement.

23. No check figures

24. **Common Cost Allocation** (LO 3)

Unique Enterprises manufactures a number of unusual yard statuary items for sale to lawn and garden stores. Two of the primary raw materials that go into the products are marble chips and decorative bricks. These materials are often delivered to Unique's facilities at the same time and in the same shipment, accompanied by a single freight bill covering both. Unique's management is concerned about the appropriate way to allocate common shipping costs to the two raw material inventory items. One option is to allocate this common cost based on relative total weights in each shipment. For example, assume that a shipment containing these two items weighs 1,000 pounds. If the chips in this shipment weigh 800 pounds, 80 percent of the shipping cost would be allocated to chips while the remaining portion of the shipping cost would be allocated to the bricks included in the shipment. Another option is to allocate based on relative total cost. The marble chips cost $500 per ton, while the bricks cost $250 per ton.

Required:

24. 1a. Chips, $100
        Bricks, $300
    1b. Chips, $160
        Bricks, $240

1. Allocate the shipping cost of $400 for a recent shipment between chips and bricks. The shipment included 5 tons of chips and 15 tons of bricks. Allocate based on the following:
    a. Total relative weight
    b. Total relative cost
2. Which allocation method would you recommend to Unique's management as best representing the actual costs of shipping chips and bricks? Explain.

25. **Effects of Industry Accounting Practice** (LO 4)
As discussed in this chapter, under previous accounting rules applicable to the savings and loan industry, losses on sales of certain securities could be deferred and written off (subtracted from income) over several years. Assume that the write-off period was five years and that a savings and loan sold a qualifying security for $1 million that had originally cost $3 million.

Required:

25. 1. −$2,000,000
    2. −$400,000

1. How much loss would the savings and loan have recognized in the year of sale had the special accounting rules *not been in effect?*
2. How much loss did the savings and loan recognize each of the five years under the special accounting rules? (Assume that an equal amount of loss was recognized each year.)
3. Write a brief memo explaining how and in what way(s) this accounting treatment may have been misleading to financial statement users.

26. **International Accounting Differences** (LO 7)
In the United States, GAAP requires that long-term assets, such as buildings and equipment, owned by a business be reported in financial statements at cost less accumulated depreciation. Accumulated depreciation represents the total "depreciation expense" recognized for an asset since it was acquired. For example, an asset that cost $10,000 and has an estimated useful life of 10 years would be depreciated $1,000 per year for 10 years. So, after three years, this asset would be reported in an entity's financial statements at $7,000—$10,000 cost less accumulated depreciation of $3,000. (Some of the finer points regarding the computation of depreciation are not discussed here but rather deferred to a later chapter.)

Long-term assets can be "written off" more rapidly if they decline in value because of obsolescence or other factors. However, in the United States, these assets cannot be increased in value for accounting purposes even if their fair market values rise. This rule does not apply in many countries, an example being Australia. In these countries, assets may be revalued upward with a related adjustment to the annual computation of depreciation expense. For example, in these countries if the asset in the present example had a fair market value of $14,000 after three years, that asset could be "written up" to $14,000. This new value would then be depreciated over the remaining seven years of the asset's useful life.

Required:

1. Consider the example presented. Assume the given asset was owned by a business operating in a country that allows long-term assets to be written up to their fair market values. If this asset had a fair market value of $14,000 after three years, how much depreciation would the business record each remaining year of the asset's life—assuming no further changes in the asset's fair market value?

2. Compare the amount computed in Part 1 to the depreciation expense allowed for an identical asset owned by a U.S. business. All other relevant variables being held constant, which of the two businesses would report the higher income for each of the next seven years?

3. "Financial decision makers must be very cautious when interpreting the financial statements of a foreign entity." Write a brief memo discussing the meaning of this statement given the example presented here and the related discussion in the text.

26. No check figures

PROBLEM SET B

27. Use of Income Statement Information (LO 3)

The following information was taken from the 1994 annual report of Winnebago Industries, Inc. The company, headquartered in Forest City, Iowa, manufactures motor homes and recreational vehicles. Amounts are in thousands.

Sales Revenue	$432,406
Service Revenue	19,710
Operating Expenses	(435,322)
Interest Expense	(661)
Other Expenses	(19,108)
Net Loss	$ (2,975)

Required:

Different financial statement users concentrate on different aspects of financial statements. For example, potential vendors (individuals or businesses that sell raw materials or services to business entities), company management, and potential lenders concentrate on different components of an income statement. Describe how each of these three groups of decision makers would use Winnebago's income statement data. Be specific in your descriptions. For example, identify the questions or issues that each type of decision maker would address with the information reported in this income statement.

27. No check figures

28. Common Cost Allocation (LO 3)

Avery Brick, Inc., manufactures stepping stones and yard ornaments from cement and stone products. Two of the primary raw materials that go into the products are ground stone chips and cement colorants. These materials are often delivered to Avery's facilities at the same time and in the same shipment, accompanied by a single freight bill covering both. Avery's management is concerned about the appropriate way to allocate common shipping costs to the two raw material inventory items. One option is to allocate this common cost based on total relative weights in each shipment. For example, assume that a shipment containing these two items weighs 4,000 pounds. If the stone chips in this shipment weigh 3,000 pounds, 75 percent (3,000 pounds/4,000 pounds) of the shipping cost would be allocated to the stone chips, while the remaining portion of the shipping cost would be allocated to the cement colorants in the shipment.

Another option is to allocate based on relative total cost. The stone chips cost $250 per ton, while the colorants cost $750 per ton.

Required:

28. 1a. Chips, $100
         Colorant, $400
     1b. Chips, $38.50
         Colorant, $461.50

1. Allocate the shipping cost of $500 from a recent shipment between chips and colorants. The shipment included 5 tons of chips and 20 tons of colorants. Allocate based on the following:
   a. Total relative weight
   b. Total relative cost
2. The two methods result in different cost allocations. Therefore, the choice of allocation method matters to anyone who uses the company's financial statements. In your opinion, which of these two methods will result in more accurate financial statements? Explain.

29. **Effects of Industry Accounting Practices** (LO 4)

Until recently in the savings and loan industry, losses on sales of certain securities could be deferred and written off (subtracted from income) over several years. Assume that the write-off period was five years under this special accounting rule and that a savings and loan sold a qualifying security for $500,000 that had cost $4 million.

Required:

29. 1. −$3,500,000
     2. −$700,000

1. How much loss would the savings and loan have recognized in the year of sale had the special accounting rule *not been in effect?*
2. How much did the savings and loan recognize each year over the five-year write-off period under the special accounting rule? (Assume it recognized an equal amount of the loss each year.)
3. Write a brief memo explaining how this accounting treatment might have affected, or influenced, financial statement users' economic decisions.

30. **International Accounting Differences** (LO 7)

Businesses in the United States must report their long-term assets, such as buildings and equipment, at cost less accumulated depreciation. Accumulated depreciation represents the total "depreciation expense" recognized for an asset since it was acquired. For example, an asset that cost $40,000 and has an estimated useful life of 10 years would be depreciated $4,000 per year for 10 years. So, after four years, this asset would be reported in an entity's financial statements at $24,000—$40,000 cost less accumulated depreciation of $16,000. (Some of the finer points regarding the computation of depreciation are not discussed here but rather deferred to a later chapter.)

Accounting principles in the United States allow long-term assets to be "written off" more rapidly if they decline in value because of obsolescence or other factors. However, these assets cannot be increased in value for accounting purposes even if their fair market values rise. This rule does not apply in many countries, an example being Sweden. In these countries, assets may be revalued upward with a related adjustment to the annual computation of depreciation expense. For example, in these countries if the asset in the present example had a fair market value of $60,000 after four years, that asset could be "written up" to $60,000. This new value would then be depreciated over the remaining six years of the asset's useful life.

Required:

30. No check figures

1. Consider the example presented. Assume the given asset was owned by a business operating in a country that allows long-term assets to be written up to their fair market values. If this asset had a fair market value of $60,000 after

four years, how much depreciation would the business record each remaining year of the asset's life—assuming no further changes in the asset's fair market value?

2. Compare the amount computed in Part 1 to the depreciation expense allowed for an identical asset owned by a United States business. All other relevant variables being held constant, which of the two businesses would report the higher income for each of the next six years?

3. This is only one example of the differences that exist between U.S. accounting rules and the accounting rules of other countries. Write a brief report discussing how knowledge of international differences in accounting rules is essential to decision makers who rely on financial statements from different countries.

CASES

31. Ethical Accounting Practices

As a first-time independent auditor of Golombay's 1995 financial statements, you are concerned that the company appears to be holding its year end "open." This means that sales actually made during 1996 are being recorded as 1995 sales.

Required:

1. How will this practice affect Golombay's financial statements for 1995 and 1996?
2. How might this practice mislead external decision makers in both years?
3. As the auditor, what should you do about this situation?

32. Ethics of Accountants

Refer to the Spotlight on Ethics vignette in this chapter titled "Doing the Right Thing . . . and Paying for It."

Required:

1. Put yourself in the position of the accountant in this case. Would you have dealt with the given situation as he did? In a brief memo, discuss how you would have responded to this situation.
2. As a private accountant, this individual may have been a member of the Institute of Management Accountants (IMA). Ask your instructor to direct you to a copy of the IMA's Code of Ethics. After reviewing the code (it's one page long), revisit your decision as to how you would have dealt with this situation. Would your approach to the situation have changed given the requirements of the IMA's Code of Ethics? Why or why not?

33. Analysis of the Auditor's Report

Review the audit report for Sears, Roebuck and Co. included in this chapter and the related discussion.

Required:

1. Based on your reading of the report, answer the following questions.
   a. What does the auditor audit?
   b. Who is ultimately responsible for a company's financial statements?
   c. What standards guide the conduct of an independent audit?
   d. What is the objective of an independent audit?
2. What role does the auditing profession play in overseeing corporate reporting?
3. What part does the SEC play in overseeing corporate reporting?
4. What is the relationship between the SEC and auditors?

PROJECTS

34. Understanding the Annual Report

Refer to Exhibit 1.1 in this chapter. Choose a recent annual report of a publicly owned company. Within the report, find the income statement (which may take on a slightly different name such as "Consolidated Statement of Income").

Required:

1. In the annual report you selected, find the following information:
   a. The exact title of the company's income statement
   b. The major income statement components (net sales, etc.).
2. Read the "footnotes" to the financial statements that pertain to the income statement and summarize any items that seem important to understanding the components of net income (loss) for the given company.
3. Prepare a brief report summarizing your answers to Parts 1 and 2.

35. Proposed Accounting Rules and Criticism of the Accounting Profession

Corporate executives are often very critical of proposed accounting rules that would negatively affect their firm's reported financial condition. In recent years, proposed new accounting rules for stock options, postretirement employee benefits, oil and gas reserves, and certain investments in marketable securities have resulted in criticism of not only the proposed rules but the accounting profession as well.

In this project, which will be completed on a team basis, you will research one of the proposed accounting rules just mentioned, or another assigned by your instructor and develop a written report summarizing the nature of the controversy involving the proposed rule. Among the items your report will cover are the following: (1) a brief summary of the proposed rule, (2) a brief overview of why the accounting profession believed the proposed rule was needed, (3) a summary of the reasons that certain parties opposed the rule, (4) a summary of the reasons that certain parties supported the rule, and (5) whether or not the rule was adopted and, if so, any major changes between the original proposed rule and the rule finally adopted.

Required:

1. Your instructor will assign you to a group or project team to complete this project. Meet briefly with your group and discuss your assigned topic. In this initial meeting, your group should decide on a strategy for allocating the responsibilities for completing this project. For example, one or more group members may have the primary responsibility to search on-line newspaper indices (*New York Times, The Wall Street Journal*, etc.) to identify articles relevant to the assigned topic. Another member may be assigned the responsibility of identifying and reviewing magazine articles related to this topic. Other tasks to be assigned individual group members include organizing and outlining the relevant materials collected, preparing the written report, critiquing the report, and presenting an in-class summary of the report.
2. Before the written report is submitted to your instructor and the in-class presentation is made, at least one additional group meeting should be arranged. In this meeting, group members should review a draft of the written report and agree on the final content of the report. The individual assigned to present the report in class should give the presentation to the group, which will then critique that presentation.

ACCOUNTING CONCEPTS AND ELEMENTS

2

After studying this chapter, you should be able to do the following:

1. Define the three financial reporting objectives of business entities

2. Describe the nature, purpose, and content of each of the four financial statements

3. Identify and define the key attributes or characteristics that accounting information should possess

4. Identify and define the fundamental concepts that underlie accounting rules and practices

The beginning of wisdom is the definition of terms.
Socrates

A Stick-to-the-Basics Approach to Business and Accounting

Jim Penney graduated from a Missouri high school in the early 1890s and immediately accepted a job as a clerk in a local dry goods store. Although he enjoyed the job, Penney was eventually caught up in the "go west, young man" fever. After moving to Colorado, Penney invested his life savings in a butcher shop, a decision he would soon regret. Penney was unfamiliar with his new line of business and totally unacquainted with the business etiquette of the Wild West. The largest customer of his butcher shop was a hotel. Unknown to Penney at the time he purchased the butcher shop, the prior owner had given the hotel's cook a bottle of whiskey each week in gratitude for the hotel's business. The principled, if not stubborn, young Penney refused to continue this practice and soon lost the hotel as a customer. Shortly thereafter, Penney was forced to close his butcher shop. Disheartened but not discouraged, Penney decided to return to the line of business that he knew best.

In 1902, Jim Penney moved north to Wyoming and opened a dry goods store in Kemmerer, a small mining town. From the beginning, Penney oriented his dry goods business around a few fundamental principles that he had learned early in his career. His "stick-to-the-basics" philosophy included four key rules: keep overhead as low as possible, offer merchandise at reasonable prices, use a cash and carry—no credit—sales policy, and allow customers to return goods if they are not totally satisfied. Almost immediately, Penney's new venture proved successful. Within a little more than two decades, there would be over one thousand J. C. Penney's stores located across the United States with total sales of more than $100 million.

Jim Penney's "stick-to-the-basics" philosophy can be successfully applied in any field, including accounting. To correctly record transactions and other events affecting organizations, accountants must understand the basic conceptual principles of accounting. The purpose of this chapter is to introduce you to those principles. This introduction will serve you well in later chapters when the more applied, or procedural, aspects of accounting are discussed.

Teaching Note
Remind students that external decision makers include investors and creditors who need information for investment and lending decisions.

In Chapter 1 you learned that the primary objective of accounting and accountants is to provide useful information to financial decision makers. The principal focus of financial accounting is the information needs of decision makers who are external to an organization. You may enroll in a subsequent course entitled Management Accounting or Managerial Accounting. In that course, you will be concerned primarily with the information needs of internal decision makers.

In this textbook, we concern ourselves principally with accounting for business entities. The phrase "business entities" refers to organizations that have a profit motive, such as Exxon, a large corporation. Most of the examples in this textbook involve corporations rather than other types of business entities such as partnerships and sole proprietorships, which are defined and discussed later in this chapter. Many organizations do not have a profit motive. Municipal hospitals, charities such as the Salvation Army, and governmental agencies are examples of not-for-profit organizations. The accounting rules and methods used by not-for-profit organizations are often quite different from the corresponding rules and methods applied by business entities. If you continue your study of accounting, you may enroll in a course entitled Governmental Accounting or Fund Accounting, which will focus on the accounting rules and methods used by not-for-profit organizations.

This chapter begins by identifying the financial reporting objectives of business entities. Next, you become acquainted with the nature, purpose, and content of the four financial statements that are prepared and issued regularly by business enterprises. The last two sections of this chapter discuss the qualitative attributes that accounting information should possess and describe the fundamental concepts that underlie accounting and financial reporting practices.

Although you may find this surprising, most financial accounting textbooks do not discuss basic accounting concepts in an early chapter. Instead, most of these textbooks focus immediately on the mechanics of accounting and relegate a discussion of accounting concepts to a chapter much farther along in the book. Here, we are going to take a different approach, a top-down approach. Beginning with a discussion of accounting concepts and the key elements of accounting can be intimidating to introductory accounting students. However, keep in mind that the purpose of this chapter is not to immediately transform you into an accounting expert. Instead, the intent of this chapter is to allow you to make sense of the many accounting rules and procedures discussed in the remainder of this textbook. You may want to think of this chapter as a user's manual for the remainder of this textbook. In particular, you will find the lengthy glossary at the end of this chapter a useful reference source for subsequent chapters.

OBJECTIVES OF FINANCIAL REPORTING

In the mid-1970s, the FASB decided that there was a need for a conceptual framework to guide the development of future accounting standards. From 1978 through 1985, the FASB issued six **Statements of Financial Accounting Concepts (SFACs)** to serve as this conceptual framework. These six statements are listed in Exhibit 2.1. Throughout Chapter 2, we will refer to these statements as we identify the basic concepts and elements of accounting.

According to *SFAC No. 1*, business enterprises have three financial reporting objectives. These objectives are listed in Exhibit 2.2. Each of these objectives directly or indirectly concerns the need for the financial reports of business entities to assist third parties in making rational and informed economic decisions.

■ **LEARNING OBJECTIVE 1**
Define the three financial reporting objectives of business entities

Statements of Financial Accounting Concepts (SFACs)

■ **EXHIBIT 2.1**
FASB's Conceptual Framework

- SFAC No. 1 Objectives of financial reporting by business enterprises
- SFAC No. 2 Qualitative characteristics of accounting information
- SFAC No. 3 Elements of financial statements of business enterprises*
- SFAC No. 4 Objectives of financial reporting by nonbusiness organizations
- SFAC No. 5 Recognition and measurement in financial statements of business enterprises
- SFAC No. 6 Elements of financial statements

*Superseded by *SFAC No. 6.*

■ **EXHIBIT 2.2**

Financial Reporting Objectives of Business Enterprises

SOURCE: Portions of various FASB documents, copyright by Financial Accounting Standards Board, 401 Merritt 7, P. O. Box 5116, Norwalk, Connecticut, 06856-5116, U.S.A., are reprinted with permission. Copies of the complete documents are available from the FASB.

1. Financial reports of business enterprises should provide information that is useful in making investment, credit, and related decisions.

2. Financial reports should provide information allowing potential investors and creditors and other parties to predict the future cash flows of business enterprises and the eventual cash flows that they will receive from those enterprises.

3. Financial reports should provide information about the assets and liabilities of given enterprises and the transactions and events that have resulted in changes in those assets and liabilities.

If investors, creditors, and other external decision makers are to make sound economic decisions involving business entities, they need a wide array of financial information regarding those entities. To prove this point, consider the Strawberry House, a bed and breakfast inn located in Cripple Creek, Colorado. Cripple Creek was a prosperous gold mining town in the early 1900s, but now the principal industry in this small mountain village is tourism. The owners of the Strawberry House rent out its three bedrooms on a nightly basis and provide their guests with breakfast each morning. If the owners of this business decide to branch out and open bed and breakfast inns in other mountain resorts in Colorado, they may require funding (loans) from a bank. A banker approached by these individuals for a loan would insist on reviewing financial statements for the Strawberry House. The banker would use these financial statements to predict the net cash flows produced by the business after its expansion, since those cash flows would be the principal source of funds used to repay the loan and the interest on the loan. The financial reporting objective most pertinent in this context would be the second objective identified by *SFAC No. 1* as shown in Exhibit 2.2.

Now, let us turn the tables on the previous situation and consider the financial reporting objectives of a banking company. First Chicago Corporation has more than $50 billion in assets and owns and operates several banks, including the First National Bank of Chicago. Since the financial crisis of the 1980s in the banking and savings and loan industries, governmental agencies such as the Federal Reserve have closely monitored the health of financial institutions. One of the items in a bank's financial statements monitored by regulatory authorities is the allowance for loan losses. This item represents a bank's best estimate of the dollar amount of its outstanding loans that will prove to be uncollectible. A bank's financial health can be jeopardized if it begins experiencing problems collecting its outstanding loans. If these problems become severe, banking regulators may force the bank to change its operating policies and procedures.

A check of recent financial statements issued by First Chicago Corporation reveals that the company's allowance for loan losses declined by nearly $100 million during the preceding twelve months. When banking regulators obtained these financial statements, you can be certain that they wanted to know exactly why First Chicago's allowance for loan losses had dropped sharply during the previous year. Here, the

Small businesses, such as the many restaurants, bed and breakfast inns, and novelty shops located in Cripple Creek, Colorado, have a need for an accounting system that will produce periodic financial statements. Among other uses, these financial statements are often included in loan applications filed with local banks by small business owners.

pertinent financial reporting objective is the third objective identified by *SFAC No. 1*. First Chicago Corporation had a responsibility to provide banking regulators and other interested third parties with information explaining the large change in its allowance for loan losses. To the credit of First Chicago Corporation, the firm's financial statements for the year in question included an extensive analysis of the large decrease in its allowance for loan losses.

Real World
Point out to students that First Chicago Corporation provided the loan loss information in its financial statement footnotes, an integral part of a set of financial statements.

FINANCIAL STATEMENTS: NATURE, PURPOSE, AND DEFINITIONS OF KEY ELEMENTS

Accountants communicate financial information regarding business entities to external decision makers principally in the form of four financial statements. These financial statements include a balance sheet, an income statement, a statement of stockholders' equity, and a statement of cash flows. In this section, we review the structure and content of each of these financial statements.

■ LEARNING OBJECTIVE 2
Describe the nature, purpose, and content of each of the four financial statements

The Balance Sheet

Shown in Exhibit 2.3 is a balance sheet as of December 31, 1995, for Small Store, Inc., a hypothetical company. Most introductory financial accounting textbooks use the balance sheet of a small hypothetical company to assist students in learning the structure and content of a balance sheet. You will find the balance sheet of Small Store useful for that purpose, since it contains all of the major elements that appear in a balance sheet and the most common terminology for those elements.

■ **EXHIBIT 2.3**

Small Store, Inc., Balance Sheet as of December 31, 1995

SMALL STORE, INC.
BALANCE SHEET
DECEMBER 31, 1995

ASSETS

Current Assets		
Cash		$ 200
Short-Term Investments		1,500
Accounts Receivable		800
Inventories		2,200
Prepaid Expenses		100
Total Current Assets		$ 4,800
Property, Plant and Equipment	$10,000	
Less: Accumulated Depreciation	(2,000)	
		8,000
Intangible Assets		600
Long-Term Investments		2,100
Other Assets		500
Total Assets		$16,000

LIABILITIES

Current Liabilities		
Accounts Payable		$ 400
Accrued Expenses		200
Notes Payable		800
Current Portion of Long-Term Debt		1,000
Total Current Liabilities		$ 2,400
Long-Term Liabilities		
Notes Payable		2,000
Mortgages Payable		3,000
Bonds Payable		2,500
Total Liabilities		$ 9,900

STOCKHOLDERS' EQUITY

Common Stock		$ 300
Additional Paid-in Capital		1,300
Retailed Earnings		4,500
Total Stockholders' Equity		6,100
Total Stockholders' Equity and Liabilities		$16,000

An example of an actual balance sheet is presented in Exhibit 2.4. The balance sheet in Exhibit 2.4 was prepared for Buffalo Don's Artesian Wells, Ltd., a Michigan-based company engaged in the bottling and distribution of distilled drinking water. In April 1993, when this balance sheet was prepared, Buffalo Don's was a publicly owned company. Any member of the public who had sufficient funds could purchase a part of the ownership interest, represented by common stock certificates, in this company.

■ **EXHIBIT 2.4**
Buffalo Don's Artesian Wells, Ltd., Balance Sheet as of April 3, 1993

BUFFALO DON'S ARTESIAN WELLS, LTD.
BALANCE SHEET
APRIL 3, 1993

ASSETS

Current Assets		
Cash		$ 79,162
Trade Accounts Receivable		407,931
Other Receivables		23,602
Inventories:		
Finished Goods		17,960
Materials and Supplies		115,834
Prepaid Expenses		87,365
Total Current Assets		$ 731,854
Equipment and Leasehold Improvements		
Leasehold Improvements	$ 140,030	
Machinery and Equipment	1,490,307	
Vehicles	43,817	
Furniture and Fixtures	71,041	
Less: Accumulated Depreciation and Amortization	(816,559)	
		928,636
Other Assets		43,989
Total Assets		$1,704,479

LIABILITIES

Current Liabilities	
Line of Credit	$ 167,185
Current Portion of Long-Term Debt	51,650
Accounts Payable	695,720
Accrued Liabilities	82,440
Total Current Liabilities	996,995
Long-Term Debt	312,000
Total Liabilities	$1,308,995

STOCKHOLDERS' EQUITY

Common stock, Par Value of $.01 Per Share:	
10,000,000 Shares Authorized, 3,000,000	
Shares Issued and Outstanding	$ 30,000
Additional Paid-in Capital	1,345,000
Retained Earnings (Accumulated Deficit)	(979,516)
Total Stockholders' Equity	$ 395,484
Total Stockholders' Equity and Liabilities	$1,704,479

SOURCE: 1993 Annual Report of Buffalo Don's Artesian Wells, Ltd.

Teaching Note

Emphasize to students that the snapshot of a company at a specific point in time is a picture of that day only. Tomorrow the company's balance sheet will have changed. For example, Buffalo Don's cash balance on April 3, 1993, was $79,162. On April 4, 1993, the company's cash balance would have been different.

Teaching Note

Use Exhibit 2.4 to illustrate the accounting equation:
Assets = Liabilities + Stockholders' Equity
($1,704,479 = $1,308,995 + $393,484).
Point out that these three components of the accounting equation make up the balance sheet.

balance sheet

accounting equation

However, in late 1993, Buffalo Don's "went private." Another company purchased all of Buffalo Don's common stock and decided that it would retain that stock indefinitely. As a result, the company's stock is no longer publicly traded. So, Exhibit 2.4 presents the final balance sheet of Buffalo Don's that was released for public consumption.

What is a balance sheet? When asked that question by a nonaccountant, accountants are prone to answer that a balance sheet is a financial snapshot of a company at a specific point in time. For the balance sheet shown in Exhibit 2.4, the snapshot date was April 3, 1993. Accountants also tend to refer to a balance sheet as a statement of financial condition or financial position. A more descriptive definition of a **balance sheet** is a financial statement that summarizes the assets, liabilities, and stockholders' or owners' equity of an entity at a specific point in time.

The title "balance sheet" is appropriate because the sum of an entity's assets must equal the sum of its liabilities and stockholders' or owners' equity. Expressed in equation form for a corporation, this relationship appears as follows:

$$\text{Assets} \quad = \quad \text{Liabilities} \quad + \quad \text{Stockholders' Equity}$$

The previous equation is known as the **accounting equation,** or the balance sheet equation. A more generic version of this equation for all business entities is as follows:

$$\text{Assets} \quad = \quad \text{Liabilities} \quad + \quad \text{Owners' Equity}$$

Notice that the only difference in the two versions of the accounting equation is in the final term. Stockholders' equity represents the collective ownership interests in a corporation of its stockholders—which are a corporation's owners. Owners' equity is a general term that refers to the collective ownership interests of any business entity.

A balance sheet provides answers to many questions that investors, creditors, and other decision makers have regarding the financial status of a business. Examples of such questions include: "How much cash does Company A have on hand?" "Is this cash balance large enough to allow the company to pay off a bank loan that comes due next month?" "How much cash or other assets have the owners of Company A invested in the business?" In later chapters, we identify a broad range of decision makers' information needs that a balance sheet satisfies. However, here, the purpose is to acquaint you with the structure and content of this financial statement. To accomplish this objective, let us "walk through" the balance sheet and identify its individual components.

assets

ASSETS   *SFAC No. 6* defines **assets** as "probable future economic benefits obtained or controlled by a particular entity as a result of past transactions or events."[1] A nonaccountant might simplify this definition to "things that a company owns." Buffalo Don's prepares a classified balance sheet, like most companies. In a classified balance sheet assets, liabilities, and stockholders' equity are subdivided into groups. Notice in Exhibit 2.4 that Buffalo Don's assets are subdivided into three groups: current assets, equipment and leasehold improvements, and other assets. Most companies have additional classes or groups of assets. Long-term investments and intangible assets are the two most common asset classes that do not appear in Buffalo Don's balance sheet shown in Exhibit 2.4. Likewise, a more common caption for "equip-

---

1. Portions of various FASB documents, copyright by Financial Accounting Standards Board, 401 Merritt 7, P.O. Box 5116, Norwalk, Connecticut, 06856-5116, U.S.A., are reprinted with permission. Copies of the complete documents are available from the FASB.

ment and leasehold improvements" is "property, plant and equipment." (Again, the balance sheet in Exhibit 2.3 lists the most common balance sheet components and the titles or captions most frequently assigned to these components.)

CURRENT ASSETS Current assets are generally listed first on a balance sheet. Included in **current assets** are cash and other assets that will be converted into cash, sold, or consumed during the next fiscal year or the normal operating cycle of a business if its operating cycle is longer than a year. An entity's **fiscal year** is the twelve-month period covered by its annual income statement. The fiscal year of most companies coincides with the calendar year. A company's **operating cycle** is that period of time elapsing from the use of cash in its normal operating, or profit-oriented, activities to the collection of cash from its customers. The operating cycle of a restaurant chain, such as Luby's Cafeterias, is usually just a few days. Luby's buys unprocessed raw materials—flour, fruit, vegetables, and so on—converts those materials into ready-to-eat food items, and then sells these items to its customers for cash. The operating cycle of a manufacturing firm, such as the La-Z-Boy Chair Company, can be several months long, if not longer.

The five most common types of current assets are cash, short-term investments, accounts receivable, inventories, and prepaid expenses. Current assets are typically listed in a balance sheet from most to least liquid—that is, in order of "nearness to cash." The line item **cash** on a balance sheet represents the collective amount of cash that an entity has on hand or on deposit with banks or other financial institutions at the balance sheet date. **Short-term investments** generally include investments that a company expects to sell or otherwise convert into cash within the coming year. Common examples of short-term investments held by businesses are corporate stocks and bonds. Buffalo Don's did not have any short-term investments as of April 3, 1993, since none were reported in its balance sheet shown in Exhibit 2.4.

Most companies that sell goods or provide services extend credit to their customers, meaning that customers are not required to pay for the goods or services immediately. Amounts owed to a business entity by its customers are referred to as **accounts receivable,** or trade accounts receivable. **Inventories** consist of goods that an entity intends to sell directly to its customers or raw materials or "in-process" items that will be converted into saleable goods. Businesses often prepay in advance for one or more months relatively minor expense items such as rent, insurance, and advertising. These amounts are reported as **prepaid expenses** in the current asset section of an entity's balance sheet.

PROPERTY, PLANT AND EQUIPMENT By definition, all assets other than current assets are long-term or noncurrent assets. The largest category of long-term assets for most companies is **property, plant and equipment.** This category of long-term assets includes buildings, machinery, furniture, and related assets used in the normal operating activities of a business.

Those property, plant and equipment assets that have limited useful lives are referred to as depreciable assets. Accounting standards require that the cost of these assets be allocated or "written off" to the time periods they benefit. The technical accounting term used to describe this cost allocation process is depreciation. Chapter 9 discusses several approaches to computing depreciation. To briefly acquaint you with this subject, suppose that Procter & Gamble buys a piece of equipment on January 1, 1998, to use in a manufacturing process. The cost of the machinery is $120,000, and its expected useful life is four years at the end of which it will have no salvage, or "scrap," value. If Procter & Gamble uses the straight-line depreciation method, it

current assets

fiscal year

operating cycle

Real World
Many companies choose a fiscal year that ends when business activity is at its lowest level. For example, many department store chains select a January 31 year end due to the large decrease in sales and lower inventory levels following the Christmas season.

cash

short-term investments

accounts receivable

inventories

prepaid expenses

property, plant and equipment

Teaching Note
Land is considered to have an unlimited useful life and, therefore, is not written off over time.

A Noncurrent Current Asset

Current assets are expected to be sold, consumed, or converted into cash within one year or less, an exception being when a company's operating cycle is longer than one year. Most companies have operating cycles shorter than twelve months. An example of a company with an operating cycle longer than one year is Philip Morris Companies, Inc., a firm best known for its tobacco products. One of Philip Morris's current assets is its inventory of leaf tobacco. Leaf tobacco requires more than one year to age properly. Since this aging process is a component of the company's operating cycle, leaf tobacco is included as a current asset in Philip Morris's balance sheet, although it may be more than one year away from being converted into cash.

will depreciate the equipment $30,000 per year from 1998 through 2001 ($120,000/4 years).

"Accumulated depreciation" is the total amount of depreciation that has been recorded on a depreciable asset or group of depreciable assets since their acquisition. For balance sheet purposes, the accumulated depreciation for property, plant and equipment assets is subtracted from the collective dollar amount of these assets, as shown in both Exhibits 2.3 and 2.4. Notice that Buffalo Don's balance sheet reports accumulated depreciation and "amortization." The latter item represents the cumulative amount of intangible assets—defined in the following section—that have been written off or amortized since their acquisition date. (Amortization is a term that accountants use to describe the cost allocation process for intangible assets.)

intangible assets

INTANGIBLE ASSETS   **Intangible assets** are long-term assets that do not have a physical form or substance. An example of an intangible asset is a patent. A patent is an exclusive right granted by the United States Patent Office to manufacture a specific product or to use a specific process. Other examples of intangible assets include copyrights, trademarks, and goodwill.

long-term investments

LONG-TERM INVESTMENTS   Investments in corporate stocks and bonds and government securities are generally considered short-term investments if they are expected to be converted into cash within the coming year. Similar investments that management intends to retain for more than one year are classified as **long-term investments** or simply investments. Land and other noncurrent assets not used in the normal operating activities of a business are often classified as long-term investments for balance sheet purposes.

other assets

OTHER ASSETS   A catch-all classification for miscellaneous long-term assets, **other assets,** is typically the last asset category appearing on a balance sheet. The total amount of these mystery assets is usually quite small compared to a business's total assets.

The operating cycle of certain companies extends beyond one year. An example is tobacco companies whose operating cycle includes the time required to harvest, age, and then process leaf tobacco.

LIABILITIES   Liabilities are amounts owed by entities to third parties. *SFAC No. 6* provides a more long-winded definition of **liabilities:** "probable future sacrifices of economic benefits arising from present obligations of a particular entity to transfer assets or provide services to other entities in the future as a result of past transactions or events."[2]

liabilities

CURRENT LIABILITIES   **Current liabilities** are listed first in the liabilities section of a balance sheet. Included in this balance sheet classification are debts and other obligations that must be paid by an entity during its next fiscal year or operating cycle, whichever is longer. Among the most common types of current liabilities are accounts payable, accrued expenses, notes payable, and the current portion of long-term debt.

current liabilities

Accounts payable represent amounts owed by a business to its suppliers. In a sense, accounts payable are the flip side of accounts receivable. For example, the amounts owed to Hershey Corporation by its customers would appear as accounts receivable in Hershey's balance sheet. Conversely, the amounts that Hershey owes to its suppliers would be reported in the company's balance sheet as accounts payable.

accounts payable

When a balance sheet is being prepared, a business entity must identify amounts it owes to third parties that have not previously been recorded as liabilities in its accounting records. Typically, these liabilities, commonly referred to as **accrued expenses** or accrued liabilities, relate to obligations incurred near the end of an accounting period. Quite often, accrued expenses must be estimated since their exact amount cannot be determined. For instance, at the end of an accounting period, a company will generally have to estimate the dollar amount of electricity it has consumed since the date of its last electric bill. This amount will then be recorded as a liability in its accounting records. Notice that Buffalo Don's balance sheet in Exhibit 2.4 reported $82,440 of accrued liabilities.

Teaching Note
Contrast prepaid expenses and accrued expenses. Prepaid expenses are paid first and recognized as expenses later. Accrued expenses are recognized as expenses first and paid later.

accrued expenses

Companies frequently borrow money from their banks on a short-term basis and sign a promissory note, which is a legally binding commitment to repay the funds

---

2. Portions of various FASB documents, copyright by Financial Accounting Standards Board, 401 Merritt 7, P.O. Box 5116, Norwalk, Connecticut, 06856-5116, U.S.A., are reprinted with permission. Copies of the complete documents are available from the FASB.

notes payable

borrowed. If due in one year or less, **notes payable** are listed as current liabilities on a company's balance sheet. To provide a readily available source of short-term loans, many companies establish a line of credit agreement with one or more banks or other financial institutions. A line of credit is simply a borrowing arrangement in which a company has access to funds on an as-needed basis. Companies usually sign a promissory note when they activate a line of credit by borrowing funds. Some companies refer to these liabilities as notes payable, while other firms simply list the dollar amount borrowed as "line of credit" on their balance sheet. As of April 3, 1993, Buffalo Don's had borrowed $167,185 on an available line of credit of $480,000.

current portion of long-term debt

Notice also that Buffalo Don's reported a $51,650 current liability for the portion of its long-term debt that was to be paid in the following year. When a company has long-term debt, or long-term liabilities, it must include in its balance sheet under current liabilities the **current portion of long-term debt.** This current liability represents the collective dollar amount of an entity's long-term liabilities that must be paid in the coming year.

long-term liabilities

LONG-TERM LIABILITIES   **Long-term liabilities** include the debts and obligations of an entity other than those classified as current liabilities. Examples of long-term liabilities include long-term notes payable, mortgages payable, and bonds payable. Quite often, a company reports the collective amount of several long-term liabilities on one balance sheet line item entitled long-term debt.

mortgages payable

Mortgages payable are long-term liabilities that are secured or collateralized by some asset, typically a building or other piece of property. If a company defaults on a mortgage payable, the lender can take possession of the secured property or force it to be sold to recover the unpaid balance of the mortgage.

The federal government periodically sells bonds and other securities to raise funds needed to finance its operations. Corporations also sell bonds, typically in $1,000 denominations, to raise funds they need for a variety of purposes. For instance, a company may sell bonds to finance a major expansion of its production facilities. When a company sells bonds, it incurs a long-term liability to repay the collective amount of those bonds to the parties who purchased them. This long-term liability is reported in an entity's balance sheet as **bonds payable.**

bonds payable

STOCKHOLDERS' EQUITY   As pointed out earlier, a balance sheet "balances" in the following sense: assets must equal the sum of liabilities and stockholders' or owners' equity. If you own a home, the difference between the value of the home and the unpaid balance of the mortgage is your ownership interest or equity, often referred to as homeowner's equity by a bank. Applying this reasoning to a corporation, total assets less amounts owed to third parties (liabilities) equals **stockholders' equity** or the stockholders' ownership interest in that corporation. The three line items most likely to appear in the stockholders' equity section of a corporate balance sheet are common stock, additional paid-in capital, and retained earnings.

stockholders' equity

common stock

COMMON STOCK   The dollar amount reported for the stockholders' equity item **common stock** on a corporation's balance sheet equals the collective par value of all common stock shares that the company has sold or otherwise issued. (Recall that ownership interests in a corporation are represented by common stock certificates.) Anticipating your next question, par value is simply a nominal value attached to each share of a corporation's common stock. Typically, par value bears no relationship to the market value of a company's stock or even the initial selling price of the stock. Most companies establish very small par values for their common stock shares. Notice in Exhibit 2.4 that Buffalo Don's common stock has a par value of one cent per share.

Teaching Note
Companies raise capital by issuing debt securities such as bonds. Corporations also raise capital by selling shares of their stock to investors.

ADDITIONAL PAID-IN CAPITAL   When a company sells stock for more than its par value, the difference between the proceeds from the sale and the collective amount of the stock's par value is commonly referred to as **additional paid-in capital.** Toastmaster Inc., a company that manufactures kitchen appliances, recently sold for $15 per share 1,875,000 shares of its common stock. This stock had a par value of $.10 per share. After subtracting transaction costs, Toastmaster received approximately $27,300,000 from the sale of the stock. The collective par value of the stock, $187,500 (1,875,000 shares × $.10), was included in the dollar amount of Common Stock reported in Toastmaster's next balance sheet. The difference between the proceeds of the sale of the stock and the stock's collective par value was included in Additional Paid-in Capital in the company's next balance sheet.

Real World
Corporations select nominal par values because most states' securities laws do not permit the sale of corporate stock below par value.

additional paid-in capital

RETAINED EARNINGS   The **retained earnings** figure on an entity's balance sheet generally represents the cumulative earnings over the life of the business less any dividends that have been distributed to its owners. Unfortunately, the cumulative earnings of Buffalo Don's through April 3, 1993, was a negative figure. In other words, since the company was established, Buffalo Don's collective losses had exceeded its collective profits. (The company had not paid any dividends to stockholders as of April 3, 1993.) When a company has negative retained earnings, that amount is typically referred to as an accumulated deficit.

retained earnings

The composition of the assets, liabilities, and stockholders' equity of corporations varies widely from company to company. However, the balance sheets of companies within the same industry tend to share certain similarities. For example, companies in certain industries tend to have most of their assets invested in property, plant and equipment, while in other industries current assets tend to be the dominant asset classification. Exhibit 2.5 depicts the asset composition of four major corporations. Shown in Exhibit 2.6 is the composition of the liabilities and stockholders' equity of these same four corporations. (The components of these firms' stockholders' equity were consolidated into one amount for purposes of Exhibit 2.6.) Notice the sizable differences in the proportionate amounts of Avon's liabilities and stockholders' equity versus those of Home Depot. Avon is a highly-leveraged company; that is, it has borrowed heavily from third parties to obtain funds to finance its operations. Home Depot, on the other hand, has relied principally on stockholders to provide funds for its operations.

The Income Statement

Exhibit 2.7 presents a recent income statement for Xylogics, Inc., a company that manufactures and sells computer networking products. An **income statement** summarizes an entity's revenues and expenses for a given accounting period. Just like a balance sheet, an income statement has a basic format. In this case, the format is revenues less expenses equals net income. Revenues result from the sale of merchandise, provision of services, and related transactions. More formally, **revenues** are increases in assets and decreases in liabilities resulting from an entity's profit-oriented activities. **Expenses** are decreases in assets and increases in liabilities resulting from these same profit-oriented activities. Employee salaries are an example of an expense incurred by most businesses.

income statement

revenues

expenses

Notice that not only is the basic format of an income statement different from that of a balance sheet, the two financial statements have different time frames as well. Recall that a balance sheet summarizes an entity's assets, liabilities, and owners' equity at one specific point in time. An income statement, on the other hand, is prepared for a period of time, typically an entity's fiscal year. Xylogics' fiscal year runs from

■ **EXHIBIT 2.5**

Asset Composition of Four Major Corporations

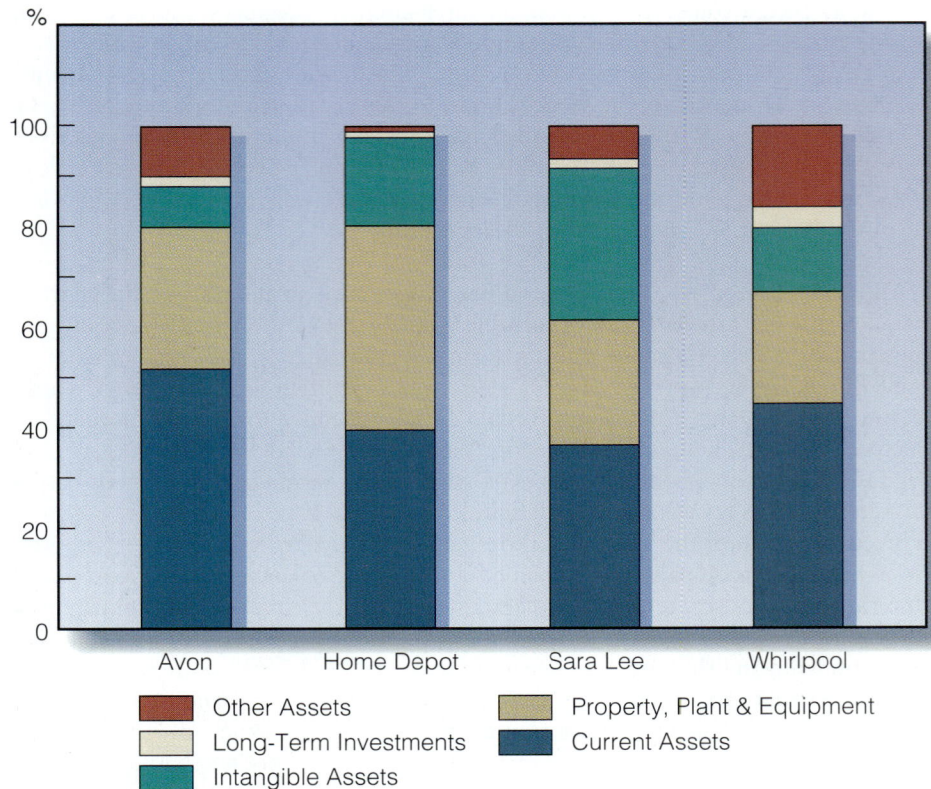

Teaching Note
Contrast the date of the balance sheet with the income statement. The balance sheet is a point-in-time statement. The income statement is a period-of-time statement. The period of time covered by the income statement must always be specified in the statement's heading. Examples are "For the Quarter Ended June 30, 1996" and "For the Year Ended September 30, 1997."

net income

gross profit

November 1 of one year through October 31 of the following year. As noted previously, most companies have a fiscal year that coincides with the calendar year.

You have probably heard someone in business or another discipline, for that matter, refer to the "bottom line." In the business world, that phrase commonly refers to the net income figure reported on an income statement. Once we subtract a business entity's total expenses from its total revenues for a given period, the difference is its profit or earnings or, best of all, **net income** for that period. ("Net loss" is the appropriate term for this difference if expenses exceed revenues.)

Like the balance sheet, decision makers have certain questions in mind when they refer to a company's income statement. Most of these questions concern that "bottom line" figure just mentioned: "Did this company earn a profit?" and if so, "How much?" Another common question answered by an income statement is, "What are this company's principal sources of revenues and expenses?" Now, let us take a closer look at the key line items appearing in a typical income statement.

GROSS PROFIT Many companies, particularly those involved in merchandising and manufacturing, begin their income statements by computing gross profit. **Gross profit** is the difference between net sales—sales revenue less any sales returns made by customers and certain other items—and the collective cost of the goods sold during a given period. Exhibit 2.7 shows that Xylogics registered a gross profit of slightly more than $24 million for the year ended October 31, 1994. Gross profit is a very

■ **EXHIBIT 2.6**

Composition of Liabilities and Stockholders' Equity of Four
Major Corporations

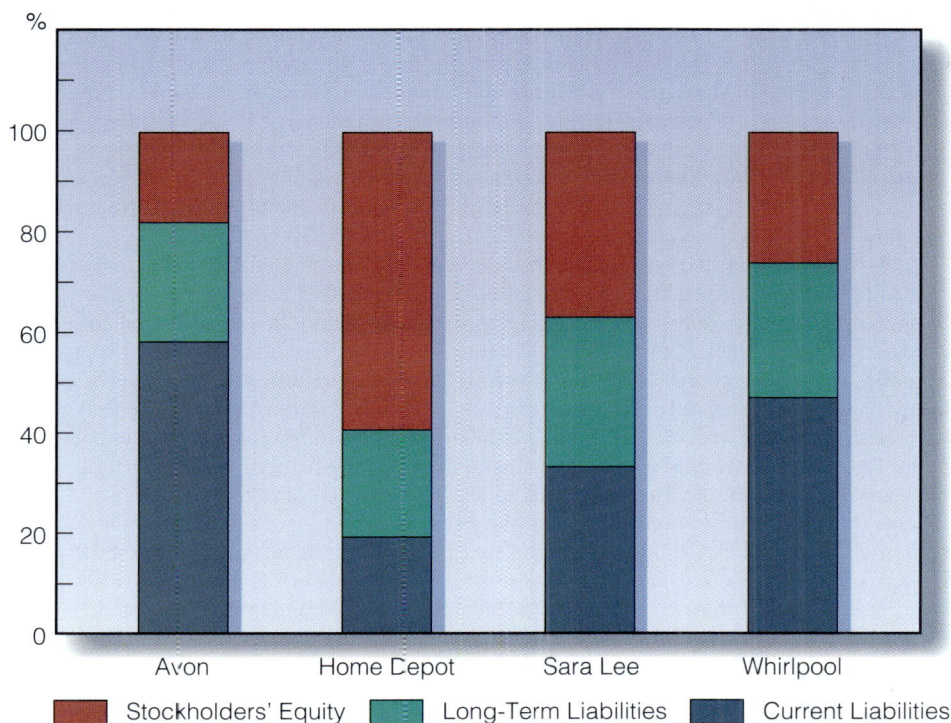

■ **EXHIBIT 2.7**

Xylogics, Inc., Income Statement for the Year Ended October 31, 1994

XYLOGICS, INC. INCOME STATEMENT FOR THE YEAR ENDED OCTOBER 31, 1994	
Net Sales	$50,421,182
Cost of Goods Sold	26,154,545
Gross Profit	24,266,637
Engineering, Research and Development Expenses	5,686,149
Sales and Marketing Expenses	9,354,244
General and Administrative Expenses	4,119,172
Operating Income	$ 5,107,072
Interest Income, Net	284,151
Foreign Exchange Loss	(9,113)
Income before Income Taxes	5,382,110
Provision for Income Taxes	1,935,559
Net Income	$ 3,446,551
Earnings Per Share	$ .63

SOURCE: 1994 Annual Report of Xylogics Inc.

| FOR YOUR INFORMATION | The Balance Sheet: Going Dutch |

The nature and purpose of accounting are much the same world-wide, although the specific accounting methods and financial reporting practices used in individual countries are often quite different. Consider the financial statements of Polygram International Ltd., an entertainment conglomerate headquartered in the Netherlands whose common stock is widely held in the United States. A comparison of Polygram's financial statements to those of comparable firms in this country reveals several distinctive differences.

Polygram's financial statements, like those of many European companies, are more condensed than the financial statements of United States firms. For instance, Polygram's 1993 balance sheet includes only six line items relating to assets and four relating to liabilities, considerably fewer than you would typically find for a large, United States–based company. Likewise, the organization of Polygram's balance sheet is quite different from that of most balance sheets prepared in this country. Instead of beginning with current assets, Polygram's balance sheet begins with "fixed assets," which is equivalent to property, plant and equipment. Polygram's balance sheet also lists stockholders' equity before long-term liabilities, while current liabilities are the final items appearing on the company's balance sheet. Finally, Polygram employs several accounting rules that are not considered generally accepted in the United States. To make the company's financial statements more informative for United States citizens, Polygram reconciles its net income under the Netherlands' accounting rules to the net income the company would have reported under GAAP.

important and informative number for financial statement users. Quite often, an early sign that a company's financial fortunes are on the decline is a decrease in its gross profit percentage, which is gross profit divided by net sales. For example, in the early 1990s, intense price competition drove down the gross profit margins of most companies in the personal computer industry. Apple Computer, in particular, was adversely affected by this cutthroat competition. When a company's gross profit margin declines, it often has to compensate by attempting to cut its operating expenses.

operating expenses

OPERATING EXPENSES   Those expenses, other than cost of goods sold, that a company incurs in its principal business operations are known as **operating expenses.** Among the more common operating expenses are selling expenses, such as sales commissions and advertising costs, and administrative expenses, such as the salaries of top management.

Income statements usually include a heading "Operating Expenses," but this is not true for Xylogics' income statement shown in Exhibit 2.7. Xylogics' operating expenses are simply listed below and then subtracted from its gross profit. The difference between gross profit and a company's operating expenses is its **operating income,** or income from operations. Operating income is another important figure for financial statement users. The remaining revenues and expenses listed on an income statement are nonoperating items that do not result from an entity's principal business operations. Decision makers tend to discount the importance of nonoperating revenues and expenses, since a company's eventual success or failure hinges on the profitability of its principal business operations.

operating income

OTHER REVENUES AND EXPENSES   Most companies have miscellaneous revenues and expenses, which they typically list under the heading Other Revenues and Expenses in their income statements. In its 1994 income statement, Xylogics reported two such items, interest income and foreign exchange loss—although the company skipped the "other revenues and expenses" heading.

EARNINGS PER SHARE   Notice in Exhibit 2.7 that income before income taxes is determined by adding or subtracting the net amount of other revenues and expenses to, or from, operating income. After subtracting the provision for income taxes (income taxes expense) from income before income taxes, we have finally arrived at net income. A corporation is required to go one step beyond net income and report an earnings per share figure for its common stock. In Chapter 13, the computation of earnings per share is discussed and illustrated.

Statement of Stockholders' Equity

The third financial statement included in an annual financial report of a corporation is the statement of stockholders' equity. (Statement of owners' equity is an alternative title used for this financial statement when prepared for unincorporated businesses.) Financial decision makers often disagree regarding which of the four financial statements is the most important or informative. However, few decision makers would disagree with the assertion that the statement of stockholders' equity is the least important financial statement. Essentially, this statement is a supporting schedule to the balance sheet. A **statement of stockholders' equity** reconciles the dollar amounts of a corporation's stockholders' equity items at the beginning and end of an accounting period, typically the entity's fiscal year. The obvious question answered by this statement is "What events or transactions accounted for the changes in a company's stockholders' equity over the previous year?" Shown in Exhibit 2.8 is a recent statement of stockholders' equity for Piccadilly Cafeterias, Inc.

Ugly Kid Joe has had several hit records produced by Polygram International, a Dutch company. Like many foreign companies, Polygram includes a schedule in its annual report that reconciles the company's net income under Dutch accounting rules to the net income the company would have reported under U.S.-based GAAP.

Statement of Cash Flows

The fourth and final financial statement is the statement of cash flows. Exhibit 2.9 presents a recent statement of cash flows for Hughes Supply, Inc., a construction supplies company. As its title implies, a **statement of cash flows** reveals how an entity generated and expended cash during a given accounting period, typically an entity's most recent fiscal year. The first three sections of a statement of cash flows summarize the cash inflows and outflows from three major types of activities engaged in by business entities: operating activities, investing activities, and financing activities. The final section of a statement of cash flows reconciles an entity's cash balance at the beginning of a period to its cash balance at the end of that period.

   When decision makers refer to a company's statement of cash flows, a question foremost in their minds is "How does the company's cash flows from its operating, or profit-oriented, activities compare to its net income?" Surprisingly to many nonaccountants, the net cash flow generated each period by an entity's operating activities

Teaching Note
Common sources of changes in stockholders' equity balances are stock transactions, payments of dividends to shareholders, and the transfer of net income or loss to retained earnings.

statement of stockholders' equity

statement of cash flows

■ **EXHIBIT 2.8**

Piccadilly Cafeterias, Inc., Statement of Stockholders' Equity for the Year Ended June 30, 1994

PICCADILLY CAFETERIAS, INC.
STATEMENT OF STOCKHOLDERS' EQUITY
FOR THE YEAR ENDED JUNE 30, 1994

	COMMON STOCK	ADDITIONAL PAID-IN CAPITAL	RETAINED EARNINGS
Balance, June 30, 1993	$18,160,000	$15,119,000	$38,913,000
Net Income	—	—	7,047,000
Cash Dividends Declared	—	—	(4,831,000)
Sales under Employee Stock Purchase Plan	188,000	843,000	—
Sales under Dividend Reinvestment Plan	48,000	242,000	—
Sales under Employee Stock Option Plan	25,000	120,000	—
Balance, June 30, 1994	$18,421,000	$16,324,000	$41,129,000

SOURCE: 1994 Annual Report of Piccadilly Cafeterias, Inc.

■ **EXHIBIT 2.9**

Hughes Supply, Inc., Statement of Cash Flows for the Year Ended January 28, 1994 (in Thousands)

Cash Flows from Operating Activities	
Cash Received from Customers	$644,667
Cash Paid to Suppliers and Employees	(638,724)
Interest and Other Investment Income Received	1,856
Interest Paid	(4,693)
Income Taxes Paid	(5,361)
Net Cash Used in Operating Activities	(2,255)
Cash Flows from Investing Activities	
Proceeds from Sale of Property, Plant and Equipment	704
Capital Expenditures	(8,257)
Business Acquisitions, Net of Cash	(3,934)
Net Cash Used in Investing Activities	(11,487)
Cash Flows from Financing Activities	
Net Borrowings under Short-Term Debt Arrangements	16,733
Principal Payments on:	
Long-Term Notes	(2,918)
Capital Lease Obligations	(660)
Proceeds from Issuance of Common Shares under Stock Option Plans	77
Purchase of Common Shares	(49)
Dividends Paid	(616)
Net Cash Provided by Financing Activities	12,567
Net Decrease in Cash and Cash Equivalents	(1,175)
Cash and Cash Equivalents, Beginning of Year	2,253
Cash and Cash Equivalents, End of Year	$ 1,078

SOURCE: 1994 Annual Report of Hughes Supply, Inc.

■ **EXHIBIT 2.10**

PMSI, Inc.: Net Income vs. Net Cash Flow from Operating Activities

SOURCE: PMSI, Inc., Annual Report

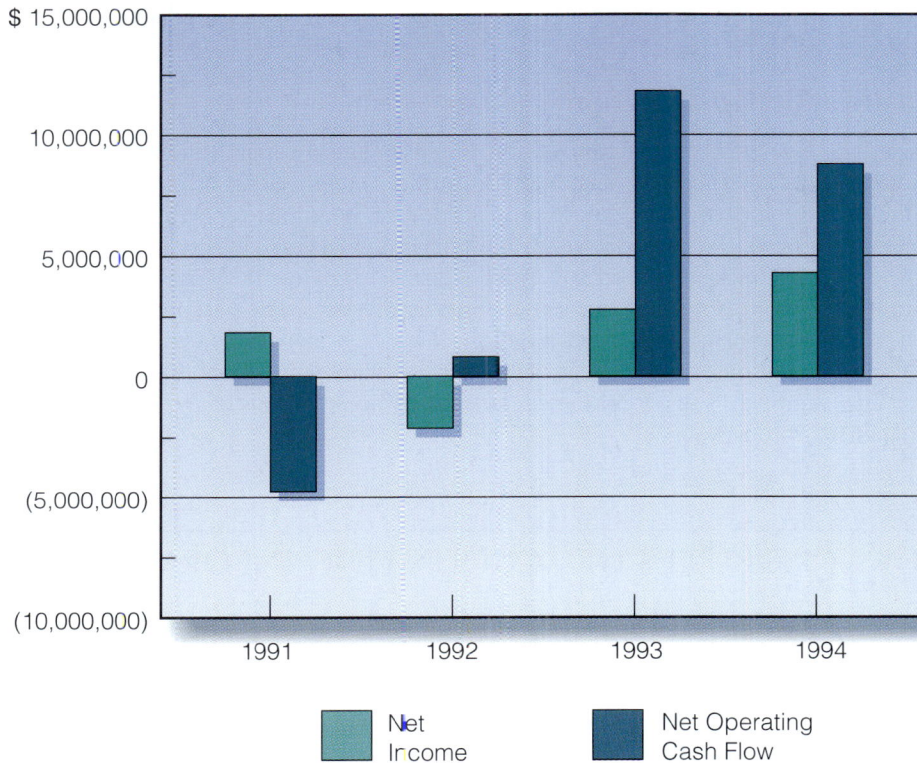

is not closely correlated, necessarily, with its net income. Consider Exhibit 2.10, which compares the net income and net cash flow from operating activities over a four-year period for PMSI, Inc., a firm that provides cost containment services. Notice that there were large differences between this company's net income and its net cash flow from operating activities for the period covered by Exhibit 2.10.

Just because a company is earning large profits each year does not mean that it is generating sufficient cash flows to sustain its operations. A very profitable company may experience severe cash-flow problems including falling behind on its debt payments and being unable to replace inventory as it is sold. Several factors could account for a profitable company failing to generate sufficient cash flows from its principal profit-oriented activities. These factors include slow-paying customers and increasing prices for raw materials and other goods and services required in its day-to-day operations.

So, there you have it. A brief—okay, not so brief—overview of the four financial statements regularly prepared by corporations and other businesses. Students new to accounting often fail to recognize that the four financial statements are closely linked although they have differing structures, contents, and objectives. For example, consider the close relationship between the balance sheet and income statement. Revenues and expenses are reported on an entity's income statement, while assets and liabilities are reported on the balance sheet. However, most of the changes in an entity's assets and liabilities during a given period of time are a direct result of an entity's

Teaching Note
The statement of cash flows reports on cash that is received and cash that is paid out by a company. In contrast, the income statement reports on revenues and expenses.

Teaching Note
Call students' attention to the fact that of the four financial statements all but the balance sheet are period-of-time statements.

revenue and expenses. Likewise, the net income figure reported in a company's income statement directly affects the retained earnings reported in the firm's balance sheet. As mentioned previously, the statement of stockholders' equity is actually just a supporting schedule to the balance sheet. Finally, consider the statement of cash flows. This financial statement accounts for the change in the amount of cash reported in a company's balance sheet at the beginning and end of a given period of time.

Financial Statement Footnotes

Besides the four financial statements, the annual financial report (often shortened to "annual report") prepared by most business entities contains other important information as well. One particularly informative section of an annual report is the **financial statement footnotes.** These footnotes assist decision makers in interpreting and drawing the proper conclusions from an entity's financial statements. Most important, the footnotes to a company's financial statements identify the specific accounting methods used by the company. Other information found in financial statement footnotes includes assumptions that underlie key financial statement amounts, financial data regarding a company's major business segments, and descriptions of any lawsuits pending against a company.

KEY ATTRIBUTES OF ACCOUNTING INFORMATION

Because of the quantitative nature of accounting, accountants and decision makers often overlook the qualitative features that accounting information should possess. The second of the FASB's six *SFACs*, "Qualitative Characteristics of Accounting Information," defines and describes the qualitative attributes that accounting information should possess. If the accounting data included in financial statements do not exhibit these attributes, the information needs of decision makers are unlikely to be satisfied. That is, those statements are unlikely to be useful to decision makers. In fact, *SFAC No. 2* observes that decision usefulness is the most important qualitative characteristic that accounting information should possess. To qualify as useful to decision makers, accounting information should be understandable, relevant, and reliable, as shown in Exhibit 2.11.

Understandability

For many years, the accounting profession debated the question of to whom accounting information should be understandable, or comprehensible. Many parties within the profession maintained that financial statements should be understandable by even naive, or unsophisticated, financial statement users. Other parties argued that financial statements should be oriented principally toward decision makers who have an in-depth understanding of financial reporting and accounting issues. *SFAC No. 1* settled this debate by stating that financial reports should be comprehensible to individuals who have a "reasonable understanding of business and economic activities" and are willing to "study the information with reasonable diligence."[3]

---

3. Portions of various FASB documents, copyright by Financial Accounting Standards Board, 401 Merritt 7, P.O. Box 5116, Norwalk, Connecticut, 06856-5116, U.S.A., are reprinted with permission. Copies of the complete documents are available from the FASB.

■ **EXHIBIT 2.11**
Key Attributes of Accounting Information

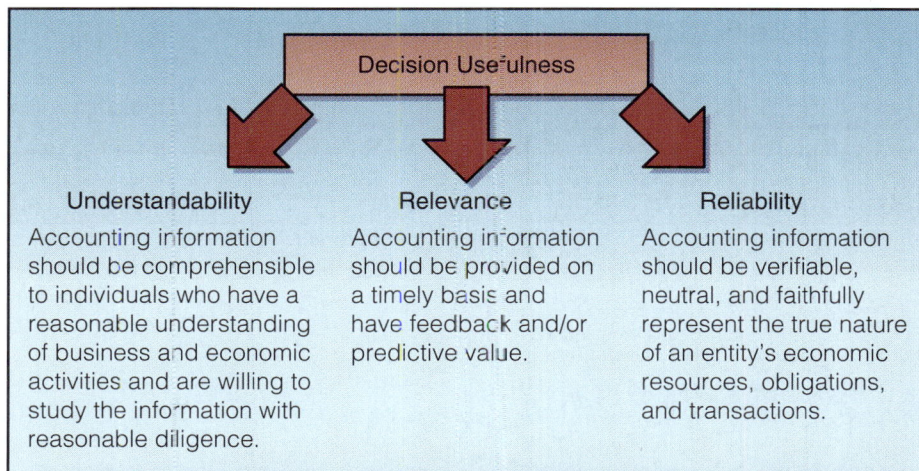

Understandability	Relevance	Reliability
Accounting information should be comprehensible to individuals who have a reasonable understanding of business and economic activities and are willing to study the information with reasonable diligence.	Accounting information should be provided on a timely basis and have feedback and/or predictive value.	Accounting information should be verifiable, neutral, and faithfully represent the true nature of an entity's economic resources, obligations, and transactions.

Relevance

For accounting information to be useful, it must possess a high degree of relevance according to *SFAC No. 2*. To qualify as relevant, accounting data must be timely and have feedback value and/or predictive value. By definition, if information is provided too late to influence financial statement users' decisions, then it is not relevant to those decisions. Feedback value is an important trait of accounting information since it allows decision makers to confirm or correct earlier expectations regarding, for instance, an entity's operating results. If accounting data has feedback value, decision makers should become more proficient, over time, in using financial information to make economic decisions.[4] Finally, predictive value is also an important trait of accounting information. For example, as suggested earlier, a banker considering a loan application should be able to use a company's financial statements to predict whether it would be able to repay the loan if it is granted.

Reliability

Accounting information must also be reliable to be useful to decision makers. *SFAC No. 2* suggests that accounting information possesses reliability if it is characterized by the following traits: verifiability, neutrality, and representational faithfulness. Accounting data do not have to be subject to precise quantification to qualify as verifiable. In fact, *SFAC No. 1* points out that most financial data are not subject to precise quantification.

> [D]espite the aura of precision that may seem to surround financial reporting in general and financial statements in particular, with few exceptions the measures are approximations, which may be based on rules and convention, rather than exact amounts.[5]

4, 5. Portions of various FASB documents, copyright by Financial Accounting Standards Board, 401 Merritt 7, P.O. Box 5116, Norwalk, Connecticut, 06856-5116, U.S.A., are reprinted with permission. Copies of the complete documents are available from the FASB.

SPOTLIGHT ON ETHICS

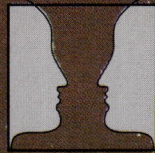

The Windbag Theory

Providing information that is comprehensible by decision makers who have a reasonable understanding of business and economic activities is an important responsibility of an entity's top management. However, critics of financial reporting suggest that business executives are not always forthright when discussing the financial status of their firms. Recently, two business journalists proposed the "windbag theory" (J. Zweig and J. Chamberlain, "Windbag Theory," *Forbes*, 3 August 1992, 43–44). This theory suggests that when a company's financial health is deteriorating, its executives become wordy and vague when discussing the company's financial status in an annual report.

To test their theory, the journalists studied the writing style and clarity of narrative disclosures in several companies' annual reports both before and after these firms began experiencing financial problems. Grammatik, a software program that analyzes writing style and clarity, was used by the authors for this purpose. Sure enough, the journalists found that business executives were prone to becoming "windy" and obscure when their company's financial health deteriorates. The journalists provided the following excerpt from an annual report as a prime example of the windbag theory in action.

> As the company continued to make the transition away from older to newer product offerings, the revenues generated by newer products and our efforts to reduce expenses was not enough to offset the severe decline in prices generally and the costs associated with designing, introducing and bringing expansive new product offerings into production.

SOURCE: Zweig and Chamberlain, "Windbag Theory," *Forbes*. Reprinted by permission of FORBES Magazine © Forbes, Inc., 1992.

To be neutral, accounting data must be presented without "bias towards a predetermined result."[6] That is, accountants should not consciously attempt to influence the decisions of the users of accounting data. Finally, the term "representational faithfulness" implies that accounting data should portray, to the greatest extent possible, the true nature of an entity's economic resources, obligations, and transactions. As suggested in Chapter 1, many savings and loans during the 1980s used accounting methods that failed to faithfully represent the economic substance of their transactions.

Attributes of Accounting Information: A Few Other Issues

So, accounting information must first and foremost be useful to decision makers. To be useful, accounting information must be understandable, relevant, and reliable. Enough said? Not quite. There are a few other issues accountants and decision makers must grasp to fully appreciate the key qualitative attributes of accounting information. In certain situations it is not necessary for accounting data to satisfy the understandability, relevance, and reliability criteria. For example, accountants do not

---

6. Portions of various FASB documents, copyright by Financial Accounting Standards Board, 401 Merritt 7, P.O. Box 5116, Norwalk, Connecticut, 06856-5116, U.S.A., are reprinted with permission. Copies of the complete documents are available from the FASB.

have to ensure that accounting data are perfectly reliable if the imprecision in that data would not be sufficiently large to "matter" to decision makers. **Materiality** is the term that accountants use when referring to the relative importance of specific items of accounting information. An item is deemed material if it is large enough or significant enough to influence the decision of a financial decision maker. The reverse is true for immaterial items.

Both preparers and users of accounting information should also recognize that the usefulness of accounting data is enhanced by comparability. **Comparability** refers to the degree to which an entity's accounting information can be easily compared with similar information reported for the entity in prior accounting periods and with similar information reported by other entities. One key threat to the comparability of accounting information is an entity's failure to use the same accounting rules from period to period. The financial statement data of a company will not be comparable from one period to the next if the company does not consistently apply the same set of accounting rules. Fortunately for decision makers, when a company changes an accounting principle, the effect of this change must be disclosed in its financial statements.

Teaching Note
Emphasize that comparability has two dimensions:
(1) comparing the financial data of one business with that of another business and
(2) comparing the financial data of a company for two or more time periods.

materiality

comparability

FUNDAMENTAL ACCOUNTING CONCEPTS

Now that we have become familiar with financial reporting objectives, the nature and content of financial statements, and the key qualitative attributes of accounting information, we are ready to tackle the basic conceptual issues that underlie accounting practices. The need for accountants to have a thorough understanding of these issues is underscored by the rapidly changing nature of the business world. New transactions and new variations of routine or familiar transactions are continually being spawned by today's volatile business environment. To record new and unusual transactions properly, accountants must have an in-depth knowledge of the fundamental conceptual principles of accounting.

Accounting concepts are not just for accountants. Financial decision makers can benefit greatly if they understand the basic concepts that dictate how accounting information is recorded and reported. Such an understanding will allow decision makers to better grasp both the uses and the limitations of accounting data. Listed in Exhibit 2.12 are the key concepts that underlie the accounting rules, procedures, and practices discussed in the remainder of this textbook.

■ **LEARNING OBJECTIVE 4**
Identify and define the fundamental concepts that underlie accounting rules and practices

■ **EXHIBIT 2.12**
Fundamental Accounting Concepts

- Entity concept
- Accounting period concept
- Going concern assumption
- Unit of measurement concept
- Historical cost principle
- Revenue and expense recognition rules
- Full disclosure principle

Entity Concept

Business enterprises operate in several different legal forms, including sole proprietorships, partnerships, and corporations. As demonstrated by Exhibit 2.13, the most common form of business organization in this country is the sole proprietorship, although corporations account for a large majority of the total business revenues generated each year in the United States. As the term implies, a **sole proprietorship** is a business owned by one individual—the proverbial "Mom and Pop" operation. Granted, if both Mom and Pop are full partners in the business, then we have a **partnership.** More generally, a partnership is an unincorporated business with two or more owners. For instance, the Boston Celtics are owned by a partnership—one consisting of several thousand partners.

Most of the largest companies in the United States operate as corporations. *Random House Webster's College Dictionary* defines a **corporation** as "an association of individuals, created by law and having an existence apart from that of its members as well as distinct and inherent powers and liabilities." As we will discover, there are several advantages of operating a business as a corporation, one of the most important being that stockholders have limited liability for the actions of a corporation. For instance, in a lawsuit against a corporation, the plaintiffs cannot recover any settlement or judgment from the personal assets of the individual stockholders. Instead, any settlement or judgment must be paid strictly from the corporation's assets.

For accounting purposes, a business enterprise is treated as a distinct and independent entity, meaning that its transactions should be accounted for separately from the personal transactions of its owners. This is true whether a business is organized as a sole proprietorship, partnership, or corporation. This **entity concept** is particularly important for sole proprietorships. The owners of one-man and one-woman firms may see no need to separate the assets and liabilities of their businesses from their personal assets and liabilities. However, a sole proprietor will find it difficult to prepare financial statements that accurately depict the financial status of his or her company if personal and business assets and liabilities are commingled.

sole proprietorship

partnership

corporation

Discussion Question

Assume an individual owns two businesses but maintains only one set of accounting records and one bank account. What potential problems does this create?

Answer: It would be difficult to prepare separate financial statements for the two businesses, which may be needed by banks, regulatory authorities, and other third parties.

entity concept

■ **EXHIBIT 2.13**

Number of Business Organizations and Their Annual Revenues

SOURCE: U.S. Bureau of the Census, *Statistical Abstract of the United States, 1994.*

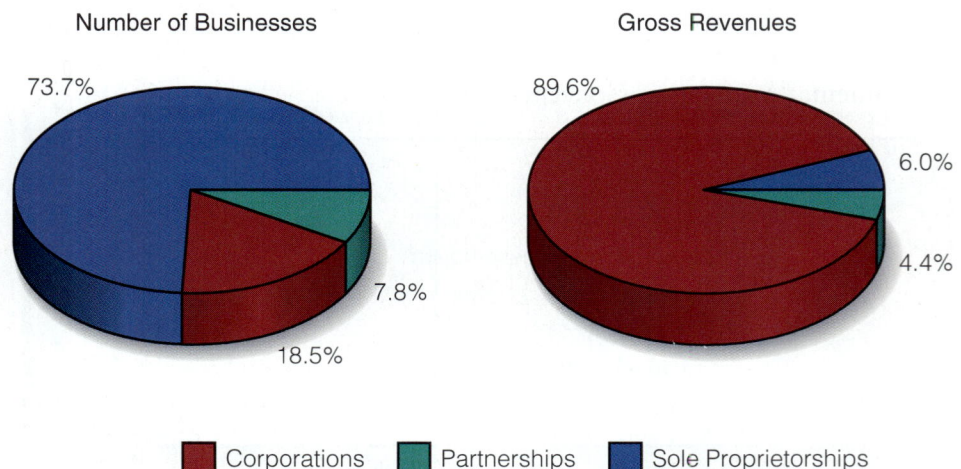

Number of Businesses: 73.7%, 18.5%, 7.8%

Gross Revenues: 89.6%, 6.0%, 4.4%

■ Corporations   ■ Partnerships   ■ Sole Proprietorships

1999, nearby urban development has caused the appraised value of the land to sky-rocket to $3 million. At what dollar amount would the land be reported in the company's balance sheet? No, not $3 million, but instead the original historical cost of $500,000.

The historical cost of an asset is often less informative or useful to third-party decision makers than the asset's current value. If you are considering buying a company, wouldn't you be more interested in the current value of that company's assets rather than their historical cost? Almost certainly. The principal justification for using historical costs instead of current values as the valuation basis for assets is the objectivity of historical costs. Historical costs are much more verifiable than current values. To determine the historical cost of the piece of land referred to in the previous paragraph, you would simply refer to the purchase contract. On the other hand, determining the current value of that property would be a much more subjective exercise. Generally, the current value of a piece of undeveloped land is established by obtaining one or more real estate appraisals. However, real estate appraising is not an exact science. Consequently, appraised values are subject to errors, sometimes very large errors.

There are several exceptions to the general rule that assets are valued for accounting purposes at their historical cost. For example, many investments in corporate stocks and bonds are reported at their current value, rather than their historical cost, in financial statements. Likewise, when there is strong evidence that the value of an asset has permanently declined to a level below its historical cost, that asset should be written down to its current value. This latter rule invokes the **conservatism principle** of accounting. More generally, when there are uncertainties regarding the valuation of assets or the magnitude of revenues, accountants are inclined to understate, rather than overstate, the recorded amounts for these items. Conversely, for liabilities and expenses the conservatism principle dictates that accountants resolve uncertainty in favor of higher recorded amounts for these items.

conservatism principle

Real World
To illustrate the problems in using current values, ask students to assume that they must determine the value of their car for a loan application. A used car salesperson estimates the value at $10,000. A bank loan officer estimates the value at $7,500. Which value should be used on the loan application and why?

Revenue and Expense Recognition Rules

One of the most important accounting issues that businesses face is when to record revenues and expenses in their accounting records. Companies would generally prefer to record revenues as quickly as possible and to postpone the recording of expenses as long as possible to enhance their apparent profitability.[7] Allowing companies to record revenues and expenses whenever they wish is certainly not in the best interests of financial statement users. Consequently, the accounting profession has established general rules to follow regarding the timing of revenue and expense recognition. These rules limit the ability of business executives to misrepresent the operating results of their firms by selectively choosing the accounting period in which to record revenues and expenses.

REVENUE RECOGNITION   *SFAC No. 5* established a two-part **revenue recognition rule** for accountants to follow in deciding when to record revenues. Before revenue is recognized (recorded) in an entity's accounting records, it should be both realized and earned.

revenue recognition rule

7. For taxation purposes, businesses prefer just the opposite. By delaying the recording of revenues and accelerating the recording of expenses, businesses minimize the amount of income taxes payable to state and federal governments.

Revenues and gains are realized when products (goods or services), merchandise, or other assets are exchanged for cash or claims to cash. . . . revenues are considered to have been earned when the entity has substantially accomplished what it must do to be entitled to the benefits represented by the revenues.[8]

For merchandising companies, both requirements of the revenue recognition rule are usually satisfied at the point of sale.

expense recognition rule

EXPENSE RECOGNITION The **expense recognition rule** established by *SFAC No. 5* requires expenditures to be recognized as expenses in the accounting period they provide an economic benefit to an entity. Typically, this rule means that an expenditure should be recorded as an expense in the accounting period when the related revenue was recorded. In other words, expenses should be "matched" with their corresponding revenues. This concept of matching revenues and expenses in the same accounting period is often referred to as the **matching principle.** Consider sales commissions. Commissions paid to a company's sales staff should be recorded as expenses in the same accounting period that the related sales were recorded as revenues. When an expenditure, such as the purchase of production equipment, provides an economic benefit to several accounting periods, the dollar amount of the expenditures should be "capitalized." (Accountants use the term "capitalize" to refer to the process of recording the cost of an asset.) Then, the cost of the asset should be gradually written off to expense—that is, depreciated over its useful life.

matching principle

Teaching Note
Emphasize the sequence of this matching process. First, revenue is recognized when both earned and realized. Second, expenses are matched with the revenue they were incurred to generate.

The expense recognition rule and related matching principle are often difficult to apply when there is no clear cause-and-effect relationship between an expenditure and the subsequent revenue that it generates. Consider the case of pharmaceutical companies, such as Abbott Laboratories and Upjohn, which engage in long-term, multimillion-dollar research programs to develop new pharmaceutical products. Matching the cost of such programs with the subsequent revenues they generate is very difficult, since these companies seldom know which research efforts are likely to result in a viable product. When there is no clear cause-and-effect relationship between an expenditure and an entity's subsequent revenues, the conservatism principle mandates that the expenditure be immediately recognized as an expense.

ACCRUAL BASIS VS. CASH BASIS OF ACCOUNTING Companies that employ the revenue and expense recognition rules just discussed are said to use the accrual basis of accounting. Under the **accrual basis of accounting,** the economic impact of a transaction is recognized (recorded) whether or not the transaction involves cash. Many business entities, very small businesses for the most part, use the **cash basis of accounting** instead of the accrual basis. These businesses record revenues when they receive cash payments from their customers and record expenses when they disburse cash to their suppliers, employees, and other parties. When decision makers use cash-basis financial statements, they must be aware that the given entity did not employ the appropriate revenue and expense recognition rules. As a result, the entity's reported net income may be unreliable.

accrual basis of accounting

cash basis of accounting

Real World
Individuals use the cash basis of accounting for income tax purposes.

Full Disclosure Principle

full disclosure principle

The **full disclosure principle** requires that all information needed to obtain a thorough understanding of a company's financial affairs be included in its financial state-

---

8. Portions of various FASB documents, copyright by Financial Accounting Standards Board, 401 Merritt 7, P.O. Box 5116, Norwalk, Connecticut, 06856-5116, U.S.A., are reprinted with permission. Copies of the complete documents are available from the FASB.

ments or accompanying disclosures. Certain information that external decision makers would find useful, if not essential, for their decision making processes does not "fit" into any of the four financial statements discussed earlier. Examples of such information include the effect that inflation may have on a company's future operations, details of profit-sharing and pension plans, and any backlog of unfilled orders. Typically, such information is presented in the footnotes to an entity's financial statements.

Consider one item of information often included in financial statement footnotes. If you are planning to invest in the stock of a manufacturing company, you should be very interested in the size of that company's backlog of orders. Generally, the future prospects of a manufacturing company are bleak if its backlog of orders are falling, since this signals that the company's sales may be declining in the future. In the defense industry, the backlog of orders for many firms fell sharply following the collapse of the USSR and the Communist bloc of Eastern Europe. As a result, many of these firms eventually had to "downsize" their business operations.

Following is an excerpt from a recent annual report of HON Industries, Inc., a manufacturer of office furniture. This excerpt comments on the size of the company's year-end backlog of unfilled orders. Notice that company management is quick to point out that a recent drop in the company's backlog of orders is not due to declining interest in its products.

> As of January 2, 1993, the Company had an order backlog of approximately $63.2 million, which compares with $70.1 million at year-end 1991 and $58.1 million at year-end 1990. This reduction in backlog is attributed to faster lead times for most of the Company's products rather than a reduction in business levels.

Real World
How much disclosure is enough?
Answer: This is a difficult decision for a company. Financial analysts, investors, and other decision makers would prefer to have unlimited access to a company's financial data.

SUMMARY

During the mid-1970s, the FASB began developing a conceptual framework to guide the development of future accounting standards. This framework was completed in 1985 and consists of six *Statements of Financial Accounting Concepts (SFACS)*. *SFAC No. 1* defines the three financial reporting objectives for business enterprises, each of which concern the need to assist third parties in making rational and informed economic decisions. Business enterprises satisfy these reporting objectives by preparing four financial statements for distribution to interested third parties.

A balance sheet summarizes an entity's assets, liabilities, and owners' equity at a specific point in time, typically the last day of an entity's fiscal year. An income statement reports on an entity's profitability for a stated period of time, usually an entity's fiscal year. Net income, the difference between an entity's revenues and expenses, is the key figure reported in an income statement. Similar to an income statement, a statement of stockholders' equity and a statement of cash flows typically present financial data for an entity's fiscal year. A statement of stockholders' equity reconciles the balances of a corporation's stockholders' equity items at the beginning and end of an accounting period. A statement of cash flows reveals how an entity generated cash and used cash during a given period.

According to *SFAC No. 2*, the key attribute that accounting information should possess is decision usefulness. For accounting information to be useful, it should be understandable, relevant, and reliable. The rapidly changing business environment continually yields new transactions and new variations of routine transactions. To properly account for new or unusual business transactions, accountants must have a thorough understanding of the conceptual principles that underlie accounting practices. Among these principles are the entity concept, the going concern assumption, the historical cost principle, and the full disclosure principles.

GLOSSARY

Accounting equation (p. 38)   The mathematical expression indicating the sum of an entity's assets must equal the collective sum of its liabilities and owners' equity.

Accounting period concept (p. 55)   An accounting principle that suggests accountants can prepare meaningful financial reports for ongoing business enterprises by dividing the lives of these entities into regular reporting intervals of equal length.

Accounts payable (p. 41)   Current liabilities that represent amounts owed by a business to its suppliers.

Accounts receivable (p. 39)   Current assets that represent amounts owed to an entity by its customers.

Accrual basis of accounting (p. 58)   A method of accounting under which the economic impact of a transaction is recognized (recorded) whether or not the transaction involves cash.

Accrued expenses (p. 41)   Current liabilities typically related to obligations incurred near the end of an accounting period; also known as accrued liabilities.

Additional paid-in capital (p. 43)   The difference between the proceeds from the sale of a corporation's common stock and the collective amount of that common stock's par value.

Assets (p. 38)   Probable future economic benefits obtained or controlled by a particular entity as a result of past transactions or events.

Balance sheet (p. 38)   A financial statement that summarizes the assets, liabilities, and owners' equity of an entity at a specific point in time.

Bonds payable (p. 42)   A long-term liability that represents the collective amount owed to the parties who purchased an entity's bonds.

Cash (p. 39)   A current asset representing the collective amount of cash that an entity has on hand or on deposit with banks or other financial institutions at a balance sheet date.

Cash basis of accounting (p. 58)   A method of accounting under which revenues are recorded when cash is received and expenses are recorded when cash is disbursed.

Common stock (p. 42)   A stockholders' equity item that represents the collective par value of all common stock shares a company has sold or otherwise issued.

Comparability (p. 53)   The degree to which an entity's accounting information can be easily compared with similar information reported for the entity in prior accounting periods and with similar information reported by other entities.

Conservatism principle (p. 57)   An accounting principle that dictates that uncertainty regarding the valuation of an asset or magnitude of a revenue should generally be resolved in favor of understating the asset or revenue; applies as well to liabilities and expenses, except that uncertainty should be resolved in favor of overstating these items.

Corporation (p. 54)   An association of individuals, created by law and having an existence apart from that of its members as well as distinct and inherent powers and liabilities.

Current assets (p. 39)   Cash and other assets that will be converted into cash, sold, or consumed during the next fiscal year or operating cycle, whichever is longer.

Current liabilities (p. 41)   Debts or other obligations of a business that must be paid during its next fiscal year or operating cycle, whichever is longer.

Current portion of long-term debt (p. 42)   A current liability representing the collective dollar amount of an entity's long-term liabilities that must be paid in the coming year.

Entity concept (p. 54)   An accounting principle that dictates that a business enterprise be treated as a distinct entity independent of its owners.

Expense recognition rule (p. 58)   An accounting rule that requires expenses to be recognized (recorded) in the accounting period that they provide an economic benefit to an entity.

Expenses (p. 43)   Decreases in assets and increases in liabilities resulting from an entity's profit-oriented activities.

Financial statement footnotes (p. 50)   A section of an annual report intended to assist decision makers in interpreting and drawing the proper conclusions from an entity's financial statements.

Fiscal year (p. 39)   The twelve-month period covered by an entity's annual income statement.

Full disclosure principle (p. 58)   An accounting principle that dictates that all information needed to obtain a thorough understanding of an entity's financial affairs be included in its financial statements or accompanying disclosures.

Going concern assumption (p. 56)   An accounting principle which dictates that entities should be treated as if they will continue to operate indefinitely, unless there is evidence to the contrary.

Gross profit (p. 44)   The difference between an entity's net sales and cost of goods sold during an accounting period.

Historical cost principle (p. 56)   An accounting principle that dictates that the primary valuation basis for most assets is their historical cost.

Income statement (p. 43)   A financial statement that summarizes an entity's revenues and expenses for a given accounting period.

Intangible assets (p. 40)   Long-term assets that do not have a physical form or substance.

Inventories (p. 39)   Goods that an entity intends to sell directly to its customers or raw materials or "in-process" items that will be converted into saleable goods.

Liabilities (p. 41)   Probable future sacrifices of economic benefits; generally amounts owed by an entity to third parties including such items as accounts payable, accrued expenses, and bonds payable.

Long-term investments (p. 40)   Ownership interests in corporate stocks and bonds and other securities that an entity intends to retain for more than one year; also includes land and other long-term assets not used in an entity's normal operating activities.

Long-term liabilities (p. 42)   Debts and other obligations of an entity other than those classified as current liabilities.

Matching principle (p. 58)   An accounting principle which suggests that expenses should be recorded in the same accounting period as the related revenues.

Materiality (p. 53)   Refers to the relative importance of specific items of accounting information; an item is material if it is large enough or significant enough to influence the decision of a third-party decision maker.

Mortgages payable (p. 42)   Long-term liabilities secured or collateralized by some asset, typically a building or other piece of property.

Net income (p. 44)   The difference between an entity's revenues and expenses for an accounting period.

Notes payable (p. 42)   Liabilities that are documented by a legally binding written commitment in the form of a promissory note; can be either current or long-term liabilities depending upon the date they must be paid.

Operating cycle (p. 39)   The period of time elapsing from the use of cash in the normal operating activities of an entity to the collection of cash from the entity's customers.

Operating expenses (p. 46)   Those expenses, other than cost of goods sold, that an entity incurs in its principal business operations.

Operating income (p. 46)   An entity's gross profit less its operating expenses; represents the income generated by an entity's principal line or lines of business.

Other assets (p. 40)   Miscellaneous assets of a business; typically long-term assets.

Partnership (p. 54)   An unincorporated business with two or more owners.

Prepaid expenses (p. 39)   Prepayments of relatively minor expense items such as rent, insurance, and advertising; reported as current assets in an entity's balance sheet.

Property, plant and equipment (p. 39)   Long-term assets such as buildings and machinery used in a business's operating activities.

Retained earnings (p. 43)   Generally, the cumulative earnings over the life of a business less any dividends distributed to its owners.

Revenue recognition rule (p. 57)   An accounting rule that requires revenues to be both realized and earned before they are recognized (recorded).

Revenues (p. 43)   Increases in assets and decreases in liabilities resulting from an entity's profit-oriented activities.

Short-term investments (p. 39)   Investments that a company expects to sell or otherwise convert into cash within the coming year.

Sole proprietorship (p. 54)   A business owned by one individual.

Statement of cash flows (p. 47)   A financial statement that reveals how a business generated and expended cash during an accounting period.

Statement of stockholders' equity (p. 47)   A financial statement that reconciles the dollar amount of a corporation's stockholders' equity items at the beginning and end of an accounting period.

Statements of Financial Accounting Concepts (SFACs) (p. 33)   Six technical pronouncements issued by the FASB from 1978 through 1985 to serve as the conceptual framework for the development of future accounting standards.

Stockholders' equity (p. 42)   The total assets of a corporation less amounts owed to third parties; represents stockholders' collective ownership interest in a corporation.

Unit of measurement concept (p. 56)   The accounting principle dictating that a common unit of measurement be used to record and report transactions and other financial statement items.

DECISION CASE

For several decades, Wilson Foods Corporation based in Oklahoma City was among the largest producers of processed pork products in the nation. One of the company's products was the Thomas E. Wilson Masterpiece Ham, which was named after the company's founder. Wilson ran a marketing promotion for this product each December for several years. Customers who purchased one of these hams could send a coupon and proof of purchase to Wilson and receive a rebate of a few dollars. The total rebates paid by Wilson each year in connection with this promotional campaign amounted to several million dollars.

Wilson's fiscal year ended on December 31, the same date that the Masterpiece Ham promotional campaign ended. However, most of the coupons that were redeemed by customers were not received until January. Near the end of each year, Wilson retained the services of the Nielsen Company to estimate the number of Masterpiece Ham coupons that would be redeemed after December 31. When this estimate was received from Nielsen, Wilson's accounting staff multiplied the estimate by the rebate amount. The resulting dollar figure was then recorded as a marketing expense for the fiscal year ending December 31.

Required: Assume that you are the controller of a company that initiated a promotional campaign identical in all key respects to the one just described. On December 31, the date the month-long promotion ends, you estimate that $1.5 million of coupons will be redeemed after the end of the year. You then notify the sales manager of the product for which this promotional campaign was run that an additional $1.5 million of marketing expense must be recorded for that product as of December 31. The sales manager immediately becomes upset. "That's ridiculous. We haven't even paid those coupons yet. They won't be paid till the next fiscal year. In fact, most customers haven't even mailed in the coupons. How can you justify making my division absorb a phantom expense like that? If you force us to take that hit, my year-end bonus and the bonus of everyone in my division will be cut by 30 percent!" A few minutes later, you receive a phone call from a senior vice-president in the marketing department. This individual also protests your decision. She insists that you write a memo justifying that decision. Write the requested memo to the senior vice-president. In your memo, refer to one or more of the accounting concepts discussed in this chapter.

QUESTIONS

1. The principal focus of financial accounting is the information needs of _____ . (Complete sentence.)

2. What is the common theme of the three financial reporting objectives for businesses?

3. Name the four basic financial statements and briefly describe the primary purpose of each.

4. Do all companies present the same four financial statements? Explain.

5. Write the accounting equation and explain its components.

6. What determines the length of a company's operating cycle?

7. In what order do companies in the United States typically list current assets in a balance sheet?

8. What is the purpose of recording depreciation expense on long-term assets?

9. What is the relationship, if any, between the par value and the market value of a company's common stock?

10. Is the income statement a "point-in-time" statement or a "period-of-time" statement?

11. Briefly describe or define the following three items including how they differ: net sales, gross profit, and net income

12. According to the classifications found in a statement of cash flows, what are the three major types of activities engaged in by businesses?

13. Identify types of information typically found in financial statement footnotes.

14. According to SFAC No. 2, what characteristics must accounting data possess to qualify as "relevant"?

15. Materiality refers to the relative importance of specific items of accounting information. How is relative importance typically determined?

16. According to SFAC No. 2, what is the most importance qualitative characteristic of accounting information?

17. How may the conservatism principle effect the valuation of the assets and liabilities of a company?

18. Comparability refers to _____ . (Complete sentence.)

19. For accounting purposes, what distinction does the entity concept draw between a business and its owners?

20. What three traits must accounting data possess to qualify as reliable?

EXERCISES

21. **Classification of Balance Sheet Items** (LO 2)
    Following are items that you may find in a balance sheet:

    Accounts Payable
    Inventories
    Retained Earnings
    Bonds Payable (due in 10 years)

Notes Payable (due in 6 months)
Prepaid Expenses
Common Stock
Intangible Assets
Cash
Accounts Receivable
Additional Paid-in Capital
Property, Plant and Equipment

Required:

21. No check figures

Determine the correct balance sheet classification for each item listed. Classification choices are: current assets, long-term assets, current liabilities, long-term liabilities, and stockholders' equity.

22. **Operating Cycle** (LO 2)

Mossback Company manufactures furniture for sale to department stores. The length of time that generally elapses from the purchase of raw materials by Mossback to the sale of an item of furniture produced from those raw materials is 90 days. All of Mossback's sales are on credit. On average, customers pay for purchases they make in 45 days.

Required:

22. 1. 135 days

1. What is the length of Mossback's operating cycle?
2. How does the length of a company's operating cycle affect the classification of items included in its balance sheet?

23. **Current Asset Classification** (LO 2)

Following are current assets of Ami Company:

Accounts Receivable
Inventories
Cash
Prepaid Rent
Short-Term Investments

Required:

23. No check figures

1. In what order would you usually find these accounts listed in the current assets section of a balance sheet?
2. Explain the significance of the ordering of these accounts.

24. **Liability Classification** (LO 2)

Martin Enterprises has reported a long-term debt of $100,000 the past five years in its balance sheet. Next year, the company will begin paying off this debt in four annual installments of $25,000 each.

Required:

24. 1. Current liabilities,
       $25,000
       Long-term liabilities,
       $75,000

1. How should Martin's $100,000 debt be included in the company's balance sheet at the end of the current year?
2. Why is the proper classification of liabilities between current and long-term items important to creditors and potential creditors?

25. **Accrued Expenses** (LO 2)

BioTechnica, an agricultural seed distribution company, reported accrued liabilities (accrued expenses) of $2,847,000 in its June 30, 1994, balance sheet.

Required:

25. No check figures

Describe the types of transactions or events that would result in the recording of accrued expenses in a company's accounting records.

26. **Balance Sheet Equation** (LO 2)

    Pylon Corporation has assets equal to twice the amount of its liabilities.

    Required:
    1. If Pylon's total stockholders' equity is $1,000,000, determine Pylon's total assets and total liabilities.
    2. If $750,000 of Pylon's stockholders' equity consists of common stock and additional paid-in capital, how much retained earnings does the company have?

    26. 1. Assets, $2,000,000
        Liabilities, $1,000,000
        2. Retained earnings, $250,000

27. **Asset Valuation on the Balance Sheet** (LO 4)

    Xenia, Inc. acquired a parcel of land 10 years ago for $100,000. Xenia's intent was to build a factory on the land. Ten years later, the factory is still not built and the land has a fair market value of $1,200,000.

    Required:
    1. Under current U.S. accounting standards, at what amount must this company report the land in its balance sheet? What principle dictates this accounting treatment?
    2. Do the current asset valuation rules mislead financial statement users regarding the true financial condition of Xenia, Inc.? Explain.

    27. 1. $100,000

28. **Stockholders' Equity in the Balance Sheet** (LO 2)

    QRS Company has sold 10,000 shares of its common stock, par value $10, for $80 per share.

    Required:
    1. Indicate how the financial data resulting from this sale of stock would appear in the company's balance sheet.
    2. Why would a potential investor be interested in the details of a company's stockholders' equity?

    28. 1. Common stock, $100,000
        Additional paid-in capital, $700,000

29. **Analyzing Balance Sheets of International Companies** (LO 2)

    The For Your Information vignette in this chapter titled "The Balance Sheet: Going Dutch" describes a recent balance sheet of Polygram International Ltd., a Dutch company. Reread that vignette if you do not recall its contents.

    Required:
    Suppose that you are considering investing in either Polygram or a similar company based in Malaysia. What problems would you likely encounter in comparing and contrasting the balance sheet data of the two firms?

    29. No check figures

30. **Preparing an Income Statement** (LO 2)

    Following are selected income statement data for Perry Corporation presented in random order:

General and Administrative Expenses	$ 45,050
Operating Income	?
Cost of Goods Sold	65,750
Net Income	?
Income Tax Expense (Provision for Income Tax)	1,500
Net Sales	115,000
Income Before Income Taxes	?
Gross Profit	?
Interest Income	5,000

    Required:
    1. Compute each missing amount.
    2. Prepare an income statement for Perry Corporation.

    30. Net income, $7,700

31. Computing Depreciation Expense (LO 4)

Assume that Tankersley Enterprises purchases a piece of machinery for $18,000 in early January of 1996. The machinery's estimated useful life is five years and it will have no salvage value at the end of its useful life.

Required:

1. Using the straight-line depreciation method discussed in this chapter, compute the yearly depreciation expense for this machinery.
2. What accounting principle or principles require companies to depreciate long-term assets over their useful lives instead of "expensing" their total cost in the year of purchase?

31. 1. $3,600

32. Gross Profit from Sales (LO 2)

In 1995, Doolan Company sold 10,000 units of inventory at twice their purchase price of $27.50 each. In 1996, Doolan had a gross profit of $200,000 and cost of goods sold of $225,000.

Required:

1. What was Doolan's gross profit in 1995?
2. What was the company's net sales in 1996?

32. 1. $275,000
2. $425,000

33. Interpreting Gross Profit (LO 2)

Company A and Company B operate in the same industry; both companies sell shoes on a wholesale basis in New Mexico. Company A had gross profit in 1995 of $400,000, while Company B had gross profit of $120,000. Sales for the two companies were nearly the same.

Required:

1. Why would the gross profits of the two companies be so different? Identify at least two causes for this large difference.
2. If you were the president of Company B, what strategies might you try to increase your firm's gross profit?

33. No check figures

34. Net Income and Net Cash Flow from Operating Activities (LO 2)

Jack's Bakery had a net income of $40,000 last year. However, the business's statement of cash flows for the year indicated a decrease in cash of $10,000. As a result, the business is short of cash in the first few weeks of the current year.

Required:

Identify specific reasons why a business can earn a profit during a year but yet have negative cash flow for that year.

34. No check figures

35. Qualitative Characteristics of Accounting Information (LO 3)

The following narratives refer to various qualitative characteristics of accounting information:

1. The relative importance of specific items of accounting information
2. Timeliness, predictive value and/or feedback value
3. Verifiability, neutrality, and representational faithfulness

Required:

Match each narrative item with one of the following terms: understandability, relevance, reliability, materiality, comparability.

35. No check figures

36. Accounting Concepts and Principles (LO 4)

The following narratives refer to various accounting concepts and principles:

1. Accountants can prepare meaningful reports for ongoing businesses by dividing the lives of businesses into regular reporting intervals of equal length.

2. Businesses are expected to continue operating indefinitely unless there is evidence to the contrary.
3. All information needed to obtain a thorough understanding of a company's financial affairs should be included in its financial statements and accompanying footnotes.
4. A means of determining the expenses to be included in an income statement.
5. Business transactions must be accounted for separately from the personal transactions of a business's owner or owners.

Required:

Match each narrative item with the appropriate accounting concept or principle. Choices are: entity, accounting period, unit of measure, and going concern concepts, and historical cost, revenue recognition, matching, and full disclosure principles.

36. No check figures

37. **Violation of Accounting Concepts** (LO 4)

Mom and Pop's Diamond Boutique carries all types of jewelry. Examples of recent transactions entered in the accounting records of the boutique are as follows:

Purchase of jewelry
Payment of employee salaries
Payment of daughter's college tuition
Sale of jewelry
Payment of store rent
Payment of insurance on Mom and Pop's house
Payment of store utility bills

Required:

1. What accounting concept are Mom and Pop apparently violating? Why?
2. Identify each transaction that prompted your answer to Part 1.

37. No check figures

PROBLEM SET A

38. **Financial Reporting Objectives** (LO 1)

Wagner Company operates a small chain of department stores in Vermont and New Hampshire. The owner of Wagner Company has decided to open two additional stores next year, but the company does not have sufficient cash to finance this project. To raise the needed funds for the expansion project, Wagner's owner has asked several friends to consider investing in the firm. She has provided these individuals with audited financial statements for Wagner's most recent fiscal year.

Required:

1. Besides the audited financial statements, what additional information do you believe the potential investors would want to obtain regarding Wagner Company before deciding whether to invest in the firm? Be specific.
2. Which financial reporting objective or objectives will Wagner's audited financial statements help satisfy in this context?
3. Which one of the four major financial statements do you believe the potential investors will find most useful? Defend your answer by writing a brief memo identifying the specific items of information from that financial statement that you believe will be particularly useful to the potential investors.

38. No check figures

39. Analyzing Balance Sheet Data (LO 2, 4)

Following is the assets section of the December 31, 1994, balance sheet of First Union Real Estate Investments. This company owns and manages real estate properties throughout the United States. Amounts are in thousands.

Investments in Real Estate

Land	$ 44,594
Buildings and Improvements	391,800
	436,394
Less: Accumulated Depreciation	(111,972)
Total Investments in Real Estate	324,422
Mortgage Loans Receivable	35,761

Other Assets

Cash	2,975
Accounts Receivable and Prepayments	4,594
Other Assets	8,437
Total Assets	$376,189

Required:

1. First Union's balance sheet is unusual in that it begins with *Investments in Real Estate* instead of *Current Assets*. Why do you believe the company uses this format for the assets section of its balance sheet?
2. If most real estate companies use this format for the assets section of their balance sheets, what accounting principle would First Union violate by using a different format?
3. Suppose that First Union is planning to apply for a large bank loan. Why would the company's bank loan officer want to know which of First Union's assets were current assets and which were long-term assets?

39. No check figures

40. Changes in Stockholder Equity (LO 2)

At the beginning of its 1995 fiscal year, Tucson Company had the following balances in its stockholders' equity accounts:

	COMMON STOCK	ADDITIONAL PAID-IN CAPITAL	RETAINED EARNINGS
January 1 Balance	$1,000,000	$200,000	$800,000

Assume the following events or transactions occurred during 1995:

1. Tucson sold 1,000 additional shares of common stock, par value $50 per share, for a price of $60 per share.
2. Tucson earned net income of $175,000.
3. Tucson paid dividends on common stock of $100,000.

Required:

1. Prepare a statement of stockholders' equity for Tucson Company for the year ended December 31, 1995.
2. How does this financial statement relate to the balance sheet?
3. What information in this financial statement is not available from a balance sheet? What decision makers might be interested in the information you identified?

40. 1. 12/31/95 balances:
Common stock,
$1,050,000
Additional paid-in
capital, $210,000
Retained earnings,
$875,000

41. Analysis of Income Statement Data (LO 2, 4)

Following is the income statement of Sizzler International, Inc., for its 1994 fiscal year. Sizzler operates a chain of family restaurants. Amounts are in thousands.

SIZZLER INTERNATIONAL, INC.
INCOME STATEMENT
FOR THE YEAR ENDED APRIL 30, 1994

Revenues

Restaurant Sales	$471,290	
Franchise Operations	16,214	
Investment Income	1,212	
Total Revenues		$488,716

Costs and Expenses

Cost of Goods Sold	170,480	
Labor and Related Expenses	143,413	
General and Administrative Expenses	171,789	
Depreciation and Amortization	33,122	
Other Operating Expenses	99,287	
Interest Expense	1,169	
Total Costs and Expenses		619,260
Income (Loss) before Income Taxes		(130,544)
Income Taxes		(35,651)
Net Income (Loss)		$(94,893)

Required:

1. Compare Sizzler's income statement to that of Xylogics, Inc., shown in Exhibit 2.7. Identify differences in the formats of these two income statements.
2. In your opinion, which of the income statement formats, Xylogics's or Sizzler's, is most informative for decision makers? Why?
3. Should all companies be required to use exactly the same format for their income statements? Defend your answer.
4. What accounting principles or concepts require business entities to prepare an annual income statement?

41. No check figures

42. Ethics and Financial Reporting (LO 1)

Tim Michael, the chief executive officer of Kokomo Corporation, is very concerned about his company's profitability for the current fiscal year. In the next few weeks, Kokomo will apply for a large loan from a local bank. This loan is needed to replace several pieces of outdated equipment on the company's production line. Michael is worried that the loan will be rejected because Kokomo's profits have been declining over the past two years. Profits are declining because Kokomo's products cost more to produce than the comparable products of the company's primary competitor. In turn, these higher production costs are a direct result of Kokomo's inefficient production equipment.

To ensure that Kokomo receives the loan, Michael decides to overstate the company's sales for the most recent fiscal year. In his own mind, Michael believes this decision is justified. Why? Because if Kokomo obtains the loan and purchases the new equipment, he is almost certain that the company will generate sufficient profits and cash flow to repay the bank loan. "Besides," Michael reasons to himself, "if we don't get this loan, the company may go under, leaving more than one hundred people without jobs."

Required:

42. No check figures
According to Tim Michael's way of thinking, the "end justifies the means." What would you do if you found yourself in Michael's shoes? If you were almost certain that your company could repay the loan in question, could you justify being dishonest to protect the jobs of the company's employees? Do you believe that any other factors have entered into Michael's decision to misrepresent Kokomo's financial data? Explain.

43. Income Statement Data for an International Company (LO 3, 4)

Following is selected information included in the 1994 income statement of The Broken Hill Proprietary Company Limited (BHP), one of Australia's largest publicly owned companies. Amounts are in millions of Australian dollars.

Sales	$16,644.1
Other Revenue	540.1
Depreciation and Amortization Expense	1,522.8

Required:

43. No check figures
1. Suppose that BHP's major competitor is a U.S. firm, Kerr-Midland Corporation. Would the income statement data of BHP and Kerr-Midland be directly comparable? Why or why not?
2. Briefly explain the unit of measurement concept. Should BHP translate its financial statements that are distributed in the United States into U.S. dollars to avoid violating the unit of measurement concept?
3. Where in BHP's annual report would you likely find information that identifies the accounting rules the company uses? Why would this information be very useful to a U.S. citizen considering investing in this company?

44. Applying Accounting Concepts (LO 4)

The following situations involve the application of accounting concepts or principles. In some cases, more than one concept or principle may be involved.

a. Logo Enterprises changed its method of computing depreciation for the third time in three years; each change was to a different depreciation method.
b. Prism Distributors sold two of its five divisions immediately after the close of its most recent fiscal year. Company executives included information regarding the sale of these two divisions in the footnotes to the company's financial statements.
c. Inventory is the largest asset of Anderson Gardening Company. Last year, Anderson's inventory was reported at its historical cost in the company's balance sheet. This year, the company intends to report its inventory at market value since the inventory's market value is significantly below its historical cost.
d. A footnote to the recent financial staements issued by Lobo, Inc., lists the cash payments that the company is required to make over the next several years as a result of its long-term lease agreements.

Required:

44. No check figures
1. Identify the accounting concepts or principles involved in each of these situations.
2. Indicate whether the given accounting concept or principle has been properly applied in each case. Explain your reasoning.

PROBLEM SET B

45. Financial Reporting Objectives (LO 1)

The owner of Roberts Greenhouse, Bud Roberts, wants to buy out a local competitor. The competitor has offered to sell her business for $400,000. Unfortunately, Roberts Greenhouse has most of its assets tied up in inventory and accounts receivable. Although the company has total assets of $822,000, its cash balance is only $12,100. To finance the purchase of the competing business, Bud Roberts has decided to apply for a $400,000 loan from a local bank. Among other items of information, the bank has requested audited financial statements for Roberts Greenhouse for the past five years.

Required:

1. What information will the bank obtain from this business's financial statements that will assist it in determining whether to grant the loan?
2. Which financial reporting objective listed in Exhibit 2.2 is most relevant in this context?

45. No check figures

46. Analyzing Balance Sheet Data (LO 2, 4)

Following are selected assets included in the December 31, 1993, balance sheet of First Union Real Estate Investments. This company owns and manages real estate properties throughout the United States. Amounts are in thousands.

Land	$ 40,284
Cash	38,523
Accounts Receivable and Prepayments	4,621
Buildings and Improvement	368,776
Mortgage Loans Receivable	35,550

Required:

1. How do businesses determine which of their assets are current assets and which are long-term assets?
2. Identify which of the listed assets of First Union are likely current assets and which are likely long-term assets.
3. What valuation basis for financial reporting purposes did First Union likely use for its investments in land? What accounting principle dictates that the company use this valuation basis?

46. No check figures

47. Stockholder Equity Changes (LO 2)

At the beginning of its 1995 fiscal year, Amazon Company had the following balances in its stockholders' equity accounts:

	COMMON STOCK	ADDITIONAL PAID-IN CAPITAL	RETAINED EARNINGS
January 1 Balance	$1,000,000	$350,000	$900,000

Assume the following events or transactions occurred during 1995:

1. Amazon sold 2,000 additional shares of common stock, par value $50 per share, for a price of $65 per share.
2. Amazon earned net income of $215,000.
3. Amazon paid dividends on its common stock of $125,000.

47. 1. 12/31/95 balances:
Common stock,
$1,100,000
Additional paid-in
capital, $380,000
Retained earnings,
$990,000

Required:

1. Prepare a statement of stockholders' equity for Amazon Company for the year ended December 31, 1995.
2. How does this financial statement relate to the balance sheet?
3. How does this financial statement relate to the income statement?

48. Analysis of Income Statement Data (LO 2, 4)

Following is information taken from the 1994 income statement of Barnes & Noble, Inc., which operates a chain of retail bookstores. Amounts are expressed in thousands.

Sales	$1,337,386
Depreciation and Amortization	29,077
Selling and Adminstrative Expenses	262,861
Rental Expenses	120,326
Cost of Goods Sold	874,038
Net Income	7,753

Required:

1. What was Barnes and Noble's gross profit in 1994?
2. Compute Barnes & Noble's gross profit percentage for 1994. Why do decision makers closely monitor a merchandising company's gross profit percentage?
3. What types of expenses are selling and administrative expenses?
4. Suppose that Barnes & Noble fails to record depreciation expense in a given year on certain of its assets. What accounting principle or concept would this oversight violate?

49. Ethics and Financial Reporting (LO 1)

Mei Wong is a loan officer employed by Capital City Bank. Recently, Mei was assigned the responsibility of processing a loan application for a local company, Kokomo Corporation. Mei is very familiar with this company, in fact her younger brother and several of her friends work on Kokomo's production line. After reviewing the loan application, Mei is disturbed. She has been told by her brother that Kokomo's sales shipments have been declining. She is also aware that the company has been suffering an excessive amount of down time on its production line due to an increasing rate of malfunctions by the company's outdated production equipment. Despite these problems, Kokomo's unaudited financial statements included in the loan application are "rosy." For the most recent year, the company's financial statements report impressive increases in sales and net income. Mei suspects that the financial statements may have been tampered with by company executives to enhance the company's apparent financial condition and operating results.

Required:

1. Does Mei have a right to question the integrity of the individuals who were responsible for the preparation of Kokomo's financial statements? Should she accept those financial statements at face value and make her loan recommendation accordingly? Explain.
2. What steps could Mei take to investigate the accuracy of Kokomo's financial statements?
3. Put yourself in Mei's position. Identify the parties who will be affected by Mei's decision regarding this loan application. What responsibility does she have to each of these parties, if any?

50. Income Statement Data for an International Company (LO 3, 4)

Following are selected items included in the 1994 income statement of Hitachi, Ltd., a Japanese electronics firm. Amounts are in millions of Japanese yen.

Other Income	104,972
Net Sales	7,400,205
Selling, General and Administrative Expenses	1,874,824
Net Income	65,279
Cost of Goods Sold	5,311,992

Required:

1. Suppose that you were considering investing in Hitachi's common stock, what types of information would you need to interpret this firm's income statement data? What information would you need to compare the company's income statement data to that of a comparable firm in the United States?
2. Determine Hitachi's gross profit and operating income for 1994.
3. Hitachi's gross profit was 2,276,807 in 1992 and 2,098,008 in 1993, while the company's 1992 net income was 127,611 and its 1993 net income was 77,289 (all amounts are expressed in millions of yen). Based only on the original data provided and these additional data, did Hitachi's financial status improve or deteriorate between 1992 and 1994? What factors may have accounted for the change in the company's financial status over this time period?

50. 2. Gross profit, 2,088,213 Operating income, 213,389

51. Applying Accounting Concepts (LO 4)

The following situations involve the application of accounting concepts or principles. In some cases, more than one concept or principle may be involved.

a. Dealer Company is being forced to discontinue its operations because of large losses it has incurred in recent years. To pay off its creditors, the company has scheduled a going-out-of-business sale for next month. The company's recently issued financial statements do not comment on this matter.

b. Luxalt Enterprises had sales of $45 million and net income of $7 million during 1995. The company inadvertently failed to record depreciation expense of $1,100 on a piece of equipment during 1995.

c. Dusny Asphalt, Inc. had several assets, principally buildings and equipment, appreciate in value during 1996 but failed to record these increases in asset value in its accounting records.

d. Madison Paving, Inc. had a poor year profit-wise in 1995, so the company's owners decided to record some January 1996 sales as if they occurred in 1995. These sales will not be "double-counted" since they will only be reflected in the company's accounting records for 1995; consequently, the company's owners believe this accounting treatment is acceptable.

Required:

1. Identify the accounting concepts or principles involved in each of these situations.
2. Indicate whether the accounting concepts and principles you identified in Part 1 were violated in the given situations.

51. No check figures

CASES

52. Information for Lending Decisions

Suppose that you are the president of a small bank in Winslow, Arizona. A group of local investors have approached you with a loan proposal. These individuals want to borrow $750,000 to build a new motel adjacent to the nearby interstate highway. Presently, there are several motels in the area where the investors intend to build the new motel. However, the investors maintain that there is more than enough business to support a new motel in this area.

Required:

1. What types of information would you require the investors to submit with their loan application? What do you hope to learn from this information?
2. Would it be appropriate for you to ask the investors to prepare projected financial statements for the first several years of the proposed motel's operations? Why or why not?
3. Suppose that the investors intend to operate their new business as a corporation. How, if at all, would this affect your decision of whether or not to grant the loan? Explain.

53. **Conflicting Accounting Principles and Concepts**

Certain of the fundamental accounting concepts and principles discussed in this chapter are not necessarily consistent. That is, one concept may dictate that a business transaction or event be recorded in one way, while another concept suggests another accounting treatment for that same item.

Required:

1. Identify two examples of accounting concepts or principles that may suggest different accounting treatments for given business transactions or events.
2. For the paired items you identified in Part 1, indicate which concept you believe should take precedence in each case. Defend your answers.

54. **Manipulation of Accounting Data**

As you will learn in a subsequent chapter, business entities can choose from among several depreciation methods to apply. Likewise, businesses often have several alternative methods to choose from in accounting for other key financial statement items such as inventory, accounts receivable, and investments.

Required:

1. Refer to the discussion of depreciation in this chapter. How might a company manipulate its depreciation expense for a given year? Be specific.
2. In general, what problem may result from allowing businessses to "pick and choose" from among different accounting methods for various financial statement items?
3. In your opinion, should business entities be allowed to choose the accounting methods to apply to their financial data, or should these accounting methods be dictated by law or a regulatory body? Write a memo supporting your stance on this issue.

PROJECTS

55. **Testing the Windbag Theory**

Reread the vignette in this chapter that is titled "The Windbag Theory." In this project, you will test the windbag theory by reviewing a recent annual report of a company.

Required:

1. Obtain a recent annual report of a large public company from your school's library or another source.

2. Review this company's four major financial statements that were discussed in this chapter.

3. Read the key narrative information included in the annual report by the company's executives. (Most companies include a "letter to stockholders," a "president's letter," or a comparable item in their annual reports.)

4. Compare and contrast the data in the company's financial statements with the information included in management's narrative disclosures in the annual report. Did you discover any apparent attempt by the company's executives to "gloss over" or downplay any negative financial information included in the company's financial statements?

5. Write a brief report summarizing your findings.

56. Analyzing Profitability

Meet with your assigned group or project team. For this project, your group should choose two large companies that are in the same industry.

Required:

1. Prepare an exhibit similar to the one in Exhibit 2.10. This exhibit should compare the net income and the net cash flow from operating activities for each selected company over a recent three-year period.

2. Prepare a second exhibit, similar in format to the first but focusing on different financial data. This exhibit should compare the total revenues, gross profit, and net income of each selected company for a recent three-year period.

3. As a group, discuss the two exhibits. Which company is more profitable? Why? How did your group reach this conclusion? Your group should prepare a brief written report, accompanied by the two exhibits, summarizing the group's findings. Be prepared to have one or more group members present a summary of this report to the class.

57. Full Disclosure Principle in Practice

Refer to the discussion of the full disclosure principle in this chapter. Reread the excerpt from the financial statements of HON Industries, Inc., which discussed the company's backlog of orders.

Required:

1. Obtain from your school's library or another source several recent annual reports of publicly owned companies.

2. Identify in one of these annual reports a good example of an application of the full disclosure principle.

3. Summarize the example you identified in Part 2 in a written report. Also include in this report a description of the company that provided the disclosure, why you believe the disclosure was made, and how the disclosure would be useful to financial decision makers such as investors and lenders.

3

ACCOUNTING SYSTEMS AND INTERNAL CONTROL

LEARNING OBJECTIVES

After studying this chapter, you should be able to do the following:

1. Define an accounting system and identify its principal components

2. Describe how an accounting system is used to process accounting data for a business each accounting period

3. Define an internal control structure and identify its primary objectives

4. Identify and describe the elements of an internal control structure

5. Discuss the need for, and nature of, internal control reports

6. Identify the key differences between manual and computer-based processing of accounting data and the related internal control implications

7. Discuss recent trends in computer processing and the related implications for organizations' accounting and control functions

8. Identify internal control issues resulting from the growing trend toward multinational business operations

The system is the solution.
American Telephone & Telegraph, Inc.

Internal Controls: Being Safe Not Sorry

Dateline: Los Angeles, California, July 1991. Federal authorities arrest sixteen individuals who stole at least $6 million in computer parts from Digital Equipment Corporation. One of the individuals was the chief of security for a large warehouse of the company.

Dateline: Long Island, New York, February 1993. Federal authorities reveal that $40 million is missing from Revere Armored, Inc., a courier company. The authorities suspect that several employees conspired with parties outside the company to steal the funds from Revere.

Dateline: New York, New York, September 1994. A social events coordinator with Salomon Brothers, Inc., admits embezzling $1.1 million from the prestigious investment banking firm.

Dateline: Boston, Massachusetts, April 1995. A former manager with Shearson Lehman Brothers, a brokerage firm, is sentenced to one year in prison for transferring nearly $100,000 from a client's brokerage account to his personal account.

Isolated instances? Hardly. Employee theft and fraud wreak havoc each year on the profits of businesses of all sizes. A recent study by the federal government estimated that annual losses due to employee theft approach $100 billion in the United States.[1] Another study found that approximately 76 percent of the largest companies in this country and 66 percent of Canadian companies suffer significant losses each year due to employee theft or fraud, the median loss being $200,000.[2]

Too often, business owners, particularly small business owners, decide to ignore the problem of employee theft. Past experience proves that this decision can be a costly one. A study reported in the early 1990s suggests that employee theft is ultimately responsible for one-third of all business failures each year.[3] To protect themselves, their firms, and the parties that rely on their firms, business owners and executives must have a strategy for dealing with this problem. The most effective approach to preventing, or at least minimizing, employee theft is a network of rigorous internal controls. Such a network is costly to establish and maintain. However, the alternative may be even more costly in the long run.

T his chapter introduces you to accounting systems and internal control concepts and issues. Chapters 4 through 6 discuss and illustrate the key procedural aspects of recording accounting information. Before focusing on accounting procedures, you will find it helpful to become acquainted with the general nature of accounting systems and internal control concepts. The introduction you receive to accounting systems in this chapter provides you with a basic framework for understanding how accounting data are systematically collected and processed. An organization's accounting system is one component of an internal control structure used by business executives to monitor and control their organizations. To fully comprehend the purpose of specific accounting procedures, you must understand the objectives and nature of an internal control structure.

---

1. L. Touby, "In the Company of Thieves," *Journal of Business Strategy*, May/June 1994, 24–35.

2. "Survey Finds Fraud a Serious and Growing Business Problem," *Journal of Accountancy*, October 1993, 20–21.

3. M. Hanif, "Making Honesty an Employee's Best Policy," *Washington Post*, 7 October 1991, WB 10.

The opening section of this chapter presents a general overview of accounting systems, while the next section discusses fundamental internal control concepts as they relate to an organization's accounting function. The final two sections of this chapter address the impact of two important trends on organizations' accounting and control functions. These trends are the growing use of computers by businesses to process accounting data and the growth in multinational business operations.

ACCOUNTING SYSTEMS: AN INTRODUCTION

Teaching Note
Help students visualize a business with a large number of transactions. Use a busy retail store, such as a Wal-Mart store, as an example of a business with thousands of sales transactions each day. Ask them to imagine the total number of transactions for all Wal-Mart stores during a given year.

How many times have you heard the now-trite expression "You gotta have a system"? The systems mentality has invaded, if not conquered, the business world in recent decades. Without exception, the purpose of every system is to help individuals or groups of individuals "attack" some problem. If anyone needs a system to help solve a problem, it has to be accountants. Consider the problem facing accountants of a large corporation that engages in millions, if not hundreds of millions, of transactions each year. To provide useful information to investors, creditors, and other decision makers, these accountants must somehow convert this massive number of transactions into the four financial statements identified in Chapter 2. Without a systematic method to approach this problem, accountants would find their task hopeless.

The Accounting Function as a System

■ **LEARNING OBJECTIVE 1**
Define an accounting system and identify its principal components

system

accounting system

The unabridged version of the *Random House Dictionary* provides more than a dozen definitions for the term "system." Paraphrasing and merging several of those definitions, a **system** is a coordinated network of plans and procedures designed to achieve a stated goal in an orderly, effective, and efficient manner. Not surprisingly, this definition applies very well to the typical accounting system. For our purposes, let us define an **accounting system** as a systematic approach to collecting, processing, and communicating financial information to decision makers.[4]

Like most types of systems, accounting systems come in varying degrees of complexity and sophistication. Some small businesses still use manual accounting systems. A manual accounting system relies strictly on a "pen and paper" mode of processing financial data. Most business entities, including small businesses, have integrated computer processing into their accounting systems. Keep in mind as you progress through this course that the fundamental concepts and methods of accounting apply equally well to both manual and computer-based accounting systems.

Real World
Accounting systems are customized for the needs of each business. Deciding on the components of a specific accounting system should involve an analysis of the cost of each component versus the benefits each component would provide.

Now, let us briefly "walk through" the principal components of an accounting system. In the next three chapters, we examine accounting systems in much more detail. Here, the primary purpose is to provide you with an overview of accounting systems and how they convert raw financial data into financial statements useful to decision makers.

---

4. This definition varies slightly from the following "official" definition of an accounting system included in *Statement on Auditing Standards No. 55*, "Consideration of the Internal Control Structure in a Financial Statement Audit" (New York: American Institute of Certified Public Accountants, 1988).

   The accounting system consists of the methods and records established to identify, assemble, analyze, classify, record, and report on an entity's transactions and to maintain accountability for the related assets and liabilities.

Notice that the latter part of this definition indicates that an accounting system has an "accountability" or control feature.

Accounts

Accounts are the basic storage units for financial data in an accounting system. Financial data related to the assets, liabilities, and other financial statement items of a business are recorded and stored in accounts either electronically or manually. Some primitive accounting systems used a very simple account format, a so-called T-account, which derived its name from its shape. Although not used in modern accounting systems, accountants often use T-accounts for illustration or analytical purposes.

Shown in Exhibit 3.1 is a T-account that summarizes a series of hypothetical cash transactions for the Strawberry House, the bed and breakfast inn mentioned in Chapter 2. This T-account summarizes the cash transactions of the Strawberry House during January 1996 and reveals the cash balance at the beginning and end of that month for the business. Chapter 4 identifies the double-entry bookkeeping rules that dictate how accounting information is recorded in individual accounts. Although

accounts

Teaching Note
Point out to students that T-accounts should be helpful to them as they begin to analyze the effects of transactions on specific accounts.

Many small businesses located on Main Street in Smalltown, USA, use an accounting system in which accounting data are manually recorded by the business owner. Large corporations, on the other hand, have sophisticated computer-based accounting systems and accounting staffs consisting of hundreds of employees.

■ **EXHIBIT 3.1**
T-Account for Cash

		Cash			
Balance	1/1/96	525			
	1/8/96	200	1/10/96		250
	1/15/96	430	1/17/96		120
	1/22/96	350	1/30/96		760
	1/29/96	440			
Balance	1/31/96	815			

we are jumping the gun slightly, let us briefly consider two of these rules so that you can better appreciate the nature and purpose of an account. When recording financial data in a T-account for an asset such as cash, transactions and other events that increase the dollar amount of the asset are recorded on the left-hand or "debit" side of the account. Transactions and other events that decrease the dollar amount of an asset are recorded on the right-hand or "credit" side of the asset's T-account. (If you are not familiar with the common bookkeeping terms "debit" and "credit," do not be concerned. In the next few chapters, you will become very familiar with those terms.)

Notice that the Strawberry House began the month of January 1996 with a $525 balance in its Cash account. By the end of the month, this account had a balance of $815. This figure was determined by adding four bank deposits made during January to the beginning-of-the-month cash balance and then subtracting from this total three checks written during the month. The four bank deposits, such as the $200 deposit on January 8, were entered on the left-hand side of the T-account. Why? Because bank deposits increase a business's cash and the relevant bookkeeping rule dictates that increases in asset accounts be entered on the left-hand side of a T-account. The three checks written during January 1996 by the Strawberry House were entered on the right-hand side of the Cash account shown in Exhibit 3.1. For example, on January 17 the Strawberry House issued a $120 check.

Your life will be much easier over the next several weeks or months if you recognize and accept one key feature of bookkeeping rules. Bookkeeping rules are arbitrary. That is, we could just as easily record increases in assets on the right-hand side of an asset account and decreases in assets on the left-hand side of an asset account. But someone in the Middle Ages decreed that increases in assets should be entered on the left-hand side of an asset account, while decreases in assets should be entered on the right-hand side of an asset account. Ever since, accountants have followed this rule or convention.

As noted previously, the T-account format is not used in modern accounting systems, not even those systems in which accounting data are processed manually. Instead, the four-column account format shown in Exhibit 3.2 is commonly used. The data included in the T-account shown in Exhibit 3.1 have been entered in the

■ **EXHIBIT 3.2**
Four-Column Account Format

Cash							Account No. 101	
Date		Explanation	Post Ref.	Debit	Credit	Balance		
						Debit	Credit	
1996								
Jan.	1	Balance Forward				525	
	8	Deposit		200		725	
	10	Check No. 112			250	475	
	15	Deposit		430		905	
	17	Check No. 113			120	785	
	22	Deposit		350		1,135	
	29	Deposit		440		1,575	
	30	Check No. 114			760	815	
	31	Balance				815	

four-column account in Exhibit 3.2. A key advantage of the four-column account format is that it provides an updated account balance after each transaction has been entered. (In a later chapter, the purpose of the "post reference" column in the four-column account format is explained.)

Chart of Accounts

A **chart of accounts** is a numerical listing, by account number, of an entity's accounts. Think of a chart of accounts as an address book. When recording a transaction, an accountant refers to the chart of accounts to identify the proper "address" for each account affected by the transaction. A chart of accounts speeds up the recording of transactions and minimizes the risk that transaction data will be recorded in the wrong accounts. Shown in Exhibit 3.3 is a partial chart of accounts that a small business might use—assuming it is organized as a corporation rather than as a sole proprietorship or partnership.

Notice that accounts appear in a chart of accounts in the same general order they appear in a balance sheet and income statement, respectively: assets, liabilities, stockholders' equity, revenues, and expenses. Most companies use a numbering system for a chart of accounts derived from the fact that there are five types or groups of accounts. For instance, asset accounts are typically assigned an account number beginning with the numeral one. Revenues, the fourth of the five groups of accounts, are generally assigned an account number beginning with the numeral four.

The General Journal and General Ledger: The Basic Accounting "Books"

When referring to the process of recording transactions, accountants often use the term "book," as in "Dennis, go ahead and book that sale to the Beresford Corporation." The principal accounting "books" or records for most business enterprises are its journals and ledgers. The general journal, sales journal, cash receipts journal, and cash disbursements journal are the journals most commonly used by businesses. The ledgers typically integrated into an accounting system include the general ledger, the accounts receivable ledger, and the accounts payable ledger.

When our friend Dennis, the accountant, was instructed to "book" the sale to the Beresford Corporation, he would have initially recorded this transaction in a journal.

chart of accounts

Teaching Note
Point out that the "address" is the account number. The address specifies the account's location in the general ledger, where accounts are arranged in consecutive, numerical order.

■ **EXHIBIT 3.3**
Partial Chart of Accounts for a Small Business

101. Cash	203. Taxes Payable
102. Accounts Receivable	250. Mortgage Payable
103. Supplies	300. Common Stock
104. Prepaid Insurance	320. Additional Paid-in Capital
151. Furniture and Fixtures	320. Retained Earnings
152. Equipment	401. Rental Revenue
153. Buildings	501. Repair Expense
201. Accounts Payable	502. Cleaning Expense
202. Unearned Rent	

■ EXHIBIT 3.4
General Journal Format and Representative Journal Entry

General Journal					Page 12
Date		**Description**	**Post Ref.**	**Debit**	**Credit**
1996 Apr.	19	Cash		1,274	
		Sales			1,274
		To record sale made to Beresford Corporation			

journalizing

general journal

general ledger

posting

Journalizing is the term used by accountants when referring to the process of recording in a journal financial data resulting from transactions or other events affecting a business. Assume for the time being that Dennis recorded the sale in his firm's general journal. Shown in Exhibit 3.4 is a general journal format and a general journal entry illustrating how a company might book or record a sales transaction.

Think of a journal as a financial diary in which accountants initially record the transactions and other events that affect the financial status of a business. Some of these events are recorded simultaneously. For instance, a small grocery store that uses a manual accounting system does not individually record each sale made to customers. Instead, the daily cash sales of such a business are typically recorded in one lump sum at the end of the day. Businesses that maintain only one journal initially record transactions and other financial events in a **general journal,** which is sometimes referred to as the "book of original entry."

The **general ledger** is the accounting record that contains each of the individual accounts for an entity's assets, liabilities, owners' or stockholders' equity, revenues, and expenses. Recording transactions and other events in a journal serves the purpose of establishing a historical record of the transactions and events affecting a business. However, accountants would have considerable difficulty preparing financial statements directly from the several hundred—or several million—journal entries recorded for a business during a given accounting period. To expedite the preparation of financial statements at the end of an accounting period, accountants transcribe or copy accounting data from the general journal and other journals used by a business to the individual accounts in the general ledger.

Posting is the term used by accountants when referring to the process of transferring accounting data from a journal to the appropriate general ledger accounts. Posting can be done daily, weekly, or monthly. In a computerized accounting system, the posting of transactions is often done simultaneously with the journalizing of transactions.

At the end of an accounting period, accountants prepare a listing of the general ledger account balances of a business. The account balances in this listing, known as a trial balance or working trial balance, are eventually incorporated into the appropriate financial statements. For financial statement purposes, several account balances are often consolidated into one item. If a company has a dozen cash accounts, the balances in those accounts would be added and the resulting total listed on the balance sheet line item Cash.

■ **EXHIBIT 3.5**
Basic Steps in the Accounting Cycle

Task		Accounting Activity
Record financial data	→	Journalize transactions
Collate financial data	→	Post transactions to general ledger
Organize account balances	→	Prepare trial balance
Consolidate and classify account balances	→	Prepare financial statements

The Accounting Cycle

Embedded in the preceding section is a condensed summary of the **accounting cycle,** which is the set of recurring accounting procedures that must be performed for a business each accounting period. First, financial information resulting from transactions and other events affecting a business must be journalized. Second, this information must be posted to the appropriate general ledger accounts. Third, the period-ending general ledger account balances must be organized into a trial balance. Finally, the account balances must be consolidated and incorporated into the appropriate financial statements. Exhibit 3.5 summarizes these four general tasks and the related accounting procedures or activities required to accomplish them. In a subsequent chapter, we discuss additional accounting procedures that must be performed each accounting period. However, Exhibit 3.5 lists the key steps in the accounting cycle.

■ **LEARNING OBJECTIVE 2**
Describe how an accounting system is used to process accounting data for a business each accounting period

accounting cycle

Teaching Note
The accounting cycle is the same for all types and sizes of businesses. Emphasize that the steps in the accounting cycle are repeated every accounting period.

INTERNAL CONTROL CONCEPTS AND ISSUES

An accounting system is one component of an overall control system that business executives use to monitor and control their organizations. For small companies, this control system is often quite informal. The principal method a sole proprietor may use to control his or her business is involvement in the day-to-day operations of the firm. Employees have less opportunity to take unfair advantage of their employer if he or she is working side by side with them. On the other hand, large corporations typically have extensive manuals documenting and defining the various aspects of their control systems. These manuals often describe in tedious detail the specific responsibilities of each job position, the chain of command within each department, the individuals who have the authority to purchase goods and services, and on and on. In this section, we focus on control concepts and issues, particularly as they relate to the accounting function of a business entity.

Internal Control Structure: Definition and Objectives

■ LEARNING
OBJECTIVE 3
Define an internal control
structure and identify its primary
objectives

internal control structure

Real World
Large companies frequently hire
public accounting firms to
review their system of controls
to identify and eliminate specific
control weaknesses.

Discussion Question
Ask students to describe specific
security measures that they have
observed in retail stores to
prevent shoplifting.

Businesses use different terms to label and describe their overall control systems. **Internal control structure** is the phrase that accountants use when referring to the system of controls that a business entity has established. An internal control structure is defined as follows:

> An entity's internal control structure consists of the policies and procedures established to provide reasonable assurance that specific entity objectives will be achieved.[5]

Two of the phrases in the previous definition—"specific entity objectives" and "reasonable assurance"—are particularly important. From an accounting perspective, two entity objectives that an internal control structure should aid an organization in accomplishing are the maintenance of reliable financial records and the safeguarding of its assets. Accountants are clearly the individuals within an organization best equipped to develop and implement controls to provide for reliable financial records. Likewise, because of their thorough understanding of control concepts, accountants typically assume responsibility for developing specific procedures, or internal controls, to minimize the risk that a business's assets will be stolen or misused.

The concept of reasonable assurance suggests that the costs of internal controls should not exceed the benefits they provide to organizations. For instance, elaborate security measures to prevent or minimize shoplifting losses in a retail store may be very effective. However, if the cost of such measures exceeds the shoplifting losses they prevent, these measures are not cost-effective and, as a general rule, should be discontinued.

Elements of an Internal Control Structure

■ LEARNING
OBJECTIVE 4
Identify and describe the
elements of an internal control
structure

control environment

The accounting profession has identified three elements of an internal control structure: an accounting system, a control environment, and a set of control procedures.[6] Since accounting systems have been discussed earlier, we focus here on the other two elements of an internal control structure.

CONTROL ENVIRONMENT   The phrase **control environment** refers to the degree of control consciousness within an organization. Executives of a company must impress upon their subordinates the importance of strong internal controls. If top executives exhibit a lack of concern regarding internal controls, their subordinates will likely follow suit. Even when an organization's executives establish strong internal controls, they may inadvertently undercut the effectiveness of those controls. For instance, if executives impose too much pressure on their subordinates to reach periodic revenue and profit goals, the subordinates may bypass the organization's controls to accomplish those financial objectives. Similarly, incentive or bonus compensation

---

5. *Statement on Auditing Standards No. 55*, "Consideration of the Internal Control Structure in a Financial Statement Audit" (New York: American Institute of Certified Public Accountants, 1988).

6. As this textbook is being written, the accounting profession is rethinking its definition of an internal control structure. The profession will apparently redefine an internal control structure as consisting of five "components" instead of three "elements." The five proposed components of an internal control structure are: control environment, risk assessment, control activities, information and communication, and monitoring. The changes being considered do not affect the nature of internal control structures. Consequently, the discussion included here of the three elements of internal control structures will serve the purpose of acquainting you with basic internal control concepts and issues.

Cashing in on Weak Internal Controls

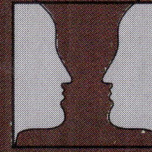

E. F. Hutton & Co. was the second largest brokerage firm in the United States during the early 1980s and a company with a long and proud history. During 1985 and 1986, a congressional investigation revealed that many of Hutton's branch managers were using illegal cash management practices to inflate the interest revenue of their individual branches. The most abusive cash management practice involved overdrawing bank accounts that were non-interest-bearing and depositing these amounts in interest-bearing accounts. Not surprisingly, a sizable portion of the interest revenue of each retail branch was paid to the branch manager as a year-end bonus. Many, if not most, banks affected by this scheme were aware of its existence. These banks apparently chose not to report the scheme to banking authorities because they did not want to lose Hutton as a client. Why? Because E. F. Hutton was typically among the most prestigious banking clients in the communities in which the firm's branch offices were located.

By 1983, the abusive cash management practices were so widespread within the Hutton firm that its bank accounts were overdrawn by $500 million. The congressional committee that investigated this scandal was stunned to learn that Hutton's top executives were unaware of the illegal cash management practices. Hutton's executives had apparently failed to establish a strong sense of control consciousness within the firm. These executives had also neglected to establish a reliable network of internal controls to monitor the activities of their subordinates. For example, despite the prominence and size of the Hutton firm, the company did not have an organizational chart that graphically depicted the chain of command within the organization.

The absence of a strong internal control structure proved fatal for E. F. Hutton & Co. After the firm pleaded guilty to two thousand counts of mail and wire fraud and paid a multimillion-dollar fine, it was never able to regain the confidence of the public. A few years later, the firm was on the brink of bankruptcy when it was taken over by one of its major competitors.

SOURCE: M. C. Knapp, "E. F. Hutton & Co., Inc." *Contemporary Auditing: Issues and Cases*, 2d ed. (Minneapolis/St. Paul: West Publishing Co., 1996).

plans that focus subordinates' attention on maximizing profits for their personal benefit can result in internal controls being undercut.

An example of a company in which executives failed to establish a strong control environment was E. F. Hutton & Co., one of the nation's largest brokerage firms until the late 1980s. The Spotlight on Ethics vignette accompanying this section describes a financial scandal within the Hutton firm that was a result of its inadequate internal control structure.

CONTROL PROCEDURES   The final element of an internal control structure is a set of control procedures. **Control procedures** are specific rules established by an entity to help ensure that its primary organizational objectives are accomplished. Shown in Exhibit 3.6 are several examples of specific control procedures. One of the most important control procedures is the segregation of key functional responsibilities or duties within an organization, particularly within the organization's account-

control procedures

■ **EXHIBIT 3.6**

Examples of Control Procedures

- Segregation of key functional responsibilities
- Proper authorization of transactions
- Use of prenumbered accounting documents
- Periodic counts of inventory
- Clerical tests of the mathematical accuracy of invoices and other accounting documents
- Periodic reconciliation of general ledger controlling accounts with balances of subsidiary ledgers

■ **EXHIBIT 3.7**

Key Duties That Should Be Segregated in an Accounting System

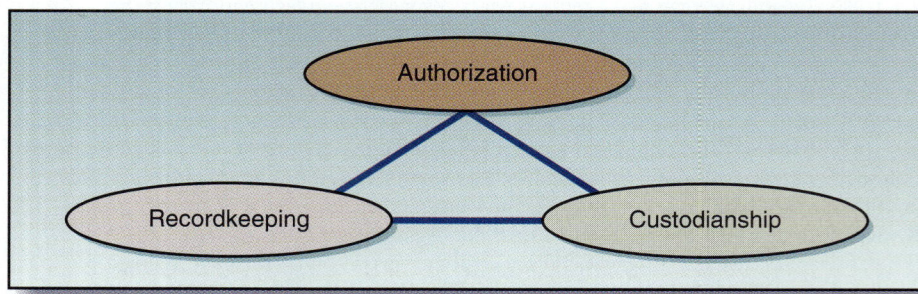

ing system. To minimize the potential for employee theft and undetected errors, the three types of duties shown in Exhibit 3.7—authorization, recordkeeping, and custodianship—should be segregated within each major segment of an accounting system. For instance, an employee should not have both custodial and recordkeeping responsibility for cash. An individual with both of those responsibilities could steal cash and then conceal the theft by making the appropriate entries in the accounting records.

In the late 1970s, the Hermetite Corporation, a manufacturing firm, learned first-hand about the risks posed by assigning incompatible responsibilities to an employee.[7] Hermetite's office manager also served as the company's bookkeeper. This individual had access to the company's blank checks, its check writing machine, the facsimile signature plate used to impress authorized signatures on checks, and the cash disbursements journal in which checks were recorded. The office manager also received the company's monthly bank statements and prepared the monthly bank reconciliations. Over a five-year period, the office manager stole more than $200,000 from Hermetite by writing and then cashing bogus checks. To conceal the scheme, the office manager

Discussion Question
Nonfinancial clues may indicate the existence of employee fraud. Ask students if they can think of "red flags" that might have signaled that the office manager was embezzling money from the company.
Example: The office manager began living beyond his salary level—expensive clothes, expensive car, and so on.

7. See Securities and Exchange Commission, *Accounting and Auditing Enforcement Release No. 2,* 18 August 1992.

recorded the embezzled amounts as purchases of raw materials and then destroyed the canceled checks when they were returned by the company's bank.

Any of a number of control procedures would have prevented or detected the office manager's embezzlement scheme. For instance, assume that another employee had been responsible for receiving the company's monthly bank statements and preparing the monthly bank reconciliations. This individual would have discovered the suspicious checks that the office manager had written to himself.

Another standard internal control procedure is clerical tests of the mathematical accuracy of invoices and other accounting documents, as indicated in Exhibit 3.6. Sounds reasonable and obvious, right? However, consider the embarrassment suffered by executives of the world's largest mutual fund, the Magellan Fund of Fidelity Investments, when an accountant made a clerical error in a tax computation. The error converted a $1.3 billion loss into a $1.3 billion gain. Magellan's shareholders were provided with a significantly overstated estimate of the fund's 1994 earnings because of the error. In January 1995, Fidelity Investments's executives had to relay the bad news to Magellan's shareholders, which, as you can imagine, was an unpleasant experience for both the executives and the shareholders.

Internal Control Reports

Okay, let's assume that you make it through college and land a great job. Because you are a forward-looking individual, you immediately begin planning for your retirement. You decide to make your initial nest egg investment in a company that sells arts and crafts items for do-it-yourself home decorators. Reportedly, the common stocks of such companies are "hot tickets" because a growing number of affluent yuppies prefer to do their own home decorating. Your broker has recommended the common stock of Rag Shops, Inc., a small but rapidly growing arts and crafts retailer. Now, the connection to internal control reports: Would you, as a prospective investor, be interested in information regarding the internal control structure of this company? Almost certainly. You have read about companies such as Hermetite and E. F. Hutton that suffered severe economic problems because of weak internal controls. As a result, one of your primary investment criteria is to buy stocks only of companies that have strong internal controls. To your disappointment, you discover that the most recent annual report of Rag Shops, Inc., does not contain information regarding the company's internal controls.

The issue of whether companies should be required to report on their internal control structures has been hotly debated in recent years. Presently, only certain financial institutions are required to include in their annual reports information concerning their internal control structures. Nevertheless, many companies voluntarily include such information in their annual reports. Each year, the American Institute of Certified Public Accountants (AICPA) analyzes the accounting and financial reporting practices of six hundred publicly owned companies. The results of this annual study are reported in a publication entitled *Accounting Trends & Techniques.* The 1994 edition of *Accounting Trends & Techniques* indicated that approximately 60 percent of public companies included a "Report of Management" in their most recent annual report. This document nearly always contains at least brief disclosures regarding a company's internal control structure. These voluntary disclosures are a step in the right direction. Hopefully, companies will become even more responsive in the future to decision makers' demand for information regarding internal controls. A vignette accompanying this section presents a Report of Management included in the 1994 annual report of Mesa Laboratories, Inc., a company that manufactures electronic measurement instruments.

■ **LEARNING OBJECTIVE 5**
Discuss the need for, and nature of, internal control reports

Real World
A procedure required on all independent audits is the evaluation of a company's internal controls. A company's auditors decide on the nature, timing, and extent of their tests of a client's accounting data after evaluating the client's control system.

Real World
Auditors typically issue a report to management listing recommendations for changes in control procedures based upon situations noted during the course of the audit. Companies with good control environments typically welcome these comments and quickly take steps to implement the recommendations.

Accounting Trends & Techniques

1994 Report of Management, Mesa Laboratories, Inc.

The management of Mesa Laboratories, Inc. is responsible for the integrity of the financial information presented in the annual report. The financial statements have been prepared in accordance with generally accepted accounting principles appropriate in the circumstances, and they include amounts that are based on management's best estimates and judgment.

Management relies heavily upon the company's system of internal controls in meeting its responsibilities for maintaining reliable financial records. This system is designed to provide reasonable assurance that assets are safeguarded and that transactions are properly recorded and executed in accordance with management's intentions. Judgments are required to assess and balance the relative cost and expected benefits of such controls.

The Board of Directors meets regularly with management, with the company's internal accounting staff and with its independent auditors, to discuss audit scope and results, internal control evaluations, and other accounting, reporting, and financial matters. The independent auditors have access to the Board of Directors without management's presence.

SOURCE: 1994 Annual Report of Mesa Laboratories, Inc.

COMPUTER PROCESSING AND INTERNAL CONTROL

■ LEARNING OBJECTIVE 6
Identify the key differences between manual and computer-based processing of accounting data and the related internal control implications

Remember the scene from the hit movie *Jurassic Park* when the dinosaurs are about to crash into the control room and devour some human flesh? To the rescue came a teenage girl who navigated through a computer-based, three-dimensional representation of the electronic security system for the imaginary amusement park. Using a mouse to click her way through the various screens of the system, the teenager finally discovered what she was looking for and activated the locking mechanism for the door of the control room. Fantasy? Yes. At least the part about the dinosaurs. With the aid of computer visualization software, a company can construct a three-dimensional map of its corporate headquarters' security system—a map that would be considered an important feature of the company's internal control structure.

Computers have dramatically influenced the methods used by business executives and their accountants to manage and control the day-to-day operations of businesses. In this section, we consider some of the key implications that computer processing has for an organization's accounting and control functions.

Integrating Computers into Accounting and Control Functions

Accountants increasingly rely on computers and computer software packages to develop more effective internal control structures and to eliminate many tedious manual aspects of the monthly accounting cycle. No businesses are too small to benefit from the computerization of accounting systems. With a small investment in a personal computer and an accounting software package, such as the popular *Profit* software originally developed by Microsoft, even a "Mom and Pop" operation can

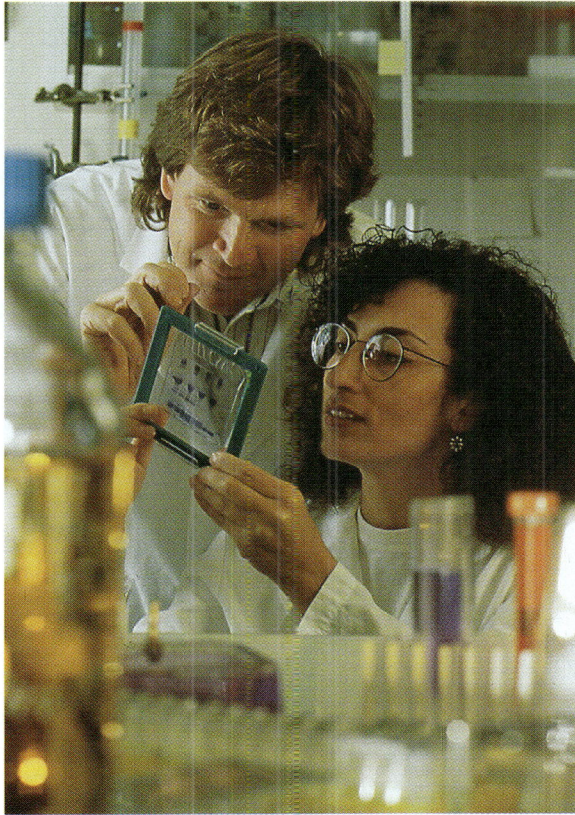

The nature of a company's operations dictates the specific policies and procedures that are necessary for management to maintain effective control over its operations. For example, the internal controls for a medical research firm are much different than the controls appropriate for a retail brokerage firm.

have a fully computerized accounting system up and running in a matter of days. Once financial data are properly formatted and entered in such a system, the accounting software does most of the work for accountants. Among other tasks, accounting software packages can automatically post data from journals to the general ledger, print accounting documents, test the clerical accuracy of those documents, and generate a complete set of financial statements.

Sounds as if computer-based accounting systems may eventually eliminate the need for accountants, right? Wrong. Despite the widespread introduction of computers into accounting systems over the past few decades, the need for accounting professionals has continued to grow each year. Similarly, the computer has not diminished the importance of the five-hundred-year-old double-entry bookkeeping system popularized by Pacioli. At the core of any multimillion-dollar, computerized accounting system are the five-hundred-year-old mechanics of double-entry bookkeeping.

The computer has changed the nature of accountants' work environment and the nature of their job responsibilities. The availability of powerful, low-cost computer resources provides accountants with the opportunity to allocate more of their time to challenging assignments. With the aid of a computer, accountants can easily develop financial forecasts based upon a variety of economic assumptions. In a matter of seconds, accountants can use a computer to analyze complex cost behavior patterns both mathematically and graphically. Computers can also be used by accountants to develop and implement more effective and efficient internal controls for an organization. A three-dimensional representation of a company's security system is just one such example, an internal control that is particularly helpful when a company is attempting to thwart a dinosaur attack!

Focus on Ethics

Assume that your small business has just acquired a personal computer. A friend offers to let you copy an accounting software package that he uses in his business. The software package has a site license that limits its use to his computer only. What do you do?

Teaching Note

No matter how sophisticated the accounting software package, the analysis of many financial transactions requires human input.

Many businesses have incorporated computers into all phases of their internal control structures, including their physical security systems. You may recall the computer-based security system that was featured in the movie *Jurassic Park*.

Computerized vs. Manual Processing of Accounting Data: Internal Control Implications

When companies switch from manual to computer-based accounting systems, they should be aware of the important implications this change has for their internal control structures. Shown in Exhibit 3.8 are six features that distinguish computer processing from manual processing of accounting data. Each of these features affects, to some degree, the ability of business executives to exercise effective control over their firm's operations.

UNIFORMITY IN THE PROCESSING OF TRANSACTIONS   The use of computers in an accounting system increases the degree of uniformity with which similar transactions are processed and recorded. On the downside, computer processing of accounting data means that thousands (or millions) of similar transactions may be incorrectly processed if there is a "bug" in a computer program.

INITIATION AND EXECUTION OF TRANSACTIONS   Computer processing can greatly expedite the initiation and execution of business transactions. For example, many retail stores use optical scanners to read bar-coded information from the price tags of merchandise. In a matter of moments, information scanned by a salesclerk is processed by a sales terminal, resulting in a quickly completed sale and thus a happy customer. The information scanned by the salesclerk is also fed into the store's accounting system via the sales terminal, resulting in the store's inventory records being updated immediately.

EXISTENCE OF TRANSACTION TRAILS   As transactions are processed in a manual accounting system, they leave a trail of paper documentation such as sales invoices, purchase orders, and receiving reports. A complete and visible transaction trail typically does not exist in a computer-based accounting system, making it more difficult to unravel errors when they occur.

■ **EXHIBIT 3.8**

Computer Processing vs. Manual Processing of Accounting Data:
Distinguishing Features

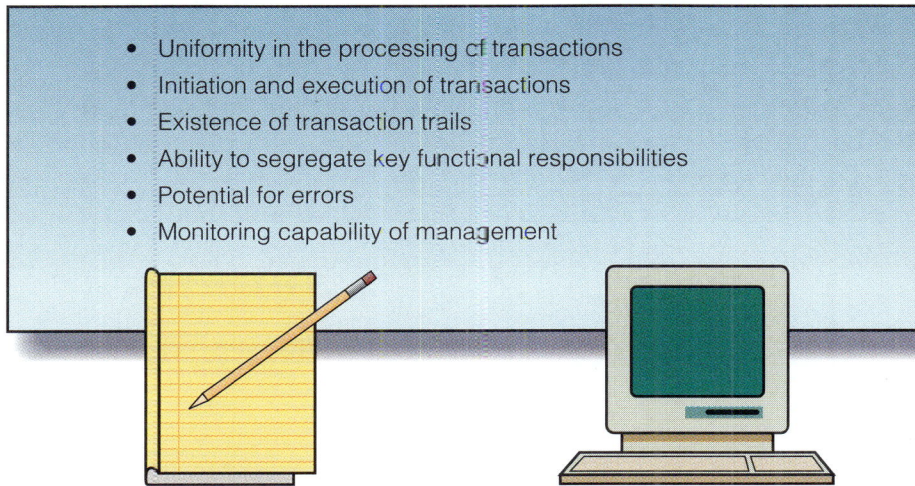

- Uniformity in the processing of transactions
- Initiation and execution of transactions
- Existence of transaction trails
- Ability to segregate key functional responsibilities
- Potential for errors
- Monitoring capability of management

ABILITY TO SEGREGATE KEY FUNCTIONAL RESPONSIBILITIES   In a manual accounting system, organizations minimize the potential for employee theft and undetected errors by properly segregating authorization, recordkeeping, and custodianship responsibilities. Such segregation of responsibilities is much more difficult to accomplish in a computer-based accounting system without forfeiting many of the cost-saving benefits of computer processing.

POTENTIAL FOR ERRORS   The potential for errors exists in both manual and computer-based accounting systems. However, computer processing is generally perceived to be less prone to errors than manual processing. For instance, computer processing eliminates the occasional random errors that occur in a manual system due to human fatigue or oversight. Of course, if a computer operator becomes tired or distracted, the result may be thousands of "systematic" random errors. Likewise, computer processing is perceived to be less subject than manual processing to errors resulting from unauthorized access to an entity's accounting records. However, when an unauthorized party obtains a valid password for a firm's computer system, the result may be devastating for the firm.

MONITORING CAPABILITY OF MANAGEMENT   Computer processing provides business executives and managers with a much greater ability to monitor the operating activities of their firms. Consider a retail store that has a fully computerized accounting system. At any point during a business day, the manager of the hardware department of this store can step up to a computer terminal and obtain a wide range of information regarding his or her department. For example, the manager can immediately determine how many electric sanders are in inventory, how many are on order, and whether the wholesale price of that item has been changed recently by the supplier. Business executives and managers can also utilize the speed and power of a

Real World

A major growth area for large accounting firms is designing and implementing computerized information systems for their clients.

■ **EXHIBIT 3.9**

Examples of Control Procedures for Computer-Based Accounting Systems

- Maintain back-up copies of key computer programs
- Periodically process test transactions to determine whether computer programs are properly functioning
- Establish controls to determine that data are not lost or modified when input into the computer
- Limit access to computer facilities to authorized personnel
- Establish procedures to identify parties accessing and operating each computer
- Limit access to key data files and computer programs by establishing a password access procedure

computer to monitor buying trends at different stores in given sales districts or regions. Products that sell well in retail stores near urban areas may not necessarily appeal to customers who frequent stores in the heart of the suburbs. With the assistance of a computer, more informed decisions can be made regarding the sales strategies that are likely to be most successful for specific stores.

Exhibit 3.6 lists examples of control procedures that can be integrated into both manual and computer-based accounting systems. Shown in Exhibit 3.9 are additional control procedures that can be incorporated into computer-based accounting systems.

Computer Processing: What the Future Holds for Accountants and Accounting

■ **LEARNING OBJECTIVE 7**
Discuss recent trends in computer processing and the related implications for organizations' accounting and control functions

The rate of technological change in both computer hardware and software has been phenomenal over the past two decades. If companies fail to monitor technological advances in the computer industry, they will find themselves at a distinct disadvantage to competitors who exploit these advancements. Given their knowledge of computers and their experience in using them, accountants are often designated the computer experts within an organization. As such, accountants assume the primary responsibility within many firms for monitoring new product offerings and technological changes in computer and information processing technologies. This monitoring may include informal activities such as reading computer periodicals, examples being *Byte* and *Computers in Accounting*. More formal responsibilities along these lines may include attending computer trade shows and identifying vendors to make in-house presentations regarding their products.

Among the advancements in computer and information processing that businesses have utilized in recent years are on-line real-time processing, database management systems, local area networks (LANs), and microcomputer-based accounting packages. In subsequent business courses, you will be introduced to these technologies and recent refinements to them. Two trends in computer and information technology that have particularly important implications for the accounting and control functions of organizations are the outsourcing of information systems and the use of electronic data interchange (EDI).

OUTSOURCING OF INFORMATION SYSTEMS   In recent years, there has been a growing trend for businesses to "outsource" or transfer their information systems to large consulting companies specializing in information processing services. One consulting company heavily involved in these services is Electronic Data Systems Corporation (EDS), now a subsidiary of General Motors but founded by Texas financier and politician Ross Perot. Shown in Exhibit 3.10 is an excerpt from the 1992 annual report of Bethlehem Steel Corporation that describes an outsourcing contract signed by that company with EDS. Over the ten-year period of this contract, EDS will be paid approximately $500 million by Bethlehem Steel.

Besides Bethlehem Steel, other major corporations that have outsourced their information systems in recent years include Del Monte Foods, Continental Bank, and General Dynamics. The outsourcing of a company's information system has important implications for the accounting and control functions of the organization. An information system includes many components of a company's internal control structure. As a result, when a firm's information system is outsourced, its accountants must subsequently coordinate their control activities with an outside agency. The need for this coordination raises complex and often difficult-to-resolve issues. Duplication of effort and disputes over assigned areas of responsibilities, so-called turf wars, are among the problems that accountants face in these situations.

Will accounting systems be outsourced in the future by large public companies? Almost certainly. In fact, for decades, many companies, primarily small businesses, have outsourced components of their accounting functions to data processing firms and computer service bureaus. Accounting for payroll is the segment of the accounting function that is most frequently outsourced. The largest firm providing payroll services is Automatic Data Processing, Inc. (ADP). By the early 1990s, ADP provided payroll accounting services for nearly three hundred thousand companies and processed weekly or monthly payroll checks for more than 16 million employees. A

Businesses establish local area networks (LANs) to allow their employees to work more efficiently In a LAN, employees of a large firm can transmit messages and data electronically to each other from their work stations and share access to large databases.

■ **EXHIBIT 3.10**

Description of Recent Outsourcing Agreement between Bethlehem Steel and EDS

> In December 1992, Bethlehem entered into an information technology partnership agreement with Electronic Data Systems Corporation (EDS), under which EDS will provide all of Bethlehem's information technology services over the next 10 years. EDS will provide Bethlehem with all the necessary resources for data center management, applications development and support, personal computers and telecommunications, and will provide additional resources for Bethlehem's existing process control activities. The new agreement will provide Bethlehem with increased access to diverse information technologies and a broad base of critical technical skills, increase its ability to stay current with rapidly changing technologies and result in reduced capital requirements. Under the agreement, substantially all of Bethlehem's 450 information technology professionals became employees of EDS effective January 1, 1993.
>
> SOURCE: 1992 Annual Report of Bethlehem Steel Corporation.

When in Rome . . .

In the mid-1970s, Congress began a series of investigations into the international business practices of several hundred United States companies. Congress was concerned by allegations that these companies were paying bribes and kickbacks to obtain lucrative business contracts overseas. Eventually, more than 450 companies were identified by one means or another as having made such payments.

Among the most prominent of these companies was Lockheed Aircraft Corporation. After repeated denials, officials of that company finally admitted in August 1975 that they had approved nearly $150 million in illicit overseas payments. These payments had been made to government officials and other "business consultants" in several foreign countries, principally Saudi Arabia, Indonesia, Iran, and the Philippines. In most cases, the purpose of these payments had been to obtain large aerospace contracts. Top Lockheed executives argued that these payments were justified since they were considered a normal business practice in the countries where they were made.

As a result of the congressional investigations of the 1970s, Congress passed new laws calling for stiff penalties and sanctions for companies that make illicit inducements to obtain business overseas. One of these laws was the Foreign Corrupt Practices Act of 1977.

very recent trend is for companies to outsource their internal audit functions to public accounting firms that also provide their independent audits.[8] This arrangement raises the critical question of whether a public accounting firm can retain its independence if it provides both types of audit services simultaneously to a client.

ELECTRONIC DATA INTERCHANGE   Each year, U.S. businesses generate an enormous amount of paper documents. Corporations, alone, issue an estimated 12 billion checks annually.[9] The cost of processing checks and other business documents is estimated to be as high as $100 billion per year.[10] A large "hidden" expense related to transacting business on paper is the cost resulting from lost documents. In late 1994, the *Journal of Accountancy* reported that 7.5 percent of all business documents are lost and that $350 is spent recreating the typical lost document.[11]

The use of paper documents is not only costly to businesses but also adds significantly to the amount of time required to consummate business transactions. To remedy the shortcomings of paper-based transactions, many companies are switching to a "paperless" mode of transacting business. To date, the most successful of these approaches has been electronic data interchange (EDI), which involves the cooperative exchange of financial data via a computer network among companies that trans-

---

8. K. Rankin, "SEC's Schuetze Warns Against Audit Outsourcing," *Accounting Today*, 12 December 1994, 4 & 70.

9. F. R. Bleakley, "Electronic Payments Now Supplant Checks at More Large Firms," *The Wall Street Journal*, 13 April 1994, A1 & A9.

10. W. C. Symonds, "Getting Rid of Paper Is Just the Beginning," *Business Week*, 21 December 1992, 88–89.

11. M. J. Weiss, "The Paperless Office," *Journal of Accountancy*, November 1994, 73–76.

act business with each other. By the early 1990s, an estimated thirty-seven thousand U.S. companies were using EDI.[12]

EDI is particularly useful for merchandising companies that require large amounts of inventory. Companies such as Wal-Mart, J. C. Penney's, Dayton-Hudson Corporation, and Sears allow their suppliers to access their inventory records through EDI. As a result, the cost of processing purchase transactions and lost sales due to inventory shortages are greatly reduced. For example, when the inventory of 501 Jeans in a retail store participating in an EDI system falls to a certain level, an electronic purchase order is automatically transmitted to Levi Strauss, which manufactures 501 Jeans.

Many EDI systems involve dozens of firms, each of which can potentially access the accounting records of the other companies in the system. Companies involved in these computer networks must establish controls to minimize the likelihood of unauthorized access and use of their accounting records. The companies involved in an EDI network must also cooperate to develop standard methods of coding and transmitting financial data. If such methods are not developed and used consistently by all participants in an EDI network, numerous errors may be introduced into the accounting records of these companies.

Discussion Question

Computers can sometimes make a company's information system less subject to control by management. Do you agree or disagree with this statement?

INTERNAL CONTROL ON AN INTERNATIONAL SCALE

Each year, more U.S. companies become involved in international trade. Involvement in international trade poses several challenges to a company's accountants including designing an effective internal control structure for the firm. The procedures that are necessary to establish effective control over domestic business operations may not necessarily be effective or appropriate for business operations in other countries.

Cultural differences across the world translate into varying definitions of acceptable and ethical business practices. Bribes, kickbacks, and related payments made by companies to obtain unfair advantage over their competitors are certainly not unheard of in this country. Nevertheless, most large companies in this country have established control procedures to discourage executives and employees from making such payments and to detect such payments if they are made. A different attitude exists toward these types of inducements in many countries. For instance, although not encouraged by governmental authorities, bribes paid by businesses in France and Germany are tax-deductible expenses. In both Japan and Mexico there is a long history of "under-the-table" payments to facilitate major business transactions. Over the past two decades in Japan, the disclosure of such payments to several high-ranking governmental officials abruptly ended those individuals' political careers. In Mexico, companies that refuse to pay *mordida* (a little bite) to governmental officials often have difficulty closing major transactions.

So, what are U.S. companies to do when faced with transacting business in a foreign country that has a much different view of acceptable business practices than the prevailing view in this country? Should these companies ignore the control proce-

■ **LEARNING OBJECTIVE 8**
Identify internal control issues resulting from the growing trend toward multinational business operations

---

12. Symonds, "Getting Rid of Paper," 89.

Focus on Ethics
When in Rome do as the
Romans do? Ask students to
discuss the pros and cons of the
Foreign Corrupt Practices Act.

dures they have established to prevent and detect illegal inducements paid by their personnel to third parties? Definitely not. The Foreign Corrupt Practices Act of 1977 expressly prohibits U.S. companies from paying bribes, kickbacks, or related inducements to officials of foreign countries to acquire business or maintain business relationships. This law also requires publicly owned companies, including those that do not have international operations, to establish internal control structures that have a high likelihood of preventing and detecting bribes, kickbacks, and similar payments.

SUMMARY

Systems technology is used extensively by businesses in the design of their accounting and control functions. An accounting system can be defined as a systematic approach to collecting, processing, and communicating financial information to decision makers. Financial data for a business entity are initially recorded in a journal. Then, these data are transferred or posted to the appropriate accounts in the general ledger. At the end of an accounting period, summary financial data drawn from the general ledger are used to prepare an entity's financial statements.

The policies and procedures a business establishes to help ensure that it achieves key organizational objectives are referred to as its internal control structure. An internal control structure consists of three elements: an accounting system, a control environment, and a set of control procedures. The phrase "control environment" refers principally to the degree of control consciousness within an organization. A primary responsibility of an organization's top executives is to ensure that their subordinates have an awareness and appreciation of the need for strong internal controls. An example of an important control procedure is the segregation of authorization, custodianship, and recordkeeping responsibilities within each major component of an entity's accounting system.

The integration of computers into the internal control structure of a business significantly affects, both positively and negatively, the ability of that entity to maintain effective control over its operations. Accountants must be aware of the key differences between manual and computerized processing of accounting data and the related internal control implications. Two fairly recent developments in information processing and computer technology have important implications for the accounting and control functions of business entities. These developments are the outsourcing of information systems and electronic data interchange (EDI) among companies that transact business with each other.

U.S. companies that have international operations often encounter very different attitudes toward acceptable or ethical business practices in foreign countries. These differing attitudes affect the ability of these companies to exercise effective control over their foreign business operations. Accountants must be aware of the requirements of the Foreign Corrupt Practices Act of 1977 when establishing internal control policies and procedures for their companies. This law prohibits the payment of illegal inducements to obtain overseas business. Additionally, this law requires publicly owned companies in this country to establish internal control structures that have a high likelihood of preventing or detecting bribes, kickbacks, and similar payments.

GLOSSARY

Accounting cycle (p. 83)   The set of recurring accounting procedures that must be performed for a business each accounting period.

Accounting system (p. 78)   A systematic approach to collecting, processing, and communicating financial information to decision makers.

Accounting Trends & Techniques (p. 87)   An annual publication of the AICPA that analyzes the accounting and financial reporting practices of six hundred publicly owned companies.

Accounts (p. 79)   The basic storage units for financial data in an accounting system.

Chart of accounts (p. 81)   A numerical listing, by account number, of an entity's accounts.

Control environment (p. 84)   An element of an internal control structure that refers to the degree of control consciousness within an organization.

Control procedures (p. 85)   Specific rules established by an entity to help ensure that its primary organizational objectives are accomplished.

General journal (p. 82)   The accounting record in which transactions and other events are initially recorded by businesses that maintain only one journal.

General ledger (p. 82)   The accounting record that contains each of the individual accounts for an entity's assets, liabilities, owners' or stockholders' equity, revenues, and expenses.

Internal control structure (p. 84)   The policies and procedures established to provide reasonable assurance that specific entity objectives will be achieved.

Journalizing (p. 82)   The process of recording in a journal financial data resulting from transactions or other events affecting an entity.

Posting (p. 82)   The process of transferring accounting data from a journal to the appropriate general ledger accounts.

System (p. 78)   A coordinated network of plans and procedures designed to achieve a stated goal in an orderly, effective, and efficient manner.

DECISION CASE

McGuire's Irish Pub and Brewery in Pensacola, Florida, has a particularly vexing internal control problem. Why? Because much of the restaurant's cash is stapled to its walls or hanging from its rafters. A long-standing tradition of this establishment is for customers to write personal notes on dollar bills with a black magic marker. These bills are then displayed within the restaurant. Although the customers provide the dollar bills, they become the property of the restaurant when they are stapled to a wall or a rafter or a wooden handrail. "Hi Mom, stuck in Pensacola over spring break, send cash," "Seminoles Eat Gator Meat," "Roll Tide," and "Rock Chalk Jayhawk" are just a few samples of notes you will find sprawled on the monetary assets of McGuire's.

The internal control problem McGuire's management faces should be obvious: discouraging would-be bill-snatchers. This is not a small problem since there is approximately $100,000 literally "hanging around" the restaurant.

Required: Assume that you accept a job in the near future with a restaurant that has a tradition identical to that of McGuire's Irish Pub and Brewery. On your first day of work, the owner of the restaurant approaches you. He mentions that the restaurant has been suffering an increasing number of bill-snatching incidents over the past few months. The owner knows that you are enrolled in an accounting course at a nearby university. Since he is aware that internal controls are taught in accounting courses, he asks you to develop a system of policies and procedures to safeguard the restaurant's "exposed" cash. The owner does not want to influence your report, so he does not inform you of the controls that have been used in the past in this regard. Develop a system to safeguard the restaurant's inventory of dollar bills. (You should first review the definition of a system included in this chapter.) Integrate at least four specific control procedures into this system.

QUESTIONS

1. Why is it necessary for businesses to develop a comprehensive strategy for dealing with employee theft and fraud?

2. Define an accounting system.

3. "Bookkeeping rules are arbitrary." Explain this statement.

4. What is the principal advantage of the four-column account format over the T-account format?

5. What is the purpose of a chart of accounts? How are numbers typically assigned to accounts in a chart of accounts?

6. Identify the principal accounting books (or records) for most business enterprises.

7. Why are accounting data posted to the general ledger from the general journal?

8. Identify the four key steps in the accounting cycle.

9. Define the phrase "internal control structure."

10. Identify the key elements of an internal control structure

11. An internal control structure should aid an organization in accomplishing two key entity objectives. What are they?

12. In reference to an organization's internal control structure, what is a control environment? Control procedures?

13. Where in a corporate annual report may you find information about a company's internal control structure?

14. What do multimillion-dollar computerized accounting systems have in common with the recordkeeping system popularized by Pacioli in the fifteenth century?

15. How have computers changed the accountant's work environment and job responsibilities?

16. List three advantages of computerized accounting systems over manual accounting systems. List three disadvantages.

17. Explain what it means for a company to "outsource" its information system. What segment of the accounting function is most frequently outsourced, especially by smaller companies?

18. In general, how does electronic data interchange (EDI) work? What problems does an EDI system create for an organization's accountants?

19. How does a company's involvement in international trade affect the nature and design of its internal control structure?

20. What does the Foreign Corrupt Practices Act of 1977 require of U.S. companies?

EXERCISES

21. **Purpose of an Accounting System** (LO 1)
    You have recently designed an accounting system for Amini's Art Gallery, a new business. The owner of this business, Alex Amini, intends to maintain its accounting records. However, after reviewing the accounting system you designed, Alex is having second thoughts. Alex does not understand why his small business must have a complete accounting system. "Why can't I just maintain a checkbook for my business?" an exasperated Alex has asked you.

Required:

Write a brief memo to Alex in which you describe the nature and purpose of an accounting system. Attempt to convince Alex that his idea of maintaining only a checkbook for his new business is a poor one.

21. No check figures

22. **Reasonable Assurance and Internal Controls** (LO 3)

Karen and Kelli Casteel own and operate Curly's Hamburger Shop on Campus Corner. The two partners have recently hired four college students to work part-time in the popular late-night hangout for college students. From 8 P.M. until closing at midnight, the hamburger shop will be staffed completely by college students. Because the two partners are concerned that they may be "ripped off" by their employees, they have decided to hire a security guard to watch over the restaurant in their absence.

Required:

1. Explain how the internal control concept of "reasonable assurance" may be relevant in this context.
2. Identify alternative control procedures that the owners of this business could consider implementing to minimize the likelihood of being ripped off by their employees.

22. No check figures

23. **Elements of an Internal Control Structure** (LO 4)

Joseph Dredd owns a company that provides security and investigative services. Dredd employs ten security guards, three detectives, and four office workers. Dredd has never paid much attention to internal control issues. He is much more interested in helping his detectives work on the latest "hot" case. Dredd's philosophy of internal control is simply to hire honest employees. However, recently, Dredd has become more interested in internal control issues. Over the past few months, the cash inflows of Dredd's business have declined considerably. Apparently, one or more of his employees is stealing cash from the business.

Required:

1. Identify the three elements of an internal control structure.
2. Which of these elements involves the degree of control consciousness within a business? How does Dredd's attitude toward internal controls affect this element of his business's internal control structure?

23. No check figures

24. **Analysis of a T-Account** (LO 1)

Consider the following T-account for the machinery owned by Rico Construction Company:

Machinery

Balance	4/1/95	125,000			
	4/15/95	15,000			
			4/18/95	100,000	
Balance	4/30/95	40,000			

Required:

Describe a transaction that would have resulted in the item posted to this account on April 15. What type of transaction might have resulted in the April 18 posting?

24. No check figures

25. **Creating a T-Account**

Barb's Bike Shop engaged in the following transactions in May:

1. Sold a bike stand for $60 cash
2. Bought three bikes from Trek for $900 on credit
3. Sold a Trek bike for $500 on credit

4. Paid an employee's wages, $50 cash
5. Sold a bike bell for $20 cash
6. Paid the electric bill of $70 by check

Required:

Prepare a T-account for Barb's Bike Shop reflecting the transactions that affected the business's cash during May. The business's Cash account had a balance of $720 on May 1.

25. 5/31 balance, $680

26. **Creating Four-Column Accounts** (LO 1)

Required:

Prepare a four-column Cash account for Barb's Bike Shop using the information in Exercise 25.

26. 5/31 balance, $680

27. **Analysis of a Four-Column Account** (LO 1)

Consider the following four-column account of Von Sydow Enterprises:

Inventory						Account No. 103	
			Post			Balance	
Date		Explanation	Ref.	Debit	Credit	Debit	Credit
1995							
March	1	Balance Forward				2,000	
	5			6,000		8,000	
	25				3,000	5,000	
	31	Balance				5,000	

Required:

27. No check figures

Notice that the explanation column was left blank for the postings made to Von Sydow's Inventory account on March 5 and March 25. Describe a transaction that would have led to each of these postings.

28. **Internal Control Procedures** (LO 4)

Following are selected control procedures established by the owner of Eddie's Ice Cream Shop:

1. Employees must collect cash for all sales.
2. All transactions must be recorded in the cash register.
3. Ice cream inventory must be counted weekly.
4. Managers must approve all purchases of ice cream inventory.
5. Cash registers must be locked when not in use.

Required:

28. No check figures

Briefly describe the purpose of each of these control procedures.

29. **Internal Control Weaknesses** (LO 4)

Diane Hershey and Ray Assante are accountants for a small company, Leisure Time, that manufactures and sells hot tubs and spas. The owner of the business has assigned these two accountants the following responsibilities:

Diane: Maintains all inventory accounting records, authorizes inventory purchases, maintains physical control of inventory by serving as supervisor of inventory warehouse.

Ray: Maintains accounts receivable accounting records, decides which customers will be granted credit, processes cash received from customers, prepares monthly bank reconciliation.

Required:

1. What benefit is realized by assigning one individual all key accounting and control responsibilities related to a given type of asset, such as inventory?
2. Identify potential problems that Leisure Time may experience as a result of the job responsibilities assigned to Diane and Ray.

29. No check figures

30. Internal Control for International Businesses (LO 8)

The owners of Zipf Productions, Inc., a manufacturing company, are presently considering building several distribution facilities in foreign countries. Each of these new facilities would be staffed with as many as 50 to 100 employees hired from the local community, including a small accounting staff of six to eight individuals for each facility.

Required:

1. What general types of internal control issues and problems will Zipf face if the company proceeds with its expansion plan?
2. How will the Foreign Corrupt Practices Act affect Zipf's foreign operations?

30. No check figures

31. Computer Control Procedures (LO 6)

Sue Thompson owns Thompson's Homebuilders, a local construction company. Because of a significant increase in the volume of her business in recent years, Sue has decided to computerize her business's accounting system. Sue, who serves as the accountant for her business, is not sure how incorporating a computer into the accounting system will affect the business's internal control structure. Sue is particularly concerned about unauthorized access to the computer system.

Required:

1. Write a brief memo to Sue explaining key differences in manual and computer-based accounting systems that have internal control implications for a business.
2. In your memo, identify one or more specific control procedures that Sue could adopt to minimize the risk of unauthorized access to her new computer system.

31. No check figures

32. Computer Controls (LO 6)

Review Exhibit 3.9 from this chapter.

Required:

1. Of the six controls listed, which two do you think are probably the least expensive to implement?
2. Which two controls are likely the most expensive to implement?
3. What role does cost play in a company's decision to implement (or not implement) a specific control?

32. No check figures

33. Reasonable Assurance and Internal Controls (LO 3)

John, the owner of Corso Cake & Cream, estimates that his store loses the equivalent of one cake (retail value $12.50, cost $6.00) and one gallon of ice cream (retail value $10.00, cost $7.50) each day to employee theft. John is so disturbed about the problem that he is considering hiring a worker at $4.00/hour for four hours per day just to "manage" (keep an eye on) the employees when he is out of the store. The worker would receive a $50.00 bonus for each employee who was caught stealing cake or ice cream.

Required:

Should John implement the new control procedure? Explain.

33. No check figures

34. Computerizing an Accounting System (LO 6)

The owner of Sheila's Auto Repair is considering converting its manual accounting system to a computerized system. Sheila, the owner, does not presently receive accounting information on a timely basis. Sheila believes that a computer-based accounting system will be free of errors and that she will receive financial statement information much more quickly with such a system.

Required:

34. No check figures

Write a brief memo to Sheila summarizing the main strengths and weaknesses of a manual versus a computerized accounting system focusing principally on the following issues:
1. Uniformity of processing transactions
2. Potential for errors
3. Monitoring capability of management

35. Updating an Information System (LO 7)

Rivera Corporation is a large publicly owned company that operates a chain of convenience stores in the eastern United States. Recently, Rivera's chief executive hired a consulting firm to perform an extensive review and critique of the company's information system including its accounting and control functions. The report prepared by this consulting firm suggests that Rivera consider outsourcing certain components of its accounting system, particularly the company's payroll function. The report also suggests that Rivera join an electronic data interchange (EDI) system involving several large convenience store chains and their major suppliers.

Required:

35. No check figures

1. Briefly explain the key advantages a business realizes by (a) outsourcing components of its information system and (b) participating in an EDI system.
2. What new internal control issues or problems may Rivera encounter if it adopts the two recommendations made by the consulting firm?

PROBLEM SET A

36. Using T-Accounts (LO 1)

The following transactions were engaged in during a recent month by Jane's Violets, a business that sells flowering plants.

June 4: Sold $300 of plants on credit
June 6: Collected $100 from a customer for credit sale made in April
June 7: Sold $850 of plants for cash
June 20: Paid $750 for June rent
June 28: Paid salaries of $3,200 to employees

Required:

36. 1. 6/30 balance, $7,000
2. 6/30 balance, $7,000

1. Prepare a T-account for cash as of June 30. The balance of the Cash account on June 1 was $10,000.
2. Prepare a four-column account for cash as of June 30.
3. What is the principal function of accounts in an accounting system?

37. Internal Controls for Small Businesses (LO 4)

Anderson Gardening is a retail garden store. The store has eight employees who are directly supervised by the business's owner. Five employees work as sales clerks. These employees also restock the store's departments when time permits.

One of the three remaining employees operates the cash register—the owner operates a second cash register during peak business hours. Another employee serves as the business's accountant. The final employee is responsible for the purchasing function for the business. All purchases exceeding $100 must be personally approved by the owner. The owner also decides which customers will be granted credit, approximately 50 percent of the store's sales are made on a credit basis. Each month, the owner reconciles the store's bank statement balance with the amount of cash reported in the accounting records. Once per month, the inventory of each department is counted to determine whether the amount of inventory on hand agrees with the amount reported in the accounting records. The business also uses prenumbered accounting documents for all sales, purchases, and miscellaneous transactions such as merchandise returned by customers.

Johnson Gardening Supply is another retail garden store which is located across town from Anderson Gardening. Johnson's owner is a local doctor who acquired the business two years ago. The owner has never been inside the store although he has driven by it occasionally. The owner's business manager visits the store twice per month to make sure that everything is "okay." The day-to-day operations of the store are co-managed by its four full-time employees; the store also has four part-time employees. Each full-time employee has complete responsibility for one of the store's four departments including making all purchase decisions for that department and maintaining the department's inventory records. The cash register is operated by a part-time employee. The store does not have a full-time accountant. Once per month, the owner's bookkeeper drops by the store to update the accounting records other than the inventory accounting records. The owner of Johnson Gardening Supply has a very simple internal control strategy: "hire honest employees." The owner believes that if an employee wants to steal cash or inventory, he or she will find some way to subvert any existing controls. As a result, the owner does not require the use of prenumbered accounting documents, instructs the employees to count inventory only once per year for tax purposes, and does not require a monthly bank reconciliation to be prepared.

Required:
1. Identify and define the three key elements of an internal control structure.
2. Which of the two businesses has a stronger control environment? Explain.
3. What is the purpose of internal control procedures? Identify specific control procedures being used by Anderson Gardening.
4. Identify three examples of internal control weaknesses that exist at Johnson Gardening Supply. Identify one or more potential problems that the business may experience as a result of each internal control weakness.

37. No check figures

38. **Internal Control Procedures: Benefits vs. Costs** (LO 3, 4)

Following is a list of internal control procedures that the owner of Goodner's Grocery Store has implemented.

1. A timeclock is used to establish a record of the hours worked by each employee. Employees must "punch in" at the beginning of a work shift and "punch out" at the end of the shift.
2. Invoices submitted by suppliers are double-checked for mathematical accuracy before being paid.
3. Customers who want to purchase merchandise on credit are required to complete a credit application and provide three credit references. Approximately 25 percent of all credit applications are rejected.

4. A monthly statement is mailed to each customer who purchases merchandise on credit.
5. Out-of-state checks are not accepted for merchandise purchases.
6. Employees are allowed to purchase food from the store and eat it in the break room. However, if requested by a supervisor, an employee eating food must provide a sales register receipt for the merchandise.
7. The store is closed on the first Monday of every third month to allow employees to count the store's inventory. The owner reconciles the resulting dollar value of the inventory to the store's inventory accounting records.
8. Employees caught stealing merchandise are immediately fired.

Required:

38. No check figures

Prepare a table with the following headings: Key Benefit of Control Procedure and Costs Associated with Control Procedure. Complete this table for the eight control procedures listed for Goodner's Grocery Store. When identifying the costs associated with a given control procedure, describe not only the monetary cost related to that procedure but also any hidden or "opportunity" cost related to the procedure. For example, a given control procedure may result in fewer losses due to customer theft in a retail store while at the same time discouraging customers from shopping in that store.

39. **Integrating Computers into an Accounting System** (LO 6)

Celeste's Arts & Crafts is a large retail store located in a rapidly growing suburb of Houston, Texas. By far, the largest asset of this business is inventory. Typically, the store has more than $250,000 of merchandise on hand in its ten departments. The store sells more than 1,000 types of merchandise, most of which have a retail sales value of less than $10. All sales are made on a cash basis. Recently, Celeste Ritchey, the owner of this business, has been considering purchasing a computer-based accounting system for the store. She is particularly interested in the internal control implications that the acquisition of a computer-based accounting system would have for her store.

Required:

39. No check figures

Write a memo to Celeste that analyzes the control-related advantages and disadvantages of a computer-based accounting system, compared with a manual accounting system. When writing this memo, keep in mind the nature of Celeste's business. Finally, in your memo, focus particular attention on how a computer-based accounting system would allow Celeste to improve control over her store's inventory.

40. **An International Focus on Internal Controls**

Gonzales Chili, Inc., a firm headquartered in El Paso, Texas, has recently begun selling frozen chili and other frozen food products in Central America. Company executives have learned that local custom in certain Central American countries dictates that a business must pay bribes to local officials to thrive.

Required:

40. No check figures

1. If Gonzales pays bribes to governmental officials in Central America, would this be considered an illegal activity in the United States?
2. Recommend specific control procedures that Gonzales's management could implement to discourage the company's sales representatives from paying bribes to increase sales. Would these procedures be cost effective?
3. If businesspeople in foreign countries believe that bribes are an acceptable business practice, do you believe that it is appropriate for U.S. companies to

challenge those beliefs when doing business in those countries? Defend your answer.

PROBLEM SET B

41. Using T-Accounts (LO 1)

Following are transactions engaged in during a recent month by Hilderbrandt Wholesalers, a small company that sells tools to retail stores.

July 5:   Sold $400 of tools to Denco Retailers on credit
July 7:   Wrote check for $150 in payment for monthly electricity bill
July 16: Collected $500 from customer for credit sale made in June
July 17: Sold $600 of tools to Eufaula Supply for cash
July 24: Received tax refund of $600

Required:

1. Prepare a T-account for cash as of July 31. The balance of the Cash account on July 1 was $4,300.
2. Prepare a four-column account for cash as of July 31.
3. Comment on the differing uses of the two types of accounts. Does a business typically use both types of accounts in its accounting system?

41. 1. 7/31 balance, $5,850
2. 7/31 balance, $5,850

42. Internal Controls for a Small Business (LO 4)

Tilt, Inc., is a small business that Scott Tway is considering purchasing. The business consists of a game arcade located in a large mall. Tway has little time to devote to the business since he is a practicing attorney. Besides, Tway does not believe that the business requires much attention. Tway told a friend of his that the business must be like owning your own mint. "Kids come in with five or ten bucks and don't leave until they have spent their very last quarter. And, there's almost no overhead. Sure, you have to pay rent for the floor space and on the machines, but other than that the only major expense is the minimum wage salaries paid to the highschool students you hire to run the place."

Tilt's operations are similar to those of most game arcades. Customers either obtain quarters from a store employee in exchange for currency or obtain quarters directly from one of the store's two bill-changing machines. Coupons earned by playing the games can be exchanged for prizes at Tilt's redemption booth. The prizes range from rubber snakes (10 coupons) to small televisions (5,000 coupons). Tilt has five part-time employees who are all highschool seniors. Unknown to Tway, the current owner is selling Tilt because of the constant headaches he has encountered attempting to prevent the employees from "stealing him blind." Besides ripping off handfulls of quarters and occasional $20 bills, the employees often give away prizes to their friends.

Required:

1. Suppose that Tway purchases Tilt. The owner of a small business has the primary responsibility for establishing an appropriate control environment for a business. What type of control environment do you believe Tway would create for Tilt? Explain.
2. What is the purpose of internal control procedures?
3. Identify several internal control procedures that could be implemented to minimize the employee theft problem that Tilt has historically experienced. Would these control procedures be cost-effective?

42. No check figures

43. **Internal Control Procedures: Benefits vs. Costs** (LO 3, 4)

    Following is a list of internal control procedures that Claire Jameson, the owner of Claire's Bookstore, has established.

    1. On a weekly basis, Claire compares the price lists of book distributors for newly issued books.
    2. Customers are allowed to pay for their purchases with personal checks if they provide two forms of personal identification.
    3. Claire approves all purchase orders that exceed $100.
    4. A daily time log is maintained of the individuals operating the store's two cash registers.
    5. Invoices submitted by suppliers are double-checked for mathematical accuracy before being paid.
    6. Sales clerks are not allowed access to the store's inventory records.
    7. Customers who want to purchase merchandise on credit are required to complete a credit application and provide three credit references. Approximately 25 percent of all credit applications are rejected.
    8. When a customer returns a book, a prenumbered credit memo must be completed by a sales clerk. A refund is mailed to the customer only after Claire has reviewed the credit memo.

    Required:

43. No check figures

    Prepare a table with the following headings: Key Benefit of Control Procedure and Costs Associated with Control Procedure. Complete this table for the eight control procedures listed for Claire's Bookstore. When identifying the cost associated with a given control procedure, describe not only the monetary cost related to that procedure but also any hidden or "opportunity" cost related to the procedure. For example, a given control procedure may result in fewer losses due to customer theft in a retail store while at the same time discouraging customers from shopping in that store.

44. **Integrating Computers into an Accounting System** (LO 6)

    Regina's Fine Jewelry is a jewelry store located in a suburb of St. Louis. The largest asset of this business is accounts receivable; practically all of the business's sales are made on a credit basis. At any point in time, the company typically has more than $3 million of outstanding receivables from as many as five hundred customers. Recently, Regina Break, the owner of this business, has been considering purchasing a computer-based accounting system for the store. She is particularly interested in the internal control implications that the acquisition of a computer-based accounting system would have for her store.

    Required:

44. No check figures

    Write a memo to Regina that analyzes the control-related advantages and disadvantages of a computer-based accounting system compared with a manual accounting system. When writing this memo, keep in mind the nature of Regina's business. Finally, in your memo, focus particular attention on how a computer-based accounting system would allow Regina to improve control over her business's receivables.

45. **An International Focus on Internal Controls** (LO 8)

    Becker Brothers, Inc., is an international distributor of cosmetic products. Executives of the company are aware that the payment of bribes to obtain business is a common practice in many countries in which it operates. However, Becker Brothers has a strict written policy prohibiting sales personnel from paying bribes to generate sales. The company compensates its sales personnel on a commission basis. Commission rates are 10 percent on all domestic sales, and 15 percent on all foreign sales. The higher commission for foreign sales is a result of the company's strategy to expand its share of the international sales market for cosmetics which is growing much more rapidly than the domestic sales market.

Required:

1. Does Becker Brothers' commission rate structure conflict with the company's policy against the payment of bribes? Explain.
2. Other than the written policy against the payment of bribes, Becker Brothers does not have any specific control procedures to prevent or detect bribes paid by employees. What signal may the absence of such procedures send to the company's sales personnel?
3. Identify specific internal control procedures that Becker could implement to reinforce its written policy regarding the payment of bribes.

45. No check figures

CASES

46. Ethics and Internal Control

Lee Venturi owns a large propane and fuel oil supply business. Venturi supplies propane and fuel oil to hundreds of farmers and ranchers in West Texas. Besides approximately twenty truck drivers, Venturi employs ten individuals in his business office in Amarillo. Recently, Venturi has begun suspecting that one or more of his office employees is stealing cash from the business. Although the volume of deliveries is higher than ever before, the business's monthly net cash flow has declined considerably in the past few months. In an effort to determine which of his employees is dishonest, Venturi has arranged to periodically have a third party offer bribes to individual employees. Venturi intends to dismiss any employee that fails to report a bribe offered to him or her.

Required:

Evaluate Venturi's plan for testing the honesty of his employees. In your opinion, is this plan ethical? Why or why not?

47. Recording Financial Data

Mark's Raspberry Farms supplies raspberries and other fruits to restaurants and grocery stores in a large southwestern city. Mark, the company's owner, maintains his own financial records. His financial records include a checkbook—he has set up a separate checking account for the business—and two notebooks. In one notebook, Mark records the sales made to his customers (all of his sales are on a credit basis). When he makes a sale to a customer, Mark records the date, amount, customer name, and a brief description of what was purchased. In the second notebook, Mark enters similar information for each purchase that he makes on a credit basis. When Mark receives a payment from a customer or pays a bill that he owes, he places a large check beside the original entry for that item in the appropriate notebook.

Required:

1. Does Mark have an "accounting system"? Why or why not?
2. A primary product of most accounting systems is a set of monthly or annual financial statements. Does Mark's "system" provide sufficient information to allow him to prepare periodic financial statements that document his business's assets, liabilities, and so on?
3. Other than providing the means to develop periodic financial statements, what other benefits do accounting systems typically provide to business owners or managers?

48. Financial Implications of Internal Control Weaknesses

In 1978, Harper & Row, a large publishing company was negotiating to purchase a smaller competitor, J. B. Lippincott Company. Before finalizing the offer for Lippincott, Harper & Row's executives retained their independent audit firm to review Lippincott's accounting records. As a result of this review, numerous errors were discovered in Lippincott's accounting records. Most of these errors resulted from poor or absent internal controls. For example, Lippincott's accounts receivable were materially overstated by such simple errors as the duplicate recording of customer sales, failure to record credit memos issued to customers, and failure to test the clerical accuracy of the company's accounting records. Eventually, Harper & Row agreed to purchase Lippincott but at a price considerably below the original offer price.

Required:

1. What individuals in an organization are ultimately responsible for the integrity of its control system? Explain.
2. Why should an organization's accountants have a significant role in the design and periodic review of the internal control structure of the organization?

PROJECTS

49. Internal Control Reporting

As indicated in the text, the issue of whether companies should report on their internal controls has been hotly debated in recent years. In this project, you will research this subject.

Required:

1. Review recent accounting periodicals such as the *Journal of Accountancy, Management Accounting, Internal Auditor,* and others recommended by your instructor and identify articles focusing on the subject of internal control reporting. Other sources of articles on this subject may include *The Wall Street Journal* and the business sections of major metropolitan newspapers.
2. Summarize in a written report the key arguments both in support of internal control reporting by companies and the arguments opposed to such reporting.
3. In your report, indicate which arguments are most persuasive, in your opinion, and why.

50. Analyzing Actual Internal Controls

In this project, your project group will study the accounting and control procedures that an actual business applies to its cash transactions.

Choose any local business of interest to your group. One member of your group should contact the owner or manager of this business and obtain a signed permission to use information regarding the business to complete this project.

Required:

1. Interview an individual in the business you have selected who is familiar with the business's accounting function. (All group members should attend this interview.) Among the items of information your group should obtain from this individual are the following:
   a. A brief history of the business.
   b. An overview of the nature of the business's operations, including the products it sells or services it provides.

    c. A summary of the methods used by the company to process cash receipts and cash disbursements transactions.

    d. The control procedures the company has established over its cash and cash processing transactions

2. Following the interview, the group should meet and discuss the information collected to ensure that there is a group consensus regarding the meaning or interpretation of that information.

3. Prepare a written report documenting the information collected in Part 1. One group member should be prepared to present an overview of this report to the class.

51. Accounting Software Packages

Visit one or more local computer software stores and identify the accounting software packages that are available in that store or stores.

Required:

1. For each accounting software package you identified, collect the following information:

    a. The name of the package.

    b. The firm that developed the package.

    c. The retail price of the package.

    d. A summary of the software's key selling features which will be listed on the outside packaging.

2. What features seem to be the most important when it comes to successfully marketing an accounting software package?

3. Document your completion of Parts 1 and 2 in a written report.

II

THE ACCOUNTING MODEL

The first three chapters introduced you to the accounting profession, the fundamental concepts and elements of accounting, and the nature of accounting systems and internal control. Chapters 4 through 6 acquaint you with the recordkeeping and data processing aspects of accounting, including the basics of double-entry bookkeeping. Chapter 4 illustrates the procedures used to record financial data, with an emphasis on journalizing transactions and other events affecting businesses. In Chapter 4 you will become very familiar with debits and credits; mastering the use of debits and credits is the key to understanding the scheme accountants use to record financial data.

Chapter 5 presents a sequential and comprehensive walk-through of the accounting cycle, the set of recurring accounting procedures that a business must complete each accounting period. Chapter 5 demonstrates how business transactions are recorded, processed, and summarized into a set of financial statements each accounting period.

Finally, Chapter 6 illustrates the accounting cycle for a merchandising company. Merchandising companies are among the most common types of business enterprises and pose particularly challenging accounting issues.

4 THE MECHANICS OF DOUBLE-ENTRY ACCOUNTING

LEARNING OBJECTIVES

After studying this chapter, you should be able to do the following:

1. Analyze business transactions in reference to the accounting equation

2. Determine whether increases and decreases in specific general ledger accounts are recorded as debits or credits

3. Identify the normal balance, debit balance or credit balance, of individual general ledger accounts

4. Prepare general journal entries

5. Post general journal entries to the general ledger

6. Prepare a trial balance of a general ledger

Double-entry bookkeeping is one of the most beautiful discoveries of the human spirit. . . . It came from the same spirit which produced the systems of Galileo and Newton and the subject matter of modern physics and chemistry.

Johann Wolfgang von Goethe

The Evolution of Accounting: From Clay Tokens to Computers

Accounting historians typically trace the beginning of the accounting profession to 1494 when Pacioli published a mathematics textbook that included a section on double-entry bookkeeping. In reality, the origins of accounting go back much farther in time, before the beginning of recorded history.

Well before journals, ledgers, and accounting software packages, decision makers had a need for a recordkeeping system to help them make informed economic judgments and to maintain control over their assets. From approximately 8,000 B.C. to 3,000 B.C., a method of financial recordkeeping that relied upon heat-baked clay tokens evolved in the Middle Eastern cradle of civilization, located in what is now Iraq.[1] These tokens were of varying shapes and sizes. A cylindrical token represented one sheep, while a triangular token represented a certain quantity of grain. Eventually, property owners, or their accountants, made the important realization that a one-to-one correspondence did not have to exist between individual assets and tokens. For example, a cylindrical token etched with five horizontal lines could be used to represent five sheep.

Cuneiform writing, a method of recording information on clay tablets, developed in Sumeria around 3,000 B.C. Initially, cuneiform writing was used exclusively to maintain financial records for wealthy merchants. For the next several thousand years, there would be few major advancements in the technology of financial recordkeeping. The earliest known example of financial records employing a form of double-entry bookkeeping has been traced to the mid-fourteenth century in Genoa, Italy. Of course, Pacioli in the late fifteenth century would set the stage for the widespread adoption of double-entry bookkeeping across Europe and eventually the world.

Now that you have been acquainted with the accounting profession, basic accounting concepts, and the nature of accounting and control systems, you are ready to tackle the procedural aspects of accounting. This chapter provides you with a set of skills that you need in the remaining chapters of this text. In this chapter, you learn how to journalize transactions, post transactions to the general ledger, and prepare a trial balance from the general ledger. Once you acquire these skills, you will be prepared to "walk through" the entire accounting cycle for a business in Chapter 5.

THE ACCOUNTING EQUATION

In Chapter 2, you learned that a balance sheet balances in the sense that the assets of a business must equal the sum of its liabilities and owners' equity. This relationship, known as the accounting equation, is graphically illustrated in Exhibit 4.1 for a corporation. Every transaction of a business must be recorded in such a way that the accounting equation for that business remains in balance. In this section, we consider several transactions of a hypothetical business to become familiar with the accounting

---

1. For an excellent discussion of prehistoric accounting methods, see the following article: R. Mattesich, "Prehistoric Accounting and the Problem of Representation: On Recent Archeological Evidence of the Middle-East From 8000 B.C. to 3000 B.C.," *The Accounting Historians Journal*, Fall 1987, 71–91.

■ **EXHIBIT 4.1**

The Accounting Equation

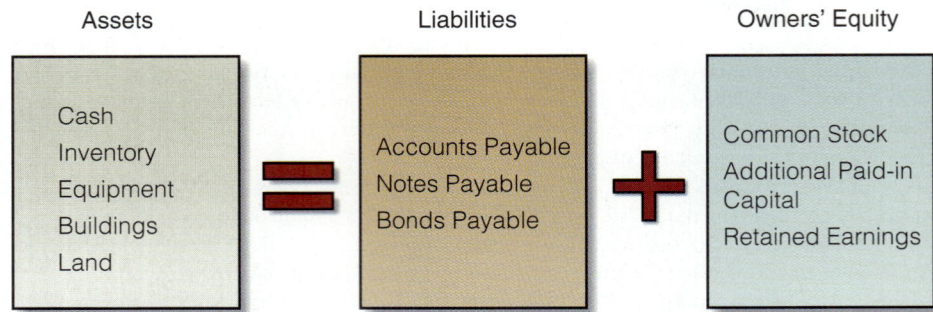

■ **LEARNING OBJECTIVE 1**

Analyze business transactions in reference to the accounting equation

Discussion Question

Ask students to identify the dual nature of each of these transactions. For example, Peg and Ted give up cash and receive an ownership interest in a pizza shop.

equation and how accountants analyze business transactions in reference to this equation.

Peg Stussi and Ted Jefferson have been friends since grade school. After graduating from Temple University with political science degrees, Peg and Ted have decided to try their hand at business. The two friends have scraped together $20,000 to establish a pizza shop a few blocks from the university campus. Following are the first five transactions of this new business venture.

1. Opened a checking account for Peg and Ted's Pizzeria at a local bank and deposited $20,000.
2. Purchased $12,000 of equipment, paying $5,000 in cash and signing a note payable for the balance.
3. Purchased $1,000 of baking supplies.
4. Purchased $2,500 of cooking utensils.
5. Sold twenty pizzas to a local fraternity for a rush party. Consumed $50 of baking supplies in producing these pizzas, which were sold for $200. (Although the pizza shop was not officially opened for business, Peg and Ted decided to accept this order to get their business off to a fast start.)

We can use the following equation format to record the first five transactions of this new business. We will refer to Peg and Ted's ownership interest in their business as "Peg & Ted's Equity." A column has been established in the following format for each specific asset or liability involved in these five transactions. For the time being, think of these columns as simple accounts. Following each transaction, we will compute a new balance for the accounts affected by that transaction.

		Assets				**Liabilities**	**Owners' Equity**
		Baking	Cooking			Note	Peg & Ted's
Cash	+	Supplies	+ Utensils	+ Equipment	=	Payable	+ Equity

Our objective for each transaction is to analyze its impact on the three major balance sheet components of Peg & Ted's Pizzeria. If we incorrectly analyze a transaction, the result will likely be an unbalanced accounting equation for this business. The first transaction is quite simple. By depositing $20,000 in a checking account for their new business, Peg and Ted increased the pizza shop's assets from zero to $20,000.

Even the smallest businesses need a reliable accounting system to process their financial data and provide a means for preparing periodic financial statements.

This transaction also established an equal amount of equity or ownership interest for Peg and Ted in the pizza shop. Following this initial transaction, the accounting equation for Peg & Ted's Pizzeria would appear as follows:

		Assets				**Liabilities**	**Owners' Equity**
		Baking	Cooking			Note	Peg & Ted's
Cash	+	Supplies	+ Utensils	+ Equipment	=	Payable	+ Equity
$20,000					=		$20,000

When Peg and Ted purchased the equipment for their shop, they made a down payment of $5,000 and signed a note promising to pay the balance of the $12,000 purchase price by a specified date. This transaction affected three of the accounts that we established for this business: (1) the balance of the Cash account decreased by $5,000, (2) the Equipment account increased from zero to $12,000, and (3) the Note Payable account increased from zero to $7,000. Notice that although two asset accounts and only one liability account were affected by this transaction, the net effect on each side of the accounting equation was $7,000: total assets and total liabilities both increased by that amount. So, our accounting equation for the pizza shop remains in balance.

		Assets				**Liabilities**	**Owners' Equity**
		Baking	Cooking			Note	Peg & Ted's
Cash	+	Supplies	+ Utensils	+ Equipment	=	Payable	+ Equity
$20,000					=		$20,000
−5,000				+ 12,000	=	+7,000	
$15,000	+			$12,000	=	$7,000	+ $20,000

Since the third and fourth transactions of Peg & Ted's Pizzeria are similar, we will deal with them simultaneously—accountants must always attempt to be as efficient as possible. Peg and Ted purchased baking supplies at a cost of $1,000 and cooking utensils costing $2,500. This transaction only affected the assets component of the accounting equation, which is true of many business transactions. Two asset accounts, Baking Supplies and Cooking Utensils, increased from zero to $1,000 and $2,500, respectively, while another asset account, Cash, decreased from $15,000 to $11,500. Following this transaction, the total assets of this new business remained at $27,000, which was also the sum of the company's liabilities and owners' equity.

	Assets				**Liabilities**	**Owners' Equity**
Cash +	Baking Supplies +	Cooking Utensils +	Equipment =		Note Payable +	Peg & Ted's Equity
$15,000 +			$12,000	=	$7,000 +	$20,000
−3,500 +	1,000 +	2,500				
$11,500 +	$1,000 +	$2,500 +	$12,000	=	$7,000 +	$20,000

The final transaction for Peg & Ted's Pizzeria is quite different from the previous transactions. Peg and Ted consumed $50 of baking supplies in producing ten pizzas, which they sold for $200. On the left-hand side of the accounting equation, cash increased by $200 while baking supplies decreased by $50, meaning that there was a net increase in assets of $150. To balance the accounting equation impact of this transaction, we increase owners' equity by $150. Make sense? Sure, since the owners of a business are entitled to any profits (revenues less expenses) that it earns. As discussed later, in an actual accounting system, revenue and expense amounts are temporarily stored in separate revenue and expense accounts. Then, at the end of each accounting period, the balances of all revenue and expense accounts are transferred to owners' equity. To simplify matters for purposes of this illustration, the difference between the revenue and expense related to Peg & Ted's first sale is entered directly in the owners' equity account. After this final transaction, the updated accounting equation for Peg & Ted's Pizzeria would appear as follows:

	Assets				**Liabilities**	**Owners' Equity**
Cash +	Baking Supplies +	Cooking Utensils +	Equipment =		Note Payable +	Peg & Ted's Equity
$11,500 +	$1,000 +	$2,500 +	$12,000	=	$7,000 +	$20,000
+ 200	− 50			=		+150
$11,700 +	$ 950 +	$2,500 +	$12,000	=	$7,000 +	$20,150

DOUBLE-ENTRY BOOKKEEPING RULES

■ LEARNING OBJECTIVE 2
Determine whether increases and decreases in specific general ledger accounts are recorded as debits or credits

Theoretically, it would be possible to use the accounting "system" illustrated in the previous section for a business entity. However, that simple system becomes very cumbersome when the number of columns (accounts) becomes quite large. As you learned in Chapter 3, businesses record financial information in accounting systems consisting of journals and ledgers. The rules of double-entry bookkeeping dictate how financial information is recorded. This section presents the bookkeeping rules for each major type of account. Before these rules are presented, the important bookkeeping terms "debit" and "credit" are discussed.

Debits and Credits?

Accountants are often asked, "Exactly what is a debit and a credit?" An accountant steeped in the history of the profession might go into a long discourse regarding the original Latin terms from which "debit" and "credit" evolved. For our purposes, simply remember that **debit** refers to the left-hand side of a T-account, while **credit** refers to the right-hand side of a T-account. When an accountant refers to a debit, he or she is typically referring to an amount entered on the left-hand side of an account. For instance, the following T-account for cash contains a debit of $600. As a verb, "debit" means to enter a given amount on the left-hand side of an account: "Vicki, debit cash $600." So, we could state that the following cash account was debited $600 on September 5.

■ LEARNING
OBJECTIVE 3
Identify the normal balance, debit balance or credit balance, of individual general ledger accounts

debit

credit

Teaching Note
Point out that debits and credits are neither good nor bad. Debits and credits are simply procedural components of bookkeeping.

Teaching Note
Point out the importance of learning to classify accounts into one of the five major categories: assets, liabilities, owners' equity, revenues, and expenses. Failure to properly classify a transaction will result in incorrect financial statements.

	CASH	
Balance 9/1/96	500	
9/5/96	600	

In a four-column account format, the term "debit" refers to an amount entered in the debit column or to the process of entering an amount in the debit column. The phrase "debit balance" indicates that the net balance of an account is a debit rather than a credit. Accountants use the term "credit" to refer to an amount entered on the right-hand side of a T-account or an amount entered in the credit column of a four-column account. Likewise, as a verb, "credit" refers to the process of entering an amount on the right-hand side of a T-account or in the credit column of a four-column account.

Accountants use debits and credits to define the bookkeeping rules and normal balances for each type of general ledger account. Exhibit 4.2 summarizes these bookkeeping rules and normal account balances. As shown in Exhibit 4.2, assets and expenses normally have debit balances, while liabilities, owners' equity items, and revenues are expected to have credit balances. Notice that Exhibit 4.2 identifies assets, liabilities, and owners' equity accounts as "permanent accounts," while revenues and expenses are identified as "temporary accounts." Shortly, the underlying meaning of these terms is explained.

Recall a key point made regarding bookkeeping rules in Chapter 3, namely, that these rules are arbitrary. Many analogies to the arbitrary rules used by accountants

■ **EXHIBIT 4.2**
Debit and Credit Rules

	PERMANENT ACCOUNTS			TEMPORARY ACCOUNTS	
	Assets	Liabilities	Owners' Equity	Revenues	Expenses
To Increase	Debit	Credit	Credit	Credit	Debit
To Decrease	Credit	Debit	Debit	Debit	Credit
Normal Account Balance	Debit	Credit	Credit	Credit	Debit

SPOTLIGHT ON ETHICS

The Pen Is Greater Than the Pistol

Al Capone's bookkeeper once bragged that he could steal much more with his bookkeeping tools—pen and paper, debits and credits—than Capone's henchmen could with their arsenal of guns. A common method that organized crime syndicates have historically used to misappropriate funds from legitimate businesses they own is a so-called skimming operation. This scheme involves avoiding taxes of all types on business revenues by systematically understating or "skimming" the cash receipts taken in by a business.

Federal authorities uncovered and prosecuted a classic example of a large-scale skimming operation in the early 1980s. This fraud involved several popular nightclubs and bars in New York City including the Peppermint Lounge, the Mardi Gras, the Haymarket, and the Grapevine. Over a three-year period, federal prosecutors proved that the nightclubs' owners failed to report more than $2 million taken in by the Mardi Gras alone. A key figure in the skimming operation was an accountant who regularly made bookkeeping entries understating the cash receipts taken in by these Big Apple watering holes. Federal authorities indicted this individual on charges of preparing fraudulent financial statements and false tax returns for the nightclubs. Eventually, nine participants in the crime ring, including the accountant, were convicted of fraud.

can be drawn to the sports world—apologies to those of you who are nonsports types. For instance, in baseball why is first base to the right of the home plate umpire, while third base is to his (or her) left? That is, wouldn't it make just as much sense for first base to be third base, and vice versa? Likewise, why are horse races run in a counterclockwise direction in this country, while they are run in a clockwise direction in Great Britain? The answers to these and other probing questions will have to be examined later. For now, simply accept, and imprint into your long-term memory, the debit and credit rules summarized in Exhibit 4.2.

Asset Accounts

Chapter 3 briefly introduced the bookkeeping rules for asset accounts. If you have forgotten those rules, Exhibit 4.2 will refresh your memory. Increases in assets are recorded as debits, while decreases in assets are recorded as credits. Also notice in Exhibit 4.2 that asset accounts normally have debit balances. Is it possible for asset accounts to have credit balances? Yes, but only under unusual circumstances. For example, assume that a company overdraws its bank account by $250 and that its general ledger Cash account reflects a credit balance of that same amount. (As you will learn in a subsequent chapter, the balance of a company's bank account and its corresponding Cash account in the general ledger are not necessarily equal.) Under these circumstances, the company owes its bank $250. If the company prepares a balance sheet at this point, it would not list the $250 as a negative cash item on its balance sheet. Instead, that amount would be listed as an account payable under current liabilities on the balance sheet.

Liability Accounts

Liability accounts are, in a sense, mirror images of asset accounts. Accounts payable, notes payable, and other liability accounts normally have credit balances. Likewise, increases in liability accounts are recorded as credits, while decreases are recorded as debits—just the opposite of the bookkeeping rules for asset accounts. Like asset accounts, individual liability accounts may occasionally have an abnormal balance. As you would expect, a debit balance is considered abnormal for liability accounts.

Owners' Equity Accounts

Before discussing the bookkeeping rules for owners' equity accounts, we should first define the terms "permanent accounts" and "temporary accounts." As indicated earlier, during each accounting period the dollar amounts associated with revenue and expense transactions are stored temporarily in revenue and expense accounts. Then, at the end of each accounting period, after a business's net income has been determined, the balances of all revenue and expense accounts are transferred or closed to an owners' equity account. As a result, revenue and expense accounts begin each new accounting period with a zero balance. For this reason, these accounts are referred to as **temporary accounts.** Accounts that are included in a balance sheet are referred to as permanent accounts. The period-ending balances of **permanent accounts** are carried forward to the next accounting period.

The bookkeeping rules for owners' equity accounts, such as common stock, additional paid-in capital, and retained earnings, are identical to the bookkeeping rules for liabilities. Increases in these accounts are recorded as credits, while decreases are recorded as debits. Likewise, these accounts normally have credit balances.

Recall from Chapter 2 that Retained Earnings, an owners' equity account of corporations, represents the cumulative earnings over the life of a company less any dividends distributed to stockholders. It is not uncommon for relatively new companies to have negative retained earnings, that is, a debit balance in their Retained Earnings account. As noted previously, asset accounts that have credit balances at the end of an accounting period are reclassified as liabilities for balance sheet purposes. Likewise, liability accounts that have debit balances at the end of an accounting period are listed as assets on an entity's balance sheet. When an owners' equity account, such as retained earnings, has an abnormal (debit) balance, the account is not reclassified into another section of the balance sheet. Instead, businesses typically report such amounts in parentheses in the owners' equity section of the balance sheet to indicate that the balance is opposite of the expected or normal balance.

Temporary Accounts

Increases in revenue accounts are recorded as credits, and increases in expense accounts are recorded as debits. Very seldom do either revenue or expense accounts have abnormal balances. Revenue accounts nearly always have credit balances, while expense accounts nearly always have debit balances. In fact, it is very uncommon to make debit entries to revenue accounts or credit entries to expense accounts. One exception would be closing entries, referred to earlier, that are required at the end of each accounting period.

Besides revenue and expense accounts, there is one additional temporary account not listed in Exhibit 4.2. For corporations, this account is typically entitled Dividends.

During the 1920s and 1930s, Al Capone was among the most infamous criminals in the U.S. Although known for his violent tendencies, the principal means Capone used to finance his crime syndicate's operations was "creative" bookkeeping. In fact, Capone was eventually sentenced to prison on tax evasion charges stemming from his organization's innovative bookkeeping practices.

temporary accounts

permanent accounts

Many corporations regularly distribute a portion of their earnings to stockholders. These distributions are referred to as dividends. For bookkeeping purposes, dividends are recorded similarly to expenses, that is, as debits. Likewise, a Dividends account normally has a debit balance, and the period-ending balance of this account is transferred or closed to retained earnings. However, dividends paid by a corporation to its stockholders are *not* expenses and thus have no impact on the corporation's net income. These amounts are reported as a reduction in retained earnings in a company's statement of stockholders' equity.[2] In a subsequent chapter, we examine in more depth accounting issues related to the payment of dividends to stockholders.

Exhibit 4.2 summarizes bookkeeping rules in a tabular format. Exhibit 4.3 presents these same rules in a format integrated with the accounting equation and with the format of T-accounts. Exhibit 4.3 also includes an expanded analysis of bookkeeping rules for owners' equity accounts and temporary accounts whose balances are eventually closed to an owners' equity account.

■ **EXHIBIT 4.3**

Summary of Bookkeeping Rules Integrated with the Accounting Equation and T-Accounts

Accounting Equation:	ASSETS		=	LIABILITIES		+	OWNERS' EQUITY	
Bookkeeping Rules:	Debit for Increases	Credit for Decreases		Debit for Decreases	Credit for Increases		Debit for Decreases	Credit for Increases

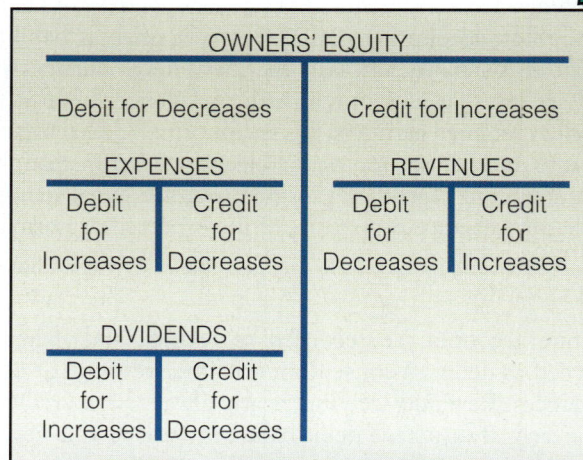

OWNERS' EQUITY

Debit for Decreases	Credit for Increases

EXPENSES

Debit for Increases	Credit for Decreases

REVENUES

Debit for Decreases	Credit for Increases

DIVIDENDS

Debit for Increases	Credit for Decreases

---

2. Quite often, companies invest in the common stock of other firms. For instance, on any given date, Exxon may own several hundred or several thousand shares of common stock in dozens of other companies. Dividends paid by one company to another are typically recorded in a revenue account entitled Dividend Revenue and reported on the income statement under Other Revenues and Expenses.

Contra Accounts

One final type of account should be mentioned before we wrap up our overview of bookkeeping rules. **Contra accounts** are created as offsets or reductions to related accounts for financial statement purposes. These accounts are maintained independently during an accounting period, but then their balances are subtracted from related account balances in the appropriate financial statement. An example of a contra account is Accumulated Depreciation, which was discussed briefly in Chapter 2. There are numerous contra accounts, but most are either contra asset or contra liability accounts. Accumulated Depreciation is a contra asset account because its balance is subtracted from an asset account—Property, Plant and Equipment—for balance sheet purposes.

From a bookkeeping perspective, this is what you need to know about contra accounts at this point: the normal account balances and basic bookkeeping rules for contra accounts are exactly the reverse of those shown in Exhibit 4.2 for the related type of account. For instance, contra asset accounts normally have credit balances, and they are increased by credits and decreased by debits. One more? Contra liability accounts normally have debit balances, and they are increased by debits and decreased by credits.

contra accounts

JOURNALIZING TRANSACTIONS: APPLYING THE BOOKKEEPING RULES

The journalizing of transactions and other events is the starting point of the accounting cycle that must be completed for a business each accounting period. If the journal entries prepared by an organization's accountants are incorrect or incomplete, these errors will be carried through the remainder of the accounting cycle. The eventual result will be inaccurate financial statements and potentially improper decisions by the parties relying on those statements. Consequently, it is very important that the journalizing process be done correctly.

Journalizing: Easy as 1, 2, 3 . . .

To illustrate the mechanical aspects of making a general journal entry, consider a purchase of cleaning supplies by the owners of the Strawberry House. Assume that on February 1, 1996, cleaning supplies costing $250 were purchased by the Strawberry House. The following is the general journal entry reflecting this transaction.

■ **LEARNING OBJECTIVE 4**
Prepare general journal entries

Teaching Note
Journalizing is a key step in the accounting cycle because it requires a great deal of judgment. The other steps are primarily procedural and involve reorganizing and summarizing information from journal entries.

General Journal				Page 2
Date	**Description**	**Post Ref.**	**Debit**	**Credit**
1996 Feb. 1	Cleaning Supplies		250	
	Cash			250
	Purchased cleaning supplies			

Mechanically, the following steps are required to prepare a general journal entry that involves two accounts.

1. Enter the year, month, and date of the entry in the columns on the left-hand margin of the general journal as just shown. Typically, the year and month are recorded only at the top of each page of the general journal.
2. Refer to the chart of accounts to identify the appropriate titles for the accounts affected by the transaction.
3. Enter the title of the account to be debited in the description column on the same line that the date was entered.
4. On the following line, indent two spaces and enter the title of the account to be credited.
5. Insert in the debit column—on the line on which the title of the account to be debited was entered—the amount of the transaction, and insert in the credit column—on the line on which the title of the account to be credited was entered—the same amount.
6. In the description column, two lines below the title of the account credited, write a brief explanation describing the nature of the transaction. This explanation may be omitted if the nature of the transaction is obvious.

compound journal entry

An entry that involves more than two accounts is known as a **compound journal entry.** The procedure for recording a journal entry involving only two accounts must be modified, but only slightly, when recording a compound journal entry. To illustrate a compound journal entry, assume that on March 1, 1996, the owners of the Strawberry House purchased $150 of cleaning supplies and $200 of office supplies. Also assume that the owners paid cash of $100 and "charged" the remaining cost of these supplies. The following is the general journal entry to record this transaction.

Discussion Question
Ask students to classify the four accounts listed in this journal entry as assets, liabilities, and so on.

			General Journal			Page 2
Date			Description	Post Ref.	Debit	Credit
1996 Mar.	1		Cleaning Supplies		150	
			Office Supplies		200	
			Cash			100
			Accounts Payable			250
			Purchased cleaning and office supplies; terms: $100 down, remainder due in 30 days			

Discussion Question
If debits equal credits, the accounting equation must be in balance. Does this mean that the accounts are correct?
Answer: No, the transactions could have been misclassified.

Compound journal entries may have several debits and one credit, several credits and a single debit, or multiple debits and multiple credits. Like all journal entries, the dollar amount of debits and the dollar amount of credits in a compound journal entry must be equal. If this rule is not violated, then a journal entry will leave an entity's accounting equation in balance. For the compound journal entry just shown, the net increase in assets was $250—an increase in supplies of $350 offset by a decrease in cash of $100. Liabilities, specifically accounts payable, increased by $250 as well. Consequently, this transaction is balanced in reference to the accounting equation.

$$\begin{array}{ccccc} \text{Assets} & = & \text{Liabilities} & + & \text{Owners' Equity} \\ +250 & = & +250 & & \end{array}$$

Knowing When to Dial "B" for Bookkeeper

Many small business owners make the mistake of attempting to establish and maintain their firm's accounting records, although they have little or no accounting experience. Chaos is often the result. Described in the following article are the experiences of one small business owner who discovered that the secret to reliable accounting records is to retain the services of an accounting firm.

When Scott Shaw, the co-owner of two restaurants in Miami, bought a majority interest in a local ice cream wholesaler named Gelato di Roma, he made an unorthodox but eminently practical decision. "I soon came to realize that the company just wasn't ready to invest in the time and accounting know-how necessary to handle bookkeeping internally," he recalls.

Shaw learned that lesson the hard way. "My first company was a small ice cream business in Texas, and we—meaning me—did the bookkeeping ourselves," he says, "We were always at least a month late with our books, and I never truly had confidence that everything was right." Once he saw the benefits of well-run bookkeeping operations, which his restaurants were successful enough to support, he saw no reason to step back into the Dark Ages.

Gelato now contracts with a local firm called Bookkeepers Inc., which, in return for a $120 monthly fee, updates the company's financial records. "They've done everything they could to McDonaldize the process for us, which reduces our margin for error," he says. "We provide them with basic information, like employees names, jobs, and salaries. They worry about all the complicated things."

Shaw still writes and codes all checks, but it's now the outside bookkeepers' responsibility to organize and prepare the journals that then are passed on to the company's tax accountants at tax time.

When shopping for an outside bookkeeper, compare price, client recommendations, and educational credentials. (Shaw's bookkeepers are CPAs by training.) You can expect to pay about $15 to $20 an hour for outside bookkeeping services, a good bit less than CPAs would charge to clean up any bookkeeping disasters.

SOURCE: Used with permission, *Inc. Magazine*, January 1992. Goldhirsch, Inc., 38 Commercial Wharf, Boston, MA 02110.

Accounting Illustrated: Eight Real-World Journal Entries

How do you learn to ride a bicycle or twirl a baton or do the Texas two-step? Practice! Practice! Practice! The same is true for accounting, particularly when it comes to the basic bookkeeping rules that dictate how transactions should be journalized. To help you sharpen your journalizing skills, this section presents several business transactions for which journal entries are developed. These transactions were drawn from recent annual reports of companies from a variety of industries.

For each transaction presented in this section, a "transaction analysis" is first performed. This analysis involves the following steps: identify the accounts affected by the transaction (since we do not have access to these companies' charts of account, an appropriate title is provided for each account); determine whether these accounts are asset accounts, liability accounts, and so on; determine whether the transaction increased or decreased these accounts; and determine whether these increases or decreases should be recorded as debits or credits. After completing the transaction analysis, the effect of the transaction on the company's accounting equation is analyzed. Finally, a general journal entry is prepared for the transaction. To promote truth in advertising (and accounting), several of the journal entries discussed in this section were not recorded exactly as they are depicted. For example, in some cases, numerous individual transactions have been consolidated into one mega-transaction.

The tasks just listed are completed for you for each of the real-world business transactions considered here; however, you may want to attempt them yourself before reviewing the completed solutions. The format of the general journal entry developed for each transaction is a simplified version of the format illustrated earlier. This format contains only the titles of the accounts affected by the entry and the dollar amounts of each debit and credit. For instance, the compound journal entry discussed earlier would be recorded as follows using this simplified format.

Cleaning Supplies	150	
Office Supplies	200	
Cash		100
Accounts Payable		250

Notice that in this format the accounts debited are listed first, followed by the accounts credited, which are indented two spaces. On the right-hand side of this format are two imaginary columns, one for debit amounts and one for credit amounts.

Smith Corona Corporation

Smith Corona is a company best known for producing and selling typewriters. This company has historically relied heavily on borrowed funds to finance its operations. During a recent year, Smith Corona paid $5,018,000 of interest expense on its outstanding loans.

Teaching Note
In analyzing a financial transaction, think of its dual impact on a business's financial status.

Transaction Analysis:

Account	Type	Increase/ Decrease	Debit or Credit	Amount
Interest Expense	Expense	Increase	Debit	$5,018,000
Cash	Asset	Decrease	Credit	5,018,000

Effect on Accounting Equation:

Assets	=	Liabilities	+	Owners' Equity
−5,018,000				−5,018,000

Teaching Note
Point out the effect on owners' equity of entries to revenue and expense accounts.

Journal Entry:

Interest Expense	5,018,000	
Cash		5,018,000

Allou Health & Beauty Care, Inc.

Allou wholesales more than eight thousand health and beauty aid products and more than seven thousand fragrance products. The company's principal markets are in the eastern United States. During the early 1990s, Allou received $425,694 after winning a legal judgment against a computer firm. The judgment was awarded to Allou after a court ruled that the computer firm had violated a contract to provide Allou with a functional computer software package.

Transaction Analysis:

Account	Type	Increase/ Decrease	Debit or Credit	Amount
Cash	Asset	Increase	Debit	$425,694
Miscellaneous Revenue	Revenue	Increase	Credit	425,694

Effect on Accounting Equation:

Assets = Liabilities + Owners' Equity
+425,694   +425,694

Journal Entry:

Cash 425,694
    Miscellaneous Revenue   425,694

United Rayore Gas Ltd.

United Rayore Gas is a Canadian company headquartered in Calgary. United Rayore is subject to several different taxes in Canada. These taxes include a large corporations tax, a provincial income tax, and a national corporate income tax. During 1993, United Rayore had total income tax expense of $1,560,000—in Canadian dollars.

Transaction Analysis:

Account	Type	Increase/ Decrease	Debit or Credit	Amount
Income Tax Expense	Expense	Increase	Debit	$1,560,000
Cash	Asset	Decrease	Credit	1,560,000

Effect on Accounting Equation:

Assets = Liabilities + Owners' Equity
−1,560,000   −1,560,000

Journal Entry:

Income Tax Expense 1,560,000
    Cash   1,560,000

Excalibur Technologies Corporation

The core business of Excalibur Technologies is adaptive pattern recognition processing. This technology allows organizations to index and retrieve information electronically and to eliminate considerable paper-based documentation. One important source of revenue for Excalibur is the provision of professional services related to the installation and operation of their products. These service revenues totaled approximately $540,000 during a recent year.

Transaction Analysis:

Account	Type	Increase/ Decrease	Debit or Credit	Amount
Cash	Asset	Increase	Debit	$540,000
Service Revenues	Revenue	Increase	Credit	540,000

Effect on Accounting Equation:

Assets	=	Liabilities	+	Owner's Equity
+540,000				+540,000

Journal Entry:

Cash	540,000	
Service Revenues		540,000

Honda Motor Co., Ltd.

Like most large companies, Honda Motor Co. invests much of its excess cash in short-term certificates of deposits and other interest-yielding investments. A recent annual report of this company disclosed that it earned interest revenue of 11,050,000,000 yen, which translated to $95,013,000. (The financial statements that Honda distributes in the United States express monetary amounts in both yen and U.S. dollars.)

Transaction Analysis:

Account	Type	Increase/ Decrease	Debit or Credit	Amount
Cash	Asset	Increase	Debit	$95,013,000
Interest Revenue	Revenue	Increase	Credit	95,013,000

Effect on Accounting Equation:

Assets	=	Liabilities	+	Stockholders' Equity
+95,013,000				+95,013,000

Journal Entry:

Cash	95,013,000	
Interest Revenue		95,013,000

Dell Computer Corporation

Dell Computer's financial success has been largely attributable to its "direct end user" marketing strategy. By selling computer hardware and software directly to end users, the company can price its products very competitively relative to other computer firms. Many of the products sold by Dell Computer include a warranty. Because of the matching principle, Dell must estimate the expenditures it will incur in future years under these warranty contracts. These estimated expenditures must be recognized as an expense in the year the products are sold. In a recent year, the company recorded an expense at year-end of $20,588,000 for estimated warranty expenditures to be paid in the future.

Transaction Analysis:

Account	Type	Increase/ Decrease	Debit or Credit	Amount
Warranty Expense	Expense	Increase	Debit	$20,588,000
Accrued Expenses	Liability	Increase	Credit	20,588,000

Effect on Accounting Equation:

Assets	=	Liabilities	+	Owners' Equity
		+20,588,000		−20,588,000

Journal Entry:

Warranty Expense 20,588,000

    Accrued Expenses   20,588,000

The Valley Fair Corporation

This company operates a large chain of retail drug and beauty aid stores in the northeastern and midwestern United States. To help finance its operations, Valley Fair annually borrows funds from several banks. During a recent year, the company repaid a $2,125,000 note payable owed to one of its banks.

Transaction Analysis:

Account	Type	Increase/ Decrease	Debit or Credit	Amount
Notes Payable	Liability	Decrease	Debit	$2,125,000
Cash	Asset	Decrease	Credit	2,125,000

Effect on Accounting Equation:

Assets	=	Liabilities	+	Owners' Equity
−2,125,000		−2,125,000		

Journal Entry:

Notes Payable 2,125,000

    Cash   2,125,000

Groundwater Technology, Inc.

Groundwater Technology provides environmental consulting and remediation services, principally to large oil companies. Remediation involves the restoration of soil and water contaminated by petroleum products accidentally released into the environment. To motivate employees and executives to perform at a high level, this company has established a bonus performance plan. During a recent year, Groundwater Technology paid out $283,000 under the terms of this plan.

Transaction Analysis:

Account	Type	Increase/ Decrease	Debit or Credit	Amount
Salary Expense	Expense	Increase	Debit	$283,000
Cash	Asset	Decrease	Credit	283,000

Effect on Accounting Equation:

Assets	=	Liabilities	+	Owners' Equity
−283,000				−283,000

Journal Entry:

Salary Expense 283,000

    Cash   283,000

Entries, Entries, and More Entries

Most of the journal entries illustrated in this chapter have been for typical business transactions. Besides these normal, recurring journal entries, there are several "special" entries that accountants record either at regular intervals or whenever appropri-

correcting entries

adjusting entries

closing entries

reversing entries

ate. These special entries include correcting entries, adjusting entries, closing entries, and reversing entries.

Correcting entries amend errors in previously recorded journal entries. For example, if a company paid cash of $3,500 for a piece of equipment but debited the Equipment account and credited the Cash account for $5,300, a correcting entry would be required. This entry would include a debit to the Cash account of $1,800 and an equal credit to the Equipment account. Correcting entries are typically made shortly following the discovery of bookkeeping errors.

Adjusting entries and closing entries are made at the end of each accounting period. **Adjusting entries** are required to ensure that the revenue recognition and expense recognition rules are properly applied at the end of each accounting period. For example, adjusting entries are required to recognize expenses that a business has incurred at the end of an accounting period but not yet paid or recorded. **Closing entries** are made at the end of each accounting period to close out the period-ending balances of all temporary accounts including revenues, expenses, and dividends. As mentioned earlier, the balances in temporary accounts are transferred to an owners' equity account at the end of each accounting period.

Reversing entries are made at the beginning of an accounting period to reverse, or cancel out, the effect of certain adjusting entries made at the end of the prior accounting period. These entries are an optional accounting procedure that accountants can use to simplify the recording of subsequent transactions or events.

Journalizing: A Few Helpful Hints and Reminders

"Hints from Heloise" is a column that has appeared in international newspapers for decades. Heloise provides her readers, of all ages, with assorted helpful hints. These hints range from six ways to turn an empty milk carton into a Christmas gift for Grannie to six hints for college students—involving everything from money management to doing their laundry. Exhibit 4.4 contains a few helpful hints and reminders for accountants-in-training who want to perfect their journalizing skills.

The most effective method of preventing or detecting journalizing errors is to review each journal entry carefully before turning your attention to another entry or accounting task. Even in the relatively simple situations included in the homework problems in this text, one small error in a journal entry can cost you an hour or two of increasing frustration and mounting blood pressure. When reviewing a journal entry, one useful technique is to ask yourself whether the entry "makes sense" from the standpoint of the given entity's normal operating activities. For example, a journal entry that involves a debit to Salary Expense and a credit to Bonds Payable is immediately suspect for any business and should be reviewed carefully.

Another helpful review technique is to analyze journal entries in reference to the accounting equation. Remember that the net dollar effect of a transaction on each side of the accounting equation must be equal. When all of the accounts affected by a transaction are on one side of the accounting equation, the net effect of the transaction on that side of the equation must be zero. For instance, a transaction that affects only assets must result in an increase in one or more asset accounts that is exactly equal to the decrease in one or more other asset accounts.

The most obvious and thus least helpful hint when it comes to booking journal entries is that debits must equal credits. In entries involving only two accounts, violations of this fundamental rule are quite rare—but they still occur. Students are more prone to overlook this type of error when making compound journal entries, particularly compound journal entries that have several debits and several credits. Keep in mind that an entry may have an unequal number of debits and credits as long as the cumulative dollar amount of the debits is equal to the cumulative dollar amount of the credits. Also recognize that just because an entry has an equal dollar amount of debits and credits does not mean that it is free of error. For example, a "balanced" entry may contain a debit and/or credit to the wrong account or an equal but incorrect dollar amount for both debits and credits.

Among the more common journalizing errors are transposition errors and "slipped" decimals. Distracted or fatigued accountants often transpose two consecutive numerals in a journal entry. For instance, if an entry calls for a debit of $3,159 to Inventory and an equal credit to Cash, the journal entry may actually be recorded with a debit of $3,519 to Inventory and a credit of $3,519 to Cash. An example of a slipped decimal would be recording a $42,300 decrease in Notes Payable as a decrease (debit) of $4,230.

Finally, you should be cautious when comparing the impact of debits and credits on the financial affairs of businesses with the implications those terms have for your own financial affairs. For a business, a debit to an asset account indicates that the given asset has increased, which is generally good news for the business. However, when you open your monthly bank statement and a "debit memo" falls out, that is not good news. A debit memo in your bank statement for a monthly service charge increases the bank's cash balance and decreases your cash balance. If you maintain a set of double-entry accounting records to keep track of your personal finances, you would credit, not debit, your cash account when you find a debit memo in your bank statement. Likewise, when you make a deposit and the bank clerk "credits" your savings account, your account balance will increase, not decrease. Why does the bank clerk credit your account? Because your savings account is a liability from the bank's perspective and your deposit has increased that liability.

When Sears "credits" your credit card account after you return a pair of jeans that are a couple of sizes too small, the outstanding balance on your credit card decreases, not increases. From Sears' standpoint, your credit card account is an asset. Consequently, when you return merchandise you owe Sears less money, meaning

hints from Heloise

Heloise has provided readers of her newspaper column with helpful hints of all types for several decades. Taking a "page" from Heloise's column, Exhibit 4.4 provides several hints that you can use to refine your journalizing skills.

■ **EXHIBIT 4.4**

Journalizing: A Few Helpful Hints and Reminders

- Review the accounts affected by a journal entry to determine whether they "make sense" from the perspective of the business's normal operating activities.
- Determine that a journal entry is balanced in reference to the accounting equation and in terms of debits and credits.
- Review a journal entry for transposition errors and "slipped" decimals.
- Recognize that businesses use the terms "debit" and "credit" in reference to the impact that transactions have on their financial records instead of the impact those transactions have on the personal financial records of their customers.

Candy's Tortilla Factory

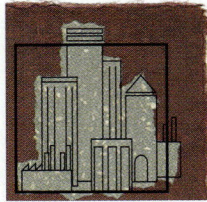

Most business transactions are routine, "everyday" transactions. Sales of merchandise, cash receipts from customers, and cash payments to suppliers are examples of frequently occurring transactions that account for most businesses' bookkeeping entries. However, the everyday transactions of some businesses are not quite so routine. For instance, it is becoming more common for companies to engage in barter transactions. These transactions involve the exchange of goods for services, goods for other goods, or services for other services. An example of a company engaging in barter transactions is Candy's Tortilla Factory, a publicly owned company headquartered in Pueblo, Colorado.

Candy's pays for its radio and billboard advertising with tortillas. Clearly, Candy's accountants cannot debit the Advertising Expense account for three hours of radio advertising and credit the Inventory account for six thousand tortillas. When recording barter transactions, accountants must analyze the value of the goods or services exchanged and establish appropriate dollar amounts to attach to both the debit and credit sides of these transactions.

Teaching Note
To record barter transactions, the accountant determines the fair value of what was given up (tortillas) or the fair value of what was received (advertising).

that your account on the company's books should be credited. If you maintain personal financial records, your outstanding credit card account balance would be a liability. A merchandise return would require a debit to that liability account, since the return decreases the amount you owe Sears. The moral here is that when companies use the terms "debit" and "credit," they use those terms in reference to the impact that transactions have on their financial records—not the financial records of their customers.

POSTING AND PREPARATION OF THE TRIAL BALANCE

■ **LEARNING OBJECTIVE 5**
Post general journal entries to the general ledger

Besides journalizing, several other procedures must be performed each accounting period in the accounting cycle. To set the stage for a discussion of the entire accounting cycle in Chapter 5, let us review two more of these procedures, the posting of data to the general ledger and the preparation of a trial balance.

Posting

Teaching Note
Posting is essentially a copying process. All the general journal entries are copied to the general ledger accounts.

The posting of financial data from the general journal and other journals of a business to its general ledger serves the purpose of summarizing that data. This summarized data can then be used to prepare financial statements at the end of an accounting period for the business. In this section, the specific steps that should be followed in posting information from general journal entries to the appropriate general ledger accounts are identified.

Discussion Question
Since each journal entry will be posted to the general ledger, why not record all entries directly in the general ledger?

Following is the compound journal entry referred to earlier in this chapter that will be used to illustrate the posting process. This entry affects four different accounts. Consequently, we will need to post information from this journal entry to four general ledger accounts.

General Journal				Page 2
Date	**Description**	**Post Ref.**	**Debit**	**Credit**

1996
Feb. 1
	Cleaning Supplies
	Office Supplies
	   Cash
	   Accounts Payable
	
	Purchased cleaning and office
	supplies; terms: $100 down,
	remainder due in 30 days
			150
			200
				
				100
				250

Following are the general ledger accounts for each item affected by the previous journal entry. Inserted in each account is its beginning-of-the-month balance for February 1996, that is, the balance of each account carried over from the previous accounting period.

Cash					Account No. 101	
Date	**Explanation**	**Post Ref.**	**Debit**	**Credit**	**Balance Debit**	**Credit**
1996 Feb. 1	Balance Forward				705	

Cleaning Supplies					Account No. 131	
Date	**Explanation**	**Post Ref.**	**Debit**	**Credit**	**Balance Debit**	**Credit**
1996 Feb. 1	Balance Forward				355	

Office Supplies					Account No. 132	
Date	**Explanation**	**Post Ref.**	**Debit**	**Credit**	**Balance Debit**	**Credit**
1996 Feb. 1	Balance Forward				145	

Accounts Payable					Account No. 201	
Date	**Explanation**	**Post Ref.**	**Debit**	**Credit**	**Balance Debit**	**Credit**
1996 Feb. 1	Balance Forward					690

The following steps should be followed in posting the information from the general journal entry for the purchase of supplies transaction to the general ledger accounts affected by that transaction.

1. In the date column of each account, record the date of the transaction (February 1 in this case).
2. In the explanation column, enter a brief description of the transaction.
3. In the initial debit and credit columns, enter the amount of the transaction affecting each account. If the amount affecting an account is a debit, that amount is entered in the debit column. Likewise, credit amounts are entered in the credit column.
4. Compute the new balance of each account and enter that amount in either the debit or credit balance column. (The new balance of the Cash account in the present example is a debit balance of $605, which is the original debit balance of $705 less the credit posted to that account of $100.)

Teaching Note
Post reference information makes a transaction easier to trace. With this information available, errors in accounting data can be corrected more easily.

5. In the post reference column of each general ledger account, indicate the journal from which the amount was posted and the page number of that journal. (In our example, "GJ2" is inserted in the post reference column to indicate that each amount was posted from page 2 of the general journal.)
6. For each account included in the journal entry, record in the post reference column of the general journal the number of that account to indicate that the appropriate debit or credit amount was posted to that general ledger account.

Shown next are the general journal entry for the purchase of supplies transaction and the general ledger accounts affected by this entry following the completion of the posting process.

General Journal				**Page 2**
Date	**Description**	**Post Ref.**	**Debit**	**Credit**
1996 Feb. 1	Cleaning Supplies	131	150	
	Office Supplies	132	200	
	Cash	101		100
	Accounts Payable	201		250
	Purchased cleaning and office supplies; terms: $100 down, remainder due in 30 days			

Cash						**Account No. 101**	
						Balance	
Date		**Explanation**	**Post Ref.**	**Debit**	**Credit**	**Debit**	**Credit**
1996 Feb.	1	Balance Forward				705	
	1	Purchase of Supplies	GJ2		100	605	

Cleaning Supplies   Account No. 131

Date			Explanation	Post Ref.	Debit	Credit	Balance Debit	Balance Credit
1996 Feb.	1		Balance Forward				355	
	1		Purchase	GJ2	150		505	

Office Supplies   Account No. 132

Date			Explanation	Post Ref.	Debit	Credit	Balance Debit	Balance Credit
1996 Feb.	1		Balance Forward				145	
	1		Purchase	GJ2	200		345	

Accounts Payable   Account No. 201

Date			Explanation	Post Ref.	Debit	Credit	Balance Debit	Balance Credit
1996 Feb.	1		Balance Forward					690
	1		Purchase of Supplies	GJ2		250		940

Preparation of a Trial Balance

At the end of each accounting period, an entity's accountants must "close the books" for the purpose of preparing a set of financial statements. One of the initial steps in this process is the preparation of a trial balance. A **trial balance** is a two-column listing of all general ledger account balances, one column for accounts with debit balances and one column for accounts with credit balances. One purpose of a trial balance is to establish that the total debits and credits entered in the general ledger accounts are equal. Unfortunately, even if the trial balance "balances," there may be errors in the individual accounts. For instance, if the debits and credits of a journal entry were posted to incorrect accounts, the debit and credit columns of the trial balance would be equal although at least two of the accounts would have improper balances.

To illustrate the preparation of a trial balance, consider a small company, the Sunshine Travel Agency, that has ten general ledger accounts. Each of these accounts is listed next. To simplify matters, only the period-ending balances of these accounts—prior to the posting of adjusting and closing entries—are shown.

Cash   Account No. 101

Date			Explanation	Post Ref.	Debit	Credit	Balance Debit	Balance Credit
1996 June	30		Balance				4,020	

■ **LEARNING OBJECTIVE 6**
Prepare a trial balance of a general ledger

trial balance

Teaching Note
The term "trial" balance highlights the fact that this item is a tool for testing whether the accounts are in balance (that is, whether the total debits equal the total credits).

Teaching Note
Only accounts with a debit or credit balance at the date of the trial balance are included. Accounts with zero balances are excluded from the trial balance.

Miscellaneous Supplies   Account No. 125

Date		Explanation	Post Ref.	Debit	Credit	Balance Debit	Balance Credit
1996 June	30	Balance				575	

Office Equipment   Account No. 151

Date		Explanation	Post Ref.	Debit	Credit	Balance Debit	Balance Credit
1996 June	30	Balance				24,570	

Accumulated Depreciation, Office Equipment   Account No. 152

Date		Explanation	Post Ref.	Debit	Credit	Balance Debit	Balance Credit
1996 June	30	Balance					6,200

Accounts Payable   Account No. 201

Date		Explanation	Post Ref.	Debit	Credit	Balance Debit	Balance Credit
1996 June	30	Balance					1,200

Common Stock   Account No. 301

Date		Explanation	Post Ref.	Debit	Credit	Balance Debit	Balance Credit
1996 June	30	Balance					2,000

Retained Earnings   Account No. 350

Date		Explanation	Post Ref.	Debit	Credit	Balance Debit	Balance Credit
1996 June	30	Balance					18,850

Commission Revenue					Account No. 401	
		Post			Balance	
Date	Explanation	Ref.	Debit	Credit	Debit	Credit
1996						
June 30	Balance					3,200

Salary Expense					Account No. 501	
		Post			Balance	
Date	Explanation	Ref.	Debit	Credit	Debit	Credit
1996						
June 30	Balance				1,960	

Miscellaneous Expenses					Account No. 509	
		Post			Balance	
Date	Explanation	Ref.	Debit	Credit	Debit	Credit
1996						
June 30	Balance				325	

Following is the trial balance of the Sunshine Travel Agency's general ledger as of June 30, 1996. Fortunately for the company's accountants, the totals of the debit and credit columns are equal.

Real World
Accountants frequently refer to adding a column of numbers as "footing" the column.

SUNSHINE TRAVEL AGENCY
TRIAL BALANCE
JUNE 30, 1996

	DEBIT	CREDIT
Cash	$ 4,020	
Miscellaneous Supplies	575	
Office Equipment	24,570	
Accumulated Depreciation, Office Equipment		$ 6,200
Accounts Payable		1,200
Common Stock		2,000
Retained Earnings		18,850
Commission Revenue		3,200
Salary Expense	1,960	
Miscellaneous Expenses	325	
	$31,450	$31,450

So, what is an accountant to do when he or she is faced with an unfriendly (unbalanced) trial balance? The first step would be a reminder to be more diligent when journalizing and posting transaction data. After completing this mental scolding, the accountant can try the following steps to identify the source of the error or errors in the accounting records.

Focus on Ethics
Management has requested a trial balance for a 4 P.M. meeting on Thursday afternoon. Unfortunately, the trial balance doesn't balance. It is off by $200. The company's accountant decides to "plug" the $200 to Miscellaneous Expense. What should the accountant have done? Suppose the amount was "immaterial" to the given company. Is the accountant's action acceptable given this assumption?

1. Re-add the debit and credit columns of the trial balance to make certain that each column was added correctly.
2. Divide the amount of the difference between the totals of the debit and credit columns by nine. If the difference is divisible by nine, there may be either a single transposition error or slipped decimal error in the trial balance or the accounting records—which must then be found. (The numerical errors caused by each of these mistakes are always divisible by nine.)
3. Divide the amount of the difference between the totals of the debit and credit columns by two. If the difference is divisible by two, it is possible that a debit has been posted as a credit, or vice versa, in the general ledger. The amount of the incorrect posting would be equal to one-half of the difference between the totals of the two columns of the trial balance. (A similar error results if an account balance is listed in the wrong column of the trial balance. For instance, if a debit balance is included in the credit column, the total of the credit column will be greater than the total of the debit column by an amount equal to twice the misplaced account balance.)
4. Trace the account balances included in the trial balance to the general ledger to determine whether errors were made in listing the account balances in the trial balance.
5. Recompute the balance of each account in the general ledger.
6. Trace the amounts posted to each general ledger account to the general journal or other journals to determine whether errors were made in the posting process.
7. Review all entries in the general journal and other journals to determine whether one or more journal entries have unequal debit and credit amounts.

SUMMARY

The accounting equation expresses the mathematical relationship between the assets, liabilities, and owners' equity of a business. When journalizing transactions and other events affecting the financial status of a business, accountants must ensure that each journal entry is balanced in reference to the accounting equation. Double-entry bookkeeping rules dictate how individual transactions and events are recorded. The key to understanding and applying these rules is the meaning and use of the terms "debit" and "credit." Debit refers to the left-hand side of a T-account, while credit refers to the right-hand side of a T-account. Likewise, to debit an account is to enter an amount on its left-hand side—or in the debit column of a four-column account. To credit an account is to enter an amount on its right-hand side—or in the credit column of a four-column account. Asset and expense accounts normally have debit balances and increases in these accounts are recorded as debits, while decreases are recorded as credits. Liability, owners' equity, and revenue accounts normally have credit balances. Increases in these accounts are recorded as credits, while decreases are recorded as debits.

When analyzing a transaction or event for the purpose of preparing a journal entry, a useful approach to follow is to first identify the type of each account (asset, liability, and so on) affected by the transaction. Next, determine whether the transaction increased or decreased these accounts. Then, after referring to the bookkeeping rules, determine whether these changes should be recorded as debits or credits. Finally, determine that the transaction has an equal dollar effect on each side of the accounting equation.

The financial data recorded in the journals of a business should be transferred or posted periodically to the appropriate general ledger accounts. At the end of each accounting period, a trial balance of the general ledger accounts is prepared. A primary purpose of a trial balance is to determine whether the total debits and credits entered in the entity's accounting records are equal.

GLOSSARY

Adjusting entries (p. 128)   Journal entries made at the end of an accounting period to ensure that the revenue recognition and expense recognition rules are properly applied.

Closing entries (p. 128)   Journal entries made at the end of each accounting period to close out or transfer the balances of temporary accounts to the appropriate owners' equity account.

Compound journal entry (p. 122)   A journal entry that involves more than two accounts.

Contra accounts (p. 121)   Accounts that are treated as offsets or reductions to related accounts for financial statement purposes; an example is accumulated depreciation.

Correcting entries (p. 128)   Journal entries made to correct errors in previously recorded journal entries.

Credit (p. 117)   The right-hand side of an account, an entry made on the right-hand side of an account, or to record an amount on the right-hand side of an account.

Debit (p. 117)   The left-hand side of an account, an entry made on the left-hand side of an account, or to record an amount on the left-hand side of an account.

Permanent accounts (p. 119)   Accounts whose period-ending balances are carried forward to the following accounting period.

Reversing entries (p. 128)   Journal entries made at the beginning of an accounting period to reverse or cancel out the effect of certain adjusting entries made at the end of the prior accounting period.

Temporary accounts (p. 119)   Accounts whose period-ending balances are transferred or closed to the appropriate owners' equity account.

Trial balance (p. 133)   A two-column listing of all general ledger account balances, one column for debit balances and one column for credit balances.

DECISION CASE

In the late 1970s, Chrysler Corporation was floundering. Stagnant sales, a poor public image of its products, and ineffective management were just a few of the problems facing Chrysler. In 1978, Chrysler's board of directors realized that the company needed a new direction and turned to a top executive of Ford Motor Company to provide that direction. Lee Iacocca had enjoyed a long and successful career at Ford when he was hired as Chrylser's chief executive. Many questioned Iacocca's decision to give up his comfortable and high-paying position at Ford to take over Chrysler, which many industry experts believed was doomed to failure. His judgment was questioned even more when the details of his employment contract were released. Iacocca's compensation package included a $1 annual salary and 400,000 stock options.

When a company grants stock options to an executive, it is giving that individual the right to purchase a certain number of shares of its common stock at a predetermined price over some specified period of time. For example, assume that DeBarger Corporation has just hired a new chief executive officer (CEO) and granted this individual 100,000 stock options. These stock options entitle the new CEO to purchase 100,000 shares of the company's common stock at a price of $20 any time over the next ten years. The "catch" is that DeBarger's stock is currently trading at only $8 per share on the New York Stock Exchange. Obviously, the new CEO will not exercise her stock options unless DeBarger's stock price rises above $20 per share.

Large corporations include stock options in their executives' compensation packages to motivate them to increase the value of the company by profitable operations. In the present example, if the new CEO is successful, the company's profits will increase in future years, resulting in the value of its common stock increasing as well. For example, if over the next five years this company posts record profits, its common stock price may rise to $40 per share. At this point, the CEO can purchase 100,000 shares of the company's stock at a price of $20 and then immediately sell those shares at a price of $40. Result: a quick profit of $2 million.

In recent years, corporate executives, particularly those who turn around financially troubled companies, have earned huge profits on the stock options included in their compensation packages. Lee Iacocca is one such example. In the 1980s, after successfully turning around Chrysler, Iacocca cashed in his Chrysler stock options for a profit of more than $40 million.

Required: Assume that you are the chief payroll accountant of DeBarger Corporation. Given your position, you have the responsibility for determining how to account for the new CEO's compensation package. The individual's annual salary is $200,000, paid on a monthly basis. In addition to the 100,000 stock options mentioned earlier, this individual's compensation package includes a $250,000 interest-free loan. As long as the CEO remains with the company, this loan does not have to be repaid. Analyze each component of the new CEO's compensation package in reference to the accounting equation and the bookkeeping rules introduced in this chapter. Write a brief report recommending how to account for each component of the compensation package, including examples of appropriate bookkeeping entries. You may want to justify your recommendations by referring to specific accounting concepts discussed in Chapter 2.

QUESTIONS

1. List two examples of each of the following components of the accounting equation: assets, liabilities, and owners' equity.

2. Explain how it is possible for a transaction to affect only one side of the accounting equation. Provide an example of such a transaction.

3. What types of transactions affect the owner's equity of a business? Provide two examples.

4. What are the debit and credit rules for assets? For liabilities? For owners' equity? For revenues? For expenses?

5. Define the terms "permanent accounts" and "temporary accounts." In which financial statement is each type of account found?

6. What happens to revenue and expense accounts at the end of each accounting period? Why?

7. Where is the retained earnings account presented in a set of financial statements and what does it represent?

8. What are "dividends" and where do they appear in a set of financial statements?

9. How are contra accounts treated in financial statements?

10. As discussed in this chapter, what is "skimming"?

11. What accounting activity represents the starting point of the accounting cycle?

12. Briefly identify the steps required to prepare a general journal entry that involves two accounts.

13. What is a compound journal entry? What must be true with regard to the dollar amount of debits and credits in a compound journal entry?

14. Identify the steps involved in performing transaction analysis as described in this chapter.

15. In addition to normal, recurring journal entries, what other types of entries do accountants typically prepare periodically or on an as-needed basis? What is the purpose of each of these types of entries?

16. Identify common errors made during the journalizing process.

17. Barter transactions involve what kinds of exchanges? What problems do transactions of this type create for accountants?

18. Identify the steps involved in the posting process, and explain the purpose of posting information from the general journal and other journals to the general ledger.

19. What is a trial balance and what is its purpose?

20. What are the steps to take in finding the cause(s) for an out-of-balance trial balance?

EXERCISES

21. **Business Transactions and the Accounting Equation** (LO 1)
    Lewis and Clare opened a tropical fish store on January 1. Following are the first four transactions of L&C's Fish Shop:
    1. Borrowed $30,000 from a local bank on a five-year note payable
    2. Paid $10,000 for fish tanks and other merchandise that was to be sold to customers
    3. Paid $8,000 for equipment to be used in the store
    4 Paid $500 for advertising expenses to publicize store's grand opening

    Required:
    1. Using the format illustrated in this chapter for Peg and Ted's Pizzeria, record the first four transactions of L&C's Fish Shop.
    2. Determine the total assets, liabilities and owners' equity of this business following its first four transactions.

    21. 2. Assets, $29,500
    Liabilities, $30,000
    Owners' Equity, −$500

22. **Using T-Accounts** (LO 2)
    Refer to the information in Exercise 21.

    Required:
    1. Prepare T-accounts for L&C's Fish Shop and post the business's first four transactions to these T-accounts.
    2. Determine the balance of each account.
    3. Identify each account you established as either a temporary account or a permanent account. Explain the difference between the two types of accounts.

    22. 2. Cash bal., $11,500 Dr.
    Inv. bal., $10,000 Dr.
    Equip. bal., $8,000 Dr.
    N. P. bal., $30,000 Cr.
    Adv. Exp. bal., $500 Dr.

23. **Analyzing General Journal Entries** (LO 2)
    The following general journal entries (presented in a simplified format) were made recently by the bookkeeper of Chandlers' Hilltop Texaco:

1. Supplies	400	
Cash		400
2. Interest Expense	270	
Cash		270
3. Equipment	4,000	
Notes Payable		4,000

23. 2. Understated by $8,000

Required:
1. Briefly describe the nature of the transactions that resulted in these journal entries.
2. Suppose that the bookkeeper inadvertently recorded the third entry by debiting Notes Payable and crediting Equipment, each for $4,000. How would this error have affected the assets and liabilities of Chandlers' Hilltop Texaco?

24. **Recording Barter Transactions** (LO 4)
Refer to the For Your Information vignette in this chapter regarding Candy's Tortilla Factory, which discusses barter transactions.

   Lillian Condit owns the local newspaper and needs to acquire a laptop computer for use in her business. Coy's Grocery Store, which regularly places ads in Lillian's newspaper, owns a laptop computer that it no longer needs. Lillian has offered the owner of Coy's Grocery Store five months of newspaper ads in exchange for the computer. The approximate fair market value of the computer is $2,700, while the monthly cost of newspaper ads for Coy's Grocery Store is $550.

24. No check figures

Required:
1. Should Coy's Grocery Store accept Lillian's offer? Why or why not?
2. Assume that Coy's Grocery Store accepts Lillian's offer, how would you suggest that Lillian record this barter transaction in the accounting records of her business?

25. **The Accounting Equation** (LO 6)
Following are the balance sheet accounts of a small business.

Cash	$2,500
Accounts Payable	700
Retained Earnings	?
Supplies	?
Land	8,200
Common Stock	1,000
Notes Payable	2,400

25. 1. Supplies, $300
2. Retained Earnings, $8,800

Required:
1. Fill in the missing amounts assuming that the business has total assets of $11,000.
2. Fill in the missing amounts assuming that the business has total liabilities and owners' (stockholders') equity of $12,900.

26. **Transaction Analysis** (LO 1, 2, 4)
The Walt Disney Company owns theme parks and resorts around the world. In 1993, the company spent $793.7 million to expand its theme parks.

26. 3. Dr. PP&E $793,700,000
Cr. Cash $793,700,000

Required:
Using the method presented in the text for developing "real-world" journal entries, complete the following tasks for this set of facts:
1. Transaction analysis.
2. Identify the effects on the accounting equation of the Walt Disney Company.
3. Prepare a journal entry for this transaction using the simplified journal entry format shown in the text.

27. **Transaction Analysis** (LO 1, 2, 4)
Centex Corporation builds housing subdivisions and supplies homebuilders with building materials. The following transactions (in thousands of dollars) are from Centex's 1994 annual report:

1. Interest paid on outstanding debt $ 68,856
2. Revenue from homes sold   1,871,627

Required:

Using the method presented in the text for developing "real-world" journal entries, complete the following tasks for each of the two transactions listed:

1. Transaction analysis.
2. Identify the effects on the accounting equation of Centex Corporation.
3. Prepare the journal entry for each of these transactions using the simplified journal entry format shown in the text.

27. 3. Dr. Int. Exp. $68,856
    Cr. Cash $68,856
    Dr. Cash $1,871,627
    Cr. Sales $1,871,627

28. **Correction of an Accounting Error (LO 4)**

Syllable, Inc., recently acquired a piece of equipment for $2,190. The entry for this transaction was recorded in Syllable's accounting records as follows:

Equipment	219	
Cash		219

Required:

1. What type of error was made in recording this transaction?
2. What effect does this error have on the two accounts involved and on Syllable's total assets? Explain.
3. Prepare the journal entry needed to correct the accounting records of Syllable, Inc.

28. 3. Dr. Equip. $1,971
    Cr. Cash $1,971

29. **Analyzing T-accounts (LO 2)**

Consider the following T-accounts for cash and accounts payable:

Cash		Accounts Payable	
10,000	14,000	7,000	6,000
9,000	9,000	5,000	8,000
8,000	2,000	1,000	1,000

Required:

1. Compute the balance of each of these accounts.
2. How would each of these accounts be classified in a balance sheet?
3. Identify a transaction that would have resulted in the $8,000 posting to the Cash account.
4. Identify a transaction that would have resulted in the $5,000 posting to the Accounts Payable account.

29. 1 Cash bal., $2,000 Dr.
    A.P. bal., $2,000 Cr.

30. **Analyzing T-accounts (LO 2)**

Considering the following T-accounts for interest expense and revenue:

Interest Expense		Interest Revenue	
4,000			180
4,000			290
4,000			240
4,000			

Required:

1. Compute the balance of each of these accounts.
2. Where in a set of financial statements would each of these accounts appear?
3. Would you ever expect the Interest Expense account to have a credit balance? Why or why not?

30. 1. Int. Exp. bal., $16,000 Dr.
    Int. Rev. bal., $710 Cr.

31. Trial Balance Errors (LO 6)

The following year-end trial balance was hurriedly prepared by the accountant of Salter Company:

	DEBIT	CREDIT
Cash	$10,250	
Accounts Receivable	5,000	
Inventory	7,500	
Property, Plant & Equipment	13,000	
Accumulated Depreciation, Property, Plant & Equipment		$ 6,100
Accounts Payable		6,500
Common Stock	10,000	
Retained Earnings		4,050
Retained Earnings		4,050
Sales Revenue		20,000
Cost of Goods Sold		12,000
Other Revenue	500	
Depreciation Expense	1,200	
Totals:	$47,450	$52,700

Required:

31. 1. Trial Bal. Total, $47,150

1. Prepare a corrected trial balance for Salter Company. The proper balance of the Inventory account is $5,700. (Hint: You may need to refer to Chapter 2 to determine whether certain accounts are assets, liabilities, and so on.)
2. If a trial balance's total debits and credits are equal, can you assume that each account balance is correct? Explain.

32. Posting General Journal Entries (LO 5)

Following are several general journal entries of the Houseman Corporation during a recent month (the journal entry descriptions have been omitted):

General Journal					Page 2
Date		Description	Post Ref.	Debit	Credit
1996 Jan.	2	Office Supplies		320	
		Cash			320
	5	Inventory		7,500	
		Accounts Payable			7,500
	12	Cash		5,750	
		Accounts Receivable			5,750
	17	Accounts Payable		4,300	
		Cash			4,300
	31	Utilities Expense		2,000	
		Cash			2,000

Following are the account number and the January 1 balance of each of the accounts affected by the listed journal entries.

	ACCOUNT NUMBER	JANUARY 1 BALANCE
Cash	101	$12,400
Accounts Receivable	111	9,300
Inventory	116	6,100
Office Supplies	121	840
Accounts Payable	201	14,200
Utilities Expense	505	0

Required:

1. What is the purpose of posting general journal entries to general ledger accounts?
2. Prepare a four-column account for each of the accounts affected by the listed transactions of the Houseman Corporation. Enter the January 1 balance into each of these accounts.
3. Post the general journal entries to the appropriate accounts.

32. 3. Cash bal., $11,530 Dr.
A.R. bal., $3,550 Dr.
Inv. bal., $13,600 Dr.
Off. Sup. bal., $1,160 Dr.
A.P. bal., $17,400 Cr.
Util. Exp. bal, $2,000 Dr.

33. **Trial Balance** (LO 6)

Moonlight Distributors has twelve general ledger accounts. Following are these accounts as of December 31, 1996. (Only the year-end balance is included in each account.)

Cash   **Account No. 101**

Date		Explanation	Post Ref.	Debit	Credit	Balance Debit	Balance Credit
Dec	31	Balance				2,075	

Accounts Receivable   **Account No. 111**

Date		Explanation	Post Ref.	Debit	Credit	Balance Debit	Balance Credit
Dec.	31	Balance				1,750	

Inventory   **Account No. 121**

Date		Explanation	Post Ref.	Debit	Credit	Balance Debit	Balance Credit
Dec.	31	Balance				925	

Property, Plant & Equipment   **Account No. 151**

Date		Explanation	Post Ref.	Debit	Credit	Balance Debit	Balance Credit
Dec.	31	Balance				5,100	

Accumulated Depreciation, Property, Plant & Equipment   Account No. 152

Date		Explanation	Post Ref.	Debit	Credit	Balance Debit	Credit
Dec.	31	Balance					1,200

Accounts Payable   Account No. 201

Date		Explanation	Post Ref.	Debit	Credit	Balance Debit	Credit
Dec.	31	Balance					1,850

Common Stock   Account No. 301

Date		Explanation	Post Ref.	Debit	Credit	Balance Debit	Credit
Dec.	31	Balance					3,000

Retained Earnings   Account No. 321

Date		Explanation	Post Ref.	Debit	Credit	Balance Debit	Credit
Dec.	31	Balance					1,800

Sales Revenue   Account No. 401

Date		Explanation	Post Ref.	Debit	Credit	Balance Debit	Credit
Dec.	31	Balance					12,000

Cost of Goods Sold   Account No. 501

Date		Explanation	Post Ref.	Debit	Credit	Balance Debit	Credit
Dec.	31	Balance				7,000	

Salaries Expense   Account No. 541

Date		Explanation	Post Ref.	Debit	Credit	Balance Debit	Credit
Dec.	31	Balance				2,000	

Depreciation Expense					Account No. 571	
Date	Explanation	Post Ref.	Debit	Credit	Balance Debit	Balance Credit
Dec. 31	Balance				1,000	

Required:

1. What is the purpose of a year-end trial balance?
2. Prepare a December 31, 1996, trial balance for this company.

33. 2 Trial Bal. total, $19,850

PROBLEM SET A

34. Journalizing and Posting Transactions (LO 4, 5)

Orlando opened a hair salon recently. During the first week he operated his new business, Orlando did not maintain a formal set of accounting records. Instead, he simply maintained a checkbook for the business. Following are the entries included in Orlando's checkbook for the period January 2–8.

January 2: Bank loan	$20,000
January 3: Rent to landlord	(500)
January 3: Hair styling fees earned	650
January 4: Bought inventory	(7,000)
January 4: Bought inventory	(3,500)
January 8: Hair styling fees earned	800

Required:

1. Prepare the necessary general journal entries for Orlando's Hair Salon for the period January 2–8.
2. Prepare T-accounts for Orlando's Hair Salon and post the journal entries for the period January 2–8 to these accounts. Compute the account balances as of January 8.
3. In a short memo to Orlando, explain why his current method of recordkeeping does not provide him with the information he needs to monitor and evaluate the financial status of his business.

34. 2. Cash bal., $10,450 Dr.
Inv. bal., $10,500 Dr.
N.P. bal., $20,000 Cr.
Fees Earn bal., $1,450 Cr.
Rent Exp. bal., $500 Dr.

35. Journal Entries and Analysis of Transactions (LO 4)

Price Gardening Supply had the following transactions during August:

1. Purchased four lawnmowers for $1,200
2. Purchased office supplies for $320
3. Paid income taxes of $400
4. Received $450 for lawn care services provided
5. Paid salaries of $500
6. Paid $1,000 of interest on a bank loan

Required:

1. Prepare general journal entries for these transactions of Price Gardening Supply.
2. You have presented the journal entries you prepared in Part 1 to the owner of Price Gardening Supply. He is concerned after reviewing them. He is convinced that each transaction is being double-counted. Write a short memo to the owner explaining why each entry requires at least one debit and one credit and why this procedure does not double-count the transactions.

35. 1. Dr. Inv. $1,200
3. Dr. Inv. Tax. Exp. $400
4. Cr. Serv. Rev. $450

36. Corrections of Accounting Errors (LO 1, 4)

Lispert Company's inexperienced bookkeeper puts question marks next to all journal entries he prepares if he is not certain that they are correct. Question marks appear next to each of the following entries.

1. Cash	2,000	
Accounts Receivable		2,000

   To record daily cash sales

2. Property, Plant & Equipment	800	
Cash		800

   To record purchase of office supplies for cash

3. Accounts Payable	100	
Cleaning Supplies		100

   To record purchase of cleaning supplies on credit; terms: balance due in 30 days

Required:

36. 2. 1. Dr. A.R. $2,000
      Cr. Sales $2,000
   2. Dr. Off. Sup. $800
      Cr. PP&E $800
   3. Dr. Clean. Sup. $200
      Cr. A.P. $200

1. Given each entry and its explanation, identify the nature of the error in the entry, if any, and how the entry should have appeared.
2. Given your responses to Part 1, prepare any necessary correcting entries.
3. Analyze each of the noted errors in reference to the accounting equation. How would these errors have affected the accounting equation for Lispert Company, if at all?

37. Trial Balance (LO 6)

Following are the general ledger account balances of Beckwith Construction as of April 30, 1996:

Cash	$ 25,000
Accounts Receivable	150,000
Inventory	150,000
Property, Plant & Equipment	425,000
Accumulated Depreciation,	
Property, Plant & Equipment	55,000
Accounts Payable	350,000
Income Taxes Payable	50,000
Common Stock	45,000
Retained Earnings	50,000
Sales Revenue	300,000
Operating Expenses	100,000

Required:

37. 1. Trial Bal. total, $850,000

1. Prepare a trial balance for Beckwith Construction as of April 30, 1996.
2. As you read in the text, the accounts of a company may contain errors even if a trial balance "balances." Provide a few examples of such errors.
3. What action(s) could the management of Beckwith Construction take to help ensure that its accounts are error-free? Write a brief memo to management describing your suggestions.

38. Accounting, Canadian Style (LO 3)

Bombardier, Inc., is a Canadian company that designs, manufactures, and distributes transportation equipment. Following is a listing of certain of the company's accounts that appeared in a recent set of financial statements.

	CLASSIFICATION	NORMAL BALANCE	INCREASES RECORDED AS
Term Deposits			
Revenues from Subsidiary			
Income Taxes Payable			
Accounts Receivable			
Fixed Assets			
Short-Term Borrowings			
Provision for Pension Costs			
Property under Lease			
Income Taxes			

Required:

Classify each of the listed accounts as one of the following: asset, liability, own-ers' equity, revenue, or expense. Also identify for each account what you would expect its "normal balance" (debit or credit) to be. Finally, indicate whether increases in each account would be recorded with debits or credits.

38. No check figures

39. **Journalizing, Posting, and Preparing a Trial Balance** (LO 4, 5, 6)

Georgian Enterprises uses the following accounts in its accounting system. The account number and balance as of January 1, 1996, are shown for each account.

	ACCOUNT NO.	BALANCE
Cash	101	$ 60,000
Supplies	121	10,000
Office Equipment	151	170,000
Accumulated Depreciation, Office Equipment	152	45,000
Accounts Payable	201	70,000
Common Stock	301	90,000
Retained Earnings	350	35,000
Fee Revenue	401	0
Selling Expenses	501	0
Salary Expense	511	0
Depreciation Expense	531	0

In January, 1996, Georgian Enterprises engaged in the following transactions:

1. Paid $30,000 on accounts payable
2. Purchased supplies of $1,100 for cash
3. Paid salaries of $5,200
4. Purchased office equipment for $2,700 cash
5. Earned and received fees (revenues) from customers of $16,400
6. Paid selling expenses of $7,100

Required:

1. Why do some of Georgian's accounts have zero balances at the beginning of January?
2. Prepare a journal entry for each of the transactions listed.
3. Set up four-column accounts for Georgian Enterprises as of January 1, 1996. Post the journal entries from Part 2 to these accounts.
4. Prepare a trial balance for Georgian Enterprises as of January 31, 1996.

39. 3. Cash bal., $30,300 Dr.
Sup. bal., $11,100 Dr.
Of. Equip. bal.,
$172,700 Dr.
Ac. Dep. bal., $45,000 Cr.
A.P. bal., $40,000 Cr.
Com. St. bal., $90,000 Cr.
R.E. bal., $35,000 Cr.
Fee Rev. bal., $16,400 Cr.
Sell Exp. bal., $7,100 Dr.
Sal. Exp. bal., $5,200 Dr.
Dep. Exp. bal., $0 Dr.
4. Trial Bal. total $226,400

PROBLEM SET B

40. **Journalizing and Posting Transactions** (LO 4, 5)

Priscilla recently opened a hair salon. Because she is unfamiliar with double-entry bookkeeping, Priscilla decided to maintain only a checkbook for her new business. Following are the entries made in this checkbook for the first week the new business was open.

April 2: Personal investment	$15,000
April 5: Paid assistant wages	(200)
April 6: Hair styling fees earned	900
April 6: Bought hair styling supplies	(800)
April 8: Bought store furniture	(4,000)
April 10: Hair styling fees earned	900

Required:

1. Prepare the necessary general journal entries for Priscilla's Hair Salon for the period April 2–10.
2. Prepare T-accounts for Priscilla's Hair Salon and post the journal entries from Part 1 into these accounts. Compute the account balances as of April 10.
3. In a short memo to Priscilla, explain why her current method of recordkeeping does not provide her with the information she needs to determine how well her business is doing financially.

41. **Journal Entries and Analysis of Transactions** (LO 4)

Laura's Flower Shop had the following transactions during August:

1. Paid $500 for newspaper ads
2. Purchased equipment for $3,500
3. Paid salaries of $500
4. Borrowed $5,000 from a local bank (signed a two-year note payable)
5. Received payment on account receivable from customer of $400
6. Paid utility bill of $90

Required:

1. Prepare general journal entries for Laura's Flower Shop for the transactions listed.
2. After reviewing the journal entries prepared in Part 1, Laura, the business's owner, is confused. Laura does not understand the meaning of the terms "debit" and "credit" nor how those items affect the recording of business transactions. Write a brief memo to Laura explaining the meaning and use of the terms "debit" and "credit" from an accounting standpoint.

42. **Correction of Accounting Errors** (LO 1, 4)

John's Towing Company has a new and inexperienced bookkeeper. The bookkeeper places a question mark next to a journal entry if she is uncertain that it is correct. Question marks appear next to each of the following entries.

1. Cash 300
   Interest Expense 300

   To record interest paid on a bank loan

2. Utilities Expense 100
   Cash 100

   To record payment of monthly electric bill

3. Office Supplies 200
   Cash 100

   To record purchase of office supplies for cash

Margin notes:

40. 2. Cash bal., $11,800 Dr.
Sup. bal., $800 Dr.
Furn. bal., $4,000 Dr.
Equity bal., $15,000 Cr.
Fees Earn. bal., $1,800 Cr.
Wages Exp. bal., $200 Dr.

41. 1. 1. Dr. Adv. Exp. $500
2. Dr. PP&E $3,500
4. Cr. N.P. $5,000
5. Cr. A.R. $400

Required:

1. Given each entry and its explanation, identify the nature of the error in the entry, if any, and how the entry should have appeared.
2. Given your responses to Part 1, prepare any necessary correcting entries.
3. Analyze each of the noted errors in reference to the accounting equation. How would these errors have affected the accounting equation for John's Towing Company, if at all?

42. 2. 1. Dr. Int. Exp. $600
Cr. Cash $600
3. Dr. Of. Sup. $100
Cr. Cash $100

43. **Trial Balance** (LO 6)

Following are the general ledger account balances of Goldblum's Mercantile as of June 30, 1996:

Cash	$10,000
Accounts Receivable	700
Inventory	3,000
Equipment	2,000
Accumulated Depreciation, Equipment	400
Accounts Payable	800
Income Taxes Payable	200
Common Stock	1,000
Retained Earnings	3,600
Sales Revenue	20,000
Operating Expenses	10,300

Required:

1. Prepare a trial balance for Goldblum's Mercantile as of June 30, 1996.
2. What is the purpose of a trial balance?
3. Identify errors that can cause a trial balance not to balance.

43. 1. Trial Bal. total, $26,000

44. **Accounting, British Style** (LO 3)

British Airways plc is a London-based airline. Following is a list of certain of the company's accounts that appeared in a recent set of financial statements.

	CLASSIFICATION	NORMAL BALANCE	INCREASES RECORDED AS
Fleet			
Trade Investments			
Convertible Capital Bonds			
Equipment			
Administrative Expenses			
Borrowings			
Profit and Loss Account			
Provisions for Liabilities and Charges			

Required:

Classify the listed accounts as one of the following: asset, liability, owners' equity, revenue, or expense. Also identify for each account what you would expect its "normal balance" (debit or credit) to be. Finally, indicate whether increases in each account would be recorded with debits or credits.

44. No check figures

45. **Journalizing, Posting, and Preparing a Trial Balance** (LO 4, 5, 6)

Mt. Horeb Company is a small real estate agency. The company uses the following accounts in its accounting system. The account number and balance as of January 1, 1996, are shown for each account.

	ACCOUNT NO.	BALANCE
Cash	101	$30,000
Supplies	131	4,000
Accounts Receivable	132	9,000
Office Equipment	152	36,000
Accumulated Depreciation,		
Office Equipment	153	35,000
Accounts Payable	201	9,000
Common Stock	301	10,000
Retained Earnings	350	25,000
Fee Revenue	401	0
Selling Expenses	501	0
Salary Expense	511	0
Depreciation Expense	531	0

45. 3. Cash bal., $28,400 Dr.
Sup. bal., $4,400 Dr.
A.R. bal., $9,000 Dr.
Of. Equip. bal.,
$36,000 Dr.
Ac. Dep. bal., $35,000 Cr.
A.P. bal., $6,500 Cr.
Com. St. bal., $10,000 Cr.
R.E. bal., $25,000 Cr.
Fee Rev. bal., $5,000 Cr.
Sell. Exp. bal., $1,100 Dr.
Sal. Exp. bal., $2,600 Dr.
Dep. Exp. bal., $0 Dr.
4. Trial Bal. total $81,500

In January, Mt. Horeb engaged in the following transactions:
1. Earned and received fees (real estate commissions) of $5,000
2. Purchased $400 of supplies for cash
3. Paid selling expenses of $1,100
4. Paid employee salaries of $2,600
5. Paid $2,500 on accounts payable

Required:
1. Why do some of Mt. Horeb's accounts have zero balances at the beginning of January?
2. Prepare journal entries to record Mt. Horeb's January 1996 transactions.
3. Set up four-column accounts for Mt. Horeb as of January 1, 1996, and then post the journal entries from Part 2 to the appropriate accounts.
4. Prepare a trial balance for Mt. Horeb as of January 31, 1996.

CASES

46. **Friends, Partners, and Accounting Records**
Mary Jane's Shoes is co-owned by Mary Johnson and Jane Kleven. Mary and Jane trust each other completely in all matters regarding the store. The two co-owners work at the store together Monday through Friday, while Mary works alone on Saturday. Mary also maintains the accounting records for the small business.

Recently, Mary has been going through some hard times financially. To help resolve her financial problems, Mary has been "skimming" receipts from the business each Saturday. Over the past several weeks, she has stolen approximately $5,000 from the business. So far, Mary has concealed the theft from Jane because Jane knows little about accounting and very seldom even reviews the accounting records.

Yesterday, Jane happened to pick up the most recent trial balance that Mary had prepared. Jane was shocked to see that the company's cash balance was so low since customer traffic and sales have been booming in recent weeks. She realizes that either the accounting records must be wrong or someone, almost certainly Mary, has been stealing cash from the business. Jane is concerned by the latter possibility because she knows her friend and partner has been experiencing significant financial problems recently.

Required:

1. Assume the role of Jane Kleven. What would you do at this point? Would you ask your friend directly regarding your suspicions? Would you take the accounting records to a local accountant and ask him or her to review them? What factors would you consider in making this decision?

2. At a minimum, what should a co-owner of a small business know about accounting and internal control issues to minimize the possibility of becoming involved in a situation similar to that facing Jane Kleven? Be specific.

47. Chart of Accounts

Your best friend, Chris, has just dropped out of college and gone into business for himself. Chris's new business, Pizzas to Go, is located across the street from your college campus. Chris enrolled in a course in financial accounting but dropped the course. Why? Because he did not believe he would ever make use of the material in the course. Chris has now come to you and asked that you help him set up an accounting system for his new business. To this point, he has only created a chart of accounts for Pizzas to Go. Following is his chart of accounts.

ACCOUNT NO.	ACCOUNT TITLE
1.	Accounts Payable
2.	Accounts Receivable
3.	Accumulated Depreciation, Equipment
4.	Cash
5.	Cleaning Supplies
6.	Delivery Fees
7.	Electricity
8.	Equipment
9.	Insurance
10.	Miscellaneous
11.	Taxes

Required:

Chris has asked you for suggestions regarding his chart of accounts. Review the chart of accounts and write a short memo to Chris recommending how he should change it. (Note: You may find it helpful to review the discussion of the nature and purpose of a chart of accounts in Chapter 3 before completing this case.)

48. "Debit" This

A college classmate who is enrolled in your financial accounting course recently received her monthly bank statement. When she opened the bank statement she discovered a "debit memo" for $12. This debit memo was for services the bank provided to her during the month. Your classmate is confused. "I don't understand this," she says. "Didn't our accounting instructor say that assets are increased with debits? Well, my checking account at the bank is an asset to me, yet there was this debit memo in my bank statement indicating that my account had been decreased by $12! What is going on here? Doesn't the bank know its debits from its credits?"

Required:

Write a brief memo to your classmate explaining the apparent inconsistency in the use of the term "debit."

PROJECTS

49. Accounting Terms Used by Foreign Companies

In this project, your project group will study the annual report of a foreign company to become acquainted with the differing account titles and other financial statement terms used by foreign companies compared with U.S. firms.

Required:

1. Obtain a recent annual report of a foreign company other than a Canadian firm. Each group member should review this annual report to become familiar with the company and its financial statements.
2. Meet as a group to discuss the selected annual report. The focus of your discussion should be the differing account titles and other financial statement terms used by the given company compared with the comparable terms you have been introduced to in this course and in other business courses. The group should attempt to determine the meaning of the unusual terms identified in the annual report. For example, "stocks" is a term found in many foreign annual reports. This term is usually synonymous with the term "inventory" in the annual reports of U.S. firms. To interpret unusual terms identified in the selected annual report, it will be helpful to refer to the financial statement footnotes included in the annual report and/or to other sources such as international accounting textbooks.
3. The group should prepare a written report that includes a brief description of the company whose annual report was selected for this project. This description should indicate where the company is located, the types of products it sells or services it provides, and so on. Also include in this report the unusual financial statement terms identified by the group in the annual report and the group's interpretation of the meaning of each of those terms.
4. One group member should be prepared to present a brief overview of the group's written report to the remainder of the class.

50. History of Accounting

Using an accounting history journal or other appropriate source, select and read an article dealing with the development and/or history of double-entry bookkeeping. (Your instructor may wish to assign several articles from which to choose.)

Required:

1. Identify and summarize the main points of the article and note its key contribution to your understanding of the historical development of accounting.
2. Prepare a brief report of your findings from Part 1 to be presented in class or turned in to your instructor.

51. Accounting for You

In this project, you will develop a chart of accounts that you could use to account for your personal financial affairs.

Required:

1. Identify the major categories of your personal assets. For example, your assets may include a car, a computer, a bike, and so on. You may "lump" similar assets into one category. For instance, you may define clothes as one of your asset categories. Similarly, identify your major types of liabilities, revenues, and expenses. Interest revenue, salaries or wages earned, college tuition, and utilities are examples of revenue and expense categories that you may define.

2. Develop a chart of accounts for your personal financial affairs using the information you developed in Part 1 and the organizational scheme discussed in Chapter 3 for a chart of accounts. You will need to include one "equity" account in your chart of accounts such as "Jennifer Doe, Net Worth."

3. Identify five recent financial transactions in which you have engaged, such as, payment of college tuition, purchase of a new car, and so on. Using the chart of accounts you developed and your knowledge of double-entry bookkeeping rules, prepare journal entries to record these five transactions.

5

THE ACCOUNTING CYCLE

LEARNING OBJECTIVES

After studying this chapter, you should be able to do the following:

1. Identify the nine steps in the accounting cycle

2. Prepare a work sheet

3. Develop period-ending adjustments to general ledger account balances

4. Prepare financial statements from a work sheet

5. Journalize and post adjusting entries

6. Journalize and post closing entries

7. Prepare a post-closing trial balance

It is best to do things systematically, since we are only human, and disorder is our worst enemy.
Hesiod

Keeping the Books for Uncle Sam: Accounting for Gridlock

The federal government requires publicly owned companies to maintain their accounting records on an accrual basis in conformity with generally accepted accounting principles (GAAP). Many of the procedures that these companies must perform in their monthly accounting cycles—the subject of this chapter—are necessary to ensure that the accrual basis of accounting is properly applied. If the federal government requires public companies to use accrual accounting, then it certainly imposes the same requirement on its hundreds of agencies. Right? Wrong.

Just like thousands of small "Mom and Pop" businesses, the enormous, multitrillion-dollar federal government employs cash-basis rather than accrual-basis accounting. Under this system of accounting, the federal government records revenues and expenses only when cash is received or paid. For example, assume that in 1998 the United States Navy invests $90 million in a battleship expected to be in service for thirty years. That $90 million investment will not be capitalized and treated as an asset in the federal government's accounting records. Instead, the $90 million will be written off completely as an expense in 1998. The same is true for other investments made by the federal government in interstate highways, administrative buildings, and so on.

The key objective of accounting is to provide decision makers with information they need to make informed judgments regarding the allocation of scarce economic resources. Deciding in which projects and programs to invest the huge tax revenues of the federal government is one of the most important responsibilities of the United States Congress. Unfortunately, Congress and other decision makers at the federal level are often hamstrung by the government's inadequate accounting system. For example, because the federal government uses cash-basis accounting, legislators are reluctant to fund programs that require large, up-front cash outlays even though these expenditures are economically justified. Instead, legislators are inclined to establish programs that require little up-front financing, although these programs may obligate the federal government to make large cash expenditures in the future.

Budgeting decisions at the federal level are also affected by a lack of reliable data regarding the federal government's true financial status. Take the case of the national debt. The size of the national debt is difficult, if not impossible, to determine given the federal government's outmoded accounting system. A recent study by an international accounting firm estimated that the reported national debt was understated by two to three trillion dollars, or by approximately 50 percent.[1] Given the absence of reliable financial data for the federal government, it is not surprising that Congress often suffers gridlock.

This chapter focuses exclusively on the accounting cycle, the set of recurring accounting procedures that must be completed for a business each accounting period. Even those of you who will not pursue a career in accounting need to understand how accounting data are collected, processed, summarized, and reported. Accounting data are central to many, if not most, major decisions made within organizations. Production supervisors, sales managers, and other nonaccountants who understand the accounting cycle are better prepared to "hold their ground" when accounting data are the central issue in important meetings with customers, bankers, and other parties.

Teaching Note
Remind students that the end product of the accounting cycle is a set of financial statements.

---

1. J. J. DioGuardi, *Unaccountable Congress* (Washington, D.C.: Regnery Gateway, 1992), 33.

THE ACCOUNTING CYCLE: AN OVERVIEW

In Chapter 3, an abbreviated version of the accounting cycle was discussed. Shown in Exhibit 5.1 is the complete accounting cycle and the documents or accounting records that are used or produced by accountants during each step of this cycle.

The accounting cycle begins with an analysis of a business's transactions. One purpose of this analysis is to identify the accounts affected by these transactions. Once these accounts have been identified, accountants must determine whether they were increased or decreased by the transactions and whether these increases or decreases should be recorded as debits or credits.

Most of the information needed by accountants to analyze business transactions is drawn from **source documents.** Source documents identify the key features or parameters of business transactions and thus minimize the potential for misunderstanding between the parties to those transactions. Among common types of source documents are invoices, bank statements, legal contracts, daily cash register tapes, checks, and purchase orders. Typically, there are multiple source documents for a business transaction. For example, a sales transaction may involve, among other documents, a purchase order, a sales order, and various shipping documents. A purchase order is prepared by a company buying goods and identifies the type, quantity, per unit price, and other pertinent information regarding those goods. A sales order contains much of the same information as a purchase order; however, a sales order is prepared by the company selling goods rather than purchasing them. Finally, a bill of lading is an example of a shipping document for a sales transaction. A bill of lading typically indicates the type and quantity of goods shipped and the date of the shipment.

In the next section of this chapter, we "walk" through the accounting cycle for a small company, Snow Mountain Retreat, which operates a bed and breakfast inn.

■ **EXHIBIT 5.1**
The Accounting Cycle

Accounting Activity	Document or Accounting Record
1. Analyze Transactions	Source Documents
2. Journalize Transactions	Journals
3. Post Journal Entries	General Ledger
4. Prepare Trial Balance	Work Sheet
5. Adjust the General Ledger Accounts	Work Sheet
6. Prepare Financial Statements	Financial Statements
7. Journalize and Post Adjusting Entries	Journals and General Ledger
8. Journalize and Post Closing Entries	Journals and General Ledger
9. Prepare Post-Closing Trial Balance	Post-Closing Trial Balance

The accounting cycle for a business such as Snow Mountain Retreat begins with an analysis of individual transactions each accounting period and concludes with the preparation of a post-closing trial balance. The principal product of the accounting cycle is a set of financial statements.

Shown in Exhibits 5.2 and 5.3 are examples of source documents for transactions of Snow Mountain Retreat. Exhibit 5.2 contains an invoice issued by Snow Mountain Retreat to bill a customer for a three-day stay, while Exhibit 5.3 contains an example of a purchase order. In subsequent chapters, you will become familiar with additional source documents as we consider a wide range of business transactions.

Once a transaction has been analyzed, the key information needed to prepare a journal entry is available. Posting of journal entries, the third step of the accounting cycle, involves transferring journal entry data to the appropriate general ledger accounts. In modern accounting systems, the first three steps of the accounting cycle are typically performed on a daily basis.

Quite often, accountants refer to "closing the books" at the end of the month. This closing process involves the final six steps of the accounting cycle shown in Exhibit 5.1. The initial step of the closing process is the preparation of a trial balance, sometimes referred to as a working trial balance. The final step of the closing process is the preparation of a post-closing trial balance. Between the preparation of these two trial balances, accountants adjust the general ledger accounts, prepare financial statements, and journalize and post both adjusting entries and closing entries. The most important product of the accounting cycle is a set of financial statements. Recall that publicly owned companies must submit annual as well as quarterly financial statements to the Securities and Exchange Commission (SEC). These financial statements are made available to the public. For the remaining months of the year, publicly owned companies usually prepare financial statements but only for internal decision makers.

Privately owned companies may prepare a formal set of financial statements only once per year. Typically, these financial statements are used in the preparation of income tax returns and are submitted to banks and other lending institutions.

Real World

During the closing process, a business's accounting department is extremely busy. Quite often, accountants must work overtime to complete the monthly closing process within the time constraints established by management.

■ **EXHIBIT 5.2**
Invoice Issued by Snow Mountain Retreat

Snow Mountain Retreat 1212 Fremont Road Castle Rock, Colorado 81302	INVOICE

	Invoice #: 4313 Date: 2/12/96 Customer ID: 999-21-0340

Bill To:

Mr. John W. William
326 Willow Drive
Murray, Oklahoma 73052

SALES REP	TERMS
Jessica Coleman	Balance due in 60 days

ITEM	UNITS	DESCRIPTION	UNIT PR	TOTAL
Hope Room, double occupancy	3 days	February 7–9, 1996	$125 per day	$ 375.00

	BAL DUE	$ 375.00

THE ACCOUNTING CYCLE ILLUSTRATED

As noted earlier, Snow Mountain Retreat, a small company that operates a bed and breakfast inn, is used in this chapter to illustrate the accounting cycle. This company is a corporation rather than a partnership or a sole proprietorship. Most accounting procedures for corporations, partnerships, and sole proprietorships are identical. However, there are differences across these three types of businesses in accounting for owners' equity. Chapter 15 will highlight some of these differences.

Shown in Exhibit 5.4 are Snow Mountain Retreat's transactions for the first month of its existence, January 1996. If we are to record the business transactions of this

■ **EXHIBIT 5.3**
Purchase Order of Snow Mountain Retreat

Snow Mountain Retreat	PURCHASE ORDER
1212 Fremont Road	
Castle Rock, Colorado 81302	

Date: March 6, 1996

To:

Charles Office Supplies
2412 Artesian Boulevard
Colorado Springs, Colorado 81406

Ship To:

Snow Mountain Retreat
1212 Fremont Road
Castle Rock, Colorado 81302

REQ BY	SHIP VIA	FOB	TERMS
Will Daniels	Barnes Delivery Service	Shipping Point	2/10, net/30

QTY	ITEM	DESCRIPTION	UNIT PR	TOTAL
6	A62-3	100-count boxes of fax forms	6.50	$ 39.00
2	C21-1	Imaging cartridges for laser printer	115.00	230.00

BAL DUE	$ 269.00

company, we need a chart of accounts. Snow Mountain Retreat's chart of accounts is shown in Exhibit 5.5.

Accounting Cycle, Step 1: Analyze Transactions

We begin our journey through Snow Mountain Retreat's accounting cycle by analyzing the company's January 1996 transactions. Accountants use their professional expertise to analyze business transactions and determine how they should be journal-

The SEC: Just Say No to Foreign Financial Statements

This chapter identifies and explains the key steps in the accounting cycle as applied by businesses in the United States. The principal product of the accounting cycle is a set of financial statements. Although the accounting cycle concept is used around the world, the resulting financial statements vary considerably from one country to the next, as suggested in earlier chapters. Why? Because accountants of different countries apply different accounting rules and procedures within the accounting cycle.

Companies in countries with significantly different accounting standards from those used in the United States are generally precluded from selling their common stock and other securities in this country. The Securities and Exchange Commission (SEC) has stubbornly resisted allowing foreign companies to "tap" the pocketbooks of U.S. investors unless these firms make certain modifications to their financial statements. This federal agency's principal concern is that U.S. citizens may be misled by the non-GAAP financial statements of foreign firms. The following table documents the number of European companies registered with the SEC and thus allowed to sell their securities in the United States as of March 1995.

United Kingdom	52
Netherlands	10
France	8
Spain	7
Italy	7
Sweden	6
Ireland	6
Norway	3
Portugal	2
Denmark	2
Germany	1

SOURCE: Gumbel, P. and G. Steinmetz, "German Firms Shift to More-Open Accounting," *The Wall Street Journal*, March 15, 1995, pp. C1 & C10. Reprinted by permission of *The Wall Street Journal*, © 1995 Dow Jones & Company, Inc. All Rights Reserved Worldwide.

ized. Here, we use a condensed version of the analytical format introduced in Chapter 4 to develop journal entries from transaction data. Following are Snow Mountain Retreat's transactions for January 1996 and the accompanying analyses.

Transaction 1, January 1: Snow Mountain Retreat was incorporated by its owners. Owners obtained a corporate charter and bought 4,000 shares of stock in Snow Mountain Retreat for $40,000. The par value of this stock is $10.

Account	Type	Increase/ Decrease	Debit or Credit	Amount
Cash	Asset	Increase	Debit	$40,000
Common Stock	Owners' Equity	Increase	Credit	40,000

Transaction 2, January 1: Rented a large, partially furnished four-bedroom house in Castle Rock, Colorado, to be operated as a bed and breakfast inn. Rent of $18,000 for one year was paid in cash.

■ **EXHIBIT 5.4**

Transactions of Snow Mountain Retreat during January 1996

1. January 1: Snow Mountain Retreat was incorporated by its owners. Owners obtained a corporate charter and bought 4,000 shares of stock in Snow Mountain Retreat for $40,000. The par value of this stock is $10 per share.
2. January 1: Owners rented large, partially furnished four-bedroom house in Castle Rock, Colorado, which will be operated as a bed and breakfast inn. Rent of $18,000 for one year was paid in cash.
3. January 1: Purchased one-year renter's insurance policy on rental property for $1,200.
4. January 1: Purchased furniture for $4,800, paying cash. The furniture is expected to have a useful life of two years and no salvage value at the end of its useful life.
5. January 3: Purchased $500 of supplies on credit.
6. January 8: Received $1,000 advance payment for two one-week rentals, January 22–28 and February 19–25.
7. January 19: Rented four rooms for the weekend, received cash of $1,500.
8. January 22: Rented two rooms for three-day stay, January 22–24, received cash of $750.
9. January 22: Paid part-time maintenance employee two-week salary of $400. Individual began working on January 8.
10. January 24: Rented one room for one week, received cash of $500.
11. January 26: Rented two rooms for weekend, received cash of $750.
12. January 30: Paid one-half of amount owed for supplies purchased on January 3.
13. January 31: Received $390 bill for utilities expenses for month of January.
14. January 31: Owners declared and paid themselves a dividend of $500.

■ **EXHIBIT 5.5**

Chart of Accounts for Snow Mountain Retreat

Balance Sheet Accounts		Income Statement Accounts	
101	Cash	401	Rental Revenue
102	Interest Receivable	402	Interest Revenue
103	Supplies	501	Rent Expense
104	Prepaid Rent	502	Salaries Expense
105	Prepaid Insurance	503	Utilities Expense
106	Furniture	504	Insurance Expense
107	Accumulated Depreciation,	505	Supplies Expense
	Furniture	506	Depreciation Expense, Furniture
201	Accounts Payable	507	Income Taxes Expense
202	Unearned Rental Revenue		
203	Salaries Payable		
204	Income Taxes Payable		
301	Common Stock		
302	Retained Earnings		
303	Dividends		
304	Income Summary		

Account	Type	Increase/ Decrease	Debit or Credit	Amount
Prepaid Rent	Asset	Increase	Debit	$18,000
Cash	Asset	Decrease	Credit	18,000

Transaction 3, January 1: Purchased one-year renter's insurance policy on rental property for $1,200.

Account	Type	Increase/ Decrease	Debit or Credit	Amount
Prepaid Insurance	Asset	Increase	Debit	$1,200
Cash	Asset	Decrease	Credit	1,200

Transaction 4, January 1: Purchased furniture for $4,800, paying cash. The furniture is expected to have a useful life of two years and no salvage value at the end of its useful life.

Account	Type	Increase/ Decrease	Debit or Credit	Amount
Furniture	Asset	Increase	Debit	$4,800
Cash	Asset	Decrease	Credit	4,800

Transaction 5, January 3: Purchased $500 of supplies on credit.

Account	Type	Increase/ Decrease	Debit or Credit	Amount
Supplies	Asset	Increase	Debit	$500
Accounts Payable	Liability	Increase	Credit	500

Transaction 6, January 8: Received $1,000 advance payment for two one-week rentals, January 22–28 and February 19–25. This advance payment was refundable in full if the reservations were canceled. (Note: Revenue received before it is earned is recorded in a liability account. In this case, an appropriate title for such a liability account is Unearned Rental Revenue.)

Account	Type	Increase/ Decrease	Debit or Credit	Amount
Cash	Asset	Increase	Debit	$1,000
Unearned Rental Revenue	Liability	Increase	Credit	$1,000

Transaction 7, January 19: Rented four rooms for the weekend, received cash of $1,500.

Account	Type	Increase/ Decrease	Debit or Credit	Amount
Cash	Asset	Increase	Debit	$1,500
Rental Revenue	Revenue	Increase	Credit	1,500

Transaction 8, January 22: Rented two rooms for January 22–24, received cash of $750.

Account	Type	Increase/ Decrease	Debit or Credit	Amount
Cash	Asset	Increase	Debit	$750
Rental Revenue	Revenue	Increase	Credit	750

Transaction 9, January 22: Paid part-time maintenance employee two-week salary of $400. Individual began working on January 8.

Account	Type	Increase/ Decrease	Debit or Credit	Amount
Salaries Expense	Expense	Increase	Debit	$400
Cash	Asset	Decrease	Credit	400

Transaction 10, January 24: Rented one room for one week, received cash of $500.

Account	Type	Increase/ Decrease	Debit or Credit	Amount
Cash	Asset	Increase	Debit	$500
Rental Revenue	Revenue	Increase	Credit	500

Transaction 11, January 26: Rented two rooms for weekend, received cash of $750.

Account	Type	Increase/ Decrease	Debit or Credit	Amount
Cash	Asset	Increase	Debit	$750
Rental Revenue	Revenue	Increase	Credit	750

Transaction 12, January 30: Paid $250 of the $500 owed for the supplies purchased on January 3.

Account	Type	Increase/ Decrease	Debit or Credit	Amount
Accounts Payable	Liability	Decrease	Debit	$250
Cash	Asset	Decrease	Credit	250

Transaction 13, January 31: Received $390 bill for utilities expenses for month of January.

Account	Type	Increase/ Decrease	Debit or Credit	Amount
Utilities Expense	Expense	Increase	Debit	$390
Accounts Payable	Liability	Increase	Credit	390

Transaction 14, January 31: Owners declared and paid themselves a dividend of $500. (Note: Recall from Chapter 4 that Dividends is a temporary account. More specifically, Dividends is a temporary contra owners' equity account. Also recall that the bookkeeping rules for Dividends are identical to those for expense accounts.)

Account	Type	Increase/ Decrease	Debit or Credit	Amount
Dividends	Owners' Equity	Increase	Debit	$500
Cash	Asset	Decrease	Credit	500

Accounting Cycle, Step 2: Journalize Transactions

The second step of the accounting cycle is the journalizing of transactions. In Chapter 4, the six specific steps to follow in preparing a journal entry were identified. Applying these steps to the January 1996 transactions of Snow Mountain Retreat results in the general journal entries shown in Exhibit 5.6.

Accounting Cycle, Step 3: Post Journal Entries

The third step of the accounting cycle is the posting of journal entries to the general ledger accounts. Recall that a principal purpose of posting accounting data from journals to the general ledger is to summarize that data so that financial statements can be more easily prepared at the end of each accounting period. The specific steps to follow in posting data from the general journal to the general ledger were listed in Chapter 4.

■ **EXHIBIT 5.6**

General Journal Entries for Snow Mountain Retreat, January 1996

		General Journal			Page 1
Date		Description	Post Ref.	Debit	Credit
1996 Jan.	1	Cash Common Stock		40,000	40,000
		Purchase of 4,000 shares of Snow Mountain Retreat stock by company owners			
	1	Prepaid Rent Cash		18,000	18,000
		Paid one year's rent in advance on rental property			
	1	Prepaid Insurance Cash		1,200	1,200
		Purchased one-year insurance policy on rental property			
	1	Furniture Cash		4,800	4,800
		Purchased furniture			
	3	Supplies Accounts Payable		500	500
		Purchased supplies on credit			
	8	Cash Unearned Rental Revenue		1,000	1,000
		Received advance payment for two one-week rentals			
	19	Cash Rental Revenue		1,500	1,500
		Received payment for weekend rentals of four rooms			
	22	Cash Rental Revenue		750	750
		Received payment for two three-day rentals			

■ **EXHIBIT 5.6**
(Continued)

	General Journal			Page 1
Date	**Description**	**Post Ref.**	**Debit**	**Credit**
22	Salaries Expense		400	
	Cash			400
	Paid two-week salary of maintenance employee			
24	Cash		500	
	Rental Revenue			500
	Received payment for one-week rental			
26	Cash		750	
	Rental Revenue			750
	Received payment for weekend rentals of two rooms			
30	Accounts Payable		250	
	Cash			250
	Paid one-half of amount due on January 3 purchase of supplies			
31	Utilities Expense		390	
	Accounts Payable			390
	Received bill for January utilities expenses			
31	Dividends		500	
	Cash			500
	Declared and paid dividend			

Shown in Exhibit 5.7 are the individual accounts of Snow Mountain Retreat after the journal entry data were posted to the general ledger. In Exhibit 5.8 (p. 169), the company's general journal entries for January are listed again. Notice that in Exhibit 5.8 the appropriate account numbers are included in the post-reference column indicating that the journal entries have been posted to the general ledger.

Teaching Note
Posting references are an important part of the audit trail created for business transactions in an accounting system.

Accounting Cycle, Step 4: Prepare Trial Balance

To begin the process of closing the books at the end of an accounting period, accountants prepare a trial balance of a business's general ledger accounts. As you learned in

■ **EXHIBIT 5.7**
General Ledger Accounts of Snow Mountain Retreat Following Posting of January 1996 Transactions

Cash							Account No. 101
			Post			**Balance**	
Date	**Explanation**		**Ref.**	**Debit**	**Credit**	**Debit**	**Credit**
1996							
Jan. 1			GJ1	40,000		40,000	
1			GJ1		18,000	22,000	
1			GJ1		1,200	20,800	
1			GJ1		4,800	16,000	
8			GJ1	1,000		17,000	
19			GJ1	1,500		18,500	
22			GJ1	750		19,250	
22			GJ1		400	18,850	
24			GJ1	500		19,350	
26			GJ1	750		20,100	
30			GJ1		250	19,850	
31			GJ1		500	19,350	

Supplies							Account No. 103
			Post			**Balance**	
Date	**Explanation**		**Ref.**	**Debit**	**Credit**	**Debit**	**Credit**
1996							
Jan. 3			GJ1	500		500	

Prepaid Rent							Account No. 104
			Post			**Balance**	
Date	**Explanation**		**Ref.**	**Debit**	**Credit**	**Debit**	**Credit**
1996							
Jan. 1			GJ1	18,000		18,000	

Prepaid Insurance							Account No. 105
			Post			**Balance**	
Date	**Explanation**		**Ref.**	**Debit**	**Credit**	**Debit**	**Credit**
1996							
Jan. 1			GJ1	1,200		1,200	

Furniture							Account No. 106
			Post			**Balance**	
Date	**Explanation**		**Ref.**	**Debit**	**Credit**	**Debit**	**Credit**
1996							
Jan. 1			GJ1	4,800		4,800	

■ **EXHIBIT 5.7**
(Continued)

Accounts Payable — Account No. 201

Date		Explanation	Post Ref.	Debit	Credit	Balance Debit	Balance Credit
1996 Jan.	3		GJ1		500		500
	30		GJ1	250			250
	31		GJ1		390		640

Unearned Rental Revenue — Account No. 202

Date		Explanation	Post Ref.	Debit	Credit	Balance Debit	Balance Credit
1996 Jan.	8		GJ1		1,000		1,000

Common Stock — Account No. 301

Date		Explanation	Post Ref.	Debit	Credit	Balance Debit	Balance Credit
1996 Jan.	1		GJ1		40,000		40,000

Dividends — Account No. 303

Date		Explanation	Post Ref.	Debit	Credit	Balance Debit	Balance Credit
1996 Jan.	31		GJ1	500		500	

Rental Revenue — Account No. 401

Date		Explanation	Post Ref.	Debit	Credit	Balance Debit	Balance Credit
1996 Jan.	19		GJ1		1,500		1,500
	22		GJ1		750		2,250
	24		GJ1		500		2,750
	26		GJ1		750		3,500

(Exhibit 5.7 continues)

■ **EXHIBIT 5.7**
(Continued)

Salaries Expense						Account No. 502	
Date	Explanation	Post Ref.	Debit	Credit	Balance Debit	Credit
1996 Jan. 22		GJ1	400		400	

Utilities Expense						Account No. 503	
Date	Explanation	Post Ref.	Debit	Credit	Balance Debit	Credit
1996 Jan. 31		GJ1	390		390	

■ LEARNING
OBJECTIVE 2
Prepare a work sheet

Teaching Note
Point out the benefits of using a
computer-based spreadsheet
package to prepare a work sheet.

Teaching Note
Point out that it is not necessary
to prepare a trial balance
independent of the work sheet.
The original trial balance can be
prepared directly on the work
sheet.

■ LEARNING
OBJECTIVE 3
Develop period-ending
adjustments to general ledger
account balances

Teaching Note
Emphasize that adjusting
journal entries help ensure that
an entity's financial statements
have been prepared in
conformity with generally
accepted accounting principles
(GAAP).

Chapter 4, a trial balance is a two-column listing of general ledger account balances, one column for accounts with debit balances and another column for accounts with credit balances. A primary purpose of a trial balance is to determine whether journalizing or posting errors have resulted in unequal debits and credits being entered in the accounting records. Accountants want to uncover and correct any such errors before they prepare period-ending financial statements for a business.

Accountants can use a work sheet to assist them in closing a business's accounting records at the end of an accounting period. We will use the work sheet shown in Exhibit 5.9 to close Snow Mountain Retreat's accounting records at the end of January 1996. The format of a work sheet varies from company to company, but the ten-column version—eleven if you count the first column—illustrated in Exhibit 5.9 (p. 172) is probably the most common. Accountants enter the trial balance of a business's general ledger in the first two columns of a work sheet. The account balances included in the trial balance in Exhibit 5.9 were taken from the general ledger accounts of Snow Mountain Retreat listed in Exhibit 5.7. Notice that only those general ledger accounts that have nonzero balances are included in a trial balance. If you refer to Exhibit 5.5, you will find that Snow Mountain Retreat had several accounts that had not been used during January 1996, at least to the point that the trial balance shown in Exhibit 5.9 was prepared.

Accounting Cycle, Step 5: Adjust the General Ledger Accounts

At the end of each accounting period, many general ledger account balances of a business must be adjusted. These adjustments are necessary to ensure that all of the revenues and expenses of a business are recognized (recorded) each accounting period. If appropriate adjusting journal entries are not entered in a business's accounting records, the revenue recognition rule and/or the expense recognition rule discussed in Chapter 2 will be violated.

THE FOUR TYPES OF PERIOD-ENDING ADJUSTMENTS Accountants must identify the specific circumstances and events that require adjustments to a business's

■ **EXHIBIT 5.8**
General Journal Entries for Snow Mountain Retreat, January 1996
Following the Posting of These Entries to the General Ledger

				General Journal			Page 1
Date			**Description**	**Post Ref.**	**Debit**	**Credit**
1996 Jan.	1		Cash	101	40,000	
			Common Stock	301		40,000
			Purchase of 4,000 shares of Snow Mountain Retreat stock by company owners			
	1		Prepaid Rent	104	18,000	
			Cash	101		18,000
			Paid one year's rent in advance on rental property			
	1		Prepaid Insurance	105	1,200	
			Cash	101		1,200
			Purchased one-year insurance policy on rental property			
	1		Furniture	106	4,800	
			Cash	101		4,800
			Purchased furniture			
	3		Supplies	103	500	
			Accounts Payable	201		500
			Purchased supplies on credit			
	8		Cash	101	1,000	
			Unearned Rental Revenue	202		1,000
			Received advance payment for two one-week rentals			
	19		Cash	101	1,500	
			Rental Revenue	401		1,500
			Received payment for weekend rentals of four rooms			
	22		Cash	101	750	
			Rental Revenue	401		750
			Received payment for two three-day rentals			

(Exhibit 5.8 continues)

■ **EXHIBIT 5.8**
(Continued)

	General Journal				Page 1
Date	**Description**	**Post Ref.**	**Debit**		**Credit**
22	Salaries Expense	502	400		
	Cash	101			400
	Paid two-week salary of maintenance employee				
24	Cash	101	500		
	Rental Revenue	401			500
	Received payment for one-week rental				
26	Cash	101	750		
	Rental Revenue	401			750
	Received payment for weekend rentals of two rooms				
30	Accounts Payable	201	250		
	Cash	101			250
	Paid one-half of amount due on January 3 purchase of supplies				
31	Utilities Expense	503	390		
	Accounts Payable	201			390
	Received bill for January utilities expenses				
31	Dividends	303	500		
	Cash	101			500
	Declared and paid dividend				

Focus on Ethics

Individuals within a company may pressure accountants to inaccurately record accruals and deferrals to make the company's financial statements more impressive. Typically, accountants are pressured to either "speed up" the recognition of revenues or delay the recognition of expenses. How should accountants deal with this kind of pressure?

general ledger account balances at the end of an accounting period. Accountants identify such items by talking to management, scanning the accounting records, reviewing prior periods' adjusting entries, and, most important, using their intuition and accounting expertise. The following are the four general types of adjustments to general ledger accounts that are required at the end of an accounting period.

1. Recognition of expenses related to a business's assets. Example: depreciation expense on property, plant and equipment.
2. Recognition of revenues related to a business's liabilities. Example: advance payments of revenues by customers that have been earned by the end of an accounting period.

Beyond the Accounting Cycle: "Nonaccounting" Information Needs of Decision Makers

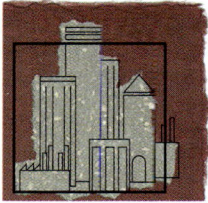

Accountants collect, process, summarize, and then report in financial statements data needed by decision makers to make informed decisions regarding the allocation of scarce resources. However, much of the information that decision makers need does not necessarily "fit" into any of the four financial statements. Typically, the accountants of an organization have the responsibility for designing methods of capturing and communicating the full range of information needed by decision makers. Following are examples of important data items drawn from recent annual reports of public companies—data items that were not included in these companies' financial statements.

American Greetings Corporation closely monitors the greeting card buying habits of the public. This company's 1994 annual report disclosed that individuals from fifty-five to sixty-four years old buy more greeting cards than any other age group. This age group buys nearly fifty-five greeting cards per year, while individuals who are twenty-five to thirty-four years old buy approximately thirty-eight greeting cards per year. These data assist American Greetings in deciding how to allocate its advertising expenditures.

Eateries, Inc., a restaurant chain based in Oklahoma City, collects data regarding its average lunch check, dinner check, "table turn," and the percentage of meal checks that consists of purchases of alcoholic beverages. These data allow management to make more informed decisions regarding such matters as the items to include on lunch and dinner menus. The company's average lunch check per person is $7.17, and sales of alcoholic beverages account for 24 percent of the company's revenues.

Circuit City Stores, Inc., retails a wide range of home appliances and electronic products. In its 1994 annual report, the company disclosed the market share that it controls for three major product lines: audio/video, major appliances, and telecommunications. In the geographical areas in which its stores are located, Circuit City accounts for approximately 20 percent of audio/video sales, 11 percent of the sales of major home appliances, and 9 percent of the sales of telecommunications products. This information allows Circuit City's executives and investors to monitor how effectively the company is competing against other companies in its industry.

The most important asset of service companies is their employees. These companies constantly evaluate whether their employees are being utilized efficiently and effectively. In 1992, the Charles Schwab Corporation, a large retail brokerage firm, had total revenues per employee of $166,200 versus $150,000 per employee the prior year. Schwab processed 5.56 transactions per customer account in 1992 and earned an average commission of $75.71 on these transactions.

3. Recognition of expenses incurred but not yet paid at the end of an accounting period. Example: unpaid wages that employees have earned at the end of an accounting period.
4. Recognition of revenues earned but not yet received. Example: interest revenue earned on bank accounts but not yet received.

One important fact to store away in your memory bank is that each journal entry resulting from a period-ending adjustment involves at least one income statement account and at least one balance sheet account. For example, an adjusting journal

■ **EXHIBIT 5.9**

Snow Mountain Retreat Work Sheet for the Month Ended January 31, 1996

	SNOW MOUNTAIN RETREAT WORK SHEET FOR THE MONTH ENDED JANUARY 31, 1996									
	Trial Balance		Adjustments		Adjusted Trial Balance		Income Statement		Balance Sheet	
Account Title	**Debit**	**Credit**	**Debit**	**Credit**	**Debit**	**Credit**	**Debit**	**Credit**	**Debit**	**Credit**
Cash	19,350									
Supplies	500									
Prepaid Rent	18,000									
Prepaid Insurance	1,200									
Furniture	4,800									
Accounts Payable		640								
Unearned Rental Revenue		1,000								
Common Stock		40,000								
Dividends	500									
Rental Revenue		3,500								
Salaries Expense	400									
Utilities Expense	390									
	45,140	45,140								

entry to record depreciation involves a debit to Depreciation Expense and a credit to Accumulated Depreciation, a contra asset account appearing on the balance sheet.

DEFERRALS AND ACCRUALS   Before we analyze the period-ending adjustments for Snow Mountain Retreat, it will be helpful to define several terms that accountants frequently use when referring to these adjustments. Assets such as prepaid rent and liabilities such as unearned rental revenue are often referred to as deferrals or, more specifically, as deferred expenses and deferred revenues, respectively. A **deferred expense** is an asset that represents a prepayment of an expense item. When a deferred expense is paid (prepaid), an asset account is debited and the Cash account credited. For example, when rent is prepaid for a six-month period, the appropriate entry would be to debit Prepaid Rent and credit Cash. At the end of this six-month period, the economic benefit of the rent prepayment has expired. As a result, the amount of the prepayment should be debited to Rent Expense with an equal credit to Prepaid Rent. At the risk of being redundant, do not be misled by the phrase "deferred *expense.*" This term refers to an asset, *not* an expense. Granted, such assets are eventually recognized or written off as expenses. But when they are initially recorded, these items are assets.[2]

deferred expense

2. Although not discussed here, you should be aware that there is an alternative approach to recording deferred expenses. Some businesses debit these expenses directly to expense accounts when they are paid. This is an acceptable accounting method as long as the appropriate adjusting entry is made at the end of an accounting period to record the "unexpired" portions of these items as assets. Similarly, deferred revenues, discussed shortly, may be recorded directly to revenue accounts as long as the appropriate adjusting entries are made at the end of each accounting period.

The terms "deferred expense" and "prepaid expense" are interchangeable. When these items are incorporated in a balance sheet, they are most often referred to as prepaid expenses. Many companies consolidate several deferred expenses into a single balance sheet amount, as suggested in Chapter 2. For instance, Big Rock Brewery, a small brewing company headquartered in Calgary, Alberta, reported $72,763 of "Prepaid Expenses" in a recent balance sheet.

deferred revenue

A **deferred revenue** is a liability resulting from an amount paid to a business for a service or product that it will provide or deliver in the future. When the earnings process is completed, a deferred revenue account is debited with an offsetting credit to a revenue account. The Unearned Rental Revenue account of Snow Mountain Retreat is an example of a deferred revenue account. Why are deferred revenues treated as liabilities for balance sheet purposes? Because they are, in fact, liabilities: something is owed to the customer, either a product or a service or a refund. For example, although there are exceptions,

amounts paid in advance on hotel, airline, and other reservations are generally refundable to customers if the reservations are canceled. In a recent annual report, Southwest Airlines reported a $42 million deferred revenue liability. This amount represented payments received for tickets purchased in advance. Southwest Airlines included this liability in the current liabilities section of its balance sheet on a line item labeled "Air Traffic Liability."

Airline passengers typically purchase their tickets several days or weeks in advance of taking a flight. Advance payments for airline tickets must be reported as current liabilities in the balance sheets of airline companies.

Accountants use the term "accruals" to refer to asset and liability accounts that are entered in a business's accounting records as a result of period-ending adjusting journal entries. Accrued revenues and accrued expenses are the more specific terms used to refer to these asset and liability items, respectively. An **accrued revenue** is a receivable resulting from revenue that has been earned but not yet received. At the end of fiscal 1993, Morgan Stanley, a large investment banking company, reported Fees Receivable of more than $291 million on its balance sheet. The total of this accrued revenue account represented fees for services that Morgan Stanley had provided to customers but which it had not collected by the end of 1993. The offsetting credit for the $291 million debit to Fees Receivable was to a revenue account such as Fees Earned.

accrued revenue

Teaching Note
Deferred revenues are not recognized even though the cash has been received; deferred expenses are not recognized even though the cash has been paid.

Teaching Note
Southwest's deferred revenue liability represents an obligation to provide transportation services in the future.

Accrued expenses were defined in Chapter 2 as current liabilities related to obligations incurred near the end of an accounting period. As noted in Chapter 2, a synonymous term for accrued expenses is accrued liabilities. A common accrued expense is salaries payable. The end of a company's accounting period often does not coincide with the end of a payroll period. As a result, the company's employees have earned salaries or wages at the end of an accounting period for which they have not been paid. These amounts are recognized via an adjusting entry by debiting an expense account, such as Salaries Expense, and crediting a liability account, such as Salaries Payable. Again, do not be confused by the term "accrued *expense.*" An accrued expense is a liability, *not* an expense. Granted, when an accrued expense is recorded, the offsetting debit is to an expense account.

Teaching Note
Accrued revenues are recognized before any cash is received; accrued expenses are recognized before any cash is paid.

ADJUSTING JOURNAL ENTRIES FOR SNOW MOUNTAIN RETREAT   Now that we have become familiar with the purpose, types, and terminology associated with adjusting journal entries, we can go about the task of adjusting the general ledger accounts of Snow Mountain Retreat. Following are eight events or circumstances requiring adjustments to the company's general ledger account balances as of January 31, 1996. Since period-ending general ledger adjustments can be difficult for accountants-in-training to grasp, these eight items are analyzed by using the detailed format employed in Chapter 4 to acquaint you with the journalizing process.

ADJUSTMENT A: Expiration of Prepaid Rent

At the beginning of January 1996, the owners of Snow Mountain Retreat paid one year's rent, $18,000, in advance on the four-bedroom house used in their bed and breakfast inn business. By the end of January, one-twelfth, or $1,500, of this prepaid expense had been "used up," since one month of the twelve-month term of the lease had expired. The decrease in this prepaid expense should be recognized so that the company's assets are not overstated. Likewise, to satisfy the matching principle, an expense equal to the decline in the balance of the Prepaid Rent account should be recorded. This expense was one of many that the company's owners incurred to generate revenue during January 1996.

To decrease the balance of the Prepaid Rent account, an asset account, it must be credited. The offsetting debit is to Rent Expense, an expense account. Technically, the owners of Snow Mountain Retreat incurred rent expense on a daily basis. However, it is not practical to adjust the general ledger accounts each day. Consequently, the balance of the Prepaid Rent account is adjusted only at the end of each month.

Discussion Question
Suppose that Snow Mountain Retreat failed to make this adjusting journal entry. What would be the impact on the company's financial statements? Answer: Assets, net income, and owners' equity would be overstated.

Analysis:

Account	Type	Increase/ Decrease	Debit or Credit	Amount
Rent Expense	Expense	Increase	Debit	$1,500
Prepaid Rent	Asset	Decrease	Credit	1,500

Effect on Accounting Equation:

Assets	=	Liabilities	+	Owners' Equity
−1,500				−1,500

Journal Entry:

Rent Expense	1,500	
Prepaid Rent		1,500

ADJUSTMENT B: Expiration of Prepaid Insurance

At the beginning of January 1996, the owners of Snow Mountain Retreat paid $1,200 for a one-year renter's insurance policy. As was true for the rent pre-payment, one-twelfth of this asset had been used up, or consumed, by the end of January. An economist might say that $100 of the economic utility or economic benefit associated with the $1,200 insurance prepayment had expired by January 31. Again, the matching principle dictates that the decrease in this asset be recognized as an expense and thus matched with the rental revenue generated during January 1996.

Analysis:

Account	Type	Increase/ Decrease	Debit or Credit	Amount
Insurance Expense	Expense	Increase	Debit	$100
Prepaid Insurance	Asset	Decrease	Credit	100

Effect on Accounting Equation:

Assets	=	Liabilities	+	Owners' Equity
−100				−100

Journal Entry:

Insurance Expense	100	
Prepaid Insurance		100

ADJUSTMENT C: Depreciation of Furniture

On January 1, 1996, the owners of Snow Mountain Retreat purchased furniture at a cost of $4,800 to place in their rental property. Recall from Chapter 2 that long-lived assets such as buildings, equipment, and furniture must be depreciated. Also recall that depreciation is the process of systematically allocating the cost of assets to the accounting periods that they provide an economic benefit to a business. There are several alternative methods of computing depreciation. One common depreciation method is the straight-line method, the method adopted by Snow Mountain Retreat. Under this method, the depreciable cost of an asset, total cost less any estimated salvage value at the end of its useful life, is written off in equal amounts to the accounting periods that the asset is expected to be in service.

The depreciable cost of the furniture purchased by Snow Mountain Retreat is $4,800: purchase cost of $4,800 less a zero estimated salvage value. Since the furniture is estimated to have a useful life of two years or twenty-four months, depreciation expense of $200 ($4,800/24) should be recognized each monthly accounting period on this asset. Recall that the offsetting credit to depreciation expense is not made directly to the account of the asset being depreciated. Instead, this credit is recorded in a contra asset account, Accumulated Depreciation, so that the historical cost of the asset is preserved or maintained in its general ledger account.

Real World
Students may think that accounting is a very precise, accurate process. Point out that depreciation is one of many estimates that accountants must make.

Analysis:

Account	Type	Increase/ Decrease	Debit or Credit	Amount
Depreciation Expense, Furniture	Expense	Increase	Debit	$200
Accumulated Depreciation, Furniture	Contra Asset	Increase	Credit	200

Effect on Accounting Equation:

Assets	=	Liabilities	+	Owners' Equity
−200				−200

Discussion Question
When a company pays expenses, a check is usually issued. Who receives the check for depreciation expense? Answer: There is no check. Depreciation is a non-cash expense.

Journal Entry:

Depreciation Expense, Furniture	200	
Accumulated Depreciation, Furniture		200

ADJUSTMENT D: Consumption of Supplies

At the end of January 1996, the owners of Snow Mountain Retreat counted or "inventoried" the business's supplies. As a result, the owners determined that $80 of the $500 of supplies purchased earlier in the month were used during January.

Analysis:

Account	Type	Increase/ Decrease	Debit or Credit	Amount
Supplies Expense	Expense	Increase	Debit	$80
Supplies	Asset	Decrease	Credit	80

Effect on Accounting Equation:

Assets	=	Liabilities	+	Owners' Equity
−80				−80

Journal Entry:

Supplies Expense	80	
Supplies		80

ADJUSTMENT E: Recognition of Portion of Advance Rental Payment Earned during January 1996

On January 8, 1996, an individual paid $1,000 to Snow Mountain Retreat for two one-week room rentals, January 22–28 and February 19–25. When this amount was received, an entry debiting Cash for $1,000 and crediting the liability account Unearned Rental Revenue for the same amount was made. By the end of January, one-half of this $1,000 advance payment had been earned by Snow Mountain Retreat, since the customer had used her reservation for the week of January 22–28. To recognize this revenue, the Rental Revenue account must be credited $500 with an offsetting debit in the same amount to Unearned Rental Revenue.

Analysis:

Account	Type	Increase/ Decrease	Debit or Credit	Amount
Unearned Rental Revenue	Liability	Decrease	Debit	$500
Rental Revenue	Revenue	Increase	Credit	500

Effect on Accounting Equation:

Assets	=	Liabilities	+	Owners' Equity
		−500		+ 500

Real World
The preparation of adjusting journal entries typically requires the expertise of an accountant. Normal, recurring transactions are often recorded by a bookkeeper or an accounting clerk.

Journal Entry:

Unearned Rental Revenue	500	
Rental Revenue		500

ADJUSTMENT F: Recognition of Interest Revenue

During January 1996, Snow Mountain Retreat had cash on deposit in a bank account. By the end of the month, the company had earned interest revenue of $120 on this bank account, interest that had not been paid to Snow

Mountain Retreat. To recognize this revenue, Interest Revenue is credited $120 with an equal debit to the asset account Interest Receivable.

Teaching Note
Interest revenue accumulates with the passage of time. The longer the bank has your money, the more interest you receive.

Analysis:

Account	Type	Increase/ Decrease	Debit or Credit	Amount
Interest Receivable	Asset	Increase	Debit	$120
Interest Revenue	Revenue	Increase	Credit	120

Effect on Accounting Equation:

Assets	=	Liabilities	+	Owners' Equity
+ 120				+ 120

Journal Entry:

Interest Receivable   120
    Interest Revenue   120

ADJUSTMENT G: Recognition of Unpaid Salary at the End of January
On January 8, 1996, the owners of Snow Mountain Retreat hired a part-time maintenance employee. This individual is paid $400 every two weeks, which translates to $40 per day for Monday through Friday. (For the time being, we ignore payroll taxes and other deductions that affect the employee's take-home pay.) The employee received his first paycheck on January 22 and is scheduled to receive his second paycheck on February 5. As of January 31, the employee had worked eight days for which he had not yet been paid (January 22–26 and January 29–31), meaning that Snow Mountain Retreat owed this individual $320 at the end of January. Likewise, the company had an unrecorded expense in the same amount.

Analysis:

Account	Type	Increase/ Decrease	Debit or Credit	Amount
Salaries Expense	Expense	Increase	Debit	$320
Salaries Payable	Liability	Increase	Credit	320

Effect on Accounting Equation:

Assets	=	Liabilities	+	Owners' Equity
		+ 320		−320

Journal Entry:

Salaries Expense   320
    Salaries Payable   320

ADJUSTMENT H: Recognition of Estimated Income Tax Expense
At the end of each year, Snow Mountain Retreat is required to pay a corporate income tax on any profit that it earns during that year. On January 31, 1996, the owners of Snow Mountain Retreat did not know how much their company would earn during 1996. Consequently, they could not determine exactly how much income tax, if any, the company would be required to pay at the end of the year. Nevertheless, a business must estimate its income tax expense each accounting period because of the expense recognition rule. The owners of Snow Mountain Retreat estimated that $200 in corporate income tax would eventually be paid on the profit earned by the company during January.

Analysis:

Account	Type	Increase/ Decrease	Debit or Credit	Amount
Income Taxes Expense	Expense	Increase	Debit	$200
Income Taxes Payable	Liability	Increase	Credit	200

Effect on Accounting Equation:

Assets	=	Liabilities	+	Stockholders' Equity
		+ 200		−200

Journal Entry:

Income Taxes Expense	200	
Income Taxes Payable		200

UPDATING SNOW MOUNTAIN RETREAT'S WORK SHEET   Now that we have analyzed the period-ending adjustments for Snow Mountain Retreat's general ledger accounts, we can update the work sheet shown in Exhibit 5.9. Each adjustment is entered in the Adjustments columns of the work sheet, as illustrated in Exhibit 5.10. If an account affected by an adjustment is not included in the original trial balance listed on the work sheet, the title of that account is entered below the accounts that were included in the trial balance.

To minimize the likelihood of errors on the work sheet, accountants code each adjustment. In this case, the adjustments are coded with the alphabetical references that were used to label them in the prior section. For example, notice in Exhibit 5.10 that adjustment "a" involves the $1,500 debit to the Rent Expense account and the equal credit to the Prepaid Rent account. After entering all of the adjustments on the work sheet, the debit and credit Adjustments columns are "footed"—an accounting term that means to add a column of numbers—and the totals are entered at the bottom of those columns. If these two totals are unequal, an error has been made in developing the adjustments or entering them on the work sheet.

After each adjustment has been entered on the work sheet, the appropriate additions and subtractions are made to determine the adjusted account balances. ("Crossfooting" is the term used by accountants when adding or subtracting amounts horizontally.) These revised account balances are entered in the Adjusted Trial Balance columns of the work sheet, as shown in Exhibit 5.10. Notice that there were no adjustments affecting the Cash account. So, the original trial balance amount for that account is simply entered in the Adjusted Trial Balance debit column. After entering each adjusted account balance in the Adjusted Trial Balance columns of the work sheet, those columns are footed. These totals are entered at the bottom of the Adjusted Trial Balance debit and credit columns. Again, these totals should be equal.

Next, the account balances in the Adjusted Trial Balance columns are sorted to the appropriate Income Statement and Balance Sheet columns on the work sheet. When completing this task, if you have difficulty remembering which accounts appear on the income statement and which appear on the balance sheet, refer to the chart of accounts. As shown in Exhibit 5.5, a chart of accounts segregates income statement and balance sheet accounts. Notice in Exhibit 5.5 that Dividends is listed as a balance sheet account. So, for work sheet purposes the balance of that account is included in the Balance Sheet debit column. However, a word of caution is appropriate here. Technically, Dividends does not appear explicitly on the balance sheet. Instead, the

■ EXHIBIT 5.10

Snow Mountain Retreat Work Sheet for the Month Ended January 31, 1996

SNOW MOUNTAIN RETREAT
WORK SHEET
FOR THE MONTH ENDED JANUARY 31, 1996

Account Title	Trial Balance Debit	Trial Balance Credit	Adjustments Debit	Adjustments Credit	Adjusted Trial Balance Debit	Adjusted Trial Balance Credit	Income Statement Debit	Income Statement Credit	Balance Sheet Debit	Balance Sheet Credit
Cash	19,350				19,350					
Supplies	500			(d) 80	420					
Prepaid Rent	18,000			(a) 1,500	16,500					
Prepaid Insurance	1,200			(b) 100	1,100					
Furniture	4,800				4,800					
Accounts Payable		640				640				
Unearned Rental Revenue		1,000	(e) 500			500				
Common Stock		40,000				40,000				
Dividends	500				500					
Rental Revenue		3,500		(e) 500		4,000				
Salaries Expense	400		(g) 320		720					
Utilities Expense	390				390					
	45,140	45,140								
Rent Expense			(a) 1,500		1,500					
Insurance Expense			(b) 100		100					
Depreciation Expense, Furniture			(c) 200		200					
Accumulated Depreciation, Furniture				(c) 200		200				
Supplies Expense			(d) 80		80					
Interest Receivable			(f) 120		120					
Interest Revenue				(f) 120		120				
Salaries Payable				(g) 320		320				
Income Taxes Expense			(h) 200		200					
Income Taxes Payable				(h) 200		200				
			3,020	3,020	45,980	45,980				

balance of this account is eventually used in determining Snow Mountain Retreat's period-ending retained earnings, which will appear on the company's balance sheet. More on this later.

The completed work sheet for Snow Mountain Retreat is shown in Exhibit 5.11. Notice that the totals of the Income Statement debit and credit columns are not equal—at least initially. The initial total of the debit column, $3,190, represents the total expenses of Snow Mountain Retreat for January 1996. The total of the credit column, $4,120, represents the company's total revenues during January 1996. The company's net income for January 1996 is the difference between these two amounts, $930.

To balance the two Income Statement columns, we add the net income figure to the debit column. This amount is also added to the Balance Sheet credit column, as shown in Exhibit 5.11, to bring the debit and credit columns for that financial state-

Teaching Note
Point out that net income is not an account.

■ **EXHIBIT 5.11**

Snow Mountain Retreat Work Sheet for the Month Ended January 31, 1996

SNOW MOUNTAIN RETREAT										
WORK SHEET										
FOR THE MONTH ENDED JANUARY 31, 1996										
	Trial Balance		**Adjustments**		**Adjusted Trial Balance**		**Income Statement**		**Balance Sheet**	
Account Title	**Debit**	**Credit**	**Debit**	**Credit**	**Debit**	**Credit**	**Debit**	**Credit**	**Debit**	**Credit**
Cash	19,350				19,350				19,350	
Supplies	500			(d) 80	420				420	
Prepaid Rent	18,000			(a) 1,500	16,500				16,500	
Prepaid Insurance	1,200			(b) 100	1,100				1,100	
Furniture	4,800				4,800				4,800	
Accounts Payable		640				640				640
Unearned Rental Revenue		1,000	(e) 500			500				500
Common Stock		40,000				40,000				40,000
Dividends	500				500				500	
Rental Revenue		3,500		(e) 500		4,000		4,000		
Salaries Expense	400		(g) 320		720		720			
Utilities Expense	390				390		390			
	45,140	45,140								
Rent Expense			(a) 1,500		1,500		1,500			
Insurance Expense			(b) 100		100		100			
Depreciation Expense, Furniture			(c) 200		200		200			
Accumulated Depreciation, Furniture				(c) 200		200				200
Supplies Expense			(d) 80		80		80			
Interest Receivable			(f) 120		120				120	
Interest Revenue				(f) 120		120		120		
Salaries Payable				(g) 320		320				320
Income Taxes Expense			(h) 200		200		200			
Income Taxes Payable				(h) 200		200				200
			3,020	3,020	45,980	45,980	3,190	4,120	42,790	41,860
Net Income							930			930
							4,120	4,120	42,790	42,790

Teaching Note
Net income by definition is equal to revenues minus expenses. On the work sheet, net income is the difference between the total of the income statement credit column (total revenues) and the total of the income statement debit column (total expenses).

ment into balance. This apparent trickery causes the debit and credit columns for the two financial statements to have equal totals, but we are not "cheating" to bring these paired columns into agreement. The entry of $930 in the Income Statement debit column and the equivalent entry in the Balance Sheet credit column transfers Snow Mountain Retreat's net income to owners' equity for work sheet purposes. Recall that the balances of revenue and expense accounts must be transferred to a corporation's Retained Earnings account at the end of each accounting period. You do not actually see these transfers to the Retained Earnings account on the work sheet. However, when we prepare Snow Mountain Retreat's balance sheet, its period-ending retained earnings will be $430. This amount is the sum of retained earnings at the beginning of the period (zero) plus the net income for January 1996 ($930) less the dividends paid during the month ($500).[3]

If Snow Mountain Retreat had realized a net loss for January 1996, the balancing procedure described in the prior paragraph would have been modified slightly. When a business has a net loss, that amount is inserted in the Income Statement credit column and the Balance sheet debit column of a work sheet, which results in the paired financial statement columns having equal totals.

Accounting Cycle, Step 6: Prepare Financial Statements

Once we complete the work sheet, we have all of the data needed to prepare an entity's income statement, statement of owners' or stockholders' equity, and balance sheet. (The mechanics of preparing a statement of cash flows are discussed in Chapter 16.) Shown in Exhibit 5.12 is Snow Mountain Retreat's income statement for January 1996. In this case, the revenues and expenses of Snow Mountain Retreat are listed on its income statement in the order in which they appear on the work sheet. In Chapter 13, we review an income statement format that is more commonly used by corporations.

■ **LEARNING OBJECTIVE 4**
Prepare financial statements from a work sheet

■ **EXHIBIT 5.12**
Income Statement for Snow Mountain Retreat for the Month Ended January 31, 1996

SNOW MOUNTAIN RETREAT
INCOME STATEMENT
FOR THE MONTH ENDED JANUARY 31, 1996

REVENUES		
Rental Revenue	$4,000	
Interest Revenue	120	
Total Revenues		$4,120
EXPENSES		
Salaries Expense	720	
Utilities Expense	390	
Rent Expense	1,500	
Insurance Expense	100	
Depreciation Expense, Furniture	200	
Supplies Expense	80	
Income Taxes Expense	200	
Total Expenses		3,190
Net Income		**$ 930**

---

3. Since Snow Mountain Retreat is a new business, its Retained Earnings account had a zero balance until the completion of the closing procedures at the end of January. For an existing company, the Retained Earnings account is included in the initial trial balance on the work sheet. The balance of the Dividends account and a company's net income or net loss are not combined with an existing Retained Earnings account balance on the work sheet. Instead, the new balance of the Retained Earnings account is computed initially in the company's balance sheet or its statement of stockholders' equity.

■ **EXHIBIT 5.13**

Statement of Stockholders' Equity for Snow Mountain Retreat for the Month Ended January 31, 1996

SNOW MOUNTAIN RETREAT STATEMENT OF STOCKHOLDERS' EQUITY FOR THE MONTH ENDED JANUARY 31, 1996	COMMON STOCK	RETAINED EARNINGS
Balance, January 1, 1996	$ -0-	$-0-
Sale of Common Stock	40,000	
Net Income		930
Dividends		(500)
Balance, January 31, 1996	$40,000	$430

Exhibit 5.13 presents Snow Mountain Retreat's statement of stockholders' equity for January 1996. As indicated in Chapter 2, a statement of stockholders' equity reconciles the beginning-of-the-period and end-of-the-period balances of a corporation's stockholders' equity accounts. Since Snow Mountain Retreat opened for business in January 1996, the beginning balances of its two equity accounts, Common Stock and Retained Earnings, were zero at the beginning of that month.

Snow Mountain Retreat's January 31, 1996, balance sheet is shown in Exhibit 5.14. The company's balance sheet is unclassified, that is, there are no subheadings within each major section. Companies with numerous asset and liability accounts prepare classified balance sheets as illustrated in Chapter 2. Recall that in a classified balance sheet, assets are commonly sorted into the following major groups: current assets; property, plant and equipment; intangible assets, long-term investments; and other assets. In a classified balance sheet, liabilities are typically segregated into current and long-term items.

Accounting Cycle, Step 7: Journalize and Post Adjusting Entries

■ **LEARNING OBJECTIVE 5**
Journalize and post adjusting entries

In step 5 of the accounting cycle, a business's accountants identify the necessary period-ending adjustments to the general ledger accounts. After the work sheet has been completed and the financial statements prepared, the work sheet adjustments are journalized and posted to the general ledger. Journalizing period-ending adjustments is a simple task, since the work sheet contains the information needed to prepare the adjusting journal entries. For instance, adjustment "a" shown in Snow Mountain Retreat's work sheet in Exhibit 5.11 requires a journal entry debiting Rent Expense for $1,500 and crediting Prepaid Rent for the same amount.

Shown in Exhibit 5.15 are the adjusting journal entries for Snow Mountain Retreat for the accounting period ending January 31, 1996. After the period-ending adjustments have been journalized, they must be posted to the appropriate accounts in the general ledger. Exhibit 5.15 indicates that the posting has been completed, since account numbers have been entered in the post-reference column of the general journal. (After the journalizing and posting of closing entries has been completed—step 8 of the accounting cycle—the updated general ledger accounts are illustrated.)

■ **EXHIBIT 5.14**
Balance Sheet for Snow Mountain Retreat as of January 31, 1996

SNOW MOUNTAIN RETREAT
BALANCE SHEET
JANUARY 31, 1996

ASSETS

Cash		$19,350
Interest Receivable		120
Supplies		420
Prepaid Rent		16,500
Prepaid Insurance		1,100
Furniture	$4,800	
Less: Accumulated Depreciation	(200)	4,600
Total Assets		$42,090

LIABILITIES

Accounts Payable		$ 640
Unearned Rental Revenue		500
Salaries Payable		320
Income Taxes Payable		200
Total Liabilities		1,660

STOCKHOLDERS' EQUITY

Common Stock		40,000
Retained Earnings		430
Total Stockholders' Equity		40,430
Total Liabilities and Stockholders' Equity		$42,090

Teaching Note
Remind students that the reported balance sheet value for furniture does not represent the asset's market value.

Accounting Cycle, Step 8: Journalize and Post Closing Entries

The temporary accounts of a business must begin each accounting period with a zero balance. This is particularly important for revenue and expense accounts because it allows an entity's net income to be easily determined each accounting period. Recall that the balances in temporary accounts are not simply erased at the end of each accounting period but instead are transferred to an owners' equity account. For a corporation, such as Snow Mountain Retreat, this owners' equity account is Retained Earnings. As pointed out in Chapter 4, closing entries are used to transfer the balances of temporary accounts to the Retained Earnings account. To facilitate this process, most companies establish an **Income Summary** account, a temporary account that is used only during the journalizing and posting of closing entries.

■ **LEARNING OBJECTIVE 6**
Journalize and post closing entries

Income Summary

THE FOUR TYPES OF CLOSING ENTRIES   The following are the four closing entries that businesses make at the end of an accounting period.

1. An entry to transfer credit balances of income statement accounts to the Income Summary account

Adjusting General Journal Entries for Snow Mountain Retreat, January 1996

General Journal						Page 2
Date		Description	Post Ref.	Debit		Credit
1996 Jan.	31	Rent Expense	501	1,500		
		Prepaid Rent	104			1,500
		To record rent expense for January				
	31	Insurance Expense	504	100		
		Prepaid Insurance	105			100
		To record insurance expense for January				
	31	Depreciation Expense, Furniture	506	200		
		Accumulated Depreciation, Furniture	107			200
		To record depreciation expense for January				
	31	Supplies Expense	505	80		
		Supplies	103			80
		To record supplies used in January				
	31	Unearned Rental Revenue	202	500		
		Rental Revenue	401			500
		To recognize the portion of an advance payment of revenue earned in January				
	31	Interest Receivable	102	120		
		Interest Revenue	402			120
		To recognize interest revenue earned in January				
	31	Salaries Expense	502	320		
		Salaries Payable	203			320
		To record amount of salary owed maintenance employee at the end of January				
	31	Income Taxes Expense	507	200		
		Income Taxes Payable	204			200
		To record estimated income tax expense for January				

2. An entry to transfer debit balances of income statement accounts to the Income Summary account
3. An entry to transfer the balance of the Income Summary account to the Retained Earnings account
4. An entry to transfer the balance of the Dividends account to the Retained Earnings account

The information needed to make these closing entries can be found in the Income Statement and Balance Sheet columns of the work sheet.

CLOSING ENTRIES FOR SNOW MOUNTAIN RETREAT   The work sheet of Snow Mountain Retreat shown in Exhibit 5.11 has two income statement accounts with credit balances, Rental Revenue and Interest Revenue. The following entry, in simplified general journal format, closes these two revenue accounts. After posting this entry, the balances of the two revenue accounts will be zero, while the Income Summary account will have a credit balance of $4,120.

Rental Revenue	4,000	
Interest Revenue	120	
Income Summary		4,120

The following entry closes the income statement accounts with debit balances on Snow Mountain Retreat's work sheet. Following the posting of this entry, each of the expense accounts of Snow Mountain Retreat will have a zero balance, while the Income Summary account will have a credit balance of $930. This $930 credit balance is the difference between the $4,120 credit to Income Summary included in the original closing entry just shown and the $3,190 debit to Income Summary included in the following closing entry.

Income Summary	3,190	
Salaries Expense		720
Utilities Expense		390
Rent Expense		1,500
Insurance Expense		100
Depreciation Expense, Furniture		200
Supplies Expense		80
Income Taxes Expense		200

The $930 balance in the Income Summary account following the posting of the first two closing entries represents Snow Mountain Retreat's net income for January 1996. By transferring the period-ending balances of all revenue and expense accounts to the Income Summary account, a business's accountants can confirm that the proper net income amount was determined. The next step in closing the temporary accounts of Snow Mountain Retreat is to close the Income Summary account by transferring its balance to the Retained Earnings account which is accomplished by the following entry.

Income Summary	930	
Retained Earnings		930

Teaching Note
Emphasize that after this entry, the Income Summary account will have a zero balance.

Discussion Question
Why is the Dividends account closed directly to Retained Earnings?
Answer: Because it is not a revenue or an expense account.

The final closing entry made at the end of an accounting period transfers the balance of the Dividends account to the Retained Earnings account. Since many companies do not pay dividends or pay dividends infrequently, this final closing entry is not always required. Following is the entry to close the Dividends account of Snow Mountain Retreat at the end of January 1996.

Retained Earnings	500	
Dividends		500

The closing entries for Snow Mountain Retreat are shown in Exhibit 5.16 as they would appear in the company's general journal. The account numbers appearing in the post reference column indicate that the closing entries have been posted to the appropriate general ledger accounts. Snow Mountain Retreat's general ledger accounts, after the posting of the adjusting and closing entries, are shown in Exhibit 5.17.

EXHIBIT 5.16

Closing Entries for Snow Mountain Retreat at the End of January 1996

General Journal					Page 3
Date		Description	Post Ref.	Debit	Credit
1996					
Jan.	31	Rental Revenue	401	4,000	
		Interest Revenue	402	120	
		Income Summary	304		4,120
		To close the revenue accounts			
	31	Income Summary	304	3,190	
		Rent Expense	501		1,500
		Salaries Expense	502		720
		Utilities Expense	503		390
		Insurance Expense	504		100
		Supplies Expense	505		80
		Depreciation Expense, Furniture	506		200
		Income Taxes Expense	507		200
		To close the expense accounts			
	31	Income Summary	304	930	
		Retained Earnings	302		930
		To close the Income Summary account			
	31	Retained Earnings	302	500	
		Dividends	303		500
		To close the Dividends account			

■ **EXHIBIT 5.17**

General Ledger Accounts of Snow Mountain Retreat Following the
Posting of Adjusting and Closing Entries for January 1996

Cash					Account No. 101	
		Post			Balance	
Date	Explanation	Ref.	Debit	Credit	Debit	Credit
1996						
Jan. 1		GJ1	40,000		40,000	
1		GJ1		18,000	22,000	
1		GJ1		1,200	20,800	
1		GJ1		4,800	16,000	
8		GJ1	1,000		17,000	
19		GJ1	1,500		18,500	
22		GJ1	750		19,250	
22		GJ1		400	18,850	
24		GJ1	500		19,350	
26		GJ1	750		20,100	
30		GJ1		250	19,850	
31		GJ1		500	19,350	

Interest Receivable					Account No. 102	
		Post			Balance	
Date	Explanation	Ref.	Debit	Credit	Debit	Credit
1996						
Jan. 31	Adjusting	GJ2	120		120	

Supplies					Account No. 103	
		Post			Balance	
Date	Explanation	Ref.	Debit	Credit	Debit	Credit
1996						
Jan. 3		GJ1	500		500	
31	Adjusting	GJ2		80	420	

Prepaid Rent					Account No. 104	
		Post			Balance	
Date	Explanation	Ref.	Debit	Credit	Debit	Credit
1996						
Jan. 1		GJ1	18,000		18,000	
31	Adjusting	GJ2		1,500	16,500	

(Exhibit 5.17 continues)

■ **EXHIBIT 5.17**
(Continued)

Prepaid Insurance						Account No. 105	
Date		Explanation	Post Ref.	Debit	Credit	Balance Debit	Balance Credit
1996							
Jan.	1		GJ1	1,200		1,200	
	31	Adjusting	GJ2		100	1,100	

Furniture						Account No. 106	
Date		Explanation	Post Ref.	Debit	Credit	Balance Debit	Balance Credit
1996							
Jan.	1		GJ1	4,800		4,800	

Accumulated Depreciation, Furniture						Account No. 107	
Date		Explanation	Post Ref.	Debit	Credit	Balance Debit	Balance Credit
1996							
Jan.	31	Adjusting	GJ2		200		200

Accounts Payable						Account No. 201	
Date		Explanation	Post Ref.	Debit	Credit	Balance Debit	Balance Credit
1996							
Jan.	3		GJ1		500		500
	30		GJ1	250			250
	31		GJ1		390		640

Unearned Rental Revenue						Account No. 202	
Date		Explanation	Post Ref.	Debit	Credit	Balance Debit	Balance Credit
1996							
Jan.	8		GJ1		1,000		1,000
	31	Adjusting	GJ2	500			500

Salaries Payable						Account No. 203	
Date		Explanation	Post Ref.	Debit	Credit	Balance Debit	Balance Credit
1996							
	31	Adjusting	GJ2		320		320

■ **EXHIBIT 5.17**
(Continued)

Income Taxes Payable					Account No. 204		
Date		Explanation	Post Ref.	Debit	Credit	Balance Debit	Balance Credit
1996	31	Adjusting	GJ2		200		200

Common Stock					Account No. 301		
Date		Explanation	Post Ref.	Debit	Credit	Balance Debit	Balance Credit
1996 Jan.	1		GJ1		40,000		40,000

Retained Earnings					Account No. 302		
Date		Explanation	Post Ref.	Debit	Credit	Balance Debit	Balance Credit
1996 Jan.	31	Closing	GJ3		930		930
	31	Closing	GJ3	500			430

Dividends					Account No. 303		
Date		Explanation	Post Ref.	Debit	Credit	Balance Debit	Balance Credit
1996 Jan.	31		GJ1	500		500	
	31	Closing	GJ3		500	-0-	

Income Summary					Account No. 304		
Date		Explanation	Post Ref.	Debit	Credit	Balance Debit	Balance Credit
1996 Jan.	31	Closing	GJ3		4,120		4,120
	31	Closing	GJ3	3,190			930
	31	Closing	GJ3	930			-0-

(Exhibit 5.17 continues)

■ **EXHIBIT 5.17**
(Continued)

Rental Revenue							Account No. 401
			Post			**Balance**	
Date		Explanation	Ref.	Debit	Credit	Debit	Credit
1996							
Jan.	19		GJ1		1,500		1,500
	22		GJ1		750		2,250
	24		GJ1		500		2,750
	26		GJ1		750		3,500
	31	Adjusting	GJ2		500		4,000
	31	Closing	GJ3	4,000			-0-

Interest Revenue							Account No. 402
			Post			**Balance**	
Date		Explanation	Ref.	Debit	Credit	Debit	Credit
1996							
Jan.	31	Adjusting	GJ2		120		120
	31	Closing	GJ3	120			-0-

Rent Expense							Account No. 501
			Post			**Balance**	
Date		Explanation	Ref.	Debit	Credit	Debit	Credit
1996							
Jan.	31	Adjusting	GJ2	1,500		1,500	
	31	Closing	GJ3		1,500	-0-	

Salaries Expense							Account No. 502
			Post			**Balance**	
Date		Explanation	Ref.	Debit	Credit	Debit	Credit
1996							
Jan.	22		GJ1	400		400	
	31	Adjusting	GJ2	320		720	
	31	Closing	GJ3		720	-0-	

Utilities Expense							Account No. 503
			Post			**Balance**	
Date		Explanation	Ref.	Debit	Credit	Debit	Credit
1996							
Jan.	31		GJ1	390		390	
	31	Closing	GJ3		390	-0-	

■ **EXHIBIT 5.17**
(Continued)

Insurance Expense							Account No. 504	
			Post				Balance	
Date		Explanation	Ref.	Debit	Credit	Debit	Credit	
1996								
Jan.	31	Adjusting	GJ2	100		100		
	31	Closing	GJ3		100	-0-		

Supplies Expense							Account No. 505	
			Post				Balance	
Date		Explanation	Ref.	Debit	Credit	Debit	Credit	
1996								
Jan.	31	Adjusting	GJ2	80		80		
	31	Closing	GJ3		80	-0-		

Depreciation Expense, Furniture							Account No. 506	
			Post				Balance	
Date		Explanation	Ref.	Debit	Credit	Debit	Credit	
1996								
Jan.	31	Adjusting	GJ2	200		200		
	31	Closing	GJ3		200	-0-		

Income Taxes Expense							Account No. 507	
			Post				Balance	
Date		Explanation	Ref.	Debit	Credit	Debit	Credit	
1996								
Jan.	31	Adjusting	GJ2	200		200		
	31	Closing	GJ3		200	-0-		

Accounting Cycle, Step 9: Prepare Post-Closing Trial Balance

The final step of the accounting cycle is the preparation of a **post-closing trial balance,** which is a general ledger trial balance following the posting of adjusting and closing entries. Accountants prepare a post-closing trial balance to determine whether the general ledger is in balance upon completion of the accounting cycle. If the totals of the debit and credit columns of this trial balance are equal, the presumption is that the adjusting and closing entries have been entered correctly in the accounting records. Shown in Exhibit 5.18 is the January 31, 1996, post-closing trial balance of Snow Mountain Retreat. Notice that only the company's permanent or

■ LEARNING
OBJECTIVE 7
Prepare a post-closing trial balance

post-closing trial balance

■ **EXHIBIT 5.18**
Post-Closing Trial Balance for Snow Mountain Retreat, January 31, 1996

SNOW MOUNTAIN RETREAT
POST-CLOSING TRIAL BALANCES
JANUARY 31, 1996

	DEBIT	CREDIT
Cash	$19,350	
Interest Receivable	120	
Supplies	420	
Prepaid Rent	16,500	
Prepaid Insurance	1,100	
Furniture	4,800	
Accumulated Depreciation, Furniture		$ 200
Accounts Payable		640
Unearned Rental Revenue		500
Salaries Payable		320
Income Taxes Payable		200
Common Stock		40,000
Retained Earnings		430
	$42,290	$42,290

Discussion Question

A manual accounting system was used to illustrate the accounting cycle in this chapter. In the real world, many, if not most, accounting systems are computerized. So, why study a manual accounting system? Answer: A manual accounting system is easier to illustrate and visualize than a computerized accounting system. All the steps in the accounting cycle discussed in this chapter apply to a computerized accounting system; however, many of the steps are completed automatically by the computer.

balance sheet accounts are listed in this trial balance. At this point, each of the temporary accounts has been closed and thus has a zero balance.

So, there you have it. The complete accounting cycle as illustrated for Snow Mountain Retreat during January 1996. You should recognize that there is considerable diversity among businesses in how accounting principles and procedures are applied. This is true of even the accounting cycle. In practice, you will find many different variations of the accounting cycle. For example, the first step in the accounting cycle for some companies is the journalizing and posting of reversing entries. Recall that in Chapter 4 reversing entries were defined as journal entries made at the beginning of an accounting period to cancel out the effect of certain adjusting entries made at the end of the prior accounting period. Reversing entries is an optional accounting procedure. If you pursue further study of financial accounting, you will be acquainted with reversing entries in the future.

FOR YOUR INFORMATION

Unaccountable Accounting by State and Local Governments

The opening vignette for this chapter pointed out that the federal government has been criticized for using cash-basis instead of accrual-basis accounting. This criticism stems from the fact that financial data produced by a cash-basis accounting cycle are less conceptually sound than financial data produced by applying accrual-basis accounting. State and local governments have also been criticized for failing to adopt accrual-basis accounting. Recently, a new accounting rule under consideration would have imposed accrual-basis accounting on state and local governments. However, as noted in the following article, that proposed rule was rejected.

Under pressure from local political officials, accounting rule makers scuttled a plan for a sweeping reform of state and local government financial practices.

The Governmental Accounting Standards Board (GASB) voted 3–2 to delay indefinitely the effective date of Statement 11, which mandates accrual accounting standards for all non-federal government agencies, jurisdictions, and funds. The GASB said it needed more time to develop a comprehensive financial reporting model.

But organizations of local cities, towns and counties vigorously opposed the accrual accounting plan because they would have been forced to account today for the explosive costs of employee retirements in the future, throwing many, if not most, solvent government units into the red.

"This really goes to the question of the credibility of the GASB," said Philip T. Calder, an Ernst & Young partner and chairman of the American Institute of CPAs' committee on government accounting and auditing. "We thought they ought not delay but should go forward. It has been studied since the first days of GASB."

At the core of the problem is the issue of so-called compensated absences. Most local governments fail to account on an accrual basis for the substantial cash payouts they are obligated to make in the future to retiring employees for their accumulated sick leaves and vacations.

"I guess it's clear that I'm disappointed," said GASB chairman James Antonio, who has spent most of his 10-year board term pushing for accrual accounting. "It [the adoption of accrual-basis accounting] is fundamental to accountability."

SOURCE: "GASB Votes Down Accrual Accounting," *Accounting Today*, June 7, 1993, pp. 1, 61.

State and local governments and their agencies generally do not use accrual basis accounting, which diminishes the reliability and credibility of their published financial data.

SUMMARY

Each accounting period, accountants for a business must complete a set of accounting procedures referred to as the accounting cycle. These procedures convert financial data resulting from a business's transactions during an accounting period into a set of financial statements. The accounting cycle begins with an analysis of these transactions. Key information regarding business transactions is obtained from source documents such as invoices, bank statements, and purchase orders. After transactions have been analyzed, they are journalized and then posted to the appropriate general ledger accounts.

At the end of each accounting period, accountants often complete a ten-column work sheet to assist them in preparing financial statements for their organization. A trial balance of all general ledger accounts is entered in the first two columns of this work sheet. In the next two columns, adjustments to the general ledger accounts are entered. These adjustments reflect events and circumstances that have not yet been recognized in the accounting records. Next, an adjusted trial balance of the general ledger accounts is entered in the fifth and sixth columns of the work sheet. Finally, the account balances from the adjusted trial balance are sorted to the final four columns of the work sheet: two columns for income statement accounts and two columns for balance sheet accounts. An entity's income statement, statement of stockholders' equity, and balance sheet can be prepared directly from the final four columns of a completed work sheet.

After the completion of the work sheet, the adjustments are journalized and then posted to the appropriate general ledger accounts. Next, the balances of all temporary accounts must be transferred or closed to the Retained Earnings account or other owners' equity account. Following the journalizing and posting of closing entries, a post-closing trial balance is prepared to determine whether the general ledger is in balance upon completion of the accounting cycle.

GLOSSARY

Accrued revenue (p. 173)   A receivable resulting from revenue that has been earned but not yet received.

Deferred expense (p. 172)   An asset that is a prepayment of an expense item.

Deferred revenue (p. 173)   A liability that represents an amount paid to a business for a service or product that it will provide or deliver in the future.

Income Summary (p. 183)   A temporary account used only during the journalizing and posting of closing entries.

Post-closing trial balance (p. 191)   A trial balance of general ledger accounts following the posting of adjusting and closing entries.

Source documents (p. 156)   Documents that identify the key features or parameters of business transactions; examples include invoices, bank statements, and purchase orders.

DECISION CASE

Many small business owners borrow from banks or other financial institutions to obtain funds needed by their businesses. Let us assume that the owners of Snow Mountain Retreat decide to expand and open another bed and breakfast inn in a nearby town. However, they do not have sufficient funds of their own to finance this expansion. So, they turn to a local bank. They provide the bank loan officer with Snow Mountain Retreat's financial statements that were prepared in this chapter. The owners hope that the profitable operations of Snow Mountain Retreat during January 1996 will convince this individual to loan them $20,000.

JOANN ROSE (LOAN OFFICER): I see that you had a profitable month in January. Net income of $930, correct?

BUD HEARST (PART-OWNER): Yes ma'am, Ms. Rose. We did very well, thank you.

MS. ROSE: You are keeping your accounting records on an accrual basis, correct?

MR. HEARST: Well . . . I guess so. A local accountant who is a friend of mine is keeping the books for us.

MS. ROSE: I see.

MR. HEARST: She's not a CPA or anything. But she sure knows her debits and credits.

MS. ROSE: Oh, really. Okay. Let's see here. You and your two friends invested $40,000 in this business. correct?

MR. HEARST: Yes ma'am, Ms. Rose, $40,000 hard-earned dollars.

MS. ROSE: And you ended the month with less than $20,000?

MR. HEARST: Uh . . . yes ma'am.

MS. ROSE: So, let me get this straight. You earned $930 in January but your cash balance decreased by more than $20,000 during the month, correct?

MR. HEARST: Uh, well . . . yeah, uh . . . yes ma'am, that's correct.

MS. ROSE: And now, you want me to loan you another $20,000?

MR. HEARST: Uh . . .

MS. ROSE: Appears to me that at the rate you're going through your cash, you will be back in here in a couple of months asking for another loan, correct?

MR. HEARST: Well, I don't think so.

MS. ROSE: You "don't think so"?

MR. HEARST: Uh . . .

MS. ROSE: Did you prepare a statement of cash flows for me to review?

MR. HEARST: Statement of cash flows?

MS. ROSE: Mr. Hearst, do you understand the difference between cash flow and profit?

MR. HEARST: Well, they're basically the same thing, aren't they?

Required: Not surprisingly, the owners of Snow Mountain Retreat were turned down for the $20,000 loan they requested. They have decided to approach a second bank for this loan but realize they must be better prepared this time. Assume that they have appointed you, one of the co-owners, to negotiate this loan. To prepare for your meeting in the next few days with a bank loan officer, one of your co-owners hands you the following partially completed statement of cash flows that he has been working on for January 1996. This statement of cash flows has the same format as the one presented in Exhibit 2.9.

CASH FLOWS FROM OPERATING ACTIVITIES

Cash received from customers	$
Cash paid to employees	
Cash paid for rent, insurance, and supplies	
Net cash used in operating activities	———

CASH FLOWS FROM INVESTING ACTIVITIES

Purchase of furniture	(4,800)
Net cash used in investing activities	(4,800)

CASH FLOWS FROM FINANCING ACTIVITIES

Purchase of common stock by owners	
Dividends paid	
Net cash provided by financing activities	39,500

Net Increase in Cash	$
Cash Balance, January 1, 1996	
Cash Balance, January 31, 1996	$19,350

By referring to the accounting data included in this chapter for Snow Mountain Retreat, complete the business's statement of cash flows for January 1996. If the business's operations in February are similar to its operations in January, estimate Snow Mountain Retreat's cash balance at the end of February 1996. Make any assumptions you believe are necessary.

QUESTIONS

1. What types of "source" documents do accountants use when analyzing business transactions for the purpose of journalizing them?

2. Identify the nine steps in the accounting cycle.

3. What is the purpose of posting journal entries to general ledger accounts?

4. Explain why the preparation of a trial balance is an important step in the accounting cycle.

5. Where do accountants obtain the information needed to prepare adjusting journal entries at the end of an accounting period?

6. Why is a deferred expense an asset? Provide two examples of deferred expenses.

7. Why are adjusting entries generally required at the end of an accounting period for deferred expenses?

8. Why is a deferred revenue a liability? Provide two examples of deferred revenues.

9. Why are adjusting entries generally required at the end of an accounting period for deferred revenues?

10. Why is an accrued revenue an asset? Provide two examples of accrued revenues.

11. Why is an accrued expense a liability? Provide two examples of accrued expenses.

12. Explain the role of an adjusted trial balance in the accounting cycle.

13. Explain how accountants use the terms "foot" and "crossfoot."

14. How does a company's net income for a given accounting period affect its period-ending balance sheet?

15. Explain the difference between a classified balance sheet and an unclassified balance sheet.

16. Why do accountants use an Income Summary account when closing revenue and expense accounts rather than simply transferring the proper amounts directly into the Retained Earnings account?

17. Why is it necessary to prepare a post-closing trial balance?

18. Explain the purpose of a post-closing trial balance.

19. What is the most significant difference between an adjusted trial balance and a post-closing trial balance?

20. Do all companies use the same accounting cycle? If not, identify one variation from the accounting cycle discussed in this chapter that certain companies integrate into their accounting cycles.

EXERCISES

21. **General Journal Entries** (LO 1)
    Grady Real Estate Company engaged in the following transactions recently:
    1. Received $24,000 for one year's advance rent on an office building
    2. Paid $6,000 in advance for six months of newspaper advertising

    Required:
    1. Prepare a general journal entry to record each of these transactions in Grady's accounting records.
    2. Prepare a general journal entry for each transaction from the point of view of the other party (company) to the transaction.

21. 1. 1. Cr. Unearn. Rent. Rev. $24,000
       2. Dr. Pre. Adv. $6,000
    2. 1. Dr. Pre. Rent. $24,000
       2. Cr. Unearn. Adv. Rev. $6,000

3. Are Grady's total assets increased, decreased, or unchanged as a result of each of these transactions?

22. **Adjusting Journal Entries** (LO 3)

Fisher, Jones and Bottomley is a local law firm. Following are several transactions engaged in by this law firm during January 1996.

January 1: Purchased a laptop computer for $3,200
January 1: Received a $4,000 advance payment from Smith Brothers, Inc., for legal services to be provided during the current month
January 16: Paid $450 for newspaper ad that ran for the three-day period January 12–14
January 24: Prepaid February rent of $1,300 on leased office space
January 31: Wrote a will for John Darden; Darden will be billed $300 for this service in February

Required:

1. Prepare a general journal entry for each of these transactions in the law firm's accounting records.
2. Which of the items recorded in the journal entries in Part 1 will require an adjusting journal entry on January 31, 1996? Why?

23. **General Journal Entries** (LO 1)

Following are several transactions engaged in by Saxe Detective Agency during March 1996.

March 2: Purchased a van for $20,000 cash
March 4: Paid the prior month's electric bill of $400 which had previously been recorded as an account payable
March 15: Received payment of $1,300 for investigative services provided to a client for the period March 1–14
March 19: Received advance payment of $4,000 for services to be provided in June 1996 to a client
March 21: Purchased office supplies of $200 on credit
March 24: Prepaid premium of $2,000 on insurance policy for an office building for the period April 1–October 1, 1996
March 31: Received interest revenue of $350 that had been earned in February; an appropriate adjusting entry had been made on February 29 to record this item

Required:

1. Prepare a general journal entry to record each of these transactions in the accounting records of Saxe Detective Agency.
2. Identify the accounts affected by the journal entries you prepared in Part 1 that qualify as an: accrued expense, accrued revenue, deferred expense, or deferred revenue.

24. **Accrued Expenses vs.** *Accrued Expenses* (LO 3)

The following conversation took place between Erica Cain, an accountant for Seminole Freight Company, and Stuart Whitman, a senior vice president recently hired by the firm.

Stuart: "Erica, why did you include $12,700 of expenses in our company's year-end balance sheet?"
Erica: "What are you talking about?"
Stuart: "I'm talking about this line item 'Accrued Expenses, $12,700' right here in the current liabilities section of our year-end balance sheet."

22. 1. 1/1 Dr. Equip. $3,200
1/1 Cr. Unearn. Rev. $4,000
1/11 Dr. Adv. Exp. $450
1/24 Dr. Pre. Rent $1,300
1/31 Cr. Fee Rev. $300

23. 1. 3/2 Dr. Autos $20,000
3/4 Dr. A.P. $400
3/15 Cr. Rev. $1,300
3/19 Cr. Unearn. Rev. $4,000
3/21 Cr. A.P. $200
3/24 Dr. Pre. Ins. $200
3/31 Cr. Int. Rec. $350

Erica: "Those aren't *expenses.*"

Stuart: "What do you mean? You referred to them as *expenses* in the balance sheet."

Erica: "Stuart, accrued expenses aren't *expenses.*"

Stuart: "Huh?"

Required:

24. No check figures

Write a brief memo to Stuart explaining to him why the $12,700 of "accrued expenses" were included in Seminole Freight Company's balance sheet.

25. **Adjusting Journal Entries for Balance Sheet Accounts** (LO 3)

Following are several balance sheet accounts of Brookhaven Square Inc., on December 31, 1996, prior to the preparation of year-end adjusting journal entries.

Property, Plant and Equipment	$1,530,200
Cash	120,600
Unearned Rental Revenue	72,000
Common Stock	30,000
Prepaid Rent	5,400
Land	340,500
Note Payable	50,000
Retained Earnings	770,100

Required:

25. No check figures

1. Identify the listed accounts that will likely require year-end adjusting journal entries.
2. Briefly describe the nature of the adjusting journal entries for the accounts you identified in Part 1.

26. **Adjusting Journal Entries for Liability Accounts** (LO 3)

Following is the liabilities section of Thiokol Corporation's balance sheet as of June 30, 1994. Among other products, Thiokol produces solid rocket motors for aerospace and defense applications. (All amounts are in millions.)

Liabilities

Current Liabilities:		
Short-Term Debt	$27.1	
Accounts Payable	40.3	
Accrued Compensation	46.4	
Other Accrued Expenses	28.9	
Income Taxes	2.6	
Current Portion of Long-Term Debt	.1	
Total Current Liabilities		$145.4
Noncurrent Liabilities:		
Long-Term Debt	87.9	
Accrued Retiree Benefits Other Than Pensions	76.0	
Deferred Income Taxes	16.9	
Accrued Interest and Other	89.8	
Total Noncurrent Liabilities		270.6
Total Liabilities		$416.0

Required:

26. No check figures

1. Identify the current liabilities in Thiokol's balance sheet that may have been recorded in period-ending adjusting entries.
2. What type of adjusting entry related to Long-Term Debt may have been required in Thiokol's accounting records?

3. Assume that the Accrued Compensation liability was recorded in a period-ending adjusting entry. Prepare that entry.

27. **Adjusting Journal Entries** (LO 3)

Laura Designs, Inc., is an interior decorating firm. The company requires that customers pay 50 percent of their bill before any work is performed. In November, Laura Designs received $5,000 in partial payment for a new job. The entire job was to cost the customer $10,000. As of December 31, 1996, the job was 90 percent complete. No further payments had been received by that date from the customer nor had any additional entries relating to this customer's job been recorded.

Required:
1. Prepare the entry to record the November partial payment.
2. Prepare any necessary adjusting journal entry as of December 31, 1996, in the accounting records of Laura Designs, Inc.

27. 1. Cr. Unearn. Rev. $5,000
    2. Cr. Fee Rev. $9,000

28. **Failure to Record Year-end Adjusting Journal Entry** (LO 3)

Silverman & Sachs is a large investment banking firm. In December 1996, Silverman & Sachs earned $4.1 million of fees for investment banking services for which the firm had not been paid as of December 31, 1996.

Required:
1. Given the facts provided, prepare an appropriate adjusting journal entry as of December 31, 1996, in Silverman & Sachs accounting records.
2. Suppose that Silverman & Sachs's accountants fail to record the adjusting journal entry you prepared in Part 1. Which accounting principles or concepts would be violated by this oversight?

28. 1. Cr. Fee Rev. $4,100,000

29. **Adjusting Journal Entries** (LO 3)

In December, Ken's Cleaning Service, a new business, bought $6,500 of cleaning supplies. At the end of December, the business had $3,400 of supplies on hand.

Required:
1. Prepare the entries to record the initial purchase of the cleaning supplies and the adjustment needed to record the supplies used during December.
2. Suppose that neither of the entries in Part 1 were made. Indicate how the business's December 31 financial statements would be affected. Consider only the firm's balance sheet and income statement.

29. 1. Dr. Supplies Exp. $3,100

30. **Closing Entries** (LO 6)

Following are selected account balances included in the December 31, 1996, adjusted trial balance of Hernandez Brothers Supply Company.

Cash	$ 2,000
Accounts Receivable	3,000
Prepaid Insurance	4,500
Unearned Rental Revenue	6,100
Accounts Payable	1,500
Utilities Expense	3,000
Income Tax Expense	4,000
Sales Revenue	25,000
Selling Expenses	6,000

Required:
1. Assuming that all of the company's temporary accounts are included in the listed accounts, prepare the appropriate December 31 closing entries for Hernandez Brothers.
2. How much net income did the company earn during the period in question?

30. 1. Cr. Inc. Sum. $25,000
    Dr. Inc. Sum. $13,000
    Cr. Ret. Earn. $12,000
    2. Net Income, $12,000

31. **Need for Adjusting and Closing Entries** (LO 5, 6)

Theo's Tailors is a small business operated by Alex Theodorius. The accounting records for this business are maintained by Markey & Michaels, CPAs. Recently, Alex questioned the monthly accounting bill submitted to him by the CPA firm. Included in the bill were the following line items, among others:

Adjustment of year-end account balances	5 hours × $60 per hour	$300
Closing of year-end balances of revenue and expense accounts	1 hour × $60 per hour	60

Alex does not understand why his accounting records must be adjusted at year-end. In a recent telephone conversation, he complained to a partner of Michaels & Markey. "If you guys did my accounting records right the first time, you wouldn't have to adjust them at year-end." Alex went on to complain that he could see no need for the $60 charge to close his revenue and expense acounts at year-end. "Why do you close those accounts, anyway? You use them every year. I think you're just closing them to run up my bill."

Required:

31.   No check figures

Write a memo to Alex Theodorius explaining the purpose of, and need for, period-ending adjusting and closing journal entries.

32. **Closing Process** (LO 6)

Selected year-end adjusted account balances for Random Access, Inc., appear as follows:

Cash	$100,000
Interest Revenue	5,000
Accounts Payable	40,000
Accumulated Depreciation, Equipment	36,000
Rental Revenue	152,000
Dividends	15,000
Salaries Expense	45,000
Depreciation Expense	12,000

Required:

32. 3. Cr. Inc. Sum. $157,000
        Dr. Inc. Sum. $57,000
        Cr. Ret. Earn. $100,000
        Cr. Div. $15,000

1. For each account, indicate whether the balance would normally be a debit or a credit.
2. Indicate which accounts are permanent accounts and which are temporary accounts.
3. Given the information provided, prepare all appropriate closing entries for Random Access.

33. **Preparation of an Income Statement** (LO 4)

Following is the adjusted trial balance of Jeffrey Consultants, Inc., that was drawn from a work sheet prepared for the company for the year ended December 31, 1996.

	DEBIT	CREDIT
Cash	$ 24,000	
Accounts Receivable	71,000	
Inventory	125,000	
Prepaid Insurance	6,000	
Equipment	242,000	
Accumulated Depreciation, Equipment		$ 31,000
Accounts Payable		17,000

Interest Payable		4,000
Notes Payable		67,000
Common Stock		15,000
Retained Earnings		91,000
Consulting Fees Revenue		460,000
Interest Revenue		3,000
Salaries Expense	176,000	
Advertising Expense	22,000	
Utilities Expense	6,000	
Interest Expense	5,000	
Depreciation Expense, Equipment	10,000	
Interest Receivable	1,000	
Income Taxes Expense	90,000	
Income Taxes Payable		90,000
	$778,000	$778,000

Required:

Prepare an income statement for Jeffery Consultants, Inc., for the year ended December 31, 1996.

34. Preparation of Balance Sheet (LO 4)

Refer to the information in Exercise 33.

Required:

Prepare an unclassified balance sheet for Jeffrey Consultants, Inc., as of December 31, 1996.

33. Tot. Rev., $463,000
     Net Income, $154,000

34. Total Assets, $438,000
     Ret. Earn., $245,000

PROBLEM SET A

35. General Journal Entries (LO 3)

The following transactions were engaged in by Hans and Heidi Dolls, Inc., during December 1996:

1. December 1:   Purchased supplies for $300
2. December 15: Paid December rent on store, $400
3. December 16: Paid employee salaries, $1,200
4. December 16: Recorded receipt of interest from bank, $600; the related interest revenue had been recorded in an adjusting entry at the end of November
5. December 22: Received $1,700 cash from customer in payment of account receivable
6. December 26: Paid January rent on store, $400
7. December 30: Received $2,500 advance payment of revenue from customer
8. December 31: Purchased sewing machine on credit for $3,000

Required:

1. Prepare general journal entries for these transactions.
2. Identify the accounts affected by the journal entries prepared in Part 1 that are a deferred expense, a deferred revenue, an accrued revenue, or an accrued expense.

35. 1. 1. Dr. Sup. $300
        2. Dr. Rent. Exp. $400
        3. Dr. Sal. Exp. $1,200
        4. Cr. Int. Rec. $600
        5. Cr. A.R. $1,700
        6. Dr. Pre. Rent $400
        7. Cr. Unearn. Rev. $2,500
        8. Dr. Equip. $3,000

36. Adjusting Journal Entries (LO 3)

Suppose you are an accountant for Kelberg, Inc., an advertising agency. You are presently preparing to close Kelberg's accounting records for the current year since December 31 is only a few days away. The owner of this business is planning to apply for a loan from a local bank in early January. Because the owner is worried that the bank will not approve the loan, he instructs you to credit a

$31,000 advance payment received from a customer on December 27 to a revenue account. Kelberg will provide the services paid for in advance by this customer in March of next year. The owner also instructs you to ignore the unpaid December rent of $7,500 that Kelberg owes on the office building it is leasing.

Required:

1. If you comply with the owner's instructions, how will the business's December 31 balance sheet for the current year be affected? How will the company's income statement for the current year be affected?
2. What accounting principles will be violated if you comply with the owner's instructions?
3. What will you do in this situation? Identify the parties who may be affected by your decision to comply or not comply with the owner's instructions and indicate how each of these parties may be affected by your decision.

37. **Adjusting Journal Entries** (LO 3)

    The following information pertains to the operations of Story Investigating, a private detective agency, for the month of December.

    1. The employees of Story earn $420 of salary collectively each day. The employees work Monday through Friday and are paid each Friday. This year, December 31 falls on a Tuesday.
    2. On December 31, Story's owner estimates that the business's electric bill for December will be $240.
    3. Story's owner also estimates that the firm will have income tax expense of $800 for the month of December. This expense will not be paid until March of the following year.
    4. On December 1, Story received and recorded a $300 payment from a customer. This payment was for services to be rendered by Story during December, January, and February. By December 31, one-third of these services had been provided.
    5. Story received $680 from a new client on December 28. No services had been provided to this client as of December 31. This item was properly recorded by Story's bookkeeper on December 29.
    6. Bonocher, Inc., owes Story $1,400 for services provided during December. No entry pertaining to these services has been recorded in Story's accounting records.

    Required:

    1. For each transaction or event identified, prepare any necessary adjusting journal entry as of December 31 in Story's accounting records.
    2. Suppose that Story Investigating employs the cash basis of accounting instead of the accrual basis. That is, the company records revenues when it receives cash payments from customers and records expenses when it disburses cash to suppliers, customers, and other parties. Analyze the six items listed and determine how Story's revenues and expenses for December would be affected by using the cash basis instead of the accrual basis of accounting.
    3. Write a brief memo indicating which method of accounting, cash basis or accrual basis, better portrays the results of Story Investigating's operations for December.

38. **"Nonaccounting" Financial Statement Disclosures** (LO 4)

    The For Your Information vignette in this chapter titled "Beyond the Accounting Cycle: 'Nonaccounting' Information Needs of Decision Makers" discusses the role of nonaccounting information in the decisions of financial

---

Margin notes:

36. No check figures

37. 1. 1. Dr. Sal. Exp. $840
       2. Dr. Util. Exp. $240
       3. Dr. Inc. Tax. Exp. $800
       4. Cr. Fee Rev. $100
       6. Cr. Fee Rev. $1,400
    2. Cash basis shows $1,360 more pre-tax profit

statement users. Consider the following nonaccounting disclosures from the 1992 annual report of Volvo, the Swedish automobile manufacturer.

Beginning in 1992, Volvo Truck Corporation has been able to deliver a complete program of engines that fulfill the new, strict environmental demands that become fully effective in the European Community in 1993. Additionally, Volvo Buses began deliveries in 1993 of environmentally compatible natural-gas buses to the city of Göteborg.
   Environmental audits were also conducted in seven plants in 1992. The audits show that conditions are satisfactory and that responsible personnel in each Volvo subsidiary are conscientiously following Volvo's environmental guidelines.

Required:

Write a brief report addressing the following topics relating to Volvo's nonaccounting financial statement disclosures.

1. What do you believe was Volvo's objective in disclosing this information in its annual report?
2. Do you believe this objective was accomplished? Why or why not?
3. Do you believe that Volvo's internal accountants or independent auditors should have reviewed these disclosures to determine that they were accurate before they were included in the company's annual report? Why or why not?

38.   No check figures

39. **Completing the Accounting Cycle for a New Business** (LO 2–7)
Following is a trial balance for a new business, Resultan Corporation, as of January 31, 1996, prior to the closing of the company's books. Resultan rents various types of equipment to manufacturing companies.

	DEBIT	CREDIT
Cash	$10,000	
Accounts Receivable	2,000	
Supplies	900	
Prepaid Insurance	1,200	
Equipment	48,000	
Accounts Payable		$ 200
Unearned Rental Revenue		700
Common Stock		12,000
Additional Paid-in Capital		46,000
Dividends	500	
Rental Revenue		8,000
Salaries Expense	3,200	
Utilities Expense	1,100	
	$66,900	$66,900

Following is additional financial information pertaining to Resultan Corporation.

a. By January 31, the company had earned $500 of the $700 balance of the Unearned Rental Revenue account.
b. On January 31, the company owed its employees $800 for salaries they had earned in the last few days of January.
c. On January 31, the company was owed $50 of interest revenue by its local bank.
d. Resultan uses the straight-line depreciation method for its equipment. The equipment was purchased on January 1 for $48,000, has a four-year useful life, and is expected to have no salvage value at the end of its useful life.

e. On January 1, Resultan purchased and paid for a one-year insurance policy on its equipment. The cost of this policy was $1,200 and was debited to Prepaid Insurance.

Required:

1. Prepare four-column accounts or T-accounts for Resultan and enter the January 31 account balances in these accounts from the company's trial balance.
2. Enter Resultan's trial balance on a work sheet and complete the work sheet.
3. Prepare an income statement for the month of January 1996, an unclassified balance sheet as of January 31, 1996, and a statement of stockholders' equity for the month of January 1996 for Resultan.
4. Prepare all necessary adjusting journal entries for Resultan as of January 31, 1996. Post these adjusting entries to the appropriate accounts. When necessary, create new accounts.
5. Prepare closing entries as of January 31, 1996. Post the closing entries to the appropriate accounts.
6. Prepare a post-closing trial balance for Resultan as of January 31, 1996.

40. **Closing Entries** (LO 6)

Following is a list of certain account balances drawn from the adjusted trial balance of Sharon's Shoe Repair Shop as of December 31, 1996. This list includes all of the business's revenue and expense accounts as well as selected additional accounts.

Prepaid Insurance	$ 5,500
Accounts Payable	8,200
Utilities Expense	1,000
Cash	12,000
Accounts Receivable	3,000
Shoe Repair Revenue	35,000
Prepaid Rent	4,500
Unearned Repair Revenue	700
Salaries Expense	12,000
Salaries Payable	900
Bonds Payable	1,500
Income Taxes Expense	8,000

Required:

1. Given the account balances just shown, prepare all appropriate closing entries for Sharon's Shoe Repair Shop on December 31, 1996.
2. What was the company's net income (loss) for 1996?
3. Explain how closing entries allow accountants to more easily determine the net income of a business each accounting period.

41. **Income Statement Preparation** (LO 4)

Following is an adjusted trial balance for Socks Yarns Company for the year ended December 31, 1996.

	DEBIT	CREDIT
Cash	$112,500	
Accounts Receivable	95,000	
Supplies	12,000	
Prepaid Advertising	18,000	
Prepaid Rent	40,000	
Equipment	90,500	
Accumulated Depreciation, Equipment		$ 71,000

Margin notes:

39. 2. Adjustments, $2,450
        Adjusted Trial Balance, $68,750
    3. Net Income $2,350
        Retained Earnings, $1,850
        Total Assets, $61,050
    5. Cr. Inc. Sum. $8,550
        Dr. Inc. Sum. $6,200
        Cr. Ret. Earn. $2,350
        Cr. Div. $500
    6. Post-Closing Trial Balance, $62,050

40. 1a. Cr. Inc. Sum. $35,000
    1b. Dr. Inc. Sum. $21,000
    1c. Cr. Ret. Earn. 14,000
    2. Net Income, $14,000

Accounts Payable		38,000
Salaries Payable		2,400
Unearned Knitting Revenue		75,000
Common Stock		34,000
Retained Earnings		20,000
Rent Expense	69,500	
Income Taxes Expense	35,000	
Salaries Expense	75,000	
Depreciation Expense, Equipment	17,000	
Interest Revenue		9,100
Knitting Revenue		315,000
Totals	$564,500	$564,500

Required:

1. Prepare an income statement for Socks Yarns Company for the year ended December 31, 1996.
2. Prepare an unclassified balance sheet for Socks Yarns Company as of December 31, 1996.
3. Identify three general classes of financial statement users that might make economic decisions based upon Socks Yarns' financial statements. How might errors in these financial statements affect such decisions?

41. 1. Net Income, $127,600
2. Retained Earnings, $147,600
Total Assets, $297,000

PROBLEM SET B

42. **General Journal Entries** (LO 3)

The following transactions were engaged in by Lynn's Decorators, Inc., during December 1996.

1. December 1:   Purchased supplies for $400
2. December 3:   Received $4,000 from customer for services to be provided in January
3. December 6:   Recorded receipt of interest from bank, $3,600; the related interest revenue had been recorded in an adjusting entry at the end of November
4. December 20: Purchased equipment on credit for $2,500
5. December 22: Received $2,500 from customer in payment of account receivable
6. December 23: Paid employee salaries, $1,200
7. December 30: Paid December rent on store, $800
8. December 31: Paid January rent on store, $900

Required:

1. Prepare general journal entries for these transactions.
2. Identify the accounts affected by the journal entries prepared in Part 1 that are a deferred expense, a deferred revenue, an accrued revenue, or an accrued expense.

42. 1. 1. Dr. Sup. $400
2. Cr. Unearn. Ser. Rev. $4,000
3. Cr. Int. Rec. $3,600
4. Dr. Equip. $2,500
5. Cr. A.R. $2,500
6. Dr. Sal. Exp. $1,200
7. Dr. Rent Exp. $800
8. Dr. Pre. Rent $900

43. **Adjusting Journal Entries** (LO 3)

Suppose that you are a local CPA and that once per month you update the accounting records of Pinpoint Printing Company. You also close this client's accounting records at the end of each year and prepare the firm's annual financial statements. After arriving at Pinpoint's headquarters office on December 31 of the current year, the business owner asks to meet with you privately. The owner explains that she is attempting to sell the company to a much larger competitor. Because she wants to receive "top dollar" for the business, she asks you to ignore several unpaid expenses of Pinpoint at year-end. These expenses include a $1,400 advertising bill, a $2,100 electric bill, and $1,100 of salaries earned by Pinpoint's employees during the last few days of the year. She assures you that these items will be paid in January and that you can record them as expenses then. "You know, since we haven't paid these bills, I don't see any reason that we should have to book them as expenses in the current month," the owner comments to you.

Required:

1. If you comply with the owner's request, how will Pinpoint's balance sheet as of December 31 of the current year be affected? How will the company's income statement for the year ended December 31 of the current year be affected?
2. Will you comply with the owner's request? Identify the parties who may be affected by your decision. Indicate how each of these parties may be affected by your decision to comply or not comply with the owner's request.
3. Will the fact that you are a CPA influence your decision of whether or not to comply with the owner's request? Why or why not?

44. Adjusting Journal Entries (LO 3)

The following information pertains to the operations of Steeplechase Consultants, a large architectural firm, for the month of December.

1. On December 31, Steeplechase's accountant estimates that the firm's water bill for December will be $2,100.
2. Steeplechase's accountant also estimates that the firm will have income tax expense of $7,700 for the month of December. This expense will be paid in March of the following year.
3. Steeplechase received and recorded a $30,000 payment on December 2 from a customer. This payment was for services to be rendered by Steeplechase during December and January. By December 31, one-half of these services had been provided.
4. The employees of Steeplechase earn $12,000 of salary collectively each day. The employees work Monday through Friday and are paid each Friday. This year, December 31 falls on a Thursday.
5. Tarkanian, Inc., owes Steeplechase $13,400 for services provided during December. No entry pertaining to these services has been recorded in Steeplechase's accounting records.
6. Steeplechase received a $4,900 advance payment from a new client on December 29. No services have been provided to this client as of December 31. This item was properly recorded by Steeplechase's accountant on December 30.

Required:

1. For each transaction or event identified, prepare any necessary adjusting journal entry as of December 31 in Steeplechase's accounting records.
2. Suppose that Steeplechase employs the cash basis of accounting instead of the accrual basis. That is, the company records revenues when it receives cash payments from customers and records expenses when it disburses cash to suppliers, customers, and other parties. Analyze the six items listed and determine how Steeplechase's revenues and expenses for December would be affected by using the cash basis instead of the accrual basis of accounting.
3. Write a brief memo indicating which method of accounting, cash basis or accrual basis, better portrays the results of Steeplechase's operations for December.

43. No check figures

44. 1. 1. Dr. Utili. Exp. $2,100
    2. Dr. Inc. Tax Exp. $7,700
    3. Cr. Ser. Rev. $15,000
    4. Dr. Sal. Exp. $48,000
    5. Cr. Ser. Rev. $13,400
  2. Cash basis shows $64,300 more profits

45. **Nonaccounting Financial Statement Disclosures** (LO 4)

The For Your Information vignette in this chapter titled "Beyond the Accounting Cycle: 'Nonaccounting' Information Needs of Decision Makers" discusses the role of nonaccounting information in the decisions of financial statement users. Consider the following nonaccounting disclosure from the 1994 annual report of Cott Corporation, a Canadian-based supplier of soft drink beverages. Cott supplies beverage products to Royal Crown, Cadbury, and Wal-Mart, among others.

Overall, sales increased by 101 percent or $334 million [Canadian dollars] in 1994 over 1993. Of this, 76 percent or $252 million represents additional sales to existing customers, and 24 percent or $82 million represents sales to new customers.

As always, it is account penetration that is most important to us. I [the CEO] believe that this measure best confirms that consumers are responding well to our offerings and that our customers value our products.

Required:

Write a brief report addressing the following topics relating to Cott's nonaccounting financial statement disclosures.

1. What do you believe was Cott's objective in disclosing this information in its annual report?
2. Do you believe this objective was accomplished? Why or why not?
3. Do you believe that Cott's internal accountants or independent auditors should have reviewed these disclosures to determine that they were accurate before they were included in the company's annual report? Why or why not?

45. No check figures

46. **Completing the Accounting Cycle for a New Business** (LO 2–7)

Following is a trial balance for a new business, Norman Enterprises, as of January 31, 1996, prior to the closing of the company's books. Norman rents furniture, principally to college students.

	DEBIT	CREDIT
Cash	$ 17,000	
Accounts Receivable	4,500	
Supplies	1,800	
Furniture	90,000	
Accounts Payable		$ 1,600
Unearned Rental Revenue		2,200
Common Stock		40,000
Additional Paid-in Capital		64,000
Rental Revenue		12,800
Utilities Expense	1,500	
Salaries Expense	4,800	
Dividends	1,000	
	$120,600	$120,600

Following is additional financial information pertaining to Norman Enterprises.

a. By January 31, the company had earned $800 of the $2,200 balance of the Unearned Rental Revenue account.
b. On January 31, the company had $500 of supplies on hand; $1,800 of supplies were purchased during the month.
c. At the end of January, the company was owed $100 of interest revenue by its local bank.
d. On January 31, the company owed its employees $900 for salaries they had earned but not yet been paid.

e. Norman uses the straight-line depreciation method for its furniture. The furniture was purchased on January 1 for $90,000, has a six-year useful life, and is expected to have no salvage value at the end of its useful life.

46. 2. Adjustments, $4,350
Adjusted Trial Balance,
$122,850
3. Net Income $3,950
Retained Earnings,
$2,950
Total Assets, $110,850
5. Cr. Inc. Sum. $13,700
Dr. Inc. Sum. $9,750
Cr. Ret. Earn. $3,950
Cr. Div. $1,000
6. Post-Closing Trial
Balance, $112,100

Required:
1. Prepare four-column accounts or T-accounts for Norman and enter the January 31 balances in these accounts from the company's trial balance.
2. Enter Norman's trial balance on a work sheet and complete the work sheet.
3. From the work sheet completed in Part 2, prepare an income statement for the month of January 1996, an unclassified balance sheet as of January 31, 1996, and a statement of stockholders' equity for the month of January 1996 for Norman.
4. Prepare all necessary adjusting journal entries for Norman as of January 31, 1996. Post these adjusting entries to the appropriate accounts. When necessary, create new accounts.
5. Prepare closing entries as of January 31, 1996. Post the closing entries to the appropriate accounts.
6. Prepare a post-closing trial balance as of January 31, 1996.

47. Closing Entries (LO 6)

Following is a list of certain account balances drawn from an adjusted trial balance for Beckwith Advertising Agency as of December 31, 1996. This list includes all of the business's revenue and expense accounts as well as selected additional accounts.

Salaries Expense	$ 5,500
Notes Payable	8,200
Utilities Expense	2,000
Cash	12,000
Accounts Receivable	3,000
Advertising Revenue	55,000
Prepaid Insurance	4,500
Unearned Advertising Revenue	6,100
Prepaid Rent	22,000
Salaries Payable	900
Accounts Payable	1,500
Income Taxes Expense	10,000

47. 1a. Cr. Inc. Sum. $55,000
1b. Dr. Inc. Sum. $17,500
1c. Cr. Ret. Earn. $37,500
2. Net Income, $37,500

Required:
1. Given the account balances just shown, prepare all appropriate closing entries for Beckwith on December 31, 1996.
2. What was Beckwith's net income (loss) for 1996?
3. Suppose the company's adjusted trial balance included the following two additional items: Dividends—$400; Dividend Revenue—$600. Recompute the company's net income (loss).

48. Income Statement Preparation (LO 4)

Following is an adjusted trial balance for Sue's Sew Shop as of December 31, 1996.

	DEBIT	CREDIT
Cash	$115,500	
Accounts Receivable	92,000	
Inventory	16,000	
Prepaid Insurance	20,000	
Prepaid Rent	40,000	
Machinery	85,500	

Accumulated Depreciation, Machinery		$ 20,000
Unearned Sewing Revenue		46,100
Accounts Payable		3,400
Income Tax Payable		19,000
Common Stock		9,000
Retained Earnings		45,000
Depreciation Expense, Machinery	14,500	
Rent Expense	50,000	
Income Taxes Expense	40,000	
Salaries Expense	80,000	
Utilities Expense	22,000	
Interest Revenue		8,000
Sewing Revenue		425,000
Totals	$575,500	$575,500

Required:

1. Prepare an income statement for Sue's Sew Shop for the year ended December 31, 1996.
2. Prepare a balance sheet for this business as of December 31, 1996.
3. Suppose this company is publicly owned and you are considering purchasing 100 shares of its common stock. Identify three questions pertaining to either the company's balance sheet or income statement that you would want to ask of the company's chief executive officer before you decide whether to invest in the company.

48. 1. Net Income, $226,500
    2. Retained Earnings, $271,500
       Total Assets, $349,000

CASES

49. Analyzing Current Liabilities

K.C. is a college student at State University. Thanks to his grandparents, K.C. has a large investment portfolio. One day, K.C. was browsing through the annual reports of several public companies in which he owns common stock. K.C. noticed the following information for Van Vleet Corporation.

	DECEMBER 31, 1994	DECEMBER 31, 1995
Accounts Payable	$17,200,000	$ 8,300,000
Salaries Payable	12,500,000	1,200,000
Income Taxes Payable	10,000,000	8,000,000
Interest Payable	1,200,000	200,000
Total Current Liabilities	$40,900,000	$17,700,000

K.C., who enrolled in an introductory financial accounting course but dropped out after the first exam, turns to his roommate and observes, "What a crooked company! Look at this. Over $40 million in current liabilities one year and less than half that the next. You know this company has been playing around with its financial statements. I'm calling my stockbroker and telling him to unload my stock in this company."

Required:

Write a brief report explaining to K.C. legitimate reasons that could account for the differences in Van Vleet Corporation's current liability account balances at the end of 1994 and 1995.

50. Year-end Expense Accruals

Sawyer Brown is the bookkeeper for the Daniels Manufacturing Company. Recently, Daniels was audited for the first time by a public accounting firm. The auditors discovered that Brown never accrues expenses for such items as unpaid salaries and unpaid utilities at year-end. When asked, Brown explained that there is no need to accrue such expenses at year-end. "Every December 31 we have approximately the same amount of unpaid salaries, unpaid utility bills, etc., etc. So, why go to the trouble of recording such expenses since they net out each year?"

Required:

1. Explain Brown's reasoning. What does he mean when he maintains that the items in question "net out each year"? Use a numerical example involving an accrued expense item in your explanation.
2. What is wrong, if anything, with Brown's method of accounting (or not accounting) for unpaid expenses at year-end?

51. Adjusting Entries and Accounting Concepts

In 1970, a large warehouse of Mattel, the toy manufacturer, was destroyed by a fire. The contents of the warehouse were fully insured. In fact, Mattel's insurance policy contained a $10 million "business interruption" clause that compensated the company for business profits lost as a result of a fire or other calamity. Near the end of 1970, Mattel recorded an adjusting entry debiting a receivable account for $10 million related to this clause of its insurance policy. The offsetting credit was to a revenue account. As it turned out, Mattel was overly optimistic in booking the receivable and revenue related to the insurance claim. Nearly seven years passed before Mattel collected on the insurance claim and then it received only $4.4 million. The Securities and Exchange Commission (SEC) subsequently criticized Mattel for its accounting treatment of the insurance claim. The SEC maintained that Mattel knew it was entitled to collect much less than $10 million from its insurance company related to the business interruption clause of its insurance policy.

Required:

What accounting concepts or principles did Mattel violate when it recorded the $10 million adjusting entry in 1970? Explain how these concepts or principles were violated. How were Mattel's subsequent financial statements affected by its improper accounting for the insurance claim.

PROJECTS

52. Prepaid Expenses and Accrued Expenses in Corporate Balance Sheets

Meet with the project team to which you have been assigned by your instructor. Each member of your team should select a public company from a different industry that has the following two items reported in its balance sheet each year for the past three years: "Prepaid Expenses" and "Accrued Expenses" (or "Accrued Liabilities"). Each member should identify the dollar amount of these two items each year for the most recent three years. For each company each year, the following percentages should be computed: Prepaid Expenses/Current Assets; Prepaid Expenses/Total Assets; Accrued Expenses/Current Liabilities; Accrued Expenses/Total Liabilities. (Note: Some companies report several accrued expenses in their balance sheet. For these companies, it will be necessary to compute total accrued expenses by adding such items as "Salaries

Payable" or "Accrued Compensation," "Income Taxes Payable," and "Other Accrued Expenses.")

Required:

Meet as a group and compare your findings. Discuss the factors that may account for any major differences or similarities in the computed percentages across the companies selected by individual group members. Prepare a written report summarizing these factors. Include in your report the financial data collected for each company.

53. Unearned Revenues in Corporate Balance Sheets

Identify three companies that report unearned revenues in their annual balance sheets. You may select these companies from annual report files available in your library or from other sources.

Required:

1. Write a brief description of each of the three companies you selected.
2. Determine whether the individual companies' financial statement footnotes describe the accounting method used for unearned revenues. If so, write a brief summary of each of these accounting methods.
3. Record the dollar amount of unearned revenues reported by each company over at least the most recent three years. Is there a definite trend in these amounts? That is, have the unearned revenue amounts of individual companies steadily increased or decreased in recent years? Provide an explanation for any obvious trends in these data.
4. Why do some companies have very large amounts of unearned revenues, while others have little or none?

54. Reconstructing an Adjusted Trial Balance

Select a large public company and obtain a recent balance sheet, income statement, and statement of stockholder's equity for the firm.

Required:

1. Reconstruct the company's adjusted trial balance at the end of the year for which you have the company's financial statements. Make sure that the totals of each column of the trial balance are in agreement.
2. Prepare the closing entries that would have been necessary for this company for the year in question.

6

ACCOUNTING FOR MERCHANDISING COMPANIES

LEARNING OBJECTIVES

After studying this chapter, you should be able to do the following:

1. Discuss the nature of merchandising operations including the operating cycle of merchandising companies

2. Compute the gross profit percentage and the profit margin percentage

3. Compare and contrast a periodic inventory system and a perpetual inventory system

4. Account for merchandise sales, purchases, and transportation costs in a periodic inventory system

5. Determine cost of goods sold in a periodic inventory system

6. Prepare a work sheet and complete the period-ending closing procedures for a merchandising company that uses a periodic inventory system

7. Prepare an income statement for a merchandising company

8. Discuss key internal control issues and procedures for a merchandising company

9. Journalize transactions in special journals and post transaction data from special journals to the general ledger and subsidiary ledgers

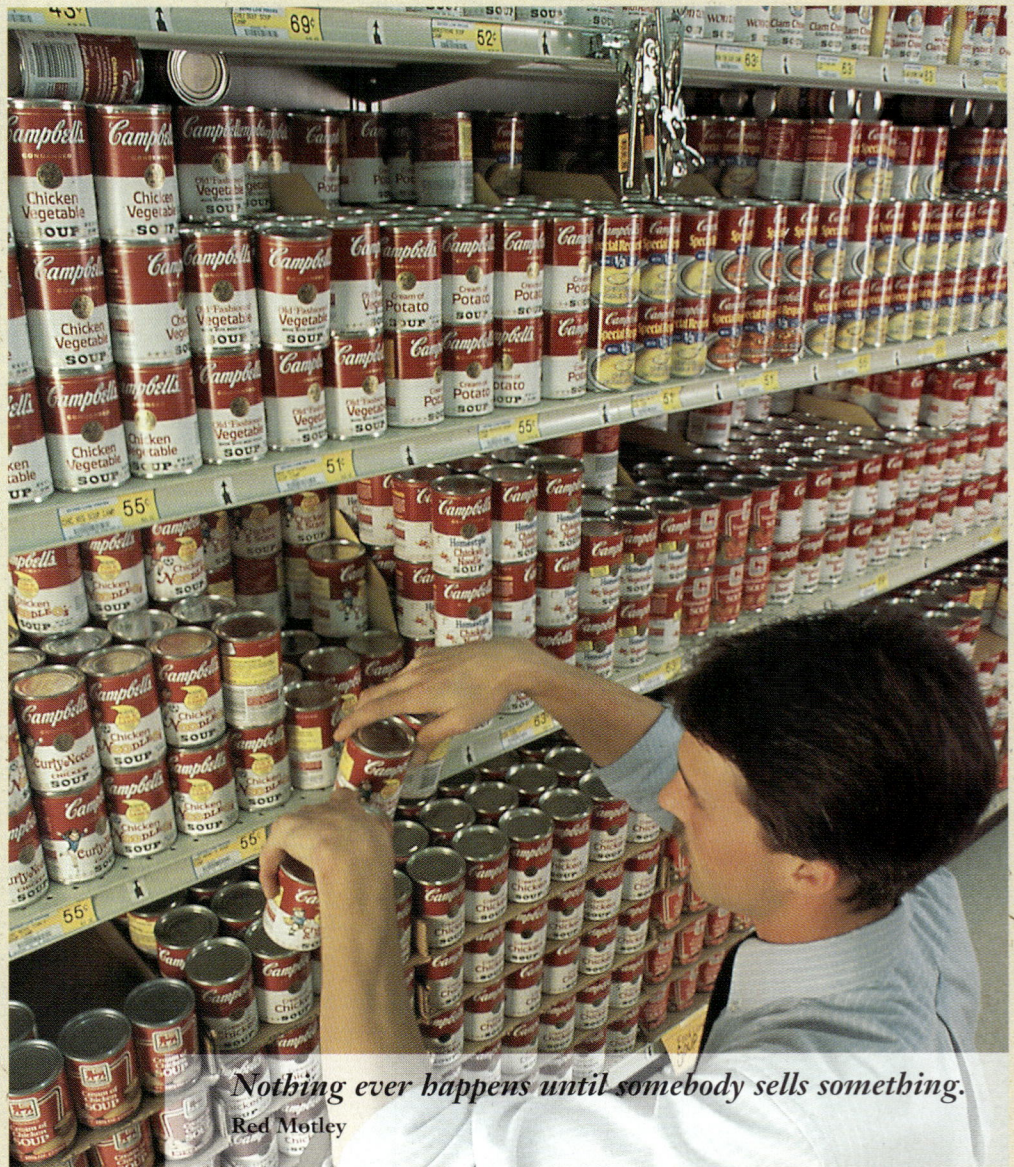

Nothing ever happens until somebody sells something.
Red Motley

Marketing by the (Accounting) Numbers

Two trillion dollars, $2 trillion, or $2,000,000,000,000, regardless how you write it, is a lot of money. What does that figure represent? The total retail sales rung up by U.S. businesses each year during the early 1990s. Economists track retail sales to gain insight on the health of the national economy. Stagnant or declining retail sales send a clear signal to economists that the nation's economy is in the doldrums or headed in that direction. Likewise, "flat" or falling sales are generally a reliable indicator that an individual company's financial future is less than promising.

The degree of financial success a company experiences is heavily influenced by how well it manages the selling or marketing process. There are several components to a company's marketing strategy, one of the most important being the product or products it offers for sale. Microsoft, General Motors, and Hershey Foods have all thrived financially in large part because each has a line of products demanded by the public. Promotion is another important component of a marketing strategy. A company that makes a "better mousetrap" may fail miserably unless it effectively promotes that product to potential customers. Then, we come to price. If the "price isn't right," a company with a tremendous product supported by extravagant advertising efforts will soon be relegated to the corporate graveyard.

Although accountants are not perceived as marketing types, they provide invaluable information to corporate executives responsible for developing a company's marketing strategy. This is particularly true for the pricing component of a company's marketing strategy. Take the case of the Standard Candy Company of Nashville, Tennessee, which sells Goo Goo Clusters, a very popular candy item in the South. In 1983, Standard Candy's executives decided to boost sales by doubling the purchase discounts they offered to retail stores, the company's principal customers. Within a matter of weeks, the company's accounting department was feeding data to these executives regarding the financial implications of the new pricing strategy. These data revealed that the discounting tactic had been successful in one respect and a disappointing failure in another. The new pricing strategy caused the sales of Goo Goo Clusters to increase dramatically. However, profits dropped even more dramatically because the company realized a much smaller "profit margin" on its sales due to the larger price discounts. After reviewing the relevant accounting data, management quickly reverted to its former pricing structure.

This chapter focuses on accounting for merchandising companies, which are among the most common and important types of business entities. The chapter begins with an overview of merchandising operations including how merchandising companies differ from other types of businesses. Then the key accounting procedures for merchandisers are presented. The chapter concludes with a discussion of internal control considerations for merchandising companies.

AN OVERVIEW OF MERCHANDISING OPERATIONS

Before we consider accounting issues related to merchandising companies, it will be helpful for you to become better acquainted with these types of businesses. This section begins by introducing you to the nature of merchandising operations and the operating cycle of merchandising companies. Next, a typical income statement for a

■ **LEARNING OBJECTIVE 1**
Discuss the nature of merchandising operations including the operating cycle of merchandising companies

merchandising company is reviewed. This section concludes with a discussion of two financial ratios that can be used to provide insight on the financial health of merchandising companies.

Nature of Merchandising Operations

Business entities are often segregated into three broad groups: service companies or organizations, manufacturing companies, and merchandising companies. Businesses that provide professional, technical, or other types of services to their customers are referred to as service companies or organizations. Law firms, airlines, and advertising agencies are examples of this type of business entity, as is Snow Mountain Retreat, the company used to illustrate the accounting cycle in Chapter 5. Manufacturing firms such as Dow Chemical, Goodyear Tire & Rubber, and Bethlehem Steel convert raw materials of some type into finished products. These finished products are then sold, typically to wholesale merchandising companies. Wholesale merchandising companies are commonly referred to as wholesale distributors or simply wholesalers. An example of a wholesale distributor is United Stationers, Inc., the largest wholesaler of office supply products in the United States. United Stationers purchases office supply products from more than four hundred manufacturing companies. Then the company resells these products to retail office supply stores from thirty regional distribution centers scattered across the United States.

Retail merchandising firms such as Sears, J. C. Penney's, and Wal-Mart buy products principally from wholesalers and then resell these products to the public from retail outlets. Some retail merchandisers sell their goods through mail-order operations, while a few futuristic companies market their goods via televised home shopping clubs. In recent years, it has become more common for large retailers to skip the so-called middleman and purchase their goods directly from manufacturers. Wal-Mart, in particular, has used this strategy to reduce the acquisition cost of the merchandise it sells. Accounting for wholesale and retail merchandising operations is very similar. This chapter focuses principally on accounting decisions and issues related to retail merchandising operations. Accounting for manufacturing operations is more complex and will be discussed in subsequent accounting courses.

The Operating Cycle for Merchandising Companies

Teaching Note
To reinforce students' understanding of the operating cycle concept, contrast the operating cycle of a business with a short operating cycle such as a florist shop with the operating cycle of a business with a longer operating cycle such as a jewelry store.

Like most businesses, merchandising firms engage in a recurring series of transactions referred to as an operating cycle. Recall from Chapter 2 that an operating cycle begins with the use of cash in the normal operating activities of a business and ends with the collection of cash from the business's customers. The two most common and important transactions in a merchandising company's operating cycle are the purchase of goods from suppliers and the sale of those same goods to customers.

The key source document for purchases and sales transactions of a merchandising company is an invoice. In Chapter 5, an invoice for Snow Mountain Retreat, a service company, was presented. The invoices used by merchandising companies are similar to those used by service companies. Shown in Exhibit 6.1 is an invoice for a sale of merchandise by Kelley Faye Fashions, a wholesaler, to Bonney's Dress Shop, a retail business used to illustrate various merchandising transactions later in this chapter. This invoice would serve as the basis for recording a sales transaction in Kelley Faye's accounting records and as the basis for recording a purchase transaction in Bonney's accounting records.

■ **EXHIBIT 6.1**
Invoice for Sale of Merchandise

Kelley Faye Fashions
1212 Laurence Way
Buffalo Falls, New York 10055

invoice

Invoice #:	**3421**
Date:	**4/1/96**
Customer ID:	**1348-12**

Bill To:

Bonney's Dress Shop
1114 East Main
Norman, OK 73073

Ship To:

Same

YOUR #	SALES REP	FOB	SHIP VIA	TERMS
1348-12	Ted Charles	Shipping Point	UPS	2/10, n/30

QTY	ITEM	DESCRIPTION	UNIT PR	TOTAL
12	672-1	Jump suit, sizes 3-5-7-9, 3 each	25.00	$ 300.00
			BAL DUE	$ 300.00

After receiving the merchandise purchased from Kelley Faye Fashions, Bonney's would ticket that merchandise and display it in the appropriate department. Eventually, that merchandise would be sold on either a cash or a credit basis. The operating cycle would be completed when Bonney's collected cash from the customers who purchased the merchandise. Besides merchandise purchases, sales, and cash receipts transactions, a merchandising company's operating cycle may include other transactions as well. Purchases returns and allowances, sales returns and allowances, and payments of freight charges for the delivery of merchandise are examples of other merchandising transactions considered in this chapter.

Merchandising businesses, such as Bonney's Dress Shop, purchase goods at wholesale prices from their suppliers and sell these goods at retail prices to their customers.

Income Statement for a Merchandising Company

Except for the income statement, the financial statements of a merchandising company are very similar to the financial statements of service companies. Shown in Exhibit 6.2 is a recent income statement for The Home Depot, a firm that bills itself as the world's largest home improvement retailer. Notice that The Home Depot's income statement is very similar to the income statement discussed in Chapter 2 for Xylogics, Inc., a manufacturing company. Nevertheless, there are differences between the income statements of merchandising companies and manufacturing companies. These differences will become more apparent when, or if, you study accounting for manufacturing companies in a subsequent accounting course.

net sales

A merchandising company's income statement begins with net sales. **Net sales** represent a merchandiser's total sales during an accounting period less sales returns and allowances and sales discounts—the latter items are discussed later in this chapter. The key difference between a service company's income statement and that of a merchandising company is the inclusion of cost of goods sold in a merchandiser's income statement. As the term implies, **cost of goods sold** is the cost of inventory sold to customers during an accounting period. Since service companies do not sell goods or products, cost of goods sold does not appear on their income statements. The difference between net sales and cost of goods sold is referred to as gross profit, as shown in Exhibit 6.2.

cost of goods sold

Real World
Point out that cost of goods sold is typically the largest expense of most merchandising companies.

Operating expenses, the major expenses that a merchandising company incurs in its day-to-day operations other than cost of goods sold, are subtracted from gross profit to arrive at income from operations or operating income. The income statement of The Home Depot in Exhibit 6.2 lists three such expenses: selling and store operating, pre-opening, and administrative. After operating income, a merchandising company's income statement lists nonoperating or "other" revenues and expenses. These are revenues and expenses not directly related to the company's merchandising operations. Interest income (revenue) and interest expense are the most common nonoperating revenues and expenses. Income before income taxes is computed by adding or

■ **EXHIBIT 6.2**

Recent Income Statement for The Home Depot, a Merchandising Company (in thousands)

Teaching Note
Using Exhibit 6.2, point out both the similarities and differences between the income statement of a service company and a merchandising company.

THE HOME DEPOT INCOME STATEMENT FOR THE YEAR ENDED JANUARY 30, 1994		
Net Sales		$9,238,763
Cost of Goods Sold		6,685,384
Gross Profit		$2,553,379
Operating Expenses:		
Selling and Store Operating	$1,624,920	
Pre-Opening	36,816	
Administrative	184,954	
Total Operating Expenses		1,846,690
Operating Income		706,689
Interest Income (Expense):		
Interest Income	60,896	
Interest Expense	(30,714)	
Interest, Net		30,182
Income before Income Taxes		736,871
Income Taxes Expense		279,470
Net Income		$457,401

SOURCE: The Home Depot's 1994 Annual Report.

subtracting the net nonoperating revenues and expenses to, or from, operating income. Finally, net income is the difference between income before income taxes and income taxes expense. Keep in mind that the income statement of The Home Depot is just one example of an income statement for a merchandising company. Although most merchandisers have income statements similar to the one shown in Exhibit 6.2, you will find many variations from this basic format.

Analyzing the Financial Health of Merchandising Companies

An excellent way to learn about an industry is to assume the role of a financial analyst and become familiar with key financial indicators for the companies within that industry. Turn to any recent edition of *Forbes*, *The Wall Street Journal*, or other major business publication and you are certain to find experts or supposed experts analyzing the financial status and future prospects of specific companies. The major focus of these experts' attention is financial ratios. **Financial ratios** express the relationship or interrelationships between two or more financial statement items. Financial ratios can be used by all types of internal and external decision makers to obtain important insight on the financial status of business entities. Numerous financial ratios are

■ **LEARNING OBJECTIVE 2**
Compute the gross profit percentage and the profit margin percentage

financial ratios

gross profit percentage

introduced in this textbook. Exhibit 6.3 presents two closely watched financial ratios, gross profit percentage and profit margin percentage, for several diverse merchandising companies.

GROSS PROFIT PERCENTAGE Merchandising companies are in the business of buying goods at one price and selling them at a higher price. If a company buys a product for $60 and resells that same product for $100, it has earned a gross profit of $40. Decision makers closely monitor the **gross profit percentage,** gross profit divided by net sales, of merchandising companies since this ratio is a key indicator of these companies' financial health. Operating problems facing a merchandising company are often quickly reflected in its gross profit percentage. For instance, if a merchandiser lowers its selling prices to meet the prices of a competitor, the result will be a smaller gross profit percentage and usually a smaller net income for the company.

Notice that the gross profit percentages of merchandising companies vary considerably. As shown in Exhibit 6.3, Drug Emporium, a drugstore chain, has a gross profit percentage less than one-half that of Lands' End and MacFrugal's. Although the latter two firms have similar gross profit percentages, the nature of their operations is distinctly different. Lands' End markets high-quality apparel merchandise via a mail-order operation, while MacFrugal's sells a wide assortment of "closeout merchandise" including housewares, tools, and toys. Lands' End sustains a high gross profit percentage because consumers are willing to pay a premium for the exclusive, brand name products that the company sells. On the other hand, MacFrugal's maintains a high gross profit percentage by selling discontinued merchandise at bargain basement prices, but prices that are nearly twice what the company paid to acquire that merchandise.

Wal-Mart, The Home Depot, and other large merchandising companies have two major categories of expenses reported in their periodic income statements: cost of goods sold and operating expenses.

profit margin percentage

Real World

Both management and investors are concerned with the trend in a company's gross profit percentage. The significance of this ratio as a measure of financial health is apparent in most annual reports of merchandising companies. Company executives generally discuss in an annual report the factors that accounted for changes in their firm's gross profit percentage from period to period.

PROFIT MARGIN PERCENTAGE Another closely monitored financial ratio for merchandising companies is the **profit margin percentage,** which is a company's net income divided by its net sales. This financial statistic indicates the percentage of each sales dollar that contributes to a company's net income. You might expect that the gross profit and profit margin percentages would be closely correlated for merchandising companies. That is not necessarily the case. For example, MacFrugal's has a high gross profit percentage compared to three of the other four merchandising companies included in Exhibit 6.3. In fact, MacFrugal's gross profit percentage is high compared to most merchandisers. Nevertheless, MacFrugal's profit per sales dollar (profit margin percentage) is not nearly as impressive. Why? Because MacFrugal's has relatively high operating expenses.

Again, financial ratios can provide important clues to decision makers regarding the financial health of individual companies. However, financial ratios can also be misleading, particularly if a decision maker focuses exclusively on one or a limited number of these ratios for a given company. To obtain a comprehensive understand-

■ **EXHIBIT 6.3**

Gross Profit and Profit Margin Percentages for Several Merchandising Companies

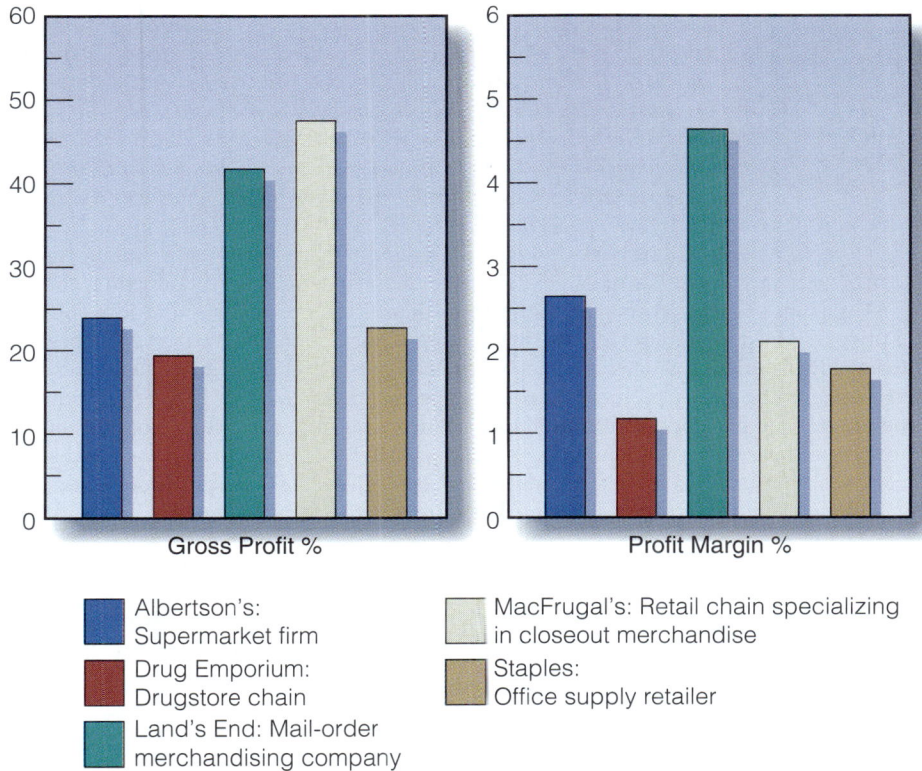

Legend:
- Albertson's: Supermarket firm
- Drug Emporium: Drugstore chain
- Land's End: Mail-order merchandising company
- MacFrugal's: Retail chain specializing in closeout merchandise
- Staples: Office supply retailer

ing of a company's financial health, a wide range of financial ratios that focus on each major dimension of the company's financial status must be analyzed.

ACCOUNTING FOR MERCHANDISING OPERATIONS

This section examines key accounting issues and procedures for merchandising companies. The section begins by comparing and contrasting the two types of inventory accounting systems used by merchandisers. Next, accounting procedures for sales, purchases, transportation costs, and cost of goods sold are discussed. This section concludes with a brief overview of the period-ending closing process for merchandising companies.

Inventory Systems Used by Merchandising Companies

Inventory is the most important asset of merchandising companies. As a result, the accounting systems of these companies are oriented around the Inventory account. Merchandising companies generally use one of two types of inventory accounting systems, either a perpetual inventory system or a periodic inventory system. In a

■ LEARNING OBJECTIVE 3
Compare and contrast a periodic inventory system and a perpetual inventory system

50-OFF Stores, Inc.

Regardless of the product or products they sell, merchandising companies engage in a never-ending battle of wits with companies offering competing products. To make their company stand out from competitors, corporate executives often identify a unique sales pitch or marketing tactic. 50-OFF Stores, Inc., operates a chain of retail stores offering a wide range of products including housewares, toys, and health and beauty aids. In the following excerpt from the company's 1992 annual report, a company executive describes the unique pricing strategy of 50-OFF Stores.

The Company employs a strategy designed to differentiate itself from other retail stores while making it easy for its customers to recognize the savings achieved by shopping at 50-OFF. Merchandise is offered every day at prices 50% off the approximate non-discounted retail prices charged by traditional department stores. This pricing policy is possible because the Company maintains low operating costs and purchases merchandise at favorable prices.

Every item in the store has a ticketed price which lists the retail price with the statement on the ticket: "You pay one-half of this amount." At the register, the cashier rings up the non-discounted price for each item being purchased. After the register totals the purchase, a discount key is pushed and the sale is reduced by 50%. This simple process provides dramatic and immediate evidence of the value being offered to the customer.

perpetual inventory system

periodic inventory system

Real World
The decision of whether to adopt a periodic inventory system or a perpetual system involves an analysis of the costs versus the benefits associated with each system. For companies in the 1990s, profitability is often a function of the speed with which management decisions can be made. Information collected at point-of-sale cash registers enables companies to quickly determine the rate of sale of products and to make more informed inventory pricing and repurchase decisions.

perpetual inventory system, the revenue and cost of goods sold associated with sales transactions are recorded simultaneously when sales are made. Additionally, in a perpetual inventory system a "perpetually" updated record of the quantity of individual inventory items and their per unit costs is maintained. In a **periodic inventory system,** the revenue from sales transactions is booked when sales are made, but cost of goods sold is not. A merchandiser that uses a periodic inventory system does not maintain a Cost of Goods Sold account or records documenting the quantity of each inventory item. Under a periodic inventory system, a company's merchandise is counted at the end of an accounting period. Then the quantity of each item is multiplied by its per unit cost to arrive at the dollar value of ending inventory. After that figure has been determined, the company's cost of goods sold can be computed.

A key advantage of most perpetual inventory systems is a continually updated record of the quantity of each inventory item on hand. A key disadvantage of perpetual inventory systems is their cost. Small businesses that process a few transactions each day, such as a retail store that sells large kitchen appliances, can easily maintain a manually based perpetual inventory system. However, a "pen and paper" perpetual inventory system is not cost effective for small businesses, such as grocery stores, that may process several hundred or more sales transactions each day.

During the past decade, the declining cost of computer-based perpetual inventory systems has convinced many merchandising companies to begin using them. Among other features of these inventory systems are optical scanners at checkout stands that update the quantity of individual inventory items on hand following each sales transaction. Despite the declining cost of computer-based perpetual inventory systems and the internal control advantages they offer, they are still too costly for many small merchandising companies. As a result, periodic inventory systems continue to be widely used. This chapter focuses on the accounting methods used in a periodic inventory system. In Chapter 8, the accounting methods used in a perpetual inventory system are illustrated.

Accounting for Sales Transactions in a Periodic Inventory System

SALES   Recall from Chapter 2 that the revenue recognition rule dictates that businesses should record revenues only when they have been both realized and earned.

> Revenues are realized when products (goods or services), merchandise, or other assets are exchanged for cash or claims to cash. . . . [R]evenues are considered to have been earned when the entity has substantially accomplished what it must do to be entitled to the benefits represented by the revenues.[1]

For most merchandising companies, sales revenue is both realized and earned at the point of sale when a customer pays for an item at a checkout stand or sales terminal. Occasionally, the earnings process is not completed at the point of sale, meaning that the recognition of the revenue should be postponed. For instance, assume that a wholesaler sells merchandise to a retail store but agrees to take back any goods that the store is unable to resell to its customers. Generally, the wholesaler should postpone recognition of the sales revenue on such a transaction until the retail store has sold the goods.

Most merchandising companies have both cash sales and credit sales, each of which are recorded in the revenue account Sales. Assume that a local hardware store, such as Payless Cashways, sells $200 of merchandise to an electrical contractor who pays cash for the goods. The following entry, in simplified general journal format, would be appropriate for this transaction.

Jan. 17	Cash	200	
	Sales		200

Cash sale to Daly Contractors, invoice no. 2751

If the customer purchased the merchandise on credit, the following journal entry would be necessary.

Jan. 17	Accounts Receivable	200	
	Sales		200

Credit sale to Daly Contractors, invoice no. 2751

SALES RETURNS AND ALLOWANCES   Most merchandising companies give customers a full refund for damaged or defective merchandise they return. Customers may be granted an "allowance"—price reduction—to persuade them to keep the damaged or defective merchandise. Collectively, these refunds and price reductions are referred to as **sales returns and allowances.** Assume that a customer of the Shamrock Shoppe purchases a $120 dress, only to discover a flaw in the dress a few days later. When the customer returns the dress to the store, the store manager may offer to "knock" $60 off the original selling price to encourage the customer to keep the dress. If the customer accepts this offer, the store manager would prepare a credit memorandum similar to the one shown in Exhibit 6.4. This credit memorandum

LEARNING OBJECTIVE 4
Account for merchandise sales, purchases, and transportation costs in a periodic inventory system

Teaching Note
Emphasize that the Sales account should only be used to record sales of merchandise. Sales of assets such as furniture or equipment should not be recorded in the Sales account.

Real World
The maintenance of a separate Sales Returns and Allowances account provides information for implementing the concept of management by exception, i.e. the manager's attention is directed to those areas of the organization which are outside the norm. When sales returns and allowances are excessive, management will want to determine the source of the problem.

sales returns and allowances

---

1. Portions of various FASB documents, copyrighted by Financial Accounting Standards Board, 401 Merritt 7, P. O. Box 5116, Norwalk, Connecticut, 06856-5116, U.S.A., are reprinted with permission. Copies of the complete documents are available from the FASB.

■ **EXHIBIT 6.4**
Example of a Credit Memorandum

Shamrock Shoppe
3133 Oak Tree Avenue
Turlock, California 90544

CREDIT MEMO

Customer		No.:	288
		Date:	2/18/96
Charlotte Wilkins		Customer ID:	3481
Rural Route 3			
Modesto, CA 90044			

ITEM	DESCRIPTION	TOTAL
32-5a	Dress returned by customer due to fabric flaw (size 7, Style 624, Crown Weavers). Customer kept dress but was granted an allowance of $60.	$ 60.00

REFUND DUE	$ 60.00

would serve as the source document for this sales allowance transaction and would be the basis for the following journal entry.

Feb. 18	Sales Returns and Allowances	60	
	Cash (or Accounts Receivable)		60
	Sales allowance granted, credit memo no. 288		

Teaching Note
Remind students that a contra account always has a related account with the opposite balance.

Sales Returns and Allowances is a contra revenue account. For income statement purposes, the balance of Sales Returns and Allowances is subtracted from sales to arrive at net sales.

SALES DISCOUNTS Many merchandising companies that sell goods on credit offer **sales discounts** to customers to entice them to pay their receivable balances on

sales discounts

a timely basis.[2] When customers take advantage of these discounts, they are recorded in a contra revenue account, Sales Discounts.

The **credit terms** for a sales transaction express the agreement between the buyer and seller regarding the timing of payment and any discount available to the buyer for early payment. Among the most common credit terms for merchandising transactions are n/30 and 2/10, n/30. Credit terms of n/30, which reads as "net 30," require the buyer to pay the full invoice amount within thirty days following the invoice date—in other words, no discount is available to the buyer for early payment.[3] This thirty-day period is referred to as the credit period and does not include the date of the invoice. For example, a customer that buys goods on May 1 with credit terms of n/30 would have until May 31 to pay for the goods. Credit terms of 2/10, n/30 allow buyers to subtract 2 percent from the invoice amount if payment is made within ten days following the invoice date. This ten-day period is referred to as the discount period and begins the day following the invoice date. With credit terms of 2/10, n/30, if payment is not made within the ten-day discount period, the full amount of the invoice is due thirty days following the invoice date.

To illustrate accounting for sales discounts, assume that a company sells $400 of merchandise on March 1 with credit terms of 2/10, n/30. At the time the sale is made, the company does not know whether the customer will take advantage of the discount. Consequently, the sales transaction is recorded at the amount reported on the sales invoice, $400.

Mar. 1	Accounts Receivable	400	
	Sales		400
	Credit sale to Johnson Brothers, invoice no. 189, credit terms 2/10, n/30		

If the customer does not take advantage of the sales discount and pays the gross invoice amount of $400 on March 31, the following entry would be required.

Mar. 31	Cash	400	
	Accounts Receivable		400
	Payment made on Mar. 1 sale, invoice no. 189, discount not taken		

Assuming the customer takes advantage of the available discount and makes payment on March 11, the last day of the discount period, the following entry would be appropriate.

Discussion Question
Ask students to list examples from their own experience of credit terms they have been granted on personal transactions involving the purchase of merchandise.

---

2. In addition to these discounts for early payment, some merchandising companies offer "trade discounts" to certain of their customers. For instance, large volume customers may be offered a 30 percent discount off selling prices quoted in a company's sales catalog or other price list. Typically, when merchandise is sold in this manner, the invoice amount of the sale is recorded net of the trade discount. That is, the trade discount does not appear on the invoice, nor does the selling firm record the trade discount in its accounting records.

3. The term "net" seems inappropriate since the customer is actually paying the full amount of the invoice. However, this term is widely used because often a trade discount (see footnote 2) has been subtracted from a price quoted by the selling firm in a catalog or other price list to arrive at the invoiced sales amount.

Mar. 11	Cash	392	
	Sales Discounts	8	
	Accounts Receivable		400

Payment made on Mar. 1 sale, invoice no. 189, 2% discount taken

Accounting for Purchases Transactions in a Periodic Inventory System

PURCHASES   When a merchandising company uses a periodic inventory system, purchases of merchandise for resale, both cash purchases and purchases made on credit, are recorded in an account entitled Purchases. Assume that on December 14 a retail company purchases $5,200 of merchandise from a wholesaler and pays cash. This transaction would require the following journal entry.

| Dec. 14 | Purchases | 5,200 | |
| | Cash | | 5,200 |

Purchase from Kwon Wholesalers, invoice no. 361

Assuming the merchandise was purchased on credit, the transaction would be journalized as follows:

| Dec. 14 | Purchases | 5,200 | |
| | Accounts Payable | | 5,200 |

Purchase from Kwon Wholesalers, invoice no. 361

PURCHASES RETURNS AND ALLOWANCES   Just like their customers, merchandising companies are sometimes dissatisfied with the goods they purchase. Merchandise received is occasionally not the goods ordered, is defective, or was damaged when it was packaged. When merchandisers return goods to suppliers or are granted price concessions for damaged or defective goods, the resulting reductions in the amounts owed to the suppliers are referred to as **purchases returns and allowances.** These items are recorded in a contra expense account, Purchases Returns and Allowances.

Assume that a merchandising company purchases $2,300 of goods on credit on August 8 and makes the appropriate entry debiting Purchases and crediting Accounts Payable. A few days later, an inventory clerk discovers that $250 of the goods are defective. The merchandising company promptly notifies the supplier, which informs the company to simply dispose of the goods. The supplier also informs the company that its receivable balance will be reduced accordingly. To document this event in the merchandising company's accounting records, a debit memorandum similar to the credit memorandum shown in Exhibit 6.4 would be prepared. (Recognize that the credit memorandum in Exhibit 6.4 served as the source document for a sales allowance instead of a purchases allowance.) The following entry would be made to record this purchases allowance.

| Aug. 11 | Accounts Payable | 250 | |
| | Purchases Returns and Allowances | | 250 |

Allowance granted on Aug. 8
purchase from Cremmins Corp.,
debit memo no. 56

PURCHASES DISCOUNTS   Merchandising companies typically purchase goods from their suppliers on credit. To encourage prompt payment of these credit purchases, many wholesalers and manufacturers offer **purchases discounts.** When a merchandising company takes advantage of such a discount, the related dollar amount is recorded in an account entitled Purchases Discounts. Unlike Sales Discounts, which is a contra revenue account, Purchases Discounts is a contra expense account.

Assume that a merchandising company purchases $1,600 of goods on September 16 with credit terms of 2/10, n/30. On September 16, the merchandising company would debit Purchases $1,600 and credit Accounts Payable for the same amount. If the company takes advantage of the discount and pays its supplier for these goods on September 26, the last day of the discount period, the following entry would be made.

purchases discounts

Focus on Ethics
A company routinely writes all checks to its suppliers on the last day of the discount period but does not mail the checks for an additional seven days. Is this practice ethical? Is anyone harmed?

Sep. 26	Accounts Payable	1,600	
	Cash		1,568
	Purchases Discounts		32

Paid for Sep. 16 purchase from Larsen
Supply, invoice no. 32, less 2% discount

If the company does not take advantage of the discount, it would be required to pay for the goods by the last day of the credit period, October 16. Assuming payment is made on October 16, the following entry would be appropriate.

| Oct. 16 | Accounts Payable | 1,600 | |
| | Cash | | 1,600 |

Paid for Sep. 16 purchase from
Larsen Supply, invoice no. 32

To complicate matters slightly, assume the company in the prior illustration returned $200 of goods on September 21 and then paid the supplier the appropriate amount on September 26. These facts would require the following two entries.

| Sep. 21 | Accounts Payable | 200 | |
| | Purchases Returns and Allowances | | 200 |

Return of merchandise purchased from
Larsen Supply, debit memo no. 212

Sep. 26	Accounts Payable	1,400	
	Cash		1,372
	Purchases Discounts		28

Paid for Sep. 16 purchase from Larsen Supply,
invoice no. 1032, less $200 purchases return,
debit memo no. 212, and less 2% discount

Notice that the purchases discount in this case is not based upon the original invoice amount of $1,600, but rather $1,400, which is the original invoice amount less the purchases return of $200.

Accounting for Transportation Costs in a Periodic Inventory System

■ LEARNING
OBJECTIVE 4
Account for merchandise sales, purchases, and transportation costs in a periodic inventory system

FOB shipping point

**FOB destination
transportation in**

Delivery charges are often a significant element of the cost of merchandise. The shipping terms for a merchandising transaction determine which party, the buyer or seller, is responsible for paying the delivery charges.

When a merchandising company purchases goods from a wholesaler or manufacturer, the two parties must agree which will be responsible for the transportation costs incurred to deliver the goods. The point at which the legal title to goods transfers from the seller to the buyer typically dictates which party will be responsible for paying the transportation charges. In turn, the shipping terms for a merchandising transaction determine when legal title to merchandise transfers between a buyer and seller.

The most common shipping terms for merchandising transactions are FOB shipping point and FOB destination. Under shipping terms of **FOB shipping point,** the seller delivers the goods "free on board" to the shipping point, such as the seller's loading dock. There, a freight company usually takes physical possession of the goods and delivers them to the buyer. With these shipping terms, the buyer is responsible for paying the transportation charges, since the title to the goods transfers to the buyer at the shipping point. When goods are shipped **FOB destination,** the seller delivers the goods to the destination point, typically the receiving dock of the buyer. Under these shipping terms, the seller retains the legal title to the goods until they reach the destination point. As a result, the seller is responsible for paying the transportation charges. The following table summarizes what you need to know about shipping terms.

SHIPPING TERMS	WHEN TITLE TO GOODS TRANSFERS FROM SELLER TO BUYER	PARTY RESPONSIBLE FOR TRANSPORTATION COSTS
FOB shipping point	When delivered to freight company at seller's place of business	Buyer
FOB destination	When delivered to buyer	Seller

To illustrate accounting for transportation costs, assume that on March 30 a merchandising company purchases goods costing $2,500. This transaction has credit terms of 2/10, n/30, and shipping terms of FOB shipping point. The freight charges for the delivery of these goods are $120 and are the responsibility of the buyer, given the shipping terms. Freight charges paid by a merchandising company for the delivery of goods it has purchased are typically referred to as **transportation in** and recorded in an account with the same title. Following is an example of a journal entry that would be appropriate when a merchandising company receives an invoice for such freight charges.

Apr. 4	Transportation In	120	
	Accounts Payable		120

Freight charges on goods received
Mar. 30, invoice no. 19 of RTD Freight

In some industries, the company selling goods prepays the freight charges even though the shipping terms are FOB shipping point. Under these circumstances, the buyer is responsible for reimbursing the seller for the freight charges. If the seller in the situation just described prepaid the freight charges, the buyer would make the following entry on receipt of the goods.

Mar. 30	Purchases	2,500	
	Transportation In	120	
	Accounts Payable		2,620
	Purchase from Jennings Company, invoice no. 314, freight charges prepaid by Jennings		

Assuming the buyer pays for these goods within the ten-day discount period, the purchase discount would be based only upon the invoiced amount of the goods, as shown in the following entry.

Apr. 9	Accounts Payable	2,620	
	Cash		2,570
	Purchases Discounts		50
	Paid for goods purchased on Mar. 30 from Jennings Company, invoice no. 314, less 2% discount on cost of merchandise (.02 × $2,500 = $50)		

When the selling company prepays the freight charges and the shipping terms are FOB shipping point, two entries are normally made in the seller's accounting records. The first entry records the sales transaction, while the second entry records the freight prepayment. For example, assume that on May 17 a company sells $3,100 of merchandise. The credit terms for this transaction are 2/10, n/30, while the shipping terms are FOB shipping point. If the company prepays the freight charges of $210, the following entries would be appropriate in its accounting records.

May 17	Accounts Receivable	3,100	
	Sales		3,100
	Credit sale to Butler Company, invoice no. 288		
May 17	Accounts Receivable	210	
	Cash		210
	Prepayment of freight charges on credit sale to Butler Company, invoice no. 155 of Chae's Trucking Company		

When goods are sold FOB destination by a business, it is responsible for the freight charges. These freight charges are typically referred to as **transportation out** and are recorded in an account with the same title. Both Transportation In and Transportation Out are expense accounts. However, Transportation Out is an operating expense,

transportation out

while Transportation In is a component of cost of goods sold. Refer to the prior illustration in which a company sold $3,100 of merchandise and paid freight costs of $210. Now, assume that the shipping terms are FOB destination for that transaction. Under this assumption, the following entries would be appropriate.

May 17	Accounts Receivable	3,100	
	Sales		3,100
	Credit sale to Butler Company invoice no. 288		
May 17	Transportation Out	210	
	Cash		210
	Payment of freight charges on credit sale to Butler Company, invoice no. 155 of Chae's Trucking Company		

Summarized in Exhibit 6.5 are the appropriate journal entries for several common merchandising transactions. Notice that Exhibit 6.5 identifies for each transaction the accounts that should be debited and credited in the accounting records of both the seller and the buyer.

Determining Cost of Goods Sold in a Periodic Inventory System

Cost of goods sold is usually the largest expense item on a merchandising company's income statement. As mentioned previously, companies that employ the periodic inventory system do not maintain a Cost of Goods Sold account in their general ledger. Under the periodic inventory system, cost of goods sold is computed by consolidating several account balances at the end of an accounting period. Shown in Exhibit 6.6 is a schedule in which Bonney's cost of goods sold is computed for the year ending December 31, 1996.

Notice in Exhibit 6.6 that cost of goods available for sale is the sum of beginning inventory, net purchases for the year, and the balance of the Transportation In account. At the end of a given year, the goods that were available for sale during the year were either (1) sold, in which case their cost should be included in cost of goods sold, or (2) unsold, in which case their cost should be included in ending inventory. To determine the dollar amount of Bonney's ending inventory, the store's employees counted the inventory after the close of business on December 31, 1996. Then, the per unit cost of each item of inventory was multiplied by its quantity. The sum of these amounts was $26,230, which is the December 31, 1996, inventory value reported in Exhibit 6.6. Once a company has determined its year-end inventory value, that figure is subtracted from cost of goods available for sale to determine cost of goods sold.

Period-Ending Closing Procedures for a Merchandising Company That Uses a Periodic Inventory System

The period-ending closing procedures for merchandising and service companies are very similar. Since closing procedures for a service company were discussed in Chapter 5, it is not necessary to rehash in detail each step of the closing process for a merchandising company.

■ **EXHIBIT 6.5**
Summary of Journal Entries for Various Merchandising Transactions, Seller and Buyer

	SELLER'S ACCOUNTING RECORDS		BUYER'S ACCOUNTING RECORDS	
Transaction	Debit	Credit	Debit	Credit
Sale of merchandise on credit	Accounts Receivable	Sales	Purchases	Accounts Payable
Return of merchandise previously purchased on credit	Sales Returns & Allowances	Accounts Receivable	Accounts Payable	Purchases Returns & Allowances
Payment, no cash discount	Cash	Accounts Receivable	Accounts Payable	Cash
Payment, cash discount taken	Cash, Sales Discounts	Accounts Receivable	Accounts Payable	Cash, Purchases Discounts
Payment of freight charges, FOB shipping point	No entry	No entry	Transportation In	Cash
Sale of merchandise on credit, FOB shipping point, freight charges prepaid by seller	Accounts Receivable	Sales, Cash	Purchases, Transportation In	Accounts Payable
Sales of merchandise on credit, FOB destination, freight charges prepaid by seller	Accounts Receivable, Transportation Out	Sales, Cash	Purchases	Accounts Payable

■ **EXHIBIT 6.6**
Cost of Goods Sold Schedule for Bonney's Dress Shop, for the Year Ended December 31, 1996

Inventory, January 1, 1996			$23,980
Purchases		$48,740	
Less: Purchases Returns and Allowances	$4,240		
Purchases Discounts	1,200	5,440	
Net Purchases			$43,300
Transportation In			3,320
Cost of Goods Available for Sale			$70,600
Less: Inventory, December 31, 1996			26,230
Cost of Goods Sold			$44,370

Teaching Note
Suggest to students that they focus on the following major components of the cost of goods computation:
    beginning inventory
+ cost of goods purchased
− ending inventory
─────────────────────
= cost of goods sold

Cadbury Schweppes plc

Cadbury Schweppes plc (public limited company) markets an extensive line of merchandise consisting principally of candy and beverage products. Although Cadbury is based in London and prepares its annual report in English, United States investors and creditors likely have difficulty interpreting the company's financial statements. For instance, Cadbury's Income Statement is not an income statement at all but rather a "Profit and Loss Account." Likewise, instead of presenting a Statement of Stockholders' Equity, the company's annual report includes a financial statement entitled "Movements in Shareholders Funds." Even novice accountants that skim Cadbury's annual report would likely conclude that "stocks" is the British term for inventory and that "turnover," since it is the first line item on the company's Profit and Loss Account, likely refers to sales. However, "called up share capital," the "gearing ratio," and "trading profit" are other terms in Cadbury's annual financial statements that likely stump even the most experienced accountants in this country.

WORK SHEET OF A MERCHANDISING COMPANY   Exhibit 6.7 contains the chart of accounts used by Bonney's Dress Shop. Those accounts used by merchandising companies but not by service companies are boldfaced. (Notice that the chart of accounts for Bonney's Dress Shop does not include a Transportation Out account. Retail merchandisers very seldom pay transportation charges for the delivery of goods to customers.) Included in Exhibit 6.8 is a completed work sheet for Bonney's Dress Shop for the year ended December 31, 1996. Unlike Snow Mountain Retreat, Bonney's closes its books only once per year, on December 31. The basic structure of Bonney's work sheet is identical to that of the work sheet illustrated in Chapter 5.

TREATMENT OF INVENTORY ON THE WORK SHEET OF A MERCHANDISING COMPANY   Notice in Exhibit 6.8 that when the adjusted trial balance amounts were sorted into the financial statement columns, $23,980 was placed in the Income Statement debit column for the Inventory account. This amount represents the January 1, 1996, balance of the Inventory account. In a periodic inventory system, no entries are made in the Inventory account until the end of an accounting period when the closing procedures are performed. As a result, Bonney's beginning-of-the-year Inventory account balance remained unchanged until December 31 when its books were closed. Also note that a $26,230 figure for the Inventory account was inserted in the Income Statement credit column and the Balance Sheet debit column of the work sheet. This figure represents the year-end balance of Bonney's Inventory account that was determined following the counting of the store's inventory on December 31, 1996.

You will probably agree that it makes sense to include the $26,230 figure for the Inventory account in the Balance Sheet debit column of Bonney's work sheet, since that column includes the company's year-end account balances for assets. A more interesting question is why the $23,980 beginning-of-the-year Inventory account balance is included in the Income Statement debit column. For that matter, why is the $26,230 end-of-the-year Inventory balance included in the Income Statement credit column? First recognize that all items involved in the computation of net income must be included in the income statement columns of a work sheet. Both the begin-

■ **EXHIBIT 6.7**
Bonney's Dress Shop, Chart of Accounts

BALANCE SHEET ACCOUNTS	INCOME STATEMENT ACCOUNTS
101 Cash	**401 Sales**
102 Accounts Receivable	**402 Sales Returns and Allowances**
103 Interest Receivable	**403 Sales Discounts**
104 Inventory	404 Interest Revenue
105 Prepaid Insurance	**501 Purchases**
106 Supplies	**502 Purchases Returns and Allowances**
107 Furniture and Fixtures	**503 Purchases Discounts**
108 Accumulated Depreciation, Furniture and Fixtures	**504 Transportation In**
201 Accounts Payable	505 Sales Salaries Expense
202 Salaries Payable	506 Advertising Expense
203 Income Taxes Payable	507 Rent Expense
301 Common Stock	508 Supplies Expense
302 Retained Earnings	509 Insurance Expense
303 Dividends	510 Depreciation Expense, Furniture and Fixtures
304 Income Summary	511 Income Taxes Expense

ning and ending Inventory account balances of a merchandising company figure into the computation of cost of goods sold, an expense item; however, cost of goods sold does not appear on a merchandiser's work sheet if a periodic inventory system is used. Consequently, the accounts used to determine cost of goods sold must be included in the Income Statement columns of the work sheet. Prove to yourself that each amount included in the cost of goods sold schedule shown in Exhibit 6.6 appears in either the Income Statement debit or credit column in Exhibit 6.8.

PREPARATION OF AN INCOME STATEMENT FOR A MERCHANDISING COMPANY   Once we have completed Bonney's work sheet, we have all the information needed to prepare an income statement, statement of stockholders' equity, and balance sheet for the company. Since the statements of stockholders' equity and balance sheets of merchandising and service companies are very similar, those two financial statements of Bonney's Dress Shop are not presented. Shown in Exhibit 6.9 is Bonney's income statement for the year ended December 31, 1996. Many merchandising companies prepare an income statement similar to the one included in Exhibit 6.9 but in condensed form. For example, refer to the income statement of The Home Depot included in Exhibit 6.2. In the condensed income statement format, gross sales, sales returns and allowances, and sales discounts are consolidated into "net sales." Likewise, the cost of goods sold section is often reduced to one line item, Cost of Goods Sold.

ADJUSTING AND CLOSING ENTRIES FOR A MERCHANDISING COMPANY
After completing the work sheet and preparing financial statements, the next step of the accounting cycle is to journalize and post adjusting entries. For Bonney's Dress Shop, this step would require the six adjustment items listed on the work sheet in Exhibit 6.8 to be journalized and then posted. The next-to-last step of the accounting cycle is the preparation and posting of closing journal entries. Since closing entries are a little different for merchandising and service companies, it will be useful to review Bonney's closing entries for 1996. These entries are included in Exhibit 6.10 (p. 234).

■ **LEARNING OBJECTIVE 7**
Prepare an income statement for a merchandising company

Discussion Question
Ask students which of the two income statement formats, Bonney's or that of The Home Depot, is more informative for decision makers. Then, ask students whether there are any disadvantages associated with the more detailed income statement format used by Bonney's.

■ EXHIBIT 6.8
Bonney's Dress Shop, Work Sheet for the Year Ended December 31, 1996

BONNEY'S DRESS SHOP
WORK SHEET
FOR THE YEAR ENDED DECEMBER 31, 1996

Account Title	Trial Balance Debit	Trial Balance Credit	Adjustments Debit	Adjustments Credit	Adjusted Trial Balance Debit	Adjusted Trial Balance Credit	Income Statement Debit	Income Statement Credit	Balance Sheet Debit	Balance Sheet Credit
Cash	12,110				12,110				12,110	
Accounts Receivable	14,840				14,840				14,840	
Inventory	23,980				23,980		23,980	26,230	26,230	
Prepaid Insurance	2,800			(a) 300	2,500				2,500	
Supplies	1,260			(b) 810	450				450	
Furniture and Fixtures	65,200				65,200				65,200	
Accumulated Depreciation, Furniture & Fixtures		20,680		(c) 4,200		24,880				24,880
Accounts Payable		6,890				6,890				6,890
Common Stock		10,000				10,000				10,000
Retained Earnings		42,480				42,480				42,480
Dividends	2,000				2,000				2,000	
Sales		132,270				132,270		132,270		
Sales Returns & Allowances	1,150				1,150		1,150			
Sales Discounts	420				420		420			
Purchases	48,740				48,740		48,740			
Purchases Returns & Allowances		4,240				4,240		4,240		
Purchases Discounts		1,200				1,200		1,200		
Transportation In	3,320				3,320		3,320			
Sales Salaries Expense	28,610		(d) 420		29,030		29,030			
Advertising Expense	2,840				2,840		2,840			
Rent Expense	8,820				8,820		8,820			
Insurance Expense	1,670		(a) 300		1,970		1,970			
Interest Receivable			(e) 250		250				250	
Interest Revenue				(e) 250		250		250		
Supplies Expense			(b) 810		810		810			
Depreciation Expense, Furniture & Fixtures			(c) 4,200		4,200		4,200			
Salaries Payable				(d) 420		420				420
Income Taxes Expense			(f) 6,100		6,100		6,100			
Income Taxes Payable				(f) 6,100		6,100				6,100
	217,760	217,760	12,080	12,080	228,730	228,730	131,380	164,190	123,580	90,770
Net Income							32,810			32,810
							164,190	164,190	123,580	123,580

■ **EXHIBIT 6.9**
Income Statement for Bonney's Dress Shop, for the Year Ended December 31, 1996

BONNEY'S DRESS SHOP
INCOME STATEMENT
FOR THE YEAR ENDED DECEMBER 31, 1996

SALES REVENUE

Sales			$132,270
Less: Sales Returns and Allowances		$ 1,150	
Sales Discounts		420	1,570
Net Sales			$130,700

COST OF GOODS SOLD

Inventory, January 1, 1996		$ 23,980	
Purchases	$48,740		
Less: Purchases Returns and Allowances	$ 4,240		
Purchases Discounts	1,200	5,440	
Net Purchases		$ 43,300	
Transportation In		3,320	
Cost of Goods Available for Sale		$ 70,600	
Less: Inventory, December 31, 1996		26,230	
Cost of Goods Sold			44,370

GROSS PROFIT ON SALES | | | | $ 86,330 |

OPERATING EXPENSES

Selling Expenses:

Sales Salaries Expense	$ 29,030		
Advertising Expense	2,840		
Total Selling Expenses		$ 31,870	

General and Administrative Expenses:

Rent Expense	$ 8,820		
Insurance Expense	1,970		
Supplies Expense	810		
Depreciation Expense, Furniture and Fixtures	4,200		
Total General and Administrative Expenses		15,800	
Total Operating Expenses			47,670

INCOME FROM OPERATIONS | | | | $ 38,660 |

OTHER REVENUES AND EXPENSES

Interest Revenue			250

INCOME BEFORE INCOME TAXES | | | | $ 38,910 |

Income Taxes Expense | | | | 6,100 |

NET INCOME | | | | $ 32,810 |

Teaching Note
Using the data from Exhibit 6.10, put the Inventory T-account on the board:

Inventory	
Beg. Bal. 23,980	Closing 23,980
Closing 26,230	
End. Bal. 26,230	

Explain that following the posting of closing entries, the balance in the Inventory account is the ending inventory amount.

Teaching Note
Remind students that under the periodic inventory system no entries are made to the Inventory account during the year. Beginning inventory remains on the books all year until the completion of the closing process at year end.

EXHIBIT 6.10
Closing Entries for Bonney's Dress Shop, December 31, 1996

General Journal					**Page 3**
Date		**Description**	**Post Ref.**	**Debit**	**Credit**
1996					
Dec.	31	Inventory	104	26,230	
		Sales	401	132,270	
		Purchases Returns and Allowances	502	4,240	
		Purchases Discounts	503	1,200	
		Interest Revenue	404	250	
		Income Summary	304		164,190
		To record the ending inventory value and to close income statement accounts with credit balances			
	31	Income Summary	304	131,380	
		Inventory	104		23,980
		Sales Returns and Allowances	402		1,150
		Sales Discounts	403		420
		Purchases	501		48,740
		Transportation In	504		3,320
		Sales Salaries Expense	505		29,030
		Advertising Expense	506		2,840
		Rent Expense	507		8,820
		Supplies Expense	508		810
		Insurance Expense	509		1,970
		Depreciation Expense, Furniture & Fixtures	510		4,200
		Income Taxes Expense	511		6,100
		To remove the beginning inventory value and to close income statement accounts with debit balances			
	31	Income Summary	304	32,810	
		Retained Earnings	302		32,810
		To close the Income Summary account			
	31	Retained Earnings	302	2,000	
		Dividends	303		2,000
		To close the Dividends account			

The first entry shown in Exhibit 6.10 inserts the appropriate year-end balance into the Inventory account and closes the temporary accounts with credit balances listed in the Income Statement columns of the work sheet. The second closing entry eliminates the beginning-of-the-year balance of the Inventory account and closes out the temporary accounts with debit balances listed in the Income Statement columns of the work sheet. Finally, the third and fourth closing entries transfer the net income for the year from the Income Summary account to the Retained Earnings account and close the Dividends account to the Retained Earnings account, respectively. After the journalizing and posting of closing entries has been completed, a post-closing trial balance would be prepared for Bonney's Dress Shop.

INTERNAL CONTROL FOR MERCHANDISING OPERATIONS

Merchandising companies pose challenging internal control problems and issues for accountants. The large volume of transactions processed by many of these businesses increases the risk that errors will be introduced into their accounting records. Another internal control risk factor for merchandising companies is their exposure to losses due to theft of inventory. In Chapter 3, you learned that two key objectives of a business's internal control structure are to provide for reliable financial records and to safeguard the entity's assets. This section discusses control procedures and accounting methods that can be implemented to accomplish these two objectives for merchandising firms.

■ **LEARNING OBJECTIVE 8**
Discuss key internal control issues and procedures for a merchandising company

General Control Procedures for Merchandising Operations

Exhibit 3.6 in Chapter 3 lists examples of general control procedures that organizations can incorporate into their internal control structures. Here we consider how these control procedures can be adapted to merchandising companies. (The final control procedure included in Exhibit 3.6 of Chapter 3, "periodic reconciliation of general ledger controlling accounts with balances of subsidiary ledgers," is discussed briefly in the final segment of this section.)

SEGREGATION OF KEY FUNCTIONAL RESPONSIBILITIES Limiting the opportunity of employees and other parties to take unfair advantage of an organization is a fundamental principle of internal control. One way businesses accomplish this objective is to segregate or separate key responsibilities within their accounting and control systems. For example, an employee should not be allowed to both process cash receipts and maintain cash receipts accounting records. A business that learned the importance of this general control procedure was Howard Street Jewelers, as discussed in the Spotlight on Ethics vignette accompanying this section.

PROPER AUTHORIZATION OF TRANSACTIONS As a young public accountant employed by a large accounting firm, an individual who is now an author of an accounting textbook was assigned to audit a client's cash disbursements. After several

8 great new Tunic Tops that ease you into Fall. pp. 2-9

PLUS:
Our biggest selection ever of authentic yarn-dyed Denims! pp. 24-40
"Vanishing America" concludes p. 87
Special kids' "back to school" mini-catalog inside!
Now faster 2-day standard delivery by UPS!

Internal control procedures vary significantly among merchandisers. For example, the key internal controls for Land's End, a mail-order merchandiser, differ significantly from the internal controls for J. C. Penney, a large department store chain.

days of working on this assignment, "AuditMan" realized that one of the client's purchasing agents had the same last name as the principal owner of a major supplier of the client. (A purchasing agent is an individual responsible for buying goods or services for an organization.) One day, AuditMan casually asked the purchasing agent if he was related to the other individual. "Sure. He's my brother," was the purchasing agent's candid response. When AuditMan asked if his superiors were aware of this fact, the purchasing agent replied that they were not.

As it turned out, the several million dollars of purchases the purchasing agent had authorized from his brother's firm were legitimate in all respects. Nevertheless, this situation could have resulted in huge losses for the organization. Proper authorization of transactions is a critical internal control procedure in any organization but particularly so in the purchasing departments of merchandising firms. Merchandising companies should establish strict control procedures to ensure that purchasing agents are aware of the types and sizes of purchases they can authorize. Just as important, these control procedures should identify the circumstances under which purchasing agents are strictly prohibited from authorizing purchase transactions.

USE OF PRENUMBERED ACCOUNTING DOCUMENTS   Merchandising companies should use prenumbered invoices, purchase orders, and other accounting documents to maintain effective control over their operations. The use of prenumbered accounting documents minimizes the likelihood that unauthorized transactions will be processed. This control procedure also increases the likelihood that all authorized transactions will be processed correctly and on a timely basis. Assume during a given month that a salesclerk of a merchandising company misplaces and thus fails to process invoices for ten sales transactions. The invoices for these transactions are numbered J-4144 through J-4153. This oversight will be discovered if the company has a control procedure requiring a complete accounting for the numerical sequence of sales invoices used each month.

PERIODIC COUNTS OF INVENTORY   Inventory accounts for a sizable proportion of the total assets of most merchandising companies. For instance, a recent balance sheet of Drug Emporium revealed that inventory accounted for 71 percent of that company's total assets. Given their large investments in inventory, merchandisers must establish effective control procedures for this asset. One such control procedure is the periodic counting of inventory. Under the periodic inventory system, merchandising companies count their inventory at least once annually. However, many retail firms that use the periodic inventory system count their inventories much more frequently for control purposes.

Under the perpetual inventory system, a business's accounting records are updated following each purchase and sales transaction. However, just because a company's perpetual inventory records indicate that there are sixty-three VCRs in the warehouse does not mean that there are exactly sixty-three VCRs in the warehouse. A dishonest employee may have permanently "borrowed" one or two of those VCRs. To provide effective control over inventory, companies using the perpetual inventory system should periodically count their inventories and compare the results with their inventory records.

CLERICAL TESTS OF THE MATHEMATICAL ACCURACY OF ACCOUNTING DOCUMENTS   You have probably been "shorted" a few cents or even a few dollars by a frazzled cashier at the local convenience store or supermarket. In the business

Betty the Cashier: A Case of Misplaced Trust

SPOTLIGHT ON ETHICS

For more than four decades, Lore and Julius Levi owned and operated the Howard Street Jewelers. The jewelry store was very profitable until the late 1970s and early 1980s. During that time frame, the business's financial condition began to slowly deteriorate. Mrs. Levi spent countless hours going over accounting and sales records trying to explain the downward trend in the store's net cash flow. Eventually, she developed a theory regarding the financial problems of Howard Street Jewelers. This theory focused on Betty the cashier, who had been a trusted and reliable employee for nearly twenty years.

Mrs. Levi concluded that Betty was stealing cash from the store's cash register. Besides working as a part-time sales clerk, Betty handled all of the cash that came into the business and maintained the cash receipts and sales records. Reluctantly, Mrs. Levi approached her husband about her theory. Mrs. Levi pointed out to Julius that Betty had unrestricted access to the cash receipts and accounting records of the business. Additionally, over the past few years, Betty had developed a taste for more expensive clothes and had begun taking more frequent and costly vacations than she had previously. Julius paid little attention to his wife's speculation regarding Betty. To him, it was preposterous to even consider the possibility that Betty could be stealing from the business.

Unfortunately, Julius's trust in Betty was misplaced. A few years later, the Levis accidentally uncovered an embezzlement scheme that Betty had used for years to steal from the business. Although she stole only $10 here and $20 there, over the period she was employed by the Levis, Betty's thefts accumulated to an estimated $350,000.

SOURCE: M. C. Knapp, "Howard Street Jewelers," in *Contemporary Auditing: Issues and Cases*, 2d ed. (Minneapolis/St. Paul: West Publishing Co., 1996)

---

world where transactions are often denominated in millions of dollars, these unintentional shortages can be very material amounts. To minimize the likelihood that such errors go undetected, merchandising companies should routinely test the mathematical accuracy of all internally and externally prepared source documents.

The Net Method of Accounting for Purchases

Earlier in the chapter, accounting for purchases discounts was illustrated. Although not mentioned at that point, the method illustrated is commonly known as the **gross method of accounting for merchandise purchases** because purchases are recorded at their total or gross invoice amount.[4] To provide for more effective control over purchases discounts, many merchandising companies use the **net method of accounting for merchandise purchases.** Under this method, purchases are recorded net of any discount that a company is permitted to deduct from the original invoice amount if it makes payment during the discount period. For illustration purposes,

gross method of accounting for merchandise purchases

net method of accounting for merchandise purchases

---

4. Use of the term "gross" to describe the total invoice amount of a merchandise purchase is ironic (and confusing to beginning accounting students) since the shipping terms for merchandising transactions, such as 2/10, n/30, refer to this same figure as a *net* amount. (Refer to footnote 3 for a related discussion of this issue.)

assume that a company purchases $1,000 of goods on October 7 with credit terms of 2/10, n/30. Given these facts, a $20 purchase discount is available to this company ($1,000 × 2%). If the net method is used, this purchase would be recorded as follows:

| Oct. 7 | Purchases | 980 | |
| | Accounts Payable | | 980 |

Purchase from Simmons Supply, invoice no. 344

Under the gross method, this purchase transaction would be recorded as a $1,000 debit to Purchases and an equal credit to Accounts Payable.

Assume that the company in the previous illustration pays for the purchased goods on the last day of the discount period, October 17. The following entry would be made under the net method of accounting for merchandise purchases.

| Oct. 17 | Accounts Payable | 980 | |
| | Cash | | 980 |

Payment for goods purchased on Oct. 7 from Simmons Supply, invoice no. 344

Under the gross method, this payment would be recorded with a $1,000 debit to Accounts Payable, a $20 credit to Purchases Discounts, and a $980 credit to Cash.

Now, assume that because of lack of funds or simple oversight, this company fails to pay for the purchased goods within the discount period. Instead, the company pays for these goods on the last day of the credit period, November 6. Under the gross method, the payment on November 6 would require an entry debiting Accounts Payable for $1,000 and crediting Cash for $1,000. Under the net method of accounting for purchases, the comparable entry would include a $20 debit to an expense account entitled Discounts Lost, as follows:

Nov. 6	Accounts Payable	980	
	Discounts Lost	20	
	Cash		1,000

Payment for goods purchased on Oct. 7 from Simmons Supply, invoice no. 344

Notice that the use of the net method highlights the fact that a purchase discount was forfeited in the situation described. If this was a conscious decision by management, it was a poor one. By not paying the invoice within the discount period, management had the use of $980 for an additional twenty days. But in exchange, a $20 discount was forfeited. Essentially, management borrowed $980 for a twenty-day period at an interest charge of $20. The true, or effective, interest rate on this "loan" is more than 36 percent: ($20/$980) × (360 days/20 days) = 36.73%. Clearly, there is a need to focus attention on situations in which a company has paid such a high interest rate. The net method of accounting for purchases discounts does just that by entering forfeited discounts in the expense account Discounts *Lost*. Consequently, the net method provides for more effective control and review of financing decisions made within an organization. As a point of information, the balance of Discounts

Lost is typically classified as an operating expense; however, some companies include the balance of this account in Cost of Goods Sold.

Special Journals and Subsidiary Ledgers

Many merchandising companies integrate special journals and subsidiary ledgers into their accounting systems. These accounting records enhance the degree of control over key assets and liabilities and provide for more efficient processing of financial data. A **special journal** is an accounting record in which a business journalizes a single type of transaction that it engages in repeatedly. When a company has several special journals, few entries will be made in its general journal. In fact, only those entries that cannot be recorded in a special journal will be recorded in the company's general journal. A **subsidiary ledger** is an accounting record that contains the detailed support for an account balance in the general ledger. When a subsidiary ledger is used, the corresponding general ledger account is referred to as a controlling account.

Special journals and subsidiary ledgers are used by all types of companies, but they are particularly beneficial to merchandisers that generate a large volume of purchase and sales transactions. The types and formats of special journals and subsidiary ledgers vary from company to company. An organization's accountants design these accounting records after considering the information needs of management, the frequency of different types of transactions, and internal control issues. Here, the special journals and subsidiary ledgers commonly used by merchandising companies are illustrated.

SALES JOURNAL   Merchandising companies typically record all credit sales of merchandise in a **sales journal.** Shown in Exhibit 6.11 is a one-day "window" of the sales journal of Bonney's Dress Shop. On May 1, 1996, three credit sales of merchandise were recorded in Bonney's sales journal. Since credit sales of merchandise require an equivalent debit and credit to Accounts Receivable and Sales, respectively, only one column for dollar amounts is necessary in a sales journal.

Periodically, the financial data recorded in journals must be posted to the general ledger and, if necessary, to the appropriate subsidiary ledger. A small company such as Bonney's generally posts sales journal data on a weekly or monthly basis. For illus-

■ LEARNING OBJECTIVE 9
Journalize transactions in special journals and post transaction data from special journals to the general ledger and subsidiary ledgers

special journal

subsidiary ledger

Teaching Note
Emphasize to students that transactions are recorded in either the general journal or a special journal, but not in both.

sales journal

■ EXHIBIT 6.11
Entries in Sales Journal of Bonney's Dress Shop on May 1, 1996

Sales Journal				Page 18
Date	Customer	Post Ref.	Invoice No.	Accounts Receivable Dr. Sales Cr.
1996				
May 1	Becky Orebel	√	171	255
1	Paula Hardy	√	172	522
1	Suzan Elliot	√	173	305
				1,082
				(102) (401)

tration purposes, assume that Bonney's posts journal data on a daily basis. The two three-digit numbers shown in parentheses at the bottom of the final column of Exhibit 6.11 indicate that the total credit sales for May 1, $1,082, have been posted to Accounts Receivable, account number 102 in Bonney's chart of accounts (see Exhibit 6.7), and to Sales, account number 401. The check marks in the post reference column in Exhibit 6.11 indicate that the individual sales transactions have been posted to the accounts receivable ledger.

An **accounts receivable ledger** is a subsidiary ledger in which a record (account) is maintained of the amount owed to a company by each of its customers. Shown in Exhibit 6.12 are the pages from Bonney's accounts receivable ledger for the three customers to whom credit sales were made on May 1, 1996. The credit sales made to these customers resulted in debits being posted to each of their accounts on May 1. The "S18" entry in the Post Reference column indicates that these transactions were posted from page 18 of the sales journal. Notice that two of the three accounts had transactions posted to them earlier in 1996.

accounts receivable ledger

■ **EXHIBIT 6.12**

Selected Customer Accounts Included in the Accounts Receivable Ledger of Bonney's Dress Shop

NAME: SUZAN ELLIOT
ADDRESS: 612 PERSIMMON WAY, ALEX SPRINGS, OK 73151
CUSTOMER ACCOUNT NO.: 62   PAGE 15

Date		Explanation	Post Ref.	Debit	Credit	Balance
1996						
Feb.	2		S3	230		230
Feb.	26		CR11		230	-0-
May	1		S18	305		305

NAME: PAULA HARDY
ADDRESS: 515 PRAIRIE DOG DRIVE, PENN VALLEY, OK 73048
CUSTOMER ACCOUNT NO.: 129   PAGE 24

Date		Explanation	Post Ref.	Debit	Credit	Balance
1996						
May	1		S18	522		522

NAME: BECKY OREBEL
ADDRESS: 808 COTTONWOOD LANE, HUGHES, OK 73060
CUSTOMER ACCOUNT NO.: 155   PAGE 61

Date		Explanation	Post Ref.	Debit	Credit	Balance
1996						
Jan.	1	Balance Forward				600
Jan.	4		CR2		400	200
Feb.	3		CR9		200	-0-
Apr.	17		S15	120		120
May	1		S18	255		375

Keep in mind that Bonney's Dress Shop maintains both an accounts receivable ledger and a general ledger controlling account, Accounts Receivable. For control purposes, Bonney's accountant periodically reconciles the total of the customer account balances included in the accounts receivable ledger to the balance of the general ledger controlling account. Any difference between these two accounting records is then investigated and eliminated. The information in the accounts receivable ledger also serves as the basis for the preparation of monthly billing statements. To encourage prompt payment of outstanding receivables, merchandising companies typically mail a monthly statement of account to each of their customers.

PURCHASES JOURNAL   Shown in Exhibit 6.13 is the purchases journal used by Bonney's Dress Shop. A company records credit purchases of merchandise in a **purchases journal.** For example, notice in Exhibit 6.13 that every transaction recorded in Bonney's purchases journal results in a debit to Purchases and an equal credit to Accounts Payable, meaning that cash purchases of merchandise are *not* recorded in this journal. The account numbers in parentheses at the bottom of the final column of Bonney's purchases journal indicate that the total credit purchases for December 5, 1996, were posted to the appropriate general ledger accounts. These accounts were Purchases (501) and Accounts Payable (201).

purchases journal

Bonney's also maintains an **accounts payable ledger,** a subsidiary ledger in which a record (account) is maintained of the amount owed by a company to each of its suppliers. A key control function of an accounts payable ledger is to ensure that a company does not pay its suppliers any more than they are owed. An accounts payable ledger has a format similar to that of an accounts receivable ledger. The check marks in the post reference column of Bonney's purchases journal shown in Exhibit 6.13 indicate that the individual purchase transactions were posted to the appropriate accounts in the accounts payable ledger.

accounts payable ledger

As noted earlier, accountants design special journals with the needs of their organization in mind. As an organization grows or its operations change, accountants may decide that the organization's special journals need to be reformatted. For example, Bonney's accountants could easily reformat the purchases journal shown in Exhibit 6.13 to accommodate transactions other than credit purchases of merchandise. Shown in Exhibit 6.14 is such a purchases journal. The purchases journal in Exhibit 6.14 is referred to as a multicolumn purchases journal since it contains multiple columns for recording dollar amounts. Besides credit purchases of merchandise, credit

■ **EXHIBIT 6.13**
Entries in Purchases Journal of Bonney's Dress Shop on December 5, 1996

			Purchases Journal			Page 39
Date		Account Credited	Post Ref.	Invoice No.	Terms	Purchases Dr. Accounts Payable Cr.
1996 Dec	5	Branch Supply	√	202	2/10, n/30	1,800
	5	McCaleb Bros.	√	203	n/30	320
	5	Arnett Stores	√	204	2/10, n/30	440
						2,560
						(501) (201)

■ **EXHIBIT 6.14**

Example of a Multicolumn Purchases Journal

								Other Accounts Dr.		
Purchases Journal										**Page 1**
Date	Account Credited	Terms	Post Ref.	Accounts Payable Cr.	Purchases Dr.	Supplies Dr.		Account	Post Ref.	Amount

■ **EXHIBIT 6.15**

Cash Receipts Journal for Bonney's Dress Shop

					Other Accounts Cr.	Sales Cr.	Accounts Receivable Dr.	Cash Dr.
Cash Receipts Journal								**Page 9**
Date		Account Credited	Post Ref.					
1996								
Feb.	3	Carol Jenkins	√				140	140
Feb.	3	Becky Orebel	√				200	200
Feb.	3	Interest Revenue	404		40			40
Feb.	3	Renee Daniels	√				210	210
Feb.	3	Cash Sales	√			160		160
					40	160	550	750
					(401)	(102)	(101)	

purchases of supplies and any other purchases that result in a credit to Accounts Payable can be entered in the purchases journal shown in Exhibit 6.14.

CASH RECEIPTS JOURNAL The cash receipts journal used by Bonney's Dress Shop is shown in Exhibit 6.15. A **cash receipts journal** is a special journal in which all cash receipt transactions of a business are recorded. Like the purchases journal shown in Exhibit 6.14, Bonney's cash receipts journal is a multicolumn journal. Every transaction entered in a cash receipts journal, by definition, must include a debit to Cash. The number and type of credit columns to include in a cash receipts journal is a matter of choice by an entity's accountants. Since most of Bonney's cash receipts involve collections of accounts receivable or cash sales, credit columns are included in its cash receipts journal for Accounts Receivable and Sales—credit sales will be recorded in Bonney's sales journal since they are noncash transactions. The other credit column included in Bonney's cash receipts journal is a column for miscellaneous cash receipts, such as interest revenue, tax refunds, and cash receipts from the sale of long-term assets. Merchandising companies that have a large volume of sales discounts, which is not true of Bonney's, include a debit column for Sales Discounts in their cash receipts journal.

cash receipts journal

■ **EXHIBIT 6.16**

Cash Disbursements Journal for Bonney's Dress Shop

		Ck. No.	Account Debited	Post Ref.	Other Accounts Dr.	Accounts Payable Dr.	Purchases Discounts Cr.	Cash Cr.
Date								
1996								
Nov.	6	471	Purchases	501	400			400
Nov.	6	472	Aaron Supply	√		320		320
Nov.	6	473	Smith Supply	√		400	8	392
Nov.	6	474	Supplies	106	130			130
Nov.	6	475	XT Distributors	√		500	10	490
					530	1,220	18	1,732
						(201)	(503)	(101)

Cash Disbursements Journal   Page 67

The numbers in parentheses at the bottom of the Sales, Accounts Receivable, and Cash columns in Exhibit 6.15 indicate that the totals of those columns have been posted to the appropriate general ledger accounts. The total of the Other Accounts credit column cannot be posted since that figure typically involves credits to several different accounts. When the individual amounts in the Other Accounts column are posted to the general ledger, the appropriate account numbers are inserted in the Post Reference column. For instance, by inserting "404," the account number for Interest Revenue, in the Post Reference column, Bonney's accountant has indicated that he or she has posted the $40 credit to the Interest Revenue account in the general ledger. The check marks in the Post Reference column indicate that the appropriate postings have been made to the accounts receivable ledger. For instance, the cash receipt of $200 from Becky Orebel was posted to her account in the accounts receivable ledger, as shown in Exhibit 6.12.

CASH DISBURSEMENTS JOURNAL   Bonney's cash disbursements journal is illustrated in Exhibit 6.16. A **cash disbursements journal** is a special journal in which all cash disbursement transactions of a business are recorded. Notice that the final column of Bonney's cash disbursements journal includes only credits to the Cash account. Since most of Bonney's cash disbursements involve payments to suppliers, one column of its cash disbursements journal is reserved for debits to Accounts Payable. Likewise, since Bonney's regularly takes advantage of the purchases discounts made available by its suppliers, a credit column for Purchases Discounts is also included in its cash disbursements journal. Miscellaneous cash payments are entered in the Other Accounts debit column of Bonney's cash disbursements journal.

cash disbursements journal

The numbers in parentheses at the bottom of the Accounts Payable, Purchases Discounts, and Cash columns in Exhibit 6.16 indicate that the collective dollar amount of debits or credits affecting each of those accounts has been posted to the general ledger. After posting the individual debit amounts in the Other Accounts column to the appropriate general ledger accounts, Bonney's accountant inserts the three-digit numbers of those accounts in the Post Reference column. Finally, the check marks in the Post Reference column indicate that those amounts affecting

Discussion Question
Ask students to summarize the
key advantages of using special
journals and subsidiary ledgers.

individual suppliers' accounts in the accounts payable ledger have been posted to that subsidiary ledger.

As suggested earlier, cash receipts and cash disbursements journals take precedence over other special journals. For example, consider a $500 sales transaction in which a $100 down payment is made by the customer and $400 is charged to the customer's receivable account. That transaction would be recorded in the cash receipts journal. Likewise, if a purchase transaction includes even a small down payment, that transaction must be recorded in the cash disbursements journal, not the purchases journal.

SUMMARY

Retail merchandising firms buy products from wholesalers or manufacturing companies and then resell these products to their customers. As is true for any type of business, the accountants of a merchandising firm must design an accounting system that yields information useful to internal and external decision makers. The key difference in the financial statements of merchandising companies and service companies lies in the structure of a merchandising company's income statement. Cost of goods sold, the largest expense item for most merchandising companies, is not found in the income statements of service companies. The difference between a merchandising firm's net sales and costs of goods sold is its gross profit. Decision makers compute and track a merchandiser's gross profit percentage (gross profit divided by net sales) and its profit margin percentage (net income divided by net sales) to monitor the company's financial health.

Because inventory is the most important asset in a merchandising operation, the accounting systems of merchandising companies are oriented around the Inventory account. The two basic inventory accounting systems that can be used by merchandising firms are the periodic inventory system and the perpetual inventory system. In a periodic inventory system, revenue from sales transactions is recorded when sales are made, but the corresponding cost of goods sold is not. Instead, cost of goods sold in a periodic inventory system is computed at the end of each accounting period and then inserted into a merchandising company's income statement.

Among the most common types of transactions for merchandising firms are sales, sales returns and allowances, purchases discounts, purchases, purchases returns and allowances, and payments of transportation costs. Two key parameters of merchandising transactions are their credit terms and shipping terms. Failure to correctly identify and interpret these parameters of a merchandising transaction may result in the transaction being recorded improperly.

The period-ending closing procedures for a merchandising company are similar to those for a service company. One key difference is the need to establish the period-ending Inventory account balance in a merchandising company's accounting records via its closing entries.

Internal control considerations are very important for merchandising companies. The high volume of transactions in many merchandising operations and the risk of inventory theft are among the factors that accountants must consider when developing internal control procedures for these businesses. Although most companies utilize special journals and subsidiary ledgers, merchandising firms can make particularly effective use of these accounting records. Special journals and subsidiary ledgers enhance the degree of control that merchandisers can maintain over key assets and liabilities and provide for more efficient processing of financial data.

GLOSSARY

Accounts payable ledger (p. 241)   A subsidiary ledger in which a record (account) is maintained of the amount owed by a company to each of its suppliers.

Accounts receivable ledger (p. 240)   A subsidiary ledger in which a record (account) is maintained of the amount owed to a company by each of its customers.

Cash disbursements journal (p. 243)   A special journal in which all cash disbursement transactions of a business are recorded.

Cash receipts journal (p. 242)   A special journal in which all cash receipts transactions of a business are recorded.

Cost of goods sold (p. 216)   The cost of inventory sold to customers during an accounting period.

Credit terms (p. 223)   The agreement between a buyer and seller regarding the timing of payment by the buyer and any discount available to the buyer for early payment.

Financial ratios (p. 217)   Measures that express the relationship or interrelationships between two or more financial statement items.

FOB destination (p. 226)   Shipping terms under which the seller delivers goods to the destination point; the seller is responsible for paying the transportation charges.

FOB shipping point (p. 226)   Shipping terms under which the seller delivers goods to the shipping point; the buyer is responsible for paying the transportation charges.

Gross method of accounting for merchandise purchases (p. 237)   A method of accounting for merchandise purchases under which purchases are recorded at their total or gross invoice amount.

Gross profit percentage (p. 218)   Gross profit divided by net sales.

Net method of accounting for merchandise purchases (p. 237)   A method of accounting for merchandise purchases under which purchases are recorded net of any available discount.

Net sales (p. 216)   A merchandising company's total sales during an accounting period less sales returns and allowances and sales discounts.

Periodic inventory system (p. 220)   An inventory accounting system in which the dollar value of ending inventory is determined by counting the merchandise on hand at the end of each accounting period and then multiplying the quantity of each item by its per unit cost.

Perpetual inventory system (p. 220)   An inventory accounting system in which a perpetually updated record of the quantity of individual inventory items and their per unit costs is maintained.

Profit margin percentage (p. 218)   Net income divided by net sales.

Purchases discounts (p. 225)   Discounts offered by suppliers to encourage prompt payment of credit purchases.

Purchases journal (p. 241)   A special journal in which credit purchases of merchandise are recorded; if a multicolumn format is used, other credit purchases can be recorded in this journal as well.

Purchases returns and allowances (p. 224)   Reductions in amounts owed to suppliers as a result of returned goods or price concessions granted by suppliers for damaged or defective goods.

Sales discounts (p. 222)   Discounts offered to customers to entice them to pay their receivable balances on a timely basis.

Sales journal (p. 239)   A special journal in which credit sales of merchandise are recorded.

Sales returns and allowances (p. 221)   The sum of refunds paid to customers who return damaged or defective merchandise and price reductions granted to customers to persuade them to keep such merchandise.

Special journal (p. 239)   An accounting record in which a business journalizes a single type of transaction that it engages in repeatedly.

Subsidiary ledger (p. 239)   An accounting record that contains the detailed support for an account balance in the general ledger.

Transportation in (p. 226)   Freight charges paid by a business for the delivery of goods it has purchased.

Transportation out (p.227)   Freight charges paid by a business for the delivery of goods it has sold.

DECISION CASE

In 1988, Burroughs Wellcome, a British firm acquired in March 1995 by Glaxo plc, developed and patented AZT. This drug had been proven in extensive clinical trials to be effective in slowing the progression of AIDS-related symptoms in HIV-positive individuals. Initially, Burroughs Wellcome charged approximately $10,000 for a one-year supply of AZT, a price which reportedly yielded a large gross profit on the sales of this product. Critics claimed that Burroughs Wellcome was engaging in price-gouging behavior of the worst kind by charging AIDS patients an exorbitant price for the drug. In testimony before Congress, Burroughs Wellcome's chief executive defended the high price of AZT by pointing out that his company had invested heavily in the development and marketing of the drug. He maintained that the pricing structure the company had established for AZT allowed Burroughs Wellcome to earn no more than a "reasonable" rate of return on this large investment. However, when pressed to disclose the accounting data regarding the costs associated with AZT, the chief executive refused. The chief executive maintained those data were confidential and that releasing the data might be beneficial to competing companies.

In response to heavy criticism of its AZT pricing policy, Burroughs Wellcome gradually reduced the price of the drug. By the mid-1990s, the average price of a one-year supply of AZT had declined to approximately $2,000.

Required: Assume that you are the chief executive of a biotechnology company that has developed a lifesaving drug for a rare and incurable disease. This disease is so rare that fewer than five hundred new cases are diagnosed each year in the United States. The total cost incurred by your firm to produce, package, and distribute a one-year supply of this drug is approximately $4,000. The New Product Committee of your firm, which includes two sales managers, a pharmacist, a cost accountant, and a research scientist, has recommended that the price for a one-year supply of this drug be established at $20,000.

When the price of this new drug is publicly announced, your company faces a storm of criticism. Similar to the Burroughs Wellcome case, critics demand that you release accounting data regarding the costs related to this product. How would you respond to this demand? Does your firm have a responsibility to defend its pricing decision for this new drug by releasing the relevant accounting data? Has your firm behaved unethically by pricing this drug at such a level that the individuals who need the drug will be forced to make a huge economic sacrifice to acquire it? Explain.

QUESTIONS

1. What is gross profit? What transactions of a company affect its gross profit?
2. What are financial ratios and how are they used by financial decision makers?
3. How are the gross profit percentage and profit margin percentage computed?
4. What is the difference between "gross" sales and net sales?
5. What significant expense item is found in the income statement of a merchandising company but not in the income statement of a service company?
6. Explain the key differences between a perpetual and periodic inventory system.
7. Identify one advantage and one disadvantage of a perpetual inventory system. Do the same for a periodic inventory system.
8. How does a company that uses a periodic inventory system determine how much inventory it has on hand at any one time?

9. What is the difference between sales returns and sales allowances? Do merchandising companies always have both?

10. Why do many merchandising companies grant their credit customers discounts for early payment?

11. Define the shipping terms FOB shipping point and FOB destination. From the standpoint of the *buyer*, which terms are more advantageous? Why?

12. Which of the following accounts would generally be found in the accounting records of a retail store: Transportation In or Transportation Out? Why?

13. Identify the accounts that generally figure into the computation of cost of goods sold in a periodic inventory accounting system.

14. Why are the Sales Returns and Allowances, and Purchases Returns and Allowances accounts closed at the end of each period?

15. Most companies use prenumbered checks. Why?

16. Which of the general control procedures described in the chapter do you believe is most important for a merchandising company to implement? Choose only one and defend your choice.

17. Why are internal control measures for inventory so important for merchandising companies?

18. How does the net method of accounting for purchases discounts provide more effective control over purchases discounts than the gross method?

19. Explain the key purpose of (a) special journals and (b) subsidiary ledgers.

20. Identify the special journals and subsidiary ledgers that a small retail business might maintain.

EXERCISES

21. **Gross Profit** (LO 2)
    Following are selected financial data for Jones Plumbing Supply for March 1997.

Sales	$520,000
Sales Discounts	10,000
Purchases Discounts	12,000
Sales Returns & Allowances	30,000
Purchases Returns & Allowances	18,000
Cost of Goods Sold	360,000

    Required:
    1. Determine Jones Plumbing Supply's gross profit for March 1997.
    2. Assume that plumbing supply companies historically have a gross profit percentage of 30 percent and that Jones Plumbing Supply's gross profit percentage averages 27 percent. Comment on the business's gross profit percentage for March 1997 relative to these two benchmarks. If you were a potential investor in this business, would this information have a favorable or unfavorable influence on your investment decision?

    21. 1. Net sales, $480,000
        CGS, $360,000
        Gross Profit, $120,000
        2. Gross Profit %, 25%

22. **Profitability Ratios for a Merchandising Company** (LO 2)
    The following information was drawn from the income statement of Quixote Corporation, a public company, for the year ended June 30, 1994. Amounts are in thousands.

Net Sales	$176,938
Cost of Goods Sold	111,328
Income Taxes	65,000
Net Income	11,644

Required:

1. Using the information provided, compute the gross profit percentage and profit margin percentage for Quixote Corporation.
2. Suppose that one goal of Quixote management for 1994 was to have its products priced so that each dollar of net sales would contribute $.10 to net income. Did the company achieve this goal?

23. Profitability Ratios for a Merchandising Company (LO 2)

Following are selected financial data included in the 1994 annual report of Conner Peripherals, Inc. Conner markets computer disk drives and related products.

	DECEMBER 31, 1992	DECEMBER 31, 1993	DECEMBER 31, 1994
Net Sales	$2,238,423	$2,151,672	$2,365,152
Gross Profit	458,464	237,954	468,649
Operating Income	153,530	(446,430)	166,564
Net Income	121,072	(445,314)	109,687

Required:

1. Compute Conner's gross profit percentage and profit margin percentage for each year listed.
2. Identify factors that may have accounted for Conner's net loss in 1993.

24. Journal Entries for a Merchandising Company (LO 4)

Following are a few transactions engaged in by William & Wallace, a men's clothes store, during September.

September 1: Sold merchandise for cash, $350
September 7: Sold $400 of merchandise on credit with terms of n/30
September 15: Customer who purchased merchandise on September 7 was granted a sales allowance of $80
September 16: Sold $2,000 of excess merchandise to Welsh Stores with terms of 2/10, n/30, FOB shipping point
September 21: Collected $800 on account from a customer
September 26: Received amount due from Welsh Stores for merchandise sold on September 16
September 29: Received amount due from customer who purchased merchandise on September 7

Required:
Prepare general journal entries for these transactions.

25. Sales vs. Purchases (LO 4)

Galahad Manufacturers sold $32,000 of merchandise to Percival Import Retailers on July 1. The cost of delivering this merchandise was $1,400 and was prepaid by Galahad. Percival uses the gross method of accounting for merchandise purchases.

Required:
Prepare the appropriate journal entries related to this transaction and the subsequent payment in the accounting records of Galahad and Percival under each of the following assumptions (do not include explanations in the journal entries):

Margin notes:

22. 1. Gross Profit, $65,610
Gross Profit %, 37.1%
Profit Margin %, 6.6%

23. 1992 Gross Profit %, 20.5%
1992 Profit Margin %, 5.4%

24. 9/15 Dr. Sales Ret. $80
Cr. A.R. $80
9/26 Dr. Cash $1,960
Dr. Sales Disc. Lost $40
Cr. A.R. $2,000

25. 1. Percival 7/1 Dr. Purch. $32,000
Dr. Trans. In $1,400
Cr. A.P. $33,400
2. Galahad 7/1 Dr. Trans. Out $1,400
Cr. Cash $1,400
3. Galahad 7/11 Dr. Cash $32,760
Dr. Sales Disc. $640

CREDIT TERMS	SHIPPING TERMS	PAYMENT DATE
1. 1/10, n/30	FOB shipping point	July 31
2. 1/10, n/30	FOB destination	July 31
3. 2/10, n/30	FOB shipping point	July 11

Cr. A.R. $33,400
Percival 7/11 Dr. A.P.
$33,400
Cr. Purch. Disc. $640
Cr. Cash $32,760

26. **Purchases and Related Entries, Gross Method of Recording Merchandise Purchases** (LO 4)

Robert Bruce Clothiers, a clothes wholesaler, engaged in the following transactions, among others, during August.

August 1: Purchased $5,000 of merchandise from Edward Tailors with terms of 2/10, n/30, FOB shipping point

August 1: Purchased $2,400 of merchandise from Crain Designs with terms of 1/10, n/30, FOB destination

August 2: Received freight bill of $170 from Scot's Trucking for merchandise purchased on August 1 from Edward Tailors

August 4: Returned $400 of the merchandise purchased on August 1 from Edward Tailors due to fabric flaws

August 11: Paid amount due Edward Tailors for merchandise purchased on August 1

August 14: Purchased $4,000 of merchandise from York Manufacturing with terms of 2/10, n/30, FOB destination

August 15: Paid freight bill received on August 2

August 19: Purchased $3,200 of merchandise with terms of 1/10, n/30, FOB shipping point, from Gibson Fashions; freight bill of $110 was prepaid by Gibson

August 24: Paid amount due York Manufacturing for merchandise purchased on August 14

August 29: Paid amount due Gibson Fashions for August 19 merchandise purchase

August 31: Paid amount due Crain Designs for merchandise purchased on August 1.

Required:

Prepare general journal entries for these transactions assuming that Robert Bruce Clothiers uses the gross method of accounting for merchandise purchases.

26. 8/2   Dr. Trans In $170
    8/4   Cr. Purch. Ret. $400
    8/11   Cr. Purch. Disc. $92
    8/24   Cr. Purch. Disc. $80
    8/29   Cr. Purch. Disc. $32

27. **Purchases and Related Entries, Net Method of Recording Merchandise Purchases** (LO 4)

Refer to the factual information provided for Exercise 26.

Required:

Assume that Robert Bruce Clothiers uses the net method of accounting for merchandise purchases. Prepare journal entries for the transactions listed for that business in August.

27. 8/1   Dr. Purch. $4,900
    8/1   Dr. Purch. $2,376
    8/4   Cr. Purch. Ret. $392
    8/11   Dr. A.P. $4,508
    8/14   Dr. Purch. $3,920
    8/19   Dr. Purch. $3,168
    8/31   Dr. Disc. Lost $24

28. **Closing Entries for a Merchandising Company** (LO 6)

Following is information drawn from the accounting records of Asp Music Stores for the year ended December 31, 1996.

Sales	$3,000,000
Purchases	1,500,000
Advertising Expense	400,000
Salaries Expense	220,000
Transportation In	30,000
Interest Revenue	5,000
Income Taxes Expense	140,000

Purchases Returns and Allowances	120,000
Sales Returns and Allowances	50,000
Purchases Discounts	30,000
Sales Discounts	10,000
Inventory on January 1, 1996	340,000
Inventory on December 31, 1996	440,000

Required:

1. Prepare the closing entries for this business at the end of 1996.
2. What was this business's net income for 1996?

29. **Computation of Cost of Goods Sold** (LO 5)

Following is information relating to the cost of goods sold for the Trojan Cove, a Los Angeles convenience store, for the year ending December 31, 1996.

Sales	$485,000
Sales Discounts	1,100
Sales Returns and Allowances	750
Inventory, January 1	26,400
Purchases Discounts	4,500
Purchases Returns and Allowances	6,100
Inventory, December 31	4,300
Transportation In	2,900
Purchases	390,400

Required:

Prepare a cost of goods sold schedule for the Trojan Cove for the year ending December 31, 1996.

30. **Reconstructing Missing Accounting Data for a Merchandiser** (LO 5)

Your friend Bob is spending the weekend at the beach. Bob is the accountant for Boston-based Haymarket Square, Inc., a company that markets sports-related products in New England. Unfortunately for Bob, he has brought along some work. Bob is hoping to complete his company's period-ending work sheet over the weekend.

Required:

As Bob is soaking up the rays on Marconi Beach in Cape Cod, he realizes that he has lost some of the data he brought with him. Help Bob out by determining the missing amounts in the following list.

Sales	$1,136,000
Purchases Returns and Allowances	?
Net Purchases	754,000
Total Operating Expenses	?
Transportation In	16,000
Inventory, January 1	?
Purchases Discounts	14,000
Gross Profit	?
Sales Returns and Allowances	32,000
Net Sales	1,100,000
Purchases	802,000
Cost of Goods Available for Sale	894,000
Sales Discounts	?
Inventory, December 31	138,000
Cost of Goods Sold	?
Income from Operations	142,000

Margin notes:

28. 2. Net Income, $905,000

29. CGS, $404,800

30. CGS, $756,000
    Gross Profit, $344,000

31. Use of Special Journals (LO 9)

The accountant for a local bookstore, Books-n-More, maintains the following special journals: cash receipts journal, cash disbursements journal, purchases journal, and sales journal. Both the purchases journal and sales journal are "single-column" journals.

Required:

Indicate in which of Books-n-More's five journals—four special journals plus its general journal—the following items would be recorded.

a. Cash sale of old office equipment
b. Credit purchase of merchandise
c. Sale of merchandise in which the customer paid $50 down and "charged" the remainder of his purchase
d. Receipt of interest revenue from the local bank
e. Payment of quarterly income taxes
f. Cash purchase of merchandise
g. Monthly closing entries
h. Payment of salaries to employees
i. Entry to correct error in depreciation expense entry made in previous month
j. Credit sale of merchandise
k. Purchase of equipment on credit—signed a six-month promissory note at the local bank
l. Income tax refund

31. No check figures

32. Internal Controls for Merchandising Operations (LO 8)

Following are selected internal controls for Koh Imports, a retail store that sells household items such as rugs and lamps imported from South Korea.

a. Salesclerks are not allowed access to accounting records.
b. The inventory of each of the store's five departments is counted once per quarter.
c. Each week the store's accountant determines the numerical sequence of purchase orders used during the week and identifies the purchase transaction related to each purchase order completed that week.
d. Store owner must approve all purchases exceeding $100.
e. Before purchase invoices are processed for payment, the store's accountant tests the mathematical accuracy of each invoice.
f. Salesclerks are not allowed to extend credit to customers; all credit-granting decisions are made by the store owner.

Required:

Identify the purpose of each internal control listed. That is, comment on the potential problem or problems that each control is designed to avoid or minimize.

32. No check figures

33. Theft at the Supermarket (LO 8)

Over a period of a few years, a large supermarket suffered several thousand dollars of losses resulting from a scam perpetrated by the store's assistant managers. One of the responsibilities of the store's assistant managers was to periodically empty and count each cash register till. One of the assistant managers pointed out to his colleagues that the cash count and the total of the cash register tape was nearly always different by some small amount. As a result, this individual convinced two of the other assistant managers to take a quarter from each cash till that they counted each day—on a daily basis each assistant manager might make as many as twenty to thirty till counts. "Who's going to miss a quarter here and a quarter there?" was the argument of the master schemer.

Required:

33. 1. $11,250

1. Suppose that each of the three assistant store managers counted twenty cash tills daily and that each worked 250 days per year. Determine the supermarket's theft loss over a period of three years.
2. Identify internal controls that might have prevented or detected this theft ring.

34. Impact of Errors on a Merchandiser's Financial Statements (LO 2, 5, 7)

Caitlin O'Regan has just completed preparing the 1996 year-end financial statements for her employer, Rourke Merchandising. Following are several of the key amounts included in these financial statements.

Total Assets	$2,530,000
Inventory	400,000
Retained Earnings	310,000
Net Sales	$1,880,000
Gross Profit	460,000
Total Operating Expenses	140,000
Net Income	255,000

Caitlin was putting her work papers away for the night when she made the disappointing discovery that there were two errors in the financial statements she had just spent three days completing. First, she found a memo from the warehouse accountant indicating that the warehouse inventory was overstated by $24,000 due to a computer glitch. Second, she found a unpaid bill for an operating expense of $12,000. This bill is not due until January, but it is for an expense incurred in 1996.

Required:

34. 1. Correct Gross Profit %, 23.2%

Correct Profit Margin %, 12.4%

1. Suppose that Caitlin does not make the appropriate corrections in the financial statements. Indicate how the financial statements will be in error. Also determine the impact on the company's gross profit percentage and profit margin percentage. (Assume that Rourke's income taxes average 40 percent of net income.)
2. How might the uncorrected errors affect the decisions of those parties relying on Rourke Merchandising's financial statements?

PROBLEM SET A

35. Merchandising Income Statement (LO 1, 7)

Following are selected account balances drawn from a recent adjusted trial balance of Lynn's Violets, Inc., a company that operates a chain of florist shops.

Sales	$4,080,000
Purchases Discounts	75,000
Cash	105,000
Transportation In	125,000
Sales Discounts	22,000
Accounts Receivable	155,000
Sales Returns and Allowances	26,000
Purchases Returns and Allowances	144,000
Inventory, January 1	100,000
Purchases	2,000,000
Depreciation Expense	75,000
Accumulated Depreciation, Equipment	280,000
Accounts Payable	77,000
Sales Salaries Expense	333,000
Inventory, December 31	130,000

Income Taxes Expense	295,000
Advertising Expense	40,000

Required:

1. Given the information provided, prepare an income statement for Lynn's Violets, Inc. (Note: Certain of the account balances listed will not be included in the income statement.)
2. Identify the items included in the income statement of Lynn's Violets that would typically not be found in the income statement of a service company.

35. 1. CGS, $1,876,000
Net Income, $1,413,000

36. **Journal Entries for a Merchandising Company** (LO 4)

Following are selected transactions of Jenkins, Inc., which sells household appliances. Jenkins uses the gross method of accounting for merchandise purchases.

June 1: Purchased $6,000 of merchandise from Lindsey Corporation with terms of 1/10, n/30, FOB shipping point. Lindsey prepaid the freight charges of $300.

June 3: Cash sales for the day totaled $1,100.

June 4: Sold $2,000 of merchandise to another appliance retailer, JLK Company, with terms of 2/10, n/30. The merchandise was picked up on Jenkins' freight dock by JLK employees.

June 6: Sold $300 of merchandise to Jae Lee, terms n/20.

June 8: Purchased $4,000 of merchandise from CET Company with terms of 2/10, n/20, FOB destination.

June 11: Paid Lindsey Corporation amount due for June 1 purchase.

June 12: JLK Company returned $500 of the merchandise purchased on June 4—the merchandise was defective.

June 14: JLK Company paid Lindsey the amount due for the June 4 sale.

June 17: Returned $400 of defective merchandise purchased from CET Company on June 8.

June 19: Purchased $6,000 of merchandise from Kaye Enterprises with terms of 2/10, n/30, FOB shipping point. Kaye prepaid the freight charges of $400.

June 20: Sold $950 of merchandise to Larissa Rodriguez with terms of n/20.

June 22: Purchased $3,200 of merchandise from Cosier Wholesalers with terms of 2/10, n/30, FOB shipping point.

June 26: Received payment from Jae Lee for merchandise sold to him on June 6.

June 26: $800 of merchandise purchased from Kaye Enterprises on June 19 was found to be defective and returned.

June 28: Paid CET Company amount due for June 8 purchase.

June 29: Paid amount due Kaye Enterprises for purchases made on June 19.

June 29: Received and paid $200 freight bill for goods purchased on June 22 from Cosier Wholesalers.

Required:

1. Prepare general journal entries for these transactions.
2. Prepare the necessary journal entries for the June 8 purchase from CET Company and the June 19 purchase from Kaye Enterprises under the assumption that Jenkins, Inc., uses the net method of accounting for merchandise purchases.

36. 1. 6/1   Dr. Trans. In $300
6/11   Cr. Purch. Disc.
        $60
6/14   Dr. Sales Disc. $30
6/29   Cr. Purch. Disc.
        $104
2. 6/8   Dr. Purch. $3,920
6/17   Cr. Purch. Ret.
        $392
6/28   Dr. Disc. Lost $72
6/29   Dr. A.P. $5,496

37. **Profitability Ratios** (LO 2)

Dixie Yarns, Inc., is headquartered in Chattanooga, Tennessee, and sells a wide range of carpet and textile products. The following information (in thousands) was reported in the company's 1994 annual report issued in April 1995.

QUARTER	NET SALES	GROSS PROFIT	NET INCOME
1st, 1993	$120,777	$15,407	$ 907
2nd, 1993	161,439	23,288	2,062
3rd, 1993	152,530	24,673	841
4th, 1993	159,855	20,855	874
1st, 1994	164,750	19,522	(4,342)
2nd, 1994	178,318	27,559	118
3rd, 1994	173,924	26,907	501
4th, 1994	171,453	18,815	496

Required:

37. 1st Q 1993 Gross Profit %, 12.8%

1st Q 1993 Profit Margin %, 0.8%

1. Compute Dixie Yarns' gross profit percentage and profit margin percentage for each quarter in 1993 and 1994.
2. Can you discern any definite trends in these data? If so, comment on them.
3. Suppose that in early 1995 you were considering investing in this company's common stock. Identify three questions you would want to ask of the company's chief executive officer before you decide whether to invest in this company.

38. **Delivery Costs and Gross Profit** (LO 2, 5)

Following is selected financial information for 1996 for the Buchanan Street Bikery, which operates a small chain of retail stores that sell bicycles and related items.

Inventory as of January 1, 1996	$3,400,000
Sales	4,500,000
Inventory as of December 31, 1996	3,300,000
Purchases	3,400,000
Transportation In	350,000
Purchases Returns and Allowances	20,000
Sales Returns and Allowances	120,000
Purchases Discounts	70,000
Sales Discounts	20,000

Required:

38. 1. Net Purchases, $3,310,000

CGS, $3,760,000

2. Gross Profit with, $600,000

Gross Profit without, $950,000

1. Compute cost of goods sold for 1996.
2. Suppose this business had not been required to pay delivery costs for the merchandise it purchased during 1996. Given this assumption, recompute the business's gross profit for 1996.
3. The owner of the Buchanan Street Bikery is unaware of the impact delivery costs have on the business's profitability. Using your answers to Parts 1 and 2, write a short memo to the owner explaining how delivery costs affected the business's profitability during 1996. Include in your memo any recommendations you have regarding how the business could lower its delivery costs.

39. **Work Sheet for a Merchandising Company** (LO 6)

Following is a trial balance for Owens-Field Distributors for the year ending December 31, 1996.

OWENS-FIELD DISTRIBUTORS
TRIAL BALANCE
DECEMBER 31, 1996

	DEBIT	CREDIT
Cash	$ 4,000	
Accounts Receivable	12,000	
Supplies	700	
Inventory	41,000	

Equipment	84,000	
Accumulated Depreciation, Equipment		$ 20,000
Accounts Payable		7,000
Common Stock		10,000
Retained Earnings		66,800
Sales		164,000
Sales Returns and Allowances	4,300	
Sales Discounts	1,200	
Purchases	74,000	
Purchases Returns and Allowances		7,000
Purchases Discounts		1,500
Transportation In	1,900	
Transportation Out	500	
Salaries Expense	46,000	
Advertising Expense	3,200	
Income Taxes Expense	3,500	
	$276,300	$276,300

Other information:
a. The company has inventory of $34,500 on hand at December 31, 1996.
b. The company has supplies on hand of $400 at December 31, 1996.
c. Owens-Field owes its employees $600 of salaries that they have earned in the last few days of the year.
d. Unrecorded depreciation expense at December 31, 1996, is $2,200.

Required:
1. Enter Owens-Field's trial balance on a work sheet and complete the work sheet.
2. Prepare a balance sheet as of December 31, 1996, and an income statement for the year ended December 31, 1996, for Owens-Field.
3. Prepare and journalize all adjusting and closing entries.

39. 1. Adjustments, $3,100
    Adjusted Trial Balance, $279,100
2. Retained Earnings, $95,100
   Assets, $112,700
   Net Income, $28,300

40. **Internal Controls for a Merchandiser** (LO 8)
Almost certainly, either you or a relative or a close friend has worked for, or is presently working for, a merchandising company or business. Use one of these sources of information to identify the internal controls of a merchandising company, past or present.

Required:
Identify and briefly describe the merchandising company for which you, a close friend, or a relative has worked or is presently working. Identify at least five internal controls of the given company relating to its merchandising operations. Be specific. Briefly describe the key purpose of each control identified.

40. No check figures

PROBLEM SET B

41. **Merchandising Income Statement** (LO 1, 7)
Following are selected account balances drawn from a recent adjusted trial balance for Mark's Office Supply, a retail merchandising firm.

Advertising Expense	$	40,000
Purchases Discounts		24,000
Sales Returns and Allowances		12,000
Transportation Out		9,000
Salaries Expense		130,000
Cash		65,000

Sales Discounts	17,000
Inventory, January 1	110,000
Purchases	1,320,000
Accounts Receivable	35,000
Utilities Expense	22,000
Accounts Payable	45,000
Transportation In	55,000
Purchases Returns and Allowances	121,000
Depreciation Expense	185,000
Accumulated Depreciation	360,000
Sales	2,020,000
Inventory, December 31	120,000
Income Taxes Expense	41,000

Required:

41. 1. CGS, $1,220, 000

    Net Income, $344,000

1. Prepare an income statement for this merchandising company. (Note: Certain of the accounts listed will not be included in this income statement.)
2. Identify the items included in the income statement of Mark's Office Supply that would typically not be found in the income statement of a service company.

42. **Journal Entries for a Merchandising Company** (LO 4)

Following are selected transactions of Chautauqua, Inc., which sells construction supplies. Chautauqua uses the gross method of accounting for merchandise purchases.

December 1: Purchased $6,000 of merchandise from Kelso Wholesalers with terms of n/30, FOB shipping point. Kelso prepaid the freight charges of $300.

December 1: Sold supplies of $700 to a local homebuilder, Gene Harrison, with terms of 1/10, n/30.

December 3: Purchased $5,000 of merchandise from Wren Brothers with terms of 2/10, n/20, FOB shipping point. Freight charges of $200 were prepaid by Wren Brothers.

December 8: Sold merchandise of $1,600 to Kasulis Homes with terms of 2/10, n/30, FOB destination. Prepaid freight charges of $80.

December 10: Purchased $8,500 of merchandise from Willinger, Inc., with terms of 2/10, n/30, FOB shipping point.

December 11: Paid Kelso Wholesalers amount due for December 1 purchase.

December 12: $1,000 of merchandise purchased from Wren Brothers on December 3 was returned because it was defective.

December 16: Sold $1,800 of merchandise to another construction supply company, Alonso Supply, with terms of 2/10, n/30, FOB shipping point. Prepaid the freight charges of $300.

December 17: Cash sales for the day totaled $550.

December 17: Received and paid $200 freight bill from Mi-Han Trucking for merchandise purchased on December 10 from Willinger, Inc.

December 18: Received payment from Kasulis Homes for sale of merchandise on December 8.

December 20: Paid Willinger, Inc., for merchandise purchased on December 10.

December 23: Paid Wren Brothers amount due for December 3 purchase.

December 23: Alonso Supply returned $400 of the merchandise purchased on December 16 because it was defective.

December 26: Received payment from Alonso Supply for merchandise purchased on December 16.

December 31: Received payment from Gene Harrison for merchandise he purchased on December 1.

Required:
1. Prepare general journal entries for these transactions.
2. Prepare the necessary journal entries for the December 3 purchase from Wren Brothers and the December 10 purchase from Willinger, Inc., under the assumption that Chautauqua uses the net method of accounting for merchandise purchases.

43. **Profitability Ratios** (LO 2)

Kellogg Company, headquartered in Battle Creek, Michigan, is the largest producer of cereal products worldwide. The following information (in millions) was included in Kellogg's 1994 annual report

QUARTER	NET SALES	GROSS PROFIT	NET INCOME
1st, 1993	$1,518.4	$793.4	$179.2
2nd, 1993	1,541.6	785.7	142.7
3rd, 1993	1,669.2	897.3	209.3
4th, 1993	1,566.2	830.0	149.5
1st, 1994	1,611.2	879.2	183.9
2nd, 1994	1,616.9	888.2	151.5
3rd, 1994	1,741.9	985.7	216.7
4th, 1994	1,592.0	858.2	153.3

Required:
1. Compute Kellogg's gross profit percentage and profit margin percentage for each quarter in 1993 and 1994.
2. Can you discern any definite trends in these data? If so, comment on them.
3. Suppose that in early 1995 you were considering investing in this company's common stock. Identify three questions you would want to ask of the company's chief executive officer before you decide whether to invest in this company.

44. **Purchases Discounts and Gross Profit** (LO 2, 5)

Following is selected financial information for 1997 for Boyd Street Electronics.

Inventory as of January 1, 1997	$1,000,000
Sales	2,300,000
Inventory as of December 31, 1997	1,100,000
Purchases	2,100,000
Transportation In	50,000
Purchases Returns and Allowances	20,000
Sales Returns and Allowances	120,000

Required:
1. Compute cost of goods sold for 1997.
2. The owner of Boyd Street Electronics has a policy of not offering discounts to customers and not taking advantage of discounts offered by the business's suppliers. Suppose that the business could have received $45,000 of purchases discounts during 1997. Recompute the business's gross profit for 1997 given this assumption.
3. The owner of Boyd Street Electronics is unaware of the impact that not taking advantage of purchases discounts has on the business's gross profit. Write a short memo to the owner addressing this issue. Also include in your memo how offering sales discounts could potentially increase the business's profits.

42. 1. 12/1   Dr. Trans. In $300
12/8   Dr. Trans. Out $30
12/18 Dr. Sales Disc. $32
12/20 Cr. Purch. Disc. $170
12/26 Dr. Sales Disc. $28
2. 12/3   Dr. Purch. $4,900
12/12 Cr. Purch Ret. $980
12/23 Dr. Disc. Lost $80
12/20 Dr. A.P. $8,330

43. 1st Q 1993 Gross Profit %, 52.2%
1st Q 1993 Profit Margin %, 11.3%

44. 1. Net Purchases, $2,080,000
GCS, $2,030,000
2. Gross Profit without, $150,000
Gross Profit with, $195,000

45. Work Sheet for a Merchandising Company (LO 6)

Following is a trial balance for Kraettli Corporation for the year ending December 31, 1996.

KRAETTLI CORPORATION
TRIAL BALANCE
DECEMBER 31, 1996

	DEBIT	CREDIT
Cash	$ 1,200	
Accounts Receivable	9,000	
Prepaid Rent	1,800	
Inventory	43,300	
Equipment	66,300	
Accumulated Depreciation, Equipment		$ 12,000
Accounts Payable		17,600
Common Stock		11,000
Retained Earnings		63,400
Sales		133,000
Sales Returns and Allowances	1,700	
Sales Discounts	1,300	
Purchases	69,000	
Purchases Returns and Allowances		5,900
Purchases Discounts		3,400
Transportation In	1,200	
Salaries Expense	45,700	
Utilities Expense	4,700	
Income Taxes Expense	1,100	
	$246,300	$246,300

Other information:

a. Kraettli has inventory of $31,200 on hand at December 31, 1996.

b. Rent expense of $600 related to the Prepaid Rent account should be recorded as of December 31, 1996.

c. Unrecorded depreciation expense at December 31, 1996, is $1,400.

d. Kraettli owes its employees $300 of salaries that they have earned in the last few days of the year.

Required:

1. Enter Kraettli's trial balance on a work sheet and complete the work sheet.
2. Prepare a balance sheet as of December 31, 1996, and an income statement for the year ended December 31, 1996, for Kraettli.
3. Prepare and journalize all necessary adjusting and closing entries.

46. Internal Controls for a Merchandising Business (LO 8)

Identify six merchandising businesses that you have visited in the past year. Make sure that each sells a different type of merchandise. Possibilities include the following, to name just a few: grocery store, computer software store, campus bookstore, furniture store, large department store, and a pet shop.

Required:

1. List the six merchandisers you identified and briefly describe the nature of their operations.
2. Identify a major internal control risk factor for each business. These risk factors may have the potential of jeopardizing the business's assets, imposing unexpected liabilities on the business, or economically damaging the business in some other way.

45. 1. Adjustments, $2,300
        Adjusted Trial Balance,
        $248,000
    2. Retained Earnings,
        $66,600
        Assets, $95,500
        Net Income, $3,200

46. No check figures

3. Identify an internal control procedure to minimize the internal control problem posed by each risk factor you identified in Part 2.

CASES

47. Ethics in Merchandising

Karla Cartier owns a small jewelry store near Campus Corner. The principal supplier for Karla's business is a large jewelry wholesaler, Gems-R-Us, located several hundred miles away. This supplier grants its customers year-end rebates based upon the volume of purchases customers make each year. The rebate program is structured as follows:

TOTAL PURCHASES	YEAR-END REBATE
$0–$100,000	1% of total purchases
$100,001–$300,000	2% of total purchases
$300,001–$500,000	4% of total purchases
$500,000+	6% of total purchases

Karla generally purchases $170,000 to $180,000 of merchandise from Gems-R-Us each year. A friend of Karla's, who owns a jewelry store in a nearby town, has suggested that they pool their purchases in the coming year to earn a larger rebate from Gems-R-Us. The friend's store purchases approximately $240,000 to $250,000 of merchandise each year from Gems-R-Us.

The offer made by her friend sounds enticing. However, Karla is unsure and wants to ask a sales representative of Gems-R-Us if pooling of purchases is allowed under the program. Her friend discourages her. "Oh, come on, Karla. Don't be so goody-goody. That company makes millions every year and it's not going to miss a few hundred here or there."

Required:

1. Determine the approximate increase in Karla's annual rebate from Gems-R-Us assuming she accepts her friend's offer.
2. Suppose you were in Karla's position. What would you do? If you go along with your friend's plan, have you acted unethically? Why or why not?

48. Merchandising Scams and Accountants

In an earlier chapter, the financial schemes of certain key executives of Regina Company, Inc., during the late 1980s were briefly discussed. Regina, which marketed vacuum cleaners and related products, was eventually forced into bankruptcy after the financial shenanigans were discovered. Regina's executives also concocted a marketing scam to increase the company's sales. In a commercial for one of the company's vacuum cleaners, a senior company executive spread crushed cereal on a carpet and then demonstrated how the Regina vacuum cleaner was much superior to the comparable product of Hoover, Regina's principal competitor. However, it was later discovered that the demonstration model used in the commercial had an industrial-strength suction that was not available on the model sold to the public.

Required:

The accountants of a business are responsible for ensuring that the financial statements and other financial data they prepare are free of material errors. However, what responsibility, if any, does an accountant of an organization have when he or she discovers unethical conduct in some other area of the organization? Suppose you were the controller (chief accountant) of Regina in the late

1980s and discovered the fraudulent nature of the commercial just described. What would you have done at that point? Why?

49. **Discounts Lost**

A company that uses the net method of accounting for merchandise purchases maintains a Discounts Lost account. As suggested in this chapter, the balance of the Discounts Lost account can be either listed as a separate operating expense or "buried" in cost of goods sold.

Required:

Write a brief report indicating which alternative treatment of discounts lost would be most informative for external decision makers and why. Why might a company choose the financial statement presentation of this item that is least informative to external decision makers?

PROJECTS

50. **Developing Internal Controls for a Merchandising Business**

Reread the Spotlight on Ethics vignette in this chapter regarding Betty the cashier. Your objective in this group project is to develop a set of internal controls for a local merchandising business to lessen the risk of employee theft that the business faces.

Required:

1. Your group should first meet and select a small merchandising business to be the focal point of this group project. Next, each member of the group should visit the business, paying particular attention to any apparent opportunities that employees may have to steal assets of the business or otherwise take unfair advantage of the business or its owner. After visiting the business, each group member should document his or her key observations in a series of notes.
2. Meet as a group and compare notes. Then, after reviewing the material relating to internal controls that you have studied to date in this course, develop specific internal controls that the given business could implement to lessen the risk of employee theft. Be certain that these controls are cost effective.
3. Your group should prepare a written report that (a) briefly describes the local business, (b) identifies internal control weaknesses related to employee theft that were observed by group members, and (c) summarizes several internal controls the business could adopt to lessen the risk of employee theft.
4. One group member should be prepared to give a brief oral presentation in class of the group's report. In this presentation, the identity of the local business should not be disclosed.

51. **International Merchandising Companies**

Using investment advisory services such as Value Line, Standard & Poor's, or Moody's, select three foreign-based companies that sell merchandise of some type in the United States.

Required:

Write a report that contains the following information for each foreign company that you selected:

a. A brief description of the nature of the company's principal line or lines of business, the location of its corporate headquarters, and the principal countries in which it markets merchandise.

b. Identify one or more U.S. companies that compete directly with each foreign company you identified.
c. After reviewing available information regarding the foreign companies and their U.S. competitors in the investment advisory services mentioned earlier and in other business publications, such as *The Wall Street Journal*, assess how well each foreign firm is doing relative to its U.S. competitors. If possible, identify the factors accounting for each foreign company's relative financial performance in this latter respect.

52. Analyzing Profitability

Comparisons of profitability between companies in the same industry can help investors determine which companies' common stocks are better investments. In this project, you compare the relative profitability of companies operating in several different merchandising lines of business.

Required:

1. Identify two public companies in three of the following general merchandising lines of business: supermarkets, hardware supply, convenience stores, furniture retailers, bookstores, women's apparel, and men's apparel.
2. For each company, obtain the following data for the three most recent years for which data are available: net income, earnings per share, gross profit, gross profit percentage, and profit margin percentage.
3. Given the data you collected and your "professional" insight, identify which company in each matched pair has been most profitable in recent years. Defend your choice in each case.

III

ACCOUNTING FOR ASSETS

Chapters 1 through 6 acquainted you with fundamental accounting concepts and with the basic accounting procedures that dictate how business transactions and events are recorded. Now you are prepared to consider in more depth accounting issues related to specific financial statement items. The series of chapters in Part III focus on accounting for assets. Chapter 7 examines accounting for cash and receivables, Chapter 8 discusses accounting issues related to inventory, while Chapter 9 illustrates accounting for long-term assets.

The key theme of this text is that an organization's accounting function should be responsive to the information needs of internal and external decision makers. Consequently, as accounting issues are considered in this sequence of chapters, the focus is on decision makers' information needs concerning specific types of assets. Among issues raised in Chapters 7 through 9 are the following. What financial disclosures do investors and creditors demand regarding cash and receivables? How can inventory accounting methods influence the reported profits of a business? What valuation methods for long-term assets provide bankers with the most insight on their clients' long-range viability?

The treatment of each major asset category in Chapters 7 through 9 begins with an overview of the relevant assets including an introduction to key terms. Then information needs of decision makers regarding that category of assets are identified. The third element of coverage is procedural accounting issues. Next, financial ratios are presented that can be used by decision makers to interpret accounting data related to the assets being discussed. Finally, important internal control procedures for those assets are identified and discussed.

CASH AND RECEIVABLES

No man's credit is as good as his money.
Ed Howe

LEARNING OBJECTIVES

After studying this chapter, you should be able to do the following:

1. Define the key information needs of decision makers regarding cash and accounts receivable

2. Account for the major types of transactions affecting cash and accounts receivable

3. Compute and interpret the quick ratio

4. Discuss key internal control issues related to cash and accounts receivable

5. Prepare a bank reconciliation

6. Use the aging method to estimate uncollectible accounts expense

7. Compute and interpret the accounts receivable turnover ratio and the age of receivables

8. Define the key characteristics of notes receivable

9. Account for the major types of transactions involving notes receivable

Giving Credit to Whom Credit Is Due

The opening vignette of Chapter 2 profiled Jim Penney, the founder of the large retail merchandising firm, J. C. Penney Company. As suggested in that vignette, Penney was a hard-nosed businessman who believed that the secret to success in business was focusing on a few fundamental principles and implementing those principles more effectively than competitors. Keeping overhead as low as possible, offering merchandise at reasonable prices, and a cash-and-carry (no credit) sales policy were the principles around which Penney built his company. The frugal—some would say tight-fisted—Penney was particularly adamant about the cash-and-carry sales policy. What else would you expect from a man whose middle name was literally Cash? Long after most retailers had begun extending credit to their customers, Penney refused to even consider selling merchandise on anything but a cash basis.

By the late 1950s, J. C. Penney's strict cash-basis sales policy was hurting the firm. Credit sales by competing retailers, Sears and Montgomery Ward in particular, were cutting into J. C. Penney's market share. Company executives realized that they had to break with tradition and begin offering their customers credit or risk losing even more ground to their competitors. By 1962, all J. C. Penney's stores were offering credit to their customers. Five years later, J. C. Penney had 12 million credit accounts and more than one-third of the company's annual sales were made on credit.

The decision to begin extending credit to customers significantly affects a business's subsequent operations. No longer do daily sales figures translate into equivalent bank deposits. Immediately, a credit department must be established. This new department must decide which customers will be extended credit, whether discounts for early payment will be offered, and the length of the discount period. Likewise, management must become concerned with collection activities. A collections department may be necessary to track down slow-paying customers. Alternatively, past-due accounts may be turned over to a collection agency, which will take a hefty cut of the amounts it collects as the fee for its services.

The decision to extend credit to customers also imposes new responsibilities on an organization's accountants. Among these responsibilities are providing management with the data needed to monitor the collectibility of receivables. Revised cash forecasting techniques may be necessary to furnish management with reliable cash-flow projections. An extensive set of control procedures must be developed and implemented for the credit-granting function. Finally, the entity's accounting records and procedures may need to be redesigned to accommodate several types of new transactions.

No doubt, the grand old gentleman of merchandising would be more than a little annoyed with the extensive use of credit by modern merchandising companies. Imagine Jim Penney's chagrin if he picked up a copy of his namesake firm's financial statements in the early 1990s and saw outstanding receivables from customers of more than $3.5 billion! Then again, imagine the frustration that plastic-toting customers would experience if merchandisers decided to return to the olden days and invoke the sales policy that worked so well for so many decades for James Cash Penney.

This chapter focuses on accounting issues related to cash, accounts receivable, and notes receivable. These three types of assets are closely related. For example, a business's cash and accounts receivable balances are often negatively correlated. When economic conditions deteriorate, accounts receivable balances tend to increase as customers delay paying their debts. Naturally, such an increase in receivables, everything else held constant, translates into reduced cash receipts and a smaller cash balance for a business. When an account receivable becomes overdue, a company may require the customer to sign a promissory note equal to the balance of the past-due receivable. Such promissory notes can then be "discounted" or converted into cash at a bank or other financial institution to relieve the company's cash-flow problems.

CASH

This first section of Chapter 7 focuses on accounting issues related to cash. As indicated earlier, the discussion of each major financial statement item in this chapter and the following several chapters begins with a brief overview of that item. Next, key information needs of decision makers regarding the given item are identified, followed by a discussion of procedural accounting matters. The treatment of each financial statement item concludes with a review of relevant financial ratios and internal control procedures.

Cash, Cash Equivalents, and Cash Flows

Most businesses list cash as the first line item on their balance sheet. The most common caption for cash in corporate balance sheets is "cash and cash equivalents." The 1994 edition of *Accounting Trends & Techniques* reported that three-fourths of all public companies use that balance sheet caption or its first cousin, "cash and equivalents." **Cash equivalents** are funds that companies have invested in short-term securities such as certificates of deposit (CDs), money market funds, and U.S. treasury bills. To qualify as cash equivalents, these investments must have ninety days or less to maturity when purchased.

Why has cash historically been the first line item on the balance sheet? Probably because cash has long been considered one of the most important assets of business entities. An old business axiom goes something like this: "Profit is an estimate, but cash is a fact." Although a company is posting large profits, it may find itself on shaky ground if those profits do not translate into positive cash flows. Recall from Chapter 2, specifically Exhibit 2.10, that a company's net income and net cash flow from its normal, profit-oriented activities are not necessarily closely correlated. For example, assume that the Suarez Corporation is realizing impressive increases in sales each accounting period. This growth in sales volume is causing the company's cash outflows to increase due to larger payments to suppliers and higher operating expenses. Unfortunately, many of the Suarez Corporation's customers are slow-paying. As a result, the increase in the company's cash outflows is not being offset, at least immediately, by an increase in cash inflows from customers. If this trend continues, the company may be forced to borrow funds so that it will not fall behind on payments to its suppliers and other creditors.

A recent study found that cash accounts for 4.2 percent of all corporate assets.[1] However, the cash balances of companies vary significantly from industry to industry and company to company. In April 1995, Sears, the large merchandiser, and Xylogics, a company discussed briefly in Chapter 2, issued their 1994 annual reports. Sears reported total cash of $1.4 billion, representing 1.5 percent of the company's total assets. On the other hand, Xylogics's cash balance of nearly $11 million accounted for 31 percent of its total assets.

cash equivalents

Teaching Note
Students frequently think of accounting as an accurate and precise process. Point out that a business's reported profit for a given accounting period is, in reality, an estimate.

Real World
Companies that maintain large cash balances can become targets of outside takeover attempts. Another company may actually use a takeover candidate's large amount of cash to help finance the takeover.

---

1. Copyright 1995 by the Treasury Management Association, all rights reserved. Used with permission of the Treasury Management Association. Reprinted from Treasury Management Association's *Journal of Cash Management*.

■ **EXHIBIT 7.1**

Length of Operating Cycle for Selected Industries

SOURCE: L. A. Soenen, "Cash Conversion Cycle and Corporate Profitability," *Journal of Cash Management*, July/August 1993, 55.

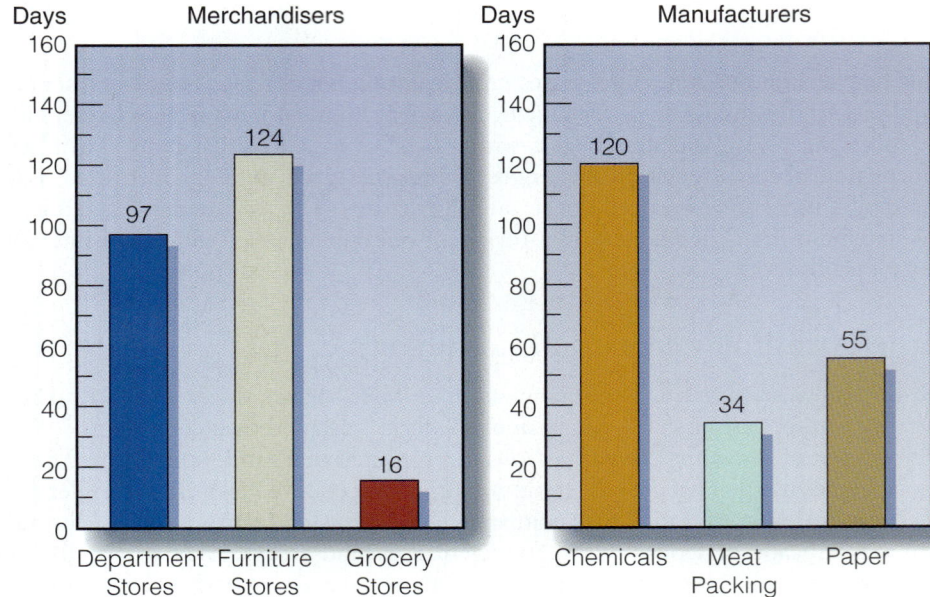

One factor that significantly influences the cash needs of a company is the length of its operating cycle. Exhibit 7.1 reports the average length of the operating cycle in six industries. (Recall that an operating cycle is the period of time elapsing between the use of cash in a business's normal operating activities and the collection of cash from customers.) As you would expect, grocery stores have short operating cycles since their inventory turns over quickly and since most of their sales are on a cash basis. On the other hand, furniture stores, although they are merchandising operations like grocery stores, have a much longer operating cycle. Apparently, convincing Joan and John Q. Public to buy a La-Z-Boy recliner requires more time than selling the couple a jar of Skippy peanut butter or a dozen farm fresh eggs.

Cash: Information Needs of Decision Makers

■ **LEARNING OBJECTIVE 1**

Define the key information needs of decision makers regarding cash and accounts receivable

As pointed out repeatedly in this text, the key role of accounting and accountants is to provide information needed by decision makers. By continually focusing on the information needs of decision makers, accountants are better prepared to select the most appropriate accounting procedures for specific financial statement items. In this section, key information needs of decision makers regarding cash and cash equivalents are identified.

CASH BALANCES   Decision makers should be informed of a business's total cash and cash equivalents as of each balance sheet date. This information is necessary to determine whether a business has sufficient cash resources to meet its short-term operating needs. For instance, potential investors may be concerned whether a company has sufficient cash to pay off a large note payable maturing shortly after its fiscal year-end. Just as important is information regarding any restrictions that a company has on the use of its cash funds. Many loan agreements require companies to deposit with the lending institution a certain portion of the proceeds of a loan. Since such an amount, known as a **compensating balance,** is not freely available for use, companies should disclose this fact in their financial statements. For example, Oneida Ltd., the world's largest manufacturer of stainless steel flatware, disclosed in its 1994 annual report a compensating balance restriction on the use of its cash. This restriction required Oneida to maintain approximately 5 percent of certain borrowed funds on deposit with the lending institution.

CASH-FLOW INFORMATION   Decision makers also need and demand information regarding the cash flows of business entities. Of prime interest to financial statement users is how a company both generated and expended cash during a given period. For example, consider a company that realized a significant increase in its cash resources during a recent year. If this increase resulted from profitable operations, this is a positive signal of the company's financial health. However, if the increase in cash resulted from the sale of productive assets, the implications for the company are quite different. If the company intends to remain an operating entity, it cannot continue to sell off its productive assets to raise cash.

Statement of Financial Accounting Standards No. 95, "Statement of Cash Flows," requires business entities to classify cash flows into three categories for financial statement purposes. These three categories are cash flows from operating activities, investing activities, and financing activities. Operating activities involve the normal, profit-oriented activities of a company such as the collection of cash from customers and cash payments to suppliers. Investing activities involve such transactions as the acquisition and disposal of property, plant and equipment assets. An example of a financing activity is the sale of common stock. Financial statement users tend to focus on cash flows related to operating activities. Why? Because over the long run, a company's financial success and viability are dependent on its day-to-day, profit-oriented activities.

FUTURE CASH FLOWS   No doubt, what decision makers really want is information about future cash flows. Forecasts of cash flows, revenues, and earnings are rarely included in annual reports. Business executives are reluctant to include financial forecasts in their companies' annual reports because of the risk of being sued if their projections are not achieved. For example, Monsanto Chemical Corporation was sued recently when it released sales and profit projections and then saw its actual operating results fall short of the projected amounts. Thankfully for Monsanto, the suit against the company was unsuccessful. The judge hearing the case ruled that Monsanto was not liable because its forecasts had been based upon reasonable assumptions.

In 1979, the Securities and Exchange Commission (SEC) attempted to encourage the release of more financial forecasts by adopting a "safe harbor" rule. Under this rule, the SEC pledges to help protect a company from subsequent lawsuits if a financial forecast prepared by the firm in good faith proves to be a poor predictor of future operating results.[2]

---

2. "Safe-Harbor Rule for Projections," *SEC Release No. 5993* (Washington, D.C.: SEC, 1979).

Accounting for Cash

■ **LEARNING OBJECTIVE 2**
Account for the major types of transactions affecting cash and accounts receivable

You may be surprised and happy to learn that there are not many "sticky" procedural accounting issues to discuss for cash. Most businesses use cash receipts and cash disbursements journals to process the bulk of their cash transactions. As indicated in Chapter 6, the accounting data from these special journals are periodically posted to the general ledger and, if necessary, to a subsidiary ledger as well. A few situations require nonroutine journal entries to the general ledger Cash account. One of these situations involves the recording of daily cash receipts for a retail business, while another concerns accounting for a petty cash fund.

Discussion Question
A sign posted beside the checkout stand of a convenience store reads, "If you do not receive a receipt, your purchase is free." Why does the store make this offer?
Answer: One reason is to encourage the cashier to ring up each sale. If a sale is not rung up, there is no record of that sale and the cash can be pocketed by the cashier.

CASH OVER & SHORT   Assume that a retail store's cash register tape indicates $2,402.17 of cash sales for a given day of business. However, only $2,389.02 is found when the cash till is counted. What happens in this case? Naturally, this situation raises internal control issues, particularly if such shortages are common, significant in size, or correlated with the presence of certain employees. Putting the internal control issues aside, the following entry, in simplified general journal format, would be appropriate to record the cash sales and related cash shortage.

Mar. 17	Cash	2,389.02	
	Cash Over & Short	13.15	
	Sales		2,402.17
	To record daily cash sales		

If the cash count had exceeded the total sales reflected by the cash register tape, the difference would have been credited to Cash Over & Short. At the end of each accounting period, the balance of Cash Over & Short is treated as a miscellaneous revenue or expense for financial statement purposes. Since this account typically has a debit balance, it is most often classified as an expense account.

petty cash fund

ACCOUNTING FOR A PETTY CASH FUND   Most businesses maintain a **petty cash fund** from which minor expenses and other miscellaneous amounts are paid. These disbursements include payments of delivery fees, postage costs, and cash purchases of minor office supplies. When a petty cash fund is established, an entry similar to the following one is made.

May 12	Petty Cash Fund	100	
	Cash		100
	To establish a petty cash fund for the headquarters office		

Real World
Petty cash funds maintained by most companies are small and immaterial. The funds exist out of practical necessity. For example, when the postal carrier delivers mail with postage due, it is necessary to have available cash to pay the postal charges. In the absence of a petty cash fund, it would be necessary to issue a check, a process that could take several hours.

For each disbursement made from a petty cash fund, the individual responsible for the physical security of the fund, the petty cash custodian, completes a petty cash voucher. Shown in Exhibit 7.2 is a common format for a petty cash voucher. Among the data items recorded on a petty cash voucher are the date and amount of the disbursement, the party to whom the disbursement was made, the goods or services acquired, and the account to which the disbursement amount will eventually be debited.

Periodically, a petty cash fund must be replenished. For example, suppose that the fund just referred to has only $15 remaining on June 17. At this point, the petty cash

■ **EXHIBIT 7.2**
Common Format for Petty Cash Voucher

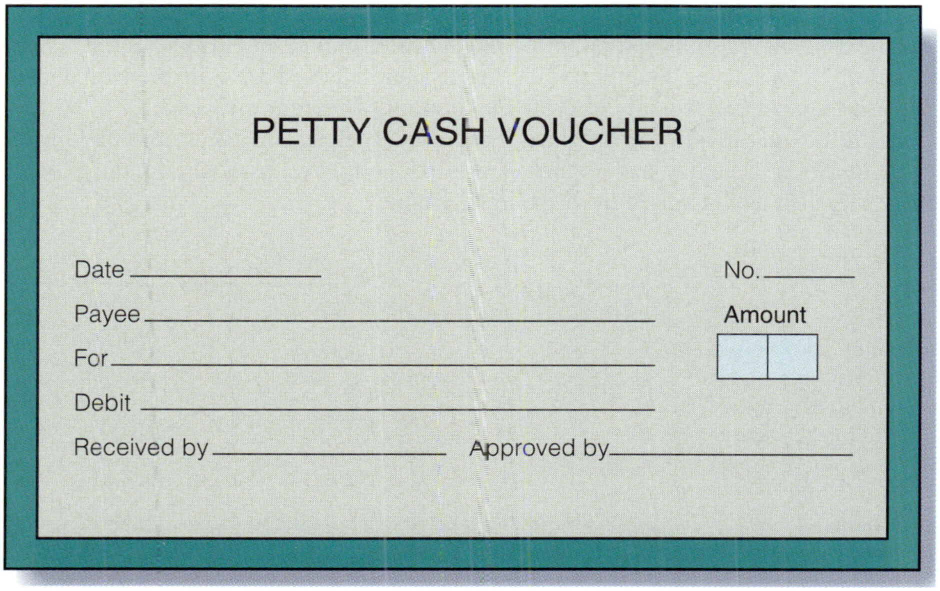

PETTY CASH VOUCHER

Date _____   No. _____

Payee _____   **Amount**

For _____

Debit _____

Received by _____   Approved by _____

custodian might prepare a request for replenishment of the fund. In this request, the custodian would list the expenditures that account for the $85 of disbursements paid from the fund since it was established. Assume that the $85 of disbursements involved the following items: delivery expenses—$32, postage costs—$41, and purchases of supplies—$12. Following approval of the petty cash custodian's request, an $85 check would be written against a company bank account, cashed, and the proceeds turned over to the petty cash custodian. The following entry would be made to record the replenishment of the petty cash fund.

Teaching Note
Point out that at any point in time the amount of cash in a petty cash fund plus the dollar amount of completed petty cash vouchers must equal the balance of the Petty Cash Fund account.

Jun. 17	Delivery Expense	32	
	Postage Expense	41	
	Supplies Expense	12	
	Cash		85
	To reimburse petty cash fund for expenses paid		

Notice that the previous entry records the miscellaneous expenditures made from the petty cash fund in the appropriate expense accounts. Also notice that this entry credits Cash instead of the account Petty Cash Fund. Entries are made to the Petty Cash Fund account only when the fund is established, increased, decreased, or eliminated.

Analyzing Cash

Recall that in Chapter 6 financial ratios were defined as measures that express the relationship or interrelationships between two or more financial statement items. A key financial ratio relating to cash is the quick ratio, which is used to assess a business's

■ **LEARNING OBJECTIVE 3**
Compute and interpret the quick ratio

liquidity

quick ratio

liquidity. Liquidity refers to a business's ability to finance its day-to-day operations and to pay its liabilities as they mature. Liquidity is heavily influenced by the amount of cash a business has on hand and the amount of cash it can raise in a short period of time, such as by selling short-term investments. The **quick ratio,** sometimes referred to as the acid-test ratio, is computed by dividing the sum of an entity's "quick" assets by the sum of its current liabilities. Quick assets generally include cash and cash equivalents, short-term investments, and the net amount of current receivables.

Piccadilly Cafeterias, Inc., operates a chain of cafeterias in the southern United States. In 1993, Piccadilly had a quick ratio of .5, compared with a quick ratio of .39 one year earlier, as illustrated in the following table.

| | AT FISCAL YEAR-END* | |
	1993	1992
Cash and Cash Equivalents	$14,094	$7,839
Short-Term Investments	—	1,599
Accounts Receivable (Net)	837	1,065
Total Quick Assets	$14,931	$10,503
Current Liabilities	$29,893	$27,214
Quick Ratio	.50	.39

*Amounts are presented in thousands

Teaching Note
The trend of a company's quick ratio over a period of time reveals if the ratio is improving or deteriorating. A deteriorating quick ratio may signal impending liquidity problems for a company.

These data suggest that Piccadilly's liquidity improved from the end of 1992 to the end of 1993. Nevertheless, the company's .5 quick ratio at the end of 1993 was low compared with one common rule of thumb. As a general rule, financial analysts suggest that businesses should attempt to maintain a quick ratio of at least 1.0.[3]

If an investor was concerned by the level of Piccadilly's quick ratios in the early 1990s, he or she could have gone one step further and compared those ratios to the norm for the restaurant industry. The significant differences in the nature of business operations cause the norms for financial ratios to vary significantly from industry to industry. Although a 1.0 quick ratio may be a desirable level for most industries, a lower quick ratio may be normal or acceptable for a specific industry.

Robert Morris Associates (RMA), a financial services firm, annually publishes key financial ratios for a large number of industries. Within each industry, RMA reports these financial ratios for companies segregated by total assets and by total sales. In 1993, RMA reported that the median quick ratio for restaurant firms the size of Piccadilly ($100–$250 million in assets) was .4.[4] Historically, firms in this industry have operated with an abnormally low quick ratio compared with firms in other industries. One reason is that most of a restaurant's daily sales are on a cash basis. So, there is no need to wait weeks or months to collect customer receivables—or face the risk of not collecting those receivables.

In summary, although Piccadilly's quick ratio appeared to be low in 1993 and 1992 compared with the quick ratio of most companies, that ratio compared favorably with the industry norm. As a result, a financial statement user would most likely have concluded that Piccadilly did not have a liquidity problem in the early 1990s.

---

3. J. E. Kristy, "Conquering Financial Ratios: The Good, the Bad, and the Who Cares?" *Business Credit*, February 1994, 14–19.

4. *RMA Annual Statement Studies, 1993* (Philadelphia: RMA, 1993).

Running a Business Without Cash

Imagine operating a billion-dollar business without cash. Sound impossible? In fact, many large companies practice what is known as "zero cash management." These companies make every effort to end each business day flat broke—in terms of cash, that is. One such firm is Northeast Utilities, the largest electric utility in the northeastern United States.[5]

To practice zero cash management, companies must make extensive use of electronic funds transfers on a daily basis to move cash out of bank accounts and into higher income-producing investments. A key to successful zero cash management is reliable cash forecasting techniques. Firms in the highly regulated electric utility industry, such as Northeast Utilities, have very predictable cash inflows and outflows. Companies that have highly variable cash flows, which is true of most merchandisers, have more difficulty practicing zero cash management.

The financial rewards associated with zero cash management can be impressive. Executives of Northeast Utilities estimate that their company adds millions of dollars each year to net income because of this innovative cash management strategy.

Teaching Note
Point out that idle cash is a nonearning asset.

Key Internal Control Procedures for Cash

A recent study by KPMG Peat Marwick, a large accounting firm, found that the two most common frauds perpetrated on businesses are the theft of cash and check forgery.[6] It should come as no surprise, then, that providing effective internal control over cash and related assets is a top priority of most businesses. In this section, three general types of internal control procedures for cash are considered. These procedures include physical security measures, cash processing controls, and periodic independent checks and reconciliations of cash balances.

PHYSICAL SECURITY MEASURES   Although businesses make every effort to hire honest individuals to work in cash-handling functions, they should also obtain fidelity bonds for these employees. Fidelity bonds are essentially insurance policies companies purchase to protect themselves from theft and other fraudulent activities by employees. Limiting the number of individuals who have access to cash and near-cash items is probably the most important physical security measure for these assets. A seemingly contradictory internal control is the policy that banks have regarding access to a vault or other secured area where large quantities of cash and securities are stored. Typically, a minimum of two people, each of whom has proper authorization and security clearance, must enter such areas. This policy minimizes the ability of one dishonest employee to "rip off" the bank.

■ LEARNING OBJECTIVE 4
Discuss key internal control issues related to cash and accounts receivable

Discussion Question
Many students work at jobs in which they handle cash. Ask students what cash controls their employers use.

---

5. Copyright 1995 by the Treasury Management Association, all rights reserved. Used with permission of the Treasury Management Association. Reprinted from Treasury Management Association's *Journal of Cash Management*.

6. KPMG Peat Marwick, *Fraud Survey Results, 1993* (New York: KPMG Peat Marwick, 1993).

CASH PROCESSING CONTROLS   The use of standardized accounting procedures for cash transactions minimizes the likelihood that errors will occur in the processing of these transactions. Take the case of cash receipts. Shown in Exhibit 7.3 is a common approach to assigning responsibilities for processing customer remittances (checks) received in the mail.

The multiple copies of key accounting documents in the tasks outlined in Exhibit 7.3 increase the likelihood that errors made in processing cash receipts will be detected. Just as important, the division of responsibilities and system of checks allow a business to pinpoint when such errors occur and the party who most likely made them.

PERIODIC INDEPENDENT CHECKS AND RECONCILIATIONS OF CASH BALANCES Despite rigorous and comprehensive physical security and cash processing controls, there is always some risk that a business's cash will be stolen. Consequently, businesses should periodically count their cash funds and reconcile the resulting totals to the amounts reflected by their accounting records. For example, companies that maintain a petty cash fund typically require internal auditors to count that fund at irregular intervals. This procedure is performed in the presence of the petty cash custodian—to discourage any sticky-fingered internal auditors. The sum of the cash in the fund and the total dollar amount of expenditures documented on completed petty cash vouchers should equal the fund's permanent balance.

Most cash resources of a business are maintained on deposit with banks and other financial institutions. Banks provide businesses with monthly statements that document the beginning and end-of-the-month balances of their bank accounts and the transactions affecting those accounts during the month. Companies should not rely exclusively on the honesty and competence of their bank's personnel. Each month, a

Banks establish extensive internal control procedures to protect their cash resources. Nevertheless, two or more dishonest bank employees can often collaborate to override a bank's control procedures.

Discussion Question
A mail clerk pockets a cash receipt from a customer. How could this theft be discovered? Answer: It could be discovered if the customer complains about not receiving credit for a payment on his or her account. Many companies try to reduce this potential problem by requesting that customers pay by check or money order.

■ **EXHIBIT 7.3**

Assignment of Key Accounting and Control Responsibilities for Processing Cash Receipts

Responsibility 1	On a daily basis, a mail clerk opens customer remittances and prepares a list of the checks for deposit. Three copies of this list are made, one of which is retained by the mail clerk. One copy of the list, along with the checks, is sent to the cashier, while the remaining copy is forwarded to the accounting department.
Responsibility 2	The cashier prepares a daily deposit slip listing the checks received from customers, makes the deposit, and then sends a duplicate copy of the deposit ticket to the accounting department.
Responsibility 3	An accounting clerk determines that the listing of receipts prepared by the mail clerk and the receipts reflected by the duplicate copy of the deposit ticket agree. Then the clerk makes the appropriate entries to record the receipts.

company's accounting staff should prepare a **bank reconciliation.** A bank reconciliation is an accounting document that reconciles the cash balance reported on a bank statement to the corresponding cash balance reflected in a company's accounting records.

Shown in Exhibit 7.4 is a bank statement for Hunt Brothers, Inc., for the month ended February 29, 1996. Although the formats of bank statements vary, the key elements or components of bank statements do not. The account summary in the Hunt Brothers bank statement lists the beginning and ending balances of the company's bank account for February 1996 and the total additions and deductions to the account during that month. Also included in this bank statement is a daily listing of the checks and other deductions made to the company's bank account, a similar listing for deposits and other additions to the account, and the daily account balances. Notice

bank reconciliation

Real World
Although "Cash" typically appears as one line item on a balance sheet, most companies have several bank accounts and maintain separate general ledger accounts for each bank account. Separate general ledger accounts facilitate the monthly reconciliation process.

Discussion Question
Ask students to compare the monthly bank statements they receive from their banks with the Hunt Brother's bank statement. Students' statements should be very similar.

■ **EXHIBIT 7.4**
Bank Statement for Hunt Brothers, Inc., February 1996

LINCOLN NATIONAL BANK
OF WALLVILLE

MEMBER FDIC
Wallville, OK 73000-3333

Hunt Brothers, Inc.   Statement of Account
2122 Turner Avenue   Account #441-230
Wallville, OK 73052-2122   From 2/1/96 To 2/29/96

```
Account Summary:

    Opening Balance                        5,254.19

    Plus Deposits and Other Credits       13,518.55

    Minus Checks and Other Debits         14,403.93

    Ending Balance                         4,368.81
```

CHECKS & OTHER DEBITS			DEPOSITS & OTHER CREDITS	DATE	DAILY BALANCE
1,106.77	212.59		2,429.66	02-01	6,364.49
345.78				02-03	6,018.71
55.43				02-06	5,963.28
101.44	352.21	49.03	3,021.18	02-08	8,481.78
22.13				02-09	8,459.65
2,986.42	707.53			02-10	4,765.70
112.09			2,783.91	02-15	7,437.52
984.25	101.78			02-16	6,351.49
565.02				02-17	5,786.47
3,476.82			2,141.17	02-22	4,450.82
202.88				02-23	4,247.94
1,190.31				02-24	3,057.63
789.52NSF	22.34		14.32INT	02-26	2,260.09
1,002.00	17.59SVC		3,128.31CM	02-29	4,368.81

```
    CM—Credit Memo              NSF—Not Sufficient Funds
    DM—Debit Memo               CD—Overdraft
    INT—Interest Credited       SVC—Service Charge
```

that a legend at the bottom of the bank statement provides brief descriptions for unusual or infrequent items appearing on the bank statement.

SOURCES OF DIFFERENCES BETWEEN BANK STATEMENT AND GENERAL LEDGER CASH BALANCES   The cash balance reported on a company's bank statement nearly always differs from the corresponding cash balance in the company's general ledger. One source of such differences is the time required for cash transactions to be processed by the banking system. Checks may take from a few days to more than one week to be processed. During the time that a check is "floating" through the banking system, it is referred to as an outstanding check. **Outstanding checks** have been deducted from a company's cash balance in its general ledger but were not subtracted from the company's cash balance in its most recent bank statement. Recognize that outstanding checks create only temporary differences between a general ledger cash balance and the corresponding bank statement balance. When these checks clear the bank, these differences are eliminated.

outstanding checks

deposits in transit

Deposits in transit also result in temporary differences between a general ledger cash balance and the corresponding bank statement balance. These amounts are deposits made near the end of an accounting period that have been added to the general ledger cash balance but were not included in the entity's most recent bank statement balance. Among other sources of differences between a general ledger cash balance and a bank statement balance are the following:

Bank service charges deducted from the bank statement balance but not from the general ledger balance.

Amounts collected for a company by its bank which have been added to the bank statement balance but which have not yet been added to the general ledger balance. (For example, banks sometimes collect notes receivable for their customers.) Errors made in either a company's accounting records or its bank's accounting records.

STANDARD FORMAT FOR A BANK RECONCILIATION   Shown in Exhibit 7.5 is a format commonly used when reconciling a general ledger cash balance to a bank statement balance. Notice that when using this format, the objective is to arrive at the same adjusted balance in each column of the bank reconciliation. If a reconciliation does not result in the same adjusted balance at the bottom of each column, it is "back to the drawing board" to figure out why. As shown in Exhibit 7.5, there are four types of reconciling items in a bank reconciliation. These items include additions and deductions to the bank statement balance to arrive at the adjusted balance, and additions and deductions to the general ledger balance to arrive at the adjusted balance. As a point of information, errors in a company's accounting records can appear as either additions or deductions to the general ledger balance in the bank reconciliation format shown in Exhibit 7.5. Similarly, errors in the accounting records of a company's bank can appear as either additions or deductions to the bank statement balance in a bank reconciliation.

STEPS IN PREPARING A BANK RECONCILIATION   The following list details the steps that are normally followed in preparing a monthly bank reconciliation. For control purposes, a bank reconciliation should be prepared by an individual who does not have access to cash or blank checks. Additionally, this individual

■ **EXHIBIT 7.5**

Standard Bank Reconciliation Format

Balance per bank statement	$XX	Balance per general ledger
Add: Deposits in transit and other items included in the general ledger balance but not yet included in the bank statement balance	XX	Add: Amounts included in the bank statement balance, such as notes receivable collections, that have not been added to the general ledger balance
Less: Outstanding checks and other reductions in the general ledger balance that have not yet been deducted from the bank statement balance	XX	Less: Items deducted from the bank statement balance, such as service charges, that have not yet been deducted from the general ledger balance
Adjusted balance	$XX	Adjusted balance

should not maintain cash accounting records or have authorization responsibilities for cash transactions.

■ **LEARNING OBJECTIVE 5**
Prepare a bank reconciliation

1. Compare deposits listed on the bank statement with the deposits included in the accounting records for the given month. Add any deposits in transit to the bank statement balance. Also review the deposits in transit included in the previous month's bank reconciliation to determine that those deposits appear in the most recent bank statement. If they do not, these are additional deposits in transit. The bank should be contacted immediately to determine why these deposits have not been processed.

2. List returned checks included in the bank statement in numerical order. Compare this listing with the checks recorded in the accounting records for the given month and with the list of outstanding checks included in the previous month's bank reconciliation. Identify outstanding checks and deduct them from the bank statement balance.

3. Review the bank statement and identify any additions to the bank statement balance that have not yet been added to the general ledger balance, such as the proceeds of a note receivable collected by the bank. Add these amounts to the general ledger balance.

4. Review the bank statement and identify any deductions to the bank statement balance, such as bank service charges, that have not yet been subtracted from the general ledger balance. Subtract these amounts from the general ledger balance.

5. While preparing the bank reconciliation, review the accounting records and the bank statement for any errors affecting either the general ledger balance or the bank statement balance. Make the appropriate additions to, or deductions from, the general ledger balance or the bank statement balance on the bank reconciliation.

6. Make any necessary journal entries for items included in the bank statement balance that have not been added to, or subtracted from, the general ledger balance.

Focus on Ethics
Bill's bank statement shows that his bank charged his account only $10 for a $100 check that he had written. Bill decides not to notify the bank of the error. Discuss the ethics of Bill's decision.

ILLUSTRATION OF A BANK RECONCILIATION   To illustrate the preparation of a bank reconciliation, return to the bank account maintained by Hunt Brothers, Inc., at the Lincoln National Bank of Wallville, Oklahoma. (In the interest of full disclosure, there is no Lincoln National Bank in the great metropolis of Wallville, Oklahoma, which had a population of fifty-two at last count.) The bank statement for the Hunt Brothers account for the month ended February 29, 1996, reports a cash balance of $4,368.81, as shown in Exhibit 7.4. However, the general ledger cash balance was $1,213.14 on February 29, 1996. So, the objective here is to reconcile these two amounts. Assume that the following information was collected by a Hunt Brother's employee as that individual completed the first five steps of the six-step process for completing a bank reconciliation.

Outstanding checks as of February 29:

No. 667	$423.12	
No. 689	891.02	
No. 690	112.29	$1,426.43

Deposit made February 29 but not reflected in bank statement	606.28
Interest revenue earned in February but not recorded in accounting records as of February 29	14.32
Note collected by bank on February 29 but not recorded in accounting records as of that date	3,128.31
NSF (not sufficient funds) check charged against bank balance on February 26 but not recorded in accounting records as of February 29	789.52
Service charge for February, charged against bank balance on February 29 but not recorded in accounting records as of that date	17.59

Exhibit 7.6 contains the completed bank reconciliation for the Hunt Brothers bank account. Notice that the reconciliation was successful. After making the necessary adjustments to the bank statement balance and the general ledger balance, the two columns of the bank reconciliation "footed" to the same adjusted balance. One item included in the bank reconciliation may need some clarification. The NSF check is a "rubber" check that Hunt Brothers received from one of its customers. That is, the check was deposited by Hunt Brothers and added to the company's account balance at Lincoln National Bank. However, a few days later, the amount of this check was subtracted from that account. Why? Because Lincoln National Bank was informed by the customer's bank that the individual did not have $789.52 in his or her account at that bank. So, the customer's bank refused to transfer $789.52 to Lincoln National Bank. Realize that Hunt Brothers had previously recorded this check by debiting Cash and crediting Accounts Receivable. The company was not aware that the check had "bounced" until it received the February 1996 bank statement. As a result, on February 29, 1996, the $789.52 was included in the general ledger cash balance.

After completing a bank reconciliation, it is usually necessary to prepare several journal entries to adjust the general ledger cash balance. For the bank reconciliation shown in Exhibit 7.6, the four entries that follow were needed. Entries were not required for the reconciling items involving outstanding checks and deposits in transit included in the Hunt Brothers bank reconciliation. When these items were processed by the bank the following month, the appropriate additions or deductions were made to the Hunt Brothers bank account. The reconciling items for which journal entries must be prepared are those items necessary to reconcile the general ledger balance to the adjusted balance. These are items that had not been entered in the accounting records at the point the bank reconciliation was prepared. Notice that an

■ **EXHIBIT 7.6**
Bank Reconciliation for Hunt Brothers, Inc., February 29, 1996

HUNT BROTHERS, INC.
BANK RECONCILIATION
FEBRUARY 29, 1996

Balance per bank, 2/29	$4,368.81	Balance per general ledger, 2/29	$1,213.14
Add: Deposit in transit, 2/29	606.28	Add: Note receivable collected on 2/29	3,128.31
		Interest revenue for February	14.32
Less: Outstanding checks			
		Less: NSF check	(789.52)
No. 667 $423.12		Service charge for February	(17.59)
No. 689 891.02			
No. 690 112.29	(1,426.43)		
Adjusted balance, 2/29	$3,548.66	Adjusted balance, 2/29	$3,548.66

NSF check from a customer is recorded by debiting Accounts Receivable and crediting Cash. This entry is necessary to reestablish the customer's receivable balance on a company's books—obviously, an NSF check does not satisfy a customer's debt to a company. The debit amount of such an entry is posted to the general ledger controlling account, Accounts Receivable, and to the customer's account in the accounts receivable subsidiary ledger.

Feb. 29	Cash	3,128.31	
	Notes Receivable		3,128.31
	To record the collection by Lincoln National of a note receivable from Ed Jones		
Feb. 29	Cash	14.32	
	Interest Revenue		14.32
	To record interest earned in February on bank account at Lincoln National		
Feb. 29	Accounts Receivable	789.52	
	Cash		789.52
	To record NSF check (from Lyn Wiggins) charged back to bank account at Lincoln National on 2/26		
Feb. 29	Miscellaneous Expense	17.59	
	Cash		17.59
	To record service charge for February on bank account at Lincoln National		

Teaching Note
Point out that the objective of these journal entries is to adjust the Cash account to the February 29 adjusted balance of $3,548.66. Only the adjustments on the right-hand side of the bank reconciliation in Exhibit 7.6 are necessary to adjust the Cash account to this amount.

ACCOUNTS RECEIVABLE

This section addresses accounting issues related to accounts receivable. Notes receivable are closely related to accounts receivable but are discussed later in a separate section of this chapter.

Credit Makes the (Business) World Go Around

When you graduate from college, expect your mailbox to be deluged with credit applications. VISA, American Express, and, yes, even J. C. Penney will somehow discover your new earnings potential. These firms and many others will invite you to join, assuming you have not already, the hoards of fully "ac-credited" American consumers. Increased sales and larger market shares await those companies that allow their customers to "charge" purchases of goods and services. As pointed out in the opening vignette for this chapter, the decision to extend credit to customers has its drawbacks. The biggest problem stemming from this decision can be summarized in two words: bad debts. Unlike a sale made on a cash basis, two key activities are associated with a credit sale: making the sale and collecting the resulting receivable. Quite often, the latter task is the more challenging and frustrating of the two.

The 1994 edition of *Accounting Trends & Techniques* reported that all six hundred companies surveyed for that publication had receivables listed on their balance sheets under current assets. Approximately 87 percent of these companies used one of the following captions for those assets: "accounts receivable," "receivables," or "trade accounts receivable." These receivables represent amounts owed to businesses by their customers who have purchased either goods or services on credit. Many companies also have miscellaneous current receivables reported on their balance sheets. For example, nearly 10 percent of the companies surveyed for the 1994 edition of *Accounting Trends & Techniques* reported current receivables from various taxing agencies.

The nature of a business's operations significantly influences the composition of its assets, including the proportion of its total assets "tied up" in accounts receivable. Shown in Exhibit 7.7 is selected financial information for three public companies. Notice that Churchill Downs, the company that operates the racetrack where the Kentucky Derby is run each year, has a relatively small amount of accounts receivable

The composition of a company's assets is heavily influenced by the nature of its operations. For example, you would not expect Churchill Downs, a company that owns and operates a thoroughbred racetrack, to have a significant amount of accounts receivable. Why? Just try "charging" a bet the next time you visit a racetrack.

■ **EXHIBIT 7.7**

Cash, Accounts Receivable, and Current Assets as a Percentage of Total
Assets for Selected Companies

SOURCE: Recent annual reports.

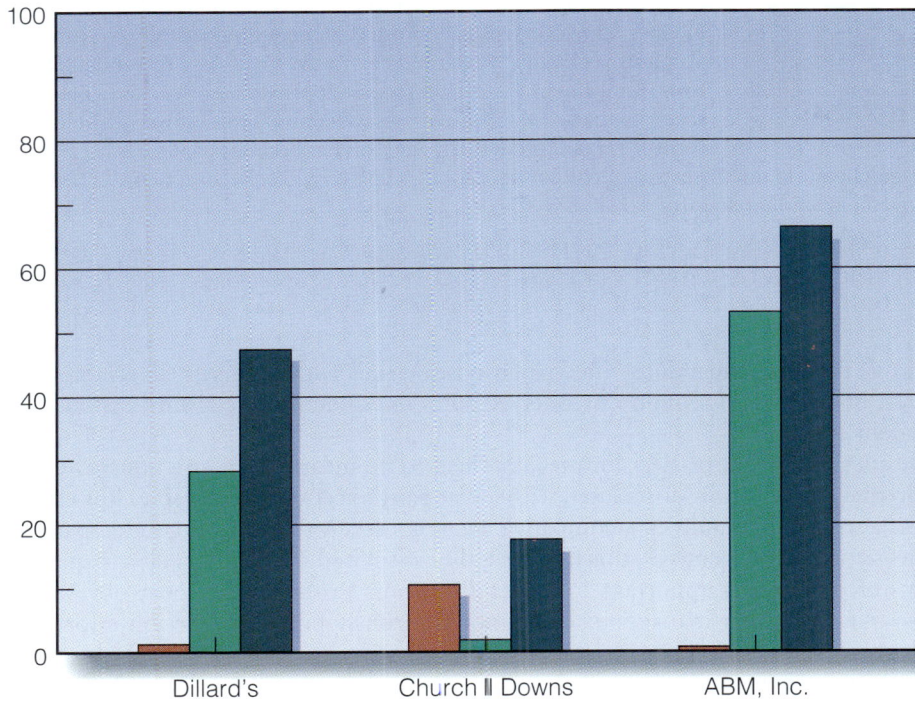

Dillard's: Operates a chain of large department stores
Churchill Downs: Operates a thoroughbred racetrack
ABM, Inc.: Provides janitorial and related services

■ Cash   ■ Accounts Receivable   ■ Current Assets

on its balance sheet. Churchill Down's executives do not allow customers to charge
their bets—clearly a wise policy. On the other hand, ABM, a janitorial services company, and Dillard's, a large department store chain, make extensive use of credit.
Why? Principally because it has become common practice in these companies' industries to extend credit to customers. Companies in these industries that do not allow
their customers to purchase goods and services on credit will find themselves at a significant competitive disadvantage.

Accounts Receivable: Information Needs of Decision Makers

When a company has a material amount of receivables on its balance sheet, the first
issue decision makers raise is whether those receivables are collectible. Business entities are required by generally accepted accounting principles to report accounts
receivable at their approximate net realizable value. For balance sheet purposes, companies must subtract from their reported receivables the dollar amount that will like-

■ **LEARNING
OBJECTIVE 1**
Define the key information
needs of decision makers
regarding cash and accounts
receivable

Foreign Receivables: Far Away and Tough to Collect

In 1993, the National Association of Credit Management reported that the average time required to collect an account receivable was 42 days. However, collection times increase dramatically for foreign accounts receivable. For instance, if your firm has a receivable due from Kenya, you can expect to wait approximately 143 days before receiving payment. The average collection period for receivables from Syria is 175 days. If your firm has recently made a sale to an Iranian client, do not expect payment anytime soon. The average collection period for a receivable from that country is 310 days.

SOURCE: "Foreign Firms Take Their Time Paying Up," *Christian Science Monitor*, 14 September 1993, 8.

uncollectible accounts expense

Teaching Note
Point out that the net realizable value of accounts receivable is computed as follows:
    Accounts Receivable
  − Allowance for Doubtful
      Accounts
  = Net Realizable Value

ly prove to be uncollectible. The expense associated with accounts receivable that cannot be collected is commonly referred to as **uncollectible accounts expense** or bad debt expense.

Besides collectibility, decision makers need to be informed of any unusual characteristics or conditions associated with a company's accounts receivable. For example, if a material amount of a company's accounts receivable is from related parties, such as company executives, this fact should be disclosed in the financial statements. This information is important for several reasons. Probably the most obvious of these reasons is that management may not vigorously pursue collection efforts on such receivables.

A company that becomes trapped in a liquidity crisis in which it is short of cash may be forced to sell its receivables to third parties. Another alternative is for a company to pledge its accounts receivable as collateral for a new loan. If a company defaults on such a loan, the lender is entitled to recover the amount it is owed from the subsequent cash collections on the company's receivables. If a company has pledged its receivables as collateral, this fact should be disclosed in the financial statements. Such disclosure alerts decision makers that the company has one less financing alternative available in the future.

Accounting for Accounts Receivable

■ LEARNING OBJECTIVE 2
Account for the major types of transactions affecting cash and accounts receivable

In prior chapters, some basic transactions involving accounts receivable were discussed along with the appropriate journal entries for those transactions. Recall that a credit sale of merchandise is recorded as a debit to Accounts Receivable and a credit to Sales. The journal entry for the collection of an account receivable involves a debit to Cash and a credit to Accounts Receivable. If a customer takes advantage of a discount for early payment, the latter entry would also include a debit to Sales Discounts. In this section, additional procedural accounting issues for accounts receivable are discussed and illustrated.

DIRECT WRITE-OFF METHOD VS. THE MATCHING PRINCIPLE
Companies that extend credit must establish some means for assessing the ability and intent of prospective customers to pay their debts. As suggested in the opening vignette for this chapter, this task is the primary responsibility of a company's credit

department. Despite the activities of a credit department, most companies do not collect all of their credit sales. When it appears that a receivable will not be collected, that receivable should be "written off." Companies that use the **direct write-off method** debit Uncollectible Accounts Expense and credit Accounts Receivable when they determine that a specific receivable is unlikely to be collected. For example, assume that in November 1995 a small retail company sold $300 of merchandise on credit to a customer. For whatever reason, the customer was unable to pay the $300. In September 1996, after vigorous collection efforts had failed, the company decided to write off the $300 receivable. If this company uses the direct write-off method, the following entry would have been appropriate.

direct write-off method

Sep. 17	Uncollectible Accounts Expense	300	
	Accounts Receivable		300
	To record write-off of receivable from D. R. Donaho		

Notice that the prior entry was made in September 1996, while the credit sale resulting in the receivable was recorded in November 1995. Expressed another way, the revenue from the sale was recorded in 1995, while the related uncollectible accounts expense was recorded the following year. Something is amiss here. Recall the matching principle discussed in Chapter 2. The matching principle dictates that a company should attempt to "match" revenues with the related expenses incurred to generate those revenues. Clearly, uncollectible accounts expense is a common expense that companies incur and expect to incur when they make sales on a credit basis. Consequently, companies should estimate the uncollectible accounts expense they will eventually realize from credit sales made during an accounting period and then record that estimate as an expense *in that same period.*

The direct write-off method is not considered a generally accepted accounting principle because it does not match uncollectible accounts expense with the related sales revenue. The next question is obvious: Why waste your time illustrating an unacceptable accounting method? Answer: Companies that do not have a material, or significant, amount of receivables are allowed to use this shortcut method of accounting for bad debts. Second answer: The direct write-off method must be used for federal taxation purposes by most businesses although it "flies in the face" of the matching principle and the accrual basis of accounting. You should recognize that federal taxation rules are intended to raise revenue for the federal government, not to provide for the most defensible method of accounting for business transactions.

Thousands of U.S. companies market their products and services around the world. However, collecting international receivables poses a major challenge and headache for these firms. For example, a recent study indicated that a U.S. firm can expect to wait nearly five months to collect outstanding receivables from Kenya.

■ **LEARNING OBJECTIVE 6**
Use the aging method to estimate uncollectible accounts expense

allowance method

Allowance for Doubtful Accounts

ALLOWANCE METHOD OF ACCOUNTING FOR UNCOLLECTIBLE ACCOUNTS EXPENSE   Because of the matching principle, most companies use the allowance method of accounting for uncollectible accounts expense. Under the **allowance method,** a business estimates its uncollectible accounts expense at the end of each accounting period. The period-ending adjusting entry for estimated uncollectible accounts includes a debit to Uncollectible Accounts Expense and an equal credit to the contra asset account **Allowance for Doubtful Accounts.** For balance sheet purposes, the Allowance for Doubtful Accounts is subtracted from Accounts Receivable to reduce that asset to its approximate net realizable value.[7] The key to understanding the allowance method is to recognize that when uncollectible accounts expense is recorded, *no specific accounts* have been identified as uncollectible. Under the allowance method, uncollectible accounts expense is simply an estimate of a company's accounts receivable that will never be collected.

Uncollectible accounts expense varies dramatically from industry to industry and from company to company. Shown in Exhibit 7.8 is the allowance for doubtful accounts for six companies expressed as a percentage of those firms' accounts receivable. As you might expect, a company such as Caesar's World, which operates several large casinos, has a particularly difficult time collecting its receivables. Even compared with other companies in the casino industry, Caesar's has a poor track record of collecting its receivables. Many of Caesar's patrons are so-called high rollers from other countries. Once these individuals return to their home countries, they are prone not to render unto Caesar's what is Caesar's. Conversely, the rigorous credit policies of the fiscally conservative Wrigley Company result in few losses on accounts receivable for that firm.

■ **EXHIBIT 7.8**

Allowance for Doubtful Accounts as a Percentage of Accounts Receivable, Selected Companies

SOURCE: Recent annual reports.

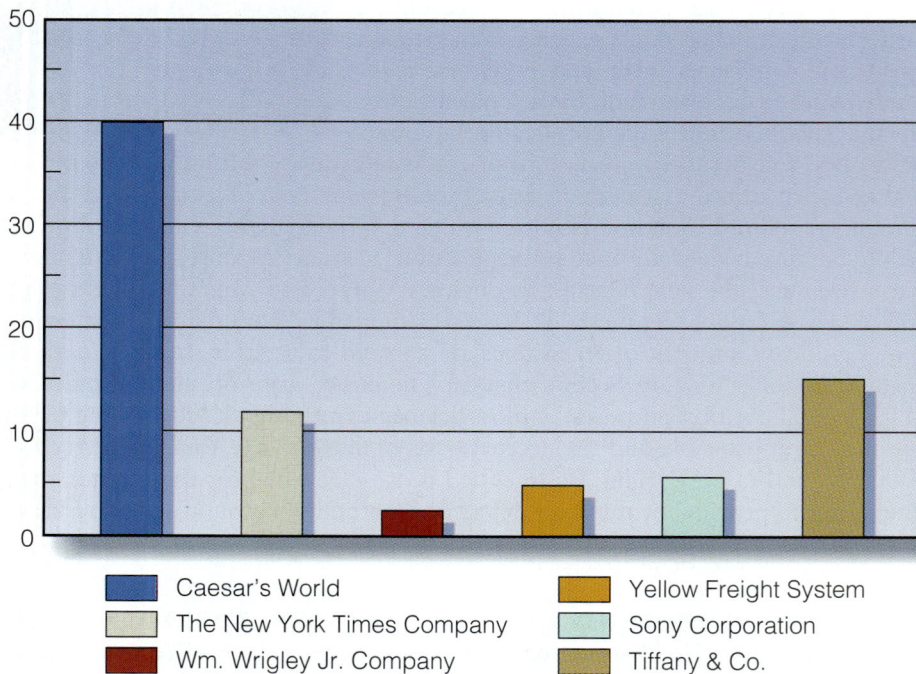

Caesar's World
The New York Times Company
Wm. Wrigley Jr. Company
Yellow Freight System
Sony Corporation
Tiffany & Co.

---

7. Most accounting textbooks use the title "Allowance for Uncollectible Accounts" for this account. However, *Accounting Trends & Techniques* reports that "Allowance for Doubtful Accounts" is a more common title. Consequently, this latter title is used in this textbook.

When it comes to estimating uncollectible accounts, one of two alternative approaches to applying the allowance method is commonly used. The net sales (allowance) method is an easy-to-use technique of estimating uncollectible accounts. This method is used by many businesses to estimate uncollectible accounts each month until the final month of the year. At year-end, when it is necessary to prepare annual financial statements, the aging (allowance) method is commonly applied. The aging method is used to prepare a year-end adjusting entry that both establishes the proper balance of the Allowance for Doubtful Accounts and adjusts the uncollectible accounts expense for the year to a more appropriate figure. Here, only the aging method is illustrated. Those of you who pursue further accounting studies will become acquainted with the net sales method in a future course.

Businesses realize that the likelihood of collecting accounts receivable is inversely related to the age of those receivables. The aging method of estimating uncollectible accounts is based upon this realization. Under the **aging method,** a business classifies its accounts receivable into several age categories. (In this context, "age" refers to the amount of time that has passed since a receivable was recorded.) Then, based upon historical experience and possibly other factors, the dollar amount of the receivables in each age group that will not be collected is estimated.

Exhibit 7.9 presents an accounts receivable aging schedule for Hunt Brothers, Inc. In an aging schedule, a company typically classifies its outstanding receivables either as being current or as past due by a certain number of days. The number and width of aging categories vary from company to company, but those shown in Exhibit 7.9 are fairly common.

Notice at the bottom of the Hunt Brothers' aging schedule that historical bad debt percentages for each aging category are listed. To estimate Hunt Brothers' uncollectible accounts as of December 31, 1996, these percentages are multiplied by the

aging method

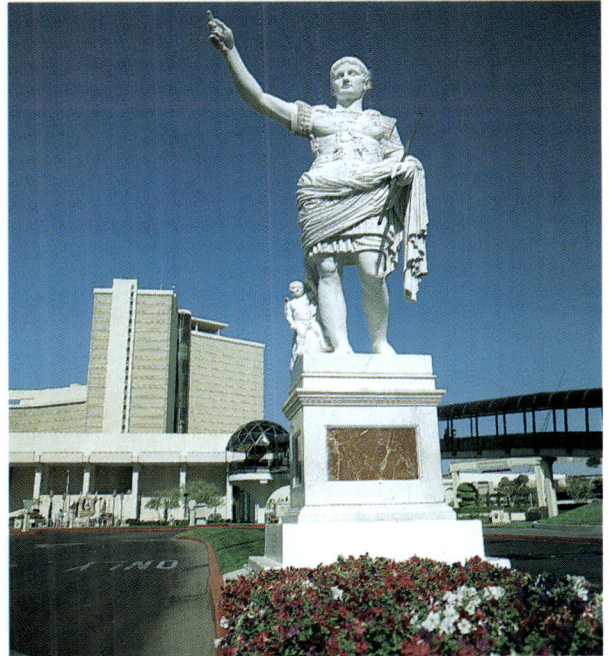

Gaming companies, such as Caesar's World, which owns the Caesar's Palace casino in Las Vegas, tend to have more difficulty collecting their receivables than other types of businesses.

■ EXHIBIT 7.9
Example of an Accounts Receivable Aging Schedule

Real World
An aging schedule can be prepared in a matter of moments in a computerized accounting system. Without a computer, preparing an aging schedule is a tedious, time-consuming process.

HUNT BROTHERS, INC.
ACCOUNTS RECEIVABLE AGING SCHEDULE
DECEMBER 31, 1996

| Customer | Balance | Current | Days Past Due | | | |
			1–30	31–60	61–90	91+
Bud Kay	$ 850	$ 220		$ 400		$230
Bess Penn	670	500			$170	
Dan Quinn	320		$ 320			
Gary Young	440	440				
Others	13,850	10,040	1,800	1,160	550	300
Totals	$16,130	$11,200	$2,120	$1,560	$720	$530
Historical Bad Debt Percentages		.5	2.5	7.5	20.0	50.0

total amount of receivables within each aging category. These computations are as follows:

Teaching Note
Point out that the older an account receivable of Hunt Brothers becomes, the less likely the company is to collect it, as documented in this schedule.

Current Receivables	$11,200 × .005 = $ 56
Past Due Receivables:	
1–30 Days	2,120 × .025 = 53
31–60 Days	1,560 × .075 = 117
61–90 Days	720 × .200 = 144
91+ Days	530 × .500 = 265
Total	$635

This analysis suggests that Hunt Brothers' Allowance for Doubtful Accounts should have a balance of $635 on December 31, 1996. So, the appropriate adjusting entry is to debit Uncollectible Accounts Expense $635 and credit the Allowance for Doubtful Accounts $635. Right? Wrong. An aging analysis reveals the proper year-end balance of an allowance account, *not* the required dollar amount of the year-end adjusting entry for uncollectible accounts expense.

Under the aging method, to determine the proper amount of the year-end adjusting entry to the Allowance for Doubtful Accounts, one must first refer to the preadjustment balance of that account. Following is the allowance account for Hunt Brothers on December 31, 1996, before the posting of the year-end adjusting entry to that account.

Allowance for Doubtful Accounts						**Account No. 131**	
			Post			**Balance**	
Date		**Explanation**	**Ref.**	**Debit**	**Credit**	**Debit**	**Credit**
1996							
Dec.	31	Balance Forward					140

Teaching Note
Remind students that one objective of adjusting the allowance account at year-end is to report a business's accounts receivable at their net realizable value.

Since the preadjustment balance of Hunt Brothers' allowance account is $140, a credit entry of $495 is necessary to establish the proper year-end balance in that account of $635 ($635 − $140 = $495). The offsetting debit in this adjusting entry is made to Uncollectible Accounts Expense. This adjusting entry is shown next, followed by Hunt Brothers' allowance account after the posting of this entry.

Dec. 31	Uncollectible Accounts Expense	495
	Allowance for Doubtful Accounts	495
	To record the year-end adjusting entry for uncollectible accounts expense	

Allowance for Doubtful Accounts						**Account No. 131**	
			Post			**Balance**	
Date		**Explanation**	**Ref.**	**Debit**	**Credit**	**Debit**	**Credit**
1996							
Dec.	31	Balance Forward					140
Dec.	31	Adjusting	GJ5		495		635

As indicated earlier, estimates of uncollectible accounts expense are often recorded on a monthly basis prior to year-end by applying the net sales method. Again, by using the aging method to adjust the year-end balance of the allowance account, a company automatically adjusts its uncollectible accounts expense to a more reasonable estimate for the year.

WRITE-OFFS AND RECOVERIES OF DOUBTFUL ACCOUNTS   Recall that under the direct write-off method, individual accounts receivable are written off when it is determined that they are unlikely to be collected. Write-off entries are also required under the allowance method. Under either variation of the allowance method, the period-ending adjustments to record uncollectible accounts expense are based upon estimates. When these estimates are made, no specific accounts have been identified as uncollectible. Later, when actual accounts are identified as uncollectible, they should be written off against the allowance account.

Assume that a customer of Hunt Brothers files for personal bankruptcy shortly after the close of the company's fiscal year on December 31, 1996. This customer, Dan Quinn, owes Hunt Brothers $320, an amount the company expects it will never collect given Quinn's financial problems. Under such circumstances, the following entry would be appropriate to write off the receivable from Dan Quinn.

Jan. 20	Allowance for Doubtful Accounts	320	
	Accounts Receivable		320
	To write off receivable from		
	D. Quinn		

Notice that this entry does not include a debit to Uncollectible Accounts Expense. Why? Because the December 31, 1996, adjusting entry for uncollectible accounts expense took into consideration the likelihood that certain of the company's year-end receivables would not be collected. That adjusting entry resulted in the uncollectible accounts expense related to those receivables being booked in 1996. Subsequently, when specific receivables existing at the end of 1996 prove to be uncollectible, it would be inappropriate to record an additional expense when such accounts are written off. Instead, such receivables are charged off to the allowance account.

Now, assume that on March 21, 1997, Hunt Brothers unexpectedly receives a check for $320 from Dan Quinn. Two entries would be required in Hunt Brothers' accounting records to record the receipt of this check. First, the receivable from Dan Quinn would be reinstated in the accounting records. Second, the collection of this reinstated receivable would be recorded. Following are these two entries in general journal format. (Note: Each of the following entries as well as the original write-off entry would be posted to Quinn's account in the accounts receivable subsidiary ledger.)

Mar. 21	Accounts Receivable	320	
	Allowance for Doubtful Accounts		320
	To reinstate the receivable from		
	D. Quinn written off on Jan. 20		
Mar. 21	Cash	320	
	Accounts Receivable		320
	To record payment by		
	D. Quinn of reinstated		
	receivable		

Focus on Ethics
A CPA provides accounting services to both the Hunt Brothers and Dan Quinn (a regular customer of the Hunt Brothers). The CPA has become aware of Quinn's financial problems. Should the CPA warn the Hunt Brothers of Quinn's financial problems?

Teaching Note
Point out that the write-off of individual accounts receivable only affects balance sheet accounts.

THE SPECIAL CASE OF CREDIT CARD RECEIVABLES   Many retail businesses allow, if not encourage, their customers to pay for purchases with major credit cards, such as VISA, MasterCard, and American Express. Retailers realize several important benefits by having their customers make purchases with a credit card. One of these benefits is that credit card companies accept the responsibility for bad debts resulting from credit card sales. Likewise, credit card companies relieve retail businesses of the need to do "credit checks" on prospective customers. Finally, credit card companies generally pay amounts owed to retailers on a more timely basis than do individual customers. As you would expect, credit card companies charge for the services they provide. These companies typically deduct a 1 to 5 percent fee from the gross receipts they collect for retailers. So, for every $1,000 of credit card sales, a retailer may receive only $950 in payments from credit card companies.

To illustrate accounting for credit card receivables, suppose that Bonney's Dress Shop had $450 of credit card sales on May 5 of a given year. To simplify matters, assume that all of these sales were charged on PlasticCard credit cards. The following entry would be made to book these sales, assuming PlasticCard charges Bonney's a 4 percent fee for its services.

May 5	Accounts Receivable—PlasticCard	432	
	Credit Card Fees Expense	18	
	Sales		450
	To record credit card sales		

When Bonney's receives payment for the receivable from PlasticCard, the company's accountant would debit Cash for $432 and credit Accounts Receivable—PlasticCard for the same amount.

Many companies that use the services of VISA or MasterCard have a special bank account into which they deposit sales charged to these credit cards. Retailers typically deposit credit card receipts (sales slips) on a daily basis into these bank accounts. The amount of such a deposit, less the service fee, is treated as a cash deposit by the bank. As a result, the journal entry on a retailer's books to record daily VISA or MasterCard credit card sales may involve a debit to Cash instead of Accounts Receivable.

Analyzing Accounts Receivable

Ask a financial analyst what he or she first considers when evaluating a company's accounts receivable and that individual will likely reply the "quality" of those receivables. The quality of a company's receivables is largely a function of their collectibility. In turn, as suggested earlier, the collectibility of receivables is principally a function of their age. Shown in Exhibit 7.10 is a graph that plots the likelihood of collecting receivables of varying ages. Obviously, a strong negative correlation exists between the age of receivables and the likelihood that they will be converted into hard, cold cash.

Determining the age of a company's receivables is a two-step process. First, the accounts receivable turnover ratio is computed.

$$\textbf{Accounts Receivable Turnover Ratio} = \text{Net Credit Sales/Average Accounts Receivable}$$

Then, the accounts receivable turnover ratio is divided into 360 days, the number of days in a business year. (To simplify the computation of financial ratios and other

■ **EXHIBIT 7.10**

Likelihood of Collecting Past-Due Accounts Receivable

SOURCE: "Annual Collectibility Survey," Commercial Collection Agency Section of the Commercial Law League of America, New Providence, N.J., April 1993.

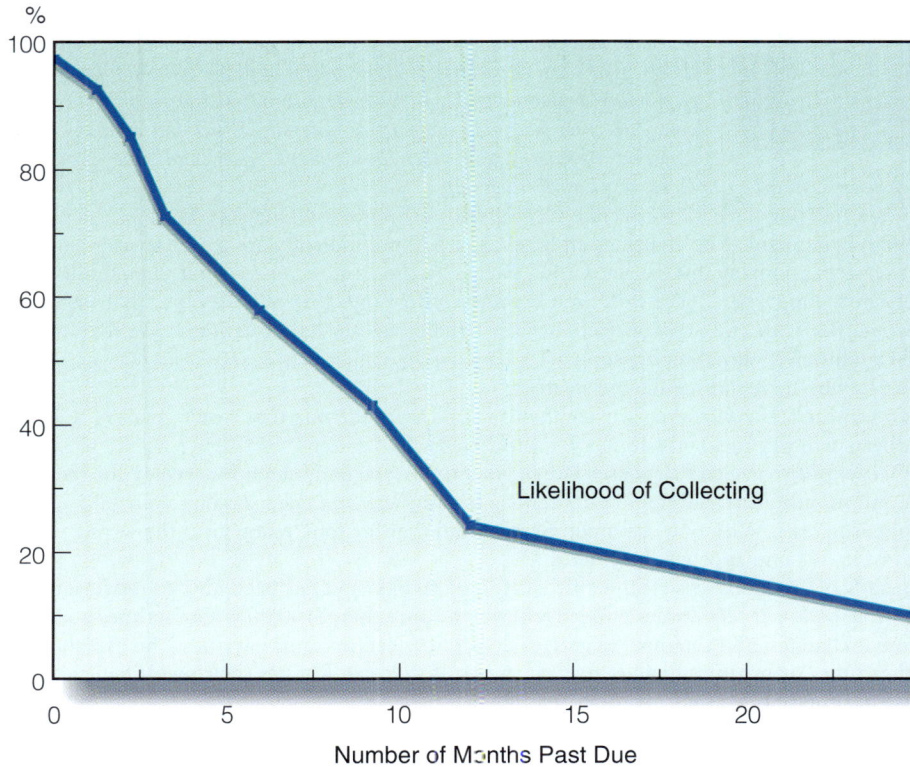

financial measures, many financial analysts and other financial statement users define a "business" year as consisting of 360 days.

$$\text{Age of Receivables} = \frac{360 \text{ days}}{\text{Accounts Receivable Turnover Ratio}}$$

age of receivables

To illustrate the computation of the age of receivables, consider the following data for Jensen Supply Company.

Accounts Receivable, January 1, 1996	$ 82,000
Accounts Receivable, December 31, 1996	74,500
Net Credit Sales, 1996	500,800

Listed next are the calculations to compute Jensen's age of receivables at the end of 1996.

$$\begin{aligned} \text{Average Accounts Receivable} &= (\$82,000 + \$74,500)/2 \\ &= \$78,250 \end{aligned}$$

StarPak's Motto: Don't Give Up, Don't Ever Give Up

Attempting to collect a past-due account receivable can be a frustrating experience. A company works hard to make a sale, books the revenue from that sale, and then waits month after month for the customer to pay for the goods or services purchased. After dozens of phone calls and nasty letters, many companies will say, "To heck with it," and write off the receivable. Not so for one small company in Colorado. When this company has a past-due receivable that is other than a small "nickel and dime" amount, the customer can expect to be harassed until it pays up.

When he's pursuing long-overdue receivables, A. Emmet Stephenson, Jr., doesn't believe he'll never get paid. The chairman of StarPak, a $20 million software manufacturer and support services company in Greeley, Colo., swears by the strategy of tracking unpaid bills "for a very, very long time." "We won't put executive effort into tiny bills, because that isn't cost-effective. But with any overdue account over $5,000, we're pretty relentless. We'll be their worst nightmare," says Stephenson.

Here's why he recommends the strategy:

It's unique. "If you make your company stand out as the one that won't go away, a lot of deadbeats will pay their bills to get you off their backs."

It's inexpensive. StarPak chases late payments by mail and telephone weekly for the first year and monthly thereafter. "For 29 cents a month, why not keep sending your bill?" Stephenson asks. With one customer, StarPak did that for four years, until the wrong executive got its bill and approved payment.

It pays off. Popular wisdom notwithstanding, Stephenson has been able to retrieve two and three-year-old receivables collectively worth more than $100,000. "Sometimes a management changes, and the new executives decide to clean up their payables," he explains. "Other times, companies genuinely *want* to pay, if they can just get their own financial house in order. So we wait for them."

SOURCE: Used with permission, *Inc. Magazine*, October 1993. Goldhirsh, Inc., 38 Commercial Wharf, Boston, MA 02110.

Accounts Receivable Turnover Ratio	=	$500,800/$78,250
	=	6.4
Age of Receivables	=	360 days/6.4
	=	56.25 days

Discussion Question

Ask students to compute the accounts receivable turnover ratio and age of receivables for Michaels Stores. (A recent annual report for this company is included as an appendix to this text.) Does this average time to collect a receivable seem reasonable for this type of business?

The accounts receivable turnover ratio measures the number of times that a company collects or "turns over" its receivables each year. Companies want to convert their receivables into cash as quickly as possible. Consequently, the higher the accounts receivable turnover ratio, the better. The age of receivables indicates the average number of days that a company's receivables have been outstanding. Viewed another way, age of receivables indicates the average period of time required for a company to collect a receivable resulting from a credit sale.

Shown in Exhibit 7.11 is the age of receivables for four companies. As suggested earlier, an important consideration in interpreting a specific financial measure for a company is the industry norm for that item. Take the case of Body Drama, a company that contracts for the manufacture of women's apparel and then wholesales these products to retail outlets across the United States. Exhibit 7.11 indicates that the

■ **EXHIBIT 7.11**

Age of Receivables, Selected Companies

SOURCE: Recent annual reports.

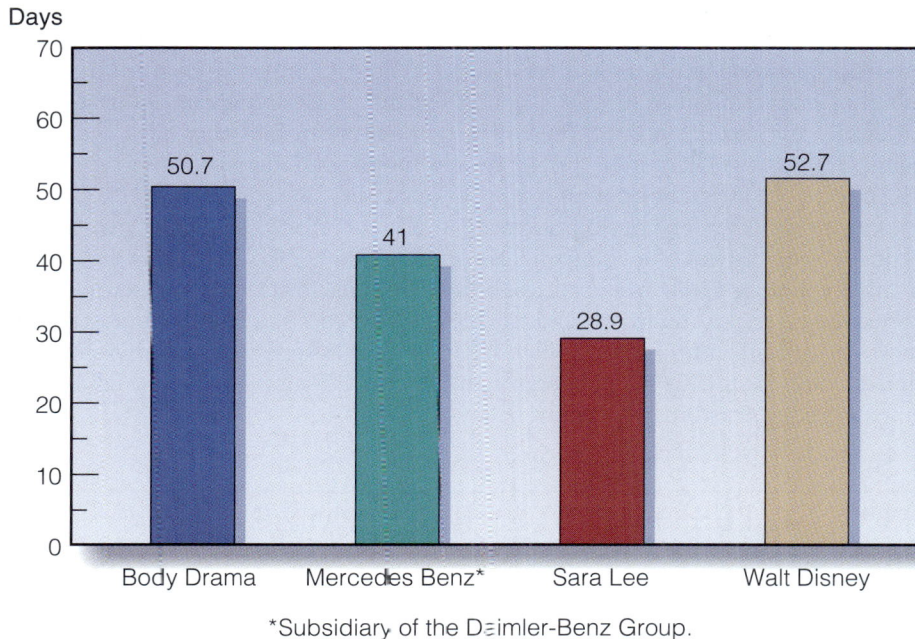

*Subsidiary of the Daimler-Benz Group.

average age of Body Drama's receivables is nearly 51 days. The median age of receivables for companies that operate businesses similar to that of Body Drama is 39.5 days,[8] while the average age of receivables across all industries is approximately 42 days, as indicated earlier in the chapter. Given these data, Body Drama's receivables appear to be somewhat "elderly," which suggests that the company will likely experience higher bad debt losses than its competitors.

Key Internal Control Procedures for Accounts Receivable

Several internal control procedures and strategies related to accounts receivable have been discussed, at least briefly, in this and earlier chapters. An important control procedure for accounts receivable is the maintenance of a subsidiary ledger. An accounts receivable subsidiary ledger provides the detailed information a company needs to prepare monthly billing statements. The mailing of such statements is one not-so-subtle way that a company can remind its customers of their unpaid account balances. A subsidiary ledger also provides the detailed support for the general ledger controlling account, Accounts Receivable. Periodically, the total of the accounts receivable subsidiary ledger should be reconciled to the balance of the controlling account and any difference investigated and eliminated.

■ **LEARNING OBJECTIVE 4**
Discuss key internal control issues related to cash and accounts receivable

---

8. This figure was computed from information found in the following source: *RMA Annual Statement Studies, 1993* (Philadelphia: RMA, 1993).

Discussion Question
What are the consequences for a company if its credit policy is "too" tight?
Answer: Lower sales.

To maintain proper control over accounts receivable, management must have a strong credit function. The most effective way to minimize uncollectible accounts expense is to withhold credit from potential customers who pose excessive credit risks. Likewise, a company should have a strategy for collecting accounts receivable. Mailing monthly statements to customers is just one aspect of such a strategy. Another important control procedure related to receivables collection activities is the periodic preparation and review of an aging schedule. Companies that use the aging method of estimating uncollectible accounts expense must prepare an aging schedule periodically for accounting purposes. However, all companies that have a material amount of accounts receivable should closely monitor the age of those receivables both collectively and individually for control purposes.

Segregation of key responsibilities is an internal control concept that relates to practically every aspect of a company's accounting and control functions. For example, an accounting clerk who processes cash receipts from accounts receivable, a recordkeeping responsibility, should not be allowed to issue credit memos to customers, an authorization responsibility. An individual assigned both of these responsibilities could steal cash receipts and then conceal the theft by issuing false credit memos to reduce customers' account balances.

A FEW NOTES ON NOTES RECEIVABLE

note receivable

Notes receivable are assets very similar to accounts receivable, with one key exception. Both accounts and notes receivable represent promises made by third parties to pay a certain amount to a business entity by a certain date. However, for a **note receivable** this promise is expressed in a formal document known as a promissory note. Since notes receivable are similar to accounts receivable, we will consider only accounting issues and procedures unique to notes receivable. Notes receivable can be classified as either current or long-term assets depending upon when they come due. Here, we focus strictly on current notes receivable. Accounting procedures for long-term notes receivable are identical, in most respects, to the procedures applied to current notes receivable.

Notes Receivable: Characteristics and Terminology

■ **LEARNING OBJECTIVE 8**
Define the key characteristics of notes receivable

Many notes receivable are initially accounts receivable. When a customer cannot pay an account receivable by the due date, the company to whom the receivable is owed may ask the customer to sign a promissory note for the unpaid balance. A promissory note documents the customer's receivable more formally and typically requires the customer to begin paying interest on his or her unpaid receivable balance. A promissory note also provides a company a better opportunity to convert a customer's receivable into cash. Companies sometimes sell their accounts receivable to banks or finance companies; however, these sales are usually made at a price considerably below the recorded amount of the receivables. Notes receivable, on the other hand, can be converted into cash at a modest cost by "discounting" them at a bank or other financial institution.

NOTES RECEIVABLE ILLUSTRATED   There is no standard format for promissory notes. Occasionally, a promissory note is nothing more than a scribbled "note" on a piece of paper. Shown in Exhibit 7.12 is an example of a promissory note. When

maker

he signs this note, Robert Brown, the **maker** of the note, is promising to pay $2,000,

■ **EXHIBIT 7.12**
Example of a Promissory Note

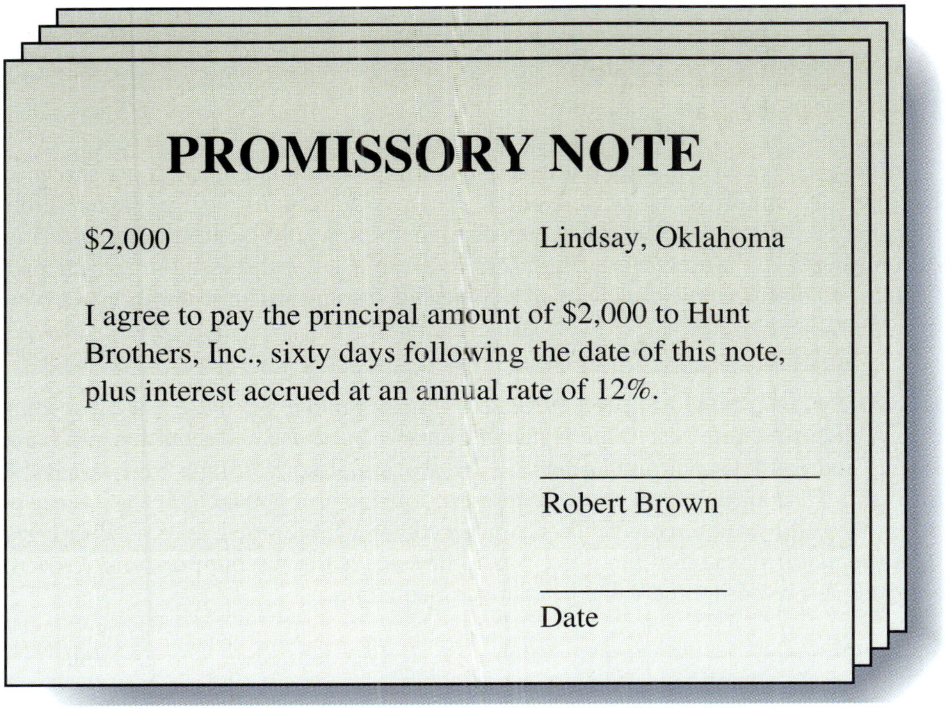

PROMISSORY NOTE

$2,000   Lindsay, Oklahoma

I agree to pay the principal amount of $2,000 to Hunt
Brothers, Inc., sixty days following the date of this note,
plus interest accrued at an annual rate of 12%.

_____
Robert Brown

_____
Date

plus interest, to Hunt Brothers, Inc., sixty days from the date of the signing. Hunt
Brothers is the payee of this note. A **payee** is the party identified in a promissory note   **payee**
to whom payment will eventually be made. (Recognize that the promissory note
shown in Exhibit 7.12 is a note receivable for Hunt Brothers, Inc., but a note payable
for Robert Brown.)

The amount initially owed by a maker of a note is the **principal** or principal amount.   **principal**
The **term of a note,** sometimes referred to as its duration, is the number of days from   **term of a note**
the date a note is signed, not counting the signing date, to the date the note matures.
For example, if the note shown in Exhibit 7.12 is signed on July 15, its 60-day term
would run from July 16 through September 13: 16 days in July, 31 days in August, and
13 days in September for a total of 60 days. Under this assumption, September 13
would be the **maturity date,** the date a note must be paid. Finally, the **maturity value**   **maturity date**
of a note is the total amount the maker must pay the payee on the maturity date. The   **maturity value**
maturity value of a note is equal to the sum of its principal and any interest that accrues
or accumulates on the note over its term. For the note shown in Exhibit 7.12, the
maturity value is $2,040, which is the principal of $2,000 plus interest of $40. (The
computation of the interest on this note is illustrated in the next section.)

COMPUTING INTEREST ON A NOTE RECEIVABLE   Following is the **interest**   **interest equation**
equation used to compute interest revenue or expense on a promissory note or, more
generally, on any type of interest-bearing financial instrument.

$$\text{Interest} \quad = \quad \text{Principal} \quad \times \quad \text{Rate} \quad \times \quad \text{Time}$$

The "rate" in the interest equation refers to the annual interest rate identified in a promissory note. The time component of the interest equation is expressed as a fraction, with the term of the note as the numerator and 360 days as the denominator. Following is the computation of the interest on the note shown in Exhibit 7.12.

Interest	=	Principal	×	Rate	×	Time
$40	=	$2,000	×	.12	×	60 days/360 days

Some notes receivable are noninterest-bearing. For example, if the note shown in Exhibit 7.12 simply stated that Robert Brown was responsible for paying Hunt Brothers $2,000 on the note's maturity date, the note would be noninterest-bearing. Accounting for noninterest-bearing notes receivable is not discussed in this chapter. Chapter 10 discusses the closely related subject of accounting for noninterest-bearing notes payable.

DISCOUNTING NOTES RECEIVABLE One advantage of converting an account receivable into a note receivable is that the latter can be easily discounted at a bank. In this context, "discounting" refers to the process of converting a note receivable into cash. Discounting is an appropriate term for this process since the cash received in exchange for a note receivable, the proceeds of a discounted note, is always less than the maturity value of the note. This difference is the discount on a note receivable and can be computed with the following equation.

Discount	=	Maturity Value	×	Discount Rate	×	Time

Notice that the equation for computing a discount is very similar to the interest equation. To convert the interest equation into the equation for computing a discount, the maturity value of a note is substituted for the principal. Next, the interest rate charged by a bank or other financial institution for a discounting transaction, referred to as the discount rate, is substituted for the interest rate. Finally, the time component in the discount equation is the fraction of a year remaining in the term of a note when it is discounted. Recall that in the interest equation, the time component refers to the term of the note expressed as a fraction of a year.

To illustrate the discounting of a note receivable, assume that a company acquires a note receivable with a principal amount of $1,000, a term of 120 days, and an interest rate of 9 percent. Since the company is short of funds, it decides to immediately convert the note receivable into cash by discounting it at a local bank. The company's bank agrees to discount the note but not at the 9 percent interest rate the customer is paying on the note. Instead, the bank discounts the note at an interest rate of 12 percent. By applying a discount rate higher than the interest rate the maker of the note is paying, the bank increases the profit (interest revenue) it realizes on the discounting transaction.

Determining the proceeds a company will receive from discounting a note receivable is a three-step process: (1) compute the maturity value of the note, (2) compute the discount on the note, and (3) compute the proceeds of the note. Each of these three steps is illustrated next for the note receivable described in the prior paragraph. Recall that this note is being discounted on the date it was obtained from the maker. Consequently, the numerator of the time component in the discount equation is 120 days, which equals both the term of the note and the number of days remaining in the term when the note is discounted.

1. Compute the maturity value:
    Maturity Value = Principal + Interest
    Maturity Value = $1,000 + ($1,000 × .09 × 120/360)
    Maturity Value = $1,000 + $30
    Maturity Value = $1,030
2. Compute the discount:
    Discount = Maturity Value × Discount Rate × Time
    Discount = $1,030 × .12 × 120/360
    Discount = $41.20
3. Compute the proceeds:
    Proceeds = Maturity Value − Discount
    Proceeds = $1,030 − $41.20
    Proceeds = $988.80

Accounting for Notes Receivable

To illustrate accounting procedures for a note receivable, the note shown in Exhibit 7.12 is used. Accounting for notes receivable can be quite complex. Here, only the basic journal entries for notes receivable are illustrated.

■ LEARNING
OBJECTIVE 9
Account for the major types of
transactions involving notes
receivable

INITIAL RECORDING AND PAYMENT OF A NOTE RECEIVABLE   Assume that Robert Brown is a customer of Hunt Brothers who was unable to pay his receivable balance of $2,000 by the end of the credit period. When the receivable became past due, the company asked Brown to sign a sixty-day, 12 percent promissory note with a principal amount of $2,000. Assume that Brown signs the note shown in Exhibit 7.12 on May 1. As a result, the note's maturity date is June 30. To record the conversion of the account receivable from Brown to a note receivable, the following journal entry would be made.

May 1	Notes Receivable	2,000	
	Accounts Receivable		2,000
	To record conversion of account receivable from Robert Brown to a note receivable		

Assuming Brown pays the maturity value of the promissory note on the maturity date, the following entry would be made in Hunt Brothers' accounting records.

June 30	Cash	2,040	
	Notes Receivable		2,000
	Interest Revenue		40
	To record payment of note receivable by Robert Brown including interest		

ADJUSTING ENTRIES FOR NOTES RECEIVABLE   Now, assume that Hunt Brothers prepares financial statements on May 31 of the year in which it is holding the note receivable from Robert Brown. Under this assumption, an adjusting entry

Discussion Question
Ask students how Hunt Brothers financial statements would be affected if the company failed to accrue interest on the note receivable at the end of an accounting period.
Answer: Net income, retained earnings, and current assets would all be understated.

would be made in Hunt Brothers' accounting records on May 31 to recognize the $20 of interest revenue earned on the note during May 1996. Shown next is the computation of that interest revenue followed by the appropriate adjusting entry.

$$\begin{array}{ccccccc}
\text{Interest} & = & \text{Principal} & \times & \text{Rate} & \times & \text{Time} \\
\$20 & = & \$2,000 & \times & .12 & \times & 30/360
\end{array}$$

May 31	Interest Receivable	20	
	Interest Revenue		20

To recognize interest earned on note receivable from Robert Brown during May 1996

The following entry would be made to record the payment of the note receivable by Robert Brown on June 30.

Jun. 30	Cash	2,040	
	Notes Receivable		2,000
	Interest Receivable		20
	Interest Revenue		20

To record payment of note receivable by Robert Brown including interest

Notice that the previous entry includes both a credit to Interest Receivable and a credit to Interest Revenue. The $20 credit to Interest Receivable is necessary to recognize the collection of the $20 debited to that account in the May 31 adjusting entry. The $20 credit to Interest Revenue recognizes the interest earned during June on the note receivable.

Teaching Note
Remind students that the term of a note extends from the day following the date it is signed through the maturity date.

RECORDING THE DISCOUNTING OF A NOTE RECEIVABLE Assume on May 16, when there are forty-five days left in the term of the note receivable from Robert Brown, that Hunt Brothers decides to discount the note at a local bank. This bank offers to discount the note at a discount rate of 15 percent. To determine the proceeds from the discounted note and to collect the information necessary to record this transaction, the three-step process identified earlier would be followed.

Step 1: Compute the maturity value of the note:

$$\begin{array}{rcl}
\text{Maturity Value} & = & \text{Principal} + \text{Interest:} \\
\text{Maturity Value} & = & \$2,000 + (\$2,000 \times .12 \times 60/360) \\
\text{Maturity Value} & = & \$2,000 + \$40 \\
\text{Maturity Value} & = & \$2,040
\end{array}$$

Step 2: Compute the discount:

$$\begin{array}{rcl}
\text{Discount} & = & \text{Maturity Value} \times \text{Discount Rate} \times \text{Time} \\
\text{Discount} & = & \$2,040 \times .15 \times 45/360 \\
\text{Discount} & = & \$38.25
\end{array}$$

Step 3: Compute the proceeds:

Proceeds = Maturity Value − Discount
Proceeds = $2,040 − $38.25
Proceeds = $2,001.75

Notice that the proceeds from discounting the note receivable from Robert Brown exceed the principal of that note by $1.75, which is the difference between an interest revenue amount and an interest expense amount. The interest revenue is the $40 that would have been earned by Hunt Brothers if the note had been held to maturity. The interest expense is the $38.75 discount charged Hunt Brothers by its bank for discounting the note. Since the revenue amount exceeds the expense amount, the difference is recorded as interest revenue. If the reverse had been true, the difference would have been recorded as interest expense. Following is the entry that would be made in Hunt Brothers' accounting records to book the discounting of the note receivable from Robert Brown.

May 16	Cash	2,001.75	
	Notes Receivable		2,000
	Interest Revenue		1.75

To record the discounting of
the note receivable from
Robert Brown

When a company (payee) discounts a note receivable at a bank, a company executive endorses the note on the reverse side—that is, signs the company's name—and delivers the note to the bank. The maker of the note is then instructed to pay the note's maturity value directly to the bank on the maturity date. A key feature of these transactions is that the payee of the note is usually liable to the bank for the note's maturity value if the maker defaults on the note. Because of this feature, a discounted note receivable is referred to as a **contingent liability.** A contingent liability is a potential debt or obligation that may become an actual liability if one or more events occur or fail to occur. In the interest of full and fair disclosure, companies should disclose all material contingent liabilities in the footnotes to their financial statements.

contingent liability

Real World
Frequently, companies will list as a line item in the liabilities section of the balance sheet "Contingencies" without a related dollar amount. This puts the reader on notice that contingent liabilities exist, and that information regarding these items can be found in the accompanying financial statement footnotes.

SUMMARY

Decision makers need and demand information regarding the major assets, liabilities, and other financial statement items of businesses. These information needs include any restrictions on the use of an entity's cash resources. Decision makers also need information concerning the primary sources and uses of cash for a business each accounting period. Collectibility is the key information need of decision makers regarding a business's accounts receivable. Decision makers realize that to provide a reliable source of cash for a business, accounts receivable must be collectible on a timely basis.

Cash typically does not pose complex accounting issues. Most cash transactions are recorded in either a cash receipts or cash disbursements journal. For accounts receivable, the key accounting issue is arriving at a reliable estimate of uncollectible accounts. For financial reporting purposes, business entities are required to use the allowance method to estimate uncollectible accounts expense each accounting period.

A common approach to applying the allowance method is to prepare an aging schedule of accounts receivable at the end of an accounting period. Then, historical bad debt percentages for the various age groups of receivables are used to arrive at a collective estimate of uncollectible accounts.

Decision makers use financial ratios to assess the financial health of business entities. Liquidity is one aspect of a business's financial health that decision makers closely monitor. Liquidity refers to a business entity's ability to finance its day-to-day operations and to pay its liabilities as they mature. A commonly used measure of liquidity is the quick ratio. This ratio is computed by dividing total quick assets—cash and cash equivalents, short-term investments, and net current receivables—by total current liabilities. A financial ratio used to monitor the collectibility of accounts receivable is the age of receivables. As the average age of a company's accounts receivable increases, the percentage of those receivables that will have to be written off as uncollectible tends to increase as well.

The susceptibility of cash to being stolen or otherwise misused makes internal control issues for this asset an important concern within most organizations. Control policies and procedures must be established to provide for the physical security of cash funds and to ensure that cash transactions are processed correctly. Cash balances in accounting records should also be reconciled periodically to physical counts of those cash funds or to bank statement balances. To maintain effective control over accounts receivable, a business should establish strong credit and collection functions. The mailing of monthly statements to customers is an example of a routine, but effective, control procedure to increase the likelihood that accounts receivable will be collected.

Companies that acquire notes receivable sometimes convert these assets into cash by discounting them at a bank or other financial institution. To account properly for discounting transactions and other transactions affecting notes receivable, one must first be familiar with the key terms associated with notes receivable. For example, the maturity value of a note receivable is the amount that must be paid by one party, the maker of the note, to another party, the payee of the note.

GLOSSARY

Accounts receivable turnover ratio (p. 288)   Net credit sales divided by average accounts receivable; indicates how often a business collects or "turns over" its accounts receivable each year.

Age of receivables (p. 289)   360 days divided by the accounts receivable turnover ratio; a measure of the collectibility of accounts receivable.

Aging method (p. 285)   One approach to applying the allowance method of estimating uncollectible accounts expense; under this method, an estimate of uncollectible accounts expense is determined by performing an aging analysis of accounts receivable.

Allowance for Doubtful Accounts (p. 283)   A contra asset account subtracted from accounts receivable to reduce those receivables to their net realizable value.

Allowance method (p. 283)   An accounting method used to estimate uncollectible accounts expense for an accounting period.

Bank reconciliation (p. 275)   An accounting document that reconciles the cash balance reported on a bank statement to the corresponding cash balance reflected in a company's accounting records.

Cash equivalents (p. 267)   Investments in short-term securities, such as certificates of deposit (CDs), money market funds, and U. S. treasury bills, that have ninety days or less to maturity when purchased.

Compensating balance (p. 269)   A portion of the proceeds of a loan that must be maintained on deposit with the lending institution.

Contingent liability (p. 297)   A potential liability that may become an actual liability if one or more events occur or fail to occur.

Deposits in transit (p. 276)   Deposits made near the end of an accounting period that have been added to the general ledger cash balance but were not included in the most recent bank statement balance.

Direct write-off method (p. 283)   An accounting method under which uncollectible accounts expense is recorded when it is determined that a specific account receivable is unlikely to be collected; this non-GAAP alternative to the allowance method is used for taxation purposes.

Interest equation (p. 293)   The equation used to compute interest revenue or expense on a promissory note or other interest-bearing financial instrument: interest = principal × rate × time.

Liquidity (p. 272)   Refers to a business entity's ability to finance its day-to-day operations and to pay its liabilities as they mature.

Maker (p. 292)   The party who has signed a promissory note and is thus obligated to pay a certain amount to another party by a certain date.

Maturity date (p. 293)   The date that the maker of a promissory note must pay its maturity value to the payee.

Maturity value (p. 293) The sum of the principal and interest due on a promissory note on the maturity date.

Note receivable (p. 292)   An asset that represents a promise made by one party to pay another a certain amount on a certain date; evidenced by a formal document known as a promissory note.

Outstanding checks (p. 276)   Checks that have been deducted from a company's cash balance in its general ledger but that were not subtracted from the company's cash balance in its most recent bank statement.

Payee (p. 293)   The party to whom the maker of a promissory note must eventually pay the maturity value of that note.

Petty cash fund (p. 270)   A small cash fund from which a business pays minor expenses and other miscellaneous amounts.

Principal (p. 293)   The amount initially owed by the maker of a promissory note.

Quick ratio (p. 272)   Quick assets (cash and cash equivalents, short-term investments, and net current receivables) divided by current liabilities; measures a business entity's liquidity.

Term of a note (p. 293)   The number of days from the date a promissory note is signed, not counting the signing date, to the date the note matures.

Uncollectible accounts expense (p. 282)   The expense associated with accounts receivable that cannot be collected; sometimes referred to as bad debt expense.

DECISION CASE

In early 1993, Warnaco Group, a firm in the clothing industry, appeared to be a company on the move. Sales were up more than 20 percent compared with the previous year and earnings were on the rise. Over the next several years, the company was expected to realize annual increases in sales of 15 percent. The company was also expanding its product line, allowing it to move into new markets. For years, the bulk of the company's sales had been generated by a few high-profile and high-priced product lines. Christian Dior, Hathaway, and Ralph Lauren were a few of the prestigious brand names under which the company's products were sold. In the early 1990s, the company began selling products under less prestigious brand names to expand its market share. These products were marketed to major discount chains such as Wal-Mart and Kmart.

Despite the impressive sales and earnings numbers being reported by Warnaco, a June 1993 article in *The Wall Street Journal* painted a less-than-rosy picture of the company's financial health. The article pointed out that although the company had annual sales exceeding $600 million, its cash balance was a measly $35,000. Apparently, the company's poor cash position stemmed principally from a large increase in accounts receivable over the previous few years. In 1991, the age of the company's accounts receivable was fifty-one

days. That figure increased to fifty-six days in early 1992 and leaped to more than seventy days in early 1993. Making matters worse for Warnaco's cash position were large interest and principal payments required on the company's $300 million of long-term debt.

Required: Assume that you are a stockholder of a company facing circumstances identical to those faced by Warnaco Group in early 1993. Recently, the value of your investment has declined by 25 percent as the company's stock has "taken a beating" in the stock market. You will be attending the company's annual stockholders' meeting within a few weeks. You are aware that company officials representing its major departments, including production, sales, finance, and accounting, will be present at the meeting and available to answer questions from stockholders. (This is a common practice at stockholders' meetings.) Additionally, representatives of the company's independent auditing firm will be present. Prepare a list of questions that you would address to these individuals. Also, identify additional accounting data that you would request from company officials or obtain on your own to provide further insight on the company's financial health.

NOTE: Much of the information for this decision case was drawn from the following article: J. E. Dorfman and T. Agins, "Warnaco Short-Sellers Cite Receivables, Debt, Paltry Cash Level Despite Analysts' Support," *The Wall Street Journal*, 22 June 1993, C2.

QUESTIONS

1. Identify three general types of internal control procedures that businesses can implement to provide effective control over their cash resources.
2. Define cash equivalents.
3. What is a "compensating balance," and who is being compensated?
4. Identify the three types of cash flows reported in a statement of cash flows.
5. Why are companies reluctant to provide information about future cash flows?
6. What types of decision makers would be particularly interested in information about a given business's future cash flows? Why?
7. Define the term "operating cycle." What determines the length of a company's operating cycle?
8. How does the length of a company's operating cycle affect its "cash management" practices?
9. Define liquidity.
10. What types of decision makers are most interested in a company's liquidity and why?
11. Identify the equation used to compute the quick ratio. How is a company's quick ratio used and interpreted by decision makers?
12. How is the accounts receivable turnover ratio and the age of receivables helpful in analyzing the collectibility of a company's accounts receivable?
13. Why would a company choose to sell on credit rather than strictly on a cash-and-carry basis?
14. What is the purpose of a bank reconciliation?
15. Identify the four types of reconciling items included in a bank reconciliation and provide an example of each.

16. What accounting concept requires businesses to estimate their uncollectible accounts expense each accounting period?

17. List two key internal control measures commonly applied to accounts receivable. Explain how these measures enhance an entity's control over its accounts receivable.

18. Briefly describe the difference between accounts receivable and notes receivable.

19. Define the following notes receivable terms: maker, payee, principal, term, and maturity value.

20. Why is a discounted note receivable considered a "contingent liability"?

EXERCISES

21. **Cash and Cash Equivalents** (LO 1)

    The 1994 annual report of Herman Miller, Inc., a furniture manufacturer, contained the following footnote:

    The company invests in certain debt and equity securities as part of its cash management function. Due to the short-term maturities and high liquidity of these securities, they are included in the balance sheet as cash equivalents.

    Required:

    Why would the management of Herman Miller invest in short-term securities rather than maintain the company's cash in a bank account?

    21. No check figures

22. **Cash Flow Forecasts** (LO 1)

    The owner of Jim's Bike Shop has applied for a loan from a local bank to finance a planned expansion of his repair shop. The bank has requested financial statements for the business for the past three years.

    Required:

    1. Describe how the bank might use recent financial statements of Jim's Bike Shop to predict whether the business will generate sufficient future cash flows to repay a loan if granted.
    2. Since many external decision makers are interested in future cash-flow data, why don't companies include a cash-flow forecast in their annual financial reports?

    22. No check figures

23. **Cash Over and Short** (LO 2)

    At the end of the day, Count Company's summary cash register tape indicated total sales of $1,342, but the cash and cash items in the register totaled only $1,325.

    Required:

    1. Prepare the journal entry to record Count Company's sales for the day in question.
    2. What factors may explain the difference between the sales reflected by the summary cash register tape and the total cash in the register at day's end?

    23. Dr. Cash Short $17

24. **Petty Cash Fund** (LO 2)

    Party Favors Company found itself needing small amounts of cash on hand periodically to pay for minor expenses. As a result, the business's owner set up a petty cash fund at the beginning of January in the amount of $250. During January, the following amounts were paid from the fund. The expense account to which each item applies is indicated parenthetically.

Flowers for an employee in the hospital (Miscellaneous)	$15.00
Postage stamps (Postage)	50.00
Office supplies (Supplies)	80.00
Cost of taking customers to lunch (Selling)	60.00

24. Cr. Cash $205

Required:

Prepare the entry needed on January 31 to replenish the petty cash fund.

25. **Bank Reconciliation** (LO 5)

The following information is available for Lasher Company on June 30:

General ledger cash balance	$13,504.03
Deposit in transit	2,676.62
Outstanding checks	3,222.19

The following information was included in Lasher's monthly bank statement as of June 30:

Account balance	14,012.10
Monthly service charge	55.50
Interest earned	18.00

25. 1. Adj. Bal., $13,466.53
    2. Dr. Misc. Exp. $55.50
        Cr. Int. Rev. $18.00

Required:

1. Prepare a bank reconciliation for Lasher Company as of June 30.
2. Prepare any necessary journal entries in Lasher Company's accounting records related to this bank reconciliation.
3. Why should a business prepare a monthly bank reconciliation?

26. **Bank Reconciliation** (LO 5)

The following bank reconciliation for Dinero Enterprises is incomplete.

Balance per bank statement, October 31	$15,577.66
Add: Deposits in transit	?
Less: Outstanding checks	2,200.05
Adjusted balance, October 31	?
Balance per general ledger, October 31	$ 9,769.36
Add: One-year note receivable collected	
for Dinero by the bank on October 24	5,400.00
Less: Service charge for October	?
Adjusted balance, October 31	$15,128.11

26. 1. Dep. in transit, $1,750.50
        Adj. Bal., $15,128.11
        Serv. Ch, $41.25
    2. Cr. N.R. $5,400
        Dr. Misc. Exp. $41.25

Required:

1. Complete the bank reconciliation.
2. Prepare any necessary journal entries related to Dinero's bank reconciliation.

27. **Journal Entries for Accounts and Notes Receivable** (LO 2)

Following are recent transactions and other events involving Rodman's Rainbow, a company that markets hair-care products.

June 1: A customer purchased $400 of merchandise on credit with terms of n/60.

June 5: Wrote off an uncollectible account receivable of $350.

June 7: Converted a customer account receivable of $1,000 to an interest-bearing, sixty-day note receivable with a stated interest rate of 10 percent.

June 14: Received maturity value of ninety-day, 10 percent note with a principal amount of $2,000.

June 15: Customer purchased $1,200 of merchandise, signing a thirty-day, 10 percent promissory note in payment for the merchandise.

June 17: Customer who purchased merchandise on June 1 returned $60 of that merchandise because it was defective.

June 22: Discounted the note receivable acquired on June 7 at a local bank at a discount rate of 12 percent.

June 29: Received payment in full from customer whose account balance had been written off on June 5.

June 30: Received amount due from customer who purchased merchandise on June 1.

Required:

1. Prepare journal entries to record each of these transactions or events.
2. Prepare the appropriate adjusting entry as of June 30 for the note receivable acquired by Rodman's Rainbow on June 15.

28. **Aging Method of Estimating Uncollectible Accounts Expense** (LO 6)

Payne Company has a $250,000 balance in Accounts Receivable at year-end. Payne uses the aging method to determine the proper year-end balance of its Allowance for Doubtful Accounts. Following is a year-end aging schedule for Payne's accounts receivable.

AGING CATEGORY	AMOUNT	PERCENTAGE ESTIMATED TO BE UNCOLLECTIBLE
1–30 days (current)	$175,000	1
31–60 days	50,000	2
61–90 days	20,000	10
More than 90 days	5,000	25

Required:

1. If Payne's Allowance for Doubtful Accounts had a credit balance of $1,500 at year-end before the posting of any adjusting entries, prepare the appropriate year-end adjusting entry to record uncollectible accounts expense for this company.
2. Now assume that Payne's Allowance for Doubtful Accounts had a debit balance of $200 at year-end before the posting of adjusting entries. Prepare the appropriate year-end adjusting entry to record uncollectible accounts expense under this assumption.

29. **Subsequent Collection of Written-Off Accounts Receivable** (LO 2)

Deadline Enterprises had a $10,000 credit balance in Allowance for Doubtful Accounts at the beginning of the year. During the year, Deadline wrote off $6,500 in accounts receivable. Near the end of the year, one of the customers whose account balance of $750 had been written off earlier in the year unexpectedly paid that balance in full.

Required:

1. Prepare a summary journal entry to record the accounts receivable written off by Deadline during the year.
2. Prepare the journal entries necessary to record the recovery of the previously written off account balance.
3. What was the balance of Allowance for Doubtful Accounts at year-end prior to the preparation and posting of any adjusting entries?
4. Deadline Enterprise's chief executive officer (CEO) has questioned the company's controller regarding the allowance method of accounting for uncollectible accounts. The CEO believes that it would be more efficient to simply

27. 1. 6/5 Dr. All Doubt. Ac. $350
         Cr. A.R. $350
     6/14 Dr. Cash $2,050
         Cr. N.R. $2,000
         Cr. Int. Rev. $50
     6/22 Dr. Cash $1,001.42
         Cr. N.R. $1,000.00
         Cr Int. Rev. $1.42
     6/29 Dr. A.R. $350
         Cr. All. Doubt. Ac. $350
         Dr. Cash $350
         Cr. A.R. $350
   2. Int. Rev. $5

28. 1. Dr. Uncol. Ac. Exp. $4,500
       Cr. All. Doubt. Ac. $4,500
   2. Dr. Uncol. Ac. Exp. $6,200
       Cr. All Doubt. Ac. $6,200

29. 1. Dr. All. Doubt. Ac. $6,500
       Cr. A.R. $6,500
   2. Dr. A.R. $750
       Cr. All. Doubt. Ac. $750
       Dr. Cash $750
       Cr. A R. $750
   3. All. Doubt. Ac. bal., $4,250 Cr.

write off individual receivables when it is determined that a customer will not pay. How should the controller respond to the CEO?

30. Credit Card Sales (LO 2)

Payton Place is a retail dress shop. This business makes most of its sales via credit cards. Following is a summary of July's total sales by credit card and the service fee each charges Payton Place.

	PLASTICCARD	BANCARD	BIGCARD
July credit card sales	$10,500	$22,000	$37,250
Service fee	3%	3%	5%

Required:

1. Record these July credit card sales in Payton Place's accounting records and the subsequent collections from each credit card company.
2. Given the higher fee charged by BigCard, what factors may account for Payton Place choosing to honor that card at its stores? More generally, why do retail stores honor credit cards? Doesn't allowing customers to pay for their purchases with credit cards effectively reduce a business's gross sales revenue? Explain.

31. Analyzing Accounts Receivable (LO 7)

Consider the following comparative information for two otherwise similar companies, A and B, for a recent year:

	COMPANY A	COMPANY B
Cash sales for the year	$ 20,000	$ 40,000
Net credit sales for the year	80,000	60,000
Total sales	$100,000	$100,000
Average accounts receivable for the year	$ 60,000	$ 30,000

Required:

1. Compute each company's accounts receivable turnover ratio and age of receivables.
2. Which of these companies is better managing its accounts receivable? Explain.

32. Establishing a Credit Policy (LO 4)

Recently, the owner of Erica's Electronics, Erica Lovell, decided to begin allowing her customers to purchase merchandise on credit. Customers who buy on credit will be given sixty days to pay for their purchases. Erica believes this new policy will increase her store's sales because her principal competitor in town has a strict cash-and-carry sales policy.

Required:

Write a brief memo to Erica describing some of the problems her business may experience as a result of the new credit policy. Include in your memo internal control issues that Erica will need to consider following the implementation of this policy.

33. Notes Receivable (LO 8, 9)

Consider the following two independent cases:

a. On January 15, Company X sells goods to Company Y accepting in payment a $5,000, ninety-day, 8 percent promissory note.
b. On February 5, Company P borrows $10,000 from Company Q by signing a sixty-day, 6 percent promissory note.

Margin notes (check figures):

30. 1. PlastiCard fee, $315
    BanCard fee, $660
    BigCard fee, $1,862.50

31. 1. A.R. turnover Co. A, 1.33
    A.R. turnover Co. B, 2.0
    Age of Rec. Co. A, 271
    Age of Rec. Co. B, 180

32. No check figures

Required:

1. For each case, identify the maker, payee, principal amount, term, maturity date, and maturity value.
2. Suppose that Company X discounts the note from Company Y on January 30 at a discount rate of 10 percent. Prepare the appropriate entry on Company X's books. Will an entry be necessary on Company Y's books? Why or why not?
3. Why might Company X choose to discount the note receivable from Company Y?

34. Converting Accounts Receivable to Notes Receivable (LO 9)

On March 18, Sellers Company sold goods to Byers Company on account (on credit) for $8,000 with terms of n/30. On April 17, Byers notified Sellers that it could not pay the amount due and offered to sign an $8,000, 120-day promissory note with a stated interest rate of 10 percent. Sellers agreed to convert the account receivable into a note receivable.

Required:

1. Prepare all journal entries necessary on Sellers' books on March 18, April 17, and the maturity date of the note, assuming Byers pays the full amount due on the maturity date.
2. Assume that the note is discounted on May 11 at a local bank at a discount rate of 15 percent. Prepare the appropriate entry in Sellers' accounting records.
3. Refer to Part 2. Suppose that Sellers Company prepares financial statements on June 30. How will the discounted note be reflected in those financial statements, if at all?

35. Notes Receivable and Year-End Interest Accrual (LO 9)

On December 16, 1997, East Exchange Company converted a customer's account receivable into a thirty-day, 9 percent note receivable. The principal amount of the note is $20,000. East Exchange's year-end is December 31.

Required:

1. Prepare the entries necessary in the accounting records of East Exchange on the following dates:
   a. December 16
   b. December 31
   c. The maturity date of the note assuming the maker pays the note in full on that date
2. How will East's financial statements be misstated in 1997 and 1998 if no adjusting entry related to this note is recorded on December 31, 1997?

PROBLEM SET A

36. Cash Management (LO 1)

Flower Company is a new company that will begin operations on June 1 with a $25,000 cash balance. All of the company's sales will be on a credit basis with terms of n/60. The company will not grant discounts for early payment. Flower Company expects to collect its credit sales (accounts receivable) as follows:

Month of sale	50%
First month following sale	30%
Second month following sale	15%
Uncollectible	5%

Margin notes:

33. 1a. Maturity value, $5,100
    1b. Maturity value, $10,100
    2. Proceeds, $4,993.75

34. 1. 8/17 Dr. Cash $8,266.67
            Cr. N.R. $8,000.00
            Cr. Int. Rev.
            $266.67
    2. Proceeds, $7,936

35. 1. 12/31 Dr. Int. Rec. $75
            Cr. Int. Rev. $75

36. 1. June Cash Collections,
$45,000
July Cash Collections,
$67,000
Aug. Cash Collections,
$87,500

Required:

1. If Flower Company forecasts sales of $90,000 in June, $80,000 in July, and $100,000 in August, what are its expected cash collections from credit sales for June, July, and August?
2. Identify reasons that a company might need to prepare a forecast of expected cash collections from credit sales.
3. Suppose that at the end of July, Flower Company projects that it will have a zero cash balance because it will have heavy advertising and other promotional expenses during June and July. What arrangements can the company begin making now to address this "problem"?

37. Credit Sales Policy and Internal Control (LO 4)

Katie O'Reilly owns Mowers-n-More, a large store that sells lawn mowers and related products. Katie has recently tightened the business's credit policy. A written application and a credit check must be completed before a customer is extended credit. Katie has placed Matt Kilroy, her top salesman, in charge of the new credit department. Matt will continue working in sales since his new responsibilities will require no more than ten hours per week.

Like the other members of the sales staff, Matt is compensated principally on a commission basis. Given Matt's new responsibilities, Katie has restructured Matt's compensation. Matt will receive the normal 15 percent commission on sales he makes plus an additional 3 percent commission on the sales of other members of the sales staff. This additional compensation is intended to make up for the commissions that Matt will lose as a result of the time he commits to his new responsibilities.

As Katie's accountant, you are glad to see that she has finally changed her credit policy. Previously, practically any customer who asked for credit was granted it "on the spot."

Required:

37. No check figures

1. Comment on how the new credit policy adopted by Katie O'Reilly will likely affect her business, both positively and negatively.
2. How will the new policy affect the business's internal controls, both positively and negatively?

38. Bank Reconciliation (LO 5)

Following is the bank statement received by Farquay Imports for the month of January.

DATE	TRANSACTION	AMOUNT	BALANCE
1/1	Balance		$16,750.57
1/2	Deposit	$5,002.20	21,752.77
1/3	Check (#513)	(2,017.50)	19,735.27
	Check (#520)	(1,612.12)	18,123.15
1/6	Check (#521)	(506.73)	17,616.42
1/9	Check (#518)	(102.10)	17,514.32
	Check (#523)	(45.85)	17,468.47
	Deposit	7,310.19	24,778.66
1/11	Check (#522)	(6,214.70)	18,563.96
1/13	Deposit	4,440.13	23,004.09
	Check (#525)	(190.21)	22,813.88
1/16	Check (#524)	(12.00)	22,801.88
	Check (#526)	(63.17)	22,738.71
1/17	Check (#528)	(276.71)	22,462.00
1/18	Check (#519)	(712.93)	21,749.07
	Check Returned NSF	(1,500.00)	20,249.07

1/20	Deposit	2,612.52	22,861.59
	Note Collection	275.00	23,136.59
1/23	Check (#516)	(4,254.08)	18,882.51
	Check (#527)	(3,206.61)	15,675.90
1/25	Check (#517)	(408.04)	15,267.86
	Deposit	3,667.75	18,935.61
1/27	Check (#530)	(881.00)	18,054.61
	Check (#532)	(65.18)	17,989.43
1/31	Check (#533)	(1,129.33)	16,860.10
	Service Charge	(22.50)	16,837.60
	Interest Earned	72.15	16,909.75

Listed next is additional information regarding Farquay's cash transactions during January and its month-end general ledger cash balance.

a. Outstanding checks as of January 31:

#514	$ 754.27
#515	512.12
#529	400.00
#531	2,361.48
#534	1,052.14

b. Check #523 was recorded by Farquay as a credit to Cash for $48.45 rather than $45.85, the correct amount (as cleared by the bank).
c. On January 31, there was a deposit in transit of $7,500.00.
d. The January 31 balance of the general ledger Cash account was $20,502.49.

Note: Farquay does not become aware of any reductions to its bank account balance for such items as service charges or additions to its bank account balance for such items as note receivable collections until it receives its monthly bank statement.

Required:

1. Prepare Farquay's bank reconciliation for January.
2. Prepare any necessary journal entries on Farquay's books as a result of the bank reconciliation.

38. 1. Adj. Bal., $19,329.74
    2. Cr. N.R. $275
       Cr. A.P. $2.60
       Cr. Int. Rev. $72.15
       Dr. A.R. $1,500
       Dr. Misc. Exp. $22.50

39. **Bank Reconciliation** (LO 5)

American Pillow Company is a firm struggling to develop a market for its principal product, duck feather pillows. The company is also struggling to maintain control over its cash accounting activities. Part of the problem is a new bookkeeper who cannot quite grasp how to prepare a monthly bank reconciliation. The following is the latest partially completed effort for the month of February:

Balance per bank statement on 2/28	$17,406.67
Balance per general ledger on 2/28	16,415.28
Difference	$ 991.39

The following note appeared beneath this computation: "These two amounts still don't balance—it's hopeless." Attached to this sheet of paper is another with the heading "Bank Reconciliation Problems." It contains the following scribbled notes and dollar amounts.

1. Checks that we wrote and the bank seems to have lost:

#488	$ 623.14
#529	476.50
#530	1,100.00

2. I deposited $780.75 at the bank myself at 3:50 P.M. on February 28, but the deposit isn't listed in the bank statement.
3. There is a $27.50 service charge listed in the bank statement this month.
4. What is this $400 item in the bank statement for an "NSF check"?

Required:

1. Given the information provided, complete the bank reconciliation for American Pillow Company for the month of February.
2. Prepare any journal entries needed as a result of this reconciliation.
3. Briefly describe the internal control objectives related to the preparation of a monthly bank reconciliation.

39. 1. Adj. Bal., $15,987.78
2. Dr. A.R. $400
Dr. Misc. Exp. $27.50

40. **Uncollectible Accounts Expense and Related Journal Entries** (LO 1, 6)
Following are the December 31, 1995, balances of Accounts Receivable and Allowance for Doubtful Accounts of Easton Hammer Corporation (EHC). These balances are prior to the preparation of any year-end adjusting entries.

Accounts Receivable	$3,200,000
Allowance for Doubtful Accounts (credit balance)	112,500

During the year, EHC wrote off several uncollectible accounts. Among these accounts and the dates they were written off are the following:

May 15	Jim Cantore, $1,425
July 6	Mike Bono, $930

Required:

40. 1. 5/15 Dr. All. Doubt. Ac.
$1,425
Cr. A.R. $1,425
11/1 Dr. A.R. $1,425
Cr. All. Doubt. Ac.
$1,425
Dr. Cash $1,425
Cr. A.R. $1,425
2. Dr. Uncol. Acc. Exp.
$250,500

1. On November 1, EHC unexpectedly received payment in full from Jim Cantore of his previously written off account balance. Prepare the journal entries to record the write-offs of the Cantore and Bono accounts and the recovery of Cantore's account balance.
2. Suppose an accountant for Easton performs an aging analysis of the company's accounts receivable at year-end. Based upon this analysis, the accountant estimates that EHC has $363,000 of uncollectible accounts receivable at year-end. Prepare the appropriate adjusting journal entry to record uncollectible accounts expense at year-end.
3. Suppose that the accountant was too conservative in his estimate. Instead of uncollectible accounts receivable of $363,000, the company actually has uncollectible accounts of $278,000. Indicate how the accountant's overestimate of year-end uncollectible accounts affected EHC's 1995 income statement and balance sheet. How may this overstatement have affected the decisions of third parties, such as bankers and investors, who relied on EHC's 1995 financial statements?
4. Would the assumed overstatement referred to in Part 2 have affected EHC's 1996 financial statements? If so, explain how.
5. Is it ever permissible to intentionally overstate expenses in a company's financial statements? Defend your answer.
6. What accounting concepts or principles does the overstatement of expenses violate?

41. **Liquidity Analysis** (LO 3)
Following are selected balance sheet data pertaining to Campbell Soup Company. The amounts reported are in millions and represent year-end figures for the indicated years.

	1994	1993
Cash and Cash Equivalents	$ 94	$ 63
Short-Term Investments	2	7
Accounts Receivable (Net)	578	646
Inventories	786	804
Property, Plant & Equipment (Net)	2,401	2,265
Current Liabilities	1,665	1,851
Long-Term Liabilities	1,338	1,343

Required:

1. Explain the significance of the quick ratio. How is that ratio used by decision makers when interpreting a company's financial statements?
2. Compute Campbell's quick ratio for both years. In which year is the company's liquidity position stronger, based only on this ratio?
3. If the average quick ratio in Campbell's industry is 1.25, how does Campbell's quick ratio compare with the industry norm?
4. Identify factors that could account for Campbell's quick ratio being significantly different from the industry norm.

41. 2. Quick Ratio 1994, 0.40
Quick Ratio 1993, 0.39

42. **Notes Receivable** (LO 9)

Nebulous Notes, a greeting card company specializing in offbeat greeting cards for offbeat occasions, often accepts short-term notes receivable from customers who are having difficulty paying their accounts receivable. Nebulous Notes typically discounts these notes at its local bank. A typical sequence of such transactions follows:

January 1: Sells on credit a large order of merchandise to a retailer for $10,000 with terms of n/30.

February 1: Accepts in exchange for the $10,000 account receivable a sixty-day, 8 percent promissory note. Immediately discounts the note at a local bank; the bank's discount rate is 10 percent.

Required:

1. Prepare the journal entries on the dates indicated to record these transactions of Nebulous Notes.
2. Assume that rather than discounting the note immediately, Nebulous Notes holds the note for fifteen days before discounting it at the bank. Prepare the entry necessary to record this discounting transaction.
3. The owner of this company is interested in how, if at all, the practice of discounting notes affects the company's profitability. Write a brief memo to the owner describing how this practice impacts the company's profitability. Use numerical examples in your memo if necessary. Comment in your memo on how the company's profitability may be affected if it refuses to do business with any customer that may be unable to pay its accounts receivable balance within the designated credit period of thirty days.

42. 1. 2/1 Proceeds, $9,964.44
2. Proceeds, $10,006.66

43. **Receivables: An International Perspective** (LO 1)

Suppose that you are an investor and that you want to diversify your portfolio by investing in a foreign company. KLM Royal Dutch Airlines is one foreign company that a broker has recommended as a strong "buy." Being a conservative investor, you want to obtain a second opinion. You happen to be in luck because one of your best friends is a Dutch exchange student who also happens to be an accounting major. In flipping through a recent annual report of KLM, you have noticed that the company has accounts receivable of 2,540 million Dutch guilders.

43. No check figures

Required:

1. Identify at least three questions that you would ask your friend regarding the Dutch accounting methods and financial disclosure rules for accounts receivable.
2. Suppose that another foreign company you have identified as a potential investment uses the direct write-off method of accounting for uncollectible accounts expense. How would this fact affect your comparison of that company's financial statements and those of a comparable U.S. company? Explain.

PROBLEM SET B

44. **Cash Management** (LO 1)

The owners of Adams & Hall Fine Furniture are planning their furniture store's grand opening for September 1. This fall, the owners plan to do extensive advertising of their store in the surrounding metropolitan area. They realize that a large percentage of new businesses fail in their first year and want to avoid adding to that percentage. One problem, though. The owners are unsure whether they have sufficient cash to finance their large-scale advertising program. Following is a schedule of their planned cash expenditures for advertising this fall:

September	$20,000
October	30,000
November	42,000
December	80,000

The owners hope that collections of accounts receivable (credit sales) in each month will be sufficient to pay for that month's advertising expenditures. Following are the store's expected credit sales for September through December. All of the store's sales will be on credit and customers will be granted terms of n/60.

September	$70,000
October	40,000
November	50,000
December	100,000

The owners expect that each month's credit sales will be collected as follows: 30 percent in the month of sale and 65 percent in the following month. Uncollectible accounts are expected to average 5 percent.

Required:

44. 1. Sep. Cash Collections, $21,000
Oct. Cash Collections, $57,500
Nov. Cash Collections, $41,000
Dec. Cash Collections $62,500

1. Determine the store's cash collections from accounts receivable for each month September through December.
2. Compare the projected cash collections with each month's planned advertising expenditures. In which months, if any, will cash collections from accounts receivable be less than the projected advertising expenditures?
3. Why is effective cash management and planning so important for businesses? How can accountants help business owners and executives properly manage an entity's cash resources?

45. **Credit Sales Policy and Internal Control** (LO 4)

Big Mike's Florist Shop has recently begun allowing his customers to purchase flowers and other merchandise on credit. Customers are not allowed to charge purchases on a credit card but are granted credit terms of n/30 by the florist shop. This policy has helped Mike, the business's owner, increase his sales while at the same time avoiding the charges that credit card companies would deduct from credit card sales.

Mike files each credit sales ticket by date sold. Once per week, he mails a bill to each customer who has an outstanding receivable. Once per month, Mike goes through the file of receivables and removes the sales tickets that have been paid. Already, Mike is encountering problems with his new credit policy and his method of keeping track of his receivables. He now has more than two hundred receivables in his file. In the past few weeks, several irate customers have called and complained that although they have paid for their credit purchase, they are still receiving a weekly bill in the mail. Additionally, Mike has several "deadbeat" customers who have not paid for credit purchases made more than two months ago.

Required:

Help out Mike. Write him a memo in which you suggest a few basic internal control procedures to improve his credit-granting function and his accounting for unpaid credit sales (accounts receivable).

45. No check figures

46. **Bank Reconciliation** (LO 5)

Following is information needed to prepare the monthly bank reconciliation for Swank & Hill, Associates, a law firm, for the month of October.

General ledger balance, October 31	$39,808.61
Bank statement balance, October 31	42,102.85
Outstanding checks, October 31	616.45
Deposits in transit, October 31	1,200.00
NSF check charged against bank balance on October 29	194.71
Bank service charge for October	37.50
Interest earned during October, credited to bank account balance on October 31	110.00
Note receivable collected by bank for Swank & Hill on October 30	3,000.00

Required:

1. Prepare a bank reconciliation for Swank & Hill for the month of October.
2. Prepare any necessary journal entries in Swank & Hill's accounting records as a result of this bank reconciliation.

46. 1. Adj. Bal., $42,686.40
   2. Cr. N.R. $3,000
       Cr. Int. Rev. $110
       Dr. A.R. $194.71
       Dr. Misc. Exp. $37.50

47. **Bank Reconciliation** (LO 5)

Linne Company has an inexperienced bookkeeper attempting to prepare the firm's December 31 bank reconciliation. Following is his effort to date:

Balance per books	$14,218.94
Add: Bank service charge	47.12
Add: Checks outstanding	2,491.29
Subtract: Deposit in transit	(3,506.38)
Subtract: Note receivable collected by the bank for Linne	(1,100.00)
NTB (needed to balance)	2,105.76
Balance per bank statement	$14,256.73

Required:

1. Prepare a proper bank reconciliation for Linne Company as of December 31.
2. Prepare any journal entries needed following the completion of the bank reconciliation.
3. Briefly describe the internal control objectives related to the preparation of a monthly bank reconciliation.

48. Uncollectible Accounts Expense (LO 1, 6)

Before the preparation of year-end adjusting entries, Chewels Company had a $70,500 debit balance in Accounts Receivable and a $4,250 credit balance in Allowance for Doubtful Accounts. Following is a year-end aging analysis of Chewels' accounts receivable.

AGE OF RECEIVABLES	AMOUNT	PERCENTAGE ESTIMATED TO BE UNCOLLECTIBLE
1–30 days (current)	$40,500	4
31–60 days	20,000	6
61–90 days	10,000	12
Over 90 days	5,000	20

Required:

1. Prepare the year-end adjusting entry to record uncollectible accounts expense for Chewels given the results of the company's aging analysis of its accounts receivable.
2. Suppose that Chewels wrote off the following two accounts during the year in question: Jeanetta Jones, $1,250 (April 3); Vivian Brown, $3,100 (November 28). Prepare the entries to write off these accounts. Also prepare the necessary entry, or entries, to record the unexpected payment by Jeanetta Jones on December 7 of her previously written-off account balance.
3. What accounting concept or concepts dictate that Chewels use the allowance method of accounting for uncollectible accounts expense?
4. Why is the direct write-off method not considered a generally accepted accounting principle? Under what circumstances can businesses use the direct write-off method?

49. Liquidity Analysis (LO 3)

Melville Corporation is a retail company that sells merchandise ranging from prescription drugs to toys to household furnishings. The following selected financial information (in thousands) was included in Melville's 1993 balance sheet:

	1993	1992
Cash and Cash Equivalents	$ 80,971	$ 145,138
Accounts Receivable (Net)	243,998	245,204
Inventories	1,858,772	1,806,550
Prepaid Expenses	214,649	244,780
Total Current Assets	$2,398,390	$2,441,672
Total Assets	$4,272,400	$4,214,062
Total Current Liabilities	$1,328,097	$1,380,919

Required:

1. Compute Melville's quick ratio for both 1992 and 1993. Did the company's liquidity improve or weaken between the end of 1992 and the end of 1993?
2. A common rule of thumb is that a company should maintain a quick ratio of 1.0. How do Melville's quick ratios in 1992 and 1993 compare with this

benchmark? Instead of this general rule of thumb, identify a better measure to evaluate a company's quick ratio in any given year.

3. Notice that Melville's cash and cash equivalents declined by more than $64 million between the end of 1992 and the end of 1993. Which financial statement of Melville's would be particularly helpful in identifying the reasons for this large drop in the company's cash resources over this twelve-month period?

50. Notes Receivable (LO 9)

Scales Company is a keyboard and piano shop that accepts short-term notes receivable in payment for most of the merchandise sold to customers. When Scales is short of cash, it discounts some of its notes receivable at a local bank. Otherwise, it holds the notes to maturity. The following transactions are typical of those the company engages in during a given year:

March 8:   Sold a piano for $11,000 accepting a 120-day, 12 percent note in exchange.

April 1:   Sold a piano for $7,500 accepting a 180-day, 10 percent note in exchange.

May 1:   Discounted the $7,500 note at a local bank at a discount rate of 14 percent.

June 30:   Prepared an adjusting entry to recognize interest revenue earned on the $11,000 note for the period March 8 through June 30.

July 6:   Collected the $11,000 note plus interest.

October 3:   Was notified by bank that the maker of the $7,500 note had paid the bank the maturity value of the note.

Required:

1. Prepare the entries required in Scales' accounting records to reflect the transactions and events listed.

2. Scales prepared a set of financial statements on June 30. What disclosure was required in the company's financial statement footnotes regarding its notes receivable transactions during the year? What is the purpose of this disclosure?

50. 1. 5/1 Proceeds, $7,415.62
6/30 Cr. Int. Rev. $418

51. Receivables: An International Perspective (LO 1)

In 1994, Sotheby's Holdings, Inc., celebrated its 250th anniversary. The London-based Sotheby's is the leading auction house worldwide. Each year, Sotheby's auctions millions of dollars of art, jewelry, rare books, and related items. The largest line item in Sotheby's periodic balance sheets is a current asset, Accounts and Notes Receivable. Each year, this line item accounts for approximately one-half of Sotheby's total assets. For reporting purposes, Sotheby's segregates its current receivables into the following three items: Auction Operations, Finance Operations, and Other.

Following are selected disclosures regarding Sotheby's current receivables that were included in the financial statement footnotes of a recent annual report. Sotheby's financial data in this annual report were denominated in U.S. dollars.

Auction receivables included $5.3 million and $1.8 million at December 31, 1993 and 1992, respectively, relating to the purchase of art objects at auction by employees, officers, directors and other related parties.

In certain situations, when the purchaser takes possession of the property [following a Sotheby's auction] before payment is made, the Company is liable to the seller for the net sale proceeds. As of December 31, 1993 and 1992, accounts and notes receivable included approximately $80.1 million and $41.4 million, respectively, of such sales.

The average interest rates charged on finance receivables were 6.8% and 9.2% at December 31, 1993 and 1992, respectively.

Presently, credit losses on the client loan portfolio [included in finance receivables] are accounted for through the allowance for doubtful accounts, which is adequate to absorb losses inherent in this portfolio.

Required:

51. No check figures

For each disclosure listed, indicate why external decision makers, such as investors and bankers, would need the information provided.

CASES

52. Analyzing Receivables

Hee-Kyung Boutiques, Inc., (HBI) began selling Asian sportswear in the southwestern United States approximately five years ago. The management of HBI wishes to obtain a better understanding of the quality of its accounts receivable before expanding its operations throughout this geographic area. Selected financial information for the chain for the past three years follows.

	YEAR 5	YEAR 4	YEAR 3
Net Credit Sales	$10,500,000	$9,000,000	$8,000,000
Year-End Accounts Receivable, Net	6,000,000	4,000,000	3,000,000

(Note: HBI's net accounts receivable at the beginning of Year 3 was $2,000,000.)

HBI is pleased with its growth in sales but experienced some cash-flow problems (shortages) in Year 5 and is investigating to determine why. Some additional information is available to you:

1. When HBI began operations five years ago, it chose not to accept credit cards of any kind, preferring to bill and collect its own receivables. Initially, the company granted credit terms of n/60 to its customers. Late in Year 3, the company switched to credit terms of n/120 to increase its sales.
2. HBI's uncollectible accounts expense was approximately 2 percent of credit sales during the first two years of its existence. However, uncollectible accounts expense as a percentage of credit sales increased to 4 percent in Year 3, 5 percent in Year 4, and 6 percent in Year 5.
3. If HBI begins accepting credit cards, its service fees from the credit card companies will average 4 percent.

Required:

1. Compute HBI's accounts receivable turnover ratio and its age of receivables for Years 3 through 5. Given these data, analyze the quality of HBI's receivables over this period. As suggested in the text, the "quality" of accounts receivable is primarily a function of their collectibility.
2. Write a memo to HBI's president that comments on how the company's credit policy may have contributed to its cash-flow problems in Year 5. Include in your memo recommendations on how the company might resolve the cash-flow problems related to its receivables collections.

53. Understanding the Allowance for Doubtful Accounts

In the early 1980s, IFG Leasing was one of many subsidiaries of IFG, Inc., a Minneapolis-based corporation. IFG Leasing was engaged in the "small ticket" leasing industry. Small ticket leasing companies generally lease assets such as farm equipment, office furniture, and construction equipment to individuals and small businesses. Typically, the cost of the assets leased by small ticket leasing companies range from $2,000 to $13,000. In the late 1970s and early 1980s, IFG Leasing experienced a huge increase in revenues. This period of time was characterized by steadily increasing interest rates—interest rates that eventually "topped out" at more than 20 percent in the early 1980s. Since many individuals and businesses could not "qualify" for loans from banks and other financial institutions during this period, they turned to small ticket leasing companies to acquire assets they needed.

As IFG Leasing's volume of business increased dramatically in the early 1980s, it began experiencing a high rate of default on its lease receivables. By early 1982, more than 20 percent of the company's receivables were past-due. Since lease receivables accounted for more than 95 percent of the company's total assets, this situation posed a major problem for the firm. To purchase new assets for their leasing business, IFG Leasing's executives regularly borrowed funds from local banks. Because the company's executives were worried that their loan applications might be rejected, they began understating the percentage of their lease receivables that were past-due in IFG Leasing's quarterly and annual financial statements. For example, in September 1982, IFG Leasing's accounting records indicated that the company had nearly $90 million of past-due lease receivables. However, the company's financial statement footnotes reported that past-due receivables totaled less than $34 million.

Allegedly, the chief executive of IFG Leasing threatened to fire any employee who reported the actual amount of the company's past-due receivables to anyone outside the company. Nevertheless, in late 1982, the chief accounting officer of IFG Leasing contacted an executive of IFG, Inc., and disclosed the actual dollar amount of the past-due receivables.

[Note: The facts of this case were drawn from the following source: Michael C. Knapp, "IFG Leasing," in *Contemporary Auditing: Issues and Cases*, 2d ed. (Minneapolis/St. Paul: West Publishing Co., 1996.)]

Required:

1. Refer to the definition of the internal control element "control environment" that was discussed in Chapter 3. Explain why or how the control environment was flawed at IFG Leasing.

2. At one point, an executive of IFG Leasing maintained that the company's independent audit firm had the responsibility for ensuring that the company's past-due receivables were properly accounted for and disclosed in the company's financial statements. Is this true? If not, who has the final responsibility for ensuring that a company's financial statements are fairly presented? What is the role of an independent audit firm relative to an audit client's financial statements?

3. The chief accounting officer of IFG Leasing eventually ignored his superior's orders and disclosed the magnitude of the company's past-due receivables to a top executive of IFG, Inc. Identify the general circumstances under which an accountant, or other company employee, should intentionally ignore a superior's orders.

54. Imprecise Accounting

Many students are attracted to accounting by its apparent precision: debits and credits must be equal in each journal entry, the balance sheet balances, the financial statements must "tie" together, and so on. On the first day of an introductory financial accounting course, one student was startled to hear her instructor stress how imprecise accounting can be.

Required:

Using the allowance for doubtful accounts as an example, write a short memo to this new accounting student, explaining the imprecision that exists in that financial statement item and the related item, uncollectible accounts expense. Then provide other examples of imprecision in accounting that you have discovered so far in this course.

PROJECTS

55. Controls Over Cash

You are an accounting major at a local college and are currently working as an accounting intern at a large store in a shopping center. Some of your activities involve internal control evaluations. Recently, your departmental manager asked you to review sales and cash receipts transactions and related accounting entries since the beginning of the year, a time period of approximately six months. For each sales transaction, a salesclerk enters the amount of the sale in a sales terminal, the type (cash, check, or credit card) and amount of payment made by the customer, and any change given to the customer. To date, you have reviewed computer printouts for each sales terminal in your department, related journal entries, and deposit slips for each day's sales.

After reviewing several months of the department's cash and sales records, you begin to notice a pattern for one particular sales terminal. On weekday evenings, during the 5:00 P.M. to 9:00 P.M. shift, you discover that there is frequently a $5 to $10 difference between the total cash balance reported by the sales terminal and the total cash and cash items (checks and credit card sales slips) included in the sales terminal cash till at the end of the shift. Occasionally there are cash overages for this terminal, but very rarely. Over the past six months, the collective cash shortage for this sales terminal is more than $500. The other four sales terminals also have a collective cash shortage over the same time period, but the largest of these is less than $50.

There is no indication that this particular sales terminal is malfunctioning. Each sales terminal is checked regularly with any needed maintenance performed immediately. You have discovered that this terminal is operated by the same employee on the work shifts when the cash shortages regularly occur.

This employee was hired shortly after the beginning of the year. A quick check of last year's data for this sales terminal indicates no pattern similar to the one you have found.

Required:

1. Meet with your project group and discuss this scenario, focusing specifically on internal control issues. Your group should prepare a written report addressed to the departmental manager in this scenario. In this report, include a list of specific internal control procedures that could be adopted to strengthen the degree of internal control over this department's cash processing activities.
2. Also include in your report a recommendation to the departmental manager regarding how he or she should deal with the frequent cash shortages occurring in one of the department's sales terminals.

56. Allowance for Doubtful Accounts

Select two public companies in the same industry that regularly have a large amount of accounts receivable reported in their annual balance sheets.

Required:

1. For each of the past five years, obtain the following data items for these companies from their annual reports.
   a. Total accounts receivable
   b. Allowance for doubtful accounts*
   c. Total current assets
   d. Total assets
   e. Net sales
2. For the companies you have selected, compute the following items for each of the five years that you obtained the relevant data:
   a. Allowance for doubtful accounts/total accounts receivable
   b. Net accounts receivable/total current assets
   c. Net accounts receivable/total assets
   d. Net accounts receivable/net sales
3. Write a brief report containing the following:
   a. A brief description of each company's principal line or lines of business.
   b. The data you computed in Part 2.
   c. Your analysis of any trends apparent in the data computed in Part 2; to interpret these trends, you will likely need to review narrative information included in the companies' annual reports.

57. Credit Policies

As a group, meet and identify three local businesses that extend credit to their customers. Make sure that the three businesses are quite different. If possible, include one service firm, one merchandiser, and one manufacturing firm in the businesses you select. Each business should be contacted by a member of the group—one member per business. The group member should ask to visit with the credit manager of the business or the individual, such as the business owner, responsible for making credit-related decisions. Obtain from this individual information allowing your group to document the objective and key features of the business's credit policy. For example, does the business accept credit cards? If so, which ones? Does the business manage its own credit function? If so, what credit terms are granted to customers, and what type of credit application, if any, must be completed? (Obtain a copy of this application, if possible.) Among other questions your group may pose to the appropriate individual are the following: How often is the business's credit policy reevaluated? Has the credit policy been changed recently? If so, how and why? What percentage of the business's sales are on credit?

Required:

A written report should be prepared by the group documenting the objective and key features of the credit policies of the three selected businesses. This report should begin with a brief overview of the nature of each business. The final section of this report should be an analysis of factors that may account for the different credit policies established by the three businesses.

---

*Some companies report a "net" accounts receivable figure in their balance sheets. The allowance for doubtful accounts for these companies is often reported in their financial statement footnotes. To determine total accounts receivable for such a company, add the allowance for doubtful accounts to the net accounts receivable figure reported in the company's balance sheet.

8

INVENTORY

LEARNING OBJECTIVES

After studying this chapter, you should be able to do the following:

1. Identify and define the key accounting terms related to inventory and inventory transactions

2. Discuss the impact that inventory errors have on a business's financial statements

3. Define the key information needs of decision makers regarding inventory

4. Apply the four major inventory costing methods

5. Discuss the financial statement and taxation implications of the different inventory costing methods

6. Apply the lower-of-cost-or-market rule to inventory

7. Estimate period-ending inventories using the gross profit method

8. Account for inventory in a perpetual inventory system

9. Compute the inventory turnover ratio and the age of inventory

10. Define key internal control procedures for inventory

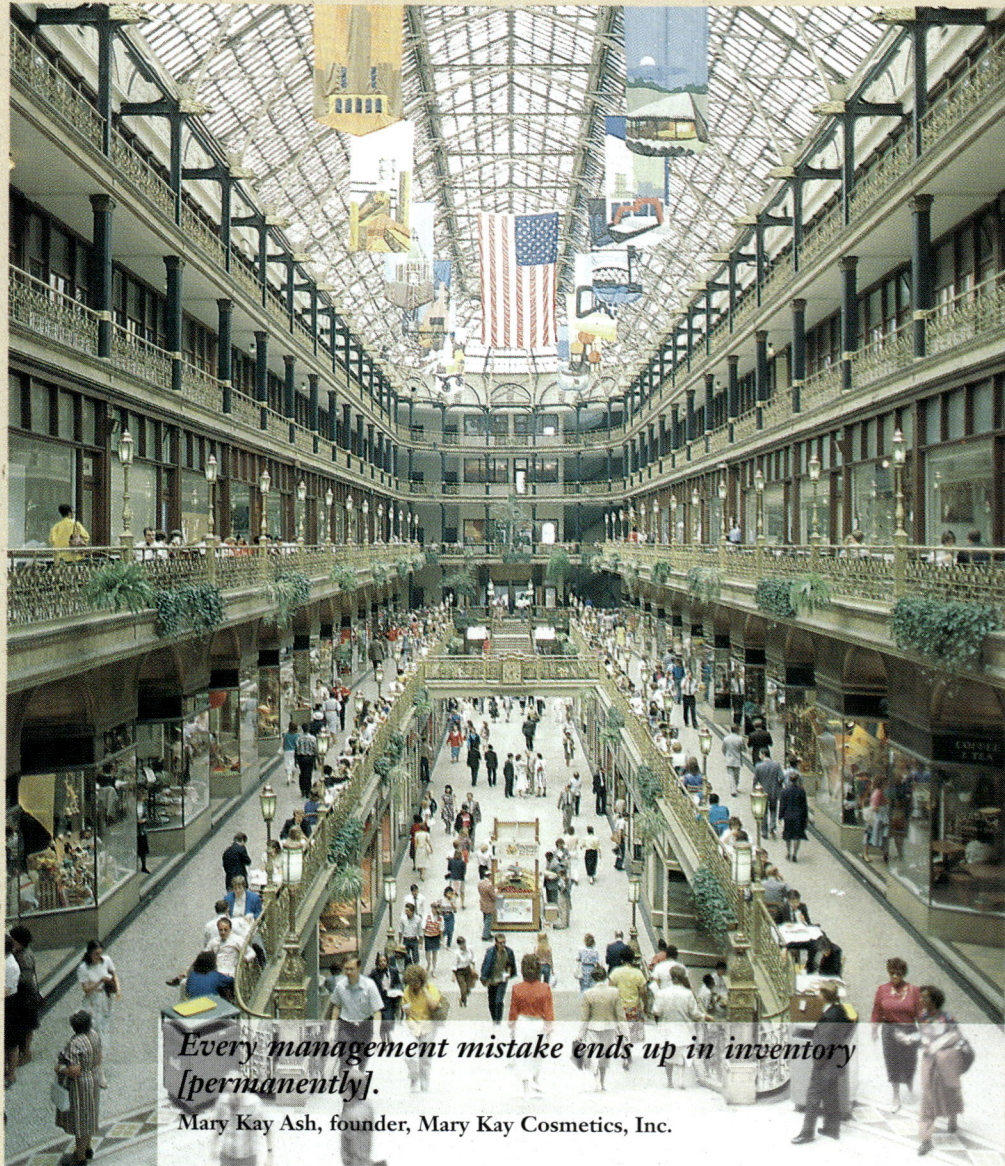

Every management mistake ends up in inventory [permanently].

Mary Kay Ash, founder, Mary Kay Cosmetics, Inc.

Managing Inventory: Cabbage Patch Kids, Hot Wheels, and the Corporate Accountant

In the early 1980s, first Mattel and then Fisher-Price were approached by an individual who wanted the toy manufacturers to market a line of "Little People" dolls he had developed. Both companies quickly rejected the proposal. Marketing experts within the two firms perceived the pudgy dolls as unattractive and unlikely to appeal to young children. The following year, Coleco Industries, another toy manufacturer, decided to take a chance on the dolls, which had been renamed by this time. During the fall of 1983, the dolls were placed on the market. Over the next several months, Cabbage Patch Kids took the country by storm.

The public's demand for the adoptable dolls greatly surpassed Coleco's ability to produce them. The result was chronic shortages at toy stores across the nation. Yelling and shoving matches between irate customers fighting over the scarce dolls were common, as were underground black markets in the dolls. Finally, Coleco was forced to suspend its advertising campaign for Cabbage Patch Kids to quell the nationwide furor. Despite the shortage, Coleco sold more than 2.5 million Cabbage Patch Kids in the fall of 1983, generating total revenues of nearly $50 million.

In the early 1970s, Mattel faced a much different crisis for one of its toys that had previously been a best-seller. In 1972, young boys' interest in Mattel's Hot Wheels plummeted unexpectedly, leaving the company with a large inventory of the toy. Mattel eventually sold nearly 6 million Hot Wheels en masse to a large oil company, which used them as a promotional item. In the process, Mattel was nailed with a whopping loss of $11 million.

Accountants play a key role in monitoring inventory levels and assisting management in making appropriate inventory-related decisions. For a hot-selling item such as Coleco's Cabbage Patch Kids, accountants can assist management by preparing weekly or daily sales reports for each sales region. The limited inventory of such a product can then be diverted to those regions where the demand is highest and inventory is lowest.

Monitoring sales and inventory levels for slow-moving items is also an important responsibility of accountants. In the early 1970s, Mattel's accounting department was responsible for tracking the weekly sales data for each of the company's toys. Based upon these data, the company's accountants were to write down the inventory values of those products that were selling poorly. For whatever reason, Mattel's accountants did not write down the company's inventory of Hot Wheels. Instead, those toys remained on the company's books at values well in excess of the prices for which they could be sold, a clear violation of generally accepted accounting principles. When this and other accounting oversights were disclosed, Mattel's management was sued by angry stockholders. Eventually, Mattel and its executives were required to pay more than $30 million to settle the lawsuits stemming from the company's sloppy accounting practices.

This chapter explores accounting for inventory. As the opening vignette suggests, a key responsibility of accountants is to supply business executives with the data they need to make proper and timely decisions regarding inventory. A company's accountants also have a responsibility to communicate information regarding this important asset to external decision makers. Investors, creditors, and other third-party decision makers realize that inventory greatly influences a company's operating results and financial condition. As a result, these decision makers closely monitor financial disclosures for inventory.

INVENTORY: AN INTRODUCTION

■ **LEARNING OBJECTIVE 1**
Identify and define the key accounting terms related to inventory and inventory transactions

Chapter 6 acquainted you briefly with merchandise inventory and related accounting decisions. This initial section of Chapter 8 provides you with a more in-depth introduction to this asset. We begin by exploring key terms and expressions that accountants use when referring to inventory.

Inventory Terms

Recall from Chapter 2 that inventories consist of goods businesses intend to sell to their customers, or raw materials or in-process items that will be converted into saleable goods or merchandise. For balance sheet purposes, inventory is classified as a current asset. Like many accounting terms, "inventory" has several different meanings. For example, it is common for accountants and nonaccountants to refer to their company's inventory of equipment or its supplies inventory. In these contexts, the term "inventory" does not refer to saleable goods but is being used in a more general way to refer to a group of assets. Accountants also frequently use the phrase "take inventory," as in, "We plan to take inventory on September 30." The phrase "take inventory" or "take a physical inventory" typically refers to an intention to count a company's saleable goods on a specific date. On the other hand, you can also "take inventory" of supplies, equipment, investments, or any other type of asset.

"Inventory cost flow" is another common expression used by accountants. Exhibit 8.1 depicts the inventory cost flow for a merchandising company. A merchandiser begins an accounting period with a certain amount of inventory and then makes additional purchases throughout the period. Taken together, the cost of beginning inventory and merchandise purchases represent cost of goods available for sale for an accounting period. (As Exhibit 8.1 indicates, cost of goods available for sale also

---

■ **EXHIBIT 8.1**
Inventory Cost Flow for a Merchandising Company

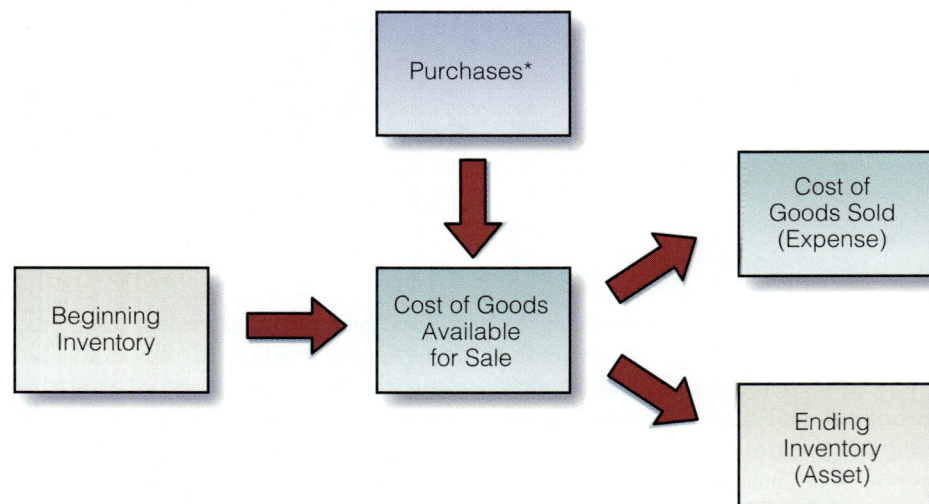

*Including delivery costs incurred to acquire merchandise (transportation in).

includes the delivery expenses incurred to acquire inventory. To simplify matters, in subsequent illustrations in this chapter we generally ignore this component of cost of goods available for sale.) The costs associated with merchandise that is sold during an accounting period flow out of cost of goods available for sale and into cost of goods sold. Cost of goods sold is the largest expense item of most merchandising companies. At the end of a period, the costs attached to unsold merchandise are designated as ending inventory and included as a current asset on a merchandiser's balance sheet. This cost flow cycle is repeated each accounting period.

The flow of inventory costs through the accounting records of a manufacturing company is more complex than for a merchandising firm. One factor complicating a manufacturer's inventory cost flow is the existence of multiple types of inventory. Merchandisers typically have only one type of inventory—the goods they sell to their customers. Manufacturers generally have three types of inventory: raw materials, in-process or work-in-process inventory, and finished goods. This chapter focuses principally on accounting for the inventory of merchandising concerns. Subsequent accounting courses illustrate inventory accounting for manufacturing companies.

Recall from Chapter 6 that there are two general types of inventory systems that can be used by merchandising companies: the periodic and perpetual inventory systems. Also recall that inventory purchases and sales of merchandise are accounted for differently in these two systems. In a periodic inventory system, merchandise purchases and sales do *not* result in entries to the Inventory account. Instead, the beginning inventory of an accounting period remains on the books until the end of the period, when a new inventory value is determined via a physical inventory. In a perpetual inventory system, merchandise purchases result in increases (debits) to the Inventory account, while merchandise sales result in decreases (credits) to the Inventory account. Later in this chapter, the differences between these two inventory systems are discussed in more detail. Unless noted otherwise, the examples used in this chapter assume that a periodic inventory system is being employed.

Inventory: Size Equals Importance

One could easily argue that inventory is the most important asset of merchandising and manufacturing companies. These firms generate nearly all of their revenues from the sale of inventory: no inventory, no sales . . . no company. The large investment most companies have in inventory is another factor that accounts for the considerable attention decision makers focus on inventory. Inventory often accounts for more than one-half of a business's total assets.

Exhibit 8.2 documents the inventories of four companies as a percentage of their total assets and current assets. Notice that both Best Buy, a consumer electronics and home appliances retailer, and the Original Sixteen to One Mine, a gold mining company, have approximately 60 percent of their assets invested in inventory. You might expect a company such as Nippon Steel, a Japanese steelmaker, to have a large amount of inventory. In terms of U.S. dollars, Nippon Steel reported nearly $7 billion of inventory in a recent balance sheet. However, Exhibit 8.2 documents the size of inventory *relative* to a company's total assets and current assets. Nippon Steel, like most steelmakers, has a huge investment in buildings and machinery that reduces, on a relative basis, the size of its inventory. Finally, Electronic Arts, which develops and markets Sega Genesis and Super Nintendo games, has a relatively small amount of inventory. Why? One reason is that the company has several "hot" products that are sold almost as quickly as they are produced.

The major problem faced by most retailers is selling their inventory. Occasionally, a very different problem faces retailers. For example, toy retailers often have difficulty obtaining a sufficient quantity of the "hottest" Sega and Nintendo games.

■ **EXHIBIT 8.2**

Inventory as a Percentage of Total Assets and Current Assets for Selected Companies

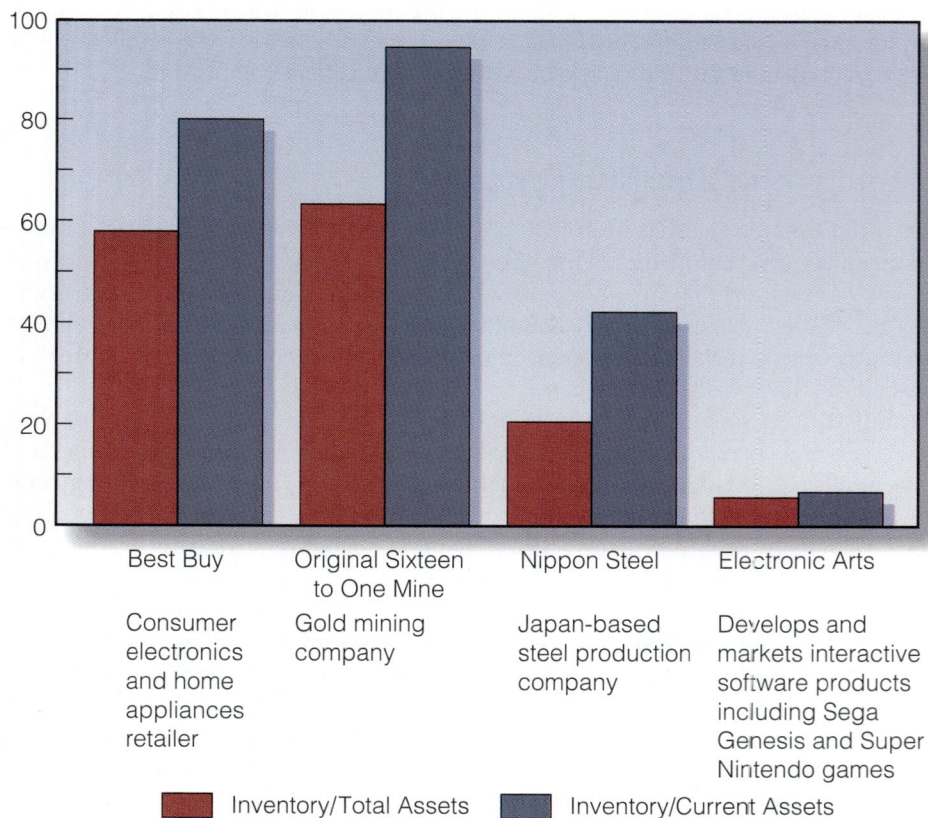

	Best Buy	Original Sixteen to One Mine	Nippon Steel	Electronic Arts
	Consumer electronics and home appliances retailer	Gold mining company	Japan-based steel production company	Develops and markets interactive software products including Sega Genesis and Super Nintendo games

■ Inventory/Total Assets   ■ Inventory/Current Assets

Inventory Errors and the Bottom Line

You will find very few accountants who discount the importance of inventory and inventory accounting decisions. Accountants realize that improper inventory accounting decisions can significantly distort a company's balance sheet and income statement. A misstatement of inventory often translates into a much larger error, on a percentage basis, in a company's net income. Compounding this problem is that most inventory errors affect a business's financial statements for two consecutive years.

For illustration purposes, assume that a company's ending inventory for 1995 was overstated by $10,000 due to a simple clerical error that went undetected. This overstatement would have affected the company's 1995 and 1996 financial statements. Why? Because the ending inventory of one accounting period is the beginning inventory of the following period. Shown in Exhibit 8.3 are side-by-side income statements for this company for 1995 and 1996. The first pair of income statements assumes that

■ **LEARNING OBJECTIVE 2**
Discuss the impact that inventory errors have on a business's financial statements

Focus on Ethics
A company's sales and operating income are down for the year. Management has decided to take whatever measures are necessary to ship all orders received in the last two weeks of the year before midnight on December 31 in an effort to improve operating results. Special arrangements have been made for employees to work overtime and for the freight company to pick up shipments on New Year's Eve. Is this policy ethical?

■ **EXHIBIT 8.3**
Income Statement Effects of an Inventory Error

	1995 INCOME STATEMENT (ASSUMING $10,000 OVERSTATEMENT OF ENDING INVENTORY)		1996 INCOME STATEMENT (ASSUMING $10,000 OVERSTATEMENT OF BEGINNING INVENTORY)	
Sales		$80,000		$86,000
Cost of Goods Sold:				
Beginning Inventory	$38,000		$44,000	
Net Purchases	52,000		54,000	
Cost of Goods Available for Sale	90,000		98,000	
Ending Inventory	44,000		38,000	
Cost of Goods Sold		46,000		60,000
Gross Profit		34,000		26,000
Operating Expenses		10,000		11,000
Operating Income		24,000		15,000
Income Taxes Expense (40%)		9,600		6,000
Net Income		$14,400		$ 9,000

	1995 INCOME STATEMENT (ASSUMING CORRECT ENDING INVENTORY)		1996 INCOME STATEMENT (ASSUMING CORRECT BEGINNING INVENTORY)	
Sales		$80,000		$86,000
Cost of Goods Sold:				
Beginning Inventory	$38,000		$34,000	
Net Purchases	52,000		54,000	
Cost of Goods Available for Sale	90,000		88,000	
Ending Inventory	34,000		38,000	
Cost of Goods Sold		56,000		50,000
Gross Profit		24,000		36,000
Operating Expenses		10,000		11,000
Operating Income		14,000		25,000
Income Taxes Expense (40%)		5,600		10,000
Net Income		$ 8,400		$15,000

Rocky Mount Accounting Horror

Near the end of 1985, top executives of Rocky Mount Undergarment Company (RMUC), a firm based in Rocky Mount, North Carolina, were unhappy with the company's operating results for the year. Shortly after year-end, these executives met with several accounting employees. The executives encouraged the accountants to overstate RMUC's ending inventory for 1985 so the company could report a larger profit for the year. The accountants were warned that if they did not cooperate, RMUC might eventually go out of business, resulting in "pink slips" for the company's employees.

After considerable goading, the accountants began falsifying RMUC's accounting records. In total, approximately $1 million of nonexistent inventory was entered in the company's accounting records. The resulting 9 percent overstatement of inventory translated into a 134 percent overstatement of RMUC's 1985 net income. Instead of its actual net income of $452,216 for 1985, RMUC reported a profit of $1,059,216. Following an investigation by the Securities and Exchange Commission (SEC), the individuals involved in the fraud were sanctioned by the federal agency.

SOURCE: Securities and Exchange Commission, *Accounting and Auditing Enforcement Release No. 212*, 9 January 1989.

the ending inventory for 1995 was overstated by $10,000. This error also resulted in beginning inventory of 1996 being overstated by the same amount. (Assume that at the end of 1996, the proper ending inventory value was determined.) The second pair of income statements reflects how the company's 1995 and 1996 income statements would have appeared had the inventory error not occurred.

Notice in Exhibit 8.3 that the assumed inventory error resulted in a significant misstatement of the company's net income for both 1995 and 1996. The company's net income for 1995 was actually $8,400 but was reported as $14,400, an overstatement of more than 70 percent. Likewise, the company's net income for 1996 was actually $15,000, but was reported as $9,000. Notice that the total profit for the two-year period was unaffected: with or without the inventory error the 1995–1996 earnings totaled $23,400. Nevertheless, the error could have affected the decisions of bankers, investors, and other parties who relied on the company's 1995 and 1996 financial statements.

Occasionally, inventory errors are not due to carelessness or oversight. Because misstating inventory is an effective way to manipulate reported profits, many fraudulent financial reporting cases involve intentionally misrepresented inventory balances. A classic example of a financial fraud involving inventory can be found in the Spotlight on Ethics vignette included in this section.

Discussion Question
Ask students what financial statements other than the income statement are affected by an inventory error.
Answer: The balance sheet and the statement of owners' equity.

INVENTORY: INFORMATION NEEDS OF DECISION MAKERS

Earnings per share is no doubt the financial statement item most closely followed by decision makers. However, when it comes to the balance sheet, inventory probably garners more attention than any other asset, at least for merchandising and manufacturing companies. In this section, key information needs of decision makers regarding this important asset are identified.

Inventory Balances

"How much?" is the first question that internal and external decision makers pose regarding a company's inventory. Instead of focusing strictly on the reported dollar amount of inventory for the most recent accounting period, decision makers also relate that figure to the comparable figure for one or more earlier periods. Decision makers also compare any significant change in inventory from one period to the next with changes in related financial statement items. An unusual or unanticipated change in inventory often provides definite clues regarding a company's future prospects.

AnnTaylor Stores Corporation markets women's apparel from more than two hundred retail outlets across the nation. In November 1994, the company reported that its net income for the third quarter of that year was nearly twice the net income reported for the comparable period in 1993.[1] Surprisingly, the company's quarterly financial report was followed by a sharp drop in the price of its common stock. Was Wall Street disappointed with the earnings report? Apparently not. AnnTaylor's reported earnings were in line with analysts' predictions. The problem was that investors zeroed in on the company's reported inventory in its balance sheet. There had been a disproportionately high increase in the company's inventory during the third quarter of 1994 compared with the increase in sales. Quite often, an unexpected buildup in inventory is a signal of approaching bad times for a company. Investors apparently concluded that AnnTaylor's new additions to its inventory were not particularly appealing to consumers, suggesting that the company's sales would be "soft" in the coming months.

Information Regarding Inventory Accounting Methods

Companies include in their financial statement footnotes a summary of the accounting methods applied to inventory and other major accounts. These disclosures are very important to financial statement users. As you will learn in a subsequent section of this chapter, there are a number of alternative inventory accounting methods that companies can employ. These different methods can significantly affect the reported dollar value of a firm's inventory. As suggested earlier, differences in the dollar value of beginning or ending inventory generally have a much greater impact, on a percentage basis, on net income. Differences in an inventory balance can also affect key financial ratios derived from balance sheet data. Consequently, it is critical that decision makers be aware of the specific inventory accounting methods that a company is using.

Included in Exhibit 8.4 are excerpts from recent annual reports that describe the inventory accounting methods of several companies. These descriptions will be more meaningful to you after you have studied the inventory accounting methods discussed later in this chapter.

---

1. "AnnTaylor Shares Fall on Inventory and Cost Report," *New York Times*, 9 November 1994, D5.

■ **EXHIBIT 8.4**

Inventory Disclosures Made by Selected Companies in Recent Annual Reports

Substantially all inventories are stated at cost determined by the last-in, first-out method, which is less than market.

Dixie Yarns

Inventories are valued at the lower of cost or market using the first-in, first-out method.

Duracell

Finished products, semi-finished products and raw materials are valued at cost which is determined by the last-in first-out method. Other inventories are valued at the lower of cost or market, cost being determined by (i) the job order cost method with respect to work in process, and (ii) the first-in first-out method or the periodic average method with respect to supplies.

Nippon Steel

Inventories are stated at the lower of cost or market using the first-in, first-out valuation method. Costs of the production and publication of products are included in inventory and charged to operations when sold or otherwise disposed. Costs of abandoned publishing projects and appropriate provisions for inventory obsolescence and decreases in market value are charged to operations on a current basis.

Thomas Nelson Publishers

"What If" Information

What may be most striking about the financial statement disclosures companies make regarding their inventories is the brief nature of those disclosures. For example, take the case of Duracell International Inc. Here is a company that regularly has several hundred million dollars of inventory reported on its balance sheet. However, in a recent year, the key narrative information the company included in its annual report regarding inventory was the brief description shown in Exhibit 8.4. Unfortunately, most companies include very limited information in their annual reports regarding this important asset.

Decision makers would clearly benefit from additional information related to inventory. Particularly helpful would be "what if" disclosures revealing how companies' reported inventory values would have been affected had they used another accounting method. In fact, the SEC requires public companies to disclose such data in certain circumstances. An example of a company that includes this type of data in its annual reports is FoxMeyer Corporation, the nation's third largest distributor of pharmaceutical products. FoxMeyer's principal inventory accounting method is LIFO (last-in, first-out), a method discussed later in this chapter. Critics of the LIFO method maintain that it often results in inventory values that are misstated. Although used by many companies, LIFO is not as popular as the FIFO (first-in, first-out) inventory accounting method. FoxMeyer discloses in its financial statement footnotes the dollar values that would have been assigned to its ending inventory under the FIFO method. With this information, decision makers can make more meaningful comparisons between FoxMeyer's financial data and that of competing companies that use the FIFO method. In 1994, FoxMeyer reported that its ending inventory of $571 million would have been approximately $635 million had it used the FIFO method.

ACCOUNTING FOR INVENTORY

In this section, accounting procedures for inventory are discussed and illustrated. We begin by examining how businesses determine their year-end inventory quantities. Next, the four most common inventory costing methods are illustrated. In some cases, companies must value their inventories at other than cost or must estimate their period-ending inventories. The required accounting procedures for these two situations are presented in this section. This section concludes with an overview of accounting issues related to the perpetual inventory system. Keep in mind that, unless indicated otherwise, the examples and illustrations in this chapter assume that a periodic inventory system is being used.

Determining Year-End Inventory Quantities

In a periodic inventory system, the first step in determining a year-end dollar value for inventory is to count the quantity of each inventory item. When a company has a large amount of inventory, taking a physical inventory is not a simple or inexpensive task. To increase the likelihood of obtaining an accurate count of inventory, many merchandisers close their retail outlets and suspend shipping operations while the counting is being done.

When taking a physical inventory, a company must consider merchandise that is in transit. Recall that in a merchandising transaction, the legal title to goods transfers between the buyer and seller at some specific point. Goods purchased with shipping terms of FOB shipping point are the property of the purchaser when the goods leave the seller's place of business. Goods purchased with shipping terms of FOB destination remain the property of the seller until they arrive at the purchaser's place of business. Consequently, a merchandiser must include in its year-end inventory in transit goods purchased from suppliers with shipping terms of FOB shipping point. In transit goods being shipped to customers with shipping terms of FOB destination must also be included in a merchandiser's year-end inventory.

Another issue that companies must consider when taking a physical inventory is the need to exclude those items that they do not own. Sounds obvious, right? Nevertheless, many merchandising companies have consigned inventory in their stores—that is, inventory owned by another party. For instance, supermarkets often have displays of hosiery products, greeting cards, and other goods that are owned by vendors. Albertson's, A&P, Safeway, and other supermarket chains receive a "cut," or commission, from the sale of these consigned goods. However, when taking a physical inventory, supermarkets must be careful to exclude consigned goods since they do not own those items. Including such items in inventory would overstate a supermarket's ending inventory, understate its cost of goods sold, and overstate its net income.

Inventory Costing Methods

Like most assets, cost is the primary valuation basis for inventory. After completing a physical inventory, a business must "cost out" its inventory quantities by multiplying them by the appropriate per unit prices. Assume that a small retail store has 620 units of a particular item at year end. If each of these units cost $7, the cost basis of this item's ending inventory would be $4,340 (620 × $7). Typically, inventory costing is not quite so simple. For example, assume that the store purchased this item several different times during the year at wholesale prices ranging from $5.43 to $8.77. Under this assumption, what purchase price or prices should the store use to determine

Real World

Because of its susceptibility to manipulation, inventory is considered a high-risk account by independent auditors. One procedure auditors use to test a client's inventory is to be present and perform independent, random test counts during a client's annual physical inventory.

Real World

Most companies ship their goods FOB shipping point and prepay the freight.

■ LEARNING OBJECTIVE 4
Apply the four major inventory costing methods

■ **EXHIBIT 8.5**

Inventory Data for Jude & Jody's for a Recent Fiscal Year

January 1	Beginning Inventory	35 pairs @ $14 each	=	$ 490
March 15	Purchase	30 pairs @ $16 each	=	480
June 30	Purchase	20 pairs @ $17 each	=	340
December 30	Purchase	25 pairs @ $18 each	=	450
Cost of Goods Available for Sale		110 pairs		$1,760
Total Sales January 1 through December 31		80 pairs @ $29 each	=	$2,320
Ending Inventory on December 31		30 pairs @ $? each	=	$?

the cost basis of the 620 units of this item in ending inventory? This section illustrates several methods that businesses can use to cost out ending inventories.

Assume that Jude & Jody's is a small retail shop in Amarillo, Texas. This business is so small that it sells only one item, 707 Jeans, a type of jeans popular among west Texas cowboys. At the end of a recent fiscal year, the store's two co-owners counted their inventory and determined that thirty pairs of 707 Jeans were on hand. Now the issue facing the co-owners is how to cost out these thirty pairs of 707 Jeans. Shown in Exhibit 8.5 are additional accounting data for Jude & Jody's.

Exhibit 8.5 documents that Jude & Jody's total cost of goods available for sale was $1,760 during the year in question. Now, refer to Exhibit 8.1. Notice that a business's total cost of goods available for sale for an accounting period must be "chopped up" into two amounts: cost of goods sold and ending inventory. By assigning a dollar value to ending inventory, the remaining portion of cost of goods available for sale is automatically allocated to cost of goods sold. This apportionment of cost of goods available for sale is dictated by the inventory costing method used by a business. The four most common inventory costing methods are the specific identification method, the weighted-average method, the FIFO (first-in, first-out) method, and the LIFO (last-in, first-out) method.

Teaching Note
Call attention to the fact that beginning inventory + net purchases = cost of goods available for sale.

specific identification method

SPECIFIC IDENTIFICATION METHOD   Under the **specific identification method,** items in ending inventory are costed out at their actual per unit cost. To use this method, a business must be able to determine the price paid for each unit of merchandise in ending inventory. Even companies that use a periodic inventory system may have access to such information. For instance, price tags often contain actual cost data concealed in a bar code or other encoded message. Assume that Jude & Jody's includes on the price tag of each pair of 707 Jeans, in an encoded format, the wholesale cost of the jeans. When the store's co-owners take a physical inventory at year-end, they record the quantity of unsold jeans and the per unit cost of each pair. Following are the per unit costs of the 707 Jeans in Jude & Jody's ending inventory multiplied by the appropriate quantities.

3 pairs @	$14	=	$ 42
2 pairs @	16	=	32
4 pairs @	17	=	68
21 pairs @	18	=	378
			$520

Given the previous data, Jude & Jody's ending inventory would be assigned a total cost of $520 under the specific identification method. Cost of goods sold would be $1,240, computed as follows:

Cost of Goods Available for Sale	$1,760
Cost Assigned to Ending Inventory	520
Cost of Goods Sold	$1,240

Discussion Question
Ask students for other examples of merchandisers that probably use the specific identification method.
Examples: Automobile dealerships, home appliance retailers, and computer retailers.

The specific identification method is ideal for many businesses that use a periodic inventory system, Jude & Jody's being an example. Businesses, such as jewelry stores, that sell high-priced merchandise use the specific identification method to enhance their control over inventory. However, for many businesses this method is impractical. For example, consider a grain mill that buys thousands of tons of corn each year, which are stored in silos. During a given year, the mill may purchase corn at dozens of different prices per bushel. Once corn that has been purchased at $2.47 per bushel is dumped into a silo, it is indistinguishable from corn purchased for $2.73 per bushel. So, it is impossible for such a business to apply the specific identification method of inventory costing.

Given the nature and size of Jude & Jody's business, its co-owners would probably use the specific identification method of costing ending inventory. Nevertheless, for comparison purposes, Jude & Jody's inventory data are used to illustrate the three remaining inventory costing methods.

WEIGHTED-AVERAGE METHOD Under the **weighted-average method** of inventory costing, an average per unit cost is computed for each type of inventory item that was available for sale during an accounting period. Then, these per unit costs are multiplied by the quantity of each inventory item that remains unsold at the end of the period to arrive at the total cost of ending inventory. For the year in question, Jude & Jody's had 110 pairs of 707 jeans available for sale at a total cost of $1,760. Given this information, the weighted-average cost of these jeans was $16 ($1,760/110 pairs). This weighted-average cost yields an ending inventory value of $480 and cost of goods sold for the year of $1,280 as follows:

Cost of Goods Available for Sale	$1,760
Ending Inventory: 30 pairs × $16	480
Cost of Goods Sold	$1,280

For financial reporting purposes, retailers must determine the cost of their year-end inventory. Many small retailers, such as the O.K. Boot Corral, use the specific identification inventory costing method.

weighted-average method

FIFO (FIRST-IN, FIRST-OUT) METHOD When your local grocer restocks the dairy display, he or she moves the "old" milk forward and places the "new" milk near the back of the dairy display. The grocer's intention is to create a "first-in, first-out" inventory flow. A first-in, first-out inventory flow minimizes the risk of any given carton remaining on the shelves until its expiration date. Granted, customers often thwart the grocer's strategy by reaching to the back of the dairy display to find a carton of new milk.

As you may have surmised, the **FIFO (first-in, first-out) method** of inventory costing assumes that the oldest merchandise is sold first. The per unit costs of the

FIFO (first-in, first-out) method

most recently acquired goods are used to establish the cost of ending inventory when the FIFO method is used. To illustrate this inventory costing method, refer again to Exhibit 8.5. Under the FIFO method, Jude & Jody's would assume that the thirty most recently purchased pairs of jeans remain unsold at the end of the year. Given this assumption, the twenty five pairs purchased on December 30 and five of the pairs purchased on June 30 would make up ending inventory. As shown in the following schedule, the resulting cost assigned to ending inventory would be $535. The remaining cost of goods available for sale of $1,225 would be allocated to cost of goods sold.

Cost of Goods Available for Sale		$1,760
Ending Inventory (30 pairs):		
From December 30 Purchase:	25 pairs @ $18 = $450	
From June 30 Purchase:	5 pairs @ $17 = 85	
Total Ending Inventory		535
Cost of Goods Sold		$1,225

This allocation of cost of goods available for sale between ending inventory and cost of goods sold can be quickly checked. The eighty pairs of jeans assumed sold under the FIFO method and their per unit costs are listed below. Notice that the total cost of goods sold in this schedule agrees with the figure in the previous schedule.

Cost of Goods Sold:		
From Beginning Inventory:	35 pairs @ $14 =	$ 490
From March 15 Purchase:	30 pairs @ $16 =	480
From June 30 Purchase:	15 pairs @ $17 =	255
Total		$1,225

LIFO (LAST-IN, FIRST-OUT) METHOD   The **LIFO (last-in, first-out) method** of inventory costing assumes that the most recently acquired goods are sold first, while the oldest units remain in inventory. In other words, the per unit costs of the earliest acquired goods are used to establish the cost basis of ending inventory. For Jude & Jody's, the earliest acquired goods shown in Exhibit 8.5 are the thirty-five pairs of jeans in beginning inventory. So, under the LIFO method, Jude & Jody's would assume that ending inventory consists of thirty of those thirty-five pairs in beginning inventory. Given this assumption, Jude & Jody's cost of goods available for sale would be segregated into ending inventory of $420 and cost of goods sold of $1,340.

Cost of Goods Available for Sale		$1,760
Ending Inventory (30 pairs):		
From Beginning Inventory:	30 pairs @ $14	420
Cost of Goods Sold		$1,340

This apportionment of cost of goods available for sale can be checked by computing costs of goods sold directly. The following schedule lists the jeans assumed sold under the LIFO method and their per unit costs. Notice that the total cost of goods sold in this schedule agrees with the figure just computed.

Cost of Goods Sold:		
From December 30 Purchase:	25 pairs @ $18 =	$ 450
From June 30 Purchase:	20 pairs @ $17 =	340
From March 15 Purchase:	30 pairs @ $16 =	480
From Beginning Inventory	5 pairs @ $14 =	70
Total		$1,340

You may have noticed that when the FIFO and LIFO methods were being described, the term "assume," or variations of it, was often used in these descriptions. In fact, the FIFO and LIFO methods are often referred to as "inventory cost flow assumptions." A business is allowed to use an inventory cost flow assumption that is at variance with the actual physical flow of its goods. For example, although a company sells goods in a first-in, first-out (FIFO) pattern, generally accepted accounting principles allow the firm to use the LIFO inventory costing method. A business whose inventory flows in a last-in, first-out (LIFO) pattern may elect to use the FIFO inventory costing method. Similarly, a merchandiser that can identify the actual per unit costs of the items in ending inventory may still use the FIFO, LIFO, or the weighted-average inventory costing method.

COMPARISON OF INCOME STATEMENT EFFECTS OF INVENTORY COSTING METHODS   Shown in Exhibit 8.6 are four condensed income statements for Jude & Jody's. Each of these income statements was prepared applying a different inventory costing method. Besides the data presented in Exhibit 8.5, the income statements shown in Exhibit 8.6 were based upon two additional items of information: (1) Jude & Jody's incurred $500 of operating expenses during the year in question, and (2) Jude & Jody's is subject to an average income tax rate of 40 percent. Notice that the net income amounts in Exhibit 8.6 range from $288 for the LIFO method to $357 for the FIFO method, a difference of approximately 24 percent. In absolute terms, these differences are quite small. However, in a similar exercise for a large firm, such as Sears or IBM, the differences in the "bottom line" amounts shown in Exhibit 8.6 would be much more impressive.

You may have noticed that the prices Jude & Jody's paid to suppliers for the 707 Jeans increased steadily throughout the year. As shown in Exhibit 8.5, the jeans in beginning inventory cost $14 a pair, while subsequent purchases were made at $16, $17, and $18 per pair, respectively. The United States economy has been characterized by steadily increasing prices over the past several decades. In an inflationary economic environment, the FIFO method results in a higher net income (or lower net

■ **EXHIBIT 8.6**
Comparison of Income Statement Effects of Different Inventory Costing Methods

	SPECIFIC IDENTIFICATION		WEIGHTED AVERAGE		FIFO		LIFO	
Sales		$2,320		$2,320		$2,320		$2,320
Cost of Goods Sold:								
Cost of Goods Available for Sale	$1,760			$1,760		$1,760		$1,760
Ending Inventory	520			480		535		420
Cost of Goods Sold		1,240		1,280		1,225		1,340
Gross Profit		1,080		1,040		1,095		980
Operating Expenses		500		500		500		500
Operating Income		580		540		595		480
Income Taxes Expense (40%)		232		216		238		192
Net Income		$ 348		$ 324		$ 357		$ 288

loss) than the LIFO method when these methods are applied to the same financial data. This result is evident in the Jude & Jody's example. Net income is higher under the FIFO method because the more costly jeans, the pairs purchased later in the year, are assumed to be in ending inventory. This leaves the cost of the merchandise that was purchased earlier in the year at lower prices assigned to cost of goods sold. Just the reverse is true under the LIFO method. The jeans assumed to be in ending inventory are the relatively low cost ($14 per unit) pairs included in beginning inventory. This leaves the cost of the higher-priced jeans purchased later in the year assigned to cost of goods sold. Result: higher cost of goods sold and lower net income compared with the scenario in which FIFO was used.

The weighted-average method typically yields a net income between the net income figures produced by the FIFO and LIFO methods. Although not always true, the specific identification method usually results in a net income figure that approximates the net income produced by applying the weighted-average method.

FIFO VS. LIFO: BALANCE SHEET VALUATION VS. INCOME DETERMINATION   As shown in Exhibit 8.7, FIFO is the most popular inventory costing method among public companies. However, just because FIFO is the most widely used inventory costing method does not mean it is the method that yields the most useful information for decision makers. The question of whether FIFO or LIFO is the most informative (best) method for decision makers has been debated for years. The problem in resolving this debate is that there are two conflicting issues that must be considered. Which of the two methods results in the more appropriate balance sheet valuation for ending inventory is the first of these issues. The second issue is which method does a better job of matching a business's expenses with its revenues.

■ **EXHIBIT 8.7**
Inventory Costing Methods: Frequency of Use by Publicly Owned Firms

SOURCE: *Accounting Trends & Techniques*, 1994.

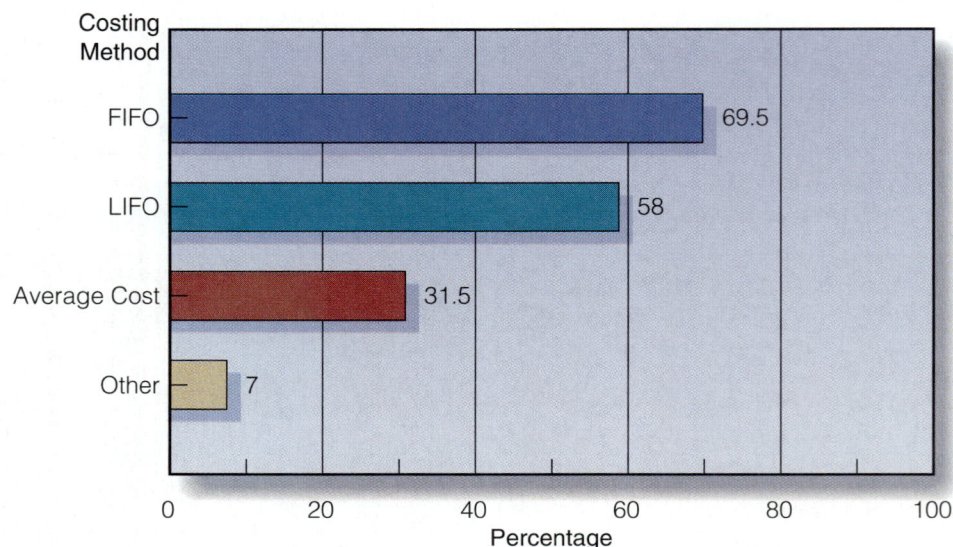

Note: Since some companies do not use the same inventory costing method for different classes of inventory, the percentages in the above table total more than 100 percent.

For balance sheet purposes, FIFO results in the per unit costs of the most recently acquired merchandise being assigned to ending inventory. LIFO, on the other hand, results in "old" per unit costs being assigned to ending inventory. For this reason, FIFO is generally perceived to yield a more appropriate balance sheet valuation for ending inventory. Return to the Jude & Jody's example for a moment. Under the FIFO method, the thirty pairs of jeans in ending inventory were costed out principally at $18 per pair, the wholesale cost of the jeans in December. As a result, the FIFO cost of ending inventory approximated the current cost, or replacement cost, of the jeans at year-end. Under the LIFO method, the ending inventory was costed out at $14 per pair, which was significantly below the jeans' replacement cost at year-end. Again, this comparison suggests that FIFO yields a more appropriate balance sheet value for ending inventory.

The next question is which of the two most popular inventory costing methods yields a more defensible cost of goods sold figure. Consider the situation facing Jude & Jody's near the end of the year for which the data in Exhibit 8.5 were presented. Each time this store sold a pair of jeans, the owners realized they would eventually have to replace those jeans if they were to continue in business. For example, when a pair of jeans was sold in December for $29, the owners recognized that they would pay $18 to replace that pair of jeans. So, after selling and replacing a pair of jeans in December, the owners "cleared" $11 on the transaction—before considering other expenses such as income taxes. This analysis assumes that business owners adopt a LIFO mentality in viewing the cost of merchandise associated with each sales transaction. That is, business owners mentally compute the gross profit on a sales transaction by subtracting from the sales price the merchandise's replacement cost, which generally approximates the cost of the most recently acquired inventory.

After considering the previous illustration, a nonaccountant remarks, "Wait a minute. What if the pair of jeans that was sold *actually* cost $14 because it was one of the pairs on hand at the beginning of the year? Then, the gross profit on the sale was actually $15 ($29 − $14) not $11 ($29 − $18)!" This individual has probably never operated a business and thus has difficulty accepting the LIFO mind-set that business owners generally adopt. Keep in mind that businesses are most concerned with their future operations, not with what has happened in the past. In the present example, when a pair of jeans was sold for $29 in December, Jude & Jody's had to spend $18 to replace those jeans. As a result, only $11 was available for other uses *regardless* of the wholesale price actually paid for that pair of jeans.

In summary, most accountants maintain that the LIFO costing method does a better job of matching revenues and expenses than the FIFO method. Consequently, when income determination is considered a more important issue than balance sheet valuation, the LIFO method is preferable to the FIFO method. Since most decision makers consider income determination a more critical issue than balance sheet valuation, they generally prefer businesses to use the LIFO method.

FIFO VS. LIFO: TAX CONSEQUENCES   Tax consequences are an important consideration when choosing an inventory costing method. Refer to Exhibit 8.6. Notice that the income taxes expense in the Jude & Jody's example was at a minimum when the LIFO method was used. As pointed out earlier, LIFO yields a lower net income than FIFO in a period of steadily rising prices. During the highly inflationary period of the late 1970s and early 1980s, hundreds of firms switched from FIFO to LIFO to reduce their income taxes. If a company uses the LIFO method for federal taxation purposes, it must also use LIFO for financial reporting purposes. Companies prefer to use LIFO for taxation purposes because that method generally minimizes their

■ LEARNING
OBJECTIVE 5
Discuss the financial statement
and taxation implications of the
different inventory costing
methods

Inventory Costing Methods in Europe

As noted earlier, FIFO is the most widely used inventory costing method in the United States although LIFO is nearly as popular. Across Europe, the popularity of inventory costing methods varies from country to country. In Great Britain, FIFO is commonly used for both financial reporting and taxation purposes since LIFO is not permitted for taxation purposes. The Republic of Ireland allows firms to use either the FIFO or weighted-average methods for financial reporting purposes but expressly forbids use of the LIFO method. Finland's "Bookkeeping Law" requires Finnish firms to use the FIFO method. Finally, Greece and Poland allow businesses wide latitude in choosing inventory costing methods, meaning that FIFO, LIFO, and other reasonable costing methods are permissible.

Inventory accounting practices vary considerably from country to country. In Great Britain, for example, LIFO is seldom used for financial accounting and reporting purposes since it cannot be used for taxation purposes.

Real World
LIFO's popularity has declined along with the decline in inflation rates in recent years.

taxes. However, FIFO is preferred for financial reporting purposes because it results in a higher net income.

Apparently, many firms forfeit the considerable tax savings yielded by LIFO so that they can report more impressive profits on their annual income statements. Again, notice in Exhibit 8.7 that the FIFO method is more widely used than the LIFO method. Dr. Gary Biddle, an accounting professor at the University of Chicago, addressed this subject in an article appearing several years ago in *The Wall Street Journal.*[2] In that article, competing companies in the same industry were classified by whether they used FIFO or LIFO. Then the resulting tax consequences for these firms were analyzed. For example, Professor Biddle reported that Minnesota Mining & Manufacturing, "The 3M Company," used FIFO at the time. Because the company used FIFO rather than LIFO, it paid $118 million more in federal taxes. On the other hand, one of 3M's major competitors, Eastman Kodak, used the LIFO method. Kodak's use of the LIFO method reduced its federal taxes, compared with what it would have paid under FIFO, by $204 million. Professor Biddle suggested, tongue in cheek, that companies using the FIFO method must consider the federal government their favorite charity.

Valuing Inventory at Other Than Cost

Cost is the primary valuation basis for inventory for accounting and financial reporting purposes. However, occasionally businesses must depart from the cost basis of valuing inventory to prevent their financial statements from being misleading to decision makers. For example, consider a situation recently facing the Callaway Golf Company. Callaway manufactures golf clubs and is best known for its popular driver, "Big Bertha." In 1991, this company wrote down the value of its inventory of golf clubs by approximately $1 million. Why? Because the company introduced a new line

2. G. C. Biddle, "Paying FIFO Taxes: Your Favorite Charity?" *The Wall Street Journal,* 19 January 1981, 18.

of clubs in that year which made much of its existing inventory obsolete and thus difficult to sell. In such circumstances, inventory generally must be reduced to its **net realizable value,** which is its sales value less any expected disposal costs.

The **lower-of-cost-or-market (LCM) rule** requires businesses to value their ending inventories at the lower of cost, as determined by FIFO or some other costing method, and current market value. Occasionally, net realizable value qualifies as the market value in the LCM rule. However, current replacement cost more commonly qualifies as market value for purposes of the LCM rule. **Current replacement cost** is the per unit amount that a business must pay to replace inventory items sold to customers. In the Jude & Jody's example, the current replacement cost of the 707 Jeans near the end of the year was $18 (see Exhibit 8.5).

The LCM rule can be applied in three different ways: on an item-by-item basis, by major classes of inventory, or on a total inventory basis. To illustrate this rule, assume that Exhibit 8.8 summarizes the cost and market value data for the year-end inventory of Anthony's Department Store.

In the item-by-item version of the LCM rule, the lower of cost or market value is identified for each inventory item. Then these amounts are added to determine the dollar amount of ending inventory for accounting and financial reporting purposes. Using the item-by-item variation of the LCM rule, the year-end inventory of Anthony's Department Store would be valued at $2,120 as shown in the following table.

ITEM	LOWER OF COST OR MARKET
727 Jeans	$ 420
757 Jeans	340
Rockaway Shirts	800
Sparrow Shirts	560
Total	$2,120

Under the second version of the LCM rule, the total cost and total market value of each major class of inventory is determined. For example, in Anthony's jeans department, the total cost of the inventory is $900: $420, the cost of the 727 jeans, plus $480, the cost of the 757 Jeans. The total market value of the inventory in the jeans department is $880 ($540 + $340). Next, the LCM rule is applied by selecting the lower of each of these paired amounts. Under this version of the LCM rule, Anthony's inventory would be valued at $2,400, as shown in the following schedule.

net realizable value

lower-of-cost-or-market (LCM) rule

current replacement cost

■ LEARNING OBJECTIVE 6
Apply the lower-of-cost-or-market rule to inventory

Focus on Ethics
Assume you are an accountant for a retailer with a large stock of hula hoops. Although hula hoops were very popular in the 1960s, kids in the 1990s aren't interested in hula hoops. Management refuses to write down the inventory to net realizable value. The impact of this decision on the financial statements is material. What can you or should you do?

■ **EXHIBIT 8.8**
Cost and Market Value Data for Year-End Inventory of Anthony's Department Store

ITEM	QUANTITY	COST PER UNIT	MARKET VALUE (REPLACEMENT COST) PER UNIT	TOTAL COST	TOTAL MARKET
Jeans Department:					
727 Jeans	30	$14	$18	$ 420	$ 540
757 Jeans	20	24	17	480	340
Shirt Department:					
Rockaway Shirts	50	16	20	800	1,000
Sparrow Shirts	40	18	14	720	560
				$2,420	$2,440

INVENTORY CLASS	TOTAL COST	TOTAL MARKET VALUE	LOWER OF COST OR MARKET
Jeans	$ 900	$ 880	$ 880
Shirts	1,520	1,560	1,520
Total			$2,400

Teaching Note
Any of the three ways of applying the LCM rule are acceptable under GAAP. Typically, cost considerations are a key factor that influence a company's decision of which version of the LCM rule to apply.

Finally, the LCM rule can be applied on a total inventory basis. In this case, a total cost and total market value are determined for inventory. Then the lower of these two amounts is selected. Exhibit 8.8 indicates that the total cost of Anthony's year-end inventory is $2,420, while the collective market value of the inventory is $2,440. So, under the final version of the LCM rule, Anthony's inventory would be valued at $2,420.

An inventory write-down resulting from application of the LCM rule is typically not reported separately in the income statement. Instead, such a reduction results in a larger portion of cost of goods available for sale being allocated to cost of goods sold. For example, assume that NBS Wholesalers has cost of goods available for sale of $12,400 during a given year. The company's ending inventory has a cost basis of $3,800. After applying the LCM rule, the firm's accountants determine that the ending inventory should be reduced to $3,400, resulting in cost of goods sold of $9,000. If the LCM rule had not been applied, the company's cost of goods would have been $8,600, as shown in the following schedule.

Cost of Goods Available for Sale	$12,400	$12,400
Ending Inventory (LCM rule not applied)	3,800	
Ending Inventory (LCM rule applied)		3,400
Cost of Goods Sold	$ 8,600	$ 9,000

Estimating Inventory

■ LEARNING OBJECTIVE 7
Estimate period-ending inventories using the gross profit method

Recall that under the periodic inventory system, a physical inventory is generally taken only at the end of a business's fiscal year. The resulting inventory dollar value remains in the accounting records until the end of the following year. Also recall that under a periodic inventory system, a Cost of Goods Sold account is not maintained in the general ledger. Instead, cost of goods sold is computed at year-end after the taking of a physical inventory. The absence of immediately available inventory and cost of goods sold data presents a problem to companies using a periodic inventory system. For example, what if such a company has a sudden need for financial statements in the middle of June to file with a loan application? Likewise, if such a company wants to prepare monthly financial statements, it must have some cost-effective means for determining cost of goods sold and ending inventory on a monthly basis. Taking a physical inventory each month is generally impractical because of the expense and time required.

gross profit method

When a company using the periodic inventory system needs to prepare financial statements but does not want to take a physical inventory, it can use the **gross profit method** to estimate its inventory. This method can also be used to estimate inventory losses due to fire or other causes. To use the gross profit method of estimating inventory, four items of information must be available. First, the beginning inventory must be known for the interim period. The interim period is generally the period of time that has elapsed since the taking of the previous physical inventory and also the time period for which an income statement will be prepared. The other necessary items of information are the given entity's normal gross profit percentage and its sales and net purchases for the interim period.

Teaching Note
Remind students that:
   Gross Profit = Sales − Cost of Goods Sold; and
   Gross Profit Percentage = Gross Profit/Sales.

■ **EXHIBIT 8.9**
Illustration of Gross Profit Method of Estimating Inventory

Inventory, January 1		$70,000
Net Purchases, January 1–June 30*		65,000
Cost of Goods Available for Sale		$135,000
Less: Estimated Cost of Goods Sold		
Sales, January 1–June 30	$150,000	
Estimated Gross Profit (40%)	60,000	
Estimated Cost of Goods Sold		90,000
Estimated Inventory, June 30		$45,000

*Transportation in, or delivery expenses, for merchandise purchases, has been included in this figure.

Assume that the owner of Reba Jo's Fashions, a retail store, needs to prepare a set of interim financial statements for her business. These financial statements are needed for the period January 1 through June 30. The owner intends to submit these financial statements with a loan application for the business. Reba Jo's uses a periodic inventory system and has historically realized a gross profit of 40 percent on sales. On December 31 of the prior year, store personnel took a physical inventory that yielded an inventory value of $70,000. During the first six months of the current year, the store has had net purchases of $65,000 and net sales of $150,000. Exhibit 8.9 presents a schedule in which the June 30 inventory of Reba Jo's Fashions is estimated using the gross profit method.

The four steps in applying the gross profit method are as follows:

1. Determine cost of goods available for sale for the interim period by adding beginning inventory to net purchases and transportation in.
2. Estimate gross profit by multiplying the business's normal gross profit percentage by its sales during the interim period.
3. Estimate cost of goods sold by subtracting gross profit from sales.
4. Determine the estimated inventory dollar value by subtracting cost of goods sold from cost of goods available for sale.

Companies that employ the gross profit method to estimate ending inventory should use this method cautiously. The key limitation of this method stems from the assumption that an entity's gross profit percentage is stable over time. If a company's gross profit percentage is highly variable, the gross profit method may not yield a reliable estimate of its inventory at a given point in time.

Real World
Auditors often use the gross profit method to test the overall reasonableness of a client's ending inventory.

The Perpetual Inventory System

The illustrations and examples to this point in the chapter have assumed that a periodic inventory system was being used by the given businesses. Now the perpetual inventory system is discussed with a particular focus on how it differs from the periodic inventory system.

A perpetual inventory system is generally more costly to implement and maintain than a periodic inventory system. However, as pointed out in Chapter 6, the declining cost of computer technology in recent years, has resulted in many firms installing computer-based perpetual inventory systems. A key advantage of a perpetual inventory system is that it allows internal decision makers to access current inventory and

■ **LEARNING OBJECTIVE 8**
Account for inventory in a perpetual inventory system

cost of goods sold data at any point during an accounting period. Easy access to these data enhances the ability of executives to react quickly to sudden changes in their firm's competitive environment. One company that capitalizes on the information advantages of a perpetual inventory system is the discount retailer 50-OFF Stores, Inc. Following is a brief excerpt from a recent annual report of that company.

> The Company's computerized management information system, featuring point-of-sale cash registers and a computerized perpetual inventory system, permits management to review each store's inventory on a current basis. This system enables the Company to tailor its purchasing and to buy selected items of merchandise on an as-needed basis.

BOOKKEEPING MECHANICS FOR A PERPETUAL INVENTORY SYSTEM To compare and contrast the bookkeeping mechanics for perpetual and periodic inventory systems, it is helpful to review journal entries within each system for several routine transactions. The following are descriptions of five transactions for a small retail business, Marcia's Boutique. Following these descriptions are the journal entries that would be appropriate for each of these transactions in a perpetual and a periodic inventory system.

1. Marcia's purchased twelve dresses from a supplier at a cost of $50 each, $600 in total, with credit terms of 2/10, n/30, and shipping terms of FOB destination. Marcia's uses the gross method to record merchandise purchases.
2. One of the dresses was discovered to have a fabric flaw and was returned to the supplier.
3. Three of the dresses were sold on credit at a retail price of $110 each.
4. A customer returned one of the dresses and was given a full refund. The dress was returned to inventory.
5. Marcia's paid the net amount due to the supplier on the last day of the discount period.

Perpetual Inventory System			Periodic Inventory System		
1. Inventory	600		Purchases	600	
Accounts Payable		600	Accounts Payable		600
2. Accounts Payable	50		Accounts Payable	50	
Inventory		50	Purchases Returns		
			and Allowances		50
3. Accounts Receivable	330		Accounts Receivable	330	
Sales		330	Sales		330
Cost of Goods Sold	150		No entry		
Inventory		150			
4. Sales Returns and	110		Sales Returns and		
Allowances			Allowances	110	
Accounts Receivable		110	Accounts Receivable		110
Inventory	50		No entry		
Cost of Goods Sold		50			
5. Accounts Payable	550		Accounts Payable	550	
Cash		539	Cash		539
Inventory		11	Purchases Discounts		11

Notice that in a perpetual inventory system every transaction affecting inventory results in an entry to the Inventory account. Consequently, in a perpetual inventory system there is no need for several accounts used in a periodic inventory system. For example, notice that merchandise purchases are debited directly to the Inventory account in a perpetual inventory system instead of being debited to a Purchases account. Likewise, merchandise returned to a supplier is credited to the Inventory account instead of to Purchases Returns and Allowances.

Also notice that sales transactions require two entries in a perpetual inventory system. One entry is necessary to record the sale: debit Cash or Accounts Receivable and credit Sales. A second entry is necessary to transfer the cost of merchandise sold from the Inventory account to the Cost of Goods Sold account. Again, firms that use a periodic inventory system do not maintain a Cost of Goods Sold account. Instead, these firms compute their cost of goods sold at the end of each accounting period after taking a physical inventory.

Teaching Note

Remind students that the Inventory account is used to record purchases of goods for resale. Purchases of assets such as supplies should not be recorded in the Inventory account.

PERIOD-ENDING CLOSING PROCEDURES FOR A PERPETUAL INVENTORY SYSTEM   The period-ending closing procedures for a perpetual inventory system are slightly different from the closing procedures illustrated in Chapter 6 for a periodic inventory system. For example, in a perpetual inventory system, accounts such as Purchases and Purchases Returns and Allowances do not have to be closed because they do not exist. Then again, the expense account Cost of Goods Sold, which does not exist in a periodic inventory system, must be closed each period in a perpetual inventory system.

In a periodic inventory system, the beginning inventory balance is eliminated with a closing entry. This closing entry includes a credit to the Inventory account and an offsetting debit to the Income Summary account. The ending inventory balance is established on the books by debiting Inventory and crediting Income Summary. Neither of these entries is needed in a perpetual inventory system since the appropriate inventory balance is already "on the books." In a perpetual inventory system, a physical inventory is usually taken near or at the end of each fiscal year. Any difference between the inventory value resulting from the physical inventory and the balance of the Inventory account is eliminated with an adjusting entry. For example, suppose a firm's Inventory account reflects a $46,000 balance, but that a physical inventory indicates that only $44,000 of goods are on hand. This difference would require an adjusting journal entry debiting Cost of Goods Sold $2,000 and crediting Inventory the same amount.

Teaching Note

A perpetual inventory system indicates the inventory that should be on hand. A physical inventory must be taken to verify that the inventory actually exists.

INVENTORY COSTING METHODS AND THE PERPETUAL INVENTORY SYSTEM   Earlier in this chapter, four inventory costing methods were discussed with particular attention focused on the two most popular of these methods, FIFO and LIFO. The four inventory costing methods can be used in either a periodic or a perpetual inventory system. When these methods were illustrated earlier, the assumption was that a periodic inventory system was being used. In a perpetual inventory system, inventory costing methods must be applied within the framework of the records maintained for each inventory item. These records are usually included in an **inventory ledger,** a subsidiary ledger that serves as the detailed support for the Inventory account in the general ledger.

Shown in Exhibit 8.10 is one page of a computer software store's inventory ledger. This ledger page summarizes the increases, decreases, and current balance, both in

inventory ledger

■ EXHIBIT 8.10
Perpetual Inventory Record, FIFO Costing Method

ITEM: QUIKWRITER, VERSION 3.4

Date	#	Received Unit Cost	Total	#	Sold Unit Cost	Total	#	Balance Unit Cost	Balance
May 1							10	$55	$550
5				2	$55	$110	8	55	440
8				3	55	165	5	55	275
12	7	$60	$420				5	55	
							7	60	695
17				2	55	110	3	55	
							7	60	585
22	6	65	390				3	55	
							7	60	
							6	65	975
26				3	55	165	6	60	
				1	60	60	6	65	750
31				2	60	120	4	60	
							6	65	630

■ EXHIBIT 8.11
Perpetual Inventory Record, LIFO Costing Method

ITEM: QUIKWRITER, VERSION 3.4

Date	#	Received Unit Cost	Total	#	Sold Unit Cost	Total	#	Balance Unit Cost	Balance
May 1							10	$55	$550
5				2	$55	$110	8	55	440
8				3	55	165	5	55	275
12	7	$60	$420				5	55	
							7	60	695
17				2	60	120	5	55	
							5	60	575
22	6	65	390				5	55	
							5	60	
							6	65	965
26				4	65	260	5	55	
							5	60	
							2	65	705
31				2	65	130	5	55	
							5	60	575

dollar terms and unit quantity, of a word processing package sold by the store. This store uses the FIFO inventory costing method in its perpetual inventory system.

Notice in Exhibit 8.10 that on May 22 the computer software store had three "layers" of the QuikWriter product: three units at a cost of $55 each, seven units at a cost of $60 each, and six units at a cost of $65 each. On May 26, when four units of this product were sold, the FIFO concept was followed in determining the per unit costs assigned to those units. The cost of goods sold for that sale consisted of the total cost of the three units in the "oldest" layer ($165) and the cost of one unit from the next oldest layer ($60).

The computer software store could apply the LIFO method in its perpetual inventory system. Exhibit 8.11 illustrates how the perpetual inventory record for the QuikWriter product would appear assuming the store uses the LIFO method. You can use the data presented in Exhibit 8.10 to prove to yourself that periodic FIFO and perpetual FIFO result in the same period-ending inventory balance and cost of goods sold figure when applied to the same inventory data. Likewise, you can use the data in Exhibit 8.11 to prove to yourself that this is not true of periodic LIFO and perpetual LIFO.

ANALYZING INVENTORY

As noted in Chapter 7, decision makers closely monitor the age of a business's accounts receivable. Decision makers have a similar interest in inventory. As a company's inventory "ages," it becomes more subject to valuation concerns due to obsolescence, spoilage, and related problems.

Computing the age of inventory is a two-step process. First, the inventory turnover ratio must be computed.

> **Inventory Turnover** = Cost of Goods Sold/Average Inventory
> **Ratio**

■ **LEARNING OBJECTIVE 9**
Compute the inventory turnover ratio and the age of inventory

inventory turnover ratio

Then, the inventory turnover ratio is divided into 360 days, the number of days in a business year.

> **Age of Inventory** = 360 days/Inventory Turnover Ratio

age of inventory

To illustrate the computation of the age of inventory, consider the following data for the Shapiro Mercantile Company.

Inventory, January 1, 1996	$ 232,200
Inventory, December 31, 1996	184,600
Cost of Goods Sold, 1996	1,563,000

Listed next are the calculations to compute Shapiro's age of inventory at the end of 1996.[3]

---

3. The preferred but more time-consuming approach to computing average inventory is to add the beginning-of-the-year inventory balance to the twelve end-of-the-month balances and divide by thirteen. This approach minimizes the impact on the inventory turnover ratio of an abnormally high or low inventory balance at the beginning or end of a year.

Teaching Note
Ask students to compute
Michaels Stores' inventory
turnover and age of inventory
for 1994. Do these measures
seem reasonable for that type of
business?

Average Inventory	=	($232,200 + $184,600)/2
	=	$208,400
Inventory Turnover Ratio	=	$1,563,000/$208,400
	=	7.5
Age of Inventory	=	360 days/7.5
	=	48 days

The inventory turnover ratio indicates the number of times that a company sells or "turns over" its inventory each year. As you would expect, businesses attempt to turn over their inventory as quickly as possible. A high rate of inventory turnover reduces the risk of inventory spoilage and obsolescence and minimizes the costs of carrying inventory such as insurance and handling costs.

Schwartz Bookshops operates several bookstores in the Milwaukee area. A January 1995 article in *Inc.* profiled this business and the problems its owners had encountered in keeping it afloat.[4] In the late 1980s, the company had an inventory turnover ratio of less than 2.0, very low by industry standards. After installing a computerized inventory system, the owners could readily identify the types of books that were their best-sellers. The owners used this information to revamp their purchasing strategy and thereby eliminate slow-moving titles that were cluttering store shelves. Within a few years, the business's inventory turnover ratio increased to 3.7. More important, the higher turnover ratio translated into a higher sales volume and larger profits.

The age of inventory statistic indicates the average period of time required to sell an item of inventory. Unlike the inventory turnover ratio, lower is better when it comes to the age of inventory. Exhibit 8.12 reports the average age of inventory for six industries. Shown in Exhibit 8.13 is the age of inventory over a recent eight-year period for Best Buy, the consumer electronics and home appliances retailer. Notice that the general trend in Best Buy's age of inventory was downward over this period, which indicates that the company was selling its inventory more quickly. In Best Buy's industry, the median age of inventory has generally hovered between eighty and ninety days in recent years. By 1994, Best Buy's age of inventory was considerably lower than the industry norm, a positive reflection on the company's inventory management practices. One key implication of this trend for decision makers is that Best Buy is likely to have fewer inventory write-offs and write-downs compared to its competitors.

KEY INTERNAL CONTROL PROCEDURES FOR INVENTORY

■ LEARNING
OBJECTIVE 10
Define key internal control procedures for inventory

In Chapter 7, the importance of physical security controls for cash was discussed. The cash resources of a business are nearly always kept under "lock and key." Merchandise inventory, on the other hand, is accessible to customers and employees and thus more susceptible to being stolen or otherwise misused. Additionally, inventory typically accounts for a much larger percentage of a business's total assets than cash. As a result, physical security controls are at least as important for inventory as they are for cash.

Business Week reported in 1994 that retailers' losses due to customer and employee theft of inventory average approximately 2 percent of annual sales.[5] Many retailers

---

4. T. Ehrenfeld, "The New and Improved American Small Business," *Inc.*, January 1995, 34–45.

5. W. Zellner, "Sticky Fingers Are Rifling Through Retail," *Business Week*, 28 March 1994, 36.

■ **EXHIBIT 8.12**

Age of Inventories, Selected Industries

SOURCE: *RMA Annual Statement Studies, 1994* (Philadelphia: RMA, 1994).

RMA cautions that the studies be regarded only as a general guideline and not as an absolute industry norm. This is due to limited samples within categories, the categorization of companies by their primary Standard Industrial Classification (SIC) number only, and different methods of operations by companies within the same industries. For these reasons, RMA recommends that the figures be used only as general guidelines in addition to other methods of financial analysis.

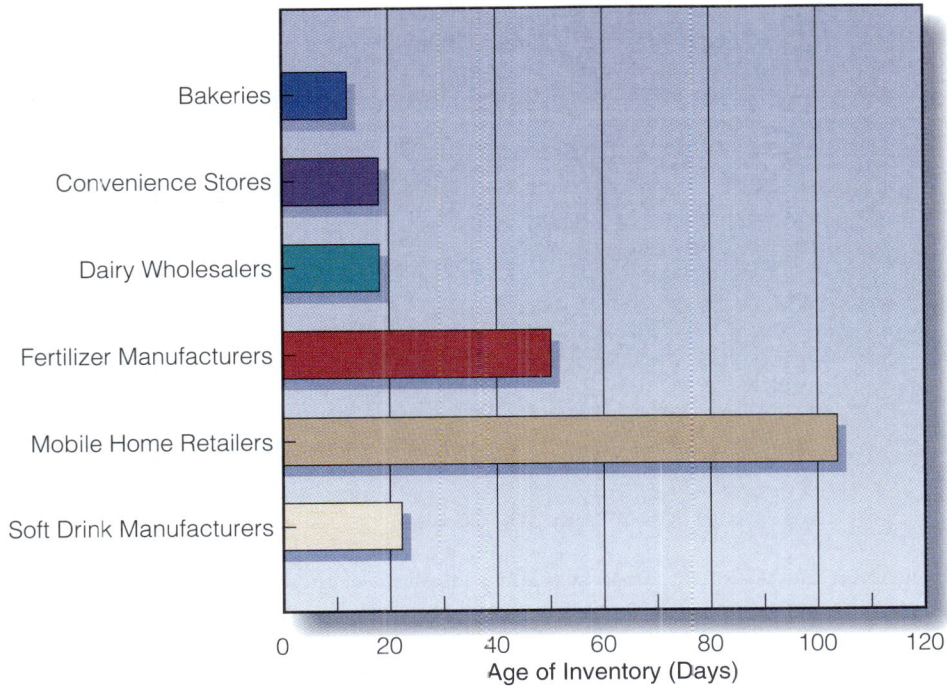

■ **EXHIBIT 8.13**

Best Buy Co., Inc.: Age of Inventory, 1987–1994

SOURCE: Recent annual reports.

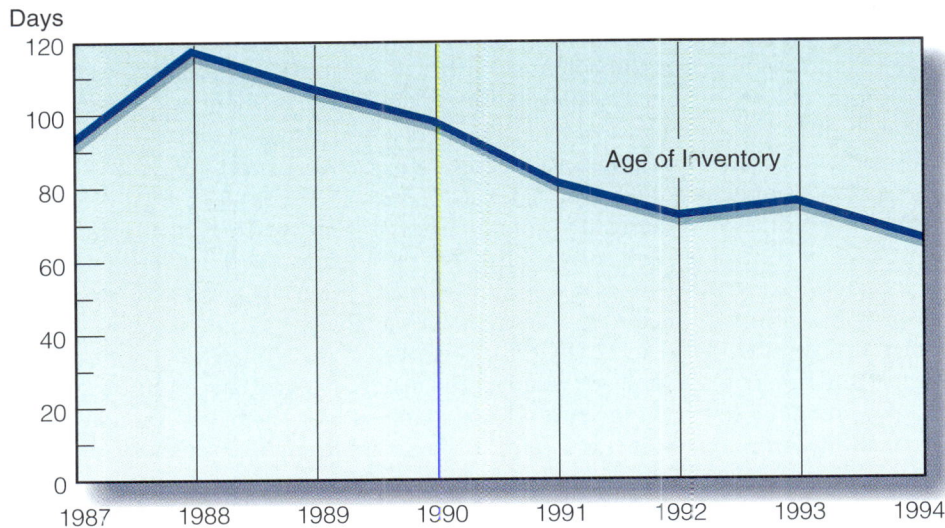

Large manufacturing companies, such as General Motors, have spent millions of dollars developing and implementing computerized inventory systems to assist them in controlling and managing their huge investments in inventory.

Discussion Question
Ask students to list other examples of how retailers safeguard their inventory.

experience much larger theft losses. For example, take the case of Tuesday Morning, a retail discount chain. That firm's theft losses in a recent year approached 4 percent of its annual sales.[6] Apparently, thieves realized that the low-overhead discount chain did not have the sophisticated security controls used by many retailers. However, that has changed. To reduce its large theft losses, Tuesday Morning has spent several million dollars recently to implement an extensive security system for each of its stores.

Most merchandisers have an array of physical security controls to minimize inventory losses due to theft. A common and very effective security measure for retail stores is inventory tagging mechanisms that set off an alarm when merchandise is not "de-tagged" before it leaves the store. Related controls include remote-controlled surveillance cameras, uniformed and plainclothes security guards, and a policy that restricts high-priced merchandise, such as jewelry, to locked displays.

Manufacturing firms and wholesalers that maintain much of their inventory in large warehouses also face the potential for heavy inventory losses. In these settings, segregation of key functional responsibilities is a particularly important internal control procedure. For example, a warehouse supervisor who has custodial responsibility for inventory should not maintain the warehouse's inventory accounting records or be allowed to authorize inventory transactions.

Many companies have developed computerized inventory management systems to enhance their control over inventory. PICOS is the acronym used by General Motors for its extensive inventory management system. (For you trivia buffs, PICOS is short for "purchased input concept optimization for supply.") A recent General Motors annual report disclosed that its PICOS system had reduced inventory levels by 47 percent. Additionally, floor space reserved for inventory was reduced by 35 percent and time required to obtain inventory from suppliers by 52 percent. Another example of an inventory management system is the Smart Response system of American

---

6. Ibid.

Inventory Management: Howard Knows Best

Six years ago, Howard Skolnick bought a sleepy, middle-aged company in Chicago that manufactured steel containers for use in the storage and disposal of hazardous materials. He had big plans for growth but knew his newly renamed Skolnick Industries, Inc., lacked the financial systems to support expansion. "No one in the old company understood how the costs associated with excessive inventory were hurting profits," he says.

Growing companies typically tie up more unnecessary cash in their inventories than in any other part of their business with the exception of accounts receivable. "If you can free up the cash from inventory," Skolnick says, "you can spend it on growth instead." That strategy becomes even more compelling in recessionary times when strong cash buildups become a company's best line of defense against order slowdowns and credit freezes.

Today $10 million Skolnick Industries maintains one of the best controlled inventory operations in its industry, enabling the company to ship most products to customers within twenty-four to forty-eight hours of orders. At the same time, inventory levels are leaner than they were when the company was half its size.

To get there, the company switched from the quarterly inventory updates the previous owner had used to a computerized inventory control system that continually updates warehousing records on a product-by-product basis. Then, with the help of Cecil Levy, a principal at the accounting firm of Miller, Cooper & Co., Skolnick set up a financial reporting system that tracks certain financial trends or ratios within his company. Together these function as an early warning system against potential inventory problems. Included in these key trends and ratios are inventory turnover, percentage of orders shipped on time, length of time to fill back orders, and percentage of customer complaints to shipped orders.

In summarizing his approach to inventory management, Skolnick observes, "When your inventory is well maintained, you can keep your customers happy, and still afford to pay for your growth."

SOURCE: Used with permission, *Inc. Magazine*, February 1991, 81–82. Golchirsh, Inc., 38 Commercial Wharf, Boston, MA 02110.

Greetings. One important feature of the Smart Response system is its ability to capture "point of sale" data directly from the sales terminals of American Greetings' customers. Direct access to these data has allowed American Greetings to reduce the time needed to restock customers' inventories. Additionally, American Greetings can now determine its future production needs much more accurately.

Most small businesses do not have the financial resources to develop and maintain elaborate inventory control systems. Nevertheless, there are several low-cost procedures that small companies can implement to manage and control their inventories more effectively. An example of an inventory control strategy implemented by the owner of one small business is described in a vignette included in this section.

SUMMARY

Inventory is a focal point of attention for decision makers when they analyze a business's financial statements. A key information need of decision makers regarding inventory is the specific method or methods used to account for this important asset.

The inventory accounting methods adopted by a business can significantly influence its apparent financial condition and reported operating results. Also helpful to decision makers are financial statement disclosures indicating how a company's financial data would have been affected had it used a different inventory accounting method.

When a business uses a periodic inventory system, the first step in determining a period-ending inventory value is a physical inventory. Once the quantity of each inventory item has been established, these quantities are multiplied by the appropriate per unit costs to determine the dollar value of ending inventory. There are four major methods that businesses can use to "cost out" their ending inventories: the specific identification method, the weighted-average method, the FIFO (first-in, first-out) method, and the LIFO (last-in, first-out) method. Cost is the principal valuation basis used for inventory; however, businesses must occasionally value their inventories at other than cost. When the cost of inventory exceeds its market value, the lower-of-cost-or-market (LCM) rule requires the inventory to be written down to market value. Generally, current replacement cost is defined as market value for purposes of the LCM rule.

When preparing monthly or quarterly financial statements, many companies use the gross profit method to estimate their period-ending inventories. A key advantage of using an inventory estimation method is the cost savings realized by not being required to take a physical inventory.

The two basic types of inventory accounting systems are the periodic inventory system and the perpetual inventory system. Typically, a periodic inventory system is less costly to establish and maintain than a perpetual inventory system. A key advantage of a perpetual inventory system is the availability of information regarding inventory balances and cost of goods sold at any point during an accounting period. From a bookkeeping perspective, there are several differences between a periodic and a perpetual inventory system. The key difference is that all transactions involving inventory require an entry to the Inventory account in a perpetual inventory system, which is not true in a periodic inventory system. Any of the major inventory costing methods can be used in either a periodic or a perpetual inventory system.

Decision makers monitor a business's age of inventory. As a company's inventory ages, it becomes more subject to obsolescence, spoilage, and related problems. Computing the age of inventory is a two-step process. First, the inventory turnover ratio is computed by dividing cost of goods sold by average inventory. Then age of inventory is determined by dividing the inventory turnover ratio into 360 days, the number of days in a business year.

The susceptibility of inventory to theft by customers and employees makes physical security controls an important consideration for this asset. Segregation of key functional responsibilities is also an important internal control for companies that maintain large quantities of inventory. Individuals who have direct access to inventory should not be permitted to maintain inventory records or authorize transactions involving inventory.

GLOSSARY

Age of inventory (p. 341)   360 days divided by the inventory turnover ratio.
Current replacement cost (p. 330)   The per unit cost that a business must pay to replace inventory items sold to customers.
FIFO (first-in, first-out) method (p. 329)   An inventory costing method under which the per unit costs of the most recently acquired goods are used to establish the cost basis of ending inventory.

Gross profit method (p. 336)   A method of estimating period-ending inventory in which the key factor is a business's normal gross profit percentage.

Inventory ledger (p. 339)   A subsidiary ledger that serves as the detailed support for the balance of the general ledger Inventory account.

Inventory turnover ratio (p. 341)   Cost of goods sold divided by average inventory; indicates how often a business sells or turns over its inventory each year.

LIFO (last-in, first-out) method (p. 330)   An inventory costing method under which the per unit costs of the earliest acquired goods are used to establish the cost basis of ending inventory.

Lower-of-cost-or-market (LCM) rule (p. 335)   An accounting rule that requires businesses to value their ending inventories at the lower of cost or market value, the latter typically being defined as current replacement cost.

Net realizable value (p. 330)   The sales value of inventory, or other assets, less any expected disposal costs.

Specific identification method (p. 328)   An inventory costing method under which actual per unit costs are used to establish the cost basis of ending inventory.

Weighted-average method (p. 329)   An inventory costing method under which average per unit costs are computed for goods available for sale during an accounting period; these average per unit costs are then used to establish the cost basis of ending inventory.

DECISION CASE

In the late 1970s, Bill Nashwinter accepted a sales position with Doughtie's Foods. Nashwinter impressed his superiors with his hard work and dedication to his job and was eventually rewarded with a promotion. His new position was general manager of a wholesale division of Doughtie's. Nashwinter soon realized that managing a large wholesale operation was much more complicated and stressful than working a sales route. Within a short time after his promotion, he was being criticized by corporate headquarters for failing to meet what he perceived were unrealistic profit goals. After several rounds of such criticism, Nashwinter decided to take matters into his own hands and began fabricating fictitious inventory on his monthly financial reports to headquarters. By inflating his division's inventory each month, he lowered the division's cost of goods sold and inflated its gross profit. After several years, Nashwinter finally confessed his misdeeds to corporate management and was fired.

Bill Nashwinter's story is not an uncommon one. A young person joins an organization with his or her sights set on a promotion to a position with more responsibility. When that promotion comes, new pressures and problems that were not anticipated are suddenly imposed on the individual. The result is often frustration and, occasionally, shortsighted and unethical conduct similar to that of Nashwinter's.

Assume that you were recently promoted to general manager of a sales division of a large corporation. Your first responsibility was to analyze your division's operations and prepare a three-year financial forecast of its operating income. The forecast you prepared is as follows:

	YEAR 1	YEAR 2	YEAR 3
Sales	$4,000,000	$4,400,000	$4,600,000
Cost of Goods Sold	2,000,000	2,100,000	2,200,000
Gross Profit	2,000,000	2,300,000	2,400,000
Operating Expenses	800,000	850,000	900,000
Operating Income	$1,200,000	$1,450,000	$1,500,000

After analyzing your division's operations, you realize that approximately one-third of the division's existing inventory is obsolete and unsaleable at any price. This obsolete inventory has never been written down and has a book value of $100,000. You estimate that the insurance, handling, and other operating expenses associated with this obsolete inventory total $20,000 annually—expenses included in your financial forecast. These expenses affect you personally since you are entitled to a bonus each year equal to 10 percent of the amount that your division's operating income exceeds $1 million.

Your immediate superior is the vice-president of sales. This individual served several years as manager of the division that you now oversee. The two of you were promoted to your new positions at the same time. The vice-president is unhappy with your suggestion to write down your division's inventory by $100,000. Such a write-down would reflect poorly on his performance while he was divisional manager. Finally, he authorizes you to make the write-down if you insist. But he points out that the write-down will be included in cost of goods sold for Year 1, meaning that your bonus for that year will be significantly reduced. You immediately respond, "But that's not fair." At this point, the vice-president shrugs his shoulders indifferently and walks away.

Required: Compute your division's operating income and your bonus for the next three years under two assumptions: (1) the $100,000 write-down is taken for the obsolete inventory in Year 1 and (2) you retain the obsolete inventory without writing it down. Which of these two alternatives would be best for you? Which would be best for the company? (Ignore all tax and time value of money considerations. Assume that the obsolete inventory can be disposed of at a nominal cost.) Do you believe the vice-president of sales has handled this matter properly? Explain. Would you discuss this matter with your company's chief executive? Why or why not?

NOTE: Some of the information for this case was drawn from the following source: M. C. Knapp, "Doughtie's Foods," in *Contemporary Auditing: Issues and Cases,* 2d ed. (Minneapolis/St. Paul: West Publishing Co., 1996).

QUESTIONS

1. Why is inventory such an important asset of retailing, wholesaling, and manufacturing firms?

2. Provide examples of how accountants can help their companies manage inventory.

3. Why is inventory always considered a current asset?

4. How do errors in a business's ending inventory for a given year affect its financial statements for that year? For the following year?

5. How is the cost of goods available for sale determined for a given accounting period under the periodic inventory system?

6. For which type of companies, merchandisers or manufacturers, is inventory accounting more complex? Why?

7. Describe what is meant by the phrase "inventory cost flow."

8. How do shipping terms determine whether a company should include merchandise it has purchased or sold near the end of a given year in that year's ending inventory?

9. What is consigned inventory?

10. Identify the four most common inventory costing methods. Briefly describe each.

11. Define what is meant by the phrase "inventory cost flow assumption."

12. In a period of rising prices, which inventory costing method, FIFO or LIFO, generally yields the higher ending inventory value? Why?

13. Which inventory costing method, FIFO or LIFO, is generally considered the more appropriate method for balance sheet valuation purposes? Why?

14. Which inventory costing method, FIFO or LIFO, is generally considered the more appropriate method for income determination purposes? Why?

15. Briefly describe the lower-of-cost-or-market (LCM) rule.

16. Define "current replacement cost."

17. Define "net realizable value." When is a company's inventory reported at its net realizable value?

18. List the steps in applying the gross profit method of estimating inventory.

19. Why is the gross profit method of inventory estimation sometimes used to determine the dollar value of a business's inventory? Identify one key limitation of the gross profit method.

20. Identify the key differences between the periodic and perpetual inventory systems.

21. Identify advantages and disadvantages of both the periodic inventory system and the perpetual inventory system.

22. List the equations used to compute the inventory turnover ratio and the age of inventory.

23. How do decision makers use the inventory turnover ratio and the age of inventory when analyzing a company's financial data?

24. Describe three internal control procedures commonly applied to inventory.

EXERCISES

Note: Unless indicated otherwise, the homework materials in this chapter assume that a periodic inventory system is in use.

25. **Cost of Goods Available for Sale and Cost of Goods Sold** (LO 2)
Following is selected financial information for 1995 for Ederington Enterprises, a merchandising company.

January 1, Inventory	$150,000
Net Purchases	625,000
December 31, Inventory	110,000

Required:
1. Compute costs of goods available for sale and cost of goods sold.
2. Suppose that Ederington's correct ending inventory for 1995 was $125,000, but that errors in counting the company's inventory resulted in the ending inventory value of $110,000. Determine the business's actual cost of goods sold for 1995.
3. Indicate how the error identified in Part 2 affected Ederington's income statement and balance sheet for 1995 and 1996.

25. 1. CGS, $665,000
    2. CGS, $650,000

26. **In Transit Inventory** (LO 2)
Victoria's Supply, a retail office supply company, both buys and sells goods on credit. Following are several merchandise transactions engaged in by Victoria's near the end of a recent year. The merchandise that Victoria's either bought or sold in these transactions is in transit at December 31.

a. Purchased goods on December 30, FOB shipping point.

b. Sold goods on December 29, FOB shipping point.

c. Sold goods on December 30, FOB destination.

d. Purchased goods on December 28, FOB destination.

Required:

26. No check figures

Which in transit items listed should be included in Victoria's December 31 inventory?

27. **Errors in Ending Inventory** (LO 2)

Countertop Industries reported $120,000 of ending inventory for the year ended December 31, 1995. Excluded from ending inventory was $10,000 of goods purchased from a supplier by Countertop on December 28 and shipped that day FOB shipping point. Also, one section of Countertop's warehouse was overlooked by the inventory counting teams at year-end. As a result, $15,000 of inventory was not counted.

Required:

27. 1. NI understated $17,500
2. NI overstated $17,500

1. Indicate how each of the listed errors affected Countertop's 1995 ending inventory, cost of goods sold, and net income. Countertop's effective income tax rate is 30 percent.

2. Also, how did these errors affect the same items in Countertop's 1996 financial statements?

28. **Inventory Costing Methods** (LO 4)

Little Joe's T-Shirts is a retail store specializing in one-size-fits-all "Super T's." Information regarding Little Joe's inventory during 1995 follows:

January 1	Beginning Inventory	100 T's @ $9 ea.	$ 900
March 15	Purchase	150 T's @ $10 ea.	1,500
July 20	Purchase	70 T's @ $9 ea.	630
December 10	Purchase	50 T's @ $11 ea.	550
Cost of Goods Available for Sale		370 T's	$3,580
Total Sales during the Year		260 T's @ $20	$5,200
Ending Inventory on 12/31		110 T's @ $? each	$?

Required:

28. 1a. Inv., $1,150
CGS, $2,430
1b. Inv., $1,064.36
CGS, $2,515.64

1. Compute ending inventory and cost of goods sold for Little Joe's under each of the following assumptions:

a. Little Joe's uses the specific identification method. Ending inventory consists of 60 T-shirts purchased on March 15 and 50 T-shirts purchased on December 10.

b. Little Joe's uses the weighted-average inventory costing method.

2. The nature of a business often dictates the type of inventory costing method it uses. Identify two types of businesses that might use the specific identification costing method and two types of businesses that might use the weighted-average costing method.

29. **Inventory Costing Methods** (LO 4)

Refer to the information presented in Exercise 28.

Required:

29. 1a. Inv., $1,090
CGS, $2,490
1b. Inv., $1,000
CGS, $2,580

1. Compute ending inventory and costs of goods sold assuming that Little Joe's uses the:

a. FIFO inventory costing method.

b. LIFO inventory costing method.

2. Comment briefly on the advantages and disadvantages commonly associated with the FIFO and LIFO costing methods.

30. **Net Realizable Value** (LO 6)

Mega Computers produces a wide array of products used in the manufacture of personal computers. Recently, one of Mega's products became obsolete because a technologically advanced product was introduced by a competitor. Presently, Mega has 5,000 units of these products in inventory at a collective (FIFO) cost of $1,500,000. Mega can sell these products for $110 each to a foreign firm that manufactures "clones" of U.S.-made personal computers. However, Mega will have to pay the freight charges to deliver these items. Delivery cost per unit will be $14.

Required:
1. Compute the net realizable value of Mega Computers' obsolete product.
2. Compute the total dollar amount of the write-down that Mega Computers must record for this product.
3. What accounting principle dictates that inventory be written down to its net realizable value? Explain.

30. 1. $480,000
    2. $1,020,000

31. **Lower-of-Cost-or-Market Rule** (LO 6)

Following is information regarding the December 31, 1996, ending inventory of Madison County Steelworks.

Item	Quantity	Original Unit Cost	Replacement Unit Cost
Exgots	125	$17	$14
Ingots	100	$12	$13
Ongots	200	$15	$13
Ungots	50	$20	$19

Required:
Apply the lower-of-cost-or-market (LCM) rule to Madison County's ending inventory under each of the following assumptions:
1. The company uses the item-by-item version of the LCM rule.
2. The company applies the LCM rule by major classes of inventory. (Madison County has two inventory classes: Exgots and Ingots; Ongots and Ungots.)
3. The company applies the LCM rule on a total inventory basis.

31. 1. $6,500
    2. $6,600
    3. $6,600

32. **Gross Profit Method of Estimating Inventory** (LO 7)

Countess Company's inventory was destroyed on October 1 of this year as a result of a fire. For insurance purposes, Countess must estimate the dollar value of the inventory that was destroyed. Following is information obtained from Countess's accounting records.

Inventory, January 1	$100,000
Net Purchases through October 1	350,000
Sales through October 1	600,000
Historical Gross Profit Percentage	60%

Required:
Using the gross profit method, estimate the amount of inventory that Countess Company lost in the fire.

32. $210,000

33. **Journal Entries in a Perpetual Inventory System** (LO 8)

Art's Auto Repair had the following transactions during July of this year:

July 1: Purchased ten car mirrors from Prisms, Inc., for $25 each, terms 2/10, n/30.

July 5: Sold six car mirrors on credit for $40 each, terms 1/10, n/30.

July 7: Two of the car mirrors sold on July 5 were returned by the customers because they were flawed.

July 9:   Returned the two flawed car mirrors to Prisms, Inc.

July 11: Paid the amount due Prisms, Inc., for the car mirrors purchased on July 1.

July 15: Received full amount due from customer who purchased car mirrors on July 5.

Required:

1. Prepare the journal entries for each of the transactions listed, assuming that Art's Auto Repair uses the perpetual inventory system.
2. Prepare the journal entries for each of the transactions listed, assuming that Art's Auto Repair uses the periodic inventory system.
3. Suppose that Art's Auto Repair is a new business and has not yet selected an inventory accounting system. Write a brief memo to Art, the owner of the business, that identifies the factors he should consider in choosing between a periodic and perpetual inventory system.

33. 1. 7/1 Dr. Inv. $250
         Cr. AP $250
         7/5 Dr. AR $240
         Cr. Sales $240
         Dr. CGS $150
         Cr. Inv. $150
     2. 7/1 Dr. Purch, $250
         Cr. AP $250
         7/5 Dr. AR $240
         Cr. Sales $240

34. **Analyzing Inventory** (LO 9)

Francesca Johnson owns and operates a sporting goods store. Following are selected financial data regarding Francesca's business over the past three years:

	1994	1995	1996
Net Sales	$280,000	$300,000	$330,000
Cost of Goods Sold	168,000	195,000	224,400
Net Income	37,100	38,500	39,600
Ending Inventory	80,000	110,000	130,000

Required:

1. Compute the inventory turnover ratio and age of inventory for Francesca's store each year from 1994 through 1996. (Note: On January 1, 1994, the store's inventory was $60,000.)
2. Given the data provided and the ratios you computed in Part 1, evaluate Francesca's management of inventory over this three-year period.
3. Francesca is concerned by the slow growth in her business's net income over this three-year period. Identify factors related to Francesca's inventory that may be adversely affecting her business's profitability.

34. 1. 1994 Inv. Turn., 2.40
         1994 Age Inv., 150

35. **Income Statement Impact of Inventory Errors** (LO 2)

Robert Kincade is the owner and manager of Winterset Manufacturing Company. Following is the business's income statement for its most recent fiscal year.

Sales		$89,000
Cost of Goods Sold:		
Beginning Inventory	$28,000	
Net Purchases	42,000	
Cost of Goods Available for Sale	70,000	
Ending Inventory	39,000	
Cost of Goods Sold		31,000
Gross Profit		58,000
Operating Expenses		10,000
Income from Operations		48,000
Income Taxes Expense (30%)		14,400
Net Income		$33,600

Shortly after the company's financial statements were prepared, Kincade's accountant discovered that the company's ending inventory had been inadvertently overstated by $12,000.

Required:

1. Compute the effect of the inventory error on Winterset's net income, gross profit percentage, and profit margin percentage.
2. Kincade told his accountant to ignore the inventory error. "Why bother? The financial statements are already out, and besides it was an honest error." Evaluate Kincade's decision. Has he behaved unethically? Why or why not?

35. 1   NI overstated $8,400

36. **Analyzing Inventory** (LO 9)

Thiokol Corporation is one of the leading firms in the aerospace and defense industry. Thiokol's 1994 annual report described one of the company's major products as "high-technology solid rockets for aerospace, defense, and commercial launch applications." Following are selected financial data (in millions) taken from that annual report.

	1992	1993	1994
Net Sales	$1,311.7	$1,201.7	$1,043.9
Cost of Goods Sold	1,122.4	996.4	860.4
Net Income	63.0	63.8	63.0
Ending Inventory	164.0*	118.4	121.9

*Estimated based upon data included in 1994 annual report.

Required:

1. Compute the inventory turnover ratio and age of inventory for Thiokol for 1992–1994. The company's approximate inventory balance at the beginning of 1992 was $153 million.
2. Did Thiokol's inventory ratios improve or deteriorate between 1992 and 1994? Explain.
3. In the early 1990s, many companies in the aerospace and defense industries were forced to "downsize." How did this downsizing affect Thiokol's financial statements?

36. 1. 1992 Inv. Turn., 7.08
            1992 Age Inv., 51

PROBLEM SET A

37. **Effects of Inventory Errors** (LO 2, 10)

Maxwell Machinery is a wholesale distributor of engine parts. This company is privately owned by two sisters, Laura Lambert and Jean Campeaux. Following are Maxwell's income statements for 1995 and 1996. Maxwell has a $300,000 loan outstanding from a local bank. The loan agreement requires the company to submit annual financial statements to the bank for its review.

	1995		1996	
Sales		$620,000		$655,000
Cost of Goods Sold:				
Beginning Inventory	$122,000		$154,000	
Net Purchases	331,000		368,000	
Cost of Goods Available for Sale	453,000		522,000	
Ending Inventory	154,000		131,000	
Cost of Goods Sold		299,000		391,000
Gross Profit		321,000		264,000
Operating Expenses		127,000		130,000
Operating Income		194,000		134,000
Income Taxes Expense (40%)		77,600		53,600
Net Income		$116,400		$ 80,400

In early 1996, shortly before Maxwell's 1995 financial statements were completed, the owners of the company discovered a large theft of inventory by a warehouse supervisor. This individual stole approximately $40,000 of goods and then sold them to an individual who allegedly smuggled the goods into Mexico. The theft occurred in June but went undetected until the results of the December 31, 1995, physical inventory had been tabulated. Maxwell's accountant failed to discover the theft because the warehouse supervisor also maintained the warehouse's perpetual inventory records.

The owners did not prosecute the warehouse supervisor who had stolen the goods to obtain funds needed to support his drug habit. The owners agreed not to prosecute the supervisor on the condition that he would check himself into a drug rehabilitation center. By settling the matter privately, the owners avoided publicly disclosing the incident. On the advice of their accountant, the owners also decided not to adjust the perpetual inventory records to agree with the dollar value of inventory determined by the annual physical inventory. "There's no need to correct the error," the accountant observed. "This is a self-correcting error. By the end of next year, the books will be right on the mark."

Required:

1. Prepare corrected income statements for Maxwell Machinery for 1995 and 1996. Recognize that the company's December 31, 1996, inventory balance is correct.
2. Compute Maxwell's gross profit and profit margin percentages for 1995 and 1996 based both on the income statement data released by the company and on the corrected income statement data you prepared in Part 1.
3. What effect did the overstatement of inventory have on Maxwell's 1995 and 1996 balance sheets and statements of owners' equity?
4. What internal control procedures might have prevented or led to more timely disclosure of the inventory theft?
5. Did the owners behave ethically by failing to correct their company's accounting records at the end of 1995? Does the fact that their accountant advised them to ignore the error affect your answer? Why or why not?

38. **Inventory Costing Methods** (LO 3, 4)

Brooks Enterprises had the following inventory purchases and sales during the year just ended:

	Units	Per Unit Cost	Per Unit Selling Price
Beginning Inventory	400	$20	
Purchase, January 2	200	22	
Sales, First Quarter	300		$40
Purchase, April 1	200	24	
Sales, Second Quarter	350		45
Purchase, July 1	200	25	
Sales, Third Quarter	150		45
Purchase, October 1	500	26	
Sales, Fourth Quarter	450		50

Required:

1. Determine Brooks' ending inventory, cost of goods sold, and gross profit for the year in question assuming the company uses a periodic inventory system and the following inventory costing methods:

37. 1. 1995 NI, $92,400
      1996 NI, $104,400
    2. 1995 GP%, 45.3%
      1995 PM%, 14.9%
      1996 GP%, 46.4%
      1995 PM%, 15.9%
      (Based on corrected data)

38. 1a. Inv., $6,500
      CGS, $28,700
      GP, $28,300
   1b. Inv., $5,000
      CGS, $30,200
      GP, $26,800
   1c. Inv., $5,866.50
      CGS, $29,333.50
      GP, $27,666.50

   a. FIFO
   b. LIFO
   c. Weighted-average
2. Given your answers to Part 1, which of the three inventory costing methods yields the most impressive financial data for Brooks? Explain.
3. What factors should a company take into account when choosing an inventory costing method? In making this choice, should a company consider which costing method would be preferred by the decision makers who will be using its financial statements?

39. **Perpetual LIFO Inventory Costing Method** (LO 4, 8)
Refer to the data presented in Problem 38 for Brooks Enterprises.

Required:
1. Determine Brooks' ending inventory, cost of goods sold, and gross profit assuming the company uses a perpetual inventory system and the LIFO inventory costing method.
2. Briefly describe the comparative advantages and disadvantages of a periodic and perpetual inventory system.

39. 1. Inv., $5,550
       CGS, $29,650
       GP, $27,350

40. **Lower-of-Cost-or-Market Rule** (LO 3, 6)
Best Plumbing, Inc., sells plumbing fixtures. The company had the following year-end inventory quantities, per unit costs, and per unit market values (current replacement costs) for its inventory at the end of a recent fiscal year. These data are segregated by item within each of the company's major inventory classes.

	UNITS	PER UNIT COST	PER UNIT MARKET VALUE
Industrial Strength			
Item A	100	$160	$150
Item B	150	200	205
Medium Strength			
Item C	75	120	125
Item D	110	140	125
Low Strength			
Item E	80	80	80
Item F	130	75	70

Required:
1. Compute Best Plumbing's ending inventory by applying the following versions of the lower-of-cost-or-market (LCM) rule:
   a. Item-by-item
   b. By major class of inventory
   c. On a total inventory basis
2. In your view, which of the following inventory valuation methods would provide the most relevant and reliable accounting data for external decision makers: valuing inventories strictly on a cost basis, valuing inventories strictly on a market basis, or valuing inventories on a lower-of-cost-or-market basis? Defend your choice.

40. 1a. $83,250
     1b. $84,375
     1c. $84,375

41. **Gross Profit Method of Estimating Inventory** (LO 7)
Louisa's Books is a large bookstore located in a local mall. The owner of this business, May Alcott, and her employees perform an annual physical inventory on December 31. At the end of each quarter, other than year end, Ms. Alcott

uses the gross profit method to estimate the business's inventory. The following information is available for a recent quarter ending on September 30:

Beginning Inventory, July 1	$ 72,000
Net Purchases	123,000
Net Sales	154,000
Normal Gross Profit Percentage	40%

Required:

1. Compute Louisa's cost of goods sold for the quarter ending September 30 and the inventory on that date using the gross profit method.
2. May Alcott has determined that it costs her approximately $800 to take a physical inventory of her store at the end of each year. So, she is considering using the gross profit method to determine her year-end inventory. Is this a good idea? Why or why not?

42. **Perpetual Inventory System** (LO 8)

Roth, Inc., is a jewelry wholesaler specializing in diamond pendants, bracelets, and earrings. Because of the nature of its inventory, Roth uses a perpetual inventory system. Roth also uses the gross method of recording merchandise purchases. The company's inventory is maintained in a warehouse located near its corporate headquarters. Following are selected transactions of Roth for November.

November 2:   Sold three diamond pendants for $450 each to Loew's Jewelry with terms of 3/10, n/60; the pendants cost $200 each.

November 5:   Purchased ten diamond bracelets for $250 each from Horne Diamonds with terms of 2/10, n/30.

November 8:   Returned two of the diamond bracelets purchased on November 5 due to flaws.

November 9:   Sold five of the diamond bracelets purchased on November 5; selling price was $550 per unit with terms of n/30.

November 10: Purchased thirty pairs of diamond earrings for $100 each from Gems Unlimited with terms of 3/10, n/60.

November 12: Received payment in full from Loew's Jewelry for November 2 sales transaction.

November 14: Sold ten diamond pendants for $500 each to Carr's Jewelry Stores with terms of 2/10, n/60; the pendants cost $200 each.

November 15: Paid amount due Horne Diamonds for bracelets purchased on November 5.

November 19: Carr's Jewelry Stores returned five of the pendants purchased on November 14, since they were not the style ordered.

November 20: Paid amount due Gems Unlimited for earrings purchased on November 10.

November 24: Received payment in full from Carr's Jewelry Stores for November 14 sales transaction.

Required:

a. Prepare the journal entries necessary to record the November transactions of Roth, Inc.
b. On November 30, Roth's perpetual inventory records reflected a balance of $1,564,200. Following the taking of a physical inventory on that date, Roth's accountant determined that there was $1,511,900 of inventory on hand. Given this information, prepare the appropriate adjusting journal entry on November 30.

---

41. 1. CGS, $92,400
Inv., $102,600

42. 1a. 11/2   Dr. AR $1,350
Cr. Sales $1,350
Dr. CGS $600
Cr. Inv. $600
11/19   Dr. Sales Ret.
$2,500
Cr. AR $2,500
Dr. Inv. $1,000
Cr. CGS $1,000

43. **Internal Controls for Inventory** (LO 10)

    Refer to the facts presented in Problem 42. The chief executive of Roth is concerned by the large difference between the dollar value of inventory as determined by the physical inventory and the corresponding dollar value reflected by the perpetual inventory records. He has retained you to develop a general strategy for safeguarding the inventory maintained in the company's warehouse and minimizing the risk that the perpetual inventory records will contain errors.

    Required:

    Write a memo to Roth's chief executive in which you describe a general control strategy that he can implement for the warehouse. The owner is willing to totally overhaul the internal controls related to the warehouse and the nature of the warehouse's operations. Because he does not want to influence your suggestions, he does not provide you with any information regarding the present controls that exist at the warehouse or the nature of the warehouse's operations.

    43. No check figures

44. **Analyzing Inventory** (LO 3, 9)

    Cracker Barrel Old Country Store, Inc., is a Tennessee-based company that operates a large chain of restaurants. The following information was taken from the company's 1994 annual report.

	1992	1993	1994
Net Sales	$400,577,451	$517,616,132	$640,898,529
Cost of Goods Sold	130,885,297	171,708,439	215,071,169
Net Income	33,942,348	46,652,485	57,947,446
Ending Inventory	23,192,110	28,426,408	41,989,546

    Required:

    1. Compute Cracker Barrel's inventory turnover ratio and age of inventory for each year 1992 through 1994. (The company's beginning inventory for 1992 was $15,746,448.)
    2. Comment on the ratios you computed in Part 1. Are there any definite trends in these ratios? If so, are these trends generally favorable or unfavorable? Explain.
    3. Why do decision makers pay particularly close attention to the age of inventory measure for companies in the restaurant industry?

    44. 1992 Inv. Turn., 6.72
         1992 Age Inv., 54

PROBLEM SET B

45. **Effects of Inventory Errors** (LO 2)

    Drexel & Clyde, Inc., operates a small chain of specialty stores that sell greeting cards, ceramic dolls, stuffed animals, and novelty gift items. Competition has been stiff in recent years for Drexel & Clyde, a company owned for the past forty years by two longtime friends. Over the past five years, a publicly owned company has begun building stores in Drexel & Clyde's market area. These new stores have caused Drexel & Clyde's annual sales to drop by nearly 40 percent during that period.

    During early 1995, the two owners began negotiations to sell Drexel & Clyde to their competitor. To improve their chances of obtaining a reasonable price for their company, the owners decided to "doctor" the firm's 1995 income statement by overstating ending inventory for the year by $60,000. They justified this decision to themselves by observing that if the competitor hadn't moved into their market area, their company's financial statements would have been much more impressive. "Besides," remarked one of the owners, "a large company like that is not going to be hurt by paying a little more than they should for our business."

Finally, in late 1996, the two owners were about to finalize a buy-out agreement with their competitor. Before closing the deal, the other firm insisted on an audit of Drexel & Clyde's financial statements as of the end of 1996. Shown next are Drexel & Clyde's 1995 income statement, which contained the overstated ending inventory, and the audited 1996 income statement. (Although the beginning inventory was in error in the 1996 income statement, the ending inventory was correct.)

		1995		1996
Sales		$904,300		$862,000
Cost of Goods Sold:				
Beginning Inventory	$232,000		$307,000	
Net Purchases	501,000		489,000	
Cost of Goods Available for Sale	733,000		796,000	
Ending Inventory	307,000		259,000	
Cost of Goods Sold		426,000		537,000
Gross Profit		478,300		325,000
Operating Expenses		241,000		221,000
Operating Income		237,300		104,000
Income Taxes Expense (40%)		94,920		41,600
Net Income		$142,380		$62,400

Required:

1. Prepare corrected income statements for Drexel & Clyde for 1995 and 1996.
2. Compute Drexel & Clyde's gross profit and profit margin percentages for 1995 and 1996 based both on the income statement data released by the company and on the corrected income statement data you prepared in Part 1. Also compute the percentage decrease in the company's net income between 1995 and 1996 and the percentage decrease or increase it would have realized in the absence of the inventory error.
3. Do you believe the two owners' plan to increase the selling price of their business worked, or did it likely backfire on them? Explain.
4. Consider the tax consequences of the two owners' scheme. How did this scheme affect the taxes paid by the company during 1995 and 1996?
5. Analyze the reasons used by the owners to justify their scheme. Do you believe those reasons justified the owners' actions? Why or why not?

45. 1. 1995 NI, $106,380
       1996 NI, $98,400
    2. 1995 GP%, 46.3%
       1995 PM%, 11.8%
       1996 GP%, 44.7%
       1995 PM%, 11.4%
       (Based on corrected data)

46. **Inventory Costing Methods** (LO 3)

J. Austin Enterprises (JAE) had the following inventory purchases and sales during the year just ended:

	UNITS	PER UNIT COST	PER UNIT SELLING PRICE
Beginning Inventory	400	$20	
Purchase, January 2	200	24	
Sales, First Quarter	300		$40
Purchase, April 1	200	22	
Sales, Second Quarter	350		45
Purchase, July 1	200	25	
Sales, Third Quarter	150		45
Purchase, October 1	500	23	
Sales, Fourth Quarter	450		50

Required:

1. Determine JAE's ending inventory, cost of goods sold, and gross profit for the year in question assuming the company uses a periodic inventory system and the following inventory costing methods:
   a. FIFO
   b. LIFO
   c. Weighted-average
2. Given your answers to Part 1, which of the three inventory costing methods yields the most impressive financial data for JAE? Explain.
3. If a company uses LIFO for federal taxation purposes, it must also use LIFO for financial reporting purposes. What is the purpose of this rule? Why isn't there a similar rule for FIFO?

47. Perpetual LIFO Inventory Costing Method (LO 4, 8)

Refer to the data presented in Problem 46 for J. Austin Enterprises (JAE).

Required:

1. Determine JAE's ending inventory, cost of goods sold, and gross profit assuming the company uses a perpetual inventory system and the LIFO inventory costing method.
2. Briefly explain why periodic FIFO and perpetual FIFO yield the same ending inventory and cost of goods sold figures when applied to the same set of data. Likewise, explain why this is not true for periodic LIFO and perpetual LIFO.

48. Lower-of-Cost-or-Market Rule (LO 6)

Don Monroe owns and operates Opie's, Inc., a beverage supply distributor. Opie's had the following inventory quantities, per unit costs, and per unit market values (current replacement costs) for its inventory at the end of a recent fiscal year. These data are segregated by item within each of the company's major inventory classes.

	UNITS	PER UNIT COST	PER UNIT MARKET VALUE
Colas			
Item A	600	$180	$170
Item B	800	170	190
Non-colas			
Item C	450	120	130
Item D	500	140	150
Diet Drinks			
Item E	700	70	75
Item F	550	85	65

Required:

1. Compute Opie's ending inventory by applying the following versions of the lower-of-cost-or-market (LCM) rule:
   a. Item-by-item
   b. By major class of inventory
   c. On a total inventory basis
2. What accounting concept or principle underlies the LCM rule? Explain.

49. Gross Profit Method of Estimating Inventory (LO 7)

Grass Point Lighthouse Supplies operates out of an old lighthouse facility on the coast of Maine. A once-in-a-century high tide has wiped out most of the business's inventory at midyear. Grass Point uses a periodic inventory system and

Side margin answers:

46. 1a. Inv., $5,750
CGS, $27,950
GP, $29,050
1b. Inv., $5,000
CGS, $28,700
GP, $28,300
1c. Inv., $5,616.50
CGS, $28,083.50
GP, $28,916.50

47. 1. Inv., $5,400
CGS, $28,300
GP, $28,700

48. 1a. $466,250
1b. $475,750
1c. $489,250

keeps good accounting records, which fortunately were not lost in the flood. However, a physical count of inventory has not been taken since the beginning of the year.

The insurance company has told Grass Point's owner that it will reimburse the company for the inventory loss only if that loss can be adequately documented. Following is information regarding Grass Point's inventory at the beginning of the year and inventory-related transactions from that point through the date of the loss:

Inventory, January 1	$ 75,000
Purchases	250,600
Purchases Returns and Allowances	8,100
Purchases Discounts	4,200
Sales	364,400
Sales Returns and Allowances	3,200

Note: Grass Point's gross profit percentages for the past three years are 42 percent, 48 percent, and 33 percent, respectively.

Required:

1. Compute the amount of inventory lost by Grass Point using the gross profit method. Use the business's average gross profit for the past three years in making this computation.
2. Recompute the amount of inventory lost by Grass Point using its highest gross profit percentage (48 percent) for the past three years and its lowest (33 percent) gross profit percentage over that period.
3. Given your answers to Parts 1 and 2, comment on the reliability of the inventory data yielded by the gross profit method.

50. **Perpetual Inventory System** (LO 8)

House of Jeans is a retail store that specializes in denim jeans. Bob Goldstein owns and operates House of Jeans in the small Arizona town of Ash Fork. Bob employs one full-time salesclerk, three high school seniors as part-time salesclerks, and a college senior, who is an accounting major, to maintain the business's accounting records. Besides the House of Jeans, Bob also owns two other businesses in town, a convenience store and a hamburger stand located across the street from the high school. Typically, Bob spends ten to fifteen hours per week at each business, helping with sales, resolving employee problems, and so on. Bob's accountant, the accounting major, has established a perpetual inventory system for the House of Jeans and uses the gross method of recording inventory purchases. Since the House of Jeans does not have a large volume of transactions, Bob's accountant updates the accounting records when the in-basket on his desk is full of purchase invoices, return memos, and other source documents. Following are selected transactions of the House of Jeans for a recent month.

April 6:   Purchased thirty pairs of 404 Jeans with terms of 2/10, n/30; the per unit cost was $22.

April 9:   Returned ten pairs of the 404 Jeans purchased on April 6 due to fabric flaws.

April 13:   Sold two pairs of 303 Jeans for cash; the per unit cost of these jeans was $21. (Goldstein has a "one price fits all" pricing strategy. All jeans are sold for $35 per pair.)

April 17:   Purchased twelve pairs of 606 Jeans with terms of 2/10, n/30; the per unit cost was $18.

April 20:   Sold one pair of 909 Jeans on credit; the cost of this pair was $24.

April 21:   A customer returned a pair of 808 Jeans because they were the wrong size; the jeans, which cost $20, were returned to inventory.

49. 1. CGS, $213,108
        Inv., $100,192
    2a. CGS, $187,824
        Inv., $125,476
    2b. CGS, $242,004
        Inv., $71,296

April 27: Sold two pairs of 101 Jeans on credit; the per unit cost of these jeans was $17.

Note: House of Jeans does not have a formal credit policy. Bob has given his salesclerks the following instructions when customers ask for credit: "If you know them, then give them credit."

On April 30, House of Jeans took a physical inventory. Bob was shocked to find that his store's inventory was only $12,080. The store's perpetual inventory records indicated that $15,600 of inventory should have been on hand. Two years earlier, when the last physical inventory was taken, the perpetual inventory figure had exceeded the physical inventory dollar value by less than $100.

Required:
a. Prepare the journal entries necessary to record the April transactions of House of Jeans.
b. Prepare the entry necessary on April 30 to adjust the perpetual inventory records following the taking of the physical inventory.

50. No check figures

51. **Internal Controls for Inventory** (LO 10)

Refer to the facts presented in Problem 50. Bob Goldstein is very concerned by the large difference between the dollar value of inventory as determined by the physical inventory and the corresponding dollar value reflected by the perpetual inventory records. He has retained you to develop a report identifying inventory-related internal control weaknesses existing at the House of Jeans. Bob has also asked you to identify specific internal control procedures that he could adopt to tighten the business's control over inventory. Bob is willing to totally revamp the operating policies and procedures related to inventory to achieve more control over this important asset.

Required:
Write the report that Bob Goldstein has requested.

51. No check figures

52. **Analyzing Inventory** (LO 9)

Dress Barn, Inc., is a public company based in New York. The company's 1994 annual report described the nature of its business as follows: "The Dress Barn, Inc., operates a chain of off-price women's apparel stores. The stores, operating principally under the name 'Dress Barn,' offer in-season, moderate to better quality fashion apparel. Dress Barn emphasizes department store quality merchandise, primarily with nationally recognized brand names at substantial discounts from department store prices."

The following financial information was taken from the Dress Barn's 1994 annual report.

	1992	1993	1994
Net Sales	$363,089,914	$419,585,581	$457,324,621
Cost of Goods Sold	231,829,749	266,867,616	291,937,984
Net Income	16,194,118	19,039,260	16,153,216
Ending Inventory	66,332,215	73,403,238	79,601,016

Required:
1. Compute Dress Barn's inventory turnover ratio and age of inventory for each year 1992 through 1994. (The company's beginning inventory for 1992 was $48,427,296.)
2. Comment on the ratios you computed in Part 1. Are there any definite trends in these ratios? If so, are these trends generally favorable or unfavorable? Explain.

52. 1992 Inv. Turn., 4.04
1992 Age Inv., 89

3. Consider the nature of the women's apparel industry. How may sudden changes in fashion trends be reflected in the inventory ratios of a company within this industry? Explain.

CASES

53. Inventory Errors and Job Protection

Reread the Spotlight on Ethics vignette in this chapter entitled "Rocky Mount Accounting Horror."

Required:

1. Place yourself in the position of the accountants who were being pressured by company executives to misrepresent RMUC's ending inventory. What would you have done in that situation?
2. Again, place yourself in the position of RMUC's accountants, but assume the following additional facts:
   a. The executives were correct that the company would eventually fail and the company's employees would lose their jobs unless ending inventory was overstated.
   b. You were almost certain that the inventory overstatement would not be discovered or disclosed outside the company.
   c. You were almost certain that the company would earn sufficient profits in the future to "wipe out" the illicit profits resulting from the intentional inventory overstatement.

   Given these additional facts, would your answer to Part 1 change? Why or why not?

54. Inventory Errors and Materiality

Following are financial data (in thousands) taken from the 1994 annual report of Wm. Wrigley Jr. Company, the "chewing gum" company.

Net Sales	$1,596,551
Cost of Goods Sold	697,442
Net Income	230,533
Inventory	221,109
Total Quick Assets	368,795
Total Current Liabilities	209,898
Total Assets	978,834

Listed next are the comparable data (in thousands) drawn from the 1994 annual report of Whole Foods Market, a food retailer based in Austin, Texas.

Net Sales	$401,684
Cost of Goods Sold	272,176
Net Income	8,638
Inventory	17,187
Total Quick Assets	7,954
Total Current Liabilities	26,035
Total Assets	136,135

Note: For purposes of this case, assume that both companies have an effective income tax rate of 40 percent.

Required:

1. Suppose that the 1994 ending inventory of both Wrigley and Whole Foods was overstated by 5 percent. Refer to the concept of materiality discussed in Chapter 2 before responding to the following questions:

    a. Did the (assumed) inventory error result in a material misrepresentation of either company's profitability for 1994? Explain.

    b. Did the (assumed) inventory error cause either company's liquidity position to be materially misrepresented at the end of 1994? Explain.

2. Suppose that the 1994 ending inventory of both Wrigley and Whole Foods was overstated by $7 million.

    a. Did the (assumed) inventory error result in a material misrepresentation of either company's profitability for 1994? Explain.

    b. Did the (assumed) inventory error cause either company's liquidity position to be materially misrepresented at the end of 1994? Explain.

55. Meeting Profit Expectations

Morehead Company did not meet its profit goal for Year 1, the year just ended. At the previous stockholders' meeting, Morehead's chief executive officer (CEO) practically guaranteed that the firm would earn at least $1.2 million in Year 1. Unfortunately, preliminary indications are that the company will earn only $850,000. Since Year 1 has just ended, there is nothing Morehead can do to change the situation . . . or is there?

    Morehead's annual physical inventory, which requires three days to complete, is in progress for Year 1. Morehead's independent auditors are busy going from warehouse to warehouse monitoring the counting of thousands of cartons and crates of merchandise. However, under cover of darkness, several Morehead officers, including the CEO, are moving a significant number of unmarked cartons and crates from warehouses that have been counted to warehouses that will be counted the following day.

Required:

1. How will the treachery of Morehead's officers affect the company's financial statements for Year 1?

2. Suppose the inventory scam goes undetected and Morehead reports a net income of slightly more than $1.2 million for Year 1 at the next stockholders' meeting. Also, assume that Morehead's CEO guarantees at the next stockholders' meeting that the company will earn $1.5 million during Year 2. How will the inventory scam perpetrated by Morehead's officers at the end of Year 1 affect the company's likelihood of legitimately reaching its profit objective for Year 2?

3. Identify how Morehead's independent auditors might have prevented or detected the inventory scam.

PROJECTS

56. International Inventory Accounting Practices

Refer to the For Your Information vignette titled "Inventory Costing Methods in Europe." You and your project group will research the inventory accounting rules and practices of at least three countries, using your college library as your principal source of information. These countries will be assigned to you by your instructor or selected by your group—do not choose countries mentioned in the vignette.

Required:

As a group, prepare a brief written report that summarizes the inventory accounting rules and practices of the countries studied by your group. Comment in your report on key similarities and differences in the inventory accounting rules and practices of these countries, and identify factors that may account for these similarities and differences. Be prepared to present an oral summary of your report to the class.

57. **Ethics, Inventory Controls, and College Students**

Suzette Washington financed her college education by working as an inventory clerk for Bertolini's, a clothing store chain located in the southeastern United States. Bertolini's caters primarily to "fashion-conscious" young men and women. The Bertolini's store for which Suzette worked is located a few blocks from the campus of the large state university that she attended. Except for management personnel, most of Bertolini's employees are college students. Suzette's best friend and roommate, Paula Kaye, worked for Bertolini's as a salesclerk. Paula majored in marketing, while Suzette was an accounting major.

During Suzette's senior year in college, Bertolini's began experiencing abnormally high inventory shrinkage in the store's three departments that stocked men's apparel. Over lunch one day in the student union, Suzette casually mentioned the inventory problem to Paula. Paula quickly changed the subject by asking Suzette about her plans for the weekend.

"Paula, rewind for just a second. Do you know something that I don't?"

"Huh? What do you mean?"

"Missing inventory . . . shrinkage . . . theft?"

After a few awkward moments, Paula responded to her friend. "Suzette, I don't know if it's true, but I've heard a rumor that Alex and Matt are stealing a few things each week—polo shirts, silk ties, jeans. Every so often, they take something expensive, like a sports jacket."

"How are they doing it?"

"I've heard—and don't repeat any of this, now—I've heard that a couple of times per week, Alex stashes one or two items at the bottom of the trash container beneath the number two cash register. Then Matt empties the trash every night in the dumpster out in the alley, takes the items out, and puts them in his car."

"Paula, we can't let them get away with this. We have to tell someone."

"No 'we' aren't. Remember, this is just a rumor. I don't know that it's true. If you tell a manager, there will be questions. And more questions. Maybe even the police will be brought in. You know that eventually someone is going to find out who told."

"So, don't get involved? Just let those guys keep stealing?"

"Suze, you work in inventory. You know the markup they put on those clothes. They expect to lose a few things here and there to employees."

"Maybe the markup wouldn't be so high if theft wasn't a problem."

Now there was no doubt in Paula's mind that Suzette was going to tattle. "Two months, Suze. Two months till we graduate. Can you wait till then to spill the beans? Then we can move out of state before our cars are spray-painted."

One week following Suzette and Paula's conversation, a Bertolini's store manager received an anonymous typed message informing her of the two-person theft ring allegedly operating within the store. Bertolini's immediately retained a private detective. Over a four-week period, the detective documented the theft by Alex and Matt of merchandise with a retail value of approximately $500. After the police were notified, criminal charges were filed against the two young men.

Note: This vignette was adapted from an actual situation documented in the following source: M. C. Knapp, "Suzette Washington, Accounting Major," in *Contemporary Auditing: Issues and Cases*, 2d ed. (Minneapolis/St. Paul: West Publishing Co., 1996).

Required:

1. After reading this vignette, meet with the members of your group to discuss the following questions:

   a. What would you do if you found yourself in Suzette's position?

   b. Would it have been unethical for Suzette to report to a store manager what she had been told, considering that it was only a rumor? Would it have been unethical for Suzette not to report what she had heard to a store manager?

   c. Accounting majors are preparing to enter a profession recognized as having one of the strongest and most rigorously enforced ethical codes. Given this fact, do you believe that accounting majors have a greater responsibility than other business majors to behave ethically?

   d. Discuss internal control procedures that might have prevented the theft losses suffered by Bertolini's.

2. One member of your group should be prepared to present a brief oral summary of the group's discussion of this vignette and the accompanying questions.

58. **Inventory Disclosures**

    Identify four companies in four different industries. Obtain for each of these companies the most recent annual report that is available. Identify in each annual report the financial statement footnote disclosures relating to inventory.

    Required:

    1. Summarize in a written report the inventory accounting policies of each company you selected.

    2. Comment in your written report on factors that may account for the different inventory accounting policies used by these firms. Also comment on how the inventory accounting policies of the companies you selected may affect their reported profits.

PROPERTY, PLANT & EQUIPMENT, AND INTANGIBLE ASSETS

LEARNING OBJECTIVES

After studying this chapter, you should be able to do the following:

1. Identify the key information needs of decision makers regarding property, plant & equipment

2. Determine the acquisition cost of property, plant & equipment assets

3. Compute depreciation expense using each of the three major depreciation methods

4. Distinguish between and account for revenue and capital expenditures

5. Account for disposals of property, plant & equipment

6. Compute return on assets and the total asset turnover ratio

7. Discuss key internal control procedures for property, plant & equipment

8. Identify major types of intangible assets and the key accounting issues related to these assets

It is said that one machine can do the work of fifty ordinary men. No machine, however, can do the work of one extraordinary man.
Tehyi Hsieh

Avoiding Edsel-Land

Suppose we used the *Family Feud* game show format and asked one hundred people to identify a corporate asset. "Machinery" would likely be the most popular response. The fastest-growing sector of the U.S. economy is service industries. Nevertheless, the public still largely equates corporate America with towering smokestacks, long assembly lines, and noisy machinery.

The last few decades have been unkind to many manufacturing firms in the United States. Rapid advancements in technology, increasing competition from foreign firms, and fast-paced changes in consumer preferences have caught many manufacturers flat-footed. A major problem manufacturing firms have historically faced is a lack of flexibility. When manufacturers purchase long-lived assets, such as machinery, they commit themselves to producing a particular product or line of products. This commitment cannot be changed easily or inexpensively. During the 1950s, Ford Motor Company invested heavily in production facilities for the Edsel. Within a few years, it was obvious that the public simply did not like the futuristic car. After discontinuing the model in late 1959, Ford was forced to scrap most of the machinery used in the Edsel production line. The final price tag for the unsuccessful Edsel project exceeded $200 million.

By constantly monitoring and evaluating alternative uses of long-term productive assets, corporate managers can overcome, to a degree, the inflexibility inherent in manufacturing operations. Consider the case of B&D Instruments & Avionics, a small Kansas-based manufacturing company. In the late 1980s, B&D's principal product was an electronic navigation system. Since the demand for this product was not growing, the company's future prospects were dismal. In 1990, the company learned that the market for cockpit voice recorders would be expanding dramatically because of a new regulation issued by the Federal Aviation Agency. B&D had never produced that product. Nevertheless, company executives believed that with a few changes and additions to production-line equipment, their firm could produce a lightweight and inexpensive cockpit voice recorder. B&D's executives acted quickly on this belief and within a few years captured a significant and profitable slice of the newly expanded market for cockpit voice recorders.

In this chapter, we focus on accounting issues related to long-term assets such as production-line equipment. Business executives rely on accountants to provide them with important data regarding long-term assets. This information allows management to make better decisions regarding the utilization of these assets. For instance, B&D's accountants were likely called upon to develop estimates of the costs necessary to retool the firm's production equipment to manufacture cockpit voice recorders. Developing cash-flow and profit forecasts for this new product was likely another responsibility assigned to B&D's accountants. Finally, B&D's accountants were almost certainly responsible for analyzing the tax implications of the changes in the company's production line. Accountants can help management structure transactions involving the acquisition and disposal of long-term assets to provide for the most favorable tax treatment of these transactions.

R ecall from Chapter 2 that assets are defined as "probable future economic benefits obtained or controlled by a particular entity as a result of past transactions or events."[1] In Chapters 7 and 8, we became familiar with accounting issues related to current assets, such as cash, accounts receivable, and inventory. Now we turn our

---

1. *Statement of Financial Accounting Concepts, No. 6*, "Elements of Financial Statements" (Stamford, Conn.: FASB, 1985), para. 25.

Discussion Question
As a review, ask students to
define an operating cycle.

attention to long-term assets. The key difference between current and long-term assets is the time frame over which these assets provide economic benefits to a business. Current assets provide economic benefits to a business over the coming twelve months or operating cycle, whichever is longer. Long-term assets typically provide economic benefits to a business for several years, if not several decades.

Those of you with an excellent long-term memory will recall that in Chapter 2, four general types of long-term or noncurrent assets were identified: property, plant & equipment; intangible assets; long-term investments; and other assets. This chapter principally concerns property, plant & equipment. The last section of this chapter provides a brief overview of accounting issues related to intangible assets. Long-term investments are discussed in Chapter 14. We do not consider in this text "other assets," a catchall classification for miscellaneous and minor long-term assets.

PROPERTY, PLANT & EQUIPMENT: FORMERLY FIXED ASSETS

Most businesses classify the long-term assets used in their day-to-day operations as property, plant & equipment on their balance sheets. "Plant assets" and "operating assets" are among other balance sheet captions for this broad class of long-term assets. For our purposes, the cumbersome phrase "property, plant & equipment" is often shortened in this chapter to "PP&E," a term commonly used by accountants. Until a few decades ago, "fixed assets" was the most common balance sheet heading for these assets. However, the accounting profession in the United States decided that caption was too vague and encouraged businesses to replace it with a more descriptive term. Nevertheless, many stubborn accountants still refer to fixed assets in everyday conversation. Likewise, the annual reports of many foreign companies refer to fixed assets. For example, Telecom Corporation of New Zealand recently reported "Fixed Assets" with a balance sheet value expressed in United States currency of nearly $4 billion.

Teaching Note
Remind students that
accumulated depreciation is a
contra asset account to PP&E.

Following is a representative example of a PP&E section of a balance sheet. This example was drawn from a recent annual report of Community Psychiatric Centers, a California-based firm. The heading used for this balance sheet section was Property, Buildings and Equipment. Notice that the accumulated depreciation related to the company's PP&E assets was subtracted from their total cost to arrive at the assets' net balance sheet value of approximately $339 million.

Land	$ 55,685,000
Buildings and Improvements	282,027,000
Furniture, Fixtures and Equipment	70,855,000
Construction in Progress	8,362,000
	$416,929,000
Less Accumulated Depreciation	(77,851,000)
Total Property, Buildings and Equipment, at Cost, Less Accumulated Depreciation	$339,078,000

The proportion of total assets invested in PP&E varies significantly across industries. Shown in Exhibit 9.1 is the average percentage of total assets represented by PP&E in six industries tracked by the Dun & Bradstreet investment advisory firm.

■ **EXHIBIT 9.1**

Property, Plant & Equipment as a Percentage of Total Assets, Selected
Industries

SOURCE: *Dun & Bradstreet's Industry Norms & Key Business Ratios, 1993–1994* (New York: Dun &
Bradstreet, Inc., 1994).

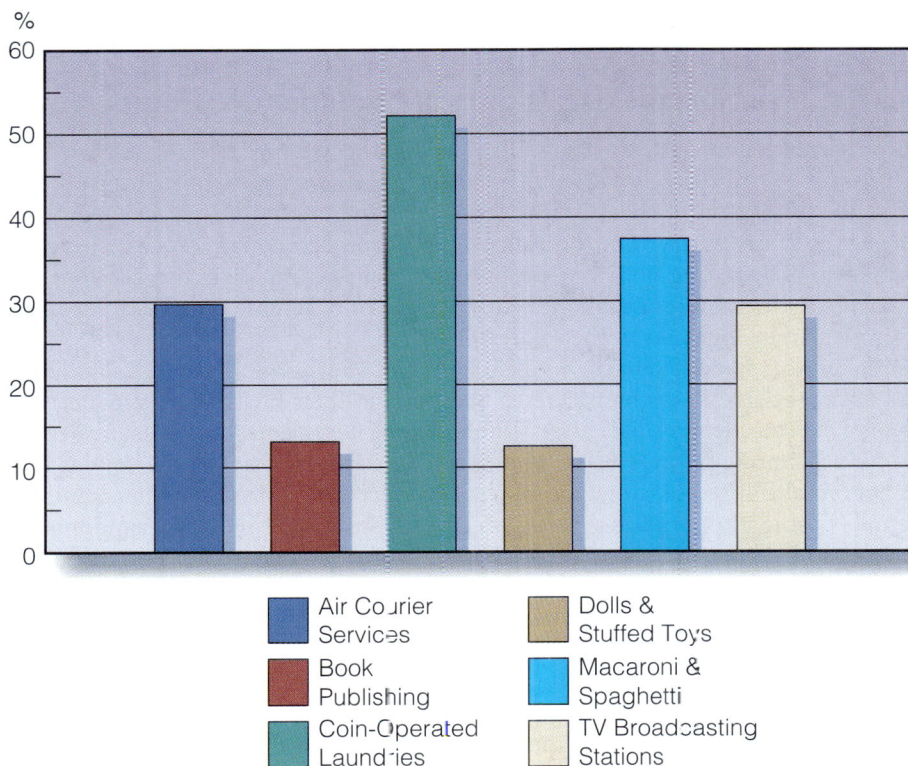

PROPERTY, PLANT & EQUIPMENT:
KEY INFORMATION NEEDS OF DECISION MAKERS

Take your average man or woman on the street who picks up an annual report of
GetanGo Convenience Stores and discovers the balance sheet line item "Buildings
. . . $20,994,038." This individual will probably interpret that line item very liter-
ally. Uncle Jack, who has little or no formal training in the world of high finance,
will likely assume that GetanGo's buildings could be sold for $20,994,038. When
Jack discovers the line item "Accumulated Depreciation, Buildings," more confusion is likely. Even worse, assume that GetanGo uses the phrase "Allowance for
Depreciation" instead of "Accumulated Depreciation." At this point, Aunt Wilma
may explain to her husband that GetanGo has obviously set aside a fund to provide
for the replacement of its buildings or for future repairs to them. Finally, assume
that Jack and Wilma turn to GetanGo's income statement and discover the line
item "Depreciation Expense, Buildings . . . $1,050,264." Here, the logical, but

■ **LEARNING
OBJECTIVE 1**
Identify the key information
needs of decision makers
regarding property, plant &
equipment

Real World
Point out that many companies have buildings and other PP&E assets with substantial market values but zero book values.

Discussion Question
Ask students to list PP&E accounts of a dental practice and a McDonald's restaurant. Examples: Dental practice— examination chair, x-ray machine, drill, office building; McDonald's—hamburger grill, deep-fryer, refrigerator/freezer, playground equipment.

Discussion Question
Ask students why land is not depreciated and land improvements are depreciated. Answer: Land does not wear out; land improvements are not permanent, and, thus, have a limited useful life.

incorrect, conclusion is that the value of GetanGo's buildings decreased by more than $1 million over the past year.

Of all the items appearing in financial statements, PP&E may be responsible for the most misconceptions in the minds of financial statement users. For this reason, it is very important that accountants include user-friendly information concerning PP&E and related accounting decisions in a business entity's annual report. This section identifies several general types of information decision makers need regarding a business's PP&E.

Disclosures of Specific Types of Property, Plant & Equipment

Decision makers demand information regarding the composition of a business's PP&E assets. Recall that Community Psychiatric Centers classified its total PP&E assets into five balance sheet line items, including accumulated depreciation. Disclosure of PP&E assets by major categories provides decision makers with insights on a company's operating policies and strategies. This information also allows decision makers to draw more meaningful comparisons of different companies' financial data, particularly companies in the same industry.

Generally accepted accounting principles require businesses to disclose "major classes of depreciable assets by nature or function" in their financial statements.[2] As you would expect, "depreciable" assets are those long-term assets that must be depreciated for accounting purposes. The only major PP&E item that is not a depreciable asset, land, is also listed separately in the balance sheet. Only land used in an entity's principal business operations is included in property, plant & equipment. Undeveloped land that is being held for investment or other purposes is classified as a long-term investment on an entity's balance sheet. Among the most common types of depreciable assets reported on balance sheets are buildings, machinery and/or equipment, and land improvements. The latter category includes such assets as parking lots and driveways. Because land improvements are depreciable assets, they must be recorded separately from land. Construction in progress, furniture and fixtures, and automobiles are examples of other PP&E balance sheet classifications reported in the 1994 edition of *Accounting Trends & Techniques*.

Valuation Issues

PP&E assets are nearly always among the largest items, in dollar terms, on a balance sheet. This is particularly true for manufacturing firms. Because PP&E typically accounts for a large proportion of a business's total assets, decision makers demand information regarding the valuation methods used for these assets. As suggested earlier, the valuation of PP&E is a source of much confusion for naive financial statement users. In fact, sophisticated financial statement users often do not fully understand how accountants assign dollar amounts to PP&E assets. At a minimum, decision makers should be aware of two important issues related to the balance sheet valuation of PP&E assets. First, decision makers need to understand that historical cost is the principal valuation basis for PP&E assets in the United States. Second, decision makers must recognize that in inflationary periods, the relevance of historical cost data for PP&E assets is undermined.

---

2. *Accounting Principles Board, Opinion No. 12*, "Omnibus Opinion—1967" (New York: AICPA, 1967), para. 5.

HISTORICAL COST   Nearly all businesses in the United States report their PP&E assets at historical cost less accumulated depreciation because of the historical cost principle. As noted in Chapter 2, a key advantage of historical costs is their objectivity. The historical cost of an asset is a "matter of record," while the current value of that same asset is a "matter of opinion." Businesses must occasionally depart from the historical cost principle in valuing their long-term assets. For example, the conservatism principle requires businesses to write down long-term assets when their value has been permanently impaired. In March 1995, Ben & Jerry's Homemade, Inc., the company that produces and distributes Ben & Jerry's ice cream products, wrote down the value of newly acquired equipment used to pack ice cream. The more than $4 million write-down was necessary because the new equipment failed to "perform up to expectations."[3]

INFLATION'S IMPACT ON THE VALUATION OF PROPERTY, PLANT & EQUIPMENT   Inflation undermines the information value of historical cost data. For example, a factory that cost $4 million to construct in 1967 may presently have a sales value of $40 million and a replacement cost of $80 million. However, for balance sheet purposes, that asset will be reported at its historical cost of $4 million, less accumulated depreciation. Since historical cost data tend to become outdated, you might reasonably expect business entities to provide decision makers with inflation-adjusted financial data. Are such data provided to decision makers? As a general rule, no.

During the highly inflationary period of the late 1970s, regulatory authorities recognized the negative impact that inflation was having on the information value of historical cost data. To address this problem, the Financial Accounting Standards Board (FASB) began requiring many companies to include "price-level adjusted" data in their financial statement footnotes. When inflation abated in the mid-1980s, this requirement was dropped. Although the FASB encourages businesses to include inflation-adjusted data in their financial statement footnotes, few companies have done so in recent years.

Depreciation Methods

Generally accepted accounting principles require businesses to depreciate long-term assets. **Depreciation** is the process of allocating, or writing off, the cost of a long-term asset over its useful life in a rational and systematic manner. A long-term asset's useful life is that period of time it provides economic benefits to a business. Depreciating long-term assets is one method businesses use to match revenues recognized each accounting period with the expense incurred to generate those revenues—recall the matching principle discussed in Chapter 2.

Later in this chapter, several different depreciation methods are discussed and illustrated. Similar to the choice of an inventory accounting method, the choice of a depreciation method can significantly influence a company's apparent financial condition and reported profits. Take the case of Sears. In April 1995, Sears reported that it had depreciation expense of nearly $650 million in 1994, compared with a net income for that year of $1.4 billion. Sears uses the straight-line depreciation method for financial reporting purposes. If Sears had used a different depreciation method, its financial data for 1994 would almost certainly have been materially different. To

---

3. Stipp, D. "Ben & Jerry's Reports Loss, Write-Down," *The Wall Street Journal*, March 7, 1995, p. B5. Reprinted by permission of *The Wall Street Journal*, © 1995 Dow Jones & Company, Inc. All Rights Reserved Worldwide.

Discussion Question
Why would the FASB drop a reporting requirement once it has been established? Answer: Accounting information must be useful and its benefit to users must be greater than the cost to provide it. In the case of price-level adjusted data, when inflation abated, its usefulness did not justify its cost.

depreciation

Focus on Ethics
A company has recently acquired a costly piece of equipment. The controller believes that an accelerated depreciation method should be applied to this asset because its usefulness declines in the later years of its life. The vice-president of finance instructs the controller to use straight-line depreciation so that the firm's net income will not be as greatly affected in the first few years of the asset's life. Comment on the appropriateness of the vice-president's decision.

International Differences in Valuing Long-Term Assets

Decision makers must be cautious when analyzing the long-term assets of foreign companies since asset valuation rules vary widely across the world. In many countries, long-term assets are regularly "revalued." Take the case of Australia. A recent study reported that each year, approximately one-fourth of Australian companies restate at least some of their long-term assets to current market values (G. Whittred and Y. K. Chan, "Asset Revaluations and the Mitigation of Underinvestment," *Abacus* 28 [1992]: 58–74). Certain European countries also allow businesses to value their long-term assets at other than historical cost. In the Netherlands, current value accounting has been used by many firms since the early 1950s.

enhance the comparability of financial data across business entities, accounting standards require that businesses disclose in their financial statement footnotes the depreciation method or methods they use.

Restrictions on Use

When there are restrictions on the use of a long-term asset, that fact should be disclosed in an entity's financial statements. For example, many long-term assets are pledged as collateral for loans. In a recent year, Maxtor Corporation, a manufacturer of disk drives and other computer products, reported that certain of its loans were "secured" by equipment. In other words, equipment owned by Maxtor serves as the collateral for those loans. Maxtor cannot dispose of this equipment without the prior approval of the lender.

Future Property, Plant & Equipment Needs

Times Mirror Company publishes the *Los Angeles Times* and several other newspapers. In February 1995, this firm announced that it would spend millions of dollars in coming years to upgrade several of its long-term assets.[4] Much of the cash to pay for these improvements would be provided by the company's sale of a cable television subsidiary. Disclosures of the type made by Times Mirror are very beneficial to decision makers. Information regarding an entity's long-term asset needs and management's strategy for satisfying those needs provides important insight on the entity's long-run viability. Unfortunately, candid disclosures of this type are fairly rare in annual reports.

Australian companies are permitted to periodically revalue, or "write up," long-term assets to their current values. One result of this practice is that the financial data of Australian and U.S. firms are not necessarily comparable.

---

4. F. Rose, "Times Mirror Stock Tumbles on Forecast of Lower 1st-Quarter Operating Profit," *The Wall Street Journal*, 3 February 1995, B5.

ACCOUNTING FOR PROPERTY, PLANT & EQUIPMENT

Property, plant & equipment assets pose four general types of accounting issues. First, accountants must determine the acquisition cost of these assets. Second, depreciation expense must be computed on these assets each accounting period. Third, expenditures related to PP&E assets following their acquisition must be analyzed and properly recorded. Finally, accountants must decide how to record the disposal of individual PP&E assets. In this section, each of these issues is considered.

Acquisition of Property, Plant & Equipment

The acquisition cost of a PP&E asset includes all *reasonable* and *necessary* expenditures incurred to obtain the asset and to prepare the asset for use. Shown in Exhibit 9.2 are examples of common acquisition costs for PP&E assets. Suppose that Kinko's, the copyshop company, purchases a large copier. The original invoice price of the copier was $40,000. However, the vendor granted a 10 percent discount to Kinko's to "close the deal," resulting in a net invoice cost of $36,000. Freight charges for the delivery of the copier were $550, and installation expenses totaled $320. During installation, a Kinko's employee accidentally damaged the copier, resulting in repair expenses of $410. The total acquisition cost of the copier is $36,870:

Net Invoice Cost	$36,000
Freight Charges	550
Installation Expenses	320
Total	$36,870

■ **EXHIBIT 9.2**

Common Acquisition Costs of Property, Plant & Equipment Assets

- Buildings (constructed): Cost of construction materials and labor, architectural fees, building permits, interest on loans obtained to finance construction,* insurance costs during construction

- Buildings (purchased): Purchase price, real estate commissions, attorneys' fees, title fees, repair and remodeling expenses necessary to put into a usable condition

- Equipment: Net invoice cost, transportation charges including in transit insurance expense paid by purchaser, sales taxes, assembly and installation expenses, costs incurred to test once installed

- Land: Purchase price, real estate commissions, attorneys' fees, title fees, surveying fees, accrued property taxes assumed by purchaser, cost to drain and otherwise prepare as a building site including the net cost of removing buildings or other structures

- Land Improvements: All reasonable and necessary costs associated with the construction or installation of parking lots, driveways, fences, lighting systems, and irrigation systems

*Only interest incurred on these loans during construction can be capitalized.

■ LEARNING
OBJECTIVE 2
Determine the acquisition cost of property, plant & equipment assets

Notice that the repair expenses are not considered a component of the copier's acquisition cost. Why? Because they were not reasonable or necessary costs to obtain the copier or to ready it for use. The repair costs would be recognized as an expense in the period incurred.

The following entry would be made to record the purchase of the copier. Included in the description for this entry is an asset number. Businesses, particularly large corporations, typically assign an asset number to each major PP&E asset for control purposes. More on this in a later section.

Apr. 19	Copier	36,870	
	Cash		36,870

To record the acquisition of copier
(asset No. 231–7)

Businesses often make basket purchases of long-term assets. For example, a company may purchase for one lump sum an entire production facility including land, land improvements, production equipment, and buildings. In such cases, the purchase price must be allocated to the specific assets acquired. This allocation is most commonly made on the basis of the relative market values of the individual assets. Suppose that Hodnett Company makes a basket purchase of assets A, B, and C for $600,000 at a court-ordered auction of a bankrupt firm's assets. The collective market value of these assets is $800,000. Individually, the assets have market values as follows: A—$160,000, B—$400,000, and C—$240,000. Given this information, the total cost of these assets would be allocated as follows based upon their relative market values.

■ **LEARNING OBJECTIVE 3**
Compute depreciation expense using each of the three major depreciation methods

salvage value

depreciable cost

book value

Real World
Determining an asset's useful life is a matter of judgment. Companies in the same industry often use different estimated useful lives for the same types of assets. What impact does establishing longer estimated useful lives for depreciable assets have on a company's financial statements compared with the financial statements of competitors?
Answer: Reduces depreciation expense and increases net income and total assets in the early years of the assets' lives.

ASSET	MARKET VALUE	PERCENTAGE OF TOTAL MARKET VALUE	ALLOCATION OF PURCHASE PRICE		COST ASSIGNED TO EACH ASSET
A	$160,000	20% ($160,000/$800,000)	20% × $600,000	=	$120,000
B	400,000	50% ($400,000/$800,000)	50% × 600,000	=	300,000
C	240,000	30% ($240,000/$800,000)	30% × 600,000	=	180,000
	$800,000	100%			$600,000

Depreciation of Property, Plant & Equipment

Again, recall that depreciation is the process of systematically allocating the cost of an asset over its useful life. Three factors must be considered when depreciation expense is computed for a depreciable asset: the asset's cost, its estimated useful life, and its **salvage value,** or residual value. Salvage value is the estimated value of an asset at the end of its useful life. When computing depreciation, accountants often refer to the **depreciable cost,** or depreciation base, of an asset, which is the asset's acquisition cost less its salvage value. An asset's salvage value is *not* considered a part of its depreciable cost since that portion of the asset's original value is not expected to be consumed or "used up" over its useful life. Another phrase often used when referring to depreciable assets is book value. The **book value,** or "carrying value," of a depreciable asset is the difference between the asset's cost and the balance of its Accumulated Depreciation account. In nearly all cases, the balance of an asset's Accumulated Depreciation account at any point in time reflects the total amount of the asset's original cost that has been expensed (depreciated).

ILLUSTRATION OF DEPRECIATION METHODS Exhibit 9.3 documents the depreciation methods commonly used by public companies. As indicated in that

■ **EXHIBIT 9.3**

Depreciation Methods: Frequency of Use by Publicly Owned Companies

SOURCE: *Accounting Trends & Techniques, 1994.*

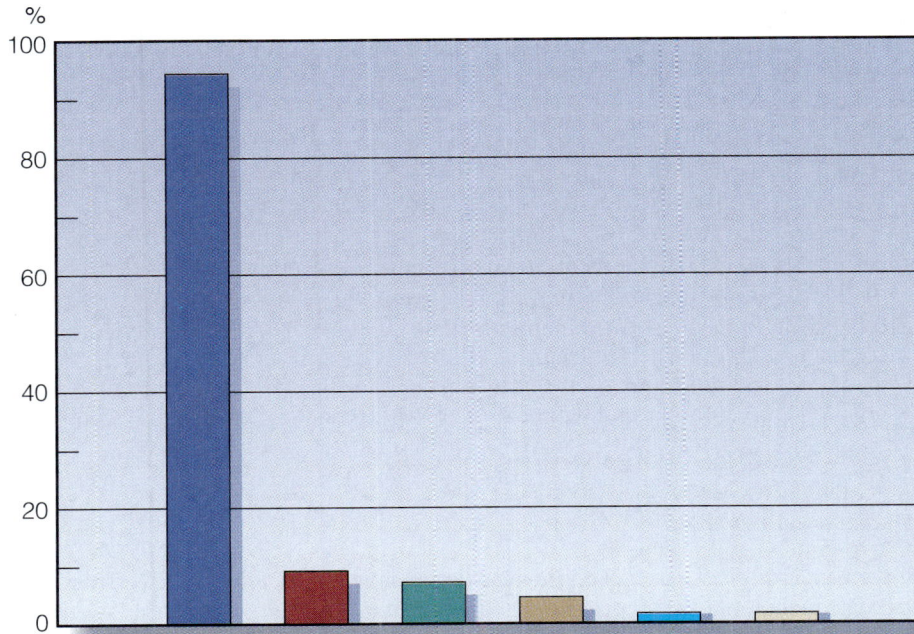

Note: Some companies use different depreciation methods for different types of depreciable assets. As a result, the percentages in this graph accumulate to more than 100 percent.

■ Straight-Line   ■ Declining-Balance
■ Accelerated Method, Unspecified   ■ Sum-of-the-Years'-Digits
■ Units-of-Production   ☐ Other

exhibit, the straight-line method is by far the most popular of these methods. Besides the straight-line method, the units-of-production and declining-balance depreciation methods are discussed here. To illustrate these three depreciation methods, let us use the following data for a depreciable asset acquired recently by the Riverside Construction Company.

Asset:	Drill Press, asset No. 14–27B
Acquisition Date:	January 1, Year 1
Acquisition Cost:	$68,000
Useful Life:	4 years
Salvage Value:	$8,000
Depreciable Cost:	$60,000 ($68,000 − $8,000)

STRAIGHT-LINE METHOD   Under the **straight-line method,** a business allocates an equal amount of depreciation expense to each year of an asset's estimated useful life. The premise underlying this method is that an asset is equally productive during each year of its useful life. Annual depreciation expense under the straight-line depreciation method can be computed by using either of the following two equations.

Discussion Question
Ask students for examples of assets that are equally productive during each year of their useful lives.
Examples: File cabinets, bookshelves, desks.

straight-line method

$$\begin{array}{lcl} \text{Annual Depreciation} \\ \text{Expense, Straight-Line Method} &=& \text{Depreciable Cost/Useful Life in Years} \end{array}$$

$$\begin{array}{lclcl} \text{Annual Depreciation} && \text{Depreciable} && \text{Straight-Line} \\ \text{Expense, Straight-Line Method} &=& \text{Cost} & \times & \text{Depreciation Rate} \end{array}$$

Applying the first equation to the drill press acquired by Riverside Construction Company yields an annual depreciation expense of $15,000 ($60,000/4). Alternatively, annual depreciation expense under the straight-line method can be computed by multiplying the depreciable cost of an asset by the appropriate depreciation rate. The depreciation rate represents the percentage of an asset's depreciable cost to be charged off to depreciation expense each year. For the drill press, the annual depreciation rate is 25 percent (100%/four years). Multiplying this percentage by the drill press's depreciable cost of $60,000 results, again, in an annual depreciation expense of $15,000. The following adjusting journal entry would be required to record depreciation expense at the end of the drill press's first year of service.

| Dec. 31 | Depreciation Expense, Drill Press | 15,000 | |
| | Accumulated Depreciation, Drill Press | | 15,000 |

To record annual depreciation expense on drill press (asset No. 14–27B)

Teaching Note

Emphasize that an asset is never depreciated below its salvage value.

Shown in Exhibit 9.4 is a straight-line depreciation schedule for Riverside's drill press that documents the depreciation computation for each year of the asset's life. Also included in this depreciation schedule is the balance of the asset's Accumulated Depreciation account and its book value at the end of each year. Notice in Exhibit 9.4 that at the end of Year 4, the drill press will have a book value of $8,000, an amount exactly equal to its salvage value. At this point, the depreciable cost of the asset will have been completely written off to depreciation expense. However, the machine will not necessarily be taken out of service. Unless the asset is unreliable or should be replaced for other reasons, it will be kept in service indefinitely. This is true even when a depreciable asset has a zero book value.

If the drill press was acquired in midyear, Riverside would likely compute depreciation expense for Year 1 by multiplying $15,000 by the fraction of the year the drill press was owned during Year 1. For example, if the drill press was purchased on

■ **EXHIBIT 9.4**

Depreciation Schedule for Drill Press of Riverside Construction Company, Straight-Line Method

| | Depreciation Computation | | | | Year-End Balance | |
Year	Depreciation Rate	×	Depreciable Cost	Depreciation Expense	of Accumulated Depreciation	Year-End Book Value*
1	25%	×	$60,000	$15,000	$15,000	$53,000
2	25%	×	60,000	15,000	30,000	38,000
3	25%	×	60,000	15,000	45,000	23,000
4	25%	×	60,000	15,000	60,000	8,000

*Computed as follows: Original cost of asset ($68,000) less year-end balance of Accumulated Depreciation account.

March 1 of Year 1, the appropriate depreciation expense would be $12,500 ($15,000 × 10/12). (Some businesses do not record depreciation expense for a partial year on newly acquired assets. Instead, these companies record a full year's depreciation expense for assets acquired in the first one-half of a year and no depreciation expense for assets acquired during the second one-half of a year.)

UNITS-OF-PRODUCTION METHOD   Under the **units-of-production method,** an asset's useful life is expressed in terms of a given number of units of production or use. The depreciation expense for any given period is a function of the level of usage of the asset during that period. The units-of-production method is particularly well suited for a manufacturing environment. In most factories, the useful life of machinery is primarily a function of how much the machinery is used instead of the passage of time. For example, a piece of production equipment may have a useful life of ten years under normal conditions, which would typically involve one eight-hour work shift each day. However, if this equipment is used continually during three eight-hour work shifts each day, it is unlikely to be in service ten years from its purchase date.

Suppose now that Riverside applies the units-of-production method to its drill press. When the drill press is acquired, a production supervisor estimates that it will produce 30,000 units of finished product over its useful life. Since the drill press's depreciable cost is $60,000, the per unit depreciation expense is $2: $60,000/30,000 units. For any given year, the asset's depreciation expense under the units-of-production method is determined by multiplying the per unit depreciation cost by the number of units produced that year.

units-of-production method

$$
\begin{array}{lcl}
\text{Annual Depreciation} & & \text{Per Unit} \qquad \text{Total Units} \\
\text{Expense, Units-of-Production} & = & \text{Depreciation Cost} \times \text{Produced} \\
\text{Method} & & \text{During Year}
\end{array}
$$

The depreciation schedule shown in Exhibit 9.5 documents the expected depreciation expense for the drill press, assuming the asset is used for four years and that the following number of units are produced each year.

Year 1   10,000 units
Year 2   8,000 units
Year 3   5,000 units
Year 4   7,000 units

■ **EXHIBIT 9.5**
Depreciation Schedule for Drill Press of Riverside Construction Company, Units of Production Method

	Depreciation Computation				Year-End Balance	
Year	Depreciation Cost Per Unit ×	Expected Production		Depreciation Expense	of Accumulated Depreciation	Year-End Book Value
1	$2	×	10,000 units	$20,000	$20,000	$48,000
2	$2	×	8,000 units	16,000	36,000	32,000
3	$2	×	5,000 units	10,000	46,000	22,000
4	$2	×	7,000 units	14,000	60,000	8,000

DECLINING-BALANCE METHOD   A few companies use "accelerated" methods to compute depreciation expense on PP&E assets. Under accelerated depreciation methods, larger amounts of depreciation are recorded in the early years of an asset's life compared with later years. The premise underlying this method is that proportionately more of the economic benefit of depreciable assets is consumed during the early years of their useful lives. Machinery, for example, generally becomes less productive over time due to increasing breakdowns and more extensive maintenance requirements.

declining-balance method

Under the **declining-balance method,** annual depreciation expense is computed by multiplying an asset's book value at the beginning of a year by an accelerated depreciation rate:

$$\begin{array}{c} \text{Annual Depreciation} \\ \text{Expense, Declining-Balance} \\ \text{Method} \end{array} = \begin{array}{c} \text{Book Value} \\ \text{(Beginning of} \\ \text{the Year)} \end{array} \times \begin{array}{c} \text{Accelerated} \\ \text{Depreciation Rate} \end{array}$$

double declining-balance method

Accelerated depreciation rates under the declining-balance method are a multiple of the straight-line depreciation rate. If a company uses the **double declining-balance method,** the annual depreciation rate for an asset is twice the straight-line rate. The annual straight-line depreciation rate for an asset with a ten-year useful life is 10 percent (100%/10). Under the double declining-balance method, the annual depreciation rate for this asset would be 20 percent (2 × 10%).

For Riverside's drill press, the accelerated depreciation rate under the double declining-balance method is 50 percent, or twice the straight-line rate of 25 percent. At the beginning of Year 1, the asset's book value is equal to its cost of $68,000. So, Year 1 depreciation expense would be $34,000: $68,000 × 50%. For Year 2, the drill press's book value at the beginning of the year would be $34,000 (cost of $68,000 less accumulated depreciation of $34,000). As a result, the depreciation expense for Year 2 would be $17,000: $34,000 × 50%.

A common mistake students make in applying the declining-balance method is multiplying the appropriate accelerated depreciation rate times the asset's depreciable cost *instead of* its book value. Another tricky aspect of the declining-balance method is that one must remember to stop depreciating an asset once its book value equals its salvage value. Recall that for both the straight-line and units-of-production methods, an asset's salvage value is subtracted from its original cost to determine its depreciable cost. Then, a systematic method is used to allocate this latter amount over the asset's useful life. Under the declining-balance method, the salvage value of an asset is ignored, at least initially, when computing periodic depreciation expense. However, once the asset's book value is equal to its salvage value, no further depreciation is recorded on the asset.

Shown in Exhibit 9.6 is a depreciation schedule for Riverside's drill press based upon the double declining-balance method. Notice in the fourth year of the asset's life that the depreciation computation yields a depreciation expense of $4,250 ($8,500 × 50%). However, since the book value of the asset at the beginning of Year 4 exceeds its salvage value by only $500 ($8,500 − $8,000), the depreciation expense for that year is limited to $500.

COMPARISON OF DEPRECIATION METHODS   The graphic in Exhibit 9.7 summarizes the annual depreciation charges for Riverside's drill press under each of the three major depreciation methods. The straight-line and double declining-balance methods result in the general depreciation patterns shown in Exhibit 9.7 regardless of

■ **EXHIBIT 9.6**

Depreciation Schedule for Drill Press of Riverside Construction Company, Double-Declining Balance Method

	Depreciation Computation			Depreciation Expense	Year-End Balance of Accumulated Depreciation	Year-End Book Value
Year	Depreciation Rate	×	Book Value			
1	50%	×	$68,000	$34,000	$34,000	$34,000
2	50%	×	34,000	17,000	51,000	17,000
3	50%	×	17,000	8,500	59,500	8,500
4	50%	×	8,500	500*	60,000	8,000

*Depreciation expense in Year 4 would be $4,250 applying the appropriate equation. However, since the asset's remaining depreciable cost is only $500 at the beginning of the year, depreciation expense for Year 4 is limited to that amount.

■ **EXHIBIT 9.7**

Annual Depreciation Expense for Drill Press of Riverside Construction Company under Three Major Depreciation Methods

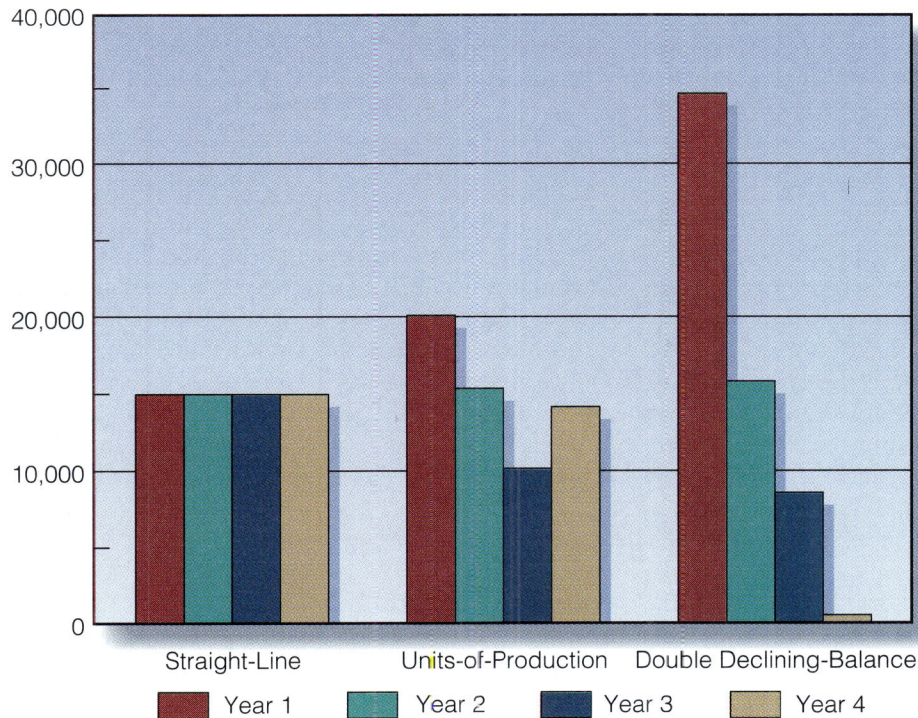

the length of an asset's useful life. Naturally, the depreciation pattern for the units-of-production method varies from case to case. Realize that whichever depreciation method is used for Riverside's drill press, the final result is the same: $60,000 of depreciation expense is recorded over the asset's useful life.

Even a Whale of an Asset Must Be Depreciated

Shamu, the killer whale that appears in advertisements for the Sea World aquarium parks, is only mortal, its new owner has concluded. Until Harcourt Brace Jovanovich Inc. sold its five Sea World parks to the Anheuser-Busch Companies last year, the whale and other similar live attractions were considered long-lived assets whose value did not have to be depreciated or reduced each year on the company's books. The new owners, however, are taking a more conservative view. Based on their expected lifespans, Shamu and other such animals are now being depreciated like everything else in the parks.

(Note: Apparently, the previous owner of the Sea World parks wrote off the cost of Shamu and friends as an expense upon their demise instead of depreciating the animals over their useful lives.)

SOURCE: "Killer Whale a Write-Down," *New York Times*, 8 February 1990, D8.

DEPRECIATION: OTHER ISSUES Besides the most common methods of computing depreciation expense, decision makers should be acquainted with certain other procedural accounting issues related to the depreciation of PP&E assets. Among these issues are changes in estimates affecting periodic depreciation expense, accounting for the depletion of natural resources, and depreciation methods used for federal taxation purposes.

CHANGES IN ESTIMATES AFFECTING DEPRECIATION COMPUTATIONS
The computation of depreciation for a PP&E asset is dependent on two key estimates: the asset's useful life and its salvage value. After an asset has been in service for a period of time, a business's accountants may realize that one or both estimates are materially wrong. For example, assume Riverside uses the straight-line depreciation method for the drill press. At the beginning of Year 3, the company's accountants realize that the drill press will likely be in service for three more years instead of two. Additionally, the accountants estimate that the drill press will have a $2,000 salvage value in three years when it is taken out of service. Based upon this information, Riverside's accountants would revise the annual depreciation computations for the drill press.

The first step in revising the depreciation computations for the drill press is to determine the asset's remaining depreciable cost. According to Exhibit 9.4, the drill press will have a book value of $38,000 at the end of Year 2. Naturally, that figure will also be the asset's book value at the beginning of Year 3. Subtracting from that amount the revised estimate of the asset's salvage value, $2,000, Riverside's accountants determine that the drill press has a remaining depreciable cost of $36,000:

Book Value at Beginning of Year 3	$38,000
Revised Estimate of Salvage Value	2,000
Remaining Depreciable Cost	$36,000

The straight-line method will be used to allocate this remaining depreciable cost over the three years that the drill press will be in service. Using the following equation,

Riverside's accountants determine that an annual depreciation charge of $12,000 is appropriate for each of the remaining years of the asset's life.

Annual Depreciation
Expense, Straight-line Method   =   Depreciable Cost/Useful Life in Years
                                = $36,000/3 years
                                = $12,000

Teaching Note
Changes in estimates of useful lives or salvage values only change *future* depreciation computations. Previously recorded depreciation is not corrected.

DEPLETION OF NATURAL RESOURCES

For some companies, the most important property, plant & equipment assets are natural resource properties. **Natural resources** include long-term assets such as coal deposits, oil and gas reservoirs, and tracts of standing timber that are extracted or harvested from the earth's surface or from beneath the earth's surface. Natural resource properties are clearly the most important assets of mining and petroleum companies. The annual report released by Barrick Gold Corporation in March 1995 reported more than $1 billion of investments in natural resource properties, including a $44 million investment in the Bullfrog Mine of Beatty, Nevada. Union Texas Petroleum Holdings, Inc., an oil and gas exploration company, recently reported that more than two-thirds of its $1.5 billion of assets were invested in oil and gas properties.

Certain industries are said to be "capital-intensive." Long-term assets, such as PP&E, typically account for a very high percentage of the total assets of firms in capital-intensive industries. An example of such an industry is oil and gas exploration.

Natural resources are known as wasting assets because the value of these properties gradually declines or "wastes away" as timber, gems, petroleum, and so on are extracted or harvested from these properties. Instead of depreciation, **depletion** is the term used to describe the allocation of the cost of natural resources to the periods they provide economic benefits to a business entity. Most companies, including Barrick and Union Texas, use the units-of-production concept to record depletion expense on natural resource properties. To compute depletion expense each period, the following adaptation of the units-of-production depreciation equation is used.

natural resources

depletion

Annual Depletion   Per Unit   Total Units Recovered
Expense, Units-of-   =   Depletion Cost   ×   and Sold During Year
Production Method

Suppose Union Texas purchases an oil and gas property for $20 million that is estimated to have 2 million barrels of recoverable oil. The depletion expense per barrel of oil recovered and sold will be $10: $20,000,000/2,000,0000 barrels. If the company recovers and sells 300,000 barrels from this property in a given year, the depreciation expense for that year would be $3 million, as shown in the following computation.

Real World
How are barrels of recoverable oil estimated? Companies employ a specialist to estimate oil and gas reserves. The reserve estimate is critical to the computation of depletion. A reserve study is prepared annually and the per unit depletion cost revised accordingly.

Annual Depletion   Per Unit   Total Units Recovered
Expense, Units-of-   =   Depletion Cost   ×   and Sold During Year
Production Method
                     = $10 × 300,000
                     = $3,000,000

This depletion expense would be recorded with the following year-end adjusting entry.

| Dec. 31 | Depletion Expense | 3,000,000 | |
| | Accumulated Depletion | | 3,000,000 |

To record depletion expense on
reservoir B4–62 (300,000 barrels
× $10 per barrel)

Suppose now that 100,000 barrels of the recovered oil was unsold at the end of the year. Under this assumption, the following entry would be appropriate:

Dec. 31	Depletion Expense	2,000,000	
	Inventory	1,000,000	
	Accumulated Depletion		3,000,000

To record recovery of 300,000 barrels
from reservoir B4–62 (300,000 barrels
× $10 per barrel); 100,000 barrels
remain unsold and in inventory

DEPRECIATION FOR FEDERAL TAXATION PURPOSES The accounting methods businesses use for financial reporting purposes are often very different from the accounting methods used for federal taxation purposes. The tax laws dictating the depreciation methods to be used for PP&E have been revised numerous times in recent decades and at this point are quite complex. Here, the purpose is simply to acquaint you briefly with the acceptable depreciation methods for taxation purposes.

For PP&E assets acquired before 1981, businesses typically use one of the major depreciation methods illustrated previously. In 1981, Congress enacted a law that created the Accelerated Cost Recovery System (ACRS). The ACRS introduced a new approach to computing depreciation for federal taxation purposes. This taxation system, used for assets acquired between 1981 and 1986, established "cost recovery periods" over which most major types of PP&E were to be depreciated. Generally, the cost recovery period assigned to a group of assets was much shorter than the useful lives of those assets.

Congress established the Modified Accelerated Cost Recovery System (MACRS) in 1987. This depreciation system is used for assets acquired in 1987 and beyond. Under MACRS, depreciable assets are assigned to one of eight classes, each of which has a different cost recovery period. Certain types of equipment, for example, are assigned a useful life of seven years. The allowable depreciation methods under the MACRS vary across the eight classes of depreciable assets. For instance, the double declining-balance method is typically used for assets with short lives, while the straight-line method is mandated for certain long-lived assets.

The ACRS and MACRS allow companies to write off the cost of depreciable assets for tax purposes more rapidly than they had in the past. Congress hoped that by allowing these more liberal approaches to computing depreciation for tax purposes, businesses would purchase new or additional PP&E assets and thus stimulate the economy. Generally, neither the ACRS or MACRS can be used for financial accounting or financial reporting purposes. Why? Because they violate certain of the fundamental conceptual principles of accounting discussed in Chapter 2. For example, these methods of computing depreciation typically violate the matching principle since they overstate the depreciation expense recorded during the early years of an asset's life.

Depreciation, Harvard Style

SPOTLIGHT
ON ETHICS

Until recently, colleges and universities were not required to record depreciation expense on their long-term assets. When a new rule requiring these organizations to depreciate their assets was enacted, one prominent university developed a unique approach to computing depreciation. This approach is discussed in the following excerpt from an article appearing in Forbes.

Harvard doesn't figure depreciation the way Generally Accepted Accounting Principles say. GAAP says depreciation should be based on what a building or piece of equipment cost originally. Now Harvard has some fine old ivy-covered buildings that cost a fraction of what it would cost to build them today. So, the university decided, the heck with GAAP, we'll figure depreciation our own way. Using GAAP rules, Harvard's depreciation last year would have been $29 million, not the $76 million actually recorded.

If Harvard had depreciated its buildings the way companies are required to do, it would have ended the year with a surplus of $6 million not a deficit of $42 million. Whatever else it is, the new Harvard accounting may come in handy in persuading alumni to be more generous. Harvard denies that was its intention, but a touch of red ink could certainly help loosen the purse strings a bit.

SOURCE: Khalaf, R., "Customized Accounting." *Forbes*, May 25, 1992. Reprinted by permission of FORBES Magazine © Forbes, Inc., 1992.

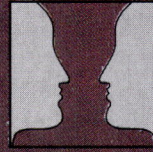

Revenue Expenditures vs. Capital Expenditures

Following the acquisition of PP&E assets, businesses incur a wide range of expenditures related to these assets. Accountants generally classify such expenditures as either revenue expenditures or capital expenditures. **Revenue expenditures** provide economic benefits to only one accounting period and, as a result, are treated as expenses in the period incurred. Examples of common revenue expenditures are maintenance expenses and minor repairs for PP&E assets. Expenditures to obtain, expand, or improve long-term assets or to extend their useful lives are known as **capital expenditures.** Unlike revenue expenditures, capital expenditures provide economic benefits to a business entity for more than one year. Because of the matching principle, capital expenditures should be debited to an asset account and then written off as an expense over the appropriate number of accounting periods.

Besides the acquisition cost of new PP&E assets, common types of capital expenditures related to these assets include additions, improvements, and extraordinary repairs. **Additions** are extensions or expansions of existing PP&E assets. For example, a new wing added to a production facility would qualify as an addition. **Improvements** are capital expenditures that enhance an existing asset's operating efficiency or reduce its operating costs. An example of an improvement is a new and more powerful engine installed on a piece of production machinery that increases the machinery's productive capacity by 20 percent. Generally, the cost of improvements and additions is debited to the existing asset's general ledger account. (Recall that improvements made to land are recorded in Land Improvements instead of the Land account.)

Additions and improvements increase the depreciable cost of PP&E assets and thus require revisions in the annual depreciation computations for these assets. Suppose

■ **LEARNING OBJECTIVE 4**
Distinguish between and account for revenue and capital expenditures

Real World
Some assets have long lives but are expensed immediately because of their insignificant cost. Trash cans and small tools are examples of such assets. Typically, most companies have a policy requiring an asset to exceed a certain dollar amount before it is capitalized.

revenue expenditures

capital expenditures

additions

improvements

extraordinary repairs

that a company owns a building that cost $2.4 million to construct ten years ago. The building is being depreciated over an estimated useful life of forty years, $60,000 per year, and is expected to have a zero salvage value. The balance of the building's Accumulated Depreciation account is $600,000. Now, assume that a new wing is added to the building at a cost of $1.2 million. This addition does not affect the useful life or salvage value of the building. The revised annual depreciation expense for the building would be $100,000, as shown by the following schedule.

Cost of Addition		$1,200,000
Cost of Existing Building	$2,400,000	
Less: Accumulated Depreciation	600,000	1,800,000
Total Depreciable Cost		$3,000,000
Useful Life		÷30 years
Revised Annual Depreciation		$ 100,000

A final type of capital expenditure is **extraordinary repairs.** Extraordinary repairs are major repair costs that extend the useful life of a PP&E asset but typically do not improve its operating efficiency or reduce its operating costs. An example of an extraordinary repair is a major overhaul of a piece of production machinery. The cost of extraordinary repairs is usually debited to an asset's Accumulated Depreciation account. This accounting treatment serves to "erase" a part of the asset's Accumulated Depreciation account balance, which is similar to the impact that extraordinary repairs have on an asset. That is, extraordinary repairs "turn back the clock" by extending an asset's useful life.

To illustrate accounting for extraordinary repairs, assume that Knutson Engineering removes a piece of machinery from its production line shortly after the beginning of a new fiscal year. This machine is given a major overhaul at a cost of $3,000. The overhaul is expected to extend the machine's useful life by two years. The following journal entry records the cost of the overhaul as an extraordinary repair.

Jan. 4 Accumulated Depreciation, Machinery	3,000	
Accounts Payable (and/or Cash)		3,000

To record expenditures incurred during the overhaul of perforating machine (asset No. 419–A51)

In recent years, major changes have been adopted in the accounting rules for nonprofit organizations. For example, Harvard University and other private educational institutions must now *book* depreciation expense on their long-term depreciable assets.

Now, assume that this machine originally cost $44,000, was estimated to have a ten-year useful life and a $4,000 salvage value, and has been depreciated under the straight-line method. The machine has been in service for seven years, resulting in accumulated depreciation of $28,000 before the overhaul ($4,000 annual depreciation × 7 years). Finally, assume that the overhaul did not affect the machine's salvage value. As shown below, the machine would have a remaining depreciable cost of $15,000 after the extraordinary repairs are debited to Accumulated Depreciation.

Original Cost		$44,000
Accumulated Depreciation:		
Balance Prior to Overhaul	$28,000	
Cost of Overhaul	(3,000)	
Revised Balance		(25,000)
Salvage Value		(4,000)
Remaining Depreciable Cost		$15,000

Since the remaining useful life of this machine has been extended from three years to five years by the overhaul, the revised annual depreciation expense would be $3,000 under the straight-line method ($15,000/5 years).

Disposal of Property, Plant & Equipment Assets

Businesses dispose of PP&E assets in several ways. These assets may simply be removed from service and "junked," sold for cash, or exchanged for other assets. In this section, the accounting procedures for disposals of PP&E assets are considered. To illustrate these procedures, the now very familiar drill press of Riverside Construction Company is used. Recall that the drill press was purchased for $68,000, had an estimated useful life of four years, and an estimated salvage value of $8,000. The examples used here to illustrate disposals of PP&E assets assume that Riverside applied the straight-line depreciation method to this asset. Because these examples require you to refer occasionally to the straight-line depreciation schedule included in Exhibit 9.4, that schedule is reproduced in Exhibit 9.8.

RETIREMENT OF PROPERTY, PLANT & EQUIPMENT ASSETS   Assume that Riverside's drill press suddenly becomes obsolete at the end of its third year of service because a new and more efficient model becomes available. The book value of the drill press at the end of year 3 is $23,000, as indicated in Exhibit 9.8. Unfortunately, the drill press has only a minimal salvage value, given the new technology available. So, Riverside "cuts a deal" with the local junkyard. The junkyard will haul away the drill press for no charge in exchange for the scrap metal that can be recovered from the machine. Disposing of the drill press in this manner results in a loss equal to the asset's book value of $23,000. Following is the entry to record the retirement of the drill press under this assumption.

Jan. 4	Accumulated Depreciation, Drill Press	45,000	
	Loss on Retirement of Long-Term Assets	23,000	
	Drill Press		68,000
	To record the retirement of drill press (asset No. 14–27B)		

Teaching Note
Emphasize that additions, improvements, and extraordinary repairs all require revised estimates of depreciation.

■ **LEARNING OBJECTIVE 5**
Account for disposals of property, plant & equipment

■ **EXHIBIT 9.8**
Depreciation Schedule for Drill Press of Riverside Construction Company, Straight-Line Method

| | Depreciation Computation | | | | Year-End Balance | |
Year	Depreciation Rate	×	Book Value	Depreciation Expense	of Accumulated Depreciation	Year-End Book Value
1	25%	×	$60,000	$15,000	$15,000	$53,000
2	25%	×	60,000	15,000	30,000	38,000
3	25%	×	60,000	15,000	45,000	23,000
4	25%	×	60,000	15,000	60,000	8,000

*Computed as follows: Original cost of asset ($68,000) less year-end balance of Accumulated Depreciation account.

This entry removes from Riverside's accounting records both the cost of the drill press and its accumulated depreciation. Gains and losses on the disposal of long-term assets are generally classified as other revenues and expenses in an income statement.

CASH SALES OF PROPERTY, PLANT & EQUIPMENT ASSETS   Suppose now that at the end of Year 3, Riverside sells the drill press for $50,000. In this case, Riverside would realize a gain of $27,000, which is the difference between the selling price of the drill press and its book value ($50,000 − $23,000). The following entry would be needed to record this scenario.

Jan. 4	Accumulated Depreciation, Drill Press	45,000	
	Cash	50,000	
	Drill Press		68,000
	Gain on Sale of Long-Term Assets		27,000

To record the sale of drill press (asset No. 14–27B)

When a long-term asset is sold for less than its book value, a loss must be recorded. To illustrate this possibility, assume that Riverside's drill press is sold for $10,000 on June 30 of Year 4. Here, we have an additional factor complicating the disposal of the drill press. If a depreciable asset is disposed of at midyear, an adjusting entry is required to record depreciation expense on that asset before the disposal of the asset is recorded. This adjusting entry is needed to record depreciation expense on the asset for that period elapsing since the most recent adjusting entry for depreciation expense. Riverside records depreciation expense at the end of each year. So, on June 30 of Year 4 when the drill press is sold for $10,000, six months would have passed since the previous adjusting entry for depreciation. Riverside would make the following journal entry to record depreciation expense of $7,500, one-half of the annual straight-line depreciation amount, before recording the sale of the drill press.

Jun. 30	Depreciation Expense, Drill Press	7,500	
	Accumulated Depreciation, Drill Press		7,500

To record depreciation expense on drill press (asset No. 14–27B) for period January 1–June 30, Year 4

Following this adjusting entry, the book value of the drill press would be $15,500.

Original Cost of Drill Press		$68,000
Less: Accumulated Depreciation		
Accumulated Depreciation, End of Year 3	$45,000	
Adjusting Entry, June 30, Year 4	7,500	
Accumulated Depreciation, June 30, Year 4		52,500
Book Value, June 30, Year 4		$15,500

Given the assumed selling price of $10,000 and the book value of $15,500, Riverside would record a loss of $5,500 on the sale of the drill press under this scenario.

Jun. 30	Accumulated Depreciation, Drill Press	52,500	
	Cash	10,000	
	Loss on Sale of Long-term Assets	5,500	
	Drill Press		68,000

To record the sale of drill press (asset
No. 14–27B)

EXCHANGES OF PROPERTY, PLANT & EQUIPMENT ASSETS   Businesses sometimes exchange existing PP&E assets for new models of those assets. Even when an asset is still functioning reliably, a business may decide to upgrade that asset for competitive reasons. A company that uses outdated equipment on its production line or in its merchandising distribution facilities may find itself lagging behind competitors in terms of operating efficiency and profits. Accounting for asset exchanges can be quite complex. Here, only two fairly simple scenarios involving exchanges of similar assets are discussed. A comprehensive discussion of accounting for asset exchanges, including the accounting rules for exchanges involving dissimilar assets, is deferred to advanced accounting courses.

ASSET EXCHANGES INVOLVING A LOSS   Assume that Riverside Construction Company decides to replace its drill press after using it for two years. At this point, the drill press has a $38,000 book value, $68,000 cost less $30,000 of accumulated depreciation, as shown in Exhibit 9.8. The replacement drill press is sold by a local equipment dealer at a cash price of $54,000. Besides trading in its original drill press on the new model, Riverside is required to pay the equipment dealer $20,000. In other words, the dealer grants Riverside a $34,000 trade-in allowance on the old drill press, as shown by the following schedule.

Discussion Question
Ask students why an asset's trade-in allowance often differs from its book value.
Answer: The trade-in allowance is based on the asset's market value; an asset's book value is simply cost minus accumulated depreciation.

Cash Price of New Drill Press	$54,000
Cash Paid in Exchange by Riverside	20,000
Trade-in Allowance for Old Drill Press	$34,000

The $38,000 book value of the old drill press exceeds the trade-in allowance of $34,000. So, Riverside incurs a $4,000 loss on this asset exchange. As a general rule, when a loss is incurred on an exchange of *similar* assets, the loss is recognized and the newly acquired asset is recorded at its fair market value, which is typically its cash price. To record this asset exchange and the resulting loss, Riverside would make the following entry in its accounting records.

Jan. 1	Drill Press (New)	54,000	
	Accumulated Depreciation, Drill Press	30,000	
	Loss on Exchange of Assets	4,000	
	Drill Press (Old)		68,000
	Cash		20,000

To record exchange of drill press
(asset No. 14–27B) for new drill press
(asset No. 14–51A)

ASSET EXCHANGES INVOLVING A GAIN   Assume the same facts as in the previous example, with one difference: Riverside is required to pay the dealer only $10,000 in the exchange of the two drill presses. In this case, Riverside has received a trade-in allowance of $44,000 for the old drill press.

Cash Price of New Drill Press	$54,000
Cash Paid in Exchange by Riverside	10,000
Trade-in Allowance for Old Drill Press	$44,000

Riverside's trade-in allowance for its old drill press exceeds that asset's book value by $6,000 ($44,000 − $38,000). However, generally accepted accounting principles do not allow gains on exchanges of *similar* assets to be recorded. Instead, the unrecognized gain of $6,000 is subtracted from the $54,000 cash price of the new asset in determining its acquisition cost. Alternatively, the $48,000 recorded cost of the new asset can be determined by adding the book value of the old asset ($38,000) and the amount of cash paid ($10,000). In either case, the asset exchange is recorded as follows:

Jan. 1	Drill Press (New)	48,000	
	Accumulated Depreciation, Drill Press	30,000	
	Drill Press (Old)		68,000
	Cash		10,000

        To record exchange of drill press
        (asset No. 14–27B) for new drill press
        (asset No. 14–51A)

At this point, the obvious question is why accounting standards require losses on exchanges of similar assets to be recognized, while gains on such transactions are not. One reason for this differing treatment is the conservatism principle. Recognizing losses and not recognizing gains both qualify as conservative accounting treatments. If you pursue further study of financial accounting, you will encounter additional rationale for these differing treatments of apparent gains and losses on exchanges of similar assets.

The economic benefit of a gain on the exchange of similar assets is not totally ignored for accounting purposes. Instead, this gain is deferred and recognized over the life of the new asset. Take the last example just discussed. In that case, the $6,000 unrealized gain on the exchange of the two drill presses is subtracted from the recorded cost of the new drill press. As a result, the depreciation expense recorded on the new drill press will be reduced by $6,000 over its useful life. So, instead of recognizing an "up front" gain of $6,000 on this exchange, this gain is recognized gradually over the life of the new drill press in the form of lower depreciation expense.

ANALYZING TOTAL ASSETS

■ LEARNING
OBJECTIVE 6
Compute return on assets and the total asset turnover ratio

Since PP&E is the last major asset category considered in Part III of this text, it is appropriate at this point that we consider two financial ratios related to the total assets of business entities. These ratios are return on assets and the total asset turnover ratio.

Return on Assets

A few years into the future when you are the chief executive officer (CEO) of a multibillion-dollar firm, one of your major responsibilities will be performance appraisal. Granted, you will not be responsible for evaluating the work performance of production-line personnel. However, you will be responsible for assessing the job performance of those individuals who manage your firm's major operating units. For example, if your company has three divisions, you will need some basis for measuring and comparing the job performance of the three divisional managers. A key measure often used to evaluate the job performance of divisional managers, departmental supervisors, and CEOs, for that matter, is return on assets. **Return on assets** measures the overall rate of return earned on a business's total assets or on the total assets of a segment of a business. This ratio is computed by dividing the sum of an entity's net income and interest expense for an accounting period by its average total assets for that period.

Return on Assets = (Net Income + Interest Expense) / Average Total Assets

Why is interest expense added to net income when computing return on assets? When return on assets is being used as a job performance measure, financing costs, such as interest expense, generally should be ignored. The issue in this context is how effectively an individual has managed the total assets in his or her area of responsibility regardless of how those assets were financed.

To illustrate the computation of return on assets, consider the following data for the Shipman Manufacturing Company. These data are for the company's fiscal year ending December 31, 1996.

Net Sales	$7,200,000
Net Income	320,000
Interest Expense	24,000
Total Assets, January 1	4,200,000
Total Assets, December 31	4,400,000

Following is the computation of Shipman's return on assets for 1996.

$$\text{Average Total Assets} = (\$4,200,000 + \$4,400,000)/2$$
$$= \$4,300,000$$

$$\text{Return on Assets} = (\$320,000 + \$24,000)/\$4,300,000$$
$$= 8\%$$

Return on assets fluctuates greatly across industries. Exhibit 9.1 of this chapter reported the average percentage of total assets represented by PP&E for companies in six industries. Shown in Exhibit 9.9 is the average return on assets for these same industries during a recent year.

Discussion Question
Ask students to compute Michaels Stores' return on assets (ROA). Does this ROA seem reasonable for a business in this industry?

Total Asset Turnover Ratio

Another measure of how effectively business executives are utilizing the total assets under their control is the **total asset turnover ratio.** This ratio is computed by dividing a company's net sales by its average total assets during an accounting period.

Total Asset Turnover Ratio = Net Sales / Average Total Assets

In 1996, Shipman Manufacturing Company had net sales of $7.2 million and average total assets of $4.3 million, yielding a total asset turnover ratio of 1.67.

The total asset turnover ratio can be used to gauge managers' success in generating revenues relative to their organization's total asset base. Suppose that two companies in the same industry each had total sales of $10 million during a recent year.

■ **EXHIBIT 9.9**
Return on Assets, Selected Industries

SOURCE: *Dun & Bradstreet Industry Norms & Key Business Ratios, 1993–1994*. Dun & Bradstreet Information Services. (New York: Dun & Bradstreet, Inc., 1994)

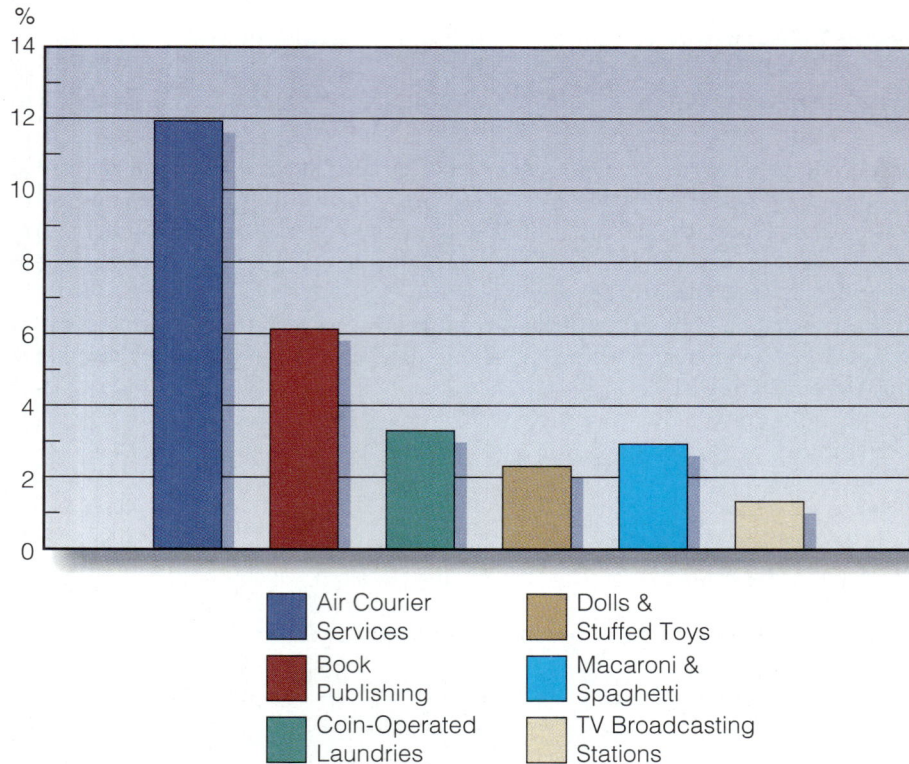

Air Courier Services
Book Publishing
Coin-Operated Laundries
Dolls & Stuffed Toys
Macaroni & Spaghetti
TV Broadcasting Stations

However, Company X had total assets of $9 million, while Company Y had total assets of only $5 million. Focusing on this fact alone, Company Y's executives appear to be better asset managers than Company X's executives. In more concrete terms, Company Y's executives generated $2.00 in revenue for every $1.00 investment in assets, while Company's X's executives produced only $1.11 in revenues for each dollar invested in assets. Shown in Exhibit 9.10 are the total asset turnover ratios for the six industries highlighted in Exhibits 9.1 and 9.9.

KEY INTERNAL CONTROL PROCEDURES FOR PROPERTY, PLANT & EQUIPMENT

■ **LEARNING OBJECTIVE 7**
Discuss key internal control procedures for property, plant & equipment

Property, plant & equipment pose different types of internal control issues compared with current assets such as cash and inventory. For the latter two assets, physical security controls are especially important. However, the risk of someone walking off with a ten-story office building or a five-ton drill press is not very great. On the other hand, physical security controls must be established for PP&E assets such as personal computers.

■ **EXHIBIT 9.10**

Total Asset Turnover, Selected Industries

Source: *Dun & Bradstreet's Industry Norms & Key Business Ratios, 1993–1994*. Dun & Bradstreet Information Services. (New York: Dun & Bradstreet, Inc., 1994).

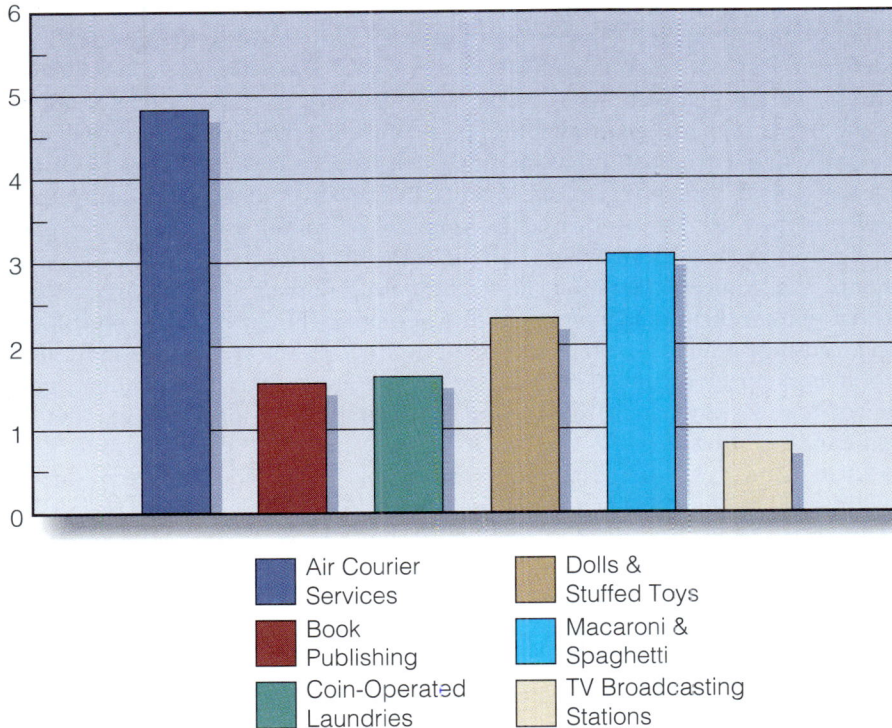

Legend:
- Air Courier Services
- Book Publishing
- Coin-Operated Laundries
- Dolls & Stuffed Toys
- Macaroni & Spaghetti
- TV Broadcasting Stations

An important internal control for PP&E is adequate insurance coverage, particularly for small companies that would be devastated by a major fire or other calamity. Proper authorization controls are also critical for long-term assets. A business should have a strict policy that requires top executives to approve the acquisition and disposal of high-priced PP&E assets. Many companies require that long-term assets be purchased through a competitive bidding process. The intent of this control procedure is to ensure that long-term assets are acquired at the lowest possible cost.

Businesses that have numerous PP&E assets usually maintain a property ledger. A **property ledger** is a subsidiary ledger in which key data are maintained for each PP&E asset. These data include date of acquisition, acquisition cost, location, intended use, insurance coverage, maintenance record, and the employee primarily responsible for the asset. The property ledger is typically organized or indexed by asset identification numbers. When a company acquires a PP&E asset, the asset is typically assigned an identification number. This number may be stamped on the asset, or a metal plate containing the number may be affixed permanently to the asset. Periodically, businesses take a physical inventory of PP&E assets by identification number. This physical inventory is intended to ensure that each asset is in the appropriate department or operating unit, is being used in the intended manner, and is being properly maintained.

Real World
Many companies require approval by the Board of Directors for major PP&E transactions.

property ledger

Real World
Some companies use bar codes to identify their PP&E assets. A physical inventory of PP&E can be performed quickly by using a scanner device to read the bar codes.

A FEW NOTES ON INTANGIBLE ASSETS

Intangible assets are long-term assets that do not have a physical existence. Given their nature, the importance of these assets is often discounted by decision makers. However, the financial success of many corporations stems largely from their intangible assets.

An example of an intangible asset is a patent, an exclusive right granted by the federal government to produce a product or to use a specific type of production process. In the pharmaceutical industry, patents are particularly important. A patent allows a pharmaceutical company to prevent other firms from producing and marketing a drug that it has developed. In January 1995, Glaxo plc, a British pharmaceutical company, announced a planned takeover of a smaller competitor, Wellcome plc, formerly known as Burroughs Wellcome. A key issue that arose during this takeover effort was the approaching expiration of one of Wellcome's patents. Wellcome's patent on its best-selling drug Zorivax would expire in 1997. At that point, other companies could produce and sell their own versions of that drug, causing an almost certain and significant decline in Wellcome's more than $1.5 billion dollars of annual sales of Zorivax. Because of the approaching expiration of the Zorivax patent, Glaxo paid considerably less for Wellcome than it would have otherwise.

Shown in Exhibit 9.11 are examples of intangible assets listed in recent annual reports of several publicly owned companies. The 1994 edition of *Accounting Trends & Techniques* reported that, except for goodwill, most types of intangible assets are quite rare, appearing on 10 percent or less of corporate balance sheets.

Accounting for Intangible Assets: An Overview

Intangible assets pose the same general types of accounting issues as their close cousins, long-term depreciable assets. For example, accountants must first determine the cost to assign to an intangible asset. Then, this cost must be systematically allocated to the accounting periods that the asset provides economic benefits to a business. For intangible assets, this allocation process is referred to as **amortization** instead of depreciation. Certain intangible assets, such as trademarks and copyrights,

A corporate trademark allows a company to quickly and efficiently identify its products to customers and other parties. Although trademarks are often developed at a minimal cost, they can be among the most valuable assets of a company.

■ **LEARNING OBJECTIVE 8**
Identify major types of intangible assets and the key accounting issues related to these assets

Discussion Question
Students are very familiar with logos (an intangible asset) associated with certain brands of clothing. Ask students to name items they are willing to pay a premium for because of the logo.

amortization

■ **EXHIBIT 9.11**
Intangible Assets of Selected Companies

SOURCE: Recent annual reports.

Company	Intangible Asset	Dollar Value
• Harvey Comics Entertainment	Trademark and Copyrights	$ 7,422,130
• Molecular Biosystems	Patents and License Rights	1,107,000
• National Pizza Company	Franchise Rights	21,778,000
• Nextel Communications	Customer Lists	74,473,000
• Physician Corporation of America	Organizational Costs	522,075
• Sound Advice	Goodwill	244,241
• Video Advice Technologies	Noncompete Agreements	4,679,863

have indefinite useful lives. Other intangible assets, such as patents, have a useful life that is limited by federal statute or a contractual agreement. The general rule is that intangible assets should be amortized over their legal life, their useful life, or forty years, whichever is shorter.

To illustrate accounting for intangible assets, assume that a record company purchases the copyright to a song for $100,000. Under federal law, the legal life of a copyright runs for the life of the creator plus fifty years. However, assume that the record company believes its newly acquired copyright will have a useful life of only five years. Amortization of intangible assets is typically computed using the straight-line method. For the copyright, the annual amortization expense under the straight-line method would be $20,000 ($100,000/5 years). Following is the entry to record the acquisition of this copyright and the first year-end adjusting entry to record amortization expense on this asset.

Jan. 3	Copyrights	100,000	
	Cash		100,000
	To record purchase of copyright to Garth Woods' song, "Headed for Nashville But Wound Up Flipping Burgers in Ash Flat, Arkansas"		
Dec. 31	Amortization Expense	20,000	
	Copyrights		20,000
	To record annual amortization expense on copyright to the song "Headed for Nashville But Wound Up Flipping Burgers in Ash Flat, Arkansas"		

Notice in the second entry that the offsetting credit to Amortization Expense is made to the Copyrights account instead of to Accumulated Amortization, Copyrights, as you might expect. Some businesses use accumulated amortization accounts for intangible assets similar to the accumulated depreciation accounts used for depreciable assets. However, a more common practice is to credit amortization expense directly to the appropriate intangible asset account.

Disposals of intangible assets are accounted for much like disposals of depreciable assets. If an intangible asset is sold, the gain or loss on the asset is computed by subtracting the unamortized cost of the asset from the selling price. Because of their nature, intangible assets are prone to losing their value rapidly. For instance, a patent held by a company may become worthless because a competitor develops a technologically advanced product. In such a case, the unamortized cost of the patent should be immediately written off as a loss.

Specific Types of Intangible Assets

Dozens of different types of intangible assets can be found on the balance sheets of business entities. In this section, the major types of intangible assets are discussed, beginning with the most common: goodwill.

GOODWILL   The 1994 edition of *Accounting Trends & Techniques* reported that approximately 64 percent of public companies listed goodwill as an asset on their

goodwill

balance sheets. What is goodwill? For John Q. Public, goodwill represents that "warm, fuzzy feeling" that makes him patronize Big Bill's Corner Grocery instead of Discount MegaMarkets USA. Superior service, excellent location, family ties to the community, and numerous other factors go into determining the goodwill associated with a business. However, just because Big Bill's Corner Grocery has accumulated a considerable amount of goodwill does not mean that goodwill can be "booked."

For accounting purposes, goodwill is generally recorded only when one business entity is purchased by another. In this context, **goodwill** is defined as the excess of the cost of a group of assets over the collective market value of those assets. Suppose that Exxon purchases for $25 million a company that operates a chain of service stations. If the collective market value of that company's assets is only $20 million, the remaining $5 million of the purchase price would be attributed to goodwill. Exxon must amortize this goodwill over a period not to exceed forty years. The 1994 edition of *Accounting Trends & Techniques* reported that forty years was the most common amortization period for goodwill.

patent

PATENTS   The United States Patent Office grants patents on both new products and new processes. The holder of a **patent** has an exclusive right to manufacture a specific product or to use a specific process for seventeen years.

copyright

trademark

COPYRIGHTS AND TRADEMARKS   The federal government grants the creators of songs, books, films, and other works of art the exclusive right to produce and sell those items. Such a grant is known as a **copyright.** Copyrights generally have a useful life of no more than a few years, although their legal lives extend fifty years beyond the life of the creator. The amortization period for a copyright cannot exceed forty years. Unlike patents and copyrights, trademarks have indefinite legal lives. A **trademark** is a distinctive word, symbol, or logo used to identify a specific business entity or one of its products. A trademark that is familiar to computer jockeys is the catchy two-word logo used by Intel Corporation. This logo is printed on adhesive labels that are applied to millions of personal computers to indicate that an Intel product is "inside." The next time you are sitting in front of a computer that displays Intel's logo, lean forward and you will discern a circled, upper-case *R*, which indicates the trademark is registered with the United States Patent Office. Although trademarks can be registered with the Patent Office, companies have the exclusive right to use the trademarks they have developed whether or not they are registered.

organizational costs

ORGANIZATIONAL COSTS   Sizable start-up or organizational costs must often be incurred by new businesses, particularly corporations. For accounting purposes, **organizational costs** include certain promotional expenditures, attorneys' fees to file articles of incorporation with a state government, and printing costs for a corporation's original stock certificates. Organizational costs qualify as intangible assets and are typically amortized over a short period of time, such as five years, the minimum period that these costs can be written off for tax purposes.

leasehold

LEASEHOLDS AND LEASEHOLD IMPROVEMENTS   Many businesses find that it makes sense to lease rather than purchase long-term assets. For example, a company may not have sufficient funds to purchase a large production facility that it needs. Instead, the company may lease that facility for an extended period. A company that leases an asset, the lessee, acquires a **leasehold,** which is a legal right to use a leased asset for a specified period subject to any restrictions in the lease agreement. Technically, leaseholds are intangible assets. As you will learn in Chapter 11, not all leaseholds are recorded as assets. Those leaseholds that are recorded are usually classified as PP&E assets for balance sheet purposes instead of being reported as intangible

Goodwill With an Attitude

Generally accepted accounting principles (GAAP) dictate accounting and financial reporting practices in the United States. However, accountants and business executives often disagree with the requirements of these rules. The following excerpt from the 1992 annual report of Capital Cities/ABC, Inc., a large entertainment conglomerate, expressed the company's displeasure with the accounting rules for goodwill.

At December 31, 1992, the Company's intangible assets, before accumulated amortization, totaled $2,516,793,000, which account for approximately 36% of the Company's total assets . . . . In accordance with *Accounting Principles Board Opinion No. 17*, the Company amortizes substantially all intangible assets over periods of up to 40 years. This practice is arbitrarily mandated by *Opinion No. 17* without regard to whether these assets have or have not declined in value.

All of the Company's intangible assets have resulted from the acquisition of broadcasting and publishing properties. Historically, such intangible assets have substantially increased in value and have long and productive lives. We believe that the Company's intangible assets have appreciated in value, and that the requirements of *Opinion No. 17*, when applied to such broadcasting and publishing assets understate net income and stockholders' equity. The amortization of intangible assets had the effect of reducing 1992 net income by $58,568,000, or $3.53 a share. [Note: Capital Cities/ABC, Inc., reported a net income of $14.82 per share in 1992.]

assets. Regardless of the balance sheet classification of a lease, its cost should be amortized over the term of the lease.

Companies that lease office buildings, retail stores, and production facilities often modify the leased properties to accommodate their operations. Expenditures for such modifications are referred to as **leasehold improvements.** Leasehold improvements revert to the owner of the property, the lessor, at the end of the lease term. Like leaseholds, leasehold improvements qualify as intangible assets. The cost of leasehold improvements should be amortized over their useful life or the term of the lease, whichever is shorter.

leasehold improvements

SUMMARY

Many financial decision makers have misconceptions about property, plant & equipment (PP&E). The most common misconception concerns the basis for determining the balance sheet values of these assets. In the United States, the historical cost principle dictates that PP&E generally be reported at historical cost, less accumulated depreciation. Besides valuation issues related to an entity's PP&E assets, decision makers should be informed of the specific types of these assets that an entity owns, the depreciation methods being applied to these assets, and any restrictions on their use. Disclosures regarding planned future acquisitions of PP&E and the intended methods of financing these acquisitions are also very informative for decision makers.

The starting point in accounting for PP&E assets is determining their acquisition cost. Only those costs that are reasonable and necessary to acquire these assets and make them ready for use should be capitalized, that is, debited to an asset account. Following their acquisition, the depreciable cost of PP&E assets should be allocated to the accounting periods that they will provide economic benefits to a business. The three major approaches to computing depreciation are the straight-line method, the units-of-production method, and the declining-balance method.

Accountants distinguish between two types of expenditures related to PP&E assets after they have been acquired: revenue expenditures and capital expenditures. Revenue expenditures, such as maintenance costs, should be treated as expenses in the period incurred. Capital expenditures, such as additions and improvements, should generally be capitalized. A special type of capital expenditures, extraordinary repairs, involves major repairs that extend the useful life of an asset. Instead of capitalizing extraordinary repairs, these expenditures are typically debited to an asset's Accumulated Depreciation account.

PP&E assets can be disposed of in several ways, including retirements, cash sales, and exchanges for other assets. A disposal of a PP&E asset usually results in a gain or loss being recorded. However, when similar PP&E assets are exchanged, gains are not recorded. Instead, the unrecognized gain on such an exchange is subtracted from the cash price of the newly acquired asset to determine its acquisition cost for accounting purposes.

Two key financial ratios related to a business's total assets are return on assets and the total asset turnover ratio. These ratios can be used to analyze how effectively business executives have utilized an entity's assets during an accounting period.

Given the nature of PP&E, the key internal controls for these assets are generally quite different from the comparable controls for other types of assets. Among internal controls for PP&E are adequate insurance coverage and procedures to ensure appropriate authorization for the acquisition and disposal of these assets. Another internal control for PP&E is the use of a property ledger to maintain important data regarding individual PP&E assets.

Intangible assets are long-term assets that do not have a physical existence. Among the major types of intangible assets are goodwill, patents, copyrights and trademarks, leaseholds, and leasehold improvements. The cost of intangible assets must be systematically allocated to the accounting periods that they provide economic benefits to a business entity. Instead of depreciation, this cost allocation process for intangible assets is referred to as amortization.

GLOSSARY

Additions (p. 383)   Capital expenditures that extend or expand existing property, plant & equipment assets.

Amortization (p. 392)   The allocation of the cost of an intangible asset to the accounting periods that it provides economic benefits to an entity.

Book value (p. 374)   For a depreciable asset, the difference between the asset's cost and the balance of its Accumulated Depreciation account; also referred to as carrying value.

Capital expenditures (p. 383)   Expenditures to obtain, expand, or improve long-term assets or to extend their useful lives.

Copyright (p. 394)   An exclusive right granted by the federal government to produce and sell works of art such as songs, books, and films.

Declining-balance method (p. 378)   A depreciation method under which annual depreciation expense is computed by multiplying an accelerated depreciation rate, which is a multiple of the straight-line rate, by an asset's book value at the beginning of the year.

Depletion (p. 381)   The allocation of the cost of natural resources to the periods these assets provide economic benefits to an entity.

Depreciable cost (p. 374)   The acquisition cost of a depreciable asset less its salvage value.

Depreciation (p. 371)   The process of allocating, or writing off, the cost of a long-term asset over its useful life in a rational and systematic manner.

Double declining-balance method (p. 378)   A variation of the declining-balance depreciation method under which the annual depreciation rate for an asset is twice the straight-line rate.

Extraordinary repairs (p. 384)   Expenditures that extend the useful life of a property, plant & equipment asset.

Goodwill (p. 394)   The excess of the cost of a group of assets over the collective market value of those assets.

Improvements (p. 383)   Capital expenditures that enhance an existing asset's operating efficiency or reduce its operating costs.

Leasehold (p. 394)   A legal right to use a leased asset for a specified period subject to any restrictions in the lease agreement.

Leasehold improvements (p. 395)   Improvements to a leased property made by a lessee that revert to the lessor at the end of the lease

Natural resources (p. 381)   Long-term assets, such as coal deposits, oil and gas reservoirs, and tracts of standing timber, that are extracted or harvested from the earth's surface or from beneath the earth's surface.

Organizational costs (p. 394)   Expenditures incurred during the formation of a business including certain promotional expenditures, attorneys' fees, and printing costs for a corporation's original stock certificates.

Patent (p. 394)   An exclusive right granted by the United States Patent Office to manufacture a specific product or use a specific process.

Property ledger (p. 391)   A subsidiary ledger in which key data are maintained for individual property, plant & equipment assets.

Return on assets (p. 389)   The sum of net income and interest expense divided by average total assets for an accounting period.

Revenue expenditures (p. 383)   Expenditures that provide economic benefits to only one accounting period and, as a result, are expensed in the period incurred.

Salvage value (p. 374)   The estimated value of an asset at the end of its useful life.

Straight-line method (p. 375)   A depreciation method that allocates an equal amount of depreciation expense to each year of an asset's estimated useful life.

Total asset turnover ratio (p. 389)   Net sales divided by average total assets for an accounting period; a measure of how effectively an entity's total assets are being utilized.

Trademark (p. 394)   A distinctive word, symbol, or logo used to identify a specific business entity or one of its products.

Units-of-production method (p. 377)   A depreciation method under which an asset's useful life is expressed in terms of a given number of units of production or use; depreciation expense for any given period is a function of the level of usage of the asset during that period.

Renee Jenkins is the CEO of Marsh Industries, Inc., a manufacturing company that has two divisions. One of Ms. Jenkins's responsibilities each year is to evaluate the job performance of the two divisional managers. Following are financial data for the most recent fiscal year for this firm and its two divisions.

DECISION CASE

	EASTERN DIVISION	WESTERN DIVISION	TOTAL
Sales	$6,000,000	$9,000,000	$15,000,000
Operating Income	620,000	730,000	1,350,000
Corporate Headquarters			
Expenses	80,000	80,000	160,000
Interest Expense	50,000	50,000	100,000
Income Taxes Expense	150,000	150,000	300,000
Net Income	430,000	560,000	990,000
Average Book Value of			
Total Assets During Year	4,200,000	8,300,000	12,500,000
Average Market Value of			
Total Assets During Year	7,100,000	8,400,000	15,500,000

Notice in the prior schedule that Marsh Industries had total interest expense of $100,000 and total income taxes expense of $300,000. Additionally, notice that the company's corporate headquarters incurred expenses of $160,000 during the year. Historically, Ms. Jenkins has allocated each of these expenses equally to the two divisions. The interest expense is on a long-term loan that was obtained to construct a new factory in the Eastern Division five years ago. The market value of the Eastern Division's assets is considerably above their book value. That division's new factory is located near the planned site for a major metropolitan airport that was announced within the past year. As a result, the value of the property on which the factory was built has increased dramatically in recent months.

Required: Assume that you are a corporate accountant for Marsh Industries. Ms. Jenkins asks you to compute return on assets and the total asset turnover ratio for the Eastern and Western Divisions and to provide a brief assessment of each divisional manager's job performance. She specifically asks that you indicate in your report which manager did a better job managing the assets assigned to his or her division.

What additional information do you believe would be helpful in evaluating the performance of the two managers? What recommendations would you make to Ms. Jenkins regarding the use of return on assets and the total asset turnover ratio to evaluate the divisional managers' job performance? Explain.

QUESTIONS

1. Define long-term assets and identify the major types of these assets.
2. Describe specific ways that accountants assist business executives in making decisions involving long-term assets.
3. Identify key information needs that financial decision makers have regarding the long-term assets of business entities.
4. Identify advantages and disadvantages of using historical costs as the primary valuation basis for long-term assets.
5. Under what circumstances can businesses depart from the historical cost principle for long-term assets?
6. What alternative valuation basis is used for long-term assets in certain countries?
7. Identify the four general issues that accountants must address in accounting for property, plant & equipment (PP&E) assets.
8. What types of expenditures are included in the acquisition cost of PP&E assets?
9. Describe the general method used to allocate the cost of a "basket purchase" of long-term assets to the individual assets acquired.
10. What is the objective of recording depreciation expense each accounting period on depreciable assets?
11. Identify the three key factors that must be identified to compute depreciation expense on a depreciable asset.
12. Identify three common methods of computing depreciation expense. Briefly describe how each of these methods is applied.
13. Which depreciation method is most popular among publicly owned companies and why?

14. How do members of the public often interpret the meaning of the term "depreciation expense"?

15. How is the "book value" of a depreciable asset computed? How does an asset's book value change from one accounting period to the next?

16. Define the terms "revenue expenditures" and "capital expenditures" and provide examples of each.

17. How is the gain or loss on the disposal of a depreciable asset determined?

18. Can a gain or loss be recorded when a business entity exchanges a depreciable asset for a similar asset? Explain.

19. How is return on assets computed? What does this ratio tell us about a business entity's operations?

20. How is the total asset turnover ratio computed? What does this ratio tell us about a business entity's operations?

21. Identify key internal control procedures for PP&E assets.

22. Define "intangible assets."

23. Provide examples of the "probable future economic benefits" that intangible assets provide to business entities.

24. Define the term "amortization" as it applies to intangible assets.

25. What is the difference between the legal life and the useful life of an intangible asset?

EXERCISES

26. **Financial Statement Reporting of PP&E Assets** (LO 1)

Wiggins Corporation is a manufacturing firm that was established in 1990. Since that time, the company has acquired several long-term assets used in its operations at a collective cost of $3,600,000. Listed in the following schedule is the acquisition cost of each of these assets and the total depreciation expense recorded on them through the end of 1996.

DESCRIPTION	ACQUISITION COST	DEPRECIATION EXPENSE THROUGH 1996
Office Building	$1,400,000	$230,000
Production Equipment	1,200,000	112,000
Office Furniture	250,000	61,000
Land	350,000	0
Delivery Trucks	400,000	125,000

Required:

1. Prepare the PP&E section of Wiggins Corporation's balance sheet at the end of 1996.

2. Why has no depreciation expense been recorded on the land owned by Wiggins?

3. Besides the information you developed in Part 1, what other information regarding Wiggins' PP&E assets is needed by decision makers who use the company's financial statements?

26. 1. Net PP&E, $3,072,000

27. **Acquisition Cost of PP&E Assets** (LO 1, 2)

Fain Enterprises recently purchased new computer equipment for its company headquarters. Following is information regarding the various expenditures related to the acquisition of this equipment.

a. The original invoice price of the computer equipment was $400,000; however, Fain's owner negotiated a 15 percent price reduction.
b. The delivery cost for the equipment was $2,300 and was paid by Fain.
c. Three computer consultants were retained by Fain to install and test the new equipment at a cost of $1,500.
d. Supplies costing $200 were used in installing and testing the equipment.
e. The day following the installation of the equipment, Fain's owner decided to move the equipment to the floor on which her office was located. An additional $600 of costs were incurred in moving the equipment.

Required:

27. 1. $344,000

1. Determine the acquisition cost of the computer equipment for accounting purposes.
2. Prepare an appropriate journal entry to record the acquisition of the computer equipment. (Assume the expenditures listed were paid in cash.)
3. A computer purchased for several thousand dollars may have little resale value one year later because of technological changes in the computer industry. Given that the resale value of computers and computer equipment can decline rapidly, is historical cost the proper valuation basis to use for such assets? Defend your answer.

28. **Basket Purchase of PP&E Assets** (LO 2)

Scott & Linn's Garden Supply recently bought a greenhouse for $360,000 from Fred's Flowers, which was going out of business. Also included in the deal was a recently installed irrigation system, a forklift, and the land on which the greenhouse is located.

Following are the individual market values of the assets required by Scott & Linn's in this "basket" purchase:

ASSET	MARKET VALUE
Greenhouse	$250,000
Irrigation System	50,000
Forklift	50,000
Land	50,000

Required:

28. 1. Greenhouse, $225,000
Irrigation, $45,000
Forklift, $45,000
Land, $45,000

1. Allocate the $360,000 basket purchase price among the four assets acquired by Scott & Linn's.
2. Why is it important to allocate the collective purchase price to the four individual assets instead of recording that amount in one aggregate asset account?

29. **Basket Purchase of PP&E Assets** (LO 1, 2)

John Anderson, the owner of Anderson Landscaping, is considering buying out a competitor who is retiring. The principal assets of the competitor's business are several large pieces of equipment and the land on which the business is located. John knows that land is not depreciated. As a result, he plans to acquire the business for one lump sum and allocate all of the cost to the land. By not assigning any cost to the equipment, John will avoid recording depreciation expense on that equipment in the future, thus increasing his business's net income. John sees nothing wrong with this plan, since he views the recording of depreciation expense as an accounting "gimmick" anyway.

Required:

29 No check figures

Write a memo to John Anderson. Explain to John in this memo why his planned method of accounting for the basket purchase is inappropriate. Comment in this memo on how his method of accounting for the basket purchase may be detrimental to third parties who will be relying on his business's financial statements.

30. **Computing Depreciation** (LO 3)

Michelman Manufacturing purchased a piece of production equipment on January 1, 1995. The equipment cost $6,500 and was estimated to have a salvage value of $500 at the end of its six-year life.

Required:

1. Compute depreciation expense on the production equipment for both 1995 and 1996 and prepare the appropriate journal entries under the following two assumptions:
   a. Michelman uses the straight-line depreciation method.
   b. Michelman uses the double declining-balance depreciation method.
2. Suppose now that Michelman uses the units-of-production method. The new production equipment is expected to have a useful life of 12,000 hours. Compute the depreciation expense on the production equipment for 1995 and 1996 and prepare the appropriate journal entries, assuming the equipment is used 2,500 hours in 1995 and 1,900 hours in 1996.

30. 1a. 1995, $1,000
        1996, $1,000
    1b. 1995, $2,166.67
        1996, $1,444.44
    2. 1995, $1,250
        1996, $950

31. **Choosing a Depreciation Method** (LO 3)

Albuquerque Stairs, which manufactures stairway railings, purchased a new lathe on January 1, 1996. The lathe cost $15,000 and was estimated to have a salvage value of $1,000 at the end of its five-year useful life. Presently, the company's owner is trying to decide on a depreciation method to use for this new asset.

Required:

1. Compute depreciation expense on the new lathe for 1996 and 1997 assuming that Albuquerque Stairs uses:
   a. the straight-line method.
   b. the double declining-balance method.
2. Suppose the new lathe will be used to produce approximately 3,500 units of finished product over its five-year useful life. Compute the depreciation expense on the lathe for 1996 and 1997 assuming that it is used to produce 550 units of finished product in 1996 and 670 units of finished product in 1997.
3. Which of the three depreciation methods best satisfies the matching principle discussed in Chapter 2? Defend your choice.
4. Under which of the three methods will the company have the highest net income for 1996? For 1997?

31. 1a. 1996, $2,800
        1997, $2,800
    1b. 1996, $6,000
        1997, $3,600
    2. 1996, $2,200
        1997, $2,680

32. **Changes in Estimates Affecting Depreciation Expense** (LO 3)

Tanner Company purchased a delivery truck on January 1, 1995, for $28,000. Tanner estimated the truck's salvage value to be $3,000 at the end of its five-year useful life. Because of unexpected growth in Tanner's volume of business, the delivery truck was used much more than expected. By January 1, 1997, Tanner's accountant determined that the delivery truck would be in usable condition for only two more years. The accountant estimates the truck will have a salvage value of $3,600 at the end of 1998. Tanner uses the straight-line depreciation method.

Required:

1. Compute the depreciation expense that would have been recorded each year of the useful life of the delivery truck had the original estimates of its useful life and salvage value been correct.
2. Compute the depreciation expense that will actually be recorded each year of the truck's useful life.

32. 1. $5,000
    2. $7,200 (1997 and 1998)
    3. $6,100

3. Compute the depreciation expense that would have been recorded each year of the truck's useful life had Tanner's accountant known exactly how long it would be in usable condition when it was acquired.
4. Why is it important for accountants to make every effort to accurately estimate a depreciable asset's useful life and salvage value?

33. **Depletion of Natural Resources** (LO 3)

On March 1, 1995, Smiley Corporation acquired a large oil reservoir that geologists estimated contained 3 million barrels of crude oil. Smiley paid $7.2 million for the reservoir, which is expected to have no salvage value after the oil has been extracted. During 1995, Smiley extracted and sold 1.2 million barrels of crude oil from the reservoir. During 1996, 1 million barrels of oil were extracted, of which 700,000 barrels were sold by year-end.

Required:

33. 1. $2.40
2. 1995 Depl. Exp.
$2,880,000
1996 Depl. Exp.
$1,680,000

1. Compute the depletion cost per barrel of oil expected to be contained in the reservoir.
2. Prepare the appropriate journal entries in Smiley Corporation's accounting records for 1995 and 1996, given the information provided.
3. If the reservoir contains only 2.5 million barrels of oil, what will happen to the remaining book value of this asset after all the oil has been extracted?

34. **Identifying Revenue and Capital Expenditures** (LO 4)

On April 1, 1986, Dodson Enterprises acquired four bulldozers to be used in its construction and land development business. The bulldozers cost $246,000. Dodson chose to depreciate the bulldozers over useful lives of ten years. Over the first several years the bulldozers were in use, Dodson incurred the following additional costs related to them:
a. Monthly oil changes and lubrication of valves, $250 per month.
b. Replaced broken steering mechanism, $1,800.
c. Replaced the engine cooling system of each bulldozer at a total cost of $14,000 to significantly improve their operating efficiency.
d. Repaired a homeowner's fence that was accidentally destroyed by a bulldozer, $2,100.
e. Paid annual state licensing fees on the bulldozers, $1,440 per year.
f. Paid $49,400 for a major overhaul of the bulldozers after they had been in service eight years; these expenditures were estimated to extend the useful lives of the bulldozers by four years.

Required:

34. No check figures

1. Identify those expenditures that are revenue expenditures and those that are capital expenditures. For those items that are capital expenditures, indicate the specific type of capital expenditure.
2. Why is it important for a business to properly distinguish between revenue and capital expenditures related to its long-term assets?

35. **Extraordinary Repairs** (LO 4)

In early January 1995, Talley & Hassee, a manufacturing firm, acquired a new hydraulic press. Talley & Hassee estimated that the machine would be in service for eight years. The machine cost $8,000 and was estimated to have a salvage value of $1,400 at the end of its useful life. The company uses the straight-line depreciation method.

On January 3, 1998, Talley & Hassee spent $2,000 overhauling the hydraulic press. This major overhaul was expected to extend the useful life of the asset by two years (to a total of ten years).

Required:

1. Prepare the appropriate journal entry to record the $2,000 spent to overhaul the hydraulic press in January 1998.
2. Compute the depreciation expense on the hydraulic press for 1998 and prepare the entry to record this depreciation.

35. 1. Dr. Accum. Dep. $2,000
2. $875

36. **Sale of a PP&E Asset** (LO 5)

On June 30, 1995, Newsom Company sold a computer for $1,250 that had been acquired on January 1, 1993. Newsom had originally estimated that the computer would have a five-year useful life and a $500 salvage value. The original cost of the computer was $2,500. Newsom uses the straight-line depreciation method. The company's fiscal year ends on December 31 and it records depreciation expense on its depreciable assets at the end of each fiscal year.

Required:

1. Determine the book value of the computer on June 30, 1995.
2. Prepare all entries needed to properly account for the disposal of the computer.

36. 1. $1,500
2. Loss, $250

37. **Disposals of PP&E Assets** (LO 5)

Chandra Corporation traded in a 1992 Ford van on a new 1995 Chevy van in late December 1995. Chandra purchased the Ford van for $24,000 in early January 1992. Chandra recorded $4,000 of depreciation expense on the van each year from 1992 through 1995. The Chevy dealer had given Chandra the option of either paying $23,500 cash for the new Chevy van, or paying $17,500 plus trading in the Ford van.

Required:

1. Prepare the entry necessary to record this exchange transaction in Chandra's accounting records.
2. Suppose the cash price of the new Chevy van was $23,500 but that the deal negotiated by Chandra to acquire the new van involved a $14,500 cash payment plus the Ford van. Prepare the entry to record the exchange transaction under these circumstances.
3. Why are losses on exchanges of similar assets recorded but gains on such exchanges are not?

37. 1. Loss, $2,000
2. New Van, $22,500

38. **Accounting for Fully Depreciated Assets** (LO 3)

Jim's Bike Shop purchased an air compressor four years ago at a cost of $2,400. The air compressor was estimated to have a four-year useful life when it was acquired. At the end of its useful life, it was projected to have no salvage value. This air compressor is now fully depreciated with a zero book value. Surprisingly to the business owner, the air compressor "works like new" and he has no plans to replace it.

Required:

1. Should this business continue to record depreciation expense on the air compressor each year? Why or why not?
2. Can a business keep a fully depreciated asset on its books indefinitely as long as the asset is being used in the business?
3. Explain how the matching principle was violated by Jim's Bike Shop and how this violation affected the financial statements of the business. Was this violation intentional?

38. No check figures

39. **Disposals of PP&E Assets** (LO 5)

On January 1, 1993, Landers Company purchased ten washing machines to be used in its coin-operated laundry. Each washer cost $400 and had an estimated salvage value of $40 at the end of its eight-year useful life. On September 30, 1996, Landers decided to purchase more efficient machines and sold the ten washers for $2,200. Landers Company uses the straight-line depreciation method for its depreciable assets and records depreciation expense at the end of each year.

Required:

1. Prepare the appropriate journal entry to record depreciation expense on the washers prior to their disposal. What is the book value of the washers following the posting of this journal entry?
2. Prepare the journal entry to record the sale of the washers.
3. Suppose that rather than being sold, the washers were simply hauled off to the junkyard. Prepare the journal entry to record the disposal of the washers under this assumption.
4. Suppose now that the old washers were exchanged for ten new washers that had a collective cash price of $5,100. In addition to trading in the old washers, Landers was required to pay cash of $3,300. Prepare the journal entry to record the disposal of the old washers under this assumption.

40. Analyzing Total Assets (LO 6)

The following information was taken from a recent annual report of TCBY Enterprises, Inc., which sells yogurt and other food items.

	YEAR 1	YEAR 2
Net Sales	$107,633,301	$109,525,036
Interest Expense	1,751,266	1,311,958
Net Income	5,072,924	6,408,811
Average Total Assets	131,925,142	128,691,136

Required:

1. Compute TCBY's return on assets for Years 1 and 2. Given these ratios, in which year did the company use its assets more effectively? Explain.
2. Compute TCBY's total asset turnover for Years 1 and 2. Given these ratios, in which year did TCBY use its assets more effectively? Explain.
3. What other information would decision makers find useful in analyzing how effectively TCBY's management used the company's assets in Years 1 and 2?

41. Intangible Assets (LO 8)

Hulsey Company, a sporting goods manufacturer, began operations on January 1, 1996. On that date, the firm purchased two intangible assets from a competitor that was going out of business. The first patent involved a golf ball that corrects hooks and slices. Husley paid $300,000 for this patent, which had a remaining legal life of twelve years and a remaining estimated useful life of five years. The second intangible asset acquired by Hulsey was a trademark for a running shoe. Hulsey paid $100,000 for this trademark, which has an indefinite legal life and an estimated useful life of ten years.

Required:

1. Prepare the journal entries to record the acquisition of the patent and trademark by Hulsey. Prepare journal entries to record amortization expense on these two assets in 1996.
2. What is a key difference in the procedures used by businesses to account for depreciation expense and amortization expense on depreciable assets and intangible assets? What likely accounts for this difference?

Margin answers:

39. 1. Deprec. Exp. $337.50
       BV, $2,312.50
    2. Loss, $112.50
    3. Loss, $2,312.50
    4. Loss, $512.50

40. 1. Year 1, 5.2%
       Year 2, 6.0%
    2. Year 1, 0.82
       Year 2, 0.85

41. 1. Amort. Exp., $70,000

42. **Internal Controls for PP&E Assets** (LO 7)

Eddie Garcia owns a small but rapidly growing plumbing business. Most of Garcia's assets are long-term assets including plumbing tools, several service vehicles, and office furniture and equipment. Collectively, the net book value of Garcia's long-term assets exceeds $300,000. Garcia has never developed a set of internal controls for his long-term assets.

Required:

Write a brief memo to Eddie Garcia that emphasizes the importance of every business having a reliable and cost-effective internal control structure. Identify in your memo internal control risks relating specifically to Garcia's long-term assets. Conclude your memo with examples of internal control procedures Garcia should consider implementing for his long-term assets.

42. No check figures

PROBLEM SET A

43. **Acquisition of PP&E Assets** (LO 2, 3)

In 1995, Kare Corporation acquired several PP&E assets for its manufacturing operations. Following are descriptions of costs incurred by Kare during 1995 related to these assets. Unless indicated otherwise, all amounts were paid in cash.

a. On January 1, 1995, Kare purchased a warehouse and the land on which it was located for $2,600,000. The land's appraised value was $700,000, while the warehouse had an appraised value of $2,100,000. The estimated useful life of the warehouse is twenty years and its estimated salvage value is $200,000. Remodeling costs on the warehouse of $250,000 were completed on January 7, 1995. On January 8, title fees of $1,200 were paid on the land and $4,000 on the warehouse.

b. On January 3, 1995, Kare purchased production equipment by signing a six-month, 10 percent note payable for $1,000,000. The equipment had an estimated useful life of five years and an estimated salvage value of $60,000. Delivery costs of $4,200 were paid by the seller of the equipment. Costs to repair the equipment after it was damaged during installation totaled $2,700.

c. On April 2, Kare purchased office furniture and fixtures for $400,000. These assets have an estimated useful life of ten years and an estimated salvage value of $30,000.

d. On July 1, Kare purchased four used delivery trucks at a cost of $12,000 each. Each truck had an estimated remaining useful life of four years and an estimated salvage value of $2,400. Expenses paid to deliver the trucks totaled $900, while insurance paid on the trucks while they were in transit amounted to $300. Kare immediately installed an alarm system on each truck at a cost of $600 per truck.

Required:

1. Prepare the journal entries to record the acquisitions of PP&E assets by Kare Corporation during 1995.
2. Kare records depreciation on its PP&E assets each December 31. Assuming that the company uses the straight-line method, prepare the December 31, 1995, adjusting entries for depreciation expense on the assets it acquired during 1995.

43. 1a. 1/1/95 Land, $650,000
Warehouse, $1,950,000
1d. Trucks, $51,600
2. Depreciation:
Warehouse, $100,200
Prod. Equip., $188,000
Office Furn., $27,750
Trucks, $5,250

44. **Alternative Depreciation Methods** (LO 3)

Roslyn and Jimmy recently decided to open a restaurant specializing in Georgian cuisine. They purchased an existing restaurant on January 1, 1996, at a cost of $650,000. The two co-owners paid 10 percent of the purchase price in cash and financed the balance of the cost by obtaining a mortgage. The restaurant has an estimated salvage value of $150,000 and an estimated useful life of twenty-five years. Also on January 1, 1996, Roslyn and Jimmy paid cash of $80,000 for used kitchen equipment. The equipment has an estimated useful life of four years and an estimated salvage value of $8,000.

Required:

1. Compute depreciation expense for 1996 and 1997 on the restaurant using the following methods:
   a. Straight-line
   b. Double declining-balance
2. Prepare year-end adjusting journal entries to record the depreciation expense amounts computed in Part 1.
3. Compute depreciation expense on the kitchen equipment for each year of its useful life, 1996 through 1999, assuming that the following depreciation methods are used:
   a. Straight-line
   b. Double declining-balance
4. Prepare year-end adjusting journal entries to record the depreciation expense amounts computed in Part 3.
5. Roslyn and Jimmy wanted to use every means possible to maximize the cash flows generated by their restaurant in the first few years of its operations. With this objective in mind, which depreciation method should the owners have selected—straight-line or double declining-balance?

45. **Alternative Depreciation Methods** (LO 3)

Midori Airlines is a small charter airline company that operates between San Francisco and Los Angeles. On January 1, 1996, Midori purchased a small jet. The jet cost $1,600,000 and is estimated to have a salvage value of $100,000 at the end of its five-year useful life. Midori expects that the jet will be flown the following number of miles over the course of its useful life:

1996	100,000	miles
1997	120,000	miles
1998	130,000	miles
1999	90,000	miles
2000	60,000	miles

Required:

1. Prepare a depreciation schedule similar to the one shown in Exhibit 9.4, assuming that Midori uses the following depreciation methods:
   a. Straight-line
   b. Double declining-balance
   c. Units-of-production
2. In your opinion, which of these three depreciation methods is most consistent with the matching principle? Defend your answer.

46. **Revenue and Capital Expenditures** (LO 4)

On April 1, 1994, Krempler Enterprises bought a new book binding machine for its manufacturing facility. The machine cost $241,000 plus sales taxes of 5 percent and a delivery charge of $2,200. Following are selected expenditures incurred by Krempler in the next few years relating to this machine.
   a. Valve adjustments on the machine were made in September 1994 at a cost of $600.

Answer column (left margin):

44. 1a. 1996, $20,000
    1997, $20,000
  1b. 1996, $52,000
    1997, $47,840
  3a. 1996, $18,000
  3b. 1996, $40,000
    1997, $20,000
    1998, $10,000
    1999, $2,000

45. 1a. Year-End BV:
    1996, $1,300,000
    1997, $1,000,000
    1998, $700,000
    1999, $400,000
    2000, $100,000
  1b. Year-End BV:
    1996, $960,000
    1997, $576,000
    1998, $345,600
    1999, $207,360
    2000, $124,416
  1c. Year-End BV:
    1996, $1,300,000
    1997, $940,000
    1998, $550,000
    1999, $280,000
    2000, $100,000

b. In September 1995, Krempler bought a special attachment for the machine to increase its operating efficiency. The attachment cost $8,000 plus $600 for installation. During installation, a Krempler employee damaged the attachment, resulting in repair costs of $240.

c. In December 1996, Krempler spent $24,000 overhauling the binding machine. This overhaul was estimated to extend the machine's useful life by two years.

d. Periodic maintenance expenses incurred in 1997 for the binding machine totaled $3,200.

e. In January 1998, the machine's cutting mechanism was replaced to accommodate special-order binding materials. This new mechanism, which cost $7,100, significantly reduced the costs to operate the machine.

Required:

1. For each expenditure related to the book binding machine, indicate whether the item is a revenue expenditure or a capital expenditure.
2. For the capital expenditures, indicate how each item should be recorded in Krempler's accounting records.
3. Suppose that all of the listed expenditures were recorded as capital expenditures. What accounting principles or concepts would be violated and why?

46. 1. Capital (b,c,e)

47. Changes in Depreciation Computations (LO 3)

Adcox Company purchased a packaging machine on January 1, 1994, at a cost of $98,000. The machine was estimated to have a salvage value of $8,000 at the end of its useful life of five years. Adcox uses the straight-line depreciation method. At the beginning of 1996, Adcox's accountant discovered information reported by the Packaging Industry Association that indicated that the original estimate of the packaging machine's useful life was in error. Instead of five years, the machine's useful life will likely be eight years. The salvage value at the end of the machine's newly determined useful life will be $2,000.

Required:

1. Compute the annual depreciation expense recorded on the packaging machine during 1994 and 1995
2. Given the revision of the packaging machine's useful life, compute the depreciation expense that will be recorded over the remaining years of the asset's useful life beginning in 1996.

47. 1. 1994, $18,000
     1995, $18,000
  2. 1996, $10,000

48. Depletion of Natural Resources (LO 3)

On February 12, 1995, Thayer Mining Corporation (TMC) acquired a large tract of land for $1,800,000. Geological reports indicate that this property contains 800,000 tons of ore. TMC estimates that the property can be sold for $360,000 following removal of the ore.

Required:

1. Assume that the following amounts of ore are recovered and sold during 1995 and 1996 from the TMC property:

48. 1. 1995, $198,000
     1996, $324,000
  2. 1995, $286,000
     1996, $468,000

	1995	1996
Tons of Ore Recovered	120,000	170,000
Tons of Ore Sold	110,000	180,000

Determine the depletion expense recorded by TMC during 1995 and 1996.

2. Suppose that the property acquired by TMC actually has a negative salvage value of $280,000 because of large reclamation expenditures required to

rehabilitate the property after the ore is extracted. Recompute the depletion expense for 1995 and 1996 given the data provided in Part 1.

3. What accounting principle dictates the accounting treatment given the reclamation expenditures referred to in Part 2?

49. Disposals of PP&E Assets (LO 5)

On January 1, 1993, Lein Phan Vending purchased five vending machines to place in a high school. Each vending machine cost $3,100 and was estimated to have a six-year useful life. The estimated salvage value of the vending machines was $400 each. Lein Phan uses the straight-line depreciation method. On April 1, 1996, the company decided to replace the vending machines and sold them collectively for $8,200.

Required:

1. Prepare the journal entry to record the depreciation expense on the vending machines for the first three months of 1996.
2. Determine the book value of the vending machines following the posting of the journal entry prepared in Part 1.
3. Prepare the journal entry to record the sale of the vending machines.
4. Prepare the journal entry to record the sale of the vending machines, assuming they were sold for $11,300.
5. Suppose now that rather than selling the vending machines, the company traded them in on six new machines that had a collective cash price of $25,300. In addition to trading in the old vending machines, Lein Phan was required to pay cash of $16,700. Prepare the appropriate journal entry to record this exchange transaction.

50. Analyzing Total Assets (LO 6)

Cardinal Health, Inc., and Herman Miller, Inc., are two companies in very different industries. Cardinal Health is a major distributor of pharmaceuticals, while Herman Miller markets office furnishings and related products. Following is selected financial information for each of these companies. (Amounts are presented in thousands.)

	CARDINAL HEALTH, INC.		HERMAN MILLER, INC.	
	1993	1994	1993	1994
Net Sales	$4,709,085	$5,790,411	$855,673	$953,200
Interest Expense	26,174	18,140	2,089	1,828
Net Income	39,298	33,931	22,054	40,373
Average Total Assets	1,048,752	1,273,013	477,805	509,044

Required:

1. Compute the return on assets and total asset turnover ratios for each company in both 1993 and 1994.
2. Based strictly upon the data you computed in Part 1, which of these companies did a better job of managing its assets in 1993 and 1994? Defend your answer.
3. How may the nature of a company's industry affect the two ratios you computed in Part 1? Explain by comparing the two industries represented by Cardinal Health and Herman Miller.

51. Accounting for Intangible Assets (LO 8)

Coleman Pharmaceuticals is a leading manufacturer and distributor of pharmaceutical products. Following are several recent transactions or events involving Coleman's intangible assets.

Margin answer key:

49. 1. Deprec. Exp., $562.50
    2. $8,187.50
    3. Gain, $12.50
    4. Gain, $3,112.50
    5. Dr. Vending Machines (new) $24,887.50

50. 1. Cardinal	1993	1994
ROA	6.2%	4.1%
Turnover	4.49	4.55
Miller	1993	1994
ROA	5.1%	8.3%
Turnover	1.79	1.87

a. On January 4, 1995, purchased a patent on the drug Zorcerin for $1,500,000.
b. On February 9, 1995, sold a patent with a book value of $753,000 to a competitor for $800,000.
c. On June 30, 1995, a competitor introduced a new drug that made a patent held by Coleman obsolete; the book value of the patent was $607,000 at the time.
d. On December 31, 1995, recorded amortization expense on goodwill of $300,000.
e. On December 31, 1995, recorded amortization expense on the Zorcerin patent, which had a legal life of twelve years when acquired on January 4, 1995, and an estimated useful life at the time of five years.

Required:

1. Prepare the appropriate journal entry for each transaction or event listed for Coleman Pharmaceuticals.
2. What accounting principles or concepts prevent a business from recording goodwill it has developed? In your opinion, would allowing businesses to record goodwill they have developed result in more useful financial statements for decision makers? Why or why not?

51. 1b. Gain, $47,000
    1c. Loss, $607,000
    1d. Amort., $300,000
    1e. Amort., $300,000

PROBLEM SET B

52. **Acquisition of PP&E Assets** (LO 2, 3)

Beckwith Construction Corporation acquired several assets for its production operations during 1996. Following are descriptions of costs incurred by Beckwith related to these asset acquisitions. Unless indicated otherwise, all amounts were paid in cash.

a. On January 4, 1996, Beckwith purchased a small factory, the land on which it was located, and the accompanying land improvements for $9,000,000. A real estate commission of $50,000 was also paid on this basket purchase. The factory had an appraised value of $8,000,000 versus an appraised value of $1,200,000 and $800,000 for the land and land improvements, respectively. The factory is expected to have a zero salvage value at the end of its estimated useful life of forty years. At the end of their estimated useful life of ten years, the land improvements are expected to have a salvage value of $20,000. Renovation of the factory, which was begun by Beckwith before the purchase agreement was officially signed, was completed on January 7, 1996. Costs to renovate the factory totaled $1,600,000.

b. On July 1, 1996, Beckwith purchased a piece of used machinery at a cost of $320,000. At the end of its five-year useful life, the machinery is expected to have a salvage value of $40,000. Immediately after the machinery was acquired, Beckwith replaced its engine at a cost of $20,000.

c. On September 2, 1996, Beckwith purchased new furniture for its corporate headquarters. The furniture cost $9,600 and is expected to have a zero salvage value at the end of its three-year useful life.

d. On October 31, 1996, Beckwith purchased a flatbed truck at a cost of $26,000 by signing a two-year, 12 percent promissory note. The truck has an estimated useful life of four years and an estimated salvage value of $2,000. The company paid $1,400 to install a bed liner and sideboards on the truck immediately after it was purchased. An additional $450 was spent to repair damage to the truck's paint job during the installation of the sideboards. Beckwith's name and logo were painted on the doors of the truck at a cost of $200.

52. 1a. 1/4/96   Land,
        $1,086,000
      Land Impr. $724,000
      Factory, $7,240,000
   1d. Truck, $27,600
   2. Depreciation:
      Land Impr., $70,400
      Factory, $221,000
      Machinery, $30,000
      Furniture, $1,066.67
      Truck, $1,066.67

Required:

1. Prepare the journal entries to record the acquisitions of PP&E assets by Beckwith Construction Corporation during 1996.
2. Beckwith records depreciation on its PP&E assets each December 31. Assuming that the company uses the straight-line method, prepare the December 31, 1996, adjusting entries for depreciation expense on the assets it acquired during 1996.

53. Alternative Depreciation Methods (LO 3)

Wayne and Garth recently decided to open a comedy club. They rented a building on January 1, 1996, and immediately furnished the building at a cost of $100,000. The furniture has an expected useful life of five years and a salvage value of $10,000.

Also on January 1, 1996, Wayne and Garth purchased $40,000 of sound equipment that has an estimated useful life of ten years. The salvage value of this equipment is estimated to be $4,000.

Required:

53. 1a. 1996, $18,000
       1997, $18,000
       1998, $18,000
       1999, $18,000
       2000, $18,000
    1b. 1996, $40,000
       1997, $24,000
       1998, $14,400
       1999, $8,640
       2000, $2,960
    3a. 1996, $3,600
       1997, $3,600
    3b. 1996, $8,000
       1997, $6,400

1. Compute the depreciation expense on the furniture for each year of its useful life, 1996 through 2000, assuming that the following depreciation methods are used:
   a. Straight-line
   b. Double declining-balance
2. Prepare year-end adjusting journal entries to record the depreciation expense amounts computed in Part 1.
3. Compute the depreciation expense for 1996 and 1997 on the sound equipment using the following methods:
   a. Straight-line
   b. Double declining-balance
4. Prepare year-end adjusting journal entries to record the depreciation expense amounts computed in Part 3.
5. Suppose that Wayne and Garth came to you shortly after they opened the comedy club. They were seeking advice on which depreciation method, straight-line or double declining-balance, they should use for their assets. What factors would you have suggested that Wayne and Garth consider in making this decision?

54. Alternative Depreciation Methods (LO 3)

54. 1a. Year-End BV:
       1996, $52,000
       1997, $42,000
       1998, $32,000
       1999, $27,000
       2000, $12,000
    1b. Year-End BV:
       1996, $37,200
       1997, $22,320
       1998, $13,392
       1999, $12,000
       2000, $12,000
    1c. Year-End BV:
       1996, $48,000
       1997, $36,000
       1998, $26,000
       1999, $18,000
       2000, $12,000

Faramarz Freight Lines recently purchased a new truck for local deliveries. The truck was purchased on January 3, 1996, at a cost of $62,000. The truck is estimated to have a $12,000 salvage value at the end of its five-year useful life. The owner of the company expects the truck to be driven the following number of miles over the course of its useful life:

1996 70,000 miles
1997 60,000 miles
1998 50,000 miles
1999 40,000 miles
2000 30,000 miles

Required:

1. Prepare a depreciation schedule similar to the one shown in Exhibit 9.4, assuming that Faramarz uses the following depreciation methods:
   a. Straight-line
   b. Double declining-balance
   c. Units-of-production

2. In your opinion, which of these three depreciation methods is most consistent with the matching principle? Defend your answer.

55. **Revenue and Capital Expenditures** (LO 4)

On March 1, 1993, Audas & Ayres, a law firm, purchased a new computer system at a cost of $24,000, plus sales taxes of 8 percent. The computer system was estimated to have a five-year useful life and a salvage value of $3,000. Following are selected expenditures Audas & Ayres incurred in the next few years related to the computer system.

a. In September 1993, $200 was spent to replace a disk drive that had gone haywire.

b. In March 1994, a computer consultant was brought in to develop a local area network for the Audas & Ayres office. The law firm spent $3,200 for this project, which did not extend the life of the computer system but made it much more efficient.

c. In January 1995, the annual computer checkup was performed by a local computer technician. This annual checkup included vacuuming the inside of each computer to remove dust and checking for any malfunctioning parts. The cost of the checkup was $250.

d. In March 1995, an electrical malfunction damaged a computer monitor, resulting in a repair bill of $90.

e. In July 1995, several compact disk (CD) drives were added to the computer system at a cost of $3,800.

f. In December 1995, a computer consultant was brought in to reconfigure Audas & Ayres' computer system and its local area network at a cost of $8,200. Several additional components were added to the system and several existing components were upgraded. Audas & Ayres estimated that the reconfiguration would extend the life of the computer system for two years beyond its original estimated useful life of five years.

Required:

1. For each expenditure related to the computer system, indicate whether the item is a revenue expenditure or a capital expenditure.

2. For the capital expenditures, indicate how each item should be recorded in Audas & Ayres' accounting records.

3. Suppose that Audas & Ayres spend $65 on a new computer component that technically satisfies the definition of an "improvement" discussed in the text. Instead of capitalizing this expenditure, Audas & Ayres charge the $65 to an expense account. The firm's accountant justifies this treatment by maintaining that the expenditure is not "material." Explain the reasoning of the accountant.

55. 1. Capital (b,e,f)

56. **Changes in Depreciation Computations** (LO 3)

Ghosh Paving, Inc., purchased a steamroller on July 2, 1991, at a cost of $210,000. Industry statistics suggested that the steamroller would have a useful life of ten years and a $42,000 resale value at the end of that length of time. During the first week of January 1996, Ghosh performed a major overhaul of the steamroller. The overhaul cost $60,000 and was estimated to extend the asset's useful life by two and one-half years. Following the overhaul, the steamroller's estimated salvage value was revised to $26,400. Ghosh uses the straight-line depreciation method.

Required:

1. Compute the depreciation expense recorded on the steamroller each year from 1991 through 1995.

56. 1. 1991, $8,400
      1992, $16,800
      1993, $16,800
      1994, $16,800
      1995, $16,800
   2. 1996, $21,000

2. Given the major overhaul of the steamroller, determine the annual depreciation expense for this asset for the remaining years of its useful life, beginning in 1996.

57. Depletion of Natural Resources

On April 19, 1994, Gist Mining, Inc. (GMI), purchased a mining property that contains an estimated 30,000 ounces of the mineral lasordite. GMI paid $2,800,000 for the property and will incur another $800,000 digging a mine shaft. The property will have a salvage value of approximately $240,000 following the removal of the lasordite.

Required:

1. Assume that GMI recovers and sells the following amounts of minerals from the mine during 1994 and 1995:

	1994	1995
Ounces Recovered	6,000	14,000
Ounces Sold	4,500	12,000

Determine the depletion expense recorded by GMI during 1994 and 1995.
2. Suppose that the property acquired by GMI actually has a negative salvage value of $150,000 because of reclamation expenditures required to rehabilitate the property after the lasordite is extracted. Recompute the depletion expense for 1994 and 1995, given the data provided in Part 1.
3. What accounting principle dictates the accounting treatment given the reclamation expenditures referred to in Part 2?

58. Disposals of PP&E Assets (LO 5)

On January 1, 1992, W & J Cabs purchased five new taxis. The taxis cost $20,000 each and were estimated to have a five-year useful life and a salvage value of $2,000 each. W & J uses the straight-line depreciation method. On September 30, 1995, W & J decided to replace the five taxis and sold them to an automobile wholesaler at a collective price of $24,200.

Required:

1. Prepare the journal entry to record the depreciation expense on the five taxis for the first nine months of 1995.
2. Determine the book value of the taxis following the posting of the journal entry prepared in Part 1.
3. Prepare the journal entry to record the sale of the taxis.
4. Prepare the journal entry to record the sale of the taxis, assuming they were sold for $39,400.
5. Suppose now that rather than selling the taxis, the company traded them in on five new taxis that had a collective cash price of $119,000. In addition to trading in the old taxis, W & J was required to pay cash of $47,300. Prepare the appropriate journal entry to record this exchange transaction.

59. Analyzing Total Assets (LO 6)

Presented in the following table are selected financial data for two companies that operate in two very different industries. Clothestime, Inc., is a discount retailer of women's apparel, while Toll Brothers, Inc., is a home builder. (Amounts are presented in thousands.)

	CLOTHESTIME, INC.		TOLL BROTHERS, INC.	
	1993	1994	1993	1994
Net Sales	$315,164	$347,569	$392,560	$501,822

Margin notes (left column):

57. 1. 1994, $504,000
   1995, $1,344,000
2. 1994, $562,500
   1995, $1,500,000

58. 1. Deprec. Exp., $13,500
2. $32,500
3. Loss, $8,300
4. Gain, $6,900
5. New Taxis, $79,800

Interest Expense	0	71	17,129	18,195
Net Income	8,652	8,167	28,058	36,177
Average Total Assets	108,146	93,771	531,445	430,417

Required:

1. Compute the return on assets and total asset turnover ratios for each company in both 1993 and 1994.
2. Based strictly upon the data you computed in Part 1, which of these companies did a better job of managing its assets in 1993 and 1994? Defend your answer.
3. How may the nature of a company's industry affect the two ratios you computed in Part 1? Explain by comparing the two industries represented by Clothestime and Toll Brothers.

60. Economic Benefits Associated with Intangible Assets (LO 8)

Refer to Exhibit 9.11, which lists specific intangible assets of several companies. Recall the following definition of an asset: Probable future economic benefits obtained or controlled by a particular entity as a result of past transactions or events.

Required:

For each intangible asset listed in Exhibit 9.11, briefly describe the "probable future economic benefit" it provides to the given entity.

59. Clothestime	1993	1994
ROA	8.0%	8.8%
Turnover	2.91	3.71
Toll Bros.	1993	1994
ROA	8.5%	12.6%
Turnover	0.74	1.17

60. No check figures.

CASES

61. Errors in Depreciation Computations

Jake Johannson is an accounting major at the local university and the accountant for Donnie's Delivery Service. The principal asset of this company is a fleet of ten identical delivery trucks. This fleet was purchased two years ago when the business was established. Jake has served as the accountant for this business since its inception, having been hired by Donnie, the business's owner and the father of Jake's best friend.

Lately, Jake has been losing sleep over a matter involving his job. Jake was responsible for selecting a depreciation method to use for the fleet of delivery trucks. Given the nature of the business, he chose to use the units-of-production method. Jake recently discovered that he has been misapplying this method. Jake was under the misunderstanding that the salvage value of a depreciable asset is not considered when computing the per unit depreciation cost under the units-of-production method. Following are the data Jake used two years ago to compute the per unit depreciation cost for the fleet of delivery trucks.

Total cost of fleet	$320,000
Divided by estimated number of miles that the fleet will be driven over its useful life (80,000 miles × 10 trucks)	800,000
Per mile depreciation expense	$ .40

As you can see, Jake ignored the fleet's estimated salvage value of $129,600 when he made this computation.

Jake is worried that if he tells Donnie about his oversight, he may lose his job. Additionally, he is concerned that Donnie may be in trouble for issuing incorrect financial statements the past two years to the bank that provided the financing for the fleet. (Note: The truck fleet was driven 200,000 miles in Year 1 and 250,000 miles in Year 2.)

Required:

1. Compute the depreciation expense that was included each of the past two years, Year 1 and Year 2, in the financial statements of Donnie's Delivery Service. Compute the depreciation expense that should have been included in the business's financial statements each of the past two years.
2. What information would you need to determine whether the financial statements of this business were "materially" misstated for the past two years? Explain.
3. Place yourself in Jake's shoes. One option is to say nothing; Jake will be graduating soon and moving out of state. Another option would be to go directly to the bank loan officer and admit the error and tell him that the misstated financial statements are his (Jake's) responsibility. Evaluate these and other options that Jake has. What would you do and why?

62. International Differences in Asset Valuation

Hanson Corporation is a Minnesota-based firm whose principal operating activities are carried on by three subsidiaries located in Ireland, France, and Sweden. You are the banker for Hanson Corporation. Recently, Hanson applied for a large loan. To supplement the company's loan application, you requested consolidated financial statements for Hanson and separate financial statements for each subsidiary for the past year. In reviewing these financial statements, you notice that each subsidiary earned approximately the same net income last year. However, you are somewhat concerned since you realize that certain countries allow businesses to periodically restate long-term assets to their current values. You are wondering whether revenues from such restatements are "buried" in Hanson's financial statements.

Required:

1. Research the accounting standards for the three countries in which Hanson's subsidiaries are located. Do the accounting rules of those countries permit revaluations of long-term assets? If so, under what general conditions or circumstances are such revaluations permitted?
2. Explain how an asset revaluation affects a company's financial statements in the year of the revaluation and in subsequent years.

63. Human Resource Accounting

The most important long-term assets of most businesses are people. How long would a major corporation survive without a skilled sales staff, financial planning experts, product development specialists, and, yes, accountants to capture and record all of that financial data? The same is true of those successful Mom-and-Pop businesses that survive and thrive primarily because Mom and Pop are dedicated and hardworking. Surprisingly, these "human resource" assets very seldom appear on a balance sheet. In recent decades, there was a brief surge of interest in human resource accounting. However, the alleged difficulty of accounting for human resources discouraged most companies from seriously considering "booking" their people assets.

Required:

Refer to the discussion of fundamental accounting concepts in Chapter 2. Prepare a brief report identifying the conceptual principles that could be used to defend the inclusion of human resource assets in the balance sheets of business entities. Also identify in your report conceptual principles that could be used to argue against inclusion of human resource assets in balance sheets. Conclude your report by presenting a coherent argument either for or against the inclusion of human resources in the balance sheets of business entities.

PROJECTS

64. **Valuation Adjustments for PP&E Assets**

Last week, the accountant of LeBaron Enterprises, Jennifer Chavez, submitted a draft of the company's financial statements for its 1996 fiscal year, which ended less than two weeks ago, to the firm's owner. Unfortunately, 1996 was not a good year for LeBaron, a company that wholesales foreign auto parts. Sales declined by more than 15 percent in the past twelve months, and the company had a net loss for the first time in its history. The net loss of $37,000 is small compared with the company's sales, which exceeded $30,000,000. Nevertheless, it is still a loss, breaking a string of more than twenty-five straight years in which the company posted a profit.

Today, H. R. Holliday, LeBaron's owner and a prominent member of the local business community, approached Jennifer with a plan to improve the reported operating results of LeBaron. Five years ago, LeBaron purchased a large tract of land on the outskirts of the city. Property values have skyrocketed in the past few years in the area where that land is located, since several residential developments have been started nearby. Holliday has obtained three real estate appraisals recently that indicate that the value of the property now exceeds $2 million—it was purchased for only $350,000.

"Jennifer, you know, I have never asked you to do something like this before," Holliday said quietly after entering Jennifer's office and closing the door behind him. "But I just can't stand to see our financial statements go out with a loss reported on them." Jennifer sat stoically behind her desk, realizing what was coming next. "I have three appraisals here in my hand proving that the Brookhaven property has increased in value by more than $1.5 million since we purchased it and by at least $600,000 in just the past year. Can't you find some way to squeeze some of this unreported gain into our income statement? All we need is $100,000 to wipe out that loss. I know that we are going to get back on track this year. This will be a one-time thing only, I promise you."

"Mr. Holliday, accounting rules don't allow us to report unrealized gains like that in our income statement."

"Jennifer, I'm not asking you to report this as an unrealized gain on a real estate property. Just make up some vague type of miscellaneous revenue to hide this item in." Jennifer frowned and looked away. "Come on, Jenny. We're talking nickels and dimes here. Look, we have $30 million in revenues. Converting a small net loss into a small net income is not going to mislead anybody." Holliday opened Jennifer's door and then turned and added, "I want you to think about it overnight. Then, come into my office first thing tomorrow so that we can make our plans."

Required:

1. Break into your project groups to discuss this vignette. In discussing the vignette, identify the factors that Jennifer should consider in deciding how to respond to Mr. Holliday's request. Also identify the parties who will be affected by Jennifer's decision. You should also discuss the short-term and long-term implications that Jennifer's decision will have for her, both in terms of her employment situation and otherwise.

2. As a group, attempt to reach a consensus regarding (a) how Jennifer will likely respond to Mr. Holliday's request and (b) how Jennifer should respond to Mr. Holliday's request.

3. Identify other information that would be helpful in analyzing Jennifer's dilemma.

4. One member of the group should be prepared to present a summary overview to the class of the group's discussion of this vignette.

65. Accounting for Research and Development Expenditures

One of the most debated accounting issues among accountants and business executives is the accounting treatment of so-called research and development expenditures. Many large companies spend millions of dollars each year researching and attempting to develop lifesaving drugs, faster and more efficient computers, fertilizers that are more effective and less dangerous to the environment, and so on. However, as a general rule, such expenditures must be written off in the period incurred instead of being capitalized.

Required:

1. Research the technical accounting rules relating to research and development expenditures. Also research accounting and business literature to identify articles and other publications focusing on the controversy regarding the accounting treatment of research and development expenditures.

2. Write a report that includes the following items:
   a. A brief summary of the accounting rules relating to research and development expenditures
   b. The arguments for capitalizing research and development expenditures
   c. The arguments against capitalizing research and development expenditures
   d. Your conclusion regarding whether the current accounting rules for research and development expenditures should be changed

66. Analyzing Total Assets

Identify three large companies with which you are familiar: one merchandising firm, one manufacturing firm, and one service firm. Obtain annual reports or other sources of financial data for these three companies for the past three years.

Required:

Compute the return on assets and total asset turnover ratios for the three companies that you selected for each of the years that you obtained data. Write a report addressing the following issues:

a. What factors likely account for the differences in these two financial measures across these three companies?
b. What trends are evident in these data for each company?
c. Are these trends favorable or unfavorable?
d. Given your familiarity with these companies, attempt to explain the reasons underlying these trends.

IV

ACCOUNTING FOR LIABILITIES

The two chapters in this section introduce you to accounting issues related to liabilities. Chapter 10 focuses principally on current liabilities; it also includes an overview of contingent liabilities and a discussion of the time value of money. Accountants use the time value of money concept to account for certain assets and liabilities, particularly bonds payable, which is the primary subject of Chapter 11. Chapter 11 also discusses accounting for obligations under capital leases and liabilities stemming from pension plans and other postretirement employee benefit plans.

The organizational scheme used in Chapters 7 through 9 is also used in Chapters 10 and 11. Each major topical area focusing on a specific liability account or group of liability accounts has the following features:

1. An overview of that account(s) including a discussion of key terms and definitions
2. Identification of the information that decision makers need about the relevant account or accounts
3. A discussion of accounting procedures
4. A description of financial ratios that decision makers can use to interpret financial data related to given liability accounts
5. A discussion of relevant internal control procedures

10

CURRENT LIABILITIES, CONTINGENT LIABILITIES, AND THE TIME VALUE OF MONEY

LEARNING OBJECTIVES

After studying this chapter, you should be able to do the following:

1. Define the key information needs of decision makers regarding current liabilities

2. Account for the major types of transactions and events affecting current liabilities

3. Compute and interpret the current ratio and working capital

4. Describe internal control procedures applied to an organization's payroll function.

5. Define the key characteristics of, and account for, contingent liabilities

6. Use the time value of money concept to compute the present value and future value of single amounts and annuities

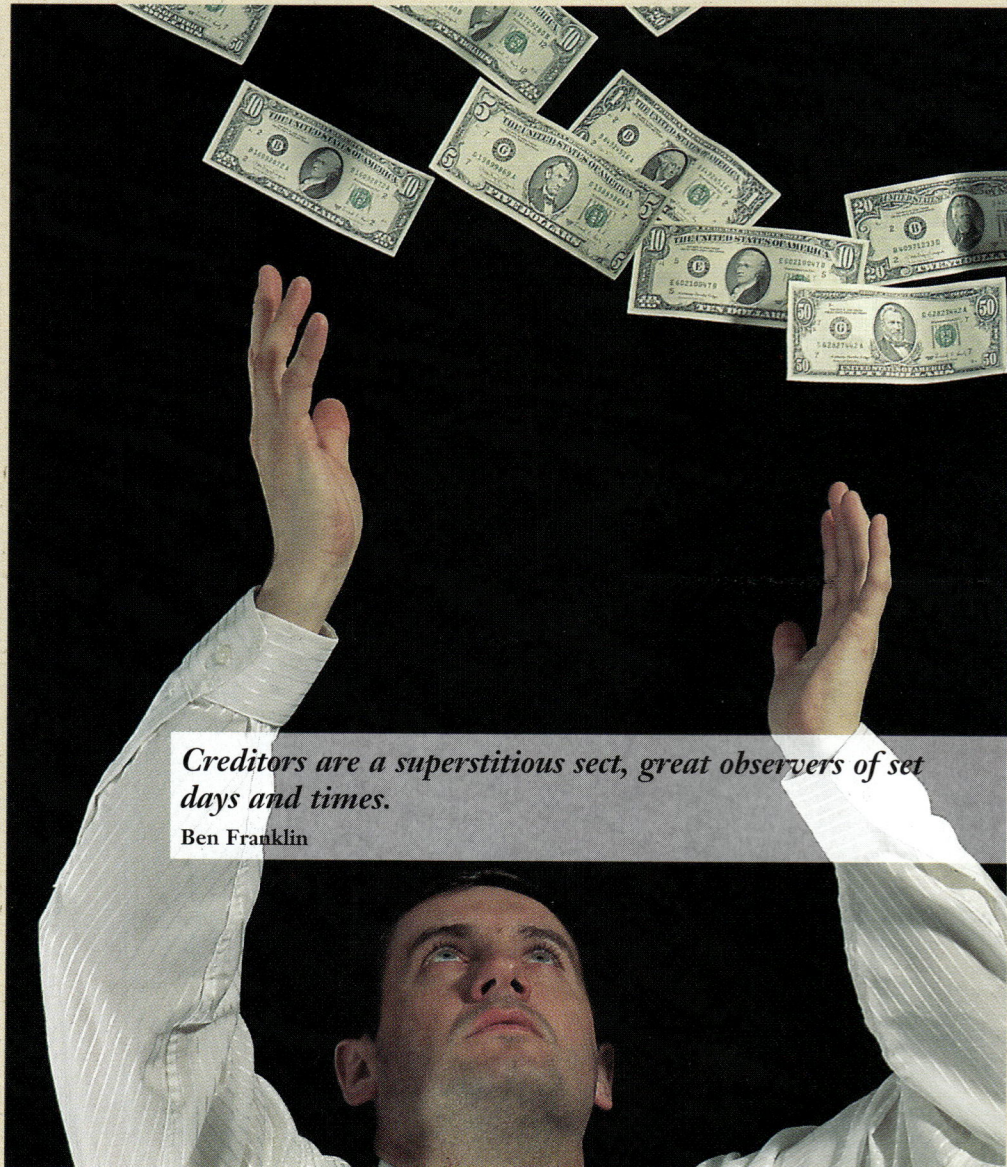

> *Creditors are a superstitious sect, great observers of set days and times.*
> Ben Franklin

Accounts Payable: A Nine-Point Management Plan

Accounts payable consume a large portion of the cash resources of most businesses and are the largest current liability of many firms. As a result, businesses should develop a comprehensive strategy to manage their accounts payable. The following excerpt from an article appearing in Inc. *summarizes a nine-point plan that businesses can use to establish and maintain effective control over their accounts payable.*

1. **Evaluate cash flow.** Every accounts payable strategy should be rooted in a company's current cash flow realities. If it takes 90 days to collect accounts receivable, it's financially destructive for you to pay your own bills within 15 days.
2. **Set goals.** Once you've evaluated your cash flow, establish written payment goals so that there can be no confusion among your bill payers. Avoid a situation in which accounting clerks make the decisions about which bills are to be paid and when—usually suppliers who yell loudest are paid the fastest, regardless of the overall benefit to the firm.
3. **Establish payment priorities.** Every company should have a two-tiered list of payment priorities that becomes a part of its formal disbursement strategy. Tier one, the group that should be paid at all costs and at whatever terms have been agreed upon, should include major vendors and, most important, state and federal tax authorities.
4. **Aggressively negotiate payment terms.** There's not much room for negotiation with bankers or tax collectors, but once they're taken care of, everything else on the payables front should be open to discussion.
5. **Forecast cash needs.** A company's CEO or controller should be able to predict exactly how much cash the company will need—and when—to fulfill its payables obligations. That forecast then becomes an important tool in averting cash-flow problems.
6. **Keep good payables records.** These records should include weekly updates about the aging of every outstanding bill; documentation that matches each bill paid with its original sales order, delivery records, and payment invoice; and total cost records, including interest penalties paid on each bill.
7. **Review payables records regularly.** Generally speaking, you should review payables-aging schedules weekly.
8. **Recognize warning signs.** One approach is to draw up a "payables problems" checklist, which breaks down average bill age, promptness of tax payments, any interest charges, and other warning factors that come up for your company.
9. **Fraud-proof the payables operation.** To minimize the risk of payables fraud, you should formalize payment procedures that include double checks at each step of the process: bills should be paid only when they can be matched against purchase orders and delivery confirmations; one person should write or authorize checks while another signs them; computerized bill-payment systems should be accessed only by computer code. If you rely on manual check-writing systems, keep blank checks under lock and key and track all numbers, including voided checks. The best defense against payables fraud, however, is simply to reconcile the checkbook balance each month with the bank statement balance.

SOURCE: Used with permission, *Inc. Magazine,* March 1991, 72–78. Goldhirsch, Inc., 38 Commercial Wharf, Boston, MA 02110.

This chapter addresses three primary topics: accounting for current liabilities, accounting for contingent liabilities, and the time value of money concept. The major focus of this chapter is current liabilities, including short-term notes payable, accrued expenses, and related accounts. Contingent liabilities can be either current or long-term liabilities. Since these liabilities pose unique and often complex accounting issues, they are discussed independently of other liabilities. The time value of money concept is the last topic covered in this chapter. This concept has implications for numerous financial statement items, including current and contingent liabilities. However, the time value of money is most often associated with long-term liabilities, such as bonds payable, which are discussed in Chapter 11. So, consider the coverage of the time value of money, at least in part, as a "prep" for the following chapter.

CURRENT LIABILITIES: AN INTRODUCTION

The Financial Accounting Standards Board defines liabilities as "probable future sacrifices of economic benefits arising from present obligations of a particular entity to transfer assets or provide services to other entities in the future as a result of past transactions or events."[1] In Chapter 2, a more concise but less precise definition of liabilities was presented: amounts owed to other parties. Those liabilities that must be paid by a business within one year or its operating cycle, whichever is longer, are classified as current liabilities.

The two general types of current liabilities are those whose dollar amounts are defined by a contractual or implied contractual agreement and those whose dollar amounts must be estimated. An example of the first type of current liability is a customer deposit on an apartment. When Joe College of Corvallis, Oregon, or Orono, Maine, signs a nine-month lease on a one-bedroom townhouse, he must make a security deposit. The apartment complex will report Joe's $200 deposit as a current liability on its balance sheet. Assuming Joe does not rip up the carpet or poke holes in the wall, the apartment complex will be obliged to return his $200 dollar deposit at the end of the lease.

The dollar amount of some current liabilities must be estimated. For example, Dell Computer Corporation guarantees the personal computers that it sells to be free of defects for one year. If a Dell computer malfunctions during the warranty period, the company will repair or replace the computer at no cost. At the end of each year, Dell must estimate and record in an adjusting entry the total warranty-related expense that it will incur in the future as a result of computers sold that year. The offsetting credit to estimated warranty expense is recorded in a current liability account such as Product Warranty Liability.

Dell Computer Corporation was founded by Michael Dell when he was 19. Dell attaches a one-year warranty to the computers it sells. At the end of each year, Dell's accountants must estimate and record as an expense and current liability the future warranty-related expenditures the company will incur as a result of the computers sold that year.

The individual line items included in the current liabilities section of a balance sheet vary from company to company. Exhibit 10.1 lists the current liabilities reported recently by two public companies. ShopKo Stores operates a chain of retail stores stretching from the company's home base in Wisconsin to the West Coast. Whole Foods Market, based in Austin, Texas, is the largest retailer of organic foods in the nation. As for most companies, the largest current liabilities of ShopKo Stores and Whole Foods Market are accounts payable and various accrued liabilities, or accrued expenses.

1. Portions of various FASB documents, copyright by Financial Accounting Standards Board, 401 Merritt, P.O. Box 5116, Norwalk, Connecticut, 06856-5116, U.S.A., are reprinted with permission. Copies of the complete document are available from the FASB.

■ **EXHIBIT 10.1**

Current Liabilities on the Corporate Balance Sheet: Two Examples

SOURCE: Recent annual reports.

ShopKo Stores, Inc.	
Accounts Payable—Trade	$ 147,152
Accrued Compensation and Related Taxes	21,851
Accrued Other Liabilities	42,812
Accrued Income and Other Taxes	12,849
Short-Term Debt	26,200
Current Portion of Long-Term Obligations	879
Total Current Liabilities	$ 251,743

Whole Foods Market, Inc.	
Current Installments of Long-Term Debt and Capital Lease Obligations	$ 1,222
Trade Accounts Payable	10,644
Accrued Payroll, Bonus and Employee Benefits	7,808
Other Accrued Expenses	6,361
Total Current Liabilities	$ 26,035

Note: Amounts reported are in thousands.

CURRENT LIABILITIES: KEY INFORMATION NEEDS OF DECISION MAKERS

Providing information useful to decision makers is the key objective of the accounting function in an organization. As a result, accountants must continually focus on the information needs of decision makers when deciding how to account for specific financial statement items. In this section, key information needs of decision makers regarding current liabilities are identified.

Completeness

In 1987, the Securities and Exchange Commission (SEC) scolded Windsor Holding Corporation, a company that markets ceiling fans, for omitting certain current liabilities from its financial statements. According to the SEC, "Windsor lacked adequate procedures for logging in invoices and processing them as they were received. As a result, there was untimely and inaccurate recording of such invoices."[2] Because of Windsor's poor controls over its unpaid invoices, third-party decision makers may have made inappropriate decisions based upon the company's financial statements.

The most important information need of decision makers when it comes to current liabilities is completeness. Decision makers must have confidence that an entity's balance sheet reflects all outstanding, or unpaid, current liabilities. A company should establish appropriate internal controls to ensure that its accounting records and financial statements "capture" all current liabilities.

---

2. Securities and Exchange Commission, *Accounting and Auditing Enforcement Release No. 137*, 22 June 1987.

FOR YOUR INFORMATION

Classification of Liabilities in Other Countries

Accounting and financial reporting rules for liabilities are fairly consistent in developed countries across the world. Nevertheless, there are some unconventional rules and practices. For instance, Sweden's approach to distinguishing between current and long-term liabilities is slightly different from that used in the United States. In the United States, liabilities that must be paid within the following year or operating cycle of a business, whichever is longer, are classified as current liabilities. Sweden does not recognize the operating cycle concept when classifying liabilities. Instead, Swedish companies strictly classify liabilities as current or long-term depending upon their maturity date. Liabilities due within one year are considered current liabilities, while all other obligations are treated as long-term liabilities.

The Republic of Ireland and the Netherlands are examples of other countries that use an unconventional classification scheme for liabilities. Both of these countries require business entities to classify certain obligations as "provisions" in their balance sheets. In the Netherlands, provisions generally include items that would be classified as estimated or contingent liabilities in the United States. The Dutch entertainment conglomerate, Polygram, segregates its debts and other obligations into long-term provisions, short-term provisions, long-term liabilities, and current liabilities. Included in Polygram's long-term provisions in a recent annual report were amounts the firm expected to pay other entertainment companies under profit-sharing agreements for certain music albums.

Valuation Methods

As is true for other assets and liabilities, financial statement users need to be informed of the methods used to value, or assign dollar amounts to, individual current liabilities. Decision makers who use financial data regularly know that the dollar amounts of many current liabilities are precisely defined by contractual or implied contractual agreements. For balance sheet purposes, these current liabilities are valued at the amount of hard, cold cash that must be paid when they come due. Occasionally, current liabilities are liquidated, or extinguished, by the delivery of goods or services. Included in a recent annual report of The Boeing Company was a $600 million current liability that represented advance payments received from its customers. Boeing would eventually extinguish that liability by delivering completed goods (airplanes) to its customers. When the method used to assign a dollar amount to a current liability is obvious, or should be obvious, a business entity does not have to discuss that method in its financial statements.

Information regarding valuation methods for estimated current liabilities are of particular interest to decision makers. A company should provide adequate disclosures in its financial statement footnotes to allow decision makers to decide whether those liabilities have been estimated in good faith. For example, consider a current liability reported in the 1994 annual report of Sonic Corporation, a fast-food restaurant chain. This current liability stemmed from litigation costs the company expected to incur in the future. A footnote to the company's financial statements described the nature of the litigation matter and why the company believed it was necessary to record a current liability related to that matter.

Unusual Circumstances

When unusual circumstances affect a major account balance or financial statement line item, those circumstances should be disclosed in an entity's financial statements. For current liabilities, an example of such a circumstance is an inability or potential inability to pay these liabilities as they come due. Of course, a company that is unable to pay its current liabilities as they mature may face bankruptcy proceedings.

American Nuclear Corporation of Casper, Wyoming, was formed in 1955 and was one of the earliest publicly owned companies engaged in the mining of uranium. In the early 1990s, American Nuclear began experiencing severe financial problems because of a low demand for uranium. The company's 1992 annual report alerted third parties to these financial problems. In particular, the company pointed out that it might be unable to pay current liabilities as they came due. The following excerpts concerning this situation were taken from American Nuclear's 1992 annual report.

> As of December 31, 1992, the Company's current liabilities exceed current assets by approximately $1,600,000 and the Company has incurred significant operating losses during recent years. As discussed in Note 4, the Company's current liabilities are primarily notes payable, and accrued interest due to its major shareholder during 1993. . . . The Company's ability to continue as a going concern is dependent upon its ability to obtain additional financing or extend the due date of its notes payable, both of which are uncertain at this time.

Discussion Question
How would American Nuclear's 1992 annual report disclosure impact investors' and creditors' decisions?

ACCOUNTING FOR CURRENT LIABILITIES

This section discusses accounting procedures for several current liabilities. Although there are dozens of different types of current liabilities, accounting decisions for most of them are fairly similar. We will focus on accounting procedures for the most common current liabilities.

■ **LEARNING OBJECTIVE 2**
Account for the major types of transactions and events affecting current liabilities

Accounts Payable

Chapter 2 introduced accounts payable and subsequent chapters described several types of transactions involving this current liability. Refer to Exhibit 6.5 to reacquaint yourself with the most frequently occurring of these transactions and the appropriate journal entries for them.

Notes Payable

Notes payable are obligations documented by a legally binding written commitment in the form of a promissory note. As pointed out in Chapter 2, notes payable can be either current or long-term. Short-term promissory notes, both notes receivable and notes payable, can be either interest-bearing or non-interest-bearing. Chapter 7 briefly discussed interest-bearing notes receivable. Here, we consider both interest-bearing and non-interest-bearing notes payable. For reporting purposes, *Accounting Trends & Techniques* combines short-term notes payable and loans payable, both of which are usually documented by a promissory note or similar legal document. According to the 1994 edition of *Accounting Trends & Techniques*, approximately 36 percent of public companies report notes or loans payable as current liabilities in their balance sheets.

INTEREST-BEARING NOTES PAYABLE   To illustrate accounting for interest-bearing notes payable, assume that Bonney's Dress Shop borrows $5,000 from a local bank on October 2 of a given year. On that date, Bonney's chief executive signs a promissory note with a 120-day term obligating her firm to repay the $5,000 loan as well as interest on the loan at a 12 percent annual rate. The maturity date of this note is January 30 of the following year. (Remember that the term of a note includes the maturity date but not the date the note is signed.) The entry to record the receipt of the $5,000 loan is as follows:

Oct. 2	Cash	5,000	
	Notes Payable		5,000

To record note payable to First Bank of Rush Springs with terms of 120 days and 12 percent interest

At year-end, Bonney's will record interest expense on this note payable for the period October 2 through December 31. Recall that the interest equation, shown next, is used to compute interest expense (or revenue).

$$\text{Interest} = \text{Principal} \times \text{Rate} \times \text{Time}$$

Since this note payable will have been outstanding for 90 days by December 31, $150 of interest expense should be recorded in a year-end adjusting entry in Bonney's accounting records.

$$\text{Interest} = \text{Principal} \times \text{Rate} \times \text{Time}$$
$$\text{Interest} = \$5,000 \times 12\% \times 90/360$$
$$\text{Interest} = \$150$$

Dec. 31	Interest Expense	150	
	Interest Payable		150

To record interest expense on note payable to First Bank of Rush Springs

On January 30, the date the note payable matures, Bonney's will repay the bank the $5,000 loan plus interest at a 12 percent annual rate for the 120-day term of the note. The amount of interest due the bank will be $200 ($5,000 × 12% × 120/360). However, only $50 of interest expense will be recorded on the note's maturity date. This $50 is the amount of interest expense on the note for the 30-day period January 1 through January 30. The remaining $150 of the interest paid to the bank will be debited to the current liability account Interest Payable, as shown in the following entry.

Jan. 30	Notes Payable	5,000	
	Interest Expense	50	
	Interest Payable	150	
	Cash		5,200

To record payment of note payable and interest to First Bank of Rush Springs

NON-INTEREST-BEARING NOTES PAYABLE The term "non-interest-bearing note" conjures up notions of the mythical free lunch. Of course, economists continually attempt to convince us that there is no such thing as a free lunch. More to the point in this context, seldom will you find a promissory note or loan on which no interest, in any form, must be paid. This is especially true when the payee of the note is a bank or other financial institution. When a business borrows funds from a bank on a non-interest-bearing promissory note, the bank discounts the note. That is, the bank subtracts the interest on the loan from the principal amount when the loan is made.

To illustrate accounting for non-interest-bearing notes payable, return to the earlier example involving Bonney's Dress Shop. Now, assume that on October 2, Bonney's chief executive signs a non-interest-bearing note obligating the firm to pay exactly $5,000 to the bank on the note's maturity date of January 30. If the bank charges an implied interest rate, or discount rate, of 12 percent on this loan, Bonney's will receive $4,800, rather than $5,000, from the bank on October 2. The $200 difference between the principal amount of the note and the cash received by Bonney's is the discount on the note. In Chapter 7, the following equation was used to compute a discount on a note receivable. This same equation can be used to compute a discount on a non-interest-bearing note payable.

$$\text{Discount} = \text{Maturity Value} \times \text{Discount Rate} \times \text{Time}$$

The $200 discount on the non-interest-bearing note signed by Bonney's chief executive is computed as follows:

$$
\begin{aligned}
\text{Discount} &= \text{Maturity Value} \times \text{Discount Rate} \times \text{Time} \\
\text{Discount} &= \$5,000 \times 12\% \times 120/360 \\
\text{Discount} &= \$200
\end{aligned}
$$

On October 2, Bonney's would make the following entry to record the loan from its bank.

Oct. 2	Cash	4,800	
	Discount on Notes Payable	200	
	Notes Payable		5,000
	To record non-interest-bearing, 120-day note payable to First Bank of Rush Springs		

Discount on Notes Payable is a contra-liability account that is subtracted from Notes Payable for balance sheet reporting purposes. Suppose that Bonney's prepares a balance sheet at the close of business on October 2 of the year in question. Under current liabilities, Bonney's would report notes payable of $4,800, which is the difference between the $5,000 balance of Notes Payable and the $200 balance of Discount on Notes Payable.

The discount on a non-interest-bearing note payable is equal to the amount of interest expense that will be recognized on the note over the period that it is outstanding. On December 31, Bonney's fiscal year-end, an adjusting entry will be needed to recognize the interest expense on its note payable for the period October 2 through

Teaching Note
Emphasize that interest is charged on a non-interest-bearing note payable by the lender on an "up-front" basis, that is, by subtracting the interest from the proceeds of the note. For example, Bonney's must repay $5,000 but receives only $4,800.

December 31. Since 90 days of the note's 120-day term will have elapsed by December 31, three-fourths of the $200 discount on the note payable, or $150, should be recognized as interest expense. Following is the year-end adjusting entry to record interest expense on this non-interest bearing note.

Dec. 31	Interest Expense	150	
	Discount on Notes Payable		150
	To record interest expense on the non-interest-bearing note payable to First Bank of Rush Springs		

On January 30, the date the note payable matures, Bonney's will pay the bank the $5,000 principal amount of the note. The following entry will be made to record this payment.

Jan. 30	Notes Payable	5,000	
	Interest Expense	50	
	Cash		5,000
	Discount on Notes Payable		50
	To record payment of non-interest-bearing note payable to First Bank of Rush Springs		

Notice that on January 30, the remaining amount of the discount on this note will be charged off as interest expense. This $50 amount represents the interest expense on the note for the 30-day period January 1 through January 30.

Discussion Question
Ask students to compare the interest expense on the interest-bearing note payable and on the non-interest-bearing note payable illustrated in the text. What is the difference between the two?
Answer: On the interest-bearing note, Bonney's paid $200 interest for the use of $5,000. On the non-interest-bearing note, Bonney's paid $200 interest for the use of $4,800. Consequently, there was a higher effective interest rate on the non-interest-bearing note.

Current Portion of Long-Term Debt

For balance sheet purposes, businesses must classify the portion of any long-term liability that matures within the coming twelve months as a current liability. For instance, refer to Exhibit 10.1. Notice that Shopko included in its current liabilities $879,000 as the "Current Portion of Long-Term Obligations." The reclassification of the current portion of a long-term debt to current liabilities is generally not done with an accounting entry. Instead an entity's accountants simply subtract such amounts from long-term debt and include them in current liabilities when preparing a set of financial statements.

Deferred Revenues

Teaching Note
Remind students that Unearned Revenues is a liability not a revenue account.

Businesses are often paid in advance by their customers for products and services. Since such amounts have not been earned when they are received, they should initially be recorded as liabilities. Typically, these amounts are debited to Cash and credited to a liability account such as Deferred Revenues or Unearned Revenues, as discussed in Chapter 5. These advance payments are usually classified as current liabilities since the products or services that have been purchased will be delivered or provided to customers within twelve months. For example, Jenny Craig, Inc., a company that operates a chain of weight-loss centers, reported $3,944,000 of deferred service revenues as a current liability in a recent balance sheet. That amount represented membership fees paid by the company's customers for the following year.

Sales Taxes Payable

When you purchase a Tootsie Roll or Snickers bar at the local convenience store, you are well aware that you must pay not only the retail price of the candy but also a certain amount of sales tax. Most retailers collect sales taxes on the products they sell. Such taxes are levied by nearly all states and many municipalities. Retailers must periodically remit the sales taxes they collect to the appropriate governmental agency.

Sales taxes collected from customers represent a current liability and should be accounted for separately from sales revenues. Typically, sales tax collections are credited to an account entitled Sales Taxes Payable. In a recent balance sheet, Tuesday Morning Corporation, a discount retailer, reported a current liability of $1,760,000 for sales taxes payable. Suppose that a Tuesday Morning store rings up $5,200 of cash sales on a given day and collects an additional $364 of sales taxes. These receipts would be recorded as follows:

Real World
Most retail businesses have sales tax formulas programmed into their cash registers. When a customer makes a purchase, sales taxes are automatically computed and printed out on the cash register receipt.

Mar. 17	Cash	5,564	
	Sales		5,200
	Sales Taxes Payable		364
	To record daily sales and sales tax collections		

When this store remits its sales tax collections to a government agency, Sales Taxes Payable will be debited and Cash will be credited.

Accrued Expenses

Each accounting period, businesses must attempt to match the revenues earned that period with the expenses incurred to generate those revenues. Many of these expenses will not have been paid by the end of a given accounting period. Nevertheless, these items must be recognized as expenses via adjusting entries in a business's accounting records, otherwise the matching principle will be violated. When these unpaid expenses are recorded in adjusting entries, one or more expense accounts are debited and one or more "accrued expense" accounts are credited. Recognize that when the term "accrued expenses" appears in a set of financial statements, it refers to a group of current liabilities, *not* to a group of expenses. Again, when accrued expenses are recorded, the offsetting debits are to expense accounts. But these expenses are combined with similar expenses in an income statement instead of being listed separately on an income statement as "accrued expenses." To eliminate the confusion caused by the term "accrued expenses," many businesses refer to these items as accrued liabilities. Nevertheless, we will use "accrued expenses" since it is the more widely used of the two terms.

Several accrued expenses have been discussed in earlier chapters, such as income taxes payable, which was considered in Chapter 5. Interest payable, which was discussed earlier in this chapter, is also an accrued expense. In this section, other accrued expenses are considered, including product warranty liability, vacation pay liability, and several related accrued expenses referred to collectively as accrued payroll expenses.

Teaching Note
Remind students that an accrued expense is expensed first and paid later.

PRODUCT WARRANTY LIABILITY Many companies provide a warranty for the goods or services that they market. For instance, A. T. Cross, the manufacturer of Cross pens (you have probably received several as graduation gifts), attaches a "forever guarantee" to its products. If a Cross pen malfunctions for any reason, the company will either repair the pen or replace it free of charge. Clearly, there is a cost associated with such guarantees or warranties. In the late 1980s, for example, A. T. Cross disclosed that it annually spent approximately $1 million repairing or replacing its eternally guaranteed pens.[3]

Since a warranty helps a company sell its products, warranty-related costs should be matched with sales revenue each accounting period. That is, businesses should estimate the total warranty costs they will eventually incur as a result of the products sold during an accounting period and record this amount as an expense in that period. As indicated earlier, the offsetting credit to this expense is typically entered in a liability account entitled Product Warranty Liability.

Real World
A company does not know how many of the products it has sold will prove to be defective when it records warranty expense, so it must estimate that amount. Typically, a company bases this estimate on prior experience.

Historically, A. T. Cross repairs or replaces approximately 2 percent of the pens it sells. For illustration purposes, assume that the average repair or replacement cost for a Cross pen is $15. In a given month, if A. T. Cross sells 80,000 pens, it can expect to eventually repair or replace 1,600 (80,000 × 2%) of these pens at a total cost of $24,000 (1,600 × $15). Given these facts, the adjusting entry to book warranty expense for the month in question would be as follows:

Jan. 31	Warranty Expense	24,000	
	Product Warranty Liability		24,000
	To record estimated warranty expense		

Assume that A. T. Cross records repairs and replacements of its pens on a weekly basis. If during a one-week period in March of a certain year the company incurs $6,200 of such costs, the following entry would be appropriate.

Mar. 17	Product Warranty Liability	6,200	
	Cash (or Inventory or Accounts Payable)		6,200
	To record the repair and replacement of products sold under warranty		

For products with warranties that extend longer than one year, such as Cross pens, the product warranty liability should be segregated into current and long-term components. The current component represents the amount of warranty-related costs a company expects to incur in the coming twelve months, while the long-term component represents warranty costs expected to be incurred beyond one year.

Discussion Question
Many companies allow employees to accumulate and carry forward to future years unused vacation days. What are the implications of this policy for a company's financial statements?
Answer: The Vacation Pay Liability account may be composed of both a current amount and long-term amount.

VACATION PAY LIABILITY Besides earning their base salary or wages each payroll period, most employees also earn, or accumulate, a certain amount of vacation pay. For instance, an employee who is paid $400 per week and is entitled to an annual two-week paid vacation actually earns $20,800 (52 × $400) for 50 weeks of work. That is, over a 50-week period, this employee accumulates two weeks of vacation pay, or $800 ($400 × 2 weeks). Expressed another way, this employee accumulates $16 of

---

3. I. Magaziner and M. Patinkin, *The Silent War* (New York: Vintage Books, 1990), 177.

Insufficient Warranty Expense for an Exploding Product

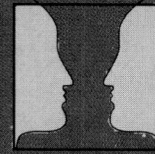

Companies typically base the estimated warranty expense they record each accounting period on their historical experience. However, companies must also consider any unusual circumstances that may cause their historical experience to be a poor predictor of the eventual warranty-related costs they will incur. One company that did not consider such circumstances in estimating its warranty expense was Poloron Products, Inc., a government contractor.

In 1989, Poloron was investigated by the SEC for allegedly failing to record a sufficient warranty expense for several million grenades sold to the United States Army. Over the term of a four-year contract, the army purchased more than 50 million grenades from Poloron—grenades on which Poloron provided a 180-day warranty. During the warranty period, the army had the right to reject and return for full credit any grenades found to be defective. In fact, several batches of the grenades, more than 8 million in total, were defective due to a design flaw. Company executives were apparently aware of this problem but chose not to take it into consideration in estimating warranty expense. The SEC charged that this faulty decision resulted in material errors in the firm's financial statements.

SOURCE: Securities and Exchange Commission, *Accounting and Auditing Enforcement Release No. 223*, 17 April 1989.

---

vacation pay ($800/50 weeks) for each week he or she works. Because of the matching principle, businesses should recognize the cost of vacation pay earned by their employees each payroll period. Vacation Pay Liability is the current liability account to which vacation pay earned by employees is typically credited. Pinkerton Security & Investigation Services, one of the largest security companies in the world, reported a vacation pay liability of $6.5 million in a recent annual report.

To illustrate accounting for vacation pay, assume that Jessica Linton & Co., Architects, provides each of its employees a two-week paid vacation. Each payroll period, the incremental cost related to vacation pay for Linton & Co. is 4 percent: 2 weeks/50 weeks. If this company's payroll is $350,000 for its most recent two-week payroll period, the amount of vacation pay earned by its employees is $14,000 ($350,000 × 4%). A portion of the vacation pay accumulated by a company's work force is usually forfeited because of employee turnover. Assume that in a typical year, 10 percent of all vacation pay accumulated by the employees of Linton & Co. is forfeited. Given this fact, the company would record only $12,600 ($14,000 × 90%) of vacation pay expense for its most recent payroll period, as shown in the following entry:

Feb. 16	Vacation Pay Expense	12,600	
	Vacation Pay Liability		12,600
	To record vacation pay liability for two-week payroll period ending Feb. 14		

When this company's employees take their vacations, Vacation Pay Liability will be debited for the cost of the vacation pay. For example, assume that several employees collectively receive $12,000 of vacation pay during a payroll period in May. The following entry would be made to record this payment.

May 18	Vacation Pay Liability	12,000	
	Cash		12,000
	To record vacation pay		

ACCRUED PAYROLL EXPENSES   Typically, the end of a business's fiscal year does not coincide with the end of a payroll period. For instance, assume that a company with a December 31 fiscal year-end pays its employees every two weeks. If December 23 is the last day of a two-week payroll period, by December 31 the employees will have worked several days for which they have not been paid. Like any other unpaid expense at the end of an accounting period, unpaid payroll expenses at year-end must be accrued.

As you are probably well aware, there is often a significant difference between a worker's gross pay and his or her net or take-home pay. The difference between gross pay and net pay is due to various payroll deductions. Among these deductions are an employee's portion of the Social Security tax, officially known as the Federal Insurance Contributions Act (FICA) tax,[4] federal and state income tax withholdings, union dues, and health insurance premiums. When accruing payroll expenses at the end of an accounting period, a business must also consider employee payroll deductions.

To illustrate the accrual of payroll expenses, assume that as of December 31 of a given year, the employees of Cathy's Engineering Services have worked one week for which they have not been paid. The gross pay earned by Cathy's employees for this one-week period is $4,240, while the net pay they are entitled to receive is $2,720, as shown by the following schedule.

Gross Pay		$4,240
Less: Payroll Deductions		
FICA Taxes	325	
Federal Income Taxes	810	
State Income Taxes	205	
Health Insurance Premiums	180	
Total Payroll Deductions		1,520
Net Pay		$2,720

Given the previous information, Cathy's would record the following year-end adjusting journal entry to recognize unpaid salaries expense and the related amounts for employee payroll deductions.

Dec. 31	Salaries Expense	4,240	
	FICA Taxes Payable		325
	Employee Federal Income Taxes Payable		810

---

4. As of the writing of this book, the FICA tax rate is 7.65 percent on employee earnings. This tax has two components: an old-age, survivors, and disability insurance (OASDI) component and a Medicare component. For 1995, the OASDI tax rate was 6.2 percent of an employee's first $61,200 in annual earnings. The Medicare tax rate for 1995 was 1.45 percent of the total annual earnings of an employee. Some companies account for these two components of FICA taxes separately. Here, they are combined into one item.

Employee State Income Taxes Payable	205	
Employee Health Insurance Premiums Payable	180	
Salaries Payable	2,720	

To record unpaid salaries expense and
related employee payroll deductions
at year-end

Businesses incur other payroll-related expenses besides wages and salaries paid to employees. For example, employers must contribute to the Social Security program an amount equal to the FICA taxes paid by their employees. In the previous adjusting entry, Cathy's Engineering Services recorded $325 of FICA taxes owed by its employees at year-end. Cathy's should record an equivalent amount to recognize the FICA taxes it must pay on the employees' year-end accrued wages. Employers are also required to pay state and federal unemployment taxes on the earnings of their employees. Assume that Cathy's will eventually pay state unemployment taxes of $80 and federal unemployment taxes of $20 related to the $4,240 of salaries expense recorded in the prior entry. Shown next is the adjusting entry to record Cathy's unpaid payroll taxes at year-end.

Dec. 31	Payroll Taxes Expense	425	
	FICA Taxes Payable		325
	State Unemployment Taxes Payable		80
	Federal Unemployment Taxes Payable		20

To record unpaid payroll taxes
expense at year-end

The final major component of payroll-related expenses for employers is fringe benefits expense. Fringe benefits include such items as an employer's contributions to an employee pension fund and the portions of employees' health and other insurance premiums that an employer pays. Assume that Cathy's Engineering Services contributes an amount equal to 5 percent of employees' gross pay to a pension fund. Since the unpaid payroll at year-end in our example is $4,240, Cathy's should recognize $212 ($4,240 × 5%) of employee fringe benefits expense for this item. Additionally, Cathy's pays one-half of its employees' health insurance premiums and 100 percent of their life insurance premiums. Assume these items total $180 and $90, respectively. Given these facts, the following year-end adjusting entry would be necessary to record Cathy's unpaid fringe benefits expense at year-end. (Cathy's should also accrue an expense for any vacation pay earned during the final few days of the fiscal year by its employees.)

Dec. 31	Fringe Benefits Expense	482	
	Pension Contributions Payable		212
	Health Insurance Premiums Payable		180
	Life Insurance Premiums Payable		90

To record unpaid fringe benefits
expense at year-end

ANALYZING CURRENT LIABILITIES

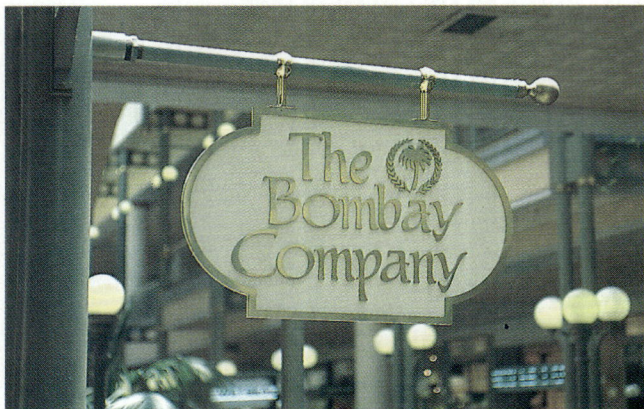

As noted in Chapter 7, liquidity refers to a business's ability to finance its day-to-day operations and to pay its liabilities as they come due. One measure of liquidity, the quick ratio, was discussed in Chapter 7. Another more widely used measure of liquidity is the current ratio. The current ratio measures the relationship between a business's total current assets and its total current liabilities at a given point in time, as expressed by the following equation.

$$\textbf{Current Ratio} \; = \; \frac{\text{Current Assets}}{\text{Current Liabilities}}$$

Another financial measure in which current liabilities figure prominently is working capital, which is the difference between an entity's current assets and current liabilities.

$$\textbf{Working Capital} \; = \; \text{Current Assets} \; - \; \text{Current Liabilities}$$

The availability of sufficient working capital—current assets less current liabilities—is a major concern of executives of merchandising firms, including those of The Bombay Company, a furniture and housewares retailer.

Besides tracking the quick and current ratios, decision makers monitor the magnitude of a company's working capital from period to period to gauge the firm's liquidity. A company that has a minimal amount of working capital, or, worse yet, a negative working capital, is at risk of defaulting on its current liabilities as they come due.

The Bombay Company, Inc., sells furniture and housewares from nearly four hundred retail stores in the United States and Canada. Shown in the following schedule is this firm's working capital and current ratio for each year from 1992 through 1994.

■ **LEARNING OBJECTIVE 3**
Compute and interpret the current ratio and working capital

current ratio

working capital

Real World
Creditors are especially interested in a company's liquidity. As discussed earlier, completeness is the most important information need of decision makers with regard to liabilities. Unrecorded liabilities result in unreliable liquidity measures.

Teaching Note
Because the Bombay Company's liquidity was strong in 1993 and 1994, the firm probably experienced little difficulty satisfying its current obligations.

	AT FISCAL YEAR-END (IN THOUSANDS)		
	1994	1993	1992
Current Assets	$118,695	$110,609	$45,015
Current Liabilities	29,305	24,078	17,371
Working Capital	$ 89,390	$ 86,531	$27,644
Current Ratio	4.05	4.59	2.59

The Bombay Company's liquidity improved considerably between 1992 and 1994. Notice that the company's working capital increased during both 1993 and 1994, while its current ratio increased significantly in 1993, followed by a small decrease in 1994. A common rule of thumb across all industries is that a company should maintain a current ratio of at least 2.0. An even better benchmark for interpreting a company's current ratio is the industry norm for that ratio. In 1994, the median current ratio for furniture retailers, such as the Bombay Company, was 2.7.[5] Compared with this industry norm, the firm's current ratios in 1993 and 1994 were very strong.

---

5. Dun & Bradstreet's *Industry Norms & Key Business Ratios, 1993–1994*. Dun & Bradstreet Information Services. (New York: Dun & Bradstreet, 1994).

KEY INTERNAL CONTROL PROCEDURES FOR CURRENT LIABILITIES

The opening vignette for this chapter presents a nine-point plan that businesses can use to manage their accounts payable. That plan actually describes a comprehensive internal control strategy for accounts payable, including several control procedures that can be applied to a wide range of current liabilities. Here, we consider internal controls that relate specifically to accrued payroll expenses.

Payroll and payroll-related expenses are among the largest expense items reported in most businesses' annual income statements and are typically the source of large year-end accrued expenses. For these reasons, businesses should establish rigorous internal control procedures for the payroll function. The most important of these procedures is the maintenance of a payroll register. A **payroll register** is an accounting record in which key payroll data, such as gross pay, payroll deductions, net pay, and payroll check number, are entered each payroll period for each employee. Shown in Exhibit 10.2 is a simple example of a payroll register. Most payroll registers have several additional columns for payroll deductions; and as you would expect, the amounts in a payroll register nearly always include dollars and cents. (As a point of information, notice that the payroll register in Exhibit 10.2 distinguishes between wages expense and office salaries expense. Typically, businesses refer to compensation paid to hourly employees as wages expense and to compensation paid to salaried employees as salaries expense.)

The maintenance of a payroll register allows a company's management to exercise effective control over the payroll function. For example, the use of a payroll register helps management ensure that the appropriate amounts are withheld each pay period from employees' paychecks. Companies face stiff fines and criminal penalties for failing to withhold the correct amounts from employees' paychecks for such items as federal and state income taxes and FICA taxes. A payroll register can also be used to ensure that only legitimate employees are receiving paychecks. Periodically, a firm's internal auditors should determine that the employees listed in the payroll register for each department are actually working in those departments. A dishonest supervisor

■ **LEARNING OBJECTIVE 4**
Describe internal control procedures applied to an organization's payroll function

payroll register

Real World
The maintenance of a payroll register helps a company satisfy the recordkeeping responsibilities imposed on employers by the Fair Labor Standards Act of 1938.

■ **EXHIBIT 10.2**
Weekly Payroll Register

WEEK ENDED JANUARY 20, 1995												
		EARNINGS			DEDUCTIONS				PAYMENT		DISTRIBUTION	
Employee	*Hours*	*Regular*	*Over-time*	*Gross*	*FICA Tax*	*Federal Income Tax*	*Union Dues*	*Total*	*Net Pay*	*Check No.*	*Wages Expense*	*Office Salaries Expense*
Choo, L. T.	40	400		400	31	60	10	101	299	421	400	
Davis, Tom	40	400		400	31	44	10	85	315	422	400	
Earl, Will	41	480	12	492	38	60		98	394	423		492
Elliot, Jo	40	400		400	31	60	10	101	299	424	400	
Howe, Mimi	47	560	98	658	50	88		138	520	425		658
Martin, Sue	40	600		600	46	81	10	137	463	426	600	
Wills, M. W.	44	480	48	528	41	68	10	119	409	427	528	
Totals		3,320	158	3,478	268	461	50	779	2,699		2,328	1,150

SPOTLIGHT ON ETHICS

Payroll Padding: A Case of Dodger Blue

Teaching Note
An important internal control procedure is to require employees to take vacations. Required vacations may prevent employees from permanently concealing irregularities.

Edward Campos accepted a position with the Los Angeles Dodgers in the late 1960s. By 1986, the industrious Campos had worked his way up the organization's employment hierarchy to become the operations payroll chief. After taking charge of the Dodgers' payroll department, Campos designed and implemented a new payroll system—a system that only he fully understood. Campos controlled the payroll system so completely that he personally filled out the weekly payroll cards for each of the Dodgers' more than four hundred employees. Even when he was on vacation, Campos would return to the Dodgers' accounting office once per week to complete the weekly payroll.

Unfortunately, the high level of trust that the organization's executives placed in Campos was not warranted. Over a period of a few years, Campos embezzled several hundred thousand dollars from the Dodgers. According to court records, Campos padded the Dodgers' payroll by adding fictitious employees to various departments. In addition, Campos inflated the number of hours worked by several employees and then split the resulting overpayments fifty-fifty with those individuals.

Campos's fraudulent scheme came unraveled when he was unable to work for a short time due to illness and his responsibilities were assumed by the Dodgers' controller. While completing the payroll one week, the controller noticed that several employees, including ushers, security guards, and ticket salespeople, were being paid unusually large amounts. In some cases, employees earning $7 per hour were receiving weekly paychecks approaching $2,000.

After pleading guilty to embezzlement charges, Campos was sentenced to eight years in state prison and was required to make restitution to the Dodgers. Another of the conspirators also received a prison sentence, while the remaining individuals involved in the fraud made restitution and were placed on probation.

SOURCE: M. C. Knapp, "The Trolley Dodgers," in *Contemporary Auditing: Issues and Cases*, 2d ed. (Minneapolis/St. Paul: West Publishing Co., 1996).

who oversees a department of several hundred employees might attempt to maintain one or more former employees on the payroll and then obtain and cash their payroll checks.

A payroll register, if properly designed, also provides the information needed to record periodic payroll disbursements to employees. For instance, for the data presented in Exhibit 10.2, the following entry would be made to record the given entity's weekly payroll.

Jan. 20	Wages Expense	2,328	
	Office Salaries Expense	1,150	
	FICA Taxes Payable		268
	Employee Federal Income Taxes Payable		461
	Employee Union Dues Payable		50
	Cash		2,699
	To record payroll for week ended January 20		

Rigorous control procedures are a necessity for the payroll function as proven by a recent payroll fraud perpetrated by an employee of the Los Angeles Dodgers.

A payroll register can also be designed to capture the data needed to record employer payroll taxes and employee fringe benefits each payroll period.

Finally, the maintenance of a payroll register helps ensure that the appropriate data are available each accounting period to determine period-ending accrued payroll expenses. As suggested earlier, these amounts can be substantial. At the end of fiscal 1994, Hechinger, Inc., a retailer in the home improvement industry, owed more than $35 million to its employees. That amount was almost twice the company's year-end cash balance.

The Spotlight on Ethics vignette accompanying this section describes a payroll fraud perpetrated on the Los Angeles Dodgers professional baseball club. That fraud highlights the need for businesses to have effective control procedures for their payroll function. Among the internal control weaknesses evident in the Dodgers' payroll function was the vesting of too much authority in one individual. The Dodgers' operations payroll chief had such complete control over the organization's payroll system that he could steal almost at will from his employer.

CONTINGENT LIABILITIES

We all remember several years ago when Saddam Hussein's Iraqi troops invaded Kuwait. That invasion had financial implications for most firms engaged in the oil industry in the Middle East. One such firm was the Oklahoma-based Halliburton Company, an oil well servicing company. Shortly after Iraq invaded Kuwait,

■ LEARNING
OBJECTIVE 5
Define the key characteristics of,
and account for, contingent
liabilities

Real World
Contingent liabilities may
require disclosure but not the
recording of an actual expense.
When this is the case, the term
"Contingencies" typically
appears as a line item on the
balance sheet with a reference
to the appropriate footnote.

Discussion Question
Ask students to indicate specific
likelihoods that something is
"probable" and that something
is "reasonably possible." Is it
"probable" that accountants will
uniformly interpret these terms?

Halliburton recorded a $16.5 million expense—and a corresponding liability in the same amount—to recognize losses that it might incur as a result of the Iraqi occupation. Accountants refer to such potential losses as loss contingencies. Again, related to every loss contingency is a contingent liability. Recall from Chapter 7 that a contingent liability is defined as a potential liability that may become an actual liability if one or more events occur or fail to occur.

The most common contingent liabilities included in financial statements are those stemming from lawsuits pending against business entities. A company involved as a defendant in a lawsuit may eventually be forced to pay a legal judgment or settlement to a third party. Contingent liabilities can also result from potential impairments or losses of assets. For example, the contingent liability recorded by Halliburton primarily involved the possible destruction of oil field equipment. Another common type of contingent liability is discounted notes receivable, which were discussed in Chapter 7.

The guidelines that should be followed in accounting for loss contingencies and the related contingent liabilities are summarized in Exhibit 10.3. The two factors to consider in determining how to account for loss contingencies are (1) how likely it is that an actual loss will eventually occur as a result of the contingency, and (2) whether the amount of the potential loss can be reasonably estimated. If it is *probable* that a contingency will result in an actual loss and that loss can be *reasonably estimated*, the contingency should be recorded. When a loss contingency is recorded, an appropriate expense or loss account is debited with an offsetting credit to a liability account. If it is probable that a contingency will result in an actual loss but the dollar amount of that loss cannot be reasonably estimated, the contingency should be disclosed in an entity's financial statement footnotes. If it is *reasonably possible* that a loss contingency will result in an actual loss, the contingency should be disclosed in an entity's financial statement footnotes whether or not its dollar amount can be reasonably estimated.

Finally, loss contingencies that have only a *remote* chance of resulting in actual losses should generally be ignored. For example, many large corporations regularly face nuisance lawsuits. In February 1995, a dispute arose between Nintendo Company and a

■ **EXHIBIT 10.3**
Accounting Treatment of Contingent Losses and Related Contingent Liabilities

LIKELIHOOD OF AN ACTUAL LOSS	POTENTIAL LOSS SUBJECT TO REASONABLE ESTIMATION	ACCOUNTING TREATMENT
Probable	Yes	Recorded by debiting an expense account and crediting a liability account
Probable	No	Disclosed in financial statement footnotes
Reasonably Possible	Yes/No	Disclosed in financial statement footnotes
Remote	Yes/No	Ignored

foreign competitor. The dispute concerned copyright infringement of Nintendo's popular video game Donkey Kong Country. Nintendo had collected evidence that the foreign competitor was participating in a large-scale counterfeiting scheme to produce and distribute the video game in the Far East. When these allegations surfaced, the foreign competitor quickly filed a large lawsuit against Nintendo, charging Nintendo with defaming its good name by making the counterfeiting allegations. A Nintendo executive responded to the lawsuit by describing it as "Absolutely looney. . . . This is nothing but a crook suing his innocent victim."[6]

The key to accounting for loss contingencies is interpreting the meaning of the terms "probable," "reasonably possible," "remote," and "reasonably estimated." Accounting standards do not provide definite guidelines regarding how these terms should be interpreted. Consequently, accountants must arrive at their own good faith interpretation of what each of these terms means.

Contingent liabilities can be current or long-term or can have a component of each. For instance, take the case of General Public Utilities (GPU). This large electric utility operated the Three-Mile Island nuclear facility, which was damaged in 1979 and leaked radioactive materials into the environment. GPU faced numerous contingent liabilities because of the Three-Mile Island incident. Some of these contingent liabilities were current liabilities. An example was the estimated cost of an environmental remediation, or cleanup, program following the accident. Other contingent liabilities stemming from the accident were long-term in nature. In 1993, more than two thousand lawsuits were still pending against GPU because of the Three-Mile Island incident. Many of these lawsuits alleged personal injuries due to the radioactive emissions from the nuclear facility.

The 1994 edition of *Accounting Trends & Techniques* reported that most companies disclose contingent liabilities in their annual reports. There are two key sources of contingent liabilities. Approximately 64 percent of the public companies surveyed by *Accounting Trends & Techniques* in 1994 reported contingent liabilities stemming from litigation. Another 45 percent of these companies disclosed contingent liabilities related to environmental issues or problems.

Contingent liabilities can occasionally threaten the existence of companies. For several years, the survival of General Public Utilities (GPU), which owned and operated the ill-fated Three-Mile Island nuclear facility, was in doubt. Nevertheless, GPU survived and today is a financially healthy company.

THE TIME VALUE OF MONEY

In October 1994, four lucky individuals literally hit the jackpot when they won the New York State lottery.[7] These individuals split the $73 million Lotto jackpot that, at the time, was the largest in New York history. So, let's see, $73 million divided four ways means each of these winners walked away with approximately $18.2 million. Right? Wrong. Like most lottery prizes, this huge jackpot was not paid out in a sin-

■ **LEARNING OBJECTIVE 6**
Use the time value of money concept to compute the present value and future value of single amounts and annuities

---

6. Carlton, J. "Samsung Countersues Nintendo in Fight Over Chip Sales to Game Counterfeiters," *The Wall Street Journal*, February 2, 1995 p. B10. Reprinted by permission of *The Wall Street Journal*, © 1995 Dow Jones & Company, Inc. All Rights Reserved Worldwide.

7. "Four Hit the Lottery for $73 Million Pot," *Los Angeles Times*, 3 October 1994, A15.

gle amount. Instead, the jackpot is being distributed in a series of equal payments stretching over twenty-one years. Each of the four winners receive annual payments of approximately $863,000. Assuming an income tax rate of 50 percent for these individuals—they have to pay federal, state, and municipal income taxes on their winnings—each pockets less than $440,000 annually.

If we go one step further and apply the "time value of money concept," we can determine the present value of each $18 million share of the lottery prize. The **time value of money concept** suggests that the economic value of a sum of cash to be received or paid is largely a function of the timing of that payment or receipt. In simple terms, the time value of money concept is based upon the premise that $1 in your pocket today is worth more than $1 you will receive sometime in the future. Applying the appropriate mathematical equation derived from the time value of money concept, the "present value" of each winner's share of the Lotto jackpot, again after taxes, is approximately $5 million. So, there you have it. Instead of winning $18 million each, these individuals were actually enriched to the tune of only $5 million, hardly enough to make an effort to collect. Right? Wrong.

Scenarios involving the time value of money abound in the business world. For example, the owner of a hardware store may be approaching retirement and intending to sell his business. The individual has the accounting records to prove that his business generates a positive net cash flow of $80,000 per year. How much should someone be willing to pay for this indefinite stream of cash flows? A different type of time value of money scenario faces a small corporation with a long-range expansion plan that includes building a new production facility in five years. The company intends to accumulate a $10 million building fund by making equal annual deposits in a savings account over the next five years. How large must these deposits be to allow the company to achieve its goal?

In this section, we consider the time value of money and the implications it has for business entities. The time value of money concept can be used to analyze a variety of financial transactions and to assign dollar values to several different types of assets and liabilities, including certain current liabilities. In this textbook, the time value of money is used primarily to illustrate accounting decisions for bonds payable in Chapter 11. But you will also find several opportunities to apply your understanding of the time value of money in other accounting and business courses.

The first topic addressed in the remainder of this section is the concept of interest, including the two methods of computing interest. Then, the four basic types of time value of money scenarios are discussed and illustrated.

Simple Interest vs. Compound Interest

In Chapter 7, we used the interest equation (interest = principal × rate × time) to compute interest on notes receivable. Earlier in this chapter, that equation was used to compute interest on notes payable. The key to understanding the time value of money is interest and the methods of computing interest. In an economic sense, **interest** is the expense of borrowing money for a specified period or, alternatively, the revenue earned from lending money for a specified period. If you borrow $1,000 from a bank for one year at an annual (simple) interest rate of 10 percent, the cost you will incur to use the bank's money is $100. That is, you will pay $100 of interest on the borrowed funds. Likewise, if you deposit money with a bank, that bank will pay you for its use of your money (but at an interest rate lower than the one it charges on loans).

Banks and other lenders have two choices when computing interest. They can charge interest on either a simple or a compound basis. **Simple interest** on a loan is

---

Margin notes:

time value of money concept

Discussion Question
Ask students if they would be willing to pay $1,000 today for the right to receive $1,000 in one year. How much would they be willing to pay today for the right to receive $1,000 in one year?

Teaching Note
Emphasize to students that the time value of money is an investment concept. The underlying assumption is that money can and will be invested to yield a return. That is why a dollar today is worth more than a dollar in a year.

interest

simple interest

computed only on the principal amount. **Compound interest** is interest computed on the principal amount of a loan plus any unpaid interest that has accumulated on the loan since its inception. For instance, assume that rather than borrowing $1,000 for one year from your local bank, you borrow that amount for two years. If this bank charges you simple interest, at the end of two years you must pay the bank the $1,000 principal amount plus $200 of interest—$100 for each year that the loan was outstanding. Alternatively, assume that the bank charges you interest on a compound basis—which is much more likely. In that case, $210 of interest will accrue, or accumulate, on your loan over its two-year term, as shown in the following schedule.

compound interest

	PRINCIPAL AMOUNT OF LOAN PLUS UNPAID INTEREST AT BEGINNING OF YEAR		INTEREST RATE		INTEREST
Year 1	$1,000	×	10%	=	$100
Year 2	1,100	×	10%	=	$110
Total					$210

Future Value of a Single Amount

In many situations, businesses need to know the future value of a single amount. In this context, **future value** refers to the sum of an invested amount plus any interest that will accumulate on that amount on a compound basis over a specified period of time. Suppose that a young woman has been given $3,000 by her grandmother, and she intends to invest this amount in a four-year certificate of deposit (CD) that pays 10 percent interest compounded annually. The young woman plans to use the accumulated balance of the CD at the end of four years to purchase a small business on Campus Corner. In four years, ignoring tax considerations, the value of the gift will accumulate to $4,392.30, as shown by the following schedule.

future value

	CD BALANCE AT BEGINNING OF THE YEAR		INTEREST RATE		INTEREST REVENUE	CD BALANCE AT END OF THE YEAR
Year 1	$3,000	×	10%	=	$300.00	$3,300.00
Year 2	3,300	×	10%	=	330.00	3,630.00
Year 3	3,630	×	10%	=	363.00	3,993.00
Year 4	3,993	×	10%	=	399.30	4,392.30

Using this approach to compute future values is quite tedious when a lengthy period is involved. For instance, if the young woman in our illustration plans to invest the $3,000 gift for a period of ten years before acquiring a business, we would have to extend the previous schedule for six additional years.

Fortunately, there are two quick and easy approaches to computing future values. The first approach involves using the following equation.

$$\text{Future Value of a Single Amount} = \text{Present Value of the Amount} \times (1 + \text{Interest Rate})^t$$

where t represents the number of periods over which interest is to be compounded

More often than not, you will find this equation expressed as follows:

$$FV = FV \times (1 + R)^t$$

Following are the computations to determine the value of the $3,000 gift both four years and ten years into the future.

Teaching Note
Call students' attention to the fact that the difference between an amount's future value and its present value is interest.

$$\text{Four Years:} \quad \begin{aligned} FV &= PV \times (1 + R)^t \\ FV &= \$3,000 \times (1 + .1)^4 \\ FV &= \$3,000 \times (1.4641) \\ FV &= \$4,392.30 \end{aligned}$$

$$\text{Ten Years:} \quad \begin{aligned} FV &= PV \times (1 + R)^t \\ FV &= \$3,000 \times (1 + .1)^{10} \\ FV &= \$3,000 \times (2.59374) \\ FV &= \$7,781.22 \end{aligned}$$

The second approach to computing future values involves the use of a table such as Table 10.1 on page 441. Included in Table 10.1 are numerical values that can be used to compute the future value of $1 amounts invested for a specified number of periods at a specified interest rate. These numerical values are referred to as future value factors. To find the future value factor for the combination of four years and 10 percent, locate the 10 percent column in Table 10.1 and then slide your finger down that column until it intersects with the 4 period row. At that intersection point, you will find the future value factor of 1.4641, which is the figure we arrived at previously when we solved for the following term in the four-year scenario: $(1 + R)^t$. What does 1.4641 represent? Answer: the future value (approximately $1.46) of $1 invested at an interest rate of 10 percent for four years. At the intersection of the 10 percent column and 10 period row is the future value factor of 2.59374. So, $1 invested at a 10 percent interest rate for ten years will accumulate to the grand total of $2.59, approximately.

If you prefer to use Table 10.1 to compute future values, you can use the following simplified future value equation. In this equation, FVF represents the appropriate future value factor drawn from Table 10.1.

$$FV = PV \times FVF$$

For the four-year assumption in our illustration, the future value is computed as follows:

$$\begin{aligned} FV &= PV \times FVF \\ FV &= \$3,000 \times 1.4641 \\ FV &= \$4,392.30 \end{aligned}$$

Quite often, interest is compounded on other than an annual basis. Fortunately, the "period" in Table 10.1 can represent any length of time, such as one year, six months, or one quarter (three months). Returning to our hypothetical scenario, suppose the granddaughter invests the $3,000 for four years in a CD earning interest at a 10 percent annual rate but that the interest is compounded twice per year, or semiannually. In this case, there are eight six-month periods over which interest is compounded at one-half the annual interest rate, or 5 percent. According to Table 10.1, the appropriate future value factor for eight compounding periods and a 5 percent interest rate is 1.47746. The appropriate future value factor for the ten-year assumption is 2.6533 if interest is compounded semiannually. Given these future value factors, the granddaughter would have the following amounts on deposit in her CD account under the four-year and ten-year assumptions.

Table 10.1
Future Value Factors for a Single Amount

PERIOD	2.5%	3%	3.5%	4%	4.5%	5%	5.5%	6%	7%	8%	9%	10%	12%	15%
1	1.02500	1.03000	1.03500	1.04000	1.04500	1.05000	1.05500	1.06000	1.07000	1.08000	1.09000	1.10000	1.12000	1.15000
2	1.05063	1.06090	1.07123	1.08160	1.09203	1.10250	1.11303	1.12360	1.14490	1.16640	1.18810	1.21000	1.25440	1.32250
3	1.07689	1.09273	1.10872	1.12486	1.14117	1.15762	1.17424	1.19102	1.22504	1.25971	1.29503	1.33100	1.40493	1.52088
4	1.10381	1.12551	1.14752	1.16986	1.19252	1.21551	1.23882	1.26248	1.31080	1.36049	1.41158	1.46410	1.57352	1.74901
5	1.13141	1.15927	1.18769	1.21665	1.24618	1.27628	1.30696	1.33823	1.40255	1.46933	1.53862	1.61051	1.76234	2.01136
6	1.15969	1.19405	1.22926	1.26532	1.30226	1.34010	1.37884	1.41852	1.50073	1.58687	1.67710	1.77156	1.97382	2.31306
7	1.18869	1.22987	1.27228	1.31593	1.36086	1.40710	1.45468	1.50363	1.60578	1.71382	1.82804	1.94872	2.21068	2.66002
8	1.21840	1.26677	1.31681	1.36857	1.42210	1.47746	1.53469	1.59385	1.71819	1.85093	1.99256	2.14359	2.47596	3.05902
9	1.24886	1.30477	1.36290	1.42331	1.48610	1.55133	1.61909	1.68948	1.83846	1.99900	2.17189	2.35795	2.77308	3.51788
10	1.28008	1.34392	1.41060	1.48024	1.55297	1.62889	1.70814	1.79085	1.96715	2.15892	2.36736	2.59374	3.10585	4.04556
11	1.31209	1.38423	1.45997	1.53945	1.62285	1.71034	1.80209	1.89830	2.10485	2.33164	2.58043	2.85312	3.47855	4.65239
12	1.34489	1.42576	1.51107	1.60103	1.69588	1.79586	1.90121	2.01220	2.25219	2.51817	2.81266	3.13843	3.89598	5.35025
13	1.37851	1.46853	1.56396	1.66507	1.77220	1.88565	2.00577	2.13293	2.40985	2.71962	3.06580	3.45227	4.36349	6.15279
14	1.41297	1.51259	1.61869	1.73168	1.85194	1.97993	2.11609	2.26090	2.57853	2.93719	3.34173	3.79750	4.88711	7.07571
15	1.44830	1.55797	1.67535	1.80094	1.93528	2.07893	2.23248	2.39656	2.75903	3.17217	3.64248	4.17725	5.47357	8.13706
16	1.48451	1.60471	1.73399	1.87298	2.02237	2.18287	2.35526	2.54035	2.95216	3.42594	3.97031	4.59497	6.13039	9.35762
17	1.52162	1.65285	1.79468	1.94790	2.11338	2.29202	2.48480	2.69277	3.15882	3.70002	4.32783	5.05447	6.86604	10.76126
18	1.55966	1.70243	1.85749	2.02582	2.20848	2.40662	2.62147	2.85434	3.37993	3.99602	4.71712	5.55992	7.68997	12.37545
19	1.59865	1.75351	1.92250	2.10685	2.30786	2.52695	2.76565	3.02560	3.61653	4.31570	5.14166	6.11591	8.61276	14.23177
20	1.63862	1.80611	1.98979	2.19112	2.41171	2.65330	2.91776	3.20714	3.86968	4.66096	5.60441	6.72750	9.64629	16.36654
21	1.67958	1.86029	2.05943	2.27877	2.52024	2.78596	3.07823	3.39956	4.14056	5.03383	6.10881	7.40025	10.80385	18.82152
22	1.72157	1.91610	2.13151	2.36992	2.63365	2.92526	3.24754	3.60354	4.43040	5.43654	6.65860	8.14027	12.10031	21.64475
23	1.76461	1.97359	2.20611	2.46472	2.75217	3.07152	3.42615	3.81975	4.74053	5.87146	7.25787	8.95430	13.55235	24.89146
24	1.80873	2.03279	2.28333	2.56330	2.87601	3.22510	3.61459	4.04893	5.07237	6.34118	7.91108	9.84973	15.17863	28.62518
25	1.85394	2.09378	2.36324	2.66584	3.00543	3.38635	3.81339	4.29187	5.42743	6.84848	8.62308	10.83471	17.00006	32.91895
26	1.90029	2.15659	2.44596	2.77247	3.14068	3.55567	4.02313	4.54938	5.80735	7.39635	9.39916	11.91818	19.04007	37.85680
27	1.94780	2.22129	2.53157	2.88337	3.28201	3.73346	4.24440	4.82235	6.21387	7.98806	10.24508	13.10999	21.32488	43.53531
28	1.99650	2.28793	2.62017	2.99870	3.42970	3.92013	4.47784	5.11169	6.64884	8.62711	11.16714	14.42099	23.88387	50.06561
29	2.04641	2.35657	2.71188	3.11865	3.58404	4.11614	4.72412	5.41839	7.11426	9.31727	12.17218	15.86309	26.74993	57.57545
30	2.09757	2.42726	2.80679	3.24340	3.74532	4.32194	4.98395	5.74349	7.61226	10.06266	13.26768	17.44940	29.95992	66.21177
35	2.37321	2.81386	3.33359	3.94609	4.66735	5.51602	6.51382	7.68609	10.67657	14.78534	20.41397	28.10244	52.79962	133.17552
40	2.68506	3.26204	3.95926	4.80102	5.81636	7.03999	8.51331	10.28572	14.97445	21.72452	31.40942	45.25926	93.05097	267.86355

$$
\begin{aligned}
\text{Four Years:} \quad FV &= PV \times FVF \\
FV &= \$3{,}000 \times (1.47746) \\
FV &= \$4{,}432.38
\end{aligned}
$$

$$
\begin{aligned}
\text{Ten Years:} \quad FV &= PV \times FVF \\
FV &= \$3{,}000 \times (2.6533) \\
FV &= \$7{,}959.90
\end{aligned}
$$

Notice that for both the four-year and ten-year assumptions, the future value is greater when interest is compounded semiannually than when it is compounded annually. In fact, that is always the case. The more frequently interest is compounded, the greater the resulting future value.

Future Value of an Annuity

annuity

An **annuity** is a series of equal payments made, or received, at equal intervals on which interest is computed on a compound basis. The lucky winners of the Lotto jackpot described earlier receive their winnings in the form of an annuity. In the business world, many financial transactions are structured as annuities. For instance, assume that a company purchases a piece of property for $2,000,000. The payment terms include a $200,000 down payment and equal monthly payments spread over ten years. This series of equal monthly payments is an annuity.

In the previous section, we computed the future value of a single amount that was left on deposit with a bank. Now, let us tackle the slightly more complex problem of computing the future value of an annuity. Assume that on January 1 of Year 1, a young man sells his prized 1969 Chevy to his best friend. In total, the friend agrees to pay $1,500 for the car in three $500 installments on December 31 of Year 1, Year 2, and Year 3. To make the deal official, the friend signs a sales contract documenting the payment terms. The former Chevy owner intends to deposit each of the three $500 payments in a bank account that earns interest at an 8 percent rate compounded annually. The young man wants to know exactly how much cash he will have in his account after the final payment is deposited on December 31 of Year 3. That is, he wants to determine the future value of a three-year, $500 annuity with interest compounded annually at 8 percent.

Shown in Exhibit 10.4 is a diagram of this annuity. As indicated in that exhibit, the future value of the annuity is $1,623.20. In other words, by December 31, Year 3, the individual who sold the car will have received the $1,500 in payments from his friend and earned interest of $123.20 on those payments.

Refer to the following schedule for a year-by-year analysis of the activity in the young man's bank account. This schedule indicates that no interest will be earned during Year 1. The initial deposit will not be made in the bank account until the final day of that year. During Year 2, $500 will be on deposit until the last day of the year, resulting in interest revenue of $40 ($500 × 8%). During Year 3, the bank account balance will be $1,040 until December 31, resulting in interest revenue of $83.20 ($1,040 × 8%). Final result: a $1,623.20 bank account balance on December 31 of Year 3.

	BALANCE OF BANK ACCOUNT AT BEGINNING OF YEAR	INTEREST EARNED AT 8%	DECEMBER 31 DEPOSIT	BALANCE OF BANK ACCOUNT AT END OF YEAR
Year 1	$ 0	$ 0.00	$500	$ 500.00
Year 2	500	40.00	500	1,040.00
Year 3	1,040	83.20	500	1,623.20

■ **EXHIBIT 10.4**

Diagram of the Future Value of a Three-Year, $500 Annuity with Interest
Compounded at 8 Percent

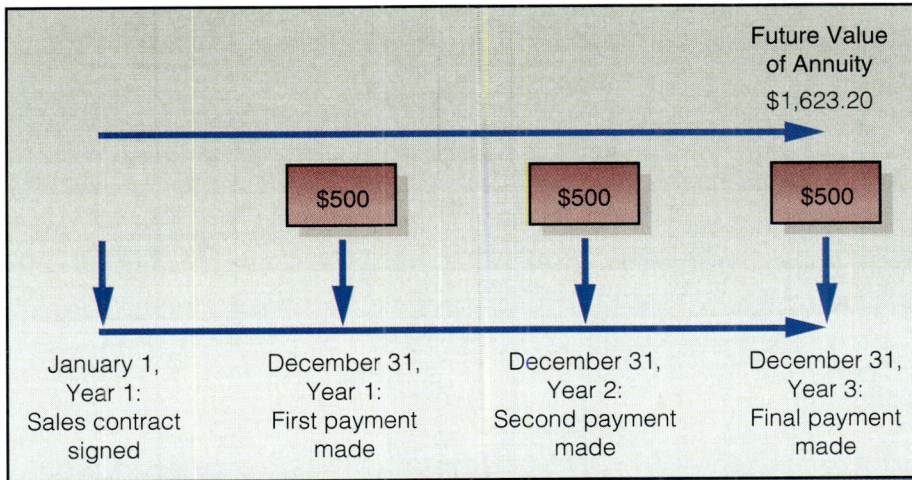

| January 1, Year 1: Sales contract signed | December 31, Year 1: First payment made | December 31, Year 2: Second payment made | December 31, Year 3: Final payment made |

Again, the schedule approach to computing a future value (here, the future value of
an annuity) is cumbersome. Shown next is the future value of an annuity (FVA) equation, which can be used instead.

$$\text{FVA} = A \times \{[(1 + R)^t - 1]/R\}$$

$$\text{where} \quad A = \text{the dollar amount of the annuity}$$
$$R = \text{interest rate}$$
$$t = \text{the number of periods}$$

If you have access to a future value of an annuity table, such as Table 10.2, you can
use a much simpler equation to determine the future value of an annuity. Included in
Table 10.2 are future value of an annuity factors (FVAFs). These factors represent the
following component of the future value of an annuity equation: $[(1 + R)^t - 1]/R$.
The two parameters of the factors included in Table 10.2 are an assumed interest rate
and a given number of time periods. For the scenario just described, the appropriate
future value of an annuity factor, 3.2464, can be found at the intersection of the 8 percent column and the 3 period row. What does that figure represent? Answer: the
amount of cash (approximately $3.24) you will have in three years if you invest $1 at
the end of each of those years at an interest rate of 8 percent.

When a future value of an annuity table is available, the following simplified version of the future value of an annuity equation can be used:

$$\text{FVA} = A \times \text{FVAF}$$

For the annuity involving the sale of the 1969 Chevy, the future value is computed as
follows:

$$\text{FVA} = A \times \text{FVAF}$$
$$\text{FVA} = \$500 \times 3.2464$$
$$\text{FVA} = \$1,623.20$$

Table 10.2
Future Value of an Annuity Factors

PERIOD	2.5%	3%	3.5%	4%	4.5%	5%	5.5%	6%	7%	8%	9%	10%	12%	15%
1	1.00000	1.00000	1.00000	1.00000	1.00000	1.00000	1.00000	1.00000	1.00000	1.00000	1.00000	1.00000	1.00000	1.00000
2	2.02500	2.03000	2.03500	2.04000	2.04500	2.05000	2.05500	2.06000	2.07000	2.08000	2.09000	2.10000	2.12000	2.15000
3	3.07562	3.09090	3.10622	3.12160	3.13702	3.15250	3.16802	3.18360	3.21490	3.24640	3.27810	3.31000	3.37440	3.47250
4	4.15252	4.18363	4.21494	4.24646	4.27819	4.31012	4.34227	4.37462	4.43994	4.50611	4.57313	4.64100	4.77933	4.99337
5	5.25633	5.30914	5.36247	5.41632	5.47071	5.52563	5.58109	5.63709	5.75074	5.86660	5.98471	6.10510	6.35285	6.74238
6	6.38774	6.46841	6.55015	6.63298	6.71689	6.80191	6.88805	6.97532	7.15329	7.33593	7.52333	7.71561	8.11519	8.75374
7	7.54743	7.66246	7.77941	7.89829	8.01915	8.14201	8.26689	8.39384	8.65402	8.92280	9.20043	9.48717	10.08901	11.06680
8	8.73612	8.89234	9.05169	9.21423	9.38001	9.54911	9.72157	9.89747	10.25980	10.63663	11.02847	11.43589	12.29969	13.72682
9	9.95452	10.15911	10.36850	10.58280	10.80211	11.02656	11.25626	11.49132	11.97799	12.48756	13.02104	13.57948	14.77566	16.78584
10	11.20338	11.46388	11.73139	12.00611	12.28821	12.57789	12.87535	13.18079	13.81645	14.48656	15.19293	15.93742	17.54874	20.30372
11	12.48347	12.80780	13.14199	13.48635	13.84118	14.20679	14.58350	14.97164	15.78360	16.64549	17.56029	18.53117	20.65458	24.34928
12	13.79555	14.19203	14.60196	15.02581	15.46403	15.91713	16.38559	16.86994	17.88845	18.97713	20.14072	21.38428	24.13313	20.00167
13	15.14044	15.61779	16.11303	16.62684	17.15991	17.71298	18.28680	18.88214	20.14064	21.49530	22.95338	24.52271	28.02911	34.35192
14	16.51895	17.08632	17.67699	18.29191	18.93211	19.59863	20.29257	21.01507	22.55049	24.21492	26.01919	27.97498	32.39260	40.50471
15	17.93193	18.59891	19.29568	20.02359	20.78405	21.57856	22.40866	23.27597	25.12902	27.15211	29.36092	31.77248	37.27971	47.58041
16	19.38022	20.15688	20.97103	21.82453	22.71934	23.65749	24.64114	25.67253	27.88805	30.32428	33.00340	35.94973	42.75328	55.71747
17	20.86473	21.76159	22.70502	23.69751	24.74171	25.84037	26.99640	28.21288	30.84022	33.75023	36.97370	40.54470	48.88367	65.07509
18	22.38635	23.41444	24.49969	25.64541	26.85508	28.13238	29.48120	30.90565	33.99903	37.45024	41.30134	45.59917	55.74971	75.83636
19	23.94601	25.11687	26.35718	27.67123	29.06356	30.53900	32.10267	33.75999	37.37896	41.44626	46.01846	51.15909	63.43968	88.21181
20	25.54466	26.87037	28.27968	29.77808	31.37142	33.06595	34.86832	36.78559	40.99549	45.76196	51.16012	57.27500	72.05244	102.44358
21	27.18327	28.67649	30.26947	31.96920	33.78314	35.71925	37.78608	39.99273	44.86518	50.42292	56.76453	64.00250	81.69874	118.81012
22	28.86286	30.53678	32.32890	34.24797	36.30338	38.50521	40.86431	43.39229	49.00574	55.45676	62.87334	71.40275	92.50258	137.63164
23	30.58443	32.45288	34.46041	36.61789	38.93703	41.43048	44.11185	46.99583	53.43614	60.89330	69.53194	79.54302	104.60289	159.27638
24	32.34904	34.42647	36.66653	39.08260	41.68920	44.50200	47.53800	50.81558	58.17667	66.76476	76.78981	88.49733	118.15524	184.16784
25	34.15776	36.45926	38.94986	41.64591	44.56521	47.72710	51.15259	54.86451	63.24904	73.10594	84.70090	98.34706	133.33387	212.79302
26	36.01171	38.55304	41.31310	44.31174	47.57064	51.11345	54.96596	59.15638	68.67647	79.95442	93.32398	109.18177	150.33393	245.71197
27	37.91200	40.70963	43.75906	47.08421	50.71132	54.66913	58.98911	63.70577	74.48382	87.35077	102.72313	121.09994	169.37401	283.56877
28	39.85980	42.93092	46.29063	49.96758	53.99333	58.40258	63.23351	68.52811	80.69769	95.33883	112.96822	134.20994	190.69889	327.10408
29	41.85630	45.21885	48.91080	52.96629	57.42303	62.32271	67.71135	73.63980	87.34653	103.96594	124.13536	148.63093	214.58275	377.16969
30	43.90270	47.57542	51.62268	56.08494	61.00707	66.43885	72.43548	79.05819	94.46079	113.28321	136.30754	164.49402	241.33268	434.74515
35	54.92821	60.46208	66.67401	73.65222	81.49661	90.32031	100.25136	111.43478	138.23688	172.31680	215.71076	271.02437	431.66350	881.17016
40	67.40255	75.40126	84.55027	95.02552	107.03032	120.79977	136.60561	154.76197	199.63511	259.05652	337.88245	442.59256	767.09142	1779.09031

Present Value of a Single Amount

When we compute the future value of a single amount or of an annuity, we are looking forward in time. Another type of time value of money problem requires us to do just the reverse. To compute a present value, we must discount a future value or a series of future values to their current dollar equivalent. A **present value** represents an amount that must be invested currently at a stated compound rate of interest to produce a given future value. For instance, assume that two members of a three-person partnership are buying out the third partner. One feature of the buy-out agreement is a $100,000 payment to the withdrawing partner in three years. The two remaining partners want to know how much they must invest currently to accumulate a fund of $100,000 in three years. The two partners assume that the invested funds will earn an annual compounded rate of return of 9 percent.

As in future value scenarios, we could use a year-by-year or schedule approach to find the solution to this present value problem. But by now, you realize that there are more efficient and easier approaches to solving time value of money problems. To compute the present value of a single amount to be received or paid in the future, we can use the following equation.

Teaching Note
Point out that an amount's future value is always greater than its present value.

present value

$$\text{Present Value of a Single Amount} = \text{Future Value of the Amount} \times \frac{1}{(1 + \text{Interest Rate})^t}$$

Where t represents the number of periods over which the future value is to be discounted.

The shorthand version of the prior equation is as follows.

$$PV = FV \times [1/(1 + R)^t]$$

Applying this equation to the scenario described in the previous paragraph, we arrive at a present value of $77,218. That is, the two remaining partners must invest $77,218 currently at an annual compound interest rate of 9 percent to accumulate the $100,000 needed in three years.

$$PV = \$100,000 \times [1/(1 + .09)^3]$$
$$PV = \$100,000 \times (1/1.29503)$$
$$PV = \$100,000 \times .77218$$
$$PV = \$\ 77,218$$

The shortcut approach to computing present values involves the use of an appropriate present value factor (PVF) from Table 10.3. Following is the present value equation to apply when using Table 10.3.

$$PV = FV \times PVF$$

For the partnership scenario, the appropriate present value factor of .77218 can be found at the intersection of the 9 percent column and the 3 period row. This present value factor indicates that the current value of $1 to be paid three years in the future is approximately $.77. Multiplying this present value factor by $100,000, we again arrive at $77,218 as the amount that the two remaining partners must invest to accumulate the funds needed to pay off the retiring partner.

Table 10.3
Present Value Factors for a Single Amount

PERIOD	2.5%	3%	3.5%	4%	4.5%	5%	5.5%	6%	7%	8%	9%	10%	12%	15%
1	0.97561	0.97087	0.96618	0.96154	0.95694	0.95238	0.94787	0.94340	0.93458	0.92593	0.91743	0.90909	0.89286	0.86957
2	0.95181	0.94260	0.93351	0.92456	0.91573	0.90703	0.89845	0.89000	0.87344	0.85734	0.84168	0.82645	0.79719	0.75614
3	0.92860	0.91514	0.90194	0.88900	0.87630	0.86384	0.85161	0.83962	0.81630	0.79383	0.77218	0.75131	0.71178	0.65752
4	0.90595	0.88849	0.87144	0.85480	0.83856	0.82270	0.80722	0.79209	0.76290	0.73503	0.70843	0.68301	0.63553	0.57175
5	0.88385	0.86261	0.84197	0.82193	0.80245	0.78353	0.76513	0.74726	0.71299	0.68058	0.64993	0.62092	0.56743	0.49718
6	0.86230	0.83748	0.81350	0.79031	0.76790	0.74622	0.72525	0.70496	0.66634	0.63017	0.59627	0.56447	0.50663	0.43233
7	0.84127	0.81309	0.78599	0.75992	0.73483	0.71068	0.68744	0.66506	0.62275	0.58349	0.54703	0.51316	0.45235	0.37594
8	0.82075	0.78941	0.75941	0.73069	0.70319	0.67684	0.65160	0.62741	0.58201	0.54027	0.50187	0.46651	0.40388	0.32690
9	0.80073	0.76642	0.73373	0.70259	0.67290	0.64461	0.61763	0.59190	0.54393	0.50025	0.46043	0.42410	0.36061	0.28426
10	0.78120	0.74409	0.70892	0.67556	0.64393	0.61391	0.58543	0.55839	0.50835	0.46319	0.42241	0.38554	0.32197	0.24718
11	0.76214	0.72242	0.68495	0.64958	0.61620	0.58468	0.55491	0.52679	0.47509	0.42888	0.38753	0.35049	0.28748	0.21494
12	0.74356	0.70138	0.66178	0.62460	0.58966	0.55684	0.52598	0.49697	0.44401	0.39711	0.35553	0.31863	0.25668	0.18691
13	0.72542	0.68095	0.63940	0.60057	0.56427	0.53032	0.49856	0.46884	0.41496	0.36770	0.32618	0.28966	0.22917	0.16253
14	0.70773	0.66112	0.61778	0.57748	0.53997	0.50507	0.47257	0.44230	0.38782	0.34046	0.29925	0.26333	0.20462	0.14133
15	0.69047	0.64186	0.59689	0.55526	0.51672	0.48102	0.44793	0.41727	0.36245	0.31524	0.27454	0.23939	0.18270	0.12289
16	0.67362	0.62317	0.57671	0.53391	0.49447	0.45811	0.42458	0.39365	0.33873	0.29189	0.25187	0.21763	0.16312	0.10686
17	0.65720	0.60502	0.55720	0.51337	0.47318	0.43630	0.40245	0.37136	0.31657	0.27027	0.23107	0.19784	0.14564	0.09293
18	0.64117	0.58739	0.53836	0.49363	0.45280	0.41552	0.38147	0.35034	0.29586	0.25025	0.21199	0.17986	0.13004	0.08081
19	0.62553	0.57029	0.52016	0.47464	0.43330	0.39573	0.36158	0.33051	0.27651	0.23171	0.19449	0.16351	0.11611	0.07027
20	0.61027	0.55368	0.50257	0.45639	0.41464	0.37689	0.34273	0.31180	0.25842	0.21455	0.17843	0.14864	0.10367	0.06110
21	0.59539	0.53755	0.48557	0.43883	0.39679	0.35894	0.32486	0.29416	0.24151	0.19866	0.16370	0.13513	0.09256	0.05313
22	0.58086	0.52189	0.46915	0.42196	0.37970	0.34185	0.30793	0.27751	0.22571	0.18394	0.15018	0.12285	0.08264	0.04620
23	0.56670	0.50669	0.45329	0.40573	0.36335	0.32557	0.29187	0.26180	0.21095	0.17032	0.13778	0.11168	0.07379	0.04017
24	0.55288	0.49193	0.43796	0.39012	0.34770	0.31007	0.27666	0.24698	0.19715	0.15770	0.12640	0.10153	0.06588	0.03493
25	0.53939	0.47761	0.42315	0.37512	0.33273	0.29530	0.26223	0.23300	0.18425	0.14602	0.11597	0.09230	0.05882	0.03038
26	0.52623	0.46369	0.40884	0.36069	0.31840	0.28124	0.24856	0.21981	0.17220	0.13520	0.10639	0.08391	0.05252	0.02642
27	0.51340	0.45019	0.39501	0.34682	0.30469	0.26785	0.23560	0.20737	0.16093	0.12519	0.09761	0.07628	0.04689	0.02297
28	0.50088	0.43708	0.38165	0.33348	0.29157	0.25509	0.22332	0.19563	0.15040	0.11591	0.08955	0.06934	0.04187	0.01997
29	0.48866	0.42435	0.36875	0.32065	0.27902	0.24295	0.21168	0.18456	0.14056	0.10733	0.08215	0.06304	0.03738	0.01737
30	0.47674	0.41199	0.35628	0.30832	0.26700	0.23138	0.20064	0.17411	0.13137	0.09938	0.07537	0.05731	0.03338	0.01510
35	0.42137	0.35538	0.29998	0.25342	0.21425	0.18129	0.15352	0.13011	0.09368	0.06763	0.04899	0.03558	0.01894	0.00751
40	0.37243	0.30656	0.25257	0.20829	0.17193	0.14205	0.11746	0.09722	0.06678	0.04603	0.03184	0.02209	0.01075	0.00373

Present Value of an Annuity

To illustrate the computation of the present value of an annuity, return to the scenario involving the 1969 Chevy. Previously, we determined that the future value of the series of three $500 payments is $1,623.20, as shown in Exhibit 10.4. Now, consider this scenario from the perspective of the buyer of the car. That individual would like to determine the cash equivalent price he is paying for the 1969 Chevy. Shown in Exhibit 10.5 is another diagram of this three-year annuity. In this case, the focus is on finding the present value, rather than the future value, of the annuity. Given an 8 percent interest rate, or discount rate, the present value of the payments to be made by the purchaser of the car is $1,288.55, an amount that we will confirm not once, but twice.

The present value of an annuity (PVA) can be computed using the following equation:

$$PVA = A \times (\{1 - [1/(1 + R)^t]\}/R)$$

where A = the dollar amount of the annuity
R = interest rate
t = the number of periods

We can apply this equation to our present scenario as follows:

$$PVA = \$500 \times (\{1 - [1/(1 + .08)^3]\}/.08)$$
$$PVA = \$500 \times \{[1 - (1/1.259712)]/.08\}$$
$$PVA = \$500 \times 2.5771$$
$$PVA = \$1,288.55$$

A simple version of the prior equation involves multiplying the annuity amount by the present value of an annuity factor (PVAF), as shown next.

Real World
Financial calculators are available with future value and present value function keys, which make the computation of future values and present values a matter of pushing a few buttons.

■ **EXHIBIT 10.5**
Diagram of the Present Value of a Three-Year, $500 Annuity
Applying a Discount Rate of 8 Percent

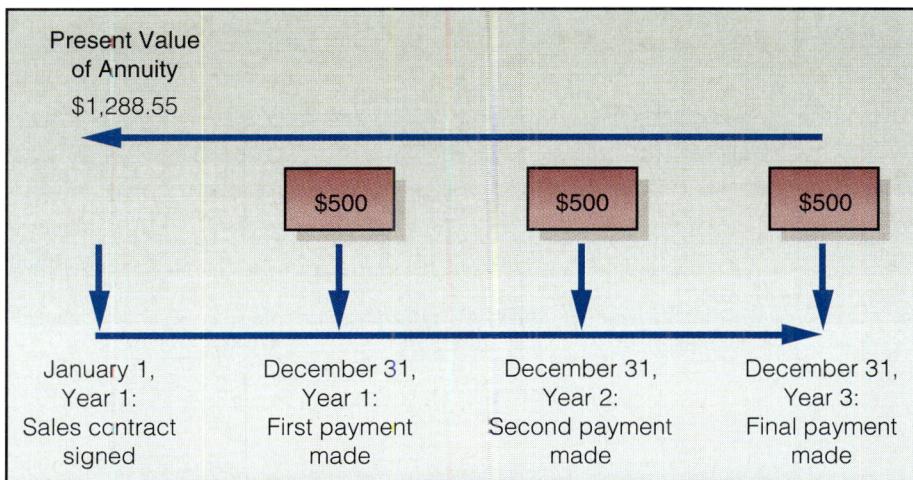

Present Value of Annuity $1,288.55			
	$500	$500	$500
January 1, Year 1: Sales contract signed	December 31, Year 1: First payment made	December 31, Year 2: Second payment made	December 31, Year 3: Final payment made

Table 10.4
Present Value of an Annuity Factors

PERIOD	2.5%	3%	3.5%	4%	4.5%	5%	5.5%	6%	7%	8%	9%	10%	12%	15%
1	0.97561	0.97087	0.96618	0.96154	0.95694	0.95238	0.94787	0.94340	0.93458	0.92593	0.91743	0.90909	0.89286	0.86597
2	1.92742	1.91347	1.89969	1.88609	1.87267	1.85941	1.84632	1.83339	1.80802	1.78326	1.75911	1.73554	1.69005	1.62571
3	2.85602	2.82861	2.80164	2.77509	2.74896	2.72325	2.69793	2.67301	2.62432	2.57710	2.53129	2.48685	2.40183	2.28323
4	3.76197	3.71710	3.67308	3.62990	3.58753	3.54595	3.50515	3.46511	3.38721	3.31213	3.23972	3.16986	3.03735	2.85498
5	4.64583	4.57971	4.51505	4.45182	4.38998	4.32948	4.27028	4.21236	4.10020	3.99271	3.88965	3.79079	3.60478	3.35216
6	5.50813	5.41719	5.32855	5.24214	5.15787	5.07569	4.99553	4.91732	4.76654	4.62288	4.48592	4.35526	4.11141	3.78448
7	6.34939	6.23028	6.11454	6.00205	5.89270	5.78637	5.68297	5.58238	5.38929	5.20637	5.03295	4.86842	4.55376	4.16042
8	7.17014	7.01969	6.87396	6.73274	6.59589	6.46321	6.33457	6.20979	5.97130	5.74664	5.53482	5.33493	4.96764	4.48732
9	7.97087	7.78611	7.60769	7.43533	7.26879	7.10782	6.95220	6.80169	6.51523	6.24689	5.99525	5.75902	5.32825	4.77158
10	8.75206	8.53020	8.31661	8.11090	7.91272	7.72173	7.53763	7.36009	7.02358	6.71008	6.41766	6.14457	5.65022	5.01877
11	9.51421	9.25262	9.00155	8.76048	8.52892	8.30641	8.09254	7.88687	7.49867	7.13696	6.80519	6.49506	5.93770	5.23371
12	10.25776	9.95400	9.66333	9.38507	9.11858	8.86325	8.61852	8.38384	7.94269	7.53608	7.16073	6.81369	6.19437	5.42062
13	10.98318	10.63496	10.30274	9.98565	9.68285	9.39357	9.11706	8.85268	8.35765	7.90378	7.48690	7.10336	6.42355	5.58315
14	11.69091	11.29607	10.92052	10.56312	10.22283	9.89864	9.58965	9.29498	8.74547	8.24424	7.78615	7.36669	6.68217	5.72448
15	12.38138	11.93794	11.51741	11.11839	10.73955	10.37966	10.03758	9.71225	9.10791	8.55948	8.06069	7.60608	6.81086	5.84737
16	13.05500	12.56110	12.09412	11.65230	11.23402	10.83777	10.46216	10.10590	9.44665	8.85137	8.31256	7.82371	6.97399	5.95423
17	13.71220	13.16612	12.65132	12.16567	11.70719	11.27407	10.86461	10.47726	9.76322	9.12164	8.54363	8.02155	7.11963	6.04716
18	14.35336	13.75351	13.18968	12.65930	12.15999	11.68959	11.24607	10.82760	10.05909	9.37189	8.75563	8.20141	7.24967	6.12797
19	14.97889	14.32380	13.70984	13.13394	12.59329	12.08532	11.60765	11.15812	10.33550	9.60350	8.95011	8.36492	7.36578	6.19823
20	15.58916	14.87747	14.21240	13.59033	13.00794	12.46221	11.95038	11.46992	10.59401	9.81815	9.12855	8.51356	7.46944	6.25933
21	16.18455	15.41502	14.69797	14.02916	13.40472	12.82115	12.27524	11.76406	10.83553	10.01680	9.29224	8.64869	7.56200	6.31246
22	16.76541	15.93692	15.16712	14.45112	13.78442	13.16300	12.58317	12.04158	11.06124	10.20074	9.44243	8.77154	7.64465	6.35866
23	17.33211	16.44361	15.62041	14.85684	14.14777	13.48857	12.87504	12.30338	11.27219	10.37106	9.58021	8.88322	7.71843	6.39884
24	17.88499	16.93554	16.05837	15.24696	14.49548	13.79864	13.15170	12.55036	11.46933	10.52876	9.70661	8.98474	7.78432	6.43377
25	18.42438	17.41315	16.48151	15.62208	14.82821	14.09394	13.41393	12.78336	11.65358	10.67478	9.82258	9.07704	7.84314	6.46415
26	18.95061	17.87684	16.89035	15.98277	15.14661	14.37519	13.66250	13.00317	11.82578	10.80998	9.92897	9.16095	7.89566	6.49056
27	19.46401	18.32703	17.28536	16.32959	15.45130	14.64303	13.89810	13.21053	11.98671	10.93516	10.02658	9.23722	7.94255	6.51353
28	19.96489	18.76411	17.66702	16.66306	15.74287	14.89613	14.12142	13.40618	12.13711	11.05108	10.11613	9.30657	7.98442	6.53351
29	20.45355	19.18845	18.03577	16.98371	16.02189	15.14107	14.33310	13.69072	12.27767	11.15841	10.19828	9.36961	8.02181	6.55088
30	20.93029	19.60044	18.39205	17.29203	16.28889	15.37245	14.53375	13.76483	12.40904	11.25778	10.27365	9.42691	8.05518	6.56598
35	23.14516	21.48722	20.00066	18.66461	17.46101	16.37419	15.39055	14.49825	12.94767	11.65457	10.56682	9.64416	8.17550	6.61661
40	25.10278	23.11477	21.35507	19.79277	18.40158	17.16909	16.04612	15.04830	13.33171	11.92461	10.75736	9.77905	8.24378	6.64178

$$PVA = A \times PVAF$$

Table 10.4 lists present value of annuity factors. For the 1969 Chevy illustration, the appropriate PVAF of 2.5771 can be found at the intersection of the 8 percent column and the 3 period row. Again, be sure you understand the literal meaning of that factor. That factor indicates that the present value of a series of $1 payments made at the end of each of the following three years and discounted at an 8 percent rate is equal to approximately $2.57. As you would expect, we arrive at the same present value for this annuity using the complex and simple versions of the present value of an annuity equation. Following is the computation of the present value of the annuity using the simple version of that equation.

$$PVA = A \times PVAF$$
$$PVA = \$500 \times 2.5771$$
$$PVA = \$1,288.55$$

Teaching Note
Point out that the present value of annuity factors in Table 10.4 are the sum of individual present value factors in Table 10.3. For example, the present value of an annuity factor for 5 periods at 5% in Table 10.4 is the sum of the first five present value factors in the 5% column of Table 10.3.

SUMMARY

Current liabilities are obligations that must be paid or otherwise extinguished by a business entity within one year or the entity's operating cycle, whichever is longer. Among the more common types of current liabilities are accounts payable, notes payable, the current portion of long-term debt, deferred revenues, and accrued expenses.

The primary concern of decision makers regarding current liabilities is completeness. Decision makers need to be assured that a business entity has disclosed all of its current liabilities in its financial statements. A related information need of decision makers is the valuation of current liabilities, particularly estimated current liabilities. Decision makers should be provided with sufficient information to determine that such liabilities have been reasonably estimated. Finally, decision makers need to be aware of any unusual and material circumstances related to current liabilities. For instance, if there is substantial doubt that an entity can pay off its current liabilities as they come due, this fact should be disclosed in the entity's financial statement footnotes.

The dollar amount of many current liabilities, such as accounts payable, is defined by a contractual or implied contractual agreement. Generally, such current liabilities do not pose complex accounting issues. Accounting procedures for notes payable differ depending upon whether the notes are interest-bearing or non-interest-bearing. The discount on a non-interest-bearing note is recorded in a contra-liability account when the note is created. Then the discount is written off to interest expense over the term of the note. An example of a current liability that must be estimated is a product warranty liability. When a business sells goods or provides services under a warranty, the entity must rely upon its historical experience to estimate the amount of warranty expense that should be recognized each accounting period. If warranty expense is not reasonably estimated each period, the matching principle is violated.

The current ratio is the primary financial measure that decision makers use to evaluate the liquidity of a business entity. This ratio is computed by dividing current assets by current liabilities. Although current ratios vary considerably from industry to industry, a current ratio of 2.0 is typically considered an average or normal current ratio across all industries.

Many businesses have significant accrued payroll expenses at the end of an accounting period. To provide effective control over payroll-related expenses and liabilities, a payroll register should be used. A payroll register is an accounting record in which a business records key payroll data, such as gross pay, payroll deductions, and net pay, for each employee each payroll period.

Contingent liabilities are not existing liabilities but are instead potential liabilities. Certain contingent liabilities must be recorded as if they are actual liabilities. Other contingent liabilities are simply disclosed in the footnotes of an entity's financial statements or ignored for financial statement purposes.

Accountants can use the time value of money concept to analyze a wide range of transactions and to assign appropriate balance sheet values to certain assets and liabilities. When using the time value of money, accountants compute the present or future value of a single dollar amount or an annuity. An annuity is a series of equal payments made, or received, at equal intervals on which interest is computed on a compound basis.

GLOSSARY

Annuity (p. 442)   A series of equal payments made, or received, at equal intervals on which interest is computed on a compound basis.

Compound interest (p. 439)   Interest computed on the principal amount of a loan (or other financial instrument) and any unpaid interest that has accumulated on the loan since its inception.

Current ratio (p. 432)   Current assets divided by current liabilities; a widely used measure of liquidity.

Future value (p. 439)   The sum of an invested amount plus any interest that will accumulate on that amount on a compound basis over a specified period of time.

Interest (p. 438)   The expense of borrowing money for a specified period, or alternatively, the revenue earned by lending money for a specified period.

Payroll register (p. 433)   An accounting record in which key payroll-related data, such as gross pay, payroll deductions, and net pay, are entered each payroll period for each employee.

Present value (p. 445)   An amount that must be invested currently at some compound rate of interest to produce a given future value.

Simple interest (p. 438)   Interest computed only on the principal amount of a loan (or other financial instrument).

Time value of money concept (p. 438)   The concept that the economic value of a sum of cash to be received or paid is largely a function of the timing of that receipt or payment.

Working capital (p. 432)   The difference between an entity's current assets and current liabilities.

DECISION CASE

Pick up a handful of annual reports and turn to the financial statement footnotes. For most companies, you will find at least a brief description of pending litigation cases. Typically, these disclosures indicate that the pending legal matters are not expected to have a material impact on the company's financial condition or its future operations. However, there are exceptions: In the early 1990s, Shoney's, Inc., agreed to pay more than $100 million over a five-year period to settle several lawsuits alleging that the company had discriminated against racial minorities. At the time, Shoney's had total assets of approximately $470 million.

Assume that you are the CEO of Threlkeld Corporation. Your company has recently been sued for $50 million by a competitor. This competitor alleges that your firm has infringed on certain patents that it owns. Attorneys for your firm believe that there is a fifty-fifty chance that the courts would rule in favor of the competitor if the case goes to trial. The attorneys inform you that your firm will be required to pay either $20 million or $50 million in damages if the competitor wins the case. The amount of the settlement will depend on the court's interpretation of a legal technicality regarding how damages should be computed in such cases. The attorneys believe that the $20 million judgment is much more likely. If damages are awarded to the competitor, the attorneys estimate that there is an 80 percent chance the awarded damages will total $20 million and a 20 percent chance that the damages will total $50 million. Given the probable length of the trial and subsequent appeals, such damages would not be paid for five years.

The CEO of your competitor has recently contacted you. She has offered to resolve this dispute by having your firm immediately pay her company $7 million. Alternatively, she has agreed to resolve the matter by having your firm pay $10 million in $2 million installments. These installments would be made at the end of each of the following five years.

Required: Ignoring taxes and other considerations, which of the following three alternatives is preferable from an economic standpoint for Threlkeld Corporation: taking the matter to court and assuming the risk of paying either $20 million or $50 million in damages five years from now; paying $7 million immediately to settle the dispute; or paying $10 million in $2 million installments over the next five years? (Use an 8 percent interest rate for any time value of money computations.) Defend your answer with the appropriate computations. Besides taxes, what other issues should you consider in making this decision? What type of accounting or financial statement treatment should be given this matter, assuming that Threlkeld Corporation decides against settling the case? Explain.

QUESTIONS

1. Define "liabilities."

2. Define "current liabilities." List several examples of common current liabilities.

3. Identify the two major types of current liabilities.

4. Describe the effects on a company's financial statements when one or more current liabilities are not recorded.

5. Identify key information needs of decision makers regarding current liabilities.

6. What is the difference between an account payable and a note payable?

7. Explain how an interest-bearing note payable and a non-interest-bearing note payable differ.

8. What type of account is Discount on Notes Payable? What is the purpose of this account?

9. Why are deferred revenues considered current liabilities?

10. Do "accrued expenses" appear on the balance sheet, the income statement, or both? Explain.

11. What is the purpose of a product warrant liability?

12. Provide at least two examples of companies you are familiar with that likely have a product warranty liability included in their balance sheets.

13. Briefly describe how a company's vacation pay liability at the end of an accounting period is determined.

14. Describe the items that employers commonly deduct from their employees' paychecks.

15. Besides salaries expense and wages expense, what additional payroll-related costs do companies commonly incur?

16. List the equation used to compute the current ratio. How is the current ratio typically used?

17. What constitutes a company's working capital? Explain briefly why decision makers closely monitor the amount of working capital maintained by a company.

18. Describe the information commonly found in a company's payroll register. How does a payroll register help a business maintain control over its payroll function?

19. Define "contingent liabilities."

20. Identify the two factors that must be considered when determining how to account for a contingent liability.

21. What are the two most common types of contingent liabilities reported by public companies?

22. Define the "time value of money concept."

23. Provide several specific examples of situations involving businesses in which the time value of money concept is relevant.

24. Define "interest." Distinguish between simple interest and compound interest.

25. What is a "future value"? A "present value"?

26. "The more frequently interest is compounded, the greater the resulting future value." Explain the meaning of this phrase.

27. What is an annuity? Identify the two key parameters of a future value of an annuity table and a present value of an annuity table.

EXERCISES

28. Accounting for Current Liabilities (LO 2)

FreeWheelers is a bike shop located near the campus of the University of Tennessee. FreeWheelers rents bikes on a nine-month basis. When a student rents a bike, he or she pays a security deposit equal to 50 percent of the bike's value. Typically, a bike is returned damaged in some way, causing some portion of the security deposit to be forfeited. When a security deposit is received, FreeWheelers' accountant debits Cash and credits Miscellaneous Revenue. If a bike is returned damaged, the accountant debits Repairs Expense and credits Cash or another appropriate account when the bike is repaired. Any portion of the deposit that was not required to repair the bike is returned to the student. Deposit amounts returned to students are recorded with a debit to Miscellaneous Expense and a credit to Cash.

Required:

28. No check figures

Write a brief memo to FreeWheelers' accountant regarding the accounting treatment given security deposits on bike rentals. Explain why this accounting treatment is incorrect and how it may introduce errors into the business's financial statements. Also recommend a more appropriate method of accounting for security deposits.

29. Liability Classification (LO 1, 2)

Hamilton's Bakery borrowed $50,000 on January 1, 1993. The repayment terms require Hamilton's to repay $5,000 of the principal amount of the loan on December 31 of each year, beginning December 31, 1993, plus 10 percent interest on the unpaid principal at the beginning of each year.

Required:

1. How will this debt be reported on Hamilton's December 31, 1996, balance sheet? How much interest expense related to this debt will be reported on Hamilton's income statement for the year ended December 31, 1996?
2. What distinguishes current liabilities from long-term liabilities under generally accepted accounting principles?
3. Suppose that Hamilton's fails to classify any portion of the outstanding bank loan as a current liability in its December 31, 1997, balance sheet. How will this error affect decision makers' analysis of the company's financial statements? Explain.

29. 1. Interest, $3,500

30. **Accounting for an Interest-Bearing Note Payable** (LO 2)

Lasiter Homebuilders borrowed $10,000 from a local bank on October 2. On that date, Lasiter's chief executive signed a 10 percent, 180-day interest-bearing promissory note.

Required:

Prepare the appropriate journal entries in Lasiter's accounting records on the following dates:

1. October 2
2. December 31, the business's fiscal year-end
3. March 31, the date the note matures

30. 1. 12/31 Interest Exp., $250
3/31 Interest Exp., $250

31. **Accounting for a Non-Interest-Bearing Note Payable** (LO 2)

Chong & Lewis, Computer Consultants, borrowed $40,000 from a local bank on August 15. The promissory note signed by Chong & Lewis's chief executive was non-interest-bearing and had a term of 120 days. The discount rate charged Chong & Lewis by the bank was 12 percent.

Required:

Prepare the appropriate journal entries in Chong & Lewis's accounting records on the following dates:

1. August 15
2. October 31, the final day of Chong & Lewis's fiscal year
3. The maturity date of the note

31. 1. 8/15 Discount, $1,600
10/31 Interest Exp., $1,026.67
12/13 Interest Exp. $573.33

32. **Accounting for an Interest-Bearing Note Payable** (LO 2)

On December 1, 1995, Andersen Gardening bought a new computer for $4,000 from Computer Village. In exchange, Andersen signed a $4,000, 12 percent promissory note with a 180-day term. Andersen's fiscal year coincides with the calendar year.

Required:

1. Prepare the appropriate journal entries related to this computer purchase in Andersen's accounting records on the following dates: December 1, December 31, 1995, and the date the note matures.
2. On the date that Andersen purchased the computer, the business had a cash balance of $8,000 on which it was earning interest at an annual rate of approximately 5 percent. What may have prompted Andersen to sign a 12 percent promissory note in payment for the computer instead of paying cash?

32. 1. 12/31 Interest Exp., $40
5/29 Interest Exp., $200

33. **Recording Sales Taxes** (LO 2)

In Bullhead City there is an 8 percent sales tax applicable to all retail sales. Suppose that Price Department Store in Bullhead City has total receipts, including sales taxes, of $16,200 on September 28.

Required:

33. 1. Sales Tax, $1,200

1. Determine the amount of sales revenue and sales taxes included in the $16,200.
2. Prepare the summary journal entry in Price's accounting records to record the September 28 receipts.
3. Why are sales taxes collected by a retailer not considered revenue?

34. Recording Warranty Expense (LO 2)

The bikes sold by Jim's Bike Shop carry a one-year warranty on labor and parts. Since Jim, the bike shop's owner, has experienced craftspeople assembling and fine-tuning the bikes, he expects very few warranty claims. Last year, Jim's Bike Shop sold two hundred bikes and made warranty repairs on three bikes at a total cost of approximately $500.

Required:

34. No check figures

1. If Jim's Bike Shop fails to record a product warranty liability at the end of each fiscal year, how will the business's financial statements be affected? What accounting concepts or principles will be violated?
2. Under what condition or conditions could Jim reasonably argue that his business does not have to record a product warranty liability at year-end?

35. Accounting for Vacation Pay Liability (LO 2)

Hobbs Company grants its employees two weeks of paid vacation each year. As a general rule, 80 percent of the vacation pay earned by Hobbs's employees is eventually paid. Hobbs's payroll was $512,400 for the most recent two-week payroll period, which ended March 9.

Required:

35. 1. $16,396.80

1. Compute the amount of vacation pay earned by the employees of Hobbs Company for the payroll period ending on March 9.
2. Prepare the journal entry to record vacation pay expense for the payroll period ending on March 9.
3. Suppose that the actual vacation pay received by Hobbs's employees for the payroll period ending on August 8 totaled $82,300. Prepare the journal entry to record this vacation pay.

36. Payroll Accounting (LO 2)

Khalid Company pays its employees every two weeks. The firm just completed its fiscal year on September 30. Prior to year-end, the company last paid its employees on September 20. For the last ten days of the fiscal year, the employees of Khalid Company earned gross pay (salaries) of $8,200. Listed next are total employee payroll deductions and Khalid's payroll-related expenses, other than salaries paid to employees, for the period September 21–30.

	EMPLOYEE PAYROLL DEDUCTIONS	EMPLOYER PAYROLL- RELATED EXPENSES
FICA Taxes	$ 627	$627
Federal Income Taxes	2,010	
State Income Taxes	311	
Health Insurance	225	225
State Unemployment Taxes		190
Federal Unemployment Taxes		50
Contribution to Employee Pension Fund		410

Required:

36. 1. Net Pay, $5,027
  2. Payroll Tax Exp., $867
    Fringe Ben. Exp., $635

1. Prepare the adjusting journal entry required on September 30 to record the unpaid salaries expense of Khalid on that date and the related employee payroll deductions.

2. Prepare the adjusting journal entries required on September 30 to record Khalid's unpaid payroll taxes and unpaid fringe benefits.
3. Why aren't payroll taxes withheld from employees' salaries considered an expense by Khalid Company?

37. Recognizing Warranty Expense (LO 2)

Haroldson, Inc.'s, revenues for the current year are nearly 20 percent below last year's level. As year-end approaches, the company president has instructed the accounting department not to record a December 31 adjusting entry for warranty expense on product sales. "We can recognize that expense next year when we actually pay those costs. That makes more sense anyway. Why go to the trouble of estimating additional expenses at year-end? We have more than enough of the real thing."

Required:

In a written memo, remind Haroldson's president why it is necessary to recognize estimated warranty expense at the end of an accounting period. In your memo, point out how the company's financial statements will be misrepresented if this expense is not recorded.

37. No check figures

38. Working Capital and the Current Ratio (LO 3)

Following are the current assets and current liabilities of the Laoretti Cigar Company for the fiscal years ending December 31, 1994 and 1995.

	DECEMBER 31,	
	1994	1995
Cash and Cash Equivalents	$ 54,817	$ 48,902
Accounts Receivable	63,295	59,748
Inventories	116,528	121,277
Other Current Assets	18,605	15,691
Total Current Assets	$253,245	$245,618
Accounts Payable	$ 71,430	$ 73,819
Accrued Payroll	26,608	28,456
Income Taxes Payable	12,089	11,572
Total Current Liabilities	$110,127	$113,847

Required:

1. Determine this company's working capital and current ratio as of December 31, 1994 and 1995.
2. Did the company's liquidity position improve or deteriorate between the end of 1994 and the end of 1995? Explain.

38. 1.   1994   1995
Working Cap.
    $143,118 $131,771
Current Ratio,
    2.3   2.2

39. Working Capital and the Current Ratio (LO 3)

The following table contains selected financial information for Conestoga, Inc. for the fiscal years ending December 31, 1995 and 1996.

	DECEMBER 31,	
	1995	1996
Current Assets	$250,000	?
Current Liabilities	?	$150,000
Working Capital	110,000	?
Current Ratio	?	2.15

Required:

1. Determine the missing amounts in this table.
2. Is the quick ratio, the current ratio, or working capital the best measure of a company's liquidity? Defend your answer.

39. 1.   Current Liab., $140,000
     Current Ratio, 1.79
     Current Assets, $322,500
     Working Cap., $172,500

40. Accounting for Contingent Liabilities (LO 5)

Saddleback Sporting Goods, Inc., manufactures and sells a unique recreational footwear product, a convertible ice skate/roller blade. Periodically, the company is sued because someone using this product is injured. Saddleback is currently the defendant in one such lawsuit. The damages requested by the plaintiff in this lawsuit total $2,400,000. The company's net income for its fiscal year just ended was $460,000; the company's total assets at year-end were $1,232,000.

Required:

40. No check figures

1. What factors should Saddleback consider in determining the accounting and financial statement treatment of this lawsuit?
2. In reference to the pending lawsuit against Saddleback, identify the conditions under which:
   a. Saddleback would be required to record an expense and a liability in its accounting records.
   b. Saddleback would be required to disclose the lawsuit in the footnotes to its financial statements.
   c. Saddleback could ignore the lawsuit for accounting and financial reporting purposes.

41. Internal Controls over Payroll (LO 4)

Reread the Spotlight on Ethics vignette in this chapter titled "Payroll Padding: A Case of Dodger Blue."

Required:

41. No check figures

Write a brief memo to the management of the Dodgers that identifies at least three specific internal control procedures that might have prevented or detected the fraud perpetrated against the organization. You may find it helpful to review the internal control material in Chapter 3 before drafting this memo.

42. Compound Interest (LO 6)

Suppose that you have $5,000 to invest for five years. Because you are a conservative investor, you decide to purchase a certificate of deposit (CD) with your nest egg. You have identified the following five-year CDs being offered by local banks.

Jefferson Bank:	10 percent, interest compounded annually
Lincoln Bank:	11 percent, simple interest
Truman Bank:	9 percent, interest compounded semiannually
Washington Bank:	10 percent, interest compounded quarterly

42. FV
Jeff. 8,052.55
Lincoln 7,750.00
Trum. 7,764.85
Wash. 8,193.10

Required:

In which CD will you invest? Why?

43. Future Value of an Annuity (LO 6)

Ben Campbell is the sole owner of Nighthorse Industries, a manufacturing firm. Campbell wants to double Nighthorse's production capacity by building another factory. His plan is to begin making annual deposits in a money market fund to accumulate the $4 million needed to finance the construction of the new factory. Suppose that Campbell needs to have the $4 million available at the end of seven years and that he can earn 7 percent compound interest on deposits made in the money market fund.

Required:

43. 1. $462,212.94 per year

1. Ignoring other considerations, how much must Campbell deposit in the money market fund each year for the next seven years to accumulate the $4 million needed to build the factory?

2. How would income taxes that Campbell must pay on interest revenue earned on the money market fund affect his plan to accumulate the $4 million within seven years? Explain.

44. Present Value of a Single Amount (LO 6)

Jim Gilliam is a major league baseball player. In the salary contract Jim's agent just negotiated, Jim will receive an annual salary plus a one-time payment of $1 million on his fortieth birthday—Jim recently celebrated his twenty-eighth birthday.

Required:

Compute the present value of the lump sum payment to be made to Jim Gilliam on his fortieth birthday using a discount rate of 10 percent.

44. $318,630

45. Present Value of an Annuity

Wally Moon, the sole owner of Ebbets Enterprises, recently lost a lawsuit filed against him by a competitor, Cyndy Garvey. The judge in this case ruled that Wally must pay Cyndy $7,500 at the end of each of the following ten years.

Required:

Cyndy needs cash now, so she has offered Wally a deal. Rather than Wally paying her $75,000 over the next ten years, Cyndy has offered to accept a lump sum payment of $55,000. How can Wally determine whether this is a "good deal" for himself? Identify the specific circumstances under which this arrangement qualifies as a good deal for Wally.

45. No check figures

46. Use of a Payroll Register (LO 4)

Dick and Lucy Tracewski own a small trucking company that they established ten years ago. Initially, Dick and Lucy were not only the owners of the company but also represented its entire work force. Now the company has two office employees, ten drivers, and six dockworkers. Lucy has maintained the company's accounting records since the firm was established. At first, Lucy's accounting system for the trucking company consisted only of a general journal and a general ledger. Over the years, she has gradually added other accounting records, including a cash receipts journal and a cash disbursement journal. One accounting record she does not maintain is a payroll register. In recent years, Lucy has experienced increasing difficulty keeping track of all the data needed to prepare the weekly payroll for the company's sixteen employees.

Required:

Write a memo to Lucy explaining the nature of a payroll register and how one is usually formatted. Also include in your memo a discussion of how a payroll register can enhance a business's control over its payroll function. In this discussion, identify specific errors or problems that a payroll register can help prevent.

46. No check figures

PROBLEM SET A

47. Accounting for Interest-Bearing vs. Non-Interest-Bearing Note Payable (LO 2)

On April 1, a local bike club, Canadian River Racing Club (CRRC), approached Jim's Bike Shop with a proposal to buy on credit ten racing bikes with a cash price of $750 each. CRRC offered the bike shop two alternative payment plans. Under the first payment plan, CRRC would make a down payment of $2,000. The remainder of the purchase price would be satisfied with a non-interest-bearing one-year note with a principal amount of $6,000. (For accounting purposes, CRRC would use an 8 percent discount rate to record this note payable.)

The second payment plan involved a $2,000 down payment and a $5,500, 8 percent interest-bearing note. The interest and principal on this note would be due in one year.

Required:

1. Prepare the appropriate journal entries in the accounting records of CRRC on the following dates, assuming that the first payment plan is accepted.
   a. April 1, the date the sales agreement is finalized
   b. December 31, the final day of CRRC's fiscal year
   c. April 1 of the following year when the note matures
2. Prepare the appropriate journal entries in the accounting records of CRRC on the following dates, assuming that the second payment plan is accepted.
   a. April 1, the date the sales agreement is finalized
   b. December 31, the final day of CRRC's fiscal year
   c. April 1 of the following year when the note matures

48. **Current Ratio and Working Capital** (LO 1, 3)

Following are the current assets and current liabilities for two recent years of two companies involved in food-related industries. Hormel Foods Corporation is a major manufacturer and distributor of prepared foods. Bob Evans Farms, Inc., operates more than three hundred restaurants located in nineteen states.

Hormel Food Corporation:

	1993	1994
	(IN THOUSANDS)	
Cash and Cash Equivalents	$157,558	$248,599
Short-Term Marketable Securities	14,862	11,360
Accounts Receivable	218,487	228,369
Inventories	208,101	199,243
Deferred Income Taxes	12,393	14,213
Prepaid Expenses	8,503	6,431
Total Current Assets	$619,904	$708,215
Accounts Payable	$ 98,357	$112,851
Accrued Expenses	30,212	29,320
Accrued Advertising	24,587	31,863
Employee Compensation	40,195	41,989
Taxes, Other than Federal Income Taxes	14,011	17,606
Dividends Payable	8,434	9,585
Federal Income Taxes	11,262	21,303
Current Portion of Long-Term Debt	0	400
Total Current Liabilities	$227,058	$264,917

Bob Evans Farms, Inc.:

	1993	1994
	(IN THOUSANDS)	
Cash	$ 8,241	$ 6,699
Investments	1,947	1,399
Accounts Receivable	12,545	15,445
Inventories	14,814	15,799
Deferred Income Taxes	4,249	4,585
Prepaid Expenses	3,371	3,514
Total Current Assets	$45,167	$47,441

Answer key (margin):

47. 1a. Dr. Discount $480
    1b. Dr. Int. Exp. $360
    1c. Dr. Int. Exp. $120
    2a. Dr. Bikes $5,500
    2b. Dr. Int. Exp. $330
    2c. Dr. Int. Exp. $110

Line of Credit	$ 0	$ 9,500
Accounts Payable	9,530	12,200
Dividends Payable	2,618	2,839
Federal and State Income Taxes	7,597	6,160
Accrued Wages and Related Liabilities	10,163	10,830
Other Accrued Expenses	17,185	18,023
Total Current Liabilities	$47,093	$59,552

Required:

1. Compute the following items for both companies for 1993 and 1994:
   a. Working Capital
   b. Current Ratio
   c. Quick Ratio (discussed in Chapter 7)
2. Which of these two companies has the stronger liquidity position in 1993 and 1994, given the data computed in Part 1? Why?
3. In your opinion, which of the three measures you computed is the best measure of liquidity? Defend your answer.
4. Review the data presented for each company. Are there any unusual items or unusual relationships in either company's data that a decision maker might want to investigate further? If so, identify these items and the issues or questions that decision makers would likely raise.

49. **Accounting for Contingent Liabilities** (LO 1, 5)

Consider the following three scenarios involving publicly owned companies in the United States.

Scenario A:

One of the four wholly owned subsidiaries of Option Plastics, Inc., is located in the South American country of San Turcia. Recent elections in the country have brought to power a political party that intends to nationalize all major businesses. The new president of San Turcia has indicated that the government will pay a "reasonable price" for these businesses. The manager of the San Turcia subsidiary estimates that Option Plastics will suffer a loss, based upon U.S. accounting standards, of between $4 million and $6 million when the government buys out the subsidiary sometime in the next several years.

Scenario B:

Charles Ironworks has just been slapped with a $5.5 million fine by the Environmental Protection Agency (EPA). The company's legal counsel intends to contest the fine. When asked to evaluate the company's chances of overturning the EPA fine, the company's chief legal counsel responded, "I think there's a 50–50 chance that we can get the fine reduced. But I have no idea if we can reduce the fine by $2 or by $2 million."

Scenario C:

Joy's Toys manufactures a wide range of toys designed for children one to four years of age. This past week, Joy's Toys was sued for $17.2 million by a competitor for allegedly infringing on that company's patent on a very popular toy. In a press release, the chief executive of Joy's Toys observed, "This suit is complete nonsense. Our competitor knows that we haven't infringed on its patent. Our toy is different in several respects than theirs. All this company is trying to do is harass us."

Required:

1. Evaluate each of the three scenarios in reference to the accounting and financial reporting guidelines for contingent liabilities. How would you recom-

48. 1a.	1993	1994
Hormel	$392,846	$443,298
Bob Evans	-$1,926	-$12,111
1b.	1993	1994
Hormel	2.73	2.67
Bob Evans	0.96	0.80
1c.	1993	1994
Hormel	1.72	1.84
Bob Evans	0.48	0.40

49. No check figures

mend that each company account for each item and/or report each item in its financial statements? Support your recommendation for each scenario.

2. Do companies have an incentive to intentionally downplay the significance of contingent liabilities and thus exclude them from their financial statements? Explain. If this occurs, what is the impact on decision makers who rely on financial statement data?

50. **Accounting for Product Warranty Liability** (LO 2)
Cool Air, Inc., wholesales air conditioners and related products to retail stores. The company's products are sold with a one-year warranty covering parts and labor. The following table lists the company's three major product lines, the percentage of the products sold in each product line that are returned while under warranty, and the average warranty-related cost incurred on each returned item.

PRODUCT LINE	PERCENTAGE OF PRODUCTS SOLD THAT ARE RETURNED WHILE UNDER WARRANTY	WARRANTY COST PER RETURNED ITEM
Air Conditioners	8%	$120
Air Compressors	6%	50
Fans	3%	18

During the month of April, the following number of products were sold by product line:

Air Conditioners	2,400
Air Compressors	1,650
Fans	1,500

Required:
1. Compute the estimated product warranty expense that should be recorded at the end of April and prepare the appropriate adjusting entry to record this expense and the related product warranty liability.
2. Suppose that during one week in May, the company pays warranty-related costs of $7,100. Prepare the entry to record these payments.

51. **Time Value of Money Applications: Single Amounts** (LO 6)
Following are three scenarios involving time value of money applications for single dollar amounts. In each scenario, interest is compounded annually. Ignore tax considerations.

Scenario A:
Today, Roseboro Farms lost a lawsuit. The business has been ordered to pay the plaintiff $200,000 two years from today's date and $300,000 four years from today's date.

Scenario B:
Phyllis Regan replaces the delivery truck for her retail furniture store every five years. Phyllis estimates that the truck she will purchase in five years will cost approximately $30,000.

Scenario C:
Wes Parker recently decided to sell the convenience store he owns. Parker believes that the business is worth $90,000. Joe Pepitone wants to purchase Parker's convenience store. Pepitone has offered to sign a $120,000 non-interest-bearing promissory note in payment for the store.

Required:
1. Scenario A: Roseboro Farms would prefer to resolve this matter immediately by paying the plaintiff the present value of the judgment rendered against

50. 1. $28,800

51. 1. $403,558
2. $20,417.40
3. No. PV = $89,671.20

it by the court. How much should the plaintiff be willing to accept as a lump sum payment from Roseboro if the appropriate interest rate for this scenario is 7 percent?

2. Scenario B: How much must Phyllis deposit in an 8 percent certificate of deposit presently to accumulate the $30,000 she will need to purchase a new delivery truck in five years?

3. Scenario C: If the appropriate interest rate in this scenario is 6 percent and Pepitone has suggested a five-year term for the promissory note, is this a "good deal" for Parker? Explain.

52. **Time Value of Money Applications: Annuities** (LO 6)

Following are three scenarios involving time value of money applications for annuities. In each scenario, interest is compounded annually. Ignore tax considerations.

Scenario A:

Tommy Davis owns a local plumbing supply business. Tommy plans to build a second store on the other side of town but does not have sufficient cash to finance the project and he doesn't want to borrow the required funds.

Scenario B:

Lou Johnson is retiring after working forty years as a dentist in the small town of Purdy. Lou wants to sell his practice to another dentist and believes that a fair price for the practice is $140,000.

Scenario C:

Maurine Wills is planning to purchase the local hardware store. She has offered to pay the present owner of the store either $100,000 in cash, or $10,000 per year at the end of each of the next fifteen years.

Required:

1. Scenario A: If Tommy needs $100,000 to build the store, how much must he deposit in his savings account at the end of each year over the next five years to accumulate the needed funds? Tommy's bank pays him interest of 7 percent annually on his savings account.

2. Scenario B: Assume that another dentist agrees to purchase Lou's practice for $140,000. However, the total amount received by Lou for his practice will exceed $140,000, since the two parties agree on a ten-year payment plan. The other dentist will pay for the practice in a series of equal annual installments over the next ten years. (The first payment is to be made one year from the date the sales agreement is finalized.) If the two parties agree that an 8 percent interest rate should be applied to this transaction, determine how much Lou will receive at the end of each of the following ten years.

3. Scenario C: Suppose that the appropriate interest rate for this scenario is 5.5 percent. Should the hardware owner accept the $100,000 lump sum payment, or the payment plan structured as an annuity? Will your answer change if the appropriate interest rate for this scenario is 7 percent? Explain.

52. 1. $17,389.07 per year
2. $20,864.13 per year
3. PV Pmt. Plan 5.5%,$100,375.80 PV Pmt. Plan 7.0%, $91,079.10

PROBLEM SET B

53. **Accounting for Interest-Bearing vs. Non-Interest-Bearing Note Payable** (LO 2)

On September 30 of the current year, Jim Ed Brown, owner of B & B Farms, was negotiating with the owner of the local John Deere dealership to purchase a tractor. Presently, the dealer is running a special on the few remaining tractors from the previous model year. For these tractors, the dealer is offering his customers one year of free interest. If a customer makes a 20 percent downpayment, he or she will be allowed to pay the remaining balance of the purchase price one year from the date of purchase. Customers will be required to sign a promissory note formally recognizing this obligation. For the tractors of the current model year, customers must also make a 20 percent downpayment. The balance of the purchase price of one of these tractors is placed on a 9 percent, one-year interest-bearing promissory note with both principal and interest due on the note's maturity date.

Jim Ed Brown has narrowed his choices down to two tractors. The first tractor, Model T, is from the previous model year. This tractor has a list price of $21,500, but the dealer will sell it for $20,000. The second tractor, Model A, is from the current model year. This tractor has a list price of $21,800. Since Jim Ed seems particularly interested in the Model A, the dealer offers to make a "sacrifice" just because Jim Ed is such a good customer. He will sell the Model A to Jim for $19,000. (Note: If Jim Ed purchases the Model T, he will apply a 9 percent discount rate for accounting purposes to the non-interest-bearing note he signs.)

Required:

1. Prepare the appropriate journal entries in the accounting records of B & B Farms on the following dates, assuming that Jim Ed purchases the Model A and makes a 20 percent downpayment.
   a. September 30, the date the sales agreement is finalized
   b. December 31, the final day of B & B Farms' fiscal year
   c. September 30 of the following year when the note matures
2. Prepare the appropriate journal entries in the accounting records of B & B Farms on the following dates, assuming that Jim Ed purchases the Model T and makes a 20 percent downpayment.
   a. September 30, the date the sales agreement is finalized
   b. December 31, the final day of B & B Farms' fiscal year
   c. September 30 of the following year when the note matures

53. 1a. Dr. Equip. $19,000
1b. Dr. Int. Exp. $342
1c. Dr. Int. Exp. $1026
2a. Dr. Discount $1,440
2b. Dr. Int. Exp. $360
2c. Dr. Int. Exp. $1,080

54. Current Ratio and Working Capital (LO 1, 3)

Following are the current assets and current liabilities of Biogen, Inc., a leading biotechnology company, at the end of each year from 1991 through 1994. Amounts presented are in thousands.

	1991	1992	1993	1994
Cash and Cash Equivalents	$ 56,647	$ 85,863	$ 74,546	$ 54,682
Short-Term Investments	129,343	142,025	195,805	213,120
Accounts Receivable	18,389	33,415	31,695	18,502
Other	4,785	7,144	7,378	8,480
Total Current Assets	$209,164	$268,447	$309,424	$294,784
Accounts Payable	3,169	3,896	2,916	9,991
Accrued Expenses	10,907	22,343	28,860	37,937
Total Current Liabilities	$ 14,076	$ 26,239	$ 31,776	$ 47,928

Required:

1. Compute the following items for Biogen for each year from 1991 through 1994.

a. Working Capital
b. Current Ratio
c. Quick Ratio (discussed in Chapter 7)
2. Evaluate this company's liquidity over this four-year period. Was it strong or poor, improving or deteriorating? What other information would be helpful in evaluating Biogen's liquidity over this time period?
3. Suppose that in early 1995 you were an investor considering a purchase of Biogen's common stock. What questions would you have wanted to pose to Biogen's executives, given the financial data presented and the financial measures you computed?

54. 1a.   1991, $195,088
        1992, $242,208
        1993, $277,648
        1994, $246,856
    1b.   1991, 14.86
        1992, 10.23
        1993, 9.74
        1994, 6.15
    1c.   1991, 14.52
        1992, 9.96
        1993, 9.51
        1994, 5.97

55. **Accounting for Contingent Liabilities** (LO 1, 5)
Consider the following three scenarios involving publicly owned companies in the United States.

Scenario A:
The financial consulting firm of Kasulis & Kenderine has been sued recently for $4.4 million for failing to provide a safe workplace for its employees. One month ago, an employee of the firm slipped and fell on a banana peel near the front door of the firm. The chief executive of Kasulis & Kenderine maintains that her firm has no liability to the individual since three witnesses have testified that the employee "staged" the accident.

Scenario B:
Jameson Exploration, Inc., an oil and gas exploration company, has been sued by a group of shrimp fishermen for an oil spill off the coast of Louisiana. The suit is asking for damages of $3.3 million; however, Jameson's chief executive has publicly stated that his company will likely settle the suit for between $2 and $2.5 million.

Scenario C:
Louis & Fred's Diners has been named as the defendant in a class action lawsuit filed by representatives of an ethnic group who allegedly have been systematically discriminated against by the firm. In responding to this lawsuit, the company's chief executive observed, "We are totally innocent of these charges. Nevertheless, our firm may have to spend several million dollars fighting this lawsuit in court."

Required:
1. Evaluate each of the three scenarios in reference to the accounting and financial reporting guidelines for contingent liabilities. How would you recommend that each company account for each item and/or report each item in its financial statements? Support your recommendation for each scenario.
2. Do companies have an incentive to intentionally downplay the significance of contingent liabilities and thus exclude them from their financial statements? Explain. If this occurs, what is the impact on decision makers who rely on financial statement data?

55. No check figures

56. **Accounting for Product Warranty Liability** (LO 2)
Standridge Farm Supply sells farm equipment through several retail outlets in western Kansas. Several of the company's products are sold with a one-year warranty covering parts and labor. Listed in the following table are the products sold under warranty, the percentage of each type of product sold that is returned while under warranty, and the average warranty-related cost incurred on each returned item.

PRODUCT LINE	PERCENTAGE OF PRODUCTS SOLD THAT ARE RETURNED WHILE UNDER WARRANTY	WARRANTY COST PER RETURNED ITEM
Tractors	20%	$ 600
Plows	4%	130
Combines	25%	1,300
Irrigation Equipment	10%	450

During the month of March, Standridge sold the following number of items covered by a warranty:

Tractors	45
Plows	125
Combines	12
Irrigation Equipment	70

Required:

56. 1. $13,100

1. Compute the estimated product warranty expense that should be recognized at the end of March. Also prepare the appropriate adjusting journal entry to record this expense and the related product warranty liability.
2. Suppose that during one week in June, Standridge pays total warranty-related costs of $2,800. Prepare the entry to record these costs.

57. Time Value of Money Applications: Single Amounts (LO 6)

Following are three scenarios involving time value of money applications for single dollar amounts. In each scenario, interest is compounded annually. Ignore tax considerations.

Scenario A:

Richardson Real Estate, Inc., leases the present building in which its offices are located. The company wants to construct an office building of its own and believes that $164,000 will be required for this project. The company presently has $100,000 that it can invest in a savings account earning interest at 7 percent.

Scenario B:

Tresh Lumberyard Company is selling a used forklift on credit to a local home-builder. The customer is currently strapped for cash and would like to pay for the forklift in three years after she completes a residential development project. She agrees to sign a three-year, non-interest-bearing promissory note in payment for the forklift. (The cash price of the forklift is $15,000.)

Scenario C:

Ford Electric Contractors is selling five used service vehicles. The company has received two bids for these vehicles. The first bid is a cash offer of $64,000 from Kubek Supply. The second bid is from Skowron Used Cars. Skowron has offered to pay Ford $90,000 for the service vehicles in a series of three payments. The first payment would be $20,000 in two years, the second payment would be $30,000 in three years, and the final payment would be $40,000 in four years.

Required:

57. 1. 7–8 years
   2. $18,895.65
   3. Skowron's; PV = $68,336.20

1. Scenario A: If Richardson immediately invests the $100,000 in the savings account, how many years will it take for the savings account to have a balance of $164,000?
2. Scenario B: If Tresh charges its customers interest at 8 percent on their unpaid balances, what should be the maturity value of the three-year, non-interest-bearing note that the customer will sign in payment for the forklift?

3. Scenario C: If the appropriate interest rate in this scenario is 9 percent, which bid should Ford accept? Besides time value of money considerations, what other factors should Ford consider in making this decision?

58. Time Value of Money Applications: Annuities (LO 6)

Following are three scenarios involving time value of money applications for annuities. In each scenario, interest is compounded annually. Ignore tax considerations.

Scenario A:

Berra Bookstores has a "balloon payment" due on a loan that it obtained several years ago from a local finance company. The balloon payment is $80,000 and is due in four years. Berra has created a savings account in which it will make annual deposits at the end of each of the following four years for the purpose of accumulating the $80,000 needed to make this payment.

Scenario B:

Cleta Boyer owns the Bronx Carloading Company (BCC). Recently, Cleta decided to retire. She has received the following three bids for her company:

Bid A $50,000 down payment plus 20 annual payments of $15,000
Bid B $70,000 down payment plus 15 annual payments of $14,000
Bid C $90,000 down payment plus 10 annual payments of $10,000

In each case, the down payment would be made on the date the sales agreement is finalized. The first annual payment under each bid would be made one year following that date.

Scenario C:

Elston Howard was seriously injured while working for his employer, Pinstripe Suit Manufacturers. He is presently negotiating to resolve this matter. The employer has offered to pay Elston $40,000 per year for the remainder of his life. Mortality tables used by the insurance industry indicate that Elston should live approximately twenty-five more years. Elston prefers to receive a lump sum payment.

Required:

1. Scenario A: If Berra earns 10 percent interest on its savings account, how much must it deposit in that account each year to accumulate the $80,000 needed for the balloon payment coming due in four years?
2. Scenario B: Suppose that the appropriate interest rate for this scenario is 10 percent. Which offer should Cleta accept?
3. Scenario C: What lump sum payment would be equivalent to the present value of the annuity offered to Elston by his employer assuming that a 9 percent interest rate is appropriate for this scenario? What other factors should Elston consider in choosing between the annuity and a lump sum payment? Explain.

58. 1. $17,237.66 per year
    2. Bid A
       PV Bid A, $177,703.70
       PV Bid B, $176,485.12
       PV Bid C, $151,445.70
    3. $392,903.20

CASES

59. Non-Interest-Bearing Note Payable

Howard Metzen recently purchased a used, twin-engine Cessna from a plane dealer, Baum's & Whey, in Cleveland. To finance the deal, Howard borrowed $100,000 from a Cleveland bank. Howard signed a $100,000, non-interest-bearing promissory note that comes due in one year. The discount rate applied to the note was 12 percent, meaning that Howard received only $88,000. A few days after signing the promissory note, Joel, a friend of Howard's, informed him that he had been "ripped off" by the bank. Why? Because according to Joel the true, or effective, interest rate on the bank loan is greater than 12 percent.

Required:
1. Explain Joel's reasoning, using a numerical example.
2. Was Howard "ripped off" by his bank? Explain.

60. **International Classification of Liabilities**

In the United States, current liabilities are debts and other obligations of a business that must be paid during the coming year or operating cycle, whichever is longer. As noted in this chapter, in Sweden current liabilities are simply those liabilities that must be paid in the coming year. Swedish accounting rules generally do not recognize the operating cycle concept when classifying current assets or current liabilities.

Assume that two shipbuilding companies have similar operations, except that one is located in the United States and one is located in a foreign country. In this latter country, current assets generally include cash and other short-term assets that will be converted into cash in the coming year; current liabilities are those short-term liabilities that must be paid in the coming year. That is, the operating cycle concept is not recognized when classifying current assets and current liabilities. Each company complies with the accounting principles of its own country and each company has an operating cycle of three years. These companies have approximately the same annual revenues each year and approximately the same amount of total assets. Following are selected financial data for these companies.

	YANKEE SHIPBUILDERS*	VIKING SHIPS*	VIKING SHIPS**
Current Assets:			
Cash	$ 3,040,000	$ 5,276,000	$ 5,276,000
Short-Term Investments	9,222,000	$ 8,322,000	6,703,000
Accounts Receivable	68,609,000	72,555,000	33,808,000
Inventories	111,278,000	103,392,000	33,067,000
Prepaid Expenses	8,231,000	16,449,000	4,611,000
Total	$200,380,000	$205,994,000	$ 83,465,000
Current Liabilities:			
Accounts Payable	$ 55,242,000	$ 51,002,000	$ 47,224,000
Accrued Expenses	32,139,000	38,864,000	34,375,000
Notes Payable	107,878,000	91,053,000	62,630,000
Total	$195,259,000	$180,919,000	$144,229,000

* Compiled in accordance with GAAP.
**Compiled in accordance with the accounting rules of Viking Ships' home country.

Required:
1. Analyze the liquidity of both companies by computing their current ratio, quick ratio, and working capital. Analyze the foreign company's liquidity using both the data based upon its home country's accounting rules and the GAAP-based data.
2. How does the difference in the accounting rules between the United States and the foreign country affect the conclusions you draw about the liquidity of the foreign company?
3. Which accounting rule for current assets and current liabilities do you believe is more appropriate? Defend your answer.

61. Secret Payroll Account

Jim and Tammy Bakker founded the PTL Club, a religious broadcasting network, in 1974. A little more than one decade later, the PTL Club had more than five hundred thousand members and annual revenues of almost $130 million. Bakker and his close associates came under intense scrutiny in 1987 when it was disclosed that PTL funds had been used to pay a former church secretary to remain silent concerning a brief liaison involving herself and Bakker. In March 1987, Bakker was forced to resign as PTL's chairman. Two years later, he was convicted of fraud and conspiracy charges, fined $500,000, and sentenced to prison.

Prior to 1987, Bakker's critics had persistently called for greater disclosure of PTL's financial affairs. Bakker resisted these demands, repeatedly asserting that such disclosure was not appropriate or necessary, since PTL had strong financial controls. Bakker also often reminded his critics that "[PTL] had excellent accountants and . . . external audits by reputable [CPA] firms." However, the results of numerous investigations of PTL during 1987 and 1988 by the FBI, IRS, and other agencies suggested that the organization's internal controls were extremely weak, and nonexistent in many cases. Investigators found that paychecks had been written to individuals who could not be identified, that large sums were paid to consultants who had not provided any services to PTL, and that there was no supporting documentation for millions of dollars of construction costs entered in PTL's accounting records.

The most troubling internal control problem that investigators uncovered in PTL's accounting system was the existence of a secret payroll bank account that was used to disburse funds to Bakker and his closest aides. This account was so secretive that the organization's chief financial officer was not informed of the nature of the expenses being paid through it. The members of PTL's board of directors were totally unaware of this payroll account. Surprisingly, the check register for the account was maintained by a partner of Laventhol & Horwath, PTL's independent audit firm. In fact, that individual was the audit partner responsible for supervising the PTL audit engagement. Bakker, or one of his aides, would telephone the Laventhol partner when a check was written on the account. The partner would also be called periodically to determine whether PTL needed to deposit additional funds into the account.

Note: This vignette was adapted from the following source: M. C. Knapp, "The PTL Club," in *Contemporary Auditing: Issues and Cases*, 2d ed. (Minneapolis/St. Paul: West Publishing Co., 1996).

Required:

1. Many large-scale financial frauds have involved the illicit use of an organization's payroll function. List the specific internal control weaknesses related to the secret payroll bank account of PTL. Also identify internal control procedures that would have prevented or detected the use of this account.
2. How do independent auditors enhance the credibility of an organization's periodic financial statements? In the PTL case, many critics questioned whether PTL's audit firm was truly independent of its client. Explain the reasoning underlying this allegation.

PROJECTS

62. Environmentally-Related Contingent Liabilities

In this project, your group will be assigned to research several companies in an industry in which contingent liabilities related to environmental issues commonly arise. Examples of such industries include many types of manufacturing companies, such as manufacturers of steel and iron products, chemicals, and fertilizers. Other industries in which environmentally-related contingent liabilities are common include oil and gas exploration, mining, and electric utilities.

Required:

1. For the industry assigned to your group, each group member should identify a company in that industry that has reported a major environmentally-related contingent liability in recent years in its financial statements or accompanying financial statement footnotes. Each member should write a summary of the contingent liability he or she identified. This summary should include a brief description of the source or cause of the contingent liability, its potential monetary effect on the given company, and management's conclusion regarding the likelihood that the contingent liability will eventually become an actual liability.

2. Meet as a group to discuss the information collected by each group member in Part 1. Among the issues you should address are the most common types of environmental problems apparently faced by companies in this industry, the apparent degree of candor or openness of each company in discussing these items, and the financial implications that these types of contingent liabilities have for companies in that industry. Regarding the latter issue, discuss whether these contingent liabilities may threaten the existence of individual companies or even the entire industry. Finally, discuss whether you believe that financial decision makers find disclosures of environmentally-related contingent liabilities useful in their decision-making processes.

3. Prepare a written report summarizing the information collected by individual group members in Part 1 and the results of the group discussion in Part 2. One group member should be prepared to make a brief presentation to the class regarding the group's report.

63. **Interpreting Current Ratios**

Identify five different industries. Make sure that a variety of different types of industries are represented in your sample. For instance, your sample should not include only manufacturing firms or only merchandising firms.

Required:

Referring to recent data published by Dun & Bradstreet, Robert Morris Associates, or another investment advisory or financial services firm, identify the average or median current ratio for each industry included in your sample. Write a brief report that begins by identifying the five industries you selected and each industry's current ratio norm. Analyze the nature of each industry in your sample and other relevant variables to explain the differences between and among the current ratio norms for these industries. For example, if one industry has a very high current ratio norm compared with the other four industries, investigate and then explain the underlying reasons for this difference. Typically, such differences will be related to one or more key characteristics or facets of the given industries and to economic conditions that differentially affect individual industries.

64. **Litigation-Related Contingent Liabilities**

Review the index of *The Wall Street Journal* or a major metropolitan newspaper such as *The New York Times* or *Los Angeles Times* for the past three years. Identify a major lawsuit filed against a public company by another firm, a group of investors, a bank, or a governmental agency. (Note: Do not select a lawsuit involving an environmental issue related to the given company.)

Required:

1. In a written report, summarize the nature of the lawsuit filed against the company. Identify the plaintiff, the major allegations, the damages requested, and other key facts.

2. Also include in your report an assessment of the financial statement implications of this lawsuit. That is, evaluate whether or not the lawsuit should be ignored for accounting and financial reporting purposes by the company or should be included in some manner in the company's financial statements. If the company has issued an annual report since the lawsuit was filed, attempt to determine whether the item was incorporated in the financial statements or accompanying footnotes included in that annual report.

11

LONG-TERM LIABILITIES

LEARNING OBJECTIVES

After studying this chapter, you should be able to do the following:

1. Define the key information needs of decision makers regarding long-term liabilities

2. Define the key terms related to and important characteristics of corporate bonds

3. Account for the issuance of bonds payable and subsequent transactions including the payment of interest expense

4. Amortize bond discount and premium using the effective-interest method

5. Account for long-term lease obligations

6. Discuss the key accounting issues related to long-term liabilities stemming from pension and other postretirement employee benefit plans

7. Compute and interpret the long-term debt to equity and times interest earned ratios

8. Define key internal control procedures for long-term liabilities

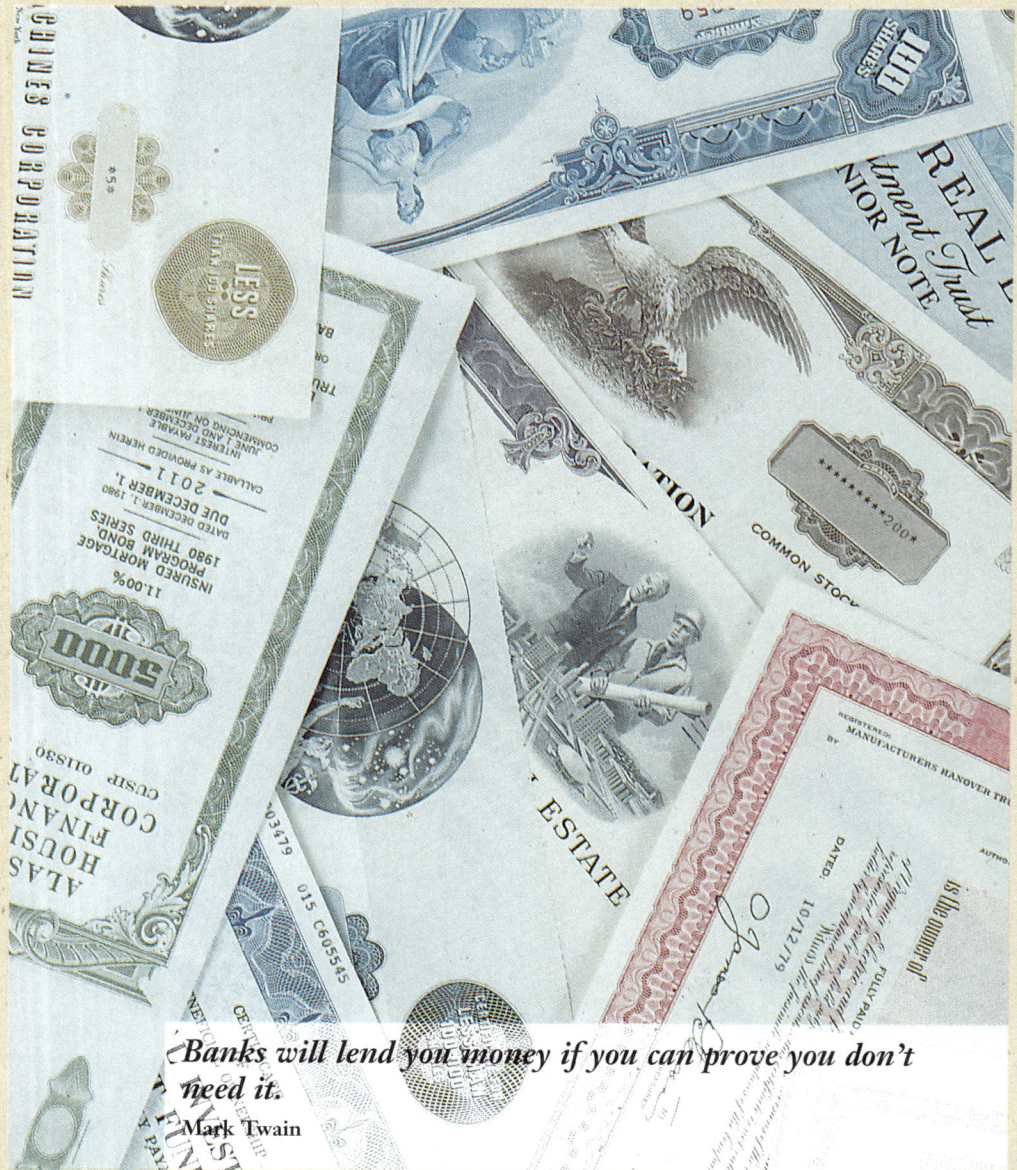

> *Banks will lend you money if you can prove you don't need it.*
> Mark Twain

A Mickey Mouse Organization
Built on Mickey Mouse Loans

In 1922, an artistic young man established Laugh-O-Gram Films, Inc., an animated film production company based in Kansas City. Only twenty-one years old at the time, the young man's artistic ability greatly exceeded his business skills. Within one year, the company was bankrupt. After considerable pleading, the young entrepreneur convinced his creditors to allow him to keep one camera and one film he had produced. With fifty dollars in his pocket, his camera, and the film, Walt Disney boarded a train for California, hoping that Hollywood would have a better appreciation for his animation skills than Kansas City.

Walt and his brother Roy, who joined him in California, scraped together enough funds to rent a small studio in Los Angeles. Most of these funds were provided by loans from friends and family members. An uncle loaned $500, Roy's fiancée $25, while a friend from Kansas City chipped in $275. The first few years for the brothers were difficult financially. It was not until 1928 that they got the break they had been looking for when Walt sketched an animation character, Mortimer the Mouse. Walt's wife, Lillian, liked the character but suggested what she thought was a more appealing name: Mickey. In less than twelve months, animated cartoons featuring Mickey Mouse were playing in movie theaters nationwide. The cartoons were so popular that they often received equal billing on theater marquees with feature films. With the profits produced by Mickey Mouse, the Disney brothers were on their way to building Walt Disney Company, a firm with more than $10 billion of assets by the mid-1990s.

The initial financing for many small companies is provided by loans from friends and family members. As companies grow, they must turn to more substantial sources of financing. It should come as no surprise that Disney is a leading company when it comes to the development of creative approaches to borrowing funds. In 1993, Disney startled Wall Street by announcing that it was selling $150 million of bonds with a one-hundred-year term. The normal term for corporate bonds is much shorter, thirty years being a common term. The following year, Disney announced that it was planning to sell an additional $400 million of bonds. These bonds are unique in that the interest rate paid to bondholders is linked to the profitability of certain Disney films.

In seven decades, the Walt Disney Company has gone from financing its operations with small loans from friends and relatives to borrowing hundreds of millions of dollars on exotic debt instruments. Would the founder of the company be impressed? Probably not. Once, when asked about the financial empire he had built, Walt Disney simply replied, "Always remember that this whole thing was started by a mouse."

In this chapter, we focus on accounting for long-term liabilities. The opening section of this chapter introduces you to the two basic types of long-term liabilities and provides examples of each. Next, the key information needs of decision makers regarding long-term liabilities are identified. Then, specific accounting procedures are illustrated for bonds payable, a common long-term liability for large public companies. Accounting for other long-term liabilities is discussed in the following section. The final two sections of this chapter discuss financial ratios and internal control procedures related to long-term liabilities.

Bill Gates, the founder of Microsoft Corporation, was declared the richest person in the United States in 1995. Gates' multibillion-dollar fortune stems largely from the stock he owns in Microsoft. In a recent balance sheet, Microsoft reported zero long-term liabilities, which is very unusual for a large public company.

LONG-TERM LIABILITIES: AN OVERVIEW

Long-term liabilities include the debts and obligations of a business entity other than those classified as current liabilities. Generally, long-term liabilities are of two types: amounts borrowed on a long-term basis and long-term accrued expenses. Included in the first category are bonds payable, notes payable due more than one year from a balance sheet date, and mortgages payable. Certain obligations incurred under long-term leases are usually included in this first category of long-term liabilities, although these obligations technically do not involve borrowed funds. Examples of long-term accrued expenses are the obligations stemming from pension and other postretirement benefit plans that many companies have established for their employees.

There is considerable variability in the types and dollar amounts of long-term liabilities reported by large public companies. For example, consider two very successful and well-known companies, Microsoft Corporation and Campbell Soup Company. In 1994, Microsoft had total assets of $5.3 billion, while Campbell Soup had total assets of $5.0 billion. Microsoft reported no long-term liabilities in its 1994 balance sheet. On the other hand, Campbell Soup reported more than $1.3 billion in long-term liabilities at the end of fiscal 1994. Included in Campbell Soup's long-term liabilities were more than $500 million of borrowed funds, including both notes and bonds payable, and more than $800 million of long-term accrued expenses. Most public companies have a significant amount of long-term liabilities. Microsoft is one of those fortunate companies that has not been forced to borrow on a long-term basis to satisfy its financing needs. Instead, the company has been able to generate sufficient funds through profitable operations to meet those needs. The company has also successfully avoided incurring other long-term obligations.

LONG-TERM LIABILITIES: KEY INFORMATION NEEDS OF DECISION MAKERS

In Chapter 10, we identified three primary types of information that decision makers need regarding current liabilities. These information needs include completeness or disclosure of all such liabilities, information regarding valuation methods, and disclosure of any unusual and material circumstances involving current liabilities. As you might expect, these same general types of information needs apply to long-term liabilities.

Completeness

Investors, creditors, and other decision makers have a need and a right to expect businesses to disclose all of their long-term liabilities. Surprisingly to most nonaccountants, certain long-term obligations of businesses are not reported on their balance sheets. These unreported liabilities result from "off–balance sheet" financing techniques used by many businesses. **Off–balance sheet financing** generally involves the acquisition of assets or services by incurring long-term obligations that are not included in an entity's balance sheet. For example, certain long-term leases qualify as off–balance sheet financing techniques.

Many companies use long-term leasing as an alternative to borrowing funds and then purchasing a needed asset. These two methods of financing the acquisition of an asset are very similar. In both cases, an asset that is needed by a business is obtained; in both cases, a business is typically obligated to make a series of payments over several years. However, long-term lease obligations are not necessarily booked as liabilities in a business's accounting records. In fact, until fairly recently, long-term lease obligations were almost never recorded as liabilities and were generally ignored for financial reporting purposes. Under present accounting rules, when an asset is leased under conditions that are equivalent to purchasing that asset with borrowed funds, both the leased asset and the long-term lease obligation must be reported in an entity's balance sheet. Other long-term leases continue to be accounted for on an off–balance sheet basis. However, existing accounting rules generally require businesses to disclose obligations stemming from off–balance sheet leasing transactions in the footnotes to their financial statements.

Requiring that long-term lease obligations be recorded as liabilities, or at least disclosed in financial statement footnotes, is just one step taken recently by the accounting profession to require businesses to account more thoroughly for long-term liabilities. Additional examples of long-term liabilities that were accounted for on an off–balance sheet basis until recently are discussed later in this chapter.

Valuation Methods

Proper valuation is a concern to decision makers for most financial statement items. Valuation issues are particularly important for long-term liabilities that must be estimated with the help of the time value of money concept discussed in Chapter 10. An

■ **LEARNING OBJECTIVE 1**
Define the key information needs of decision makers regarding long-term liabilities

off–balance sheet financing

Real World
Business executives often structure lease terms to ensure that the lease qualifies as an operating lease and, thus, does not have to be recorded on the balance sheet.

example of such a long-term liability is the obligation that many businesses incur because of their employee pension plans. Companies with employee pension plans often face complex computations each year to determine their pension-related liabilities. For example, these companies must project the future salaries of their employees, since pension benefits are usually tied directly to employee compensation in the final few years before retirement. A company that wants to minimize its pension-related expenses and the present value of its related liabilities might intentionally underestimate employee pay raises to be granted in the future. To guard against this possibility, accounting standards require businesses to disclose the key assumptions underlying their pension-related expense and liability computations. Comparable financial statement disclosures are generally required for other material long-term liabilities that must be estimated.

Unusual Circumstances

When a business borrows funds on a long-term basis, a debt agreement or contract is usually signed by representatives of the borrower and the lender. These agreements generally include restrictive debt covenants or conditions. Since restrictive debt covenants often impose significant constraints on a borrower's future operations, they should be disclosed in the entity's financial statements. Probably the most common restrictive debt covenant is a limitation on the payment of dividends. Following is a restrictive debt covenant disclosed in a recent annual report of Aaron Rents, Inc.

> The Company's credit agreement with the two banks restricts cash dividend payments and stock repurchases to 25% of net earnings since April 1, 1991, and places other restrictions on additional borrowings and requires the maintenance of certain financial ratios.

When a company is in danger of defaulting on long-term debt, this fact should be disclosed in its financial statements. Clearly, a prospective investor or lender needs and deserves this information. In February 1995, Healthcare America, a company based in Austin, Texas, disclosed that it was having difficulty making the interest payments on its long-term debt. The company reported that lenders had agreed to the postponement of certain interest payments while it attempted to solve its financial problems.[1]

ACCOUNTING FOR BONDS PAYABLE

In this section and the following section, we consider procedural accounting issues related to long-term liabilities. We begin by focusing on bonds payable for two reasons. First, bonds payable are among the most common and largest long-term liabilities of many companies, particularly large public companies. Second, many of the accounting issues posed by bonds payable are similar, although not identical, to the issues raised by other key long-term liabilities. Consequently, by focusing in depth on the accounting procedures for bonds payable, we can then touch only lightly on procedural accounting issues for other major long-term liabilities.

---

1. "Healthcare America Inc.," *The Wall Street Journal*, February 13, 1995, p. B6. Reprinted by permission of *The Wall Street Journal*, © 1995 Dow Jones & Company, Inc. All Rights Reserved Worldwide.

Corporate Bonds: An Introduction

Large corporations often borrow funds needed to finance the construction of new production facilities, the purchase of other companies, or the retirement of existing debt by selling bonds to the general public. For example, in early 1995, American Home Products, Inc., sold $1 billion of bonds to finance the acquisition of another company.[2] A **bond** is a long-term loan made by one party to another that is documented by a legal instrument known as a bond certificate. The sale of bonds by corporations has been a popular financing alternative in recent years when interest rates have been low by historical standards. In 1993 alone, nearly one-quarter of a trillion dollars of corporate bonds were sold, a record at the time.[3] Shown in Exhibit 11.1 is an example of a bond certificate.

Before discussing specific accounting procedures for bonds payable, it will be helpful to become better acquainted with these long-term liabilities. Here, we consider key terms related to corporate bonds, their various types, factors influencing their market price, and how the selling price of newly issued bonds is determined.

KEY TERMS   Bonds are traded like other debt and equity securities on major securities exchanges such as the New York Stock Exchange. Assume that you read in the business section of *The Wall Street Journal* that Exxon intends to sell a $300 million "bond issue." A bond issue is simply a group of identical bonds being sold at approximately the same point in time. If you want, you could call up your broker and place an order to buy one or more of Exxon's bonds. Although you are buying these bonds, you are technically lending money to Exxon, which explains why the proceeds of a bond issue are recorded in a long-term liability account entitled Bonds Payable.

Corporate bonds are usually issued in $1,000 denominations. That is, the face value or principal amount or maturity value, whichever term you prefer, of corporate bonds is typically $1,000. Most corporate bonds sell for slightly more or less than their face value. For instance, a $1,000 Exxon bond may sell for a $20 "discount" to its face value, or $980. Alternatively, a $1,000 bond that sells for a "premium" of $30 to its face value has a selling price of $1,030. In either case, the bondholder would be entitled to receive exactly $1,000 from the issuing company on the bond's maturity date.

Prior to the sale of a bond issue, a bond indenture is prepared by the company selling the bonds. A **bond indenture** is the legal contract between a bond purchaser and the issuing company and identifies the rights and obligations of both parties. For example, a bond indenture identifies the **stated interest rate** for a bond issue. The stated interest rate is the rate of interest paid to bondholders based upon the face value of the bonds. (Face interest rate and contract interest rate are terms that are interchangeable with stated interest rate.) An individual who purchases a $1,000 bond with a stated interest rate of 8 percent is entitled to receive $80 of interest each year ($1,000 × 8%). Interest on bonds is usually paid semiannually, although some bond indentures specify quarterly or annual payment of interest. A bond indenture also indicates the maturity date of a bond issue. On the maturity date of a bond issue, a company must pay the face value of the bonds to the bondholders. The term of a bond issue is the period elapsing between the date bonds are first available for sale and the date they mature.

■ **LEARNING OBJECTIVE 2**
Define the key terms related to and important characteristics of corporate bonds

bond

Discussion Question
Ask students why American Home Products would choose to sell bonds rather than borrow the $1 billion from a bank. Answer: Banks frequently are not willing to assume the risk of extremely large loans. Issuing bonds effectively spreads such risk among a large number of lenders.

Discussion Question
Bonds are generally considered a less risky investment than common stocks. Why? Answer: In the liquidation of a company, bondholders have priority to the firm's assets over stockholders. In addition, most bond indentures limit the payment of dividends to stockholders to ensure that bondholders will receive all required principal and interest payments.

bond indenture

stated interest rate

---

2. Creswell, J and L. Young, "Bond Prices Stage Broad Rally After Fed Says Manufacturing Sector Shows Signs of Slowing," *The Wall Street Journal*, February 16, 1995, p. C22. Reprinted by permission of *The Wall Street Journal*, © 1995 Dow Jones & Company, Inc. All Rights Reserved Worldwide.

3. J. E. Lebherz, "It Was a Very Big Year for Bonds," *Washington Post*, 2 January 1994, H5.

■ **EXHIBIT 11.1**

Example of a Corporate Bond Certificate

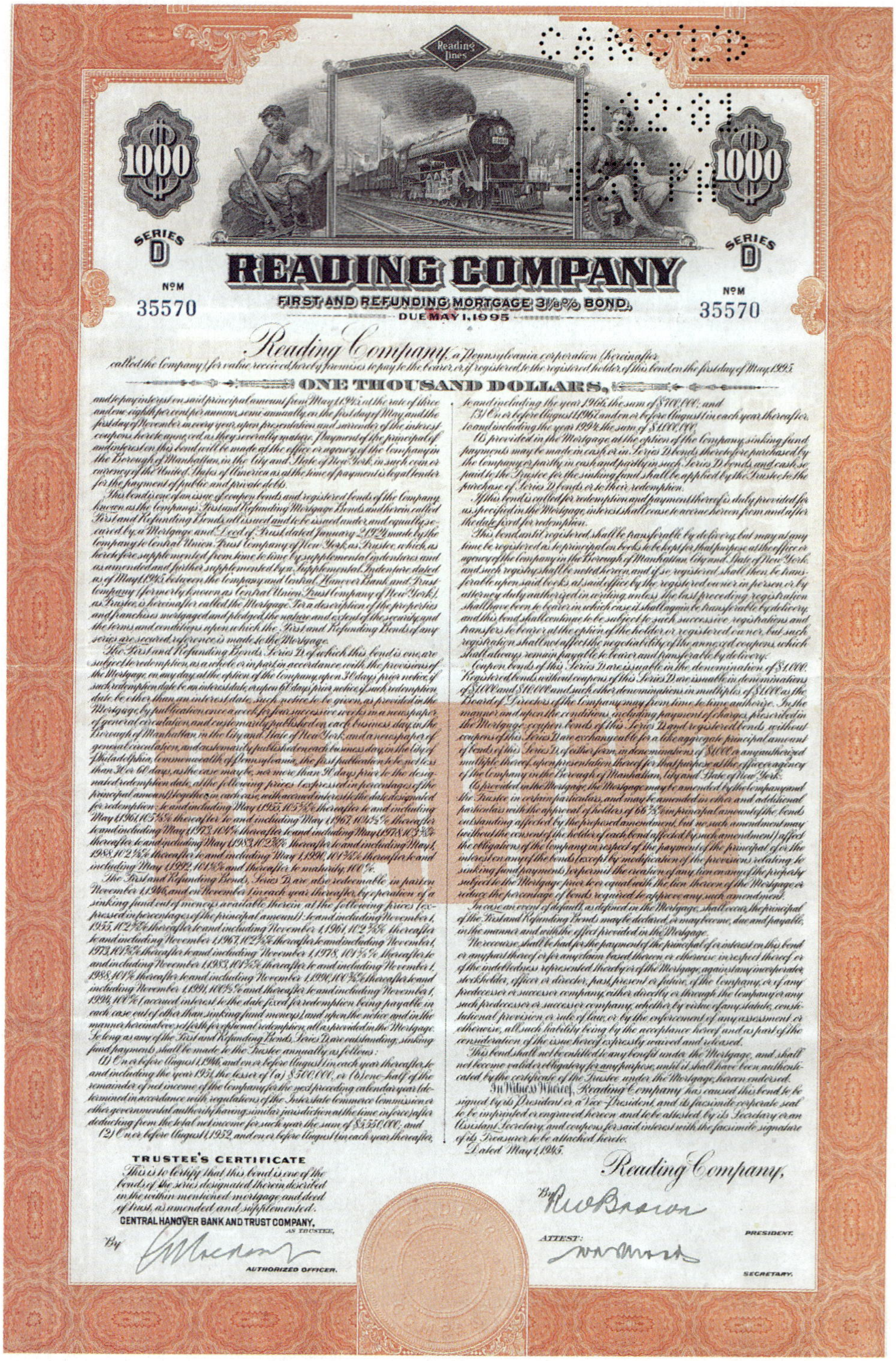

TYPES OF BONDS Bonds are often identified by one or more distinctive features that they contain. **Secured bonds,** sometimes referred to as mortgage bonds, are collateralized by specific assets of the company issuing the bonds. **Unsecured bonds,** or debentures, are backed only by the legal commitment of the issuing firm to make all required principal and interest payments. Bond indentures typically include a call option and occasionally a convertible option. **Callable bonds** can be retired or redeemed by the issuing company when one or more conditions are met. The most common condition that activates a call option is simply the passage of time. For instance, a bond issue may be callable at the option of the issuing company at any point after the bonds have been outstanding for more than five years. If a bond issue is callable, the bond indenture usually requires the payment of a call premium to the bondholders. That is, the bondholders must be paid more than the face value of the bonds. **Convertible bonds** can be exchanged at the option of bondholders for stock in the issuing company. For example, a convertible option in a bond indenture may grant bondholders the right to exchange each $1,000 bond for twenty-five shares of the issuing company's common stock.

BOND MARKET PRICES Open *The Wall Street Journal* and turn to the section entitled "New York Exchange Bonds," and you will find price quotations for several hundred individual bond issues. Following is a recent price quotation line for a bond issue of Safeway, a supermarket chain.

	Cur Yld	Vol	Close	Net Chg
Safeway 10s01	9.3	10	107 ¼	-¼

The "10s01" indicates that Safeway's bonds have a 10 percent stated interest rate and that they mature in the year 2001—the s simply separates the interest rate on the bonds from their maturity date. According to the volume column, ten of these bonds, each with a face value of $1,000, were sold on the day in question. The final or closing selling price for the Safeway bonds on this day was 107 ¼. No, these $1,000 bonds were not sold for $107.25. The selling prices of bonds are quoted as a percentage of their face value. So, a quoted selling price of 100 translates to an actual selling price of $1,000. Safeway's bonds closed the day at a price of $1,072.50 ($1,000 × 107.25%). The net change in the selling price of the Safeway bonds was a decrease of ¼ or $2.50 per bond, meaning that the previous day these bonds closed at 107 ½ ($1,075). Finally, the closing price of these bonds resulted in a current yield of 9.3 percent. Individuals who purchased a Safeway bond at a price of $1,072.50 on this particular date would earn interest on their investment at an annual rate of approximately 9.3 percent. This current yield can be computed by dividing the interest earned on the bond each year, $100 ($1,000 × 10%), by the cost of the bond, $1,072.50.

The market price of Safeway's bonds, at any point in time, is determined by several factors. These factors include Safeway's financial condition, the level of interest rates in the economy, the length of time to the bonds' maturity date, and investors' preferences. As these factors change, the market price of Safeway's bonds will fluctuate. Several investment advisory firms, including Moody's Investors Service and Standard & Poor's Corporation, monitor hundreds of bond issues and assign a risk assessment rating to each. As the factors affecting the risk associated with individual bond issues change, Moody's and Standard & Poor's upgrade or downgrade their risk assessment ratings. In late April 1995, Standard & Poor's assigned an "A+" rating to certain outstanding bonds of Lockheed Corporation and a "BB+" rating to certain

CORPORATION BONDS
Volume, $29,444,000

Bonds	Cur Yld	Vol	Close	Net Chg.
ADT Op zr10	...	127	42½	+ ¼
AMR 8.10s98	7.8	30	103½	+ ¼
AMR 9s16	8.6	46	105⅛	− ⅜
AMR 6⅞24	cv	41	105½	+ ½
ATT 6s00	6.1	90	98⅜	...
ATT 5⅛01	5.5	46	93¾	+ ¼
ATT 6¾04	6.7	65	101⅛	+ ¼
ATT 7s05	6.8	50	102⅜	...
ATT 7½06	7.1	5	106¼	+ ⅜
ATT 8⅛22	7.7	85	105	− ½
ATT 8⅛24	7.7	60	106	+ ½
ATT 8.35s25	7.7	7	108½	+ 1¼
ATT 8⅝31	7.9	10	108⅞	− ⅛
Actava 9⅞97	9.9	1	100	+ ½
Actava 9½98	9.6	65	98⅞	− ⅛
Actava 10s99	10.0	6	100	− 2
Advst 9s08	cv	14	99¼	...
AlskAr 6⅞14	cv	11	88	+ 1
AlbnyInt 5¼02	cv	32	99½	− 1
AlegCp 6½14	cv	10	106	− 1
AlldC zr98	...	6	82⅛	...
AlldC zr99	...	30	77	− ½
AlldC zr2000	...	5	71⅜	− 1⅝
Allwst 7¼14	cv	80	88¾	+ ¾
AmBrnd 9⅛16	8.7	10	105⅛	− ½
AMedia 11⅝04	11.3	30	103¼	− ¾
Amsco 2002	cv	86	95	+ ½
Ancp 13⅞02f	cv	49	40½	+ ⅛
Anhr 8⅝16	8.3	25	103½	− 1½
AnnTaylr 8¾00	9.2	208	94⅝	+ ½
Arrow 5¾02	cv	5	167	...
Arvin 7½14	cv	40	100¾	− ¼
AutDt zr12	...	38	46¼	− ¼
Bally 10s06f	cv	17	95½	− ½
Ballys 3s00f	cv	25	102	...
BkrLfe 13s02	11.6	15	112¼	+ ¾
Barnt 8½99	8.0	20	105⅝	+ ⅝
BellPa 7⅛12	7.2	20	98½	+ ½
BellPa 8⅛17	7.9	5	103	− ½
BellPa 7½13	7.5	35	100¼	+ ½
BellsoT 6½00	6.4	200	101¼	− ⅛
BellsoT 6¼03	6.4	9	98¼	− ¾
BellsoT 7s05	6.8	10	102⅝	− ¼
BellsoT 6½05	6.5	45	99¼	+ ¼
BellsoT 8¼32	7.7	30	106½	+ 1¼
BellsoT 7½33	7.5	20	100	+ ¼
BellsoT 6¾33	7.4	78	91⅝	− ⅞
BstBuy 8⅝00	8.6	32	99⅞	+ ½
BethSt 6⅞99	7.0	3	98⅝	− ¼
BethSt 8⅜01	8.5	30	98¾	...
BethSt 8.45s05	8.7	54	97½	− ⅛

Bond tables published daily in *The Wall Street Journal* allow investors to track the prices of hundreds of corporate bond issues.

secured bonds

unsecured bonds

callable bonds

convertible bonds

Teaching Note

Bondholders must relinquish callable bonds at the option of the bond issuer. In contrast, the decision to exercise the convertible feature of a bond is made strictly by individual bondholders.

Teaching Note
Bring a copy of a bond table
from *The Wall Street Journal* to
class and walk students through
several examples of bond price
quotations.

Teaching Note
Emphasize to students that risk
and interest rate (rate of return)
are positively correlated. As the
risk associated with a bond
investment increases, the
interest rate on that investment
increases.

bonds of USX Corporation. These ratings indicated that USX's bonds were perceived by Standard & Poor's to be more risky than the Lockheed bonds.

The day-to-day changes in the market price of Safeway's bonds do not have accounting implications for that firm. Most of the accounting decisions for bonds payable are resolved on the date they are initially sold. To fully appreciate the accounting procedures for bonds payable, it is important to understand how the selling price of newly issued bonds is determined.

DETERMINING THE SELLING PRICE OF NEWLY ISSUED BONDS   As noted earlier, corporate bonds typically do not sell for their face value. To illustrate how the selling price of newly issued bonds is established, suppose that Hardin Manufacturing Company plans to sell $100,000 of bonds. These bonds have a face value of $1,000 each and a five-year term that runs from April 1, Year 1, through April 1, Year 6. The stated interest rate on the bonds is 10 percent and interest on the bonds is payable semiannually on April 1 and October 1. On each of those dates, interest payments of $5,000 ($100,000 × 5%) will be made to bondholders. The initial interest payment date is October 1, Year 1.

Now, assume that Hardin's bonds are sold on April 1, Year 1, when the market interest rate is 11 percent. In this context, the market interest rate refers to the rate of return that investors can earn on bonds that pose the same general level of risk. Here, "risk" refers primarily to the likelihood that a company will eventually default on its bonds, that is, fail to make required interest or principal payments. The market interest rate represents the "yield to maturity" on a bond investment. Yield to maturity is slightly different from the "current yield" defined earlier in reference to the Safeway bonds. The current yield is simply the annual interest earned on a bond divided by the cost of that bond. The yield to maturity of a bond investment takes into account both the interest earned on the bond each year and the impact on the return on that investment of any bond discount or bond premium. On April 1, Year 1, bonds that posed the same level of default risk as Hardin's bonds were selling at a price that allowed investors to earn an 11 percent rate of return on those bonds through their maturity date. Because Hardin is paying only 10 percent interest on its bonds, compared with a market interest rate of 11 percent, the bonds will sell for less than their face value. Companies attempt to establish a stated interest rate on their bonds that is approximately equal to the market interest rate. However, several weeks or longer may be required to process a new bond issue, meaning that the market interest rate on the date bonds are sold must be predicted well in advance. As a result, the stated interest rate for a bond issue is usually different from the market interest rate when the bonds are actually sold.

To determine the selling price of Hardin's bonds, we can use the time value of money concept discussed in Chapter 10. The selling price of these bonds will be the present value of the cash outflows that Hardin will be required to pay over the five-year term of the bonds. These cash outflows consist of ten $5,000 semiannual interest payments and a $100,000 principal payment at the end of the bond term. Recall from Chapter 10 that the two key variables in a time value of money scenario are a given number of time periods and an interest or discount rate. In the present example there are ten time periods, the number of semiannual interest payment periods for Hardin's five-year bonds. The discount rate is 5.5 percent, one-half of the 11 percent market interest rate on the date the bonds are sold. *Key point to remember:* The market interest rate on the date bonds are sold, not the stated interest rate, is used to determine the present value of the future cash outflows related to a bond issue.

Shown in Exhibit 11.2 is a diagram of the present value of the cash outflows related to the Hardin bonds. On April 1, Year 1, the present value of the principal pay-

■ **EXHIBIT 11.2**

Determining the Selling Price of Five-Year Bonds With a 10 Percent Stated Interest Rate When the Market Interest Rate is 11 Percent

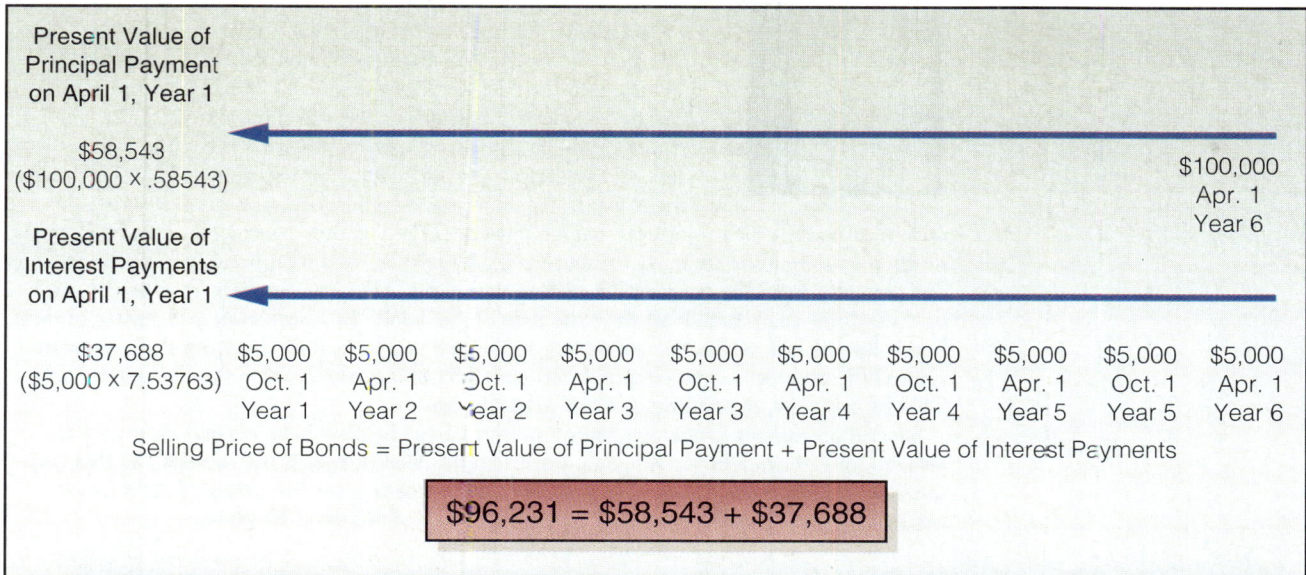

ment to be made on the bonds' maturity date (April 1, Year 6) is $58,543. This amount was determined by multiplying the bonds' $100,000 principal amount or face value by the appropriate present value factor for a single amount. That factor, .58543, is found at the intersection of the 5.5 percent column and the 10 period row in Table 10.3. To determine the present value of the series of interest payments, which is an annuity, we use the present value of an annuity table, Table 10.4. At the intersection of the 5.5 percent column and the 10 period row in Table 10.4 is the present value of an annuity factor 7.53763. When this factor is multiplied by $5,000, the result is $37,688, which is the present value of the ten semiannual interest payments on April 1, Year 1.

As shown in Exhibit 11.2, the Hardin bonds will sell for $96,231. Realize that although these bonds will sell for $96,231, Hardin will be required to pay the bondholders $100,000 on the bonds' maturity date. In essence, Hardin is being penalized by bond purchasers for selling bonds with a stated interest rate that is less than the market interest rate.

Accounting for Bonds Issued at Face Value

To illustrate the basic accounting entries for bonds payable, we can use Hardin Manufacturing's $100,000 bond issue. Assume that these bonds are sold on April 1, Year 1, the first day of the bond term, and that the market interest rate on that date is 10 percent. Under this assumption, the bonds will sell for their face value of $100,000. You can confirm this by computing the present value of the bond's future cash outflows using a 5 percent semiannual discount rate. To record the sale of the bonds, the following entry would be made in Hardin's accounting records.

■ **LEARNING OBJECTIVE 3**
Account for the issuance of bonds payable and subsequent transactions including the payment of interest expense

Teaching Note
Emphasize that when the market rate of interest is equal to the stated interest rate, bonds will sell for their face value.

Zeroes, LYONS, TIGRS, and . . . CATS?

Corporate financiers have become increasingly innovative in developing new methods of raising debt capital for large public companies. Complex borrowing arrangements create major headaches for corporate accountants who must record these transactions. One of the more popular new debt instruments is zero-coupon bonds or notes. In the early 1990s, Disney had more than $1 billion of these debt securities outstanding. "Zeroes" are comparable to the short-term non-interest-bearing notes that we considered in Chapter 10, since interest is not paid to the parties holding them. If you purchase a $1,000 zero-coupon bond, you are entitled to one payment from the corporation issuing that bond. That one payment may be ten, twenty, or even thirty years following the issue date of the bond. To compensate purchasers of these bonds for the lack of interest payments, zeroes sell at a large discount from their maturity value. For instance, a zero-coupon bond with a $1,000 maturity value may be purchased for $200 or even less, depending upon its maturity date.

Several prominent brokerage firms and investment bankers have created their own specialized long-term debt instruments. For example, Merrill Lynch has created LYONS (liquid yield option notes) and TIGRS (treasury investment growth receipts). CATS (certificates of accrual on treasury securities) are a product of Salomon Brothers.

Apr. 1	Cash	100,000	
	Bonds Payable		100,000

To record sale of five-year bonds with a stated interest rate of 10% and a maturity date of April 1, Year 6

Recall that the semiannual interest payment dates for Hardin's bonds are April 1 and October 1. The initial interest payment date is October 1, Year 1, six months following the sale of the bonds. On that date, the following entry would be made to record the first interest payment.

Oct. 1	Interest Expense	5,000	
	Cash		5,000

To record interest payment on bonds payable

On December 31, Year 1, an adjusting entry would be necessary to recognize interest expense on Hardin's bonds for the three-month period October 1 through December 31. Using the interest equation (interest = principal $\times$ rate $\times$ time), we determine that the appropriate expense accrual is $2,500 ($100,000 $\times$ 10% $\times$ 3/12) resulting in the following year-end adjusting entry.

Dec. 31	Interest Expense	2,500	
	Interest Payable		2,500

To recognize year-end interest expense on bonds payable

Three months later, on April 1, Year 2, the second interest payment would be made and recorded.

Apr. 1	Interest Expense	2,500	
	Interest Payable	2,500	
	Cash		5,000
	To record interest payment on bonds payable		

On April 1, Year 6, Hardin would make the final semiannual interest payment and pay the face value of the bonds to the bondholders. Following are the two entries in Hardin's accounting records on that date assuming the appropriate amount of interest expense was accrued on December 31, Year 5.

Apr. 1	Interest Expense	2,500	
	Interest Payable	2,500	
	Cash		5,000
	To record interest payment on bonds payable		
Apr. 1	Bonds Payable	100,000	
	Cash		100,000
	To record payment of principal amount of bonds payable		

Accounting for Bonds Issued at a Discount

Now, let us assume that on April 1, Year 1, when Hardin sells its bonds the market interest rate is 11 percent. We have already determined that Hardin's bonds will sell for $96,231 under this assumption—see Exhibit 11.2. The difference between the $100,000 face value of the bonds and the bonds' selling price would be entered in a contra-liability account, Discount on Bonds Payable, as shown in the following entry.

■ LEARNING OBJECTIVE 3
Account for the issuance of bonds payable and subsequent transactions including the payment of interest expense

Teaching Note
Emphasize that when the market rate of interest is greater than the stated interest rate for a bond issue, the bonds will sell at a discount.

Apr. 1	Cash	96,231	
	Discount on Bonds Payable	3,769	
	Bonds Payable		100,000
	To record sale of five-year bonds with a stated interest rate of 10% and a maturity date of April 1, Year 6		

If Hardin prepares a balance sheet shortly after the sale of these bonds, the company would report the bonds payable at their "carrying value," or book value, of $96,231. The carrying value of bonds that sell at a discount is the difference between their face value and the balance of the bond discount account.

When bonds are sold at a discount, the interest expense recorded each interest payment date is greater than the amount of the interest payment. In the present example, Hardin received $96,231 when it sold its bonds; however, the company will be required to pay the bondholders $100,000 when the bonds mature. The difference between these two amounts is additional interest expense that Hardin incurs on its bonds payable. This additional interest expense increases the interest rate on Hardin's bonds to 11 percent, the market interest rate when the bonds were sold. Because of the matching principle, this additional interest expense should be prorated and recognized over the term of the bonds. Two methods can be used to amortize, or write off, bond discount: the straight-line method and the effective-interest method. Here, the straight-line method is illustrated.

Under the straight-line method of amortizing a discount on bonds payable, an equal amount of the discount is written off as interest expense each interest payment period. For the present example, the amount of the bond discount is $3,769 and there are ten semiannual interest payment periods. So, Hardin would amortize $377 ($3,769/10) of bond discount each interest payment period. (The small rounding error would be corrected during the final interest payment period.) Following is the October 1, Year 1, entry to record the first interest payment by Hardin.

Oct. 1	Interest Expense	5,377	
	Cash		5,000
	Discount on Bonds Payable		377

To record interest payment on bonds payable

On December 31, Year 1, an adjusting entry would be necessary to record the interest expense on Hardin's bonds for the period October 1 through December 31. The debit to Interest Expense in this adjusting entry would be $2,689. This amount is the sum of the "normal" interest expense accrual of $2,500 for October 1 through December 31 and $189, which is approximately one-half of the $377 of bond discount amortized each six months. Since three months of the second six-month interest payment period would have elapsed by December 31, Year 1, one-half of $377 should be written off as interest expense on that date. On April 1, Year 2, the remaining one-half of the $377 would be charged off as interest expense. Following are the appropriate entries in Hardin's accounting records on December 31, Year 1, and April 1, Year 2.

Dec. 31	Interest Expense	2,689	
	Interest Payable		2,500
	Discount on Bonds Payable		189

To recognize year-end interest expense on bonds payable

Apr. 1	Interest Expense	2,688	
	Interest Payable	2,500	
	Cash		5,000
	Discount on Bonds Payable		188

To record interest payment on bonds payable

As the discount on bonds payable is amortized, the carrying value of the bonds gradually increases. In the present example, following the final interest payment on April 1 of Year 6, Hardin's bond discount account would have a zero balance. As a result, the carrying value of Hardin's bonds payable at that point would be exactly $100,000. Following is the entry that would be appropriate to record the payment of the bonds' face value to the bondholders on April 1, Year 6.

| Apr. 1 | Bonds Payable | 100,000 | |
| | Cash | | 100,000 |

To record payment of principal
amount of bonds payable

Accounting for Bonds Issued at a Premium

Now, let us consider a scenario in which Hardin's bonds will sell for more than their face value. Hardin's bonds will sell for a premium if their stated interest rate is higher than the market interest rate on the date they are sold. Assume that on April 1, Year 1, when Hardin sells its bonds, the market interest rate is 9 percent. Here again, we can use what we learned in Chapter 10 regarding the time value of money to determine the selling price of the bonds. In this case, the appropriate semiannual discount rate is 4.5 percent, or one-half the market interest rate on the date the bonds are sold. Shown next are the computations to determine the bonds' selling price under this new assumption.

■ **LEARNING OBJECTIVE 3**
Account for the issuance of bonds payable and subsequent transactions including the payment of interest expense

Teaching Note
Emphasize that when the market rate of interest is less than the stated interest rate for a bond issue, the bonds will sell at a premium.

Teaching Note
Remind students that the market interest rate is always used to compute the present value of the future cash flows related to a bond issue.

Present Value of Principal Payment: $100,000 × .64393* = $64,393
Present Value of Interest Payments: $5,000 × 7.91272** =   39,564
    Selling Price of Bonds $103,957

* Present value factor for 10 periods and 4.5%; see Table 10.3.

** Present value of an annuity factor for 10 periods and 4.5%; see Table 10.4.

Given a selling price of $103,957, the following entry would be made to record the sale of the bonds.

Apr. 1	Cash	103,957	
	Bonds Payable		100,000
	Premium on Bonds Payable		3,957

To record sale of five-year bonds with
a stated interest rate of 10% and a
maturity date of April 1, Year 6

Recognize that although Hardin sells its bonds for $103,957, the company will be required to pay its bondholders only $100,000 on the maturity date. One useful way to think of a bond premium is as a bonus payment made by bond purchasers to the company issuing the bonds. This bonus payment compensates the company for paying a higher interest rate on its bonds than the market interest rate when the bonds are sold. Bonds sold at a premium are reported on an entity's balance sheet at their carrying value, which is the sum of their face value and the balance of Premium on Bonds Payable.

The matching principle requires a bond premium to be amortized over the term of a bond issue. The amortization of a bond premium reduces the interest expense recorded each accounting period and gradually reduces the bonds' carrying value. If Hardin uses the straight-line amortization method, each semiannual interest payment period $396 ($3,957/10) of the bond premium would be amortized. Following is the entry that would be made to record the first interest payment by Hardin on October 1, Year 1, assuming the bond premium is amortized on a straight-line basis.

Oct. 1	Interest Expense	4,604	
	Premium on Bonds Payable	396	
	Cash		5,000

To record interest payment on bonds payable

Using the Effective-Interest Method to Amortize Bond Discounts and Premiums

In the previous examples, the straight-line method was used to amortize the bond discount or premium. Generally, the effective-interest method should be used to amortize discount or premium on bonds payable.[4] The straight-line method is acceptable if it does not result in material differences between the discount or premium amounts that would be amortized each period under the effective-interest method.

effective-interest method

Under the **effective-interest method,** the interest expense recorded each interest payment period is a constant percentage of the carrying value of bonds payable. This constant percentage is the market interest rate on the date the bonds were initially sold. The market interest rate on the date bonds are sold by the issuing company is often referred to as the **effective interest rate.** The effective interest rate represents

effective interest rate

the true rate of interest incurred over the term of a bond issue. As a result, that interest rate should be used to determine the interest expense on bonds payable each interest payment period.

BONDS ISSUED AT A DISCOUNT   The first step in applying the effective-interest method is typically the preparation of an amortization schedule. Among other items, an amortization schedule documents the interest expense to be recognized each interest payment period on a long-term liability. Shown in Panel B of Exhibit 11.3 is an amortization schedule for the bonds of Hardin Manufacturing Company. Panel A of Exhibit 11.3 lists the key factual data for this bond issue, which are unchanged from the original example used to illustrate accounting for bonds sold at a discount. The first column of the amortization schedule in Exhibit 11.3 lists the individual interest payment dates in chronological order. The second and third columns list the appropriate interest expense and interest payment amounts, respectively, for each interest payment period. Notice that interest expense for each six-month period is computed by multiplying the effective semiannual interest rate, 5.5 percent, by the bonds' carrying value at the end of the previous interest payment period. The interest payment, $5,000, does not vary over the bond term since it is contractually determined by the bond indenture.

The fourth column of the amortization schedule in Exhibit 11.3 indicates the amount of bond discount amortized each interest payment period. These amounts represent the difference between the interest expense each period and the interest payment. The balance of the discount account at the end of an interest payment period is determined by subtracting the discount amortized that period from the account's previous balance. Finally, the carrying value of bonds payable at the end of an interest payment period is the difference between their face value and the period-ending balance of the bond discount account. (An amortization schedule can also be prepared

---

4. *Accounting Principles Board, Opinion No. 21,* "Interest on Receivables and Payables" (New York: AICPA, 1971), para. 15.

■ **EXHIBIT 11.3**

Effective Interest Method of Amortizing Bond Discount

Panel A—Bond Data

Date Sold—April 1, Year 1
Face Value—$100,000
Stated Interest Rate—10%, paid semiannually
Market Interest Rate on Date Sold—11%
Selling Price—$96,231

Panel B—Amortization Schedule, Effective Interest Method

INTEREST PAYMENT DATE	INTEREST EXPENSE[1]	INTEREST PAYMENT[2]	DISCOUNT AMORTIZATION[3]	BOND DISCOUNT BALANCE[4]	BOND CARRYING VALUE[5]
Date Sold, Apr. 1, Year 1				$3769	$96,231
Oct. 1, Year 1	$5,293	$5,000	$293	3,476	96,524
Apr. 1, Year 2	5,309	5,000	309	3,167	96,833
Oct. 1, Year 2	5,326	5,000	326	2,841	97,159
Apr. 1, Year 3	5,344	5,000	344	2,497	97,503
Oct. 1, Year 3	5,363	5,000	363	2,134	97,866
Apr. 1, Year 4	5,383	5,000	383	1,751	98,249
Oct. 1, Year 4	5,404	5,000	404	1,347	98,653
Apr. 1, Year 5	5,426	5,000	426	921	99,079
Oct. 1, Year 5	5,449	5,000	449	472	99,528
Apr. 1, Year 6	5,472*	5,000	472	0	100,000

[1]. 5.5% × Bond Carrying Value at the end of the prior interest payment period; for the initial interest payment date, interest expense is determined by multiplying 5.5% by the original carrying value (selling price) of the bonds.
[2]. 5% × Bond Face Value of $100,000.
[3]. Interest Expense − Interest Payment.
[4]. Prior Balance − current period Discount Amortization.
[5]. Bond Face Value of $100,000 − Bond Discount Balance.
* Difference due to rounding.

when the straight-line method is used and can be prepared for other long-term liabilities as well.)

Once an amortization schedule for a bond issue has been prepared, recording the periodic interest expense is a simple task. On October 1, Year 1, the following entry would be made to record the semiannual interest payment and the interest expense on Hardin's bonds payable.

Oct. 1	Interest Expense	5,293	
	Cash		5,000
	Discount on Bonds Payable		293
	To record interest payment on bonds payable		

Accounting for Discounts on Long-Term Debt: A "Conservative" Approach

In the United States, GAAP require companies to amortize a discount on bonds or other long-term debt over the term of the liability. However, many countries allow businesses to write off the full amount of a discount on a long-term debt in the period that the debt is issued. Examples of such countries are Belgium, France, Japan, and Sweden. This method of accounting for a bond discount is justified by rule-making bodies in these countries on the grounds that it is conservative. That is, the additional interest expense associated with a bond discount is immediately recognized as an expense when a long-term debt is incurred instead of being "spread out" over the term of the debt.

On December 31, Year 1, Hardin's accountants would prepare an adjusting entry to record interest expense on the bonds payable. At this point, one-half of the second semiannual interest payment period would have elapsed. So, one-half of the $309 discount amortization amount for that period reported in Exhibit 11.3 (approximately $155) would be recognized as interest expense. Following is the adjusting entry at the end of Year 1 to record interest expense on Hardin's bonds payable.

Dec. 31	Interest Expense	2,655	
	Interest Payable		2,500
	Discount on Bonds Payable		155

To recognize interest
expense on bonds payable

BONDS ISSUED AT A PREMIUM   Shown in Panel B of Exhibit 11.4 is a second amortization schedule for the Hardin bonds based upon the effective interest method. Here, the assumption is that the bonds are sold for a premium as illustrated earlier. The structure of an amortization schedule for bonds issued at a premium is nearly identical to an amortization schedule for bonds issued at a discount. Again, interest expense each six-month period is computed by multiplying the effective semiannual interest rate by the bonds' carrying value at the end of the previous period. In this case, the effective semiannual interest rate is 4.5 percent instead of 5.5 percent. Shown next is the entry to record the initial interest payment on Hardin's bonds, assuming the effective-interest method is being used to amortize the premium.

Oct. 1	Interest Expense	4,678	
	Premium on Bonds Payable	322	
	Cash		5,000

To record interest payment on bonds
payable

In certain countries, such as France, accounting rules allow companies to immediately write off a bond discount to expense. This conservative accounting treatment can result in a violation of the matching principle.

■ **EXHIBIT 11.4**
Effective-Interest Method of Amortizing Bond Premium

Panel A—Bond Data

Date Sold—April 1, Year 1
Face Value—$100,000
Stated Interest Rate—10%, paid semiannually
Market Interest Rate on Date Sold—9%
Selling Price—$103,957

Panel B—Amortization Schedule, Effective-Interest Method

INTEREST PAYMENT DATE	INTEREST EXPENSE[1]	INTEREST PAYMENT[2]	PREMIUM AMORTIZATION[3]	BOND PREMIUM BALANCE[4]	BOND CARRYING VALUE[5]
Date Sold, Apr. 1, Year 1				$3,957	$103,957
Oct. 1, Year 1	$4,678	$5,000	$322	3,635	103,635
Apr. 1, Year 2	4,664	5,000	336	3,299	103,299
Oct. 1, Year 2	4,648	5,000	352	2,947	102,947
Apr. 1, Year 3	4,633	5,000	367	2,580	102,580
Oct. 1, Year 3	4,616	5,000	384	2,196	102,196
Apr. 1, Year 4	4,599	5,000	401	1,795	101,795
Oct. 1, Year 4	4,581	5,000	419	1,376	101,376
Apr. 1, Year 5	4,562	5,000	438	938	100,938
Oct. 1, Year 5	4,542	5,000	458	480	100,480
Apr. 1, Year 6	4,520*	5,000	480	0	100,000

[1]. 4.5% × Bond Carrying Value at the end of the prior interest payment period; for the initial interest payment date, interest expense is determined by multiplying 4.5% by the original carrying value (selling price) of the bonds.
[2]. 5% × Bond Face Value of $100,000.
[3]. Interest Payment − Interest Expense.
[4]. Prior Balance − current period Premium Amortization.
[5]. Bond Face Value of $100,000 + Bond Premium Balance.
* Difference due to rounding.

Accounting for Bonds Payable: A Few Other Issues

Before we consider accounting issues related to other long-term liabilities, we should address a few remaining topics for bonds payable. Among these topics are accounting for bonds issued at other than an interest payment date, accounting for the early retirement of bonds, and accounting for the conversion of bonds into common stock.

BONDS PAYABLE ISSUED AT OTHER THAN AN INTEREST PAYMENT DATE
Companies often sell bonds in a new bond issue on one or more dates between the first day of the bond term and the initial interest payment date. When this occurs, the bonds are typically sold on a "plus accrued interest" basis. That is, the amount paid for the bonds includes "phantom" interest accruing on them since the first day of the bond term. The bondholders are then paid a full six months of interest on the first interest payment date. Selling bonds on a plus accrued interest basis eliminates the

Teaching Note
Emphasize that when bonds are sold "plus accrued interest," on the next interest payment date the bondholders will receive a full six months of interest even if they have only owned the bonds for one month.

need for the issuing company to compute the amount of interest each bondholder is entitled to receive on the initial interest payment date.

Suppose that Hardin Manufacturing Company sells its bonds at face value on June 1, Year 1. This date is two months after the beginning of the bond term and four months before the initial interest payment date of October 1. The bond purchasers would pay $100,000 for the bonds plus $1,667 of "accrued interest." This latter amount represents the interest that would have accrued, or accumulated, on the bonds for the period April 1 through June 1 and is computed as follows: $100,000 \times 10\% \times 2/12 = \$1,667$. Following is the entry to record this transaction.

Jun. 1	Cash	101,667	
	Bonds Payable		100,000
	Interest Expense		1,667

To record sale of five-year bonds with a stated interest rate of 10% and a maturity date of April 1, Year 6, plus accrued interest of $1,667

Notice that the $1,667 of accrued interest collected from the bond purchasers is credited to the Interest Expense account. On October 1, Year 1, the initial interest payment date, the bondholders would be paid $5,000. This payment would be recorded as follows:

| Oct. 1 | Interest Expense | 5,000 | |
| | Cash | | 5,000 |

To record interest payment on bonds payable

The balance of the Interest Expense account following the posting of these two entries would be $3,333 ($5,000 − $1,667). That amount represents the interest actually earned by the bondholders for the four months the bonds were outstanding during the initial interest payment period: $100,000 \times 10\% \times 4/12 = \$3,333$.

EARLY RETIREMENT OF BONDS PAYABLE   If interest rates decline considerably after a company issues bonds, company executives may decide to retire those bonds and issue new ones that have a lower stated interest rate. Such a decision is easier to implement if a call option is included in the bond indenture. If a company's bonds are not callable, the firm may purchase them on the "open" market and then retire them. An example of a company that retired bonds before their maturity date is Fleming Companies, a large food distribution firm headquartered in Oklahoma City. In 1993, Fleming retired some of its unsecured bonds, or debentures. As often happens, Fleming's bonds were not retired at their carrying value. The difference between the carrying value of a company's bonds and the amount paid to retire them is treated as an "extraordinary" gain or loss for accounting purposes. Fleming, for example, recorded a $2.3 million extraordinary loss on the retirement of its debentures in 1993. Extraordinary gains and losses are unusual and infrequently occurring items that companies are required to report separately in their income statements. In Chapter 13, we discuss extraordinary gains and losses in more depth.

To illustrate accounting for an early bond retirement, assume that the Fleming bonds retired in 1993 had a face value of $63,000,000 and an unamortized bond discount of $1,200,000. So these bonds had a preretirement carrying value of

Corporations sometime retire outstanding bonds prior to their maturity date. A common motivation for this decision is to eliminate high interest payments being made on the bonds. In 1993, Fleming Companies, a food distributor, retired more than $60 million of bonds by purchasing them on the open market.

$61,800,000 ($63,000,000 − $1,200,000). If Fleming paid $64,100,000 to purchase these bonds, the following entry would have been appropriate to record this bond retirement.

Apr. 3	Bonds Payable	63,000,000	
	Loss on Bond Retirement	2,300,000	
	Cash		64,100,000
	Discount on Bonds Payable		1,200,000
	To record retirement of bonds payable		

Since these bonds were being retired, all account balances related to them had to be removed from Fleming's accounting records. The entry just shown eliminated the balance of the Bonds Payable account and the balance of Discount on Bonds Payable. Notice that the difference between the amount paid to retire the bonds, $64,100,000, and their carrying value, $61,800,000, was debited to the extraordinary loss account Loss on Bond Retirement.

BOND CONVERSION: A SPECIAL TYPE OF BOND RETIREMENT   Recall that some bond issues have a conversion option. When bondholders exercise such an option, they receive stock in a company in exchange for their bonds. Suppose that Holden Construction Company has convertible bonds outstanding with a collective face value of $5 million—5,000 individual bonds each with a $1,000 face value. These

Real World
Convertible bonds typically offer a lower interest rate than nonconvertible bonds. Convertible bondholders accept the lower interest rate in exchange for the opportunity to trade the bonds for shares of stock in the future.

individual bonds can be converted into 20 shares of Holden's common stock that has a $40 par value. Assume that the Holden bonds have an unamortized premium of $240,000 and that the bonds are currently selling for a quoted price of 125. Finally, assume that the current selling price of Holden's common stock is $65 per share. Summarized next is the key information for Holden's convertible bonds.

Face Value of Bonds	$5,000,000
Unamortized Premium	240,000
Carrying Value of Bonds	$5,240,000
Current Market Price of Bonds	$1,250
Conversion Option	20 shares of common stock per $1,000 bond
Current Selling Price of Common Stock	$65
Par Value of Common Stock	$40

If you own a Holden bond, you should frequently consider whether to exercise the bond's conversion option and obtain 20 shares of Holden common stock in exchange for your bond. Given the facts provided, the collective market value of 20 shares of Holden common stock is $1,300 (20 × $65), while each Holden bond has a market value of $1,250. So, you presently have an economic gain of $50 available to you. Since conversion options usually expire before the end of a bond term, bondholders often exercise a conversion option to "lock in" any gain available to them.

Let us assume that you, and the other Holden bondholders, decide to exercise the conversion option. To record the conversion of its bonds payable into common stock, Holden would make the following entry in its accounting records.

Jan. 28	Bonds Payable	5,000,000	
	Premium on Bonds Payable	240,000	
	Common Stock		4,000,000
	Additional Paid-In Capital, Common Stock		1,240,000

To record conversion of bonds
payable into common stock

Teaching Note
Contrast the different accounting treatment of callable bonds and convertible bonds. When callable bonds are retired, a gain or loss is nearly always recorded. When bonds are converted to stock, a gain or loss is not recognized.

Again, when bonds payable are retired, each account balance related to them must be eliminated from a company's accounting records. In the present example, the account balances that must be eliminated are the $5,000,000 balance of Bonds Payable and the $240,000 balance of Premium on Bonds Payable. Unlike the previous example of a bond retirement, when bonds are converted into common stock, a gain or loss is not recorded on the transaction. We have not considered accounting for stockholders' equity in any depth to this point in the text. For now, simply recognize that in a bond conversion the total carrying value of the converted bonds is credited to stockholders' equity accounts. The collective par value of the stock issued in a bond conversion is credited to the Common Stock account. Holden's 5,000 bonds would each be exchanged for 20 shares of common stock, resulting in a total of 100,000 shares being issued. The collective par value of these shares, $4 million ($40 × 100,000), would be credited to Common Stock, as shown in the previous entry. The $1,240,000 difference between the bonds' carrying value and the collective par value of the stock issued would be credited to another stockholders' equity account. For Holden, this account is Additional Paid-In Capital, Common Stock.

ACCOUNTING FOR LONG-TERM LIABILITIES OTHER THAN BONDS PAYABLE

Now that we have "nailed down" accounting procedures for bonds payable, let us briefly examine accounting issues related to other long-term liabilities. In this section, we consider long-term notes payable, long-term lease obligations, pension liabilities, and other postretirement benefit liabilities.

Long-Term Notes Payable

In Chapter 10, accounting for short-term notes payable was discussed. The accounting procedures for long-term notes payable are very similar to the procedures used for short-term notes payable. So, there is no need to rehash those procedures at this point. But let us consider briefly a special type of long-term notes payable.

Real World
Most lenders reduce the risk associated with lending money by requiring some form of collateral.

Many long-term notes payable are actually mortgage notes payable. A company that borrows $10 million to purchase a new building may be required by the lender to sign a mortgage note. This note will likely pledge the building as security or collateral for the loan. If the company defaults on the mortgage note, the lender can obtain legal title to the building or force it to be sold to satisfy the unpaid mortgage. Mortgage notes payable usually require equal monthly payments consisting of both principal and interest. For financial statement purposes, mortgage notes are often reported as "mortgages payable." Calton Inc., a home-building company, reported $7.7 million of mortgages payable in a recent balance sheet. The portion of mortgages payable that matures in the coming year must be reported as a current liability in an entity's balance sheet.

Long-Term Lease Obligations

In Chapter 9, leaseholds were discussed in the context of intangible assets. Recall that a leasehold is a legal right to use a leased asset for a specified period subject to any restrictions in the lease agreement. The two parties to a lease agreement are the lessor, the owner of the asset being leased, and the lessee, the party leasing the asset. Leasing has become a popular method used by businesses to finance the acquisition of a wide range of assets including buildings, equipment, and automobile fleets.

■ **LEARNING OBJECTIVE 5**
Account for long-term lease obligations

As suggested earlier, leased assets and the long-term obligations stemming from lease agreements were largely ignored by lessees for accounting and financial reporting purposes until fairly recently. Fortunately for decision makers, the accounting profession converted certain leasing arrangements from off-balance sheet to "on-balance sheet" financing methods in the mid-1970s. Many companies now regularly report on their balance sheets large long-term liabilities related to lease agreements. These long-term liabilities are commonly known as long-term lease obligations or capital lease obligations. Carl Karcher Enterprises, a fast-food chain, reported $45.8 million of "Capital Lease Obligations" in its 1994 financial statements.

OPERATING VS. CAPITAL LEASES   Accounting standards distinguish between operating leases and capital leases. An **operating lease** is usually cancelable by the lessee, has a relatively short term, and does not transfer ownership rights or risks to the lessee. A **capital lease** is generally noncancelable, long-term, and transfers at least some ownership rights or risks to the lessee. More technically, leases that meet one or more of the following criteria qualify as capital leases.

operating lease

capital lease

1. The lease agreement transfers legal title to the leased asset to the lessee at the end of the lease term.
2. A "bargain purchase option" that can be exercised by the lessee is included in the lease agreement.
3. The term of the lease covers 75 percent or more of the economic life of the leased asset.
4. The present value of the lease payments is equal to 90 percent or more of the market value of the leased asset.

Accounting for operating leases is quite simple. The leasehold obtained by the lessee is not recorded as an asset, nor is a long-term liability related to the lease recorded in the lessee's books. When the lessee makes a lease payment, Rental Expense or Lease Expense is debited and Cash is credited.

ACCOUNTING FOR CAPITAL LEASES   The economic substance of business transactions, instead of their legal form, should dictate how they are recorded. In substance, capital leases are equivalent to purchases of long-term assets that are financed by long-term loans. Consequently, a capital lease should result in both a long-term asset and a long-term liability being recorded in a lessee's accounting records.

Suppose that Holden Construction Company leases a bulldozer from Adams Equipment Supply at the beginning of a year and this lease qualifies as a capital lease. The term of the lease is five years. At the end of each year, Holden is required to make a $20,000 payment to Adams. The first step in recording this lease is to determine the present value of the payments to be made over the term of the lease. The present value of the payments under a capital lease is recorded as both an asset and a long-term liability in the lessee's accounting records.

For purposes of our example, assume that a discount rate of 10 percent is appropriate to determine the present value of the lease payments. Given this discount rate, the present value of the lease payments can be computed by using the present value of an annuity equation.

$$\begin{matrix} \text{Present Value} & & \text{Annuity} & \text{Present Value of} \\ \text{of an Annuity (PVA)} & = & \text{Amount (A)} \times & \text{an Annuity Factor (PVAF)} \end{matrix}$$

Here, the appropriate present value of an annuity factor is 3.79079, which can be found in Table 10.4 at the intersection of the 10 percent column and the five-year row. The present value of the lease payments can now be computed as follows:

$$\begin{aligned} \text{PVA} &= \text{A} \times \text{PVAF} \\ \text{PVA} &= \$20,000 \times 3.79079 \\ \text{PVA} &= \$75,815.80 \end{aligned}$$

Shown next is the entry to record the present value of the lease payments in Holden's accounting records as both an asset and a long-term liability.

Jan. 1	Leased Equipment, Bulldozer	75,816	
	Capital Lease Obligation		75,816
	To record capital lease of bulldozer (asset No. 1–28)		

Over the term of a capital lease, the leased asset is depreciated similar to depreciable assets owned by the lessee. Besides adjusting entries to record depreciation, an

Leasing vs. Borrowing: A Tough Decision for Small Businesses

Leasing is generally a more costly method of financing the acquisition of an asset than borrowing funds and then purchasing the asset. Despite this fact, many small business owners choose leasing over borrowing. In the following excerpt of an article appearing in The Wall Street Journal, *Michael Selz explains why small business owners often make this choice.*

Roger Wolfanger didn't even call a banker this year when he needed business equipment. He says banks had rejected his Wilcox Collision Repair Center in Rochester, N.Y., for a loan two years ago, and he was too discouraged to go through the whole approval process again.

He chose instead to lease the equipment. Doing so required filling out only a simple one-page application. Two days later, his company was taking delivery on a $4,000 machine that straightens auto frames.

One problem, though: the effective interest rate on the lease is 21.7%. And Wilcox is stuck with it for two years.

Countless companies are in the same position. Having been rebuffed by banks in recent years they turn to equipment leasing. And now, they are saddled with onerous lease commitments. In many cases, the effective rates on the leases exceed those on the business owner's personal VISA card.

[Nevertheless] small business financial advisers say leasing often makes good sense. It conserves a company's borrowing power. It requires less upfront cash than a purchase because the security deposit is usually much smaller than a loan's down payment. Leasing also offers better protection against technological change. Trading in an old machine for a new one when the lease expires is simpler than getting rid of obsolete equipment that a company owns. And for numerous small businesses that found credit tight in recent years, leasing was the only way to finance new equipment.

SOURCE: M. Selz, "Many Small Businesses Are Sold on Leasing Equipment," *The Wall Street Journal,* 27 October 1993, B2.

entry is required each year to record the lease payment to the lessor. Examples of these entries are not presented here, but instead are deferred to advanced accounting courses.

Like other long-term liabilities, a long-term lease obligation should be segregated for balance sheet purposes into its current and long-term portions. Additionally, for both operating and capital leases, lessees must disclose in their financial statements future minimum lease payments over the next five years. For example, in its 1994 annual report, Cracker Barrel Old Country Store, Inc., disclosed the future minimum payments it would be required to make under operating and capital leases for the period 1995–1999.

Pension Liabilities

Most large companies, and many smaller ones as well, have established pension plans to provide a monthly retirement income for their employees. These pension plans come in two varieties: defined benefit plans and defined contribution plans.

■ LEARNING OBJECTIVE 6
Discuss the key accounting issues related to long-term liabilities stemming from pension and other postretirement employee benefit plans

FOR YOUR INFORMATION

Abe Lincoln on Accounting for Postretirement Employee Benefits

Warren Buffett, chief executive officer of Berkshire Hathaway, Inc., and reportedly among the wealthiest individuals in the world, has been an outspoken critic of the accounting profession for many years. In his company's 1992 annual report, Mr. Buffett commented on the profession's tardiness in requiring companies to record liabilities for the postretirement health benefits promised to their employees.

Another major accounting change, whose implementation is required by January 1, 1993, mandates that businesses recognize their present-value liability for postretirement health benefits. Though GAAP has previously required recognition of pensions to be paid in the future, it has illogically ignored the costs that companies will then have to bear for health benefits. The new rule will force many companies to record a huge balance-sheet liability (and a consequent reduction in net worth) and also henceforth to recognize substantially higher costs when they are calculating annual profits.

I believe that part of the reason for this reckless behavior was that accounting rules did not, for so long, require the booking of postretirement health costs as they were incurred. Instead, the rules allowed cash-basis accounting, which vastly understated the liabilities that were building up. In effect, the attitude of both managements and their accountants toward these liabilities was "out-of-sight, out-of-mind." Ironically, some of these same managers would be quick to criticize Congress for employing "cash-basis" thinking in respect to Social Security promises or other programs creating future liabilities of size.

Managers thinking about accounting issues should never forget one of Abraham Lincoln's favorite riddles: "How many legs does a dog have if you call his tail a leg"? The answer: "Four, because calling a tail a leg does not make it a leg." It behooves managers to remember that Abe's right even if an auditor is willing to certify that the tail is a leg.

Real World
Frequently, employees have an option of receiving their retirement benefits in either a lump-sum payment or in a series of equal installments. An understanding of the time value of money concept allows retirees to make this decision on a more informed basis.

Under a defined contribution plan, employers make periodic contributions to a pension fund. These contributions are typically a percentage of each employee's gross earnings. Individual pension accounts are usually maintained for each employee. Following retirement, an employee receives a monthly, quarterly, or annual benefit based upon the size of his or her pension account. Accounting for a defined contribution plan is quite simple. When an employer determines the proper periodic contribution to the pension fund, Pension Expense is debited and Cash or a liability account is credited.

Defined benefit pension plans are much more complex and cumbersome to account for, compared with defined contribution plans. Under a defined benefit plan, employees are promised a monthly pension benefit. The size of this benefit depends on such factors as an employee's length of employment, age at retirement, and salary level over the last few years of employment. Until recently, businesses typically accounted for the costs stemming from defined benefit pension plans on a cash basis. That is, the expense associated with a defined benefit pension plan was not recognized or accrued in an entity's accounting records as employees accumulated retirement benefits. Instead, when retirement benefits were paid to employees, an expense account was debited and a cash account credited. This approach to accounting for defined benefit pension plans violated the matching principle by not recording a significant employment-related expense each accounting period. This approach also

General Motors employs several hundred thousand workers in plants like this across the nation. Each year, GM pays billions of dollars of health care costs for present and former employees and their dependents. Since 1991, GM has accounted for these costs on an accrual basis.

resulted in an often huge long-term liability going unreported on the balance sheets of companies having a defined benefit pension plan.

Extensive criticism of cash basis accounting for defined benefit pension plans resulted in a series of lengthy studies of this topic by the accounting profession. Finally, in 1985, *Statement of Financial Accounting Standards No. 87*, "Employers' Accounting for Pensions," was adopted. This accounting standard requires companies that have a defined benefit pension plan to recognize pension expense on an accrual basis each accounting period. If a company's pension fund assets are less than the present value of the pension benefits owed to employees, this difference must be reported as a liability. For example, Puritan-Bennett Corporation, a small manufacturing company, reported an $8 million long-term liability in its 1994 balance sheet stemming from its "underfunded" pension plan.

Other Postretirement Benefit Liabilities

Many businesses provide some type of nonpension postretirement benefits to their employees, probably the most common being health care benefits. Similar to pension benefits, these "other postretirement benefits" (OPBs) were accounted for principally on a cash basis until recently. In the early 1990s, businesses were required to adopt the accrual basis of accounting for OPBs. This new accounting treatment was mandated by *Statement on Financial Accounting Standards No. 106*, "Employers' Accounting for Postretirement Benefits Other Than Pensions."

Many companies apparently did not realize the magnitude of the off–balance sheet liabilities they had accumulated because of OPBs earned by their employees. When IBM implemented the new accounting rule in 1991 for OPBs, it took a more than $2 billion "hit" on its income statement. That expense item caused IBM to report its first ever quarterly loss. Likewise, consider the case of General Motors. General Motors

■ **LEARNING OBJECTIVE 6**
Discuss the key accounting issues related to long-term liabilities stemming from pension and other postretirement employee benefit plans

Real World
When Exxon Corporation adopted *SFAS No. 106* in 1992, it reported the cumulative effect of the accounting change on years prior to 1992 as an $800 million reduction in net income.

reported in its 1992 annual report that it was paying the health care costs of 386,000 employees, 358,000 retirees, and approximately 1 million dependents. In 1992 alone, General Motors paid $3.7 billion for health care expenses of these individuals. Even more staggering is the $35 billion long-term liability that General Motors reported in its 1992 balance sheet for OPBs.

The recent moves to require accrual basis accounting for defined benefit pension plans and OPBs provide decision makers with a truer "picture" of the financial condition of business entities. Nevertheless, many critics of the accounting profession complain that these new rules were too long in the making. Included in a vignette in this section is one critic's analysis of the profession's belated decision to impose accrual basis accounting on postretirement employee benefits.

ANALYZING LONG-TERM LIABILITIES

■ LEARNING OBJECTIVE 7
Compute and interpret the long-term debt to equity and times interest earned ratios

When analyzing a business's long-term liabilities, the principal concern of decision makers is whether the entity can pay off those liabilities as they come due. Two financial ratios that are used to analyze long-term liabilities are the long-term debt to equity ratio and the times interest earned ratio. Shown in Exhibit 11.5 is a four-year comparison of these ratios for two public companies, Harris Corporation and XTRA

■ **EXHIBIT 11.5**
Long-Term Debt to Equity and Times Interest Earned Ratios: Harris Corporation vs. XTRA Corporation

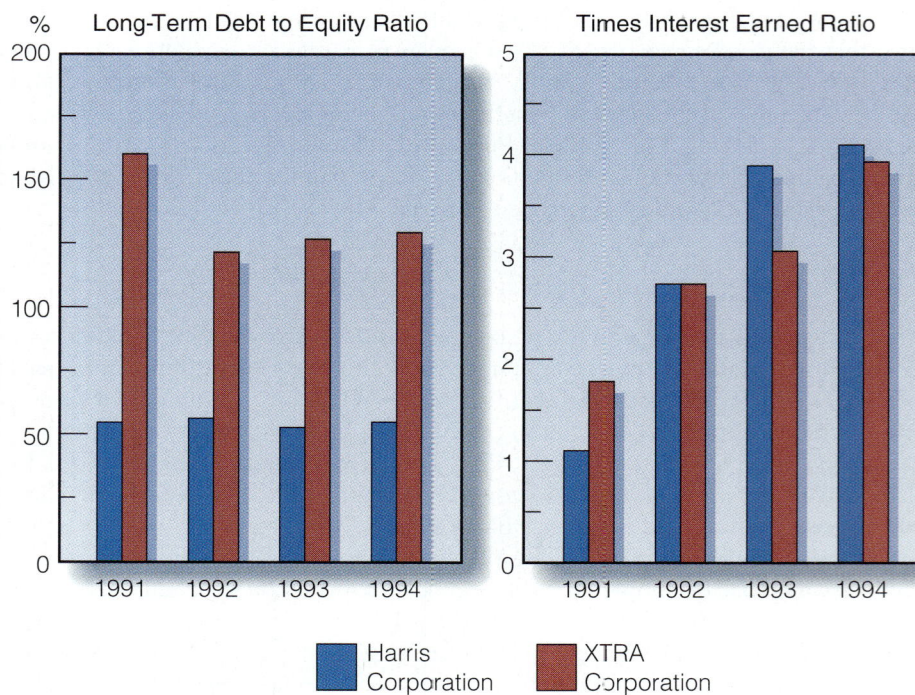

Corporation. Harris's major product lines include communication equipment and office systems, while XTRA is a truck and trailer leasing company.

Long-Term Debt to Equity Ratio

A company that makes extensive use of long-term debt to meet its financing needs is said to be highly leveraged. Such companies are generally at a higher risk of "going under" than firms that have little long-term debt on their balance sheet. If a company fails to make required interest or principal payments on its long-term debt, it may face legal action including the initiation of bankruptcy proceedings. Firms do not have a legal obligation to make regular payments to their stockholders or other owners.

A common measure of financial leverage is the **long-term debt to equity ratio,** which is computed by dividing a company's total long-term liabilities by its total stockholders' equity. Notice in Exhibit 11.5 that XTRA Corporation had a much higher long-term debt to equity ratio than Harris Corporation in the early 1990s. XTRA Corporation consistently had more long-term liabilities than stockholders' equity on its balance sheet. On the other hand, Harris Corporation's total long-term liabilities averaged approximately 50 percent of its stockholders' equity during the same period.

Shown in Exhibit 11.6 are average long-term debt to equity ratios for six industries in 1994. Included in these industries are communication equipment, the industry of Harris Corporation, and truck rental and leasing, XTRA Corporation's industry. Notice that both companies utilized more financial leverage than their industries as a whole. The average long-term debt to equity ratio for the communication equipment industry was approximately 20 percent in 1994. Compare that ratio with Harris's long-term debt to equity ratio of approximately 50 percent in the same year as shown in Exhibit 11.5. The norm for the long-term debt to equity ratio in the truck rental and leasing industry was slightly less than 60 percent in 1994. XTRA's long-term debt to equity ratio was more than double that level. Conclusion? Compared with industry norms, both Harris and XTRA were more highly leveraged in the early 1990s than competing firms in their industries. Consequently, both firms faced a higher risk than their competitors of being forced out of business if they encountered financial problems.

Times Interest Earned Ratio

A company that is highly leveraged is not necessarily in danger of defaulting on its long-term debt. The **times interest earned** ratio helps decision makers evaluate the ability of companies, particularly highly leveraged companies, to make their interest payments as they come due. Following is the equation used to compute the times interest earned ratio.

$$\text{Times Interest Earned Ratio} = \frac{\text{Net Income} + \text{Interest Expense} + \text{Income Taxes Expense}}{\text{Interest Expense}}$$

The times interest earned ratio indicates the number of times that earnings before interest expense and income taxes "covers" a company's interest expense during a given period. The lower this ratio, the more risk a company faces of being unable to make interest payments on its long-term debt. As is true for most financial ratios, there is not complete agreement on what represents a reasonable level for the times

Discussion Question
What impact does recording a lease as a capital lease instead of an operating lease have on a company's long-term debt to equity ratio?
Answer: It increases the long-term debt to equity ratio.

long-term debt to equity ratio

Focus on Ethics
A company needs to borrow money to purchase an expensive piece of equipment. Recording additional long-term debt on the balance sheet will cause the company to be in violation of some of its debt covenants. Company executives decide to lease the equipment and carefully structure the lease agreement to ensure that the lease does not qualify as a capital lease. Is this ethical? Why or why not?

times interest earned ratio

Discussion Question
Compute the times interest earned ratio for Michaels Stores. What does this ratio imply about the company's ability to make its interest payments?

■ **EXHIBIT 11.6**
Long-Term Debt to Equity Ratio, Selected Industries

SOURCE: Dun & Bradstreet's *Industry Norms & Key Business Ratios, 1993–1994.* Dun & Bradstreet Information Services. (New York: Dun & Bradstreet, 1994).

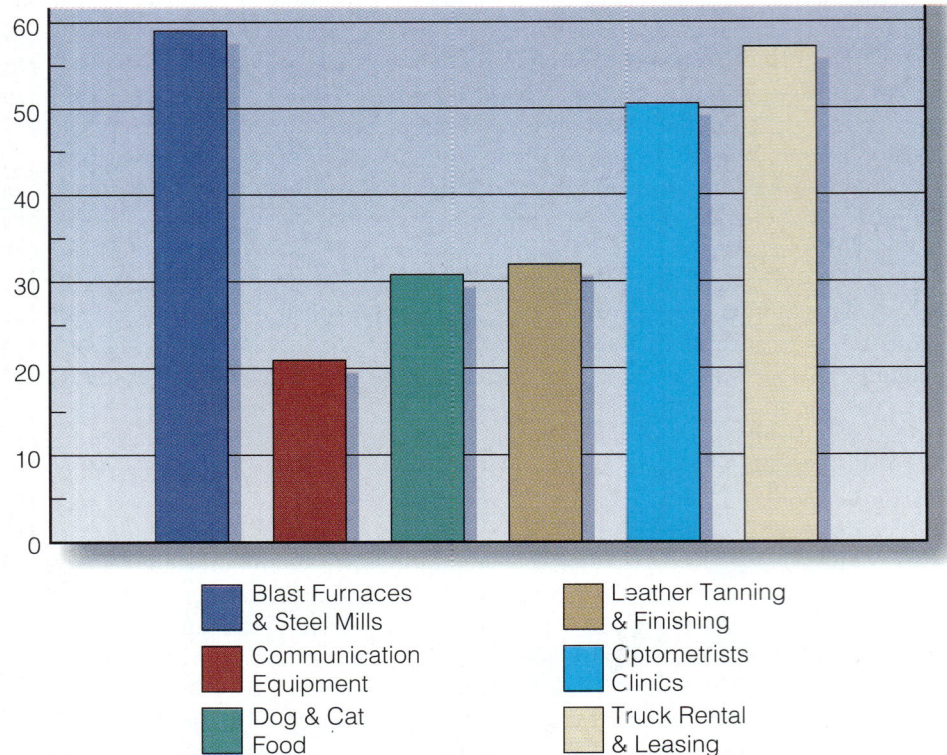

Blast Furnaces & Steel Mills
Communication Equipment
Dog & Cat Food
Leather Tanning & Finishing
Optometrists Clinics
Truck Rental & Leasing

interest earned ratio. Generally, somewhere between 4.0 to 6.0 is considered a comfortable level for this ratio. Exhibit 11.5 illustrates that the times interest earned ratio of both Harris and XTRA gradually improved (increased) during the early 1990s. By 1994, these companies faced a much lower risk of defaulting on their long-term debt interest payments than they did in 1991.

KEY INTERNAL CONTROL PROCEDURES FOR LONG-TERM LIABILITIES

■ **LEARNING OBJECTIVE 8**
Define key internal control procedures for long-term liabilities

The first step in achieving adequate control over long-term liabilities is to establish procedures for ensuring that long-term financing decisions are properly authorized. Decisions to sell corporate bonds, to borrow large sums on long-term promissory notes, or to create a pension plan must be approved by an organization's top executives. Once these transactions have been properly authorized, adequate documentation must be developed to meet all tax-related, financial reporting, and other regulatory requirements for the resulting long-term liabilities. For instance, federal regulations relating to the establishment, maintenance, and recordkeeping for employee pension plans are extensive and complex. A company that fails to meet these requirements faces a risk of large fines and sanctions. Adequate documentation for bonds payable is also critical. Bond indentures must be written with extreme precision to protect the rights and privileges of both the company issuing bonds and the parties that subsequently purchase those bonds.

Control procedures should also be established to ensure that interest and principal payments on long-term debt are made promptly, in the proper amounts, to the appropriate individuals, and are recorded correctly. One such control procedure is the preparation of an amortization schedule. As you learned earlier, an amortization schedule documents, among other items, the amounts to be included in the entries to record periodic interest payments on long-term debt.

Large public companies that have bonds payable outstanding often hire outside agencies to help them control these long-term liabilities. For example, a company that has bonds outstanding may retain a bank to serve as its transfer agent. A transfer agent maintains a continually updated record of a company's bondholders and their addresses. This record serves as the basis for determining the individuals entitled to receive periodic interest payments on the bonds.

Finally, a business entity should establish control procedures to monitor compliance with any restrictive covenants included in a bond indenture or other long-term debt agreement. If a company violates one or more of these conditions, the entire long-term debt may become immediately due and payable.

Real World

Pension plans that have a tax-exempt status must have an annual independent audit. Public accounting firms typically audit their clients' pension plans in addition to their financial statements.

SUMMARY

Long-term liabilities include debts and other obligations of a business other than those classified as current liabilities. Among the more common long-term liabilities are bonds payable, notes payable, and capital lease obligations. The key information needs of decision makers regarding long-term liabilities parallel those for current liabilities. Most important, decision makers need to be assured that all long-term liabilities are included in an entity's financial statements. Several recent accounting standards have reduced the number of "off–balance sheet" long-term liabilities. As a result, decision makers now obtain a more accurate picture of the financial condition of business entities. Decision makers also need to be informed of the valuation methods used to assign dollar amounts to long-term liabilities, particularly those that must be estimated. Finally, any material and unusual circumstances related to long-term liabilities, such as the existence of restrictive debt covenants, should be disclosed in an entity's financial statement footnotes.

A key to accounting properly for bonds payable is an understanding of how bond selling prices are established. Newly issued bonds usually sell for more or less than their face value because their stated interest rate is either higher or lower than the market interest rate on the date they are sold. A bond discount or premium should be amortized over the term of a bond issue. The amortization of a bond discount increases the interest expense recognized on a bond issue. The amortization of a bond premium reduces the interest expense recognized on a bond issue. Generally, the effective-interest method should be used to amortize bond discounts and premiums.

When accounting for a long-term lease, the key issue that must be addressed is whether the lease qualifies as an operating lease or a capital lease. For a capital lease, a lessee must record both an asset and a long-term liability in its accounting records. Accounting standards adopted recently require companies to record long-term liabilities stemming from commitments they have made to provide postretirement benefits to employees. These liabilities are often enormous and have dramatically affected large public companies' reported financial condition.

When analyzing long-term liabilities, decision makers monitor the degree of financial leverage used by a business and its ability to make its periodic interest payments. A key ratio used to analyze financial leverage is the long-term debt to equity ratio. An entity's ability to make periodic interest payments has historically been assessed by computing and tracking the times interest earned ratio.

Proper authorization of decisions to incur long-term liabilities is a critical element of internal control for business entities. Once a long-term liability has been incurred, an entity must adequately document the liability to meet all tax-related, financial reporting, and other regulatory requirements. Control procedures are also necessary to ensure that interest and principal payments on long-term liabilities are made promptly, in the proper amounts, to the appropriate individuals, and are properly recorded. Control procedures should be implemented as well to monitor an entity's compliance with any restrictive covenants included in long-term debt agreements.

GLOSSARY

Bond (p. 475)   A long-term loan made by one party to another that is legally documented by a bond certificate.

Bond indenture (p. 475)   The legal contract between a bond purchaser and the issuing company; identifies the rights and obligations of both parties.

Callable bonds (p. 477)   Bonds that can be retired or redeemed by the issuing company when one or more conditions are met.

Capital lease (p. 491)   A lease that is generally noncancelable, long-term, and transfers at least some ownership rights or risks to the lessee.

Convertible bonds (p. 477)   Bonds that may be exchanged for stock in the issuing company at the option of the bondholders.

Effective interest method (p. 484)   A method of determining interest expense on bonds payable each interest payment period; under this method, interest expense is computed by multiplying the effective interest rate by the bonds' carrying value.

Effective interest rate (p. 484)   The market interest rate on the date bonds are initially sold; represents the true rate of interest actually incurred over the term of a bond issue.

Long-term debt to equity ratio (p. 497)   Computed by dividing an entity's total long-term liabilities by its total stockholders' equity; a common measure of financial leverage.

Off-balance sheet financing (p. 473)   Involves the acquisition of assets or services by incurring long-term obligations that are not included in an entity's balance sheet.

Operating lease (p. 491)   A lease that is usually cancelable by the lessee, covers a short-term, and does not transfer ownership rights or risks to the lessee.

Secured bonds (p. 477)   Bonds collateralized by specific assets of the issuing company; sometimes referred to as mortgage bonds.

Stated interest rate (p. 475)   The rate of interest paid to bondholders based upon the face value of the bonds; also known as the face interest rate or contract interest rate.

Times interest earned ratio (p. 497)   Computed by dividing the sum of net income, interest expense, and income taxes expense by interest expense; used to assess an entity's ability to make interest payments on long-term debt.

Unsecured bonds (p. 477)   Bonds backed only by the legal commitment of the issuing firm to make all required principal and interest payments; often referred to as debentures.

DECISION
CASE

You began your college career at Louisiana State University as a marketing major and somehow wound up graduating with an accounting degree. You have recently passed the CPA exam and are now a practicing public accountant in the small town of Hope, Arkansas. Like most small-town accountants, most of your revenue comes from preparing tax returns and performing bookkeeping services for local businesses. Occasionally, you serve as an informal financial advisor to your clients—no fees, just free, off-the-cuff advice. Recently, Virgilene Crawford, former wife of your now-deceased Uncle Rufus, came into your office and asked for advice on investing $100,000 she had recently inherited. Aunt Virgie is a strong-willed woman. A friend of hers made a "killing" in the last couple of years in the corporate bond market. So, Aunt Virgie is dead set on investing her newly found wealth in corporate bonds. A cousin on the other side of the family has suggested that she consider investing in the corporate bonds listed in the following table. The data in this table were taken from a recent edition of *The Wall Street Journal*.

COMPANY	STATED INTEREST RATE	CURRENT YIELD	MARKET PRICE	MATURITY DATE
AMR	9.0%	9.8%	91 ⅜	2016
IBM	6.375%	6.9%	92 ¼	2000
IBM	8.375%	8.6%	97	2019
U.S. Air	12.875%	14.3%	90	2000
Wendy's*	7.0%	5.3%	132	2006

*Convertible bonds.

Required: Aunt Virgie does not understand why there is such a disparity in the current yields on these bonds. In a brief report, explain to her the key factors that may account for this disparity. When identifying these factors, refer to specific examples using the data provided in the table just shown. Also, identify additional information that she needs to obtain regarding these bonds before she makes her investment decision.

   Applying the time value of money concept, illustrate to Aunt Virgie how the market price of the AMR bonds can be confirmed mathematically. Assume today's date is January 1, 1997, that the bonds mature on December 31, 2016, the interest on the bonds is paid semi-annually, and the market interest rate for comparable bonds is 10 percent. Finally, briefly explain to Aunt Virgie the difference between "current yield" and "yield to maturity."

QUESTIONS

1. Define "long-term liabilities." Provide several examples of long-term liabilities.
2. Identify the key information needs of financial decision makers regarding the long-term liabilities of business entities.
3. Define "off–balance sheet financing." Provide one example of an off–balance sheet financing technique.
4. What are restrictive debt covenants? Provide an example.
5. What is a bond issue?
6. What is a bond indenture? Identify the key items of information included in a bond indenture.
7. Briefly describe callable and convertible bonds.
8. What factors influence the selling price of a corporate bond?

9. What is the actual selling price of a $1,000 bond that has a quoted market price of 97½?

10. Explain how the current yield on a bond is determined.

11. Why is a bond's stated interest rate usually different from the market interest rate on the date the bond is initially sold?

12. Will a bond with a stated interest rate of 10 percent that is issued when the market interest rate is 9 percent sell for more or less than its face value? Why?

13. Compare and contrast the straight-line and effective-interest methods of amortizing bond discount and bond premium.

14. What is the purpose of an amortization schedule for bonds payable?

15. How is the carrying value of bonds payable determined for balance sheet reporting purposes?

16. Describe the conditions that would make a bondholder want to exercise a bond conversion feature.

17. What is the advantage to a corporation of including a call option in a bond indenture?

18. What are mortgage notes payable?

19. What is a lease? Identify the two parties to a lease agreement.

20. Summarize the criteria used to determine whether a lease is a capital lease or an operating lease.

21. Identify the advantages and disadvantages of leasing assets as opposed to purchasing them.

22. How do defined benefit and defined contribution pension plans differ?

23. How did the pay-as-you-go, or cash-basis, method of accounting for defined benefit pension plans violate the matching principle?

24. Define "financial leverage." Identify one method of measuring financial leverage.

25. How is the times interest earned ratio computed? How do decision makers use this ratio?

26. Identify three internal control procedures for long-term liabilities.

EXERCISES

27. **Bond Terminology** (LO 2)
    Following are definitions or descriptions of terms relating to corporate bonds.

    _____ Bonds that may be exchanged for stock in the issuing company.
    _____ Long-term loan made by one party to another.
    _____ Legal instrument documenting a bond.
    _____ $1,000 is the typical amount for corporate bonds.
    _____ Bonds backed only by the legal commitment of the issuing company to make all required principal and interest payments.
    _____ When bond principal is repaid.
    _____ Bonds collateralized by specific assets of the company issuing the bonds.
    _____ Legal contract between a bond purchaser and the company that issued the bond.
    _____ Period elapsing between the date bonds are first available for sale and the date they mature.

_____ Rate of interest to be paid to bondholders based on the face value of the bonds.

Required:

Match each definition or description listed with the appropriate term from the following list.

1. Bond
2. Coupon bonds
3. Face value (or principal amount)
4. Maturity date
5. Bond indenture
6. Stated interest rate (or contract rate)
7. Term of the bonds
8. Serial bonds
9. Callable bonds
10. Registered bonds
11. Bond certificate
12. Term bonds
13. Secured bonds
14. Convertible bonds
15. Debentures

27. 14,1,11,3,15,4,13,5,7,6

28. **Stated Interest Rate, Current Yield, and the Market Interest Rate** (LO 2)

Suppose you purchase a corporate bond with a face value of $1,000. That has a stated interest rate of 8 percent. Interest on the bond is paid semiannually.

Required:

1. How much interest will you receive on each interest payment date?
2. Suppose that you purchased this bond when the quoted market price was 98. How much did you pay for the bond? If you pay more or less than the face value of a bond, will the amount of interest you receive be affected? Why?
3. Suppose again that you purchase this bond at a quoted market price of 98. What is this bond's "current yield"? Why is the bond's current yield different from the bond's stated interest rate? Explain.
4. If you purchase this bond at a quoted market price of 98, is the market interest rate on the purchase date higher or lower than the bond's stated interest rate? Explain.

28. 1. $40
2. $980
3. 8.16%

29. **Cash Flows Related to Bonds Payable** (LO 2)

Lomax Corporation issued $1,000,000 of six-year, 10 percent bonds on January 1 of Year 1. Interest on the bonds is payable semiannually on January 1 and July 1 of each year.

Required:

1. How much will Lomax pay its bondholders on each interest payment date? On the bonds' maturity date?
2. Do the amounts you listed in Part 1 change if the market interest rate on the date these bonds are sold differs from the bonds' stated interest rate? Explain.
3. Diagram the cash flows for this bond issue using the format illustrated in Exhibit 11.2. Assume that the market interest rate is 10 percent when the bonds are sold.
4. Determine the cash that Lomax will receive from the sale of these bonds on January 1, Year 1, if the market interest rate on that date is:
   a. 9 percent.
   b. 7 percent.

29. 1. Interest, $50,000
Maturity, $1,000,000
3. PV principal, $556,840
PV interest, $443,160
4a. $1,045,589
4b. $1,144,947

30. **Bonds Payable Journal Entries** (LO 3)

On February 1, 1994, Softique Company issued $10,000,000 of ten-year, 8 percent bonds at face value. Interest is payable semiannually on February 1 and August 1 of each year. Softique's year-end is December 31.

Required:

Prepare the appropriate journal entries in Softique's accounting records on the following dates for these bonds.
1. February 1, 1994
2. August 1, 1994
3. December 31, 1994
4. February 1, 1995

30. 2. Int. Exp. $400,000
    3. Int. Exp. $333,333
    4. Int. Exp. $66,667

31. **Straight-Line Method of Amortizing Bond Discount or Premium** (LO 3)

Peterson Company issued $200,000 of five-year, 12 percent bonds on May 1, 1992, when the market rate of interest for similar bonds was 10 percent. The bonds pay interest semiannually on May 1 and November 1 of each year. Peterson's year-end is December 31.

Required:

Prepare the journal entries necessary on each of the following dates, assuming Peterson amortizes any bond discount or premium using the straight-line method.
1. May 1, 1992
2. November 1, 1992
3. December 31, 1992
4. May 1, 1993

31. 1. Premium, $15,442.76
    2. Int. Exp. $10,455.72
    3. Int. Exp. $3,485.42
    4. Int. Exp. $6,970.48

32. **Effective-Interest Method of Amortizing Bond Discount or Premium** (LO 4)

Refer to the information in Exercise 31.

Required:

Prepare the journal entries necessary on each of the following dates, assuming Peterson amortizes any bond discount or premium using the effective-interest method:
1. May 1, 1992
2. November 1, 1992
3. December 31, 1992
4. May 1, 1993

32. 1. Premium, $15,442.76
    2. Int. Exp. $10,772.14
    3. Int. Exp. $3,570.25
    4. Int. Exp. $7,140.49

33. **Straight-Line Method of Amortizing Bond Discount or Premium** (LO 3)

Mason Company issued $700,000 of five-year, 8 percent bonds on March 1, 1991, when the market interest rate for similar bonds was 10 percent. The bonds pay interest semiannually on March 1 and September 1 of each year. Mason's year-end is December 31.

Required:

Prepare the journal entries necessary on each of the following dates, assuming Mason amortizes bond premium or discount using the straight-line method.
1. March 1, 1991
2. September 1, 1991
3. December 31, 1991
4. March 1, 1992

33. 1. Discount, $54,054.56
    2. Int. Exp. $33,405.46
    3. Int. Exp. $22,270.31
    4. Int. Exp. $11,135.15

34. **Effective-Interest Method of Amortizing Bond Discount or Premium** (LO 4)

Refer to the information presented in Exercise 33.

Required:
Prepare the journal entries necessary on each of the following dates, assuming Mason amortizes bond premium or discount using the effective-interest method.
1. March 1, 1991
2. September 1, 1991
3. December 31, 1991
4. March 1, 1992

34. 1. Discount, $54,054.56
    2. Int. Exp. $32,297.27
    3. Int. Exp. $21,674.76
    4. Int. Exp. $10,837.38

35. **Bonds Sold between Interest Payment Dates** (LO 4)
Rescue Company attempted to issue $1,000,000 of ten-year, 12 percent bonds on January 1, 1995, with interest to be paid semiannually on June 30 and December 31 of each year. Because of unfavorable market conditions, Rescue did not sell the bonds until March 1, 1995. At that time, the bonds sold at their face value plus accrued interest.

Required:
Prepare the entries (if any) on Rescue's books on the following dates.
1. January 1, 1995
2. March 1, 1995
3. June 30, 1995

35. 2. Cr. Int. Exp. $20,000
    3. Dr. Int. Exp. $60,000

36. **Key Bond Terms** (LO 2)
A. J. Coleman is a retired blacksmith who would like to invest some of his retirement funds in corporate bonds although he knows very little about the bond market. A. J. is particularly confused by the following terms associated with bonds: stated interest rate, current yield, face interest rate, and market interest rate.

Required:
Write a memo to A. J. explaining the meaning of the bond terms that have him confused. In your memo, indicate how these terms are related to each other.

36. No check figures

37. **Retirement of Bonds Payable** (LO 3)
On December 31, 1995, Rockport Enterprises had a $10 million bond issue outstanding. The carrying value of this bond issue was $10,750,000. On that date, Rockport purchased these bonds on the open market and then immediately retired them. The bonds were purchased for $10,425,000.

Required:
1. Prepare the journal entry to record the purchase and retirement of Rockport's bonds.
2. Identify possible reasons that a company might choose to retire its outstanding bonds before their maturity date.
3. Is it ethical for a company to purchase its own bonds in the open market? Why or why not?

37. 1. Gain, $325,000

38. **Convertible Bonds** (LO 3)
Refer to the information in Exercise 37. Assume that each $1,000 Rockport bond was convertible into 40 shares of Rockport's common stock that has a $20 par value.

Required:
1. Prepare the appropriate journal entry in Rockport's accounting records on December 31, 1995, assuming that all of the company's bonds were exchanged on that date for Rockport common stock.
2. What is the most likely explanation for all of Rockport's bondholders exercising the conversion option of these bonds on the exact same date?

38. 1. Add'l Paid-in Cap., $2,750,000

39. Operating Leases and Capital Leases (LO 5)

On January 11, 1995, Lonestar Gathering Hole leased a mechanical bull-riding machine for its entertainment room. The lease term is four years and the contract calls for payments of $10,000 a year at the end of each year.

Required:

1. What is the primary difference between an operating lease and a capital lease?
2. Briefly describe the different accounting treatment given operating leases and capital leases by lessees.
3. Suppose that Lonestar's lease qualifies as a capital lease and that the appropriate discount rate to determine the present value of the payments to be made over the term of this lease is 7 percent. Prepare the journal entry in Lonestar's accounting records on January 11 to record the lease of the bull-riding machine.

40. Buy vs. Lease Decision (LO 5)

Aspereen Corporation needs a particular piece of equipment for its manufacturing operations. This equipment typically has an estimated useful life of six years and a zero salvage value. Johnson Equipment Supply will sell the equipment to Aspereen for $32,000 cash. Kelvin Equipment Supply will lease the equipment to Aspereen for six years with an annual lease payment of $7,000 due at the end of each year. The appropriate discount rate to determine the present value of the lease payments is 10 percent.

Required:

1. Based strictly on the information provided, which of the two alternative methods of acquiring the equipment appears to be more attractive to Aspereen? Why?
2. Identify key factors other than acquisition cost that may influence a company's decision whether to buy or lease a long-term asset.

41. Internal Control for Bonds Payable (LO 8)

Scully Brothers is a manufacturing firm that sold $1 million of bonds two years ago. The bonds have a ten-year term, a stated interest rate of 8 percent, and pay interest semiannually. The sale of the bonds raised $950,000. Over the past five years, Scully's net income has ranged from $1.5 million to $2.1 million.

Recently, Scully's accountant, Ross Porter, was having lunch with a friend who is also an accountant of a manufacturing firm. Porter told his friend that applying the effective-interest method of accounting for his company's bonds was a real headache. "Every six months, I have to drag out all of this information regarding the bonds. Then I have to multiply this times that and subtract that from this. Man, it's a mess. It's impossible to make all of these computations without messing something up."

Required:

1. What basic internal control related to bonds payable would greatly simplify the accounting for Scully's bonds? Identify other internal control procedures related to bonds payable.
2. Suppose that Porter's friend had the following to say about his friend's complaint. "Ross, why do you go to the trouble of using the effective-interest method? You can use the straight-line method, given the circumstances. That will solve most of your problems." Is Porter's friend correct? Under what circumstances is the straight-line method an acceptable alternative to

---

Margin notes:

39. 3. PV = $33,872.10

40. 1. Lease, PV = $30,486.82

41. No check figures

the effective-interest method? Do one or more of these circumstances apply to Scully Brothers?

42. Analyzing Long-Term Liabilities (LO 7)

Following is information drawn from the 1993 and 1994 financial statements of Community Psychiatric Centers (CPC).

	1993	1994
Total Assets	$530,340	$605,404
Current Assets	150,237	183,999
Total Stockholders' Equity	422,492	440,039
Long-Term Liabilities	40,718	69,090
Net Income (Loss)	(24,892)	10,220
Interest Expense	2,420	3,545
Income Taxes Expense	(13,662)	10,220

Required:

1. Suppose that CPC has applied for a $20 million long-term loan from Lowell Bank, while Thomas Manufacturing is considering purchasing 10,000 shares of CPC's common stock. Which of these two parties, Lowell Bank or Thomas Manufacturing, would likely be most interested in evaluating CPC's financial leverage? Why?
2. Compute CPC's long-term debt to equity ratio in 1993 and 1994. Did the company become more or less leveraged between the end of 1993 and the end of 1994?
3. Compute CPC's times interest earned ratio in both 1993 and 1994. Did this ratio improve or deteriorate between the end of 1993 and the end of 1994? Explain.
4. Notice that CPC had a negative income taxes expense in 1993. How is this possible?

42. 2.	1993	1994
LTD to		
equity	9.64%	15.7%
3.	1993	1994
Times		
Int.	-14.94	6.77

PROBLEM SET A

43. Accounting for Bonds Payable, Straight-Line Method of Amortizing Bond Premium or Discount (LO 3)

The Doubleday Corporation issued $20,000,000 of five-year, 8 percent bonds on May 1, 1995. Interest payment dates are May 1 and November 1 of each year. Doubleday uses straight-line amortization for any bond premium or discount and has a December 31 fiscal year-end.

Required:

1. Prepare a diagram of the cash flows related to this bond issue similar to the diagram shown in Exhibit 11.2. (Do not compute the cash flows' present values.)
2. Determine the total proceeds Doubleday received from the sale of these bonds, assuming that the market interest rate for similar bonds on May 1, 1995, was:
   a. 6 percent.
   b. 10 percent.
3. Prepare the appropriate journal entries on the following dates for each assumption listed in Part 2:
   a. May 1, 1995
   b. November 1, 1995
   c. December 31, 1995
   d. May 1, 1996

43.2a. $21,705,960
2b. $18,455,584
3a. 6% Premium,
$1,705,960
10% Discount,
$1,544,416
3b. 6% Int. Exp., $629,404
10% Int. Exp.
$954,441.60
3c. 6% Int. Exp.,
$209,801.34
10% Int. Exp.,
$318,147.20
3c. 6% Int. Exp.,
$419,602.66
10% Int. Exp.,
$636,294.40
4. 6% LT Liab.,
$21,478,498.67

10% LT Liab.,
$18,661,506.13
5. Cr. Int. Exp.
$266,666.67

4. For each assumption in Part 2, at what carrying value were these bonds reported in Doubleday's December 31, 1995, balance sheet?
5. Suppose these bonds were sold on July 1, 1995, at face value plus accrued interest. Prepare the journal entry to record the sale of the bonds under this assumption.

44. Accounting for Bonds Payable, Effective-Interest Method of Amortizing Bond Premium or Discount (LO 4)

The Naismith Corporation sold $4,000,000 of five-year, 7 percent bonds on June 1, 1995, when the market interest rate for similar bonds was 8 percent. Interest payment dates are June 1 and December 1 of each year. Naismith uses the effective-interest method to amortize bond discount or premium and has a December 31 fiscal year-end.

Required:

44. 1. Bond Carrying Value
   6–1–95 $3,837,766
   12–1–97 $3,910,945
   6–1–2000 $4,000,000
2a. Discount, $162,234
2b. Int. Exp. $153,511
2c. Int. Exp. $25,675
2d. Int. Exp. $128,376
 3. LT Liab., $3,853,619
4a. Premium, $170,588
4b. Int. Exp. $125,118
4c. Int. Exp. $20,779
4d. Int. Exp. $103,893

1. Prepare an amortization schedule for Naismith's bonds.
2. Prepare the appropriate journal entries in Naismith's accounting records on the following dates:
   a. June 1, 1995
   b. December 1, 1995
   c. December 31, 1995
   d. June 1, 1996
3. At what carrying value were these bonds listed in the December 31, 1995, balance sheet of Naismith Corporation?
4. Suppose now that on June 1, 1995, when these bonds were sold the market interest rate for similar bonds was 6 percent. Prepare the appropriate journal entries in Naismith's accounting records on the following dates:
   a. June 1, 1995
   b. December 1, 1995
   c. December 31, 1995
   d. June 1, 1996

45. Long-Term Liabilities of an International Firm (LO 1, 7)

Many investors and other financial decision makers in this country are unaware that numerous, well-known companies are actually foreign corporations. Take the case of Nestle, probably best known for its "crunchy" candy bar. Nestle is a Swiss company whose annual financial statements are denominated in Swiss francs. Like most international companies, the accounting and financial reporting policies used by Nestle are different in several respects from those applied by United States firms. Listed next are excerpts from the general description of Nestle's accounting policies that was included in the company's 1994 annual report.

Accounting Convention and Accounting Standards

The accounting policies adopted by the [Nestle] Group are in accordance with International Accounting Standards issued by the International Accounting Standards Committee (IASC). . . . The accounts have been prepared under the historical cost convention, except that tangible fixed assets are shown at their net replacement value. The accounts are prepared on the accrual basis of accounting.

Following are selected amounts included in Nestle's 1993 and 1994 financial statements. Amounts are expressed in millions of Swiss francs.

	1993	1994
Short-Term Debts and Liabilities	18,166	17,297
Medium and Long-Term Debts and Liabilities	10,424	10,156

	1993	1994
Shareholders' Funds	16,343	17,104
Net Profit	2,887	3,250
Interest Expense	1,284	1,118
Taxes	1,669	1,647

The following components of Nestle's "medium and long-term debts and liabilities" were reported in the footnotes to the company's financial statements.

	1993	1994
Medium and Long-Term Financial Creditors:		
Loans from Financial Institutions	660	714
Bonds	3,412	3,837
Obligations under Finance Leases	109	112
Current Portion of Medium and Long-Term		
Financial Creditors	(108)	(483)
Provisions and Sundry Medium and Long-Term Creditors:		
Pensions and Retirement Benefits Provision	2,162	2,170
Taxes Payable	110	108
Deferred Tax Liabilities	172	166
Other Provisions and Sundry Creditors	3,907	3,532
Total	10,424	10,156

Required:

1. Compute Nestle's long-term debt to equity ratio and its times interest earned ratio for 1993 and 1994.
2. Compare Nestle's degree of financial leverage in 1993 and 1994 with the average degree of financial leverage for the U.S. industries listed in Exhibit 11.6. Is Nestle generally more or less leveraged than the average company in each of these industries?
3. According to the text, somewhere between 4.0 to 6.0 is generally considered a comfortable level for the times interest earned ratio. Were Nestle's times interest earned ratios in 1993 and 1994 "comfortable"?
4. Suppose that in early 1995 you were considering buying several hundred shares of Nestle's common stock. Identify three questions that you would have wanted to ask the company's controller regarding Nestle's medium and long-term debts and liabilities.

45. 1.	1993	1994
LTD to equity	63.78%	59.38%
Times Int.	4.55	5.38

46. **Analyzing Long-Term Liabilities** (LO 1, 7)

Station Casinos, Inc., is a Las Vegas–based firm that owns and operates casinos and other gaming operations. Following is selected financial information included in the company's 1993 and 1994 financial statements. Amounts are in thousands.

	1993	1994
Total Assets	$185,110	$301,486
Long-Term Liabilities	121,792	161,302
Stockholders' Equity	37,153	95,791
Interest Expense	8,949	9,179
Income Taxes Expense	4,806	6,100
Net Income	9,417	11,840

In Station Casinos' 1994 annual report, the company's executives discussed aggressive expansion plans for the future. Following are specific comments addressing the issue of how and whether the company would be able to finance these plans.

The Company's plan for the development of new gaming opportunities, as well as further expansion of existing operations, may require substantial amounts of additional capital. . . There can be no assurance that any such financing would be available to the Company or, if available, that any such financing would be available on favorable terms.

46. 1.
	1993	1994
LTD to equity	327.81%	168.39%
Times Int.	2.59	2.95

Required:

1. Compute Station Casinos' long-term debt to equity and times interest earned ratios for 1993 and 1994. Did these ratios improve or weaken between the end of 1993 and the end of 1994?
2. Considering the financial data presented for the company, what factor was apparently most responsible for the significant change in the company's long-term debt to equity ratio between the end of 1993 and the end of 1994? Explain.
3. Suppose that the average long-term debt to equity ratio for the gaming industry is 50 percent and that the average times interest earned ratio is 4.5. Evaluate Station Casinos' ratios in reference to these industry norms.
4. What purpose is served by the narrative disclosures included in Station Casinos' 1994 annual report regarding the company's potential need for additional capital to finance its expansion plans?

47. Retirement of Bonds Payable (LO 3)

CookieTown Industries of CookieTown, Oklahoma, has a $10 million bond issue outstanding. These bonds were sold on February 1, 1992, have a ten-year term, and have a stated interest rate of 12 percent. Interest on the bonds is paid semiannually on February 1 and August 1. The bonds have a current carrying value of $9,877,000.

If CookieTown sold bonds in today's market, the company would be required to pay annual interest of only 9 percent. Consequently, the company's management wants to retire its outstanding bonds and sell new bonds with a lower stated interest rate. The current market price of CookieTown's bonds is 122 ¼.

Required:

47. 1. $12,225,000
  2. Loss, $2,348,000
  4. Add'l Paid-in Cap., $2,450,000

1. At the present market price, how much will it cost CookieTown to purchase all of its outstanding bonds? What accounts for the difference between the bonds' carrying value and the amount that CookieTown must pay to reacquire the bonds?
2. Suppose that CookieTown purchases and immediately retires the bonds. Prepare the appropriate journal entry to record this transaction.
3. What stipulation could have been included in the bond indenture that would have allowed the company to retire the bonds without being forced to purchase them in the open market?
4. Suppose now that the CookieTown bonds are convertible into common stock of CookieTown Industries. The conversion ratio is 20 shares of stock for each $1,000 bond. CookieTown's stock has a $25 par value and is currently selling for $64 per share. Prepare the appropriate journal entry if 5,000 of these bonds are converted when the total carrying value of the bond issue is $9,900,000.

48. Selected Long-Term Liabilities in Corporate Balance Sheets (LO 1, 6)

Most large public companies have several long-term liabilities in their balance sheet. Suppose that a friend of yours is a social psychology major who is writing a term paper on the nature of large corporations. One feature she is studying is how corporations finance their operations. She has identified the following long-term liabilities, and related information, in corporate balance sheets.

a. 8 percent Convertible Debentures Due April 15, 2011—$19,975,000

These debentures were included in a recent balance sheet of Quixote Corporation, a firm in the computer industry.

b. Accrued Pension Costs—$12,265,000

Hormel Foods Corporation, in whose balance sheet this liability was recently reported, manufactures and markets prepared food products.

c. Unearned Portion of Paid Subscriptions—$2,700,000,000

This item was a long-term liability of Time Warner which, among other lines of business, publishes *Time*, *People*, and *Sports Illustrated*.

d. Mortgages on Property, Plant & Equipment—$4,952,000

This item is a long-term liability of Tuesday Morning Corporation, a discount retailer.

Required:

Prepare a report for your friend. Begin your report with a brief overview of the nature of liabilities and the general types of long-term liabilities. Then provide a brief description of the nature and source of each of the long-term liabilities identified by your friend. Include in these descriptions how each liability is related, or likely related if you are unsure, to the given company's profit-oriented activities.

48. No check figures

PROBLEM SET B

49. **Accounting for Bonds Payable, Straight-Line Method of Amortizing Bond Premium or Discount** (LO 3)

The Hardaway Company issued $6,000,000 of four-year, 10 percent bonds on April 1, 1995. Interest payment dates are April 1 and October 1 of each year. Hardaway uses straight-line amortization for any bond premium or discount and has a December 31 fiscal year-end.

Required:

1. Prepare a diagram of the cash flows related to this bond issue similar to the diagram shown in Exhibit 11.2. (Do not compute the cash flows' present values.)
2. Determine the total proceeds Hardaway received from the sale of these bonds, assuming that the market interest rate for similar bonds on April 1, 1995, was:
   a. 8 percent.
   b. 12 percent.
3. Prepare the appropriate journal entries on the following dates for each assumption listed in Part 2:
   a. April 1, 1995
   b. October 1, 1995
   c. December 31, 1995
   d. April 1, 1996
4. For each assumption in Part 2, at what carrying value were these bonds reported in Hardaway's December 31, 1995, balance sheet?
5. Suppose these bonds were sold on July 1, 1995, at face value plus accrued interest. Prepare the journal entry to record the sale of the bonds under this assumption.

49. 2a. $6,403,962
   2b. $5,627,397
   3a. 8% Premium, $403,962
      12% Discount, $372,603
   3b. 8% Int. Exp., $249,504.75
      12% Int. Exp., $346,575.38
   3c. 8% Int. Exp., $124,752.37
      12% Int. Exp., $173,287.69
   3d. 8% Int. Exp., $124,752.37
      12% Int. Exp., $173,287.69
   4. 8% LT Liab., $6,328,219.62
      12% LT Liab., $5,697,260.07
   5. Cr. Int. Exp. $150,000

50. Accounting for Bonds Payable, Effective-Interest Method of Amortizing Bond Premium or Discount (LO 4)

The Anfernee Corporation sold $4,000,000 of four-year, 9 percent bonds on March 1, 1995, when the market interest rate for similar bonds was 8 percent. Interest payment dates are March 1 and September 1 of each year. Anfernee uses the effective-interest method to amortize bond discount or premium and has a December 31 fiscal year-end.

Required:

1. Prepare an amortization schedule for Anfernee's bonds.
2. Prepare the appropriate journal entries in Anfernee's accounting records on the following dates:
   a. March 1, 1995
   b. September 1, 1995
   c. December 31, 1995
   d. March 1, 1996
3. At what carrying value were these bonds listed in the December 31, 1995, balance sheet of Anfernee Corporation?
4. Suppose now that on March 1, 1995, when these bonds were sold the market interest rate for similar bonds was 10 percent. Prepare the appropriate journal entries in Anfernee's accounting records on the following dates:
   a. March 1, 1995
   b. September 1, 1995
   c. December 31, 1995
   d. March 1, 1996

50. 1. Bond Carrying Value
      3–1–95 $4,134,653
      3–1–97 $4,072,596
      3–1–99 $4,000,000
   2a. Premium, $134,653
   2b. Int. Exp. $165,386
   2c. Int. Exp. $109,868
   2d. Int. Exp. $54,934
    3. LT Liab., $4,109,907
   4a. Discount, $129,262
   4b. Int. Exp. $193,537
   4c. Int. Exp. $129,476
   4d. Int. Exp. $64,738

51. Long-Term Liabilities of an International Firm (LO 1, 7)

Rolls-Royce plc is an internationally known company that is headquartered in London. As you would expect, the company prepares its annual financial statements based upon accounting principles used in Great Britain rather than GAAP.

Listed next are selected excerpts from the initial footnote to Rolls-Royce's 1994 financial statements. This footnote describes the company's principal accounting policies.

Basis of Accounting

The financial statements have been prepared in accordance with applicable accounting standards on the historical cost basis, modified to include the revaluation of land and buildings.

Pension Costs

Contributions to the Group pension schemes are charged to the profit and loss account so as to spread the cost of pensions at a substantially level percentage of payroll costs over employees' working lives with the Group.

Accounting for Leases

Assets financed by leasing agreements which give rights approximating to ownership (finance leases) have been capitalised at amounts equal to the original cost of the assets to the lessors and depreciation provided on the basis of Group depreciation policy. The capital elements of future obligations under finance leases are included as liabilities in the balance sheet. . . . The annual payments under all other lease arrangements, known as operating leases, are charged to the profit and loss account on an accrual basis.

Following is selected information drawn from the 1994 annual report of Rolls-Royce. These amounts are expressed in millions of British pounds.

	1993	1994
Creditors—Amounts Falling Due within One Year	1,263	1,173
Creditors—Amounts Falling Due after One Year	543	514
Provisions for Liabilities and Charges*	301	160
Equity Shareholders' Funds	1,225	1,242
Interest Payable (Interest Expense)	36	36
Taxation (Income Taxes Expense)	18	20
Profit Attributable to Shareholders of		
Rolls-Royce plc (Net Income)	63	81

*The largest component of this long-term liability item is the long-term portion of the company's product warranty liability.

Required:

1. Compute Rolls-Royce's long-term debt to equity ratio and its times interest earned ratio for 1993 and 1994.
2. Compare Rolls-Royce's degree of financial leverage in 1993 and 1994 with the average degree of financial leverage for the U.S. industries listed in Exhibit 11.6. Was Rolls-Royce generally more or less leveraged in 1993 and 1994 than the average company in each of these industries?
3. According to the text, somewhere between 4.0 to 6.0 is generally considered a comfortable level for the times interest earned ratio. Were Rolls-Royce's times interest earned ratios "comfortable" in 1993 and 1994?
4. Suppose that in early 1995 you were considering investing in Rolls-Royce's common stock. Identify three questions that you would have wanted to ask of the company's controller regarding Rolls-Royce's long-term liabilities.

51. 1.	1993	1994
LTD to		
equity	68.9%	54.27%
Times Int.	3.25	3.81

52. **Analyzing Long-Term Liabilities** (LO 1, 7)

Pier 1 Imports, a Texas-based corporation, operates a chain of retail stores that sell furniture, decorative household items, gifts, and related items of merchandise. Following is selected financial information included in the company's 1993 and 1994 financial statements. Amounts are in thousands.

	1993	1994
Total Assets	$460,497	$463,302
Long-Term Liabilities	167,073	169,798
Stockholders' Equity	200,494	201,093
Interest Expense	14,956	16,771
Income Taxes Expense	9,309	2,423
Net Income	23,017	5,933

Required:

1. Compute Pier 1's long-term debt to equity and times interest earned ratios for 1993 and 1994. Did these ratios improve or weaken between the end of 1993 and the end of 1994?
2. Suppose that the average long-term debt to equity ratio for Pier 1's industry is 40 percent and that the average times interest earned ratio is 5.5. Evaluate Pier 1's ratios in reference to these industry norms.
3. The following disclosure was included in a footnote titled "Current and Long-Term Debt" that accompanied Pier 1's 1994 financial statements.

52. 1.	1993	1994
LTD to		
equity	83.33%	84.44%
Times Int.	3.16	1.50

The Company's loan agreements require that the Company maintain certain financial ratios and limit specific payments and equity distributions including cash dividends, loans to shareholders, and purchases of treasury stock. At year end, the most restrictive of the agreements limits the aggregate of such payments to $10 million.

What was the purpose of this disclosure?

53. Retirement of Bonds Payable (LO 3)

Follybeach Enterprises of Folly Beach, South Carolina, sold $5,000,000 of 8 percent bonds with a twenty-year term on May 15, 1987. Interest is paid semi-annually on the bonds on May 15 and November 15. The bond indenture contains a call option that allows Follybeach to "call in" or retire the bonds on the ten-year anniversary date of their issue—May 15, 1997. This call provision requires Follybeach to pay the bondholders $1,050 for each bond.

Required:

1. Prepare the appropriate journal entry in Follybeach's accounting records if the company calls in the bonds on May 15, 1997. On that date, assume the carrying value of the bonds is $5,232,000, while the quoted market price of the bonds is 103.

2. Suppose that one of Follybeach's bondholders is very upset when he receives the notice that the bonds are being called in. He had purchased ten of the bonds six months earlier at a market price of 110. Is this person being "cheated" by Follybeach? Explain.

3. Suppose now that the Follybeach bond indenture contains a conversion feature, meaning that bondholders can exchange the bonds for Follybeach common stock. The conversion ratio is 40 shares of stock for each $1,000 bond. Follybeach's stock has a $10 par value and is currently selling for $29 per share. Prepare the appropriate journal entry if 3,000 of these bonds are converted when the total carrying value of the bond issue is $5,240,000.

54. Selected Long-Term Liabilities in Corporate Balance Sheets (LO 1, 6)

Uncle Marcelle was until recently a retired truck driver who spent most of his free time either drinking coffee at the donut shop or playing bingo at the Moose hall. However, that changed recently when a large oil reservoir was discovered beneath three hundred acres of previously "dirt cheap" land he inherited from his sister in west Texas. Now Marcelle is a "private investor." He has been studying the financial statements of dozens of corporations and has uncovered the following long-term liabilities that he wants you to explain to him.

a. Nonpension Postretirement Benefits—$486,800,000
   This long-term liability was reported in a recent balance sheet of Kellogg, the cereal company.

b. Convertible Debentures—$44,782,000
   Dixie Yarns, Inc., in whose 1994 balance sheet this liability was reported, manufactures and markets carpets, designer rugs, and yarns.

c. Long-Term Obligations under Capital Leases—$233,242
   This item was included in a recent balance sheet of Jennifer Convertibles, Inc., a company that operates a line of specialty furniture stores.

d. Deferred Service Contract Revenues—$29,058,000
   This long-term liability was included in the 1994 balance sheet of Fretter, Inc., which sells consumer electronics, appliances, and related products.

Required:

Prepare a written report for Uncle Marcelle. Begin your report with a brief overview of the nature of liabilities and the general types of long-term liabilities. Then provide a brief description of the nature and source of each of the long-term liabilities that Marcelle has identified. Include in your descriptions how each liability is related, or likely related if you are unsure, to the given company's profit-oriented activities.

53. 1. Loss, $18,000
   3. Add'l Paid-in Cap., $1,944,000

54. No check figures

CASES

55. **Violation of Restrictive Debt Covenant**

Gharst Corporation is in danger of violating a restrictive debt covenant included in its bond indenture. The debt covenant requires Gharst to maintain no higher than a .5 long-term debt to equity ratio. If this ratio is higher than .5 at the end of any fiscal year, the bond issue becomes immediately due and payable. That is, the bondholders must immediately be paid the principal amount of the bonds they hold.

At the end of the third quarter of this fiscal year, Gharst's long-term debt to equity ratio stood at .57. Gharst's management is now scrambling to find some way to reduce the ratio so that it is no higher than .5 by year-end. Several suggestions have been made by individual executives of the company.

a. One vice-president has suggested treating all new capital leases signed during the fourth quarter as operating leases. This will allow the company in the fourth quarter to avoid recording several hundred thousand dollars of capital lease obligations.

b. An assistant controller has suggested that the company sell a piece of land that it has been holding to use as the site of a new production facility. The proceeds from the sale of this land could be used to pay down the balance of a large bank loan that Gharst has outstanding.

c. The chief financial officer believes the best solution is to sell additional Gharst common stock to outside investors. Selling additional common stock will increase total stockholders' equity and thus reduce the long-term debt to equity ratio.

d. A final solution recommended by another vice-president is to simply ask a finance company to whom Gharst owes nearly $1 million on a three-year note payable to change the maturity date so that the note qualifies as a current liability. Later, the maturity date can be changed back to the original date.

Required:

1. Why do lenders insist on including restrictive debt covenants in lending agreements?
2. Evaluate each of the proposed solutions to Gharst's problem. Are any of these solutions unethical? If so, why?

56. **Times Interest Earned Ratio**

A classmate of yours, Scott O'Grady, is having difficulty understanding the times interest earned ratio. Scott does not understand why interest expense and income taxes expense must be added to net income to determine the numerator of this ratio.

Required:

Write a concise but thoughtful memo to Scott explaining the "why" underlying the equation used to compute the times interest earned ratio. In your memo, use one or more examples to make your explanation crystal clear.

57. **Financial Leverage**

Following are selected financial data for three companies of similar size that operate in the same industry. These amounts are in thousands and were taken from each firm's 1995 financial statements.

	ALLEN COMPANY	BURNS COMPANY	CAPOTE COMPANY
Total Assets	$100,600	$96,600	$105,400
Long-Term Liabilities	25,200	27,200	28,900
Stockholders' Equity	41,200	37,300	44,600
Interest Expense	4,900	3,000	3,500
Income Taxes Expense	1,600	2,500	2,700
Net Income	2,500	3,800	4,100

Required:

1. Compute the long-term debt to equity and times interest earned ratios for each of these companies.
2. Suppose you discover that Allen Company is a foreign corporation. In Allen's home country, bond discount is not amortized over the term of the bonds payable but is expensed in the year the bonds are sold. In 1995, Allen wrote off as interest expense $2 million of bond discount on a new bond issue. Under GAAP, only $200,000 of this amount would have been charged off to interest expense. Recompute Allen's interest expense, income taxes expense (assume an average tax rate of 40 percent), and net income for 1995 as these amounts would have been determined under GAAP. Also, recompute the dollar amounts of Allen's year-end long-term liabilities and stockholders' equity. Finally, recompute Allen Company's long-term debt to equity and times interest earned ratios.
3. Are Allen's original financial data and financial ratios materially different from the financial data and financial ratios that result from applying the GAAP-based approach to accounting for bond discounts? Explain.

PROJECTS

58. **Factors Affecting Bond Prices**

In this group project, each group member should identify a corporate bond listed in the daily bond tables published in *The Wall Street Journal* and other major newspapers. The members of each group should select bonds of companies from different industries.

Required:

1. Each group member will plot the quoted market price of the bond he or she selected over the most recent one-year period. After you have selected a bond, identify the market price of the bond approximately one year ago. Then identify the bond's market price at monthly intervals up to the present date. These prices can be obtained from *The Wall Street Journal* or other major newspapers stored on microfilm or in some other form in your library. Once you have identified your bond's market price for each of the past twelve months, obtain a standard sheet of graph paper, prepare an appropriate scale, and then plot these market prices.
2. Meet as a group and compare and discuss the data you have selected. Are the bond prices of the different companies closely correlated over the past twelve months? Is there a definite trend in these bond prices? If so, what factor or factors are likely responsible for this trend? For any bond whose market prices over the past year are not consistent with the general trend evidenced by the other bonds' market prices, attempt to determine what accounts for this divergence. Information useful in this regard may be found in the company's annual or quarterly financial statements or in articles focusing on the

company that have been published in the past year in *The Wall Street Journal*, *Barron's*, *Business Week*, and other business publications.

3. Each group should prepare a written report that summarizes the data collected by the individual group members in Part 1. The report should also summarize the issues discussed by the group in responding to the requirements of Part 2 and the related conclusions reached by the group. One group member should be prepared to present a brief overview of the group's written report to the remainder of the class.

59. Classifying Liabilities

Companies in certain industries are not required to prepare classified balance sheets. Examples of such companies include stock brokerages, real estate firms, and life insurance companies. Generally, accounting standards allow companies to prepare unclassified balance sheets when the distinction between current and long-term assets and current and long-term liabilities is of little or no interest to financial statement users (*Statement of Financial Accounting Standards No. 6*, "Classification of Short-Term Obligations Expected to be Refinanced").

Required:

1. Identify a company that does not prepare a classified balance sheet. List the liabilities included in this company's balance sheet and indicate those that you believe qualify as current liabilities and those that likely qualify as long-term liabilities. Next, compute the company's long-term debt to equity ratio. In your opinion, is this company highly leveraged? Why or why not?

2. Do you agree that assigning this company's assets and liabilities to current and long-term classifications would be irrelevant to financial statement users? Defend your answer.

3. Prepare a summary written report documenting your completion of Parts 1 and 2.

60. Lease Disclosures

Identify two companies that have significant capital, or long-term, lease obligations reported in their balance sheets.

Required:

1. For each company, identify the financial statement footnote that discusses the company's leasing transactions. Read this footnote and summarize the key information that it contains.

2. Compare the two companies' leasing disclosures. Are they similar? If so, in what way? Also identify any significant differences between the companies' leasing disclosures.

3. Determine for each company its capital lease obligations as a percentage of (a) long-term liabilities, (b) total liabilities, and (c) property, plant & equipment. Given these percentages, do you believe that leasing is a major financing method for one or both companies? Explain.

4. Document your completion of Parts 1, 2, and 3 in a brief written report.

ACCOUNTING FOR OWNERSHIP INTERESTS

V

Parts III and IV of this text presented the principal accounting issues and rules related to assets and liabilities. This series of chapters addresses the third of the three elements of the accounting equation: owners' equity. As we discuss accounting for owners' equity we will continually focus on the information needs of decision makers regarding the ownership interests of business entities. Because the corporation is the dominant form of business organization, our principal concern in these chapters is accounting for the stockholders' equity of corporations. Chapter 12 begins with an overview of the corporate form of business organization and then presents the fundamental accounting issues and rules for stockholders' equity. Chapter 13 discusses financial reporting practices for corporations including the structure and principal components of the corporate income statement and the statement of stockholders' equity.

Intercorporate investments and accounting for international operations are the topics of Chapter 14. Hostile takeovers, stock swaps, and other forms of intercorporate investments have become increasingly common in recent years. Another important business trend evident over the last few decades is the evolution of a global economy. To increase their revenues and profits, many United States businesses have established operating units in foreign countries or formed partnerships with foreign firms. The increasing frequency of intercorporate investments and international business operations complicate the efforts of accountants to provide useful financial data to decision makers. For example, accountants of firms with international business operations must convert transactions from one currency to another and cope with cross-cultural differences in financial reporting practices.

This section concludes with Chapter 15, which discusses accounting for the ownership interests of sole proprietorships and partnerships. These types of business organizations account for approximately 10 percent of gross business revenues each year in this country; corporations account for the remainder. Nevertheless, more than 80 percent of all businesses in this country are unincorporated. Approximately 74 percent of U.S. businesses are sole proprietorships, while approximately 8 percent are partnerships.

The Corporate Form of Business Organization: Accounting for Stockholders' Equity

A corporation is an artificial being, invisible, intangible, and existing only in contemplation of law.
Chief Justice John Marshall

LEARNING OBJECTIVES

After studying this chapter, you should be able to do the following:

1. Describe the important characteristics, advantages, and disadvantages of the corporate form of business organization

2. Identify the key rights and privileges of common and preferred stockholders

3. Define the key information needs of decision makers regarding stockholders' equity

4. Account for the issuance of corporate stock

5. Account for treasury stock transactions

6. Account for cash dividends and stock dividends

7. Account for stock splits

8. Compute and interpret return on equity

9. Define key internal control procedures for stockholders' equity

Going Public: The Price Is Right . . . Hopefully

In early 1992, Scott Beck, chief executive of Boston Chicken, Inc., realized his company needed cash, lots of cash. And fast. Boston Chicken was a small, privately owned corporation operating a chain of restaurants specializing in roasted chicken and healthy side dishes such as zucchini marinara. The company had grown rapidly since its founding in 1985. However, by the early 1990s, several larger and better financed competitors had recognized that Boston Chicken's menu items appealed to a wide cross section of health-conscious Americans. These companies were pouring millions of dollars into developing and advertising similar products. If Boston Chicken did not move quickly to expand, competitors would capture a significant portion of the company's potential market.

To raise the funds that his company needed, Scott Beck chose to do what hundreds of other owners of small but rapidly growing companies have done in recent years: sell stock to the public in an initial public offering or IPO. In 1993, more than eight hundred IPOs raised nearly $60 billion of equity capital for new or underfunded companies.

Accountants play a central role in the preparation of an IPO. An IPO involves complex accounting and financial reporting requirements. If these requirements are not met, an IPO can be delayed for weeks or months, leaving a company starving for cash. Accountants also help management collect and analyze the data needed to arrive at an initial price for a company's stock. Among the data used for this purpose are the company's projected future earnings, the relationship between similar firms' earnings and stock prices, and the company's present financial condition.

Establishing an initial selling price for a stock being sold in an IPO is a critical decision for a company "going public." If a company places an unrealistically high price on its stock, an IPO may fail because the stock sells poorly or not at all. Take the case of the 1993 IPO for Wilt Chamberlain's Restaurants. Despite the high or "tall" profile of the firm's principal owner, the company's IPO was canceled after failing to generate sufficient interest. Apparently, the "asking" price for the company's common stock was perceived to be unreasonably high. On the other hand, if the initial price for a company's common stock is too low, speculators will snap up the shares at that price and then resell them later at a higher price.

Scott Beck eventually settled on a $20 per share offering price for his company's stock. As it turned out, that price was too low, much too low. The perception that Boston Chicken was the next McDonald's of the restaurant industry sent the company's stock soaring. On the first day of trading, Boston Chicken's stock leaped from $20 per share to $51 per share. Boston Chicken raised approximately $38 million by selling 1.9 million shares in its IPO. However, if the company's stock had been initially priced at $51 per share, the company could have raised nearly $100 million.

SOURCE: Most of the facts for this vignette were drawn from Boston Chicken's 1993 annual report and the following article: W. Konrad, "Fowl Play," *Smart Money*, February 1994, 92–99.

Real World
Besides enabling a firm to raise a large amount of funds for a specific purpose, going public improves the liquidity of a company by providing it the means to obtain additional capital in the future.

Business owners who need to raise a large amount of funds to build a factory, buy another company, or establish a foreign subsidiary have two principal financing alternatives. They can raise debt capital by borrowing funds, or they can raise equity capital by selling a portion of their ownership interests to outside parties. Corporations that have a need for a large amount of funds often raise equity capital by selling stock, the approach taken by Boston Chicken as described in the opening vignette. This chapter focuses on the accounting issues and rules related to the stockholders' equity of corporations. The chapter begins with an overview of the corporate form of business organization. Next, the information needs of decision makers regarding stockholders' equity are identified, followed by a discussion of accounting procedures for major stockholders' equity transactions. The final two sections of this chapter illustrate a key financial ratio used to analyze stockholders' equity and review internal control procedures related to the ownership interests of corporations.

AN INTRODUCTION TO THE CORPORATE FORM OF BUSINESS ORGANIZATION

Although corporations have been used throughout this text to illustrate accounting issues and procedures, we have not yet examined in depth this form of business organization. This section better acquaints you with corporations by first defining a corporation and describing how one is created. Then, the advantages and disadvantages of the corporate form of business organization are identified. Finally, the major types and characteristics of corporate stock are discussed, including the rights and privileges associated with each.

■ LEARNING OBJECTIVE 1
Describe the important characteristics, advantages, and disadvantages of the corporate form of business organization

Corporations: Artificial and Invisible Beings

Chief Justice John Marshall of the Supreme Court provided a legalistic definition of a corporation in a famous litigation case of the early nineteenth century. That definition serves as the opening quote for this chapter. More recently, *Random House Webster's College Dictionary* defined a **corporation** as "an association of individuals, created by law and having an existence apart from that of its members as well as distinct and inherent powers and liabilities." When the owner or owners of a business decide to incorporate, articles of incorporation are prepared and filed with a state agency—corporations are established by individual states, not by the federal government. Among other items, articles of incorporation typically identify the organization's purpose, the location of its principal business operations, and the type and quantity of stock that it plans to issue. If all legal requirements are met, the business is granted a corporate charter by the state agency. A corporate charter is a contract between a corporation and the state in which it was organized and identifies the principal rights and obligations of the corporation.

When Jane Q. Public hears the term "corporation," names like General Motors, IBM, and Exxon are likely to pop into her head. However, most corporations are small businesses. The large majority of corporations are "closely held" corporations. The stock of closely held corporations is owned by a few individuals, often members of the same family, and is not publicly traded on a securities exchange. Many small incorporated businesses qualify as "S corporations" under the Internal Revenue Code. One requirement to qualify as an S corporation is to have thirty-five or fewer stockholders. S corporations retain most of the advantages of the corporate form of organization, but avoid a key disadvantage—namely, the double taxation of corporate profits, which is discussed shortly.

corporation

Real World
Many large firms incorporate in the state of Delaware because of legal advantages available to corporations created in that state.

Key Advantages of the Corporate Form of Business Organization

Corporations have several advantages compared with the other two principal types of business organizations, sole proprietorships and partnerships. There are also disadvantages of incorporating a business. Summarized in Exhibit 12.1 are the key advantages and disadvantages of the corporate form of business organization.

■ **EXHIBIT 12.1**

Key Advantages and Disadvantages of the Corporate Form of Business Organization

Advantages	Disadvantages
• Limited liability of stockholders	• Double taxation of corporate profits
• Continuity of existence	• Extensive regulatory oversight
• Ease of transferring ownership interests	• Potentially higher level of credit risk
• Access to equity capital	
• Professional management	

Real World

Not-for-profit organizations often organize as corporations to limit their members' legal liability.

Teaching Note

Emphasize that a corporation is both a separate legal entity and a separate accounting entity from its owners.

One important advantage of corporations is the limited liability of corporate stockholders. In practically all cases, the maximum financial loss a corporate stockholder faces is his or her original investment in a corporation. If a corporation files for bankruptcy, the unpaid debts of the firm cannot be recovered from the personal assets of its stockholders. If a partnership folds without paying all of its debts, the individual partners are individually responsible for those debts. In 1992, the public accounting firm of Laventhol & Horwath was declared bankrupt by the United States Bankruptcy Court of New York. The former Laventhol & Horwath partners were required to contribute up to $400,000 each to pay off the partnership's remaining liabilities.[1]

Unlike sole proprietorships and partnerships, the legal existence of a corporation is unaffected by the death or withdrawal of individual owners. Upon the death of a corporate stockholder, the individual's ownership interest passes directly to his or her estate or heirs. A partnership must be dissolved when one partner leaves the firm—although the remaining partners have the option of immediately forming a new partnership.

Corporations also benefit from the ease with which stockholders can transfer their ownership interests to other parties. A corporate stockholder can sell his or her ownership interest without the prior approval of the other owners, which is not true for the members of a partnership.

Generally, corporations can raise equity capital more readily and in larger amounts than unincorporated businesses. Even small corporations, as proven by Boston Chicken, can raise large amounts of capital very quickly by selling stock on a nationwide basis via an IPO.

An important advantage of large corporations is their ability to retain professional management teams. The resources of these firms allow them to employ skilled financial executives, marketing experts, professional accountants, and talented individuals in the other functional areas of business. Proprietorships, partnerships, and small corporations may also have talented individuals in their key positions. However, the limited financial resources of most small businesses make it very difficult for them to compete with large corporations in hiring skilled professionals.

---

1. L. Berton, "Laventhol Ex-Partners Face PTL Claims," *The Wall Street Journal*, 19 August 1992, B5.

Key Disadvantages of the Corporate Form of Business Organization

Double taxation of corporate profits is the key disadvantage of the corporate form of business organization. Corporations are considered taxable entities and are required to pay income taxes on their annual earnings. These profits are taxed again when corporations distribute earnings in the form of cash dividends, since stockholders must report these dividends as income on their individual tax returns. The income of sole proprietorships and partnerships—and S corporations—is not taxed. Instead, the profits of these entities "flow" through to the tax returns of their individual owners. (This is true whether or not the profits are distributed to the owners.)

All businesses are subject to some degree of regulatory oversight at the local, state, and federal levels. However, corporations are generally subject to more regulatory oversight than other business entities. For example, corporations that sell stock on an interstate basis to the public must comply with the extensive accounting and financial reporting requirements of the Securities and Exchange Commission (SEC). If these firms list their stock on a securities exchange, such as the New York Stock Exchange, they are subject to the rules and regulations of that organization as well.

Real World
Public companies are required by the SEC to have an annual audit of their financial statements by independent accountants.

Occasionally, some of the items listed previously as advantages of the corporate form of organization "backfire." For example, a small corporation that approaches a bank for a loan may be rejected because of the limited liability feature of corporations. Bank loan officers realize that only corporate assets, not the personal assets of stockholders, can be seized to satisfy unpaid principal or interest payments if a corporation defaults on a loan. As a result, small corporations often pose a higher level of credit risk than sole proprietorships and partnerships of comparable size. To overcome this problem, one or more individual stockholders of a small corporation may agree to personally guarantee a loan that the corporation has applied for from a bank or other lender.

Corporate Stock

A corporation's charter grants it the right to issue a certain number of shares of one or more classes of stock. If a corporate charter identifies only one class of stock, that stock is automatically considered the corporation's common stock. If a second class of stock is identified in a corporate charter, it is usually a preferred stock. As you will discover, individuals who own a corporation's **preferred stock** have certain "preferences" relative to the individuals who own the company's common stock.

Teaching Note
Students are often confused by the terms "authorized stock," "issued stock," and "outstanding stock." All stock has to be authorized. Authorized stock can be either (1) unissued, (2) issued and outstanding, or (3) issued and reacquired (that is, treasury stock)

For each class of a corporation's stock, **authorized stock** refers to the number of shares the firm is permitted to issue. **Issued stock** refers to the number of shares that have been sold or otherwise distributed, while **outstanding stock** is the number of shares owned by a company's stockholders. The corporate charter of The Home Depot, Inc., authorizes the company to issue up to one billion—yes, billion—shares of common stock. Home Depot's 1994 annual report disclosed that 449,364,000 shares of that stock was "issued and outstanding." Occasionally, companies reacquire some of their stock. **Treasury stock** is the term used when referring to such shares—these shares are typically maintained by a company's treasury department. When a company has reacquired some of its stock, the difference between the company's issued stock and its outstanding stock equals its treasury stock.

preferred stock

authorized stock

issued stock

outstanding stock

treasury stock

COMMON STOCK: RIGHTS AND PRIVILEGES OF COMMON STOCK-HOLDERS   A corporation's common stockholders are often referred to as its residual

■ LEARNING
OBJECTIVE 2
Identify the key rights and
privileges of common and
preferred stockholders

preemptive right

Real World
The preemptive right allows
existing stockholders of a
corporation to maintain control
of the company.

Real World
Until recently, the New York
Stock Exchange had a rule
against listing a company's
common stock if that firm had
nonvoting common stock
outstanding. The rule was
changed because one of the
world's largest corporations,
General Motors, wanted to issue
nonvoting common stock.

owners. If a corporation is liquidated, or goes out of business, common stockholders are entitled to share proportionately in its residual assets after all other claims have been satisfied. These claims include the corporation's current and long-term liabilities and any amounts that must be paid to other classes of stockholders, such as preferred stockholders. Common stockholders also have the right to share proportionately in any earnings distributed by the company. For example, assume that a company has 10,000 shares of outstanding common stock and decides to distribute a cash dividend of $50,000 to its common stockholders. Each common stockholder would be entitled to a $5 dividend ($50,000/10,000 shares) for each share he or she owns. The dividend could not be allocated exclusively to a few stockholders.

In most states, common stockholders have what is known as the **preemptive right,** or the right to retain their fractional ownership interest in a corporation. If a company issues additional common stock, each stockholder must be allowed to purchase a sufficient number of those shares to maintain his or her proportionate ownership interest in the company.

Possibly the most important legal privilege of common stockholders is the right to vote on key matters facing a corporation. Common stockholders periodically elect individuals to serve on a corporation's board of directors. A board of directors is responsible for establishing a corporation's long-range objectives and operating policies. A corporation's officers, which are selected by its board of directors, have the responsibility for implementing the board's policies. Typically, the top executives of a corporation, such as the chief executive officer and senior vice-president, also sit on the corporation's board of directors.

Some corporate charters permit the issuance of different classes of common stock. For example, a closely held corporation may go public by selling common stock that has all of the normal rights and privileges of common stock except the voting privilege. An example of a large company with two classes of common stock is Tootsie Roll Industries. Both classes of Tootsie Roll's common stock have voting privileges. However, one class of common stockholders is permitted ten votes for every share owned, while a one share–one vote rule applies to the other class of common stock. Members of the family that founded the company control large blocks of the dominant class of Tootsie Roll's common stock.

par value

stated value

COMMON STOCK: PAR VALUE, NO-PAR, AND STATED VALUE   Shown in Exhibit 12.2 is a common stock certificate. Most corporate charters establish par values for the different classes of stock that a company is permitted to issue. **Par value** is a nominal dollar value assigned to each share of a given class of stock. In certain states, the collective par value of issued common stock establishes a firm's "legal capital." Corporations in these states are generally not permitted to allow their stockholders' equity to fall below their legal capital. This requirement explains why par values are typically established at very low, or nominal, dollar amounts. For example, the par value of Home Depot's common stock is $.05, while the common stock of Charles Schwab Corporation has a par value of $.01. Although a common stock's par value typically has limited, if any, economic significance, it does influence how the sale of the stock is recorded, as we shall see later.

Some corporate charters do not establish a par value for a company's common stock. Such common stock is known as no-par stock. A no-par common stock may be assigned a **stated value** by a company's board of directors. Why go to the trouble of assigning a stated value to no-par common stock? Answer: Because some states do not allow companies to issue common stock that does not have either a par value or a stated value.

■ **EXHIBIT 12.2**

Example of a Common Stock Certificate

PREFERRED STOCK: RIGHTS AND PRIVILEGES OF PREFERRED STOCK- HOLDERS   As noted previously, preferred stockholders have certain preferences compared with a corporation's common stockholders. The two most important of these preferences involve the payment of dividends, both normal cash dividends and liquidating dividends. Preferred stockholders are usually entitled to receive an annual cash dividend per share. For example, Woolworth Corporation has preferred stock outstanding on which a $2.20 annual dividend is paid. Before Woolworth's common stockholders can receive a dividend in a given year, the company's preferred stockholders must be paid their $2.20 dividend. When a corporation is liquidated, preferred stockholders must be paid the par value or other predetermined liquidation value of their stock before common stockholders can receive any distribution of cash or other assets.

Besides preferences as to dividends, preferred stockholders have the same rights as those identified previously for common stockholders unless stated otherwise in the corporate charter. For instance, preferred stockholders generally have a right to maintain their fractional ownership interest in a corporation's outstanding preferred stock. One stockholder right that corporate charters nearly always take away from preferred stockholders is the voting right.

PREFERRED STOCK: DISTINCTIVE FEATURES   Most preferred stocks have one or more distinctive features. For example, preferred stocks are usually cumulative. If a corporation fails to pay a dividend on a **cumulative preferred stock,** that

■ **LEARNING OBJECTIVE 2**
Identify the key rights and privileges of common and preferred stockholders

Real World
A corporation generally does not have a legal obligation to pay dividends to preferred stockholders even though a stated dividend rate is listed in the preferred stock indenture and/or on the preferred stock certificates.

cumulative preferred stock

One major source of capital for Woolworth Corporation has been the sale of preferred stock. Investors who purchase a corporation's preferred stock should thoroughly investigate the key features or stipulations attached to that stock.

callable preferred stock

convertible preferred stock

Teaching Note
A conversion option on preferred stock is advantageous to the preferred stockholders; a call provision on preferred stock is advantageous to the corporation.

Real World
From an investor's standpoint, preferred stock is considered riskier than corporate bonds. Corporations have no contractual obligation to pay preferred stock dividends, but do have a legal obligation to make periodic interest payments on outstanding bonds.

dividend accumulates and must be paid in the future before common stockholders can receive a dividend. Most preferred stocks also have a call provision attached to them. **Callable preferred stock** can be reacquired, or "called in," at the option of the issuing corporation. When a company reacquires its preferred stock, a call premium must generally be paid. That is, the redemption price of a callable preferred stock usually exceeds its initial selling price. Similar to convertible bonds, **convertible preferred stock** may be exchanged at the option of preferred stockholders for the issuing corporation's common stock.

PREFERRED STOCK: DEBT OR EQUITY?   In certain respects, preferred stock is more similar to debt than equity. For example, consider bondholders and preferred stockholders. Both bondholders and preferred stockholders generally receive a fixed annual payment that does not vary from year to year. Neither of these parties typically benefits directly if a company posts large profits. In fact, large profits can work to the detriment of bondholders and preferred stockholders. A very profitable corporation may use funds generated by its operations to retire outstanding bonds or reacquire preferred stock. Both bondholders and preferred stockholders are usually entitled only to the par value or other liquidation value of their securities if a corporation goes out of business. Finally, in most cases, neither bondholders or preferred stockholders can influence a corporation's objectives or operating policies since they are not allowed to vote on key issues facing the corporation.

So, the question is, should preferred stock be included as a component of stockholders' equity? In reality, there is not much of a controversy here. Federal and state securities laws, rule-making authorities, and other regulators have firmly concluded that preferred stock is a part of stockholders' equity. Of course, there are always exceptions. If a preferred stock meets certain restrictive conditions that make it equivalent to debt, it is not included in the stockholders' equity section of a corporate balance sheet. Instead, such preferred stocks are listed separately in a corporation's balance sheet between its long-term liabilities and stockholders' equity.[2]

---

2. A. B. Afterman, *Handbook of SEC Accounting and Disclosure, 1994* (New York: Warren, Gorham & Lamont, 1994), B16–2.

Battle Mountain Gold Company's Statement of Core Values

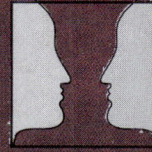

Several prominent corporations have been criticized recently for ethical lapses by key executives or employees. In response to such criticism, many corporations have adopted mission statements that expressly comment on their executives' and employees' ethical responsibilities. Following is one such mission statement, the Statement of Core Values of Battle Mountain Gold Company.

Statement of Core Values, Battle Mountain Gold Company

Our core values are keyed to the acronym **"RESPECT."**

Respect: Show concern for your fellow employees, community, environment and shareholders.

Excellence: Strive to achieve world-class status.

Safety: Promote the well-being of employees and the public.

Profit Motivation: Encourage low costs through innovation and entrepreneurship.

Cooperation: Talk with people, not about people; teamwork is the basis for achievement.

Truth: Act honestly and openly with the highest ethics.

STOCKHOLDERS' EQUITY: KEY INFORMATION NEEDS OF DECISION MAKERS

Corporate stockholders and potential stockholders represent a large and important class of financial decision makers. For these investors to make wise economic decisions, they need a wide range of financial information. Here, we consider three such items of information.

Stockholder Rights and Privileges

Assume your Uncle Bob has been given a "hot tip" by a domino-playing friend of his in the local old folks home. Because of this tip, Uncle Bob is planning to invest much of his retirement nest egg in Woolworth Corporation's preferred stock. Before calling his broker, Bob decides to ask for your advice on this matter. So, what do you do at this point? Probably first you would obtain a copy of Woolworth's most recent annual report. Being a sophisticated financial statement user, you realize that Woolworth's annual report will contain information regarding the rights and privileges of the company's preferred stock. Exhibit 12.3 contains the paragraph describing that preferred stock which was included in Woolworth's 1994 annual report.

After reading the paragraph shown in Exhibit 12.3, you know much more about the stock Uncle Bob is planning to purchase. For example, you know the stock pays a $2.20 annual dividend. After checking a recent edition of *The Wall Street Journal*, you determine that the stock is selling for $136 per share. Now, you can compute the

Many corporations have recently adopted mission statements to encourage their employees to behave ethically and responsibly. Companies in the extractive industries, such as Battle Mountain Gold Company, often comment in these statements on their responsibilities to the environment.

■ **EXHIBIT 12.3**

Disclosures in Woolworth Corporation's 1994 Annual Report Regarding the Company's Preferred Stock

> At January 29, 1994, the 109,318 outstanding shares of $2.20 Series A Convertible Preferred Stock had a liquidation value of $45.00 per share, or $4.9 million. The stock is cumulative, voting and convertible at any time at the option of the holder, at the rate of 5.68 shares of common stock for each share of preferred stock, subject to anti-dilution provisions. A total of 620,926 shares of common stock has been reserved for the conversion. At the option of the company, the preferred stock is redeemable at liquidation value, subject to a holder's right to convert such shares into shares of common stock prior to the date fixed for redemption.

■ **LEARNING OBJECTIVE 3**

Define the key information needs of decision makers regarding stockholders' equity

Focus on Ethics

Assume that Uncle Bob received his "hot tip" from a friend who is an executive of Woolworth Corporation. Has this individual behaved ethically in providing "inside information" to Uncle Bob?

stock's "dividend yield," which is its annual dividend divided by its current market price. The Woolworth preferred stock has a meager dividend yield of 1.6 percent ($2.20/$136). This surprises you, since preferred stocks typically have a dividend yield comparable to the interest rates on high-quality corporate bonds. Since the current interest rate on such bonds is 10 percent, the Woolworth preferred stock should be selling at about $22 per share, given its $2.20 annual dividend ($22 × 10% = $2.20).

Apparently, some factor other than dividend yield accounts for the current selling price of Woolworth's preferred stock. One such factor could be the stock's conversion feature. As indicated in Exhibit 12.3, each share of Woolworth's preferred stock can be converted into 5.68 shares of the company's common stock. You check the most recent price of Woolworth's common stock and discover that it is selling for $24 per share. So, the conversion feature of the preferred stock has a value of almost exactly $136 ($24 × 5.68) per share, which is also the current market price of that stock. In fact, the market price of a convertible preferred stock is often tied directly to the market price of the common stock to which it can be converted.

The disclosures included in Exhibit 12.3 provide you with other valuable information to pass along to Uncle Bob. For instance, the Woolworth preferred stock, like most preferred stocks, is cumulative. If Woolworth skips a dividend on the preferred stock, it must pay that dividend in the future before making any dividend payments to common stockholders. You will also want to explain to Uncle Bob that Woolworth has an option of redeeming the preferred stock for $45 per share. Before forcing the preferred stockholders to cash in their shares at that price, Woolworth will permit them to exchange those shares for Woolworth common stock.

The moral you should learn from the Uncle Bob tale is that investors should identify the rights and privileges attached to the different classes of a corporation's stock. This is particularly critical information for preferred stocks. The rights and privileges associated with common stock are typically consistent across corporations and well understood by most investors.

Earnings Data

Current and prospective stockholders are very interested in information that reveals the historical profitability of a corporation. Of particular interest to these parties is the earnings per share of a company's common stock. (The computation of earnings per share is illustrated in Chapter 13.) Investors often use earnings per share data to predict a firm's future earnings and stock price. Unfortunately, history does not necessarily repeat itself, especially when it comes to corporate earnings. In early 1995, both USX Corporation, the nation's largest steelmaker, and Hewlett-Packard, a computer firm, reported impressive increases in earnings.[3] Given this good news, you might predict that each company's stock price increased: increased earnings means even higher earnings in the future means a higher stock price. Right? Not necessarily. On the day USX announced a 300 percent increase in its earnings, the company's stock price dropped 5 percent. On the other hand, Hewlett-Packard's stock leaped more than seven dollars per share, approximately 7 percent, on the day it announced a 64 percent increase in earnings.

A key difference between these two cases explained the behavior of the companies' stock prices. Despite USX's impressive earnings, financial analysts predicted that demand for the company's products would decline in the future, resulting in lower earnings. The demand for Hewlett-Packard's product line was projected to become stronger in the future, resulting in even higher earnings for that firm. The moral here is that earnings per share disclosures are important but must be used cautiously when the objective is to predict a company's future profits. Besides historical earnings per share data, investors must obtain and analyze other relevant information to evaluate a company's future earnings potential.

Dividend Information

When it comes to any specific investment, the principal concern of most investors can be summarized in one brief question: "How much cash will this investment produce for me in the future?" To predict future cash flows from their investments, investors need information concerning the dividend policies of corporations and the factors that may affect those policies. Retirees, for example, often rely heavily on divided income. The common stocks of electric utilities are particularly favored investments of retirees since those stocks have historically paid high dividends. In 1994, two large electric utilities, Florida Power & Light and Southern California Edison, unexpectedly cut their dividends by 30 percent. Because of these dividend cuts, many retirees were suddenly forced to rework their cash budgets.

The SEC recognizes the importance of dividend information for decision makers. Companies subject to the SEC's regulations must disclose the cash dividends they have paid over their five most recent fiscal years. Additionally, these companies must disclose any significant restrictions on the payment of dividends, such as restrictive debt covenants included in a bond indenture. The SEC also encourages companies to discuss their dividend policies in their annual reports. Following is such a disclosure included in the 1994 annual report of The Clothestime, Inc., a company that operates a chain of apparel shops for young women.

> The Company has never paid cash dividends on its common stock. Payment of dividends is within the discretion of the Company's Board of Directors and will depend upon the earnings, capital requirements and operating and financial condition of the Company, among other factors. The Company anticipates that for the foreseeable future it will follow a policy of retaining earnings in order to finance the expansion and development of its business.

Preferred stocks typically have a predetermined annual dividend rate. However, most corporate charters do not require preferred stock dividends to be paid in any

Teaching Note
Just as past earnings are not necessarily perfect predictors of future earnings, past dividends are not necessarily perfect predictors of future dividends.

---

3. Norton, E., "USX Reports Earnings Tripled in Fourth Quarter," *The Wall Street Journal*, January 31, 1995, p. A4. Reprinted by permission of *The Wall Street Journal*, © 1995 Dow Jones & Company, Inc. All Rights Reserved Worldwide. Yoder, S. K. "H-P's Earnings Jumped 64% in First Quarter," *The Wall Street Journal*, February 17, 1995, p. A4. Reprinted by permission of *The Wall Street Journal*, ©1995 Dow Jones & Company, Inc. All Rights Reserved Worldwide.

dividends in arrears

Teaching Note
Point out that dividends in arrears do not represent liabilities. Dividends are not liabilities until they are declared by a company's board of directors.

given year. When a dividend is not paid on a cumulative preferred stock, a corporation must maintain a record of these **dividends in arrears.** As suggested earlier, before a company can pay a common stock dividend, all dividends in arrears on cumulative preferred stock must be paid. Dividends in arrears should be disclosed in the footnotes to a company's financial statements. In its 1993 annual report, Talley Industries, Inc., disclosed approximately $6 million of dividends in arrears on its outstanding cumulative preferred stock. Investors find such disclosures informative since dividends in arrears affect the ability of a company to pay dividends in the future, particularly to common stockholders.

ACCOUNTING FOR STOCKHOLDERS' EQUITY

In this section, key accounting procedures related to stockholders' equity transactions are illustrated. Among the major types of stockholders' equity transactions we consider here are the issuance of stock by a corporation, treasury stock transactions, dividends, and stock splits. Before considering procedural accounting issues for stockholders' equity, let us briefly review the stockholders' equity section of a corporate balance sheet.

Stockholders' Equity in the Corporate Balance Sheet

Teaching Note
Stockholders' equity is made up of two types of capital: capital contributed by the owners and earnings that have been retained in the corporation.

Shown in Exhibit 12.4 is the stockholders' equity section of Dollar General Corporation's 1994 balance sheet. Dollar General operates a large chain of general merchandise stores located principally in the southeastern United States. Notice that instead of "stockholders' equity," Dollar General prefers the synonymous term "shareholders' equity." Also notice that there are four components of Dollar General's stockholders' equity: common stock, additional paid-in capital, retained earnings, and treasury stock. The stockholders' equity section of a balance sheet provides brief descriptive information regarding a company's equity securities. For example, Dollar General's balance sheet identifies the par value of its common stock and the number of shares authorized and issued.

■ **EXHIBIT 12.4**
Stockholders' Equity Section of Dollar General Corporation's 1994 Balance Sheet

Teaching Note
Stress that treasury stock is deducted from stockholders' equity.

	1994	1993
	(IN THOUSANDS)	
Shareholders' Equity:		
Common Stock, par value, $.50 per share:		
Shares authorized: 100,000,000		
Issued: 1994—54,497,000; 1993—35,641,000	$ 27,248	$ 17,820
Additional Paid-In Capital	65,857	57,246
Retained Earnings	151,165	119,580
	$244,270	$194,646
Less Treasury Stock, at cost:		
Shares: 1994—1,746,000; 1993—2,900,000	3,553	4,881
Total Shareholders' Equity	$240,717	$189,765

Many companies disclose in their annual report a book value per share, or equity per share, for their common stock. **Book value per share** is computed by dividing total common stockholders' equity by the number of common shares outstanding. Dollar General's common stock had a book value per share of $4.56 and $5.84 at the end of 1994 and 1993, respectively. The book value per share at the end of 1994 was computed as follows:

book value per share

$$\text{Book Value per Share} = \frac{\text{Common Stockholders' Equity}}{\text{Shares of Common Stock Outstanding}}$$

$$\text{Book Value Per Share} = \frac{\$240,717,000}{(54,497,000 - 1,746,000)}$$

$$\text{Book Value per Share} = \$4.56$$

Notice that Dollar General's outstanding common stock was computed by subtracting its 1,746,000 shares of treasury stock from the total shares issued. When a company has preferred stock outstanding, the equity attributable to that stock should be subtracted from total stockholders' equity to determine book value per share. Again, book value per share relates only to common stockholders' equity.

Issuance of Common Stock

Many different types of transactions involve the issuance of stock by corporations. Recall that one such transaction was illustrated in Chapter 11—namely, the conversion of bonds payable into common stock. Here, we consider several of the most frequently occurring transactions resulting in the issuance of corporate stock.

■ LEARNING OBJECTIVE 4
Account for the issuance of corporate stock

SALE OF PAR VALUE COMMON STOCK   According to *Accounting Trends & Techniques*, approximately 90 percent of all common stocks have a par value. Suppose that Blue Onion Grill, Inc., a trendy restaurant chain, sells 30,000 shares of its $1 par value common stock for $12 per share. Following is the entry to record this transaction.

Teaching Note
Most stock transactions occur between investors and, thus, have no impact on a corporation's accounting records.

Mar. 9	Cash	360,000	
	Common Stock		30,000
	Additional Paid-in Capital, Common Stock		330,000
	To record sale of 30,000 shares of common stock at $12 per share		

Notice that the collective par value of the stock sold by Blue Onion Grill (30,000 shares × $1) is credited to Common Stock, while the remaining proceeds ($360,000 − $30,000) are credited to Additional Paid-in Capital, Common Stock. *Key point to remember:* Corporations are not allowed to recognize gains or losses on the sale of their stock. The sale of a corporation's own stock is a financing transaction. That is, the intent is to raise funds to meet the financing needs of the given firm, not to generate a profit. Any premium on the sale of common stock must be recorded in a permanent

■ **EXHIBIT 12.5**

Additional Paid-in Capital: Balance Sheet Captions Used by Six Hundred Firms Surveyed by *Accounting Trends & Techniques*

SOURCE: *Accounting Trends & Techniques, 1994.*

• Additional paid-in capital	40.8%
• Capital in excess of par or stated value	24.5%
• Paid-in capital	8.0%
• Additional capital, or other capital	6.9%
• Capital surplus	5.3%
• Paid-in surplus	.3%
• Other captions	2.5%
• No additional paid-in capital accounts	11.7%

stockholders' equity account. There is considerable variability across corporations in the terminology used for stockholders' equity items, particularly "additional paid-in capital." Shown in Exhibit 12.5 are the various balance sheet captions that you may encounter for this general category of stockholders' equity accounts.

EXCHANGE OF PAR VALUE COMMON STOCK FOR NONCASH ASSETS
Occasionally, corporations exchange their common stock for equipment, buildings, or other assets. Either the fair market value of the stock being issued or the asset being acquired, whichever is more evident, should be used as the basis for recording this type of transaction. Assume that Blue Onion Grill agrees to exchange 9,000 shares of its $1 par value common stock for an office building. Blue Onion's stock is publicly traded and has a market value of $14 per share on the date this exchange is made. Like most real estate, the fair market value of the building being acquired is not readily apparent. So, the total market value of the Blue Onion stock, $126,000 (9,000 shares × $14), would be used to determine the acquisition cost of the building. The following entry would be made to record this transaction.

Teaching Note
Although cash is not involved in this transaction, the receipt of the building represents contributed capital.

Nov. 21	Buildings	126,000	
	Common Stock		9,000
	Additional Paid-in Capital,		
	Common Stock		117,000

        To record exchange of 9,000 shares of
        common stock for office building
        (asset No. A–5)

Suppose now that Blue Onion's common stock does not have a readily determinable market value because it is not publicly traded. In this case, company officials would likely use the appraised value of the building as the basis for recording the exchange transaction. Assume that a real estate appraiser assigns a fair market value of $133,000 to the building. The following entry would be appropriate to record the exchange of the building for 9,000 shares of Blue Onion's common stock.

Nov. 21	Buildings	133,000	
	Common Stock		9,000
	Additional Paid-in Capital,		
	Common Stock		124,000

To record exchange of 9,000 shares of
common stock for office building
(asset No. A–5)

SALE OF NO-PAR COMMON STOCK   To illustrate the sale of no-par common
stock, assume that Baylee Almon, Inc., has no-par common stock to which a $5 stat-
ed value per share has been assigned. To record the sale of 5,000 shares of this stock
for $17 per share, the following entry would be appropriate.

Apr. 19	Cash	85,000	
	Common Stock		25,000
	Additional Paid-in Capital,		
	Common Stock		60,000

To record sale of 5,000 shares of
common stock at $17 per share

Recognize that this entry is no different from the entry that would be made if the
stock had a par value of $5 instead of a stated value of $5.

For companies whose common stock does not have a par value or a stated value,
the total proceeds from the sale of common stock are credited to the Common Stock
account. For example, if the no-par common stock of Baylee Almon does not have a
stated value, the following entry would be made to record the sale of the 5,000 shares.

| Apr. 19 | Cash | 85,000 | |
| | Common Stock | | 85,000 |

To record sale of 5,000 shares of
common stock at $17 per share

Sale of Preferred Stock

The 1994 edition of *Accounting Trends & Techniques* reported that approximately 27
percent of publicly owned companies have preferred stock outstanding. Accounting
for the issuance of preferred stock is very similar to accounting for the issuance of
common stock. For example, assume that Blue Onion Grill sells 6,000 shares of preferred stock. If this preferred stock has a $100 par value and is sold for $102, the following entry would be appropriate.

Sep. 13	Cash	612,000	
	Preferred Stock		600,000
	Additional Paid-in Capital,		
	Preferred Stock		12,000

To record sale of 6,000 shares of
preferred stock at $102 per share

Teaching Note
Each class of stock and its
related additional paid-in capital
should be reported separately in
the stockholders' equity section
of the balance sheet.

Treasury Stock Transactions

■ LEARNING
OBJECTIVE 5
Account for treasury stock
transactions

In February 1995, Polaroid Corporation announced that it intended to purchase 3.2 million shares of its own common stock on the open market.[4] Such stock "buy-back" plans are not unusual for large public corporations. If corporate executives believe their company's common stock is selling for less than its true value, the firm may purchase large blocks of that stock. These shares are typically resold at a later date when the stock's market price more accurately reflects its true value. There are other reasons, as well, why a corporation may purchase its own common stock. Many companies have an ESOP (employee stock ownership plan) through which employees periodically purchase common stock of their employer. Likewise, many corporations have a stock option plan that allows executives to purchase shares of their company's common stock at predetermined bargain prices. A corporation that does not have sufficient unissued common stock to provide for the needs of its ESOP and/or stock option plan will purchase stock in the open market to meet those needs.

To illustrate treasury stock transactions, we can use the data presented in Exhibit 12.4 for the treasury stock held by Dollar General Corporation. Like nearly all companies, Dollar General records its treasury stock at cost. On a per share basis, the average cost of Dollar General's treasury stock at the end of 1994 was approximately $2.03 ($3,553,000/1,746,000). Assuming this stock was purchased in one transaction, an entry similar to the following one would have been made in Dollar General's accounting records.

Teaching Note
Point out that Treasury Stock normally has a debit balance, while most stockholders' equity accounts normally have credit balances.

Jan. 11	Treasury Stock	3,553,000	
	Cash		3,553,000
	To record purchase of 1,746,000 shares of treasury stock		

Now, suppose that Dollar General sells 5,000 shares of the treasury stock it acquired in the previous transaction. If the treasury stock is sold for cost, which would be approximately $10,150 ($2.03 × 5,000), the following entry would be made.

Feb. 12	Cash	10,150	
	Treasury Stock		10,150
	To record sale of 5,000 shares of treasury stock at cost		

If Dollar General subsequently sells another 5,000 shares of this treasury stock at $3 per share, $15,000 in total, the following entry would be appropriate.

May 15	Cash	15,000	
	Treasury Stock		10,150
	Additional Paid-in Capital, Treasury Stock Transactions		4,850
	To record sale of 5,000 shares of treasury stock at $3 per share		

---

4. B. Carton, "Polaroid to Cut Work Force by Up to 5%," *The Wall Street Journal*, 6 February 1995, A9.

When treasury stock is sold for more than cost, the difference between the proceeds and its cost is credited to an additional paid-in capital account, as indicated in the previous entry. Many novice accountants might be tempted to credit the $4,850 in the previous entry to an account such as "Gain on Sale of Treasury Stock." However, remember that a company cannot recognize gains or losses on the sale of its own stock, including treasury stock. If Dollar General subsequently sells 2,000 shares of its treasury stock for $1.50 per share, a loss would not be recorded on this transaction. Instead, the difference between the proceeds of the sale and the cost of the treasury stock would be debited to Additional Paid-in Capital, Treasury Stock Transactions, as follows:

Jun. 12	Cash	3,000	
	Additional Paid-in Capital,		
	Treasury Stock Transactions	1,060	
	Treasury Stock		4,060
	To record sale of 2,000 shares of treasury stock at $1.50 per share		

Dollar General may not have an account equivalent to Additional Paid-in Capital, Treasury Stock Transactions because it has never sold treasury stock for more than its cost. In such a case, the $1,060 debit in the previous entry would be made to Retained Earnings.

Recognize that a company does not pay cash dividends to shares of treasury stock. Likewise, treasury stock is not entitled to receive any liquidating dividends when a corporation is dissolved. Finally, a corporation's executives or stockholders cannot exercise the voting privilege on any shares of treasury stock held by the firm.

Teaching Note
Treasury stock has no rights and privileges because it is not outstanding stock.

Dividends

Naive financial statement users often assume that the retained earnings reported on a corporate balance sheet represents a cash fund accumulated by a company over its existence. Not true. Retained earnings is simply a general ledger account in which certain entries are made each accounting period. Just because a company has a large amount of retained earnings does not mean it has the ability to pay dividends. Why? Because company executives may have chosen to reinvest those earnings into the company. A company's executives may have used the cash flows stemming from the firm's profits to purchase new equipment, develop new products, or acquire a jet aircraft to zip them to and from important meetings.

Here, our concern is not companies that choose to retain earnings indefinitely but instead those that "share the wealth" with their stockholders. Companies that have paid dividends regularly to their stockholders for an extended period generally broadcast this fact in their annual report. Tootsie Roll Industries is one such firm. Tootsie Roll's executives are proud to boast that their firm is one of the few companies to have paid quarterly cash dividends for more than fifty consecutive years.

CASH DIVIDENDS   A **cash dividend** is a proportionate distribution of a company's prior earnings to its stockholders made in the form of cash. Companies that pay cash dividends typically do so on a regular basis. Although some companies pay semi-annual or annual dividends, by far the most common approach is to pay quarterly cash dividends.

■ **LEARNING OBJECTIVE 6**
Account for cash dividends and stock dividends

Focus on Ethics
A company has a long history of paying quarterly cash dividends. The board of directors has just declared the next quarterly cash dividend, although the company has been experiencing cash-flow problems. The payment of this dividend will impair the company's ability to pay its current liabilities as they come due. Comment on the ethics of the board's action.

cash dividend

Before a company can distribute cash dividends to its stockholders, three conditions must be met. First, a company must have sufficient cash available. Second, a company must have a sufficient amount of "unrestricted" retained earnings to pay a cash dividend. Suppose a company has a $5 million balance in its Retained Earnings account and several million dollars of available cash. However, if a restrictive debt covenant prohibits the company from paying dividends while a bond issue is outstanding, the payment of cash dividends is clearly out of the question. The final condition that must be met before a cash dividend can be paid is a formal dividend declaration, or authorization, by a company's board of directors.

A corporation's accountants must consider three dates when accounting for and maintaining control over cash dividend transactions. In chronological order, these three dates are the declaration date, the record date, and the payment date. On the dividend declaration date, a company's board of directors authorizes a cash dividend. On the record date, a list of the individuals owning a company's stock is prepared. This list becomes the official record of the stockholders who are entitled to receive the cash dividend. If an individual purchases a stock after the record date but before the dividend payment date, he or she is not entitled to receive the cash dividend. Finally, on the dividend payment date, dividend checks are mailed to stockholders.

Open *The Wall Street Journal* any day of the week and you will find a large block of dividend announcements reported under "Corporate Dividend News." These announcements disclose the name of the company; whether the dividend is a quarterly, semiannual, or annual dividend payment; the dollar amount of the dividend; the dividend payment date; and, finally, the record date. For example, on June 8, 1995, *The Wall Street Journal* reported thirty-one quarterly dividend announcements. Included in these announcements was a $.05 dividend declared by Dollar General Corporation. This dividend was payable by Dollar General on September 15, 1995, to stockholders of record on August 28, 1995.

To illustrate the accounting entries for a cash dividend, assume that Charles & Edward, Inc., a stock brokerage firm, has 2 million shares of common stock outstanding. On January 16, the firm's board of directors declares a cash dividend of $.24 per share, $480,000 in total, to be paid February 16 to stockholders of record on February 2. When a cash dividend is declared, it becomes a liability of the company and should be recorded as such in its accounting records. On the declaration date, the following entry would be made to record the cash dividend declared by Charles & Edward's board of directors.

Jan. 16	Dividends	480,000	
	Dividends Payable		480,000
	To record $.24 cash dividend declared on common stock		

Discussion Question
Ask students why Dividends, a stockholders' equity account, normally has a debit balance. Answer: Dividends are distributions of earnings to the owners of a corporation, thus, dividends reduce retained earnings, an account that normally has a credit balance.

Dividends is a temporary account that is closed to Retained Earnings at the end of each accounting period, while Dividends Payable is a current liability account.

No entry would be required in Charles & Edward's accounting records on the record date, February 2. On that date, a list of the individuals who own the company's stock would be prepared. The following entry would be made on the dividend payment date to record the distribution of dividend checks to stockholders.

Feb. 16	Dividends Payable	480,000	
	Cash		480,000
	To record payment of cash dividend to common stockholders		

A Yen for Dividends

In recent years, many United States citizens have diversified their investment portfolios by purchasing the stocks of foreign companies. Investing in foreign stocks can be tricky. At a minimum, investors considering such stocks should investigate the securities laws and other applicable regulations in the relevant countries. Take the case of Japan. Historically, Japanese companies have paid only modest cash dividends. One factor affecting the ability of Japanese firms to pay dividends is restrictions imposed by the Japanese Commercial Code. This code requires Japanese companies to establish a sizable legal reserve within their retained earnings, a reserve from which dividends cannot be paid.

This example illustrates the accounting procedures for a cash dividend paid to common stockholders. The same procedures are followed in accounting for a cash dividend paid to preferred stockholders.

STOCK DIVIDENDS   Besides the impressive string of cash dividends paid by Tootsie Roll, that firm has also distributed an annual stock dividend for more than twenty-five consecutive years. A **stock dividend** is a proportionate distribution of a corporation's own stock to its stockholders. On February 21, 1995, Tootsie Roll declared a 3 percent stock dividend to be distributed on April 21, 1995, to stockholders of record on March 14, 1995. A Tootsie Roll stockholder who owned 400 shares of the firm's common stock on March 14, 1995, was entitled to receive an additional 12 shares (400 × 3%) because of the stock dividend. Stock dividends are often issued in lieu of cash dividends by companies that have a limited amount of cash or that need to conserve their cash for other uses. Alternatively, some companies, such as Tootsie Roll, simply have a policy of regularly distributing a stock dividend to their stockholders.

ACCOUNTING IMPACT OF A STOCK DIVIDEND   Stock dividends are divided into two groups for accounting purposes: small stock dividends and large stock dividends. There is not a clear line of demarcation between small and large stock dividends. However, a small stock dividend is generally one that involves a distribution of up to 20–25 percent additional stock to existing stockholders. All other stock dividends are classified as large stock dividends.

From an accounting standpoint, stockholders are no better off after the distribution of a stock dividend than they were before the stock dividend. To prove this point, refer to Exhibit 12.6. This exhibit presents the stockholders' equity of Erin Springs, Inc., both before and after the declaration and distribution of a small (5 percent) stock dividend. Also included in Exhibit 12.6 is an analysis of the stock dividend's impact on the ownership interest of an Erin Springs stockholder, Chris Jennings. (For the time being, we will ignore the technical aspects of accounting for a stock dividend.)

When considering foreign stocks, U.S. investors must be wary. Many countries impose legal restrictions on the ability of companies to pay dividends. In Japan, for example, the Japanese Commercial Code limits the ability of companies to pay dividends to their stockholders.

stock dividend

■ **EXHIBIT 12.6**

Stockholders' Equity of Erin Springs, Inc., and Ownership Interest of an Individual Stockholder Before and After the Declaration and Distribution of a 5 Percent Stock Dividend

	BEFORE 5% STOCK DIVIDEND	AFTER 5% STOCK DIVIDEND
Erin Springs, Inc., Stockholders' Equity:		
Common Stock, par value $1:		
Shares authorized—200,000;		
Shares issued and outstanding:		
100,000 before stock dividend	$100,000	
105,000 after stock dividend		$105,000
Additional Paid-in Capital	600,000	675,000
Retained Earnings	560,000	480,000
Total Stockholders' Equity	$1,260,000	$1,260,000
Book Value Per Share (total stockholders' equity/number of common shares outstanding)	$12.60	$12.00
· ·		
Chris Jennings, Erin Springs stockholder:		
Shares Owned	100	105
Percentage of Outstanding Shares Owned	.1%	.1%
Total Book Value of Shares Owned	$1,260	$1,260

Teaching Note
Point out that total stockholders' equity remains unchanged after recording a stock dividend, while the recording of a cash dividend reduces total stockholders' equity.

Notice in Exhibit 12.6 that the total stockholders' equity of Erin Springs is the same before and after the stock dividend. Likewise, notice that Chris Jennings's ownership interest in the company was unaffected by the stock dividend. If we think of stockholders' equity as a pie that is cut into several slices, a stock dividend simply cuts that pie into a larger number of smaller slices.

ECONOMIC IMPACT OF A STOCK DIVIDEND   Despite the analysis shown in Exhibit 12.6, a company's stockholders may benefit from a stock dividend. Stockholders benefit from a stock dividend if the market price of the company's stock is unaffected by the dividend. For example, assume that Erin Springs's common stock trades for $16 per share both before and after the declaration and distribution of the 5 percent stock dividend. Given this assumption, the market value of Chris Jennings's ownership interest in Erin Springs will increase from $1,600 ($16 × 100 shares) before the stock dividend to $1,680 ($16 × 105 shares) afterward. If Erin Springs's stock price remains at $16 per share following this stock dividend, many stock market experts would argue that the stock market was "fooled" by the stock dividend. In other words, the stock market, as a whole, failed to recognize that the value of the company's stock should have dropped by approximately 5 percent per share following the stock dividend.

Is the stock market fooled by stock dividends? Despite extensive research on this topic, the evidence is inconclusive. Nevertheless, small stock dividends are accounted for as if the stock market is fooled. That is, a small stock dividend is accounted for as if stockholders realize an economic benefit equal to the number of new shares they receive multiplied by the pre-dividend stock price. Large stock dividends are dealt with quite differently. Since most stock dividends are of the small variety, we concentrate here on accounting for that type of stock dividend.

ACCOUNTING FOR A SMALL STOCK DIVIDEND   To illustrate accounting for small stock dividends, return to the data presented in Exhibit 12.6, specifically, the data in the "before" column of that exhibit. Assume that Erin Springs's board of directors declares the 5 percent stock dividend on October 5 of the current year. The record date is October 25 and the distribution date is November 21. (A stock dividend is distributed rather than paid, so a stock dividend has a distribution date instead of a payment date.) To account properly for a small stock dividend, we must know the market price of the stock on the dividend declaration date. As suggested earlier, assume that the market price of Erin Springs's common stock is $16 on the declaration date.

A small stock dividend is accounted for similarly to a cash dividend. Recall that on the date a cash dividend is declared, the Dividends account is debited for the amount of cash to be paid to the stockholders. That cash amount represents the economic benefit realized by the stockholders because of the dividend declaration. For a small stock dividend, the assumed economic benefit to be realized by stockholders is the total market value of the stock to be distributed. This amount is determined by multiplying the number of shares to be issued by the stock's market price on the dividend declaration date.

On the declaration date of a stock dividend, the collective market value of the shares to be issued is debited to the Stock Dividends account. The offsetting credit in this entry consists of two amounts. First, the total par value of the shares to be issued is credited to Common Stock Dividend Distributable. Second, the difference between the market value of the stock to be distributed and its total par value is credited to Additional Paid-in Capital, Common Stock.

The Erin Springs stock dividend will result in an additional 5,000 shares (5% × 100,000) of common stock being issued by the company. Since the market price of Erin Spring's stock is $16 on the declaration date, the total market value of the 5,000 shares on that date is $80,000 Of this amount, $5,000, the collective par value of the new shares (5,000 shares × $1), is credited to Common Stock Dividend Distributable. The remaining $75,000 is credited to Additional Paid-in Capital, Common Stock, as shown in the following entry.

Oct. 5	Stock Dividends	80,000	
	Common Stock Dividend		
	Distributable		5,000
	Additional Paid-in Capital,		
	Common Stock		75,000
	To record declaration of 5 percent		
	stock dividend		

On October 25, the record date for the Erin Springs stock dividend, a list of stockholders entitled to receive the stock dividend would be prepared. As with a cash dividend, no accounting entry is necessary on the record date for a stock dividend. On the stock distribution date of November 21, the following entry would be made to record the issuance of the additional stock to Erin Springs's stockholders.

FOR YOUR INFORMATION

Stock Dividends and the Supreme Court: A Taxing Matter

When Congress established the federal income tax in the early twentieth century, a long debate ensued regarding the "taxability" of stock dividends. The issue was a simple one: Did stock dividends provide economic income to stockholders? Congress insisted that stockholders benefit from stock dividends much like cash dividends. So, stock dividends should be considered taxable income. Attorneys for corporate stockholders argued in case after case that stock dividends were not income to stockholders. Instead, they contended that the effect of a stock dividend was simply to cut the stockholders' equity "pie" into a larger number of smaller pieces—an analogy you have heard before. After nearly a decade of legal wrangling, the Supreme Court resolved this controversy in 1920 by agreeing with the "pie" argument rather than with the "income" argument.

Nov. 21	Common Stock Dividend Distributable	5,000	
	Common Stock		5,000

To record common stock issued as a result of the stock dividend declared October 5

On December 31, the balance of Erin Springs's Stock Dividends account would be closed to Retained Earnings—Stock Dividends is a temporary account similar to Dividends. Recall that Dividends Payable, the account credited when a cash dividend is declared, is a current liability account. So, Common Stock Dividend Distributable must also be a current liability account. Right? Wrong. In Chapter 2, we learned that a liability involves the probable future sacrifice of economic benefits. The declaration of a stock dividend does not involve a probable future sacrifice of economic benefits. Instead of a liability account, Common Stock Dividend Distributable is considered a stockholders' equity account. Assume that a company prepares a balance sheet after the declaration date for a stock dividend but before the distribution date. In such a case, Common Stock Dividend Distributable would be listed as a separate line item, following Common Stock, in the stockholders' equity section of the company's balance sheet.

Teaching Note
Again, emphasize that a stock dividend does not change a company's total stockholders' equity. A stock dividend simply results in certain reclassifications within stockholders' equity accounts.

■ **LEARNING OBJECTIVE 7**
Account for stock splits

stock split

Accounting for Stock Splits

On May 19, 1994, Capital Cities/ABC, Inc., announced that its board of directors had approved a 10-for-1 stock split to make the company's stock "more affordable.[5]" A **stock split** is an increase in the number of shares of a company's stock accompanied by a proportionate reduction in the stock's par value. When the stock split was announced, Capital Cities/ABC's common stock was trading on the New York Stock Exchange for $740 per share. The company's stock was the second highest priced on the New York Stock Exchange at the time, topped only by the $12,600 per share price of Berkshire Hathaway's common stock. Investors prefer to purchase common stock

---

5. "Capital Cities/ABC Approves Stock Split," *New York Times*, 20 May 1994, D4.

■ **EXHIBIT 12.7**

Stockholders' Equity of Erin Springs, Inc., and Ownership Interest of an Individual Stockholder Before and After a 2-for-1 Stock Split

	BEFORE 2-FOR-1 STOCK SPLIT	AFTER 2-FOR-1 STOCK SPLIT
Erin Springs, Inc., Stockholders' Equity:		
Common Stock, par value $1:		
Shares authorized—200,000;		
Shares issued and outstanding—100,000	$100,000	
Common Stock, par value $.50:		
Shares authorized—400,000;		
Shares issued and outstanding—200,000		$100,000
Additional Paid-in Capital	600,000	600,000
Retained Earnings	560,000	560,000
Total Stockholders' Equity	$1,260,000	$1,260,000
Book Value Per Share (total stockholders' equity/number of common shares outstanding)	$12.60	$6.30
Chris Jennings, Erin Springs stockholder:		
Shares Owned	100	200
Percentage of Outstanding Shares Owned	.1%	.1%
Total Book Value of Shares Owned	$1,260	$1,260

in multiples of one hundred shares, so-called round lots. Given the high price of Capital Cities/ABC's common stock, few individual investors could afford to purchase a minimum round lot of one hundred shares. By splitting the common stock on a 10-for-1 basis, company executives realized the stock's price would fall from $740 per share to approximately $74 per share. This lower stock price would make it easier for the company to sell additional stock to the public in the future.

When a company splits its stock, it issues new stock to stockholders and cancels the old shares. Assume that Erin Springs's board of directors declares a 2-for-1 stock split on October 5 of the current year instead of declaring a 5 percent stock dividend. Shown in Exhibit 12.7 is how the stockholders' equity section of Erin Springs's balance sheet would appear both before and after the stock split. Also included in Exhibit 12.7 is the ownership interest of Chris Jennings, the now-familiar Erin Springs stockholder, both before and after the stock split.

Notice in Exhibit 12.7 that the par value of Erin Springs's common stock is $.50 per share after the stock split instead of $1 per share. Another noticeable change in the company's stockholders' equity following the stock split is a 100 percent increase in the number of authorized, issued, and outstanding shares. The stock split also reduced the book value per share of Erin Springs's stock by one-half, from $12.60 to $6.30. Finally, notice that the Erin Springs stockholder, Chris Jennings, was largely

Teaching Note
A stock split results in the cancellation of all old stock certificates and the issuance of new stock certificates. A stock dividend results in existing stock certificates being issued to stockholders.

unaffected by the stock split. True, Mr. Jennings has twice as many shares following the stock split as before. But the collective book value of Mr. Jennings's shares is the same before and after the stock split. Unlike a small stock dividend, the market price of a company's stock typically drops proportionately following a stock split. For the present example, that would mean the market price of the Erin Springs stock would drop from $16 to $8 per share immediately following the stock split.

Because a stock split does not affect the balance of any account, a formal journal entry is not necessary to record the announcement of a stock split. However, some companies make a memorandum entry in their general journal to provide a historical record of a stock split. For example, Erin Springs might make the following memorandum entry in its general journal to record the 2-for-1 stock split.

> Oct. 5   Board of directors announced a 2-for-1 stock split for company's common stock. The 200,000 shares of $1 par value common stock will be canceled, and 400,000 shares of $.50 par value common stock will be authorized. The new shares will be issued to stockholders on October 25.

ANALYZING STOCKHOLDERS' EQUITY

■ LEARNING OBJECTIVE 8
Compute and interpret return on equity

return on equity

As suggested earlier, investors continually assess the profitability and potential future profitability of corporations whose stock they have purchased or are considering purchasing. A key financial measure used to evaluate the profitability of a corporation is return on equity. This financial ratio measures the rate of return earned on the capital invested in a firm by its residual owners, the common stockholders. **Return on equity** is computed by dividing a corporation's net income, less preferred stock dividends, by average common stockholders' equity for a given period.

$$\text{Return on Equity} = \frac{\text{Net Income} - \text{Preferred Stock Dividends}}{\text{Average Common Stockholders' Equity}}$$

Every business day, millions of shares of stock are traded by U.S. investors on the New York Stock Exchange. A key factor influencing investors' decisions are financial ratios computed for individual companies, such as the current ratio, the inventory turnover ratio, and return on equity.

Preferred stock dividends are subtracted from net income when computing return on equity because those dividends reduce a corporation's earnings available to common stockholders.

Following are the data needed to compute Cortez Corporation's return on equity for a recent year.

Net Income	$ 474,000
Preferred Stock Dividends	32,000
Common Stockholders' Equity, January 1	3,120,000
Common Stockholders' Equity, December 31	3,830,000

Given these data, Cortez's return on equity for this year is approximately 12.7 percent:

$$\text{Return on Equity} = \frac{\text{Net Income} - \text{Preferred Stock Dividends}}{\text{Average Common Stockholders' Equity}}$$

$$\text{Return on Equity} = \frac{\$474,000 - \$32,000}{(\$3,120,000 + \$3,830,000)/2}$$

$$\text{Return on Equity} = 12.7\%$$

Discussion Question
Ask students to compute Michaels Stores' return on equity. Does this return on equity ratio seem reasonable for a company in Michaels Stores' industry?

Shown in Exhibit 12.8 are the return on equity ratios over a recent five-year period for two publicly owned corporations, Lowe's Companies, Inc., and Zero Corporation. Lowe's operates a chain of do-it-yourself home improvement centers. Zero designs and manufactures engineered cases used to protect electronic equipment, artwork, and other valuable items while they are in transit. Over the five-year period covered by Exhibit 12.8, the average return on equity for these two companies

---

■ **EXHIBIT 12.8**
Return on Equity: Lowe's Companies vs. Zero Corporation

SOURCE: Recent annual reports.

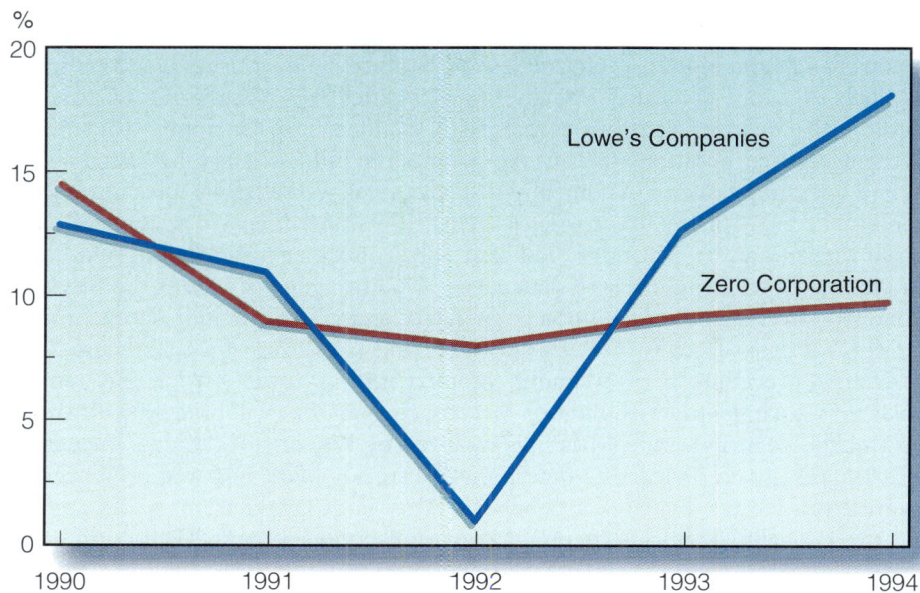

Zeroes Who Are Heroes

Most corporations encourage employees to purchase their common stock. The theory is that an employee who has an ownership interest in a company will be a more dedicated and productive member of the organization. Zero Corporation goes one step beyond by giving employees who perform "above and beyond the call of duty" common stock in the company. Each year, the company lists these employees prominently in its annual report in a section entitled "Zero Heroes."

was very comparable: 11 percent for Lowe's and 10.2 percent for Zero. However, Lowe's earnings were much more volatile over this period than Zero's. Why? One reason is because Lowe's relies more heavily on long-term debt to satisfy its financing needs than does Zero.

Generally, the more long-term debt a company has, the more volatile its earnings will be. The owners of a company benefit when the rate of return earned on assets financed by borrowed funds exceeds the interest rate being paid on those loans. But debt financing can also work to the detriment of companies. For example, when a company's sales decline, most of its expenses tend to decrease, including cost of goods sold and major operating expenses. However, interest expense is unaffected by sales volume. Interest charges must be paid regardless of the revenues realized by a business in any given year. When a company with a significant amount of long-term debt suffers a drop in revenues, its earnings are driven down even further by the large interest expense it continues to incur.

KEY INTERNAL CONTROL PROCEDURES FOR STOCKHOLDERS' EQUITY

■ **LEARNING OBJECTIVE 9**
Define key internal control procedures for stockholders' equity

Real World
Corporate directors may be held personally liable for their actions as board members. Consequently, corporate directors often purchase liability insurance to protect themselves.

The first step in achieving adequate control over stockholders' equity is to ensure that decisions to sell common or preferred stock are approved by a firm's board of directors. Such decisions are extremely important, particularly when common stock is involved. Individuals who become common stockholders have the right to vote on key matters facing a corporation and thus the potential to influence its long-range objectives and operating policies. A company that sells stock to the public must also establish internal control procedures to guard against violations of securities laws and other relevant regulations. Violations of these laws and regulations may result in significant fines and sanctions being imposed on a corporation by agencies such as the SEC.

Following the issuance of common or preferred stock, a corporation should implement control procedures to protect the rights and privileges of stockholders. One such control procedure is maintaining complete and up-to-date name and address records for stockholders. Without such records, corporations will have difficulty notifying stockholders on a timely basis, as required by law, of stockholders' meetings. These records are also needed to determine the stockholders, past and present, who are entitled to receive dividend distributions. Most large corporations retain an outside firm, typically a bank, to maintain their stockholder records. Banks and other firms providing this service are specialists in this area and thus well equipped to keep track of a given corporation's several hundred, or several thousand, widely dispersed stockholders.

SUMMARY

Corporations exist independently of their owners, which is not true of the other two principal types of business organizations, sole proprietorships and partnerships. Among the advantages of the corporate form of business organization is limited liability for its stockholders. Generally, the maximum financial loss a corporate stockholder faces is the amount he or she invested in the corporation's stock. Continuity of existence, the ease with which ownership interests can be transferred, and greater access to equity capital are other benefits of the corporate form of business organization.

The key disadvantage of the corporate form of business organization is the double taxation of corporate profits. Unlike the earnings of sole proprietorships and partnerships, corporate profits are taxed by the federal government and other governmental agencies. These profits are taxed again when they are distributed as cash dividends to stockholders.

When owners of a business decide to incorporate, they file articles of incorporation with an appropriate agency of a state government. If all legal conditions for incorporation are met, the company is granted a corporate charter. A corporation's charter authorizes it to issue a specified number of shares of one or more classes of stock. Common stock represents the residual ownership interests in a corporation. If a corporation is liquidated, its common stockholders are entitled to share proportionately in the firm's residual or remaining assets after all other claims have been satisfied.

The owners of preferred stock are granted certain preferences relative to common stockholders. For example, before common stockholders can be paid any dividends, preferred stockholders must receive the full amount of dividends to which they are entitled. Preferred stock often has one or more distinctive features. These features may include a call option that can be exercised by the issuing company or a convertible option that can be exercised by individual preferred stockholders. The most common preferred stock feature is a cumulative stipulation. If a dividend is not paid on a cumulative preferred stock, that dividend accumulates and must be paid in the future before common stockholders can receive a dividend.

Investors represent a large and important class of financial decision makers. To make rational economic decisions, investors need information regarding the stockholders' equity of individual corporations. Among these information needs are the specific rights and privileges of each class of a corporation's stock. Investors also need data allowing them to assess the profitability of corporations and information regarding corporate dividend policies.

Among the key types of stockholders' equity transactions are the issuance of common stock and the payment of cash dividends. The key to accounting correctly for the issuance of corporate stock is to segregate the proceeds from these transactions into the appropriate accounts. For example, when common stock is sold at a premium, the collective par value of the stock should be credited to the Common Stock account. The difference between the proceeds of the sale of common stock and its collective par value should be credited to Additional Paid-in Capital, Common Stock. To account properly for payments of cash dividends and to exercise effective control over these transactions, accountants must be aware of three key dates. These three dates are the declaration, record, and payment dates.

Assessing the profitability of a corporation is an important concern of its current and prospective stockholders. Return on equity is a key measure of a corporation's profitability. This financial ratio is computed by dividing net income, less any preferred stock dividends, by a corporation's average common stockholders' equity for a given period.

Proper authorization of corporate stock transactions is a key element of a firm's internal control over its stockholders' equity. After the issuance of corporate stock has been properly authorized, control procedures must be implemented to ensure compliance with all state and federal securities laws and other applicable regulations. The maintenance of accurate name and address records for stockholders is one example of an internal control procedure related to stockholders' equity.

GLOSSARY

Authorized stock (p. 525)   The number of shares of a given class of stock a company is permitted to issue under the terms of its corporate charter.

Book value per share (p. 533)   Common stockholders' equity per share for a corporation; computed by dividing total common stockholders' equity by the number of outstanding shares of common stock.

Callable preferred stock (p. 528)   Preferred stock that can be reacquired at the option of the issuing corporation.

Cash dividend (p. 537)   A proportionate distribution of a company's prior earnings to its stockholders made in the form of cash.

Convertible preferred stock (p. 528)   Preferred stock that can be exchanged at the option of preferred stockholders for common stock of the issuing corporation.

Corporation (p. 523)   An association of individuals, created by law and having an existence apart from that of its members as well as distinct and inherent powers and liabilities.

Cumulative preferred stock (p. 527)   Preferred stock on which dividends that are not paid accumulate and must be paid in the future before common stockholders can receive a dividend.

Dividends in arrears (p. 532)   Unpaid dividends on cumulative preferred stock; should be disclosed in a company's financial statement footnotes.

Issued stock (p. 525)   The number of shares of a class of stock that has been sold or otherwise distributed by a corporation; these shares may be outstanding or held as treasury stock.

Outstanding stock (p. 525)   The number of shares of a given class of stock owned by a company's stockholders.

Par value (p. 526)   A nominal dollar value assigned to each share of a class of stock.

Preemptive right (p. 526)   The right of stockholders to retain their fractional ownership interest in a corporation when additional stock is issued.

Preferred stock (p. 525)   A class of stock that has certain preferences or advantages relative to a company's common stock.

Return on equity (p. 544)   A key measure of a corporation's profitability; computed by dividing net income, less preferred stock dividends, by average common stockholders' equity for a given period.

Stated value (p. 526)   A nominal value assigned to each share of a no-par common stock.

Stock dividend (p. 539)   A proportionate distribution of a corporation's own stock to its stockholders.

Stock split (p. 542)   An increase in the number of shares of a company's stock accompanied by a proportionate reduction in the stock's par value.

Treasury stock (p. 525)   Common or preferred stock that has been issued by a corporation and then reacquired.

Suddenly, you find yourself at the advanced age of forty. For nearly two decades, you have worked for a large corporation but now want to go into business for yourself. Your plan is to start a real estate development company, Forest Pointe Enterprises (FPE). You believe that $4 million is needed to get this new company "off the ground," but you have only $1 million to invest. Presently, you are considering two alternative methods of raising the additional $3 million. The first alternative involves selling $2 million of common stock in your company to outside investors—you would purchase the remaining $1 million of the company's common stock. The other $1 million needed would be borrowed from a local bank on a long-term loan with a 10 percent interest rate. Under the second financing alternative, you would purchase all of FPE's common stock for $1 million and borrow the remaining $3 million from the local bank at an interest rate of 10 percent.

DECISION CASE

To choose the optimal financing strategy, you must predict FPE's annual earnings. You have identified two possible earnings scenarios. Under the first scenario, FPE "scores" big and posts earnings before interest expense and income taxes of $700,000 annually. Under the second scenario, the company fails to realize its full potential and earns only $350,000 annually prior to the payment of interest and taxes. Following are projected financial data for FPE's first year for each earnings scenario and financing alternative.

	SCENARIO 1: EARNINGS BEFORE INTEREST AND TAXES OF $700,000		SCENARIO 2: EARNINGS BEFORE INTEREST AND TAXES OF $350,000	
	Financing Strategy 1*	*Financing Strategy 2†*	*Financing Strategy 1*	*Financing Strategy 2*
Capital Structure:				
Owners' Equity	$3,000,000	$1,000,000	$3,000,000	$1,000,000
Debt Capital, 10% Interest Rate	1,000,000	3,000,000	1,000,000	3,000,000
Total Capital	$4,000,000	$4,000,000	$4,000,000	$4,000,000
Earnings Before Interest and Taxes	$ 700,000	$ 700,000	$ 350,000	$ 350,000
Interest Expense	100,000	300,000	100,000	300,000
Pretax Income	$ 600,000	$ 400,000	$ 250,000	$ 50,000
Income Tax Expense (40%)	240,000	160,000	100,000	20,000
Net Income	$ 360,000	$ 240,000	$ 150,000	$ 30,000

* Invest $1 million in FPE's common stock, sell $2 million of common stock to external investors, and borrow $1 million on a long-term loan with a 10 percent interest rate.

† Invest $1 million in FPE's common stock and borrow $3 million on a long-term loan with a 10 percent interest rate.

Required: Compute the return on equity and times interest earned ratio (discussed in Chapter 11) for each of the four situations presented. Which financing strategy is the most "risky"? Why? Assuming Scenario 1 is realized, which financing strategy would be most advantageous for you? Support your answer with the appropriate data. Assuming Scenario 2 is realized, under which financing strategy would you personally benefit the most? Would it be more advantageous for you under the second financing strategy to operate FPE as a corporation or as a sole proprietorship? Explain.

QUESTIONS

1. Match the letter of the appropriate percentage with the correct statement that follows.
   a. 8 percent
   b. 10 percent
   c. 74 percent
   d. 90 percent
   _____ Corporations account for approximately this percentage of gross business revenues each year in the United States.
   _____ Sole proprietorships make up approximately this percentage of businesses in the United States.
   _____ Partnerships and sole proprietorships account for approximately this percentage of gross business revenues each year in the United States.
   _____ Partnerships make up approximately this percentage of businesses in the United States.

2. Identify two methods that business owners can use to raise a large amount of funds in a short period of time.

3. What is a corporation? A closely held corporation? An S corporation?

4. Identify the significance of each of the following items to a corporation.
   a. Articles of incorporation
   b. Corporate charter

5. Identify key advantages and disadvantages of the corporate form of business organization.

6. Explain how a corporation's income is taxed twice.

7. How do the common stock and preferred stock of a corporation differ?

8. Identify the primary rights and privileges of common stockholders. Of preferred stockholders.

9. Briefly define the following terms:
   a. Authorized stock
   b. Issued stock
   c. Outstanding stock
   d. Treasury stock

10. What does the par value of a common stock represent?

11. Distinguish between and among cumulative preferred stock, callable preferred stock, and convertible preferred stock.

12. How is the book value per share of a corporation's common stock computed?

13. What are dividends in arrears? Of what significance to existing or potential common stockholders is information about a company's dividends in arrears?

14. When a corporation exchanges its common stock for an asset such as a building or a piece of equipment, how is the initial book value of the asset determined?

15. Why may a corporation decide to repurchase some of its outstanding common stock?

16. Does a corporation with a positive retained earnings balance have an equivalent balance of cash on hand? Explain.

17. What three dates are significant in the proper accounting for and control over a corporation's cash dividend transactions? On which of these three dates is a cash dividend recognized as a liability by a corporation?

18. Identify the three conditions that must be met before a corporation can distribute cash dividends to its stockholders.

19. What is a stock dividend?

20. If the declaration of a cash dividend imposes a liability on a corporation, why does the declaration of a stock dividend not result in a liability for a corporation?

21. What is a stock split? Why are journal entries not necessary to record a stock split?

22. How does a stock split make a corporation's shares more affordable to potential investors? Provide a numerical example to support your answer.

23. How is the return on equity ratio computed?

24. Identify two internal control procedures related to stockholders' equity.

EXERCISES

25. **Terms** (LO 1, 2)

Following are definitions or descriptions of terms relating to corporations and corporate stockholders' equity.

_____ First-time sale of a corporation's stock to the general public.

_____ A minimal dollar value assigned to each share of a given class of stock.

_____ An association of individuals created by law and having an existence apart from that of its members as well as distinct and inherent powers and liabilities.

_____ The total number of shares of a given class of stock that a corporation is permitted to sell.

_____ Normally the only voting stock of a corporation.

_____ Items found in this document usually include the purpose of the organization and the type and quantity of stock it can issue.

_____ The number of shares of a class of stock that has been sold or otherwise distributed by a corporation.

_____ Permits a stockholder to maintain his or her existing ownership percentage in a company's stock when new stock is issued.

_____ The number of shares of a given class of stock owned by a company's shareholders.

_____ Stock that has been issued and reacquired by a corporation.

_____ A contract between a corporation and the state in which it does business.

Required:

Match each definition or description listed with the appropriate term from the following list.

a. Corporation
b. Articles of incorporation
c. Corporate charter
d. Initial public offering
e. Stated value
f. Authorized stock
g. Issued stock
h. Outstanding stock
i. Treasury stock
j. Preferred stock
k. Common stock

25. c,m,a,f,k,b,g,l,h,i,c

l.   Preemptive right

m.   Par value

26.   Common Stockholder Rights (LO 2)

Suppose that you own 500 shares of the common stock of Cohen & Cohen Securities Brokers. The company has 50,000 shares of common stock outstanding. The par value of the stock is $40. Cohen & Cohen does not have any other classes of stock outstanding.

Required:

26. a. $300

   b. 140 shares

   c. $35,500, market value

a.   If Cohen & Cohen declares a cash dividend of $30,000, or $.60 per share, how much of this dividend can you expect to receive?

b.   If Cohen & Cohen decides to sell an additional 14,000 shares of common stock, how many of these shares will you be entitled to purchase if you so choose? Explain.

c.   Presently, Cohen & Cohen has total stockholders' equity of $3,200,000 and the company's common stock is trading for $71 per share on a major stock exchange. What is the total "value" of the Cohen & Cohen shares that you own? Explain.

27.   Preferred Stock Dividends (LO 3)

Biloxi Corporation has 10,000 shares of cumulative preferred stock outstanding. This stock has a $100 par value and an annual dividend rate of $5 per share. Biloxi has not paid any dividends to its preferred stockholders during the past three years.

Required:

27. No check figures

a.   What disclosure is Biloxi required to make in its annual report regarding the unpaid dividends on its preferred stock?

b.   Where in Biloxi's financial statements will you find this disclosure?

c.   Why is this information of interest to Biloxi's preferred and common stockholders?

28.   Sale of Common Stock for Cash (LO 4)

On January 15, Shaller Legal Services, Inc., sold 20,000 shares of common stock for $14 per share.

Required:

28. 1. Cr. Common Stock
        $100,000
     2. Cr. Common Stock
        $280,000
     3. Cr. Common Stock
        $120,000

Prepare the entry to record the sale of this stock, assuming that the stock:

1.   has a $5 par value.

2.   has no par value.

3.   has no par value but has a stated value of $6 per share.

29.   Issuance of Common Stock for Noncash Assets (LO 4)

Pincus Enterprises acquired a large tract of land from Mock Corporation. In exchange for the land, Pincus gave Mock 500 shares of its $2 par value common stock.

Required:

29. 1. Cr. Common Stock
        $1,000
        Cr. Add'l Paid-in Cap.
        $40,200
     2. Cr. Common Stock
        $1,000
        Cr. Add'l Paid-in Cap.
        $37,500

1.   Prepare the appropriate journal entry to record this transaction in Pincus's accounting records, assuming that the company's stock is not publicly traded and that the land has an appraised value of $41,200.

2.   Suppose now that Pincus's stock is actively traded on the New York Stock Exchange. Immediately before the tract of land was acquired from Mock Corporation, Pincus's stock was trading for $77 per share. Again, assume that

the land has an appraised value of $41,200. Prepare the appropriate journal entry to record this exchange transaction in Pincus's accounting records.

30. Accounting for Cash Dividends (LO 3, 6)

Karlinsky Distributors has 1,000,000 shares of common stock outstanding. On January 11 of this year, Karlinsky declared a cash dividend of $.20 per share, payable on March 9 to stockholders of record on February 12.

Required:

1. When did this dividend become a liability to Karlinsky?
2. Prepare any journal entries required in Karlinsky's accounting records relating to this cash dividend on the following dates:
   a. January 11
   b. February 12
   c. March 9
   d. December 31
3. What individual or group of individuals within the Karlinsky firm authorized the payment of this dividend?
4. What general types of information must public companies regulated by the SEC disclose in their annual reports regarding their dividend policies? Why is this information important to potential investors?

30.2a. Dr. Dividends $200,000
2c. Cr. Cash $200,000

31. Accounting for Stock Dividends (LO 6)

Savich, Inc., had 100,000 shares of $50 par common stock outstanding on April 19 when the company declared a 10 percent stock dividend. The stock dividend was distributed on June 12 to stockholders of record on May 15. The market value of the stock on the declaration date was $61 per share; on the distribution date, the stock had a market value per share of $64.

Required:

1. When did this dividend become a liability to Savich? Explain.
2. Prepare any journal entries required in Savich's accounting records relating to this stock dividend on the following dates:
   a. April 19
   b. May 15
   c. June 12
   d. December 31
3. How does a stock dividend affect the total book value of a corporation's stock controlled by an individual stockholder? How does a stock dividend typically affect the collective market value of an individual stockholder's ownership interest in a corporation? Explain.

31.2a. Dr. Stock Dividends $610,000
2c. Cr. Common Stock $500,000

32. Accounting for Preferred Stock Transactions (LO 2, 4)

The corporate charter of Mosich Motors, Inc., authorizes the company to sell up to 20,000 shares of preferred stock. This preferred stock has a $20 par value and a $1 annual dividend rate. The stock is both cumulative and convertible. Each share of the preferred stock can be exchanged for two shares of Mosich's $3 par value common stock.

In 1995, the company had the following transactions involving its preferred stock.

March 25:	Sold 5,000 shares at a price of $24 per share.
May 24:	Sold 2,000 shares at a price of $25.
August 8:	Declared a $1 preferred stock dividend payable September 13 to preferred stockholders of record on August 21.

September 13:   Paid dividend declared on August 8.

October 25:   3,000 of the shares sold on March 25 were exchanged for Mosich common stock.

Required:

1. In what sense is preferred stock "preferred" compared with a corporation's common stock?
2. Prepare the appropriate journal entries for the 1995 transactions involving Mosich's preferred stock.

33. Accounting for Treasury Stock Transactions (LO 5)

Quick & Reilly is a large discount brokerage firm. In 1994, the stockholders' equity section of the company's 1994 balance sheet indicated that 69,400 shares of the company's common stock was being held as treasury stock. This treasury stock had been acquired at a total cost of $1,930,450, or approximately $27.82 per share. The company's common stock has a par value of $.10 per share.

Required:

1. Why do companies sometimes reacquire stock that they have previously issued?
2. Suppose that Quick & Reilly purchased all of the treasury stock on January 28, 1994. Prepare the journal entry to record this transaction in the company's accounting records.
3. Assume that Quick & Reilly sold 2,000 shares of its treasury stock on April 3, 1995, at a price of $35 per share. Prepare the journal entry to record this transaction in the company's accounting records.
4. Assume that on May 31, 1995, Quick & Reilly sold another 3,000 shares of its treasury stock for $27 per share. Prepare the journal entry to record this transaction in the company's accounting records.
5. Prepare the journal entry to record the May 31, 1995, sale of treasury stock in Quick & Reilly's accounting records, assuming the company had not previously sold any treasury stock.

34. Stockholders' Equity Section of a Corporate Balance Sheet (LO 4, 6, 8)

Following is the stockholders' equity section of the balance sheets included in the 1994 annual report of Piccadilly Cafeterias, Inc. The company's fiscal year ends on June 30.

	1993	1994
	(IN THOUSANDS)	
Shareholders' Equity:		
Preferred Stock, no par value; authorized 50,000,000 shares; issued and outstanding: none	—	—
Common Stock, no par value, stated value $1.82 per share; authorized 100,000,000 shares; issued and outstanding: 9,988,189 shares at June 30, 1993, and 10,131,784 shares at June 30, 1994	$18,160	$18,421
Additional Paid-in Capital	15,119	16,324
Retained Earnings	38,913	41,129
Total Shareholders' Equity	$72,192	$75,874

Required:

1. Compute the book value per share of Piccadilly's common stock at the end of 1993 and 1994.

2. In 1994, Piccadilly had net income of $10,061,000. Compute Piccadilly's return on equity for 1994.

3. Suppose that Piccadilly sold 10,000 shares of its common stock on May 1, 1994, at a price of $9 per share. Prepare the journal entry to record this transaction.

4. During the fourth quarter of Piccadilly's 1994 fiscal year, which ended June 30, 1994, the company paid a cash dividend of $.12 per share. Prepare the appropriate journal entries on Piccadilly's books, assuming the following relevant dates for this dividend and assuming the company had 10,131,784 shares of common stock outstanding throughout the fourth quarter of 1994.
   a. Declaration date: April 5
   b. Record date: May 7
   c. Payment date: June 1

35. **Accounting for Stock Splits** (LO 7)
Refer to the information presented in Exercise 34 for Piccadilly Cafeterias. Suppose that on July 1, 1994, Piccadilly announced a 2-for-1 stock split. The new stock was to be issued on July 31, 1994.

    Required:

    1. Prepare a memorandum entry on July 1, 1994, in Piccadilly's general journal to record the announcement of this stock split.
    2. Following the stock split, how many shares of common stock would Piccadilly have authorized? Issued and outstanding?
    3. Suppose that you owned 200 shares of Piccadilly common stock following the stock split. Determine the total book value of your shares, assuming no other changes in the company's stockholders' equity during July 1994.

36. **Corporate Form of Business Organization** (LO 1)
Doyle Holder and Bill Williams own a small but rapidly growing business, Videos Unlimited. Holder and Williams have been told by their attorney that they should consider incorporating their business, which they now operate as a partnership.

    Required:

    Suppose that you are the accountant for Videos Unlimited. Write a memo to Holder and Williams that summarizes the key advantages and disadvantages of incorporating a business.

37. **Internal Controls over Dividends** (LO 9)
A company's internal control structure should address all major financial transactions of the company, including dividend declarations. Adequate controls in this area are very important. If a company's board of directors approves and pays a dividend that violates bond covenants, the directors and the company may be subject to prosecution by state and federal regulatory agencies and be held responsible for any resulting losses suffered by the bondholders. The company and its directors may also be held liable if dividends are not paid to stockholders who have a right to receive those dividends.

    Required:

    1. Identify specific internal control policies and procedures a company can adopt to ensure that bond covenants are not violated by dividend declarations.
    2. Identify specific internal control policies and procedures a company can adopt to ensure that dividends are paid to the proper stockholders and in the proper amount.

34. 1. 1993, $7.23
       1994, $7.49
    2. 13.59%
    3. Cr. Common Stock
       $18,200
       Cr. Add'l Paid-in Cap,
       Com. Stk. $71,800
   4a. Dr. Dividends
       $1,215,814.08
   4c. Cr. Cash $1,215,814.08

35. 2. Authorized, 200 million
       shares
       Issued & outstanding,
       20,263,568 shares
    3. $748

36. No check figures

37. No check figures

PROBLEM SET A

38. Accounting for Stockholders' Equity Transactions (LO 4, 6)

Arnold Manufacturing was granted a corporate charter on January 3, 1995, and began operations shortly thereafter. Arnold's corporate charter authorizes the firm to issue up to 100,000 shares of $3 par value common stock and 20,000 shares of $100 par value preferred stock. The preferred stock carries an annual dividend rate of $5, is cumulative, and can be converted into Arnold common stock through December 31, 1999. Each share of preferred stock can be converted into 2 shares of Arnold common stock. During 1995, the following events or transactions affected the stockholders' equity of Arnold:

January 10:   Sold 22,000 shares of common stock for $11 per share.

March 30:   Sold 5,000 shares of preferred stock for $101 per share.

June 12:   Exchanged 3,000 shares of common stock for a building with an appraised value of $37,000; on this date Arnold's common stock was trading at $12 per share on a regional stock exchange.

October 3:   Sold 7,000 shares of common stock for $13 per share.

November 4:   Declared a cash dividend of $5 per share on outstanding preferred stock, payable on December 6 to stockholders of record on November 21.

December 31: Net income for 1995 was determined to be $89,000.

Required:

1. Prepare all appropriate journal entries for the events and transactions listed that affected Arnold Manufacturing's stockholders' equity during 1995, including year-end closing entries.
2. Prepare the stockholders' equity section of Arnold's balance sheet as of December 31, 1995.
3. Suppose now that Arnold's common stock has no par value. Prepare the appropriate journal entries to record the January 10, June 12, and October 3 transactions.
4. Suppose now that Arnold's common stock does not have a par value but has a $4 stated value. Prepare the appropriate journal entries to record the January 10, June 12, and October 3 transactions.
5. Refer to the transaction on June 12. Assume that Arnold's common stock is not publicly traded. Prepare the appropriate journal entry for this transaction given this assumption.
6. What accounting principle dictates that Arnold include information in its financial statement footnotes regarding the specific features or stipulations attached to the company's preferred stock?

39. Analyzing Stockholders' Equity (LO 8)

King World Productions, Inc., produces and/or distributes several popular television shows. Included among these shows are *Jeopardy!*, *Wheel of Fortune*, and *The Oprah Winfrey Show*. Following is the stockholders' equity section of King World's balance sheet that was included in the company's 1994 annual report. Also listed is the company's net income for 1993 and 1994.

	1993	1994
	(IN THOUSANDS)	

Stockholders' Equity:

Preferred Stock, $.01 par value; 5,000,000
  shares authorized, none issued   —   —

Answer key (left margin):

38. 1. 1/10/95 Cr. Common Stock $66,000
    Cr. Add'l Paid-in Cap., Com. Stk. $176,000
    3/30 Cr. Preferred Stock $500,000
    Cr. Add'l Paid-in Cap., Pref. Stk $5,000
2. Retained Earnings, $64,000
    Total Stockholders' Equity, $938,000
3. 1/10/95 Cr. Common Stock $242,000
4. 1/10/95 Cr. Common Stock $88,000
    Cr. Add'l Paid-in Cap., Com. Stk. $154,000
5. Cr. Common Stock $9,000
    Cr. Add'l Paid-in Cap., Com. Stk. $28,000

Common Stock, $.01 par value; 75,000,000		
shares authorized, 49,505,363 shares and		
49,722,218 shares issued in 1993 and		
1994, respectively	$ 495	$ 497
Paid-in Capital	76,647	82,171
Retained Earnings	577,039	665,339
Treasury Stock, at cost; 12,207,79~		
shares and 12,960,894 shares in 1993		
and 1994, respectively	(260,008)	(288,930)
Total Stockholders' Equity	$394,173	$459,077
Net Income	$101,936	$ 88,300

Note: King World's total stockholders' equity at the beginning of its 1993 fiscal year was $241,655,000.

Required:

1. Compute the book value per share of King World's common stock at the end of 1993 and 1994.
2. Compute King World's return on equity for 1993 and 1994. Did this ratio improve or deteriorate in 1994 compared with the previous year's ratio?
3. Did King World declare any cash dividends during 1994? Any stock dividends? Explain.
4. Identify one reason that may explain why King World's common stock has such a low par value.

39. 1. 1993, $10.56
       1994, $12.49
    2. 1993, 32.06%
       1994, 20.70%

40. Accounting for Treasury Stock Transactions (LO 5)

Refer to the financial data presented in Problem 39 for King World Productions, Inc.

Required:

1. Compute the average cost of King World's treasury stock at the end of 1994.
2. Suppose that King World purchased 5,000 shares of treasury stock on May 1, 1994, at the average cost computed in Part 1. Prepare the appropriate journal entry to record this transaction.
3. Suppose now that 2,000 shares of the stock assumed purchased in Part 2 were sold for $27 per share on June 15, 1995. Prepare the appropriate journal entry to record this transaction.
4. Finally, suppose that the remaining 3,000 shares of treasury stock assumed purchased in Part 2 were sold for $21 per share on July 29, 1995. Prepare the appropriate journal entry to record this transaction.
5. How can the concept of an inventory cost flow assumption be applied to the sale of treasury stock? Would the application of different cost flow assumptions by a company affect how its treasury stock transactions are recorded? Explain.

40. 1. $22.29
    2. Dr. Treasury Stock
       $111,450
    3. Cr. Treasury Stock
       $44,580
       Cr. Add'l Paid-in Cap.,
       T.S.T. $9,420
    4. Dr. Add'l Paid-in Cap.,
       T.S.T. $3,870
       Cr. Treasury Stock
       $66,870

41. Accounting for Stock Dividends and Stock Splits (LO 6, 7)

Following is the stockholders' equity section of RocLee Corporation's December 31, 1995, balance sheet:

Common Stock, $2 par value; 500,000 shares authorized,	
120,000 shares issued	$240,000
Additional Paid-in Capital	90,000
Retained Earnings	310,000
Total Stockholders' Equity	$640,000

Following are events and transactions involving RocLee's stockholders' equity during 1996.

a. On January 10, 1996, RocLee declared a 5 percent stock dividend. This stock dividend was distributed on March 1, 1996, to stockholders of record on January 31, 1996. RocLee's common stock was trading for $3 per share on both January 10 and January 31. On March 1, the stock was trading for $3.75 per share.

b. On August 15, 1996, RocLee announced a 2-for-1 stock split. The new stock was issued on September 28. Immediately prior to the announcement of the stock split on August 14, the company's stock was trading for $3.50 per share. On October 1, 1996, the company's common stock was trading for $1.75 per share.

c. On December 31, 1996, RocLee's net income for the year was determined to be $64,000. The year-end market price of RocLee's common stock was $2.00.

Required:

1. Prepare all appropriate journal entries involving RocLee's stockholders' equity during 1996.

2. Prepare the stockholders' equity section of RocLee's balance sheet as of December 31, 1996.

3. Assume that you owned 100 shares of RocLee common stock on January 1, 1996. Determine the book value of your ownership interest in this company on the following dates (show your computations.)
   a. January 1, 1996
   b. March 1, 1996
   c. August 14, 1996
   d. October 1, 1996
   e. December 31, 1996

4. Refer to Part 3. Identify the collective market value of your ownership interest in RocLee on each of the indicated dates. (Show your computations.)

42. Stockholders' Equity: Management Decisions (LO 3)
In early 1986, Cardillo Travel Systems, Inc., a publicly owned company, was experiencing severe financial problems. These problems worsened considerably when a large legal judgment was imposed on the firm following the settlement of a lawsuit. Public companies are required to disclose "material events," such as the loss of a major lawsuit, to the SEC. Such disclosures are made available to the public by the SEC. Instead of immediately disclosing the large legal judgment to the SEC, Cardillo's management delayed this disclosure for three weeks. In the meantime, Cardillo's chief executive sold 100,000 shares of the company's common stock in the open market. [Note: The facts of this problem were taken from the following source: M. C. Knapp, "Cardillo Travel Systems, Inc.," in *Contemporary Auditing: Issues and Cases*, 2d ed. (Minneapolis/St. Paul: West Publishing Co., 1996.)]

Required:

1. What is the purpose of the SEC rule requiring public companies to disclose "material events"?

2. Did the management of Cardillo behave ethically in the series of events described? Explain.

3. What parties were harmed as a result of the decisions made by Cardillo's management?

43. Stockholders' Equity for an International Company (LO 3)
Telefonaktiebolaget LM Ericsson (hereinafter "Ericsson"), one of the largest telecommunications firms in the world, is a Swedish company headquartered in

Stockholm. Following is the stockholders' equity section included in the company's 1994 balance sheet. Ericsson's financial data are presented in millions of Swedish kronor. Recently, one Swedish krona was equivalent to approximately $.13. Expressed another way, a U.S. dollar was recently equivalent to approximately 8 kronor.

	1993	1994
Stockholders' Equity (note 19)		
Capital Stock	2,172	2,172
Reserves Not Available for Distribution	4,267	4,281
General Reserve	100	100
Retained Earnings	2,483	4,047
Reported Net Income	2,541	1,961
	11,563	12,561

Required:

1. Notice that one of the largest elements of Ericsson's stockholders' equity is "Reserves Not Available for Distribution." This item represents the amount that Ericsson's long-term assets have been "revalued" (written up) in excess of their cost. Would you find this item in the stockholders' equity section of a U.S. company? At the end of 1994, the revaluation reserve was equal to approximately 11 percent of the company's total assets. In your opinion, does the company's practice of periodically revaluing its long-term assets have a "material" effect on the firm's reported financial condition? Why or why not?

2. Why do you believe Sweden's federal securities laws prevent Swedish companies from paying dividends from revaluation reserves included in their stockholders' equity?

3. Swedish companies are allowed to establish "general reserves" within their stockholders' equity. Notice that Ericsson had such a reserve in both 1993 and 1994. The company's financial statement footnotes did not explain the purpose of this reserve. Identify the accounting concept or concepts that would be violated if similar practices were engaged in by a U.S. firm.

43. No check figures

PROBLEM SET B

44. **Accounting for Stockholders' Equity Transactions** (LO 4, 6)

On February 4, 1996, Moore Industries received a corporate charter. A few days later, the new company began operations. The corporate charter of Moore Industries permits the firm to issue up to 400,000 shares of $1 par value common stock and up to 50,000 shares of $50 par value preferred stock. The preferred stock is cumulative and has a $3.50 annual dividend rate. Additionally, the preferred stock can be called in at the option of Moore within the first ten years of the corporation's existence or through February 4, 2006. If the preferred stock is called in by Moore, the preferred stockholders will be paid $53 for each share they own. During 1996, the following events or transactions affected Moore's stockholders' equity:

February 16: Sold 67,000 shares of common stock for $15 per share.
February 28: Sold 3,000 shares of preferred stock for $52 per share.
May 15: Exchanged 10,000 shares of common stock for a tract of land with an appraised value of $164,000; on this date, Moore's common stock was trading for $15 per share on a national stock exchange.
August 7: Sold 7,000 shares of common stock for $17 per share.

October 22: Declared a cash dividend of $3.50 per share on outstanding preferred stock, payable on November 21 to stockholders of record on November 5.

December 31: Net income was determined to be $202,000 for 1996.

Required:

1. Prepare all appropriate journal entries for the events and transactions listed that affected Moore Industries' stockholders' equity during 1996, including year-end closing entries.
2. Prepare the stockholders' equity section of Moore's balance sheet as of December 31, 1996.
3. Suppose now that Moore's common stock has no par value. Prepare the appropriate journal entries to record the February 16, May 15, and August 7 transactions.
4. Suppose now that Moore's common stock does not have a par value but does have a $4 stated value. Prepare the appropriate journal entries to record the February 16, May 15, and August 7 transactions.
5. Refer to the transaction on May 15. Assume that Moore's common stock is not publicly traded. Prepare the appropriate journal entry for this transaction given this assumption.
6. Moore's executives considered not attaching a cumulative stipulation to the company's preferred stock. However, the company's investment banking firm informed Moore's executives that the preferred stock would likely sell for no more than $40 per share if it did not have a cumulative feature. Explain why this was the case. What other feature could Moore's management have added to the preferred stock to increase its initial selling price?

45. **Analyzing Stockholders' Equity** (LO 8)

Circus Circus Enterprises, Inc., owns and operates several Las Vegas casinos including the Luxor and the Excalibur. Following are the stockholders' equity sections of Circus Circus's balance sheets that were included in the company's 1994 annual report. Also listed is the company's net income for 1993 and 1994.

	1993	1994
	(IN THOUSANDS)	
Stockholders' Equity:		
Common Stock, $.01 ⅔ par value		
Authorized—450,000,000 shares		
Issued—95,914,143 and 96,168,179 shares in 1993 and 1994, respectively	$ 1,599	$ 1,603
Preferred Stock, $.01 par value		
Authorized—75,000,000 shares	—	—
Additional Paid-in Capital	111,516	120,135
Retained Earnings	502,257	618,446
Treasury Stock, at cost; 8,663,214 shares and 10,062,814 shares in 1993 and 1994, respectively	(125,363)	(180,234)
Total Stockholders' Equity	$490,009	$559,950
Net Income	$117,322	$116,189

Note: Circus Circus's total stockholders' equity at the beginning of its 1993 fiscal year was $326,196,000.

Answers (margin):

44. 1. 2/16/96 Cr. Common Stock $67,000
Cr. Add'l Paid-in Cap., Com. Stk. $938,000
2/28 Cr. Preferred Stock $150,000
Cr. Add'l Paid-in Cap., Pref. Stk. $6,000
2. Retained Earnings, $191,500
Total Stockholders' Equity, $1,621,500
3. 2/16/96 Cr. Common Stock $1,005,000
4. 2/16/96 Cr. Common Stock $268,000
Cr. Add'l Paid-in Cap., Com. Stk. $737,000
5. Cr. Common Stock $10,000
Cr. Add'l Paid-in Cap., Com. Stk. $154,000

Required:
1. Compute the book value per share of Circus Circus's common stock at the end of 1993 and 1994.
2. Compute Circus Circus's return on equity for 1993 and 1994. Did this ratio improve or deteriorate in 1994 compared with the previous year's ratio?
3. Why do you believe Circus Circus lists its preferred stock in the stockholders' equity section of its balance sheet even though none of that stock is outstanding?
4. Did Circus Circus declare any cash dividends during 1994? Any stock dividends? Explain.

45. 1. 1993, $5.62
1994, $6.50
2. 1993, 28.75%
1994, 22.13%

46. Accounting for Treasury Stock Transactions (LO 5)
Refer to the financial data presented in Problem 45 for Circus Circus Enterprises, Inc.

Required:
1. Compute the average cost of Circus Circus's treasury stock at the end of 1994.
2. Suppose that Circus Circus purchased 10,000 shares of treasury stock on May 1, 1994, at the average cost computed in Part 1. Prepare the appropriate journal entry to record this transaction.
3. Now suppose that 4,000 shares of the stock assumed purchased in Part 2 were sold for $24 per share on June 15, 1995. Prepare the appropriate journal entry to record this transaction.
4. Finally, suppose that the remaining 6,000 shares of treasury stock assumed purchased in Part 2 were sold for $17 per share on July 29, 1995. Prepare the appropriate journal entry to record this transaction.
5. Why are corporations prohibited from recognizing gains or losses on treasury stock transactions? Which accounting concept or concepts discussed in Chapter 2 would be violated if a company recorded the proceeds from the sale of its treasury stock as revenue?

46. 1. $17.91
2. Dr. Treasury Stock $179,100
3. Cr. Treasury Stock $71,640
Cr. Add'l Paid-in Cap., T.S.T. $24,360
4. Dr. Add'l Paid-in Cap., T.S.T. $5,460
Cr. Treasury Stock $107,460

47. Accounting for Stock Dividends and Stock Splits (LO 6, 7)
Following is the stockholders' equity section of the December 31, 1995, balance sheet of Sampson & Schnell Associates (SSA), an investment advisory firm.

Common Stock, $5 par value; 500,000 shares authorized, 80,000 shares issued	$400,000
Additional Paid-in Capital	80,000
Retained Earnings	250,000
Total Stockholders' Equity	$730,000

Following are events and transactions involving SSA's stockholders' equity during 1996.
a. On January 25, 1996, SSA declared a 10 percent stock dividend. This stock dividend was distributed on March 4, 1996, to stockholders of record on February 16, 1996. SSA's common stock was trading for $9 per share on January 25. On March 4, the stock was trading for $8.50 per share.
b. On July 7, 1996, SSA announced a 2-for-1 stock split. The new stock was issued on August 8. Immediately prior to the announcement of the stock split on July 6, the company's stock was trading for $8.00 per share. On August 9, 1996, the company's common stock was trading for $4.25 per share.
c. On December 31, 1996, SSA's net income for the year was determined to be $112,000. The year-end market price of SSA's common stock was $4.75.

47. 1. 1/25/96 Dr. Stock Dividends $72,000
Cr. Common Stock Div. Distr. $40,000

Required:

1. Prepare all appropriate journal entries involving SSA's stockholders' equity during 1996.
2. Prepare the stockholders' equity section of SSA's balance sheet as of December 31, 1996.
3. Assume that you owned 100 shares of SSA common stock on January 1, 1996. Determine the book value of your ownership interest in this company on the following dates (show your computations):
   a. January 1, 1996
   b. March 4, 1996
   c. July 6, 1996
   d. August 9, 1996
   e. December 31, 1996
4. Refer to Part 3. Identify the collective market value of your ownership interest in SSA on each of the indicated dates. (Show your computations.)

48. Stockholders' Equity: Management Decisions (LO 3, 9)

Four Seasons Nursing Centers of America was incorporated in 1967 in Oklahoma City. This company's principal line of business was the construction of nursing homes. During the first few years of its existence, the company recorded large profits, which caused the price of the firm's common stock to increase dramatically. In early 1968, Four Seasons' common stock was selling for $10 per share; eighteen months later the stock was trading for $100 per share. However, a large portion of the company's reported profits was bogus, the product of illicit accounting schemes by Four Seasons' executives. In the early 1970s, Four Seasons collapsed when the executives could no longer conceal the company's true financial condition and operating results. Nevertheless, before the company failed, several Four Seasons executives realized large gains on the sale of the company's common stock. One executive alone earned more than $10 million by selling stock he owned in the company after the stock's price had skyrocketed on the strength of the false earnings data.

Numerous lawsuits and criminal charges were filed against Four Seasons and its executives. In one legal case involving Four Seasons, an intercompany memo written by one Four Seasons executive to another was uncovered. This memo contained the following statement: "Let's get Walston's [one of Four Seasons' investment bankers] opinion as to when we could sell a sizable portion of our stock, while the stock is at a good price, to guard against having to sell after the public realizes that [our] nursing homes will not meet [profit] expectations." (Note: The facts of this problem were taken from the following source: M. C. Knapp, "Four Seasons Nursing Centers of America, Inc." in *Contemporary Auditing: Issues and Cases*, 2d ed. (Minneapolis/St. Paul: West Publishing Co., 1996.)

Required:

1. In the Four Seasons case, what parties were harmed by the decisions of the company's management?
2. Refer to the concept of a "control environment" discussed in Chapter 3. What members of an organization are responsible for establishing an adequate control environment within the organization? Briefly analyze Four Seasons' control environment.
3. Can the establishment of a corporate code of conduct or mission statement, such as the one included in the Spotlight on Ethics vignette in this chapter, help to create a strong control environment in an organization? Why or why not?

49. Stockholders' Equity for an International Company (LO 3)

San Miguel Corporation is the largest publicly owned beverage and food products company in the Philippines. San Miguel accounts for approximately 4 percent of the country's gross national product and approximately 6 percent of the tax revenues taken in by the Philippines federal government. In 1993, the company's total stockholders' equity was approximately 21 billion Philippine pesos. (Recently, the U.S. equivalent of one Philippine peso was approximately $.04.) A "Revaluation Increment" accounted for nearly 6 percent of San Miguel's 1993 stockholders' equity. This item resulted from periodic "revaluations" (write-ups) of the book values of San Miguel's long-term assets to their approximate market values.

San Miguel's 1994 annual report contained the following financial statement footnote entitled "Change in Accounting Policy":

Pursuant to the Company's internationalization thrust, effective January 1994, the management decided to adjust the recorded appraised value of certain property, plant and equipment to conform with the historical cost method of valuation. The cost method is internationally the more widely accepted accounting principle for this account. This method, as well as the appraisal valuation previously used, are both generally accepted accounting principles in the Philippines.

Required:

1. In your opinion, did San Miguel's practice of periodically revaluing its long-term assets (prior to 1994) materially affect the firm's stockholders' equity? Defend your answer.
2. What benefits may San Miguel realize as a result of adopting the historical cost principle for accounting and financial reporting purposes? Why?

49. No check figures

CASES

50. Preferred Stock Features

Larsen & O'Leary Publishing Company, a partnership, is preparing articles of incorporation to file with the state corporation commission. The present owners of the firm intend to purchase all 50,000 shares of the corporation's common stock which will have a $10 par value. The owners also plan to sell 20,000 shares of $100 par value preferred stock to outside investors. This preferred stock will pay a $6 dollar annual dividend per share and be nonvoting. The company's owners are attempting to decide what other features the preferred stock should have. Among the additional features they are considering are a call provision, a convertible option, and a cumulative stipulation. Following are brief descriptions of each of these features.

Call Provision: The preferred stock would be callable on the fifth anniversary date of its issuance. If Larsen & O'Leary exercises the call option, the preferred stockholders would receive $105 per share for the stock they own.

Convertible Option: After ten years, any preferred stock still outstanding could be converted at the option of the preferred stockholders into Larsen & O'Leary common stock. The exchange rate would be three shares of common stock for each share of preferred stock.

Cumulative Stipulation: Any annual dividend not paid on the preferred stock would accumulate as dividends in arrears. In subsequent years, before common stockholders would be entitled to receive any dividends, all dividends in arrears would have to be paid first. If the annual dividend is not paid on the preferred stock for three consecutive years, the preferred stockholders would be granted voting rights. Each share of preferred stock would be entitled to three votes. A one share–one vote rule will apply to the company's common stock.

Required:
1. What advantages will the owners of Larsen & O'Leary realize by retaining all of the common stock of the corporation and selling only preferred stock to outside investors?
2. Which of the three preferred stock features being considered would be advantageous to Larsen & O'Leary's common stockholders? Which would be advantageous to the company's preferred stockholders? Explain.
3. Why may the present owners of this firm, its future common stockholders, attach features to the company's preferred stock that would be disadvantageous to them?

51. Corporate Stock Terminology

Merle Hopkins is the only M.D. in the small town of Bitter Creek, Wyoming. Recently, Dr. Hopkins has turned to you, a summer accounting intern for a local business, for some financial advice—Dr. Hopkins is beginning to develop a financial plan for his retirement years. Next fall, you will be returning to the University of Wyoming to complete your accounting degree. Dr. Hopkins realizes that you must have learned a great deal about corporate financial statements during your three years in Laramie. The first question Dr. Hopkins poses of you concerns the different values attached to corporate stocks.

Required:

Write a brief memo to Dr. Hopkins explaining the meaning of each of the following terms and how they are related: par value, stated value, book value per share, and market value (market price of common stock). Dr. Hopkins would like to know which of these values is most important. That is, which should he pay particular attention to when deciding whether or not to invest in a given company's stock. When writing your memo, keep in mind that Dr. Hopkins literally does not know a debit from a credit.

52. Stock Split

The following footnote disclosure was included in the 1994 annual report of Circus Circus Enterprises, Inc.

In June 1993, the board of directors declared a 3-for-2 stock split on the Company's common stock, which was distributed July 23, 1993, to stockholders of record on July 9, 1993. All share data have been adjusted retroactively in the accompanying financial statements for the 3-for-2 stock split.

Required:

Interpret this footnote. Why would per share data, such as earnings per share and book value per share amounts, be adjusted retroactively—that is, restated from amounts reported in previously issued financial statements, for a stock split? Is this a dishonest practice? Or, are such restatements necessary to prevent the company's financial statements for two or more consecutive years from being misleading when the company's stock was split during the most recent of those years? Explain.

PROJECTS

53. Stockholders' Equity: Management Decisions

In early 1985, several key executives of a small biotechnology firm headquartered in Utah began negotiating a merger with the executives of another company. While this merger was being secretly negotiated, the executives of the Utah company purchased several hundred thousand shares of their firm's common stock on the open market. When the news of the merger was finally released, the market price of the Utah firm's common stock increased dramatically. At this point, the company's executives sold much of their stock at a large profit. (Note: The facts of this case were drawn from the following source: Securities and Exchange Commission, *Accounting and Auditing Enforcement Release No. 195*, 13 July 1988.)

Required:

Break into your project groups to discuss this case and the following questions.

1. Did the executives of the Utah company behave unethically? If so, who was disadvantaged by their actions?
2. In this case, corporate executives had access to "inside information" that induced them to purchase their company's common stock before that information became public. Often, just the reverse happens (see Problems 42 and 48). That is, corporate executives sell stock in their company before negative "inside information" regarding the company's financial condition or operations is released to the public. Should corporate executives be allowed to profit from inside information? If so, under what general conditions or circumstances? If not, how can corporate executives be prevented from profiting from such information?
3. Consider this scenario. You are at lunch one day and hear two business executives quietly discussing an upcoming but unannounced merger of two publicly owned companies. You realize that the market price of each company's common stock will likely increase when the merger is announced. Would it be unethical for you to act on this information by purchasing stock in these companies? Keep in mind that you did not "steal" this information. Instead, you were simply in the right place at the right time.
4. One member of your group should be prepared to present a summary overview to the class of your group's discussion of this material.

54. **Initial Public Offerings**

    Research on-line or hard copy indices of *The Wall Street Journal, Los Angeles Times, New York Times*, or other major metropolitan newspapers and identify three initial public offerings (IPOs) of common stock within the past three years. These newspapers often contain a series of articles, or at least brief commentaries, regarding major IPOs. Once you identify one article relating to an IPO, you will likely discover related articles or commentaries in the weeks and months before and/or after the publication date of that article.

    Required:

    1. In a written report, summarize the principal line of business of each company involved in the three IPOs you identified. Also, identify the principal reason that each company chose to raise funds by selling common stock. For example, was the purpose to provide funds needed to enlarge the company's production facilities, to expand overseas, or to purchase another company?
    2. Identify the initial selling price of the stock being sold in each IPO and the number of shares offered for sale.
    3. Determine whether each IPO was successful. That is, was all the stock sold? Also identify each new stock's market price one month following the IPO. How does this market price in each case compare with the original offering price? If these prices are significantly different, what factor or factors likely accounted for this difference?

55. **Corporate Dividend Policies**

Obtain a recent copy of *The Wall Street Journal* and turn to the section titled "Corporate Dividend News." Choose any five companies for which a dividend announcement was reported that day.

Required:

For each company selected, record the amount of the dividend, the payment date, the record date, and whether the dividend was a quarterly, semiannual, or annual dividend. For two of the companies selected, obtain and review their most recent annual reports. For each of these firms, identify information in the company's annual report regarding management's dividend policy or apparent dividend policy. This information may be included in a narrative disclosure within the annual report or disclosed in a tabular or graphical format. Prepare a brief written report that documents the information you obtained from *The Wall Street Journal* and the additional information regarding the dividend policies of two of the companies you selected.

THE CORPORATE INCOME STATEMENT AND STATEMENT OF STOCKHOLDERS' EQUITY

13

LEARNING OBJECTIVES

After studying this chapter, you should be able to do the following:

1. Discuss the comprehensive approach to income measurement

2. Identify the key elements of the corporate income statement

3. Compute earnings per share

4. Describe temporary differences and their impact on pretax accounting income versus taxable income

5. Account for corporate income taxes

6. Describe the structure and purpose of a statement of stockholders' equity

7. Account for prior period adjustments and appropriations of retained earnings

8. Compute and interpret the price-earnings and market price to book value ratios

Practice random acts of kindness & senseless beauty.

Bumper sticker included in 1991 annual report of Ben & Jerry's Homemade, Inc.

Mixing Social Consciousness and Corporate Profits

Probably the best-known and most successful "corporation with a conscience" is Vermont-based Ben & Jerry's Homemade, Inc. Ben & Jerry's manufactures and markets super premium ice creams and related products. Founded in 1978 by two self-proclaimed hippies, Ben Cohen and Jerry Greenfield, the company quickly outgrew the former gas station that was its original corporate headquarters. Within a few years, the company was known nationwide for its tasty and memorable flavors include Cherry Garcia, Chunky Monkey, Wavy Gravy, and Bluesberry. The public's craving for Ben & Jerry's products translated into booming sales and profits for the company.

When it comes to social causes, Ben & Jerry's puts its money where its mouth is. A long-standing corporate policy is to donate 7.5 percent of pretax profits to a nonprofit organization, Ben & Jerry's Foundation, Inc. Since the mid-1980s, this foundation has poured millions of dollars into a wide range of charitable organizations and social causes. Recipients of Ben & Jerry's Foundation grants include the Center for Immigration Rights, the Vermont Clean Water Project, the Massachusetts Coalition for the Homeless, and the Brattleboro Area AIDS Project.

Firms such as Ben & Jerry's can become so preoccupied with their social causes that they neglect the fundamental business aspects of their operations. Even a "new age" corporation must establish strict receivables collection procedures, implement inventory control measures, and closely monitor earnings and cash flows. In fact, rigorous accounting and financial controls are probably more important for these firms than most, since a sizable portion of their profits is siphoned off for charitable donations.

Economic realities caught up with Ben & Jerry's in the early 1990s. Aggressive competition from firms such as Haagen-Dazs loosened the company's stranglehold on the market for super premium ice creams. The company also had to cope with inventory control problems and disrupted production schedules stemming from the use of antiquated equipment. Collectively, these problems caused Ben & Jerry's growth rates in sales and profits to nosedive. From 1992 through mid-1994, Ben & Jerry's common stock plummeted 60 percent in value as the company's troubles mounted. Recognizing that he was not the man to rescue Ben & Jerry's from its downward spiral, Ben Cohen resigned in 1994 as the company's chief executive officer.

Not a company to ever take the conventional route to solving a problem, Ben & Jerry's launched an innovative, nationwide search for a new chief executive. In a series of advertisements, the company instructed individuals wishing to replace Ben Cohen to write a one-hundred-word essay on "Why I would be a great CEO for Ben & Jerry's." The result was more than twenty thousand essays from would-be ice cream executives of all ages and backgrounds.

Chapter 12 focused on accounting for stockholders' equity. In this chapter, we again consider stockholders' equity but concentrate principally on financial reporting issues. First, we examine the structure and content of the corporate income statement, including taxation issues. Next, the statement of stockholders' equity is discussed. Finally, two financial ratios are discussed and illustrated: the price-earnings and market price to book value ratios. Investors use these ratios when making investment decisions involving corporate common stocks.

THE CORPORATE INCOME STATEMENT

Income statements have been presented and illustrated in earlier chapters. However, we have not yet examined in depth financial reporting issues related to the income statement, particularly the corporate income statement. That is our purpose in this section. We begin by briefly identifying the information needs of decision makers that income statements address. Then, the comprehensive approach to income measurement is discussed. This approach dictates the general strategy that accountants follow in preparing a corporate income statement. Next, alternative titles and formats for, and the key elements of, corporate income statements are identified and illustrated. This section concludes with an overview of corporate income taxes.

If we are going to analyze the corporate income statement, it will be helpful to have an example to which we can refer occasionally. Most corporate income statements do not contain all of the elements that we need to discuss. So, for illustration purposes, we will use an income statement of an imaginary company, Happy Hollow Corporation. Shown in Exhibit 13.1 is a recent income statement for this firm. Notice that the line items in Happy Hollow's income statement have been numbered so that we can refer more easily to its individual components. Notice also that certain items in Happy Hollow's income statement are boldfaced. These are items on which we focus particular attention.

Corporate Income Statements: Serving the Information Needs of Decision Makers

A wide range of decision makers need and use the information found in corporate income statements. As suggested in Chapter 12, stockholders need such information to evaluate the wisdom of their investments and to decide whether to make further investments. Suppliers need to know whether their corporate customers are "money-making" operations so that they can decide whether to continue extending credit to them. Prospective employees want to identify profitable corporations that will provide a reliable source of employment income. Finally, consider executives of charitable organizations, a small subset of financial decision makers. These individuals study corporate income statements to identify profitable companies that can easily afford to donate "a few million here and there" to good causes.

Keep in mind as we study and dissect the corporate income statement that it is just one source of data regarding corporations. Decision makers must use all of a corporation's financial statements and accompanying footnotes as well as other available data to obtain a complete picture of the entity's financial status.

Teaching Note
Emphasize that the primary function of an income statement is to measure a business entity's profitability for a specific period of time.

The Comprehensive Approach to Income Measurement

Statement of Financial Accounting Concepts No. 6, "Elements of Financial Statements,"[1] suggests that businesses should use a comprehensive, or all-inclusive, approach to determining their periodic income. This approach mandates that most transactions and events affecting the owners' equity of a business be included in its periodic income statements. Clearly, certain transactions influencing the owners' equity of a

■ LEARNING
OBJECTIVE 1
Discuss the comprehensive approach to income measurement

---

1. Portions of various FASB documents, copyright by Financial Accounting Standards Board, 401 Merritt, PO Box 5116, Norwalk, Connecticut 06856-5116, U.S.A., are reprinted with permission. Copies of the complete documents are available from the FASB.

■ **EXHIBIT 13.1**

Example of a Corporate Income Statement

HAPPY HOLLOW CORPORATION INCOME STATEMENT FOR THE YEAR ENDED DECEMBER 31, 1995		
1 Net Sales		$2,100,000
2 Cost of Goods Sold		1,240,000
3 Gross Profit		860,000
4 Operating Expenses		
5 Selling	$ 80,000	
6 General	47,000	
7 Administrative	130,000	257,000
8 Operating Income		603,000
9 Other Gains or Losses		
10 Gain on Sale of Equipment		42,000
11 Income from Continuing Operations before Income Tax		645,000
12 Income Tax Expense		258,000
13 **Income from Continuing Operations**		387,000
14 **Discontinued Operations**		
15 Operating Income, $24,000, less Income Tax of $9,600	14,400	
16 Gain on Disposal, $40,000, less Income Tax of $16,000	24,000	38,400
17 Income before Extraordinary Loss and Cumulative Effect of a Change in Accounting Principle		425,400
18 **Extraordinary Loss due to Tornado, $100,000, less Income Tax Savings of $40,000**		(60,000)
19 **Cumulative Effect of a Change in Accounting Principle, $18,000, less Income Tax of $7,200**		10,800
20 Net Income		$376,200
21 **Earnings Per Share of Common Stock**		
22 Income from Continuing Operations		$3.87
23 Income from Discontinued Operations		.38
24 Income before Extraordinary Item and Cumulative Effect of a Change in Accounting Principle		4.25
25 Extraordinary Loss		(.60)
26 Cumulative Effect of a Change in Accounting Principle		.11
27 Net Income		$3.76

Teaching Note

Remind students that corporations never record gains and losses on the sale of their own stock.

business should be excluded from its income statements. For example, the sale of common stock by a corporation increases its stockholders' equity. However, this transaction is a financing activity, not a profit-oriented activity, and thus should not be included in the corporate income statement. Prior period adjustments, discussed later in this chapter, are another example of items affecting stockholders' equity that are excluded from the income statement.

Critics of the comprehensive approach to income measurement maintain that it often results in a cluttered and difficult to interpret income statement. Nevertheless, the accounting profession firmly supports this approach to income measurement. When it comes to the income statement, the profession has decided that it is better to risk that decision makers will be confused by too much information than misled by too little information.

Alternative Titles and Formats

Business entities, including corporations, do not necessarily refer to the financial statement reporting their periodic revenues and expenses as an income statement. *Accounting Trends & Techniques* reports that approximately 50 percent of all companies use a title other than "income statement." The two most common alternative titles are "statement of earnings" and "statement of operations." The latter caption is often used when a company has incurred a loss for one or more of the years for which financial data are being presented.

Corporations can use one of two alternative formats for their income statements: the single-step format or the multiple-step format. In the single-step format, a company lists its revenues followed by its expenses and then computes net income as the difference between the totals of those two items. Many companies in service industries use the single-step format, an example being Quick & Reilly, the discount brokerage firm. According to *Accounting Trends & Techniques*, approximately two-thirds of all companies use the multiple-step format for their income statements. In a multiple-step income statement, certain revenues and expenses are netted to arrive at key subtotals, such as gross profit and operating income, before net income is presented. The accountants of Happy Hollow Corporation used the multiple-step format in preparing the income statement shown in Exhibit 13.1.

Teaching Note
Remind students that an income statement is prepared for a period of time unlike a balance sheet which is prepared as of a specific point in time.

Key Elements of the Corporate Income Statement

This section introduces you to the common elements or components of a corporate income statement. As we review Happy Hollow's 1995 income statement, recognize that corporations typically present income statement data on a comparative basis—that is, for multiple years. Corporations regulated by the Securities and Exchange Commission (SEC) must generally present income statement data for their most recent fiscal year and the two preceding years.

INCOME FROM CONTINUING OPERATIONS In 1995, Happy Hollow had Income from Continuing Operations of $387,000, as shown on line 13 of Exhibit 13.1. This amount is net of income taxes of $258,000 reported on line 12. Later in this chapter, we examine several corporate taxation issues. For the time being, you should be aware of two "taxing" matters as they pertain to Happy Hollow's 1995 income statement. First, you should be aware that certain key items in a corporate income statement are presented "net of tax," such as the extraordinary loss reported on line 18 of Happy Hollow's income statement. This presentation method reveals to financial statement users the dollar effect of these items on an entity's net income. Second, corporations have different effective, or average, income tax rates. Happy Hollow's effective income tax rate in 1995 was 40 percent. So, each income tax expense item reported in Exhibit 13.1 is 40 percent of the appropriate base amount. For example, the income tax expense reported on line 12 of Exhibit 13.1 is 40 percent of Happy Hollow's Income from Continuing Operations before Income Tax (line 11).

Income from continuing operations represents the earnings produced by a corporation's principal profit-oriented activities. This figure is often used as the starting point to predict a firm's future profits. All other variables held constant, we would expect a firm to earn approximately the same amount each year from its continuing operations. Granted, the all-other-variables-held-constant assumption is huge. Numerous factors may cause a company's income from continuing operations to vary significantly from one year to the next. Nevertheless, income from continuing operations provides decision makers with a base amount for predicting future corporate earnings. Given this fig-

■ LEARNING OBJECTIVE 2
Identify the key elements of the corporate income statement

Discussion Question
Ask students why comparative income statements are useful to readers.

Real World
Effective tax rates for corporations are not uniform for a variety of reasons. One reason is that income tax rates at the state level vary considerably.

income from continuing operations

An Income Statement With a Northern Accent

Our friendly neighbors to the north, the Canadians, share most of our attitudes toward accounting and financial reporting. On certain matters of style, though, the Canadians often go their own way. Take the case of Hudson's Bay Company, Canada's largest department store chain and its oldest corporation, having been founded in 1670. Following is the company's statement of earnings for the year ended January 31, 1995. Contrast the format of Happy Hollow's income statement shown in Exhibit 13.1 with the income statement format used by Hudson's Bay. (As a point of information, The Bay and Zellers are the two major divisions of Hudson's Bay.)

HUDSON'S BAY COMPANY
CONSOLIDATED STATEMENT OF EARNINGS

	Notes	YEAR ENDED JANUARY 31, 1995 $000's
Sales and Revenues		
The Bay	2	2,353,410
Zellers	2	3,374,830
Other		101,003
		5,829,243
Operating Profit		
The Bay	2	161,301
Zellers	2	215,560
Other		(7,424)
Earnings before Interest and Income Taxes		369,437
Interest Expense	4	(100,525)
Earnings before Income Taxes		268,912
Income Taxes	5	(117,625)
Earnings before Unusual Items		151,287
Unusual Income Tax Credits	5	33,033
Net Earnings		184,320
Earnings per Common Share	6	$3.23

ure as a starting point, investors can make assumptions regarding such variables as a company's future growth rate in sales to arrive at a less naive prediction of its future earnings.

DISCONTINUED OPERATIONS   Most large corporations have more than one line of business. For example, a company that operates a large chain of discount stores may also own a regional trucking company and a minor league baseball team. When a company decides to discontinue a line of business, a separate section of its income statement entitled **discontinued operations** should be devoted to the business segment being eliminated. This section of a corporation's income statement normally includes two items: the operating income or loss of the discontinued segment and the net gain or loss resulting from the disposal of that segment.

Notice that line 15 of Happy Hollow's income statement reports operating income of $14,400, net of income tax, for a discontinued line of business. The following line discloses a $24,000 after-tax gain on the disposal of that business segment. Listing these items in this manner clearly indicates that they are not components of continuing operations and thus should not be considered when making future profit projections.

When a company has discontinued operations reported in its income statement, there is usually an accompanying reference to a financial statement footnote. That footnote will describe the nature of the discontinued operations and provide additional details of the operating results and gains or losses attributable to the discontinued business segment. McKesson Corporation, a large pharmaceutical concern, reported discontinued operations in its 1994 income statement under the following caption: "Discontinued Operations (Note 8)." McKesson's financial statement footnotes revealed that the firm had disposed of a wine and spirits production company and certain other smaller business segments. The footnote also provided a mini–income statement documenting the operating results and gains and losses attributable to the discontinued operations.

EXTRAORDINARY ITEMS   Occasionally, companies incur material gains or losses—mostly losses—due to rare events such as a catastrophic fire or the expropriation of assets by a foreign government. Because these "extraordinary items" are not normal components of a corporation's revenues and expenses, they should be shown separately in a corporate income statement. Accounting standards require that both of the following conditions must be met before a gain or loss qualifies as an **extraordinary item:**

1. *Unusual nature:* The underlying event or transaction should possess a high degree of abnormality and be of a type clearly unrelated to, or only incidentally related to, the ordinary and typical activities of the entity, taking into account the environment in which the entity operates.
2. *Infrequency of occurrence:* The underlying event or transaction should be of a type that would not reasonably be expected to recur in the foreseeable future, taking into account the environment in which the entity operates.[2]

Happy Hollow's income statement includes an extraordinary loss of $60,000 resulting from a tornado (line 18). The gross loss attributable to this tornado was $100,000; however, the company realized tax savings of $40,000 by deducting this loss on its tax return. As recommended by accounting standards, Happy Hollow reported this extraordinary item following the discontinued operations section of its income statement.

According to the 1994 edition of *Accounting Trends & Techniques*, approximately 15 percent of publicly owned companies report extraordinary items in their annual income statements. By far, the most common type of extraordinary item is a gain or loss on the early retirement of debt. Time-out. Does an early retirement of debt, such as paying off callable bonds before their maturity date, qualify as both unusual in nature and infrequent in occurrence? In most cases . . . no. Nevertheless, when it comes to the early retirement of debt, the Financial Accounting Standards Board

discontinued operations

Real World
In the AICPA's 1994 edition of *Accounting Trends and Techniques*, 45 companies out of the 600 surveyed reported discontinued operations.

extraordinary item

Discussion Question
If Happy Hollow is located in Oklahoma or Kansas (tornado alley), should the loss due to the tornado be classified as extraordinary?

---

2. *Accounting Principles Board Opinion No. 30*, "Reporting the Results of Operations" (New York: AICPA, 1973), para. 20.

(FASB) has made a specific exception to the two-requirement rule for extraordinary items. During the early 1970s, many companies were retiring outstanding debt and recording huge gains—gains included in income from continuing operations. The FASB believed this practice was misleading. So, the rule-making body declared that gains and losses from the early retirement of debt would be treated as extraordinary items and thus excluded from income from continuing operations.[3]

Teaching Note
Emphasize that for a gain or loss to be classified as extraordinary, the gain or loss must also be *material* to the financial statements.

American Stores Company, a food and drug retailer, recently reported an extraordinary loss due to the retirement of debt. This loss occurred in the company's 1993 fiscal year, which ended January 29, 1994. Following is the footnote disclosure the company provided regarding this item.

> Extraordinary Item: Earnings for 1993 were impacted by charges incurred in the early retirement of debt which are accounted for as an extraordinary item. In connection with the debt restructuring, the Company extinguished $146 million of debt and expensed the related costs of prepaying such debt and related derivatives. The restructuring resulted in an extraordinary pre-tax loss of $25 million ($15 million, net of tax) or $.11 per share.

Businesses often incur gains or losses that meet one of the two criteria for extraordinary items but not both. For example, a company that grows agricultural products in a flood-prone area may suffer material losses every five to ten years because of a flood. Since the floods occur periodically, the resulting losses do not meet the infrequency of occurrence rule for extraordinary items. On the other hand, these losses may qualify as being unusual in nature. Typically, gains or losses that meet only one of the two criteria for extraordinary items are shown as separate components of an entity's income from continuing operations. For example, the disposal of PP&E assets may qualify as an unusual or infrequently occurring transaction. Apparently, this is the case for Happy Hollow Corporation since Exhibit 13.1, line 10, reports a $42,000 gain on the sale of equipment. Notice that, unlike an extraordinary item, an unusual or infrequently occurring gain or loss is *not* presented net of taxes.

Real World
The AICPA's 1994 edition of *Accounting Trends & Techniques* reported that of 600 companies surveyed, 176 reported an accounting change for postretirement benefits during 1993.

CUMULATIVE EFFECT OF A CHANGE IN ACCOUNTING PRINCIPLE
Cascade Corporation designs and manufactures materials handling equipment. In 1994, this company reported a nearly $2 million expense item, net of tax, due to a change in an accounting principle. Cascade's change in accounting principle involved postretirement benefits other than pensions. Like most companies, Cascade accounted for these expenses on a cash basis before the adoption of *Statement on Financial Accounting Standards No. 106*. As noted in Chapter 11, this standard mandates that companies account for postretirement benefits other than pensions on an accrual basis.

A company that changes from one accounting principle to another is generally required to report a "catch-up" effect in the income statement of the year in which the accounting change is made. That is, such a company must determine the impact that using the "new" accounting principle, versus the "old" accounting principle, would have had on its earnings in previous years. This difference, or catch-up effect, is then reported in its income statement in the year in which the change is made. For example, assume that Cascade had used the accrual basis of accounting for nonpension postretirement benefits since its inception. Under that assumption, the company's cumulative, after-tax earnings before 1994 would have been nearly $2 million

---

3. Portions of various FASB documents, copyright by Financial Accounting Standards Board, 401 Merritt, PO Box 5116, Norwalk, Connecticut 06856-5116, U.S.A., are reprinted with permission. Copies of the complete documents are available from the FASB.

less. So, in 1994, when the company switched to the accrual basis of accounting for these employee benefits, a catch-up expense item for that amount was necessary.

As shown in Exhibit 13.1 (line 19), Happy Hollow Corporation reported a $10,800 net-of-tax "cumulative effect of a change in accounting principle" in its 1995 income statement. For our purposes, a **cumulative effect of a change in accounting principle** is defined as the change in an entity's collective net income for prior years assuming a newly adopted accounting principle had been used during those years. Again, thinking of this item as a catch-up effect may be more appealing to you. You might question why these items are reported in a company's current year income statement when they actually relate to preceding years. One could make a reasonable case for simply bypassing the income statement and recording these adjustments directly to retained earnings. However, recall that the comprehensive, or all-inclusive, approach to income measurement dictates that most transactions and events affecting owners' equity be reported in an entity's income statement.

As shown in Exhibit 13.1, a cumulative effect of a change in accounting principle is inserted in an income statement following any extraordinary items and immediately before net income. Recognize that the impact of a new accounting principle on an entity's *current* year revenues or expenses is included in income from continuing operations. The $10,800 cumulative effect of a change in an accounting principle shown in Exhibit 13.1 relates to Happy Hollow's pre-1995 fiscal years. The impact of the new accounting principle on Happy Hollow's 1995 operations is included in the firm's income from continuing operations for that year.

The annual surveys that are the basis for each edition of *Accounting Trends & Techniques* demonstrate that changes in accounting principles are infrequent occurrences. In recent years, most of these changes have involved companies implementing new accounting standards adopted by the FASB, an example being the accounting change made by Cascade Corporation. Examples of other accounting changes include switching from one inventory accounting method to another, changing depreciation methods, and capitalizing costs formerly expensed.

One final point. When a company makes a change in accounting principle, it must justify the change in the footnotes to its financial statements. The justification should explain why the new accounting principle is preferable to the principle that was formerly used.

EARNINGS PER SHARE   Notice that the last section of Happy Hollow's income statement presents earnings per share data. No doubt, earnings per share is the most closely monitored and eagerly awaited financial disclosure each year for most corporations. If a company's earnings per share is lower than expected, its stock price may plummet shortly following the release of that data to the investing public. Likewise, a positive earnings "surprise" can cause a company's stock price to increase sharply.

COMPUTATION OF EARNINGS PER SHARE   Corporations report an overall earnings per share figure and per share amounts for the "special" income statement items discussed previously. (Corporations are not required to report separate per share amounts for gains and losses from discontinued operations or extraordinary items. However, it is common practice to do so.) For example, notice in Exhibit 13.1 that Happy Hollow reported an overall earnings per share of $3.76, as shown on line 27, and an extraordinary loss per share of $.60 (line 25). Segmenting earnings per share into its various components allows decision makers to interpret earnings data more quickly and accurately.

Earnings per share is generally computed by dividing a company's net income by the weighted-average number of shares of common stock outstanding during the

Teaching Note
Shares of common stock that
were outstanding for only part
of a year represent capital that
was available to earn a return for
a company for only part of that
year. Thus, an accurate EPS
computation requires shares of a
company's common stock to be
weighted for the period of time
they were actually outstanding
during a given year.

year. Happy Hollow had 100,000 shares of common stock outstanding throughout all of 1995. Dividing that number of shares into Happy Hollow's net income of $376,200 for 1995 yields the earnings per share of $3.76 shown on line 27 of Exhibit 13.1. Suppose now that Happy Hollow had 80,000 shares of common stock outstanding for the first six months of 1995. Then, on July 1, the company issued an additional 20,000 shares, resulting in 100,000 shares being outstanding over the final six months of the year. The weighted-average number of shares outstanding would have been 90,000 for 1995: (80,000 × 6/12) + (100,000 × 6/12). In this case, Happy Hollow's overall earnings per share would have been $4.18 ($376,200/90,000) instead of $3.76.

The term "earnings per share" is used only in reference to common stock. There is no such "animal" as earnings per share of preferred stock. However, if a company has preferred stock outstanding, its earnings per share computation is affected. Dividends on preferred stock are subtracted from net income when computing earnings per share. Suppose that in 1995 Happy Hollow had 10,000 shares of preferred stock outstanding on which a $3 per share dividend was paid. The company's earnings per share would have been computed as follows, assuming 100,000 shares of common stock were outstanding throughout the year.

$$\text{Earnings Per Share} = \frac{\text{Net Income} - \text{Preferred Stock Dividends}}{\text{Weighted-Average Number of Shares of Common Stock Outstanding}}$$

$$\text{Earnings Per Share} = \frac{\$376,200 - \$30,000}{100,000}$$

$$\text{Earnings Per Share} = \$3.46$$

Real World
The 1994 edition of *Accounting Trends & Techniques* reported that 48 companies out of 600 had convertible preferred stock that was dilutive.

EARNINGS PER SHARE AND COMPLEX CAPITAL STRUCTURES   Corporations that have complex capital structures are generally required to report two overall earnings per share figures: primary and fully diluted earnings per share.[4] A company with a complex capital structure has convertible bonds, convertible preferred stock, or other securities that have the potential to dilute (decrease) its earnings per share. For example, assume that a corporation has convertible preferred stock outstanding. If the preferred stockholders exchange their preferred stock for common stock, the company's future earnings per share figures will typically be lower than they would have been otherwise. (The "dilutive" effect of preferred stock being converted to common stock results from the larger number of common shares being included in the denominator of the earnings per share computation.)

For companies with complex capital structures, primary earnings per share is similar to the earnings per share reported by companies with simple capital structures, such as Happy Hollow Corporation. Fully diluted earnings per share for a company with a complex capital structure is essentially earnings per share under a worst-case scenario. This earnings per share figure takes into account potentially dilutive effects that are often unlikely to occur.

---

4. At the time this book was being written, the FASB was considering certain changes in earnings per share computations and disclosures. Most of these changes concerned companies with complex capital structures. Among these proposed changes were replacing the terms "primary earnings per share" and "fully diluted earnings per share" with "basic earnings per share" and "diluted earnings per share," respectively.

Fully "Inflated" Earnings Per Share

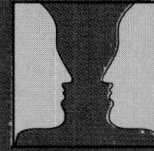

SPOTLIGHT
ON ETHICS

The SEC has proven repeatedly that it does not appreciate innovative interpretations of account-ing and financial reporting rules. One Oklahoma firm learned this lesson the hard way.

Prepaid Legal Services, Inc., a small publicly owned company headquartered in Ada, Oklahoma, reported the following earnings per share figures in 1983 and 1984.

	FISCAL YEAR ENDING DECEMBER 31,	
	1984	**1983**
Primary Earnings per Share	$.00	($.02)
Fully Diluted Earnings per Share	$.12	$.05

A company's primary earnings per share is nearly always greater than its fully diluted earnings per share. In those rare cases when fully diluted earnings per share exceed pri-mary earnings per share, companies are permitted to report *only* the latter. As shown by the previous table, Prepaid ignored this rule in both 1983 and 1984. Prepaid attempted to justify this decision in its annual report: "Management believes the [fully diluted earn-ings per share] calculation presents a more historic, consistent and meaningful view of earnings per share." The SEC did not agree with the reasoning of Prepaid's manage-ment. After publicly scolding the company, the SEC required Prepaid to amend the financial statements that contained the inappropriate earnings per share disclosures.

SOURCE: M. C. Knapp, "Full and Fair Disclosure," *Financial Accounting: Issues and Cases* (Minneapolis/St. Paul: West Publishing Co., 1994), 95–110.

Illustrating the computation of fully diluted earnings per share is beyond the scope of this text. An example of a company that recently reported primary and fully dilut-ed earnings per share is Hughes Supply, Inc., a distributor of construction supplies. Included in Hughes Supply's complex capital structure are convertible bonds. For its fiscal year ending in 1994, Hughes reported primary earnings per share of $1.35 and fully diluted earnings per share of $1.25.

Corporate Income Taxes

Before we dissect Happy Hollow's income statement shown in Exhibit 13.1, we briefly touched on the subject of corporate income taxes. Given the magnitude of income tax expense for most corporations and the resulting implications for decision makers, it seems reasonable that we examine corporate income taxes in more depth. To simplify matters, we consider only the federal income taxes that corporations pay. Recognize that most corporations pay other income taxes as well.

CORPORATE INCOME TAX RATES   A graduated, or progressive, income tax rate structure has historically been imposed on corporations—and individuals, for that matter. As corporations earn more taxable income, the percentage of the income that must be paid to the federal government gradually increases. Notice the term "taxable income." Corporations pay taxes based upon their taxable income, not their pretax

The Internal Revenue Service (IRS) oversees the collection of federal income taxes from individuals and corporations. Income taxes are typically a significant expense item for most corporations. For example, in recent years, the income tax expense of Sears, Roebuck & Co. has approached one-half billion dollars.

accounting income, which we have commonly referred to as income before income taxes. Shown in Exhibit 13.2 are the tax rates to which corporations were subject when this book was being written. Congress has a habit of revising income tax rates, so do not be surprised if the rates shown in Exhibit 13.2 are no longer effective.

Assume that a corporation has $150,000 of taxable income. Given the tax rates shown in Exhibit 13.2, this corporation would owe federal income taxes of $41,750 as demonstrated by the following computations.

$$\text{Federal Income Tax Payable} = \$22,250 + .39\,(\$150,000 - \$100,000)$$
$$\text{Federal Income Tax Payable} = \$22,250 + \$19,500$$
$$\text{Federal Income Tax Payable} = \$41,750$$

■ LEARNING OBJECTIVE 4
Describe temporary differences and their impact on pretax accounting income versus taxable income

temporary differences

Teaching Note
By postponing the payment of taxes as long as possible, companies increase the amount of cash that they have available for other uses.

TEMPORARY DIFFERENCES   A corporation's accountants often use different accounting methods for taxation purposes and financial accounting purposes. When accounting methods are selected for taxation purposes, the objective is to minimize or postpone the income taxes that a corporation must pay. When choosing accounting methods for financial accounting purposes, the objective should be to capture the economic reality of an entity's financial condition and operations.

The term **temporary differences** is often used when referring to certain differences between an entity's taxable income and its pretax accounting income. Temporary differences arise from recognizing revenues or expenses in one accounting period for taxation purposes and in another accounting period for financial accounting purposes. For example, in 1998, assume that a company has bad debt, or uncollectible accounts, expense of $25,000 for taxation purposes and $14,000 for financial accounting purposes. (Recall that the direct write-off method is used to account for bad debt expense for taxation purposes, while the allowance method is used for financial accounting purposes.) The $11,000 difference between these amounts is a temporary difference. "Temporary" is an appropriate adjective for such

■ **EXHIBIT 13.2**

Federal Income Tax Rates for Corporations

SOURCE: *1995 U.S. Master Tax Guide* (Chicago: Commerce Clearing House, 1994).

If Taxable income is:			
Over—	But not over—	Tax is—	Of the amount over—
$ 0	$ 50,000	15%	$ 0
50,000	75,000	7,500 + 25%	50,000
75,000	100,000	13,750 + 34%	75,000
100,000	335,000	22,250 + 39%	100,000
335,000	10,000,000	113,900 + 34%	335,000
10,000,000	15,000,000	3,400,000 + 35%	10,000,000
15,000,000	18,333,000	5,150,000 + 38%	15,000,000
18,333,000	—	35%	0

Note: The 39% and 38% rates are imposed to phase out the benefits of the lower brackets for higher-income corporations.

items because eventually these differences reverse. In the example just given, for instance, the firm's total bad debt expense over its entire existence will be the same for taxation and financial accounting purposes. However, in any given year, there is likely to be a difference between the bad debt expense reported on its federal income tax return and the bad debt expense reflected by its general ledger.

Temporary differences generally work to the benefit of corporations. Corporations tend to use accounting methods for taxation purposes that postpone the recognition of revenues or accelerate the recognition of expenses, thus allowing them to defer taxes owed to Uncle Sam. Recall the famous adage used for years in a series of television commercials, "You can pay me now, or you can pay me later." In the case of taxes, the latter alternative is clearly preferred.

Teaching Note
Stress that temporary differences only change the timing of the payment of taxes, not the amount.

ACCOUNTING FOR CORPORATE INCOME TAXES   Temporary differences, changes in tax rates, and the huge volume of tax laws and regulations cause accounting for income taxes to be very complex. Because of the complex nature of this subject, only a brief overview is provided here. Again, recognize that the taxes a corporation pays the federal government are based upon its taxable income; a corporation's income tax expense is based upon its pretax accounting income. Consider the following entry to record a corporation's income tax expense at year-end.

■ **LEARNING OBJECTIVE 5**
Account for corporate income taxes

Dec. 31	Income Tax Expense	143,000	
	Income Taxes Payable		106,000
	Deferred Income Taxes		37,000
	To record federal income tax expense		

Notice in this example that the corporation's income tax expense exceeds the amount of taxes currently payable to the federal government by $37,000. This difference is

Deferred Income Taxes

recorded in an account entitled **Deferred Income Taxes.** Essentially, this company has postponed $37,000 of taxes to be paid to the federal government.

Deferred Income Taxes can be either a current or long-term liability but is more often a long-term liability. Thanks to their knowledgeable tax accountants, many large corporations report huge deferred tax liabilities in their balance sheets. For example, at the end of fiscal 1994, Procter & Gamble reported a $347 million long-term liability for deferred taxes. Occasionally, Deferred Income Taxes has a debit balance, in which case it is classified as either a current or long-term asset for balance sheet purposes.

STATEMENT OF STOCKHOLDERS' EQUITY

■ LEARNING
OBJECTIVE 6
Describe the structure and
purpose of a statement of
stockholders' equity

Teaching Note
Remind students that a
statement of stockholders'
equity, like an income statement,
covers a period of time.

The statement of stockholders' equity is typically presented in a corporation's annual report immediately following the balance sheet. Many decision makers perceive this financial statement to be a supporting schedule to the balance sheet, a view similar to that expressed by the SEC. The SEC does not require companies that it regulates to prepare a statement of stockholders' equity. What the SEC does require is a reconciliation of the beginning-of-the-year and end-of-the-year balance of each stockholders' equity account. This reconciliation can be included in the financial statement footnotes but is more easily presented in a separate statement of stockholders' equity. The 1994 edition of *Accounting Trends & Techniques* reported that less than 10 percent of the six hundred companies surveyed included this reconciliation in the footnotes to their financial statements. Some corporations include a statement of retained earnings in their annual report instead of a statement of stockholders' equity. A statement of retained earnings is generally presented when the only changes in stockholders' equity during a given year were in the Retained Earnings account.

Statement of Stockholders' Equity Illustrated

Shown in Exhibit 13.3 is a recent statement of stockholders' equity for ShopKo Stores, Inc. As advertised, this statement reconciles the beginning-of-the-year balances of ShopKo's stockholders' equity accounts to the end-of-the-year balances. Companies with capital structures that include preferred stock, treasury stock, and other stockholders' equity items have more elaborate statements of stockholders' equity. However, the basic structure of those statements is the same as the format shown in Exhibit 13.3.

Notice that three items affected ShopKo's stockholders' equity during the fiscal year ended February 26, 1994. Net income of slightly more than $32 million and cash dividends of approximately $14 million were closed to the company's Retained Earnings account. The third item involved the issuance of 16,000 shares of common stock. According to Exhibit 13.3, the $185,000 proceeds from the issuance of this stock were credited in total to Additional Paid-in Capital, Common Stock. However, appearances can be deceiving. The par value of ShopKo's common stock is $.01 per share, meaning that the collective par value of the 16,000 shares issued was only $160. Since ShopKo's statement of stockholders' equity is presented in "thousands," the additional $160 of par value was not large enough to affect the reported balance of the Common Stock account. In fact, an entry similar to the following one was made when ShopKo issued the 16,000 shares of common stock.

■ **EXHIBIT 13.3**

Statement of Stockholders' Equity for ShopKo Stores, Inc., for the Year
Ended February 26, 1994 (in Thousands)

| | COMMON STOCK | | ADDITIONAL PAID-IN CAPITAL | RETAINED EARNINGS |
	Shares	Amount		
Balances at February 27, 1993	32,000	$320	$242,793	$112,367
Net Income				32,122
Issuance of Common Stock	16		185	
Cash Dividends Declared on				
Common Stock—$.44 per share				(14,081)
Balances at February 26, 1994	32,016	$320	$242,978	$130,408

Cash	185,000	
Common Stock		160
Additional Paid-in Capital, Common Stock		184,840

To record issuance of 16,000 shares of
common stock

Prior Period Adjustments

As mentioned earlier, prior period adjustments affect stockholders' equity but are
excluded from the corporate income statement. Instead, these items are reported in
the statement of stockholders' equity. A **prior period adjustment** is a correction of
a material error occurring in a previous accounting period that involves a revenue or
expense item. This correction is made to the Retained Earnings account in the
accounting period when the error is discovered. Errors that may result in prior period adjustments include fraud, mathematical mistakes, misapplication of accounting
principles, and misinterpretation of facts.

Suppose that in May 1997 a company discovers that depreciation expense on production equipment was accidentally understated by $40,000 during 1996 for both
financial accounting and taxation purposes. This company's effective tax rate for
financial accounting and taxation purposes is 40 percent. Following are the two
entries required in May 1997 to correct this error made in 1996.

May 15	Retained Earnings	40,000	
	Accumulated Depreciation, Equipment		40,000

To record prior period adjustment
related to understated depreciation
expense for 1996

May 15	Tax Refund Receivable	16,000	
	Retained Earnings		16,000

To record tax effect related to prior
period adjustment

■ LEARNING
OBJECTIVE 7
Account for prior period
adjustments and appropriations
of retained earnings

prior period adjustment

■ **EXHIBIT 13.4**

Footnote Disclosure of Prior Period Adjustment Included in 1992 Annual Report of Buffalo Don's Artesian Wells, Ltd.

> During Fiscal 1992, the Company became aware of the existence of certain financial irregularities. Upon investigation, it was discovered that in prior years certain financial accounts had been misstated, and company funds had been misappropriated.
>
> As a result, the Company restated its financial statements to reflect corrections as of March 30, 1991. These corrections were due to (1) accounts payable and accrued liabilities at March 30, 1991, that were understated by $561,049, (2) the Company's line of credit that was understated by $100,000, (3) cash that was overstated by $77,084 and (4) certain asset accounts that were overstated by $3,400. Such corrections, less insurance recoveries of $98,842, reduced the Company's prior years' results of operations before income taxes and net income by $642,691 and $536,691, respectively.

The first of these entries corrects the understatement of depreciation expense for 1996. However, notice that Retained Earnings, not Depreciation Expense, is debited in this entry. Again, a prior period adjustment is made directly to the Retained Earnings account not the relevant revenue or expense account. The second entry is necessary to recognize the tax effect of the prior period adjustment. Since this company overstated its taxable and pretax accounting income by $40,000 in 1996, it paid $16,000 more income tax than it should have and overstated its income tax expense by the same amount. This tax effect related to the prior period adjustment is recorded with a debit to a receivable account and a credit to Retained Earnings (instead of a credit to Income Tax Expense.) In this company's 1997 statement of stockholders' equity, the prior period adjustment would be reported as $24,000, $40,000 less the related tax effect of $16,000.

By design, prior period adjustments are intended to be rare. And they are. The 1993 edition of *Accounting Trends & Techniques* reported only one example of a prior period adjustment from the six hundred companies surveyed. The following year, no prior period adjustments were reported by *Accounting Trends & Techniques*. Exhibit 13.4 presents a footnote disclosure of a prior period adjustment included in the 1992 annual report of Buffalo Don's Artesian Wells, Ltd. This prior period adjustment resulted from "certain financial irregularities" (translation: fraud).

Appropriations of Retained Earnings

Occasionally, a statement of stockholders' equity includes one or more appropriations of retained earnings. An **appropriation of retained earnings** is a part of retained earnings that has been "earmarked," or restricted, for a special purpose. To illustrate an appropriation of retained earnings, assume that on December 31, 1997, the Red Horse Freight Company borrows $5 million from a bank on a five-year promissory note. One stipulation of the loan agreement is that $3 million of Red Horse's $4.5 million retained earnings balance on December 31, 1997, will be unavailable for the declaration of dividends over the note's term. This restrictive debt covenant serves to protect the economic interests of the lender by limiting Red Horse's ability to pay dividends, thus increasing the amount of cash available to make principal and interest payments on the note. Although not required to do so by GAAP, Red Horse may recognize this restriction on retained earnings in its accounting records and financial statements. If Red Horse chooses to account for this restrictive debt covenant by appropriating retained earnings, the following entry would be made on December 31, 1997.

Real World

The rare nature of prior period adjustments does not mean that companies never make accounting errors. Accounting errors, both those that are material and those that are immaterial, are typically detected and corrected by an entity's internal controls before these errors can affect reported financial statement data.

■ **LEARNING OBJECTIVE 7**

Account for prior period adjustments and appropriations of retained earnings

appropriation of retained earnings

Real World

The 1994 edition of *Accounting Trends & Techniques* disclosed that approximately 62% of the companies surveyed reported dividend restrictions related to loan agreements.

Dec. 31	Retained Earnings	3,000,000	
	Retained Earnings, Appropriated		
	due to Restrictive Debt Covenant		3,000,000

        To record appropriation of retained
earnings due to restrictive debt
covenant in loan agreement with
Altamira National Bank

Red Horse's statement of stockholders' equity for the year ended December 31, 1997, may include a column for both unrestricted retained earnings and appropriated, or restricted, retained earnings. Additionally, in its December 31, 1997, balance sheet, Red Horse would report its total retained earnings of $4.5 million, as follows:

Retained Earnings:		
Appropriated under Terms of		
Long-Term Debt Agreement	$3,000,000	
Unrestricted	1,500,000	
Total Retained Earnings		$4,500,000

This balance sheet treatment effectively communicates to decision makers that the ability of the company to pay dividends is limited. When Red Horse pays off the note payable, the appropriated retained earnings will be returned to unrestricted retained earnings by reversing the original appropriation entry.

ANALYZING CORPORATE COMMON STOCKS AS POTENTIAL INVESTMENTS: THE PRICE-EARNINGS AND MARKET PRICE TO BOOK VALUE RATIOS

■ **LEARNING OBJECTIVE 8**
Compute and interpret the price-earnings and market price to book value ratios

As noted in Chapter 12, investors are a large and important class of financial decision makers. A free market economy relies on investors to allocate their resources (investment funds) to productive business ventures. Society benefits if the savings of individuals are invested in companies that provide a stable source of income for employees, sizable tax revenues for governmental agencies, and a reasonable rate of return to stockholders.

To make optimal investment decisions, investors need relevant and reliable accounting information. Such information helps investors identify companies with good earnings potential, strong liquidity, and solid cash flow prospects. However, investors cannot rely exclusively on accounting information when analyzing common stocks for investment purposes. A company that has impressive financial statements may be a poor investment. Why? Because the market price of its stock is too high. Before closing the books on corporations, let us consider two financial ratios that investors can use to analyze the investment potential of common stocks. These ratios are the price-earnings and market price to book value ratios.

Price-Earnings Ratio

The **price-earnings (P/E) ratio** is computed by dividing the current market price of a company's common stock by its earnings per share for the most recent twelve-month period, as indicated by the following equation.

price-earnings (P/E) ratio

$$\text{Price-Earnings Ratio} = \frac{\text{Current Market Price of Common Stock}}{\text{Earnings per Share for Most Recent 12-Month Period}}$$

The P/E ratio is commonly used to assess the reasonableness of the market prices of common stocks. If a corporation's common stock has a much higher P/E ratio than its historical norm, sophisticated investors may suggest that the stock is overpriced. If a common stock is selling for an abnormally low P/E ratio, the stock may be viewed as a bargain by many investors.

Like most financial statistics, limitations of the P/E ratio can make it unreliable when used independently of other available information. For example, changes in a company's industry, the retirement of key executives, and many other factors may cause a company's normal P/E ratio to change over time. Likewise, a company's P/E ratio can be significantly distorted in any one year by extraordinary losses and other "special" income statement items discussed earlier in this chapter.

P/E ratios are particularly insightful when analyzed on a comparative basis. Shown in Exhibit 13.5 are the P/E ratios of ten well-known corporations in August 1994. Notice the large range of P/E ratios across these firms. The most striking difference is the contrast between the P/E ratio of Chrysler (6) and the P/E ratio of DuPont (41). Think of it this way. In August 1994, investors were willing to pay $6 for every

Discussion Question

Ask students to look up Michaels Stores' price-earnings ratio in a recent edition of *The Wall Street Journal*. Does the company's P/E ratio appear reasonable compared with the P/E ratios reported in Exhibit 11.5?

■ **EXHIBIT 13.5**

Price-Earnings Ratios, Selected Companies

SOURCE: *The Wall Street Journal*, August 3, 1994. Reprinted by permission of *The Wall Street Journal*, © 1994 Dow Jones & Company, Inc. All Rights Reserved Worldwide.

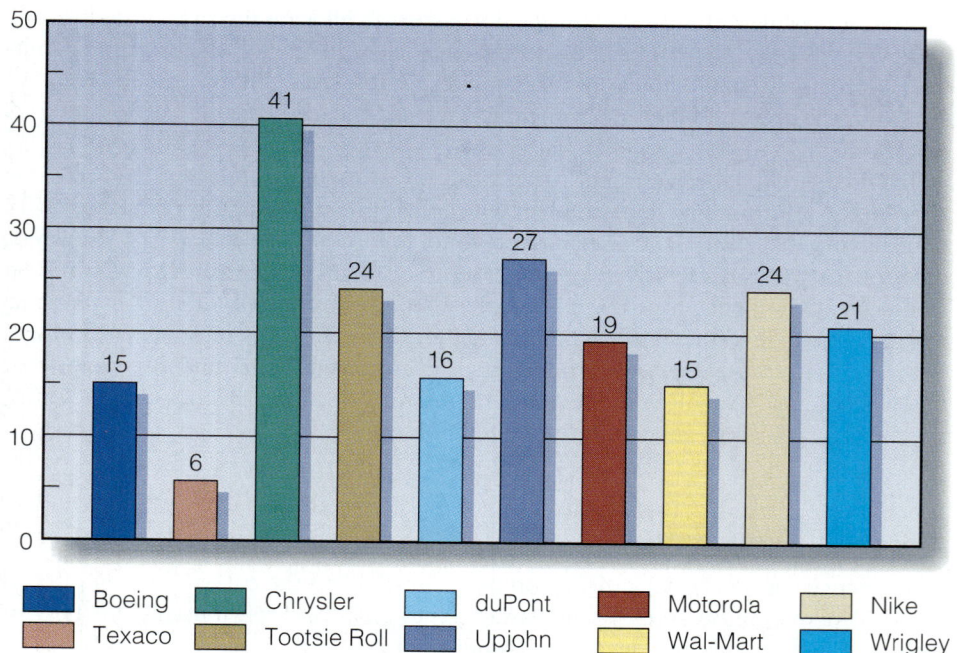

$1 of Chrysler's earnings but were willing to pay a whopping $41 for each $1 of DuPont's earnings. By comparison, the average P/E ratio for large corporations in August 1994 was 19.[5] That is, investors were willing to pay $19, on average, for every $1 of corporate earnings when Exhibit 13.5 was prepared.

Chrysler's common stock was selling for approximately $48 per share in early August 1994 when the company's earnings per share for the past twelve months was approximately $8. Given the average P/E ratio of 19 for corporate common stocks at the time, Chrysler's stock should have been selling for approximately $152 ($8 earnings per share × 19). So, why were investors pricing Chrysler at such a low P/E ratio in August 1994? One plausible explanation is that investors did not believe Chrysler could sustain the record earnings it was posting at that time. In other words, investors were discounting Chrysler's record earnings and expecting the company's future earnings to return to a more normal (lower) level. For example, assume that investors expected Chrysler to earn $3 per share in the future. If the company's stock price remained at approximately $48 per share, the company's P/E ratio would increase to a more normal level of 16 ($48/$3 earnings per share) in the future.

Well, you have the final word in this matter. Did Chrysler fail to sustain its record earnings and did the company's P/E ratio rise to a more normal level? Pick up the most recent edition of *The Wall Street Journal* or a local paper and check out Chrysler's P/E ratio and stock price.[6] While you are at it, you might as well check out the P/E ratios of the other companies shown in Exhibit 13.5. How have those companies' P/E ratios changed, if at all?

A key measure of the market strength of a company's common stock is its P/E ratio. For a large corporation, such as Motorola, the P/E ratio indicates how much investors are willing to pay at any point in time for each $1 of the company's earnings over the past 12 months.

Teaching Note
Bring a copy of *The Wall Street Journal* to class and compute Chrysler's current P/E ratio with the students.

Market Price to Book Value Ratio

Many companies regularly report a book value per share for their common stock although not required to do so by accounting standards or the SEC. As pointed out in Chapter 12, book value per share is computed by dividing total common stockholders' equity by the number of common shares outstanding. Since stockholders' equity is the difference between a corporation's total assets and total liabilities, book value per share represents a corporation's net assets per share of common stock. As noted earlier, a P/E ratio reveals how much investors are willing to pay for each $1 of a company's earnings. The **market price to book value ratio** indicates how much investors are willing to pay for each $1 of a company's net assets. This ratio is computed as follows:

$$\text{Market Price to Book Value Ratio} = \frac{\text{Current Market Price of Common Stock}}{\text{Book Value per Share}}$$

market price to book value ratio

Discussion Question
Ask students to compute Michaels Stores' market price to book value ratio using data drawn from the company's annual report included in the Appendix. What does this ratio indicate about investors' perceptions of the company's future prospects?

---

5. Gottschalk, E.C., "Investment Clubs May Be Mired in 'Stagnant' Stocks," *The Wall Street Journal*, July 28, 1994, p. C1. Reprinted by permission of *The Wall Street Journal*, © 1994 Dow Jones & Company, Inc. All Rights Reserved Worldwide.

6. As a point of information, in the spring of 1995 a hostile takeover of Chrysler was initiated by its largest stockholder, Kirk Kerkorian. Kerkorian had criticized Chrysler's management for failing to take steps to increase the company's common stock price, which he believed was much lower than it should have been given the company's strong financial condition at the time. Within a few months, Kerkorian dropped his takeover bid after failing to raise sufficient funds to finance the buyout of Chrysler.

Market Price vs. Book Value

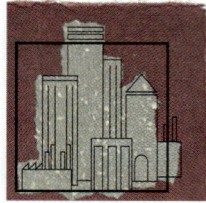

For decades, financial analysts and other financial decision makers have debated the meaningfulness of a company's book value per share. The focal point of this debate is whether there should be a close correlation between the market price of a company's common stock and its book value per share. In the following excerpt from a 1991 article appearing in the Washington Post, *this debate is analyzed. As a point of information, the terms "bulls" and "bears" are referred to in this article. These terms do not refer to Chicago sports teams. Instead, a "bull" is generally an investor or financial analyst who believes stock prices will be heading higher in the future. A "bear," on the other hand, has a more pessimistic view of future stock prices.*

With stocks at record heights, bulls and bears alike are straining mightily to defend their respective positions. If you want to start a fist-fight between the two camps, mention "book value." . . . One way to measure how high-priced the stock market has become is to look at the average stock's price relative to the average book value per share.

The price-to-book measure is typically expressed as a ratio. If a stock is priced at $10, and the company's book value is $10 a share, the stock sells for 1.0 times book. If the stock is at $20 and book is $10, the ratio is 2.0. In theory, the more you pay for stock relative to book value, the greater the risk because you're "buying" assets that aren't there.

As stock prices have soared in recent years, the price-to-book ratio of the Standard & Poor's index of 400 major industrial companies has risen dramatically from 1.3 in 1982 to 2.1 by 1987, to 2.97 in 1991. In fact, today's price-to-book ratio is higher than at virtually any point in modern history. The only other times that stocks have sold for nearly three times book value were brief periods in 1928 and 1987—just before the two greatest stock crashes of the century. No wonder the bears are adamant that prices are peaking.

If you read *The Wall Street Journal* regularly, you will often find references to bulls and bears. On Wall Street, a bull is someone who believes that stock prices are on the rise, while a bear is someone who believes that stock prices will be trending downward in the future.

How do the bulls defend paying 2.97 times book? They can offer only one argument: Book isn't what it used to be—it's better. So you're really not paying as much as it seems.

Money manager Charles Brandes at Brandes Investment Management in San Diego figures it this way: The price-to-book ratio was low in the 1970s partly because "a lot of what companies carried as 'book value' in the past wasn't real." Look at the number of plants closed, assets sold and restructuring charges incurred by major American companies in the 1980s, Brandes says. In that decade, companies took the assets that weren't producing and either wrote them off or streamlined them. Either way, the value of the assets on many companies' balance sheets was clipped to reflect what those buildings and machines were truly worth.

That caused book value to decline at many companies. But what was left on the balance sheet was the real thing—productive assets that would generate a far better rate of return.

SOURCE: From the Los Angeles Times, © 1991, Los Angeles Times. Reprinted by permission. T. Petruno, "The Bulls vs. the Bears on the Value of 'Book Value'," *Washington Post*, August 27, 1991, D11.

■ **EXHIBIT 13.6**

Market Price to Book Value Ratios, Selected Companies

SOURCE: 1994 annual reports and *The Wall Street Journal.*

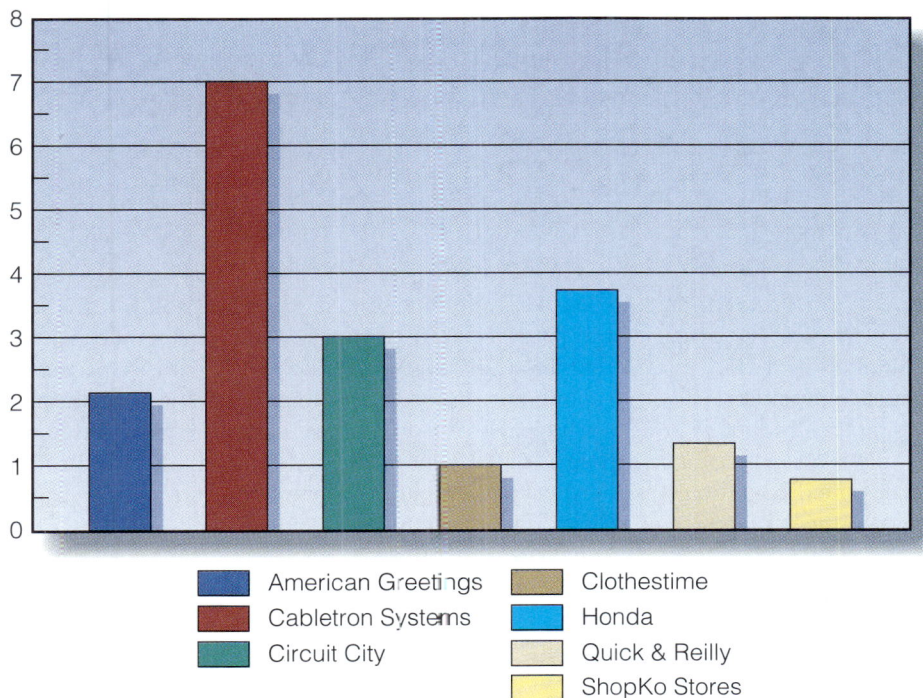

Legend:
- American Greetings
- Cabletron Systems
- Circuit City
- Clothestime
- Honda
- Quick & Reilly
- ShopKo Stores

A naive investor might assume that the market price to book value ratio for most common stocks is 1.0, or thereabouts. That is, if a company's common stock has a book value per share of $24, that stock's current market price will be approximately $24. In fact, the market price of a common stock is often considerably different from its book value per share. Why? Because the accounting-based book value, or net asset value per share, does not necessarily reflect the "true" economic value of a corporation's common stock. This point is made very clearly in the vignette accompanying this section.

Shown in Exhibit 13.6 are market price to book value ratios for the common stocks of seven companies. In 1994, investors were willing to pay $7 for every $1 of Cabletron Systems' net assets, while the "going price" for $1 of ShopKo Stores' net assets was only $.80. Some insight on the large disparity in these ratios can be gained by considering the nature of these two companies' operations and their future prospects. Cabletron is a high-tech company that designs and manufactures products used in local area computer networks. The perception in the early 1990s that Cabletron had tremendous profit potential caused investors to conclude that the true value of the company's common stock was several times its book value per share. On the other hand, ShopKo's future prospects were much dimmer in the early 1990s. ShopKo is a department store chain that competes directly with several large merchandisers, most notably Wal-Mart. In 1994, ShopKo's industry was becoming increasingly competitive, principally due to Wal-Mart driving down gross profit margins

Focus on Ethics
"Insiders" frequently have access to information that will have a significant effect on a company's future financial results. Information about large new contracts or new products in development are examples of this type of information. Discuss the ethics of an investor purchasing shares of stock based upon insider information.

with its aggressive pricing strategies. Another problem facing ShopKo in 1994 was a large buildup of inventory. Financial analysts suggested that much of the company's inventory would have to be sold at sharply discounted prices.

Recognize that neither the P/E ratio nor the market price to book value ratio indicates which stocks' market prices will definitely increase or decrease in the future. Nevertheless, these ratios provide strong clues regarding the stock market's perception of the investment potential of common stocks. If an individual investor can identify stocks for which this perception is wrong or will change in the near future, then that investor can make a bundle.

SUMMARY

The corporate income statement is an important source of information for financial decision makers. To properly interpret corporate earnings data, decision makers must be familiar with the key elements of a corporate income statement. Of particular interest to investors is a corporation's income from continuing operations that represents the earnings of an entity's principal profit-oriented activities. Investors often use this figure as the starting point for predicting a corporation's future profits. Discontinued operations, extraordinary items, and the cumulative effect of a change in accounting principle are "special" income statement items that influence a corporation's net income during any given year.

Corporations are required to disclose earnings per share data in their income statements. These data include an overall earnings per share and per share amounts for individual components of net income such as income from continuing operations. Companies with complex capital structures are generally required to report two overall earnings per share figures: primary and fully diluted earnings per share.

Federal income taxes are a large expense item for most corporations and pose complex accounting issues for corporate accountants. Corporations must report key income statement items net of their related taxes so that financial statement users can determine the impact of these items on net income. Different accounting rules are often used by corporations for taxation and financial accounting purposes. As a result, a corporation's income tax expense for a given year typically does not equal the amount of tax payable to the federal government for that year. The difference between these two amounts is recorded in the Deferred Income Taxes account. Deferred income taxes is usually a long-term liability, although occasionally it may be a current liability or even an asset.

The purpose of a statement of stockholders' equity is to reconcile the beginning-of-the-year and end-of-the-year balances of a corporation's stockholders' equity accounts. Besides net income and dividends, other items that may appear in a statement of stockholders' equity include prior period adjustments and appropriations of retained earnings. A prior period adjustment is a correction of a material error occurring in a previous accounting period that involves a revenue or expense item. This correction is made directly to the Retained Earnings account in the period when the error is discovered. An appropriation of retained earnings is a part of retained earnings that has been designated for a special purpose, such as to satisfy a legal or contractual obligation.

The price-earnings (P/E) and market price to book value ratios are two key financial statistics monitored by investors. These ratios allow investors to assess the reasonableness of the market prices of individual common stocks.

GLOSSARY

Appropriation of retained earnings (p. 582)   A part of a corporation's retained earnings that has been restricted for a special purpose; limits the ability of a corporation to pay cash dividends.

Cumulative effect of a change in accounting principle (p. 575)   The change in an entity's collective net income for prior years, assuming a newly adopted accounting principle had been used during those years.

Deferred Income Taxes (p. 580)   An account in which a corporation records the difference between its federal income tax expense and federal income tax payable each year; typically a long-term liability account.

Discontinued Operations (p. 573)   A section of a corporate income statement devoted to a business segment that is being discontinued.

Earnings per share (p. 575)   Generally, net income divided by the weighted-average number of shares of common stock outstanding during a given year.

Extraordinary items (p. 573)   A material gain or loss that is both unusual in nature and infrequent in occurrence.

Income from continuing operations (p. 571)   Represents the earnings produced by a corporation's principal profit-oriented activities.

Market price to book value ratio (p. 585)   Computed by dividing the current market price of a company's common stock by its book value per share.

Price-earnings (P/E) ratio (p. 583)   Computed by dividing the current market price of a company's common stock by its earnings per share for the most recent twelve-month period.

Prior period adjustment (p. 581)   A correction of a material error occurring in a previous accounting period that involves a revenue or expense item; the correction is made directly to the Retained Earnings account in the accounting period when the error is discovered.

Temporary differences (p. 578)   Differences between an entity's taxable income and pretax accounting income that arise from recognizing revenues or expenses in one accounting period for taxation purposes and in another accounting period for financial accounting purposes.

DECISION CASE

Ben & Jerry's Homemade, Inc., the company profiled in the opening vignette of this chapter, was sharply criticized in the early 1990s by several public interest groups. Much of this criticism stemmed from the high-fat content of Ben & Jerry's most popular products. In 1993, the Center for Science in the Public Interest placed Ben & Jerry's super premium ice creams on the top ten list of foods that you should never eat. Tobacco firms, fast-food restaurant chains, and companies producing alcoholic beverages are among other corporations that have been lambasted recently by public interest groups.

Suppose that you are the chief executive officer (CEO) of Carol Ann's Homemade Cookies, Inc. Revenues and earnings have skyrocketed over the past few years after your company introduced a new line of cookies, Donut-Dough Delites. The public simply cannot get enough of these high-fat, cholesterol-laden cookies. Although your competitors have tried, they have been unable to develop a product that mimics the taste of Donut-Dough Delites. Nevertheless, trouble is on the horizon. Several public interest groups have banded together and are calling for a nationwide boycott of your products. These groups insist that your company is profiting at the expense of your customers' health. Your accountants have been monitoring the impact of the boycott on monthly sales and profit figures. So far, the boycott's impact is minimal. But you are concerned that the boycott may eventually cut significantly into your sales.

Required: As the CEO of this company, identify the parties to whom you have a responsibility and briefly describe the nature of each of those responsibilities. Do any of these responsibilities conflict with each other? If so, explain how these conflicts should be resolved.

What accounting and/or financial reporting implications, if any, does the boycott have? Explain. Evaluate the feasibility and acceptability of the following responses to the boycott:

1. Stop producing the cookies, in which case your company's annual sales and profits will decline by approximately 35 percent.
2. Donate 10 percent of the profits from the sale of the cookies to a nonprofit group that researches heart disease.
3. Put a highly visible disclaimer on the cookies' packaging that discloses their high-fat and cholesterol content.
4. Threaten to sue the public interest groups if they continue the boycott.

QUESTIONS

1. Indicate how different types of financial decision makers use the information included in corporate income statements.
2. What general approach to measuring periodic income is suggested by accounting standards? Identify one key advantage and one key disadvantage of this approach to income measurement.
3. Briefly describe the single-step and multiple-step income statement formats.
4. Companies regulated by the SEC generally include how many years of income statement data in their annual financial reports?
5. What does "income from continuing operations" represent in a corporation's income statement? What is one important way this item is used by financial statement users?
6. Why are financial data related to discontinued lines of business reported separately in a corporate income statement?
7. What two criteria must be met for a gain or loss to be reported in the income statement as an extraordinary item?
8. If a gain or loss meets only one of the two criteria for extraordinary items, how may it be reported in a corporate income statement?
9. Define a "cumulative effect of a change in accounting principle."
10. Why is a cumulative effect of a change in accounting principle reported in the income statement instead of being charged directly to a corporation's retained earnings?
11. In general, how is earnings per share computed?
12. What is the difference between primary and fully diluted earnings per share? What types of companies are required to report both earnings per share figures?
13. What is meant by a graduated, or progressive, income tax rate structure?
14. Why do companies often use different accounting methods for taxation and financial accounting purposes?

15. Define what is meant by the term "temporary difference" in reference to corporate income taxes.

16. When does a corporation use a Deferred Income Taxes account? Is this account typically a liability or asset account? Current or long-term?

17. What is the purpose of a statement of stockholders' equity?

18. Define "prior period adjustment." Are prior period adjustments frequently found in financial statements? Why or why not?

19. What is an appropriation of retained earnings?

20. Identify the equation to use in computing the price-earnings (P/E) ratio. How is this ratio used by investors?

21. Why is the market price of a corporation's common stock often considerably different from the common stock's book value per share?

EXERCISES

22. **Terms** (LO 1, 2)

Following are definitions or descriptions of terms relating to corporate income statements or income measurement.

_____ The change in an entity's collective net income for prior years assuming a newly adopted accounting principle had been used during those years.

_____ Differences between an entity's taxable income and pretax accounting income that arise from recognizing revenues or expenses in one accounting period for taxation purposes and in another accounting period for financial accounting purposes.

_____ An account in which a corporation records the difference between its federal income tax expense and federal income tax payable each year; typically a long-term liability account.

_____ Generally, net income divided by the weighted-average number of shares of common stock outstanding during a given year.

_____ A part of a corporation's retained earnings that has been restricted for a special purpose; limits the ability of a corporation to pay cash dividends.

_____ A material gain or loss that is both unusual in nature and infrequent in occurrence.

_____ Represents the earnings produced by a corporation's principal profit-oriented activities.

_____ A correction of a material error occurring in a previous accounting period that involves a revenue or expense item; the correction is made directly to the Retained Earnings account in the accounting period when the error is discovered.

_____ A section of a corporate income statement devoted to a business segment that is being discontinued.

Required:
Match each definition or description listed with the appropriate term from the following list.
a. Discontinued Operations
b. Temporary Differences
c. Earnings Per Share
d. Income from Continuing Operations
e. Deferred Income Taxes

22. h,b,e,c,f,i,d,g,a

    f. Appropriation of Retained Earnings
    g. Prior Period Adjustment
    h. Cumulative Effect of a Change in Accounting Principle
    i. Extraordinary Item

23. Elements of a Corporate Income Statement (LO 2)

Listed next are items often reported in corporate income statements.

Operating Income
Cumulative Effect of a Change in Accounting Principle
Gross Profit
Discontinued Operations
Net Income
Extraordinary Item
Income from Continuing Operations

Required:

23. No check figures

1. List these items in their proper order in a corporate income statement.
2. Why is there a distinction in a corporate income statement between transactions and events involving "continuing operations" and transactions and events involving "discontinued operations"?
3. Why are extraordinary items included as separate components of a corporate income statement?

24. Comprehensive Approach to Income Measurement (LO 1, 2)

Jack, an accounting major, is preparing an income statement for an imaginary firm, Harrison Corporation. Jack is considering including the following items in this income statement.

Cost of Goods Sold
Income Taxes Payable
Accounts Receivable
Income Tax Expense
Net Sales
Accounts Payable
Dividends (paid to stockholders)
Gain on Sale of Equipment
Salaries Payable
Administrative Expenses

Required:

24. No check figures

1. Which of these items should be included in Harrison's income statement, assuming Jack is using the comprehensive approach to income measurement?
2. What is one major criticism of the comprehensive approach to income measurement?

25. Multiple-Step Income Statement (LO 2)

Following is information taken from the accounting records of Tarrasco Company for 1996.

Net Sales, $220,000
Operating Income from Discontinued Operations, $12,000
Cost of Goods Sold, $120,000
Gain on Sale of Assets (discontinued operations), $20,000
Operating Expenses, $60,000
Flood Loss, $25,000 (an extraordinary item)
Cumulative Effect of a Change in Depreciation Methods, $12,000 (credit)

Tarrasco had 10,000 shares of common stock issued and outstanding throughout the year. Tarrasco's effective tax rate is 40 percent of its pretax accounting income.

Required:
1. Prepare a multiple-step income statement for Tarrasco for 1996.
2. Is the single-step or multiple-step income statement format more informative for financial decision makers? Defend your answer.

25. 1. Net Income, $35,400
        Earnings per Share,
        $3.54

26. **Computation of Earnings Per Share** (LO 3)
Jericho Corporation had 100,000 shares of common stock outstanding for the first three months of the year. The company issued an additional 20,000 shares on April 1, and another 30,000 shares on September 1. Jericho reported net income of $371,250 for the year ended December 31.

Required:
1. Compute the weighted-average number of shares of common stock that Jericho had outstanding during the year.
2. Compute Jericho's earnings per share for the year.
3. Why is the weighted-average number of shares of common stock outstanding during a year used in an earnings per share computation instead of the number of shares outstanding at the end of the year?

26. 1. 125,000 shares
    2. $2.97

27. **Computation of Income Taxes Payable** (LO 5)
Refer to the federal income tax rates for corporations included in Exhibit 13.2.

Required:
1. Following is a list of taxable incomes for individual corporations. Compute the amount of federal income taxes owed in each case.
   a. $117,000
   b. $37,500
   c. $12,000,000
   d. $62,000
   e. $25,000,000
2. Define a graduated, or progressive, income tax rate structure.
3. What is the reasoning underlying a graduated income tax rate structure?

27. a. $28,880
    b. $5,625
    c. $4,100,000
    d. $10,500
    e. $8,750,000

28. **Deferred Income Taxes** (LO 4, 5)
Suppose that for the current year, Doublet Company has a $10,000 difference between pretax accounting income and taxable income as indicated in the following schedule.

	PRETAX ACCOUNTING INCOME	TAXABLE INCOME
Income before Depreciation Expense	$100,000	$100,000
Depreciation Expense	(20,000)	(30,000)
	$ 80,000	$ 70,000

Required:
1. Define the meaning of the term "temporary difference" as it applies to the pretax accounting and taxable incomes of corporations.
2. Prepare Doublet's year-end adjusting entry to record income tax expense for the current year. Assume that Doublet's effective income tax rate is 40 percent for both financial accounting and taxation purposes.
3. Suppose that Doublet pays the amount of tax due for the current year on January 15 of the following year. Record this payment.

28. 2. Dr. Income Tax Exp.
        $32,000
        Cr. Income Taxes
        Payable $28,000
        Cr. Deferred Income
        Taxes $4,000
    4. $4,000

4. How much less income tax did Doublet pay to the federal government in the entry recorded in Part 3 as a result of the temporary difference related to depreciation expense?

5. Will the amount computed in Part 4 eventually be paid by Doublet? If so, what advantage did Doublet realize as a result of this temporary difference?

29. **Temporary Differences** (LO 4)

Following are the taxable incomes and pretax accounting incomes for 1996 for two corporations that began operations in that year. Each corporation has an effective income tax rate of 40 percent for financial accounting and taxation purposes.

	TAXABLE INCOME	PRETAX ACCOUNTING INCOME
Hartman Corporation	$30,000	$35,000
Reckers Corporation	38,000	$34,000

29. No check figures

Required:

1. The difference between each company's taxable and pretax accounting incomes is due to a "temporary difference." Identify one possible source of each of these temporary differences.

2. Indicate whether the year-end balance of each company's deferred tax account will be reported as an asset or a liability in its December 31, 1996, balance sheet.

30. **Statement of Stockholders' Equity** (LO 6)

Following is an incomplete statement of stockholders' equity for Mufasa Corporation:

	COMMON STOCK		ADDITIONAL PAID-IN	RETAINED
	SHARES	AMOUNT	CAPITAL	EARNINGS
Balances, January 1	?	$500,000	$150,000	$250,000
Net Income				
Sale of Common Stock	10,000			
Cash Dividends Declared				
Balances, December 31		$	$	$

Notes:

a. Mufasa's common stock has a $10 par value.

b. Net income for the year was $40,000.

c. The common stock issued during the year was sold at $22 per share on July 1.

d. Two $1.50 cash dividends per share were declared and paid during the year. The first dividend was declared on March 1 and paid on April 11 to stockholders of record March 21. The second dividend was declared on August 6 and paid on September 4 to stockholders of record on August 21.

30.   12/31 Balances: Common Stock, $600,000 Add'l Paid-in Cap., $270,000 Retained Earnings, $125,000

Required:

Complete Mufasa's statement of stockholders' equity.

31. **Prior Period Adjustment** (LO 7)

Andersen Gardening Company had no changes in stockholders' equity in 1996 other than in retained earnings. The following schedule analyzes the changes in the company's Retained Earnings account during 1996.

Retained Earnings, January 1, 1996	$200,000
Net Income	40,000

| Dividends Declared | (10,000) |
| Retained Earnings, December 31, 1996 | $230,000 |

On March 2, 1997, Andersen Gardening discovered that depreciation expense on a piece of equipment was understated by $10,000 during 1996. Andersen's effective income tax rate is 40 percent for both financial accounting and taxation purposes.

Required:

1. How much was Andersen's net income overstated or understated in 1996?
2. Prepare the appropriate journal entries on March 2, 1997, to correct the error in depreciation expense made in 1996.
3. What would be the dollar amount of the prior period adjustment reported in Andersen's statement of stockholders' equity for 1997?

31. 1. $6,000 overstated

32. **Overlooking Prior Period Adjustments** (LO 7)
Jane Byrd, the owner of Jane's Greenhouse, hired an accountant, Mary, a few weeks ago to maintain the business's accounting records. In the past, Jane kept the books herself, although she is not an accountant. This past week, Mary discovered three errors that Jane had made in the accounting records during the previous year, 1996. These errors collectively resulted in the business's net income for 1996 being overstated by a material amount. The business's net income was reported as $83,200, when it was actually $46,300. The only external party that received a copy of the business's 1996 financial statements was the president of a local bank. Jane's Greenhouse has an outstanding loan of $50,000 from that bank.

   Since Mary has determined that the errors were not intentional and instead were the result of Jane's lack of accounting experience, she recommends to Jane that the errors be ignored. "Besides," said Mary, "these errors relate to last year. Who cares about last year anymore?"

Required:

Was Mary's advice to Jane appropriate? Does Jane have a responsibility to inform the local banker of the errors in the 1996 financial statements even if those financial statements are not corrected and reissued? Write a brief memo to Jane regarding these issues. Include in this memo your recommendation regarding how she should resolve this matter.

32. No check figures

33. **Appropriation of Retained Earnings** (LO 7)
The Pony Corporation must record an appropriation of retained earnings at the end of the current year because of a restrictive debt covenant in a new bond indenture. The amount of the appropriation is $100,000. Assume that the company will have total retained earnings of $500,000 at year end.

Required:

1. Prepare the year-end appropriation entry in Pony Corporation's accounting records.
2. Indicate how Pony's retained earnings will appear in the company's year-end balance sheet.
3. What "signal" does an appropriation of retained earnings send to users of a company's financial statements?

33. 1. Dr. Retained Earnings $100,000
Cr. Retained Earnings Appropriated $100,000

34. **Price-Earnings Ratio** (LO 8)
The following information was taken from the June 13, 1995, edition of *The Wall Street Journal.*

COMPANY	MARKET PRICE OF COMMON STOCK	P/E RATIO
Caterpillar	$60.87	12
IBM	90.25	14
Marriot International	33.62	24
PepsiCo	46.87	21
Service Merchandise	4.50	9

34. 1. Caterpillar, $5.07
IBM, $6.45
Marriot, $1.40
PepsiCo, $2.23
Service Merch., $0.50

Required:

1. For each company listed, determine the twelve-month earnings per share figure used in computing the firm's reported P/E ratio.
2. Why do large publicly owned companies often have very different P/E ratios?

35. Market Price to Book Value Ratio (LO 8)

The ratio of a stock's market price to its book value per share reveals how much investors are willing to pay for each $1 of a company's net assets per share. The following information is available for Companies A, B, and C.

	COMPANY A	COMPANY B	COMPANY C
Total Assets	$1,000,000	$750,000	$2,000,000
Total Liabilities	$250,000	$400,000	$1,500,000
Number of Shares of Common Stock Outstanding*	100,000	200,000	125,000
Year-End Stock Price	$8.00	$7.00	$24.00

35. 1. BVPS:
Co. A, $7.50
Co. B, $1.75
Co. C, $4.00
Market Price to Book Value Ratio:
Co. A, 1.07
Co. B, 4.00
Co. C, 6.00

* None of the companies have preferred stock outstanding.

Required:

1. For each of the companies listed, compute the book value per share and the market price to book value ratio.
2. How is it possible for a company's market price to book value ratio to differ significantly from 1.0?

PROBLEM SET A

36. Income Statement Preparation (LO 2, 3)

Following are key line items included in the income statement of Shaw Corporation for the year ended December 31, 1996. These items appear in no particular order.

Cost of Goods Sold	$360,000
General Expenses	18,000
Gain on Sale of Machinery	22,000
Income Tax Expense (related to Income from Continuing Operations before Income Tax)	?
Operating Income from Discontinued Line of Business, $10,000, less Income Tax of $4,000	6,000
Selling Expenses	20,000
Extraordinary Loss due to Fire, $20,000, less Income Tax Savings of $8,000	12,000
Net Sales	520,000
Administrative Expenses	19,000
Cumulative Effect of a Change in Accounting Principle, $5,000, less Income Tax of $2,000	3,000

Shaw's average income tax rate is 40 percent. Throughout 1996, Shaw had 50,000 shares of common stock outstanding.

Required:

Prepare a multiple-step income statement for Shaw Corporation including an earnings per share section.

37. Earnings Per Share Computations (LO 3)

The following income statement data are available at year-end for Ellis & Reddings Corporation:

Income from Continuing Operations before Taxes	$800,000
Income Tax Expense	320,000
Income from Continuing Operations	$480,000
Discontinued Operations:	
Operating Income, $40,000, less Income Tax	
of $16,000	$24,000
Loss on Disposal, $50,000, less Income Tax	
Savings of $20,000	(30,000)
	(6,000)
Income before Extraordinary Item	$474,000
Extraordinary Loss due to Plane Crash, $100,000,	
less Income Tax Savings of $40,000	(60,000)
Net Income	$414,000

At the beginning of the year, Ellis & Reddings had 100,000 shares of common stock outstanding. On October 1, Ellis & Reddings sold an additional 80,000 shares of common stock.

Required:

1. Compute the weighted-average number of shares of common stock that Ellis & Reddings had outstanding during the year.
2. Compute and clearly label the earnings per share figures you would expect to see in Ellis & Reddings's income statement.
3. Assume that Ellis & Reddings has a complex capital structure. Assume further that for purposes of computing fully diluted earnings per share, the weighted-average number of shares of common stock outstanding is 150,000. Compute the company's fully diluted earnings per share.
4. Explain how fully diluted earnings per share should be interpreted by financial decision makers.

38. Statement of Stockholders' Equity (LO 6, 7)

Following are the balances of the Hatlan Company's stockholders' equity accounts on January 1, 1996.

Common Stock	$ 32,000
Additional Paid-in Capital	310,500
Retained Earnings	2,664,200

On May 15, 1996, Hatlan sold an additional 11,000 shares of common stock for $24 per share. Hatlan's common stock has a $2 par value. On September 13, Hatlan declared a $2 per share cash dividend. The dividend was payable on October 25 to stockholders of record on October 3. Hatlan's net income for 1996 was $229,300.

Required:

1. Prepare a statement of stockholders' equity for Hatlan Company for the year ended December 31, 1996.
2. Suppose that on January 25, 1997, Hatlan issues bonds payable. One stipulation of the bond indenture requires Hatlan to make $1.5 million of its existing retained earnings unavailable for the declaration of dividends over the term of the bonds. Prepare the journal entry to record this appropriation of retained earnings.

---

36. Net Income, $72,000
     Earnings per Share,
     $1.44

37. 1. 120,000 shares
     2. Net income per share,
         $3.45
     3. $2.76

38. 1. 12/31/96 Balances:
         Common Stock, $54,000
         Add'l Paid-in Cap.,
         $552,500
         Retained Earnings,
         $2,839,500
     2. Dr. Retained Earnings
         $1,500,000
         Cr. Retained Earnings
         Appropriated $1,500,000
     3. Dr. Accum. Deprec.
         $20,000
         Cr. Retained Earnings
         $20,000
         Dr. Retained Earnings
         $8,000
         Cr. Income Tax Payable
         $8,000

3. Suppose that on May 1, 1997, Hatlan's accountant discovers that depreciation expense on a piece of machinery was accidentally overstated by $20,000 during 1996. Prepare the appropriate journal entries to record the prior period adjustment to correct this error, assuming that the company's effective tax rate for both financial accounting and taxation purposes is 40 percent.

39. Analyzing Stockholders' Equity (LO 8)

Thiokol Corporation's 1994 annual report contained the following description of the company's principal lines of business: "Thiokol Corporation is one of the nation's leaders in the development and production of high-technology solid rocket motors for aerospace, defense and commercial launch applications; and a major manufacturer of precision fastening systems for aerospace and industrial markets worldwide."

The early 1990s was a difficult period for Thiokol. Following the collapse of the Soviet Union, defense expenditures by the federal government declined, directly affecting the revenues of defense contractors such as Thiokol. In 1992, Thiokol had total revenues of approximately $1.32 billion; two years later, that figure had dropped to $1.06 billion. Following is selected financial information for Thiokol for the period 1992–1994.

	1992	1993	1994
Total Revenues*	$ 1.32	$ 1.21	$ 1.06
Net Income**	63.0	63.8	60.3
Earnings Per Share	3.12	3.13	(.18)
Book Value Per Share of Common Stock	19.44	21.94	20.52
Year-End Market Price of Common Stock	16.00	21.88	24.13
Cash Dividends Per Share	.36	.47	.68

* In billions.
** In millions.

Required:

1. Describe briefly the meaning of both the P/E ratio and the market price to book value ratio. How do investors use these ratios to analyze a company's common stock as a potential investment?
2. Compute Thiokol's P/E ratio and market price to book value ratio at the end of each year 1992 through 1994.
3. Analyze the ratios you computed in Part 2 relative to the financial and narrative information presented for Thiokol. Are there any unusual or unexpected relationships in these data? If so, identify these unusual and unexpected relationships and identify plausible explanations for them.
4. In 1994, Thiokol's earnings per share was reduced by a $3.20 after-tax charge related to a cumulative effect of an accounting change. Recompute Thiokol's year-end P/E ratio based upon the company's earnings per share before the cumulative effect of the accounting change. Is there any evidence which suggests that investors ignored the impact of the cumulative effect item on Thiokol's 1994 earnings? Explain.
5. What may account for Thiokol increasing its dividends in 1994 although the company's revenues and earnings decreased considerably during that year compared with the previous year?

40. Temporary Differences for Tax Purposes (LO 4, 5)

During three recent years, Timber Country Enterprises (TCE) had the following pretax accounting and taxable incomes.

Margin note:

39. 2. P/E Ratio:
1992, 5.13
1993, 6.99
Market Price to Book Value Ratio:
1992, 0.82
1993, 1.00
1994, 1.18

	PRETAX ACCOUNTING INCOME	TAXABLE INCOME
1994	$440,000	$380,000
1995	470,000	410,000
1996	370,000	490,000

For each year, the difference between TCE's pretax accounting income and its taxable income was due to the different depreciation methods the company uses for financial accounting and taxation purposes. Recently, a local attorney, who is a new member of TCE's board of directors, reviewed the company's financial records. At the next board meeting, this individual suggested that the use of different accounting methods for financial accounting and taxation purposes was, in her opinion, unethical.

Required:

1. Is it unethical to use different accounting methods for financial accounting and taxation purposes? Why or why not? Are financial statement users misled by this practice? Explain.
2. TCE's effective tax rate in recent years has been 40 percent for both financial accounting and taxation purposes. Compute the company's income tax expense and income taxes payable for 1994–1996.
3. Prepare the appropriate journal entries to record TCE's income tax expense at the end of each year 1994 through 1996.

40. 2. Income Tax Expense:
    1994, $176,000
    1995, $188,000
    1996, $148,000
  Income Tax Payable:
    1994, $152,000
    1995, $164,000
    1996, $196,000
3. 1994 Cr. Deferred
  Income Taxes $24,000
  1995 Cr. Deferred
  Income Taxes $24,000
  1996 Dr. Deferred
  Income Taxes $48,000

41. **Ethics and the Corporate Income Statement** (LO 1)

In 1984, executives of Berkshire Hathaway, Inc., a large investment company, became involved in a dispute with representatives of their independent audit firm. The focus of this dispute was a large payment received by Berkshire Hathaway during 1984 from another company. Berkshire's executives believed that this payment should be treated as a dividend for financial accounting purposes, the treatment prescribed for taxation purposes. The company's independent auditors insisted on another accounting treatment for this transaction for financial accounting purposes. This alternative treatment was not preferred by Berkshire's executives because it would reduce the company's 1984 net income by approximately 8 percent. If Berkshire's executives failed to adopt the accounting treatment for this transaction suggested by the independent auditors, the auditors would issue an unfavorable audit opinion on Berkshire's 1984 financial statements.

Eventually, Berkshire's executives agreed to the accounting treatment suggested by their independent auditors. However, the following year, company management retained another accounting firm to audit the company's financial statements. (The facts of this problem were drawn from the following source: M. C. Knapp, "Berkshire Hathaway, Inc.," in *Contemporary Auditing: Issues and Cases*, 2d ed. (Minneapolis/St. Paul: West Publishing Co., 1996).

Required:

1. Who has the final responsibility for determining the accounting methods that a company should use, its management or its independent auditors?
2. What responsibility do independent auditors have regarding the annual financial statements of their audit clients?
3. Should the prescribed treatment for a transaction for taxation purposes be used as the basis for determining its treatment for financial accounting purposes? Explain.

41. No check figures

PROBLEM SET B

42. Income Statement Preparation (LO 2, 3)

Following are key line items included in the income statement of Shank Corporation for the year ended December 31, 1996. These items appear in no particular order.

Selling Expenses	$ 29,000
Cost of Goods Sold	440,000
Income Tax Expense (related to Income from Continuing Operations before Income Tax)	?
Gain on Sale of Equipment	16,000
Operating Income from Discontinued Line of Business, $15,000, less Income Tax of $6,000	9,000
Extraordinary Loss due to Flood, $25,000, less Income Tax Savings of $10,000	15,000
General Expenses	33,000
Net Sales	810,000
Administrative Expenses	9,000
Cumulative Effect of a Change in Accounting Principle, $10,000, less Income Tax of $4,000	6,000

Shank's average income tax rate is 40 percent. Throughout 1996, Shank had 100,000 shares of common stock outstanding.

Required:

Prepare a multiple-step income statement for Shank Corporation including an earnings per share section.

43. Earnings Per Share Computations (LO 3)

The following income statement data are available at year-end for Andrew & DuPraine Corporation:

Income from Continuing Operations before Taxes		$725,000
Income Tax Expense		290,000
Income from Continuing Operations		$435,000
Discontinued Operations:		
Operating Income, $30,000, less Income Tax of $12,000	$18,000	
Gain on Disposal, $25,000, less Income Tax of $10,000	15,000	33,000
Income before Cumulative Effect of a Change in Accounting Principle		$468,000
Cumulative Effect of a Change in Accounting Principle, $35,000 less Income Tax of $14,000		21,000
Net Income		$489,000

At the beginning of the year, Andrew & DuPraine had 90,000 shares of common stock outstanding. On September 1, Andrew & DuPraine sold an additional 30,000 shares of common stock.

Required:

1. Compute the weighted-average number of shares of common stock that Andrew & DuPraine had outstanding during the year.
2. Compute and clearly label the earnings per share figures you would expect to see in Andrew & DuPraine's income statement.
3. Assume that Andrew & DuPraine has a complex capital structure. Assume further that for purposes of computing fully diluted earnings per share, the weighted-average number of shares of common stock outstanding is 150,000.

42. Net Income, $189,000
    Earnings per Share, $1.89

43. 1. 100,000 shares
    2. Net income per share, $4.89
    3. $3.26

Compute the company's fully diluted earnings per share.
4. Suppose that Andrew & DuPraine's fully diluted earnings per share was less than its "primary" earnings per share. What should the company do under these circumstances?

44. Statement of Stockholders' Equity (LO 6, 7)

Following are the balances of the Brooks Corporation's stockholders' equity accounts on January 1, 1996.

Common Stock	$ 66,000
Additional Paid-in Capital	230,800
Retained Earnings	1,243,800

Brooks sold an additional 5,000 shares of its $3 par value common stock for $17 per share on October 15, 1996. On January 1, 1996, the company had 22,000 shares of common stock outstanding. On June 12, 1996, Brooks declared a $1.50 per share cash dividend. The dividend was payable on August 8 to stockholders of record on July 16. Brooks's net income for 1996 was $101,700.

Required:
1. Prepare a statement of stockholders' equity for Brooks Corporation for the year ended December 31, 1996.
2. Assume that on January 25, 1997, Brooks obtains a large loan from a local bank. One stipulation of the loan agreement is that Brooks make $1 million of its existing retained earnings unavailable for the declaration of dividends over the term of the loan. Prepare the journal entry to record this appropriation of retained earnings.
3. Suppose that on June 24, 1997, Brooks's accountant discovers that depreciation expense on a piece of machinery was accidentally understated by $16,000 during 1996. Prepare the appropriate journal entries to record the prior period adjustment to correct this error, assuming that the company's effective tax rate for both financial accounting and taxation purposes is 40 percent.

44. 1. 12/31/96 Balances:
Common Stock, $81,000
Add'l Paid-in Cap.,
$300,800
Retained Earnings,
$1,312,500
2. Dr. Retained Earnings
$1,000,000
Cr. Retained Earnings
Appropriated $1,000,000
3. Dr. Retained Earnings,
$16,000
Cr. Accum. Deprec.
$16,000
Dr. Tax Ref. Rec. $6,400
Cr. Retained Earnings
$6,400

45. Analyzing Stockholders' Equity (LO 8)

Hudson's Bay Company was established in 1670 and is Canada's oldest corporation and its largest department store retailer. Following is a description of the company and its operations that was included in the Hudson's Bay 1994 annual report.

Through its major operating divisions, the Bay and Zellers, Hudson's Bay Company covers the Canadian retail market across all price zones and from coast to coast. It accounts for approximately 40% of Canadian department store sales; almost 8% of all retail sales other than food and automobiles.

Following is selected financial information for Hudson's Bay for the period 1992–1994.

	1992	1993	1994
Total Revenues*	$ 5.15	$ 5.44	$ 5.83
Net Income**	117.0	147.7	151.3
Earnings Per Share	2.32	2.72	2.66
Book Value Per Share			
of Common Stock	25.92	28.56	30.76
Year-End Market Price			
of Common Stock	24.00	32.00	29.25
Cash Dividends Per Share	.80	.80	.92

* In billions.
** In millions.

45. 2. P/E Ratio:
   1992, 10.34
   1993, 11.76
   1994, 11.00
   Market Price to Book
   Value Ratio:
   1992, 0.93
   1993, 1.12
   1994, 0.95

Required:

1. Describe briefly the meaning of both the P/E ratio and the market price to book value ratio. How do investors use these ratios to analyze a company's common stock as a potential investment?
2. Compute the P/E ratio and market price to book value ratio for Hudson's Bay at the end of each year 1992 through 1994.
3. Analyze the ratios you computed in Part 2 relative to the financial information presented for Hudson's Bay. Are there any unusual or unexpected relationships in these data? If so, identify these unusual and unexpected relationships and identify plausible explanations for them.
4. What factors may cause the market price of a company's common stock to be different from the common stock's book value per share?
5. Suppose that you were considering purchasing common stock of Hudson's Bay. Identify three questions that you would want to ask of the company's chief executive officer before deciding whether to invest in the company.

46. Temporary Differences for Tax Purposes (LO 4, 5)

Thunder Gulch Developers (TGD) uses the direct write-off method of accounting for bad debts for taxation purposes but the allowance method of accounting for bad debts for financial accounting purposes. Shown in the following table are TGD's bad debt expenses under each of these accounting methods for a recent three-year period.

	DIRECT WRITE-OFF METHOD	ALLOWANCE METHOD
1994	$40,000	$60,000
1995	50,000	50,000
1996	80,000	60,000

A major stockholder of TGD was surprised when she obtained these data. She immediately contacted TGD's controller. "You're the chief accountant of this organization. How can you allow TGD to keep two sets of accounting records? That's got to be illegal!"

Required:

1. Is it permissible for a company to maintain different accounting records for financial accounting and taxation purposes? Explain.
2. Is it ethical for a company to choose accounting methods for taxation purposes that minimize and/or delay the income taxes paid to governmental agencies? Why or why not?
3. Assume that for each year 1994 through 1996, the difference in TGD's pre-tax accounting income and taxable income was totally due to the different accounting methods used for bad debt expenses. Also assume that in each year, the company's pretax accounting income was $200,000 and the company's effective tax rate for both financial accounting and taxation purposes was 40 percent. Prepare the appropriate journal entries to record TGD's income tax expense at the end of each year 1994 through 1996.

46. 2. Income Tax Expense:
   1994, $80,000
   1995, $80,000
   1996, $80,000
   Income Tax Payable:
   1994, $88,000
   1995, $80,000
   1996, $72,000
   3. 1994 Dr. Deferred
   Income Taxes $8,000
   1996 Cr. Deferred
   Income Taxes $8,000

47. Ethics and the Corporate Income Statement (LO 2)

Kim Caraway is the controller of Cotton Industries, a large manufacturing firm. During the current year, Cotton suffered a $4.2 million loss, after taxes, as a result of being forced to write off a large piece of machinery that was not suited for Cotton's production process. In the preliminary financial statements that Kim has drafted for the current year, she reports this loss under "Other Gains or

Losses" on Cotton's income statement. After reviewing the preliminary financial statements, Cotton's chief executive officer (CEO) insists that the loss be reported as an extraordinary item.

Required:

1. Why would it be advantageous for Cotton Industries to have this loss reported as an extraordinary item rather than as a component of Income from Continuing Operations? Explain.
2. In your opinion, does this item qualify as an extraordinary item? Why or why not?
3. Suppose that after studying this matter, Kim decides that the accounting rules do not expressly prohibit reporting this type of loss as an extraordinary item. Given this conclusion, would it be appropriate, or ethical, for Kim to treat the item as an extraordinary loss? Why or why not?

47. No check figures

CASES

48. Statement of Added Value

Electrolux Group is a large Swedish company based in Stockholm. Electrolux's operations are segregated into four lines of business: household appliances, commercial appliances, outdoor products, and industrial products. In the United States, Electrolux is probably best known for its vacuum cleaners.

Included in Electrolux's 1994 annual report was a "Statement of Added Value." The company's annual report defined "added value" as follows:

Added value represents the contribution made by a company's production, i.e., the increase in value arising from manufacturing, handling, etc. within the company. It is defined as sales revenues less the cost of purchased goods and services.

Following is Electrolux's statement of added value for 1994. The amounts in this statement are expressed in millions of Swedish kronor. Recently, one Swedish krona was equivalent to approximately $.13.

Calculation of Added Value:

		%
Total Sales	108,004	100
Cost of Purchased Goods and Services	(70,610)	(65)
Added Value	37,394	35

Distribution of Added Value:

To Employees:		
Wages and Salaries	19,431	52
Employer Contributions	5,939	16
	25,370	68
To Central and Local Governments:		
Taxes	1,444	4
To Credit Institutions:		
Interest, etc.	1,439	4
To Shareholders:		
Dividend Payments	915	2
	3,798	10

Retained in the Group:

For Wear on Fixed Assets (Depreciation)	4,214	11
Other	4,012	11
	8,226	22
Added Value	37,394	100

Required:

1. Review Electrolux's 1994 statement of added value. What do you believe is the principal purpose of this statement?
2. What information does a statement of added value provide that is not contained in an income statement of a U.S. corporation?
3. How would the information you identified in Part 2 be used by financial decision makers? Is this information particularly useful to certain types of decision makers? If so, identify these decision makers.
4. Do you believe that U.S. corporations should be required to include a statement of added value in their annual reports? Defend your answer.

49. 1920 Income Statement

Following is an income statement of the Frederick Kahl Iron Foundry for the company's fiscal year ended May 31, 1920. This income statement is formatted as originally issued by the company's accountants.

INCOME	MAY 31–1920
Net Sales	$284,158.85
Cost of Sales	199,866.63
MANUFACTURING PROFIT	$ 84,292.22
EXPENSES	
Administrative, General and Selling	39,545.55
OPERATING PROFIT OR LOSS	$ 44,746.67
Other Deductions or Other Income—Net	5,836.15
PROFIT OR LOSS (Before Federal Taxes)	38,910.52
Provision for Federal Taxes—Estimated	10,500.00
NET PROFIT OR LOSS	$ 28,410.52

Required:

1. Identify the differences and similarities between this 1920 income statement and the income statements prepared by U.S. corporations in the 1990s.
2. What factors likely account for the evolution of the content and format of financial statements over a period of several decades?

50. Elements of Corporate Income Statements

Norton Warden has worked for many years as a state employee of Maine. With less than ten years to retirement, Norton realizes that he must begin planning for his retirement. Lately, Norton has begun reading *The Wall Street Journal* and studying the financial statements of dozens of publicly owned companies. When Norton identifies an item that he does not understand, he writes it down. Following is a list of mysterious items Norton has stumbled across in recent corporate income statements.

Orbital Sciences Corporation:
Cumulative Effect of Change in Accounting for Income Taxes $200,000

Conner Peripherals, Inc.:

Primary Earnings Per Share	$2.10
Fully Diluted Earnings Per Share	$1.77

First Union Real Estate Investments:

Extraordinary Loss from Early Extinguishment of Debt	$1,200,000

National Pizza Company:

Loss on Disposition of Underperforming Assets	$4,000,000

Occidental Petroleum Corporation:

Loss from Discontinued Operations	$622,000,000

Required:

Write a memo to Norton Warden explaining the nature of each item in his list. While writing this memo, keep in mind that Norton knows very little about accounting and financial reporting rules.

PROJECTS

51. Tracking P/E Ratios over Time

Select three industries of particular interest to you and then identify two major companies within each of these industries.

Required:

1. Using *The Wall Street Journal* or other sources, find the P/E ratios of each of the companies you selected at the end of each quarter for the past three years. (The specific dates for which you should obtain P/E ratios for these companies are March 31, June 30, September 30, and December 31.) Plot these twelve P/E ratios for each firm on a piece of graph paper with an appropriate numerical scale.
2. Study the data collected and plotted in Part 1. Among the issues you should address are the following: Are the P/E ratios of the paired companies within each industry fairly consistent over the three-year period? Are the P/E ratios of the paired companies in each industry more consistent than the P/E ratios of companies not in the same industry? Are there any apparent trends for the P/E ratios within specific industries? If so, attempt to identify factors that may account for these trends.
3. Write a brief report containing the data you collected in Part 1 and your analysis of that data in Part 2.

52. Analyzing Statements of Stockholders' Equity

To obtain the data required to complete this project, you will need to select ten companies that include a statement of stockholders' equity in their annual reports.

Required:

Prepare a brief report to be presented in class or turned in to your instructor that includes the following:

1. A list of the specific activities that affected the stockholders' equity of the ten companies you selected during the most recent year for which data are available.
2. An indication of how many of the ten companies report each of the activities identified in Part 1.

53. Income Statements of a Failing Business

For this project, your project group will identify a company that went into bankruptcy within the last three years. There are several readily available sources that can be used to identify such companies. One such source is the entries listed under the "bankruptcies" heading in the hard copy or on-line indices of *The Wall Street Journal.*

Required:

1. For the company your group selected, obtain a copy of the firm's annual income statement for each of the five years immediately preceding the bankruptcy filing. Each group member should obtain or be provided copies of these income statements. After each group member has had an opportunity to study this series of income statements, meet as a group and discuss these income statements. The key issue you want to address as a group is whether the series of income statements contains any "red flags" or warning signals regarding the company's financial problems. Examples of approaches you may use to address this issue include, but are not limited to, the following:
    a. Computing and interpreting financial ratios for this company
    b. Documenting and studying any trends apparent in the company's income statements
    c. Investigating unusual or "special" items included in the company's income statements
    d. Comparative analysis of the company's income statement data and related ratios and trends with comparable data of similar companies and the company's industry as a whole

2. A written report summarizing the group's discussion of the selected company's income statements should be prepared. This report should identify any of the "red flags" that suggested that the company might eventually fail. Your report should also contain recommendations that decision makers might use to identify companies that are in the process of failing.

3. One group member should be prepared to present a brief overview of the group's written report to the class.

INTERCORPORATE INVESTMENTS AND ACCOUNTING FOR INTERNATIONAL OPERATIONS

> *It is not the return on my investment that I am concerned about; it is the return of my investment.*
> Will Rogers

TIME WARNER

LEARNING OBJECTIVES

After studying this chapter, you should be able to do the following:

1. Define the key information needs of decision makers regarding intercorporate investments

2. Account for intercorporate investments in trading securities

3. Describe the key accounting issues related to available-for-sale securities, held-to-maturity securities, and influential but noncontrolling investments in equity securities

4. Describe the nature and purpose of consolidated financial statements for controlling investments in equity securities

5. Identify important internal control issues related to intercorporate investments

6. Discuss how intercorporate investments affect decision makers' analyses of financial statement data

7. Discuss the key issues related to accounting for international operations, including accounting for realized and unrealized gains and losses resulting from changes in foreign currency exchange rates

LBOs and CPAs

As documented in the hit film *Wall Street* starring Michael Douglas and Charlie Sheen, corporate America viewed "big as better" during the 1980s. One result of the so-called decade of greed was a record pace of business combinations, corporate takeovers, and other intercorporate investments. Many of these mega-deals were structured as leveraged buyouts, or LBOs, by the Wall Street underwriting firms that typically coordinate corporate takeovers. In an LBO, the bulk of the funds needed to finance the acquisition of one company by another is supplied by bank loans. The acquiring company generally provides 10 percent, or even less, of the required funds for an LBO.

A major problem with an LBO is the heavy burden of debt under which the post-takeover company must operate. A temporary downturn in sales or an unexpected series of expenses can jeopardize the company's ability to make its principal and interest payments. Many companies involved in LBOs during the early 1980s did fail, resulting in huge losses for the large metropolitan banks that had financed these deals. To persuade these banks to continue participating in LBOs, underwriters retained the services of the "Big Six" accounting firms. These accounting firms were asked to prepare "solvency letters" in connection with LBOs. In a solvency letter, an accounting firm would offer an opinion on the likelihood that a company emerging from an LBO would survive for at least two to five years. A solvency letter typically indicated that the post-LBO company would be financially viable over that time frame. Given this assurance, banks were much more likely to participate in an LBO.

An example of an LBO in which a solvency letter was requested was the 1987 buyout of Southland Corporation, the owner of the nationwide chain of 7-Eleven convenience stores. The prospective purchaser of Southland requested a $2 billion loan from five large banks to finance the acquisition. The underwriters negotiating the LBO asked the accounting firm of Touche Ross, now known as Deloitte & Touche, to provide the five banks with a solvency letter. Touche Ross supplied the solvency letter without which the banking syndicate reportedly would not have financed the takeover of Southland.

Solvency letters not only helped sustain the corporate takeover frenzy of the 1980s but also provided large accounting firms with a significant source of revenue. Accounting firms were typically paid several hundred thousand dollars for a solvency letter. In 1986 and 1987 alone, the Big Six accounting firms earned nearly $100 million for the solvency letters they issued. However, the solvency letter bonanza was short-lived for these firms, ending abruptly in 1988.

Critics of solvency letters maintained that accounting firms were not qualified to make the financial projections contained in these letters. Rule-making authorities within the accounting profession quickly sided with these critics. In February 1988, public accounting firms were officially prohibited from issuing solvency letters.

Discussion Question
As a review, ask students for specific examples of debt and equity securities.
Answer: Corporate bonds, common stock, preferred stock, etc.

Chapters 7 through 9 focused on accounting for assets. Two types of assets not considered in those chapters were short-term and long-term investments. Among the most common short-term and long-term investments of corporations are investments in debt and equity securities of other corporations. In this chapter, we consider accounting issues related to such intercorporate investments. First, we identify the motives for these investments and the long-standing controversy regarding the primary valuation basis that should be applied to them. Next, the key information needs of decision makers regarding these assets are discussed, followed by an overview of procedural accounting issues related to the five major types of intercorporate investments. Finally, we highlight internal controls related to intercorporate investments and describe how these investments affect decision makers' analysis of corporate financial statement data.

The second section of this chapter focuses on accounting for international operations. In recent years, an increasing number of companies have expanded their operations across international borders. Many firms expand abroad by investing in foreign companies, while other firms establish foreign subsidiaries. Regardless of the approach they have taken to enter foreign markets, multinational companies pose challenging accounting issues and problems for their accountants.

INTERCORPORATE INVESTMENTS

Corporations invest in other firms' stocks and bonds for various reasons. As you will discover, the motives for these investments often influence, if not dictate, the accounting methods used for them. Many companies invest in corporate stocks and bonds to make effective use of excess cash. Generally, the rates of return on corporate stocks and bonds are more attractive than the interest rates offered on certificates of deposit and savings accounts. Stock and bond investments also provide an opportunity for corporations to earn "trading" profits by taking advantage of short-term fluctuations in security prices. Many corporations have a long-term perspective when they purchase the stocks and bonds of other companies. Such investments are made with the hope of realizing a reasonable rate of return over an extended period. The two principal components of this rate of return are cash dividends and capital appreciation—that is, an increase in the market value of the given securities.

Another common motivation for intercorporate investments is to control, or at least influence, another firm's operations. For example, consider a company that retails large home appliances such as microwave ovens, washers, and dryers. To ensure that it has a reliable supply of such appliances, this retailer may "vertically integrate" by purchasing an appliance manufacturing company. Then again, instead of purchasing this company outright, the appliance retailer may choose to buy a controlling interest in the manufacturer's common stock. By purchasing slightly more than 50 percent of the manufacturer's outstanding common stock, the retailer can dictate the operating policies of that firm.

Accounting for investments in debt and equity securities is another subject that has generated considerable controversy within the accounting profession. For decades, the accounting profession has debated whether investments in stocks and bonds should be reported at their historical cost or at their market value for balance sheet purposes. Diehard supporters of the historical cost principle insist that these investments should be reported at their original acquisition cost similar to most other assets. Advocates of current value accounting argue just as adamantly that the historical cost of these investments is much less relevant to decision makers than their current value. This controversy became known as the "mark-to-market" debate because of the demand by many parties to "mark up" or "mark down" the acquisition cost of stock and bond investments to their market value.

The debate regarding historical costs and current values is unlikely to end soon. However, supporters of current value accounting claimed a significant victory in 1993 with the adoption of *Statement on Financial Accounting Standards No. 115*, "Accounting for Certain Investments in Debt and Equity Securities." This accounting standard requires many investments in debt and equity securities to be accounted for on a current value, or "fair value," basis.

Discussion Question
What characteristic of most investments in debt and equity securities allows them to be readily recorded at market value?
Answer: Easily accessible and objective market values.

Golden Parachutes and White Knights

The rapid pace of intercorporate investments during the 1980s spawned a colorful Wall Street dialect to describe these investments and related management strategies. An understanding of these terms is not necessary to account properly for intercorporate investments. Nevertheless, knowledge of these terms is helpful when reading The Wall Street Journal *or when your stockbroker tries to impress you with his or her latest "hot tip."*
Following are definitions of several Wall Street slang terms related to intercorporate investments that appeared in the 1993 Educational Edition of The Wall Street Journal.

Crown Jewel Defense: A management strategy to thwart a hostile takeover. The strategy centers on an agreement to sell to a third party the company's most valuable assets to make the company less attractive to the potential buyer.

Golden Parachute: When a company anticipates a future takeover, its executives may approve a lucrative termination package for themselves. If a takeover occurs, the executives can "parachute" to safety if their positions are eliminated by the new owners.

Lobster Trap: A defense mechanism used by a company that has convertible securities outstanding to prevent an unfriendly takeover. This mechanism prohibits conversion into common stock of any convertible preferred stock or bonds if the owner of those securities would control 10 percent or more of the given firm's common stock following conversion.

Raider: Any party that attempts to buy a sufficiently large percentage of a company's stock so that it can install new management. This term does not apply to parties that buy large blocks of a company's stock simply as an investment.

Toehold Purchase: Term used to describe a purchase of less than 5 percent of a company's common stock. Once the purchaser owns 5 percent or more of the company's stock, a public disclosure of the purchaser's identity and the percentage of stock that it owns must be made to the SEC.

White Knight: An individual or corporate investor that rescues a corporation from an unfriendly takeover by purchasing the company on terms more agreeable to its owners.

Intercorporate Investments: Key Information Needs of Decision Makers

■ LEARNING
OBJECTIVE 1
Define the key information
needs of decision makers
regarding intercorporate
investments

Decision makers need and demand certain information regarding a company's intercorporate investments. Most important, decision makers need to be aware of the nature of these investments. Intercorporate investments often signal a shift in the objectives and operating policies of a corporation. For example, a company that begins accumulating common stock in an unrelated business may be signaling that it plans to expand into that line of business. Decision makers also demand information regarding the market values of these investments and disclosures of the revenues and expenses related to them.

NATURE OF INTERCORPORATE INVESTMENTS   Decision makers should be aware of the general nature and purpose of a company's intercorporate investments. Such information, as just suggested, may provide important insight on an entity's plans for the future. As always, the need for external decision makers to be well informed must be balanced against an entity's need to protect its economic interests. For example, a corporation that has decided to begin slowly accumulating stock in a competitor to attempt a "hostile" takeover in the near future would not want to

A record pace of corporate takeovers in recent years has caused corporate executives to develop sophisticated strategies to protect their economic self-interests. One such strategy involves a "golden parachute," which is a lucrative termination package that a firm's executives establish for themselves in case their company is acquired and their positions eliminated.

immediately disclose this intention. Doing so would not only drive up the acquisition cost of the competitor's stock but also provide its executives with a head start in successfully resisting the takeover.

A key source of information regarding the nature of a company's intercorporate investments is the footnotes to its annual financial statements. Shown in Exhibit 14.1 is an example of a footnote disclosure regarding an intercorporate investment. This disclosure was included in the 1994 annual report of BancTec, Inc. BancTec describes itself as a leading worldwide provider of electronic and document-based financial transaction processing systems, application software, and support services. The footnote in Exhibit 14.1 does not explicitly indicate the purpose of the investment being described. Nevertheless, it should be apparent to financial statement readers that BancTec is expanding its operations into South America.

Teaching Note
Remind students that financial statement footnotes are an integral part of a set of financial statements. Footnotes allow business entities to comply with the full disclosure principle discussed in Chapter 2.

■ **EXHIBIT 14.1**

Footnote Included in 1994 Annual Report of BancTec, Inc., Describing Investment in a South American Company

During the second quarter of fiscal year 1994, BancTec contributed approximately $500,000 in cash and certain other considerations in exchange for a 33% equity interest in Servibanca, S.A., a Chilean company. Servibanca is a check processing service bureau as well as a distributor of BancTec image processing systems, document processing systems, and stand alone readers/sorters to banks, service bureaus, and other financial processors in Chile and other South American countries. BancTec's investment in and share of Servibanca's earnings have been included since September 14, 1993, and are recorded using the equity method of accounting.

MARKET VALUE INFORMATION   "What's it worth?" is a common question posed by decision makers regarding most assets of business entities. As you know, this question often goes unanswered. However, many intercorporate investments are reported at their fair value, or current market value, in an entity's balance sheet. An example is investments in "trading securities," which are discussed shortly. Investments in "held-to-maturity securities," also discussed later in this chapter, are not reported at their fair value in a balance sheet. These investments are accounted for on a cost basis. Nevertheless, companies must disclose the fair value of the latter investments in their financial statement footnotes. For example, at the end of fiscal 1994, Cracker Barrel Old Country Store reported approximately $81.2 million dollars of held-to-maturity securities in its balance sheet. A footnote to the company's financial statements revealed that the fair value of those assets was $80.8 million.

The fair value of certain investments is not reported in either an entity's balance sheet or its financial statement footnotes. Among these investments are ownership interests in common stocks accounted for via the equity method, such as the BancTec investment in Servibanca described in Exhibit 14.1. Because a company intends to retain these investments indefinitely, the profession has concluded that fair value disclosures for them are not relevant to decision makers.

Teaching Note
Generally, investment income is reported after operating income on the income statement because it does not relate to the principal profit-oriented activities of a company.

REVENUES AND EXPENSES RELATED TO INTERCORPORATE INVEST-MENTS   The net amount of revenues and expenses related to intercorporate investments is generally reported as a separate item in a corporate income statement under Other Revenues and Expenses. Reporting this item separately allows decision makers to determine its impact on a corporation's net income. Tommy Hilfiger Corporation designs and markets sportswear for men and boys. The company's 1994 income statement reported $637,000 of "investment income." A footnote to the company's financial statements listed the following components of this investment income.

Interest Income	$994,000
Net Realized Losses	(210,000)
Unrealized Losses on Short-Term Investments	(147,000)
Investment Income	$637,000

In certain cases, the income or loss associated with intercorporate investments is not reported separately in a corporate income statement. As discussed later in the chapter, if one company owns a controlling interest in another, the two companies should be treated as one economic entity for financial reporting purposes. Such companies prepare a consolidated income statement in which their sales, cost of goods sold, and other revenue and expense amounts are merged.

Accounting for Intercorporate Investments

In this section, we consider accounting and financial reporting rules for the five major types of intercorporate investments identified in the accounting standards. These investments are listed in Exhibit 14.2 along with a brief description of each.

The accounting issues posed by the five types of intercorporate investments are similar. However, the specific accounting rules applied to these investments are often considerably different. Discussing all of the "ins and outs" of accounting for intercorporate investments is beyond the scope of this text. Here, the objective is to acquaint you with the major accounting issues for intercorporate investments. The strategy used to accomplish this objective is to present a comprehensive overview of accounting for the first category of intercorporate investments, trading securities. Trading securities raise

■ **EXHIBIT 14.2**

Five Major Types of Intercorporate Investments for Accounting and Financial Reporting Purposes

Trading securities: Investments in debt and equity securities acquired principally for the purpose of selling them in the near term and thereby generating profits on short-run fluctuations in market prices. Classified as current assets for balance sheet purposes.

Available-for-sale securities: Investments in debt and equity securities that do not qualify as one of the other types of investments in these securities. Classified as either current or long-term assets depending upon the length of time that management intends to hold these securities.

Held-to-maturity securities: Investments in debt securities acquired with the positive intent and ability to hold them to maturity. Classified as long-term assets unless they mature in the coming year, in which case they are classified as current assets.

Influential but noncontrolling investments: Investments in equity securities in which the "investor" corporation generally owns at least 20 percent but not more than 50 percent of the "investee" corporation's common stock. Classified as long-term assets for balance sheet purposes.

Controlling investments: Investments in equity securities in which the "parent" company owns more than 50 percent of the common stock of the "subsidiary." Consolidated financial statements are prepared for a parent company and its subsidiaries.

trading securities

available-for-sale securities

held-to-maturity securities

influential but noncontrolling investments

controlling investments

most of the key accounting issues related to intercorporate investments. For the remaining four categories of these investments, a brief summary of the accounting issues and procedures unique to each is presented. Those of you who continue your study of accounting will be introduced in more elaborate detail to accounting procedures and rules for intercorporate investments in subsequent courses.

TRADING SECURITIES   As indicated in Exhibit 14.2, trading securities can be either debt securities, such as corporate bonds, or equity securities, such as common stock. The key defining characteristic of trading securities is management's intention to generate short-term trading profits on these investments. Since management does not intend to hold these investments for an extended period, trading securities are classified as current assets. Accounting standards require trading securities to be reported in an entity's balance sheet at fair value. The **fair value** of a debt or equity security on any given date is generally the security's closing price on that date on a securities exchange.

■ LEARNING OBJECTIVE 2
Account for intercorporate investments in trading securities

fair value

PURCHASE OF TRADING SECURITIES   To illustrate accounting for trading securities, suppose that on April 1, 1998, Exxon purchases 200 shares of IBM common stock and five corporate bonds of Apple Computer. The Apple bonds have a $1,000 face value, a 10 percent stated interest rate, and semiannual interest payment dates of April 1 and October 1. Assuming Exxon pays $50 per share for the IBM common stock and $1,000 for each Apple bond, the cost of these securities would be $10,000

Teaching Note
Point out to students that on the
date of purchase, the fair value of
a security and its historical cost
are one and the same (ignoring
transaction costs).

and $5,000, respectively. (The illustrations of purchases and sales of securities in this chapter ignore brokerage commissions and other transaction costs.) Following are the entries that would be appropriate to record these investments in Exxon's accounting records.

Apr. 1	Investment in IBM Common Stock,		
	Trading Securities	10,000	
	Investment in Apple Computer Bonds,		
	Trading Securities	5,000	
	Cash		15,000

To record stock and bond investments

RECORDING INTEREST AND DIVIDEND REVENUE ON TRADING SECURITIES   Companies that have investments in trading securities periodically receive interest and dividend revenues on these investments. For example, on October 1, 1998, Exxon will receive a $250 interest payment from Apple Computer. Shown next is the computation of this interest payment.

$$\text{Interest} = \text{Principal} \times \text{Rate} \times \text{Time}$$
$$\$250 = \$5,000 \times 10\% \times 6/12$$

Teaching Note
Emphasize that the receipt of
investment income on trading
securities has no affect on the
balance of the investment
account.

In addition to the interest payment from Apple Computer, assume that Exxon receives a dividend check from IBM of $200 on November 21, 1998. These two revenues would be recorded as shown in the following entries.

Oct. 1	Cash	250	
	Interest Revenue		250

To record receipt of semiannual
interest payment on Apple bonds

Nov. 21	Cash	200	
	Dividend Revenue		200

To record receipt of dividend on
IBM common stock

YEAR-END ADJUSTING ENTRIES FOR TRADING SECURITIES   At the end of each fiscal year, an entity records certain adjusting entries related to its investments in trading securities. Returning to our example, Exxon's accountants will record an adjusting entry at the end of 1998 to recognize $125 ($5,000 × 10% × 3/12) of interest earned on the Apple bonds but not yet received. Following is the year-end adjusting entry to record this revenue.

Dec. 31	Interest Receivable	125	
	Interest Revenue		125

To recognize interest revenue on
investment in Apple bonds

Like many large companies, IBM regularly pays dividends. Nevertheless, Exxon should not record a year-end adjusting entry to recognize dividend revenue on the

IBM investment in anticipation of a dividend declaration. IBM is not legally obligated to pay a dividend until it is declared by the company's board of directors. If IBM has declared a dividend before December 31 *and* the record date is December 31 or earlier, then Exxon should record the dividend revenue in a year-end adjusting entry.

A second adjusting entry will be required to restate the book values of the investments in IBM and Apple securities to their year-end fair values. For illustration purposes, assume that the IBM stock has a closing price on the New York Stock Exchange of $56 per share on December 31, 1998. Assume that the Apple bonds end the year at a quoted price of 97, which translates to an actual selling price per bond of $970 ($1,000 × 97%). Consequently, Exxon's investment in IBM stock will have a year-end fair value of $11,200 (200 × $56), while the fair value of the investment in Apple bonds will be $4,850 (5 × $970). The difference between the year-end fair value of trading securities and their book value is an "unrealized" gain or loss. These gains or losses are unrealized because the securities have not yet been sold. "Paper" gains or losses are common terms that investors use to describe these amounts. The following table illustrates the computation of the net unrealized gain on Exxon's trading securities at year-end.

	BOOK VALUE	FAIR VALUE AT 12/31/98	UNREALIZED GAIN OR (LOSS)
IBM Common Stock	$10,000	$11,200	$1,200
Apple Computer Bonds	5,000	4,850	(150)
	$15,000	$16,050	$1,050

To recognize the net unrealized gain on Exxon's trading securities, the following entry would be made on December 31, 1998.

Dec. 31	Investment in IBM Common Stock, Trading Securities	1,200	
	Investment in Apple Computer Bonds, Trading Securities		150
	Unrealized Gain on Trading Securities		1,050

To adjust investments in trading securities to their year-end fair values

Following this entry, the investment in IBM common stock will have a book value of $11,200, while the book value of the investment in Apple bonds will be $4,850. In its December 31, 1998, balance sheet, Exxon will include under current assets a line item such as "Short-Term Investments" with a dollar amount of $16,050 ($11,200 + $4,850).

Although the net gain of $1,050 on the trading securities owned by Exxon is unrealized at the end of 1998, that gain will be reported in the company's income statement. When these securities are sold, Exxon will record a realized gain or loss. For example, assume that on January 16, 1999, Exxon sells the 200 shares of IBM common stock for $55 per share. The following entry would be made to record this sale.

Jan. 16	Cash	11,000	
	Loss on Sale of Trading Securities	200	
	Investment in IBM Common Stock, Trading Securities		11,200

To record loss on sale of 200 shares of IBM common stock

Teaching Note
"Marketable securities" is another balance sheet caption often used for investments in trading securities.

Notice that the loss on this transaction is the difference between the investment's revised book value as of December 31, 1998, and the sales proceeds of $11,000.

AVAILABLE-FOR-SALE SECURITIES Available-for-sale securities is a "catchall," or miscellaneous, category of intercorporate investments. Investments in debt and equity securities that do not qualify as one of the other four types of investments listed in Exhibit 14.2 are considered available-for-sale securities. These securities can be classified as either current or long-term assets for balance sheet purposes. If management intends to sell these securities within the coming year, they should be classified as current assets. Otherwise, these investments should be considered long-term assets. In fact, a corporation can have two sets of available-for-sale securities: those reported as current assets and those reported as long-term assets.

The accounting procedures for available-for-sale securities are similar to those applied to trading securities. Most important, both types of investments are reported at their fair values in an entity's balance sheet. There is one major difference between the accounting methods used for trading and available-for-sale securities. Return to the previous example used to illustrate accounting for trading securities. At the end of 1998, the following entry would be made to record the net unrealized gain on Exxon's investment in trading securities.

From its headquarters in Connecticut, the Financial Accounting Standards Board deliberates on many important issues. Among the more controversial decisions made by the FASB in recent years was applying "fair value" accounting to investments in certain corporate debt and equity securities.

Dec. 31	Investment in IBM Common Stock, Trading Securities	1,200	
	Investment in Apple Computer Bonds, Trading Securities		150
	Unrealized Gain on Trading Securities		1,050

To adjust investments in trading
securities to their year-end fair values

Now, assume that Exxon's investments in IBM common stock and Apple bonds qualify as available-for-sale securities. Under this assumption, the following year-end adjusting entry would be appropriate.

Dec. 31	Investment in IBM Common Stock, Available-for-Sale Securities	1,200	
	Investment in Apple Computer Bonds, Available-for-Sale Securities		150
	Unrealized Gain on Available-for-Sale Securities		1,050

To adjust available-for-sale securities
to their year-end fair values

The key difference in these two entries is the title of the unrealized gain account. This difference is important since Unrealized Gain on Trading Securities is a *revenue* account, while Unrealized Gain on Available-for-Sale Securities is an *equity* account. An unrealized gain or loss on available-for-sale securities is included as a separate line item in the stockholders' equity section of a corporate balance sheet. An unrealized gain on available-for-sale securities increases stockholders' equity, while an unrealized loss on such an investment is treated as a reduction in stockholders' equity. Shown next is the stockholders' equity section of Foxmeyer Corporation's 1994 balance sheet that included a $565,000 unrealized loss on available-for-sale securities.

Stockholders' Equity: (in thousands)

Common Stock, par value, $.010 per share;	
60,000,000 shares authorized;	
31,350,000 shares issued	$ 314
Capital in Excess of Par Value	460,042
Net Unrealized Holding Loss on Marketable Securities	(565)
Retained Earnings	42,531
Treasury Stock, 3,150,000 shares	(40,720)
Total Stockholders' Equity	$461,602

The obvious question here is why unrealized gains and losses are treated differently for trading securities versus available-for-sale securities. Recall that management's objective in acquiring trading securities is to generate short-term profits due to fluctuations in stock prices. So, it seems reasonable that gains and losses on such investments due to fluctuations in stock prices should be recognized for income statement purposes whether they are realized or not. Management's objective in purchasing available-for-sale securities is not short-term trading profits. Consequently, the accounting profession has decided that reporting unrealized gains and losses on these investments in the income statement is inappropriate. Instead, the unrealized gains and losses on these investments are "tucked away" in the stockholders' equity section of a balance sheet. When available-for-sale securities are sold, any realized gain or loss is reported in the income statement.

HELD-TO-MATURITY SECURITIES   Trading and available-for-sale securities can be either debt or equity securities. However, only debt securities can be classified as held-to-maturity securities. (Equity securities, such as common stock, do not have a maturity date and thus cannot be "held to maturity.") Among the more common types of held-to-maturity securities are corporate bonds. According to *Statement of Financial Accounting Standards No. 115*, an entity must have both the "positive intent" and "ability" to hold debt securities until their maturity date for these investments to qualify as held-to-maturity securities. If both criteria are not met, investments in debt securities are usually classified as available-for-sale securities.

Unlike trading and available-for-sale securities, held-to-maturity securities are not accounted for on a fair value basis. Since an entity intends to hold these securities until their maturity date, fluctuations in their market values are generally ignored for accounting purposes. Nevertheless, as indicated earlier, the fair value of held-to-maturity securities must be disclosed in an entity's financial statement footnotes.

The amortized cost method is the prescribed accounting method for held-to-maturity securities under *Statement of Financial Accounting Standards No. 115*. To illustrate key features of this accounting method, we will use investments in corporate bonds. The amortized cost method of accounting for bond investments is similar to the accounting treatment applied to bonds payable. Recall from Chapter 11 that a premium or discount on bonds payable is amortized over the term of the bonds using either the effective-interest or straight-line method. Under the **amortized cost method,** an entity must amortize the premium or discount on an investment in held-to-maturity securities over the remaining term of those securities when they are purchased. For balance sheet purposes, held-to-maturity securities are reported at their original cost adjusted for any amortized premium or discount.

Focus on Ethics
A company purchased equity securities to generate short-term trading profits. Unfortunately, at year-end the securities had decreased in value resulting in a significant unrealized loss. The chief financial officer (CFO) of the company decided to classify these securities as available-for-sale rather than as trading securities. Discuss both the ethics and the financial statement implications of the CFO's decision.

■ **LEARNING OBJECTIVE 3**
Describe the key accounting issues related to available-for-sale securities, held-to-maturity securities, and influential but noncontrolling investments in equity securities

Real World
SFAS No. 115 became effective for fiscal years beginning after December 15, 1993. The 1994 edition of *Accounting Trends & Techniques* reported that 21 companies out of 600 surveyed elected to adopt *SFAS No. 115* prior to its effective date.

amortized cost method

Shown in the following table are key facts for an investment in corporate bonds that qualify as held-to-maturity securities. These bonds were issued by Drexel Corporation and purchased by Manhattan Company.

Purchase date:	April 1, Year 1
Cost:	$14,400
Face value:	$15,000
Stated interest rate:	10%
Interest payment dates:	April 1 and October 1
Maturity date:	April 1, Year 4

To record the purchase of these bonds, Manhattan would make the following entry.

Apr. 1	Investment in Drexel Bonds,		
	Held-to-Maturity Securities	14,400	
	Cash		14,400
	To record bond investment		

Recall that a discount on bonds payable is typically recorded in a bond discount account. When bonds are purchased as an investment, a discount from face value is generally not recorded in a separate account. Instead, the total cost of the bonds is simply debited to the investment account.

In the present example, the Drexel bonds were purchased at a $600 discount from their face value. Assuming Manhattan uses the straight-line method to amortize this discount, $100 of discount will be amortized each of the remaining six semiannual interest payment periods in the bonds' term. On the first interest payment date, Manhattan would make the following entry to record the $750 ($15,000 × 10% × 6/12) of interest received from Drexel and to amortize $100 of the discount on the bond investment.

Oct. 1	Cash	750	
	Investment in Drexel Bonds,		
	Held-to-Maturity Securities	100	
	Interest Revenue		850
	To record interest revenue on bond investment		

Notice that under the amortized cost method, the amortization of bond discount increases interest revenue and increases the balance of the bond investment account. (The amortization of a premium on a bond investment decreases the interest revenue recognized each interest payment period and reduces the book value of the bond investment.) By the end of the bond term, the balance of the bond investment account in the present example will be $15,000, which is the face value of the Drexel bonds purchased by Manhattan.

An example of a company reporting held-to-maturity securities in its financial statements is Cabletron Systems, Inc. In its 1994 balance sheet, Cabletron listed its investments in these securities under "Long-Term Investments." The company also included the following financial statement footnote in its annual report to describe these investments.

Held-to-maturity securities are those investments in which the Company has the ability and intent to hold the security until maturity. Held-to-maturity securities are recorded at cost

Missing the Mark in the Mark-to-Market Debate?

In recent years, several controversial accounting issues have been considered by the Financial Accounting Standards Board (FASB). One such issue, "mark-to-market" accounting, culminated in the adoption of Statement on Financial Accounting Standards No. 115, "Accounting for Certain Investments in Debt and Equity Securities." This new standard, which became effective in late 1993, established the accounting treatment for trading securities, available-for-sale securities, and held-to-maturity securities. Before new accounting standards are adopted, they must be approved by at least five of the seven members of the FASB. Statement No. 115 received the minimum majority vote of 5–2. The two dissenting votes were cast by a prominent academic, Robert Swieringa, and the former Chief Accountant of the SEC, Clarence Sampson. Following are excerpts of the dissenting views regarding Statement No. 115 that were expressed by these gentlemen and included in an addendum to that accounting standard.

This Statement requires that debt securities be classified as held-to-maturity, available-for-sale, or trading and that securities in each classification be accounted for differently. As a result, three otherwise identical debt securities could receive three different accounting treatments within the same enterprise. Moreover, classification of debt securities as held-to-maturity is based on management's positive intent and ability to hold to maturity. The notion of intent to hold to maturity (a) is subjective at best, and (b) not likely to be consistently applied.

This statement also requires that certain debt securities classified as held-to-maturity be reported at amortized cost and that certain debt and equity securities classified as available-for-sale be reported at fair value with unrealized changes in fair value excluded from earnings. Those requirements provide the opportunity for the managers of an enterprise to manage its earnings by selectively selling securities and thereby selectively including realized gains in earnings and selectively excluding unrealized losses from earnings. An impressive amount of empirical evidence indicates that many financial institutions have engaged in that behavior. That behavior undermines the relevance and reliability of accounting information.

adjusted for the amortization of premiums and discounts which approximates market value. All investments mature within a two-year period. Interest income is recognized in the period earned. Realized gains and losses are included in earnings.

INFLUENTIAL BUT NONCONTROLLING INVESTMENTS   Earlier in this chapter, a financial statement footnote included in the 1994 annual report of BancTec, Inc., was presented. That footnote, shown in Exhibit 14.1, describes an investment BancTec made in a Chilean company, Servibanca. If you refer to the BancTec footnote, you will notice that the company reported using the "equity method" of accounting for its 33 percent interest in Servibanca. The equity method is used to account for influential but noncontrolling investments. These investments generally involve ownership by an "investor" corporation of 20 to 50 percent of an "investee" corporation's common stock. Accounting standards assume that a 20 to 50 percent ownership interest allows an investor firm to exercise significant influence over the investee's operations. An ownership interest of more than 50 percent of another firm's common stock represents a "controlling interest." Accounting for controlling investments is discussed shortly.

■ **LEARNING OBJECTIVE 3**
Describe the key accounting issues related to available-for-sale securities, held-to-maturity securities, and influential but noncontrolling investments in equity securities

equity method

Under the **equity method** of accounting, the investor corporation records its investment in the common stock of the investee corporation at cost. Subsequently, the investor records its proportionate interest in the investee's periodic earnings (losses) as an addition (reduction) to the investment's book value. Any dividends received from the investee reduce the book value of the investment. This accounting treatment is appropriate because of the assumption that the investor can influence the timing and size of the investee's dividend distributions. Suppose for the moment that investor corporations were allowed to record dividends received from investee corporations as revenue. Under this condition, the investor's executives might be tempted to pressure the investee to increase its dividend distributions in those years when the investor's profits were unimpressive or nonexistent.

To illustrate the key features of the equity method, assume that on January 1 of a given year, BancTec purchases 40 percent of CheckTec Company's common stock for $300,000. During this year, CheckTec reports net income of $50,000 and distributes a cash dividend of $25,000, $10,000 of which (40% × $25,000) is paid to BancTec. Shown next are the three entries recorded by BancTec during this year for its investment in CheckTec.

Jan. 1	Investment in CheckTec Common Stock		300,000	
	Cash			300,000
	To record purchase of 40 percent of CheckTec's common stock			
Dec. 31	Investment in CheckTec Common Stock		20,000	
	Investment Revenue			20,000
	To record proportionate interest in CheckTec's earnings ($50,000 × 40%)			
Dec. 31	Cash		10,000	
	Investment in CheckTec Common Stock			10,000
	To record cash dividend received from CheckTec			

Notice that BancTec debited Investment in CheckTec Common Stock for 40 percent of CheckTec's reported earnings and then credited the investment account for the cash dividend received from CheckTec. The year-end balance of the investment account was $310,000 (300,000 + 20,000 − 10,000). That figure was the amount reported on BancTec's balance sheet for this asset. Again, because it is assumed that influential but noncontrolling investments will be held indefinitely, any unrealized gains and losses on these investments are not included in the investor's financial statements or disclosed in the investor's financial statement footnotes. If these investments are sold, the realized gain or loss is the difference between the investment's book value and the cash received from the sale.

LEARNING OBJECTIVE 4

Describe the nature and purpose of consolidated financial statements for controlling investments in equity securities

parent company
subsidiary

CONTROLLING INVESTMENTS   As indicated earlier, a controlling investment exists when one company owns more than 50 percent of another company's common stock. Here, the investor corporation is referred to as the **parent company,** while the investee company is the **subsidiary.** Large corporations typically have numerous subsidiaries, most of which are 100 percent or "wholly owned." When a parent company owns between 50 and 100 percent of a subsidiary's common stock, the subsidiary is referred to as "majority owned."

Hughes Supply, Inc., a distributor of construction supplies, has five wholly owned subsidiaries: Mills & Lupton Supply Company, One Stop Supply, Inc., Paine Supply Company, Pump & Lighting Company, and USCO, Inc. Legally, each of these subsidiaries is a corporate entity distinct from the parent company and has its own corporate charter, board of directors, and accounting records. However, the executives of Hughes Supply can dictate the operating policies of these companies. As a result, the accounting profession views Hughes Supply and its five subsidiaries as one economic entity. For financial reporting purposes, a parent company and its subsidiaries must combine their financial statements into a set of **consolidated financial statements.** To illustrate the nature and preparation of consolidated financial statements, let us focus on the balance sheet. Procedures similar to those discussed here are used to prepare other consolidated financial statements such as a consolidated income statement.

Discussion Question
Ask students for examples of parent/subsidiary companies.
Answer: Philip Morris/Kraft General Foods, Quaker Oats/Pet Foods, and Ford Motor/Jaguar.

consolidated financial statements

PREPARING CONSOLIDATED FINANCIAL STATEMENTS   Assume that on December 30, 1995, Pecos Corporation purchased all of Sunset Corporation's common stock at a cost of $66,000, which was exactly equal to the book value of Sunset's stockholders' equity. The purchase of Sunset's common stock was recorded with the following entry in Pecos' accounting records.[1]

Dec. 30	Investment in Sunset Corporation	66,000	
	Cash		66,000
	To record the purchase of all the common stock of Sunset Corporation		

This transaction did not require an entry in Sunset's accounting records since it only involved a change in that company's stockholders.

Immediately after Pecos purchased Sunset, it extended the wholly owned subsidiary a $50,000 loan. To record this transaction, an entry was made in the accounting records of both Pecos and Sunset. Following are these two entries. The first of these entries was made in Pecos' books, while the second was made in Sunset's books.

Dec. 30	Note Receivable from Sunset Corporation	50,000	
	Cash		50,000
	To record loan made to Sunset Corporation		
Dec. 30	Cash	50,000	
	Note Payable to Pecos Corporation		50,000
	To record loan received from Pecos Corporation		

---

1. Two basic methods can be used to account for "business combinations"—the purchase method and the pooling of interests method. The purchase method is by far the most commonly used of the two methods and is assumed to have been used by Pecos Corporation. Advanced accounting texts provide detailed explanations of both approaches to accounting for business combinations.

■ EXHIBIT 14.3

Balance Sheets for Pecos Corporation and Sunset Corporation as of December 31, 1995

Assets	PECOS CORPORATION	SUNSET CORPORATION
Cash	$ 10,000	$ 55,000
Accounts Receivable	72,000	16,000
Note Receivable from Sunset Corporation	50,000	—
Inventory	46,000	26,000
Property, Plant & Equipment (net)	224,000	39,000
Investment in Sunset Corporation	66,000	—
Total Assets	$468,000	$136,000
Liabilities and Stockholders' Equity		
Accounts Payable	$ 18,000	$ 20,000
Note Payable to Pecos Corporation	—	50,000
Bonds Payable	100,000	—
Common Stock	10,000	6,000
Retained Earnings	340,000	60,000
Total Liabilities and Stockholders' Equity	$468,000	$136,000

intercompany transactions

Transactions between a parent company and a subsidiary, between two or more subsidiaries, or between other operating units of a company are known as **intercompany transactions.** The note receivable and note payable accounts shown in the previous entries are referred to as intercompany accounts.

Shown in Exhibit 14.3 are separate balance sheets as of December 31, 1995, for Pecos Corporation and Sunset Corporation. If Pecos wants to distribute financial statements to external decision makers as of December 31, 1995, it must consolidate its separate financial statements with those of Sunset. Why? Because, again, for financial reporting purposes the two companies are considered one economic entity.

The most direct approach to preparing a consolidated balance sheet for Pecos and Sunset would be to add the assets, liabilities, and stockholders' equity of the two corporations shown in Exhibit 14.3. However, if the two separate balance sheets are simply added, certain items will be counted twice. For example, consider the $50,000 loan from Pecos to Sunset. If we treat Pecos and Sunset as one entity, that loan does not exist. The loan from Pecos to Sunset is comparable to an individual loaning $20 to himself by transferring that amount from one pocket to another. When consolidated financial statements are prepared, intercompany account balances must be eliminated to avoid double-counting those items.

The balance of the Investment in Sunset Corporation account on Pecos' books and Sunset's stockholders' equity must also be eliminated when a consolidated balance sheet is prepared for these entities. The $66,000 balance of the investment account represents Pecos' ownership of Sunset's net assets of $66,000 ($136,000 of assets less $70,000 of liabilities). If the balance of Pecos' investment account in Sunset is included in the consolidated balance sheet along with Sunset's individual assets, those assets would be counted twice. Similarly, Sunset's $66,000 of stockholders' equity should be eliminated in a consolidated balance sheet. Why? Because the ownership interest of Pecos' stockholders in Sunset is already reflected in the common stockholders' equi-

Focus on Ethics
The requirement to eliminate intercompany transactions when preparing consolidated financial statements helps minimize the risk that such transactions will be used to artificially inflate a consolidated entity's earnings.

■ **EXHIBIT 14.4**

Consolidated Work Sheet for Pecos Corporation and Sunset Corporation as of December 31, 1995

Assets	PECOS CORPORATION	SUNSET CORPORATION	ELIMINATIONS Debit	ELIMINATIONS Credit	CONSOLIDATED AMOUNTS
Cash	$ 10,000	$ 55,000			$ 65,000
Accounts Receivable	72,000	16,000			88,000
Note Receivable from Sunset Corporation	50,000	—		(a) 50,000	—
Inventory	46,000	26,000			72,000
Property, Plant & Equipment (net)	224,000	39,000			263,000
Investment in Sunset Corporation	66,000	—		(b) 66,000	—
Total Assets	$468,000	$136,000			$488,000
Liabilities and Stockholders' Equity					
Accounts Payable	$ 18,000	$ 20,000			38,000
Note Payable to Pecos Corporation	—	50,000	(a) 50,000		—
Bonds Payable	100,000	—			100,000
Common Stock	10,000	6,000	(b) 6,000		10,000
Retained Earnings	340,000	60,000	(b) 60,000		340,000
Total Liabilities and Stockholders' Equity	$468,000	$136,000	$116,000	$116,000	$488,000

ty of Pecos. Recall that the Pecos stockholders collectively paid $66,000 to acquire all of Sunset's common stock.

To minimize the risk that double-counting will occur when consolidated financial statements are prepared, a consolidation work sheet is used such as the one shown in Exhibit 14.4. A consolidation work sheet allows accountants to merge the accounting data of two or more entities *without making actual entries in the entities' accounting records.*

Notice in Exhibit 14.4 that only two elimination entries are needed to consolidate the accounting data of Pecos and Sunset. The first elimination entry cancels the note receivable balance on Pecos' books and the note payable balance on Sunset's books that resulted from the $50,000 intercompany loan. The second elimination entry "wipes out" the investment account on Pecos' books and Sunset's stockholders' equity. After these two entries are recorded on the consolidation work sheet, the work sheet is crossfooted to arrive at the consolidated amounts shown in the final column. The amounts in this column can then be arranged into a balance sheet format for the consolidated Pecos-Sunset entity as shown in Exhibit 14.5. Again, elimination entries are not recorded in the accounting records of either a parent or a subsidiary. Elimination entries appear only on a consolidated work sheet.

CONSOLIDATED FINANCIAL STATEMENTS: OTHER ISSUES   Suppose that Pecos Corporation acquired 80 percent, instead of 100 percent, of Sunset Corporation's common stock. In this case, Sunset would be a majority owned subsidiary of Pecos. Stockholders other than Pecos Corporation would control the remaining 20 percent of Sunset's stockholders' equity. **Minority interest** is the term used when referring to the stockholders' equity of a subsidiary that is not controlled by the parent company. In a consolidated balance sheet, minority interest is usually included between long-term liabilities and stockholders' equity.

Teaching Note
Emphasize that consolidation is simply the process of combining the financial statements of a parent company and its subsidiaries after eliminating the effects of all intercompany transactions.

minority interest

■ **EXHIBIT 14.5**

Consolidated Balance Sheet for Pecos Corporation and Sunset Corporation as of December 31, 1995

Cash	$ 65,000
Accounts Receivable	88,000
Inventory	72,000
Property, Plant & Equipment (net)	263,000
Total Assets	$488,000
Accounts Payable	38,000
Bonds Payable	100,000
Common Stock	10,000
Retained Earnings	340,000
Total Liabilities and Stockholders' Equity	$488,000

Corporations sometimes pay more for a controlling interest in another company than justified by the fair value of that company's net assets (assets less liabilities). This purchase premium may be due to any number of factors. One such factor is a perceived need by the acquiring company to close the deal quickly or risk becoming involved in a bidding war with other companies also interested in the firm being acquired.

Real World
In 1993, Hershey Foods Corporation reported goodwill of $473,408,000 on its balance sheet. Hershey amortizes goodwill on a straight-line basis over 40 years.

Suppose in the original Pecos-Sunset illustration that the fair value of Sunset's net assets was $66,000, an amount exactly equal to the company's stockholders' equity. Also assume that Pecos paid $75,000, instead of $66,000, to acquire Sunset's common stock. This $9,000 difference is referred to as "goodwill" by accountants. When resulting from the purchase of a wholly owned subsidiary, goodwill represents the amount in excess of the fair value of the subsidiary's net assets that a parent company paid to acquire the subsidiary. (Recall that in Chapter 9 goodwill was more generally defined as the excess of the cost of a group of assets over their collective market value.) Although accountants prefer the term "goodwill," a more descriptive label is usually assigned to this asset for financial reporting purposes. For example, BancTec's balance sheet caption for goodwill is "Excess of Cost Over Net Assets of Acquired Business." The 1994 edition of *Accounting Trends & Techniques* disclosed that nearly 65 percent of public companies report goodwill in their consolidated balance sheets.

Intercorporate Investments: Other Issues

Exhibit 14.6 presents summary information for the five major types of intercorporate investments. Notice that the last column of Exhibit 14.6 identifies a key accounting procedure for each type of investment. Before closing the books on intercorporate investments, let us consider two final and important issues related to these assets. First, corporations that have investments in other companies must adopt policies and procedures to maintain effective control over these investments. Second, intercorporate investments complicate the efforts of decision makers to analyze a company's financial statement data.

■ LEARNING OBJECTIVE 5
Identify important internal control issues related to intercorporate investments

INTERNAL CONTROL AND INTERCORPORATE INVESTMENTS   The extent and nature of internal controls exercised by an entity over intercorporate investments vary depending upon the size and type of those investments. For exam-

■ **EXHIBIT 14.6**

Accounting Methods for Intercorporate Investments

TYPE OF INVESTMENT	TYPE OF SECURITIES	ACCOUNTING METHOD	KEY ACCOUNTING RULE
Trading Securities	Debt and Equity	Fair Value	Unrealized Gains and Losses Reported in Income Statement
Available-for-Sale Securities	Debt and Equity	Fair Value	Unrealized Gains and Losses Reported as Component of Stockholders' Equity
Held-to-Maturity Securities	Debt	Amortized Cost	Interest Revenue Equals Interest Payments Received Plus or Minus the Periodic Amortization of Discount or Premium
Influential but Noncontrolling Investments	Equity	Equity Method	Book Value of Investment Increased (Decreased) for Investor's Proportionate Interest in Investee's Earnings (Losses) and Decreased by Dividends Received from Investee
Controlling Investments	Equity	Consolidated Financial Statements	All Intercompany Items Eliminated in Consolidated Financial Statements

ple, internal control issues are much more critical when a company purchases a controlling interest in a firm than when it purchases one hundred shares of another company's common stock.

When a controlling interest in another firm is acquired, the investor corporation should perform a comprehensive review of the subsidiary's internal control structure. This review should include such issues as whether key accounting and control responsibilities are properly segregated and whether access to assets is limited to authorized personnel. Based upon this review, the parent company will make any necessary changes in the subsidiary's internal control structure.

A common internal control procedure related to controlling investments is periodic compliance audits of a subsidiary by the parent company's internal auditors. The purpose of these audits is to ensure that the subsidiary's personnel are not violating internal control policies and procedures or other administrative rules and guidelines. An important internal control for all intercorporate investments is providing adequate physical security for bond and stock certificates. Most large corporations retain an external firm to serve as the custodian for bond and stock certificates. If investment certificates are maintained by company personnel, those individuals should be bonded to protect the company from losses due to theft. These certificates should also be counted periodically by internal auditors. Companies that have numerous intercorporate investments typically establish an investment ledger comparable to an accounts receivable ledger to enhance their control over these assets.

Real World

When a corporation uses an outside custodian to maintain its stock and bond investment certificates, the corporation's independent auditors may periodically take a "surprise" inventory of those certificates.

THE WALL STREET JOURNAL.

Millions of investors rely on *The Wall Street Journal* for price quotations for corporate securities, investment advice, and general news stories involving U. S. and international businesses.

■ **LEARNING OBJECTIVE 6**

Discuss how intercorporate investments affect decision makers' analyses of financial statement data

Real World

The 1994 edition of *Accounting Trends & Techniques* reported that 354 companies out of the 600 companies surveyed had operations in more than one industry.

FINANCIAL STATEMENT ANALYSIS AND INTERCORPORATE INVESTMENTS   Although there are exceptions, intercorporate investments other than controlling investments typically do not represent a large percentage of the total assets of individual corporations. As a result, such investments are generally not a critical consideration when analyzing the financial status of corporations. On the other hand, controlling investments tend to be much larger and thus should be carefully considered by decision makers when performing financial statement analysis.

The rapid pace of business combinations in recent years has created hundreds of large companies that have multiple lines of business. The financial statements of such companies, often referred to as conglomerates, are more difficult to analyze than the financial statements of companies that operate only one line of business. For example, suppose a furniture manufacturer acquires a chain of retail toy stores. When analyzing this entity's consolidated financial data, it would be inappropriate to focus strictly on financial ratios of either the furniture industry or the retail toy industry. Instead, decision makers would have to analyze the two segments of the company independently.

To assist decision makers in interpreting the financial data of conglomerates, the FASB in 1976 issued *Statement of Financial Accounting Standards No. 14*, "Financial Reporting for Segments of a Business Enterprise." This accounting standard requires companies with multiple business segments to disclose in their financial statement footnotes key financial data for each segment. These data allow decision makers to analyze the financial status of a company's major segments and thus reach a more reliable conclusion about the company's financial condition and future prospects.

An example of a company with multiple business segments is Stewart & Stevenson Services, Inc. Shown in Exhibit 14.7 are the descriptions of the company's three business segments included in its annual report for the fiscal year ending January 31, 1994. For each of these segments, Stewart & Stevenson disclosed sales, profit, total assets, and other key financial data in a financial statement footnote.

■ **EXHIBIT 14.7**

Description of Business Segments of Stewart & Stevenson Services, Inc.

Engineered Power Systems Segment: Includes the designing, packaging, and manufacturing and marketing of diesel and gas turbine engine-driven equipment.

Distribution Segment: Includes the marketing of diesel engines, automatic transmissions, material handling equipment, transport refrigeration units and construction equipment and the provision of related parts and service.

Tactical Vehicle Systems: Includes the designing, manufacturing and marketing of tactical vehicles, primarily 2 1/2-ton and 5-ton trucks under contract with the United States Army.

ACCOUNTING FOR INTERNATIONAL OPERATIONS

Every year, a larger share of the revenues and profits of United States companies is derived from foreign operations. As shown by Exhibit 14.8, many of this nation's largest companies already sell more goods and services abroad than they do in the United States. This trend "cuts" both ways. Honda, BASF, Sony, Michelin, Unilever, and Daimler Benz are just a few examples of foreign corporations that have strong and growing annual sales in this country. The trend toward a global economy is also confirmed by the size of equity investments each year by individuals and companies who see profit opportunities in foreign stocks. One recent study estimated that nearly $2 trillion of investment capital crosses international boundaries each year.[2]

The trend toward a global economy poses significant challenges and problems for the accounting profession. The most pressing problem this trend exposes is the lack of uniform international accounting standards. Investors, creditors, and even skilled accountants often have difficulty interpreting accounting data from certain countries. Take the case of Germany. One partner of the British affiliate of Deloitte & Touche, a large international accounting firm, observed that a German financial statement is equivalent to a "crossword puzzle where you're not given all the clues."[3] Even countries with similar economic and political systems, such as the United States and the United Kingdom, often account for identical transactions quite differently. A perfect

■ **LEARNING OBJECTIVE 7**
Discuss the key issues related to accounting for international operations, including accounting for realized and unrealized gains and losses resulting from changes in foreign currency exchange rates

Teaching Note
Point out that many industrialized countries, but not the U.S., allow companies to periodically "revalue" their long-term assets.

■ **EXHIBIT 14.8**
Ten Largest U.S. Multinational Firms

SOURCE: "Ten Largest U.S. Multinational Firms," Forbes, July 18, 1994. Reprinted by permission of FORBES Magazine © Forbes Inc., 1994.

	Foreign Sales*	As % of Total Sales
Exxon	$75.4	77.3%
General Motors	38.6	28.0
Mobil	38.5	67.5
IBM	37.0	59.0
Ford Motor	32.9	30.3
Texaco	24.2	53.5
Citicorp	20.7	64.5
duPont	16.8	51.4
Chevron	16.6	41.1
Procter & Gamble	15.9	52.1
	*In billions	

2. N. Anderson, "The Globalization GAAP," *Management Accounting*, August 1993, 52.
3. Hagerty, B., "Differing Accounting Rules Snarl Europe," *The Wall Street Journal*, September 4, 1992, p. A4A. Reprinted by permission of *The Wall Street Journal*, © 1992 Dow Jones & Company, Inc. All Rights Reserved Worldwide.

example is inventory accounting. In the United States, the LIFO inventory costing method is widely used. In the United Kingdom, LIFO is seldom used; most companies opt instead for the FIFO method.

Some progress has been made in recent years in establishing a uniform set of international accounting concepts, guidelines, and procedures. The organization leading the way in this effort is the London-based International Accounting Standards Committee (IASC). Established in the early 1970s, by 1995 the IASC had issued more than thirty accounting standards on such topics as accounting for income taxes, leases, depreciation, and business combinations. However, the IASC does not have the authority to require international companies to apply its accounting standards. As a result, the IASC's technical pronouncements have not been widely adopted. In the United States, the IASC's standards are not considered generally accepted accounting principles, nor does the SEC accept financial statements prepared according to the IASC's rules.

On a more technical level, accountants of firms with international operations must wrestle with such problems as having business transactions denominated in more than one currency. For example, consider the challenge faced by the accountants of a U.S. company that has foreign subsidiaries in several countries. This company must file consolidated financial statements with the SEC that are denominated in U.S. dollars. The company's accountants may be required to translate into U.S. dollars the assets and liabilities of subsidiaries expressed in Italian lira, Pakistani rupees, and Malaysian ringgits. In the remainder of this section, we focus on the accounting problems that multinational companies face and review disclosure requirements for these firms.

Realized Gains and Losses on Currency Exchange

Teaching Note
Emphasize that transactions between a U.S. company and a foreign company often involve an additional component not found in transactions between two U.S. companies, namely the exchange of one currency for another currency.

When U.S. firms transact business in foreign countries, they can either insist on their transactions being denominated in U.S.. dollars or can do business in the currency of the host country. The latter choice is typically a wise decision. Imagine a German company that opens a subsidiary in Ames, Iowa, or Tempe, Arizona, and insists that its customers pay their bills in deutsche marks. That company will likely have some difficulty keeping its doors open. In other words, when in Rome . . .

A U.S. company that transacts business in a foreign currency must convert those transactions into U.S. dollar equivalents for accounting purposes. For example, assume that on June 1 of a given year, a U.S. company sells goods on credit to a French firm for Fr 20,000 (Fr = francs). The payment date for these goods is June 30. To convert this transaction into a U.S. dollar equivalent, we must know the "exchange rate" for U.S. dollars and French francs on the transaction date. An **exchange rate**
exchange rate is the value of one currency expressed in terms of another. Assume that on June 1 the exchange rate for converting francs into dollars is $.25 per franc. That is, a franc brought into the U.S. by a French tourist on that date could be exchanged for $.25. Alternatively, a U.S. dollar could be exchanged for four francs on that date. Given this exchange rate, the U.S. dollar equivalent of the sales transaction involving the Fr 20,000 would be $5,000 (Fr 20,000 × $.25). This transaction would be recorded as follows in the U.S. firm's accounting records.

Jun. 1	Accounts Receivable	5,000	
	Sales		5,000

To record sale of goods to D'Boughre Farms (Fr 20,000 × $.25)

Changes in exchange rates can have significant implications for a nation's economy. In the early 1990s, the value of the Japanese yen rose compared to most other currencies. The higher value of the yen impaired the ability of Japanese firms to export their goods to other countries.

When the U.S. company receives payment on June 30, the Fr 20,000 received will be converted into U.S. dollars *at the exchange rate existing on that date*. Suppose that by June 30 the exchange rate has dropped from $.25 per franc to $.20 per franc. Consequently, the Fr 20,000 received from the French customer can be exchanged for only $4,000 (Fr 20,000 × $.20). The U.S. firm has suffered a foreign currency transaction loss of $1,000 because of the change in the dollar-franc exchange rate. A **foreign currency transaction gain or loss** results from a change in the exchange rate for a credit transaction denominated in a foreign currency before the transaction is completed by the payment or receipt of cash. Shown next is the entry made in the U.S. company's accounting records to record the payment received from the French customer and the resulting foreign currency transaction loss.

foreign currency transaction gain or loss

Jun. 30	Cash	4,000	
	Foreign Currency Transaction Loss	1,000	
	Accounts Receivable		5,000
	To record payment received from D'Boughre Farms ($.20 × Fr 20,000)		

Recognize that the change in the exchange rate would have no impact on the recording of this transaction by the French firm that purchased the goods. On June 1, an accountant of that firm would debit Purchases and credit Accounts Payable, each for Fr 20,000. On June 30, Accounts Payable would be debited and Cash credited for Fr 20,000.

U.S. firms can also realize foreign currency transaction gains and losses on purchase transactions. For example, assume that on June 16 the U.S. company in the previous illustration purchases goods on credit from a British firm. The quoted purchase price in British pounds is £3,000 and the exchange rate on the date of purchase is

$1.60 per British pound. Given this exchange rate, the U.S. dollar equivalent for this transaction is $4,800 ($1.60 × £3,000) resulting in the following entry in the U.S. firm's accounting records.

| Jun. 16 | Purchases | 4,800 | |
| | Accounts Payable | | 4,800 |

To record purchase of inventory from
Thames plc (£3,000 × $1.60)

Suppose that the payment date for this transaction is July 16 and that the exchange rate for the U.S. dollar and British pound has dropped to $1.50 per pound on that date. To pay the debt owed to the British supplier, the U.S. firm must first purchase the required £3,000. Given the change in the exchange rate, only $4,500 will be required to purchase the £3,000 ($1.50 × £3,000) on July 16. As a result, the U.S. firm will realize a $300 foreign currency transaction gain on the payment of this debt, as shown in the following entry.

Jul. 16	Accounts Payable	4,800	
	Cash		4,500
	Foreign Currency Transaction Gain		300

To record payment for June 16
purchase from Thames plc
($1.50 × £3,000)

Unrealized Gains and Losses on Currency Exchange

The foreign currency transaction gain and loss in the two previous illustrations were realized when cash exchanged hands between the U.S. company and its foreign customer or supplier. U.S. companies that engage in international commerce also have "unrealized" foreign currency transaction gains and losses. These unrealized gains and losses result from credit transactions denominated in foreign currencies that have not been completed by an entity's fiscal year-end. That is, cash has not changed hands between the parties to the transactions by year-end. Unrealized gains and losses are recorded via adjusting entries. For financial reporting purposes, a multinational company "nets" its realized and unrealized foreign currency transaction gains and losses into one amount. Consequently, all foreign currency transaction gains and losses can be recorded in the same account. The net foreign currency transaction gain or loss in an accounting period is typically reported in the income statement under the heading Other Revenues and Expenses.

To illustrate an unrealized foreign currency gain, assume that a U.S. company purchases goods from a Japanese supplier, Katsura Corporation, on December 11 of a given year. In Japanese yen, the selling price of these goods is ¥132,000. Since the exchange rate for the U.S. dollar and Japanese yen on this date is $.011 per yen, the U.S. dollar equivalent of this purchase transaction is $1,452 ($.011 × ¥132,000). The U.S. company would record this purchase as shown in the following entry.

| Dec. 11 | Purchases | 1,452 | |
| | Accounts Payable | | 1,452 |

To record purchase of inventory from
Katsura Corporation ($.011 × ¥132,000)

International Ethics and Internal Controls

Cultural differences in the definition of acceptable or ethical behavior are key stumbling blocks that must be overcome when developing internal control policies and procedures for a multinational firm. Consider the results of a recent study published in a leading academic journal of the accounting profession. This study attempted to determine whether there are cross-cultural differences in the likelihood that material accounting errors will be reported by key management personnel. The study focused on business managers from France, Norway, and the United States. The results of the study suggest that U.S. managers are more likely to report material accounting errors than their French and Norwegian counterparts. In summarizing the results of their study, the authors had the following to say.

> This study supports [earlier] claims that national culture dominates organizational culture in matters involving value judgments. This result suggests that multinational companies wishing to achieve similar levels of reliability across divisions located in different countries need to implement different control systems.

SOURCE: J. J. Schultz, D. A. Johnson, D. Morris, and S. Dyrnes, "An Investigation of the Reporting of Questionable Acts in an International Setting," *Journal of Accounting Research* 31 (Supplement 1993): 75–102.

Now, assume that on December 31, the dollar-yen exchange rate is $.01 per yen. Given this exchange rate, the liability to Katsura Corporation, expressed in U.S. dollars, is only $1,320 ($.01 × ¥132,000). The U.S. firm will record the following year-end adjusting entry to recognize the unrealized gain of $132 on the payable to Katsura Corporation ($1,452 − $1,320) and to reduce the book value of that payable to $1,320.

Dec. 31	Accounts Payable	132	
	Foreign Currency Transaction Gain		132
	To record unrealized foreign currency gain on account payable to Katsura Corporation		

Consolidation of Foreign Subsidiaries

The executives of many U.S. companies believe that the best strategy for quickly establishing a strong economic presence in a foreign country is to set up a subsidiary in that country. This strategy generally provides greater access to a foreign country's economic markets and often results in considerable tax advantages as well. In nearly all cases, a foreign subsidiary's financial statements must be consolidated with those of the U.S. parent company. Since the subsidiary's financial data will be denominated in another currency, that data must be translated into U.S. dollars before consolidated financial statements can be prepared. Illustrating the conversion of a foreign subsidiary's financial statements into U.S. dollars is deferred for advanced accounting courses.

Real World
The 1994 edition of *Accounting Trends & Techniques* reported that approximately 42% of the companies surveyed had foreign operations.

Financial Disclosures for International Operations

Statement of Financial Accounting Standards No. 14, "Financial Reporting for Segments of a Business Enterprise," requires many U.S.-based multinational companies to disclose financial data for their foreign operations. These disclosures provide decision makers with a better understanding of the nature and scope of a multinational company's operations and the business risks it faces. Generally, U.S. multinational companies must include disclosures regarding their foreign operations in their financial statement footnotes if at least one of two conditions is met:

1. The revenue generated by their foreign operations accounts for at least 10 percent of their consolidated revenues; or
2. The "identifiable" assets of their foreign operations account for at least 10 percent of the assets reported on their consolidated balance sheet.

An example of a U.S. company that has significant foreign operations is Integrated Device Technology, Inc. (IDT), which designs, manufactures, and markets high-performance integrated circuits. In a footnote to its 1994 financial statements, IDT disclosed financial data for each geographic region in which it operates, including sales, net revenue, operating income, and identifiable assets. For example, IDT provided the following breakdown of its total sales by geographic region (000s omitted).

United States	$223,600
Japan	29,959
Europe	60,064
Asia-Pacific	16,839
Total	$330,462

SUMMARY

Corporations purchase debt and equity securities of other companies for a variety of reasons. Among these reasons are generating trading profits on short-term fluctuations in the market prices of securities and obtaining a sufficiently large ownership interest in another company to control its operations. Decision makers should be informed of the general nature and purpose of intercorporate investments since this information may provide important insight on an entity's future plans. Other key items of information needed by decision makers regarding a firm's intercorporate investments include market value disclosures and investment-related revenues and expenses.

There are five major types of intercorporate investments: trading securities, available-for-sale securities, held-to-maturity securities, influential but noncontrolling investments, and controlling investments. Trading securities and available-for-sale securities can be either debt or equity securities. For balance sheet purposes, these two classes of intercorporate investments are reported at their fair values. Unrealized gains and losses on trading securities are reported in an entity's income statement, while unrealized gains and losses on available-for-sale securities are a component of stockholders' equity. The amortized cost method is used to account for held-to-maturity securities, which include only investments in debt securities. Under the amortized cost method, debt securities are reported on a balance sheet at their original cost adjusted for any amortized premium or discount.

The equity method must be used to account for influential but noncontrolling investments in equity securities. An influential but noncontrolling investment generally exists when a corporation owns 20 to 50 percent of another firm's common stock. Under the equity method, an intercorporate investment is reported in the investor corporation's balance sheet at adjusted historical cost. The original cost of the investment is increased (decreased) by the investor's proportionate interest in the investee's earnings (losses). Dividends paid to the investor by the investee reduce the investment's book value. When one company owns more than 50 percent of the common stock of another company, these firms must prepare consolidated financial statements each reporting period. A consolidation work sheet is used to merge the accounting data of a parent company and its subsidiaries.

Recent decades have witnessed a significant trend toward international business operations. A major problem faced by multinational companies is the lack of uniform accounting standards. Accountants for multinational companies must also cope with transactions denominated in different currencies and constantly changing foreign currency exchange rates. A U.S. multinational company includes in its income statement realized and unrealized gains and losses due to the conversion, or anticipated conversion, of funds from one currency to another. U.S. multinational companies must also prepare consolidated financial statements with foreign subsidiaries. Finally, U.S. companies that have significant foreign operations must include in their financial statement footnotes key financial data for each major geographical area in which they operate.

GLOSSARY

Amortized cost method (p. 617)   A method of accounting for investments in held-to-maturity securities under which any premium or discount on the purchase of these securities is amortized over their remaining term when they are purchased.

Available-for-sale securities (p. 613)   Investments in debt or equity securities that do not qualify as one of the other types of investments in these securities.

Consolidated financial statements (p. 621)   The combined financial statements of a parent company and its subsidiaries.

Controlling investments (p. 613)   Investments in equity securities in which the parent company owns more than 50 percent of the common stock of the subsidiary.

Equity method (p. 620)   The accounting method used for influential but noncontrolling investments; the investor's proportionate interest in the investee's periodic earnings (losses) is treated as an addition (reduction) to the book value of the investment, while dividends received from the investee reduce the book value of the investment.

Exchange rate (p. 628)   The value of one currency expressed in terms of another.

Fair value (p. 613)   Generally, the closing price of a debt or equity security on a given date on a securities exchange.

Foreign currency transaction gain or loss (p. 629)   A gain or loss resulting from a change in the exchange rate for a credit transaction denominated in a foreign currency before the transaction is completed by the payment or receipt of cash.

Held-to-maturity securities (p. 613)   Investments in debt securities acquired with the positive intent and ability to hold them to maturity.

Influential but noncontrolling investments (p. 613)   Investments in equity securities in which the investor corporation generally owns at least 20 percent but not more than 50 percent of the investee corporation's common stock.

Intercompany transactions (p. 622)   Transactions between a parent company and a subsidiary, between two or more subsidiaries, or between other operating units of a company.

Minority interest (p. 623)   The stockholders' equity of a subsidiary that is not controlled by the parent company.

Parent company (p. 620)   A company that owns more than 50 percent of another company's common stock.

Subsidiary (p. 620)   A company that has more than 50 percent of its common stock owned by another company.

Trading securities (p. 613)   Investments in debt and equity securities acquired principally for the purpose of selling them in the near term and thereby generating profits on short-run fluctuations in market prices.

DECISION CASE

Isis Pharmaceuticals, Inc., is a California-based company that develops and markets pharmaceuticals. In March 1995, Isis announced that a German pharmaceutical firm, Boehringer Ingelheim International (BII), had purchased nearly 2 million shares of its common stock. Isis also announced that BII might increase its ownership interest to as much as 15 percent in the future. BII provided Isis with a $40 million line of credit and agreed to work with the company to develop a new line of anti-inflammatory drugs. Approximately 6 percent of Isis's common stock was already owned by the large Swiss pharmaceutical company, Ciba-Geigy Ltd.

Suppose that you are the chief executive of Vitale, Inc., a pharmaceutical company that finds itself in the same circumstances as Isis. Two foreign competitors are your firm's largest stockholders. Together, these competitors own approximately 20 percent of Vitale's outstanding common stock and have been gradually increasing their ownership interests. Each firm has provided your company with substantial loans at interest rates well below existing market interest rates at the time the loans were made. In recent months, you have become concerned because the two companies have been working together to exert increasing influence on your company's operations. For example, executives of the firms have suggested that two of Vitale's laboratories should be moved overseas. The executives maintain that such a move would both reduce labor costs and minimize the "interference" of the FDA (Food and Drug Administration) in Vitale's operations.

In a recent conference call, the chief executives of these firms voiced displeasure with certain financial reporting requirements of the SEC. They pointed out that their countries' comparable regulatory agencies do not require the extensive financial disclosures mandated by the SEC. At one point, one of the executives suggested that certain disclosures required by the SEC would be useful to competitors and thus should not be made. The executive then explained that he was familiar with the SEC's rules and believed that the disclosures could be avoided because of loopholes in those rules.

Required: Analyze your present situation as the chief executive officer of Vitale. How may the future operations of your firm be influenced by its two largest stockholders? What actions on your part, if any, do you believe are appropriate at this point and why?

The one executive is correct in that the SEC has more extensive disclosure requirements than comparable regulatory agencies in other countries. Would it be appropriate for you to accept the executive's suggestion and avoid making certain financial disclosures because of a loophole in the SEC's rules? What factors should you consider in making this decision? Ignoring existing rules and regulations, do you believe public companies should disclose in their financial statements the identities of stockholders that control large blocks of their common stock? Explain.

QUESTIONS

1. The initials "LBO" describe what kind of business acquisition? Briefly describe the nature of an LBO.

2. Identify common reasons that corporations invest in the stocks and bonds of other corporations.

3. When a company anticipates a future takeover, its executives may approve a lucrative termination package for themselves. What is such a package called?

4. What are the five major types of intercorporate investments? Identify one key characteristic of each.

5. In what sense are available-for-sale securities a "catchall" category for intercorporate investments?

6. How is the fair value of an investment in a debt or equity security usually determined for balance sheet purposes?

7. Where is an unrealized gain or loss on trading securities reported in a set of financial statements? Where is an unrealized gain or loss on available-for-sale securities reported in a set of financial statements?

8. What is the logic underlying the different financial statement treatments of unrealized gains and losses on trading securities and available-for-sale securities?

9. Why can only investments in debt securities be classified as held-to-maturity securities?

10. When a company purchases corporate bonds at a price different from the bonds' face value, how does the company determine the periodic interest revenue to be recognized on this investment?

11. When should the equity method be used by a company to account for an investment in the common stock of another company?

12. When should two or more companies prepare consolidated financial statements? What is the justification for preparing consolidated financial statements for two or more legally separate entities?

13. Define "minority interest." Where in a consolidated balance sheet is minority interest typically disclosed?

14. Distinguish between a "wholly owned" and "majority owned" subsidiary.

15. How does "goodwill" result from a business combination?

16. Why is a company concerned with the internal controls of its subsidiaries?

17. Why do controlling investments make financial statement analysis more complicated?

18. What is the IASC and what is its objective?

19. What is a foreign currency exchange rate? How are exchange rates used in accounting for multinational business transactions?

20. How do foreign currency transaction gains and losses arise? When are these gains and losses realized? When are they unrealized?

21. U.S. multinational companies must disclose information about their foreign operations if either of two conditions are met. What are these conditions?

EXERCISES

22. **Short-Term Investments** (LO 2)

Ellen and Jason McDougal own a retail business, Shoes 'n' Boots, Inc. This corporation has excess cash of S25,000 that presently is not needed in the day-to-day operations of the business. The McDougals would like to invest this cash. However, they do not want to "tie up" the cash for an extended period, since they have plans to open another retail store within the next twelve months.

Required:

1. Identify the investment alternatives that the McDougals should consider. Identify an advantage and disadvantage of each of these alternatives.

22. No check figures

2. Suppose that the McDougals invest the $25,000 in 500 shares of a corporate common stock. What type of intercorporate investment is this stock purchase? Why?

3. How will dividends received on this investment be reported in Shoes 'n' Boots' financial statements?

4. Suppose that by the next balance sheet date, the market value of the 500 shares of stock is $3,500 less than the amount paid for the stock. Will this "paper loss" be reported in Shoes 'n' Boots' financial statements? If so, how?

23. **Accounting for Stock and Bond Investments** (LO 2, 3)

On March 31, 1996, Alpha Company acquired 1,000 shares of Omicron Company common stock for $15 a share and 25 corporate bonds of Epsilon Company for their face value of $1,000 each. The bonds have a 6 percent stated interest rate, and the interest is paid semiannually on April 1 and October 1 of each year. Omicron Company pays a dividend of $1 per share on October 31 each year. Alpha's fiscal year ends on December 31.

Required:

1. How will Alpha likely classify these investments in its year-end balance sheet if it intends to hold the stock and bonds
   a. indefinitely?
   b. for three to six months (until their market prices increase significantly)?

2. Prepare the journal entries to record Alpha's two investments under both assumptions "a" and "b" in Part 1.

3. Assuming Alpha's two investments are considered trading securities, prepare the journal entries to record the dividends and interest revenue received by Alpha during 1996.

4. Suppose that Omicron common stock is trading for $14 per share on December 31, 1996, and the Epsilon bonds have a quoted market price of 97 on that date. Prepare any necessary adjusting journal entries in Alpha's accounting records on December 31, 1996, again assuming that both investments are classified as trading securities.

24. **Accounting for Available-for-Sale Securities** (LO 3)

On March 14, 1996, Zeile Company purchased for $14.25 per share 1,000 shares of The China Fund, a mutual fund listed on the New York Stock Exchange. Zeile received a cash dividend of $.64 per share from this mutual fund on September 28. On December 31, 1996, the China Fund was trading for $11.50 per share. Zeile accounts for the investment in The China Fund as an available-for-sale security.

Required:

1. Under what conditions do intercorporate investments qualify as available-for-sale securities?

2. Prepare all necessary journal entries in Zeile Company's accounting records during 1996 related to its investment in The China Fund.

25. **Balance Sheet Treatment of Investments** (LO 3)

Following is the stockholders' equity section that was included in the December 31, 1994, balance sheet of Orbital Sciences Corporation (OSC).

Common Stock	$ 202
Additional Paid-in Capital	201,328
Unrealized Losses on Marketable Securities	(462)
Retained Earnings	978
Total Stockholders' Equity	$202,046

Margin notes:

23.2a. Dr. Invest. in Omicron Common Stock, Avail.-for-Sale Sec. $15,000
Dr. Invest. in Epsilon Bonds, Held-to-Mat. Sec. $25,000

2b. Dr. Invest. in Omicron Common Stock, Trading Sec. $15,000
Dr. Invest. in Epsilon Bonds, Trading Sec. $25,000

3. 10/1/96 Cr. Interest Revenue $750
10/3/96 Cr. Dividend Revenue $1,000

4. Dr. Unrealized Loss on Trading Securities $1,750

24. 2. 3/14/96 Dr. Invest. in The China Fund, Avail.-for-Sale Sec. $14,250
9/28 Cr. Dividend Revenue $640
12/31 Dr. Unrealized Loss on Avail.-for-Sale Sec. $2,750

Required:

1. What type of intercorporate investments resulted in the unrealized loss being reported in the stockholders' equity section of OSC's balance sheet?
2. The marketable securities referred to in the stockholders' equity section of OSC's balance sheet were reported as current assets in that same balance sheet. Does this change your answer to Part 1? Why or why not?
3. What is the rationale for reporting unrealized gains and losses of this type in the stockholders' equity section of a company's balance sheet?

25. No check figures

26. **Accounting for Trading Securities** (LO 2)

During 1996, Ashley Fay Fashions had the following transactions involving intercorporate investments.

March 11:	Purchased 2,000 shares of Maxim Co. common stock for $21 per share
May 3:	Purchased 1,200 shares of El Cortez Co. common stock for $7 per share
June 1:	Received a $.44 per share cash dividend on its investment in Maxim Co.
October 7:	Sold 1,500 shares of Maxim Co. common stock for $18 per share
November 1:	Purchased 600 shares of Binion Co. common stock for $8 per share

Following are the December 31, 1996, stock prices of the companies in which Ashley Fay Fashions has an ownership interest:

Maxim Co. $17.25
El Cortez Co.   9.50
Binion Co.   6.75

Required:

1. Under what circumstances should intercorporate investments be classified as trading securities?
2. Suppose that each of the investments made by Ashley Fay Fashions during 1996 qualifies as a trading security. Prepare the appropriate journal entries to record the investment transactions of the company during 1996.
3. Ashley Fay Fashions' fiscal year ends on December 31. Prepare any necessary year-end adjusting entries for the company's trading securities.

26. 2. 3/11/96 Dr. Invest. in Maxim Common Stock, Trad. Sec. $42,000
6/1 Cr. Dividend Revenue $880
10/7 Dr. Loss on Sale of Trad. Sec. $4,500
12/31 Cr. Unrealized Gain on Trad. Sec. $375

27. **Accounting for Held-to-Maturity Securities** (LO 3)

On March 1, 1996, Emerson, Inc., purchased 60 Branson Corporation bonds. The bonds have a 10 percent stated interest rate, pay interest semiannually on March 1 and September 1, and mature on March 1, 2006. Emerson paid $65,000 for these bonds, $5,000 more than their collective face value, and plans to hold the bonds until they mature.

Required:

1. Prepare the journal entry in Emerson's accounting records to record the acquisition of these bonds.
2. Prepare the journal entry to record Emerson's receipt of interest from Branson Corporation on September 1, 1996. Emerson uses the straight-line method to amortize any discount or premium on bond investments.
3. Emerson's fiscal year ends on December 31. Prepare any necessary adjusting journal entry at year-end in Emerson's accounting records related to this bond investment.

27. 1. Dr. Invest. in Branson Bonds, Held-to Mat. Sec. $65,000
2. Cr. Invest. in Branson Bonds, Held-to-Mat. Sec. $250
Cr. Interest Revenues $2,750
3. Cr. Invest. in Branson Bonds, Held-to-Mat. Sec. $166.67
Cr. Interest Revenue $1,833.33

28. Classification of Investments (LO 3)

On January 1, 1995, Telle Corporation purchased 30 percent of Apple & Son, Inc., common stock for $500,000. Apple & Son reported net income of $100,000 in 1995 and paid a $60,000 cash dividend to its common stockholders on November 1, 1995.

Required:

1. What accounting method did Telle likely use to account for its investment in Apple & Son? Why is this accounting method appropriate for such investments?
2. Given the accounting method identified in Part 1, prepare the appropriate journal entries in Telle's accounting records during 1995 related to the company's investment in Apple & Son common stock.

28. 2. 1/1/95 Dr. Invest. in Apple & Son Common Stock $500,000
11/1 Cr. Invest. in Apple & Son Common Stock $18,000
12/31 Dr. Invest. in Apple & Son Common Stock $30,000

29. Equity Method of Accounting for Intercorporate Investments (LO 3)

Barkley Enterprises purchased 40 percent of the common stock of Majerle Company on January 1, 1993, paying $370,000. Barkley uses the equity method to account for this investment. Following is Majerle's net income for each year 1993 through 1996 and the total cash dividends paid by the company during each of those years.

	NET INCOME	CASH DIVIDENDS PAID
1993	$ 25,000	$20,000
1994	(90,000)	10,000
1995	100,000	50,000
1996	35,000	45,000

Required:

1. Determine the balance of the Investment in Majerle Common Stock account in Barkley Enterprises' accounting records at the end of each year 1993 through 1996.
2. Prepare the appropriate journal entry in Barkley's accounting records, assuming the Marjerle common stock is sold on January 1, 1997, for $395,000.
3. How, if at all, did the issuance of *SFAS No. 115*, "Accounting for Certain Investments in Debt and Equity Securities," affect Barkley's accounting for the investment in Majerle common stock?

29. 1. 1993, $372,000
1994, $332,000
1995, $352,000
1996, $348,000
2. Cr. Invest. in Majerle Common Stock $348,000
Cr. Gain on Sale of Stock $47,000

30. Consolidated Financial Statements (LO 4)

Following are the trial balances of Parent Company and Subsidiary Company following Parent's purchase of 100 percent of Subsidiary's common stock. Parent Company loaned $5,000 to Subsidiary Company immediately after the stock purchase was completed.

Assets	PARENT	SUBSIDIARY
Cash	$ 15,000	$ 10,000
Accounts Receivable (net)	25,000	22,500
Note Receivable From Subsidiary Co.	5,000	—
Inventory	17,500	12,750
Property, Plant & Equipment (net)	72,650	55,275
Investment in Subsidiary	66,075	—
Total Assets	$201,225	$100,525
Liabilities and Stockholders' Equity		
Accounts Payable	$17,400	$9,450
Note Payable to Parent	—	5,000

Bank Loans Payable	50,000	20,000
Common Stock	110,000	60,000
Retained Earnings	23,825	6,075
Total Liabilities and Stockholders' Equity	$201,225	$100,525

Required:

1. How much did Parent Company pay for the common stock of Subsidiary Company?
2. Will any goodwill result from this acquisition assuming that the fair value of Subsidiary's assets is equal to their book value? Why or why not?
3. Will there be any "minority interest" included in the consolidated financial statements of Parent and Subsidiary? Why or why not?
4. Using the work sheet format shown in Exhibit 14.4, prepare any eliminating entries needed to consolidate the two companies' balance sheets.
5. Prepare the consolidated balance sheet for Parent and Subsidiary.

31. **Accounting for Goodwill and Minority Interest** (LO 4)

El Palacio Restaurants purchased 80 percent of the common stock of a competing firm, Casa Sol Restaurants, on May 5. El Palacio paid $3,357,000 for Casa Sol's common stock. Immediately prior to El Palacio's investment in Casa Sol, the latter had net assets—total assets less total liabilities–of $4,030,000. The book value of these assets was approximately equal to their fair market value.

Required:

1. Will El Palacio record any goodwill as a result of its purchase of Casa Sol's common stock? If so, how much?
2. Suppose that a consolidated balance sheet is prepared for El Palacio and Casa Sol on May 5. How much minority interest will be reported in this balance sheet?

32. **Accounting for Foreign Currency Transactions** (LO 7)

On April 1, Le Plume Company in France sold 100,000 pounds of perfume to a U.S. company, Ou Pew Corporation. Ou Pew agreed to pay six francs for each pound of perfume. The credit terms for the transaction are n/30. The dollar-franc exchange rates on the relevant dates for this transaction are as follows:

April 1: $.20 per franc
May 1: $.22 per franc

Required:

1. Prepare the journal entry in Ou Pew's accounting records for the purchase of merchandise from Le Plume on April 1.
2. Prepare the journal entry in Ou Pew's accounting records for the payment made to Le Plume on May 1.
3. Prepare the appropriate journal entries in Le Plume's accounting records on April 1 and May 1. Record these entries in francs, not dollars.

33. **Accounting for Foreign Currency Transactions** (LO 7)

Takaguchi Company, a Japanese firm, sold 42,000 pounds of a metal alloy to Wolverine Metals, a U.S. firm, on December 4. The price per pound was 21 yen and the credit terms were n/60. Following are the dollar-yen exchange rates on the relevant dates for this transaction.

December 4: $.11
December 31: $.10
February 2: $.12

Margin answers:

30. 1. $66,075
   4. Eliminations, $71,075
   5. Total Assets, $230,675

31. 1. Goodwill, $133,000
   2. Minority Interest, $806,000

32. 1. Cr. Accounts Payable $120,000
   2. Dr. Accounts Payable $120,000
      Dr. Foreign Currency Transaction Loss $12,000
   3. Dr. Accounts Receivable 600,000 francs

33. 1. Cr. Accounts Payable
$97,020
2. Cr. Foreign Currency
Transaction Gain $8,820
3. Dr. Accounts Payable
$88,200
Dr. Foreign Currency
Transaction Loss $17,640

Required:
1. Prepare the journal entry in Wolverine Metals' accounting records for the purchase of the metal alloy from Takaguchi on December 4.
2. Wolverine's fiscal year ends on December 31. Prepare any necessary adjusting journal entry in Wolverine's accounting records related to the December 4 purchase transaction.
3. Prepare the journal entry in Wolverine's accounting records on February 2 to record the payment made to Takaguchi.

PROBLEM SET A

34. Accounting and Financial Reporting Decisions for Intercorporate Investments (LO 1, 3)

In January 1996, Tervino Corporation purchased 41 percent of the outstanding common stock of Azle Landers, Inc., at a total cost of $7.2 million. The chief executive officer (CEO) of Tervino believed the large block of Azle Landers common stock was a bargain at that price. In the previous five years, Azle Landers' net income had averaged $2.6 million and the firm had paid out approximately $1.4 million in cash dividends each year. Tervino's CEO was so impressed with the company that she would have purchased all of its outstanding common stock. However, the remaining 59 percent of the company's common stock is owned by a foreign corporation, Resolut, Ltd, which intends to retain its ownership interest in Azle Landers indefinitely.

Unfortunately, 1996 was not a good year for Azle Landers. A strike by production personnel and problems with new machinery contributed to a 20 percent decline in Azle Landers' revenues compared with the previous year and resulted in a $400,000 loss for the year, the first in the company's twenty-five-year history. Because of the company's financial problems, the company's board of directors, which is controlled by Resolut, voted not to pay any cash dividends during 1996.

Tervino's controller prepared a draft of the company's 1996 financial statements in early January 1997. When Tervino's CEO reviewed the draft of the 1996 income statement, she "hit the roof" after discovering the $164,000 "investment loss" related to the company's ownership interest in Azle Landers. The CEO immediately stormed into the controller's office. "Are you telling me that not only did we receive no dividends from Azle Landers this past year, but we also have to report a portion of its loss in our financial statements? This can't be right. Who came up with this rule?"

Required:
34. No check figures

Write a memo to Tervino's CEO explaining the reasoning underlying the equity method of accounting for influential but noncontrolling investments. In this memo, discuss whether there may be any rationale for not applying the equity method to Tervino's investment in Azle Landers.

35. Classification of Intercorporate Investments (LO 2, 3, 4)

Thanos Corporation recently acquired the following corporate securities:

January 12:   Purchased 55,000 shares of Elektra, Inc., common stock at a cost of $12 per share. Elektra has 250,000 shares of common stock outstanding.

January 17:   Purchased 500 shares of Namor Enterprises preferred stock at a cost of $17 per share. Thanos intends to hold these shares indefinitely.

March 9:   Purchased 15 bonds of Sunfire Company at a quoted market price of 104. These bonds have a stated interest rate of 10 percent, pay interest semiannually on May 1 and November 1, and mature on May 1, 2009.

June 29:   Acquired 75 percent of the outstanding common stock of Kraven Company. The total acquisition cost was $3.2 million.

August 3:   Acquired 2,000 of the 5,000 outstanding bonds of Mephisto Enterprises. These bonds were purchased at a quoted market price of 96, have a stated interest rate of 12 percent, and pay interest semiannually on June 1 and December 1. Thanos executives believe that these bonds will provide a high rate of return and pose a low level of default risk. Consequently, a decision has been made to retain these bonds until June 1, 2002, when they mature.

Required:

Classify each of the intercorporate investments acquired by Thanos Corporation into one of the five classes or groups of these investments identified in this chapter. If there is not sufficient information to classify one of Thanos' investments, indicate the classes to which the investment could potentially be assigned and the conditions under which it would be assigned to each of those classes.

36. **Accounting for Intercorporate Investments** (LO 2, 3)
Pembroke Enterprises held the following investments in corporate securities on December 31, 1996, the company's fiscal year-end.

	COST	FAIR VALUE
Locus Corporation Common Stock	$ 65,000	$ 62,500
Excelsior Enterprises Bonds	200,000	208,000

The Locus common stock was purchased on April 4, 1996, while the Excelsior bonds were acquired a few months later on October 1. Excelsior's bonds have a stated interest rate of 8 percent paid semiannually on March 31 and September 30 of each year. Pembroke purchased the Excelsior bonds at a quoted market price of 100.

Required:

1. Prepare all necessary journal entries related to Pembroke's investments during 1996, assuming that they are considered trading securities. Include the year-end adjusting entry to record any unrealized gain or loss on these investments.
2. Prepare all necessary journal entries related to Pembroke's investments during 1996, assuming that they are considered available-for-sale securities. Include the year-end adjusting entry to record any unrealized gain or loss on these investments.
3. Indicate how any unrealized gain or loss on Pembroke's intercorporate investments would be reported in the company's December 31, 1996, financial statements, assuming these investments are classified as:
   a. trading securities.
   b. available-for-sale securities.
4. Suppose that the investment in Locus common stock is considered a trading security. Prepare the appropriate journal entry on January 11, 1997, assuming that stock is sold by Pembroke for $64,200.

37. **Classification of and Accounting for Intercorporate Investments** (LO 1, 3)
On January 1, 1996, Eggling Corporation invested in the bonds of Rinker Company. Eggling purchased 100 of Rinker's $1,000 bonds at a quoted market

35. No check figures

36. 1. 4/6/96 Dr. Invest. in Locus Common Stock, Trad. Sec. $65,000
10/1 Dr. Invest. in Excelsior Bonds, Trad. Sec. $200,000
12/31 Cr. Interest Revenue $4,000
12/31 Cr. Unrealized Gain on Trad. Sec. $5,500

2. 4/6/96 Dr. Invest. in Locus Common Stock, Avail.-for-Sale Sec. $65,000
10/1 Dr. Invest. in Excelsior Bonds, Avail.-for-Sale Sec. $200,000
12/31 Cr. Interest Revenue $4,000
12/31 Cr. Unrealized Gain on Avail.-for-Sale Sec. $5,500

4. Cr. Gain on Sale of Stock $1,700

37. 2. 1/1/96 Dr. Investment in
Rinker Bonds, Held-to-
Mat. Sec. $105,000
7/1 Cr. Investment in
Rinker Bonds, Held-to-
Mat. Sec. $500
Cr. Interest Revenue,
$4,500
12/31 Cr. Investment in
Rinker Bonds, Held-to-
Mat. Sec. $500
Cr. Interest Revenue
$4,500
3. $104,000

38. 2. 1/1/95 Dr. Invest. in
Soledad Common Stock
$4,000,000
Dr. Invest. in MultiMax
Common Stock
$2,000,000
1995 Dr Investment in
Soledad Common Stock
$350,000
Dr. Investment in
MultiMax Common
Stock $135,000
Cr. Investment Revenue
$485,000
Dr. Cash $197,500
Cr. Investment in
Soledad Common Stock
$175,000
Cr. Investment in
MultiMax Common
Stock $22,500
3. 1/1/98 Dr.
Cash
$2,250,000
Cr. Investment
in MultiMax
Common Stock
$2,180,000
Cr. Gain on Sale of
Stock $70,000

price of 105. Rinker's bonds have a 10 percent stated interest rate, semiannual interest payment dates of January 1 and July 1, and a maturity date of January 1, 2001. On December 31, 1996, Eggling's fiscal year-end, Rinker's bonds have a quoted market price of 107.

Required:

1. Under what condition or conditions would Eggling Corporation account for the investment in Rinker Company's bonds as a held-to-maturity security?
2. Assuming that the investment in Rinker bonds is treated as a held-to-maturity security by Eggling, prepare the appropriate journal entries in Eggling's accounting records during 1996 for this investment. (Eggling uses the straight-line method to amortize any premium or discount on a bond investment.)
3. At what dollar amount will the investment in the Rinker bonds be reported in Eggling's December 31, 1996, balance sheet? What other financial statement disclosures, if any, will Eggling include in its 1996 financial statements related to this investment?

38. **Classification of and Accounting for Intercorporate Investments** (LO 3)
On January 1, 1995, Grabbe Company acquired 35 percent of the outstanding common stock of Soledad Corporation for $4,000,000 and 45 percent of the outstanding common stock of MultiMax Corporation for $2,000,000. During 1995 through 1997, these two corporations reported the following net incomes (losses) and paid the following amounts of dividends:

	NET INCOME OR (LOSS)			**TOTAL DIVIDENDS PAID**		
	1995	1996	1997	1995	1996	1997
Soledad	$1,000,000	$800,000	$1,500,000	$500,000	$500,000	$800,000
MultiMax	300,000	(200,000)	500,000	50,000	50,000	100,000

Required:

1. How should Grabbe account for its investments in Soledad and MultiMax? Briefly explain the logic underlying this accounting method.
2. Prepare any entries needed in Grabbe's accounting records for 1995 through 1997 to account for its investments in Soledad and MultiMax.
3. Suppose that Grabbe sells its investment in MultiMax Corporation on January 1, 1998, for $2,250,000. Record this sale in Grabbe's accounting records.

39. **Consolidated Work Sheet for a Wholly Owned Subsidiary** (LO 4)
On December 31, 1996, Phoenix Inns purchased all of the outstanding common stock of Sabretooth Resorts for $250,000. Immediately following the acquisition of Sabretooth, Phoenix extended a loan of $100,000 to its new subsidiary. Following are the separate balance sheets of the two companies at the close of business on December 31, 1996.

Assets	PHOENIX	SABRETOOTH
Cash	$ 24,000	$112,000
Supplies	5,000	4,200
Prepaid Expenses	11,200	3,100
Note Receivable from Sabretooth	100,000	—
Buildings and Land (net)	596,000	275,000
Investment in Sabretooth	250,000	—
Total Assets	$986,200	$394,300

Liabilities and Stockholders' Equity

Accounts Payable	$ 74,100	$ 44,300
Note Payable to Phoenix	—	100,000
Bonds Payable	250,000	—
Common Stock	120,000	55,000
Additional Paid-in Capital	303,100	—
Retained Earnings	239,000	195,000
Total Liabilities and Stockholders' Equity	$986,200	$394,300

Required:

1. Assume that the fair value of Sabretooth's assets is approximately equal to their collective book value. Should any "goodwill" be included in the consolidated balance sheet of these two companies? Explain.
2. Prepare any journal entries required on December 31, 1996, in either the accounting records of Phoenix Inns or Sabretooth Resorts. Indicate in which company's accounting records each journal entry belongs.
3. Complete a post-acquisition consolidated work sheet for Phoenix and Sabretooth.
4. Prepare a consolidated balance sheet for Phoenix and Sabretooth.

40. **Accounting for Foreign Currency Transactions** (LO 7)

Vermont Creations, Inc., a U.S. firm, wholesales stuffed toys to retail companies from several warehouses located around the world. For the convenience of its customers and suppliers, the company transacts business in the currency of each customer's or supplier's home country. Following are selected transactions engaged in by Vermont Creations during 1996. The company's 1996 fiscal year ended on June 30.

March 26: Sold a shipment of stuffed toys to Colebridge Corporation, a London-based firm. The sales price was 8,000 pounds and the credit terms were n/60.

April 1: Purchased 500 cubic yards of raw materials from Chevalier Corporation, a French firm, for 15,000 francs. The credit terms were n/20.

April 21: Paid Chevalier Corporation the amount due for the April 1 purchase.

May 15: Sold a shipment of stuffed toys to Bee Choo Corporation, a Malaysian firm. The sales price was 22,000 ringgits and the credit terms were n/60.

May 25: Received payment from Colebridge Corporation for March 26 sale.

July 14: Received payment from Bee Choo Corporation for May 15 sale.

Following are the assumed foreign exchange rates that are relevant to the listed transactions of Vermont Creations.

March 26 $1.60 per pound
April 1 $.20 per franc
April 21 $.22 per franc
May 15 $.40 per ringgit
May 25 $1.55 per pound
June 30 $.42 per ringgit
July 14 $.41 per ringgit

Required:

1. Prepare the appropriate journal entries to record the listed transactions in the accounting records of Vermont Creations. Include the required journal entry

39. 2. Phoenix:
   Dr. Investment in Sabretooth $250,000
   Dr. Note Receivable from Sabretooth $100,000
   Sabretooth:
   Cr. Note Payable to Phoenix $100,000
   3. Eliminations, $350,000
   4. Total Assets, $1,030,500

40. 1. 4/21 Dr. Foreign Currency Transaction Loss $300
   5/25 Dr. Foreign Currency Transaction Loss $400
   6/30 Cr. Foreign Currency Transaction Gain $440
   7/14 Dr. Foreign Currency Transaction Loss $220
   2. $260 Loss

to record any unrealized foreign currency transaction gain or loss as of June 30, 1996. (Round all amounts to the nearest dollar.)

2. What was the net foreign currency transaction gain or loss that Vermont Creations included in its income statement for the year ended June 30, 1996, for the transactions listed?

PROBLEM SET B

41. Accounting and Financial Reporting Decisions for Intercorporate Investments (LO 1, 4)

You are the controller of Psylocke Company, a conglomerate that has two major subsidiaries, Silver Surfer Corporation and Sauron Company. The CEO of Psylocke is presently negotiating to obtain a large bank loan desperately needed by the company. He asks you to provide him with both consolidated financial statements for Psylocke and its subsidiaries and separate financial statements for Psylocke Company alone. The CEO is planning to review these two sets of financial statements and include the set that he believes is most impressive with the application for the bank loan.

Required:

41. No check figures

Write a memo to the CEO of Psylocke explaining the purpose of consolidated financial statements. In this memo, comment on whether you believe it is appropriate for the CEO to choose between the two sets of financial statements to file with the loan application.

42. Classification and Accounting for Intercorporate Investments (LO 2, 3, 4)

Recently, Gambit, Inc., acquired the following corporate securities:

January 29: Purchased 200 shares of Rhino, Inc., common stock at a cost of $3 per share. Gambit's executives believe the price of these shares will likely increase significantly in a few months, at which point they will be sold.

March 6: Purchased 20 bonds of Morbius Company. These bonds have a stated interest rate of 9 percent, pay interest annually on July 1, and mature on July 1, 2004. The bonds were purchased at a quoted market price of 92 1/2.

May 11: Purchased 100 shares of Jubilee, Inc., common stock at a cost of $29 per share. Gambit plans to hold these shares indefinitely.

June 2: Acquired 1,200 of the 4,000 outstanding bonds of Mystique Corporation. These bonds were purchased at a quoted market price of 101, have a stated interest rate of 12 percent, and pay interest semiannually on April 1 and October 1. Because these bonds have a relatively high yield to maturity, Gambit's management intends to retain these bonds until their maturity date, which is April 1, 2004.

June 12: Acquired 61 percent of the outstanding common stock of Xavier Company at a cost of $10 per share, or $5,200,000 in total.

Required:

42. No check figures

Classify each of the intercorporate investments acquired by Gambit, Inc., into one of the five classes or groups of these investments identified in this chapter. If there is not sufficient information to classify one of Gambit's investments, indicate the classes to which the investment could potentially be assigned and the conditions under which it would be assigned to each of those classes.

43. **Accounting for Intercorporate Investments** (LO 2, 3)

    Carner Enterprises held the following investments in corporate securities on its fiscal year-end of December 31, 1996.

	COST	FAIR VALUE
Steinhauer Corporation Preferred Stock	$ 77,100	$ 78,400
Sheehan Corporation Bonds	240,000	231,000

    Carner purchased the Steinhauer preferred stock on May 22, 1996, while the Sheehan bonds were purchased on September 1, 1996. Carner received a $2,200 dividend on the Steinhauer preferred stock on December 1, 1996. Sheehan's bonds have a stated interest rate of 9 percent paid semiannually on February 28 and August 31. Carner purchased the Sheehan bonds at a quoted market price of 100.

    Required:
    1. Prepare all necessary journal entries related to Carner's investments during 1996, assuming that they are considered trading securities. Include the year-end adjusting entry to record any unrealized gain or loss on these investments.
    2. Prepare all necessary journal entries related to Carner's investments during 1996, assuming that they are considered available-for-sale securities. Include the year-end adjusting entry to record any unrealized gain or loss on these investments.
    3. Indicate how any unrealized gain or loss on Carner's intercorporate investments would be reported in the company's December 31, 1996, financial statements, assuming these investments are classified as:
        a. trading securities.
        b. available-for-sale securities.
    4. Suppose that the investment in Steinhauer preferred stock is considered a trading security. Prepare the appropriate journal entry on March 15, 1997, assuming that the stock is sold by Carner for $74,300.

44. **Classification of and Accounting for Intercorporate Investments** (LO 1, 3)

    On April 1, 1996, Lopez Enterprises purchased 200 of Mocchrie Company's $1,000 corporate bonds. Lopez purchased these bonds at a quoted market price of 98. Mocchrie's bonds have an 8 percent stated interest rate and interest payment dates of March 31 and September 30. The bonds mature on March 31, 2000. On December 31, 1996, Lopez's fiscal year-end, Mocchrie's bonds have a quoted market price of 96.

    Required:
    1. Under what condition or conditions would Lopez Enterprises account for the investment in Mocchrie Company's bonds as a held-to-maturity security?
    2. Assuming that the investment in Mocchrie bonds is treated as a held-to-maturity security by Lopez, prepare the appropriate journal entries in Lopez's accounting records during 1996 for this investment. (Lopez uses the straight-line method to amortize any premium or discount on a bond investment.)
    3. At what dollar amount will the investment in the Mocchrie bonds be reported in Lopez's December 31, 1996, balance sheet? What other financial statement disclosures, if any, will Lopez include in its 1996 financial statements related to this investment?

45. **Classification of and Accounting for Intercorporate Investments** (LO 3)

    On January 18, 1995, Greystoke, Inc., purchased 30 percent of the outstanding

---

43. 1. 5/22/96 Dr. Invest. in Steinhauer Common Stock, Trad. Sec. $77,100
       9/1 Dr. Invest. in Sheehan Bonds, Trad. Sec. $240,000
       12/1 Cr. Dividend Revenue $2,200
       12/31 Cr. Interest Revenue $7,200
       12/31 Dr. Unrealized Loss on Trad. Sec. $7,700
    2. 5/22/96 Dr. Invest. in Steinhauer Common Stock, Avail.-for-Sale Sec. $77,100
       9/1 Dr. Invest. in Sheehan Bonds, Avail.-for-Sale Sec. $240,000
       12/1 Cr. Dividend Revenue $2,200
       12/31 Cr. Interest Revenue $7,200
       12/31 Dr. Unrealized Loss on Avail.-for-Sale Sec. $7,700
    4. Dr. Loss on Sale of Stock $4,100

44. 2. 4/1/96 Dr. Investment in Mocchrie Bonds, Held-to-Mat. Sec. $196,000
       9/30 Dr. Investment in Mocchrie Bonds, Held-to-Mat. Sec. $500
       Cr. Interest Revenue $8,500
       12/31 Dr. Investment in Mocchrie Bonds, Held-to-Mat. Sec. $250
       Cr. Interest Revenue $4,250
    3. $196,750

45. 2. 1/18/95 Dr. Invest. In
Weiss Common Stock
$4,500,000
Dr. Invest. in Muller
Common Stock
$1,500,000
1995 Dr. Investment in
Weiss Common Stock
$450,000
Dr. Investment in
Muller Common Stock
$200,000
Cr. Investment Revenue
$650,000
Cr. Investment in Weiss
Common Stock
$150,000
Cr. Investment in
Muller Common Stock
$20,000
3. 1/1/98
Dr. Loss on
Sale of Stock
$180,000
Cr. Investment
in Muller
Common Stock
$1,820,000

common stock of Weiss Corporation for $4,500,000 and 40 percent of the outstanding common stock of Muller Corporation for $1,500,000. During 1995 through 1997, these two corporations reported the following net incomes (losses) and dividend payments:

	NET INCOME (LOSS)			TOTAL DIVIDENDS PAID		
	1995	1996	1997	1995	1996	1997
Weiss	$1,500,000	($800,000)	$1,000,000	$500,000	$600,000	$800,000
Muller	500,000	200,000	400,000	50,000	100,000	150,000

Required:

1. What accounting method should Greystoke use to account for its investments in Weiss and Muller? Briefly explain the logic underlying this accounting method.
2. Prepare any entries needed in Greystoke's accounting records for 1995 through 1997 to account for its investments in Weiss and Muller.
3. Suppose that Greystoke sells its investment in Muller Corporation on January 1, 1998, for $1,640,000. Record this sale in Greystoke's accounting records.

46. **Consolidated Work Sheet for a Wholly Owned Subsidiary** (LO 4)

On December 31, 1995, Puppet Masters, Inc., a toy company, purchased all of the outstanding common stock of a smaller competitor, Stryfe Toys. Puppet Masters paid $200,000 for this stock and immediately loaned Stryfe $40,000. Following are the separate balance sheets of the two companies after the close of business on December 31, 1995.

Assets	PUPPET MASTERS	STRYFE
Cash	$ 12,000	$ 43,000
Accounts Receivable (net)	121,000	78,500
Note Receivable from Stryfe	40,000	—
Inventory	77,000	35,500
Property, Plant & Equipment (net)	242,000	98,000
Investment in Stryfe	200,000	—
Total Assets	$692,000	$255,000

Liabilities and Stockholders' Equity		
Accounts Payable	$154,500	$ 15,000
Note Payable to Puppet Masters	—	40,000
Bonds Payable	250,000	—
Common Stock	50,000	20,000
Additional Paid-in Capital	120,000	40,000
Retained Earnings	117,500	140,000
Total Liabilities and Stockholders' Equity	$692,000	$255,000

Required:

1. Assume that the fair value of Stryfe's assets is approximately equal to their collective book value. Should any "goodwill" be included in the consolidated balance sheet of these two companies? Explain.
2. Prepare the journal entries required on December 31, 1995, in the accounting records of both Puppet Masters and Stryfe Toys. Indicate in which company's accounting records each journal entry belongs.

46. 2. Puppet Masters:
Dr. Investment in Stryfe
Toys $200,000
Dr. Note Receivable
from Stryfe Toys
$40,000
Stryfe Toys:
Cr. Note Payable to
Puppet Masters $40,000
3. Eliminations, $240,000
4. Total Assets, $707,000

3. Complete a post-acquisition consolidated work sheet for Puppet Masters and Stryfe.
4. Prepare a consolidated balance sheet for Puppet Masters and Stryfe.

47. **Accounting for Foreign Currency Transactions** (LO 7)

Wisconsin Cheeses, Inc. (WCI), is a U.S. firm that has four large warehouses located in foreign countries. WCI wholesales cheese to retailers in more than forty countries. For the convenience of its customers and suppliers, WCI transacts business in the currency of each customer's or supplier's home country. Following are selected transactions engaged in by WCI during 1996. The company's 1996 fiscal year ended on December 31.

August 28:	Sold a shipment of 5,000 pounds of cheese to O'Shaughnessey & Sons, an Irish firm. The sales price was 4300 punts and the credit terms were n/90.
September 13:	Sold 6,000 pounds of cheese to Hansmeier Corporation, an Austrian firm. The sales price was 70,000 schillings and the credit terms were n/30.
October 13:	Received payment from Hansmeier Corporation for September 13 sale.
November 14:	Purchased 3,000 pounds of packing supplies from Troberg of Stockholm, a Swedish firm. The purchase price was 6,000 kronor and the credit terms were n/60.
November 26:	Received payment from O'Shaughnessey & Sons for August 28 sale.
January 13:	Paid amount due Troberg of Stockholm for November 14 purchase.

Following are the assumed foreign exchange rates that are relevant to the listed transactions of WCI.

August 28:	$1.65 per punt
September 13:	$ .11 per schilling
October 13:	$ .10 per schilling
November 14:	$ .14 per krona (singular of kronor)
November 26:	$1.70 per punt
December 31:	$ .13 per krona
January 13:	$ .12 per krona

Required:

1. Prepare the appropriate journal entries to record the listed transactions in the accounting records of WCI. Include the required journal entry to record any unrealized foreign currency transaction gain or loss as of December 31, 1996. (Round all amounts to the nearest dollar.)
2. What was the net foreign currency transaction gain or loss that WCI reported in its income statement for the year ended December 31, 1996, related to the transactions listed?

47. 1. 10/13 Dr. Foreign Currency Transaction Loss $700
11/26 Cr. Foreign Currency Transaction Gain $215
12/31 Cr. Foreign Currency Transaction Gain $60
1/13/97 Cr. Foreign Currency Transaction Gain $60
2. $425 Loss

CASES

48. **Preventing Hostile Takeovers**

Kowalsky Clothiers, Inc., has been a very successful company over the past two decades. The owners of this retail business began operations with one small store in Peoria, Illinois. Now, Kowalsky stores are located in twenty-two states and the company's common stock is listed on the New York Stock Exchange. The two founders of this company own 25 percent of Kowalsky's outstanding common stock. The remaining shares are widely held by individual and institutional investors. Recently, there have been rumors that another large company will attempt a hostile takeover of Kowalsky.

Required:
The two founders and principal stockholders of Kowalsky are very concerned by the rumors of the hostile takeover. Write a brief memo to these individuals identifying at least two strategies they can use to reduce the risk of a hostile takeover of their company.

49. **Classification of Intercorporate Investments**
Piazza Engineering, Inc., invested $450,000 to acquire approximately 6 percent of the outstanding common stock of Yeager Tools during the current year. Piazza's controller has determined that this investment should be classified as an available-for-sale security and reported as a long-term asset in the company's periodic balance sheets. A key factor in reaching this decision was the stated intention of Piazza's chief executive officer (CEO) to hold this stock indefinitely. As the fiscal year-end approaches, the market value of this investment has increased to nearly $1 million. Because the company's expected profit for the year is unimpressive, Piazza's CEO has suggested that the Yeager investment be classified as a trading security. When Piazza's controller asked the CEO whether he intended to sell the Yeager stock in the near term, the CEO responded, "Oh, sure," as he winked at the controller and slapped him heartily on the back.

Required:
1. Explain how the classification of the investment in Yeager common stock will affect Piazza's financial statements for the year in question.
2. Should a company allow the financial statement impact of alternative accounting methods to dictate which accounting method it selects? Why or why not?
3. Identify the parties that may be affected by Piazza's classification of the Yeager investment and how these parties may be affected.
4. Should Piazza's controller classify the Yeager investment as a trading security given the circumstances? Defend your answer.

50. **Foreign Companies and U.S. Accounting Standards**
Hitachi, Ltd., is a large Japanese company that manufactures a wide range of products including semiconductors, televisions, and large computer systems. Hitachi's common stock is traded on the New York Stock Exchange. The following footnote concerning Hitachi's accounting for investments in debt and equity securities was included in the company's 1994 annual report.

SFAS No. 115, "Accounting for Certain Investments in Debt and Equity Securities," which is effective for fiscal years beginning after December 15, 1993, was issued in May 1993. Regarding the method of implementation of *SFAS No. 115,* the Company requested the United States Securities and Exchange Commission (SEC) for special treatment, which allows the Company to provide the required *SFAS No. 115* disclosure in a footnote to its financial statements, instead of implementing it in the body of its consolidated financial statements.

This request is based upon the following reasons:

Most marketable equity securities in Hitachi's portfolio are semi-permanent investments for maintaining business relationships with investee companies and management generally has no current plans to sell such securities.

The Company files its consolidated financial statements with both the SEC and the Ministry of Finance in Japan utilizing accounting principles generally accepted in the United States. If *SFAS No. 115* is implemented, the comparability among Japanese companies' financial statements would be considerably reduced. Many Japanese companies prepare their consolidated financial statements utilizing accounting practices generally accepted in Japan which generally reflect historical cost accounting.

The SEC Division of Corporate Finance approved the Company's request in a letter dated August 16, 1993. Consequently, the Company has decided to disclose the effect of its departure from *SFAS No. 115* in an audited footnote to its consolidated financial statements and not to implement *SFAS No. 115* in the body of its consolidated financial statements.

Required:
1. Do you agree with the SEC's decision to allow Hitachi to not comply with the requirements of *SFAS No. 115?* Defend your answer.
2. If foreign companies are allowed to issue financial statements in this country that do not fully comply with GAAP, what problems may this pose for investors and other decision makers in this country who use these companies' financial statements?

PROJECTS

51. Consolidated Financial Statements

Choose any annual report available to you in which consolidated financial statements are included.

Required:

For the company whose annual report you selected, identify the names and principal line of business of each subsidiary. (Hint: If you cannot find this information in the annual report itself, obtain a copy of the company's annual 10-K report filed with the SEC.) Determine whether each subsidiary is wholly owned or majority owned. If the subsidiary is majority owned, determine the percentage of its common stock owned by the parent company. Also, determine the amount of goodwill and minority interest reported in the consolidated financial statements. Finally, review the information you collected. Briefly summarize what you believe is the parent company's strategy in acquiring other companies. For example, the parent company's acquisition strategy may be to "vertically integrate" or to achieve "economies of scale" by expanding its operations. Summarize your findings in a written report.

52. Business Combinations

Each project group will be assigned or be required to identify a major business combination that occurred between five and ten years ago. If your instructor does not assign a business combination to your group, group members can review indices of business periodicals during the relevant time period to identify several business combinations from which one can be selected for this project.

Required:
1. Each project group should obtain the following information for the business combination it has been assigned or has selected.
   a. A description of the two companies involved in the business combination including, among other items, their location and principal lines of business
   b. Key financial information for each company immediately prior to the combination (total assets, most recent annual sales, most recent net income, and so on)

c. The nature of the business combination (for instance, was the combination a mutually agreed-upon merger, a "hostile takeover," or some other type of business combination)

d. The key terms of the business combination (for example, were the stockholders of one firm "bought out" with cash payments or did they receive shares of stock in the new firm or surviving firm, were the key executives of both firms given positions in the newly created or surviving firm, were certain segments of one or both firms eliminated following the combination, and so on)

e. The stated objective or purpose of the business combination (for example, was the stated purpose of the combination to achieve economies of scale and thus reduce operating costs, to achieve stated profit or revenue goals, or to create the dominant firm in a given industry)

2. For the five- to ten-year period following the business combination, your group should research the financial condition and operating results of the new firm or surviving firm. Information sources you can use for this purpose include annual reports of the given firm and newspaper articles regarding the firm that appeared in *The Wall Street Journal* and major metropolitan newspapers.

3. After completing Parts 1 and 2, meet as a group and review and discuss the information collected. The key issue you should address is whether the business combination has apparently been a success to date. The group's decision should be supported with the appropriate financial data and other relevant information.

4. A written report documenting the research and conclusions of the group should be prepared. One group member should be prepared to present an in-class summary of this report.

53. Foreign Currency Exchange Rates

A key factor influencing the operating results of multinational companies is the foreign currency exchange rates that affect how much they must pay for goods and services obtained from foreign countries and how much they will receive for goods and services delivered in foreign countries. To complete this project, you should select three foreign countries in which you have a particular interest.

Required:

1. For the three countries you selected, identify their present currency exchange rate relative to the U.S. dollar. Then identify each country's currency exchange rate relative to the U.S. dollar one, three, five, and ten years ago. This information can be obtained from *The Wall Street Journal* and several other business publications.

2. Plot the currency exchange rates for each country on a piece of graph paper with an appropriate numerical scale.

3. Interpret the data you collected. What factor or factors account for the variations apparent in these exchange rates over the past ten years? (Research relevant articles in business periodicals if necessary to address this issue.) What implications do the changes in the exchange rates you plotted have for U.S. firms transacting business in each of these countries?

4. Document your completion of Parts 1, 2, and 3 in a written report. Be prepared to present a summary of your report in class.

PARTNERSHIPS AND PROPRIETORSHIPS

15

LEARNING OBJECTIVES

After studying this chapter, you should be able to do the following:

1. Identify the key characteristics of partnerships

2. Account for partners' initial investments in partnerships

3. Apply several methods of allocating partnership profits and losses to individual partners

4. Prepare a statement of partners' capital

5. Account for the dissolution of a partnership

6. Account for the liquidation of a partnership and prepare a statement of partnership liquidation

7. Account for the ownership interests of proprietorships

I will have no one work for me who has not the capacity to become a partner.
J.C. Penney

Sinking Partner-Ships

Until the late nineteenth century, most large businesses in the United States operated as partnerships. Corporations were rare; one reason was because the incorporation of a business generally required the approval of a state legislature. Gradually, individual states passed laws that made it easier for businesses to incorporate. These laws spurred many partnerships to reorganize as corporations to take advantage of key benefits offered by the corporate form of organization. By the early 1990s, there were more than twice as many corporations as partnerships in the United States—3.7 million corporations versus 1.6 million partnerships.[1]

The limited liability feature of corporations is the factor most responsible for large numbers of partnerships converting to the corporate form of organization. Individual stockholders face the risk of losing their total investment in a corporation if the firm goes "belly up." However, the creditors of a bankrupt corporation cannot collect their unpaid bills by filing legal claims against the personal assets of individual stockholders. If a partnership folds while it still has unpaid debts, the former partners are liable individually for the partnership's debts.

Several examples of the financial risk that partners face can be found in the accounting profession, since most accounting firms are organized as partnerships. Over the past twenty-five years, many accounting firms have suffered huge financial losses due to a dramatic increase in class-action lawsuits filed by unhappy investors and creditors. Until the late 1980s, Laventhol & Horwath was among the ten largest accounting firms in the United States. In 1990, Laventhol was forced out of business following several legal judgments imposed on the firm. When it disbanded, Laventhol owed creditors nearly $50 million. The former Laventhol partners contributed up to $400,000 each to pay off the partnership's remaining debts.

The Big Six firms that dominate the accounting profession have been the hardest hit by litigation losses in recent years. In 1992, Ernst & Young settled several lawsuits filed against it by the federal government. These lawsuits charged Ernst & Young with negligently auditing savings & loans that eventually failed, resulting in significant losses for depositors, investors, and the federal government. The price tag of the Ernst & Young settlement? $400 million. In the following two years, Deloitte & Touche and KPMG Peat Marwick paid $312 million and $186 million, respectively, to the federal government to settle similar legal claims.

I n this chapter, we consider accounting for the ownership interests of unincorporated businesses—namely, partnerships and sole proprietorships. There is no need to discuss accounting for the assets and liabilities of unincorporated businesses. The accounting rules identified in earlier chapters apply, with a few exceptions, to all types of business organizations. A key focus of this text is the information needs of financial decision makers regarding business entities. The information needs of these decision makers are very similar whether a given entity is organized as a corporation, a partnership, or a sole proprietorship. In earlier chapters, we have also identified internal control policies and procedures for a wide array of asset, liability, and equity accounts. These same general internal control concepts apply to all types of business entities.

---

1. U.S. Bureau of the Census, *Statistical Abstract of the United States, 1994* (Washington, D.C.: U.S. Government Printing Office, 1993), 539.

PARTNERSHIPS

In Chapter 2, a **partnership** was defined as an unincorporated business with two or more owners. A more formal definition of a partnership is found in the Uniform Partnership Act, a law that specifies the principal legal features of partnerships. According to this statute, which has been adopted by most states, a partnership is "an association of two or more persons to carry on as co-owners a business for profit." Some partnerships are based on a "handshake" agreement between, or among, the partners. However, to avoid misunderstandings, this agreement should be documented in writing. A **partnership agreement** identifies the contractual rights and responsibilities of each member of a partnership. Among other issues, a partnership agreement specifies how profits and losses are to be allocated to individual partners and the procedures to be followed when partners withdraw or new partners are admitted.

In the remainder of this opening section of Chapter 15, we first identify the distinguishing characteristics of partnerships. Then the technical aspects of accounting for the owners' equity of partnerships are illustrated.

partnership

partnership agreement

Teaching Note
Emphasize that a formal, written partnership agreement is not a legal requirement for the formation of a partnership.

Characteristics of Partnerships

UNLIMITED LIABILITY   As indicated in the opening vignette for this chapter, the members of a partnership are individually responsible for their firm's liabilities. If a partnership's assets are depleted before all of its debts are paid, creditors can file legal claims against the individual partners. As a result, one "deep-pocketed" partner may find herself or himself totally responsible for the liabilities of a failed partnership. For example, when a Washington, D.C., law partnership disbanded in the early 1990s, the landlord of the former partnership sued one of its partners. Suddenly, that individual found himself being held personally responsible for a $10,000 monthly rental payment on a lease contract that extended over ten years.[2]

To reduce the financial risk faced by individual partners, many large partnerships are organized as limited partnerships. Limited partnerships typically have at least one "general" partner and dozens or even thousands of "limited" partners. The unlimited liability feature applies only to the general partners of a limited partnership. The limited partners face the risk of losing their investment in the partnership, but their personal assets are not at risk if the partnership fails. Many Big Six accounting firms have recently reorganized as limited liability partnerships, a type of partnership that also reduces the financial risk faced by individual partners.

MUTUAL AGENCY   Another defining characteristic of partnerships is mutual agency, which is the authority of individual partners to enter into contracts binding on the entire partnership. For example, individual partners can sign lease agreements and employment contracts on behalf of their partnership. Many partners in business ventures have been "burned" because of poor decisions made by their fellow partners. The moral here is to make sure you trust the judgment of your prospective partners before you sign the dotted line at the bottom of the partnership agreement.

LIMITED LIFE   Recall that one feature of the corporate form of business organization is "continuity of existence." A corporation's legal existence is unaffected when

■ LEARNING OBJECTIVE 1
Identify the key characteristics of partnerships

Teaching Note
Given the mutual agency feature of partnerships, when a partner withdraws from a partnership the remaining partners often inform the public. Such a disclosure places the public on notice that the former partner can no longer enter into agreements binding on the partnership.

2. Carlson, E., "Personal Risk Becomes a Major Worry for Partnerships," *The Wall Street Journal*, January 3, 1992, p. B2. Reprinted by permission of *The Wall Street Journal*, © 1992 Dow Jones & Company, Inc. All Rights Reserved Worldwide.

Owning a (Small) Piece of the Boston Celtics

Arguably one of the most famous partnerships in the United States is the limited partnership that owns and operates the Boston Celtics. Partnership interests in the Boston Celtics Limited Partnership, which are known as "units" instead of "shares," are traded on the New York Stock Exchange. For approximately $21 in June 1995, you could brag to your friends that you owned part of an NBA franchise. Of course, you probably would not mention that your ownership interest represented .0000167 percent of the total owners' equity of the Boston Celtics.

Real World
Certain publicly owned limited partnerships are taxed as corporations.

The financial statements issued each year by large, publicly owned limited partnerships are very similar to corporate financial statements. However, there are certain differences. For example, the owners' equity section of the Boston Celtics' balance sheet consists of only two line items: "General Partner" and "Limited Partners." Likewise, the final two lines of the firm's income statement segregate net income into the following amounts: "Applicable to General Partner" and "Applicable to Limited Partners."

By definition, the Celtics' line of business is "seasonal." As a result, the limited partnership's revenues and expenses vary significantly over the four quarters of its fiscal year. The following excerpt from a recent annual report describes the Celtics' revenue and expense recognition policies.

> For financial reporting purposes, the Partnership recognizes its revenues and expenses on a game-by-game basis. Because the NBA regular season begins in November, the first quarter which ends on September 30th will generally include limited or no revenue and will reflect a loss attributable to general and administrative expenses incurred in the quarter. Based on the present NBA game schedule, the Partnership will generally recognize approximately one-third of its annual regular season revenue in the second quarter, approximately one-half in the third quarter and the remainder in the fourth quarter, and it will recognize all of its playoff revenue in the fourth quarter.

dissolution

the firm's ownership interests change hands. Partnerships do not have this feature. As a general rule, when at least one partner withdraws or one new partner is admitted, a partnership agreement becomes void and the partnership terminates. **Dissolution** is the term used to refer to the termination of a partnership. When a partnership is dissolved, its business operations do not necessarily cease. The partnership can continue operating while a new partnership agreement is being reached. If the new set of partners cannot reach a mutually acceptable agreement, the partnership will discontinue operations and be "liquidated." **Liquidation** involves the process of converting a discontinued partnership's assets into cash, paying its liabilities, and then distributing any remaining cash to the partners. Some partnership agreements limit a partnership's life to a specific length of time. On the expiration date of the partnership agreement, the partnership is automatically dissolved and the liquidation process begins.

liquidation

JOINT OWNERSHIP OF ASSETS When a partnership is formed, the individual partners contribute assets to the new firm as their initial investments. These assets may include cash, equipment, land, or other items. Once such assets have been contributed to a partnership, they are no longer the personal property of the individual partners but instead become the joint property of the partnership.

NONTAXABLE STATUS   Unlike corporations, partnerships are not taxable entities. The income of a partnership "flows through" to the tax returns of its individual partners. However, a partnership must file an "information return" annually with the Internal Revenue Service (IRS). The primary purpose of this information return is to help the IRS ensure that partners report their share of partnership income on their individual tax returns.

So, you want to become a part owner of a professional sports franchise? No problem. For much less than the price of a pair of sneakers, you can call up your local broker and purchase one "unit" of the Boston Celtics Limited Partnership.

Accounting for the Owners' Equity of a Partnership

In this section, we examine several events or transactions involving the owners' equity of a partnership and the related accounting decisions. We begin by considering the initial investments of partners in a new partnership.

INITIAL INVESTMENTS OF PARTNERS   Suppose that Chris Austen and Jane Everett decide to form a partnership to operate a sporting goods store. If each individual contributes $20,000 to this new venture, the following entry would be made in the partnership's accounting records.

Apr. 19 Cash	40,000	
C. Austen, Capital		20,000
J. Everett, Capital		20,000

To record partners' initial investments

Notice that the investments of the partners are credited to their individual "capital" accounts. The maintenance of separate capital accounts allows a partnership to easily determine the ownership interest of each partner at all times.

Partners sometimes contribute assets other than cash to a new partnership. Noncash assets contributed to a partnership should be recorded at their fair market value. In this context, "fair market value" generally means a value mutually agreed upon by the partners. Returning to the previous example, assume that Jane Everett has been operating a sporting goods store as a sole proprietorship. Everett invites Chris Austen to form a partnership to operate this store. Austen's initial investment in the partnership will be a cash contribution of $20,000, while Everett's initial investment will be the noncash assets of her business. The two individuals also agree that the partnership will assume the liabilities of Everett's business. Following are the book values of the noncash assets and liabilities of Everett's sporting goods store immediately before she struck the deal to become a partner with Austen.

■ **LEARNING OBJECTIVE 2**
Account for partners' initial investments in partnerships

Discussion Question
Why do individuals form partnerships to operate a business venture?
Answer: Principally to increase the resources, both human (personal skills) and economic (cash, buildings, land, etc.), available to the business.

Accounts Receivable	$5,400	
Less: Allowance for Doubtful Accounts	(1,200)	$ 4,200
Inventory		11,200
Prepaid Rent		1,400
Furniture & Fixtures	8,600	
Less: Accumulated Depreciation	(1,100)	7,500
Accounts Payable		(3,200)
Total Net Assets		$21,100

Austen and Everett must now agree upon the fair market value of the assets and liabilities that Everett is contributing to the partnership. This is an important decision for the partners since these values will influence how the partnership's residual assets are allocated between the partners if the firm is liquidated at some point. This decision may also influence how the partnership's profits and losses are allocated between the two partners.

Assume that the partners agree upon the following values for the assets and liabilities Everett is contributing to the partnership.

Accounts Receivable	$5,400	
Less: Allowance for Doubtful Accounts	(1,000)	$ 4,400
Inventory		8,900
Prepaid Rent		1,400
Furniture and Fixtures		10,300
Accounts Payable		(3,200)
Total		$21,800

The following entry would be made to record the partners' investments in the new business venture.

Apr. 19	Cash	20,000	
	Accounts Receivable	5,400	
	Inventory	8,900	
	Prepaid Rent	1,400	
	Furniture & Fixtures	10,300	
	Allowance for Doubtful Accounts		1,000
	Accounts Payable		3,200
	C. Austen, Capital		20,000
	J. Everett, Capital		21,800

To record partners' initial investments

Notice that the two new partners agreed that $1,000 of Everett's receivables are unlikely to be collected. The partners do not want to write off the questionable accounts just yet, since there is still some glimmer of hope that they may be collected. So, the gross amount of Everett's former receivables is debited to Accounts Receivable with an offsetting credit of $1,000 to Allowance for Doubtful Accounts. On the other hand, there is no need to establish an accumulated depreciation balance for Furniture & Fixtures. These depreciable assets will be given a "fresh start" in the new partnership by being recorded at their fair market value of $10,300.

ALLOCATION OF PARTNERSHIP PROFITS AND LOSSES   When two or more individuals decide to form a partnership, they must tackle the difficult issue of how to divide the partnership's profits and losses between, or among, themselves. Several factors may be considered in reaching this decision. Among these factors are the amount of capital contributed by each partner, the relevant skills of the individual partners, and the amount of time each partner commits to the daily operations of the firm. If the partnership agreement does not indicate how profits and losses are to be divided, then partnership profits and losses must be split equally among all partners.

PROFIT SHARING BASED UPON INITIAL CAPITAL INVESTMENTS   Assume that Tim Johnson, Sadi Karim, and Larissa Lopez form Hair Care Distributors, a partnership, on January 1, 1998, to distribute hair-care products to salons. Johnson, Karim, and Lopez agree that their initial capital investments will be $30,000, $60,000, and $90,000, respectively. The partners also agree that the profits and losses of the

A Partnership Gone Sour: The Sad Story of Claude and Harry

Partnerships and sole proprietorships rely heavily on the expertise of accountants, attorneys, and other skilled professionals. Small businesses often cannot afford to hire these professionals on a full-time basis. Instead, they periodically retain professionals in "public practice" to resolve problems and to address issues that arise in connection with their operations. The following vignette, drawn from an actual set of circumstances, illustrates the need for accountants to provide high-quality professional services and advice to their small business clients.

In 1978, two businessmen formed a partnership to operate a real estate development company. Claude contributed an undivided piece of land to the partnership that had an appraised value of $640,000, while Harry contributed an equal amount of cash. Partnerships, like other personal and business relationships, have their ups and downs. And so it was with Claude and Harry. After a few years, Harry accused Claude of squandering most of the cash he had contributed to the partnership. To settle the dispute, Claude allowed Harry to retain an accounting firm to examine the partnership's accounting records.

The young accountant assigned to review the partnership's accounting records discovered that the legal title to the partnership's principal asset, the land contributed to the firm by Claude, was still in Claude's name. At this point, the accountant "blew a fuse" and stormed into Claude's office. In the presence of Claude's secretary, the accountant accused Claude of attempting to defraud his partner. The accountant suggested that Claude intended at some point to claim that the land and the considerable improvements made to it were his personal property, leaving his partner, Harry, out in the proverbial cold. When Harry was informed of this matter, he insisted that Claude buy his share of the partnership at an inflated price. Otherwise, Harry would consider various legal alternatives. In fact, Claude had never intended to defraud his partner. However, after being convinced that his actions could be construed as fraudulent, he agreed to a buy-out deal structured by the accounting firm. Within a matter of days, Claude arranged to borrow $900,000 to purchase Harry's share of the partnership.

After the partnership with Harry collapsed, Claude lost interest in the real estate venture and eventually sold it at a large loss. Several months later, Claude was informed by another accountant that, under state law, he had not been required to transfer the legal title of the land to the partnership. According to this accountant, the stated intentions of partners are the controlling factor in determining whether a partner's personal assets have been contributed to a partnership. Claude immediately filed a large civil suit against the accounting firm that had accused him of defrauding his partner. Unfortunately, Claude's health had deteriorated rapidly following the dissolution of the partnership and he died of a heart attack before the lawsuit was resolved. Claude was later vindicated completely when the accounting firm settled the lawsuit by making a sizable payment to his estate. The accounting firm also apologized to Claude's family for the unfortunate incident.

Suppose that in the future you decide to form a partnership with a friend to build new homes, operate a sporting goods store, or market a new hair-care product. You should recognize that partnerships can be very fragile. To protect yourself, you should insist that a written partnership agreement be developed for the new venture.

SOURCE: Adapted from the following: M. C. Knapp, "Laurel Valley Estates," in *Contemporary Auditing: Issues and Cases*, 2d ed. (Minneapolis/St. Paul: West Publishing Co., 1996).

firm will be allocated in the same proportions as their initial capital investments. If Hair Care Distributors earns a net income of $135,000 during 1998, this profit will be allocated as follows to the three partners.

Johnson: ($30,000/$180,000) × $135,000 = $ 22,500
Karim: ($60,000/$180,000) × $135,000 = 45,000
Lopez: ($90,000/$180,000) × $135,000 = 67,500
Total $135,000

Teaching Note
Remind students that the Income Summary account is a temporary account used only during the period-ending closing process.

Like corporations and other business entities, partnerships close their books at the end of each accounting period. At the end of 1998, the Income Summary account of Hair Care Distributors will have a credit balance of $135,000 after the firm's revenue and expense accounts have been closed. Instead of transferring the balance of the Income Summary account to retained earnings, partnerships close this account balance directly to the partners' capital accounts. In the present example, the following entry would be appropriate to close the Income Summary account.

Dec. 31 Income Summary 135,000
T. Johnson, Capital 22,500
S. Karim, Capital 45,000
L. Lopez, Capital 67,500

To allocate net income to the
partners' capital accounts

PROFIT SHARING INCLUDES SALARY ALLOWANCES Suppose now that the three partners of Hair Care Distributors agree to a profit-sharing plan that takes into consideration the time that each devotes to the partnership's daily operations. Tim Johnson works full-time in the business, while Sadi Karim and Larissa Lopez spend approximately 50 percent and 25 percent, respectively, of each work week involved with the business. The three partners mutually decide that Johnson will be given an annual salary allowance of $40,000 to compensate him for the time he devotes to the partnership. Karim and Lopez will receive salary allowances of $20,000 and $10,000, respectively. The partners also agree that any profit or loss remaining after the allocation of the salary allowances will be divided equally. Recognize that "salary allowances" are *not* considered expenses of a partnership for accounting purposes. That is, a partnership's net income is unaffected by salary allowances. The intent of these allowances is simply to help allocate a partnership's profits in a fair manner to the individual partners.

If Hair Care Distributors earns a net income of $124,000 during 1998, the three partners would receive their salary allowances totaling $70,000 and then participate equally in the remaining profit of $54,000 ($124,000 − $70,000). The following schedule indicates the amount of profit allocated to each partner under this scenario.

	SALARY ALLOWANCE	EQUAL SHARE OF REMAINING PROFIT	PROFIT ALLOCATED TO EACH PARTNER
Johnson:	$40,000	$18,000	$ 58,000
Karim:	20,000	18,000	38,000
Lopez:	10,000	18,000	28,000
Net Income			$124,000

Instead of a $124,000 net income, assume that Hair Care Distributors earns only $62,500 during 1998. In this case, the partners' total salary allowance would exceed the company's net income by $7,500 ($70,000 − 62,500). This amount, sometimes referred to as an "income deficiency," would be allocated to the partners equally as shown in the following schedule.

	SALARY ALLOWANCE	EQUAL SHARE OF REMAINING PROFIT (INCOME DEFICIENCY)	PROFIT ALLOCATED TO EACH PARTNER
Johnson:	$40,000	$(2,500)	$37,500
Karim:	20,000	(2,500)	17,500
Lopez:	10,000	(2,500)	7,500
Net Income			$62,500

PROFIT SHARING INCLUDES SALARY ALLOWANCES AND INTEREST ALLOWANCES ON CAPITAL INVESTMENTS   The final profit-sharing plan we consider for Hair Care Distributors involves an agreement to provide each partner with a salary allowance and an interest allowance based upon his or her initial capital investment. Let us again assume that the annual salary allowances for Johnson, Karim, and Lopez are $40,000, $20,000, and $10,000, respectively. The annual interest allowance granted to each partner is 10 percent of his or her original capital investment. Given the initial investments of $30,000, $60,000, and $90,000, by Johnson, Karim, and Lopez, respectively, the following annual interest allowances would be provided to each partner under this profit-sharing agreement.

Teaching Note
Emphasize that there are an unlimited number of ways to share profits and losses among partners. To prevent disputes among partners, a partnership agreement should expressly indicate how profits and losses are to be allocated among partners.

Johnson	$30,000 × 10%	=	$ 3,000
Karim	60,000 × 10%	=	6,000
Lopez	90,000 × 10%	=	9,000
Total			$18,000

Any profit or income deficiency remaining after the salary and interest allowances will be split equally among the partners. For example, assume that the partnership earns a profit of $130,000 during 1998. After the total salary allowances ($70,000) and interest allowances ($18,000) are allocated to the partners, $42,000 ($130,000 − 88,000) will remain to be allocated equally among the partners. The following schedule indicates the profit allocation to each partner under this scenario.

	SALARY ALLOWANCE	INTEREST ALLOWANCE	EQUAL SHARE OF REMAINING PROFIT	PROFIT ALLOCATED TO EACH PARTNER
Johnson:	$40,000	$3,000	$14,000	$ 57,000
Karim:	20,000	6,000	14,000	40,000
Lopez:	10,000	9,000	14,000	33,000
Net Income				$130,000

If the sum of the salary and interest allowances had exceeded the partnership's net income, the income deficiency would have been allocated equally to the three partners. Also recognize that the salary and interest allowances would be allocated to the individual partners even if the partnership had a loss for the year. For example, assume that Hair Care Distributors suffers a loss of $11,000 in 1998. In this case, an income deficiency of $99,000 would exist after the allocation of the salary and interest allowances. This deficiency is the sum of the $11,000 loss, the salary allowances of $70,000, and the interest allowances of $18,000. For this scenario, the following allocations would be made to the partners' capital accounts at year-end.

	SALARY ALLOWANCE	INTEREST ALLOWANCE	EQUAL SHARE OF INCOME DEFICIENCY	ALLOCATION TO EACH PARTNER
Johnson:	$40,000	$3,000	($33,000)	$10,000
Karim:	20,000	6,000	(33,000)	(7,000)
Lopez:	10,000	9,000	(33,000)	(14,000)
Net Loss				$(11,000)

One final point before we move on. Like salary allowances, interest allowances are *not* considered expenses of a partnership for accounting or financial reporting purposes. The intent of these allowances is simply to help allocate a partnership's profits to the individual partners.

PARTNERSHIP DRAWING ACCOUNTS   When a partnership's profit is allocated at year-end to the individual partners, cash or other assets are not physically distributed to the partners. However, a partnership agreement usually allows partners to withdraw assets from a partnership. Quite often, the partnership agreement requires that withdrawals be approved by all partners or by an executive committee consisting of senior partners. Withdrawals made by partners are recorded in "drawing" accounts that are temporary equity accounts similar to the Dividends account for a corporation.

To illustrate the use of drawing accounts, assume that during 1998 the three partners of Hair Care Distributors withdraw the following amounts: Johnson—$5,000, Karim—$3,000, and Lopez—$12,000. To simplify matters, assume that these withdrawals are all made on December 1, 1998. Following is the compound journal entry to record these withdrawals.

Dec. 1	T. Johnson, Drawing	5,000	
	S. Karim, Drawing	3,000	
	L. Lopez, Drawing	12,000	
	Cash		20,000
	To record partner withdrawals		

At the end of an accounting period, the balances of drawing accounts are closed to the capital accounts of the individual partners. The balances of the drawing accounts for Hair Care Distributors would be closed at the end of 1998 with the following entry.

Dec. 31	T. Johnson, Capital	5,000	
	S. Karim, Capital	3,000	
	L. Lopez, Capital	12,000	
	T. Johnson, Drawing		5,000
	S. Karim, Drawing		3,000
	L. Lopez, Drawing		12,000
	To close partners' drawing accounts		

■ **LEARNING OBJECTIVE 4**
Prepare a statement of partners' capital

STATEMENT OF PARTNERS' CAPITAL   Partnership financial statements are very similar to corporate financial statements. The most noticeable differences in the financial statements of the two types of business organizations involve the owners' equity accounts. For example, as suggested previously, partnerships do not maintain

■ **EXHIBIT 15.1**

Statement of Partners' Capital for Hair Care Distributors for the Year
Ended December 31, 1998

HAIR CARE DISTRIBUTORS **STATEMENT OF PARTNERS' CAPITAL** **FOR THE YEAR ENDED DECEMBER 31, 1998**				
	JOHNSON	**KARIM**	**LOPEZ**	**TOTAL**
Balances, January 1, 1998	$ -0-	$ -0-	$ -0-	$ -0-
Add: Investments during 1998	30,000	60,000	90,000	180,000
Profit Allocations	57,000	40,000	33,000	130,000
Total	$87,000	$100,000	$123,000	$310,000
Less: Withdrawals	5,000	3,000	12,000	20,000
Balances, December 31, 1998	$82,000	$ 97,000	$111,000	$290,000

a Retained Earnings account. Likewise, capital accounts are maintained for each individual investor (partner) in a partnership, which is not true for corporations. Finally,
instead of a statement of stockholders' equity, partnerships typically prepare a **statement of partners' capital** to document the changes in partners' capital account balances for a given period of time.

 To illustrate a statement of partners' capital, return to an earlier scenario presented for Hair Care Distributors in which the firm earns $130,000 and both salary and
interest allowances are provided to each partner. The profit allocations to Johnson,
Karim, and Lopez for this scenario are $57,000, $40,000, and $33,000, respectively.
Also assume that the three partners make the December 1, 1998, withdrawals discussed previously: Johnson—$5,000; Karim—$3,000; Lopez—$12,000. Exhibit 15.1
presents a Statement of Partners' Capital for Hair Care Distributors for the year
ended December 31, 1998, based upon these assumptions.

statement of partners' capital

DISSOLUTION OF A PARTNERSHIP As noted earlier, when there is a change in
the composition of a partnership, the firm must generally be dissolved. Here, we consider several scenarios involving the dissolution of a partnership and the related
accounting decisions. As a point of information, before a new partner is admitted or
an existing partner withdraws, a partnership's assets are usually restated to their current values. The purpose of such restatements is to ensure that partners participate
only in increases and decreases in the value of the partnership's assets that occur while
they are a member of the firm. Any gain or loss resulting from a restatement of partnership assets to their current values is allocated to the existing partners according to
their profit-sharing agreement.

■ LEARNING
OBJECTIVE 5
Account for the dissolution of a
partnership

ADMISSION OF A PARTNER A new partner can be admitted to a partnership
either by purchasing the ownership interest of an existing partner or by investing
assets in the partnership. To illustrate the first of these possibilities, assume that Bill
Hardy wants to purchase an ownership interest in Cabrillo Enterprises, a partnership
with a June 30 fiscal year-end. On June 30, 1998, this partnership has total capital of
$372,000, as reflected by the following schedule.

Chad Keith	$121,000
Earl Stacy	106,000
Paul Tate	145,000
Total Partnership Capital	$372,000

Discussion Question
What is the rationale for requiring that the admission of new partners be approved by existing partners?
Answer: Since the members of a partnership must be able to work together, it is only reasonable that existing partners be allowed to determine which individuals will be admitted to their firm.

Because he is anxious to join the partnership, Hardy offers Chad Keith $140,000 for his interest in the firm, or $19,000 more than the balance of Keith's capital account. After obtaining approval from the other two partners, Keith accepts Hardy's offer. (As a general rule, a new partner cannot be admitted to a partnership without the prior approval of existing partners.) The exchange of the $140,000 between these two individuals is a personal transaction that does not affect the assets or liabilities of the partnership. The only entry required in the partnership's books is the following one that transfers the balance of Keith's capital account to Hardy.

Jul. 7	C. Keith, Capital	121,000	
	B. Hardy, Capital		121,000

To transfer ownership interest of
Chad Keith to Bill Hardy

Instead of purchasing an existing partner's ownership interest in Cabrillo Enterprises for $140,000, assume now that Bill Hardy invests that amount of cash directly into the partnership. For his cash contribution of $140,000, the three existing partners agree to assign a one-fourth ownership interest in their firm to Bill Hardy. Following the admission of Hardy, the total partnership capital of Cabrillo Enterprises will increase to $512,000, as the following schedule indicates.

Existing Partnership Capital	$372,000
Additional Capital to be Invested by Hardy	140,000
Total Partnership Capital Following Hardy's Admission	$512,000

Since Hardy is acquiring a one-fourth interest in Cabrillo Enterprises, the balance of his capital account immediately following his admission should equal $128,000, or one-fourth of the partnership's total capital ($512,000/4). This raises a question. Since Hardy is investing $140,000 to obtain $128,000 of equity, what happens to the other $12,000 that he contributes to the partnership?

The "extra" $12,000 that Hardy contributes to the partnership is treated as a "bonus" paid to the existing partners. Generally, such a bonus is allocated to existing partners in accordance with their profit-sharing agreement. Assume that the three partners of Cabrillo Enterprises shared profits and losses equally before Hardy's admission. Following is the entry to record Hardy's admission to the partnership and the allocation of the $12,000 bonus to his new partners.

May 15	Cash	140,000	
	B. Hardy, Capital		128,000
	C. Keith, Capital		4,000
	E. Stacy, Capital		4,000
	P. Tate, Capital		4,000

To record admission of Bill Hardy to
partnership

Now, consider a situation in which the existing partners of a firm are very eager to convince a specific person to join their partnership. This individual may have skills

A partnership that operates a chain of sporting goods stores would benefit from having a high-profile athlete, such as Hall of Fame basketball player Cheryl Miller, as a partner.

particularly needed by the partnership or a "high profile" that will attract additional business to the firm. For example, a partnership that operates sporting goods stores would benefit if Cheryl Miller (Hall of Fame basketball player) became a partner and appeared in occasional advertisements for the firm. As an incentive to "join up," the existing partners may offer such an individual a greater ownership interest in the partnership than justified by his or her initial investment. That is, the existing partners may offer a bonus to the prospective new partner. To illustrate this possibility, we can modify the facts of the case just presented.

Assume that the three existing partners of Cabrillo Enterprises are very interested in convincing Bill Hardy to join their partnership—so interested that they offer him a one-fourth ownership interest in the firm for $100,000. Following Hardy's investment of $100,000, the partnership will have total capital of $472,000. Because of his agreement with the existing partners, Hardy's capital account upon his admission should be credited $118,000, or one-fourth of the partnership's total capital ($472,000/4). The $18,000 bonus credited to Hardy's capital account must be allocated (debited) to the capital accounts of the existing partners. Generally, such an allocation is made in the same proportions as the profit-sharing ratios of the partners. Because the existing partners share profits and losses equally, an equal amount of the $18,000 bonus, or $6,000, should be charged to each of their capital accounts. Under this scenario, the following entry would be made to record the admission of Hardy to the partnership.

Jul. 7	Cash	100,000	
	C. Keith, Capital	6,000	
	E. Stacy, Capital	6,000	
	P. Tate, Capital	6,000	
	B. Hardy, Capital		118,000
	To record admission of Bill Hardy to partnership		

Real World
The restaurant chain Planet Hollywood is a partnership with several "high profile" partners, including Sylvester Stallone and Bruce Willis.

Teaching Note
Remind students that when a partner withdraws or a new partner is admitted, the former partnership is dissolved and a new partnership is generally created.

WITHDRAWAL OF A PARTNER   A partner may withdraw from a partnership by selling his or her ownership interest to an outside party as illustrated in the previous section. Alternatively, a partner can withdraw by "selling out" to another partner or to the partnership as a whole. In this section, we consider the latter alternative.

Partnership agreements typically dictate the payments partners are entitled to receive when they withdraw from a partnership. The most common arrangement is for a withdrawing partner to receive an amount equal to the balance of his or her capital account. For example, assume that Carla Vecchia decides to withdraw from a partnership that operates a small business, Landscape By Design. Following the restatement of the partnership's assets to their current values, the balances of the partners' capital accounts are as follows:

Lesley Jennings	$21,000
Kelly Kovich	17,000
Carla Vecchia	13,000
Total Partners' Capital	$51,000

The partnership agreement of Landscape By Design states that a withdrawing partner is entitled to receive assets equal to the balance of his or her capital account. Shown next is the entry that would be made to record the withdrawal of Vecchia from the partnership if she is paid cash for her ownership interest.

Oct. 3	C. Vecchia, Capital	13,000	
	Cash		13,000
	To record withdrawal of Carla Vecchia from partnership		

Occasionally, a partner receives more or less than the balance of his or her capital account upon withdrawing from a partnership. The difference between the amount paid to a withdrawing partner and the balance of his or her capital account is treated as a bonus to the withdrawing partner or a bonus to the remaining partners. Suppose that Landscape By Design has most of its assets invested in equipment and only $9,500 in cash when Carla Vecchia decides to withdraw. Because she does not want her friends to be forced to sell equipment to raise additional cash, Vecchia agrees to accept the $9,500 in cash for her ownership interest in the partnership. The $3,500 difference between Vecchia's capital account ($13,000) and the amount she is paid upon withdrawing from the partnership ($9,500) is treated as a bonus to the remaining partners. Assuming the partners of Landscape By Design share profits and losses equally, the two remaining partners will each be entitled to a $1,750 bonus upon Vecchia's withdrawal. Following is the entry to record Vecchia's withdrawal under these circumstances.

Oct. 3	C. Vecchia, Capital	13,000	
	Cash		9,500
	L. Jennings, Capital		1,750
	K. Kovich, Capital		1,750
	To record withdrawal of Carla Vecchia from partnership		

■ LEARNING
OBJECTIVE 6
Account for the liquidation of a partnership and prepare a statement of partnership liquidation

PARTNERSHIP LIQUIDATION   When a partnership decides to go out of business or "liquidate," for whatever reason, the firm's accountants first close the books as if it were the end of a normal accounting period. Then, a three-step liquidation process is

■ **EXHIBIT 15.2**

Newcastle Communications, Post-Closing Trial Balance as of April 1, 1995

	DEBIT	**CREDIT**
Cash	$10,000	
Accounts Receivable (Net)	56,000	
Equipment (Net)	33,000	
Accounts Payable		27,000
M. Hale, Capital		19,000
L. McGill, Capital		41,000
J. Polumbra, Capital		12,000
Total	$99,000	$99,000

generally followed. First, the partnership disposes of its noncash assets. Second, the partnership's liabilities are paid. Finally, all remaining cash is distributed to the partners.

To illustrate a partnership liquidation, consider the untimely demise of Newcastle Communications, a mail-order business operated by three partners. Like many small businesses, Newcastle Communications encountered cash-flow problems stemming principally from slow-paying customers. So, the partners decided to shut down their business as of April 1, 1995. Exhibit 15.2 contains a post-closing trial balance as of that date for Newcastle.

When a business is liquidated, the owners often suffer losses resulting from the sale of its assets. Why? One reason is that the business's assets generally have to be sold at unfavorable prices to quickly raise cash needed to pay off nervous creditors. In the present example, assume that Newcastle Communications sold its accounts receivable to a finance company for $28,000, resulting in a loss of the same amount. The equipment that had a net book value of $33,000 was sold for $21,000. In total, then, the partnership suffered a loss of $40,000 on the sale of these assets. Newcastle's partners shared profits and losses in the following proportions: Hale—20 percent, McGill—30 percent, and Polumbra—50 percent. Consequently, the loss on the disposal of Newcastle's noncash assets was allocated as follows to the partners.

Hale	$40,000 × 20% =	$ 8,000
McGill	40,000 × 30% =	12,000
Polumbra	40,000 × 50% =	20,000

Listed next are the entries to record the sale of Newcastle's accounts receivable and equipment and to allocate the resulting loss to the partners' capital accounts. When a partnership is being liquidated, losses incurred on the disposal of assets are closed directly to the partners' capital accounts instead of being funneled through the Income Summary account.

Apr. 21	Cash	49,000	
	Loss on Disposal of Assets	40,000	
	Accounts Receivable		33,000
	Equipment		56,000

To record disposal of noncash assets for the purpose of liquidating the partnership

Apr. 21	M. Hale, Capital	8,000	
	L. McGill, Capital	12,000	
	J. Polumbra, Capital	20,000	
	Loss on Disposal of Assets		40,000

To allocate loss on disposal of assets
to partners' capital accounts

statement of partnership liquidation

The liquidation of a partnership generally requires at least several weeks to complete, sometimes much longer. To keep partners informed of the status of a liquidation as it progresses, a statement of partnership liquidation may be prepared and periodically updated. A **statement of partnership liquidation** is a financial report of a partnership's account balances at various stages of its liquidation. Shown in Exhibit 15.3 is a statement of partnership liquidation for Newcastle Communications. Notice that this statement was prepared as of April 21, 1995, following the sale of the noncash assets. As demonstrated by Exhibit 15.3, one partner, Polumbra, had already seen his ownership interest in the partnership totally "wiped out" by this stage of the liquidation. In fact, Polumbra owed the partnership $8,000 at this point.

The next step in the liquidation of Newcastle Communications was to pay off its debts. The following entry was made to record the payment of Newcastle's accounts payable.

May 10	Accounts Payable	27,000	
	Cash		27,000

To pay remaining liabilities of
partnership

After the liabilities of Newcastle Communications were paid, the three partners had to resolve the matter of Polumbra's "capital deficiency." There were two possibilities at this point. Either Polumbra was solvent and would pay the $8,000 to the partnership, or he was insolvent and the $8,000 would be treated as a loss by the other two Newcastle partners. Fortunately for the other two partners, Polumbra paid the $8,000 to the partnership. This payment was recorded as follows:

■ **EXHIBIT 15.3**
Preliminary Version of Statement of Partnership Liquidation for Newcastle Communications

	NEWCASTLE COMMUNICATIONS STATEMENT OF PARTNERSHIP LIQUIDATION AS OF APRIL 21, 1995					
	CASH	**NONCASH ASSETS**	**LIABILITIES**	**HALE CAPITAL**	**MCGILL CAPITAL**	**POLUMBRA CAPITAL**
Beginning Balances	$10,000	$89,000	$27,000	$19,000	$41,000	$12,000
Sale of Noncash Assets and Allocation of Loss	49,000	(89,000)		(8,000)	(12,000)	(20,000)
Updated Balances	$59,000	-0-	$27,000	$11,000	$29,000	($8,000)

Jun. 5	Cash	8,000	
	J. Polumbra, Capital		8,000
	To record receipt of cash from		
	J. Polumbra		

If Polumbra had not paid the $8,000, his capital deficiency would have been allocated to Hale and McGill in proportion to their profit-sharing percentages. Since Hale was allocated 20 percent of the partnership's losses and McGill 30 percent, the $8,000 "loss" would have been charged to the two partners as follows:

Hale: [20%/(20% + 30%)] × $8,000 = $3,200
McGill: [30%/(20% + 30%)] × $8,000 = $4,800

The final step in the liquidation process was to distribute Newcastle's remaining cash to its partners. After updating the partnership's account balances for the two previous entries, the partnership had three nonzero account balances: Cash—$40,000, M. Hale, Capital—$11,000, and L. McGill, Capital—$29,000. The following entry recorded the distribution of the firm's cash to Hale and McGill. Shown in Exhibit 15.4 is the final version of the statement of partnership liquidation for Newcastle Communications.

Jun. 30	M. Hale, Capital	11,000	
	L. McGill, Capital	29,000	
	Cash		40,000
	To record distribution of remaining		
	cash to partners		

■ **EXHIBIT 15.4**
Final Version of Statement of Partnership Liquidation for Newcastle Communications

NEWCASTLE COMMUNICATIONS
FINAL STATEMENT OF PARTNERSHIP LIQUIDATION
APRIL 1, 1995–JUNE 30, 1995

	CASH	NONCASH ASSETS	LIABILITIES	HALE CAPITAL	McGILL CAPITAL	POLUMBRA CAPITAL
Beginning Balances	$10,000	$89,000	$27,000	$19,000	$41,000	$12,000
Sale of Noncash Assets and Allocation of Loss	49,000	(89,000)		(8,000)	(12,000)	(20,000)
Updated Balances	$59,000	-0-	$27,000	$11,000	$29,000	($8,000)
Payment of Liabilities	(27,000)		(27,000)			
Updated Balances	$32,000	-0-	-0-	$11,000	$29,000	($8,000)
Receipt of Deficiency	8,000					8,000
Updated Balances	$40,000	-0-	-0-	$11,000	$29,000	$ -0-
Distribution of Cash to Partners	(40,000)			(11,000)	(29,000)	
Final Balances	-0-	-0-	-0-	-0-	-0-	-0-

PROPRIETORSHIPS

sole proprietorship

In Chapter 2, a **sole proprietorship** was defined as a business owned by one individual. By far, proprietorships are the most common type of business entity. In the early 1990s, the U.S. Bureau of the Census reported nearly 15 million nonfarm businesses operating as proprietorships, more than twice the number of partnerships and corporations combined.[3] Nevertheless, the total revenues of proprietorships are swamped by the collective revenues of corporations. As reported in Chapter 2, approximately 90 percent of annual U.S. business revenues are produced by corporations, 6 percent by proprietorships and approximately 4 percent by partnerships. In this section, we first consider broad accounting and control issues related to proprietorships and then discuss accounting for the ownership interests of these business entities.

Proprietorships: Accounting on a "No Frills" Budget

The defining characteristic of most proprietorships is their size. Referring again to statistics published by the U.S. Bureau of the Census, proprietorships had average annual revenues in the early 1990s of approximately $49,000. The comparable figures for partnerships and corporations were $348,000 and $2.9 million, respectively.[4] The small size of most proprietorships has a pervasive influence on their accounting and control functions. For example, a small business owner typically cannot justify investing considerable resources in an accounting system. It is not unusual to find "Mom and Pop" businesses still using "pen and paper" accounting systems. However, the declining cost of personal computers and computer software has enticed many small business owners to buy computer-based accounting systems "off the shelf" in recent years. By 1995, a comprehensive set of accounting software programs for a small business could be purchased for less than $100.

Although a small business may have its own high-tech, if low-cost, accounting system, the reliability of that system largely depends upon the accounting expertise of the individual entering the debits and credits. Possibly the most common error made by small business owners who double as "do-it-yourself" accountants is the commingling of their personal assets and liabilities with those of their business. Unlike a corporation, a proprietorship is not a legal entity distinct from its owner. Nevertheless, proprietorship accounting records should reflect only the business's assets, not the personal assets and liabilities of the owner.

Quite often, a small business owner who doubles as the company bookkeeper has a sudden change of heart. When a banker rejects a loan application because accounts payable are listed under owner's equity on the firm's balance sheet or an IRS agent points out that a depreciation schedule does not balance, the owner will likely reach for the telephone and dial C-P-A.

Discussion Question

A young man has just opened a pizza shop in a strip mall. He knows how to make pizza, but he knows nothing about accounting. What course of action would you recommend? Answer: A visit to a friendly local CPA who specializes in small business clients.

Teaching Note

Failure to keep a proprietorship's financial data separate from its owner's personal financial data will make it difficult, if not impossible, to prepare reliable financial statements for the firm for use by external decision makers.

■ LEARNING OBJECTIVE 7

Account for the ownership interests of proprietorships

Accounting for the Ownership Interests of Proprietorships

Accounting for the owner's equity of a proprietorship is fairly simple since, by definition, there is only one owner. There is no need to compute earnings per share for a proprietorship or to "divvy up" earnings at year-end among several partners' capital accounts. To illustrate accounting for the owner's equity of a proprietorship, consider

---

3. U.S. Bureau of the Census, *Statistical Abstract of the United States, 1994* (Washington, D.C.: U.S. Government Printing Office, 1994), 539.
4. Ibid.

a bakery owned and operated by Rosie McNatt. Rosie established this business recently by transferring $25,000 from her personal savings account into a checking account entitled Rosie's Bakery. This initial transaction was recorded as follows:

Sep. 16	Cash	25,000	
	Rosie McNatt, Capital		25,000
	To record initial investment		

In the next few weeks, Rosie leased a shop, purchased various supplies and equipment, and placed an ad in the local paper to announce her grand opening. Accounting for the payment of rent, purchases of supplies, and other common business transactions is no different for a proprietorship than for a corporation or partnership. So, there is no need for us to examine Rosie's accounting entries for such transactions.

Similar to the owners of a partnership, a sole proprietor may "pay" herself or himself a weekly or monthly salary allowance. Again, such payments are not considered expenses for accounting purposes. If such amounts were considered expenses, a sole proprietor could easily distort the entity's profits by varying the amount of salary he or she receives each accounting period. Salary allowances and other assets withdrawn by a proprietor from a business are recorded in a drawing account. For example, assume that Rosie McNatt withdraws $2,200 from her business for personal use. The following entry would be made to record this transaction.

Oct. 25	Rosie McNatt, Drawing	2,200	
	Cash		2,200
	To record withdrawal of cash		

At the end of each accounting period, Rosie's accountant will close the business's books. First, the balances of Rosie's revenue and expense accounts will be closed to the Income Summary account. Next, the balance of the Income Summary account will be closed to Rosie's capital account. Finally, the balance of the drawing account will be closed to Rosie's capital account. To illustrate the closing process for a proprietorship, assume that the following schedule summarizes the revenues, expenses, and withdrawals of Rosie's Bakery for a recent accounting period.

Sales	$3,800
Baking Supplies Used	900
Utilities	200
Advertising	100
Withdrawals	1,100

The following entries would be necessary to close Rosie's books at the end of this accounting period.

Nov. 30	Sales	3,800	
	Income Summary		3,800
	To close the Sales account		
Nov. 30	Income Summary	1,200	
	Baking Supplies Expense		900
	Utilities Expense		200
	Advertising Expense		100
	To close expense accounts		

Teaching Note
Emphasize that the key difference between a partnership's accounting records and a sole proprietorship's accounting records is the number of capital and drawing accounts. A partnership has multiple capital and drawing accounts, while a proprietorship has one capital account and one drawing account.

International Opportunities for Small Businesses: Advice from the Accounting Profession

Real World
Indirect exporting typically allows small businesses to avoid dealing with the problems and risks posed by translating business receipts and disbursements from one currency to another.

As pointed out in Chapter 14, economic markets around the world are rapidly merging into one global economy. To remain competitive and to maximize the return on their investments, small businesses must be aware of this trend and attempt to benefit from it. Not surprisingly, when a small business owner wants to pursue international opportunities, he or she often turns to a local CPA. Besides providing a full array of accounting services to small businesses, CPAs also serve such clients as general business consultants. Recently, the AICPA published a book to assist CPAs in advising small businesses that want to expand the market for their goods and services past U.S. borders.

Excerpts from this book were published in an article in the Journal of Accountancy. *One suggestion to small businesses included in this article was the following advice on how to become involved in "indirect exporting."*

Indirect exporting is a good beginning for a company [that wants to become involved in international commerce]. It involves minimal start-up costs and low risk. The following are the three forms of indirect exporting.

1. The company passively fills orders from domestic buyers who subsequently export the product to foreign consumers.

2. The company seeks out domestic buyers—usually other U.S. companies, foreign corporations, foreign trading companies, foreign government agencies or foreign distributors and retailers—to purchase its product for export. The buyer assumes the risk as well as the responsibility for exporting.

Many small businesses have attempted to take advantage of the increasingly global nature of economic markets in recent years. To learn how to become involved in exporting their goods and services to foreign countries, small business owners often turn to their accountants.

3. The company retains a domestic intermediary, such as an export management company (EMC) or an international consultant, to identify foreign consumers for its products. The domestic company, as the actual exporter, retains control over exporting operations. Although representatives may be costly, their knowledge of products and established networks of foreign distributors make them a valuable asset to companies wanting to export their products indirectly.

SOURCE: Murray, M. F., "Answers to Small Business Questions in International Opportunities," Journal of Accountancy, August 1993, 52-53. Reprinted with permission of *The Journal of Accountancy*. Copyright © 1993 by American Institute of CPAs. Opinions of the authors are their own and do not necessarily reflect policies of the AICPA.

Nov. 30	Income Summary	2,600	
	Rosie McNatt, Capital		2,600
	To close Income Summary account		
Nov. 30	Rosie McNatt, Capital	1,100	
	Rosie McNatt, Drawing		1,100
	To close drawing account		

SUMMARY

A partnership is an unincorporated business with two or more owners. A partnership agreement defines the key features of the contractual arrangement between, or among, the partners including the method to be used in allocating profits and losses to individual partners. The characteristic that most clearly distinguishes partnerships from corporations is the unlimited liability of individual partners for a partnership's debts. Another key characteristic of the partnership form of business organization is mutual agency, which is the authority of individual partners to enter into contracts binding on the entire partnership.

For accounting purposes, a separate capital or equity account is maintained for each member of a partnership. The fair market value of the assets initially contributed by partners to a partnership should be credited to their capital accounts. Several methods can be used to allocate a partnership's profits and losses to the capital accounts of individual partners. For example, profits and losses may be allocated in proportion to the partners' initial capital investments. Partners often withdraw assets, typically cash, from a partnership. Such withdrawals are recorded in a drawing account, which is a temporary equity account. The balances of partners' drawing accounts are closed at the end of an accounting period to the partners' capital accounts. To document the changes in partners' capital accounts for a given period, a statement of partners' capital is prepared.

A partnership must be dissolved whenever a new partner is admitted or an existing partner withdraws. In such circumstances, the partnership can continue operating while a new partnership agreement is being reached between, or among, the new set of partners. A partnership's assets are usually restated to their fair market values before a partner withdraws or a new partner is admitted. Such restatements ensure that partners participate only in increases and decreases in the value of a partnership's assets that occur while they are members of the partnership. A new partner can be admitted either by purchasing the ownership interest of an existing partner or by contributing assets to the partnership. When a partner is admitted, a "bonus" may be credited to the new partner's capital account or the capital accounts of the existing partners. A partner withdrawing from a partnership typically receives a distribution of partnership assets equal to the balance of his or her capital account.

When a partnership discontinues its business operations, a three-step liquidation process is followed. First, the partnership disposes of its noncash assets, which may require the allocation of gains or losses to the partners' capital accounts. Second, the partnership pays its liabilities. Third, the remaining cash of the partnership is distributed to the partners based upon the balances of their capital accounts. A statement of partnership liquidation is often prepared to keep partners informed of the status of a liquidation as it progresses.

A sole proprietorship is a business owned by one individual. The small size of most proprietorships has important implications for their accounting and control functions. For example, proprietorships typically cannot justify investing considerable resources in an accounting system. Accounting for the owner's equity of a proprietorship is similar to accounting for a partnership's ownership interests. A capital account and drawing account are established for the owner of a proprietorship. At the end of each accounting period, the net income of a proprietorship and the balance of the drawing account are closed to the proprietor's capital account.

GLOSSARY

Dissolution (p. 654)   The termination of a partnership.

Liquidation (p. 654)   The process of converting a discontinued partnership's assets into cash, paying its liabilities, and then distributing any remaining cash to the partners.

Partnership (p. 653)   An unincorporated business with two or more owners.

Partnership agreement (p. 653)   A contract between, or among, the members of a partnership that defines the key contractual rights and responsibilities of each partner.

Sole proprietorship (p. 668)   A business owned by one individual.

Statement of partners' capital (p. 661)   A partnership financial statement that documents the changes in partners' capital accounts during a given period; equivalent to a corporation's statement of stockholders' equity.

Statement of partnership liquidation (p. 666)   A financial report of a partnership's account balances at various stages of its liquidation.

DECISION CASE

Suppose that you have recently been contacted by a friend from your home town. This individual is one of three partners who own 3D Mining, a small mining company that operates in the Powder Basin of Wyoming. 3D Mining owns a five-year lease on a mining site. When that lease expires, the partnership will be liquidated. Your friend has invited you to join the partnership by investing $100,000. The company needs the additional funds to acquire new mining equipment.

The existing partners have given you a choice between two profit-sharing agreements if you join the partnership. Under Option A, each of the other three partners would receive an annual salary allowance of $20,000. They each work in the business, while you would be a "passive" partner. Any profit remaining after the salary allowances would be allocated 50 percent to the existing partners and 50 percent to you. Any income deficiency would be allocated in the same manner. Under Option B, the three existing partners would each receive an annual salary allowance of $20,000, while you would receive a 5 percent interest allowance on your initial investment. Any profit or income deficiency following the distribution of the salary and interest allowances would be divided equally among you and the other three partners. That is, you would be allocated 25 percent of that profit or income deficiency.

The existing partners also offer you Option C, which is to borrow $100,000 from you at an annual interest rate of 10 percent. A final option available to you is to invest your $100,000 nest egg in a five-year CD (certificate of deposit) that pays interest at an annual rate of 7 percent.

Required: Suppose that you have analyzed the financial statements of 3D Mining and thoroughly investigated the company's business operations. You believe that over the next five years there is a 25 percent likelihood the company will earn $60,000 annually before any salary and interest allowances paid to partners. Likewise, the probability that the company will earn the following amounts, before salary and interest allowances, is 25 percent each: $80,000, $100,000, and $120,000. On average, which of the following investment alternatives is optimal for you: Option A, Option B, Option C, or Option D (investing the $100,000 in a 7 percent CD)? Which investment alternative has the highest potential return for you? Which alternative has the lowest potential return for you? Suppose the company actually earns $80,000 annually over its remaining five years. Under this assumption, which investment alternative is preferred? What factors, other than those specifically mentioned, should you consider in making this decision?

QUESTIONS

1. Identify the factor most responsible for large numbers of partnerships converting to the corporate form of organization.

2. What is a partnership agreement and why is it important to the proper functioning of a partnership?

3. What is a limited partnership?

4. Define the terms "dissolution" and "liquidation" as they apply to partnerships.

5. Are partnerships taxable entities? Explain.

6. What is one key difference in the method used to account for the stockholders' equity of a corporation versus the owners' equity of a partnership?

7. How should noncash assets contributed to a partnership by a new partner be valued when initially recorded in the partnership's accounting records?

8. Identify factors that partners may consider in deciding how to allocate a partnership's profits among themselves.

9. How are partnership profits and losses divided if the partnership agreement is silent on this point?

10. Why are salary and interest allowances granted to partners not considered expenses for purposes of a partnership's accounting records? What is the key purpose of salary and interest allowances?

11. What is the purpose of partnership drawing accounts?

12. Drawing accounts are equivalent to what account of a corporation?

13. Briefly describe the differences in the period-ending closing procedures for a corporation versus a partnership.

14. A statement of partners' capital is equivalent to what financial statement of a corporation?

15. Identify the two general ways that a new partner can acquire an ownership interest in an existing partnership.

16. Describe the meaning of the term "bonus" as it relates to the admission of a new partner to a partnership.

17. When a partner withdraws from a partnership, how much cash or other assets is he or she typically entitled to receive?

18. Identify the three steps typically followed in liquidating a partnership.

19. Why is it common for owners to suffer losses when a business is discontinued and its assets sold?

20. What is the purpose of a statement of partnership liquidation?

21. Which business entities collectively generate more annual revenues in the United States, partnerships or proprietorships?

22. What is the defining characteristic of most proprietorships? How does this characteristic affect the accounting function of proprietorships?

23. Compare and contrast the accounting methods used for the owner's equity of a proprietorship versus the owners' equity of a partnership.

EXERCISES

24. Partnership Characteristics (LO 1)

Following are definitions or descriptions of terms relating to partnerships.

_____ The account in which individual partners' withdrawals are recorded each period.

_____ Term indicating that the continuity of existence feature applicable to corporations is not applicable to partnerships.

_____ A financial report prepared at various points during the liquidation of a partnership.

_____ The account in which a partner's initial investment and subsequent allocations of his or her share of partnership profits are recorded.

_____ The termination of a partnership.

_____ A contract between, or among, the members of a partnership that defines the key contractual rights and responsibilities of each partner.

_____ The process of converting a discontinued partnership's assets into cash, paying its liabilities, and then distributing any remaining cash to the partners.

_____ The authority of individual partners to enter into contracts binding on the entire partnership.

_____ A partnership financial statement that documents the changes in partners' capital accounts during a given period.

_____ A feature of partnerships that makes individual partners responsible for a partnership's liabilities.

Required:

Match each definition or description listed with the appropriate term from the following list.

a. Partnership agreement
b. Statement of partnership liquidation
c. Mutual agency
d. Capital account
e. Unlimited liability
f. Liquidation
g. Statement of partners' capital
h. Drawing account
i. Limited life
j. Dissolution

25. Advantages and Disadvantages of Partnerships (LO 1)

Charles Xavier is planning to form a partnership along with several of his close friends. Xavier is unfamiliar with the specific features of partnerships and other forms of business organizations.

Required:

Write a memo to Xavier explaining how a partnership differs from a corporation and a proprietorship. In your memo, be sure to comment on the following key features of partnerships and whether these features are generally advantages or disadvantages of the partnership form of business organization: unlimited liability, mutual agency, limited life, joint ownership of assets, and nontaxable status.

26. Partnership Formation (LO 2)

John Burr and Alex Hale decide to form a partnership. Following are the book values and fair market values of the assets and liabilities contributed to this new

24. h,i,b,d,j,a,f,c,g,e

25. No check figures

partnership by each of these individuals who previously operated their own businesses as sole proprietors.

	BURR		HALE	
	Book Value	*Fair Market Value*	*Book Value*	*Fair Market Value*
Cash	$10,000	$10,000	$ 5,000	$ 5,000
Supplies	15,000	12,000	0	0
Inventory	20,000	23,500	0	0
Furniture	12,000	15,000	20,000	17,500
Building	0	0	150,000	160,000
Land	0	0	25,000	40,000
Note Payable	0	0	(110,000)	(110,000)
Totals	$57,000	$60,500	$ 90,000	$112,500

Required:
1. Prepare the entry to record the initial investment of each partner in the new partnership.
2. Suppose that because Hale was eager to have Burr as a partner, he granted Burr a 50 percent ownership interest in the net assets of the new partnership. Prepare the entry to record the formation of the partnership under this assumption.

26. 1. Cr. Burr, Capital $60,500
Cr. Hale, Capital $112,500
2. Cr. Burr, Capital $86,500
Cr. Hale, Capital $86,500

27. Allocation of Partnership Profits and Losses (LO 3)
Mathis Furniture is a retail furniture store owned by Jonetta, Kiana, and Laura, three sisters. The partners' original capital contributions to the partnership were $50,000, $30,000, and $20,000, respectively. The partnership agreement states that partnership profits and losses are to be allocated in the same proportions as the partners' initial capital investments.

Required:
1. Assume that during 1996, Mathis Furniture earned a profit of $240,000. Allocate this profit to the individual partners' capital accounts.
2. Allocate the $240,000 profit for 1996 to the three partners' capital accounts assuming that the partnership agreement is silent on how profits and losses are to be allocated.

27. 1. Jonetta, $120,000
Kiana, $72,000
Laura, $48,000
2. Jonetta, $80,000
Kiana, $80,000
Laura, $80,000

28. Allocation of Partnership Profits and Losses (LO 3)
Three individuals own and operate St. Croix Enterprises, a real estate development company. Following are the names of these individuals, their original capital investments, their annual salary allowances, and the balances of their capital accounts on January 1, 1996.

PARTNER	ORIGINAL CAPITAL INVESTMENT	ANNUAL SALARY ALLOWANCE	BALANCE OF CAPITAL ACCOUNT, JANUARY 1, 1996
R. Hearst	$ 50,000	$40,000	$105,000
C. Kane	70,000	30,000	84,000
O. Welles	100,000	20,000	110,000

In addition to an annual salary allowance, each partner is granted an annual interest allowance equal to 10 percent of his or her original capital investment. Any profit or income deficiency remaining after the allocation of the salary and interest allowances is divided equally among the partners.

28. 1. Hearst, $55,000
        Kane, $47,000
        Welles, $40,000
    2. Hearst, $42,000
        Kane, $34,000
        Welles,
        $27,000

Required:

Allocate the 1996 profit of St. Croix Enterprises to the capital accounts of its three partners assuming that profit is:

1. $142,000.
2. $103,000.

29. Allocation of Partnership Profits and Losses (LO 3)

Following is the partially completed 1996 profit allocation schedule for Four Star Partnership.

PARTNER	SALARY ALLOWANCE	INTEREST ALLOWANCE	REMAINDER	TOTAL
Star 1	$12,000	?	($4,000)	?
Star 2	16,000	?	?	?
Star 3	0	5,000	?	?
Star 4	?	?	?	?
Totals	$50,000	?	?	?

Three of the partners of this firm receive salary allowances, Star 3 being the exception. Each partner receives an annual interest allowance equal to 10 percent of his or her capital balance at the beginning of the year. Capital balances on January 1, 1996, were as follows:

Star 1	$40,000
Star 2	20,000
Star 3	50,000
Star 4	60,000

After the allocation of salary and interest allowances, the remaining profit or income deficiency is allocated in the following proportions to the partners' capital accounts:

Star 1	1/5
Star 2	1/5
Star 3	1/5
Star 4	2/5

29. Star 1, $12,000
    Star 2, $14,000
    Star 3, $1,000
    Star 4, $20,000

Required:

Complete the 1996 profit allocation schedule for Four Star Partnership.

30. Partnership Drawing Accounts (LO 4)

In accordance with their partnership agreement, the three partners of Oak Tree Developers are allowed to withdraw cash from the partnership to provide for their personal expenses. The only restriction in the partnership agreement is that a partner may not withdraw more than $5,000 per month for this purpose. The following schedule lists the withdrawals made by the partners during December 1995 and the total withdrawals for the year:

30. 1. Dr. Donahue, Drawing
        $4,500
        Dr. Jude, Drawing
        $3,500
        Dr. Thomas, Drawing
        $5,000
    2. Cr. Donahue, Drawing
        $52,500
        Cr. Jude, Drawing
        $47,000
        Cr. Thomas, Drawing
        $60,000

	DECEMBER WITHDRAWALS	TOTAL WITHDRAWALS DURING YEAR
M. Donahue	$4,500	$52,500
S. Jude	3,500	47,000
D. Thomas	5,000	60,000

Required:

1. Prepare the journal entry to record the withdrawals made by the partners during December 1995.
2. Prepare the entry to close the partners' drawing accounts at the end of 1995.

31. **Admission of a New Partner** (LO 5)

Nancy Belmont wants to purchase an interest in Seal Beach Imports, a partnership with total capital of $720,000. The partners of this firm have an explicit agreement that all profits and losses will be shared equally regardless of the number of partners within the firm. Following are the capital account balances of the firm's existing partners:

Jack Alamitos, Capital	$120,000
Katie Bolsa, Capital	350,000
Tom Chica, Capital	250,000
Total	$720,000

The existing partners of Seal Beach Imports have approved admitting Nancy to the partnership under either of two options she negotiated. The first option involves Nancy purchasing Tom Chica's ownership interest for $300,000, while the second option involves Nancy contributing $280,000 to the partnership for a one-fourth ownership interest in the firm.

Required:

1. Why is it important that all existing partners of a firm approve the admission of a new partner?
2. Prepare the journal entry necessary to record the admission of Nancy if she purchases Tom Chica's ownership interest.
3. Prepare the journal entry necessary to record the admission of Nancy if she contributes $280,000 to obtain a one-fourth ownership interest in the firm.
4. Which of the two options do you believe Nancy will choose? Why?

31. 2. Cr. Belmont, Capital
$250,000
3. Cr. Belmont, Capital
$250,000
Cr. Alamitos, Capital
$10,000

32. **Withdrawal of a Partner** (LO 5)

Sharon Regard has recently decided to withdraw from Penisula Exports, a four-person partnership. The partners in the firm share profits and losses equally. Immediately prior to Sharon's withdrawal, the balances of the partnership's capital accounts were as follows:

T. Beau, Capital	$100,000
O. Corne, Capital	150,000
S. Regard, Capital	110,000
J. Wallis, Capital	135,000
Total	$495,000

Required:

Prepare the appropriate journal entry to record the withdrawal of Sharon Regard from this partnership under each of the following assumptions:
1. She receives cash equal to the balance of her capital account.
2. She receives $120,000.
3. She receives cash of $80,000 and a short-term note receivable of $70,000 signed by the remaining three partners.

32. 1. Dr. Regard, Capital
$110,000
2. Dr. Regard, Capital
$110,000
Dr. Beau, Capital
$3,333.33
3. Dr. Regard, Capital
$110,000
Dr. Beau, Capital
$13,333.33

33. **Partnership Liquidation** (LO 6)

On June 30, 1996, the partners of the law firm Brown, McGrew & Associates decided to liquidate the partnership. The three partners of this firm share profits and losses equally. Following is the post-closing trial balance of this firm on June 30, 1996.

	DEBIT	CREDIT
Cash	$ 50,000	
Accounts Receivable (Net)	60,000	
Furniture and Equipment (Net)	80,000	

Accounts Payable		$ 25,000
Brown, Capital		70,000
Herrick, Capital		70,000
McGrew, Capital		25,000
	$190,000	$190,000

On July 15, the law firm's accounts receivable were sold to a local collection agency for $48,000. Two weeks later, the firm's furniture and equipment were sold for $44,000. On August 5, the company's outstanding liabilities were paid. Finally, on August 14, the remaining cash of the firm was distributed to the partners.

Required:

1. Prepare all journal entries necessary to record the liquidation of this partnership.
2. Prepare a final statement of partnership liquidation.
3. Notice that in each case the assets of this company were sold for a loss. Why do partnerships that are being liquidated typically incur losses when they dispose of their assets?

34. **Accounting for a Proprietorship** (LO 7)

Luther McCord went into business for himself on January 1, 1996, by opening Luther's Music Store. Following is the working or pre-closing trial balance of this business on January 31, 1996.

	DEBIT	CREDIT
Cash	$ 6,450	
Inventory	9,000	
Notes Payable		$ 5,000
L. McCord, Capital		10,000
L. McCord, Drawing	1,000	
Sales		17,500
Cost of Goods Sold	12,450	
Rent Expense	2,350	
Utilities Expense	1,200	
Interest Expense	50	
Total	$32,500	$32,500

Required:

Prepare the journal entries needed to close the accounting records of Luther's Music Store on January 31, 1996.

Margin notes:

33. 1. 7/15 Dr. Brown, Capital $4,000
7/29 Dr. Brown, Capital $12,000
8/14 Dr. Brown, Capital $54,000
Dr. Herrick, Capital $54,000
Dr. McGrew, Capital $9,000

34. Dr. Income Summary $1,450
Cr. McCord, Capital $1,450

PROBLEM SET A

35. **Partnership Formation and Allocation of Partnership Profits and Losses** (LO 2, 3, 4)

Alexis Pavin and her two brothers, Boba and Corey, set up a partnership to operate a counseling practice entitled Family Counseling Services. The firm began operations on January 1, 1996. The individual partners' initial investments in the partnership are listed in the following schedule.

	A. PAVIN	B. PAVIN	C. PAVIN
Cash	$10,000	$ 15,000	$60,000
Supplies	1,000	—	—
Equipment	9,000	30,000	—
Furniture	—	30,000	—
Building	—	105,000	—

Note Payable	—	(90,000)	—
	$20,000	$ 90,000	$60,000

Alexis will be the head counselor and general manager of Family Counseling Services. Boba will devote approximately 50 percent of his time to the business performing maintenance and janitorial services, while Corey will work full-time as an associate counselor in the business. Given the division of work responsibilities, each partner will be granted the following annual salary allowances: Alexis—$50,000, Boba—$15,000, and Corey—$40,000. Each partner will also be entitled to an annual interest allowance equal to 10 percent of the balance of his or her capital account at the beginning of the year. Any profit or income deficiency remaining after the allocation of salary and interest allowances will be divided equally among the partners.

Required:
1. Prepare the journal entry necessary on January 1, 1996, to record the partners' initial investments in Family Counseling Services.
2. Suppose that during 1996 the partnership earned a profit of $140,000. Allocate this profit to the capital accounts of the partners and prepare the entry to close the balance of the Income Summary account to the partners' capital accounts at year-end.
3. Suppose that during 1996 the partnership earned a profit of $90,000 and the three partners withdrew the following amounts of cash from the business during the year: Alexis—$7,200, Boba—$14,300, and Corey—$9,000.
    a. Allocate the partnership's profit to the capital accounts of the three partners.
    b. Prepare the entries to close the balance of the Income Summary account and the drawing accounts to the partners' capital accounts at year-end.
    c. Prepare a statement of partners' capital for 1996 for Family Counseling Services.
4. Suppose that Family Counseling Services applies for a bank loan of $50,000 in early 1997. Other than the firm's financial statements, what other financial information might a bank loan officer request from the individual partners that would not be requested from the executives of a large corporation applying for a similar loan? Explain.

36. **Allocation of Partnership Profits and Losses** (LO 3)
    The Sutter brothers, Brent, Daryl, and Rich, have recently established Ice Rinks of America, a company that operates ice skating rinks in large malls. The brothers are presently attempting to agree on a method for allocating the firm's profits and losses to their individual capital accounts—the firm is organized as a partnership. The following options are being considered.

    Option A: Salary allowance to Brent and Daryl equal to 25 percent of any partnership profit if the partnership earns a profit of at least $100,000. If the partnership suffers a loss during a given year or does not earn a profit of at least $100,000, no salary allowances will be granted. Each partner will also receive an annual interest allowance equal to 10 percent of his capital account balance at the beginning of the year. Any remaining profit or income deficiency after the allocation of salary and interest allowances will be divided equally among the partners.
    Option B: Partnership profits and losses divided equally among the three partners.

    The initial investments of the three brothers in the partnership are as follows: Brent—$0, Daryl—$50,000, and Rich—$500,000.

35. 1. Cr. A. Pavin, Capital $20,000
       Cr. B. Pavin, Capital $90,000
       Cr. C. Pavin, Capital $60,000
    2. Cr. A. Pavin, Capital $58,000
       Cr. B. Pavin, Capital $30,000
       Cr. C. Pavin, Capital $52,000
    3a. Cr. A. Pavin, Capital $41,333.33
       Cr. B. Pavin, Capital $13,333.33
       Cr. C. Pavin, Capital $35,333.34

36. 1a. Option A
        Brent, $82,916.66
        Daryl, $87,916.67
        Rich, $72,166.67
     Option B
        $81,000 each
    1b. Option A
        Brent, $12,000
        Daryl, $17,000
        Rich, $62,000
     Option B
        $30,333.33 each
    1c. Option A
        Brent, $26,666.67
        Daryl, $31,666.67
        Rich, $49,666.66
     Option B
        $36,000 each

37. 1. Dr. B. Watts, Capital
        $117,000
        Cr. Gibbs, Capital
        $117,000
    2. Cr. Gibbs, Capital
        $150,000
        Cr. B. Watts, Capital
        $3,000
    3. Dr. B. Watts, Capital
        $7,000
        Cr. Gibbs, Capital
        $140,000

38. 1a. Dr. Boosler, Capital
        $500,000
        Cr. Foxx, Capital
        $15,000
        Cr. O'Donnell, Capital
        $7,500
        Cr. Pryor, Capital
        $7,500
    1b. Dr. Boosler, Capital
        $500,000
        Dr. Foxx, Capital
        $25,000
        Dr. O'Donnell, Capital
        $12,500
        Dr. Pryor, Capital
        $12,500

Required:
1. Determine how much profit or loss will be allocated to each Sutter brother under each profit allocation scheme assuming the following profits for the business's first year of operations:
   a. $243,000
   b. $91,000
   c. $108,000
2. Suppose that Rich maintains the accounting records for the partnership. What ethical or "conflict of interest" issue may this raise if Option A is adopted? Explain. How could the partnership eliminate this conflict of interest or minimize its potential impact on the firm?

37. **Admission of a Partner** (LO 5)
Barry, Dewey, and LeRoy Watts own and operate the Eufaula Ironworks. Recently, a cousin, J. C. Gibbs, has inquired about joining the firm. The Watts brothers have agreed to admit Gibbs to the firm, which is organized as a partnership. Presently, the capital account balances of the three partners are as follows:

B. Watts	$117,000
D. Watts	161,000
L. Watts	163,000

The three Watts brothers share profits and losses equally.

Required:
Prepare the journal entry to admit J. C. Gibbs to the Eufaula Ironworks partnership under each of the following assumptions:
1. Gibbs purchases the ownership interest of Barry Watts for $132,000.
2. Gibbs invests $159,000 in the firm in exchange for a 25 percent ownership interest.
3. Gibbs invests $119,000 in the firm in exchange for a 25 percent ownership interest.

38. **Withdrawal of a Partner** (LO 5)
Foxx & Pryor, Attorneys at Law, is a law partnership. Recently, one of the partners of this firm, Ellen Boosler, has indicated that she would like to withdraw from the partnership to establish her own law firm. Following are the updated balances of the firm's capital accounts following Boosler's announcement:

E. Boosler	$500,000
R. Foxx	874,000
R. O'Donnell	604,000
R. Pryor	522,000

The partnership agreement for this law firm dictates that 50 percent of the annual profit or loss of the firm be allocated to the capital account of the firm's senior partner, R. Courtney Foxx. The remaining profit or loss is shared equally by the other partners.

Required:
1. Prepare the journal entry to record the withdrawal of Boosler from the law partnership under the following independent assumptions:
   a. Boosler is paid $470,000 for her ownership interest in the firm.
   b. Boosler receives $550,000 for her ownership interest in the firm.
2. Suppose that immediately following Boosler's withdrawal from the partnership, six clients of Foxx & Pryor inform R. Courtney Foxx that they will be

using the services of Boosler's new law firm in the future. How could Foxx & Pryor have prevented Boosler from "taking" several clients with her when she left the firm?

39. **Partnership Liquidation** (LO 6)

Green Valley Hardware is a retail store located in Green Valley, Nevada. Recently, the four partners who own and operate Green Valley Hardware decided to liquidate the business beginning July 1, 1996. Following is the partnership's post-closing trial balance as of June 30, 1996:

	DEBIT	CREDIT
Cash	$ 12,500	
Accounts Receivable (Net)	25,000	
Inventory	40,000	
Equipment & Fixtures (Net)	70,000	
Accounts Payable		$ 30,250
J. Berwanger, Capital		30,000
J. Capiletti, Capital		40,000
T. Detmer, Capital		31,250
A. Griffin, Capital		16,000
Total	$147,500	$147,500

The partners share profits and losses as follows:

J. Berwanger	30%
J. Capiletti	15%
T. Detmer	20%
A. Griffin	35%

Following is a summary of the transactions engaged in by the company during the liquidation process:

July 7:   Sold accounts receivable to a finance company for $15,000.
July 15: Sold inventory and equipment & fixtures to another hardware store for $80,000.
July 22: Paid accounts payable.
July 31: Disbursed remaining cash to partners.

Required:
1. Prepare the necessary journal entries to record the liquidation of this business.
2. Prepare a final statement of partnership liquidation.

40. **Accounting for the Owner's Equity of a Proprietorship** (LO 7)

In January 1996, Merlie O'Shea opened a plumbing supply shop. Following is the adjusted trial balance on December 31, 1996, of Merlie's Plumbing Supply Store:

	DEBIT	CREDIT
Cash	$ 25,000	
Inventory	52,000	
Supplies	4,350	
Equipment	70,000	
Accumulated Depreciation, Equipment		$ 5,000
Accounts Payable		1,750
Notes Payable		80,000
M. O'Shea, Capital		50,000
Salaries Expense	32,500	
Sales		148,250

39. 1. 7/7   Dr. Berwanger, Capital $3,000
Dr. Capiletti, Capital $1,500
Dr. Detmer, Capital $2,000
Dr. Griffin, Capital $3,500
7/15 Dr. Berwanger, Capital $9,000
Dr. Capiletti, Capital $4,500
Dr. Detmer, Capital $6,000
Dr. Griffin, Capital $10,500
7/31 Dr. Berwanger, Capital $18,000
Dr. Capiletti, Capital $34,000
Dr. Detmer, Capital $23,250
Dr. Griffin, Capital $2,000

Cost of Goods Sold	75,700	
Interest Expense	6,100	
Depreciation Expense	5,000	
Rent Expense	10,500	
Utilities Expense	3,100	
Advertising Expense	750	
	$285,000	$285,000

Merlie is not only the sole proprietor of her store but also its only employee. The salaries expense shown in the business's adjusted trial balance represents cash amounts paid by Merlie to herself.

Required:

1. Prepare the journal entry needed to correct the accounts of Merlie's Plumbing Supply as of December 31, 1996. Why is this entry necessary? Would this entry still be necessary if Merlie did not intend to provide her year-end financial statements to outside parties such as a local bank? Explain.

2. Prepare the closing entries for Merlie's Plumbing Supply Store on December 31, 1996.

3. What is Merlie O'Shea's total ownership interest in her business at the end of 1996?

40. 2. Dr. Income Summary
$47,100
Cr. O'Shea, Capital
$47,100
3. $64,600

PROBLEM SET B

41. Partnership Formation and Allocation of Partnership Profits and Losses (LO 2, 3, 4)

Josie Alou and her two brothers, Felipe and Mattie, recently created a partnership to operate an architectural firm. The firm, Alou Architects & Associates, began operations on January 1, 1996. Josie's initial investment in the partnership was a building valued at $200,000. The new partnership assumed responsibility for the $80,000 balance of the mortgage payable on the building. Felipe and Mattie contributed cash of $60,000 and $100,000, respectively, as their initial investments in the partnership.

The three Alous, all licensed architects, receive an annual salary allowance based on the number of "chargeable" hours they work for the firm each year. For 1996, each partner received $100 per chargeable hour. Each partner is also entitled to an annual interest allowance equal to 10 percent of the balance of his or her capital account at the beginning of the year. Any profit or income deficiency remaining after the allocation of salary and interest allowances is divided equally among the partners.

Required:

1. Prepare the journal entry necessary on January 1, 1996, to record the partners' initial investments in Alou Architects & Associates.

2. Suppose that during 1996, the partnership earned a profit of $424,000 and the three partners had the following number of chargeable hours: Felipe—1,200, Josie—1,500, and Mattie—1,100. Allocate the firm's profit to the capital accounts of the partners and prepare the entry to close the balance of the Income Summary account to the partners' capital accounts at year-end.

3. Suppose that during 1996, the partnership earned a profit of $265,000 and the partners had the following number of chargeable hours: Felipe—1,000, Josie—1,600, and Mattie—1,300. Additionally, the partners withdrew the following amounts of cash from the business during the year: Felipe—$60,000, Josie—$55,000, and Mattie—$68,000.

41. 1. Cr. J. Alou, Capital
$120,000
Cr. F. Alou, Capital
$60,000
Cr. M. Alou, Capital
$100,000
2. Cr. J. Alou, Capital
$167,333.33
Cr. F. Alou, Capital
$131,333.33
Cr. M. Alou, Capital
$125,333.34
3a. Cr. J. Alou, Capital
$121,000
Cr. F. Alou, Capital
$55,000
Cr. M. Alou, Capital
$89,000

a. Allocate the partnership's profit to the capital accounts of the three partners.

b. Prepare the entries to close the balance of the Income Summary account and the drawing accounts to the partners' capital accounts at year-end.

c. Prepare a statement of partners' capital for 1996 for Alou Architects & Associates.

4. Suppose that this firm applies for a bank loan of $200,000 in early 1997. Other than the firm's financial statements, what other financial information might a bank loan officer request from the individual partners that would not be requested from the executives of a large corporation applying for a similar loan? Explain.

42. **Allocation of Partnership Profits and Losses** (LO 3)

The three Fitzgerald sisters, Eunice, Jean, and Rose, have recently established Honey Fitz Enterprises, a movie production company. The sisters are presently considering two methods of allocating the annual profits and losses of this business, which will be operated as a partnership, to their capital accounts. These two profit allocation schemes are as follows:

Option A: Salary allowance of $100,000 each to Eunice and Jean if the partnership earns a profit of $500,000 or more during a given year. Rose will be a passive partner and thus not be entitled to a salary allowance. Each partner will also receive an annual interest allowance equal to 8 percent of her capital account balance at the beginning of the year. Any remaining profit or income deficiency after the allocation of salary and interest allowances will be divided equally among the partners.

Option B: Partnership profits and losses divided equally among the three partners.

The initial investments of the three sisters in the partnership are as follows: Eunice—$200,000, Jean—$100,000, and Rose—$1,000,000.

Required:

1. Determine how much profit or loss will be allocated to each Fitzgerald sister under each profit allocation scheme assuming the following profits for the business's first year of operations:
   a. $490,000
   b. $510,000
   c. $840,000

2. If the company's annual profit is expected to average slightly less than $500,000 each year, which profit allocation scheme do you believe Rose will prefer? Why?

3. Suppose that Rose maintains the accounting records for the partnership. What ethical or "conflict of interest" issue may this raise if Option A is adopted? Explain. How could the partnership eliminate this conflict of interest or minimize its potential impact on the firm?

43. **Admission of a Partner** (LO 5)

Billy, Gomer, and Steve Vessels own and operate the Uptown Athletic Club. Recently, Bud Sims has inquired about joining the firm. The Vessels brothers have agreed to admit Sims to the firm, which is organized as a partnership. Presently, the capital account balances of the three partners are as follows:

B. Vessels	$252,000
G. Vessels	188,000
S. Vessels	196,000

42. 1a. Option A
        Eunice, $144,666.66
        Jean, $136,666.67
        Rose, $208,666.67
     Option B
        $163,333.33 each
   1b. Option A
        Eunice, $184,666.66
        Jean, $176,666.67
        Rose, $148,666.67
     Option B
        $170,000 each
   1c. Option A
        Eunice, $294,666.66
        Jean, $286,666.67
        Rose, $258,666.67
     Option B
        $280,000

43. 1. Dr. S. Vessels, Capital
$183,000
Cr. Sims, Capital
$183,000
2. Dr. B. Vessels, Capital
$14,400
Dr. G. Vessels, Capital
$10,800
Dr. S. Vessels, Capital
$10,800
Cr. Sims, Capital
$200,000
3. Cr. B. Vessels, Capital
$9,600
Cr. G. Vessels, Capital
$7,200
Cr. S. Vessels, Capital
$7,200
Cr. Sims, Capital
$220,000

44. 1a. Dr. Poundstone, Capital
$60,000
Dr. Jeni, Capital $2,000
1b. Dr. Poundstone, Capital
$60,000
Cr. Jeni, Capital $1,500

Profits and losses are divided as follows among the three partners: Billy—40 percent, Gomer—30 percent, and Steve—30 percent.

Required:
Prepare the journal entry to admit Bud Sims to the Uptown Athletic Club partnership under each of the following assumptions:
1. Sims purchases the ownership interest of Steve Vessels for $183,000.
2. Sims invests $164,000 in the firm in exchange for a 25 percent ownership interest.
3. Sims invests $244,000 in the firm in exchange for a 25 percent ownership interest.

44. **Withdrawal of a Partner** (LO 5)
Jeni Leatherworks is a firm that makes and repairs leather products, including shoes, cowboy boots, and purses. The four partners of Jeni Leatherworks share equally in the annual profits and losses of the firm. Patricia Poundstone has recently announced that she will be withdrawing from the partnership. Listed next are the balances of the firm's capital accounts immediately following Poundstone's announcement:

R. Jeni	$84,000
A. Lubell	42,000
P. Poundstone	60,000
M. Smith	36,000

Required:
1. Prepare the journal entry to record the withdrawal of Poundstone from the partnership under the following independent assumptions:
   a. Poundstone is paid $66,000 for her ownership interest in the firm.
   b. Poundstone is paid $55,500 for her ownership interest in the firm.
2. Suppose that immediately following Poundstone's withdrawal from the partnership, she establishes her own firm, Poundstone Leatherworks, directly across the street from Jeni Leatherworks. How could Jeni Leatherworks have prevented Poundstone from establishing a competing business following her withdrawal from the partnership?

45. **Partnership Liquidation** (LO 6)
For several years, the Five & Dime Store of Holbrook, Arizona, was a prosperous business. However, in recent years two large retail chains have opened competing stores in Holbrook. As a result, the three partners who own the Five & Dime Store have decided to liquidate the business beginning October 1, 1996. Following is the post-closing trial balance for this business as of September 30, 1996:

	DEBIT	CREDIT
Cash	$ 23,750	
Accounts Receivable (Net)	30,000	
Inventory	52,250	
Property, Plant & Equipment (Net)	70,250	
Accounts Payable		$ 45,750
Notes Payable		25,000
M. Bogues, Capital		10,500
S. Bradley, Capital		30,000
B. Reeves, Capital		65,000
	$176,250	$176,250

The partners share profits and losses as follows:

M. Bogues	40%
S. Bradley	20%
B. Reeves	40%

Following is a summary of the transactions engaged in by the company during the liquidation process:

October 1: Sold accounts receivable to a finance company for $24,000.
October 9: Sold inventory and property, plant & equipment at a public auction for $82,500.
October 16: Paid liabilities in full.
October 31: Remaining cash disbursed to partners.

Note: Any deficiency in partners' capital accounts was paid in full by the partner(s) on October 30.

Required:
1. Prepare the necessary journal entries to record the liquidation of this business.
2. Prepare a final statement of partnership liquidation.

46.   Accounting for the Owner's Equity of a Proprietorship (LO 7)
Tillman Rollins experienced a very interesting 1996. In addition to learning how to run a business, Tillman also became very familiar with double-entry bookkeeping during 1996. On February 2, 1996, Tillman opened a small country store, the Wallville General Store. To cut down on overhead, Tillman "hired" himself as the business's bookkeeper. Following is the adjusted trial balance of the Wallville General Store's accounting records as of December 31, 1996:

	DEBIT	CREDIT
Cash	$ 2,500	
Inventory	15,000	
Accounts Receivable	10,000	
Building	18,000	
Accumulated Depreciation, Building		$1,800
Accounts Payable		4,100
T. Rollins, Capital		40,000
Sales		65,200
Cost of Goods Sold	31,600	
Salaries Expense	24,000	
Interest Expense	4,800	
Depreciation Expense	1,800	
Utilities Expense	2,400	
Advertising Expense	1,000	
	$111,100	$111,100

Tillman is disappointed by his store's operating results for 1996. According to his computations, the store had a net loss during the year. Then again, Tillman rationalizes, he did earn $24,000 working as the business's sole employee during the year. Plus, he received $4,800 of interest revenue on the $40,000 he invested in the business during the year.

Required:
1. Prepare any necessary correcting entries to the accounts of the Wallville General Store. Why are these correcting entries necessary?

45. 1. 10/1 Dr. Bogues, Capital $2,400
Dr. Bradley, Capital $1,200
Dr. Reeves, Capital $2,400
10/9 Dr. Bogues, Capital $16,000
Dr. Bradley, Capital $8,000
Dr. Reeves, Capital $16,000
10/31 Cr. Bogues, Capital $7,900
10/31 Dr. Bradley, Capital $20,800
Dr. Reeves, Capital $46,600

46. 2. Dr. Income Summary $28,400
Cr. Rollins, Capital $28,400
3. $39,600

2. Prepare the closing entries for the Wallville General Store on December 31, 1996.

3. What is Tillman's total ownership interest in his business at the end of 1996?

CASES

47. Withdrawal of a Partner

Joyce Whitmore and James Somerset have owned and operated the Dublin Brewery in south Boston for twenty-five years, sharing profits and losses equally. Somerset informed Whitmore during July 1996 that he wanted to retire from the business at the end of the year. After the partnership's accounting records had been closed at the end of the year, the partners had the following capital balances:

J. Whitmore	$490,000
J. Somerset	550,000

Two independent appraisals of the business obtained in late December 1996 established an appraised value of $1,200,000, net of liabilities, for the business as a whole. On January 2, 1997, Somerset offered to accept $600,000 as payment for his share of the business. Whitmore immediately accepted this offer. Because approximately two weeks would be required to draw up the legal documents for the buy-out agreement, the two partners decided to formally "close the deal" on January 16. On January 10, 1997, Whitmore was approached by a much larger brewery. This brewery offered Whitmore $1.4 million for the Dublin Brewery.

Required:

Whitmore decides not to inform Somerset of the buy-out offer from the larger brewery. Since Somerset had already decided to retire from the business before this buy-out offer was received, Whitmore does not believe that Somerset is entitled to profit from that offer. Do you agree with Whitmore's reasoning? Why or why not? Is this an example of a situation or issue that should be dealt with in a partnership agreement?

48. Limited Liability Partnerships

The Big Six accounting firms that dominate the public accounting profession faced a serious problem in the early 1990s. As indicated in the opening vignette for this chapter, three of these large partnerships were forced to pay hundreds of millions of dollars to settle legal claims filed against them. Faced with such large legal settlements, the Big Six firms were forced to either "close their doors" or find some way to limit their litigation losses.

In July 1994, Ernst & Young, a Big Six firm, announced that it was reorganizing as a "limited liability partnership" (LLP) to reduce its partners' exposure to litigation losses. An LLP's total capital can be wiped out by litigation judgments. However, the personal assets of an LLP's individual partners are not at risk—with one key exception. Partners who were directly involved in a "bum" audit or other professional services engagement that was negligently performed are not protected by the limited liability feature of an LLP. These partners can lose their investment in an LLP and have their personal assets seized to satisfy any remaining portion of a legal judgment imposed on the firm. Shortly after Ernst & Young announced its decision to reorganize as an LLP, several other Big Six accounting firms quickly followed suit.

Required:

1. Why do partnerships have the unlimited liability feature discussed in this chapter? If necessary, review a business law text or other relevant materials in

your school's library to address this issue. What benefit does this feature of partnerships provide to society? What disadvantage does this feature impose on the members of partnerships?

2. Do you agree that large accounting firms should be allowed to reorganize as limited liability partnerships? Defend your answer. Should all partnerships be allowed to reorganize as limited liability partnerships? Why or why not?

PROJECTS

49. Success and Failure Factors for Small Businesses

Most small businesses in the United States are either sole proprietorships or partnerships. Today's business environment poses a wide range of problems and opportunities for small businesses. In this group project, you will study these problems and opportunities.

Required:

1. Your project group should research major business publications including *Business Week*, *The Wall Street Journal*, and *Inc.* in recent years to identify several articles focusing specifically on small businesses. In particular, your group should attempt to identify small business "success" stories and, conversely, articles that discuss examples of small businesses that failed.

2. The articles collected by individual group members should be shared with other group members. After each group member has had an opportunity to read or review the articles collected by all group members, meet as a group and discuss these articles. Your discussion should focus on identifying the key "success" and "failure" factors for small businesses.

3. A written report should be prepared by each group. This report should contain a list of the articles identified in Part 1 and should briefly discuss or explain the success and failure factors related to small businesses that were identified in Part 2.

4. One group member should be prepared to present a summary of the written report in class.

50. Partnerships: An International Perspective

Reread the vignette near the end of this chapter that discusses methods small businesses can use to become involved in international commerce.

Required:

1. Review on-line and/or hard copy indices of business publications available in your library and identify articles focusing on how small businesses have become involved in international commerce. Identify at least three examples of such businesses.

2. Prepare a written report summarizing the following items, if available, for each small business you identified in Part 1:
   a. The name of the business, its location, its approximate size in terms of total assets and annual revenues, and its principal line or lines of business.
   b. The method used by the business to become involved in international commerce.
   c. How the business's operations have been favorably and/or unfavorably affected by the involvement in international commerce.
   d. Whether the business intends to expand its international operations in the future and, if so, how the business intends to accomplish this objective.

VI ANALYSIS OF ACCOUNTING DATA

This final section focuses on methods used by decision makers to analyze accounting data. Chapter 16 acquaints you with the statement of cash flows and methods used to interpret cash-flow data. Chapter 17 presents a comprehensive discussion of financial ratios and other analytical techniques that can be applied to accrual-based data.

In the late 1980s, the accounting profession responded to a long-standing demand for cash-flow data by decision makers. Since 1987, businesses have been required to include a statement of cash flows in their annual reports. Cash-flow data provide decision makers with important insights on the financial health of businesses that are not available from accrual-based data. In Chapter 16, we first become familiar with the structure, content, and preparation of a statement of cash flows. Then we discuss approaches to use in analyzing cash-flow data.

Earlier chapters have introduced numerous financial ratios and measures that can be used to analyze and interpret accrual-based data reported in an income statement and balance sheet. Chapter 17 presents a comprehensive discussion of these techniques. Included in this discussion are financial ratios and measures presented in earlier chapters as well as several additional analytical techniques.

16

STATEMENT OF CASH FLOWS

LEARNING OBJECTIVES

After studying this chapter, you should be able to do the following:

1. Identify the principal uses of the statement of cash flows

2. Identify and distinguish among operating, investing, and financing activities

3. Prepare a statement of cash flows using the indirect method

4. Prepare a statement of cash flows using the direct method

5. Interpret cash-flow data by comparatively analyzing the three components of an entity's cash flows

6. Compute and interpret cash flow per share

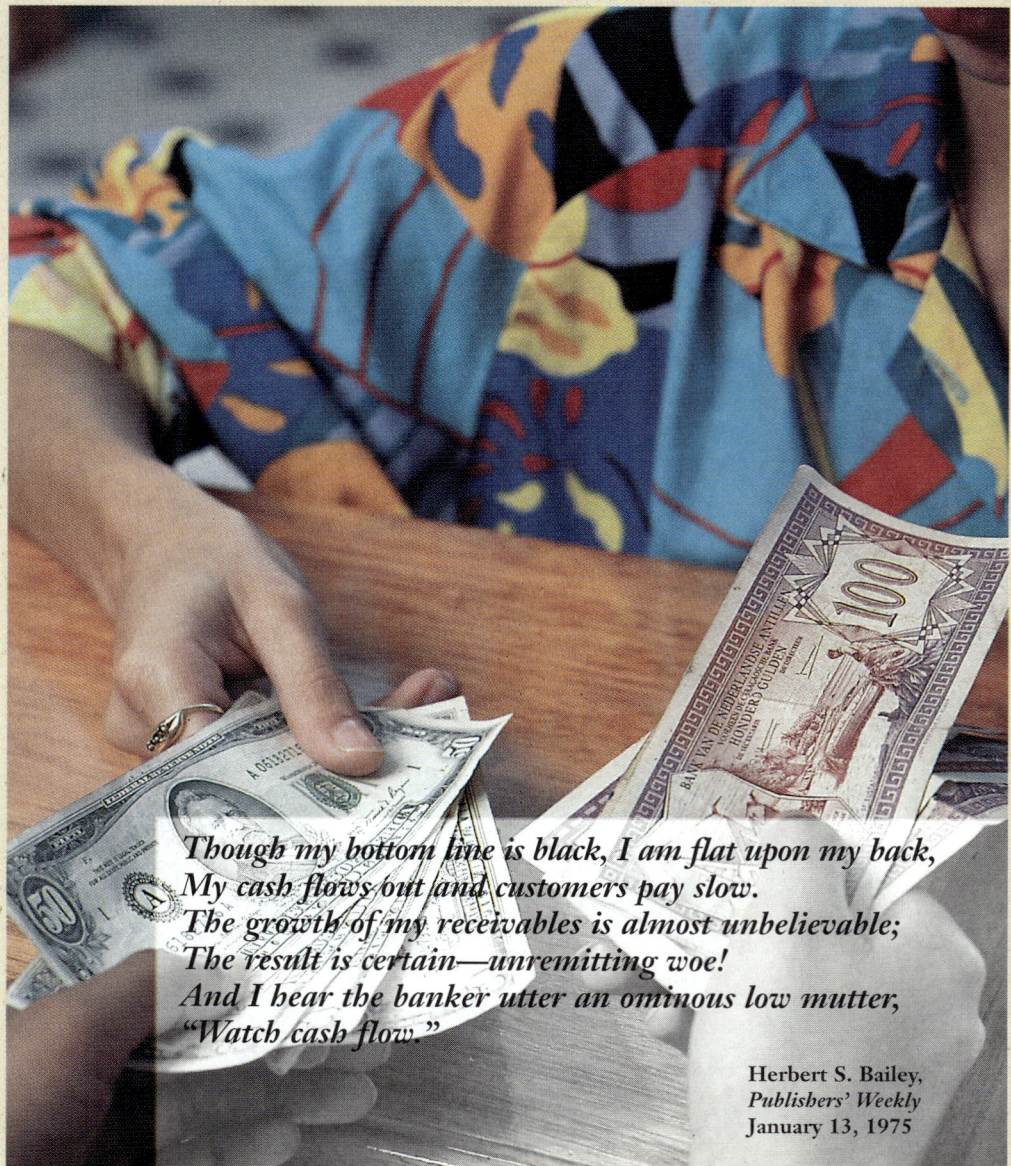

Though my bottom line is black, I am flat upon my back,
My cash flows out and customers pay slow.
The growth of my receivables is almost unbelievable;
The result is certain—unremitting woe!
And I hear the banker utter an ominous low mutter,
"Watch cash flow."

Herbert S. Bailey,
Publishers' Weekly
January 13, 1975

Slow Cash Flow: Common Nemesis of the Rapidly Growing Small Company

Many companies, particularly small companies, lose sight of the fact that posting impressive profits each accounting period does not guarantee that they will thrive or even survive. Under the accrual basis of accounting, the revenue from credit sales is generally recognized when the goods go out the front door. However, a company that cannot collect its receivables will soon find itself closing that front door—permanently. The following article profiles a small business that faced a cash-flow crisis. The owner of this business quickly learned that accrual-based profits and cash flows are two distinctively different phenomena that require different decision-making skills to manage effectively.

Douglas Roberson, president of Atlantic Network Systems, "woke up one morning and realized we were out of cash." The Cary, N.C., data- and voice-systems integrator had been growing so quickly—from $100,000 in sales during its first year to $460,000 the next—that its staff never worried about things like how to pay for supplies or how to float accounts receivable, Roberson recalls.

By the end of 1988, when Atlantic Network was two years old, "receivables had gone through the roof," says Roberson. "I actually believed that the more money companies owed us, the better shape we were in." Then, during a long collection dry spell, Roberson watched "our money go out and nothing come in. We went into the hole as far as we could, using our existing credit lines to keep us going while we waited for invoices to be paid."

Roberson gradually realized that managing cash flows is different from simply accumulating sales. "If you don't do serious projections about how much cash you'll need to handle sales—and how long it will take to collect on invoices—you can wind up out of business, no matter how fast you're growing," he says. In fact, during a cash-flow crisis, fast growth usually exacerbates problems because you're spending cash on supplies and payroll—usually at an accelerated pace—while waiting 45 days or longer to collect receivables.

Fortunately, Roberson had built up enough credibility with his banker—thanks to detailed monthly financial reports and sales growth that repeatedly exceeded projections—that he was able to win an emergency loan to help Atlantic Network hold on until it revamped its cash-flow systems. Now, Roberson and his partner perform elaborate cash-flow projections once a year, and they update them "on a reality basis" each month. The result: the company was solidly profitable last year on sales of $9.3 million. But Roberson still sets cash-flow improvement goals: "What I want to do next is figure how to collect receivables faster from our big-company and foreign accounts, which now take 45 to 60 days to pay. I want to bring them in line with our other, faster-paying accounts."

SOURCE: Used with permission, *Inc. Magazine*, August 1994, 107. Goldhirsch, Inc., 38 Commercial Wharf, Boston, MA. 02110.

Business entities have been required to include a statement of cash flows in their annual financial reports only since the late 1980s. Nevertheless, this newest of the three major financial statements is a key source of information for financial decision makers. The opening section of this chapter introduces you to the statement of cash flows. The two methods of preparing a statement of cash flows are discussed in the next section. Then, the following two sections illustrate these two methods by applying them to the financial data of a small company. This chapter concludes with an overview of two approaches that can be used to analyze and interpret cash-flow data.

691

FINANCIAL DECISION MAKING AND CASH-FLOW DATA

As the opening vignette for this chapter demonstrates, business entities must be concerned not only with generating revenues but also with managing their cash resources. Many companies that had a long history of reporting profits eventually failed because their owners or managers did not pay sufficient attention to cash flows. The classic example of such a firm is W. T. Grant Company, one of the nation's largest retail chains until the mid-1970s.

No Cash, No Company: The Case of W. T. Grant Company

W. T. Grant Company experienced dramatic growth rates in revenues and profits between 1962 and 1972. Over that decade, Grant's annual earnings increased by 340 percent, topping out at almost $40 million in 1972 on sales of nearly $2 billion. These impressive revenue and profit numbers caused Grant's common stock to be among the "hottest" investments on Wall Street. However, appearances can be deceiving. Less than three years later, Grant filed for protection from its creditors in bankruptcy court. The following year, a federal judge ordered the company to be liquidated.

Apparently, Grant's executives believed that if they could generate sufficient revenues and profits, the company's cash flows would follow suit. That was clearly not the case. Although the company was very profitable during the early 1970s, its net cash flows during that period were negative. The chief culprit was an aggressive expansion program that required huge increases in inventory and other current assets. In 1973 alone, the company had a negative cash flow of more than $100 million from its principal business operations. Suddenly, there was no cash to pay the bills. Result: bankruptcy court. The liquidation of Grant led to the closing of more than one thousand retail stores, the loss of eighty thousand jobs, and huge write-offs by Grant's creditors.

Statement No. 95 to the Rescue

The W. T. Grant debacle and several similar cases resulted in increasing demands by decision makers for business entities to report cash-flow data. In 1987, the Financial Accounting Standards Board (FASB) responded by adopting *Statement on Financial Accounting Standards No. 95*, "Statement of Cash Flows." This accounting standard requires business entities to include a statement of cash flows in their annual financial reports.

A **statement of cash flows** accounts for the net change in an entity's cash balance during a given period. This net change is explained by summarizing an entity's cash receipts and disbursements by three major types of activities: operating, investing, and financing activities. Recognize that the statement of cash flows is not intended to replace either the balance sheet or income statement. Instead, decision makers should jointly use these three major financial statements to analyze the financial condition, operating results, and future prospects of business entities.

Principal Uses of the Statement of Cash Flows

Shown in Exhibit 16.1 are the principal uses of a statement of cash flows according to FASB *Statement No. 95*. Most important, a statement of cash flows helps decision

Teaching Note
An income statement reports a company's profit (revenues less expenses) for a specific period of time. In contrast, a statement of cash flows reports on the cash received and disbursed by a company for a specific period of time.

statement of cash flows

■ LEARNING
OBJECTIVE 1
Identify the principal uses of the statement of cash flows

■ **EXHIBIT 16.1**

Four Principal Uses of the Statement of Cash Flows

SOURCE: Portions of FASB documents, copyright by Financial Accounting Standards Board, 401 Merritt 7, P. O. Box 5116, Norwalk, Connecticut 06856-5116, U.S.A., are reprinted with permission. Copies of the complete documents are available from the FASB.

- Assess an entity's ability to generate positive future net cash flows
- Assess an entity's ability to meet its obligations, its ability to pay dividends, and its needs for external financing
- Assess the reasons for differences between net income and associated cash receipts and payments
- Assess the effects on an enterprise's financial position of both its cash and noncash investing and financing transactions during the period

makers evaluate an entity's ability to generate positive future net cash flows. Economic theory tells us that the true value of an asset—or business entity—is determined by the present value of its future cash flows. Although a statement of cash flows reports historical cash-flow data, a strong correlation usually exists between a company's future cash flows and its historical cash flows.

The second use of cash-flow data noted in Exhibit 16.1 refers principally to the information needs of specific types of financial statement users. As you would expect, individual decision makers are most concerned with how an entity's cash flows will benefit them directly. For example, suppliers want to be reassured that their customers can generate sufficient cash to pay their bills when they come due. A supplier is not concerned with a customer's ability to generate sufficient excess cash each accounting period to pay dividends. Stockholders, on the other hand, are often preoccupied with the latter issue.

A statement of cash flows also allows decision makers to reconcile an entity's net income to the net cash flow resulting from its principal operating activities. As demonstrated by the opening vignette and the demise of W. T. Grant, profitable companies do not necessarily generate sufficient cash to pay their bills. If a company's net income significantly exceeds the cash generated by its principal business operations, decision makers will want to investigate this difference. Consider a company that reports a large increase in net income in a given year but a negative cash flow from its operating activities for that year. Further investigation may reveal that the firm increased its net income by adopting a more liberal credit policy that resulted in increased sales to high-risk customers. If many of these new customers are unable to pay their bills, this company has essentially inflated its reported profits over the short term by giving away inventory.

Finally, a statement of cash flows can help decision makers assess the impact of investing and financing transactions on an entity's financial position. For example, a company may be financing the cost of its operations—inventory purchases, payroll costs, and so on—by selling off long-term assets. Obviously, this source of financing is very short-lived. Take the case of Figgie International, Inc., a conglomerate with more than twenty separate lines of business in the late 1980s. To finance its operations and pay off large debts, Figgie's executives were forced to sell one business segment after another. By 1995, all but four of the company's business segments had been

Teaching Note

The income statement and balance sheet are both based upon the accrual basis of accounting. In contrast, the statement of cash flows is based upon the cash basis of accounting.

sold or were up for sale.[1] Clearly, at some point, a company such as Figgie must begin generating significant cash flows from its principal operating activities or join W. T. Grant in the corporate graveyard.

In summary, a statement of cash flows has a variety of important uses. Following are examples of specific questions decision makers can better address with the assistance of the data found in a statement of cash flows.

Will a company generate sufficient cash to make a large "balloon" payment on a long-term debt that is due in three years?

Since a company has reported record profits over the past two years, why is the firm being forced to obtain short-term loans to finance its day-to-day operations?

Will the board of directors of a company suspend dividend payments in the near future because the firm's net cash flows have recently plummeted?

Is a company producing sufficient cash flows from its principal operations to finance an aggressive expansion program, or will additional debt or equity capital be required to finance this program?

How does the composition of a company's cash flows compare with that of its principal competitors?

How does a company's cash flows this year compare with previous years? Are any important trends evident in these data?

THE STATEMENT OF CASH FLOWS: A CLOSER LOOK

Now that we are better acquainted with how decision makers use cash-flow data, we can focus on the technical features of the statement of cash flows. This section begins with two examples of statements of cash flows drawn from recent annual reports of large corporations. Then the three types of cash flows generated by business entities are discussed. This section concludes with an overview of the two methods that can be used to prepare a statement of cash flows.

The Statement of Cash Flows: Two Examples

Discussion Question
Ask students to compare Exhibits 16.2 and 16.3 and identify similarities and differences between the formats used for the direct and indirect methods of preparing a statement of cash flows.

Shown in Exhibit 16.2 and 16.3 are statements of cash flows for two public companies referred to in earlier chapters. Exhibit 16.2 contains a recent statement of cash flows for Hughes Supply, Inc., while Exhibit 16.3 (p. 696) presents a statement of cash flows for Cabletron Systems, Inc. The FASB in *Statement No. 95* specifies two acceptable methods of preparing a statement of cash flows: the direct method and the indirect method. As indicated in the captions for Exhibits 16.2 and 16.3, Hughes Supply uses the direct method, while Cabletron applies the indirect method.

From a technical standpoint, a statement of cash flows has one primary objective: explain the change in an entity's cash resources during a given accounting period. If a company's balance sheet indicates that its cash increased by $8,421,573 during 1997, its statement of cash flows for that year will account for that increase down to the last dollar. To explain the change in a business's cash balance during a given period, its accountants must identify all transactions that affected cash during that period. For purposes of the statement of cash flows, "cash" includes both cash and cash equiva-

---

1. Narisetti, R., "Figgie Plans Sale of Assets to Reduce Debt," *The Wall Street Journal*, February 16, 1995, p. A3. Reprinted by permission of *The Wall Street Journal*, © 1995 Dow Jones & Company, Inc. All Rights Reserved Worldwide.

■ **EXHIBIT 16.2**

Statement of Cash Flows—Direct Method, Hughes Supply, Inc., for the
Year Ended January 28, 1994 (in thousands)

HUGHES SUPPLY, INC.
STATEMENT OF CASH FLOWS
FOR THE YEAR ENDED JANUARY 28, 1994 (IN THOUSANDS)

Cash flows from operating activities:

Cash received from customers	$644,667
Cash paid to suppliers and employees	(638,724)
Interest and other investment income received	1,856
Interest paid	(4,693)
Income taxes paid	(5,361)
Net cash used in operating activities	(2,255)

Cash flows from investing activities:

Proceeds from sale of property, plant & equipment	704
Capital expenditures	(8,257)
Business acquisitions, net of cash	(3,934)
Net cash used in investing activities	(11,487)

Cash flows from financing activities:

Net borrowings under short-term debt arrangements	16,733
Principal payments on:	
Long-term notes	(2,918)
Capital lease obligations	(660)
Proceeds from issuance of common shares under stock option plans	77
Purchase of common shares	(49)
Dividends paid	(616)
Net cash provided by financing activities	12,567

Net Decrease in Cash and Cash Equivalents	(1,175)
Cash and Cash Equivalents, beginning of year	2,253
Cash and Cash Equivalents, end of year	$ 1,078

lents. Recall from Chapter 7 that cash equivalents are generally investments in short-term securities that have ninety days or less to maturity when purchased.

A statement of cash flows typically consists of four sections. The first three sections summarize the cash inflows (receipts) and outflows (disbursements) from an entity's operating, investing, and financing activities during a given acounting period. The final section reconciles an entity's cash balance at the beginning and end of that accounting period. This reconciliation involves adding the net cash provided or used by operating, investing, and financing activities to the beginning cash balance to arrive at the period-ending cash balance.

The reconciliation near the bottom of Exhibit 16.2 indicates that Hughes Supply had total cash of $2,253,000 on January 30, 1993. The company's next fiscal year ended on January 28, 1994. On that date, Hughes Supply had a cash balance of $1,078,000. When preparing the statement of cash flows for the fiscal year ending on January 28, 1994, the primary objective of Hughes Supply's accountants was to

Teaching Note
By definition, any transaction that results in a debit or credit to the Cash account affects a company's cash balance and thus must be included in the entity's statement of cash flows for the given accounting period.

■ **EXHIBIT 16.3**

Statement of Cash Flows—Indirect Method, Cabletron Systems, Inc., for the Year Ended February 28, 1994 (in thousands)

CABLETRON SYSTEMS, INC.
STATEMENT OF CASH FLOWS
FOR THE YEAR ENDED FEBRUARY 28,1994 (IN THOURSNDS)

Cash flows from operating activities:	
Net Income	$119,218
Adjustments to reconcile net income to net cash provided by operating activities:	
Depreciation and amortization	17,334
Provision for losses on accounts receivable	1,734
Loss on disposals of property, plant & equipment	113
Deferred taxes	(6,150)
Changes in current assets and liabilities:	
Accounts receivable	(17,707)
Inventories	(8,758)
Prepaid expenses and other assets	1,211
Accounts payable and accrued expenses	22,003
Income taxes payable	3,056
Net cash provided by operating activities	132,054
Cash flows from investing activities:	
Capital expenditures	(39,399)
Purchase of investment securities, net of maturities	(91,208)
Net cash used in investing activities	(130,607)
Cash flows from financing activities:	
Repayments of notes receivable from stockholders	66
Common stock issued to employee stock purchase plan	1,637
Proceeds from stock option exercise	7,185
Net cash provided by financing activities	8,888
Effect of exchange rate changes on cash	161
Net Increase in Cash and Cash Equivalents	10,496
Cash and Cash Equivalents, beginning of year	44,067
Cash and Cash Equivalents, end of year	$ 54,563

Teaching Note
Point out to students that the line item "Cash and Cash Equivalents, end of year . . . $1,078,000" appearing at the bottom of Hughes's statement of cash flows is the same cash balance reported on the company's January 28, 1994 balance sheet.

explain the $1,175,000 decline in the company's cash balance over that period. This change in Hughes Supply's cash balance was attributable to the following net cash flows that are boldfaced in Exhibit 16.2.

Net cash used in operating activities	$ (2,255,000)
Net cash used in investing activities	(11,487,000)
Net cash provided by financing activities	12,567,000
Net Decrease in Cash and Cash Equivalents	$ (1,175,000)

The change in Cabletron's cash balance for its fiscal year ending in 1994 is explained by the following amounts that are boldfaced in Exhibit 16.3.

Net cash provided by operating activities	$132,054,000
Net cash used in investing activities	(130,607,000)
Net cash provided by financing activities	8,888,000
Effect of exchange rate changes on cash	161,000
Net Increase in Cash and Cash Equivalents	$ 10,496,000

Notice that a fourth minor item was necessary to account for the change in Cabletron's cash balance. The year-to-year change in the cash balance of companies with international operations is often partially explained by a change in foreign currency exchange rates. Since the impact of this factor on an entity's cash balance is typically very small, we do not consider it further in this chapter.

Three Major Types of Business Activities and Related Cash Flows

Several references have been made to the three types of activities by which cash flows are classified in a statement of cash flows. Now let us define exactly what each of those activities involve. The most important of these activities are operating activities. Technically, the FASB defines operating activities as all transactions and events other than investing and financing activities. That definition is not very helpful at this point, since we have not yet defined investing and financing activities. **Operating activities** are generally those transactions and events related to the production and delivery of goods and services by business entities. In other words, operating activities are the day-to-day profit-oriented activities of a business.

The principal cash inflows from operating activities are cash receipts from customers, both cash sales and collections of accounts receivable. Notice in Exhibit 16.2 that Hughes Supply reported more than $644 million of cash receipts from its customers, which was easily the largest source of cash inflows from its operating activities. Other cash inflows from operating activities include cash dividends received, receipts of interest revenue, and cash provided by the sale of investments in trading securities. Major sources of cash outflows from operating activities include payments to suppliers, payroll expenditures, interest payments, and payments of taxes.

Investing activities include the making and collecting of loans, the acquisition and disposal of property, plant & equipment, and the purchase and sale of debt and equity securities other than trading securities and cash equivalents. Notice in Exhibit 16.2 that Hughes Supply's principal investing activities for the given year were $8 million of capital expenditures to acquire property, plant & equipment. Exhibit 16.3 indicates that Cabletron had cash outlays of approximately $39 million for capital expenditures in its comparable fiscal year.

FASB *Statement No. 95* provides the following definition of **financing activities.**

> Financing activities include obtaining resources from owners and providing them with a return on, and a return of, their investment; borrowing money and repaying amounts borrowed, or otherwise settling obligations; and obtaining and paying for other resources obtained from creditors on long-term credit.[2]

Hughes Supply's financing activities for its fiscal year ending January 28, 1994, included approximately $17 million of cash raised via loans. Cabletron realized cash receipts of more than $7 million from the exercise of stock options during its fiscal year ending February 28, 1994.

---

2. Portions of FASB documents, copyright by Financial Accounting Standards Board, 401 Merritt 7, P. O. Box 5116, Norwalk, Connecticut 06856-5116, U.S.A., are reprinted with permission. Copies of the complete documents are available from the FASB.

■ **LEARNING OBJECTIVE 2**
Identify and distinguish among operating, investing, and financing activities

operating activities

Teaching Note
Emphasize that critical to understanding and preparing a statement of cash flows is learning to classify business activities as either operating, investing, or financing.

investing activities

financing activities

Discussion Question
Ask students to review Michaels Stores' 1994 statement of cash flows included in the Appendix and identify the company's largest cash inflow or outflow related to each type of business activity: operating, investing, and financing.

■ **EXHIBIT 16.4**

Examples of Common Cash Inflows and Cash Outflows from Operating, Investing, and Financing Activities

OPERATING ACTIVITIES	
Cash Inflows	*Cash Outflows*
Receipts from customers	Payments to suppliers
Receipts of interest and dividends	Payments to employees
Receipts from the sale of investments in debt and equity securities classified as trading securities	Payments of interest
	Payments of taxes
	Purchases of debt and equity securities classified as trading securities
Miscellaneous receipts related to operating activities	Miscellaneous payments related to operating activities

INVESTING ACTIVITIES	
Cash Inflows	*Cash Outflows*
Receipts from the sale of property, plant & equipment assets	Payments to acquire property, plant & equipment assets
Receipts from the sale of investments in debt and equity securities other than trading securities and cash equivalents	Payments to acquire investments in debt and equity securities other than trading securities and cash equivalents
Receipts from the repayment of long-term loans	Loans made to other firms

FINANCING ACTIVITIES	
Cash Inflows	*Cash Outflows*
Receipts from the issuance of common stock and preferred stock	Dividend payments
	Payments to acquire treasury stock
Receipts from the issuance of bonds	Payments to retire principal amounts of bonds payable
Amounts borrowed from banks and other parties	

Exhibit 16.4 provides a summary listing of the principal cash inflows and outflows from operating, investing, and financing activities. Notice that the classification of cash flows from the sale or purchase of investments in debt and equity securities depends upon the type of investment. Cash receipts and disbursements from the sale or purchase of trading securities are reported as cash flows from operating activities. Cash receipts and disbursements from the sale or purchase of investments in debt and equity securities other than trading securities and cash equivalents are reported as cash flows from investing activities.

The cash flow classification scheme required by the FASB in *Statement No. 95* has been criticized. Much of this criticism focuses on the treatment of interest and dividend receipts as cash flows from operating activities. Many parties contend that these items are more properly classified as cash flows from investing activities. This argument is particularly valid for interest and dividend receipts on investments other than trading securities and cash equivalents. Notice in Exhibit 16.4 that the purchase and sale of investments in debt and equity securities, other than trading securities and cash equivalents, are considered investing activities. It seems reasonable, then, that the

Cabletron Systems is a "high-tech" company that in recent years has generated large positive cash flows from its operating activities. Much of this cash flow has been reinvested by company executives into PP&E assets.

cash receipts resulting from revenues on these investments should be classified as cash flows from investing activities. Nevertheless, because these items affect an entity's net income, the FASB chose to classify them as cash flows from operating (profit-oriented) activities. For the same reason payments of interest expense, which seem to qualify as financing activities, are classified as cash flows from operating activities.

Direct Method vs. Indirect Method of Preparing a Statement of Cash Flows

The only major difference between the two methods of preparing a statement of cash flows concerns how net cash flow from operating activities is determined and reported. Notice in Hughes Supply's statement of cash flows shown in Exhibit 16.2 that the initial section lists specific cash inflows and outflows from operating activities. This approach to preparing a statement of cash flows is known as the **direct method.** Now, refer to Exhibit 16.3, which presents a statement of cash flows for Cabletron Systems. Notice in this case that specific cash flows from operating activities, such as "cash received from customers," are not listed in the initial section of the statement of cash flows. When the **indirect method** is used to prepare a statement of cash flows, the net cash flow from operating activities is determined indirectly by making certain adjustments to net income. The indirect method yields the net cash flow from operating activities without revealing the individual cash inflows and outflows from those activities. Cash flows from investing and financing activities are determined and reported in the same manner under both the direct and indirect methods.

In the following two sections, we prepare statements of cash flows using both the indirect method and the direct method. Of the two methods, the indirect method is more popular. Over the last several years, *Accounting Trends & Techniques* has reported that approximately 97 percent of public companies use the indirect method to prepare their statement of cash flows. Why? Principally because the indirect method is easier and less expensive to apply than the direct method. Despite the popularity of the indirect method, the FASB expressly stated a preference for the direct method in

FOR YOUR INFORMATION

A TAD Here and a TAD There Adds Up to Real Cash

The opening vignette for this chapter discussed how a small business survived a cash-flow scare by improving its money management practices. The following excerpt from an article appearing in Inc. *concerns another small company that faced a similar problem. The solution to this company's cash-flow crisis was a financing technique widely used in many countries but seldom employed in the United States.*

Last year Edge Trucking, a Bayshore, N.Y., distribution and warehousing business, had more than $150,000 in accounts receivable but no cash to repair its truck fleet or to pay other pressing bills. Banks wouldn't offer credit to the $2 million service business, notes vice-president Jeff Chapov. "When things got really bad, we had to look for customers who could pay us fast."

Today, though, thanks to something called a trade-acceptance draft (TAD), Edge's cash troubles seem to be history. The company no longer has to sit around waiting for customers to pay invoices. Indeed, Chapov says, "We get most of our money in 48 hours."

For Edge, a TAD works like this: When an Edge truck driver makes a delivery, the customer that receives it is asked to sign a document accepting the merchandise and agreeing to make payment on a specific date. Edge then endorses the signed paper over to a financial company in New York City, Actrade International, which advances 75% of the face value within two business days. The remainder, less service fees and interest, is paid to Edge after the funds are received by Actrade from the customer.

[On the downside, the financing costs associated with TADs are typically higher than interest costs on short-term bank loans.] Actrade charges processing fees of 1.5% to 4% (depending on such factors as the creditworthiness of the client's customers and the overall volume of business), plus interest based on the client's credit and how long it takes customers to pay.

SOURCE: Used with permission, *Inc., Magazine*, April 1994, 114. Goldhirsch, Inc., 38 Commercial Wharf, Boston, MA 02110.

Statement No. 95. Because the direct method discloses specific types of operating cash flows, the FASB believes this method is more informative for financial statement users than the indirect method.

INDIRECT METHOD OF PREPARING A STATEMENT OF CASH FLOWS

■ **LEARNING OBJECTIVE 3**
Prepare a statement of cash flows using the indirect method

Now we are ready to tackle the task of preparing a statement of cash flows. In this section, we first review the general approach to preparing a statement of cash flows using the indirect method. Then, we apply what we have learned by using this method to prepare a statement of cash flows for a small business, Cherokee Station, Inc.

Source of Data for a Statement of Cash Flows

When preparing a statement of cash flows, the initial issues to address are where to obtain and how to assemble the data for this financial statement. Recall from Chapter 5 that the information needed to prepare a balance sheet and income statement are

AC *Trade Acceptance Draft*   No. 999-1002   Due Date: 10/10/xx

For Value Received

PAY TO THE ORDER OF: **ABC Corp.** $ 10,000.00

Ten Thousand only   **DOLLARS**

SPECIMEN

Company Name: **XYZ Corp**

Bank Name: **First Bank of America**
Bank Street: **123 Any St.**
City, State, Zip: **Anytown, US 00000**   Authorized Signature:

general ledger account balances. These account balances are entered on a work sheet, adjusted, and then sorted to either the balance sheet or income statement columns of the work sheet. Once the work sheet is completed, it is a simple task to prepare a balance sheet and income statement.

Unlike the balance sheet and income statement, few of the items in a statement of cash flows are general ledger account balances. Instead, cash-flow amounts must be "filtered" from the accrual-based data reported in an entity's accounting records. Several approaches can be used to develop this data. Advanced accounting textbooks often illustrate a work sheet approach to collecting and collating the data needed to prepare a statement of cash flows. However, the work sheet approach to preparing a statement of cash flows is cumbersome. The key objective of this chapter is to introduce you to the statement of cash flows while avoiding becoming "bogged down" in procedural details. Consequently, here we use a streamlined approach to collecting and organizing the data for a statement of cash flows.

The data we need to prepare a statement of cash flows for Cherokee Station for the year ended December 31, 1996, are included in Exhibits 16.5, 16.6, and 16.7. Exhibit 16.5 (p. 702) presents the company's 1996 income statement, while Exhibit 16.6 (p. 703) contains balance sheets for the firm as of December 31, 1995 and 1996. The accounting entries shown in Exhibit 16.7 (p. 704) summarize all of the company's transactions during 1996. For example, the first entry combines the journal entries made to record the company's credit sales during 1996—all of the company's sales are on a credit basis. Notice that the final column of Exhibit 16.7 indicates the type of activity—operating, investing, or financing—to which each summary journal entry relates. This information is particularly useful later when we prepare a statement of cash flows for Cherokee Station using the direct method. (Note: When you are attempting to classify a specific event or transaction as either an operating, investing, or financing activity, it will be helpful to refer to Exhibit 16.4.)

Resourceful business executives often develop or discover innovative methods of financing their firm's operations. One such method involves the use of trade acceptance drafts to accelerate cash payments from customers.

Determining Cash Flows from Operating Activities: The Indirect Method

The starting point for "indirectly" determining net cash flow from operating activities is an entity's net income. Recall that operating activities are the profit-oriented activities of a business. A company's net income for a given period seldom equals the

■ **EXHIBIT 16.5**

Cherokee Station, Inc., Income Statement for the Year Ended December 31, 1996

CHEROKEE STATION, INC. INCOME STATEMENT FOR THE YEAR ENDED DECEMBER 31, 1996		
Sales		$44,900
Cost of Goods Sold		26,200
Gross Profit		18,700
Operating Expenses:		
Selling & General Expenses	10,600	
Depreciation Expense	4,200	14,800
Operating Income		3,900
Gain on Sale of Available-for Sale Securities		700
Income before Income Tax		4,600
Income Tax Expense		1,000
Net Income		$ 3,600

Teaching Note
Ask students what accounting concept or principle calls for the recognition (recording) of interest revenue before it is received.
Answer: The revenue recognition rule.

net cash flow generated by its operating activities for that period. Why? Because net income is determined on an accrual basis, while cash flows from operating activities are, of course, cash-basis amounts. For example, take the case of interest revenue. During a given year, suppose that a company earned $2,000 of interest revenue on an investment. However, the company had received none of that interest by the end of its fiscal year. So, $2,000 of interest revenue was included in the company's income statement although the cash flow related to this revenue item was $0. If this company had no other revenues or expenses during the year in question, its net income was $2,000, while its net cash flow from operating activities was $0.

To determine an entity's net cash flow from operating activities for a given period, the entity's accountants convert net income for that period to a cash basis. That is, net cash flow from operating activities is essentially a "cash-basis" net income figure. Shown in the schedule in Exhibit 16.8 (p. 705) are the general types of adjustments necessary to convert net income to net cash flow from operating activities.

Discussion Question
Ask students for examples of amortization or amortization-related expenses.
Examples: Expenses stemming from the write-off of bond discount, goodwill and patents.

DEPRECIATION AND AMORTIZATION EXPENSES   Depreciation and amortization are noncash expenses. That is, neither of these expenses results in cash outflows. However, these expenses decrease net income. So, to arrive at a "cash-basis" net income, depreciation and amortization expenses recorded during an accounting period must be added back to net income.

Teaching Note
Emphasize to students that gains and losses result from nonoperating activities.

GAINS AND LOSSES   Several examples of gains and losses have been discussed in earlier chapters, including gains and losses on the disposal of property, plant & equipment, and on the sale of investments. As shown in Exhibit 16.8, losses should be added to net income when computing net cash flow from operating activities. Likewise, gains must be subtracted from net income for this purpose. To illustrate the rationale for this treatment of gains and losses, consider a gain realized on the sale of

■ **EXHIBIT 16.6**

Cherokee Station, Inc., Balance Sheets as of December 31, 1996, and December 31, 1995

	1996		1995	
CHEROKEE STATION, INC.				
BALANCE SHEETS				
DECEMBER 31, 1996, AND 1995				
		1996		**1995**
Assets				
Cash		$15,000		$ 6,100
Accounts Receivable		5,500		3,300
Inventory		10,800		12,000
Prepaid Expenses		2,500		1,400
Total Current Assets		$33,800		$22,800
Equipment	$35,000		$24,000	
Less: Accumulated Depreciation	10,100	24,900	5,900	18,100
Investment in Kellogg Common Stock		—		1,900
Total Assets		$58,700		$42,800
Liabilities				
Accounts Payable		$ 5,900		$ 5,600
Accrued Expenses		4,600		5,800
Total Current Liabilities		$10,500		$11,400
Stockholders' Equity				
Common Stock		3,600		3,600
Preferred Stock		18,000		3,000
Additional Paid-in Capital		12,500		12,500
Retained Earnings		14,100		12,300
Total Stockholders' Equity		$48,200		$31,400
Total Liabilities and Stockholders' Equity		$58,700		$42,800

an investment. Assume that a company sells 100 shares of Mattel common stock that had been recorded as a long-term investment in its accounting records. The cost of the stock was $2,400 and it was sold for $3,300. For illustration purposes, assume that the Mattel stock qualified as an available-for-sale security and that no unrealized gain or loss had been recorded on the investment before it was sold. The following entry would be made to record this sale.

Oct. 4	Cash	3,300	
	Investment in Mattel Common Stock,		
	Available-for-Sale Securities		2,400
	Gain on Sale of Available-for-Sale		
	Securities		900
	To record sale of 100 shares of Mattel		
	common stock		

■ **EXHIBIT 16.7**

Cherokee Station, Inc., Summary Journal Entries for the Year Ended December 31, 1996

	DEBIT	CREDIT	TYPE OF ACTIVITY
1. Credit Sales:			Operating
Accounts Receivable	44,900		
Sales		44,900	
2. Collections of Accounts Receivable:			Operating
Cash	42,700		
Accounts Receivable		42,700	
3. Cost of Goods Sold:			Operating
Cost of Goods Sold	26,200		
Inventory		26,200	
4. Credit Purchases of Merchandise:			Operating
Inventory	25,000		
Accounts Payable		25,000	
5. Payments of Accrued Operating Expenses:			Operating
Accrued Expenses	5,800		
Cash		5,800	
6. Payments of Operating Expenses:			Operating
Selling & General Expenses	3,600		
Cash		3,600	
7. Prepayments of Operating Expenses:			Operating
Prepaid Expenses	3,500		
Cash		3,500	
8. Expiration of Prepaid Expenses:			Operating
Selling & General Expenses	2,400		
Prepaid Expense		2,400	
9. Payments to Suppliers:			Operating
Accounts Payable	24,700		
Cash		24,700	
10. Purchase of Equipment:			Investing
Equipment	11,000		
Cash		11,000	
11. Sale of Long-Term Investment:			Investing
Cash	2,600		
Investment in Kellogg Common Stock, Available-for-Sale Securities		1,900	
Gain on Sale of Available-for-Sale Securities		700	
12. Sale of Preferred Stock:			Financing
Cash	15,000		
Preferred Stock		15,000	
13. Declaration and Payment of Dividends:			Financing
Dividends	1,800		
Cash		1,800	
14. Payment of Income Tax Expense:			Operating
Income Tax Expense	1,000		
Cash		1,000	
15. Accrual of Unpaid Operating Expenses at Year-End:			Operating
Selling & General Expenses	4,600		
Accrued Expenses		4,600	

■ **EXHIBIT 16.7 (continued)**

	DEBIT	CREDIT	TYPE OF ACTIVITY
16. Adjusting Entry to Record Depreciation Expense:			Investing
Depreciation Expense, Equipment	4,200		
Accumulated Depreciation, Equipment		4,200	
17. Entry to Close Net Income to Retained Earnings:			N/A
Income Summary	3,600		
Retained Earnings		3,600	
18. Entry to Close Dividends to Retained Earnings:			N/A
Retained Earnings	1,800		
Dividends		1,800	

■ **EXHIBIT 16.8**

Standard Format for Determining Net Cash Flow from Operating Activities under the Indirect Method

Net Income		$x,xxx
Plus:	Depreciation and Amortization Expenses	xxx
	Losses	xxx
	Decreases in Current Assets (other than cash)	xxx
	Increases in Current Liabilities	xxx
Less:	Gains	
	Increases in Current Assets (other than cash)	xxx
	Decreases in Current Liabilities	xxx
Net Cash Flow from Operating Activities		$x,xxx

As indicated in Exhibit 16.4, the previous transaction is considered an investing activity. So, the $3,300 cash inflow from this transaction should be reported as a component of "net cash flows from investing activities" in the statement of cash flows. This presents a problem since the $900 gain on this transaction will also be included in the entity's net income, which, again, is the starting point for determining net cash flow from operating activities under the indirect method. Without an appropriate adjustment in the statement of cash flows, the total cash flow from this transaction will be reported as $4,200: $900 included in cash flows from operating activities via net income and $3,300 included in cash flows from investing activities. To remedy this problem, the $900 gain must be subtracted from net income in the statement of cash flows to determine net cash flow from operating activities. If the Mattel stock had been sold for $2,100, the $300 loss would have been added to net income when computing net cash flow from operating activities.

CHANGES IN CURRENT ASSET AND CURRENT LIABILITY ACCOUNTS

Most of the adjustments to net income required to determine net cash flow from operating activities under the indirect method involve noncash current asset and current liability accounts. As indicated in Exhibit 16.8, changes in these accounts must be added to, or subtracted from, an entity's net income when computing net cash flow from operating activities.

Discussion Question
If this was an existing company that had accounts receivable of $12,000 on January 1, would the $7,000 change (decrease) in Accounts Receivable be added to, or deducted from, net income under the indirect method?
Answer: Added to net income.

CURRENT ASSETS   To illustrate the logic underlying the adjustments to net income shown in Exhibit 16.8 for changes in current assets, let us focus on accounts receivable. Assume that a company begins operations on January 1, 1996. At the end of the year, the company's general ledger reflects total sales of $60,000 and accounts receivable of $5,000. As a result, the company's sales produced cash flows from operating activities of only $55,000 ($60,000 − $5,000). That is, on a cash basis, the company's sales were $55,000. So, when computing net cash flow from operating activities, $5,000 must be deducted from net income. (To simplify matters, in the examples illustrated in this chapter we assume that there are no uncollectible accounts and thus no allowance for doubtful accounts.)

More generally, when accounts receivable increase during a year, this increase must be deducted from net income when computing net cash flow from operating activities. This adjustment gives recognition to the fact that the cash inflows from customers were less than the sales recorded during the year. Conversely, when accounts receivable decrease during a year, this decrease must be added to net income when computing net cash flow from operating activities. This adjustment gives recognition to the fact that the cash inflows from customers exceeded the sales recorded during the year. Similar reasoning can be applied to other noncash current assets accounts. In summary, *increases in noncash current asset accounts are deducted from net income and decreases in these accounts are added to net income when computing net cash flow from operating activities under the indirect method.*

CURRENT LIABILITIES   Now, consider income taxes payable to illustrate the treatment of current liabilities in Exhibit 16.8. Again, keep in mind that our objective is to arrive at a cash-basis net income figure for operating, or profit-oriented, activities. One of these activities is the payment of taxes, according to Exhibit 16.4. Assume that during 1996, a company paid $14,000 of income taxes and that these taxes were for the company's taxable income of 1995. This entry was booked as follows:

Mar. 15	Income Taxes Payable	14,000	
(1996)	Cash		14,000
	To pay 1995 income taxes		

At the end of 1996, the company recorded the following adjusting entry to recognize its income tax expense for 1996.

Dec. 31	Income Tax Expense	12,000	
(1996)	Income Taxes Payable		12,000
	To record income tax expense for 1996		

Given the above two entries, we can determine that the company's income tax payments during 1996 exceeded its income tax expense for that year by $2,000. So, to determine a cash-basis net income figure, this $2,000 must be subtracted from net income.

A shortcut method of determining this $2,000 adjustment would be to analyze the change in the Income Taxes Payable account during 1996. Generally, there are only two types of entries that affect Income Taxes Payable. Accruals of income tax expense are credited to this account, while income tax payments are debited to the account. The balance of Income Taxes Payable is the present example decreased by $2,000 in 1996, meaning that debits to the account exceeded credits to the account by $2,000. Consequently, we can conclude that the company's 1996 income tax payments exceeded its income tax expense for that year by $2,000. Again, this $2,000 item is deducted from net income to arrive at net cash flow from operating activities. Other current liabilities can be analyzed in the same manner using such "bookkeeping logic." As a general rule, then, *increases in current liabilities are added to net income and decreases in current liabilities are deducted from net income when computing net cash flow from operating activities under the indirect method.*

Discussion Question
If income tax expense for 1996 had been $17,000 instead of $12,000, would the change (increase) in Income Taxes Payable be added to, or deducted from, net income under the direct method? Answer: Added to net income.

Determining Cash Flows from Investing and Financing Activities: The Indirect Method

Most businesses have only a few transactions or events each year that qualify as investing or financing activities. To identify such items, an entity's accountants must be familiar with the FASB's definitions of these activities. An accountant of a small company may simply scan the company's journals and ledgers to identify transactions involving cash flows from investing and financing activities. Accountants of larger companies often use the work sheet method alluded to previously to identify these items.

Companies occasionally engage in significant noncash investing or financing activities. For example, a company might acquire a building by issuing a long-term promissory note to the seller. Although these types of transactions do not involve cash, FASB *Statement No. 95* requires that they be disclosed in an entity's financial statements. Such disclosure is required whether the indirect or direct method of preparing a statement of cash flows is used. Typically, noncash investing and financing activities are included in a schedule appended to the statement of cash flows.

Real World
Some companies narratively disclose noncash investing and financing activities at the bottom of the statement of cash flows. Other companies disclose this information in a financial statement footnote.

Cherokee Station, Inc.: The Indirect Method of Preparing a Statement of Cash Flows

Our task now is to prepare a statement of cash flows using the indirect method for Cherokee Station, Inc. Referring to Exhibit 16.6, we find that the company's cash balance increased by $8,900 during 1996. So, our objective is to identify the events and transactions during 1996 that account for the net increase in the company's cash.

CASH FLOWS FROM OPERATING ACTIVITIES   The first step in preparing Cherokee Station's 1996 statement of cash flows is to identify the adjustments that must be made to net income to derive net cash flow from operating activities. Recall that the general types of these adjustments are listed in Exhibit 16.8. Since Cherokee Station's transactions for 1996 have been summarized in journal entry form in Exhibit 16.7, we can refer to that exhibit to identify these items. One such item is the $700 gain on the sale of an investment in Kellogg common stock that was classified as an available-for-sale security (see journal entry #11 in Exhibit 16.7). As explained earlier, such a gain must be subtracted from an entity's net income to determine the firm's net cash flow from operating activities. A second adjustment item is the $4,200 of depreciation expense recorded during 1996 (see journal entry #16 in Exhibit 16.7).

Teaching Note
Remind students that the sale of
an available-for-sale security is a
nonoperating activity, which
explains why the resulting gain
must be subtracted from net
income (an amount derived
from operating activities).

This item is a noncash expense that must be added to net income to compute net cash flow from operating activities.

Next, we must analyze the changes in Cherokee Station's noncash current asset and current liability accounts during 1996 to determine their impact on the company's cash flows from operating activities. This is easily done by referring to Exhibit 16.6 and subtracting the December 31, 1995, balance of each of these accounts from the corresponding December 31, 1996, balance. Following are the resulting amounts and the type of adjustment, addition or deduction, which must be made for each item when computing net cash flow from operating activities.

		TYPE OF ADJUSTMENT TO NET INCOME TO DETERMINE NET CASH FLOW FROM OPERATING ACTIVITIES
Increase in Accounts Receivable	$2,200	Deduction
Decrease in Inventory	1,200	Addition
Increase in Prepaid Expenses	1,100	Deduction
Increase in Accounts Payable	300	Addition
Decrease in Accrued Expenses	1,200	Deduction

We now have the information needed to compute Cherokee Station's net cash flow from operating activities. Shown next is this information organized as it would appear in the company's statement of cash flows for 1996.

Cash flows from operating activities:	
Net Income	$3,600
Adjustments to reconcile net income to net cash provided by operating activities:	
Depreciation expense	4,200
Gain on sale of long-term investment	(700)
Changes in current assets and liabilities:	
Increase in accounts receivable	(2,200)
Decrease in inventory	1,200
Increase in prepaid expenses	(1,100)
Increase in accounts payable	300
Decrease in accrued expenses	(1,200)
Net cash provided by operating activities	$4,100

Teaching Note
Point out to students footnote 3,
which indicates the different
classifications of depreciation
expense for purposes of the
income statement and the
statement of cash flows.

CASH FLOWS FROM INVESTING AND FINANCING ACTIVITIES   After the net cash flow from operating activities has been determined, the next step in preparing a statement of cash flows is to identify the cash flows from investing and financing activities. Scanning the data in Exhibit 16.7, we find that Cherokee Station engaged in three investing activities during 1996. One of these investing activities, the recording of depreciation expense, did not produce a cash inflow or outflow. So, we ignore that item. (Recall that depreciation expense is added to net income when computing net cash flow from operating activities.)[3] The other two investing activities were the sale of the Kellogg common stock and the purchase of equipment costing

---

3. FASB *Statement No. 95*, paragraph 28, indicates that depreciation and amortization expenses are investing activities for purposes of the statement of cash flows. However, for income statement purposes, these items are considered operating expenses. As a result, in Cherokee Station's income statement shown in Exhibit 16.5, depreciation expense is listed under operating expenses.

$11,000. Given these two transactions, we can prepare the following schedule of Cherokee Station's cash flows from investing activities during 1996.

Cash flows from investing activities:

Sale of available-for-sale securities	$ 2,600
Purchase of equipment	(11,000)
Net cash used in investing activities	$(8,400)

During 1996, Cherokee Station also engaged in two financing activities. The company received $15,000 from the sale of preferred stock and paid dividends of $1,800. Following is a schedule that summarizes these cash flows from financing activities.

Cash flows from financing activities:

Sale of preferred stock	$15,000
Dividend payments	(1,800)
Net cash provided by financing activities	$13,200

COMPLETING THE STATEMENT OF CASH FLOWS   Recall that our objective in preparing a statement of cash flows for Cherokee Station is to account for the $8,900 increase in the company's cash balance during 1996. To ensure that we have accomplished this objective, we can add the net cash flows from Cherokee Station's operating, investing, and financing activities as shown in the following schedule.

Net cash provided by operating activities	$ 4,100
Net cash used in investing activities	(8,400)
Net cash provided by financing activities	13,200
Net increase in Cash	$ 8,900

Shown in Exhibit 16.9 is the completed statement of cash flows for this company using the indirect method. Notice that the final section of this statement reconciles the company's beginning and ending cash balances with the net cash flow generated during the year. As a point of information, if a company uses the indirect method to prepare its statement of cash flows, FASB *Statement No. 95* requires that two specific cash outflows related to operating activities be disclosed in the entity's financial statements. These two cash outflows are interest payments and income tax payments. Many companies disclose these two items in a note or schedule attached to the statement of cash flows.

Teaching Note
Ask students to compare the last line of Cherokee Station's 1996 statement of cash flows with the company's December 31, 1996 balance sheet. Again, point out that the ending cash balance on the statement of cash flows equals the cash reported on the balance sheet.

DIRECT METHOD OF PREPARING A STATEMENT OF CASH FLOWS

As mentioned previously, the only major difference between the indirect and direct methods of preparing a statement of cash flows involves the computation of net cash flow from operating activities. Under the indirect method, net cash flow from operating activities is derived from net income through a series of adjustments. Under the direct method, the specific cash inflows and outflows from operating activities must be identified and reported in the statement of cash flows. Recall that Exhibit 16.2 presents a statement of cash flows for Hughes Supply, Inc., prepared using the direct

■ LEARNING OBJECTIVE 4
Prepare a statement of cash flows using the direct method

■ **EXHIBIT 16.9**

Cherokee Station, Inc., Statement of Cash Flows—Indirect Method, for the Year Ended December 31, 1996

CHEROKEE STATION, INC.
STATEMENT OF CASH FLOWS
FOR THE YEAR ENDED DECEMBER 31, 1996

Cash flows from operating activities:

Net Income	$ 3,600
Adjustments to reconcile net income to net cash provided by operating activities:	
Depreciation expense	4,200
Gain on sale of available-for-sale securities	(700)
Changes in current assets and liabilities:	
Increase in accounts receivable	(2,200)
Decrease in inventory	1,200
Increase in prepaid expenses	(1,100)
Increase in accounts payable	300
Decrease in accrued expenses	(1,200)
Net cash provided by operating activities	4,100
Cash flows from investing activities:	
Sale of available-for-sale securities	2,600
Purchase of equipment	(11,000)
Net cash used in investing activities	(8,400)
Cash flows from financing activities:	
Sale of preferred stock	15,000
Dividend payments	(1,800)
Net cash provided by financing activities	13,200
Net increase in Cash	8,900
Cash balance, December 31, 1995	6,100
Cash balance, December 31, 1996	$15,000

---

method. Shown next is the initial section of that financial statement in which the company's cash flows from operating activities are listed.

Cash flows from operating activities:

Cash received from customers	$644,667
Cash paid to suppliers and employees	(638,724)
Interest and other investment income received	1,856
Interest paid	(4,693)
Income taxes paid	(5,361)
Net cash used in operating activities	$ (2,255)

FASB *Statement No. 95* requires companies that use the direct method to include in their financial statements a supporting schedule reconciling net income to net cash flow from operating activities. In other words, a firm that uses the direct method to prepare a statement of cash flows must also use the indirect method to prepare this supporting schedule.

Determining Cash Flows from Operating Activities: The Direct Method

To determine Cherokee Station's net cash flow from operating activities using the direct method, we will rely on the summary journal entries included in Exhibit 16.7 as our primary data source. If such data are not available, an entity's cash flows from operating activities can be determined by using an account-analysis technique. This technique involves identifying the specific accounts in which cash flows from operating activities are recorded and then analyzing the activity in these accounts to filter out the cash-flow data.

To illustrate the account-analysis technique, let us take a brief break from the financial affairs of Cherokee Station and consider instead Crimson Corporation. Suppose that we want to determine Crimson Corporation's cash inflows from customer receipts during 1995 using the account-analysis technique. The accounts that must be considered for this purpose are sales and accounts receivable. Assume that Crimson Corporation had total sales of $424,000 during 1995. On January 1, 1995, the company had accounts receivable of $34,200, while at the end of the year the firm had accounts receivable of $29,500. Given these balances, we know that cash receipts from customers exceeded sales recorded during 1995 by $4,700.[4] On a cash basis, then, Crimson's sales for the year amounted to $428,700 ($424,000 + $4,700). This process of converting accrual-basis sales to cash-basis sales is captured by the following equation:

$$\text{Sales} \left\{ \begin{array}{c} + \text{ decrease in accounts receivable} \\ \text{or} \\ - \text{ increase in accounts receivable} \end{array} \right\} = \begin{array}{c} \text{Cash} \\ \text{Received from} \\ \text{Customers} \end{array}$$

---

4. We can prove this by using the following equation:

				Collections
Year-end		Beginning	Credit	of Receivables
Receivables Balance	=	Receivables Balance	+ Sales	− during year

				Collections
Year-end		Beginning	Credit	of Receivables
Receivables Balance	−	Receivables Balance	= Sales	− during year

			Collections
		Credit	of Receivables
$29,500 − $34,200	=	Sales	− during year

			Collections
		Credit	of Receivables
($4,700)	=	Sales	− during year

By definition, cash sales cannot result in any difference between an entity's recorded sales during an accounting period and its cash receipts from customers during that period. Consequently, the above analysis ignores cash sales. Also, recall that in this chapter we assume that all receivables are collectible. Thus, the above analysis is not affected by the write-off of uncollectible receivables.

Plugging in the numbers for the example just given to the previous equation, we again arrive at cash-basis sales of $428,700.

$$\$424,000 + \$4,700 = \$428,700$$

One more example? Assume that a company had salaries expense of $356,400 during 1996. The balance of the firm's Salaries Payable account on January 1, 1996, was $4,600 and $2,800 on December 31, 1996. Using the following equation, we determine that the company paid salaries to employees during 1996 of $358,200.

$$\text{Salaries Expense} \left\{ \begin{array}{c} + \text{ decrease in salaries payable} \\ \text{or} \\ - \text{ increase in salaries payable} \end{array} \right\} = \begin{array}{c} \text{Salaries} \\ \text{Paid to} \\ \text{Employees} \end{array}$$

$$\$356,400 + \$1,800 = \$358,200$$

Discussion Question
Ask students to apply the account-analysis technique to one or more operating cash flow items of Cherokee Station.

In summary, when using the account-analysis technique, the types of cash inflows and outflows from an entity's operating activities must first be defined, such as cash received from customers. Then, the accounts in which these cash flows were recorded must be identified and analyzed using "bookkeeping logic." Again, a work sheet technique is also available to compile and organize data needed to prepare a statement of cash flows using the direct method.

Determining Cash Flows from Investing and Financing Activities: The Direct Method

Cash flows from investing and financing activities are determined and reported in the same manner under the indirect and direct methods. Again, when summary journal entry data are available, such as the data shown in Exhibit 16.7, that data can be scanned to identify the cash flows from investing and financing activities.

Cherokee Station, Inc.: The Direct Method of Preparing a Statement of Cash Flows

CASH FLOWS FROM OPERATING ACTIVITIES   To determine Cherokee Station's net cash flow from operating activities under the direct method, we identify those summary journal entries in Exhibit 16.7 that involve both operating activities and cash flows. For example, consider the initial two entries in Exhibit 16.7. The first entry summarizes the company's credit sales transactions during 1996. Although credit sales are an important operating activity, they do not directly result in cash flows. Instead, cash flows result from the collection of accounts receivable. The second summary journal entry indicates that Cherokee Station collected $42,700 of cash from its accounts receivable during 1996. Following are the summary transactions for Cherokee Station during 1996 that involved both operating activities and cash inflows or outflows.

Cash Flows: To Report or Not to Report

Unlike the balance sheet and income statement, the statement of cash flows is not universally recognized across the world as a major financial statement. In fact, most countries do not require business entities to include a statement of cash flows in their annual financial reports. Instead of requiring a statement of cash flows, accounting and financial reporting standards in some countries, Sweden being an example, require businesses to prepare a funds statement. A funds statement analyzes the changes in working capital accounts—current assets and current liabilities—during an accounting period. Several developed countries do not require business entities to prepare a statement of cash flows or a funds statement. Among these countries are Denmark, Italy, the Netherlands, and Switzerland. Even in the absence of requirements to do so, many multinational companies voluntarily include a statement of cash flows in their annual reports because of the demand for that statement by financial decision makers.

SUMMARY JOURNAL ENTRY (SJE)	CASH EFFECT	
Collections of Accounts Receivable (SJE #2)	Increase	$42,700
Payments of Accrued Operating Expenses (SJE #5)	Decrease	5,800
Payments of Operating Expenses (SJE #6)	Decrease	3,600
Prepayments of Operating Expenses (SJE #7)	Decrease	3,500
Payments to Suppliers (SJE #9)	Decrease	24,700
Payment of Income Tax Expense (SJE #14)	Decrease	1,000

Given the previous data, we can now compute Cherokee Station's net cash flow from operating activities under the direct method, as shown in the following schedule.

Cash flows from operating activities:	
Cash received from customers	$42,700
Cash paid to suppliers	(24,700)
Cash paid for operating expenses	(12,900)
Income taxes paid	(1,000)
Net cash provided by operating activities	$ 4,100

Notice that the payments of accrued operating expenses ($5,800), payments of operating expenses ($3,600), and prepayments of operating expenses ($3,500) were consolidated into one amount ($12,900). Finally, notice that the net cash provided by operating activities is the same amount determined previously under the indirect method.

CASH FLOWS FROM INVESTING AND FINANCING ACTIVITIES   As indicated previously, the net cash flows from investing and financing activities are determined in the same manner under the indirect and direct methods. Since these items were discussed earlier when the indirect method was illustrated for Cherokee Station, here we simply list the schedules for these cash flows.

Discussion Question
How would the discarding or "junking" of a piece of equipment be reported in a statement of cash flows?
Answer: The loss, if any, related to this transaction (event) would be added to net income to arrive at net cash provided (or used) by operating activities. This item would not be reported as an investing activity since it did not involve cash.

■ **EXHIBIT 16.10**

Cherokee Station, Inc., Statement of Cash Flows—Direct Method, for the Year Ended December 31, 1996

CHEROKEE STATION, INC. STATEMENT OF CASH FLOWS FOR THE YEAR ENDED DECEMBER 31, 1996	
Cash flows from operating activities:	
Cash received from customers	$42,700
Cash paid to suppliers	(24,700)
Cash paid for selling and general expenses	(12,900)
Income taxes paid	(1,000)
Net cash provided by operating activities	4,100
Cash flows from investing activities:	
Sale of available-for-sale securities	2,600
Purchase of equipment	(11,000)
Net cash used in investing activities	(8,400)
Cash flows from financing activities:	
Sale of preferred stock	15,000
Dividend payments	(1,800)
Net cash provided by financing activities	13,200
Net increase in Cash	8,900
Cash balance, December 31, 1995	6,100
Cash balance, December 31, 1996	$15,000
Reconciliation of net income to net cash flow from operating activities:	
Net Income	$ 3,600
Adjustments to reconcile net income to net cash provided by operating activities:	
Depreciation expense	4,200
Gain on sale of available-for-sale securities	(700)
Changes in current assets and liabilities:	
Increase in accounts receivable	(2,200)
Decrease in inventories	1,200
Increase in prepaid expenses	(1,100)
Increase in accounts payable	300
Decrease in accrued expenses	(1,200)
Net cash provided by operating activities	$ 4,100

Discussion Question

Instruct students to read the operating activities sections of the statements of cash flows shown in Exhibits 16.9 and 16.10. Ask students which of these two sections has the higher "information value" for decision makers.

Cash flows from investing activities:	
Sale of available-for-sale securities	$ 2,600
Purchase of equipment	(11,000)
Net cash used in investing activities	($ 8,400)
Cash flows from financing activities:	
Sale of preferred stock	$15,000
Dividend payments	(1,800)
Net cash provided by financing activities	$13,200

COMPLETING THE STATEMENT OF CASH FLOWS Exhibit 16.10 presents Cherokee Station's statement of cash flows for the year ended December 31, 1996, prepared using the direct method. Notice that the reconciliation of Cherokee Station's net income to its net cash provided by operating activities is included as a supporting schedule to the statement of cash flows. If you refer to Exhibit 16.2, you will notice that Hughes Supply did not include this reconciliation as a supporting schedule to its statement of cash flows. Instead, Hughes Supply, like many companies using the direct method, included this reconciliation in a financial statement footnote.

INTERPRETING CASH-FLOW INFORMATION

The ability to prepare a statement of cash flows is an important skill, particularly for accountants. However, a more important skill for both accountants and financial decision makers is the ability to interpret cash-flow data. For at least two reasons, the interpretation of cash-flow data is more subjective than the interpretation of accrual-basis accounting data reported in the income statement and balance sheet. First, cash flows are more susceptible to manipulation than accrual-based accounting data. For example, cash disbursements can often be shifted from one accounting period to another. Consequently, decision makers must be cautious when drawing conclusions based upon cash-flow data, since an entity's executives may have intentionally "sculpted" that data to serve some purpose. Second, there are fewer widely accepted financial ratios and measures available to interpret cash-flow data than accrual-based accounting data.

In this section, we consider two common approaches to analyzing cash-flow data. The first approach is a comparative analysis of an entity's cash flows from its operating, investing, and financing activities. The second approach focuses specifically on operating cash flows and involves computing and interpreting cash flow per share.

Comparative Analysis of an Entity's Cash Flows

Much can be learned about a company's financial status and future prospects by analyzing the three components of its cash flows. For example, refer to Exhibit 16.11, which presents cash-flow data over a three-year period for Zero Corporation, a manufacturing company discussed briefly in an earlier chapter. Notice that in each year from 1992 through 1994, Zero Corporation's operating activities generated a positive net cash flow. For a company to remain viable over the long term, its operating activities must generate positive cash flows. There is a limit to the amount of cash a company can raise by selling stocks or bonds or by taking out long-term loans—examples of financing activities. Likewise, a company cannot survive for long if it must sell equipment or other productive assets—an investing activity—to generate needed cash.

Zero's 1992–1994 statements of cash flows reveals that much of the company's cash outflows from investing activities involved the purchase of property, plant & equipment. Here again is a positive indication of the company's future prospects. The company is investing cash generated by its operating activities into additional productive assets to expand the scope of those activities. Finally, practically all of the cash outflows from Zero's financing activities for the period 1992–1994 involved dividend payments and principal payments on long-term debt. Few stockholders or potential stockholders will complain regarding those uses of a company's cash resources.

Focus on Ethics
A company recently applied for a bank loan. Several weeks before applying for this loan, the company's owner instructed her accountant to postpone all payments due suppliers until the loan application and accompanying financial statements had been completed. How would the owner's decision affect the company's statement of cash flows? Has the owner behaved unethically?

■ **LEARNING OBJECTIVE 5**
Interpret cash-flow data by comparatively analyzing the three components of an entity's cash flows

■ **EXHIBIT 16.11**
Zero Corporation:
Cash Flows, 1992–1994

SOURCE: 1994 annual report.

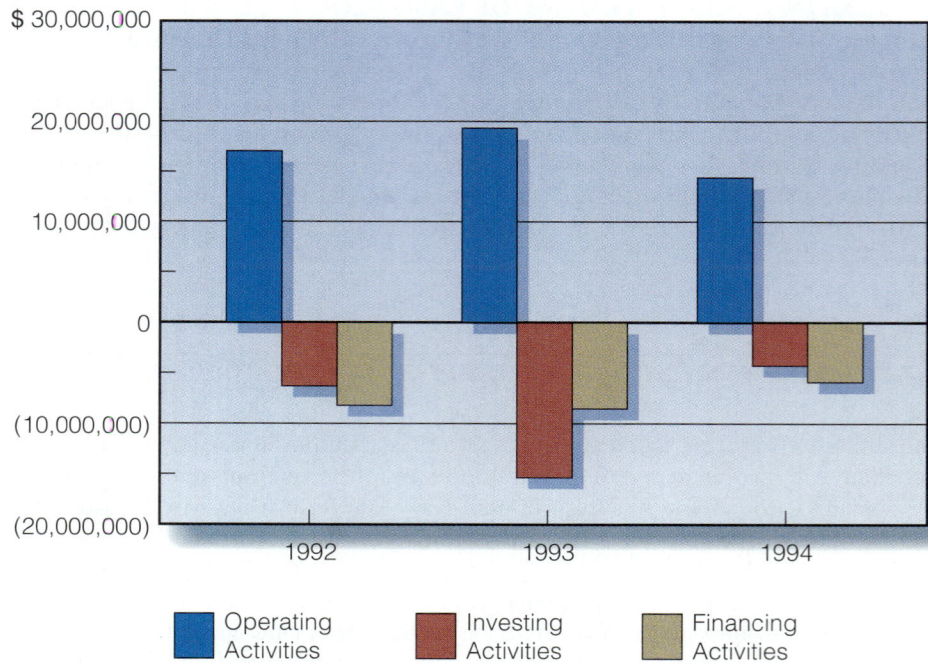

■ **EXHIBIT 16.12**
Allou Health & Beauty Care:
Cash Flows, 1992–1994

SOURCE: 1994 annual report.

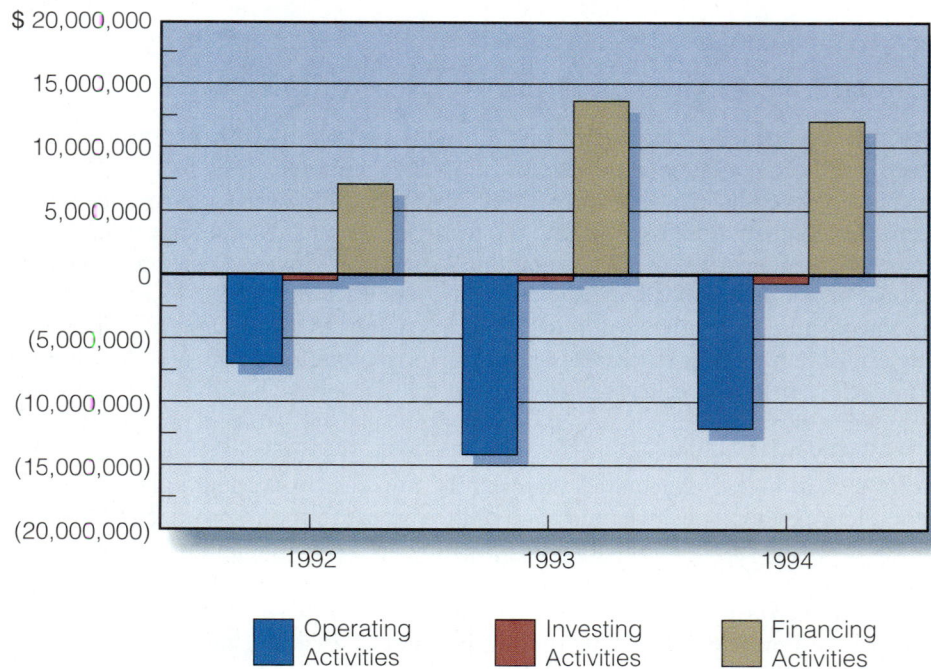

Now, consider the cash-flow data presented in Exhibit 16.12 for Allou Health & Beauty Care, Inc., which distributes health and beauty aids, fragrances, and cosmetics to thousands of retailers nationwide. Unlike Zero Corporation, Allou's operating activities did not produce positive net cash flows over the three-year period 1992–1994. This was true despite the fact that the company posted a record net income each successive year during that period. Instead of relying upon its operating activities to generate positive cash flows, this company relied heavily upon financing activities to provide for its cash needs during 1992–1994. Most of this financing resulted from bank loans and the sale of stock.

Allou's 1994 annual report reveals that a buildup of inventory was largely responsible for the company's negative net cash flow from operating activities in the early 1990s. In 1994 alone, the company saw its inventory increase by more than $13 million. Further investigation reveals that the company's inventory grew at nearly twice the rate of its sales during that year, raising the question of potential inventory obsolescence. Obviously, the earnings and future cash flows of a company will be adversely affected if it is unable to sell its inventory at normal retail prices.

Computing and Interpreting Cash Flow Per Share

Cash flow per share is another financial measure tracked by decision makers. Ironically, in *Statement No. 95* the FASB specifically prohibited business entities from reporting cash flow per share. Why? Principally because the FASB was concerned that reporting both earnings per share and cash flow per share would confuse financial statement users. A related concern was that decision makers would begin using cash flow per share as the primary measure of an entity's financial performance. Despite the important uses of cash-flow data, the accounting profession firmly believes that accrual-based earnings data are the most reliable measures of the financial performance of business entities.

Since corporations are not allowed to disclose cash flow per share amounts in their annual reports, this "service" is provided by investment advisory firms. A problem stemming from the absence of formal rules for cash flow per share disclosures is a lack of consistency in how this financial statistic is computed. For our purposes, **cash flow per share** for an accounting period is computed as follows:

$$\text{Cash Flow Per Share} = \frac{\text{Net Cash Flow from Operating Activities} - \text{Preferred Stock Dividends}}{\text{Weighted Average Number of Shares of Common Stock Outstanding}}$$

Shown in Exhibit 16.13 is a ten-year comparison of Compaq Computer's earnings per share and cash flow per share. As you might expect, these two important financial measures tend to be closely correlated. Over the period covered by Exhibit 16.13, Compaq's earnings increased significantly. This increase in profits was accompanied by a comparable increase in net cash flow from operating activities. Notice that each year Compaq's cash flows per share exceeded its earnings per share, which is true for most companies. The gap between these two amounts is usually due to noncash expenses, principally depreciation expense.

When a company's earnings per share and cash flow per share in a given year diverge from their normal relationship, decision makers want to know why. Quite often, a company's operating cash flows begin declining in advance of a decrease in earnings. For example, during the early stages of an economic recession, a company's

Discussion Question
Ask students to review the statement of cash flows for Michaels Stores and to comment on any apparent trends in the company's cash-flow data over the three-year period covered by that financial statement.

■ **LEARNING OBJECTIVE 6**
Compute and interpret cash flow per share

cash flow per share

Discussion Question
Ask students to compute the cash flow per share of Michaels Stores for each year for which sufficient data are available in the annual report included in the Appendix. How does the company's cash flow per share compare each year to its earnings per share?

To properly interpret a statement of cash flows prepared for Ohio Edison, Compaq Computer, or any other business, a financial decision maker must first understand the nature of that business.

■ **EXHIBIT 16.13**

Compaq Computer: Earnings Per Share vs. Cash Flow Per Share

SOURCE: Value Line investment advisory service.

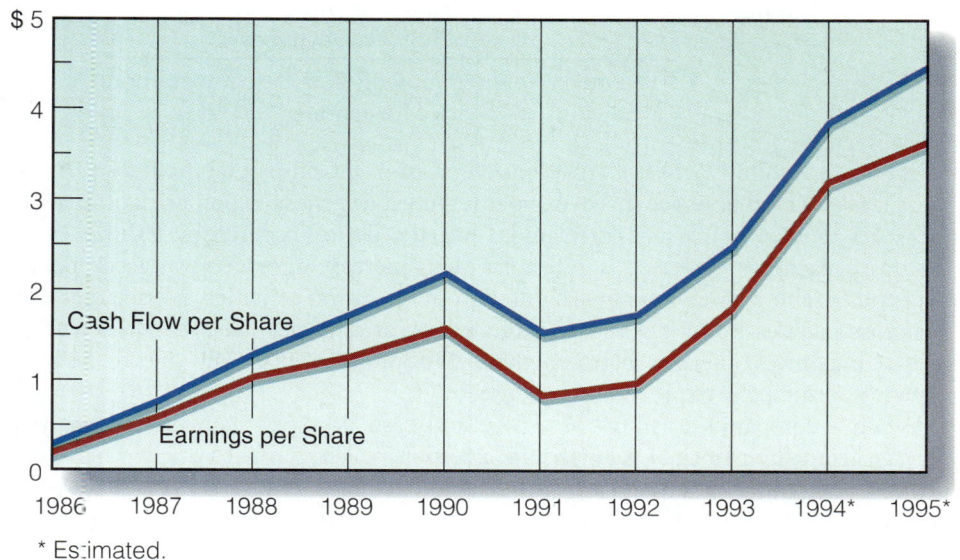

* Estimated.

In Our Employees We Trust: Safeguarding Cash in a Small Business

As suggested in earlier vignettes in this chapter, cash-flow problems are a common bugaboo of small companies. Slow-paying customers, economic downturns, and periods of tight credit are among the principal causes of depleted bank accounts for small businesses. Another major source of cash-flow problems for small firms is employee theft. Owners of small businesses often do not have the financial resources to establish a rigorous internal control structure or do not believe that an extensive system of internal controls is necessary given their close relationship with their employees. In either case, employees of such firms often find themselves in situations in which they can take unfair advantage of their employers.

Several incidents of employee theft or embezzlement have been referred to in earlier chapters. Two prominent but relatively small business organizations, by most standards, that suffered embarrassing embezzlement losses recently include the Los Angeles Dodgers and Salomon Brothers. Recall that the Dodgers suffered several hundred thousand dollars of losses due to the scheming of a dishonest payroll chief. Salomon Brothers, the investment banking firm, was ripped off for more than one million dollars by a key administrative employee. Then there was the case of Howard Street Jewelers that was highlighted in Chapter 6. Recall that Betty, the trusted but sticky-fingered cashier, stole $350,000 from her employer.

One circumstance common to these embezzlement cases was the trust that management had placed in a given employee. In each case, the employee who stole from his or her employer was a well-liked and respected individual who was perceived to be very competent and loyal to the organization. Although small business owners may be predisposed toward trusting their employees, they should never lose sight of the possibility that an employee may be quietly "stealing them blind." Again, the most effective deterrent to employee theft is a rigorous internal control structure that includes occasionally "looking over the shoulder" of even the most trusted employees within an organization.

sales may remain stable. However, the collection period on the company's credit sales will typically lengthen if the recession continues, causing cash flows from operating activities to decline. If economic conditions fail to improve, the company's earnings will likely begin declining as well. This drop in earnings may result from falling sales and/or from increases in bad debt expense and write-offs or write-downs of slow-moving inventory.

Another approach to tracking cash flow per share and earnings per share is to express one of these statistics as a percentage of the other. Under this approach, a significant divergence from the normal relationship between these two important financial measures is readily apparent. This monitoring technique also allows decision makers to more easily compare the relationship between net operating cash flows and earnings for two or more companies. Exhibit 16.14 presents a ten-year summary of the relationship between earnings per share and cash flow per share for Compaq Computer and Ohio Edison, a large electric utility. Except for 1986, Ohio Edison's earnings per share as a percentage of cash flow per share is much lower than the comparable measure for Compaq Computer. Why? Principally because electric utilities have relatively high depreciation expenses each year, resulting in their earnings being significantly less than their net cash flow from operating activities.

Teaching Note
Remind students that depreciation is a noncash expense that is added to net income to determine net cash flow from operating activities under the indirect method.

■ **EXHIBIT 16.14**

Earnings Per Share as a Percentage of Cash Flow Per Share: Compaq Computer vs. Ohio Edison

SOURCE: Value Line investment advisory service.

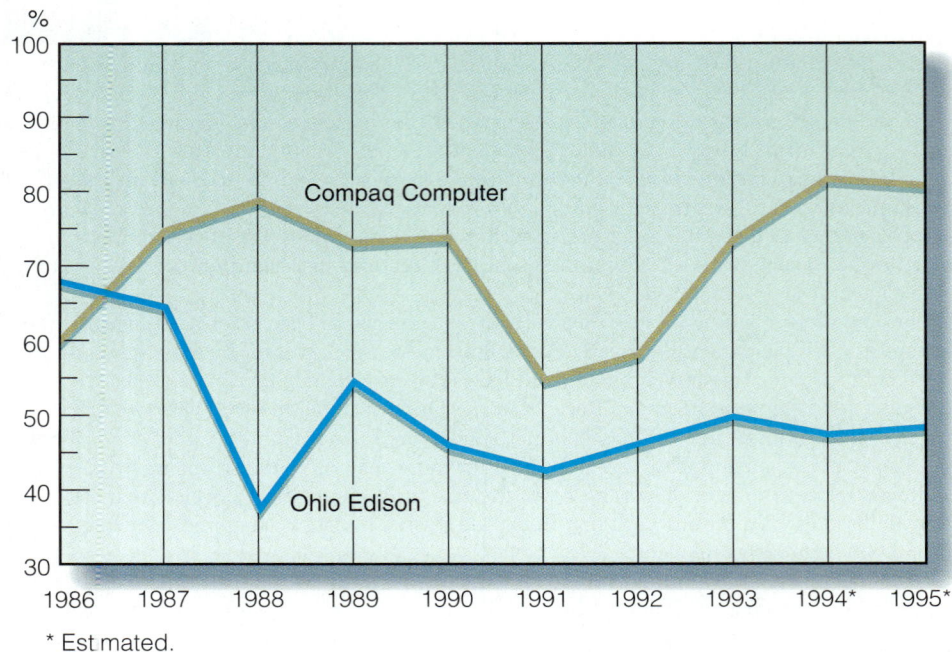

* Estimated.

SUMMARY

Recent history provides many examples of once-profitable companies that did not survive because they had insufficient cash resources. Most of these companies failed because they did not generate sufficient cash from their principal business operations. In 1987, the Financial Accounting Standards Board (FASB) issued *Statement of Financial Accounting Standards No. 95*, "Statement of Cash Flows." This accounting standard requires business entities to include a statement of cash flows in their annual financial reports. The most important objective of a statement of cash flows is to allow decision makers to evaluate an entity's ability to generate positive net cash flows in the future.

Business entities engage in three principal types of activities that result in cash inflows and outflows: operating, investing, and financing activities. Operating activities generally involve transactions and events related to the production and delivery of goods and services. Receipts from customers are typically the principal cash inflows from operating activities. The largest cash outflows from operating activities are usually payments to suppliers. The acquisition and disposal of property, plant & equipment, and the purchase and sale of investments in debt and equity securities, other than trading securities and cash equivalents, are principal sources of cash flows from investing activities. Finally, financing activities involve debt and equity capital. Examples of cash flows from financing activities include proceeds from the sale of an entity's common stock, payments of dividends, and principal payments on long-term loans.

FASB *Statement No. 95* permits business entities to use either the direct or indirect methods of preparing a statement of cash flows. The only major difference between these two methods involves the computation of net cash flow from operating activities. Under the indirect method, net cash flow from operating activities is determined by making certain adjustments to an entity's net income. These adjustments involve depreciation and amortization expenses, gains and losses, and changes in noncash current asset and current liability accounts. Under the direct method, net cash flow from operating activities is the sum of specific cash flows such as cash received from customers and cash paid to suppliers.

Interpreting cash-flow data requires the exercise of more subjective judgment than analyzing accrual-based accounting data for two reasons. First, cash-flow data are more susceptible to manipulation than accrual-based data. Second, fewer financial ratios and measures have been developed to interpret cash-flow data. One common method of analyzing cash-flow data is to compare the three components of an entity's cash flows over a period of several years. Most important, such analysis reveals any distinctive trends in an entity's cash flows.

A second method of analyzing cash-flow data is to relate an entity's cash flow per share to its earning per share. Any significant divergence from the normal relationship between these two key financial measures should be investigated. Cash flow per share for an accounting period is computed by dividing the difference between a company's net cash flow from operating activities and preferred stock dividends by the company's weighted-average number of shares of common stock outstanding during that period. FASB *Statement No. 95* specifically prohibits business entities from reporting cash flow per share. Nevertheless, investment advisory firms regularly report this financial statistic for public companies.

GLOSSARY

Cash flow per share (p. 717)   Net cash flow from operating activities for an accounting period, less preferred stock dividends, divided by the weighted-average number of shares of common stock outstanding during that period.

Direct method (p. 699)   An approach to preparing the statement of cash flows in which specific cash inflows and outflows from an entity's operating activities are identified and listed in the initial section of this financial statement.

Financing activities (p. 697)   Those activities of business entities that include obtaining resources from owners and providing them with a return on, and a return of, their investment; borrowing money and repaying amounts borrowed; and obtaining and paying for other resources obtained from creditors on long-term credit.

Indirect method (p. 699)   An approach to preparing the statement of cash flows in which net cash flow from operating activities is determined by making certain adjustments to an entity's net income.

Investing activities (p. 697)   Those activities of business entities that include the making and collecting of loans, the acquisition and disposal of property, plant & equipment, and the purchase and sale of debt and equity securities other than trading securities and cash equivalents.

Operating activities (p. 697)   Those transactions and events related to the production and delivery of goods and services by business entities.

Statement of cash flows (p. 692)   A financial statement that accounts for the net change in an entity's cash balance during a given period; this statement summarizes the cash receipts and disbursements from an entity's operating, investing, and financing activities.

DECISION CASE

Suppose that you have decided to enter the business world by becoming the sole proprietor of Acme Roadrunning Enterprises (ARE), a company that manufactures wear-resistant soles for running shoes. The major asset required by this business is a piece of production machinery. Presently, there are two models of this machinery available. Model A costs $300,000 and produces a higher-quality sole than Model B, which costs $180,000. Each machine has a three-year useful life and a zero estimated salvage value. You have sufficient resources available to purchase either Model A or Model B for cash. In either case, you will invest an additional $60,000 in your business. That is, you will transfer $60,000 from your personal bank account to ARE's bank account.

Listed in the following table are forecasted operating data, in condensed form, for the first three years of ARE's existence. Data are presented under the assumption that Model A is acquired and then under the assumption that Model B is acquired. In either case, the straight-line depreciation method will be used for the production machinery. The table does not include information on two transactions of ARE in Year 1—namely, the purchase of either Model A or Model B and your investment of an additional $60,000 in the business. You estimate that the replacement cost of Model A at the end of three years will be $410,000, while the replacement cost of Model B at that point will be $200,000. You realize that your initial decision regarding whether to purchase Model A or Model B is an important one. The products (soles) produced by the two models would be sold to different customers and require different business plans and strategies. As a result, it would not be economically feasible to switch from Model A to Model B, or vice versa, in the future.

	YEAR 1	YEAR 2	YEAR 3
Model A:			
Net Income	$ 40,000	$ 50,000	$ 85,000
Depreciation Expense	100,000	100,000	100,000
Year-End Inventory	25,000	65,000	125,000
Year-End Receivables	20,000	50,000	120,000
Year-End Payables and Accrued Expenses	10,000	25,000	50,000
Model B:			
Net Income	$ 30,000	$ 35,000	$ 40,000
Depreciation Expense	60,000	60,000	60,000
Year-End Inventory	10,000	20,000	40,000
Year-End Receivables	10,000	20,000	35,000
Year-End Payables and Accrued Expenses	5,000	10,000	20,000

Required: Prepare statements of cash flows for ARE for Years 1–3 assuming that Model A is acquired. Then prepare comparable statements of cash flows assuming Model B is acquired. Which model will produce the largest positive (net) cash flow over this period? Given the available data, which model should be purchased and why? What other factors should you consider in making this decision?

QUESTIONS

1. A statement of cash flows is intended to supplement an entity's balance sheet and income statement. True or false?

2. What is the principal use of a statement of cash flows from the perspective of financial decision makers?

3. From a technical standpoint, what is the primary objective of a statement of cash flows?

4. Identify the four sections of a typical statement of cash flows.

5. Define and provide an example of each of the following: operating activities, investing activities, and financing activities.

6. Identify one common criticism of the classification scheme that the FASB requires in a statement of cash flows.

7. Why is it important for decision makers to be provided with a reconciliation of an entity's net income and net cash flow from operating activities for a given period?

8. What is the only major difference between the direct and indirect methods of preparing a statement of cash flows?

9. Why does the FASB prefer the direct method of preparing the statement of cash flows?

10. Identify several examples of cash flows from operating activities that might be included in a statement of cash flows prepared using the direct method.

11. What factor or factors likely account for the popularity of the indirect method of preparing a statement of cash flows?

12. What is the starting point for determining an entity's net cash flow from its operating activities under the indirect method?

13. When the indirect method is being used, why is depreciation expense added to net income when determining net cash flow from operating activities?

14. How are gains and losses on the sale of property, plant & equipment dealt with in the statement of cash flows when the indirect method is being used? Why?

15. How do increases in current assets affect the determination of net cash flow from operating activities under the indirect method? What about decreases in current liabilities?

16. How are "noncash" investing and financing activities typically reported in an entity's financial statements?

17. Identify the two specific cash outflows from operating activities that a company using the indirect method of preparing a statement of cash flows must disclose in its financial statements.

18. Briefly describe how the account-analysis technique can be used to determine cash flows from operating activities when the direct method of preparing a statement of cash flows is being used.

19. Identify two reasons why cash-flow financial data are more difficult to interpret than accrual-based financial data.

20. "For a company to remain viable over the long term, its operating activities must generate positive cash flows." Explain the reasoning underlying this statement.

21. How is cash flow per share typically computed?

22. Why does the FASB prohibit business entities from reporting cash flow per share?

23. Which amount is typically larger each year for a business entity, cash flow per share or earnings per share? Why?

24. "Quite often, a company's operating cash flows begin declining in advance of a decrease in earnings." Explain this statement.

25. What is a common mistake many small businesses make relative to their internal controls over cash and cash processing activities?

26. What is the most effective deterrent to employee theft in a small business?

EXERCISES

27. **Classification of Cash Flows** (LO 2)
Following are examples of cash inflows and outflows that appear in statements of cash flows prepared by business entities.

_____ Payments to employees
_____ Loans made to other firms
_____ Payments to acquire trading securities
_____ Receipts from customers
_____ Receipts from the sale of property, plant & equipment
_____ Payments of interest
_____ Payments made to acquire controlling interests in other firms
_____ Receipts of interest and dividends
_____ Payments to retire outstanding bonds
_____ Payments to suppliers
_____ Receipts from the sale of available-for-sale securities

Required:
Classify each of the listed cash flows as one of the following:
a. Cash inflow from operating activities
b. Cash outflow from operating activities
c. Cash inflow from investing activities
d. Cash outflow from investing activities
e. Cash inflow from financing activities
f. Cash outflow from financing activities

27. b,d,b,a,c,b,d,a,f,b,c

28. **Classification of Cash Flows** (LO 2)
Following are examples of cash inflows and outflows that appear in statements of cash flows prepared by business entities.

_____ Receipts from the sale of investments in trading securities
_____ Receipts from the issuance of common stock
_____ Dividend payments
_____ Payments to acquire available-for-sale securities
_____ Payments to acquire property, plant & equipment
_____ Receipts from the sale of controlling investments
_____ Receipts from the issuance of bonds
_____ Amounts borrowed from banks
_____ Payments of taxes
_____ Payments to acquire treasury stock

Required:
Classify each of the listed cash flows as one of the following:
a. Cash inflow from operating activities
b. Cash outflow from operating activities
c. Cash inflow from investing activities
d. Cash outflow from investing activities
e. Cash inflow from financing activities
f. Cash outflow from financing activities

28. a,e,f,d,d,c,e,e,b,f

29. **Corporate Statement of Cash Flows** (LO 3)
Individual companies often have their own unique methods of preparing and presenting financial data. Take the case of Microsoft Corporation. Presented next are the exact line items, in random order, that appeared in the initial sec-

tion of Microsoft's 1994 statement of cash flows (amounts are expressed in millions of dollars):

Accounts receivable	$ (146)
Inventories	23
Current liabilities	360
Net income	1,146
Other current assets	(27)
Depreciation and amortization	237
Net cash from operations	1,593

Required:
Prepare the initial section of Microsoft's 1994 statement of cash flows using the format shown in Exhibit 16.3.

30. **Net Income vs. Net Cash Flow from Operating Activities** (LO 1)
Conner Peripherals, Inc., manufactures computer disk drives and related computer products. In 1993, Connor Peripherals suffered a loss of nearly $450 million. However, the company's 1993 statement of cash flows reported a net cash flow from operating activities of approximately $20 million.

Required:
How could Conner's incur a large loss in a given year but still have a positive cash flow from operating activities for that year?

31. **Completing a Statement of Cash Flows** (LO 3)
Following is a partially completed statement of cash flows for Brigham Company. (Amounts are expressed in thousands.)

Cash flows from operating activities:

Net Income	$ 1,433
Adjustments to reconcile net income to net	
cash provided by operating activities:	
Depreciation expense	?
Gain on sale of long-term investment	(115)
Changes in current assets and liabilities:	
Increase in accounts receivable	(863)
Decrease in inventories	350
Decrease in prepaid expenses	667
Decrease in short-term notes payable	(400)
Decrease in accrued expenses	(1,004)
Net cash provided by operating activities	?

Cash flows from investing activities:

Sale of long-term investment	?
Purchase of property, plant & equipment	(7,639)
Net cash used by investing activities	(1,113)

Cash flows from financing activities:

Sale of common stock	6,329
Dividend payments	?
Net cash provided by financing activities	4,072

Net increase in Cash	4,115
Cash balance, December 31, 1995	?
Cash balance, December 31, 1996	$11,332

29. No check figures

30. No check figures

Required:
1. What method does Brigham Company use to prepare its statement of cash flows?
2. Complete Brigham's statement of cash flows.
3. What was Brigham's largest source of cash during the year in question?

32. Classification of Cash Flows from Sales of Debt and Equity Securities (LO 2)

During 1996, Lodi Corporation had the following sales of debt and equity securities:

January 12: 300 shares of Exxon common stock classified as available-for-sale securities

March 19: 42,500 shares of a controlling investment in MacDonald Manufacturing, Inc.

June 4: 300 short-term government securities classified as cash equivalents

July 16: 500 shares of IBM common stock classified as trading securities

October 3: 11,400 shares of Othello Restaurants, Inc., classified as an influential but noncontrolling investment

Required:
Indicate how the cash flow resulting from each sale would be incorporated in Lodi's 1996 statement of cash flows.

33. Account-Analysis Technique of Determining Cash Flows (LO 4)

Micah Manufacturing, Inc., had total sales of $4,232,000 during 1996, 50 percent of which were made on credit. On January 1, 1996, Micah had accounts receivable of $237,100, while on December 31, 1996, the company had accounts receivable of $303,900.

Required:
1. Assuming that Micah collects all of its credit sales, use the account-analysis technique to determine the cash collected from its customers during 1996.
2. For which method of preparing a statement of cash flows, the direct or indirect method, is the account-analysis technique useful?

34. Account-Analysis Technique of Determining Cash Flows (LO 4)

On January 1, 1995, Nahum Corporation had salaries payable of $22,340, while the balance of this account at the end of 1995 was $17,890. Nahum's salaries expense during 1995 was $957,316.

Required:
Using the account-analysis technique, determine the amount of salaries paid by Nahum during 1995.

35. Interpreting Cash-Flow Data (LO 5)

Between 1992 and 1994, Kellogg Company's statements of cash flows indicated cumulative increases in the company's accounts receivable of $145 million.

Required:
1. How does an increase in accounts receivable affect a company's net cash flow from operating activities? Why?
2. If a company's accounts receivable balance is continually increasing from one year to the next, does that indicate, necessarily, that the firm is doing a poor job of "managing" or collecting its accounts receivable? Explain.

36. Analyzing Cash-Flow Effects (LO 3, 4)

Motta Storage Company had the following balances in its Equipment and Accumulated Depreciation, Equipment accounts at the beginning and end of 1996.

	JANUARY 1, 1996	DECEMBER 31, 1996
Equipment	$100,000	$120,000
Accumulated Depreciation, Equipment	25,000	18,000

During 1996, Motta engaged in the following transactions involving equipment:

March 9: Purchased new equipment for $40,000.

July 16: Sold for $16,500 equipment that originally cost $20,000 and had accumulated depreciation of $12,000.

Required:

1. How much depreciation expense did Motta Storage Company record on its equipment during 1996?
2. Indicate how Motta's depreciation expense and its transactions involving equipment would appear in the company's 1996 statement of cash flows.

36. 1. $5,000

37. **Comparative Analysis of Cash Flows** (LO 5)

The following data were included in the 1994 annual report of Whole Foods Market, Inc., a retailing firm headquartered in Austin, Texas.

	1992	1993	1994
Net Income	$ 3,716,084	$ 3,818,190	$ 8,638,658
Net Cash Flow from Operating Activities	7,460,501	12,556,072	15,390,336
Net Cash Flow from Investing Activities	(7,792,408)	(41,527,077)	(32,850,636)
Net Cash Flow from Financing Activities	15,113,487	17,478,816	14,982,854

Required:

1. Why is a company's net income typically less than its net cash flow from operating activities?
2. Most companies, including Whole Foods, typically have negative cash flows from investing activities. Why is this true?
3. Over the period 1992–1994, what type of activities was the largest source of funds for Whole Foods? Do business executives want these activities to be their firm's principal source of funds? Explain.

37. No check figures

38. **Cash Flow Per Share** (LO 6)

The following data were included in the 1995 annual report of the large discount retailer, Dollar General Corporation.

	1993	1994	1995
Net Income	$35,574,000	$48,557,000	$73,634,000
Net Cash Flow from Operating Activities	42,713,000	36,196,000	43,257,000
Weighted-Average Number of Shares of Common Stock Outstanding	66,306,000	67,281,000	69,009,000
Preferred Stock Dividends Paid	—	—	772,000

Required:

1. Compute Dollar General's earnings per share and cash flow per share for each year 1993 through 1995.
2. For each year, express Dollar General's earnings per share as a percentage of its cash flow per share.

38. 1.

	1993	1994	1995
Earnings per share	$0.54	$0.72	$1.06
Cash flow per share	$0.64	$0.54	$0.62

2.

	1993	1994	1995
	84%	133%	171%

3. What factors could have accounted for Dollar General's net cash flow from operating activities being less than the firm's net income in 1994 and 1995? Why would a potential investor in this firm want to identify these factors? Explain.

PROBLEM SET A

39. Classification of Cash Flows (LO 2)

Following are line items included in recent statements of cash flows issued by Tuesday Morning Corporation, a discount retailer, and America Online, Inc., a leading provider of on-line information and entertainment services.

_____ Repurchase of common stock
_____ Interest received
_____ Income taxes refunded
_____ Principal payments on long-term notes payable
_____ Cash paid to suppliers and employees
_____ Purchase of property and equipment
_____ Proceeds from (long-term) note payable
_____ Principal payments under capital lease obligations
_____ Payment of dividends on convertible redeemable preferred stock
_____ Principal payments on mortgages
_____ Proceeds from common stock offering
_____ Loans to officers
_____ Proceeds from the sale of property, plant & equipment
_____ Cash received from customers

Required:

39. f,a,a,f,b,d,e,f,f,f,e,d,c,a

Classify each of the line items listed as one of the following:
a. Cash inflow from operating activities
b. Cash outflow from operating activities
c. Cash inflow from investing activities
d. Cash outflow from investing activities
e. Cash inflow from financing activities
f. Cash outflow from financing activities

40. Corporate Statement of Cash Flows (LO 3)

Following are the line items included in a recent statement of cash flows prepared by Goody's Family Clothing, Inc. (Note: Amounts are expressed in thousands and minor changes have been made for the purpose of clarity.)

Proceeds from sale of long-term investments	$ 8,077
Depreciation and amortization	5,285
Increase in miscellaneous current assets	(1,396)
Increase in accounts payable	12,590
Purchase of long-term investments	(34,959)
Net income	16,214
Increase in accrued expenses	4,072
Proceeds from sale of property and equipment	192
Increase in inventories	(11,320)
Net advances on (long-term) notes payable	500
Reductions of long-term debt	(172)
Net gain on disposal of long-term assets	(135)
Issuance of common stock	126
Cash and cash equivalents, beginning of the year	31,350

Increase in income taxes payable		2,108
Acquisitions of property and equipment		(11,043)
Net increase (decrease) in cash and cash equivalents		?
Cash and cash equivalents, end of year		?

Required:

Prepare Goody's statement of cash flows using the indirect method.

41. **Determining Net Cash Flow from Operating Activities, Indirect Method (LO 1, 3)**

Following is an income statement of Cline Pacific Corporation for the year ended December 31, 1996, and the company's current assets and current liabilities at the end of 1995 and 1996.

40. Net cash flow provided by operating activities, $27,418 Net cash flow used by investing activities, $(37,733) Net cash flow provided by financing activities, $454 Net decrease in cash and cash equivalents, $(9,861) Cash and and cash equivalents, end of year, $21,489

CLINE PACIFIC CORPORATION
INCOME STATEMENT
FOR THE YEAR ENDED DECEMBER 31, 1996

Sales		$77,600
Cost of Goods Sold		44,400
Gross Profit		33,200
Operating Expenses:		
Selling & General Expenses	8,800	
Depreciation Expense	1,900	10,700
Operating Income		22,500
Gain on Sale of Land		5,500
Income before Income Tax		28,000
Income Tax Expense		11,200
Net Income		$16,800

	1995	1996
Cash	$11,700	$ 4,100
Accounts Receivable	4,500	9,800
Inventory	6,700	11,300
Prepaid Expenses (Operating)	3,500	800
Accounts Payable	2,900	5,600
Accrued Expenses (Operating)	1,600	2,800

Required:

1. Prepare a schedule documenting Cline Pacific Corporation's net cash flow from operating activities for the year ended December 31, 1996, using the indirect method.

2. Briefly evaluate the schedule you prepared in Part 1. Does the schedule of cash flows from operating activities provide any clues regarding the financial health of Cline Pacific? Explain.

41. 1. Net cash flow provided by operating activities, $9,900

42. **Determining Net Cash Flow from Operating Activities, Direct Method (LO 4)**

Problem 41 presents an income statement for Cline Pacific Corporation for the year ended December 31, 1996, and the company's current assets and current liabilities at the end of 1995 and 1996. Following is additional information obtained from Cline Pacific's 1996 accounting records.

a. Collections of accounts receivable		$72,300*
b. Merchandise purchases		49,000
c. Payments to suppliers (of merchandise)		46,300
d. Payments of accrued operating expenses		1,600

e. Payments of operating expenses   2,500
f. Prepayments of operating expenses   800
g. Expiration of prepaid (operating) expenses   3,500
h. Payment of 1996 income tax expense   11,200
i. Accrual of unpaid operating expenses at year end   2,800
j. Year-end adjusting entry to record depreciation expense   1,900

*All of Cline Pacific's sales and merchandise purchases are made on a credit basis.

Required:

1. Using the account-analysis technique illustrated in the text, confirm that Cline Pacific Corporation collected cash of $72,300 from its customers during 1996.
2. Prepare a schedule documenting Cline Pacific Corporation's net cash flow from operating activities for the year ended December 31, 1996, using the direct method.

42. 2. Net cash flow provided by operating activities, $9,900

43. **Preparing a Statement of Cash Flows, Indirect Method** (LO 3)
Following is the income statement of Knob Hill, Inc., for the year ended December 31, 1996, and the company's balance sheets for the years ended December 31, 1995 and 1996.

KNOB HILL, INC.
INCOME STATEMENT
FOR THE YEAR ENDED DECEMBER 31, 1996

Sales		$92,900
Cost of Goods Sold		36,800
Gross Profit		56,100
Operating Expenses:		
Selling & General Expenses	$14,600	
Depreciation Expense	5,700	20,300
Operating Income		35,800
Loss on Sale of Long-Term Investment		2,500
Income before Income Tax		33,300
Income Tax Expense		13,300
Net Income		$20,000

KNOB HILL, INC.
BALANCE SHEETS
DECEMBER 31, 1995 AND 1996

	1995		1996	
Assets				
Cash		$12,100		$36,500
Accounts Receivable		10,600		12,700
Inventory		14,700		13,000
Prepaid Expenses		1,300		700
Total Current Assets		38,700		62,900
Equipment	$52,000		$52,000	
Less: Accumulated Depreciation	16,300	35,700	22,000	30,000
Investment in LaPage Common Stock		5,100		—
Total Assets		$79,500		$92,900

Liabilities		
Accounts Payable	$ 7,100	$ 5,200
Accrued Expenses	3,300	3,700
Total Current Liabilities	10,400	8,900
Stockholders' Equity		
Common Stock	4,500	4,800
Additional Paid-in Capital	18,200	20,300
Retained Earnings	46,400	58,900
Total Stockholders' Equity	69,100	84,000
Total Liabilities and Stockholders' Equity	$79,500	$92,900

The prepaid expenses and accrued expenses included in Knob Hill's balance sheets all relate to operating (selling and general) expenses. All of Knob Hill's sales and merchandise purchases are made on a credit basis. Following is additional financial information that was obtained from Knob Hill's accounting records for 1996:

a.	Collections of accounts receivable	$90,800
b.	Credit purchases of merchandise	35,100
c.	Payments of accrued operating expenses	3,300
d.	Payments of operating expenses	9,600
e.	Prepayments of operating expenses	700
f.	Expiration of prepaid expenses	1,300
g.	Payments to suppliers	37,000
h.	Proceeds from sale of LaPage common stock	2,600
i.	Sale of 300 shares of $1 par value common stock for $8 per share	2,400
j.	Declaration and payment of cash dividends on common stock	7,500
k.	Payment of 1996 income taxes	13,300
l.	Accrual of unpaid operating expenses at year-end	3,700
m.	Year-end adjusting entry to record depreciation expense on equipment	5,700

Required:

Prepare a statement of cash flows for Knob Hill for the year ended December 31, 1996, using the indirect method.

44. Preparing a Statement of Cash Flows, Direct Method (LO 4)

Refer to the information presented in Problem 43 for Knob Hill, Inc.

Required:

Prepare a statement of cash flows for Knob Hill for the year ended December 31, 1996, using the direct method.

45. Comparative Analysis of Cash Flows (LO5)

Following are data obtained from recent financial statements of Biogen, Inc., one of the nation's leading biotechnology firms (amounts are in thousands):

	1990	1991	1992	1993	1994
Net Income	$ 7,720	$ 7,186	$38,311	$32,417	$ (4,987)
Net Cash Flow from Operating Activities	10,721	5,884	43,052	47,570	34,886
Net Cash Flow from Investing Activities	(29,551)	(48,334)	(23,869)	(66,695)	(70,295)
Net Cash Flow from Financing Activities	(1,797)	86,253	10,033	7,808	15,545

43. Net cash flow provided by operating activities, $26,900
Net cash flow provided by investing activities, $2,600
Net cash flow used by financing activities, $(5,100)
Net increase in cash and cash equivalents, $24,400

44. Net cash flow provided by operating activities, $26,900
Net cash flow provided by investing activities, $2,600
Net cash flow used by financing activities, $(5,100)
Net increase in cash and cash equivalents, $24,400

Required:

1. In 1994, Biogen's operating activities produced almost $35 million in positive cash flow although the firm had a loss of approximately $5 million for the year. How is this possible?
2. Explain how a company's net income can exceed its net cash flow from operating activities, which was the case for Biogen in 1991.
3. Biogen's total assets increased by more than 50 percent between 1990 and 1994. What activities were the largest source of the funds used to finance this growth?
4. What factor or factors likely account for the large negative net cash flows from investing activities experienced by Biogen between 1990 and 1994?

46. Cash Flow Per Share (LO 6)

Following is selected financial information for Claire's Stores, Inc., a women's apparel retailer, and Pioneer Standard Electronics, Inc., a distributor of industrial electronic supplies and components.

	1992	1993	1994
Claire's Stores:			
Net Income	$14,551,000	$23,634,000	$23,855,000
Net Cash Flow from			
Operating Activities	34,430,000	34,750,000	37,030,000
Weighted-Average Number of			
Shares of Common Stock			
Outstanding (in millions)	21.8	22.0	22.2
Pioneer Standard Electronics			
Net Income	$ 5,327,000	$12,913,000	$19,676,000
Net Cash Flow from			
Operating Activities	2,450,000	16,104,000	9,531,000
Weighted-Average Number of			
Shares of Common Stock			
Outstanding (in millions)	8.2	9.2	10.1

Between 1992 and 1994, neither Claire's Stores nor Pioneer Standard Electronics had preferred stock outstanding.

Required:

1. Compute earnings per share and cash flow per share for Claire's Stores and Pioneer Standard Electronics for each year 1992 through 1994.
2. For each year, express each company's earnings per share as a percentage of its cash flow per share.
3. Which of these two companies had a more "normal" relationship between earnings per share and cash flow per share for the period 1992 through 1994? Explain.
4. Claire's Stores had approximately $13 million of depreciation expense each year between 1992 and 1994, while Pioneer Standard had annual depreciation over this same period of approximately $5 million. Does this additional information change your answer to Part 3? Why or why not?
5. Why does the FASB prohibit companies from disclosing cash flow per share in their annual financial statements?

PROBLEM SET B

47. Classification of Cash Flows (LO 2)

Following are line items included in recent statements of cash flows issued by United States Surgical Corporation, a medical supply company, and Pacific Scientific Corporation, a company that manufactures electrical equipment.

_____ Dividends paid
_____ Acquisition of common stock for treasury
_____ Long-term borrowings under credit agreements
_____ Cash received from customers
_____ Proceeds from disposition of property
_____ Cash paid to vendors, suppliers, and employees
_____ Issuance of common stock
_____ Income tax paid
_____ Payments for business acquisitions
_____ Additions to property, plant & equipment
_____ Interest payments

Required:

Classify each of the line items listed as one of the following:
a. Cash inflow from operating activities
b. Cash outflow from operating activities
c. Cash inflow from investing activities
d. Cash outflow from investing activities
e. Cash inflow from financing activities
f. Cash outflow from financing activities

47. f, f, e, a, c, b, e, b, d, d, b

48. Corporate Statement of Cash Flows (LO 3)

Following are the line items included in a recent statement of cash flows prepared by Hormel Foods Corporation. (Note: Amounts are expressed in thousands and minor changes have been made for the purpose of clarity.)

Amortization of intangibles	$ 2,956
Loss on sale of long-term investments	4,368
Increase in accounts receivable	(9,882)
Cash and cash equivalents, beginning of the year	157,558
Decrease in income taxes payable	(5,859)
Sale of long-term investments	3,309
Acquisitions of businesses	(9,750)
Purchase of property & equipment	(65,441)
Sale of property & equipment	1,575
Depreciation	33,655
Acquisition of miscellaneous long-term assets	(3,973)
Decrease in inventories and prepaid expenses	10,930
Purchase of long-term investments	(357)
Increase in accounts payable and accrued expenses	40,686
Proceeds from long-term borrowings	5,000
Net income	117,975
Dividends paid on common stock	(38,463)
Loss on sale of idle facility	4,312
Net increase (decrease) in cash and cash equivalents	?
Cash and cash equivalents, end of the year	?

48. Net cash flow provided by operating activities, $199,141
Net cash flow used by investing activities, $(74,637)
Net cash flow used by financing activities, $(33,463)
Net increase in cash and cash equivalents, $91,041
Cash and cash equivalents, end of year, $248,599

Required:
Prepare Hormel's statement of cash flows using the indirect method.

49. **Determining Net Cash Flow from Operating Activities,
Indirect Method** (LO 1, 3)
Following is an income statement of Yates & Callahan, Inc., for the year ended
December 31, 1996, and the company's current assets and current liabilities at
the end of 1995 and 1996.

YATES & CALLAHAN, INC.
INCOME STATEMENT
FOR THE YEAR ENDED DECEMBER 31, 1996

Sales			$88,200
Cost of Goods Sold			39,800
Gross Profit			48,400
Operating Expenses:			
Selling & General		$6,200	
Depreciation Expense		2,700	8,900
Operating Income			39,500
Loss on Sale of Equipment			1,400
Income before Income Tax			38,100
Income Tax Expense			15,200
Net Income			$22,900

	1995	1996
Cash	$5,700	$6,100
Accounts Receivable	7,500	6,800
Inventory	7,700	5,300
Prepaid Expenses (Operating)	1,200	1,800
Accounts Payable	2,500	2,600
Accrued Expenses (Operating)	1,100	900

Required:
1. Prepare a schedule documenting Yates & Callahan's net cash flow from operating activities for the year ended December 31, 1996, using the indirect
method.
2. Briefly evaluate the schedule you prepared in Part 1. Does the schedule of
cash flows from operating activities provide any clues regarding the financial
health of Yates & Callahan? Explain.

50. **Determining Net Cash Flow from Operating Activities,
Direct Method** (LO 4)
Problem 49 presents an income statement for Yates & Callahan, Inc., for the
year ended December 31, 1996, and the company's current assets and current
liabilities at the end of 1995 and 1996. Following is additional information
obtained from Yates & Callahan's 1996 accounting records.

a. Collections of accounts receivable	$88,900*
b. Merchandise purchases	37,400
c. Payments to suppliers (of merchandise)	37,300
d. Payments of accrued operating expenses	1,100
e. Payments of operating expenses	4,100
f. Prepayments of operating expenses	1,800
g. Expiration of prepaid (operating) expenses	1,200
h. Payment of 1996 income tax expense	15,200

49. 1. Net cash flow provided
by operating activities
$29,400

i.   Accrual of unpaid operating expenses at year-end   900
j.   Year-end adjusting entry to record depreciation expense   2,700

*All of Yates & Callahan's sales and merchandise purchases are made on a credit basis.

Required:

1. Using the account-analysis technique illustrated in the text, confirm that Yates & Callahan collected cash of $88,900 from its customers during 1996.
2. Prepare a schedule documenting Yates & Callahan's net cash flow from operating activities for the year ended December 31, 1996, using the direct method.

50. 2. Net cash flow provided by operating activities, $29,400

51. **Preparing a Statement of Cash Flows, Indirect Method** (LO 3)

Following is the income statement of Back Bay Corporation, for the year ended December 31, 1996, and the company's balance sheets for the years ended December 31, 1995 and 1996.

BACK BAY CORPORATION
INCOME STATEMENT
FOR THE YEAR ENDED DECEMBER 31, 1996

Sales		$82,300
Cost of Goods Sold		41,800
Gross Profit		40,500
Operating Expenses:		
Selling & General Expenses	$12,600	
Depreciation Expense	2,400	15,000
Operating Income		25,500
Gain on Sale of Equipment		1,500
Income before Income Tax		27,000
Income Tax Expense		10,800
Net Income		$16,200

BACK BAY CORPORATION
BALANCE SHEETS
DECEMBER 31, 1995 AND 1996

		1995		1996
Assets				
Cash		$ 9,200		$18,700
Accounts Receivable		8,300		14,400
Inventory		12,500		14,700
Prepaid Expenses		800		300
Total Current Assets		$30,800		$48,100
Equipment	$39,200		$29,200	
Less: Accumulated Depreciation	8,000	31,200	1,400	27,800
Total Assets		$62,000		$75,900
Liabilities				
Accounts Payable		$ 7,100		$ 2,700
Accrued Expenses		3,300		3,600
Total Current Liabilities		10,400		6,300
Long-Term Note Payable		—		10,000

Stockholders' Equity

Common Stock	12,000	12,000
Additional Paid-in Capital	24,000	24,000
Retained Earnings	15,600	23,600
Total Stockholders' Equity	$51,600	$59,600
Total Liabilities and Stockholders' Equity	$62,000	$75,900

The prepaid expenses and accrued expenses included in Back Bay's balance sheets all relate to operating (selling and general) expenses. All of Back Bay's sales and merchandise purchases are made on a credit basis. Following is additional financial information obtained from Back Bay's accounting records for 1996:

a.	Collections of accounts receivable	$76,200
b.	Credit purchases of merchandise	44,000
c.	Payments of accrued operating expenses	3,300
d.	Payments of operating expenses	8,200
e.	Prepayments of operating expenses	300
f.	Expiration of prepaid expenses	800
g.	Payments to suppliers	48,400
h.	Sale of piece of equipment:	

Selling price		$ 2,500	
Original cost	$10,000		
Less: Accumulated depreciation	(9,000)		
Book value		1,000	
Gain			1,500

i.	Bank loan obtained at year-end	10,000
j.	Declaration and payment of cash dividends on common stock	8,200
k.	Payment of 1996 income taxes	10,800
l.	Accrual of unpaid operating expenses at year-end	3,600
m.	Year-end adjusting entry to record depreciation expense on equipment	2,400

51. Net cash flow provided by operating activities, $5,200
Net cash flow provided by investing activities, $2,500
Net cash flow provided by financing activities, $1,800
Net increase in cash and cash equivalents, $9,500

Required:
Prepare a statement of cash flows for Back Bay for the year ended December 31, 1996, using the indirect method.

52. Net cash flow provided by operating activities, $5,200
Net cash flow provided by investing activities, $2,500
Net cash flow provided by financing activities, $1,800
Net increase in cash and cash equivalents, $9,500

52. Preparing a Statement of Cash Flows, Direct Method (LO 4)
Refer to the information presented in Problem 51 for Back Bay Corporation.

Required:
Prepare a statement of cash flows for Back Bay for the year ended December 31, 1996, using the direct method.

53. Comparative Analysis of Cash Flows (LO 5)
The Dress Barn, Inc., operates a chain of women's apparel stores, while Tommy Hilfiger Corporation markets sportswear apparel for men and boys through department and specialty stores. In 1994, each of these companies had approximately $200 million in total assets. Following are cash-flow data for both companies for the period 1992 through 1994:

	1992	1993	1994
Dress Barn:			
Net Cash Flow from Operating Activities	$24,391,633	$29,046,893	$23,704,087

Net Cash Flow from			
Investing Activities	(21,704,345)	(25,032,079)	(27,678,458)
Net Cash Flow from			
Financing Activities	354,795	1,408,732	578,585

Tommy Hilfiger:

Net Cash Flow from			
Operating Activities	$(8,589,000)	$ 4,335,000	$ 4,326,000
Net Cash Flow from			
Investing Activities	(3,451,000)	(12,186,000)	(50,776,000)
Net Cash Flow from			
Financing Activities	14,300,000	24,116,000	65,924,000

Between 1992 and 1994, Dress Barn purchased approximately $36 million of property and equipment; during the same period, Tommy Hilfiger purchased approximately $33 million of property and equipment. Dress Barn raised approximately $2 million by issuing stock between 1992 and 1994, compared with $112 million raised in this manner by Tommy Hilfiger.

Required:

1. What activities were the principal source of funds between 1992 and 1994 for Dress Barn? For Tommy Hilfiger?
2. For each year 1992 through 1994, Dress Barn's net income was considerably less than its net cash flow from operating activities. Is this the "normal" relationship between net income and net operating cash flow? Explain.
3. In 1994, Tommy Hilfiger reported a net income of $25.3 million, which was considerably more than its $4.3 million net cash flow from operating activities for that year. What factor or factors may have accounted for the large disparity between these two amounts?
4. To remain financially viable over the long run, a company's principal source of funds must be its operating activities. Do you agree with that statement? Explain.

53. No check figures

54. **Cash Flow Per Share** (LO 6)

Following is selected financial information for two companies, Airgas, Inc., a supplier of medical and specialty gases and related equipment, and Toll Brothers, Inc., a home builder.

	1992	1993	1994
Airgas:			
Net Income	$ 7,292,000	$12,469,000	$20,290,000
Net Cash Flow from			
Operating Activities	51,682,000	58,321,000	64,798,000
Weighted-Average Number			
of Shares of Common Stock			
Outstanding (in millions)	28.0	30.9	32.4
Toll Brothers:			
Net Income	$16,538,000	$28,058,000	$36,177,000
Net Cash Flow from			
Operating Activities	(25,898,000)	(54,196,000)	(29,514,000)
Weighted-Average Number of			
Shares of Common Stock			
Outstanding (in millions)	33.2	33.5	33.6

Between 1992 and 1994, neither Airgas nor Toll Brothers had preferred stock outstanding.

Required:

1. Compute earnings per share and cash flow per share for Airgas and Toll Brothers for each year 1992 through 1994.
2. For each year, express each company's earnings per share as a percentage of its cash flow per share.
3. What factor or factors may have accounted for the large difference between Airgas's net income and its net cash flow from operating activities for the period 1992 through 1994?
4. During 1992 through 1994, Toll Brothers' inventory increased by more than $280 million. What effect did this factor have on the company's net cash flow from operating activities over this time period? Explain.
5. Over the long run, what relationship would you expect to observe between a company's net income and its net cash flow from operating activities? Why?
6. Why does the FASB prohibit companies from disclosing cash flow per share in their annual financial statements?

54. 1.

Airgas	1993	1994	1995
Earnings per share	$0.26	$0.40	$0.63
Cash flow per share	$1.85	$1.89	$2.00

Toll Brothers

	1993	1994	1995
Earnings per share	$0.50	$0.84	$1.08
Cash flow per share	$(0.78)	$(1.62)	$(0.88)

	1993	1994	1995
Airgas	14%	21%	32%
Toll Brothers	Not meaningful		

CASES

55. **Classification of Cash Flows by Foreign Companies**

As noted in this chapter, the statement of cash flows is not a mandatory financial statement in most countries. However, large multinational corporations often include a statement of cash flows in their annual reports whether or not they are required to do so by their home country's accounting standards.

Following are line items included in recent statements of cash flows issued by the following foreign-based corporations: Telecom Corporation of New Zealand, Lloyd's of London (Great Britain), Ito-Yokado Co., Ltd. (Japan), Barclay's plc (Great Britain), Thyssen AG (Germany), and San Miguel Corporation (Philippines).

_____ Disposals of fixed assets
_____ Increase in gross financial indebtedness
_____ Preference dividends paid
_____ Proceeds from issuance of long-term debt
_____ Purchase of investments
_____ Investment income
_____ Issue of ordinary shares
_____ Purchase of associated undertakings
_____ Cash received from customers
_____ Dividends paid to minority interests
_____ Redemption of (short-term) notes receivable
_____ Interest paid on debt
_____ Proceeds from sales of distribution and food center assets
_____ Payments under revolving credit facilities
_____ Redemption of preference shares
_____ Prior year cash dividend

Required:

Indicate how you believe each of the listed items would appear in a statement of cash flows prepared by a United States firm. Use the following key:

a. Cash inflow from operating activities
b. Cash outflow from operating activities
c. Cash inflow from investing activities
d. Cash outflow from investing activities
e. Cash inflow from financing activities
f. Cash outflow from financing activities

If you are unsure of the nature of a given item, list an assumption regarding your interpretation of that item and then classify the item accordingly.

56. **Safeguarding Cash in a Small Business**
Speedy Papers is a small business that provides word processing services to students of a large state university. The owner of the business supervises six typists (word processors) who work from a leased office in the university's student union. The accounting records of Speedy Papers are maintained by a part-time bookkeeper. These accounting records include a general ledger, general journal, cash receipts and cash disbursements journals, and an accounts receivable subsidiary ledger. Approximately 50 percent of the company's services are provided on a credit basis with terms of n/30. The bookkeeper is also involved in processing cash collections and cash disbursements, including making deposits and reconciling the monthly bank statement. Recently, the owner of Speedy Papers has become concerned by a downward trend in the business's net cash flows. After reviewing the business's bank statements for the past six months and those for the comparable period in the two previous years, the owner determined that the average monthly net cash inflow is down approximately 10 percent for the current year compared with the two previous years. This downward trend in cash flows has occurred despite the owner's impression that Speedy Papers has been busier than ever in recent months.

After work one night, the owner reviewed the cash receipts records of the business. For two recent months, she compared the daily cash receipts recorded in the cash receipts journal with the daily bank deposit slips, finding no differences. After flipping through the other accounting records, something did catch her eye. The business's bad debt write-offs had increased considerably in the past six months. "Aha!" the owner thought to herself. "Here's the problem. Maybe I'll have to rethink my credit policy."

Required:
Is the owner's analysis of Speedy Papers' cash-flow problem necessarily correct? Explain. Write a memo to the owner that identifies further steps she could take to investigate the cause of the company's declining cash flows. Also include in the memo several internal control procedures she could implement to enhance the degree of control over the business's cash and cash processing activities.

57. **Manipulation of Cash-Flow Data**
Suppose that you are the CEO of a major corporation. Your company's fiscal year will be ending in three weeks. This year has not been a memorable one. Your company will apparently eke out a profit this year, but just barely. You realize that financial analysts pay considerable attention to both earnings per share and cash flow per share data. There is not much you can do at this late date to improve your company's earnings per share for the year without violating GAAP. However, you have the ability to significantly improve your firm's reported cash flow per share for the year without violating GAAP. For example, you can instruct your collections department to make every effort to collect outstanding receivables even to the point of offering customers small price conces-

sions on purchases they will make next year. You can also delay the payment (prepayment) of items such as insurance premiums and rent for expenses that will not be incurred until next year.

Required:

1. It is unethical for business executives to intentionally "manage" or manipulate their firms' reported cash-flow data even though there are no explicit rules prohibiting them from doing so? Defend your answer.

2. Should rule-making bodies in the accounting profession prohibit business entities from manipulating reported cash-flow data? Again, support your answer.

PROJECTS

58. The FASB and Cash Flows

The FASB has stated that it prefers the direct method of preparing a statement of cash flows. Why? Because the direct method provides more useful information to financial decision makers than the indirect method. Nevertheless, more than 95 percent of all large corporations use the indirect method of preparing their annual statements of cash flows. On the other hand, the FASB prohibits business entities from reporting cash flow per share data. However, investors and a wide range of decision makers demand and obtain cash flow per share data from financial analysts and apparently use that data when making important financial decisions.

Required:

1. Break into your project groups for a discussion of the FASB's accounting rules for cash flows. Specifically address the following issues:

   a. Should the FASB continue to allow business entities to use either the direct or indirect method of preparing a statement of cash flows? Identify reasons supporting the FASB's present stance on this issue and reasons suggesting that the FASB should require the direct method to be used exclusively.

   b. Should the FASB allow business entities to report cash flow per share data in their periodic financial statements? Identify reasons supporting the FASB's present stance on this issue and reasons suggesting that the FASB should allow cash flow per share data to be reported by business entities.

   When discussing these issues, be sure to refer to the fundamental accounting concepts identified in Chapter 2.

2. One group member should maintain a list of the reasons or arguments identified by the group in completing Part 1. This individual should be prepared to provide a brief oral report to the other members of the class of the group's discussion and analysis.

59. Comparing Cash Flows across Industries

Select three large public companies. One of these companies should be involved in merchandising, another in manufacturing, while the final company should be a service firm.

Required:

1. Obtain the most recent annual report of each of the firms you selected. These annual reports will contain statements of cash flows for each firm for the past three years. Compare and contrast the cash-flow data of each of these firms.

2. Document in a written report the major differences and similarities you noticed in the cash-flow data of the three firms you studied. Also attempt to identify the source or sources of the major differences in these terms firms' cash-flow data.

60. **Cash Management Practices**

In recent years, "cash management" has become a hot topic among the executives of large corporations that often have hundreds of millions of dollars in cash and cash equivalents at any point in time. Effective management of cash resources is just as important, if not more important, for small businesses. One reason is that small businesses typically have much less access than large corporations to external sources of funds when they encounter liquidity problems. An example of a cash management practice is "zero cash management," which was discussed in a vignette in Chapter 7.

Required:

1. Research the topic of cash management in your school's library, focusing particular attention on recent articles in business periodicals addressing this topic.

2. Write a brief report summarizing three cash management practices, other than zero cash management, that have been used successfully in recent years by business entities of any size.

17

FINANCIAL STATEMENT ANALYSIS

LEARNING OBJECTIVES

After studying this chapter, you should be able to do the following:

1. Discuss the objectives of financial statement analysis for different types of decision makers

2. Identify the key sources of information for financial statement analysis

3. Prepare trend analyses of financial statement data

4. Prepare common-sized financial statements

5. Compute key financial ratios including liquidity, leverage, activity, profitability, and market strength ratios

6. Assess earnings quality

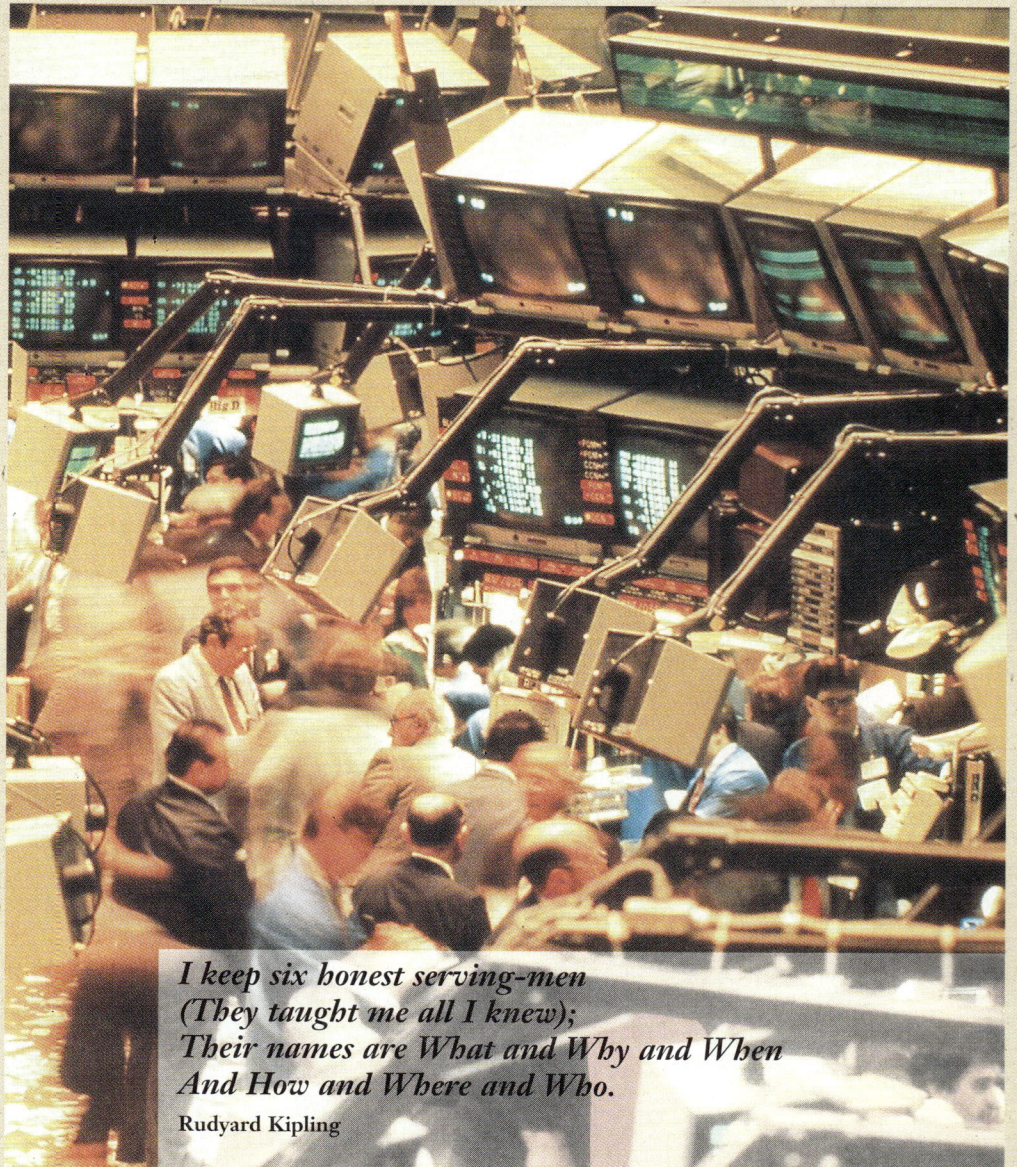

I keep six honest serving-men
(They taught me all I knew);
Their names are What and Why and When
And How and Where and Who.
Rudyard Kipling

Too-Good-to-Be-True Financial Statements Are Usually Too Good to Be True

On May 19, 1987, a short article in *The Wall Street Journal* reported that ZZZZ Best Company, Inc., had signed a contract for a $13.8 million building restoration project. This project was just the most recent of a series of such jobs obtained by ZZZZ Best (pronounced "zee best"), a leading firm in the building restoration industry. Located in the San Fernando Valley of southern California, ZZZZ Best had begun operations in the fall of 1982 as a small, door-to-door carpet cleaning operation. Under the direction of Barry Minkow, the sixteen-year-old who founded the company and initially operated it from his parents' garage, ZZZZ Best experienced explosive growth during the first few years of its existence. In the three-year period from 1984 to 1987, the company's net income surged from less than $200,000 to more than $5 million on revenues of $50 million.

When ZZZZ Best went public in 1986, Minkow became a multimillionaire overnight. By early 1987, Minkow's stock in the company had a market value exceeding $100 million. Minkow's charm and entrepreneurial genius made him a sought-after commodity on the television talk show circuit. On *The Oprah Winfrey Show* in April 1987, Minkow exhorted his peers to "Think big, be big" and encouraged them to adopt his personal motto, "The sky is the limit."

Less than two years after his appearance on *The Oprah Winfrey Show*, Barry Minkow began serving a twenty-five-year prison sentence. Tried and convicted on fifty-seven counts of securities fraud, Minkow had been exposed as a fast-talking con artist who bilked the public out of millions of dollars. Federal prosecutors estimate that, at a minimum, Minkow cost investors and creditors $100 million. The company that Minkow founded was an elaborate scam. The reported profits of the firm were nonexistent and the huge restoration contracts, imaginary. In July 1987, just three months after the company's stock reached a total market value of $220 million, an auction of its few actual assets netted only $62,000.

Minkow was able to dupe the investing public for several years because investors failed to rigorously analyze his company's financial statements when they made investment decisions regarding ZZZZ Best's stock. For example, investors failed to notice that ZZZZ Best's reported revenues exceeded the total annual revenues of the small building restoration industry. Likewise, the number of multimillion-dollar restoration jobs allegedly obtained by ZZZZ Best surpassed the total number of such jobs available during the mid-1980s according to industry statistics. Finally, ZZZZ Best's gross profit percentage was much higher than the normal gross profit percentage within the building restoration industry, again information that was available from industry sources.

The lesson to be learned from ZZZZ Best and similar financial frauds is for investors to do their homework before making a decision to invest their hard-earned savings. A careful, painstaking analysis of financial statements should reveal when a company's profits are too good to be true.

SOURCE: M. C. Knapp, "ZZZZ Best Company, Inc.," in *Contemporary Auditing: Issues and Cases*, 2d ed. (Minneapolis/St. Paul: West Publishing Co., 1996).

In prior chapters, financial ratios and other financial measures have been discussed that can be used to analyze specific components of an entity's financial statements. In this chapter, we take a "big picture" approach to financial statement analysis. Here, the purpose is to discuss approaches that can be used to comprehensively analyze the financial performance and financial condition of business entities as reported by their income statements and balance sheets, respectively. Since Chapter 16 discussed approaches to analyzing and interpreting cash-flow data, the statement of cash flows is not a major focus of this chapter.

The initial section of this chapter identifies the key objectives of financial statement analysis and the principal sources of information used in financial statement analysis. The following section discusses specific analytical techniques and illustrates how these techniques are applied. The final section of this chapter identifies the factors influencing "earnings quality" and discusses specific measures decision makers can use to analyze this important characteristic of earnings data.

FINANCIAL STATEMENT ANALYSIS: MAKING INFORMED ECONOMIC DECISIONS

Discussion Question
Ask students to identify and briefly describe another financial fraud in which investors were "duped".

Recall from Chapter 1 that accounting is principally a service activity whose primary function is to provide information useful to financial decision makers. As proven by the ZZZZ Best fraud discussed in this chapter's opening vignette and other recent financial frauds, decision makers need more than just access to financial data. Decision makers must have the skills to analyze financial data if they are to make informed economic decisions. In this section, we focus on the objectives of financial statement analysis and identify the information sources used by decision makers to obtain and analyze financial statement data.

Objectives of Financial Statement Analysis

■ LEARNING OBJECTIVE 1
Discuss the objectives of financial statement analysis for different types of decision makers

The objectives of financial statement analysis vary across different types of decision makers. Suppliers are very concerned with an entity's liquidity over the short term. A company that has a poor liquidity position may be unable to pay its accounts payable that come due in the following weeks and months. Bank loan officers, bondholders, and other long-term creditors are more concerned with an entity's ability to generate profits and cash flows over an extended number of years. The main concern of customers when it comes to financial statement analysis is which business entities will provide a reliable source of products or services. Prospective employees may analyze financial statements to identify companies that offer secure, long-term employment opportunities.

Investors are the decision makers who by necessity must take the most comprehensive approach to financial statement analysis. If you are considering becoming a part owner of IBM or Sam's Corner Deli, you should be concerned with every aspect of these entities' financial status. For example, you should be concerned with liquidity. If a company in which you invest encounters short-term cash-flow problems and cannot pay its suppliers, your investment will likely go down the proverbial drain. Investors also want to be reassured that a firm can retire its long-term debt as it matures. Bondholders and other long-term creditors can seize an entity's assets and put the firm out of business if they are not paid on a timely basis. An entity's profitability is an obvious concern of investors. Potential investors want to be assured that a company will generate sufficient profits to provide a reasonable rate of return on owners' equity.

This chapter illustrates a comprehensive approach to financial statement analysis that would be suitable to prospective investors. However, many techniques discussed in this chapter can also be used by other decision makers to focus specifically on one aspect of an entity's financial performance or financial condition.

Information Sources for Financial Statement Analysis

A recent television commercial highlights a dilemma facing a professional couple. The couple has suddenly realized that they should begin planning for their not-too-distant retirement years, but are unsure where to obtain the information they need for this purpose. Eventually, the couple turns to a local stockbroker to guide them through this planning process. Here, we identify sources of information that couples planning for retirement, stockbrokers, and a wide range of other parties, including yourself, can use to obtain financial data regarding business entities.

■ **LEARNING OBJECTIVE 2**
Identify the key sources of information for financial statement analysis

ANNUAL REPORTS   The annual reports of publicly owned companies not only contain financial statements for these firms but also are the principal source of information needed to analyze those financial statements. Publicly owned companies are required by the Securities and Exchange Commission (SEC) to file a 10-K registration statement with that agency each year. Besides financial statements, a 10-K contains other financial data and extensive nonfinancial data regarding a company. Less comprehensive financial reports must be filed with the SEC by public companies each quarter. Typically, a public company's annual report is a user-friendly version of its 10-K. Certain disclosures required in a 10-K are either eliminated or condensed in a company's annual report. Many privately owned companies also prepare annual reports for their bankers, customers, employees, and other parties.

By now, you are probably familiar with the recent annual report of Michaels Stores, Inc., that is included in an appendix to this text. The organizational scheme and content of annual reports vary from company to company. However, most annual reports contain several items of particular interest to investors and other financial decision makers. These items include the financial statements and accompanying footnotes, a financial highlights table, management's discussion and analysis (MDA) of financial condition and operating results, and the independent auditor's report.

Most companies include a financial highlights table in their annual report that tracks key financial items over the prior five- or ten-year period. The data in this table provide financial statement users with a quick overview of a company's recent financial performance and recent changes in its financial condition. The MDA section of an annual report contains a summary discussion of the factors that have recently affected a company's financial status. This section also typically includes a general overview of management's key plans for the future.

A company's independent auditor's report should be read carefully by decision makers. Included in this report are a discussion of such key items as departures from generally accepted accounting principles (GAAP) and inconsistent application of those principles. Auditors are also required to disclose in their reports any conditions that may threaten the survival of an audit client.

INVESTMENT ADVISORY SERVICES   If you browse through the business section of your college library, you will find an assortment of reference materials published by investment advisory firms. Value Line, Standard & Poor's, Moody's, Dun &

Many investors obtain investment advice and financial data in their homes by accessing on-line financial services through their personal computers.

Real World
The annual reports of public companies are available to the public free of charge. To obtain a copy of a specific annual report, simply call the company's corporate headquarters and request one. (*Standard and Poor's Directory of Corporations* publishes the telephone numbers of public companies' corporate headquarters.)

SPOTLIGHT ON ETHICS

On-Line, Real-Time Financial Fraud

As investors have become more sophisticated so too have the con artists and flimflam men—and women—who prey on them. A recent article in *Forbes* (T. Jaffe, "Cyberfraud," *Forbes*, 25 April 1994, 390) reported several instances of "cyberfraud" involving electronic bulletin boards used by subscribers to on-line computer services. This scam works something like this. A group of subscribers to an on-line computer service will purchase stock of a small but little-known company. Then one of these subscribers will post a hot tip in an electronic bulletin board regarding this stock. Shortly thereafter, the other participants in the scheme will hype that stock by posting messages confirming that it is a "can't miss" investment. If the scheme is successful, the stock's price will increase rapidly in a period of a few days. The schemers will then sell their stock at the inflated price.

Teaching Note

Emphasize to students that a company can be performing very well compared to industry norms and still be in poor shape financially. Why? Because the company's industry, as a whole, is financially troubled.

Bradstreet, and Robert Morris Associates are among the best known of these firms. The *Value Line Investment Survey*, for example, provides a detailed analysis of key financial statistics and the future prospects of nearly two thousand public companies. Included in this analysis is Value Line's best estimate of each company's stock price several years into the future. In March 1995, Value Line predicted that CBS's common stock would have a price range of $90–$105 per share between 1998 and 2000. At the time, the market price of CBS's common stock was $69 per share.

Decision makers often evaluate a company's financial data by comparing that data with the company's historical norms and with industry norms. For example, assume that a company has a current ratio of 1.2 at the end of a given year. Decision makers can better interpret that ratio if they have access to the company's current ratio in prior years and to the industry norm. Historical data for companies that do not include a financial highlights table in their annual report can be found in financial databases published by investment advisory firms. Disclosure, Inc., provides a widely used computerized financial database that contains information on several thousand companies. Industry norms for a wide range of financial ratios and other financial measures are also available. In earlier chapters, two of the more frequently used sources of industry norms have been referenced on several occasions. These annual publications are *Industry Norms & Key Business Ratios* published by Dun & Bradstreet and *RMA Annual Statement Studies* published by Robert Morris Associates.

OTHER SOURCES   Financial and nonfinancial information regarding individual companies can also be obtained from business periodicals such as *Barron's*, *Business Week*, *Forbes*, and *The Wall Street Journal*. A recent trend is for investors and other financial decision makers to access financial data through a personal computer by logging on to an on-line financial service. Among the more popular on-line financial services are those offered by Prodigy, CompuServe, and America OnLine. Do-it-yourself investors can obtain a free directory of on-line financial services and related computer software from the American Association of Individual Investors in Chicago.

ANALYTICAL TECHNIQUES

In this section, three general approaches to financial statement analysis are discussed and illustrated. These approaches are trend analysis, the preparation of common-sized financial statements, and ratio analysis. Keep in mind while we consider these methods that although financial statement analysis is a powerful tool for decision makers, it does have limitations.

Financial statement analysis is principally used as an attention-directing device. Analytical techniques identify unusual or unexpected relationships in the financial data of a business entity. Further investigation, though, is usually required to determine whether these "red flags" are a signal that an entity's financial health is changing—for the better or worse. Analytical techniques can also be used to make predictions regarding an entity's future financial performance and financial condition based upon its past financial data. However, changes in an entity's operations, its industry, and the overall economic environment can cause historical data to be less than a reliable indicator of a company's future prospects. A final limitation of financial statement analysis stems from the nature of the business entities to which it is applied. In this chapter, data drawn primarily from companies that have one line of business are used to illustrate financial statement analysis. You should recognize that financial statement analysis is more difficult for conglomerates that have two or more major lines of business. For such companies, analytical techniques are most useful if they are applied independently to the data of each major business segment.

Discussion Question
Ask students to identify some obvious "red flags" in financial statement data.
Examples: Declining sales, negative working capital, recurring losses, and negative cash flows over a period of several years.

Trend Analysis

Much can be learned about a company's financial condition and financial performance by simply tracking changes in key financial statement items over a period of time. For example, an investor might plot a company's net income for ten successive years to monitor the company's profitability and to predict the level of profits it will earn in the future. To more easily grasp the changes in individual financial statement items from period to period, these amounts are often converted into percentages. The study of percentage changes in financial statement items over a period of time is known as **trend analysis.**

To illustrate trend analysis, assume that we have an interest in monitoring the net cash flow from operating activities of American Greetings, the large greeting card company. Following are the net cash flows from operating activities reported by this company for 1992–1994.

■ **LEARNING OBJECTIVE 3**
Prepare trend analyses of financial statement data

trend analyis

$$1992 — \$\ 69,382,000$$
$$1993 — \ \ 169,280,000$$
$$1994 — \ \ \ 75,613,000$$

To apply trend analysis to these data, we must first select a base year and then express each amount as a percentage of the base-year figure. Typically, the first or earliest year for which data are available is selected as the base year. Applying this rule, 1992 becomes the base year for the present example. By dividing each of the dollar amounts in the previous schedule by the base-year figure of $69,382,000, we arrive at the following percentages.

$$1992 — 100\%$$
$$1993 — 244$$
$$1994 — 109$$

Teaching Note
Point out that one factor contributing to the higher variability of cash-flow data compared with accrual-basis data is the greater ability of business executives to manipulate cash-flow data.

As suggested earlier, trend analysis provides a simple method of predicting a future financial statement amount. Suppose that we want to predict the net cash flow from operating activities that American Greetings realized in 1995. Unfortunately, the trend percentages just computed for American Greetings are not very useful for this purpose. That is, we cannot be very confident in making an extrapolation to 1995 based upon these trend percentages since they are so volatile. Cash-flow financial data tend to be more variable and thus more difficult to predict than accrual-basis financial data.

Let us try another application of trend analysis, this time using accrual-basis financial data. The following schedule lists the annual sales of Medtronic, Inc., a medical technology company, for the period 1989–1993.

1989 — $ 765,800,000
1990 —   865,900,000
1991 —   1,021,400,000
1992 —   1,176,900,000
1993 —   1,328,200,000

Applying trend analysis, we convert the above data to percentages using 1989 as the base year.

1989 — 100%
1990 — 113
1991 — 133
1992 — 154
1993 — 173

Discussion Question
Ask students to use data included in Michaels Stores's 1994 annual report (see Appendix) to develop a five-year sales trend for the company for the period 1990–1994. Based upon this trend, ask students to predict the company's 1995 sales.

Unlike the previous example, the above percentages indicate a definite pattern in Medtronic's annual sales. By "eyeballing" this trend, we would predict the company's 1994 sales to be roughly 194 percent of its 1989 sales. Multiplying 194 percent times Medtronic's 1989 sales, we arrive at predicted sales for 1994 of $1,485,652,000. In fact, Medtronic's 1994 sales totaled $1,390,900,000. So, our prediction was off by "just" $95 million or so. The moral of this story is that trend analysis can help decision makers identify patterns in financial data. However, trend analysis is a very crude financial forecasting technique. Although beyond the scope of this text, there are several sophisticated and more reliable techniques decision makers can use to forecast financial data. You will be introduced to one such technique, regression analysis, a distant cousin of trend analysis, in subsequent business courses.

Trend analysis, and other analytical techniques for that matter, can be enhanced by using computer-based graphics. Computer software packages such as PowerPoint, Freelance Graphics, and Harvard Graphics allow decision makers to more easily analyze and interpret financial data. Shown in Exhibit 17.1 is Medtronic's sales trend for 1989 through 1994. Notice that rather than continuing the smooth, upward trend that was evident between 1990 and 1993, Medtronic's sales trend "flattened" somewhat in 1994. An investor considering a purchase of Medtronic common stock in early 1995 would almost certainly have sought an explanation for this downturn in the company's sales trend. This weakening of Medtronic's sales may have been a temporary "blip" in the financial performance of the company. On the other hand, it may have been an early warning signal of financial problems for the company. Medtronic operates in a competitive, high-technology industry. Companies in such industries are vulnerable to technological changes. A new product or technology introduced by a competitor can quickly render a high-tech company's products inferior, if not obsolete.

■ **EXHIBIT 17.1**
Medtronic, Inc., Sales Trend: 1989–1994

SOURCE: 1994 annual report.

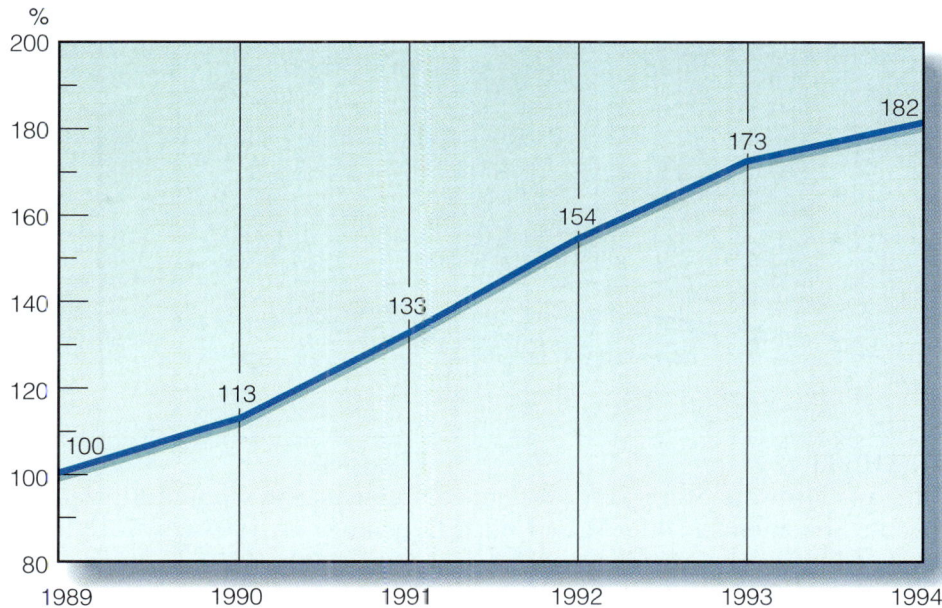

Common-Sized Financial Statements

Common-sized financial statements are used by decision makers to better grasp the relationships among the items in a financial statement or series of financial statements. In **common-sized financial statements,** each line item is expressed as a percentage of a major financial statement component. For example, in a common-sized balance sheet each line item is expressed as a percentage of total assets. In a common-sized income statement each line item is expressed as a percentage of net sales.

To illustrate common-sized financial statements, consider a hypothetical company, Lindsay Hardware Stores, Inc. Shown in Exhibit 17.2 are income statements and common-sized income statements for Lindsay Hardware Stores for the three-year period 1993–1995. Exhibit 17.3 presents year-end balance sheets and common-sized balance sheets for this company for the same period. Lindsay's common-sized income statements were developed by dividing each line item in the company's 1993–1995 income statements by the dollar amount of net sales for the given year. For example, the percentages in Lindsay's 1995 common-sized income statement were determined by dividing each income statement amount for that year by $920,000, Lindsay's net sales for the year. Lindsay's 1995 common-sized balance sheet was derived by dividing each balance sheet amount for that year by $424,000, the dollar value of the company's total assets at the end of 1995.

Common-sized financial statements can be used to identify structural changes in a company's operating results and financial condition over a period of time. Referring to Exhibit 17.2, we notice that Lindsay's cost of goods sold as a percentage of net sales steadily decreased between 1993 and 1995. The company's selling expenses increased

■ **LEARNING OBJECTIVE 4**
Prepare common-sized financial statements

common-sized financial statements

So, you are planning to purchase a hardware store? Before you sign on the dotted line, you should study the store's recent financial data and compare that data to industry norms. Key sources of financial data for individual industries include *Industry Norms & Key Business Ratios*, an annual publication of Dun & Bradstreet.

■ **EXHIBIT 17.2**

Lindsay Hardware Stores, Inc., Income Statements and Common-Sized Income Statements for the Years Ended December 31, 1993–1995

	1995	1994	1993
Net Sales	$920,000	$864,000	$704,000
Cost of Goods Sold	506,000	493,000	408,000
Gross Profit	414,000	371,000	296,000
Operating Expenses:			
Selling	144,000	95,000	74,000
General	77,000	72,000	60,000
Administrative	72,000	71,000	63,000
Operating Income	121,000	133,000	99,000
Interest Revenue	3,000	2,000	2,000
Interest Expense	12,000	11,000	8,000
Income before Income Taxes	112,000	124,000	93,000
Income Tax Expense	45,000	50,000	37,000
Net Income	$ 67,000	$ 74,000	$ 56,000

	1995	1994	1993
Net Sales	100.0%	100.0%	100.0%
Cost of Goods Sold	55.0	57.1	58.0
Gross Profit	45.0	42.9	42.0
Operating Expenses:			
Selling	15.7	11.0	10.5
General	8.4	8.3	8.5
Administrative	7.8	8.2	8.9
Operating Income	13.1	15.4	14.1
Interest Revenue	.3	.2	.3
Interest Expense	1.3	1.3	1.1
Income before Income Taxes	12.1	14.3	13.3
Income Tax Expense	4.9	5.8	5.3
Net Income	7.2%	8.5%	8.0%

■ **EXHIBIT 17.3**
Lindsay Hardware Stores, Inc., Balance Sheets and Common-Sized
Balance Sheets as of December 31, 1993, 1994, and 1995

	1995	1994	1993
Assets			
Cash	$ 8,700	$ 2,200	$ 4,300
Accounts Receivable	72,000	46,300	37,500
Inventory	243,700	188,000	151,900
Prepaid Expenses	11,200	9,700	8,300
Total Current Assets	335,600	246,200	202,000
Property, Plant & Equipment (net)	72,500	76,000	74,200
Other Assets	15,900	20,300	19,800
Total Assets	$424,000	$342,500	$296,000
Liabilities			
Accounts Payable	$ 52,000	$ 39,600	$ 26,100
Accrued Expenses	25,400	23,400	14,200
Notes Payable	20,000	18,000	17,000
Total Current Liabilities	97,400	81,000	57,300
Long-Term Debt	110,000	110,000	110,000
Total Liabilities	207,400	191,000	167,300
Stockholders' Equity			
Common Stock	5,000	5,000	5,000
Additional Paid-in Capital	85,000	85,000	85,000
Retained Earnings	126,600	61,500	38,700
Total Stockholders' Equity	216,600	151,500	128,700
Total Liabilities and			
Stockholders' Equity	$424,000	$342,500	$296,000
Assets			
Cash	2.1%	.6%	1.5%
Accounts Receivable	17.0	13.5	12.7
Inventory	57.4	54.9	51.3
Prepaid Expenses	2.6	2.9	2.8
Total Current Assets	79.1	71.9	68.3
Property, Plant & Equipment (net)	17.1	22.2	25.0
Other Assets	3.8	5.9	6.7
Total Assets	100.0%	100.0%	100.0%
Liabilities			
Accounts Payable	12.3%	11.6%	8.8%
Accrued Expenses	6.0	6.8	4.8
Notes Payable	4.7	5.3	5.7
Total Current Liabilities	23.0	23.7	19.3
Long-Term Debt	25.9	32.1	37.2
Total Liabilities	48.9	55.8	56.5

Exhibit continues

■ **EXHIBIT 17.3 (continued)**

	1995	1994	1993
Stockholders' Equity			
Common Stock	1.2	1.4	1.7
Additional Paid-in Capital	20.0	24.8	28.7
Retained Earnings	29.9	18.0	13.1
Total Stockholders' Equity	51.1	44.2	43.5
Total Liabilities and			
Stockholders' Equity	100.0%	100.0%	100.0%

significantly during this time period relative to net sales. Among other changes, the common-sized balance sheet in Exhibit 17.3 shows that between 1993 and 1995 Lindsay's accounts receivable and inventory increased as a percentage of total assets. Any significant and unexpected changes or unusual relationships uncovered by common-sized financial statements should be investigated. The purpose of such investigation is to determine whether these changes or unusual relationships are indicative of developing financial problems for the given entity. In the next section, we apply ratio analysis to Lindsay's financial data to gain further insight on changes reflected by the company's 1993–1995 common-sized financial statements.

Common-sized financial statements also allow decision makers to more easily compare and contrast the financial data of two or more companies. For example, assume that Company A and Company B are the two leading firms in an industry. However, Company A is much larger than Company B. This size difference makes it difficult to compare the companies' financial data. To minimize this "apples and oranges" problem, we can prepare common-sized financial statements for the two firms. For example, common-sized income statements will indicate the proportion of each sales dollar of the two companies that is absorbed by cost of goods sold and by operating expenses. Although Company A may have a much larger net income than its smaller competitor, inefficiencies in the company's operations may cause it to have disproportionately high expenses. Over the long run, these inefficiencies may spell serious problems for Company A—and a window of opportunity for Company B.

Another use of common-sized financial statements is to allow decision makers to more easily compare a company's financial data with industry norms. Dun & Bradstreet's annual publication *Industry Norms & Key Business Ratios* provides a common-sized balance sheet for each of several hundred industries. The percentages reflected in these common-sized balance sheets are averages for each industry. One industry tracked by Dun & Bradstreet is "hardware stores." Shown next are selected items from the common-sized balance sheet for the hardware stores industry included in the 1993–1994 edition of the Dun & Bradstreet publication. The corresponding percentages from the 1994 common-sized balance sheet of Lindsay Hardware Stores are presented for comparison purposes. (As a point of information, there were approximately 1,400 companies in the hardware stores industry when the following industry norms were computed.)

	LINDSAY HARDWARE STORES	INDUSTRY NORM
Cash	.6%	8.1%
Accounts Receivable	13.5	11.7
Inventory	54.9	52.8
Property, Plant & Equipment	22.2	11.7
Accounts Payable	11.6	11.8

The data just shown indicate that Lindsay had much less cash, on a proportionate basis, than the average hardware store company in 1994. Lindsay also had a greater percentage of its total assets invested in property, plant & equipment than the typical company in its industry. An investor considering Lindsay's common stock might investigate these differences and assess their implications for the company's future prospects before pulling out his or her checkbook.

Common-sized financial statements can be presented graphically. Exhibit 17.4 presents common-sized asset data for Lindsay Hardware Stores in a three-dimensional bar graph. In this graph, you can see that the composition of Lindsay's assets changed from 1993 to 1995. In 1995, versus 1993, the company obviously had a smaller proportion of its total assets invested in property, plant & equipment and more of its assets invested in inventory and accounts receivable.

Ratio Analysis

The most widely used method to analyze financial data is ratio analysis. **Ratio analysis** typically involves a comparison of the relationship between two financial statement items. For example, the current ratio measures an entity's liquidity at a specific point in time by comparing its current assets and current liabilities. Financial ratios are used by decision makers in two ways, on a cross-sectional and longitudinal basis. **Cross-sectional ratio analysis** involves comparing a company's financial ratios with those of competing companies and/or with industry norms. **Longitudinal ratio analysis** focuses on changes in an entity's ratios over a period of time, typically a time span measured in several years.

Several financial ratios have been introduced in earlier chapters. These ratios are presented in Exhibit 17.5 along with the equations used to compute them and a brief explanation of their purpose. Notice that the ratios have been classified into five categories. These categories represent key features of the financial status of business entities that decision makers monitor. In the following sections, we review these five categories of financial ratios. Since each ratio shown in Exhibit 17.5 has been discussed previously, we do not dwell on their computational aspects. Instead, we focus on applying these ratios to the financial data of business entities, primarily financial data of Lindsay Hardware Stores.

LIQUIDITY RATIOS   Liquidity refers to an entity's ability to finance its day-to-day operations and to pay its liabilities as they mature. The current ratio and the quick ratio are commonly used to assess the liquidity of business entities. The data from Exhibit 17.3 were used to compute the current and quick ratios for Lindsay Hardware Stores shown in the following table. Also included in this table are the approximate norms for these ratios in the mid-1990s within the hardware retailers industry.

	LINDSAY HARDWARE STORES			INDUSTRY NORM
	1995	1994	1993	
Current ratio	3.45	3.04	3.53	3.4
Quick ratio	.83	.60	.73	.8

Notice that Lindsay's liquidity ratios were closely in line with industry averages. Given these data, it appears that Lindsay Hardware Stores did not have any significant liquidity problems during the mid-1990s, at least compared with industry norms. This conclusion is tempered by one minor caution. Recall that data reported previously indicated that companies in this industry, on average, had 8 percent of

■ **EXHIBIT 17.4**

Lindsay Hardware Stores: Common-Sized Financial Statement Data for Assets

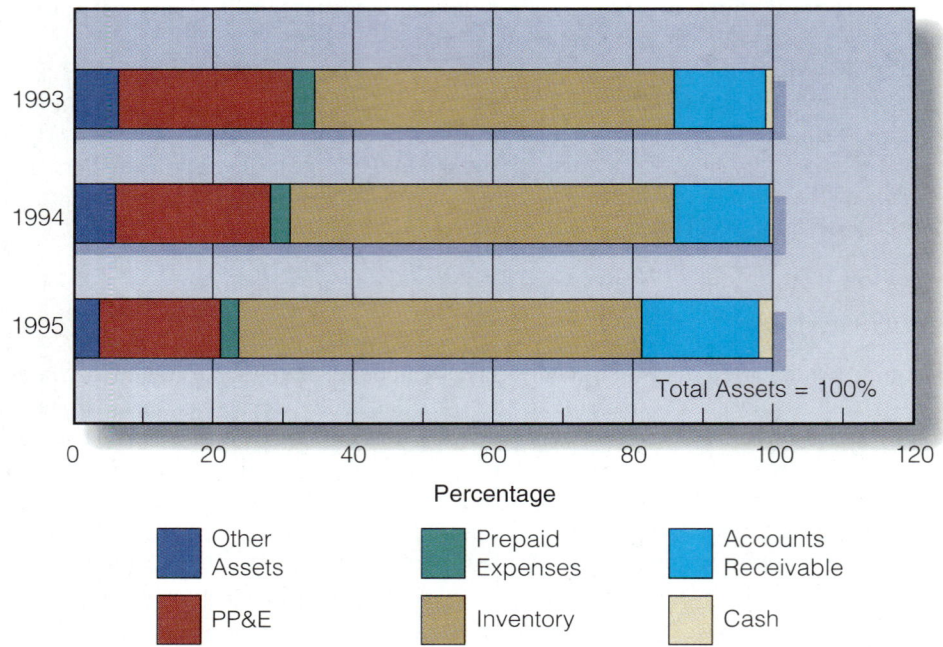

Total Assets = 100%

Legend:
- Other Assets
- PP&E
- Prepaid Expenses
- Inventory
- Accounts Receivable
- Cash

■ **EXHIBIT 17.5**

Summary of Key Financial Ratios

RATIO	EQUATION	PURPOSE
Liquidity Ratios		
Current ratio	$\dfrac{\text{Current assets}}{\text{Current liabilities}}$	Measures an entity's ability to pay its current liabilities from its current assets
Quick ratio	$\dfrac{\text{Cash + cash equivalents +}}{\text{net current receivables +}}$ $\dfrac{\text{short-term investments}}{\text{Current liabilities}}$	Measures an entity's ability to pay its current liabilities without relying on the sale of its inventory
Leverage Ratios		
Long-term debt to equity ratio	$\dfrac{\text{Long-term debt}}{\text{Stockholders' equity}}$	Measures the degree of financial leverage employed by an entity
Times interest earned ratio	$\dfrac{\text{Net income +}\ \text{interest expense +}\ \text{income taxes expense}}{\text{Interest expense}}$	Indicates the number of times that an entity's interest expense is "covered" by earnings

■ **EXHIBIT 17.5 (continued)**

RATIO	EQUATION	PURPOSE
Activity Ratios		
Accounts receivable turnover ratio	$$\dfrac{\text{Net credit sales}}{\text{Average accounts receivable}}$$	Indicates the number of times that an entity collects or turns over its accounts receivable each year
Age of receivables	$$\dfrac{360 \text{ days}}{\text{Accounts receivable turnover ratio}}$$	Indicates the length of time normally required to collect a receivable resulting from a credit sale
Inventory turnover ratio	$$\dfrac{\text{Cost of goods sold}}{\text{Average inventory}}$$	Indicates the number of times that an entity sells or turns over its inventory each year
Age of inventory	$$\dfrac{360 \text{ days}}{\text{Inventory turnover ratio}}$$	Indicates the length of time normally required to sell an inventory item
Total asset turnover ratio	$$\dfrac{\text{Net sales}}{\text{Average total assets}}$$	Measures an entity's ability to generate sales relative to its investment in assets
Profitability Ratios		
Profit margin percentage	$$\dfrac{\text{Net income}}{\text{Net sales}}$$	Indicates the percentage of each sales dollar that contributes to net income
Gross profit percentage	$$\dfrac{\text{Gross profit}}{\text{Net sales}}$$	Indicates the percentage of each sales dollar not absorbed by cost of goods sold
Return on assets	$$\dfrac{\text{Net income} + \text{interest expense}}{\text{Average total assets}}$$	Measures the rate of return an entity realizes on its investment in assets
Return on equity	$$\dfrac{\text{Net income} - \text{preferred stock dividends}}{\text{Average common stockholders' equity}}$$	Measures the rate of return on an entity's common stockholders' equity
Market Strength Ratios		
Price-earnings ratio	$$\dfrac{\text{Current market price of common stock}}{\text{Earnings per share for most recent 12-month period}}$$	Indicates the amount that investors are willing to pay for each dollar of an entity's earnings
Market price to book value ratio	$$\dfrac{\text{Current market price of common stock}}{\text{Book value per share}}$$	Indicates the amount that investors are willing to pay for each dollar of an entity's net assets

their assets invested in cash during the mid-1990s. From 1993 through 1995, cash accounted for a much smaller percentage of Lindsay Hardware Stores' total assets, as shown by the common-sized balance sheets in Exhibit 17.3. The company's relatively small cash balances during this time span could have presented a problem if a sudden and unexpected need for a significant amount of cash had arisen.

LEVERAGE RATIOS   Financial leverage refers to the degree that a business relies on debt, or borrowed, capital instead of equity, or invested, capital to finance its operations. A company's stockholders, or other owners, benefit if the rate of return earned on borrowed funds exceeds the interest rate paid on those funds. Financial leverage works to the disadvantage of a business's owners when the interest rate paid on borrowed funds exceeds the rate of return earned on those funds. The long-term debt to equity ratio is a key measure of financial leverage. As shown in Exhibit 17.5, this ratio relates a corporation's total long-term debt to its total stockholders' equity.

The second leverage ratio shown in Exhibit 17.5 does not directly measure financial leverage. Instead, the times interest earned ratio provides a margin of safety measure that is particularly useful when analyzing highly leveraged companies. This ratio indicates how many times a company's interest expense was "covered" by earnings before income taxes and interest charges for a given period. For example, if this ratio is 2.0, a company covered its interest charges twice with its earnings during the period in question. The lower this ratio, the more risk a company faces of defaulting on its periodic interest payments.

Listed next are Lindsay Hardware Stores' long-term debt to equity and times interest earned ratios for 1993–1995 and the corresponding industry norms.

	LINDSAY HARDWARE STORES			
	1995	1994	1993	INDUSTRY NORM
Long-term debt to equity ratio	.51	.73	.85	.30
Times interest earned ratio	10.3	12.3	12.6	2.5

The data just shown indicate that Lindsay became less leveraged between 1993 and 1995. If you refer to Exhibit 17.3, you will notice that Lindsay's long-term debt was unchanged during this period. However, due to profitable operations, the company's total stockholders' equity increased significantly between 1993 and 1995, causing the company's long-term debt to equity ratio to decline.

The average long-term debt to equity ratio for companies operating hardware stores was approximately .30 in the mid-1990s. Although Lindsay's long-term debt to equity ratio steadily decreased from 1993 to 1995, the company was still more highly leveraged in 1995 than the typical firm in its industry. Again, financial leverage can be good or bad. If Lindsay continually earns a higher rate of return on its borrowed funds than the interest it pays on those funds, stockholders will benefit. However, unlike most expenses, interest expense does not decline if a company's revenues fall. As a result, when a company with a heavy debt burden experiences a drop in sales, its earnings are dragged down even further by the large interest expense it continues to incur.

Lindsay's times interest earned ratio decreased from 1993 through 1995, indicating that the company's coverage of its interest payments was declining. However, this ratio was well above the industry norm during each of these years, suggesting that the company faced a minimal risk of defaulting on its interest payments.

ACTIVITY RATIOS   Activity ratios generally measure how well a company is managing its assets. For example, these ratios allow decision makers to determine how quickly a company is converting receivables into cash and how quickly it is selling or "turning over" inventory. Exhibit 17.5 lists five common activity ratios. Shown in the following schedule are these activity ratios for Lindsay Hardware Stores for 1994 and 1995 along with the corresponding industry norms.

	LINDSAY HARDWARE STORES		INDUSTRY NORM
	1995	1994	
Accounts receivable turnover ratio	15.6	20.6	20.0
Age of receivables	23.1 days	17.5 days	18 days
Inventory turnover ratio	2.3	2.9	2.6
Age of inventory	157 days	124 days	140 days
Total asset turnover ratio	2.4	2.7	2.0

Before we discuss Lindsay's activity ratios, a few explanatory comments are necessary. First, all of Lindsay's sales are on a credit basis. As shown in Exhibit 17.5, the numerator of the accounts receivable turnover ratio is net credit sales. Second, the denominator of three of the five activity ratios is an average asset amount. To determine Lindsay's activity ratios, these averages were computed by adding the appropriate beginning and end-of-the-year dollar amounts and then dividing by two. For example, Lindsay's average accounts receivable for 1995 was determined by dividing by two the sum of its December 31, 1994, receivables and its December 31, 1995, receivables. Finally, Lindsay's activity ratios are not presented for 1993. To compute those ratios we would need asset balances as of December 31, 1992.

Lindsay's accounts receivable and inventory turnover ratios declined from 1994 to 1995, meaning that the company was not collecting its receivables as quickly nor selling its inventory as rapidly in 1995 compared with 1994. In 1994, Lindsay collected a receivable, on average, in a little more than 17 days, while the company required 23 days to collect a credit sale made during 1995. The average collection period for receivables in the hardware stores industry in the early 1990s was approximately 18 days. Consequently, in 1994, Lindsay outperformed its typical competitor in terms of how quickly receivables were converted into cash. The reverse was true in 1995. In 1994, Lindsay sold its inventory more rapidly than the average hardware retailer, while in 1995 the company lagged behind its average competitor in this regard. Industry statistics during the mid-1990s revealed that approximately 140 days were required to sell a typical inventory item in a hardware store. Notice that Lindsay's average time to sell an inventory item leaped from 124 days in 1994 to 157 days in 1995.

Recall that Lindsay's common-sized balance sheets indicated that both its receivables and inventory increased as a percentage of total assets from 1993–1995. Earlier, the meaning of these increases relative to the company's overall financial health was unclear. The company's activity ratios provide further insight on these changes. These ratios suggest that the company did not manage its receivables and inventory in 1995 as effectively as it did in 1994. Receivables become more susceptible to bad debt losses the longer they go uncollected. Similarly, the longer the time required to sell inventory, the higher the risk that inventory items will become obsolete, damaged, or stolen.

Finally, Lindsay's total asset turnover ratio decreased (worsened) in 1995. This change indicates that the company did a poorer job of generating sales relative to its total assets in 1995 compared with 1994. However, the industry average for the total asset turnover ratio in the mid-1990s was approximately 2.0. So, in both 1994 and 1995, Lindsay outperformed the industry, as a whole, in producing sales relative to its asset base.

PROFITABILITY RATIOS   Profitability ratios measure a business entity's earnings performance. The most common benchmarks against which to evaluate an entity's profitability are its sales, assets, and owners' equity. Exhibit 17.5 lists four common

Real World
Many companies experience seasonal cycles in their levels of business activity each year. To reduce the distortion that "seasonality" can introduce into financial ratios, decision makers should use twelve-month averages for balance sheet items, such as account receivable, involved in the computation of these ratios.

Teaching Note
Ask students to identify the incremental costs that a retailer incurs when the length of time required to sell its inventory increases.
Answers: Higher insurance costs, increased handling costs, and larger losses due to customer and employee theft.

profitability ratios. These profitability ratios for Lindsay Hardware Stores for 1994 and 1995 and the related industry norms are listed in the following schedule. Again, since we do not have the data necessary to compute certain of these ratios for 1993, none of the ratios for that year are presented.

| | LINDSAY HARDWARE STORES | | INDUSTRY NORM |
	1995	1994	
Profit margin percentage	7.2%	8.5%	3.0%
Gross profit percentage	45.0	42.9	35.0
Return on assets	20.6	26.6	4.8
Return on equity	36.4	52.8	9.0

Notice that in both 1994 and 1995, Lindsay outperformed the typical hardware retailer across the board in terms of the four profitability ratios listed in Exhibit 17.5. In the mid-1990s, Dun & Bradstreet reported that only 25 percent of all hardware retailers had a return on assets exceeding 11 percent. Additionally, only 25 percent of these companies had a return on equity exceeding 23 percent. These additional industry statistics reveal that Lindsay's return on assets and return on equity ratios were not only impressive, they were exceptional. But are these ratios reasonable? At a minimum, when a company has very impressive financial ratios, decision makers should consider the possibility that errors, intentional or unintentional, artificially inflated those ratios.

If errors in Lindsay's financial data overstated its profitability ratios, the most likely culprit was the company's cost of goods sold. Companies frequently make mistakes in counting and pricing year-end inventory—errors that result in their reported cost of goods sold being incorrect. Firms that wish to distort their earnings data may intentionally misrepresent their year-end inventory to understate their cost of goods sold. In either case, the result is that a company's gross profit percentage and its other profitability ratios are misstated.

For illustration purposes, assume that Lindsay's year-end inventory for 1995 was overstated by $50,000, or approximately 20 percent. We know from an earlier chapter than an overstatement of year-end inventory causes an entity's cost of goods sold for that year to be understated by the same amount. The following schedule shows a side-by-side comparison of Lindsay's reported income statement data for 1995 and that same data corrected for the assumed $50,000 overstatement of year-end inventory. (Note: Lindsay's average income tax rate is approximately 40 percent.)

	REPORTED 1995 INCOME STATEMENT DATA	CORRECTED 1995 INCOME STATEMENT DATA
Net Sales	$920,000	$920,000
Cost of Goods Sold	506,000	556,000
Gross Profit	414,000	364,000
Operating Expenses	293,000	293,000
Operating Income	121,000	71,000
Other Revenues and Expenses (Net)	(9,000)	(9,000)
Income before Income Taxes	112,000	62,000
Income Taxes	45,000	25,000
Net Income	$ 67,000	$ 37,000
Gross Profit Percentage	45%	39.6%
Profit Margin Percentage	7.2%	4%

Notice the impact of the assumed inventory error on the company's gross profit and profit margin percentages. Also notice that an assumed 20 percent overstatement of inventory resulted in an 81 percent overstatement of Lindsay's net income ($67,000/$37,000 = 180%). As you can see, inventory errors typically have a greatly magnified effect, on a percentage basis, on an entity's net income.

Now, let us take an intuitive, or common sense, approach to assessing Lindsay's profitability ratios. Suppose that all hardware retailers purchase a certain type of hammer from Hammers 'n Nails, Inc., at a wholesale cost of $20. Lindsay would have to sell this item at a retail price of $36.36 to realize a 45 percent gross profit—its average 1995 gross profit percentage.[1] Conversely, a competitor that realizes the average gross profit percentage of 35 percent for hardware retailers would sell this same hammer at a price of $30.76. Question: Would Joe or Josephine "Home Improvement" pay $36.36 for this hammer at Lindsay Hardware Stores instead of driving a mile or so to a competitor to purchase the same item at less than $31? Answer: Probably not. In other words, it is quite unlikely that Lindsay Hardware Stores could realize a gross profit percentage on its sales of 45 percent when the industry norm is 35 percent. When interpreting financial statements, a decision maker must be well versed in how to compute financial ratios but must also exercise common sense in interpreting those ratios. In the final section of this chapter, we expand upon this intuitive approach to financial statement analysis when we discuss the concept of earnings quality.

MARKET STRENGTH RATIOS   The first four categories of financial ratios we have considered focus on a company's financial condition or operating results. Market strength ratios, on the other hand, provide insight on how the capital markets, as a whole, perceive a company's common stock. Despite impressive operating results and a strong financial condition, a company's common stock may fare poorly in the capital markets. In the early 1990s, the stock prices of many electric utilities plummeted when regulatory authorities took steps to introduce more competition into the electric utility industry. Investors discounted the strong financial condition and impressive operating results of these companies because they believed the firms' future prospects were uncertain.

In Chapter 13, two market strength ratios were introduced, the price-earnings (P/E) ratio and the market price to book value ratio. Recall that the P/E ratio indicates how much investors are willing to pay for each $1 of earnings reported by a company over the previous twelve months. The market price to book value ratio indicates how much investors are willing to pay for each $1 of book value of a company's net assets.

Market strength ratios tend to be more volatile than other financial ratios because they are influenced by investors' perceptions and expectations, both of which can change rapidly. The following schedule documents for 1990 through 1994 the year-end market price to book value ratio of Telxon Corporation, a company involved in the computer industry. Notice that this ratio ranged from approximately 1.1 to 3.0 over this period. If we consider the intrayear fluctuations in this ratio, we will observe even more volatility.

	1994	1993	1992	1991	1990
Market price to book value ratio, Telxon Corporation	1.55	1.19	2.71	3.00	1.11

Teaching Note
Point out to students that one key to successful investing is identifying common stocks whose market strength ratios are not strongly correlated with the given firms' true financial strength and/or future prospects.

Teaching Note
The market price of a company's stock is largely a function of investors' expectations of the future dividends and capital appreciation they will realize by acquiring that stock.

1. A selling price of $36.36 would yield a gross profit of $16.36. When this gross profit is divided by the selling price, the result is a 45 percent gross profit: $16.36/$36.36 = 45%.

■ **EXHIBIT 17.6**
Market Price vs. Book Value: Telxon Corporation, 1990–1994

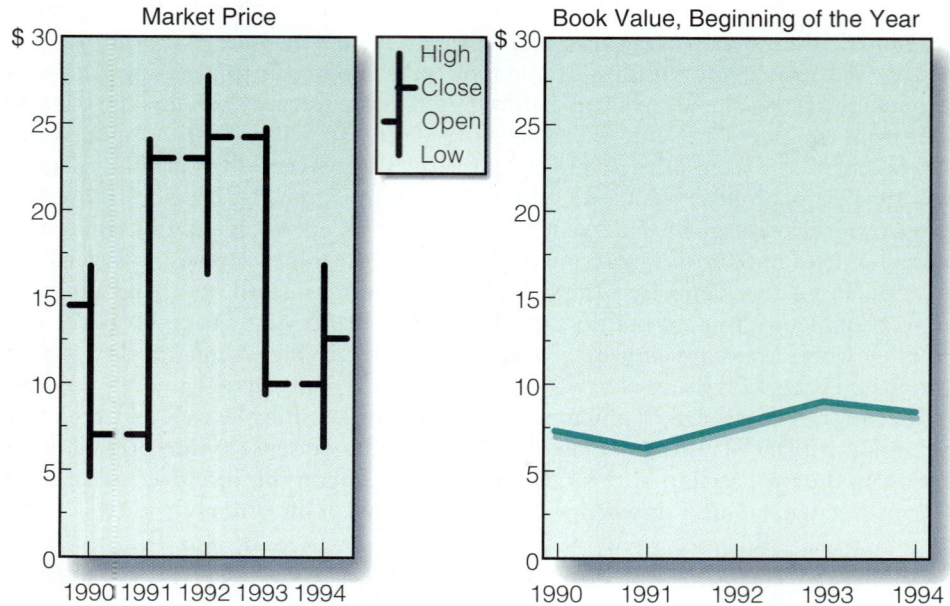

Shown in Exhibit 17.6 are two charts. The first chart depicts a graphical format used by security analysts to plot stock market prices. This chart presents four data points each year from 1990 through 1994 for Telxon's common stock: the opening price for the year, the highest price of the year, the lowest price of the year, and the stock's closing price for the year. On January 1, 1990, Telxon's common stock had a market price of approximately $15, while the stock closed the year at a price of $7. During the year, the stock topped out at nearly $17 per share and bottomed out at approximately $5 per share. The second chart presents Telxon's beginning-of-the-year book value for 1990 through 1994. Notice that unlike Telxon's stock market price, the company's book value per share was very stable over this five-year period.

What accounts for the significantly different behavior patterns of Telxon's stock price and book value per share shown in Exhibit 17.6? Again, stock prices are driven by investors' perceptions and expectations. Security analysts suggest that investors often overreact to quarterly earnings data, changes in management, and news reports regarding a company's future prospects or those of its industry. The result is volatile stock prices. On the other hand, book value per share is based strictly upon financial data methodically captured by an entity's accounting system.

ASSESSING EARNINGS QUALITY

earnings quality

In recent years, the concept of earnings quality has become increasingly important in the context of financial statement analysis. Although not rigidly defined, **earnings quality** generally refers to the degree of correlation between an entity's economic income and its reported earnings determined by GAAP. So what is "economic income"? Economic income is generally defined as the change in the total value, or

Guilders to GAAP

Foreign companies that want to market their securities in the United States must first register those securities with the SEC. The SEC requires these firms to include in their annual reports a reconciliation of the net income reported under their home country's accounting rules to the net income that they would have reported under GAAP. These companies must also reconcile their stockholders' equity as determined by their home country's accounting rules to a GAAP-based stockholders' equity figure. The starting point for decision makers who wish to compare and contrast these companies' financial data to that of similar United States firms are these two reconciliations. Often these reconciliations reveal large differences between foreign companies' reported net income and stockholders' equity and the comparable GAAP-based amounts.

In its 1993 annual report released in the United States, Polygram, the Dutch entertainment conglomerate, reported net income determined under "Dutch legal requirements" of 614 million Netherlands guilders. If the company had used GAAP, its net income would have been 534 million Netherlands guilders—the equivalent of $316 million. Under Dutch accounting rules, the company reported total stockholders' equity at the end of 1993 of 2.02 billion Netherlands guilders. Under GAAP, this figure would have been nearly 50 percent higher.

"well-offness," of a business from one point in time to another.[2] The analytical techniques illustrated in the previous section, including the profitability ratios, do not allow decision makers to comprehensively assess the quality of an entity's reported earnings. In this section, we consider the principal factors that influence earnings quality. Then we identify specific measures that can be used to assess earnings quality.

■ LEARNING OBJECTIVE 6
Assess earnings quality

Factors Influencing Earnings Quality

The opening vignette for this chapter described a large-scale financial fraud involving ZZZZ Best Company. Financial fraud obviously diminishes the correlation between an entity's economic income and its reported accounting earnings. However, business executives, or their accountants, can manipulate a firm's reported earnings without engaging in financial fraud. As you know, there are often several alternative methods that can be used to account for a specific type of transaction or event. Depreciation expense, cost of goods sold, and uncollectible accounts expense are examples of income statement items that may be materially affected by an entity's choice of accounting methods. Business executives can also influence their firms' reported earnings by modifying operating decisions. For example, if a company is having a poor year profit-wise, management may purposefully delay discretionary expenses such as advertising and maintenance. Delaying these expenditures may improve a company's reported accounting earnings for a given year, while actually diminishing the overall economic value of the business.

Focus on Ethics
Point out that economic self-interest may cause corporate executives to enhance their firm's current operating results by delaying discretionary expenditures although this decision damages the firm economically over the long run.

---

2. S. Cottle, R. F. Murray, and F. S. Block, *Graham and Dodd's Security Analysis* (New York: McGraw-Hill, 1988), 138.

The Dutch entertainment conglomerate Polygram, issues an annual report each year in the United States. In this report, Polygram reconciles its net income determined under Dutch accounting rules to the comparable net income the company would have reported under GAAP.

Teaching Note
One of the most subjective accounting estimates is the proper year-end balance of the allowance for doubtful accounts.

A company's reported profits may not be closely correlated with its economic income even if there have been no explicit efforts to distort those profits. Many financial statement items are estimates, such as warranty expenses and losses from pending lawsuits. These estimates may be materially in error although they are made honestly and objectively. Additionally, GAAP does not capture, or quantify, all events that affect the change in the economic value of a business during a given period of time. In fact, GAAP is not intended to capture all of these variables. For example, the change in the current value, or market value, of most assets is not considered a revenue item by GAAP.

Measures to Use in Assessing Earnings Quality

Analyzing the quality of a business's reported accounting earnings requires the exercise of considerable judgment. The analytical techniques described earlier in this chapter rely on quantitative data and mathematical relationships. An understanding of an entity's operations, knowledge of accounting rules and concepts, and simple intuition—common sense—are the principal tools used in analyzing earnings quality. Listed in Exhibit 17.7 are several specific methods that can be used to assess the quality of an entity's reported earnings.

The starting point for analyzing the quality of a company's earnings is the accounting methods it uses. These accounting methods are summarized in the initial footnote to an entity's financial statements. A review of this footnote should reveal whether a company tends to use income-inflating accounting methods. For example, as explained in Chapter 8, the FIFO inventory method generally results in a higher net income than the LIFO method during a period of steadily rising prices. Financial statement footnotes also disclose whether a company has changed one or more accounting methods recently and the impact of such changes on its reported earnings.

■ **EXHIBIT 17.7**

Examples of Measures to Use in Assessing the Quality of an Entity's
Reported Earnings

> Compare accounting principles employed by an entity to those used by competitors.
>
> Does the set of accounting principles used by the entity tend to inflate its reported earnings?
>
> Analyze any recent changes in accounting principles or accounting estimates to determine whether they inflated reported earnings.
>
> Read the footnotes to the financial statements to identify any unusual events that may have affected reported earnings.
>
> Read the footnotes to the financial statements to determine whether any major loss contingencies exist that could negatively affect future earnings.
>
> Review extraordinary losses included in the income statement to determine that they are actually nonoperating items.
>
> Attempt to determine whether there are any significant expenses not reflected in the income statement, such as warranty expenses on products sold.
>
> Attempt to determine whether discretionary expenditures, such as advertising and maintenance expenses, have been delayed.

A review of financial statement footnotes may also reveal unusual transactions or events that artificially inflated or deflated a company's reported accounting earnings. One such example is a "LIFO liquidation," which is the subject of the Decision Case at the end of this chapter.

Most large companies are involved in litigation. Quite often, pending litigation has the potential to significantly influence the value of a business, although this possibility may be ignored for accounting purposes. An entity's financial statement footnotes will provide a summary of the major litigation cases in which it is involved. These footnotes typically assess the likely financial statement impact of these cases as well. Decision makers should review these disclosures and determine whether they agree with management's assessment of how pending legal matters may affect a company's financial condition.

When analyzing a firm's reported earnings, decision makers tend to focus on the income generated by its continuing operations. Extraordinary gains and losses are discounted since they are nonrecurring and unusual events or transactions that are unlikely to affect an entity's future earnings. One method that business executives can use to inflate income from continuing operations is to misclassify operating expenses and losses as extraordinary losses in their firm's income statement. When assessing the quality of a company's reported earnings, decision makers should review any extraordinary losses in the entity's income statement. Footnote disclosures related to extraordinary items often provide insight on whether such items have been properly classified for income statement purposes.

Decision makers should also attempt to determine whether an entity has failed to include certain expenses in its income statement. To make this determination, decision makers must be familiar with the nature of a company's operations and its industry. A review of competitors' financial statements is one useful technique for identifying expenses that a company may have understated or omitted from its income statement. Finally, a comparison of a company's financial statements over several

Focus on Ethics
Recall that there are three levels of likelihood that may be assigned to contingent liabilities: probable, reasonably possible and remote. Management may contend that a contingent liability has only a remote chance of becoming an actual liability to justify not recording the contingency or disclosing it in a firm's financial statements.

years may reveal that discretionary expenses, such as advertising and maintenance, have been postponed in the most recent year. Again, the postponement of such expenses may increase a company's reported accounting earnings while damaging the company economically. For example, the postponement of maintenance expenses on production-line machinery may result in a higher rate of equipment breakdowns, higher repair bills in the future, and a decline in production efficiency.

A Random Walk through the Stock Market

So, you want to become rich and famous. Okay, you will be satisfied with rich. Your plan is to parlay your knowledge of accounting, financial reports, and investment analysis into a stock market "killing." Not to rain on your parade, but outsmarting the stock market is a difficult task, to say the least. Consider the "random walk" theory. This theory suggests that instead of spending hours analyzing financial data, individual investors might as well select their investments by throwing darts at daily stock market tables in a newspaper.

To test the random walk theory, *The Wall Street Journal* has conducted dozens of overlapping "experiments" since 1990. In these experiments, *The Wall Street Journal* selects four prominent financial analysts. Each of those analysts picks a stock that he or she believes will increase in price over the following six months. Then the staff of the newspaper randomly selects four stocks by throwing darts at a set of stock market tables. At the end of six months, the net gain or loss of each portfolio is determined. In April 1995, after fifty-eight such experiments, the investment professionals held a 33 to 25 lead over the darts.

Is choosing profitable stock investments a skill, an art, or simply "dumb luck"? In an ongoing experiment, *The Wall Street Journal* suggests that financial analysts, on average, can do a better job of choosing profitable stock investments than a random technique such as throwing darts at a stock market table.

SUMMARY

To make informed economic decisions, financial statement users must have the ability to analyze financial data and draw proper conclusions from such analysis. The objectives of financial statement analysis vary across different types of decision makers. This chapter focuses on financial statement analysis from the standpoint of investors, decision makers who must take a comprehensive approach to analyzing and interpreting financial data.

Annual reports are the principal source of information used in analyzing the financial statements of business entities. Key information useful in analyzing financial statement data can be found in the following sections of an annual report: the financial statement footnotes, the financial highlights table, management's discussion and analysis of financial condition and operating results, and the independent auditor's report. Other sources of information useful in financial statement analysis can be found in publications of investment advisory services and on-line financial services.

Among the principal approaches to financial statement analysis are trend analysis, the preparation of common-sized financial statements, and ratio analysis. These analytical techniques serve primarily as attention-directing devices. Unusual or unexpected variations or relationships revealed by these techniques should be investigated further to determine their cause and the related implications for a given entity.

Trend analysis is the study of percentage changes in financial statement items over a period of time. Trend analysis is often used to predict the future value of a financial statement item. However, such predictions must be used cautiously since they are not highly reliable. Common-sized financial statements allow decision makers to better grasp the relationships among the items in a specific financial statement. Common-sized financial statements also help decision makers uncover major structural changes in these relationships over a period of time. Ratio analysis typically involves a comparison of the relationship between two financial statement items. A company's financial ratios are often compared with its historical norms for those ratios and to industry norms. There are five general types of financial ratios: liquidity, leverage, activity, profitability, and market strength.

In recent years, increasing attention has been focused on the need to assess the quality of business entities' reported earnings. Earnings quality generally refers to the degree of correlation between an entity's economic income and its reported accounting earnings. Among key factors influencing earnings quality are the efforts of business executives to manipulate, or distort, their firm's financial data. The need to estimate many financial statement amounts can also negatively affect earnings quality. Specific measures that can be used to assess earnings quality include comparing a firm's accounting methods with those used by its competitors. Income-inflating accounting methods tend to diminish the quality of a company's reported earnings compared with the earnings of competitors that use more conservative accounting methods.

GLOSSARY

Common-sized financial statements (p. 749)   Financial statements in which each line item is expressed as a percentage of a major financial statement component.

Cross-sectional ratio analysis (p. 753)   Comparison of a company's financial ratios with those of competing companies and/or with the industry norms for those ratios.

Earnings quality (p. 760)   The degree of correlation between an entity's economic income and its reported earnings determined by GAAP.

Longitudinal ratio analysis (p. 753)   A variation of ratio analysis that focuses on the changes in an entity's ratios over a period of time.

Ratio analysis (p. 753)   An analytical technique that typically involves a comparison of the relationship between two financial statement items.

Trend analysis (p. 747)   The study of percentage changes in financial statement items over a period of time.

DECISION CASE

Suppose that you are the controller of DeQuasie Corporation. This company is a wholesale distributor of lasonics, an electronic component used by computer manufacturers. DeQuasie uses the periodic inventory system and the LIFO costing method to account for its inventory of lasonics. Presently, on November 1, DeQuasie has 12,000 lasonics in inventory at a per unit LIFO cost of $20. Sales forecasts indicate that DeQuasie will sell 10,000 lasonics at an average selling price of $50 per unit during the last two months of the year. The current replacement cost for lasonics is $35 per unit. DeQuasie typically stocks up on inventory during November and December to prepare for January and February, which are historically its busiest sales months. As a matter of company policy, the year-end inventory of lasonics is expected to be no less than 20,000 units. Given this policy, the company should purchase 18,000 units of inventory during the last two months of the year as determined by the following equation:

$$
\begin{array}{ccccc}
\text{Required Inventory} & & \text{Desired} & \text{Expected Sales} & \text{November 1} \\
\text{Purchases, November 1} = & \text{Inventory,} & + \text{during November} & - \text{Inventory} \\
\text{through December 31} & \text{December 31} & \text{and December} &
\end{array}
$$

$$
\begin{array}{c}
\text{Required Inventory} \\
\text{Purchases, November 1} = \quad 20{,}000 \quad + \quad 10{,}000 \quad - \quad 12{,}000 \quad = \quad 18{,}000 \\
\text{through December 31}
\end{array}
$$

Unfortunately, the current year has been a poor one for DeQuasie. Expenses are up and revenues are down. Latest projections indicate that the company's net income will be a meager $200,000, down from nearly $600,000 the previous year. At a management meeting in late October, your immediate superior, the chief financial officer (CFO), suggested delaying additional inventory purchases until after January 1. The CFO pointed out that by delaying inventory purchases, the company could record a significantly higher gross profit in the last two months of the year.

Required: Assume that your firm accepts the CFO's recommendation and delays all inventory purchases planned during November and December until after year-end. Explain how this decision will affect DeQuasie's earnings and determine the impact on the company's gross profit and net income for the year. (DeQuasie has an effective income tax rate of 40 percent.) Is your company's decision appropriate? Is it ethical? Why or why not? Identify the parties potentially affected by this decision and how they may be affected. What action, if any, should you take regarding this matter, given your position with the firm?

QUESTIONS

1. What is the primary purpose of the accounting function within a business organization?

2. Briefly explain why the objectives of financial statement analysis vary across different types of financial decision makers.

3. Why must investors take a comprehensive approach to financial statement analysis?

4. What is a 10-K registration statement? What companies are required to prepare a 10-K?

5. What is the purpose of a financial highlights table in a company's annual report?

6. What type of information is generally included in the "MDA" section of an annual report?

7. Identify several prominent investment advisory firms that publish financial data, statistical measures, and other information regarding business entities.

8. Identify two frequently used sources of industry norms for various financial ratios and other financial measures.

9. "Financial statement analysis is principally used as an attention-directing device." Explain the meaning of that statement.

10. What problem do decision makers encounter when analyzing financial data of companies with more than one line of business?

11. Define trend analysis and identify its primary purpose.

12. Define common-sized financial statements and indicate how they are used by decision makers.

13. Define ratio analysis. What are the two approaches to applying ratio analysis?

14. What are five general types or categories of financial ratios?

15. Why is it important for decision makers to monitor a company's liquidity?

16. When do a company's stockholders benefit from the use of financial leverage? When are they disadvantaged by the use of financial leverage?

17. What does the times interest earned ratio measure?

18. What aspect of a company's financial performance do activity ratios measure?

19. The benchmarks used in evaluating a company's profitability generally involve what major financial statement items?

20. How might a company manipulate its ending inventory to intentionally distort its earnings data?

21. What do market strength ratios measure?

22. Why do market strength ratios tend to be more volatile than other financial ratios?

23. Define earnings quality.

24. Identify the factors that influence the quality of a company's earnings.

25. Identify measures that decision makers can use to evaluate a company's earnings quality.

EXERCISES

26. **Terminology** (LO 1, 2)

Following are definitions or descriptions of terms relating to financial statement analysis.

_____ Involves a comparison of the relationship between two or more financial statement items.

_____ Indicates the amount that investors are willing to pay for each dollar of an entity's earnings.

_____ Involves a comparison of a company's financial ratios with those of competing companies or industry norms.

_____ Measures an entity's ability to generate sales relative to its investment in assets.

_____ Focuses on changes in an entity's ratios over a period of time.

_____ Ratios that indicate how the capital markets as a whole perceive a company's common stock.

_____ Indicates the percentage of each sales dollar that contributes to net income.

_____ Used to evaluate an entity's ability to finance its day-to-day operations and pay its liabilities as they mature.

_____ Ratios used to evaluate how well a company is managing its assets.

_____ Indicates the number of times that an entity sells or turns over its inventory each year.

_____ Measures an entity's ability to pay its current liabilities from its current assets.

26.   a, n,c,e,f,k,p,g,j,b,d

Required:

Match each definition or description listed with an appropriate term from the following list.

a.   Ratio analysis
b.   Inventory turnover ratio
c.   Cross-sectional ratio analysis
d.   Current ratio
e.   Total asset turnover ratio
f.   Longitudinal ratio analysis
g.   Liquidity ratios
h.   Gross profit percentage
i.   Leverage ratios
j.   Activity ratios
k.   Market strength ratios
l.   Age of inventory
m.   Quick ratio
n.   Price-earnings ratio
o.   Accounts receivable turnover ratio
p.   Profit margin percentage

27. **Trend Analysis** (LO 3)

Logicon, Inc., headquartered in Torrance, California, provides advanced technology systems and services to support national security, civil, and industrial needs. Shown in the following schedule are selected financial data included in

Logicon's 1994 annual report. Dollar amounts are expressed in millions except for dividends per share.

YEAR	TOTAL REVENUES	DIVIDENDS PER SHARE	TOTAL ASSETS
1990	$258.5	$.18	$102.8
1991	260.0	.18	98.4
1992	299.1	.195	113.8
1993	325.1	.24	119.8

Required:

1. Prepare a trend analysis for each of the three financial statement items listed for Logicon using 1990 as the base year.
2. Predict the 1994 figure for each financial statement item. In which of these predicted amounts do you have the most confidence? Why?
3. Logicon actually had total revenues of $320.2 million in 1994, paid dividends of $.28 per share during 1994, and had total assets at the end of 1994 of $129.3 million. Compute the percentage error between each of these actual amounts and the corresponding prediction you made in Part 2. Comment on any additional insight these results provide you regarding trend analysis.

27.	Revenues	Dividends	Total Assets
1990	100.0%	100.0%	100.0%
1991	100.6	100.0	95.7
1992	115.7	108.3	110.7
1993	125.8	133.3	116.5

28. **Common-Sized Financial Statements**

Following are balance sheets for Gabe's Shoe Repair Shop as of December 31, 1995 and 1996.

GABE'S SHOE REPAIR SHOP
BALANCE SHEETS
DECEMBER 31, 1995 AND 1996

	1995	1996
Assets		
Cash	$ 9,200	$18,700
Accounts Receivable (net)	8,300	14,400
Inventory	12,500	14,700
Prepaid Expenses	800	300
Total Current Assets	30,800	48,100
Equipment (net)	31,200	27,800
Total Assets	$62,000	$75,900
Liabilities		
Accounts Payable	$ 7,100	$ 2,700
Accrued Expenses	3,300	3,600
Total Current Liabilities	10,400	6,300
Long-Term Bank Loan	10,000	10,000
Stockholders' Equity		
Common Stock	12,000	12,000
Additional Paid-in Capital	24,000	24,000
Retained Earnings	5,600	23,600
Total Stockholders' Equity	41,600	59,600
Total Liabilities and Stockholders' Equity	$62,000	$75,900

28. 2.

	1995	1996
Cash	14.8%	24.6%
Accounts Payable	11.5%	3.6%

Required:
1. How are common-sized financial statements used by decision makers?
2. Prepare common-sized balance sheets for Gabe's Shoe Repair Shop as of December 31, 1995, and 1996.
3. What major structural changes occurred in this business's balance sheet during 1996? What factors may have accounted for these changes?

29. **Common-Sized Financial Statements** (LO 4)

Following is a recent income statement for the Cable Company (amounts are expressed in thousands). Also presented is the average common-sized income statement for Cable Company's industry.

	CABLE COMPANY	INDUSTRY
Sales	$44,900	100.0%
Cost of Goods Sold	21,700	47.3
Gross Profit	23,200	52.7
Operating Expenses	16,100	30.3
Operating Income	7,100	22.4
Other Revenue (Expense)	(1,300)	(2.9)
Income before Income Tax	5,800	19.5
Income Tax Expense	2,300	8.2
Net Income	$ 3,500	11.3

Required:
1. Prepare a common-sized income statement for Cable Company.
2. What major differences exist between the common-sized income statement of Cable and that of its industry?

29. 1.

	Cable
Cost of goods sold	48.3%
Net income	7.8%

30. **Liquidity and Leverage Ratios** (LO 5)

P. R. Williamson Company operates two small clothing stores in southeastern Idaho. Following are this company's income statements for the years ended December 31, 1994 through 1996, and the company's year-end balance sheets for 1994 through 1996.

P. R. WILLIAMSON COMPANY
INCOME STATEMENTS
FOR THE YEARS ENDED DECEMBER 31, 1994–1996

	1994	1995	1996
Sales*	$641,900	$652,000	$654,500
Cost of Goods Sold	304,500	323,700	339,200
Gross Profit	337,400	328,300	315,300
Operating Expenses	154,200	155,800	161,900
Operating Income	183,200	172,500	153,400
Other Revenue (Expense)†	13,400	(6,400)	(1,200)
Income before Income Tax	196,600	166,100	152,200
Income Tax Expense	78,600	66,400	60,900
Net Income	$118,000	$ 99,700	$ 91,300

* All of the company's sales are on a credit basis.
† Includes interest expense of the following amounts: 1994—$9,900, 1995—$7,400, and 1996—$7,100.

P. R. WILLIAMSON COMPANY
BALANCE SHEETS
DECEMBER 31, 1994–1996

	1994	1995	1996
Assets			
Cash	$ 22,000	$ 9,100	$ 3,700
Accounts Receivable (net)	72,500	103,300	116,900
Inventory	109,800	102,000	89,000
Prepaid Expenses	2,500	1,400	1,700
Total Current Assets	206,800	215,800	211,300
Property & Equipment (net)	212,000	201,500	189,400
Other Assets	3,200	2,600	1,500
Total Assets	$422,000	$419,900	$402,200
Liabilities			
Accounts Payable	$ 51,900	$ 57,200	$ 64,900
Notes Payable	25,000	15,000	12,000
Accrued Expenses	41,100	35,800	7,400
Total Current Liabilities	118,000	108,000	84,300
Bonds Payable	100,000	80,000	80,000
Stockholders' Equity			
Common Stock	50,000	50,000	50,000
Additional Paid-in Capital	130,000	130,000	130,000
Retained Earnings	24,000	51,900	57,900
Total Stockholders' Equity	204,000	231,900	237,900
Total Liabilities and Stockholders' Equity	$422,000	$419,900	$402,200

Required:

1. Compute the liquidity and leverage ratios discussed in this chapter for P. R. Williamson Company for 1994 through 1996.
2. Indicate which of the company's liquidity and leverage ratios improved and which worsened during the period 1994 through 1996.
3. Overall, did the company's liquidity improve or deteriorate between 1994 and 1996? Explain.
4. Did this company become more or less leveraged between 1994 and 1996?

31. **Activity Ratios** (LO 5)

Refer to the data presented in Exercise 30 for P. R. Williamson Company.

Required:

1. Compute the activity ratios discussed in this chapter for P. R. Williamson Company for 1995 and 1996.
2. Indicate which of these ratios improved and which worsened during 1996.
3. Overall, did the company do a better job of managing its accounts receivable, inventory, and total assets in 1996 compared with 1995? Explain.

32. **Profitability and Market Strength Ratios** (LO 5)

Refer to the information presented in Exercise 30 for P. R. Williamson Company. This company had 50,000 shares of common stock outstanding throughout the period 1994–1996. Following are the market prices of P. R. Williamson's common stock at the end of each year 1994 through 1996: 1994—$8.50, 1995—$7.75, and 1996—$6.50.

30. 1.

	1993	1994	1995
Current ratio	1.7	2.0	2.5
Quick ratio	0.8	1.0	1.4
Long-term debt to equity	0.5	0.3	0.3
Times interest earned	20.9	23.4	22.4

31. 1.

	1995	1996
Accounts receivable turnover	7.4	5.9
Age of receivables	49 days	61 days
Inventory turnover	3.1	3.6
Age of Inventory	116 days	100 days

Required:

1. Compute the profitability and market strength ratios discussed in this chapter for P. R. Williamson Company for 1994 through 1996. (Note: The company's total assets on January 1, 1994, were $425,000, while the company's total stockholders' equity on that date was $186,000.)
2. Evaluate the company's profitability ratios for the period 1994–1996. Did the company become more or less profitable over this time period? Explain.
3. Evaluate the company's market strength ratios for the period 1994–1996. What do the changes in these ratios over this period indicate?

33. **Ethics and Investment Advice** (LO 1)

Suppose that you are considering an investment in the common stock of Merck & Company, a large pharmaceutical firm. You recently read a very favorable analysis of this company's future prospects. The investment advisor who prepared this analysis indicated that, in her opinion, Merck common stock was a "strong buy."

Required:

1. Would the degree of reliance that you place on this investment advisor's analysis of Merck common stock be affected by whether or not the advisor owns Merck stock? Why or why not?
2. Should investment advisors be required to disclose whether or not they own stock in the companies they analyze and discuss in published articles and reports? Defend your answer.

34. **Accounting Errors and the Impact on Financial Ratios** (LO 5)

Moses & Stanley, Inc., is a retail company that has a large amount of obsolete inventory. The company carries this inventory at its original cost although its net realizable value is essentially zero.

Required:

1. Refer to Exhibit 17.5. Identify the financial ratios listed in Exhibit 17.5 that would be affected by the failure of a company to write off obsolete inventory.
2. Is it unethical for a company to refuse to write off or write down inventory that has little or no value to the company?
3. What accounting principle or principles would be violated by failing to write off or write down obsolete inventory?

35. **Accounting Errors and the Impact on Financial Statement Data** (LO 5)

Following is a condensed version of the 1996 income statement of Linton Supply Company.

Sales	$725,400
Cost of Goods Sold	404,300
Gross Profit	321,100
Operating Expenses	111,300
Operating Income	209,800
Other Revenue (Expense)	10,200
Income before Income Tax	220,000
Income Tax Expense	88,000
Net Income	$132,000

Linton's accountant overlooked a $3,200 utility bill at the end of 1996. This bill should have been recorded with a debit to Utilities Expense and a credit to Accrued Expenses. The company's year-end inventory account balance was also incorrect. Because of errors made during the counting of inventory, Linton's year-end inventory was listed as $174,300 in its accounting records instead of the correct figure of $151,200.

Following is other information regarding Linton Supply:

Average total assets during 1996	$820,500
Interest expense for 1996 (included in	
Other Revenue and Expense)	34,000
Average common stockholders' equity	380,000
Average income tax rate	40%

Required:

1. Ignoring the two errors discovered in Linton's accounting records, compute the company's profitability ratios for 1996.
2. Compute Linton's profitability ratios for 1996 after adjusting the company's financial data for the two errors.
3. Did the two errors have a significant effect on Linton's profitability ratios? Defend your answer.

36. Earnings Quality (LO 6)

Charlie Turner wants to begin investing in the stock market but knows very little about accounting and financial reporting practices. Recently, he stumbled across a brief article in *The Wall Street Journal* that focused on the subject of "earnings quality." After reading this article, Charlie was baffled. "How can there be a difference in the *quality* of earnings for different companies?" he asked a friend after reading the article. "Corporate earnings are hard, cold facts, right? Accountants just add numbers here and subtract numbers there to arrive at a company's net income, right? Any way you cut it, two plus two equals four . . . right?"

Required:

Write a memo to Charlie that explains the concept of earnings quality. Comment in this memo on several factors that influence earnings quality. Since Charlie is unfamiliar with accounting and financial reporting practices, include numerical examples in the memo to clarify how these factors influence earnings quality. Conclude your memo with a few suggestions to Charlie regarding how he can evaluate the quality of reported earnings data.

PROBLEM SET A

37. Trend Analysis (LO 1, 3)

Following are selected financial data for the period 1990–1994 for Whole Foods Market, Inc., a company headquartered in Austin, Texas. (Amounts are expressed in thousands of dollars except for per share data.)

	1990	1991	1992	1993	1994
Sales	$144,267	$173,164	$205,348	$322,308	$401,685
Operating Income	3,546	5,023	5,842	8,343	14,666
Earnings Per Share	.26	.31	.37	.29	.61
Book Value Per Share	.99	1.16	4.02	5.77	6.87

Required:

1. Prepare a trend analysis for each listed financial item of Whole Foods Market.
2. How is trend analysis used by decision makers? What are the limitations of trend analysis?

3. Why aren't the trend percentages you computed consistent across each financial statement item?

38. **Common-Sized Financial Statements** (LO 4)

The News Corporation Limited is a large Australian company that publishes newspapers and magazines and operates television stations. Following are the 1992 through 1994 income statements of The News Corporation. (Amounts are expressed in millions of Australian dollars.)

THE NEWS CORPORATION
INCOME STATEMENTS
FOR THE YEARS ENDED JUNE 30, 1992–1994

	1992	1993	1994
Revenues	$10,189	$10,686	$11,621
Costs and Expenses	8,373	8,753	9,788
Earnings before Interest, Taxes			
Depreciation and Amortization	1,816	1,933	1,833
Depreciation and Amortization	225	231	236
Operating Income	1,591	1,702	1,597
Other Income (Expense):			
Equity Income (Losses) of			
Associated Companies	(57)	177	394
Net Interest Expense	(932)	(737)	(667)
Other	20	19	40
Income before Income Taxes, Outside			
Equity Interests, and Abnormal Items	622	1,161	1,364
Income Tax Expense	25	110	132
Outside Equity Interests	67	72	20
Income before Abnormal Items	530	979	1,212
Abnormal Items:			
Parent Entity and Controlled Entities	(18)	(7)	105
Associated Items	(11)	(108)	18
Net Income	$ 501	$ 864	$ 1,335

Required:

1. Prepare common-sized income statements for The News Corporation for each year 1992 through 1994.
2. What major structural changes occurred between 1992 and 1994 in this company's income statement data? Are these changes apparently favorable or unfavorable? Explain.

39. **Comparative Analysis of Financial Data** (LO 5)

The following schedule provides key financial ratios for three companies in the same industry and the industry norm for each of the financial ratios.

	INDUSTRY NORM	ALONSO COMPANY	BUCKLEY, INC.	COSGROVE CORPORATION
Current Ratio	2.4	1.6	2.3	2.5
Quick Ratio	1.0	.4	1.3	1.2
Long-Term Debt				
to Equity Ratio	.5	.6	.4	.2
Times Interest				
Earned Ratio	4.5	2.4	5.6	14.9
Age of Receivables	89 days	101 days	77 days	80 days
Age of Inventory	97 days	99 days	92 days	76 days
Profit Margin				
Percentage	3.4%	2.3%	3.6%	4.7%

38. 1.

	1992	1993	1994
Operating Income	15.6%	15.9%	13.7%
Net Income	4.9%	8.1%	11.5%

Return on Assets	4.9%	3.4%	5.6%	6.0%
Return on Equity	7.1%	4.9%	7.1%	8.9%
Price-Earnings Ratio	10.2	7.5	7.7	12.7
Market Price to Book				
Value Ratio	1.8	1.3	1.2	3.2

Required:

1. Evaluate the overall financial health of these three firms. Given the informa-   tion provided, which firm do you believe is in the strongest condition finan-   cially? Explain.
2. Again, based only upon the data provided, which firm's common stock do you   believe is the most attractive investment alternative? Why?
3. List three other items of financial or nonfinancial information that you   would want to review before making an investment decision regarding the   common stocks of these companies.

39. No check figures

40. **Impact of Accounting Errors on Financial Ratios** (LO 5)

Following are examples of errors that can be made in processing accounting data. Listed next to each error is a financial ratio.

		IMPACT OF ERROR ON FINANCIAL RATIO		
ACCOUNTING ERROR	FINANCIAL RATIO	*Increase*	*Decrease*	*No Effect*
a. Recording a sales transaction twice	Total asset turnover	_____	_____	_____
b. Overstatement of ending inventory	Quick	_____	_____	_____
c. Debiting a payment of a long-term note payable to a short-term payable account	Return on assets	_____	_____	_____
d. Understating the estimated useful life of a depreciable asset	Return on equity	_____	_____	_____
e. Failing to prepare a year-end adjusting entry to record interest revenue	Price-earnings	_____	_____	_____
f. Failing to record the declaration of a cash dividend shortly before year-end	Profit margin percentage	_____	_____	_____
g. Recording purchase of long-term asset as a current asset	Market price to book value ratio	_____	_____	_____

Required:

Indicate whether each error overstates, understates, or has no impact on the financial ratio with which it is coupled.

40. No check figures

41. **Comprehensive Financial Statement Analysis** (LO 5)

Following are income statements and balance sheets for three recent years for Wichita Enterprises.

WICHITA ENTERPRISES
INCOME STATEMENTS
FOR THE YEARS ENDED DECEMBER 31, 1994–1996

	1994	1995	1996
Sales*	$685,300	$702,000	$730,900
Cost of Goods Sold	384,800	378,400	373,800
Gross Profit	300,500	323,600	357,100
Operating Expenses	124,300	158,100	179,300
Operating Income	176,200	165,000	177,800
Other Revenue (Expense)†	2,000	400	1,300
Income before Income Tax	178,200	165,900	179,100
Income Tax Expense	71,200	66,400	71,600
Net Income	$107,000	$ 99,500	$107,500

* All of the company's sales are on a credit basis.
† Includes interest expense of the following amounts: 1994—$17,940, 1995—$17,940, and 1996—$14,820.

WICHITA ENTERPRISES
BALANCE SHEETS
DECEMBER 31, 1994–1996

	1994	1995	1996
Assets			
Cash	$ 6,200	$ 1,500	$ 2,300
Accounts Receivable (net)	51,000	47,300	38,600
Inventory	132,500	188,000	251,500
Supplies	1,100	2,400	1,700
Prepaid Expenses	10,200	8,600	8,900
Total Current Assets	201,000	247,800	303,000
Property, Plant &			
Equipment (net)	512,500	511,400	520,300
Other Assets	5,700	7,300	3,600
Total Assets	$719,200	$766,500	$826,900
Liabilities			
Accounts Payable	$ 81,000	$ 99,600	$ 98,100
Accrued Expenses	55,600	43,400	32,200
Total Current Liabilities	136,600	143,000	130,300
Bonds Payable	230,000	230,000	190,000
Total Liabilities	366,600	373,000	320,300
Stockholders' Equity			
Common Stock	12,000	12,000	16,000
Additional Paid-in Capital	122,000	122,000	142,000
Retained Earnings	218,600	259,500	348,600
Total Stockholders' Equity	352,600	393,500	506,600
Total Liabilities and Stockholders' Equity	$719,200	$766,500	$826,900

During all of 1994 and 1995, Wichita Enterprises had 80,000 shares of common stock outstanding. During 1996, the company had 90,000 shares of common stock outstanding. Following are the market prices of Wichita's common stock at the end of each year 1994 through 1996: 1994–$12.50, 1995—$11.75, and 1996—$10.50.

Listed next are the norms in Wichita Enterprises' industry for key financial ratios during the period 1994–1996.

Liquidity Ratios:

Current	2.1
Quick	.8

Leverage Ratios:

Long-term debt to equity	.4
Times interest earned	7.0

Activity Ratios:

Accounts receivable turnover	10.0
Age of receivables	36 days
Inventory turnover	4.5
Age of inventory	80 days
Total asset turnover	1.2

Profitability Ratios:

Profit margin percentage	12.5
Gross profit percentage	42.1
Return on assets	11.4
Return on equity	16.1

Market Strength Ratios:

Price-earnings	12
Market price to book value	6.2

Required:

1. Compute financial ratios for Wichita Enterprises for the period 1994–1996. (Compute all of the ratios for which an industry norm is provided. For certain ratios, sufficient data will only be available to compute ratios for 1995 and 1996.)
2. Analyze the financial ratios of Wichita Enterprises on a longitudinal basis. What positive and negative trends are apparent in the company's financial data?
3. Analyze the ratios of Wichita Enterprises by comparing each with the corresponding industry norm. Comment on which of the company's ratios are significantly different from the industry norm and whether these differences are favorable or unfavorable.
4. Identify unusual or unexpected relationships in Wichita Enterprises' financial data that you believe decision makers relying on this company's financial statements would want to further investigate.
5. Comment on the overall financial status of Wichita Enterprises as of December 31, 1996. In your opinion, did the company's financial status improve or deteriorate during the period 1994 through 1996? Explain.
6. List additional financial and nonfinancial information you would want to obtain regarding Wichita Enterprises before you reach a final conclusion concerning the company's future prospects.

41. 1.

	1994	1995	1996
Current ratio	1.5	1.7	2.3
Quick ratio	0.4	0.3	0.3
Long-term debt to equity	0.7	0.6	0.4
Times interest earned	10.9	10.2	13.1
Accounts receivable turnover		14.3	17.0
Age of receivables		25 days	21 days
Inventory turnover		2.4	1.7
Age of inventory		150 days	212 days
Total asset turnover		0.9	0.9
Profit margin percentage	15.6%	14.2%	14.7%
Gross profit percentage	43.8%	46.1%	48.9%
Return on assets		15.8%	15.4%
Return on equity		26.7%	23.9%
Price-earnings	9.3	9.5	8.8
Market price to book value per share	2.8	2.4	1.9

42. **Earnings Quality** (LO 6)

Pickard Corporation and Jenkins Company are two firms in the same industry. These two firms have approximately the same annual revenues and total assets. Following is the most recent income statement of each firm.

	PICKARD CORPORATION	JENKINS COMPANY
Sales	$1,324,900	$1,337,300
Cost of Goods Sold	690,200	640,900
Gross Profit	634,700	696,400
Operating Expenses:		
Selling	90,000	86,400
General & Administrative	72,000	87,000
Depreciation	102,000	71,000
Operating Income	370,700	452,000
Other Revenue (Expense)	5,200	3,700
Income before Income Tax	375,900	455,700
Income Tax Expense	150,400	182,300
Net Income	$ 225,500	$ 273,400

Pickard Corporation uses the LIFO inventory costing method and an accelerated depreciation method, while Jenkins Company uses FIFO inventory costing and the straight-line depreciation method.

Required:

1. Define earnings quality.
2. Why is earnings quality an important consideration for financial decision makers when evaluating financial statement data?
3. Suppose that a friend of yours is considering investing in the common stock of either Pickard Corporation or Jenkins Company. Write a memo to your friend explaining the concept of earnings quality and comment on how the quality of these firms' reported earnings may be affected by their use of different accounting methods.

42. No check figures

PROBLEM SET B

43. **Trend Analysis** (LO 1, 3)

Following are recent financial data for King World Productions, Inc., which distributes *The Oprah Winfrey Show* and *Jeopardy!* (Amounts are expressed in thousands of dollars except for per share data.)

	1990	1991	1992	1993	1994
Total Revenues	$453,749	$475,909	$503,174	$474,312	$480,659
Operating Income	142,828	154,084	152,481	150,950	127,578
Total Assets	406,950	500,834	498,240	535,546	569,562
Earnings per Share	2.15	2.31	2.43	2.65	2.33

Required:

1. Prepare a trend analysis for each listed financial item of King World Productions.
2. How is trend analysis used by decision makers? What are the limitations of trend analysis?
3. Why aren't the trend percentages you computed consistent across each financial statement item?

43. 1.

	1990	1991	1992	1993	1994
Sales	100%	105%	111%	105%	106%
Operating Income	100	108	107	106	89
Total assets	100	123	122	132	140
Earnings per share	100	107	113	123	108

44. **Common-Sized Financial Statements**

The News Corporation Limited is a large Australian company that publishes newspapers and magazines and operates television stations. Following are year-end balance sheets of The News Corporation for the company's 1993 and 1994 fiscal years. (Amounts are expressed in millions of Australian dollars.)

THE NEWS CORPORATION
BALANCE SHEETS
JUNE 30, 1993 AND 1994

	1993	1994
Assets		
Current Assets		
Cash	$ 659	$ 433
Receivables	1,984	2,127
Inventories	972	984
Other	180	199
Total Current Assets	3,795	3,743
Noncurrent Assets:		
Investments	3,268	3,396
Property, Plant & Equipment (net)	3,691	3,545
Goodwill	527	457
Publishing Rights, Titles and		
Television Licenses	13,317	13,162
Long-Term Receivables	364	480
Inventories	1,751	1,635
Other	559	528
Total Noncurrent Assets	23,477	23,203
Total Assets	$27,272	$26,946
Liabilities and Shareholders' Equity		
Current Liabilities:		
Current Maturities of Long-Term Debt	$ 18	$ 112
Accounts Payable and Other	3,245	3,539
Total Current Liabilities	3,263	3,651
Noncurrent Liabilities:		
Long-Term Debt	10,162	7,793
Accounts Payable and Other	1,073	1,039
Total Noncurrent Liabilities	11,235	8,832
Redeemable Preference Shares	228	11
Outside Equity Interests	448	476
Shareholders' Equity	12,098	13,976
Total Liabilities and Shareholders' Equity	$27,272	$26,946

Required:
1. Prepare common-sized balance sheets for The News Corporation for 1993 and 1994.
2. What major structural changes occurred during 1994 in this company's balance sheet data? Are these changes apparently favorable or unfavorable? Explain.

44. 1.

	1993	1994
Receivables	7.3%	7.9%
Accounts Payable and Other	11.9%	13.1%

45. **Comparative Analysis of Financial Data** (LO 5)
The following schedule provides key financial ratios for three companies in the same industry and the industry norm for each of the financial ratios.

	INDUSTRY NORM	RAZOOK, INC.	SCHUMACHER ENTERPRISES	TERSINE CORPORATION
Current Ratio	2.2	2.0	1.8	1.3
Quick Ratio	.8	.8	.9	.5
Long-Term Debt to Equity Ratio	.3	.2	.4	.9
Times Interest Earned Ratio	6.5	11.4	12.1	3.9
Age of Receivables	72 days	73 days	76 days	80 days
Age of Inventory	83 days	75 days	79 days	97 days
Profit Margin Percentage	4.4%	5.3%	4.6%	3.1%
Return on Assets	5.7%	7.4%	6.2%	3.7%
Return on Equity	8.1%	9.2%	7.7%	4.9%
Price-Earnings Ratio	12.5	16.5	9.7	13.4
Market Price to Book Value Ratio	2.2	3.5	1.3	2.7

Required:

1. Evaluate the overall financial health of these three firms. Given the information provided, which firm do you believe is in the strongest condition financially? Explain.
2. Again, based only upon the data provided, which firm's common stock do you believe is the most attractive investment alternative? Why?
3. List three other items of financial or nonfinancial information that you would want to review before making an investment decision regarding the common stocks of these companies.

46. **Impact of Accounting Errors on Financial Ratios** (LO 5)

Following are examples of errors that can be made in processing accounting data. Listed next to each error is a financial ratio.

		IMPACT OF ERROR ON FINANCIAL RATIO		
ACCOUNTING ERROR	FINANCIAL RATIO	*Increase*	*Decrease*	*No Effect*
a. Failing to record year-end adjusting entry for amortization of discount on bonds payable	Return on equity	___	___	___
b. Understating the estimated salvage value of a depreciable asset	Gross profit percentage	___	___	___
c. Failing to prepare a year-end adjusting entry to record interest revenue	Return on assets	___	___	___
d. Overstatement of prepaid expenses	Quick	___	___	___
e. Debiting the prepayment of an insurance premium near year-end to an expense account	Times interest earned	___	___	___
f. Understating the year-end estimate of uncollectible accounts receivable	Current	___	___	___
g. Recording a sales transaction twice	Return on assets	___	___	___

Required:

Indicate whether each error overstates, understates, or has no impact on the financial ratio with which it is coupled.

45. No check figures

46. No check figures

47. **Comprehensive Financial Statement Analysis** (LO 5)
    Following are income statements and balance sheets for three recent years for
    Tulsa Corporation.

TULSA CORPORATION
INCOME STATEMENTS
FOR THE YEARS ENDED DECEMBER 31, 1994–1996

	1994	1995	1996
Sales*	$484,200	$523,000	$576,600
Cost of Goods Sold	234,300	259,200	291,000
Gross Profit	249,900	263,800	285,600
Operating Expenses	104,100	104,600	106,200
Operating Income	145,800	159,200	179,400
Other Revenue (Expense)†	12,000	5,400	11,300
Income before Income Tax	157,800	164,600	190,700
Income Tax Expense	63,100	65,800	76,200
Net Income	$ 94,700	$ 98,800	$114,500

* All of the company's sales are on a credit basis.
† Includes interest expense of the following amounts: 1994—$14,280, 1995—$11,220, and 1996—$9,180.

TULSA CORPORATION
BALANCE SHEETS
DECEMBER 31, 1994–1996

	1994	1995	1996
Assets			
Cash	$ 16,700	$ 21,500	$ 52,300
Accounts Receivable (net)	81,000	94,300	139,800
Inventory	52,500	56,000	58,200
Prepaid Expenses	6,200	4,600	5,600
Total Current Assets	156,400	176,400	255,900
Property, Plant &			
Equipment (net)	488,900	539,300	529,200
Total Assets	$645,300	$715,700	$785,100
Liabilities			
Accounts Payable	$ 71,400	$ 79,100	$ 81,200
Accrued Expenses	35,600	41,700	12,200
Total Current Liabilities	107,000	120,800	93,400
Bonds Payable	140,000	110,000	95,000
Total Liabilities	247,000	230,800	188,400
Stockholders' Equity			
Common Stock	5,000	5,000	6,000
Additional Paid-in Capital	62,000	62,000	99,000
Retained Earnings	331,300	417,900	491,700
Total Stockholders' Equity	398,300	484,900	596,700
Total Liabilities and			
Stockholders' Equity	$645,300	$715,700	$785,100

During all of 1994 and 1995, Tulsa Corporation had 100,000 shares of common stock outstanding. During 1996, the company had 120,000 shares of common stock outstanding. Following are the market prices of Tulsa's common stock at the end of each year 1994 through 1996: 1994—$17.75, 1995—$20.25, and 1996—$26.50.

Listed next are the norms in Tulsa Corporation's industry for key financial ratios during the period 1994–1996.

Liquidity Ratios:

Current	1.5
Quick	.5

Leverage Ratios:

Long-term debt to equity	.6
Times interest earned	4.5

Activity Ratios:

Accounts receivable turnover	7.5
Age of receivables	48 days
Inventory turnover	4.0
Age of inventory	90 days
Total asset turnover	1.3

Profitability Ratios:

Profit margin percentage	13.6
Gross profit percentage	52.8
Return on assets	12.4
Return on equity	16.9

Market Strength Ratios:

Price-earnings	14
Market price to book value	3.1

47. 1.

1994	1995	1996
Current ratio		
1.5	1.5	2.7
Quick ratio		
0.9	1.0	2.1
Long-term debt to equity		
0.4	0.2	0.2
Times interest earned		
12.1	15.7	21.8
Acounts receivable turnover		
	6.0	4.9
Age of receivables		
	60 days	73 days
Inventory turnover		
	4.8	5.1
Age of inventory		
	75 days	71 days
Total asset turnover		
	0.8	0.8
Profit margin percentage		
19.6%	18.9%	19.9%
Gross profit percentage		
51.6%	50.4%	49.5%
Return on assets		
	16.2%	16.5%
Return on equity		
	22.4%	21.2%
Price-earnings		
18.7	20.5	27.9
Market price to book value per share		
4.5	4.2	5.3

Required:

1. Compute financial ratios for Tulsa Corporation for the period 1994–1996. (Compute all of the ratios for which an industry norm is provided. For certain ratios, sufficient data will only be available to compute ratios for 1995 and 1996.)
2. Analyze the financial ratios of Tulsa Corporation on a longitudinal basis. What positive and negative trends are apparent in the company's financial data?
3. Analyze the ratios of Tulsa Corporation by comparing each with the corresponding industry norm. Comment on which of the company's ratios are significantly different from the industry norm and whether these differences are favorable or unfavorable.
4. Identify unusual or unexpected relationships in Tulsa Corporation's financial data that you believe decision makers relying on this company's financial statements would want to further investigate.
5. Comment on the overall financial status of Tulsa Corporation as of December 31, 1996. In your opinion, did the company's financial status improve or deteriorate during the period 1994 through 1996? Explain.
6. List additional financial and nonfinancial information you would want to obtain regarding Tulsa Corporation before you reach a final conclusion concerning the company's future prospects.

48. Earnings Quality (LO 6)

Monnett Enterprises and Page Company are two firms in the same industry. These two firms have approximately the same annual revenues and total assets. Following is the most recent income statement of each firm.

	MONNETT ENTERPRISES	PAGE COMPANY
Sales	$6,727,800	$6,638,900
Cost of Goods Sold	3,190,200	3,385,100
Gross Profit	3,537,600	3,253,800
Operating Expenses:		
Selling & General	424,600	456,700
Depreciation	305,000	394,000
Operating Income	2,808,000	2,403,100
Other Revenue (Expense)	(34,200)	53,700
Income before Income Tax	2,773,800	2,456,800
Income Tax Expense	1,109,500	982,700
Net Income	$1,664,300	$1,474,100
Earnings Per Share	$1.66	$1.47
Recent Market Price of Common Stock	$18.50	$16.75

Page Company uses the LIFO inventory costing method and an accelerated depreciation method, while Monnett Enterprises uses FIFO inventory costing and the straight-line depreciation method. If Page had used the FIFO method during this particular year, the company's cost of goods sold would have been reduced by $240,000. If Page had used the straight-line depreciation method, its depreciation expense for the year would have been reduced by $70,000. Both firms have an effective income tax rate of approximately 40 percent.

Required:

1. Define earnings quality.
2. Prepare a revised income statement for Page Company for the year in question, assuming it had used the FIFO inventory costing method and the straight-line depreciation method. Compute Page's profit margin percentage and gross profit percentage for both sets of income statement data. Also, compute Monnett Enterprises' profit margin percentage and gross profit percentage.
3. Which of these two companies was more profitable during the year in question? Explain.
4. If Page Company had issued the revised income statement you prepared, do you believe that the market price of its common stock would have been affected? Explain.

48. 2.	Profit margin %	Gross profit %
Page		
As reported	22.2%	49.0%
Revised	25.0%	52.6%
Monnett	24.7%	52.6%

CASES

49. Managing Earnings

In 1985, the Securities and Exchange Commission (SEC) charged that Oak Industries, Inc., a California-based firm, was "managing" its earnings (Securities and Exchange Commission, *Accounting and Auditing Enforcement Release No. 63*, 25 June 1985). In both 1980 and 1981, Oak Industries reported record earnings.

However, the company's earnings for those years would have been higher if company officials had not intentionally overstated certain expenses.

Required:

1. Identify reasons that a company might intentionally overstate expenses during a given accounting period.
2. Does the conservatism principle permit business entities to intentionally overstate expenses and understate revenues? Explain.
3. Is it ethical for business executives to intentionally overstate their firm's expenses or understate its revenues? Defend your answer.

50. **Analyzing International Financial Statements**

    Problems 38 and 44 present recent income statements and balance sheets, respectively, for The News Corporation, a large Australian conglomerate. As pointed out repeatedly in this text, accounting and financial reporting rules and practices vary considerably from country to country. This is true even of countries that have similar political and social systems, such as Australia and the United States.

    Required:

    1. Review the financial statements of The News Corporation that are presented in Problems 38 and 44. Prepare a list of unusual or unfamiliar features of these financial statements that you have not observed in the financial statements of U.S. companies.
    2. Research the accounting and financial reporting rules applied by Australian companies. Identify the key differences between these rules and those applied by U.S. firms.
    3. Write a brief memo to an individual who is considering investing in an Australian company. Inform this individual of key differences in the accounting and financial reporting practices of Australian and U.S. firms. Indicate in the memo how these differences may cause the financial statement data of Australian firms to differ from the financial statement data of comparable U.S. firms.

51. **Stock Market Prices and Financial Data**

    Sears, Roebuck and Co. is one of the most recognizable corporate names in the United States. This company's common stock is listed on stock exchanges around the world, including exchanges in Great Britain, Switzerland, Japan, and Germany. In the mid-1990s, the company had approximately 400 million shares of common stock outstanding which were owned by nearly 300,000 stockholders. Because of the prominence and size of this firm, its financial data and key developments affecting its operations are closely monitored by thousands of sophisticated investors such as financial analysts of large brokerage firms. Given how rigorously this company is monitored, you might expect there to be little variance in the short-term market prices of its common stock. However, in a span of less than four years in the early 1990s, Sears' common stock traded in a range of $22 per share to more than $60 per share. In 1990 alone, the company's stock traded in a range from $22 to $42 per share. The following year, the stock's price ranged from $24 to $43 per share.

    Required:

    1. Why do the market prices of common stocks of even the largest corporations fluctuate significantly over a short period of time?

2. Is it possible to identify the "true" value of large corporations and their common stocks at any given point in time? Explain.

3. How do investors use accounting data to gain insight on the economic value of a corporation and its common stock?

PROJECTS

52. The Big Bath Theory

In recent years, the "big bath theory" has been discussed in the business press. According to this theory, when companies are experiencing a very poor year profit-wise, they often overstate their expenses and losses for that year—that is, they take a "big bath." By taking all of its "lumps" in one year, a company in such a situation can more easily return to a profitable status the following year.

Required:

1. Identify articles published in recent years that directly or indirectly address the big bath theory.

2. Find at least one example of a company that apparently, or at least allegedly, took a "big bath."

3. Prepare a written report that summarizes the key issues raised in the articles you identified that focus on the big bath theory. Also include in your report the circumstances surrounding the "big bath" case you identified in Part 2. Identify the company, its location and principal line or lines of business, and the apparent or alleged activities it engaged in that were consistent with the big bath theory.

53. Financial Statement Analysis for Investors

Each member of your project group should select a publicly owned company whose common stock he or she believes is an attractive investment. Each member should select his or her company independently of the other group members.

Required:

1. Each group member will obtain a recent set of financial statements for the company he or she selected. Each group member will analyze the financial data of his or her firm by applying the techniques discussed in this chapter, including trend analysis, the preparation of common-sized financial statements, and ratio analysis.

2. Each group member should also prepare a brief summary of key nonfinancial information relevant to the company he or she selected. An impending merger, the release of new products, a move into international markets, and the hiring of new executives are a few examples of key nonfinancial items of information that should be obtained and documented for the company selected by each group member. This information may be obtained from the given firm's annual reports, from articles in recent business periodicals, from investment advisory services, or other relevant sources.

3. After each group member has obtained and analyzed the information collected in Parts 1 and 2 for his or her firm, the group should meet and review and discuss this information. The purpose of the group's discussion will be to identify one firm, among the several identified by group members, whose common stock is the most attractive investment.

4. A written report should be prepared by the group. This report should document the individual companies selected by group members and provide a

brief summary of the key financial and nonfinancial information collected for each of these companies. The final section of the report should explain how and why the group selected one of these companies' common stock as the most attractive investment alternative.

5. One group member should be prepared to present a brief overview of the group's written report to the remainder of the class.

54. Analyzing Investment Advice

Contact a stockbroker and ask him or her to identify two common stocks that are presently recommended by the broker's firm.

Required:

1. Obtain the most recent financial statements available for the firms whose common stocks were recommended by the stockbroker you contacted.

2. Analyze the financial statements of these firms using the techniques discussed in this chapter. Also, identify key nonfinancial information that provides insight on the future prospects of each firm. This information may be obtained from the firms' annual reports, from articles in recent business periodicals, from investment advisory services, or other relevant sources.

3. Write a report summarizing your research. Identify in this report the firms you researched, their locations, and their principal lines of business. Include in your report your analyses of the firms' financial data and the key nonfinancial information you collected regarding these firms. Conclude your report by indicating whether you agree that these firms' common stocks are attractive investments.

APPENDIX

MICHAELS STORES INC.
ANNUAL REPORT

MICHAELS STORES INC. ANNUAL REPORT 1994

NUMBER OF STORES AT FISCAL YEAR-END   28% CAGR

Year	Stores
94	380
93	220
92	168
91	140
90	137
89	122
88	106
87	96
86	51
85	41

NET SALES (in millions)   33% CAGR

Year	Net Sales
94	$995
93	$620
92	$493
91	$411
90	$362
89	$290
88	$250
87	$167
86	$116
85	$76

EARNINGS PER SHARE   30% CAGR

Year	Earnings Per Share
94	$1.97**
93	$1.52
92	$1.21
91	$0.87*
90	$0.57
89	$0.00
88	$0.50
87	$0.50
86	$0.35
85	$0.19

* Before extraordinary item
** Excluding store closing and conversion costs

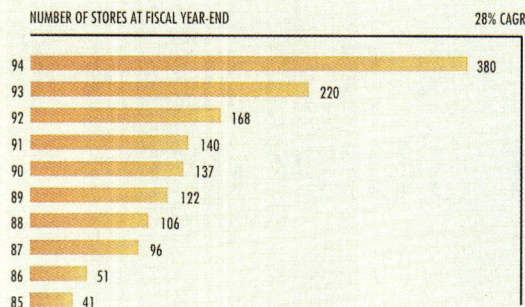

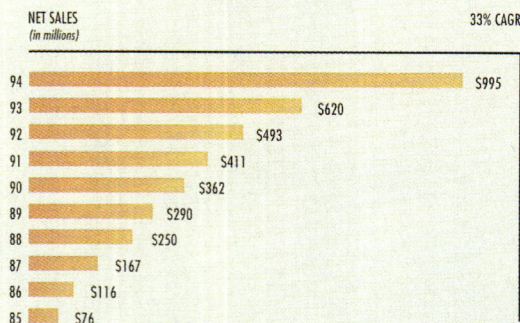

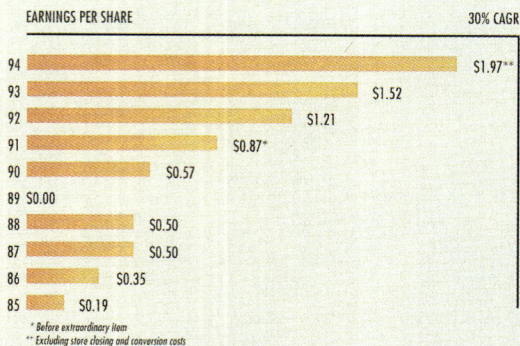

Michaels Stores, Inc. is the nation's leading specialty retailer of arts, crafts, and decorative products. Stores contain over 30,000 items, including a wide selection of picture framing materials and services, silk and dried flowers, hobby and art supplies, creative crafts, and party, seasonal and holiday merchandise.

Michaels has become the only nationwide industry player. Last year a major fall promotion featuring television ads on five cable networks took us into over 100 million homes. Our newspaper ads in 42 states are delivered to 35 million homes.

In all parts of the country, Michaels stores are imagination destinations. Knowledgeable associates and other experts conduct classes and demonstrations that both teach and provide hands-on experience and help make us a fun place to shop. Michaels Kids Club is cultivating a new generation of loyal young customers.

We became a publicly-held company in 1984 with 12 stores, mostly in Texas, and ended 1994 with 380 stores in 41 states and Canada. During that time period, the stock price rose from $2.50 to $35.00.

FINANCIAL HIGHLIGHTS

(In thousands except per share and store data)

	Fiscal Year				
	1994	*1993*	*1992*	*1991*	*1990*[1]
Results of Operations:					
Net sales	**$994,563**	$619,688	$493,159	$410,899	$362,028
Operating income	**64,036**	41,356	34,263	25,643	20,694
Income before extraordinary item	**35,647**	26,287	20,378	10,739 [2]	5,855
Earnings per share	**1.76**	1.52	1.21	.87 [2]	.57
Stores Open at End of Period	**380**	220	168	140	137
Balance Sheet Data:					
Current assets	**$418,532**	$291,012	$170,021	$125,873	$ 84,572
Total assets	**686,026**	397,830	322,099	130,913	144,238
Working capital	**232,442**	181,816	104,462	74,786	44,080
Long-term debt	**138,050**	97,750	97,750	—	52,983
Total liabilities	**330,109**	212,415	166,822	54,614	97,623
Shareholders' equity	**355,917**	185,415	155,277	126,299	46,615

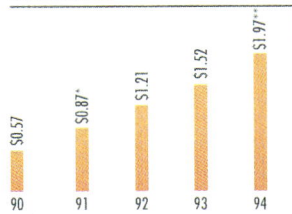

(1) Fiscal 1990 was a 53-week fiscal year.
(2) Before extraordinary item related to early retirement of debt.

NET SALES *(in millions)*
90 $362.0 | 91 $410.9 | 92 $493.2 | 93 $619.7 | 94 $994.6

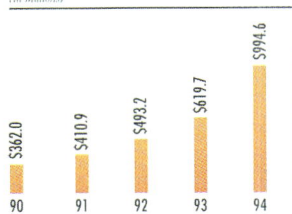

EARNINGS PER SHARE
90 $0.57 | 91 $0.87* | 92 $1.21 | 93 $1.52 | 94 $1.97**
* Before extraordinary item
** Excluding store closing and conversion costs

STORES ADDED
90 17 | 91 4 | 92 28 | 93 54 | 94 184

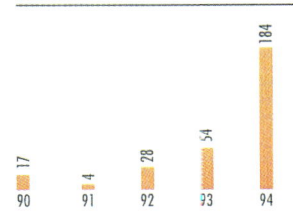

OPERATING INCOME *(in millions)*
90 $20.7 | 91 $25.6 | 92 $34.3 | 93 $41.4 | 94 $64.0

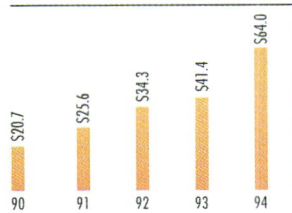

AVERAGE SALES PER FULL YEAR STORE *(in millions)*
90 $2.8 | 91 $2.9 | 92 $3.2 | 93 $3.2 | 94 $3.2

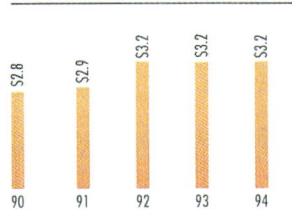

1994 DEPARTMENT SALES
20% | 22% | 10% | 14% | 15% | 19%
- Hobby, party, needlecraft, ribbon
- Picture framing
- Seasonal & promotional
- Art materials
- Silk & dried flowers & plants
- General crafts & wearable art

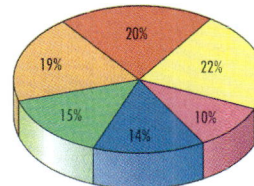

NET INCOME *(in millions)*
90 $5.9 | 91 $10.7* | 92 $20.4 | 93 $26.3 | 94 $35.6
* Before extraordinary item

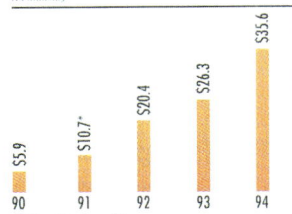

TOTAL EQUITY *(in millions)*
90 $46.6 | 91 $126.3 | 92 $155.3 | 93 $185.4 | 94 $355.9

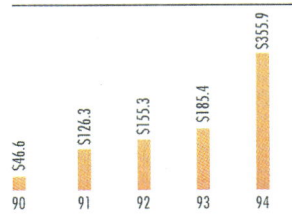

FINANCIALS — NET WORTH UP FROM $185 TO $356 MILLION

1994 sales of $995 million were up 60% over fiscal 1993 and lifted us to the billion dollar retail level. Same-store sales for 1994 were up a healthy 7%.

Operating income for the year increased 72% to $71 million before a one-time second quarter charge for store closing and conversion costs related to an acquisition. Operating margin expanded to 7.1% of sales from 6.7% last year.

Excluding the second quarter charge, income increased by 52% to $40 million and earnings per share increased by 30% to $1.97.

FORTUNE

AMERICA'S FASTEST GROWING COMPANIES

★ ★ ★ ★ ★

GROWTH — OVER 1.5 MILLION FRAMED PICTURES DELIVERED

In 1994, we grew from 220 stores to 380 in 41 states and Canada. We completed four strategic acquisitions which added 100 stores after some closings in overlapping markets and opened 61 new locations. Our acquisitions provided an immediate and substantial market presence in the Northwest and the Northeast.

Three acquisitions in early 1994 enhanced our market position in the Northwest. Treasure House, Oregon Craft, and

H&H Craft were fully converted last summer and recorded successful first-year sales as Michaels stores.

In July we acquired our largest competitor, Leewards Creative Crafts. Leewards provided Michaels with prime real estate and a market presence in the Northeast. Their store sizes were almost identical to ours, their management styles were similar, and we were fortunate to inherit over 3,000 trained associates plus Dave Bolen as a new Executive Vice President.

Sam Wyly. Jack Bush. Charles Wyly

We're proud of how we executed the challenge of absorbing a chain approximately 40% our size within the deadline imposed by the approaching Christmas selling season. 21 stores in overlapping markets conducted successful clearance sales and were closed by September 30. The remaining stores hosted "The Greatest Craft Sale Ever" to clear out merchandise that was inconsistent with the standard Michaels assortment. We simultaneously upstyled these stores to the Michaels format. We expanded the art and floral departments, hired floral designers, added demonstration booths and party departments – increasing assortments by about 10,000 items per store.

In addition to our acquisitions, we opened 61 new stores, including 6 in Toronto, bringing our Canadian store count to 8, and opened our first Alaska store in Anchorage. We added

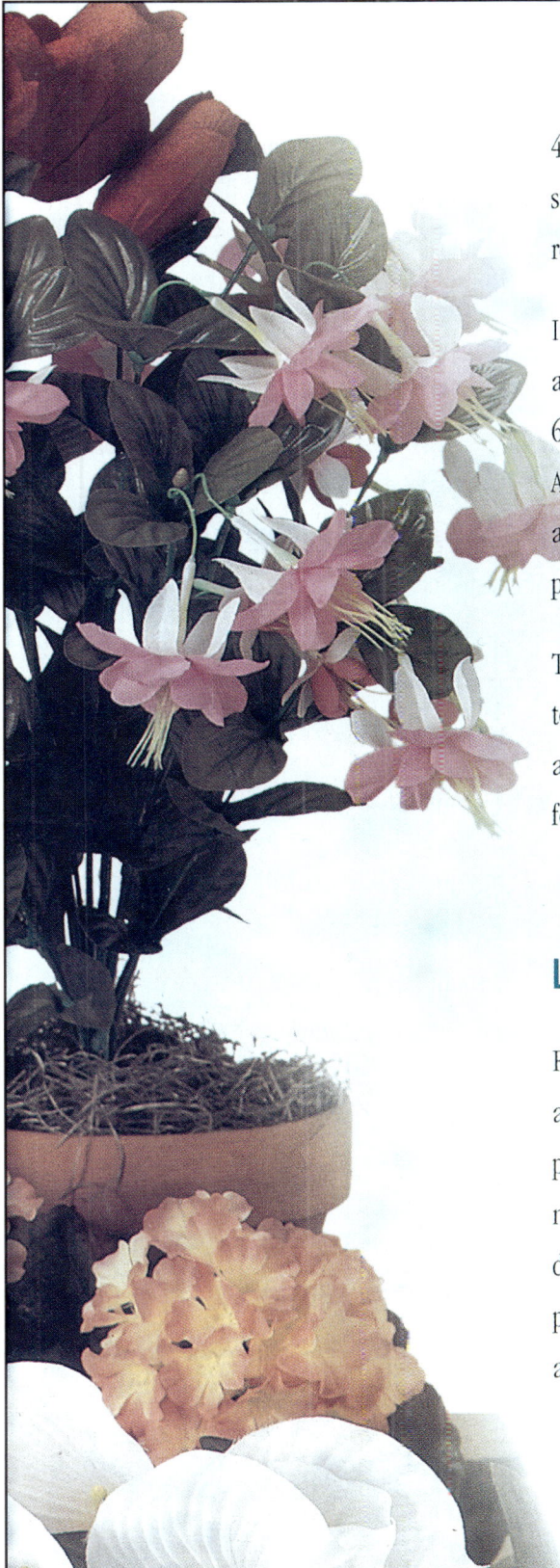

4 Craft & Floral Warehouses around the country, and to make sure our existing stores remain fresh and inviting, we relocated 6 stores and expanded another 8.

In March we announced the purchase of Aaron Brothers, a chain in California with about $60 million in sales — 65% in picture framing and 30% in art supplies. With the Aaron Brothers store format (about 7,000 selling square feet and 6,500 items), we will enter areas for which the Michaels prototype is inappropriate.

To support the additional demand for distribution we added a total of about 500,000 square feet to our Kentucky, California, and Texas distribution centers and leased a 500,000 square foot distribution center in Florida.

LEADERSHIP — MANAGERS MUST MANAGE

Rapid growth is creating new career opportunities for our associates. In 1994, 114 of our hourly associates were promoted to assistant store managers, 89 assistants to store managers, 6 store managers to district managers, and 3 district managers to regional managers. This year we will promote 125 hourly associates to assistant manager and 100 assistants to store manager.

Last year over 200 associates participated in management training and development seminars, over 11,000 in gross margin training programs, and over 1,500 in frame shop training.

During 1994 we added 11 senior executives to the Michaels team in such key areas as operations, real estate, finance, information systems, distribution, and merchandise. They bring with them excellent track records at other high growth retailers.

Technology — EDI Is Here, Scanning Is Arriving

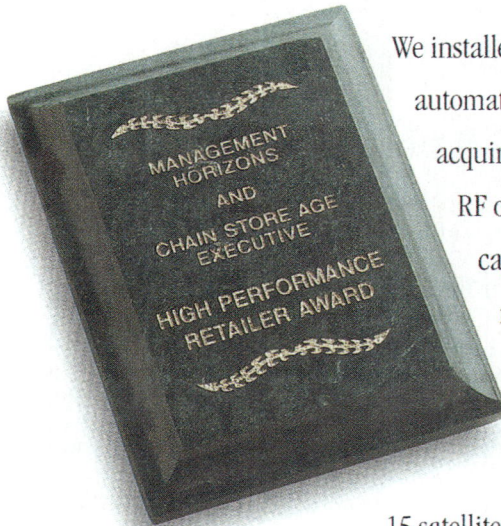

We installed in-store radio frequency (RF) ordering and automated custom framing systems in 166 new and acquired stores last year, so all stores have standardized RF ordering and automated custom framing capabilities. Each store has been converted to a new communication system that collects store orders and transmits corporate item and price changes. This provides more speed, accuracy, and flexibility in managing merchandise. 15 satellite systems that speed credit card approval and reduce phone costs were tested last year and about 250 stores will be converted in 1995.

Our new point-of-sale system with full item-level scanning, promotional price lookup, and sales audit capabilities has been tested in 23 stores. Most of our 1995 new stores will utilize these new systems, and we have selected 40 of our higher volume existing stores to be converted this summer. By the end of the year, 100 stores providing a nationwide cross-section of sales history will use this technology.

The sales information that is currently collected this way has already reduced the labor intensive sales item counting that was done manually. The new sales history will provide much better input for the purchase order and contribution analysis merchandising systems we installed in 1994. It ain't been easy, but we're getting there.

We are adding technology to our new Jacksonville, Florida distribution center that allows it to operate in a paperless environment. The first phase of a new store communication system will reduce by at least a third the number of forms our stores must complete, with an ultimate goal of a nearly paperless environment in the store. After four years of consistent technical progress by us and our vendors, we are now using EDI (electronic data interchange) for 70% of our distribution center purchases.

Service — The Purpose Of A Business Is To Create A Customer

We have worked to bond our relationship with our customers to ensure that their local Michaels store is a frequent destination. Our store layout includes a wide promotional aisle which is redesigned regularly with new attractions throughout the month. Customers seem to like the variety; our mystery shop scores (one way we audit our quality of service) in the store appearance category are consistently high.

In 1994, each Michaels store offered about 20 demonstrations a week. 30 classes are offered each month for projects requiring more detailed instruction. Each store also distributes free project sheets ("recipes" for customers to take home and follow while assembling their creations). Our Kids Club, with 260,000 members, teaches children how to create their own projects.

Demonstrations, classes, and project sheets are neither new nor unique to Michaels, so we work very hard to improve their quality and polish. The demonstration schedule is printed in each weekly Michaels newspaper ad. Vendors who recognized the value of these demonstrations provided almost a third of our demonstration materials and have even joined forces to create projects.

In 1995, we will sponsor regional seminars in which vendor representatives will train our store associates in the use of new

products and techniques, enabling our associates to quickly introduce them to our customers.

MERCHANDISING — OVER 3 MILLION SUNFLOWERS SOLD

Customer value results from how we tie together all the purchasing and sales events in the retail channel.   We are now developing about a third of our merchandise. Our buyers work up to a year in advance to help vendors develop their product lines, ensuring that Michaels receives first dibs on new products. This early involvement allows the simultaneous design and selection of coordinating accessories and a head start in creating promotional activities that fit.

Our Christmas *Holiday Elegance* collection is a good example of how we unite products and events into one seamless package. Holiday decorations, tree ornaments, silk florals, ribbons, vases, and accessories are offered in coordinated color schemes and patterns, which allow our customers to select their favorite components and combine them to produce their own unique holiday decor.

In 1992 our merchants launched the sunflower invasion which has since swept across the USA. Your local Michaels

Doug Sullivan and Don Morris

store last summer offered silk sunflowers in a wide variety of sizes and shades, complemented by vases and ribbon with sunflower motifs, and solid-color accessories in coordinating shades. We have sold over three million sunflower-themed items since their introduction.

The Stern Stewart
PERFORMANCE 1000

Product design and direct sourcing means products can be developed to our exact specifications and delivered more quickly, resulting in better prices and better quality. Direct sourcing is particularly beneficial for trend items, such as the leather trunks and antique leather books that are currently popular. We offer department store quality at half the cost, securing one-time buys delivered to the stores at the peak of the trend and in just enough quantities to sell through.

Since 1990, we have reduced the total number of Michaels vendors from 4,000 to 1,000, which allows us to focus more on individual relationships. More than 80% of our 1994 overseas purchase dollars were made on open terms, rather than letters of credit, which significantly lowers handling costs for us and our vendors. Last fall, our vendors contributed to the *Michaels Explosion*, a major marketing effort, providing dollars, product rebates,

Bob Rudman and Dave Bolen

and related promotional tie-ins featured in our newspaper ads and on national television. The Family Channel, Discovery, Lifetime, USA, and TNN network ads were seen in over 100 million homes. The promotion was so successful that vendor support in 1995 will increase by 50%.

Effective advertising helps promote craft and hobby project ideas among customers. Just as we are leaders in customer service and product development, nobody else in the industry has the strength or in-house talent to market like Michaels. Circulation of the *Michaels Arts & Crafts* magazine increased by 65%. We will invest $65 million ($3 per share) in 1995 advertising to deliver over 500 million circulars and ads in over 275 newspapers in 42 states.

THE FUTURE — TAKE THE ROAD LESS TRAVELED

Carl Steidtmann, in the March 1995 issue of *The Retail Economist* published by Management Horizons, wrote that "retailing is on the precipice of another shift in the value curve . . . [which] will shift the creation of value from distribution to planning and relationship building." We share Dr. Steidtmann's vision and have been positioning ourselves accordingly.

We will continue to emphasize customer service and to look for innovative ways to better serve our customers. Our custom floral and custom framing departments are good examples of changes we are making. We have increased the quality of both the flowers and frames offered while expanding the services offered by our floral designers and framers. Now custom floral and custom framing are two of our most profitable departments.

We will open 70 new stores in 1995 and will relocate or expand or shrink about three dozen in a continuing effort to be in the right place at the right size. Our first small-market stores (about 12,500 feet) will open in metropolitan areas of less than 100,000 people near larger cities that already have Michaels stores so that we start with name recognition. We will be participating in different markets with several different sized stores with varying assortments and varying competitive mixes of location, service, assortment, price, and advertising, seeking to deliver the best value mix in the eye of the local consumer.

Our report cards have been heavily expansion and sales driven and sensitive to same-store sales and individual store profit. We are now focusing on local market strength and return on investment in each market with whatever cannibalization called for. Our buyers and store managers will be learning more about cost of capital and economic value added.

NOVEMBER 28, 1994

FORTUNE

AMERICA'S BEST

Wealth Creators

MICHAELS STORES AS OF APRIL 28, 1995

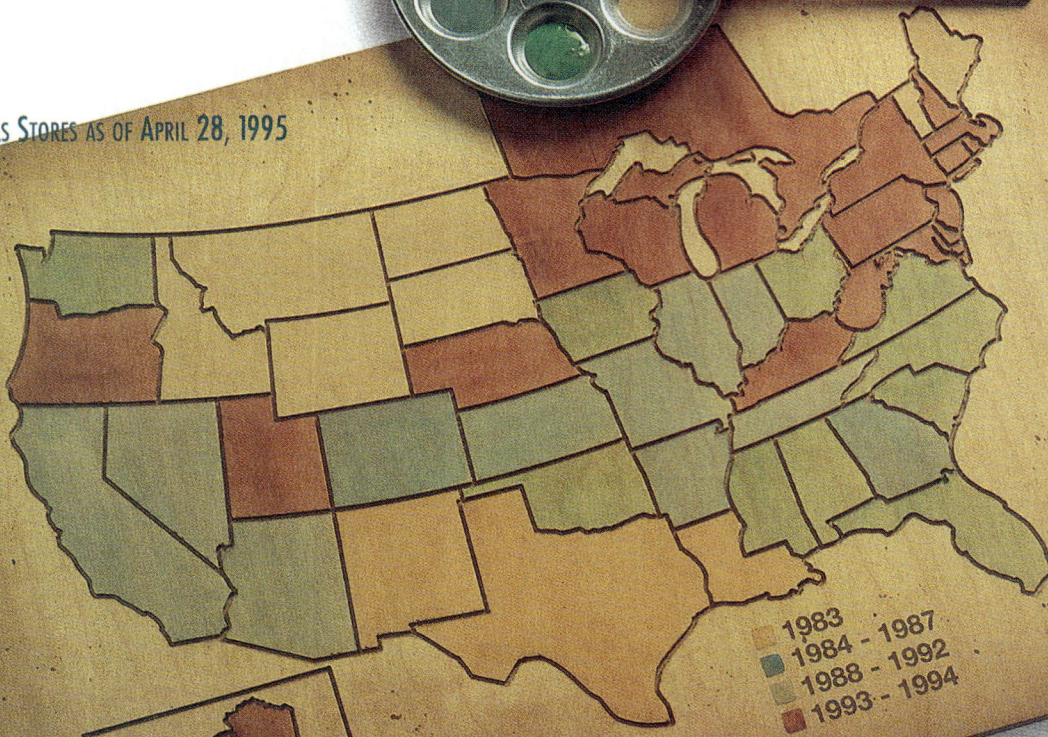

1983
1984 - 1987
1988 - 1992
1993 - 1994

395 MICHAELS STORES IN 41 STATES, CANADA AND PUERTO RICO

UNITED STATES		
ALABAMA	5	
ALASKA	1	
ARIZONA	11	
ARKANSAS	3	
CALIFORNIA	77	
COLORADO	9	
CONNECTICUT	1	
FLORIDA	14	
GEORGIA	16	
ILLINOIS	21	
INDIANA	9	
IOWA	6	
KANSAS	3	
KENTUCKY	3	

LOUISIANA	4
MARYLAND	1
MASSACHUSETTS	8
MICHIGAN	17
MINNESOTA	9
MISSISSIPPI	1
MISSOURI	11
NEBRASKA	1
NEVADA	4
NEW HAMPSHIRE	2
NEW JERSEY	7
NEW MEXICO	2
NEW YORK	10
NORTH CAROLINA	10
OHIO	19

OKLAHOMA	7
OREGON	9
PENNSYLVANIA	9
RHODE ISLAND	1
SOUTH CAROLINA	4
TENNESSEE	8
TEXAS	34
UTAH	4
VIRGINIA	5
WASHINGTON	12
WEST VIRGINIA	1
WISCONSIN	6
CANADA	
ONTARIO	8
PUERTO RICO	2

AARON BROTHERS STORE LOCATIONS

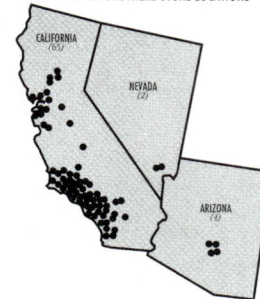

CALIFORNIA
(65)
NEVADA
(2)
ARIZONA
(4)

MANAGEMENT'S DISCUSSION AND ANALYSIS OF FINANCIAL CONDITION AND RESULTS OF OPERATIONS

GENERAL

In fiscal years 1992, 1993 and 1994, Michaels Stores, Inc. (the "Company") added 28, 54 and 184 Michaels stores, respectively, before considering store closures. During these periods, the Company obtained a substantial portion of its sales increases from stores added during, or subsequent to, the prior comparable period and thus not yet included in comparable store sales comparisons. During these periods, sales from these newer stores accounted for approximately 56%, 88% and 93%, respectively, of aggregate sales increases. The Company intends to add approximately 70 to 75 Michaels stores in fiscal 1995, of which 15 stores have been opened as of April 28, 1995. These new stores do not include the 71-store acquisition of Aaron Brothers Holdings, Inc. ("Aaron Brothers") completed in March 1995. In fiscal 1995 and beyond, sales increases from newly opened and acquired stores will depend in part on the availability of suitable store sites, the rate of development of new stores, and the Company's ability to hire and train qualified managers.

RESULTS OF OPERATIONS

The following table shows the percentage of net sales that each item in the Consolidated Statements of Income represents. This table should be read in conjunction with the following discussion and with the Company's Consolidated Financial Statements, including the related notes.

	Fiscal Year		
	1994	1993	1992
Net sales	**100.0%**	100.0%	100.0%
Cost of sales and occupancy expense	**64.9**	65.2	65.6
Selling, general and administrative expense	**28.0**	28.1	27.5
Store closing and conversion costs	**0.7**	0.0	0.0
Operating income	**6.4**	6.7	6.9
Interest expense	**0.9**	1.0	0.0
Other (income) and expense, net	**(0.2)**	(1.2)	0.1
Income before income taxes	**5.7**	6.9	6.8
Provision for income taxes	**2.1**	2.7	2.7
Net income	**3.6%**	4.2%	4.1%

In the discussion below, all percentages given for expense items are calculated as a percentage of net sales for the applicable year.

FOR FISCAL 1994 COMPARED TO FISCAL 1993

Net sales in the fiscal year ended January 29, 1995 ("1994"), increased $374.9 million, or 60%, over the fiscal year ended January 30, 1994 ("1993"). The results for 1994 included sales of 160 stores (net of 24 closures) that were opened or acquired during the year. During 1994, sales of the newer stores accounted for $348.6 million of the increase. Comparable store sales increased seven percent in 1994 compared to the prior year. The Company expects to achieve comparable store sales increases for 1995 although fluctuations in the rate of increase may occur during the year.

Cost of sales and occupancy expense for 1994 decreased by 0.3% compared to 1993 due primarily to increases in sales of higher margin custom framing and floral services, an improvement in the gross margin achieved on seasonal merchandise sales and greater margin contributions from new and acquired stores, due principally to new store volume discounts from vendors. This improvement in gross margin was partially offset by an increase in occupancy expenses driven by the Company's shift to new stores with higher average selling square footage than existing stores, coupled with the Company's expansion into states with higher occupancy costs such as New York, Massachusetts and Connecticut. This trend of higher occupancy costs in new stores will continue during 1995, and may offset improvements, if any, in cost of sales as a percentage of sales.

Selling, general and administrative expense decreased by 0.1% in 1994 from 1993. The decrease was due primarily to continued leveraging of the Company's general and administrative expenditures over a larger revenue base. Improvements in these expenses as a percentage of sales during 1995 will depend in part on the level of sales increases attained.

Interest expense for 1994 was $9.1 million compared to $6.4 million in 1993. The increase was due to higher bank borrowings coupled with higher interest rates than in 1993. The Company expects interest expense during 1995 to increase over 1994 levels.

Other income (net of other expense) was $2.2 million in 1994 compared to $7.7 million in 1993. This year's decrease from last year was due to a decline in the Company's average investment portfolio, which was used to fund the store expansion program.

The effective tax rate was reduced to 37.6% in 1994 from 38.4% in 1993 primarily due to the Company's participation in tax advantaged programs, partially offset by increases in non-deductible goodwill amortization. The Company expects the effective tax rate to increase slightly during 1995 due to higher non-deductible goodwill amortization over 1994 levels.

FOR FISCAL 1993 COMPARED TO FISCAL 1992

Net sales in 1993 increased $126.5 million, or 26%, over the fiscal year ended January 31, 1993 ("1992"). The results for 1993 included sales of 54 stores added during the year. During 1993, sales of the newer stores accounted for $111.3 million of the increase. Comparable store sales increased three percent in 1993 compared to the prior year.

Cost of sales and occupancy expense for 1993 decreased by 0.4% compared to 1992 due primarily to increases in sales of higher margin custom framing and floral services, an improvement in the gross margin achieved on seasonal merchandise sales, greater margin contributions from new stores, and an increase in new store volume discounts from vendors. This improvement in gross margin was partially offset by an increase in occupancy expenses driven by the Company's shift to new stores with higher average selling square footage than existing stores, coupled with the Company's expansion into states with higher occupancy costs such as New York, Ohio, Minnesota and Michigan.

Selling, general and administrative expense increased by 0.6% in 1993 from 1992. The increase was due to expenses associated with the Company's new store opening program and additional payroll attributed to the increase in custom framing and floral services, offset in part by a decrease in general and administrative expenditures, as a percentage of sales, which were spread over a larger revenue base in 1993.

Interest expense for 1993 was $6.4 million compared to $0.3 million in 1992. The increase was due primarily to the issuance of convertible subordinated debt in January 1993.

Other income (net of other expense) was $7.7 million in 1993 compared to other expense of $0.5 million in 1992, as the Company earned substantial interest, dividends and capital gains on its investment portfolio during 1993.

The effective tax rate was reduced to 38.4% in 1993 from 39.1% in 1992 primarily due to the Company's investments in tax-advantaged securities.

LIQUIDITY AND CAPITAL RESOURCES

The Company acquired 99 stores, net of closures, and opened 61 stores during fiscal 1994. Capital expenditures for these stores, and, to a lesser extent, the remodeling, expansion and relocation of certain existing stores, the expansion of two distribution facilities, and information system enhancements, amounted to $68.1 million in fiscal 1994.

In July 1994, the Company paid $7.9 million in cash as part of the total consideration provided to acquire Leewards Creative Crafts, Inc. ("Leewards"), and repaid $39.6 million of Leewards' outstanding debt.

Also in July 1994, the Company completed a public offering of 2,353,432 shares of Michaels common stock. The $72.2 million of net proceeds from the sale were used to reduce outstanding bank debt.

In March 1995, the Company acquired the 71-store chain operated by Aaron Brothers. In addition to this acquisition, the Company plans to add approximately 70 to 75 stores, including Craft and Floral Warehouse ("CFW") stores, additional stores in Canada, stores in Puerto Rico, and possibly stores acquired through other minor acquisitions during 1995. The Company anticipates the costs of adding stores (excluding CFW stores) to be approximately $300,000 to $400,000 per store, which includes furniture, fixtures, equipment, and pre-opening expenses. Leasehold improvement costs tend to vary among locations. The inventory investment associated with the typical new store ranges from approximately $450,000 to $600,000 depending on the store size, operating format, and date opened; however, due to the Company's typical payment terms and inventory turnover, the Company's vendors, in effect, finance a significant component of this initial inventory investment. In addition to the new store opening costs and expenses, the Company expects to spend an additional $13.0 to $16.0 million on store renovation, the continued

development of new point-of-sale and merchandising systems, and the expansion of the Company's distribution network in fiscal 1995.

Inventory per store has increased for several years. While the Company believes that this inventory trend enhances its ability to generate continued increases in comparable store sales, it intends to manage its inventories during the next year such that inventory per store in January 1996 may be lower than it was in January 1995.

At January 29, 1995, the Company had working capital of $232.4 million, compared to $181.8 million at January 30, 1994. The Company currently has a bank credit agreement ("Credit Agreement") which includes an unsecured line of credit and provides for the issuance of letters of credit. Borrowings under the Credit Agreement, which expires June 16, 1997, are limited to the lesser of $150 million or the Company's borrowing base (as defined in the Credit Agreement), in either case minus the aggregate amount of letters of credit. As of January 29, 1995, the Company had $93.5 million in available unused credit capacity under the Credit Agreement.

In March 1995, the Company paid approximately $5.3 million in cash and retired $19.7 million in outstanding debt of Aaron Brothers. The Credit Agreement has recently been amended to provide a $50 million increase in borrowing capacity, due primarily to the credit capacity used to retire the Aaron Brothers debt and fund its working capital needs of approximately $5.0 million, and to extend its term to June 1998. Management believes that the Company has sufficient working capital, operating cash flows, and available unused credit capacity to sustain current growth plans.

OTHER MATTERS

The Company's business is seasonal in nature with higher store sales in the third and fourth quarters. Historically, the fourth quarter, which includes the Christmas selling season, has accounted for approximately 37% of the Company's sales and approximately 55% of its operating income.

Management considers the effect of inflation on 1994 results and its projected effect on 1995 financial results to be nominal.

CONSOLIDATED BALANCE SHEETS

(In thousands except share data)

Michaels Stores, Inc.

	January 29, 1995	January 30, 1994
ASSETS		
Current assets:		
Cash and equivalents	$ 1,907	$ 867
Marketable securities	15,002	67,956
Merchandise inventories	375,096	206,185
Deferred income taxes	15,002	2,952
Prepaid expenses and other	11,525	13,052
Total current assets	418,532	291,012
Property and equipment, at cost	204,032	119,555
Less accumulated depreciation	(62,228)	(43,683)
	141,804	75,872
Costs in excess of net assets of acquired operations, net	117,377	23,503
Other assets	8,313	7,443
	125,690	30,946
	$686,026	$397,830
LIABILITIES AND SHAREHOLDERS' EQUITY		
Current liabilities:		
Accounts payable	$103,649	$ 42,309
Short-term bank debt	—	13,000
Income taxes payable	—	7,866
Accrued liabilities and other	82,441	46,021
Total current liabilities	186,090	109,196
Bank debt	41,100	—
Convertible subordinated notes	96,950	97,750
Deferred income taxes and other	5,969	5,469
Total long-term liabilities	144,019	103,219
	330,109	212,415
Commitments and contingencies		
Shareholders' equity:		
Preferred stock, $.10 par value, 2,000,000 shares authorized, none issued	—	—
Common stock, $.10 par value, 50,000,000 shares authorized, 21,354,167 issued and outstanding (16,697,357 in fiscal 1993)	2,135	1,670
Additional paid-in capital	244,561	107,168
Retained earnings	109,221	76,577
Total shareholders' equity	355,917	185,415
	$686,026	$397,830

See accompanying notes to consolidated financial statements.

CONSOLIDATED STATEMENTS OF INCOME
(In thousands except per share data)

Michaels Stores, Inc.

	Fiscal Year		
	1994	1993	1992
Net sales	**$994,563**	$619,688	$493,159
Cost of sales and occupancy expense	**644,737**	403,869	323,577
Selling, general and administrative expense	**278,716**	174,463	135,319
Store closing and conversion costs	**7,074**	—	—
Operating income	**64,036**	41,356	34,263
Interest expense	**9,103**	6,378	263
Other (income) and expense, net	**(2,226)**	(7,666)	538
Income before income taxes	**57,159**	42,644	33,462
Provision for income taxes	**21,512**	16,357	13,084
Net income	**$ 35,647**	$ 26,287	$ 20,378
Earnings per common and common equivalent share:			
Primary	**$1.77**	$1.53	$1.22
Assuming full dilution	**$1.76**	$1.52	$1.21
Weighted average common and common equivalent shares outstanding:			
Primary	**20,146**	17,231	16,692
Assuming full dilution	**20,807**	19,809	16,853

See accompanying notes to consolidated financial statements.

CONSOLIDATED STATEMENTS OF CASH FLOWS

(In thousands)

Michaels Stores, Inc.

	Fiscal Year		
	1994	1993	1992
Operating activities:			
Net income	$ **35,647**	$ 26,287	$ 20,378
Adjustments:			
Depreciation and amortization	**21,512**	12,490	10,160
Other	**(501)**	(3,537)	466
Change in assets and liabilities excluding the effects of acquisitions:			
Merchandise inventories	**(134,671)**	(87,885)	(27,354)
Prepaid expenses and other	**5,747**	(6,358)	(451)
Deferred income taxes and other	**7,276**	(611)	(190)
Accounts payable	**37,065**	11,545	10,474
Income taxes payable	**(8,363)**	3,304	294
Accrued liabilities and other	**(1,979)**	5,830	3,032
Net change in assets and liabilities	**(94,925)**	(64,175)	(14,195)
Net cash (used in) provided by operating activities	**(38,267)**	(28,935)	16,809
Investing activities:			
Additions to property and equipment	**(68,106)**	(46,816)	(19,796)
Net proceeds from sales of marketable securities	**44,484**	17,807	(81,633)
Acquisitions and other	**(43,685)**	—	(1,853)
Net cash used in investing activities	**(67,307)**	(29,009)	(103,282)
Financing activities:			
Net borrowings under bank credit facilities	**28,100**	13,000	—
Net proceeds from issuance of long-term debt	**—**	—	94,636
Payment of other long-term liabilities	**(89)**	(115)	(216)
Proceeds from issuance of common stock	**78,603**	3,851	6,772
Net cash provided by financing activities	**106,614**	16,736	101,192
Net increase (decrease) in cash and equivalents	**1,040**	(41,208)	14,719
Cash and equivalents at beginning of year	**867**	42,075	27,356
Cash and equivalents at end of year	$ **1,907**	$ 867	$ 42,075
Cash payments for:			
Interest	$ **7,166**	$ 5,034	$ 222
Income taxes	**17,753**	11,620	8,087

See accompanying notes to consolidated financial statements.

21

CONSOLIDATED STATEMENTS OF SHAREHOLDERS' EQUITY

For the Three Years Ended January 29, 1995
(In thousands except share data)

Michaels Stores, Inc.

	Number of shares	Common stock	Additional paid-in capital	Retained earnings	Total
Balance at February 2, 1992	15,058,756	$1,506	$ 94,881	$ 29,912	$126,299
Exercise of stock options and warrants	1,300,191	129	6,643	—	6,772
Issuance of shares in an acquisition	115,383	12	1,816	—	1,828
Net income	—	—	—	20,378	20,378
Balance at January 31, 1993	16,474,330	1,647	103,340	50,290	155,277
Exercise of stock options	223,027	23	3,828	—	3,851
Net income	—	—	—	26,287	26,287
Balance at January 30, 1994	16,697,357	1,670	107,168	76,577	185,415
Adjustments for pooling-of-interests accounting in an acquisition	—	—	—	(1,157)	(1,157)
Issuance of shares in acquisitions	1,992,268	199	58,257	—	58,456
Proceeds from stock offering	2,353,432	235	71,980	—	72,215
Adjustment for change in fair value of marketable securities	—	—	—	(1,514)	(1,514)
Exercise of stock options and other	311,110	31	7,156	(332)	6,855
Net income	—	—	—	35,647	35,647
Balance at January 29, 1995	21,354,167	$2,135	$244,561	$109,221	$355,917

See accompanying notes to consolidated financial statements.

NOTES TO CONSOLIDATED FINANCIAL STATEMENTS

SUMMARY OF SIGNIFICANT ACCOUNTING POLICIES

Michaels Stores, Inc. (the "Company") owns and operates a chain of specialty retail stores. The Company reports on a 52/53-week fiscal year which ends on the Sunday closest to January 31; thus, fiscal 1994 ("1994"), fiscal 1993 ("1993") and fiscal 1992 ("1992"), ended on January 29, 1995, January 30, 1994 and January 31, 1993, respectively.

Consolidation

The consolidated financial statements include the accounts of the Company and all wholly-owned and majority-owned subsidiaries. All intercompany accounts and transactions have been eliminated.

Cash and Equivalents

Cash and equivalents are generally comprised of highly liquid instruments with original maturities of three months or less. Cash equivalents are carried at cost which approximates fair value.

Marketable Securities

Marketable securities are carried at fair value, based on quoted market prices or dealer quotes as of the last trading day of the fiscal year.

Merchandise Inventories

Store merchandise inventories are valued at the lower of average cost (determined by a retail method) or market. Distribution center inventories are valued at the lower of cost (determined by the first-in, first-out method) or market.

Property and Equipment

Depreciation is provided on a straight-line basis over the estimated useful lives of the assets.

Costs in Excess of Net Assets of Acquired Operations

Costs in excess of net assets of acquired operations are being amortized over 40 years on a straight-line basis. Accumulated amortization was $7,295,000 and $5,182,000 as of the end of 1994 and 1993, respectively. The Company assesses the recoverability of costs in excess of net assets acquired annually based on existing facts and circumstances. The Company measures the recoverability of this asset on an on-going basis based on projected earnings before interest, depreciation and amortization, on an undiscounted basis. Should the Company's

assessment indicate an impairment of this asset in the future, an appropriate write-down will be recorded.

Store Pre-Opening Costs

Store pre-opening costs are expensed in the fiscal year in which the store opens. In 1994, 1993 and 1992, the Company incurred $6,541,000, $4,893,000 and $2,377,000, respectively, of store pre-opening costs.

Earnings Per Share

Earnings per share data are based on the weighted average number of shares outstanding, including common stock equivalents and other dilutive securities. The assumed conversion of the convertible subordinated notes was dilutive for the fourth quarter and full year of both 1993 and 1994 and was therefore included in the calculation of fully diluted earnings per share data for those periods.

DETAIL OF CERTAIN BALANCE SHEET ACCOUNTS

	1994	1993
	(In thousands)	
Property and equipment:		
Land and buildings	$ 7,640	$ 7,500
Fixtures and equipment	145,253	87,443
Leasehold improvements	51,139	24,612
	$204,032	$119,555
Accrued liabilities and other:		
Salaries, bonuses and other payroll-related costs	$ 21,527	$ 13,498
Rent	16,524	7,138
Taxes, other than income and payroll . .	13,344	9,337
Other	31,046	16,048
	$ 82,441	$ 46,021

DEBT

In January 1993, the Company issued $97.75 million of convertible subordinated notes ("Notes") due January 15, 2003. Interest, payable on January 15 and July 15, is computed at the rate of 4¾% from the date of issuance to January 15, 1996, and at 6¾% thereafter. Interest expense is accrued by the Company based on an effective interest rate of 6.38% (including amortization of deferred issuance costs) over the full term of the Notes. The Notes are redeemable at the option of the Company on or after January 24, 1996 at redemption prices ranging from 104.14% to 100%. The Notes are not entitled to any sinking fund. The Notes are convertible into the Company's common stock at any time, at a conversion price of $38 per share. A total of 2,572,368 shares of common stock were reserved for conversion. During 1994, a total of $800,000 in $1,000 Notes were converted to 21,052 shares of the Company's common stock. The fair value, based on dealer quotes, of the outstanding Notes as of January 29, 1995 and January 30, 1994 was $98.6 million and $105.6 million, respectively.

The Company has a bank credit agreement ("Credit Agreement") which includes an unsecured line of credit and provides for the issuance of letters of credit. Borrowings under the Credit Agreement, which expires in June 1997, were $41.1 million at January 29, 1995 and borrowings under the Company's prior credit agreement, which expired in April 1994, were $13.0 million at January 30, 1994. The weighted average interest rates for outstanding borrowings were 7.7% and 6.0% as of January 29, 1995 and January 30, 1994, respectively. As of January 29, 1995, the Company had $93.5 million in available unused borrowing capacity under the Credit Agreement. The Credit Agreement requires the Company to maintain various financial ratios and restricts the Company's ability to pay dividends.

INCOME TAXES

Deferred income taxes reflect the net tax effects of temporary differences between the carrying amounts of assets and liabilities for financial reporting purposes and the amounts used for income tax purposes. Significant components of deferred tax liabilities and assets as of the respective year-end balance sheets are as follows:

	1994	1993
	(In thousands)	
Deferred tax liabilities:		
Tax over book depreciation/amortization ..	$ 3,546	$3,981
Other — net	2,313	937
Total deferred tax liabilities	5,859	4,918
Deferred tax assets:		
Tax inventory in excess of book inventory ..	748	1,121
Accrued expenses not deductible until paid .	11,114	2,385
Pre-acquisition net operating loss and alternative minimum tax credit carryforwards	2,687	—
Other — net	1,582	987
Total deferred tax assets	16,131	4,493
Net deferred tax assets (liabilities)	$10,272	$ (425)

	Liability Method		Deferred Method
	1994	1993	1992
	(In thousands)		
Income tax provision:			
Current	$ 7,422	$16,210	$13,219
Deferred	14,090	147	(135)
	$21,512	$16,357	$13,084

Reconciliation of income tax provision to statutory rate:

	1994	1993	1992
	(In thousands)		
Income tax expense at statutory rate	$20,005	$14,925	$11,377
State income taxes, net of federal income tax benefit	858	1,275	1,347
Amortization of intangibles and other	649	157	360
	$21,512	$16,357	$13,084

COMMITMENTS AND CONTINGENCIES

Commitments

The Company operates stores and uses distribution and office facilities and equipment leased under noncancellable operating leases, the majority of which provide for renewal options. Future minimum rentals for all noncancellable operating leases as of January 29, 1995 are as follows:

Fiscal Year	Rent
	(In thousands)
1995	$ 70,276
1996	67,131
1997	59,408
1998	51,921
1999	44,210
2000 and thereafter	133,516
	$426,462

Rental expense applicable to operating leases was $56,181,000, $33,551,000 and $26,188,000 in 1994, 1993 and 1992, respectively.

Contingencies

The Company is a defendant from time to time in routine lawsuits incidental to its business. The Company believes that none of such current proceedings, individually or in the aggregate, will have a materially adverse effect on the Company.

STOCK OPTIONS

All full-time employees are eligible to participate in the Michaels Stores, Inc. Key Employee Stock Compensation Program (the "Program"), as amended, under which 3,000,000 shares of common stock have been authorized for issuance. Selected employees and key advisors, including directors, of the Company may participate in the 1992 and 1994 Non-Statutory Stock Option Plans of Michaels Stores, Inc. (the "Plans"), with 3,000,000 shares of common stock having been authorized for issuance under each plan. In addition stock options have been granted to certain directors and key advisors other than pursuant to the Program or the Plans. The exercise price of all options granted was the fair market value on the date of grant.

	Shares	Exercise price per share
Exercised during 1992	1 307,838	$3 to $15¼
Exercised during 1993	223,027	$3 to $27
Exercised during 1994	308,424	$3 to $27⅞
Outstanding at January 29, 1995	3 336,313	$3 to $41⅞₆
Exercisable at January 29, 1995	1 336,803	$3 to $39¼

MARKETABLE SECURITIES

The Company invests excess cash in a diversified portfolio consisting of a variety of securities including preferred stocks, mutual funds and government debt instruments, which may include both investment grade and non-investment grade securities. The Company limits its credit exposure to any one entity. Net realized gains, dividend income, and interest income were $0.1 million, $1.0 million, and $0.3 million, respectively, for 1994 and $4.1 million, $4.0 million, and $1.5 million, respectively, for 1993. Marketable securities held by the Company at January 29, 1995 were classified as available-for-sale securities and carried at fair value under SFAS No. 115, "Accounting for Certain Investments in Debt and Equity Securities," which the Company adopted in the first quarter of 1994. The aggregate fair value of marketable securities as of January 30, 1994 was $72 0 million.

During 1993 and 1994 Maverick Capital, Ltd. ("Maverick") provided investment management services for the Company. Maverick is owned and managed by a group of individuals, five of whom are directors of the Company. In May 1994, the Company terminated its investment management services agreement with Maverick.

ACQUISITIONS

In February 1994, the Company acquired Treasure House Stores, Inc. ("THSI"), a chain of nine arts and crafts stores operating primarily in the Seattle market, for 280,000 shares of Michaels common stock in a transaction accounted for as a pooling-of-interests. The transaction was not considered material to the Company's sales, net income or financial position of any previous year and therefore the Company's financial statements have not been restated. The accumulated deficit of THSI at January 31, 1994 of $1.2 million has been recorded as a decrease in the Company's retained earnings.

In April 1994, the Company acquired the affiliated arts and crafts store chains of Oregon Craft & Floral Supply Co. ("OCF"), with eight stores located primarily in the Portland, Oregon area, and H&H Craft & Floral Supply Co. ("H&H"), with eight stores located in southern California, for a total of 455,000 shares of Michaels common stock valued at $18.5 million in a transaction accounted for as a purchase. This transaction resulted in the Company recording an addition to goodwill in the amount of $22.3 million.

Effective July 10, 1994, Michaels acquired Leewards Creative Crafts, Inc. ("Leewards"), an arts and crafts retailer with 98 stores located primarily in the midwestern and northeastern United States. The acquisition consideration consisted of $7.9 million in cash and 1,257,279 shares of Michaels common stock valued at $39.9 million. Upon consummation of the Leewards acquisition, Michaels also repaid $39.6 million of Leewards' indebtedness. The cost in excess of the estimated fair value of net assets acquired was recorded as goodwill in the amount of $73.7 million.

The OCF, H&H and Leewards transactions were accounted for as purchases; accordingly, the purchase prices have been allocated to assets and liabilities based on estimated fair values as of the respective acquisition dates. The results of operations since the acquisition dates are included in the accompanying consolidated financial statements.

The following pro forma combined net sales, net income and earnings per share data summarize the results of operations for 1994 and 1993 as if Leewards had been acquired as of the beginning of 1993.

Pro Forma
(In thousands, except per share amounts)

	1994	*1993*
Net sales	**$1,050,173**	$780,302
Net income[(A)]	**$ 36,456**	$ 26,157
Earnings per share assuming full dilution[(A)]	**$ 1.71**	$ 1.41

(A) Excludes a $7.1 million charge ($4.4 million after tax or $.21 per share) for store closing and conversion costs.

The pro forma combined financial results do not purport to represent the results of operations which would have occurred had such transactions been consummated at the beginning of the period indicated or the Company's results of operations for any future period. Anticipated operational efficiencies from the integration of the acquisition are not fully reflected in the above pro forma data.

The above pro forma data includes adjustments to: eliminate net sales and related expenses of overlapping Leewards stores that have been closed; eliminate the duplicate occupancy costs of Leewards' distribution center and duplicate purchasing costs; amortize goodwill; expense pre-opening costs in the year incurred; reduce interest expense to Michaels' average borrowing rate; and reflect the tax effects of the above adjustments.

The above pro forma data does not include THSI, OCF or H&H prior to their respective acquisition dates in February 1994 and April 1994, since the acquisitions are not considered material, individually or in the aggregate, to the operating results of the Company.

SUBSEQUENT EVENT

In March 1995, the Company purchased Aaron Brothers Holdings, Inc., which operates a chain of 71 framing and art supplies stores predominantly in California for a purchase price of $25 million in cash, including the assumption of $19.7 million of debt. In 1994, the chain produced sales of approximately $60 million. The transaction will be accounted for as a purchase.

REPORT OF INDEPENDENT AUDITORS

The Board of Directors and Shareholders
Michaels Stores, Inc.

We have audited the accompanying consolidated balance sheets of Michaels Stores, Inc. as of January 29, 1995 and January 30, 1994, and the related consolidated statements of income, cash flows, and shareholders' equity for each of the three years in the period ended January 29, 1995. These financial statements are the responsibility of the Company's management. Our responsibility is to express an opinion on these financial statements based on our audits.

We conducted our audits in accordance with generally accepted auditing standards. Those standards require that we plan and perform the audit to obtain reasonable assurance about whether the financial statements are free of material misstatement. An audit includes examining, on a test basis, evidence supporting the amounts and disclosures in the financial statements. An audit also includes assessing the accounting principles used and significant estimates made by management, as well as evaluating the overall financial statement presentation. We believe that our audits provide a reasonable basis for our opinion.

In our opinion, the consolidated financial statements referred to above present fairly, in all material respects, the financial position of Michaels Stores, Inc. at January 29, 1995 and January 30, 1994, and the results of its operations and its cash flows for each of the three years in the period ended January 29, 1995, in conformity with generally accepted accounting principles.

Ernst & Young LLP

Dallas, Texas
March 6, 1995

UNAUDITED SUPPLEMENTAL QUARTERLY FINANCIAL DATA

	First Quarter	Second Quarter	Third Quarter	Fourth Quarter
	(In thousands except per share data)			
1994:				
Net sales	$159,798	$174,204	$233,069	$377,492
Cost of sales and occupancy expense	103,511	111,237	137,566	242,423
Operating income	9,071	3,076	14,827	37,062
Net income	4,967	712[1]	7,813	22,154
Fully-diluted earnings per common share	$ .28	$ .04[1]	$ .36	$ .94
Weighted average shares outstanding — assuming full dilution	17,856	18,845	21,930	24,577
1993:				
Net sales	$112,961	$115,414	$155,750	$235,563
Cost of sales and occupancy expense	73,279	74,150	101,588	154,852
Operating income	5,962	5,756	7,819	21,819
Net income	3,798	3,635	4,852	14,002
Fully-diluted earnings per common share	$ .22	$ .21	$ .28	$ .75
Weighted average shares outstanding — assuming full dilution	17,130	17,145	17,287	19,932

[1] Includes a one-time charge of $4.4 million, net of tax, or $.23 per share for store closing and conversion costs.

27

DIRECTORS AND OFFICERS

Sam Wyly
Chairman and Chief Executive Officer
(Director and Officer)

Charles J. Wyly, Jr.
Vice Chairman
(Director and Officer)

Jack E. Bush
President and Chief Operating Officer
(Director and Officer)

Jerry Andrzejewski
Vice President – Sales Promotion and
Merchandise Presentation

Mark V. Beasley
Vice President, General Counsel and Secretary

David E. Bolen
Executive Vice President

Tony J. Chron
Vice President – Real Esate

Bruce Dale
Vice President – Store Operations

William A. Dandy
Vice President – Advertising

Michael C. French (Director)
Managing Director, Maverick Capital, Ltd.

Richard E. Hanlon (Director)
Vice President – Investor Relations
America OnLine, Inc.

Phillip D. Hixon
Vice President – Store Development and Presentation

Kristen L. Magnuson
Vice President – Finance and Planning

Donald R. Miller, Jr. (Director and Officer)
Vice President – Market Development

R. Don Morris
Executive Vice President and Chief Financial Officer

Len Priode
Vice President – Information Services

John H. Rittenhouse
Vice President – Distribution

Robert H. Rudman
Executive Vice President and
Chief Merchandising Officer

Bob Sasser
Vice President – General Merchandise Manager

Douglas B. Sullivan
Executive Vice President

Dr. F. Jay Taylor (Director)
President Emeritus
Louisiana Tech University

Donald C. Toby
Vice President – Personnel

Evan A. Wyly (Director and Officer)
Managing Director, Maverick Capital, Ltd.

Stephen C. Yevich
Controller

SUBSIDIARY OFFICERS

Tony Cincotta
Aaron Brothers

Mike Hess
Puerto Rico

Don Hunt
Craft & Floral Warehouse

Annette Verschuren
Canada

CORPORATE AND SHAREHOLDER DATA

Executive Offices

5931 Campus Circle Drive
Las Colinas Business Park
Irving, Texas 75063

P.O. Box 619566
DFW, Texas 75261-9566
214/714-7000

Transfer Agent and Registrar

Society National Bank

Attorneys

Jackson & Walker, L.L.P.

Auditors

Ernst & Young LLP

Commercial Banking

NationsBank
Bank of America

Dividend Policy

The Company's present policy is to retain earnings for the foreseeable future for use in the Company's business and the financing of its growth. The Company did not pay dividends on its common stock during fiscal 1993 and 1994.

Ticker Symbol

Michaels Stores, Inc. Common Stock is quoted through The Nasdaq National Market System under the ticker symbol MIKE.

Shareholders

As of April 7, 1995, there were 1,156 shareholders of record.

Stock Prices

The following table sets forth for each quarter of the two most recent fiscal years of the Company the high and low sale prices of the Company's Common Stock.

Fiscal 1994	High	Low
First	$44¾	$31
Second	46½	30½
Third	45	29½
Fourth	45¾	32¼

Fiscal 1993	High	Low
First	$34	$26¼
Second	33	25¼
Third	39	26⅜
Fourth	36½	31⅞

Form 10-K

Copies of Michaels Stores, Inc.'s annual report to the Securities and Exchange Commission on Form 10-K are available upon request from the Investor Relations Department at the Company's executive offices.

Annual Meeting

The Annual Meeting of Shareholders will be held on June 6, 1995 at 10:00 a.m. at the Omni Mandalay Hotel, 221 East Las Colinas Boulevard, Irving, Texas.

Investor Relations

General inquiries: 214-714-7100

Analysts and portfolio managers: 214-714-7101

*To locate your nearest Michaels store,
call 1-800-MICHAELS.*

Michaels Stores, Inc.

5931 Campus Circle Drive

Las Colinas Business Park

Irving, Texas 75063

214/714-7000